Financial Accounting for Management

THIRD EDITION

PARESH SHAH

Accredited Management Teacher

OXFORD
UNIVERSITY PRESS

OXFORD
UNIVERSITY PRESS

Oxford University Press is a department of the University of Oxford.
It furthers the University's objective of excellence in research, scholarship,
and education by publishing worldwide. Oxford is a registered trade mark of
Oxford University Press in the UK and in certain other countries.

Published in India by
Oxford University Press
22 Workspace, 2nd Floor, 1/22 Asaf Ali Road, New Delhi 110 002

ISBN-13: 978-0-19-949443-9
ISBN-10: 0-19-949443-6

Typeset in Times New Roman
by E-Edit Infotech Private Limited (Santype), Chennai
Printed in India by Rakmo Press, New Delhi 110 020

Cover image: © Freedomz / Shutterstock

For product information and current price, please visit www.india.oup.com

Third-party website addresses mentioned in this book are provided
by Oxford University Press in good faith and for information only.
Oxford University Press disclaims any responsibility for the material contained therein.

Dedicated to

Tirthankar Parmatma

and Jain Gods and Goddesses

–Paresh Shah

Forewords

It gives me great pleasure to write this foreword as I have the privilege of knowing Dr Paresh Shah, for more than three decades now. Our association started as co-students of doctoral programme under Professor I. M. Pandey of IIM, Ahmedabad. Later on it has continued as professional colleagues in academia.

I feel glad to learn that his book entitled *Financial Accounting for Management*—a third edition—is forthcoming which itself is an attestation of the quality and acceptance of the two previous editions. We use his books for teaching accounting courses at G. H. Patel Post Graduate Institute of Management, Sardar Patel University, Gujarat since the 1st edition published in 2007.

Financial Accounting for Management, 2nd edition was a fantastic outcome covering the complexity of accounting involved by removing the complexity from the mind of students and readers at large. He has developed an innovative approach in discussing the core concepts of accounting in a learner friendly mode.

In this third edition, I understand that he has enriched further, based on his feedback from teaching and conducting the workshops at a number of management development programmes, faculty development programmes, and regular management courses during this period.

Readers of financial reports often get nervous about understanding the concepts such as revenue recognition, measurement, and recording of economical events that take place within a firm and with outsiders. Strangely, such references almost invariably describe the profit of the firm.

Once the sensitivity of profit and profitability is appreciated, it is clear that a managerial decision policy is needed to understand the impact of recording of economical events, in turn its recording as an accounting event, and presentation in financial statements. Paresh has approached this key issue, by considering non-commercial and commercial background of participants. His approach has been that of detailed reasoning and straightforward through the application of an accounting equation rather than using complication of Debit and Credit treatment.

Paresh's book is being published at the right time as I have a feeling that there is really no better book for non-commerical background as well as commercial students. He has made an attempt to explain and elaborate the financial accounting in simple language without going through the technical processes and jargons.

All those who work for competitive advantage realize the need for informed managerial decisions and therefore will welcome this contribution by Paresh.

Wishing all the best for this edition, and I expect this edition too will succeed as the second edition.

With best wishes,

Prof. (Dr) P.K. Priyan
Professor (Finance)
G.H. Patel Post Graduate Institute of Business Management
MBA Department
Sardar Patel University, Vallabh Vidyanagar
Gujarat

It is indeed a pleasure to write the foreword for the books authored by Prof. (Dr) Paresh Shah, which are referred in various courses taught at PDPU and at EDII.

Financial Accounting as a subject faced a key issue, especially for non-commercial and commercial based students and that is to understand the complication of accounting procedures. Dr Shah made detailed reasoning to answer the question

'Why?' This has been converted into modern approach of accounting through the first two editions of *Financial Accounting for Management*, which makes the participants understand the recognition, measurement, and recording of economic events without going into the complication of Debit and Credit, through the application of accounting equation.

This edition of the book is enriched due to his rich teaching experience and also as an outcome of conducting workshops, number of management development programmes, faculty development programmes, and regular management courses. Dr Shah's third edition of the book is relevant in the present time as I believe there is really no good book for students in this subject at national and international levels. This book explains financial accounting in a simple language without going through the technical processes and jargons and makes the subject understandable and application oriented.

Dr Shah's other books on *Financial Management* and *Management Accounting* are also well conceptualized and blended with caselets and cases covering practical applications. *Management Accounting* by Dr Shah is a text and reference book for the subject of Principles of Finance and Costing at PDPU.

All those who desire to work with the competitive advantage have realized the need for informed managerial decisions and will welcome this contribution to academia.

Wishing all the best for this edition,
With best wishes,

Prof. (Dr) D.M. Parikh
Professor and Dean, FoET
Pandit Deendayal Petroleum University, Gandhinagar
Gujarat

It gives me great pleasure to write this foreword as I have the privilege of knowing Dr Paresh Shah over a decade as he has been associated with us as faculty member of our postgraduate management programme and Master of Business Administration programme.

Som-Lalit, a name which has been synonymous in the area of management education in the state of Gujarat for more than two decades, has imbibed a philosophy of research, creativity, innovation, and empathy in its institute resulting in unlocking the potential of the students and faculty members of the institute.

As educators, our focus has been on grooming the students towards holistic development by providing learning based on knowledge dissemination through practical understanding of current socio-economic-financial-technological developments and advancements. To achieve our academic excellence level, we use the world's best academic books. In this endeavour, we have adopted the books authored by Dr Paresh Shah, *Financial Accounting for Management* (Manac-I) and *Management Accounting* (Manac-II), published by Oxford University Press. We also use two other books authored by him—*Financial Management* and *Forex Management*.

Being an educationalist for over three decades, I would like to share some of my thoughts from my own perspective and also based on reactions of the student and reader community at large. The books authored by him are being highly appreciated by the student community in addition to the teaching faculty in the institutions of SLERF. The books provide indepth knowledge in simple and lucid language, and free from complicated arithmetical formulas, etc.

My final words: Use of books authored by Dr Paresh Shah will bring enlightenment in understanding and using the language of business and it will surely bring the prosperity of knowledge, and in turn wealth to all readers and students.

Again, I extend commendation to Paresh for making his talent available in preparing manuscripts on highly complex and technical subjects.

With Best Wishes,

Pragnesh K. Shastri
Managing Trustee
Som-Lalit Education and Research Foundation, Ahmedabad
Gujarat

Preface to the Third Edition

Financial accounting is an integral part of the study of accountancy. The scope of accounting encompasses not only recording of financial transactions of companies but also information that facilitates decision-making. This in turn inspired business schools across the world to include separate courses on financial accounting. It has been acknowledged by academicians and professionals alike that the worth of financial accounting has only increased over the years and is expected to never lose its importance.

About the Book

An attempt has been made to make the third edition of *Financial Accounting for Management* the most interesting, relevant, and comprehensible financial accounting text available in the market. The objective of the current edition of the book is to prepare readers, students, and participants of management development programmes to succeed as future business or non-business managers and/or entrepreneurs. This book introduces the concepts in a lucid way and is developed with an intention to enhance the analytical capability of the readers.

Readers cannot understand financial statements in isolation. They must look at them in the context of a firm's environment. I have learnt through experience that the way to teach financial accounting is to keep reinforcing the business relevance of accounting. This can be done by teaching examples from real-life situations and/or companies. As in the previous editions, every attempt has been made to build each chapter around the most recent cases and events from real-life Indian companies.

In the latest edition of the book, accounting procedures such as transaction analysis, journalizing, and posting are given due consideration wherever appropriate, by considering state-of-the-art technology combined with the *modern approach of accounting*. Readers can develop a better understanding of the economic consequences of a firm's transactions by summarizing those transactions into journal entries and columnar accounts format, instead of the traditional T-accounts format. Effort has been made to include the latest guidelines on IFRS, Ind AS, Ministry of Corporate Affairs, ICAI, etc. for presentation of financial statements, in addition to GST accounting.

Most of the original chapters have been realigned, revised, and updated. This edition also contains extracts from published annual reports of several corporates, to provide better insights into practices adopted in financial accounting.

Key Features

- Uses modern approach of accounting throughout the book (except for indicating debit and credit terms as per traditional approach)
- Focuses on the concepts, principles, and practices that facilitate the development of accounting skills for effective decision-making
- Provides objective type questions, numerical solved illustrations, and self-evaluation exercises
- Contains conceptual and business application cases at the end of the chapters
- Focuses on the latest development in the Indian taxation system and its impact, like GST and Indian income tax provisions

New to the Third Edition

- New chapter on Modern Approach of Accounting
- Full-fledged chapter on Regulatory Framework on Accounting and Reporting
- Discussions on IFRS norms, Indian Accounting Standards (Ind AS), deferred tax assets and deferred tax liabilities, GST accounting
- Revised and updated content in existing chapters
- Specific discussion on goodwill valuation

Coverage and Structure

The book is divided into five parts, comprising 20 chapters.

Part I: Fundamentals of Accounting

The first part starts with an introduction to accounting and deals with different kinds of economic resources and claims in Chapter 1. This chapter further explains the cyclical nature of business activities, in addition to the importance of ethics in accounting. Chapter 2 provides the fundamentals of understanding the modern approach of accounting, in addition to the traditional approach of accounting. The important accounting concepts, their vertical presentation from management and legal points of view, and utility of balance sheet are covered in detail in Chapter 3. Chapter 4 deals with a detailed analysis of income statement in the vertical format. It also discusses the cash conversion cycle.

Part II: Recognition and Types of Transactions

This part starts with Chapter 5 that introduces the readers to the concept of objectively verifiable evidence, in addition to the concepts of receipt and capital maintenance. It also explains the modus operandi of electronic banking. Chapter 6 is dedicated to revenue and expense recognition and its measurements in addition to relationship between assets and expenses. Chapter 7 takes the readers through the concept of analysing transactions wherein it explains topics such as journal proper, fundamentals of accounting as per modern approach of accounting, errors in accounting, and suspense account.

Chapter 8 discusses the concept of non-current assets and their writing off values over a period of time based on time phenomenon, capacity phenomenon, and funds management phenomenon. Additionally, different goodwill valuation methods are covered in this chapter. The management of current assets in the form of cash balance, bank balance, and their different types are discussed in Chapter 9. Chapter 10 is on receivables and inventory valuation, and discusses topics such as accounting of uncollectible receivables, receivable and inventory measurement, controlling of inventories, costing of inventories, and valuation of stock and its impact on financial statements. A critical discussion and accounting treatments related to capital and liabilities and its presentations in financial statements of corporates are discussed in Chapter 11.

Part III: Financial Statements

Part III starts with Chapter 12 that deals with the need of bank reconciliation statements and their preparation as part of internal control management, and identification of causes of differences in the balance as per the firm's record as against the banker's record. Chapter 13 deals with the different types of entries used in preparing financial statements, and the concept of worksheet and its utility. It also elaborates upon GST accounting and its impact. Chapter 14 discusses accounting from incomplete records. The modus operandi to find out missing figures are covered in this chapter.

Part IV: Analytical Accounting

This part begins with Chapter 15 discussing the concepts of average due date, account current, and negotiable instruments. Bills of exchange and promissory notes are explained in this chapter. The analytical aspects of financial statements, such as common size statements, comparative financial statements, and financial ratio analysis are covered in Chapter 16. Chapter 17 discusses the concept of cash flow statement for manufacturing firms and financial enterprises. It also explains both the methods of preparation of cash flow statements.

Part V: Special Topics

The last part begins by explaining foreign exchange accounting for import–export transactions in addition to foreign branch accounting in Chapter 18. It also discusses the different ways of quotations of foreign exchange rates, hedging transactions, and treatment of exchange differences. Chapter 19 deals with the legal and regulatory aspects of accounting. Topics such as IFRS, Ind AS, and GAAP are explained in this chapter. Chapter 20, the last chapter of the book, is about contemporary accounting concepts such as inflation accounting, human resource accounting, and forensic accounting.

Acknowledgements

I would first like to thank Fenil Shah, FCA, ACMA, MIMA (practicing chartered accountant) for his comments on the topics of GST accounting, deferred tax assets, and deferred tax liabilities accounting, in addition to the legal aspects of accounting and reporting.

I would like to provide my gratitude to the following individuals for the valuable comments and remarks in their respective forewords: Prof. (Dr) P.K. Priyan, MBA Department, Sardar Patel University, Vallabh Vidyanagar, Gujarat; Prof. (Dr) D.M. Parikh, Pandit Deendayal Petroleum University, Gandhinagar, Gujarat; and Pragnesh K. Shastri, Som-Lalit Education and Research Foundation, Ahmedabad.

I would also like to thank Dr Somen Saha, Indian Institute of Public Health, Gandhinagar (IIPHG); Dr Srinivas Deshpande, Principal, Gadag Institute of Medical Sciences, Karnataka; Prof. (Dr) Janardhan Pawar, Principal and Professor, Tuljaram Chaturchand College of Arts, Science and Commerce, Baramati, Maharashtra; Prof. (Dr) Rakesh Patil, Dean, Professor and Head (MBA), Sandip Institute of Technology and Research Centre, Nashik, Maharashtra; Prof. (Dr) Rajesh Rathore, Professor and Dean, Faculty of Commerce and Management, Madhav University, Abu Road, Rajasthan; and Prof. Vivek A. Bale, Assistant Professor, Tuljaram Chaturchand College of Arts, Science and Commerce, Baramati, Maharashtra.

Without the blessings of Saraswati Mataji, Sadguru P.P. Panyaspravar Shree Vinitchandravijayji Ganivarya Maharaj, and my (late) mother Lilavatiben, it would not have been possible for me to write this third edition of the book.

I am immensely grateful to my best friend and wife, Trupti, for her selfless sacrifice and unstinted support, and the significant suggestions and views she provided from time to time. I am also extremely thankful to my son, Fenil, daughter-in-law, Roma, and my grandchildren for supporting me in my endeavour. I lack words to express my deep sense of sincere gratefulness and indebtedness to my esteemed guru, Prof. (Dr) I.M. Pandey, Professor of Finance, and Ex-Dean of Indian Institute of Management, Ahmedabad, for his profuse and perpetual praise and pep, and constant motivation and encouragement to me towards becoming a moulded researcher and teacher of management.

I deeply appreciate the painstaking efforts of the editorial team at Oxford University Press, India, who have played a pivotal role in making the book more reader-friendly.

While using information from a number of books and research publications, certain errors and omissions may have crept in. I would be happy to receive your comments, suggestions, and feedback for the further improvement of the book. You can send your feedback at my email IDs profpareshshah@yahoo.co.in and paresh@profparesh.in.

Paresh Shah

The publisher and the author would like to thank the following reviewers for their valuable feedback:

- Prof. Pinky Agarwal, ITM Group of Institutions, Kharghar, Maharashtra
- Prof. Geetanjali (Renold) Pinto, ITM Group of Institutions, Kharghar, Maharashtra
- Dr Anju Motwani, N.L. Dalmia Institute of Management Studies and Research, Mumbai, Maharashtra
- Prof. Khushboo Vora, N.L. Dalmia Institute of Management Studies and Research, Mumbai, Maharashtra
- Dr Nitin Gupta, Lovely Professional University, Jalandhar, Punjab

Praise for the Previous Editions

Financial Accounting for Management is an excellent book, balancing accounting mechanics, concepts, and practices with sufficient coverage of accounting standards and regulatory framework. It is an indispensable book for serious management students.

– Prof. (Dr) P.K. Priyan, Corporation Bank Chair, Sardar Patel University

Contents

PART III   FINANCIAL STATEMENTS

PART IV ANALYTICAL ACCOUNTING

PART V SPECIAL TOPICS

Fundamentals of Accounting

Introduction to Accounting

Learning Objectives

After studying this chapter, you will understand

- development of business enterprise and accounting
- different forms of business organization
- difference between bookkeeping, accounting, and accountancy
- functions, objectives, users, and limitations of accounting
- kinds of accounting activities
- cyclical nature of business activity
- economic resources and claims
- basic documents and records for validating transactions
- relationship of accounting with other disciplines
- role and activities of an accountant
- job descriptions of accounting positions
- important accounting standards
- importance of ethics in accounting and corporate governance
- organizational structure of accounts and the finance department

INTRODUCTION

A business is the activity of making, buying, selling, or supplying goods or services for money. It involves the investment of money and earning reasonable returns on it. A business enterprise may function in the form of a (a) proprietorship, (b) partnership, (c) company, or (d) cooperative. It may be involved in purchasing and selling activities, producing goods, or providing services. Irrespective of the nature of the business, an enterprise has to invest capital. The business must be kept completely separate from its owners. If the business has acquired money, it owes an equal amount to its owners.

Using this capital, the enterprise can acquire assets. The economic resources employed by an enterprise are called *assets*. They may be in the form of plant and machinery, furniture and fitting, land and building, motor vehicles, stock-in-trade, amount receivable from customers, etc. A business can acquire two types of assets—*fixed* assets, which are permanently held, and *current* assets, which are currently held and change constantly.

> Accounting is the language of business.

It is necessary to keep a record of production, sales, profits, etc., of any business activity. The business activity may be related to production, trade, or service and may involve some expenditure and returns. It is necessary to have proper records of such transactions to avoid confusion. The record-keeping activity of a business is known as bookkeeping. In fact, accounting is known as the language of business. Luca Pacioli, a Franciscan monk and Renaissance mathematician, is considered to be the father of the modern system of accounting known as the double-entry system of bookkeeping and accounting (Weygandt, 2006). The double-entry system involves making at least two entries for every transaction. The sum of all debits should always equal the sum of all credits. According to Pacioli (1494), 'Books should be closed each year, especially in a partnership, because frequent accounting makes for long friendship.'

People around the world use some form of accounting everyday. Customers account for the money they spend; students plan for their educational expenses; and organizations use

accounting to track performance of their operating activities. Accounting is a diverse, dynamic, and service-based discipline. An accountant's responsibility is to provide reliable and relevant information that is useful in making intelligent business decisions.

> **Accounting is a service-based discipline.**

Accounting is also a measurement discipline. It measures results, and guides managers and external users to make relevant business decisions.

According to the American Institute of Certified Public Accountants (AICPA), accounting is 'the art of recording, classifying, and summarizing in a significant manner and in terms of money; transactions and events which are, in part, at least, of a financial character,

> **Accounting is a measurement discipline.**

and interpreting the results thereof.' The various attributes of accounting are as follows:

1. Events and transactions of a financial nature are recorded while the events of a non-financial nature cannot be recorded.
2. The record should reflect the importance of the transactions so recorded both individually and collectively, which includessummarization, thereby making it amenable to analysis.
3. The users of the financial statements should be able to obtain the message encompassed in such financial statements, and it is the knowledge of accountancy which enables the user to understand the contents of the financial statements.

Accounting is the process of recording financial transactions in a proper format. It then analyses, classifies, and reports these financial transactions to the user. Accounting also provides financial information by preparing reports and statements. Thus, accounting is the art of preparing significant summaries, analysing and interpreting transactions and activities, and communicating the results to those who frame judgements and take decisions.

FORMS OF BUSINESS ORGANIZATION ▰▰▰

Human activities are broadly categorized into economic activities (employment, business, or professional practice) or non-economic activities (religious rituals, cultural and social work, etc.).

Economic activities can be of three types: business activities, professional practice, or employment.

A business may involve trading (buying and selling of finished goods), manufacturing (changing the shape of the raw material into a usable form), or providing a service. A business earns profits from the activities undertaken.

A professional may be described as a person who provides personal services of specialized and expert nature and charges fees from the client for the service(s) rendered.

Employment refers to the work performed by a person for someone else according to the contract between them. This gives rise to an employer–employee relationship, where the employee is compensated in the form of salary, or wages, or contractual payment.

Organizations can be broadly classified as *for-profit* or *non-profit*. The main purpose of organizations or firms in the first category is to earn a profit. Non-profit organizations have objectives other than generating profit. No part of the organization's income is distributed to its members, directors, or officers. Non-profit organizations include schools, charities, clinics and hospitals, legal aid societies, volunteer services organizations, and professional associations. The bookkeeping system, necessary to monitor funds, is similar in both profit-making and non-profit making organizations.

Forms or structures created for the smooth running of a business or a profession are of the following types (Fig. 1.1).

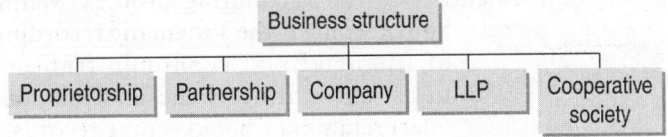

FIG. 1.1 Various business structures

Sole Proprietorship

In this structure, only one person takes all decisions related to the functioning of the business, such as purchase of goods, sale of goods, management of finance, and recruitment of staff. The sole proprietor or the one person is solely responsible for the profit or loss of the business.

Partnership

Partnership is the relation between persons who have agreed to share the profits of a business carried on by all or any of them acting for all. In this structure, two or more than two persons collaborate to take all decisions related to the business. They cooperate with each other to perform business or professional activities as co-owners, and are jointly responsible for the profit or loss of the business. The profits are shared in a certain ratio among them as per agreement.

Company

It is an association of persons, who contribute money to the common share capital of the company or joint stock. The company appoints managers or directors to run the activities related to the business. It is a separate legal entity and has a limited liability of persons who have contributed to the common share capital.

Limited Liability Partnership (LLP)

LLP is a new type of corporate structure. It combines the flexibility of a partnership and of a limited liability company. It provides the benefits of a company to its partners and at the same time does not put restrictions on them for organizing internal management, as applicable in case of a company. On account of flexibility in its management and operations, an LLP is useful for small and medium enterprises in the service sector, in particular.

Cooperative Societies

A particular group of persons with a common purpose may collaborate with one another and work together in order to achieve financial and/or social goals. Such a structure represents a united, collective front for the benefit of all members.

BOOKKEEPING

Bookkeeping is an activity concerning the recording of financial data related to business operations in a significant and orderly manner. It is the record-making phase of accounting. Accounting is based on a careful and efficient bookkeeping system. The terms 'accounting' and 'bookkeeping' are often used synonymously. In fact, bookkeeping is complementary to the accounting process. While bookkeeping is the systematic recording of financial and economic transactions, accounting is the analysis and interpretation of bookkeeping records.

> *Bookkeeping is the record-making phase of accounting.*

BOOKKEEPING, ACCOUNTING, AND ACCOUNTANCY

Bookkeeping is a part of accounting that deals with record-keeping or maintenance of books of accounting which is often routine and clerical in nature. It covers the following:

- Identifying the transactions and events
- Ceasuring the identified transactions and events
- Recording the identified and measured transactions and events in proper books of accounts
- Classifying the recorded transactions and events in a ledger

Accounting refers to the actual process of preparing and presenting the accounts of an enterprise. In addition to the aforementioned functions of bookkeeping, accounting covers the following:

- Summarizing the classified transactions and events in the form of income statements and position statements
- Analysing and interpreting the summarized results
- Communicating the interpreted information to the interested parties

Accountancy refers to a systematic knowledge of accounting. It explains the reasons and the processes of accounting. Accountancy explains the method of preparing the books of accounts, and summarizing and communicating accounting information.

> *Accounting is the process of preparing and presenting the accounts.*

An event can be considered as an accounting event if it satisfies the following four conditions:

1. There must be two parties.
2. One of the parties must have fulfilled the obligations.
3. It should be measurable in acceptable monetary terms, as per law of the land.
4. It should be legal, moral, and ethical.

FUNCTIONS OF ACCOUNTING

An entity (also referred to as an enterprise, firm, or organization) is a specific unit (i.e., individual, firm, or institution) for which the accountant records and reports economic information. As mentioned earlier, the boundaries of an accounting entity are distinct and separate from those of the owners, creditors, managers, and employees.

An accountant records and reports financial information for an entity. For example, Lakhina Traders is a business entity owned by Mr Sharma. The financial statements of Lakhina Traders will report the effect of the event on the entity, not on its owner. Accounting measures the resources held by an entity by

- ascertaining the claims and interest in the said entity;
- measuring the resources and changes in these resources;
- assigning the changes to specified period of times in terms of money;
- communicating information about an entity; and
- fulfilling the statutory requirements, particularly in respect of income tax, sales tax, etc.

From the above, it becomes clear that accounting accumulates data systemically and supplies the necessary information to the user of financial statements. The user can take proper decisions based on the financial information about an entity for a specified period. This indicates that maintaining accounts is not the primary objective of an entity. Its primary objective is to take decisions on the basis of financial facts presented by accounting statements. Thus, accounting is not an end in itself, but is a means to an end.

OBJECTIVES OF ACCOUNTING

The primary objectives of accounting are as follows.

1. Have a permanent record of each transaction and to show the financial effects on the business.
2. Ascertain the combined effects of all the transactions made during an accounting period on the financial position of the business.
3. Evaluate the earning capacity of the enterprise by supplying a statement of its financial position. A statement of periodic earnings together with a statement of financial activities is provided to the internal and external users of the information.
4. Provide necessary information about the efficiency or otherwise of the management regarding proper utilization of resources.
5. Provide necessary information for financial forecasting, formulation of overall policies, and devising remedial measures for the deviations between the actual and projected (or budgeted) performance.
6. Provide necessary data to the government for taking proper decisions related to duties, taxes, price control, etc.

USERS OF ACCOUNTING INFORMATION

Accounting information is used for making better investment and credit decisions. The demand for accounting information of any entity comes from both outside and inside the organization.

Outside Users

Accounting information is used by investors and other capital providers outside the organization. For those outside the organization, financial accounting reports constitute most of the financial information concerning the organization's status and performance.

Capital markets Investors who participate in capital markets need accounting information to make investment decisions. Investors may include equity shareholders, preference shareholders, debenture holders, brokers, etc.

Financial institutions Funding institutions such as banks, state and/or central financial institutions need accounting information for credit appraisal.

Government institutions They determine the taxes owed by the enterprise to implement a regulatory framework and to formulate economic policies.

Special interest groups Creditors, labour unions, consumer action groups, competing businesses, financial advisers, and the general public seek accounting information about an enterprise to further their own interests.

Inside Users

Accounting information is used internally by operating, marketing, and financial managers within an organization. The information provided by accounting assists the management in making pricing, product, and investment decisions.

Managers Financial information is required to control the resources of the enterprise, and to direct resources to the most promising products, sub-units, and activities of the business.

Employees They are interested in the financial performance of their company as it is their source of income. Decisions regarding wage increases and bonuses also drive employees to be on the look out for financial information.

LIMITATIONS OF ACCOUNTING

The limitations of accounting are as follows.

Financial nature The accountant measures only those events that are of a financial nature, that is, are capable of being expressed in terms of money. Non-monetary events, however, significant and important, are not measured or recorded in accounting.

Historical costs Accounting contains information related to historical costs. It does not provide day-to-day information about costs and expenses. For example, fixed assets are shown at historical cost. This value may change over time, and hence there may be a great difference between the original cost at which assets were purchased and the current replacement cost. The balance sheet, thus, may not show a true picture of the financial affairs of an enterprise on a particular date.

Measurement unit Money as a measurement unit is not stable but it changes in value. Unless changes in price levels are considered in the measurement of income, the accounting information will not show true results.

Personal judgement Accounting information is not without personal influence or bias of the accountant. In measuring income, an accountant makes a choice between different methods of inventory valuation, depreciation methods, provision for doubtful debts, etc.

Estimates Accounting data are sometimes based on estimates, and these estimates may be inaccurate. For example, the actual useful life of an asset cannot be accurately estimated for the purpose of providing and calculating depreciation.

Inexact information Accounting does not provide information to analyse losses incurred due to factors, such as idle plant and machinery, seasonal fluctuations in volume of business, etc. It is also difficult to have detailed information regarding costs relating to different departments, processes, products, jobs in the production divisions, etc. Cost control is one of the most important objectives of a firm and it cannot be achieved by using accounting processes alone.

KINDS OF ACCOUNTING ACTIVITIES

Due to growing business complexities and advanced decision processes, different kinds of accounting have been developed to serve different objectives.

Financial accounting It deals with recording and summarizing economical events and preparing financial statements in accordance with accepted accounting practices. Hence, it is also known as stewardship accounting.

Cost accounting It deals with the computation of aggregate costs of the products manufactured and/or services provided by using the same set of information used by financial accounting. In cost accounting, the production processes are broken down into financial values to calculate cost.

Taxation accounting It involves preparing records and reports necessary for filling tax returns to local, state, and central govern-ment authorities.

Management accounting It relates to the use of financial and cost data for the purpose of evaluating the performance of the enterprise, reviewing the existing policies, and making decisions about new policies.

In India, taxation accounting is merged with financial accounting, and cost accounting is merged with management accounting. Figure 1.2 depicts the pictorial presentation of the linkage between the sub-fields of accounting and the users of accounting information.

CYCLICAL NATURE OF BUSINESS

Business transactions or events form a sequence of connected and regularly repeated patterns of activity. Although these patterns or cycles vary from one business to another, broadly they involve

- receiving assets from owners and creditors;
- purchasing assets (including traded items for resale) or materials to produce saleable goods and/or services;
- selling goods or services;
- collecting cash or assets equivalent to cash-in-kind from customers; and
- repaying creditors their dues.

Financial cycle A financial cycle is the time between the receiving of assets from owners and creditors and the repayment of assets to owners and creditors. In business, the owners are repaid when the entity closes down.

Investing cycle An investing cycle indicates investing activities like the purchase of fixed or long-term or non-current assets. These expenditures are made to generate future income and cash flows for the entity.

Operating cycle The operating cycle is the average time between the purchase of assets or services and the final cash realization from that purchase. Figure 1.3 illustrates the concept of the financial cycle and the operating cycle. Usually the operating cycle is much shorter than a financial cycle. The operating cycle may exist for a year or even for a few days.

ECONOMIC RESOURCES AND CLAIMS

Economic resources are the factors of production or services used in the fulfillment of the objectives of a firm. They can be divided into human resources, such as labour and professional,

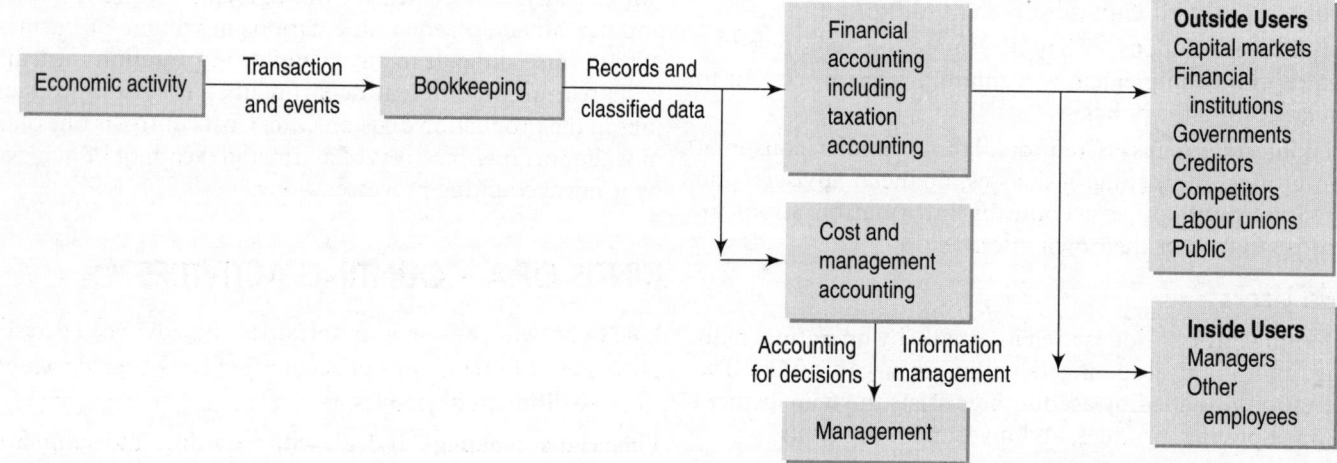

FIG. 1.2 Accounting system

Source: Adapted from C.A.P.E-I., the Institute of Chartered Accountants of India, p.8.

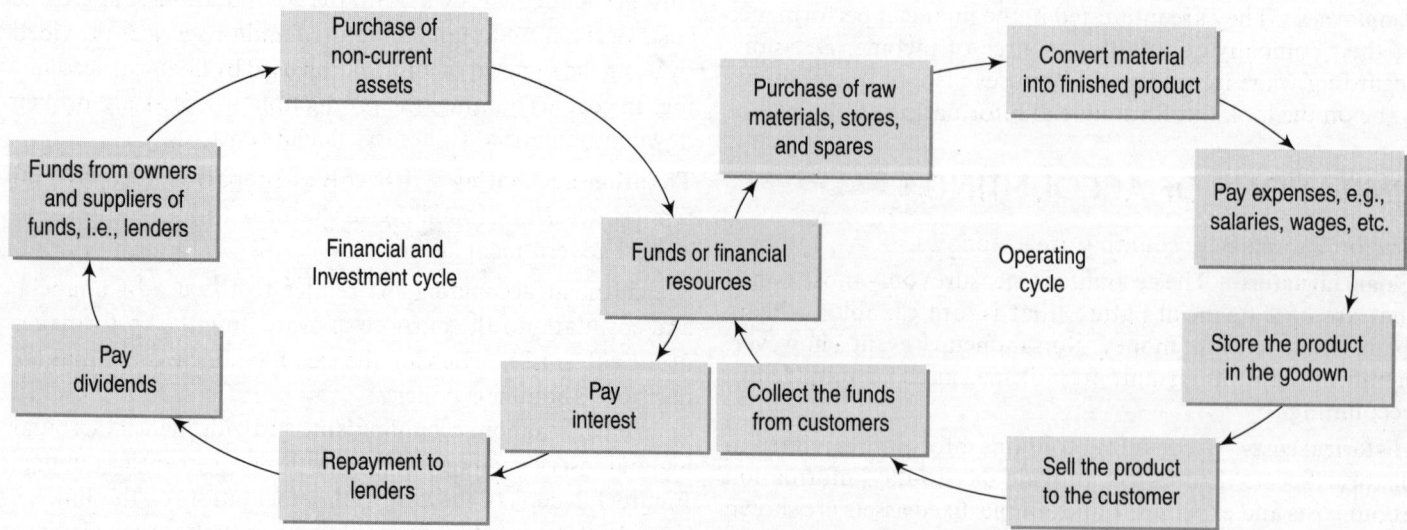

FIG. 1.3 Financial and operating cycle

and non-human resources such as land, plant, property and equipment, financial resources and technology, etc.

Economic claims arise out of contractual formal or informal relationships between parties, involving firm or enterprise or entity and outsiders. A firm's resources, that is, assets are claimed by an outsider (banks in case of bank loan, suppliers in case of credit purchases, etc.), and/or by the owners of an entity (promoters, equity shareholders in case of company, partners in case of partnership firm, etc.).

BASIC TERMINOLOGY

Due to the growing need of the spread of accounting information among its users and in order to bring uniformity in treatment of economic events in the books of accounts, the knowledge of the following terminologies is important. These terminologies can be applied in both profit-making and not-for-profit organizations.

Capital

The owner's interest in the assets of the firm, after paying off liabilities towards third parties, is known as *capital*. Capital consists of the owner's contribution in the start up of the firm's activities, additional amount brought subsequently by the owner to the firm, and also the profit (excess of income over expenses) retained in the firm. It is known as capital on the date of balance sheet. Capital is also referred to as *equity* or *net worth*.

When an owner invests personal funds in the business, such an investment is recorded in an account that carries the owner's name and is referred to as the *capital account*. In case of corporate entities, such an account is known as a share capital account, a corpus fund account, or an equity share capital account. For example, Raja Kapoor's account balance (as proprietor of the firm) in the books of Raja Associates indicates the capital balance, that is, the sum of capital contributed by Raja Kapoor at the time of start up of the firm, new capital introduced by Raja Kapoor, and profit gained from the business activities less the *withdrawals* by Raja Kapoor since the start up of the firm.

Equity

Equity refers to the right, claim, or interest in the assets of the firm by the owner or promoters or partners or shareholders. It is also known as contributed capital of an entity.

Liabilities

Liability represents the claim or right to be paid off by a firm, irrespective of the performance of the firm. If a firm fails to pay its liabilities, then the law recognizes the right of the debtor party to force recovery even by selling the firm's assets to secure the money due. For example, when RuPaltm Enterprises purchased stocks for its business from Orange Acetech on a credit period of three months, the date of receipt of goods till the date Orange is paid off is known as liability for RuPaltm.

If it avails loans from bank(s) or friends and associates, then these will also be considered as the liability of RuPaltm.

Drawings

An owner invests funds in a firm in order to generate profits. The profit is earned over a period of time, such as a year. The owner may withdraw a fixed amount each week or month for living expenses or for other personal use. These withdrawals do not constitute the salary of the firm's owner in the legal sense. When an owner uses a withdrawn amount, both the assets and the capital of the firm may reduce. To exercise control over these withdrawals, a separate account referred to as *drawings* in the name of the person is used. For example, to record the drawings of Raja Kapoor, the owner of Raja Associates, an account referred to as Raja Drawings account will be maintained in the books of the proprietory concern. Drawings are also referred to as withdrawals.

Assets

Resources such as land, building, plant and machinery, furniture, and vehicles owned by the firm with an intention to be used in the operating activities of the firm are known as *assets* of the firm. The assets may be of *tangible* or *intangible* form, which provide value to a firm.

Assets that possess a physical form are known as *tangible assets*, for example, land, plant, machinery, etc. *Intangible* assets are not present in the physical form, but are valuable as they generate cash for a business. Some of the most common *intangible* assets are legal claims or rights, such as patents, goodwill, etc.

Goods or Merchandise

A business firm earns revenue by selling goods. Merchandise refers to the aggregate of the items, commodities, or goods that are either sold in the same form or converted into saleable products by the firm. For example, if Home Furniture purchases chairs for sale to its customer, the chairs constitute goods of Home. However, if the chairs are purchased by Alia Grocery Stores, they would be referred to as that firm's *fixed assets*. To consider another example, if Home Furniture purchases wooden pieces to manufacture dining tables, these wooden pieces will be referred to as *goods* of the firm. Goods are expected to be sold within a year or during the course of one business cycle. Consequently, the merchandise not sold during this period is reported as *inventory* and is considered as part of *current assets*.

Revenue, Income, or Turnover

Revenue refers to the cash and cash equivalent received or receivable for goods and commodities supplied, services rendered, or the right given to the other party for utilization of the resources of the firm. The revenue generated by a firm for the regular operating activities is known as *business income*. For example, a grocery shopkeeper earns revenue by the sale of consumable items, such as food, soaps and detergents, and

cosmetics. The amount received on sale of goods is known as *sale income*. In the case of a practicing chartered accountant, the service fees charged from a client is covered under *consultancy income* or *service income*. If the firm is transferring the right to use the shop floor to a third party, and earns rental income, it is known as *other income* or *rental income*. Revenue is also referred to as turnover.

Expenses

When a payment is made or undertaken to be made for the services rendered by a third party, a firm, or a legal entity, no further future benefits can be availed from the third party. This payment is referred to as an *expense*. For example, the peon of Jeevan Software has paid ₹50 as auto fare for going to and returning from the bank for official work. This ₹50 will be considered as conveyance expense, because no future benefit will be available from this auto fare.

If an expense cannot provide future benefit, it is known as *revenue expense*. If an expense creates scope for future benefits, it is known as *capital expense*.

Discount

It is the concession in the amount payable offered by the seller to the buyer on the market price or listed price of the product. In business, the discount allowed by a firm is of two types: trade discount and cash discount.

Trade discount

It is offered by the seller to the retailer on the listed or printed price in order to enable the latter to earn profit. It is also sometimes offered by the seller to the customer, with an intention to maintain the relationship or to sell a bulk quantity. Trade discount being part of sales promotion efforts is not recorded in the account books. Trade discount is allowed in a business transaction irrespective of whether it involves cash or credit transaction.

Cash discount

It is a type of financing cost undertaken by the seller, with the intention to recover the money early in the transaction. It is a mechanism to encourage the prompt payment of money by customers, so that for the seller, financing from bankers and financial institutions is reduced and bad debts avoided. *Bad debt* refers to the failure to recover moneys due from customers. This is a type of financing cost and is recorded separately in the account books.

Debtors

When a firm pays a person or another firm cash or cash equivalent with future relationship in mind, such as to receive the paid amount back in cash or kind, then the receiving party of the transaction is known as the *debtor* for the person or the firm. For example, Packing Maker Stores delivered 30 boxes of packing material to Mr Jeeyu Kumar as on Monday, and Jeeyu agreed to pay ₹150 on Wednesday as consideration for purchase of the boxes of packing material. This means that as

on Monday, based on the future relationship between Packing Maker Stores and Jeeyu, the latter, will be treated as a Debtor in the books of Packing Maker Stores.

Creditors

When a firm receives support in the form of cash or in kind from another firm or any other legal entity, then the providing firm or legal entity becomes the giver to the firm and is called the *creditor*. The firm is bound to return the cash or equivalent in kind as agreed upon to the lending or providing firm. Hence, it is considered as a *future liability*. For example, Packing Maker Stores has delivered 30 boxes of packing material to Jeeyu as on Monday, and Jeeyu agreed to pay ₹150 on Wednesday as consideration of receipt of the boxes of packing material. It means that as on Monday, based on the future relationship between Packing Maker Stores and Jeeyu, the specified amount is payable by Jeeyu to Packing Maker Stores. Hence, Packing Maker Stores would be treated as a creditor in the books of Jeeyu.

Loss

When the sales revenue is lesser than the cost of goods sold, the difference is called *gross loss*. When the sum of sales revenue including the other revenues is lower than the sum of the cost of goods sold and other administrative, selling, and distribution expenses, it is called *net loss*.

Profit

When the sales revenue is greater than the cost of goods sold, the difference is called *gross profit*. When the sum of sales revenue including the other revenues is greater than the sum of cost of goods sold and other administrative, selling, and distribution expenses, it is called *net profit*.

Cost of Goods Sold

The *cost of goods sold* is equal to the sum of the cost of opening stock of raw materials, work-in-progress, and finished goods and the cost of purchase of raw materials and/or finished goods, from which the sum of the cost of closing stock of raw materials, work-in-progress, and finished goods are deducted. In addition to the above, the sum of the directly identifiable expenses necessary to complete the operating cycle are added to the cost of goods sold. In other words, it takes into account the operating expenses, such as wages, power and fuel, inward freight expenses, etc. involved in bringing the goods to a *saleable* condition.

Expenditure

Assets, goods, or commodities purchased by a firm considering the long-term benefits that they provide to the firm, are called *long-term assets* or *fixed assets*. The amount expended or agreed to be expended in future in addition to the expense incurred to make the asset workable is referred to as *capital expenditure*.

When the amount expended or agreed to be expended in future is not concerned with the value addition of the fixed

asset, but supports the firm's business activities on a day-to-day basis, it is termed as *revenue expenditure.* For example, payment of wages to workers for delivery of sold goods to customer's premises is known as revenue expenditure. If the worker is paid for installation of a newly purchased machine, then it is known as capital expenditure. Capital expenditure is capitalized. This means that the expense is booked as the value of a tangible or intangible asset of the firm. An asset provides benefits of its use over a longer period of time, that is, more than one year or one accounting period. In the said example, if the expenditure on installation of machine is not incurred, the machine cannot be made operational and put into effective and productive use over a long period.

ACCOUNTING METHODS

Cash basis accounting (also known as cash accounting) and accrual basis accounting (also known as accrual accounting) are the two principal methods of keeping track of an enterprise's income and expenses.

Accrual basis accounting is the method of recording business events or activities when they occur rather than when cash is received or paid. Thus, accrual accounting recognizes revenue and expense when goods are sold or when services are performed rather than when cash is received or paid. *Cash basis accounting* records only cash receipt and payments, and recognizes income increases and decreases when cash is received and paid.

Accrual basis accounting is superior to cash basis for measuring the performance of a business because it ties income measurement to sales. In contrast, cash basis accounting is influenced by many factors that may have little to do with the performance of the entity. Cash basis accounting is not permitted by accepted accounting principals, income tax authorities, etc.

BASIC DOCUMENTS AND RECORDS

Following are the important objectively verifiable evidences to establish the validity of the transactions recorded in the books of accounts.

Voucher

An accounting transaction is an economic event that affects an entity's assets, liabilities, or owner's equity at the time of occurrence of an event. The transaction between a firm or entity and an external party is an external transaction, whereas the transaction within a firm or entity is internal transaction. For such transactions, documentary evidence is prepared, which is known as voucher.

A voucher refers to an authorized consent of the payments made, or agreed upon to make payments of funds or receipts, or agreed upon to receive funds.

Books of Original Entry or Journal

The accounting transactions are recorded from the vouchers to the original books of accounts or journals. Transactions are recorded in chronological order. If the same type of transactions takes place a large number of times, then subsidiary books can be maintained. Subsidiary books are specialized books of original entry, and are explained in Chapters 6 to 8.

Account

An account is an accounting record that accumulates the activity of a specific item or nature of transaction and yields the balance of the specific nature of transactions. An account is the standardized record in which all the changes in each of entity's assets, liabilities, capital, income, and expenses are collected. The amount in an account at any time is called the balance of an account.

An account can take a variety of forms and accounts are traditionally shown the form of T; while in the present era, as per modern approach it is maintained in a columnar way, as explained and used throughout this book.

Ledger or Principal Books of Accounts

The accounting record in which all the accounts of the entity are kept is called the ledger in which the individual accounts are summed up to produce the aggregate amount entered in the balance sheet and income statement. In short, a ledger refers to a book or register in which financial transactions are permanently recorded after being summarized and classified. A ledger helps in preparing a trial balance, after which the final statement is prepared. A ledger is also known as a principal book.

Trial Balance

A trial balance is a listing of accounts and their balances at a specific point of time, which constitutes the first step towards the preparation of financial statement of an entity. A trial balance is generally prepared at the end of the accounting period for preparing the financial statements. It is done with the objective of checking the arithmetic accuracy of ledger positions.

RELATIONSHIP OF ACCOUNTING WITH OTHER DISCIPLINES

Accounting is closely related to several other disciplines, and thus, to acquire a good knowledge in accounting, one should understand the relevance of these disciplines. Accountants should have a working knowledge of related disciplines, so that they can understand such overlapping areas and apply the knowledge of other disciplines in their own work.

Accounting and Economics

Economics is viewed as a science of rational decisions. It deals with the efficient use of scarce resources for satisfying human wants. Accounting is viewed as a system that provides data for informed judgement and decisions. Some non-accounting data are also relevant for decision-making.

Accounting and Statistics

The use of statistics in accounting can be appreciated better in the context of the nature of accounting records. Accounting information is very precise; it is exact to the last paisa. However, for the purpose of decision-making, such precision is not necessary and hence approximations are sought.

In accounts, all values are important because they are related to business transactions. As against this, statistics involves the typical value, behaviour, or trend over a period of time, or the degree of variation over a series of observations. Therefore, whenever a need arises for generalization of relationships, statistical methods are applied in accounting data.

Statistical methods are helpful in developing and interpreting accounting data. For example, time series and cross-sectional comparisons of accounting data are based on statistical techniques. Regression analysis is useful in forecasting, budgeting, and cost control; significance tests are used in budget analysis and standard cost variances. Multiple discriminant analysis is commonly used to identify the causes of sickness in a business firm. Therefore, the study and application of statistical methods would add an extra edge to the accounting data.

Accounting and Mathematics

Double-entry bookkeeping can be converted into algebraic form. In fact, the first known book on accounting was part of a treatise on algebra.

Knowledge of arithmetic and algebra is a prerequisite for accounting computations and measurements. Calculation of interest and annuity are examples of such fundamental uses. Mathematical techniques are commonly used to calculate depreciation, installments payment transactions, loan repayment and replacement amount, lease rentals, etc. Accounting data can also be presented in ratio form.

Accounting and Law

A business entity operates within a legal environment. All transactions with suppliers and customers are governed by the Contract Act, the Sale of Goods Act, the Negotiable Instruments Act, etc. The entity itself is created and controlled by laws. For example, a partnership business is controlled by the Partnership Act. A company is created and controlled by the Companies Act.

Every country has a set of economic, fiscal, and labour laws. Laws of the land guide economic transactions and events. Often the accounting system followed is prescribed by the law. For example, the Companies Act has prescribed the format of financial statements. Banking, insurance, and electric supply undertakings have to produce financial statements as prescribed by the respective legislations controlling such entities.

Accounting and Management

Management is a broad field, which comprises many functions and encompasses applications of many disciplines. Accountants play a key role in the management team. A large portion of accounting information is prepared for decision-making by the management. Although the management relies on other data sources, accounting data are the basis for making crucial decisions. An accountant is in a better position to understand and use such data.

ROLE AND ACTIVITIES OF AN ACCOUNTANT

The training of accountants in assessing the financial implications of alternative courses of action, working with multiple constituencies, establishing systems and controls, and behaving in a responsible and credible manner, prepares them to play critical roles in organizations. The following statements list the activities of an account:

1. An accountant is engaged in accounts keeping.
2. An accountant is a functionary who aids in control.
3. An accountant keeps the conscience of an organization.
4. An accountant is a professional whose primary duties include information management for internal and external use.
5. An accountant is a financial adviser.
6. An accountant produces an income statement and a balance sheet for an accounting period, and maintains all supporting evidence and classified facts that lead to final accounting statements.
7. An accountant verifies, authenticates, and certifies the accounts of an entity.
8. An accountant provides necessary information for various managerial decisions.

Primary role Statement (1) defines the primary role of an ac- countant. Statement (6) echoes almost a similar profile, but extends an accountant's role to the production of financial statements. The work implied in these statements is that of score-keeping and the person performing such activity is known as a financial accountant (or maintenance accountant).

Decision-maker Statements (2) and (8) illustrate the accountant's role in decision-making and the management control process. These roles involve directing attention and solving problems. The functionary may be designated as a management accountant (or controller, as in the USA).

Tax planner Statement (5) underlines a narrow, specific role of an accountant. In view of high corporate tax in India, tax planning assumes a vital role in financial management. By planning the operations of the enterprise in a particular manner, the tax adviser attempts to minimize the liability of the firm by availing the concessions and incentives provided by the applicable tax laws.

External verifier Statement (7) stresses the audit, corporate watchdog, or certification role of the accountant who is not an employee of a business but who performs an external verification of the accounts. Such a functionary is a trained and qualified professional, and has an educational status and prescribed code of conduct. Chartered accountants in India, England and Wales, and certified public accountants in the USA belong to this category of accountants.

Conscience-keeper Statement (3) defines the role of an account-ant as a conscience-keeper. He/she is seen as a person whose mission is to protect and promote the interests of the enterprise. An accountant sees to it that none of the staff carries

work in an unethical way, or in a manner prejudicial to the long-term legitimate interests of the enterprise.

Manager of information Statement (4) defines an accountant as a professional and underlines his/her pre-occupation with management of information for internal use (management accounting) and for external use (financial accounting). Accounting as an information system has made it easier to comprehend the role of an accountant. Information management is not necessarily associated with the sophisticated (or high-technology) areas of computers. Small firms may 'manage' information without a substantial degree of mechanization or automation. Often, the role of accounting in a small business is not properly recognized. It is widely known that a large number of small businesses fail and do not survive beyond a few years. One of the main reasons for the failure is the lack of an adequate information system to help managers control costs, forecast cash needs, and plan growth. Organizations which have poor accounting systems often find it difficult to obtain finance from banks and outside investors.

ACCOUNTING PERSONNEL

There is hardly any organization that does not have an accountant. An accountant is involved in a wide range of activities, particularly in a large and complex organization. The exact duties of an accountant might differ in different organizations.

Accountants can be broadly divided into two categories: those who are in *public practice* and those who are in *private employment*. Public accountants are generally members of professional bodies like the Institute of Chartered Accountants of India (ICAI). In addition to conducting a financial or cost audit (in accordance with the requirements of, for example, the Companies Act), accountants also provide advisory services for designing, or improving accounting and management control systems.

Accountants in various organizations perform a variety of accounting and management control functions. Accountants at higher levels generally belong to professional accounting bodies. Accounting chiefs in different organizations, depending upon their nature of work, are designated as finance officers, internal auditors, chief accountants, or accounts officers. The term 'controller' as the head of the accounting and finance function is not very popular in India. Several large organizations, both in the public and private sectors, have controllers. This section gives the job descriptions of various positions available in the field of accounting.

Auditor

Auditors are accountants in public practice who conduct financial and/or cost audit. The auditor examines the books of accounts and reports on the company's balance sheet, profit and loss account, and profit. The auditor in a company is appointed by the shareholders to whom he/she reports.

An *internal auditor* is an employee of organization in contrast to an external auditor who is paid a fee for his/her services. An external auditor is not an employee of a company, and he/she is appointed to conduct *statutory audit*. The principal objective of a statutory audit is to ensure that the financial statements prepared by the management give a true and fair view of the company's business, and are free of discrepancies resulting from frauds and errors. The internal auditor is responsible for performing and monitoring activities, designing and operating the system of internal control, auditing the data reported to the directors of the company, and assisting external auditors. The head of the internal audit reports directly either to the chief executive or to the audit committee of the board of directors.

An internal audit includes continuous verification of entries appearing in the books of accounts with the original vouchers and proper accounting assets. Further, it attempts to ensure that the policies and procedures regarding financial matters are being complied with. Internal auditing is also concerned with administering the system of internal checks so that mistakes, innocent or intentional, are prevented from taking place.

While an internal auditor devotes his/her entire time and energy to the needs of one company, an *external auditor* serves many clients. The primary function of the external auditor is to safeguard the interests of the shareholders by an independent and impartial appraisal of the financial transactions of the company so that he/she could report on the net profit earned by the company and its financial position. An external auditor performs the role of an objective outsider. He/she expresses expert opinions on the financial condition and operating results of the client's business. Apart from shareholders, other parties such as banks, lending institutions, government agencies, etc. rely on the fairness of such financial reports in making certain decisions about a company. An auditor is bound by a set of professional regulations which include an examination on technical competence and adherence to a code of ethical conduct.

Controller

In some organizations, the chief accountant is known as the controller. The controller is the overall in-charge of financial accounting, management accounting, and tax accounting activities. He/she is responsible for internal accounting and external reporting. The external reports include reports to government revenue collection and regulatory bodies, such as the Company Law Board and the Department of Income Tax. The controller supervises the company's internal audit and control systems. In addition to processing historical data, he/she supplies accounting information to the top management concerning future operations, in line with the management's planning and control needs. Besides, he/she supplies detailed information to managers in different functional areas (such as production and marketing) and at different levels of an organization to assist them in decision-making. The responsibilities of the controller are as follows:

- Designing and operating the accounting system
- Preparing financial statements and reports
- Establishing and maintaining systems and procedures
- Supervising internal auditing and arranging for external audit

- Supervising computer applications
- Overseeing cost control
- Preparing budgets
- Making forecasts and analytical reports
- Reporting financial information to top management
- Handling tax matters and ensuring other legal compliances

Treasurer

A treasurer is the custodian and manager of all the cash and near-cash resources of the enterprise. The treasurer handles credit reviews and sets the policy for collecting receivables (from the debtors of the firm, to whom the firm has sold goods or services on credit). He/she also handles relationships with banks and other lending or financial institutions. The Financial Executive Institute (USA) makes certain distinctions between the functions of a treasurer and those of a controller (see Table 1.1).

TABLE 1.1   Distinction between the functions of a controller and a treasurer

Controller	Treasurer
Planning and control	Provision of capital
Reporting and interpreting	Investor relations
Evaluating and consulting	Short-term financing
Tax administration	Banking and custody
Government reporting	Credit and collections
Protection of assets	Investment
Economic appraisal	Insurance

Finance Director

Finance is the lifeblood of any business. Procuring financial resources and ensuring their judicious utilization are the two most important aspects of financial management. Financial management includes major decisions concerning investment, financing, dividends, and working capital.

Investment decision   It is perhaps the most important decision, because it involves the allocation of resources. It deals with assessing the risks an organization encounters in a business environment. The firm's strategy in allocating its scarce resources and planning its growth largely determines its value in the market.

Financing decision   It deals with determining the optimum financing mix, or capital structure. It examines the various methods by which a firm obtains short-term and long-term finances through alternative sources.

Dividend decision   It involves questions such as how much profit is to be retained and how much is to be distributed as dividend.

Working capital   It gives investors an idea of the company's operational efficiency. The finance director has to strike a balance between the cash requirements of the enterprise, and the needs of the shareholders for adequate returns. Working capital is calculated as:

Working Capital = Current Assets – Current Liabilities

A positive working capital indicates that the company is able to pay off its short-term liabilities. A negative working capital indicates that the company is unable to meet its short-term liabilities with its current assets.

The financial management of a large company is usually the responsibility of the finance director who may be in place of, or in addition to, the controller. Often the terms 'finance director' and 'controller' are inter-changeable, and only one of these two positions may be present in a company. The finance director is concerned with implementing the financial policy of the board of directors, managing liquidity, preparation of budgets, administration of budgetary control system, managing profitability, etc.

Though financial management is regarded as a separate area, this function is performed in several countries, including India, by the accountant (or the financial controller). Several large organizations, however, have a chief financial executive besides the chief accountant. Often, finance and accounting functions are clubbed together in small organizations.

NATURE OF ACCOUNTING FUNCTION

Accounting is a service function and the accountant's role is advisory in nature. The chief accountant holds a staff position except within the accounts department where he/she exerts authority. This is in contradiction to the roles played by the production or marketing managers who hold line authority. The role of the accountant is *advisory* in nature. He/she works through the authority of the chief executive. The accountants and or the finance department(s) do not exercise direct authority over line departments. In a decentralized structure with a number of units and divisions, the accounts manager, however, exercises functional authority over all the accounting staff deployed in different segments.

There are two facets to the role of an accountant. An accountant performs the role of a corporate watchdog for the top management, and of a helper for the middle and lower management. The accountant reports to the higher management and performs the score-keeping task of accounting. The accountant performs the role of a helper by directing managers' attention to problems, and assisting them in solving these problems. Mutual understanding and rapport between the accountant and the managers, in the tasks of attention-directing and problem-solving, can be enhanced if the accountant and the staff frequently interact with the line managers and guide them in matters concerned with preparation of budgets and control documents. This will instill confidence in line managers regarding the reliability of reports.

ACCOUNTING STANDARDS

At one time, firms and corporates followed different accounting policies and practices. It was, therefore, not possible to compare different financial statements to understand outcomes. With a view to establish reliability and comparability of financial statements prepared and presented by firms, corporates, business houses, etc., India's accounting body, that is, the Institute of Chartered Accountants of India (ICAI) developed the Accounting Standards. Accounting Standards are authoritative guidelines issued by the ICAI regarding accounting norms for measurement and treatment of accounting events and transactions. The traditional debits and credits of the accounting discipline and the modern approach of accounting equation have evolved to more reliable accounting standards and the Generally Accepted Accounting Principles (GAAP).

The US GAAP are the rules and practices of accounting applicable to firms operating in the United States. While preparing and presenting the financial statements, the US GAAP are to be followed, by all companies, whether their shares are publicly traded or are not traded in the security market. The Government Accounting Standard Board (GASB) is mandated to develop accounting standards for local and state governments. The local and state governments normally operate under a different set of assumptions, principles, and constraints. Hence, a separate set of accounting standards have been developed.

Likewise, Indian firms, corporates, companies, and business houses must adhere to the various accounting standards developed by the ICAI. In addition, Indian companies have to follow the regulations prescribed by the Companies Act, 1956. The accounting standards set by ICAI, together with the legal regulations of the Companies Act, 1956 are known as Indian GAAPs. ICAI recognized the need for harmonization of diverse accounting policies and practices, and constituted an Accounting Standard Board (ASB) in the year 1977. The specific accounting standard is mandatory from the date mentioned in the standard. Mandatory means that it is the duty of the member of the ICAI to examine that accounting standards are complied by the firm, or company, or the business entity in the presentation of financial statements.

The main aim of accounting standards is to ensure comparability, credibility, and reliability of financial statements of the firm. Comparability indicates that the financial statements of firms in the same industry are prepared in a comprehensible way, and the same accounting principles and practices are used in the preparation of financial statements. By providing uniform guidelines and structure, it creates an environment of confidence among the users of the accounting information, and also provides a true and fair view of the financial position and performance.

Advantages of Accounting Standards

A few advantages offered by accounting standards and its implementation are illustrated as follows:

1. It reduces to a reasonable extent or altogether removes confusing variations in the accounting treatment of specific items of income and expense.
2. Accounting standards look into important areas of information, which may not be required to be disclosed by law or statute, but would be useful in fair presentation.

3. It is useful to have meaningful comparisons of financial statements of different companies situated over the different places.

Disadvantages of Accounting Standards

Some important demerits or disadvantages of the accounting standards are as follows:

1. It brings rigidity in the working and does not provide the important flexibility in reporting by a particular firm.
2. The difference is reflected in the treatment of a particular transaction and its reporting, on account of difference in the traditions and legal system among the countries.
3. Accounting standards cannot override the law, Act, or any legal pronouncement.
4. The choice of better alternative of accounting treatment is eliminated.

ACCOUNTING STANDARDS AND DEVELOPMENT

To provide the benefit to all countries of the globe to achieve industrialization, to facilitate free flow of capital, merchandise, goods and commodities, etc., and to achieve the harmonization of accounting standards at the international level, the International Financial Reporting Standards (IFRS) have been introduced.

The Indian Accounting Standards are discussed in Chapter 15 (Legal and Regulatory Framework of Accounting and Auditing) in addition to the applications in respective chapters. The IFRS is explained in Chapter 18 (Contemporary Issues). The comparison between Indian Accounting Standards (Ind AS), US GAAP, and IFRS are discussed in Chapter 18 in addition to the applications in respective chapters.

The Ministry of Corporate Affairs (MCA) have notified 35 Ind AS converged with IFRS which shall be applicable to the specified class of companies. (Refer Appendix of this book)

Appendix B of this book indicates relationship between International Accounting Standards/IFRS and corresponding Ind ASs.

Appendix C of the book indicates the relationship between Ind AS (as per MCA) and AS (as per ICAI). Brief explanation of AS is provided in Appendix D of this book. Professional chartered accountants' have to adhere to the AS for professional ethics and parameters.

The detailed descriptions along with examples for each and every IFRS are given in Chapter 18 of the book.

ORGANIZATIONAL STRUCTURE OF ACCOUNTING AND FINANCE DEPARTMENT

A typical organization chart for the accounting and finance department is presented in Fig. 1.4. The person at the helm

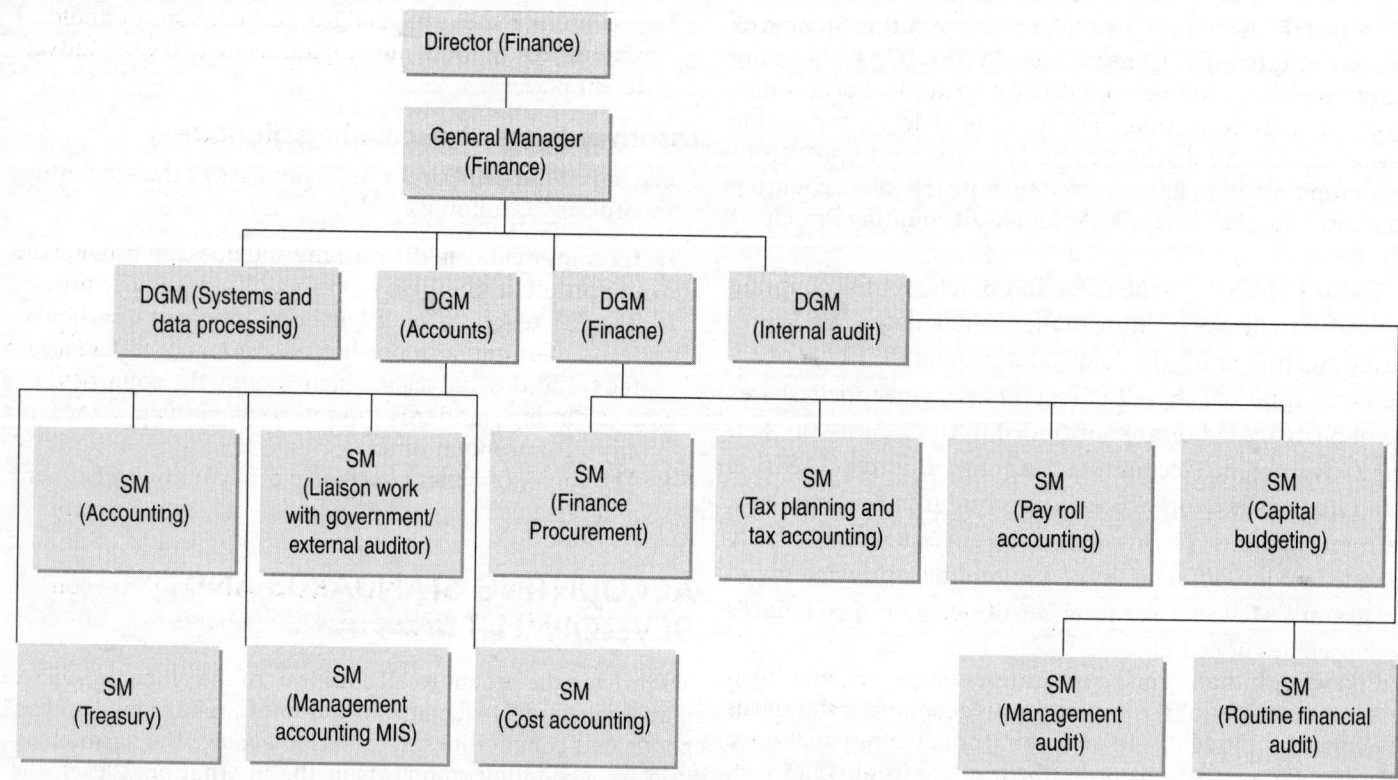

FIG. 1.4 Organization chart for accounting and finance

of affairs in the accounts and finance department is the director (finance) who is a member of the board of directors. One or more than one general manager reports to the director. Large organizations may have four or five deputy general managers in charge of different areas, such as systems and data processing, accounts, finance, and internal auditing reporting to the general manager. Some multinational companies designate general manager (finance) as president (finance or finance and accounts), and deputy general manager (finance) as vice president (finance). Each deputy general manager is assisted by a number of senior managers, who look after different components of financial accounting, tax planning and administration, management auditing, etc.

A *management audit* is a comprehensive review of the various sub-systems of the organizations, such as objectives and goals, structure, technical system, personnel policies (including succession planning), control and coordination policies and procedures, adequacy and effectiveness of communication system, etc. This type of audit is usually done by a team of people comprising the internal resource persons drawn from various functional areas and an external management consultant.

ETHICS IN ACCOUNTING AND CORPORATE GOVERNANCE

The current world economy has given rise to nearly free movement of goods, commodities, services, and capital among the countries across the globe. Hence, the commercial and economical world requires the accounting profession to provide accurate and timely financial reports, with observance of the highest standards of ethical, moral, and accounting professional code of conducts.

Professional accountants who record business transactions need to follow the guidelines based on accepted practices in accounting of their country concerned. The code of conduct has been defined and enumerated by the governing body of professional accountants with the intention to achieve the highest level of integrity by an accountant. In India, the governing body for financial accounting and auditing is the ICAI, and for cost and management accounting it is the Institute of Cost Accountants of India (ICAI). The respective code of conduct expects the members of the Institute to strictly follow the standards and maintain the highest degree of professional integrity. Integrity means honesty, impartiality, and truthfulness. It aims at the maintenance and fulfilment of professional objectivity during the performance of duties by an accountant in the role of employee, practice, business, or as an auditor. Objectivity

is the state of mind that takes into consideration all aspects relevant to a task undertaken. An accountant, according to the guideline of the Institute, should accept or perform work according to competence. He/she is required to work with skill, care, and diligence.

The ethical codes of the accounting profession have changed significantly over time due to two critical tests: first, whether the accounting rules accepted and applied are appropriate and reasonable for both the public and the firm who follow them; second, whether the practice enumerated by accounting rules are valid over the period or need to be challenged.

Corporate governance pertains to systems through which companies are directed and controlled, keeping in mind the long-term interest of stakeholders. It is a blend of good legal, regulatory, and voluntary practices that enable companies to attract financial and human capital, perform efficiently, and provide sustainable economic value to all its stakeholders.

It aims to align the interests of the company with those of its stakeholders. The incentive for companies and those who own and manage them, in adopting global governance standards, is that these standards help them to achieve a long-term sustainable partnership with their stakeholders efficiently. The principal characteristics of corporate governance are as follows:

- Transparency
- Independence
- Accountability
- Responsibility
- Fairness
- Social responsibility

The financial statements are governed by fundamental accounting assumptions of going concern, consistency, and accrual. Any deviation must be disclosed. An organization is guided by the following considerations in selecting accounting policies.

Prudence Do not recognize anticipated profits but provide for all acquired losses.

Substance over form Economic reality and financial consideration get preference over legal form in reporting.

Materiality Financial statements should disclose all material items.

Summary

- A business consists of investment of a certain amount of money in fixed assets and current assets.
- Luca Pacioli is considered to be the father of accounting.
- Accounting is the language of business.
- Accounting is the art of recording, classifying, and summarizing transactions which are of a financial nature and interpreting the results.
- Accounting is the art of recording, classifying, and summarizing transactions which are of a financial nature and interpreting the results.
- Bookkeeping is the record-keeping phase of accounting. Accounting refers to the actual process of preparing accounts. Accountancy refers to a systematic knowledge of accounting.
- Accounting provides the permanent record of each transaction.
  - Accounting information is useful to investors, financial institutions, banks, government, creditors, labour unions, managers, employees, etc.
  - Assets are valuable resources owned by an entity.
- Liabilities are measurable, future economic sacrifices arising from a company's obligations to convey assets or perform services.
- Owners' equity is the residual balance remaining after total liabilities are deducted from total assets.
- Accounts are maintained for a business entity.
- A business entity is a specific unit separate from its owner.
- Accrual basis accounting is the method of recording business events or activities when they occur.
- Cash basis accounting records transactions or business events when cash is received and paid.
- Accounting is closely related with several other disciplines such as economics, statistics, mathematics, law, and management.

Keywords

Accountancy It refers to a systematic knowledge of accounting.

Accounting It is the process of recording, analysing, classifying, and reporting of economic events in a proper manner.

Accrual basis accounting It is the method of recording business events or activities when they occur rather than when cash is received or paid.

Assets Economic resources employed by an enterprise or organization to accomplish the organization's goals are called assets.

Bookkeeping It deals with record-keeping or maintenance of books of accounting, which is often routine and clerical in nature.

Cash basis accounting It records only cash receipts and payments, recognizes increases or decreases in income only when cash is received and paid.

Cost accounting It involves the computation of the aggregate costs of products manufactured and for services provided.

Creditors The individuals, suppliers, and/or institutions who loan goods and/or services to an entity.

Entity An entity is a specific unit for which the accountant records and reports economic information.

Liabilities They are probable, measurable future economic sacrifices arising from company's obligations to provide assets or perform services to a person or other organizations outside of the company at some time in future.

Management accounting It relates to the use of financial and cost data for the purpose of evaluation of performance of the entity, reviewing policies, and planning.

Owners Those who have contributed capital for starting an enterprise. Owners have a residual interest in the enterprise.

Owner's equity It represents the stockholders' claim on the resources of the business.

 # Questions

I. Answer the following questions.

1. Define 'accounting'.
2. Who are the users of accounts?
3. State briefly the information needs of these users.
4. What are the sub-fields of accounting? Distinguish between the various sub-fields.
5. Discuss briefly the relationship of accounting with economics, statistics, mathematics, law, and management.
6. Explain in detail the role of a treasurer and a controller.
7. Explain the nature of the accounting function.

 # References

Hawkins, David F. and Jacob Cohen 2002, *The Balance Sheet*, Harvard Business School Note, pp.101–8.

Weygandt, Jerry J., Donald E. Kieso and Paul D. Kimmel 2006, *Financial Accounting,* 4th edition, Wiley-India, p.5.

Modern Approach of Accounting

Learning Objectives

After studying this chapter, you will understand

- modern approach of accounting
- accounting events and transactions
- personal and impersonal accounts
- traditional approach of accounting
- relationship between books of original entry and ledger
- meaning of an account

INTRODUCTION

The principal function of financial accounting is to furnish financial information to various interested groups. In order to supply this information, the accountant must collect and tabulate the data, summarize them, and present the results in such a way that they may be interpreted and informed managerial decisions are taken. It is necessary that adequate systematic record must be kept which will provide for the communication of the information required.

The management of an organization must rely on reports prepared by accountants for different types of information so that sound decisions can be made in the conduct of operations of the entity. Hence, it is required that each member of management should have the understanding of financial accounting, its principles, and applications of the concepts in day-to-day working of the entity. Knowledge of the fundamental principles of accounting and of the procedures followed in one type of business should contribute to an understanding of the accounting records and accounting information of others, that is, competitors, etc.

The general methods followed in recording transactions are the same for service, retail, wholesale, and manufacturing establishments, in addition to non-profit motive entities. This does not imply that there is but one accounting system which may be universally applied to all entities of whatever nature. Each business has its own peculiarities and characteristics, and modifications must be made to fit its particular requirements. The basic procedures and principles, however, are generally applicable.

To understand the significance of the financial information and the methods used for accumulating this information, it is necessary to understand the reasoning underlying the analysis of accounting transactions. Operational transactions of an entity are the basic source of financial data and the foundation on which permanent records are built.

The procedures and methods used in this chapter are intended to demonstrate the analysis of transactions to show their effect on the assets, liabilities, capital, income, and expenses. The analyses of transactions are explained keeping in mind the present state-of-the-art electronic technology and modern approach of accounting. Today, the managerial

personnel seem to get confused with the traditional approach of accounting. Majority of the software related to financial accounting and management accounting are based on the modern approach of accounting (also known as accounting equation approach or Harvard Business School approach).

MODERN APPROACH OF ACCOUNTING

Economic activities involve the transfer of existing resources from one form to another. The objective is to enhance the wealth of its owners by creating assets of greater value. The economic resources or assets belong to businesses that have lent goods, services, or assets to the enterprise.

Assets   These refer to the valuable resources owned by the entity. An entity needs cash, equipments, and other resources to operate. These resources are the assets of the entity.

Liabilities   These refer to the probable, measurable, future economic sacrifices arising from a company's obligations to transfer assets or perform services to individuals or other organizations. These are the creditor's claims on the resources of the firm (Hawkins and Cohen 2002).

Owner's equity   It is the residual balance after total liabilities are deducted from total assets. It represents the stockholders' claim on the resources of the business. There are two sources of owner's equity—(a) the amount provided by equity investors or owners, also known as capital, paid-up capital, or contributed capital, and (b) the amount retained from profits or earnings, also known as retained earnings. Any assets not claimed by creditors are claimed by equity investors. It is also known as residual equity.

An expression of the relationship between the assets and the claims is known as the accounting equation. The accounting equation (Assets = Claims) is a fundamental accounting concept.

Two distinct classes of claims are in existence in business:

- Creditors, individuals and/or institutions who loaned goods and/or services
- Owners who have invested capital in an organization and have a residual interest

In the case of liquidation or closure of the business entity, the creditors have the first claim on the assets and the residual assets become the property of the owners. Assets represent the sum of liabilities and equity.

Five Parts of Modern Approach of Accounting

The relationship can be summarized as follows:

$$
\begin{aligned}
\text{Assets} &= \text{Claims} \\
\text{Assets} &= \text{Liabilities} + \text{Owners' Equity} \\
\text{Owners' Equity} &= \text{Assets} - \text{Liabilities}
\end{aligned}
$$

Equity represents the owners' equity in a firm. Owners' equity is the residual interest in the assets of an entity that remains after deducting the liabilities from the value of the firm's assets. This description clarifies that creditors and third parties who have loaned goods, services, or funds to the firm have the first claim on the assets of the firm. It can also be depicted as

$$\text{Assets} - \text{Liabilities} = \text{Owners' Equity}$$

In case of companies, the owners' equity is known as the shareholders' funds. It consists of two components: contributed capital and retained earnings. Contributed capital refers to the capital contributed by owners' of the business or shareholders of the company. Retained earnings represent the part of the profit of the firm that is not distributed by the firm among its owners. Profit is the excess of income over expenses. The distribution of profit may be in the form of dividend (for company and co-operative societies), drawings (for partnership firm or LLP), and withdrawals (for sole-proprietorship). As the entity is separate from its owners, it is considered as one type of expense of the firm. To distinguish it from expense payable or paid to outsiders, it is treated as an implied expense, and separately treated in the Statement of Retained Earnings as explained in Chapter 3. The following equations summarize the aforementioned phrases.

$$
\begin{aligned}
\text{Owners' Equity} &= \text{Capital} + \text{Retained Earnings} \\
\text{Retained Earnings} &= \text{Income} - \text{Expenses} - \text{Drawings by Owners} \\
\text{Owners' Equity} &= \text{Capital} + (\text{Income} - \text{Expenses} - \text{Drawings}) \\
\text{Assets} &= \text{Liabilities} + \text{Capital} + \text{Retained Earnings}
\end{aligned}
$$

The following illustrations will explain the economic events that take place and their impact on the accounting equation.

■ **ILLUSTRATION 2.1**   Indicate the accounting equation following the actions taken by Raja Kapoor, during the course of his business, in the name of Raja Enterprise:

1. Started business with cash ₹20,000
2. Paid auto rickshaw charges ₹300
3. Purchased goods to sell ₹15,000
4. Sold all the goods for cash ₹16,000
5. Purchased furniture worth ₹30,000 from Shine Systems.

Everything is to be viewed as from a business concern and not from Raja Kapoor's view. This means that the person Raja Kapoor is different from the business run by him in the name of Raja Enterprises.

1. *Started business with cash: ₹20,000*
   Every transaction has two effects, because the accounting equation has to tally. Here, the two accounts are cash and Raja Kapoor's capital account. Cash is an asset account, while Raja Kapoor's capital account is a equity or capital type account. On account of this event, asset has increased by ₹20,000 and at the same time capital has also increased by the same amount.
2. *Paid auto rickshaw charges: ₹300*
   In this transaction, cash leaves the firm, and the auto rickshaw driver has received the cash for providing the services of his vehicle. The benefit of auto rickshaw charges is a one-time activity that will not provide future benefits. Hence, this expense would be considered as a revenue expense. The impact on the accounting equation would be as follows: Asset in the form of cash would decrease by ₹300 and expense would increase by ₹300.
3. *Purchased goods to sell: ₹15,000*

Goods were purchased by Raja Enterprises for selling them in future, and to earn profit from the sales activity. Hence, it is known as 'Purchases' of the firm. The goods purchased will be the asset of the firm till they are sold. Hence, the asset in the form of stock increases, and at the same time cash has been paid to the supplier of the goods resulting in decrease in the asset represented by cash balance. There is increase in assets in the form of inventory. Hence, the accounting equation tallies.

4. *Sold all the goods for cash: ₹16,000*

When the goods were sold by Raja Enterprises, the firm received cash of ₹16,000. At the same time, goods worth ₹15,000 purchased previously have been delivered to the customer. This transaction implies that the gross asset represented by cash has increased by ₹1,000. The stock is reduced by ₹15,000 and cash balance is increased to ₹16,000; hence, the net increase in the asset is ₹1,000. On the other side of the accounting equation, the outgoing of stock would be termed as expense (₹15,000) as the stock will now not be available for future benefits and the sale proceeds (₹16,000) is considered as income. Therefore, on the right-hand side of the equation, the net effect would be increased by ₹1,000.

5. *Purchased furniture from Shine Systems: ₹30,000*

Furniture is purchased by Raja Enterprises for future use. Hence, it is considered as a long-term asset of the firm. The furniture is purchased from Shine Systems, and not paid for immediately. Hence, it would be treated as a liability of the firm. This transaction results in an increase in assets in the form of furniture and also an increase in the liability of Raja Enterprises towards Shine Systems. As a result, the accounting equation is tallied.

ACCOUNTING EVENTS AND TRANSACTIONS

A *transaction* is a particular kind of economic event that involves the transfer of something between two enterprises, for example, borrowing of funds from banks.

An *accounting event* is an economic transaction that has an impact on the organization's assets, liabilities, and/or equity. The transactions may be internal, for example, using raw materials for the production of goods; or external, for example, exchanging goods with another business organization.

Effect of Financial Transactions on Accounting Equation

Business activity consists of many different events or transactions, for example, borrowing of funds, purchases of goods for business purpose, purchases of assets, and repayment of borrowed funds.

Every business transaction can be analysed by or expressed in terms of its effect on the balance sheet. Irrespective of the nature of the change, the accounting equation remains in balance. Various kinds of business transactions may result in a maximum of eight possible effects on the accounting equation. These are as follows:

1. Increase in a liability leads to decrease in another liability.
2. Increase in one item of equity leads to decrease in another item of equity.
3. Increase in equity leads to decrease in liability.
4. Increase in liability leads to decrease in equity.
5. Increase in an asset leads to increase in liability.
6. Increase in asset leads to increase in equity.
7. Decrease in asset leads to decrease in liability.
8. Decrease in asset leads to decrease in equity.
9. Decrease in one asset leads to increase in another asset.

This book blends two approaches of accounting—(a) the traditional approach of accounting (debit and credit) which is widely used in accountancy courses all over the world, and (b) the modern approach of accounting equation, which is widely used in management schools. A combination of these two approaches has been enumerated and illustrated throughout the book.

■ **ILLUSTRATION 2.2** The following table explains the direct impact of transactions on the accounting equation in the books of M/s Vivu Electricals.

Book of M/s Vivu Electricals

Transaction details	Assets	Liabilities	Capital	Income	Expense
Paid ₹500 to a creditor in cash	Decrease (–)	Decrease (–)			
Bought furniture worth ₹5,000 by paying the amount through personal cheque by Vivu	Increase (+)		Increase (+)		
Bought goods for business purpose from M/s Priya Associates for ₹2,000 but not paid for	Increase (+)	Increase (+)			
Vivu's wife invested ₹3,000 cash in the business	Increase (+)	Increase (+)			
Mr Asahi, a reputed customer, has given a cheque of ₹2,000 to clear old dues	Increase (+) and Decrease (–)				
Returned the goods purchased from M/s Aarti worth ₹1,200 not paid for till date	Decrease (–)	Decrease (–)			
Returned goods to M/s Bhavish worth ₹600 payment for which was made previously	Decrease (–) and Increase (+)				
Bought additional office premises of ₹50,000 by paying amount from the savings of Vivu	Increase (+)		Increase (+)		
Sold goods worth ₹5,000 and received cash from Francis, a customer	Increase (+)			Increase (+)	
The goods sold to Francis cost ₹4,000	Decrease (–)				Increase (+)
Given goods costing ₹2,000 to Rahim as gift	Decrease (–)				Increase (+)

PERSONAL ACCOUNTS AND IMPERSONAL ACCOUNTS

Personal accounts are generally accounts in the name of an individual (Ravi, Priety, etc.), a company or firm (Goodwill Traders, Tata Motors Limited, Oceania Builders, etc.), or a representative person's personal account (outstanding salary account, outstanding income account, prepaid expense account, etc.).

As the term indicates, impersonal accounts are generally not personal. It includes real accounts (asset type) and nominal accounts (income and expense types).

Table 2.1 displays the illustrative list of items of an event and its respective account type.

TABLE 2.1   Event types and account nature

Event type	Nature of Account	Event type	Nature of Account
Cash	Personal	Ravi's A/c	Personal
Dena Bank	Personal	Sales	Impersonal
Office supplies in stock	Personal	Office supplies used	Impersonal
Notes payable	Personal	Land	Personal
Accounts receivable	Personal	Salary paid	Impersonal
Tax payable	Personal	Income tax paid	Impersonal

According to traditional approach of accounting, accounts are classified as personal account and impersonal account. Impersonal accounts are further classified into real accounts and nominal accounts. Basic accounting equation classifies accounts into five broad categories: asset account, liability account, capital account, revenue account, and expense account. This is known as modern approach of accounting equation. Figure 2.1 presents the classification of accounts, according to the traditional and modern approaches of accounting.

TRADITIONAL APPROACH OF ACCOUNTING

According to traditional approach, the accounts maintained by an entity may be classified into (i) personal, (ii) real, or (iii) nominal. It is also known as 'Golden Rules of Accounting'.

Personal Account

It deals with accounts of individuals, such as creditors, debtors, and bank. It shows the balance due to these individuals or due from them on a particular date. The capital account is the account of the proprietor, and, therefore, it is a personal account.

Real Account

It represents assets such as plant and machinery, land and buildings, goodwill, etc. As on a particular date, this account shows the worth of the asset. These accounts are related to the assets of the firm but not to debt.

Nominal Account

It consists of different types of expense or income or loss or profit. These accounts show the amount or income earned or expense incurred for a particular period. The net result of all the nominal accounts is reflected as profit, loss, or retained earnings, which is transferred to the capital account.

Keeping in view the above classification of accounts, the rules of debit and credit are summarized in the following text by traditional accountants; which help in deciding whether an account is to be debited or credited.

The various rules of debit and credit are explained in this section. An example is also given to illustrate the concept further.

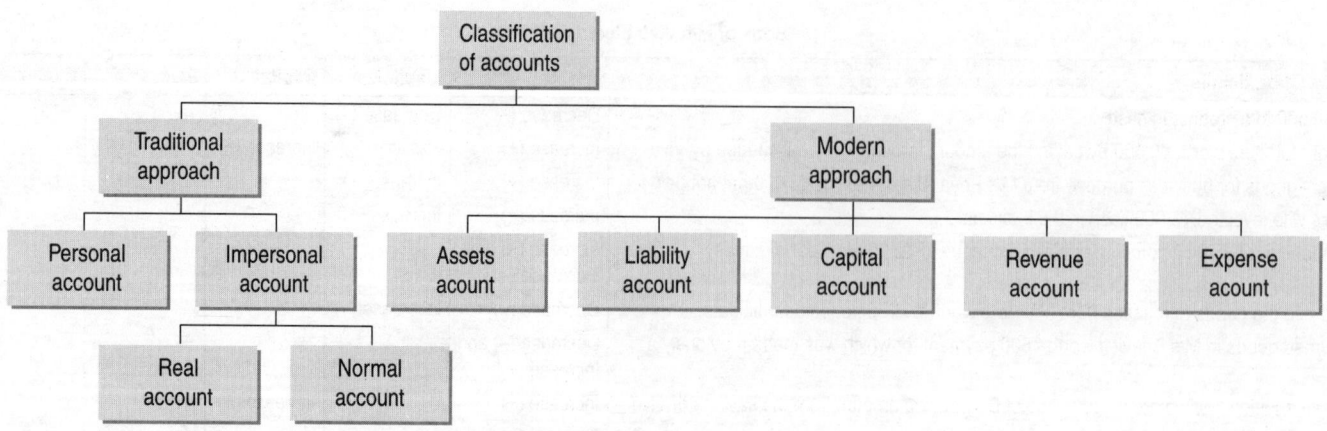

FIG. 2.1   Classification of accounts

1. For personal accounts
   Debit the receiver
   Credit the giver
2. For real accounts
   Debit what comes in
   Credit what goes out
3. For nominal accounts
   Debit all expenses and loses
   Credit all incomes and gains

■ **ILLUSTRATION 2.3** Let us apply the rules of debit and credit for a few sample transactions.

1. ABC Ltd received ₹5,000 from Gupta and Co.
   Aspect 1: • Cash of ₹5,000 is received
   • Cash account debited
   • Cash account is a real account. The rule of 'debit what comes in' applies.
   Aspect 2: The amount is given by Gupta and Co.
   • Gupta and Co. credited
   • Gupta and Co. account is a personal account
   • The rule of 'credit the giver' applies
2. PQR Ltd purchased goods worth ₹6,000 from X Co.
   Aspect 1: • Goods worth ₹6,000 are received
   • Purchase account debited
   • Purchase account is a real account
   • The rule of 'debit what comes in' applies
   Aspect 2: • The goods are supplied by X Co.

• X Co. account credited
• X Co. is a personal account
• The rule of 'credit the giver' applies

3. XYZ Ltd paid salaries worth ₹15,000 to its staff for the month through bank transfer.
   Aspect 1: • Payment of an expense of ₹15,000
   • Salaries account is debited
   • Salary account is a nominal account
   • The rule of 'debit all expenses' applies
   Aspect 2: • Bank balance is reduced by ₹15,000
   • Bank account credited
   • Bank account is a real account
   • The rule of 'credit what goes out' applies

■ **ILLUSTRATION 2.4** Determine the nature of accounts from the following transactions. State which account should be debited and which account should be credited.

1. Salary paid
2. Interest received
3. Machinery purchased for cash
4. Building sold
5. Outstanding salary
6. Received cash from Rajul
7. Proprietor introduced capital
8. Dividend received
9. Commission paid
10. Furniture purchased for cash

Solution

Transactions	Accounts Involved	Type of Account	Rules of Debit and Credit
1. Salaries	Salary A/c Cash A/c	Nominal Real	Debit all expenses and losses Credit what goes out
2. Interest received	Cash A/c Interest A/c	Real Nominal	Debit what comes in Credit all incomes and gains
3. Machinery purchase	Machinery A/c Cash A/c	Real Real	Debit what comes in Credit what goes out
4. Building sold	Cash A/c Building A/c	Real Real	Debit what comes in Credit what goes out
5. Outstanding salary	Salary A/c Outstanding salary A/c	Nominal Personal	Debit all expenses and losses Credit the giver
6. Received cash from Rajul	Cash A/c Rajul A/c	Real Personal	Debit what comes in Credit the giver
7. Capital introduced	Cash A/c Capital A/c	Real Personal	Debit what comes in Credit the giver
8. Dividend received	Cash A/c Dividend A/c	Real Nominal	Debit what comes in Credit all incomes and gains
9. Commission paid	Commission A/c Cash A/c	Nominal Real	Debit all expenses and losses Credit what goes out
10. Furniture purchased	Furniture A/c Cash A/c	Real Real	Debit what comes in Credit what goes out

■ **ILLUSTRATION 2.5** Classify the following accounts as per the traditional approach and the modern approach.

1.	Stock	2.	Loan
3.	Insurance	4.	Salary
5.	Interest	6.	Bank
7.	Cash	8.	Capital
9.	Prepaid interest	10.	Salary outstanding
11.	Drawings	12.	Bank overdraft
13.	Salary prepaid	14.	Fixtures
15.	Bills receivables	16.	Machinery
17.	Building	18.	Goodwill
19.	Sale of goods		

Solution

Transaction		Traditional approach	Modern approach
1. Stock	=	Real account	Asset
2. Loan	=	Personal account	Liability
3. Insurance	=	Nominal account	Expense
4. Salary	=	Nominal account	Expense
5. Interest	=	Nominal account	Expense
6. Bank	=	Personal account	Asset
7. Cash	=	Real account	Asset
8. Capital	=	Personal account	Capital
9. Prepaid interest	=	Personal account	Asset
10. Salary outstanding	=	Personal account	Liability
11. Drawings	=	Personal account	Capital
12. Bank overdraft	=	Personal account	Liability
13. Salary prepaid	=	Personal account	Asset
14. Fixtures	=	Real account	Asset
15. Bills receivables	=	Real account	Asset
16. Machinery	=	Real account	Asset
17. Building	=	Real account	Asset
18. Goodwill	=	Real account	Asset
19. Sale of goods	=	Nominal account	Income

RELATIONSHIP BETWEEN BOOKS OF ORIGINAL ENTRY AND LEDGER

The books of original entry and the ledger are the most important and closely interrelated books of an entity. Business transactions are recorded first in the journal (book of original entry) and then transferred to the ledger. The journal records transactions in a chronological order, while the ledger records transactions in a classified form.

A journal is not useful in answering questions such as 'What is the balance of a particular party at a certain date?' Questions such as these may be answered by referring to the ledger, which summarizes the cumulative effect of transactions recorded individually in the journal into an appropriate account in the ledger.

Both the journal and the ledger serve as important books in a firm's accounting cycle. The important points that differentiate the journal and the ledger are provided in Table 2.2.

THE ACCOUNT

A ledger is a set of accounts. It contains all accounts of the business firm—real, nominal, and personal. It may be kept in either of two forms—(a) bound ledger or (b) loose leaf ledger.

A ledger is the main or principal book of accounts. The bound ledger is inflexible, in that new accounts or old accounts must be placed where additional space for blank pages is available. The loose leaf ledger is more flexible, and permits rearrangement of the account, if necessary. A new account may be placed where desired and additional space may be provided for an account merely by inserting a new sheet along with the old.

An account is a standardized format used to maintain separate records and to accumulate data for each of the individual items to facilitate the preparation of periodical financial statements, and to provide a continuous check on the accuracy of the recording of transactions.

The account (of an item) shows

- the account title, such as machinery account;
- a place to record increases and decreases in monetary amounts in the account (may be on the left or the right of the T vertical bar);
- the date and descriptive narration; and
- cross-references to other accounting records.

The specimen format of a ledger account is presented in Exhibit 2.1.

TABLE 2.2 Difference between journal and ledger

Journal	Ledger
1. Journal is the book of original or first entry.	1. Ledger is the book of second entry.
2. It is the book of chronological record.	2. It is the book of analytical record.
3. The process of recording in a journal is known as journalizing.	3. The process of recording in ledger is known as posting.
4. Journal as a book is supported by greater sources of evidence.	4. Ledger is dependent on journal.
5. It focuses on recording transactions.	5. It focuses on the process of classification or grouping of different heads of accounts.
6. Journalizing is a continuous process.	6. The process of posting in ledger is done according to the needs of the business.

EXHIBIT 2.1 Ledger Account

Dr. (Add/ Less)				Name of Account...............			Cr. (Add/Less)
Date	Particulars	J.F.*	Amount (₹)	Date	Particulars	J.F.*	Amount (₹)
	To.....				By.......		
	To.....				By.......		
	To.....				By.......		
	Total				Total		

(*J.F. means journal folio number)

Alternatively, a ledger account can be prepared in the format as depicted in Exhibit 2.2.

EXHIBIT 2.2 Ledger Account

Name of Account............

Date	Particulars	J.F. No.	Dr. (Add/Less) (₹)	Cr. (Add/Less) (₹)	Balance Amount (₹)

Considering today's commercial and reporting culture for tabulation and summarization of accounting transactions, which are being used throughout this book, Exhibit 2.2 is being prepared.

The terms 'debit' and 'credit' are used to describe the left side and the right side of an account. The verb 'to debit' means 'to make an entry on the left side of an account', and the verb 'to credit' means 'to make an entry on the right side of an account'. The noun 'debit' is derived from the Latin word 'debitur', which means 'debtor'. The noun 'credit' is derived from the Latin word 'creditor', which means 'lender'. Apparently, the abbreviations 'Dr.' and 'Cr.' came from the first and last letters of the words 'debit' and 'credit'. In accounting, the words 'debit' and 'credit' do not mean 'debtor' and 'creditor'. The abbreviations 'Dr.' and 'Cr.' are used in place of 'debit' and 'credit'. In some accounts, increases are recorded on the left side (debit side) of the account, and decreases are recorded on the right side (credit side) of the account. In other accounts, the converse is true. It means debit and credit by themselves to a specific account does not determine whether the debits or credits represent increases or decreases.

Debit refers to entry on the left side of an account. Credit refers to entry on the right side of an account.

The double-entry system is designed so that total debits always equal total credits. The recording of transactions can be checked for accuracy by verifying that the debits and credits are equal. The entire list of accounts can be checked by verifying that the total of all debits is equal to the total of all credits.

For any given account, the difference between the debit and credit amounts is known as account balance.

The double-entry system cannot assure complete accuracy. The selection of a wrong account by an accountant at the time of recording the transaction cannot be traced. The double-entry system has proved to be effective in eliminating or reducing incomplete entries, transposed or incorrect amounts, and inaccurate entries in accounts.

Assets are equal to claims.

There are two fundamental equality requirements of the double-entry accounting system.

1. The equality of the basis accounting equation

    (Assets = Claims) must be maintained.

2. Total debits must equal total credits.

The recording rules are as follows:

1. Debit increases assets and decreases liabilities and equity.
2. Credit increases liabilities and equity and decreases assets.
3. Equity is increased by revenues and decreased by expenses.

The modern approach of accounting equation identifies the accounts and explains them in broad terms.

1. Assets are the firm's resources. Examples are cash, stock of goods, land, building, etc.
2. Liabilities are the firm's debts to outside creditors.
3. Capital, or owner's equity, is the owners' investment in the firm. It may increase or decrease.

Since capital is affected by expenses and gains, it has two more categories.

1. Expenses are accounts that show the amount spent or lost in carrying out business activities.
2. Revenues are accounts that show the amounts earned by the firm.

Retained earning is the excess of income over expense.

According to the modern approach of accounting equation, the impact of debit and credit entry is as follows:

1. Asset account: Debit side shows increases
   Credit side shows decreases
   Normal balance is debit
2. Liabilities account: Debit side shows decreases
   Credit side shows increases
   Normal balance is credit
3. Capital account: Debit side shows decreases
   Credit side shows increases
   Normal balance is credit
4. Revenue account: Debit side shows decreases
   Credit side shows increases
   Normal balance is credit
5. Expenses account: Debit side shows increases
   Credit side shows decreases
   Normal balance is debit

The following table provides a summary of the impact of a debit entry and a credit entry on all account categories. For example, an accountant will record a debit entry to increase an asset account and to decrease a revenue account. The summary of the rules are as under.

	Debit	Credit	Credit	Credit	Debit
↑	Assets	Liabilities	Capital account	Revenue	Expenses
↓	Credit	Debit	Debit	Debit	Credit

Normal balance refers to the positive balance of an account. For any account, generally speaking, the total of the increases to the account exceeds the total of decreases to the account. Generally, the resulting balance is a positive balance rather than a negative balance.

Remember that every financial transaction gives rise to two accounting entries, one is debit and the other is credit, as shown below:

To Own/Have Debit	To Owe Credit
Asset increases	Asset decreases
E.g., New office furniture	E.g., Pay out cash
Capital liability decreases	Capital liability increases

To Own/Have Debit	To Owe Credit
E.g., Pay a certificate	E.g., Buy goods on credit
Income decreases	Income increases
E.g., Cancel a sale	E.g., Make a sale
Expense increases	Expense decreases
E.g., Incur advertising costs	E.g., Cancel a purchase
Left hand side	Right hand side

The example given in this section illustrates the effect of various transactions on the accounting equation. This method is widely known as the modern approach of accounting equation.

Conceptual Transaction Analysis

The following example of thirteen transactions of Shine Ltd will aid in understanding the modern approach of accounting equation.

■ **ILLUSTRATION 2.6** On 1 January 2019, a group of individuals form a business and call it 'Shine Ltd'. The following accounting events and transactions occurred.

1. Owners provide assets: The owners contributed ₹1,00,000 in cash to Shine Ltd. The process of transferring assets to the business is referred to as an investment by the owners.

	Assets		Liabilities		+ Equity
Opening balance (OB)					
Effect of investment	+ 1,00,000		nil		+ 1,00,000
Closing balance (CB)	1,00,000	=	nil		+ 1,00,000

An owner's contribution to capital can be named as investment by the owner in the firm. It increases the balance in cash and bank account in the form of asset (debit asset account), and in turn also increases the owner's capital in case of a firm or shareholder's capital in case of a company (credit the capital account).

If the owner invested in assets such as furniture, computer equipment, stock, for the firm, the appropriate asset account balance would increase, and the capital account balance would also increase by the same amount.

2. Creditors provide assets: The business acquires inventory worth ₹60,000 from creditors.

	Assets		= Liabilities		+ Equity
OB	1,00,000		= nil		+ 1,00,000
Effect of borrowing	+ 60,000		= +60,000		+ nil
CB	1,60,000		= 60,000		+ 1,00,000

The purchase of inventory, that is, business goods on credit, increases the asset account titled purchase or stock (debit purchase or stock account) and also increases the liability account titled creditors or accounts payable (credit creditors account).

The inventory is considered as an asset because it may not be used in the current period, and hence the benefits will be available in future. Entries in creditors or accounts payable are made when there is a gap between the time of purchase and the payment.

3. Sale of business goods: The enterprise received ₹1,00,000 for selling business goods to a customer.

	Assets		= Liabilities	+ Contributed capital	+ Retained earnings
	Other assets +	Revenue	= Liabilities	+ Contributed capital	+ Retained earnings
OB	1,60,000		= 60,000	+ 1,00,000	+ nil
Effect of revenue		+ 1,00,000	= nil	+ nil	+ 1,00,000
CB	1,60,000	+ 1,00,000	= 60,000	+ 1,00,000	+ 1,00,000

Revenue received in cash will increase the asset account balance (debit cash or bank account) and also increase the retained earnings in the form of income earned (sales or revenue or income account credited). In this transaction, revenue is recognized as the firm provides their service or business goods to the customer and simultaneously receives the payment from the customer.

4. Assets used to produce revenue (expense): Shine Ltd had used ₹70,000 (consumption of stock of ₹60,000 and cash expenses paid ₹10,000) of its assets in order to earn ₹1,00,000 as revenue shown in previous transaction.

	Assets	= Liabilities	+ Contributed capital	+ Retained earnings
OB	26,000	= 60,000	+ 1,00,000	+ 1,00,000
Effect of expenses	– 70,000	= nil	+ nil	– 70,000
CB	1,90,000	= 60,000	+ 1,00,000	+ 30,000

The utilization of inventory, that is, stock, will reduce the asset account in the form of purchases or stock (credit the purchase or stock account), and also reduce the retained earnings of the firm. A reduction in the retained earnings of a firm means an increase in the expenses of the firm. Hence, the expenses account in the form of cost of goods sold will increase (debit the expense account named as cost of goods sold account).

The payment of cash of ₹10,000 to meet the transaction needs would be treated as an expense, and in turn could be charged in the cost of goods sold account or can be accounted in a separately named account to exercise better control and information availability. This will reduce the asset account balance in the form of cash or bank, and also increase the expense of the firm. Hence, the cash account balance will be reduced by ₹10,000 (credit cash account), while the cost of goods sold account balance will be increased (debit the cost of goods sold account).

When more than two accounts are involved in the transaction, the entry involved in the books of accounts is known as a compound entry.

5. Shine Ltd distributes ₹20,000 of assets to its owners.

	Assets	= Liabilities	+ Contributed capital	+ Retained earnings
OB	1,90,000	= 60,000	+ 1,00,000	+ 30,000
Effect of expenses	– 20,000	= nil	+ nil	– 20,000
CB	1,70,000	= 60,000	+ 1,00,000	+ 10,000

Payment of cash to the owners to meet their household and personal expenses decreases the retained earnings of the firm. Similarly, dividend is considered as reduction in the retained earnings of the company. This would result in a reduction in the asset account known as cash or bank balance (cash account would be credited) and also decrease the owners' equity (expenses account will be debited, in the name of drawings or withdrawal or dividend account).

It can thus be seen that no businessman will withdraw the capital to meet day-to-day personal expenses. Generally, the withdrawal is done from the excess of income over expense from the firm's activities.

6. Shine Ltd billed a customer for ₹1,00,000 towards service provided on credit terms.

	Assets		= Liabilities	+ Contributed capital	+ Retained earnings
	Other assets +	A/c receivables	= Liabilities	+ Contributed capital	+ Retained earnings
OB	1,70,000		= 60,000	+ 1,00,000	+ 10,000
Effect of credit sales		+ 1,00,000	= nil	+ nil	+ 1,00,000
CB	1,70,000	+ 1,00,000	= 60,000	+ 1,00,000	+ 1,10,000

Revenue billed to a customer increases the asset account in the form of debtors or accounts receivable (debit the debtors account) and also the retained earnings in the form of income account (credit the sales or revenue account).

A debtor account is used to indicate the future realizable from the customers to whom business goods or services are provided on credit. Revenue or income is booked at the time when the right to own is transferred to the customer, immaterial of whether payment is received or not at the time of transferring the right of business goods and services to the customer.

7. Shine Ltd collected ₹1,00,000 from a customer who had been billed in a previous transaction.

	Assets		= Liabilities	+ Contributed capital	+ Retained earnings
	Other assets +	A/c receivables	= Liabilities	+ Contributed capital	+ Retained earnings
OB	1,70,000 +	1,00,000	= 60,000	+ 1,00,000	+ 1,10,000
Effect of cash collection	1,00,000 –	1,00,000	= nil	+ nil	+ nil
CB	2,70,000 +	nil	= 60,000	+ 1,00,000	+ 1,10,000

Collection of an amount from debtors billed previously increases the balance in the asset account in the form of cash or bank balance (debit the cash or bank account). It also decreases the balance of the asset account named as debtors or accounts receivable (credit the debtors account).

The revenue related to this transaction is already recorded as revenue or income in transaction no. 6; hence, no revenue is recorded in this transaction. The business revenue is recorded when the property right of the goods is given up.

8. Shine Ltd employed one clerk on 1 January 2019 and incurred a salary obligation of ₹20,000 as on 31 January 2019.

	Assets	= Liabilities		+ Contributed capital	+ Retained earnings
	Other assets	= Other liabilities	+ Salaries payable	+ Contributed capital	+ Retained earnings
OB	2,70,000	= 60,000		+ 1,00,000	+ 1,10,000
Recognized expense/ liabilities	nil	= nil	+ 20,000	+ nil	– 20,000
CB	2,70,000	= 60,000	+ 20,000	+ 1,00,000	+ 90,000

The salary account will be debited, indicating a reduction in the retained earnings of Shine Ltd. It has to pay its employees for services rendered by them; it is therefore a type of period expense for the firm. As the payment is still not made by the firm to the employees, it would be treated as a liability of the firm. Hence, a salary payable account would be created in the form of a liability account and credited to show the increase in liability of Shine Ltd.

The expense is recorded as the benefit is received, and the amount is payable by the firm.

9. Shine Ltd paid ₹20,000 in cash to its clerk towards salary.

	Assets	= Liabilities		+ Contributed capital	+ Retained earnings
	Other assets	= Other liabilities	+ Salaries payable	+ Contributed capital	+ Retained earnings
OB	2,70,000	= 60,000	+ 20,000	+ 1,00,000	+ 90,000
Made cash payment	– 20,000	= nil	– 20,000	+ nil	+ nil
CB	2,50,000	= 60,000	+ nil	+ 1,00,000	+ 90,000

This transaction would reduce the asset account balance in the form of cash (credit the cash account) and also reduce the liability of the firm in the form of salary payable (debit the salary payable account).

The expense related to this transaction is already recorded as expense in transaction no. 8; hence, no expense in the form of salaries is recorded in this transaction.

10. Shine Ltd received ₹80,000 cash, in exchange, and it agreed to provide services after one month.

	Assets	= Liabilities		+ Contributed capital	+ Retained earnings
	Other assets + Cash	= Other liabilities	+ Unearned revenue	+ Contributed capital	+ Retained earnings
OB	2,50,000	= 60,000	+ nil	+ 1,00,000	+ 90,000
Realized cash	nil + 80,000	= nil	+ 80,000	+ nil	+ nil
CB	2,50,000 + 80,000	= 60,000	+ 80,000	+ 1,00,000	+ 90,000

Revenue received in advance from the customer increases the balance of an asset account known as a cash or bank account, and would also result in an increase in the liability of the firm. Shine Ltd would be liable to provide service to its customers in future, or refund the amount to the customer in case of failure to provide the service. Hence, it would be treated in parallel as a liability in the form of revenue received in advance. Thus, the cash account will be debited, and a pre-received revenue account would be credited.

11. Shine Ltd provided services to the customer worth ₹80,000, which was received earlier, as per transaction no. 10.

	Assets = Liabilities				+Contributed capital +Retained earnings	
	Other assets + Cash	= Other liabilities	+ Unearned revenue	+Contributed capital	+Retained earnings	
OB	2,50,000 + 80,000	= 60,000	+ 80,000	+1,00,000	+ 90,000	
Realized revenue cash	nil + nil	= nil	– 80,000	+nil	+ 80,000	
CB	2,50,000 + 80,000	= 60,000	+ nil	+1,00,000	+1,70,000	

Shine Ltd has provided services to customers from whom the amount has been received in advance as per transaction no. 10. This would result in an increase in the retained earnings, leading to an increase in the revenue or income as well as the asset account in a normal situation. However, in this transaction, the amount has already been received in advance, and hence there is a decrease in liability in the form of pre-received revenue instead of an increase in the asset account balance. Thus, the pre-received revenue account will be debited and the revenue or income account will be credited.

12. Shine Ltd paid cash to purchase ₹2,00,000 of office equipment for its business.

	Assets		= Liabilities	+ Contributed capital + Retained earnings	
	Other assets + Cash or bank A/c		= Other liabilities	+ Contributed capital	+ Retained earnings
OB	3,30,000		= 60,000	+ 1,00,000	+ 1,70,000
Purchased assets	+ 2,00,000	– 2,00,000	= nil	+ nil	+ nil
CB	5,30,000	– 2,00,000	= 60,000	+ 1,00,000	+ 1,70,000

The purchase of office equipment in cash will increase the balance in one asset account (office equipment account) and simultaneously reduce the balance in another asset account (cash or bank account).

Office equipment with a debit will increase the asset account balance, and cash with a credit will reduce the asset account balance. In short, the impact of this transaction would be noticed only on one side of the equation.

13. Shine Ltd had bought inventory worth ₹60,000 on credit (as per the second transaction). The creditors demanded ₹6,000 towards interest. Shine Ltd agreed to pay in future.

	Assets	= Liabilities		+ Contributed capital + Retained earnings	
	Other assets	= Other liabilities	+ Provision for interest	+ Contributed capital	+ Retained earnings
OB	3,30,000	= 60,000		+ 1,00,000	+ 1,70,000
Accrual of interest expenses	nil	= nil	+ 6,000	+ nil	– 6,000
CB	3,30,000	= 60,000	+ 6,000	+ 1,00,000	+ 1,64,000

This transaction involved the imposition of additional charges by a third party on the firm on account of non-fulfilment of commitment. This may be a normal business transaction or an abnormal business event. In either case, management normally creates separate expense accounts for such events to have a proper internal control and also to gain a proper understanding of financial statements. This will reduce the retained earnings of the firm, which means that it would be charged as an expense of the period. In this transaction, it would be treated as an expense named as penalty charges account (expense account will be debited). As a future payment has been agreed upon by Shine Ltd, its liability towards the supplier will be increased (credit the supplier account).

Summary of Conceptual Transaction Analysis

Transaction No.	Assets				Liabilities				Contributed Capital	Income		Expenses			
	Cash	Inventory	Accounts Receivables	Office Equipments	Creditors	Salary Payable	Unearned Revenue	Interest Payable	Capital	Sales Income	Service Income	COGS	Withdrawal	Salary	Interest
1	1,00,000								1,00,000						
2		60,000			60,000										
3	1,00,000									1,00,000					
4	(10,000)	(60,000)										70,000			
5	(20,000)												20,000		
6			1,00,000								1,00,000				
7	1,00,000		(1,00,000)												
8						20,000								20,000	
9	(20,000)					(20,000)									
10	80,000						80,000								
11							(80,000)				80,000				
12	(2,00,000)			2,00,000											
13								6,000							6,000
Total	**1,30,000**	**–**	**–**	**2,00,000**	**60,000**	**–**	**–**	**6,000**	**1,00,000**	**1,00,000**	**1,80,000**	**70,000**	**20,000**	**20,000**	**6,000**

Summarization of Value as per Accounts Type

Assets		Expenses	
Cash	1,30,000	COGS	70,000
Inventory	–	Withdrawal	20,000
Accounts receivables	–	Salary	20,000
Office equipments	2,00,000	Interest	6,000
Total Assets	**3,30,000**	**Total Expenses**	**1,16,000**

Liabilities

		Impact on Five Part of Modern Approach of Accounting	
Creditors	60,000	Assets	
Salary payable	–	**Equals to Liabilities**	**66,000**
Unearned revenue	–	**Capital**	**1,00,000**
Interest payable	6,000	**Retained Earnings**	
Total Liabilities	**66,000**	Income	2,80,000
Capital	**1,00,000**	*Less:* Expenses	1,16,000

Impact on Five Part of Modern Approach of Accounting

Assets 3,30,000

Equals to Liabilities 66,000

Capital 1,00,000

Retained Earnings — Income 2,80,000; *Less:* Expenses 1,16,000 → 1,64,000

Total 3,30,000

Hence equation talled, as per five parts.

Income

Sales income	1,00,000
Service income	1,80,000
Total Income	**2,80,000**

■ **ILLUSTRATION 2.7**   Show the effect on accounting equation and also prepare the balance sheet based on the following transactions.

Particulars	Amount (₹)
1. Ahmed started business with cash	50,000
2. Purchased goods on credit	4,000
3. Purchased goods for cash	1,000
4. Purchased furniture	500
5. Paid rent	200
6. Withdrew money for private use	700
7. Received interest	100
8. Sold goods on credit (cost ₹500) for	700
9. Paid to creditors	400
10. Paid salaries	200

Solution

Particulars	Assets									=	Liabilities	+	Capital
	Cash	+	Stock of Goods	+	Debtors	+	Furniture	=			Creditors	+	Capital
1. Ahmed started business with ₹50,000	50,000	+	0	+	0	+	0	=			0	+	50,000
2. Purchased goods on credit ₹4,000	0	+	4,000	+	0	+	0	=			4,000	+	0
3. New equation	50,000	+	4,000	+	0	+	0	=			4,000	+	50,000
4. Purchased goods for cash ₹1,000	(–)1,000	+	1,000	+	0	+	0	=			0	+	0
5. New equation	49,000	+	5,000	+	0	+	0	=			4,000	+	50,000
6. Purchased furniture ₹500	(–)500	+	0	+	0	+	500	=			0	+	0
7. New equation	48,500	+	5,000	+	0	+	500	=			4,000	+	50,000
8. Paid rent ₹200	(–)200	+	0	+	0	+	0	=			0	–	200
9. New equation	48,300	+	5,000	+	0	+	500	=			4,000	+	49,800
10. Withdrew for private use ₹700	(–)700	+	0	+	0	+	0	=			0	–	700
11. New equation	47,600	+	5,000	+	0	+	500	=			4,000	+	49,100
12. Received interest ₹100	+100	+	0	+	0	+	0	=			0	+	100
13. New equation	47,700	+	5,000	+	0	+	500	=			4,000	+	49,200
14. Sold goods on credit costing ₹500 for ₹700		–	500	+	700	+	0	=				+	200
15. New equation	47,700	+	4,500	+	700	+	500	=			4,000	+	49,400
16. Paid to creditors ₹400	(–) 400	+	0	+	0	+	0	=			(–) 400	+	0
17. Paid salaries ₹200	(–) 200	+	0	+	0	+	0	=			0	–	200
18. Total	47,100	+	4,500	+	700	+	500	=			3,600	+	49,200

 SUMMARY

- Owners' equity is the residual balance remaining after total liabilities are deducted from total assets.
- The fundamental accounting equation is
     Assets = Liabilities + Equity.
- Accounts are maintained for a business entity.
- A business entity is a specific unit separate from its owner.
- An account is a standardized format used to record information on individual transactions to facilitate the preparation of periodical financial statements and to provide a continuous check on the accuracy of the recording of the transactions.
- For any given account, the difference between debit and credit amounts is known as account balance.
- The modern approach of accounting equation classifies accounts into five types and uses the following method.

Account type	Debit side	Credit side
1. Assets	Add	Less
2. Liabilities	Less	Add
3. Capital	Less	Add
4. Revenue	Less	Add
5. Expenses	Add	Less

- The traditional approach classifies accounts into three types and uses the following method.

Account type	Debit side	Credit side
1. Real	What comes in	What goes out
2. Personal	The receiver	The giver
3. Nominal	All expenses and losses	All incomes and gains

 # KEYWORDS

Account An account is a standardized format used to record information on individual transactions to facilitate the preparation of periodical financial statements and to provide a continuous check on the accuracy of the recording of the transactions.

Credit It is an entry on the right side of an account.

Debit It is an entry on the left side of an account.

Journal It is a book that contains a chronological record of transactions.

Ledger A ledger is the grouping of accounts that are used to prepare financial statements for a business or an entity. A ledger is a principal book of entry although not an independent record.

Nominal account It consists of different types of expense, income, loss, or profit.

Personal account It deals with accounts of individuals such as creditors, debtors, bank, etc.

Prime document It is the document in which transactions are recorded; it is also called voucher document or source document.

Real account It represents accounts such as plant and machinery, land and building, goodwill, etc.

SOLVED PROBLEMS

■ **PROBLEM 2.1** Classify the following accounts as per modern approach.

1. Cash account
2. Furniture account
3. Machinery account
4. Salaries account
5. Interest account
6. Carriage account
7. Alka Stores account (Supplier)
8. Bhupen Dalal's account (Customer)
9. Mr B.S. Shah (Loan provider)
10. Loose tools
11. Bank of India's account
12. Octroi account
13. L.I.C's A/c
14. Bombay University
15. Building account
16. Rent account
17. Stock of stationery account
18. Stationery account
19. Bank loan A/c
20. Coal, gas account
21. Depreciation account
22. Sports Club account
23. Capital account
24. Drawings account
25. Bad debts account
26. Amul Dairy account
27. Freight account
28. Carriage inward account
29. Insurance premium
30. Repairs account
31. Dividend received account
32. Discount received account
33. Punjab Govt.'s account
34. Bad debt recovery account
35. Discount allowed account

Solution

Name of Account	Modern Approach	Remark
1. Cash account	Asset A/c	It is an asset
2. Furniture account	Asset A/c	It is a fixed asset
3. Machinery account	Asset A/c	It is a fixed asset
4. Salaries account	Expense A/c	It is an expense
5. Interest account	Expense A/c OR Income A/c	It is an expense OR It may be an income also
6. Carriage account	Expense A/c	It is an expense
7. Alka Stores account (Supplier)	Liability A/c	It is a trading firm from whom supplies are purchased
8. Bhupen Dalal's account (Customer)	Asset A/c	He is a natural person to whom goods are sold
9. Mr B.S. Shah (Loan/Lender)	Liability A/c	He is a lender
10. Loose tools	Asset A/c	It is an asset
11. Bank of India's account	Asset A/c OR Liability A/c	It is an artificial entity. If the amount is deposited then it would be asset account, if the amount is borrowed then it would be a liability account.
12. Octroi account	Expense A/c	It is an expense
13. L.I.C's account	Asset A/c	It is a legal entity. It is a future receivable from LIC.
14. Bombay University	Asset A/c OR Liability A/c	It is a legal entity. If the amount is receivable then it would be an asset account. If the amount is payable then it would be a liability account.
15. Building account	Asset A/c	It is an asset
16. Rent account	Expense A/c	It is an expense
17. Stock of stationery account	Asset A/c	It is an asset
18. Stationery account	Expense A/c	It is an expense

Name of Account	Modern Approach	Remark
19. Bank loan account	Liability A/c	It is an account of bank, which is a legal entity
20. Coal, gas account	Expense A/c	It is a production expense for a firm
21. Depreciation account	Expense A/c	It is a loss to business on account of utilization of asset.
22. Sports club account	Asset A/c OR Liability A/c	Club is an artificial entity. If the amount is receivable then it would be an asset account. If the amount is payable then it would be a liability account
23. Capital account	Capital A/c	It is the account of the owner of business
24. Drawings account	Expense A/c	It is the account of the owner of business
25. Bad Debts account	Expense A/c	It is a loss suffered by firm on account of non receipt of funds from the customer to whom credit sale was made.
26. Amul Dairy account	Asset A/c OR Liability A/c	Amul dairy is an artificial entity. If the amount is receivable then it would be an asset account. If the amount is payable then it would be a liability account.
27. Freight account	Expense A/c	It is an expense
28. Carriage inward account	Expense A/c	It is an expense
29. Insurance premium	Expense A/c	It is an expense
30. Repairs account	Expense A/c	It is an expense
31. Dividend received account	Income A/c	It is an income
32. Discount received account	Income A/c	It is a gain
33. Punjab Govt.'s account	Asset A/c OR Liability A/c	Punjab Govt. is an artificial entity. If the amount is receivable then it would be an asset account. If the amount is payable then it would be a liability account
34. Bad debt recovery account	Income A/c	It is an income, in the form of recovery of the amount previously accounted as an expense.
35. Discount allowed account	Expense A/c	It is an expense as firm has agreed to receive less amount from the giver on account of business parameters.

■ **PROBLEM 2.2** Give the names of accounts affected in the following transactions as per modern approach in the firm's book of Mr K. Kapoor.

1. Mr Kapoor started business with ₹10,000 cash and purchased a chair for ₹100.
2. Borrowed ₹2,000 from Mehak Poonawalla on the same day.
3. Opened a bank account with ₹2,000.
4. Purchased goods for cash of ₹1,800.
5. Purchased goods from Chirag for ₹800.
6. Sold goods to Tarun for ₹400.
7. Sold goods for cash of ₹300.
8. Paid insurance premium of the shop by a cheque for ₹50.
9. Purchased stationery for ₹30.
10. Bought a table for ₹200 from Modern Furniture Mart.
11. Paid rent of ₹100.
12. Mr Kapoor withdrew ₹200 for personal use.
13. Received in cash ₹50 for commission.
14. Paid ₹10 for carriage to Ramvilas.
15. Paid salary of ₹200 to clerk Dinesh.
16. Bought goods worth ₹500.
17. Sold goods for ₹300.
18. Purchased goods of ₹200 from Bharati for cash.
19. Sold goods for cash to Anu for ₹100.
20. Received an order for goods from Dhanraj for ₹200.
21. Sent an order for supplying goods to Pritam worth ₹300.

Solution

No.	Names of Accounts	Modern Approach
1	Cash account	Asset
	Capital account	Capital
	Furniture account	Asset
2	Cash account	Asset
	Master's loan account	Loan

No.	Names of Accounts	Modern Approach
3	Bank account	Asset
	Cash account	Asset
4	Goods account (Purchase)	Asset
	Cash account	Asset
5	Goods account (Purchase)	Asset
	Chirag's account	Liability
6	Tarun's account	Asset
	Goods account (Sales)	Income
7	Cash account	Asset
	Goods account (Sales)	Income
8	Insurance premium account	Expense
	Bank account	Asset
9	Stationery account	Asset
	Cash account	Asset
10	Furniture account	Asset
	Modern Fur. Mart account	Liability
11	Rent account	Expense
	Cash account	Asset
12	Drawings account	Expense
	Cash account	Asset
13	Cash account	Asset
	Commission account	Income
14	Carriage account	Expense
	Cash account	Asset
15	Salary account	Expense
	Cash account	Asset
16	Purchases account	Asset
	Cash account	Asset
17	Cash account	Asset
	Goods (Sales) account	Income
18	Goods (Purchases) account	Asset
	Cash account	Asset
19	Cash account	Asset
	Goods (Sales) account	Income
20	It is not a transaction	–
21	It is not a transaction	–

■ **PROBLEM 2.3** Provide explanations for effects of transactions in terms of an accounting equation as provided in the following table.

Business Activity (Transaction)	Assets	Liabilities	Owners' Equity
1. Investment by owner	Cash Dr (+)		Share capital Cr (+)
2. Borrowed money from bank	Cash Dr (+)	Notes Payable or Loan Cr (+)	
3. Purchased inventory for cash	Inventory Cash Dr (+) Cr (−)		
4. Purchased machinery on credit from Mr Y	Machinery Dr (+)	Y's A/c Cr (+)	
5. Purchased machinery for cash	Machinery Cash Dr (+) Cr (−)		

Solution

Transaction 1: Cash and capital are the two elements affected by this transaction. Since cash and capital are being brought into the business, the value of both capital and cash increases.

Transaction 2: Since money is being borrowed from the bank, cash increases and the amount payable in the form of loan also increases.

Transaction 3: Since inventory is bought by paying cash, the value of inventory increases and the cash available with the business would reduce. This transaction affects only the asset side of the Account Equation.

Transaction 4: Since machinery is being purchased on credit, th name of the party from whom the purchase is made (in this case, Mr Y) is relevant. This transaction increases both machinery and Y's account.

Transaction 5: This transaction affects only the asset account. Machinery account increases while cash account decreases.

The following table indicates the relationship between the various types of accounts and debits and credits.

Types of Account	Explanation	Results	
		Debit or Credit	Closing Balance
Assets	Increase results in	Debit	Debit
Assets	Decrease results in	Credit	Debit
Liability	Increase results in	Credit	Credit
Liability	Decrease results in	Debit	Credit
Owner's equity	Increase results in	Credit	Credit
Owner's equity	Decrease results in	Debit	Credit

■ **PROBLEM 2.4** Classify the following items of a consulting company based on the type of account each item belongs to.

1. Share capital
2. Commissions earned
3. Office supplies
4. Prepaid advertising
5. Interest income
6. Salaries expenses
7. Rent prepaid
8. Cash
9. Bills receivable
10. Proprietor's drawings
11. Creditors
12. Debtors
13. Advances from customers
14. Income tax payable
15. Electricity charges
16. Outstanding professional fees
17. Advances to customers
18. Professional fees earned and received
19. Dividends
20. Accounts payable
21. Accounts receivable
22. Retained earning
23. Buildings
24. Telephone expense
25. Prepaid insurance
26. Commission outstanding

Solution

Items	Type of Account				
	Asset	Liability	Capital	Income	Expenses
1. Share capital			✓		
2. Commissions earned				✓	
3. Office supplies	✓				
4. Prepaid advertising	✓				
5. Interest income				✓	
6. Salaries expenses					✓
7. Rent prepaid	✓				
8. Cash	✓				
9. Bills receivable	✓				
10. Proprietor's drawings					✓
11. Creditors		✓			
12. Debtors	✓				
13. Advances from customers		✓			
14. Income tax payable		✓			
15. Electricity charges					✓
16. Outstanding professional fees	✓				
17. Advances to customers	✓				
18. Professional fees earned and received				✓	
19. Dividends					✓
20. Accounts payable		✓			
21. Accounts receivable	✓				
22. Retained earning			✓		
23. Buildings	✓				
24. Telephone expense					✓
25. Prepaid insurance	✓				
26. Commission outstanding		✓			

QUESTIONS

I. Answer the following questions.

1. Equity = Assets – Liabilities. What does this equation imply? Can it be an equation?
2. Define the five parts of modern approach of accounting.
3. Explain personal account and impersonal account.
4. Define the three types of accounts as per traditional approach of accounting.
5. Establish the relationship between books of original entry and ledger account.
6. Do you think the word 'debit and credit' signifies any meaning? How it is to be interpreted?

II. Solve the following problems.

1. From the following transactions, indicate which accounts are affected and why, by presenting the same in a table in the form of an accounting equation in the books of Anant's firm.
   (a) Anant commenced the business with cash of ₹1,50,000.
   (b) Goods of ₹40,000 purchased for cash.
   (c) Credit sale of goods to Aqua Soft Solution of ₹18,000.
   (d) Paid rent of ₹1,200.
   (e) Cash received from Aqua Soft Solution on his A/c – ₹7,500.
   (f) Deposited ₹10,000 into the bank.
   (g) Salary paid ₹2,500.
   (h) Machinery of ₹50,000 purchased for cash
   (i) Credit purchase of goods from Fortune Electro worth ₹12,500.
   (j) Cash sales of ₹19,000.

2. From the following transactions, find out which accounts are affected and why, by presenting the same in a table in the form of an accounting equation in the books of Poonam's firm.
   (a) Purchase of goods costing ₹2,000 from Impel Marketing on credit.
   (b) Sales of goods to VSN Global on credit costing ₹3,000.
   (c) Cash purchase – ₹4,000.
   (d) Cash Sales – ₹6,000.
   (e) Paid cash to Impel Marketing – ₹2,000.
   (f) Received cash from VSN Global – ₹3,000.

 ## CASES

Conceptual Application Case

Effect of Transactions Anand John owns a fish farm in Goa. He sells fish to wholesalers and a large supermarket chain. His business has flourished in recent years even though the price of fish has come down. On 12 June 2012, the following business transactions were recorded by Anand:

(a) Fish sold to Naresh Singh (fish merchant) for ₹260.
(b) Fish food purchased from Dinesh Gupta for ₹78.
(c) Boat maintenance expenses paid ₹100.
(d) Fish sold to Shivraman (fish merchant) for ₹200.
(e) Equipment purchased for ₹280.

Questions

1. Distinguish between personal and impersonal accounts in the transactions.
2. How will the transactions be verified?
3. Why is it important to verify such transactions?

Business Application Case

Shidh Moka

Shidh Moka decided to operate a hot dog stand near a football stadium during the football season. The following transactions describe the financial effects of his activities in setting up the business and operating it for one week.

(a) He deposited ₹30,000 in the Second National Bank.
(b) He rented a site, paying ₹4,500 for the right to use the location on the following three Saturdays.
(c) A tent and other equipment were purchased for ₹11,000 from a bankrupt concern; a cheque was issued in payment.
(d) Merchandise was purchased from Ranjan worth ₹30,500; Moka paid ₹10,000 (by cheque) and promised to pay the balance on Monday after the first game.
(e) All the merchandise was sold for cash on the first Saturday, and Mr Moka deposited the total receipt (₹65,000) in his bank account.
(f) Moka decided that one-third of the rent payment was applicable to the business done at the first game and that the tent and equipment would have a cash value of ₹4,700 at the end of the third Saturday, which was the last game of the season. After that game, Mr Moka intended to leave this business.
(g) On Monday, Mr Moka paid the balance due to Ranjan in full.

Questions

1. Summarize the effects of these transactions on the assets, liabilities, and owner's equity of Mr Moka's hot dog business, using the format illustrated. Indicate clearly the assets, the liabilities, and the owner's equities.
2. Prepare a balance sheet as of Monday night, after all the aforementioned information has been collected.
3. Prepare an income statement for the period that ended on Monday night.

 ## REFERENCES

Anthony, Robert, N., David Hawkins, and Kenneth Merchant (2003), *Accounting Text and Cases*, 11th edn, p. 87.

Hawkins, David, F. (2004), *The Mechanics of Financial Accounting*, Harvard Business School, p. 3.

Balance Sheet

Learning Objectives

After studying this chapter, you will understand

- accounting concepts and their characteristics and utility
- how to read a balance sheet

INTRODUCTION

Manufacturing, trading, and services entities are important organs of the world's economic dimensions. In an economy, financial transactions are inherent. Entities need to communicate to the employees, investors, public, and statutory bodies about the transactions they have made and those that have financial implications for the macro economy at large. Accounting framework is an important edifice like technical, legal, and other entities. This situation has given rise to the decision-making role. Decision making is the nucleus role of promoters, managers, investors, lenders, etc. The necessary information is provided in the annual report of an entity. The annual report is prepared for the management of the entity to inform them about the performance of the firm over the preceding financial year. However, the challenge is how to read and understand the report. The current and the following chapters (Chapters 3 and 4) of the book help the readers understand how to prepare a balance sheet and an income statement, and the important financial jargons and their implications in financial statements.

ACCOUNTING CONCEPTS

Accounting concepts are concepts of accounting heads (such as cost, income, capital, debit, or credit) and are assumptions or conditions that form the basis of the science of accounting.

> Accounting concepts are assumptions or conditions.

They influence accounting procedures and practices, for example, appropriation and charge, reserves and provisions, etc. Accounting concepts are

- made and developed by accountants; since they cannot be validated or proved by reference to natural laws, as in the case of the natural sciences, they do not have the authority of universal principles;
- suggestions based on experience, reasoning, and observation;
- developed for common usage to ensure uniformity and understandability;
- in evolution, and, therefore, flexible; and

- need to be (a) useful (meaningful to users); (b) objective (supported by facts and data); and (c) feasible (practical and attainable) to be accepted.

The concepts that are most important in the preparation of financial statements may be categorized as being relevant to (1) balance sheet and (2) income statements. The concepts are (i) entity, (ii) going concern, (iii) money measurement (monetary expression), (iv) cost (historic), (v) conservatism, (vi) accounting equivalence (dual aspect), and (vii) verifiable and objective evidence.

Entity

An *entity* consists of many persons. The owners of an entity are shareholders in the case of corporations, partners in the case of partnership firms, and proprietors in the case of sole proprietorship firms. An entity, firm, or enterprise exists primarily to produce goods or services at minimum cost and sell them for a profit. Therefore, the accounting process needs to relate to the operations of an enterprise as an entity distinct from its owners. For the accounting purpose, an enterprise exists in its own right,

A business is distinct from its owners.

and accounts are maintained for an entity as distinct from all categories of persons related to it. This concept suggests that the affairs of the enterprise must not be mixed up with the private affairs of the owners or other persons associated with it.

To obtain the true picture of the performance of a firm, it is necessary to separate the affairs of business from the private affairs of the owner or proprietor. Hence, transactions between the proprietor/owner of the firm and the firm will be recorded separately in the account books of the firm, and this would be recorded as capital account. All transactions would be recorded from the perspective of the firm and not that of the owner.

Ms Trupti, the owner of Trupti Telesystems, withdrew ₹5,000 from the firm's bank account to meet her household expenses. This would not be recorded as a business expense, but as drawings made by Ms Trupti. In turn, her capital account balance in the firm's book will be reduced.

Going Concern

The *going concern* concept assumes that the entity has a continuity of life, or that the enterprise is to be prolonged or extended indefinitely, or that the activity is to be continued and that dissolution or liquidation is not intended. This concept recognizes the value of the assets and liabilities of the enterprise based on their

An entity's life is intended to be infinite.

productivity and contribution to profits, not on their current realizable values or on the assumption that they are to be disposed of.

It assumes that the resources currently available to the entity will be used in its future operations.

Sandhya Rai acquired a toothpaste making machine at a cost of ₹60,000 which is expected to be used for six years and then scrapped. Since the business is a going concern, it is assumed that it will continue its operating activities, and the machine will live out its full useful life. Hence, Sandhya will recognize a reduction in the value of the machine on account of use and/or passage of time over the next 6 years. ₹10,000 per year would be recognized as depreciation charges and the machine will be shown in the balance sheet at reduced value. At the end of the first year, the toothpaste making machine would be reported at a net book value of ₹50,000 (₹60,000 less ₹10,000).

As the asset continues to be in use and is not sold, it is appropriate to value the asset at its net book value in the accounts of the going concern.

Money Measurement

In accounting, all transactions are expressed in terms of money, i.e., money is considered the common unit of measurement. The common economic value of the assets and liabilities is expressed in monetary terms rather than in terms of any other physical dimension (e.g., area of land in square metres, quantity of furniture, etc.). However, this concept constrains accounting

Accounting measures assets and liabilities in terms of money.

from measuring assets and liabilities— such as human assets or productivity— that cannot be expressed in monetary terms accurately.

This concept provides for a common expression by means of which heterogeneous factors can be expressed in numbers that will be useful for mathematical and arithmetical workings. Money is expressed in terms of its valuation at the time an event occurs and in turn is recorded in the books of accounts.

Assume that Star Electronics Ltd owns ₹20,000 cash, 2,000 kilograms of raw materials, three delivery vans, and office space of 2,300 square feet. These amounts cannot be added together as they have different measurement units. Hence, it is necessary to convert these assets into meaningful amounts that may be measured with a common measurement unit such as Indian Rupees, US dollars, or Sterling pounds, based on the legal currency of the country concerned.

Cost

All transactions are recorded at their monetary cost of acquisition, that is, the price paid for acquiring assets or for receiving services. If an asset does not cost anything, that is, no money is paid specifically for its acquisition, it is not recorded in the books of accounts of an enterprise. Examples of such assets are built-up goodwill of the enterprise, growing teamwork in the enterprise,

Monetary or acquisition cost is important, but limited.

or the brand name of the product. The cost concept ignores the effects of excessive inflation in the economy; it is irrelevant to the purpose of valuation of assets.

This is based on the fundamental concept of a going concern. An asset is ordinarily entered in the accounting records at the price paid or agreed upon for purchase, which is also known as *cost*. The cost price forms the base for subsequent accounting of the asset. Subsequently, changes in the purchasing power of money on account of inflation or deflation would not affect the value of the asset.

Third Eye Systems has purchased on 1 January 2020 land measuring 200 square yards for ₹200 lakh. Thus, the land would be recorded in the accounts of the firm at ₹200 lakh. A year later the land could be sold for either ₹250 lakh or ₹150 lakh, no change would ordinarily be made in the accounting records to reflect this effect in its original value.

In short, the amount at which an asset would be shown in the account books of a firm does not indicate the sales value of the asset concerned.

The cost concept does not mean or subscribe to the view that all assets would be shown at their original purchase price for as long as the firm owns the same. The cost of an asset that has a long, but limited life is reduced systematically during its life time by the process of writing off, referred to as *depreciation*. This aspect is discussed in detail in the chapter on fixed assets and depreciation.

Conservatism or Prudence

Conservatism is 'playing safe', or never overstating profit (excess of income over expenses). The most common practices representative of this principle are (a) not to consider income or gain until it is realized in cash and (b) to base provision of loss or contingency on past performance. The principle of conservatism has been particularly significant in the growth of

> Provide for loss and contingency based on past performance; do not provide for expected gain or income.

industry and/or services. Net profits and assets need to be understated to protect the interest of all parties. However, conservatism may exceed necessity, result in the creation of secret reserves, and thereby contradict the convention of disclosure.

Blue Moon Enterprises had purchased wheat for ₹20,000, but because of a sudden increase in the crop yield, the firm expects that now only ₹18,000 is likely to be realized if the stock is sold. Such conservatism, which is also known as the *prudence* concept, dictates that the wheat is to be valued at ₹18,000 only. It is not advisable to wait until the stock is sold and then recognize the loss of ₹2,000.

Let us take another example: Raymond Roy started to trade on 1 January 2019, and sold goods worth ₹2,00,000 over a period of one year. As on 31 December 2019, ₹13,500 was due from Rajeev Misra, and it was uncertain whether Raymond will be able to recover the money from Rajeev. Thus, in such a situation, Raymond should make an allowance for debtors in the form of *doubtful debts*, and should consider ₹13,500 as a reduction in the profit for the year 2019.

Accounting Equivalence (Dual Aspect)

The economic resources or future benefits of an entity are called assets. The future claims of various suppliers of funds against these assets are called equities. Equities may be (a) liabilities, or claims of creditors (all other than owners) or (b) owners' equity (or shareholders' equity or shareholders' fund), which is the owners' claim.

The accounting equation used to reflect the two types of equities is

> Assets = Liabilities + Owner's Equity

The above equation may again be written as

> Assets = Liabilities + Contributed capital by proprietors or owners + Net profit retained by an entity or – Net loss retained by an entity

This concept is technically stated as 'For every debit, there is a credit'. Every transaction or event has two aspects: (a) yielding of or receiving of a benefit; and (b) giving of that benefit. For example, when a firm acquires an asset (receiving of the benefit), it must pay cash (giving the benefit). Therefore, two accounts are

affected in the books of accounts—one for receiving the benefit (acquiring of an asset) and the other for giving the benefit (payment of cash). Thus, there will be two entries for every transaction—(a) debit and (b) credit. The accounting equation

> Assets = Liabilities + Owner's Equity

> For every debit, there is an equal credit.

that is, contributed capital added with retained earnings or reduced by net losses, is based on this concept.

Verifiable and Objective Evidence

The accounting data or business transaction should be objective, that is, free from the bias of accountants or others. They are subjected to verification by independent experts. Therefore, there must always be objective, verifiable, and documented evidence of transactions reflected in accounting and financial statements and reports. Such statements and reports may be internal and/or external documents. Invoices and vouchers for purchase, sales and expenses, physical checking of stock

> Accounting should be free from any bias.

in hand, etc., are examples of objective, verifiable, and documented evidence.

BALANCE SHEET

A *balance sheet* describes the financial position of an entity at any time. A balance sheet dated 31 March implies a description of the financial position of an entity 'at the close of business on 31 March'. Its formal name is 'statement of a financial position'. It is a point-in-time measurement of assets, liabilities, and owners' equity of an entity or firm or enterprise.

A balance sheet reveals an entity's resource structure (major classes and amounts of assets) and its financial structure (major classes and amounts of liabilities and equity). A balance sheet is a detailed summary of the basic accounting equation. The proper heading of a balance sheet consists of the

- name of the organization;
- title of the statement; and
- date for which the balance sheet is prepared.

The assets and liabilities on a balance sheet may be written on either the liquidity basis or the fixity basis. The *liquidity basis* arranges assets and liabilities according to their reliability and payment preference, for example, current first and then non-current assets or fixed assets (see Exhibit 3.1). The *fixity basis* arranges assets and liabilities according to their permanence, for example, fixed assets first and then current assets (see Exhibit 3.2). The balance of many accounts are grouped in profit and loss account and balance sheet and named to signify the meanings, which they meant, and for the proper analysis and interpretation of financial statements.

A balance sheet is always prepared on the date of closure of the accounting period. The accounting period may be according to the legal prescription (for example end of March of each year) or may follow the accepted practice by the firm (such as Diwali).

The liquidity base is recommended from management view, as the fulfillment of current obligations and use of current resources are necessary for successful management of operating cycle.

EXHIBIT 3.1 Sample Balance Sheet: Liquidity Basis

Name of an Entity
Balance Sheet as at _____
(As per liquidity basis)

Particulars	Notes No.	Figures at the end of current reporting period (₹)
LIABILITIES AND EQUITY OR SOURCES OF FUNDS		
1. Current Liabilities		
(a) Bills payable		
(b) Outstanding expenses		
(c) Income received in advance		
(d) Trade payables or Creditors		
(e) Bank overdraft		
(f) Short-term loans taken		
(g) Other current liabilities		
(h) Short-term provisions		
TOTAL CURRENT LIABILITIES		
2. Non-current Liabilities		
(a) Long-term provisions		
(b) Other long-term liabilities		
(c) Deferred tax liabilities (Net)		
(d) Debentures or bonds		
(e) Long-term borrowings		
TOTAL NON-CURRENT LIABILITIES		
3. Share Application Money Pending Allotment		
4. Shareholders' Funds or Owners' Equity or Capital Funds		
(a) Share capital or Capital		
(b) Retained earnings or Reserves and Surplus		
(c) Money received against share warrants		
TOTAL SHAREHOLDERS' FUNDS		
TOTAL EQUITY AND LIABILITIES		
ASSETS OR USES OF FUNDS		
1. Current assets		
(a) Cash on hand		
(b) Cash at bank		
(c) Bills receivables		
(d) Trade receivables or Debtors		
(e) Income receivables		
(f) Prepaid expenses		
(g) Closing stock		
TOTAL CURRENT ASSETS		
2. Investments		
3. Non-current Assets		
(a) Other non-current assets		
(b) Long-term loans and advances		
(c) Deferred tax assets (Net)		
(d) Non-current investments		
(e) Fixed assets		
(i) Tangible assets		
(ii) Intangible assets		
(iii) Capital work-in-progress		
(iv) Intangible assets under development		
TOTAL NON-CURRENT ASSETS		
TOTAL ASSETS		

EXHIBIT 3.2 Sample Balance Sheet: Fixity Basis

Name of an Entity
Balance Sheet as at _____
(As per permanency basis)

Particulars	Notes No.	Figures at the end of current reporting period (₹)
LIABILITIES AND EQUITY OR SOURCES OF FUNDS		
1. Shareholders' Funds or Owners' Equity or Capital Funds		
(a) Share capital or Capital		
(b) Retained earnings or Reserves and Surplus		
(c) Money received against share warrants		
TOTAL SHAREHOLDERS' FUNDS		
2. Share Application Money Pending Allotment		
3. Non-current Liabilities		
(a) Debentures or Bonds		
(b) Long-term borrowings		
(c) Deferred tax liabilities (Net)		
(d) Other long-term liabilities		
(e) Long-term provisions		
TOTAL NON-CURRENT LIABILITIES		
4. Current Liabilities		
(a) Short-term loans taken		
(b) Bank overdraft		
(c) Outstanding expenses		
(d) Income received in advance		
(e) Bills payable		
(f) Trade payables or Creditors		
(g) Other current liabilities		
(h) Short-term provisions		
TOTAL CURRENT LIABILITIES		
TOTAL EQUITY AND LIABILITIES		
ASSETS OR USES OF FUNDS		
1. Non-current Assets		
(a) Fixed assets		
(i) Tangible assets		
(ii) Intangible assets		
(iii) Capital work-in-progress		
(iv) Intangible assets under development		
(b) Non-current investments		
(c) Long-term loans and advances		
(d) Deferred tax assets (Net)		
(e) Other non-current assets		
TOTAL NON-CURRENT ASSETS		
2. Investments		
3. Current Assets		
(a) Closing stock		
(b) Prepaid expenses		
(c) Income receivables		
(d) Trade receivables or Debtors		
(e) Bills receivables		
(f) Cash at bank		
(g) Cash on hand		
TOTAL CURRENT ASSETS		
TOTAL ASSETS		

As per the Companies Act, 2013 and MCA GSR 191 (E), the format of abridged financial statements are provided as part of Form AOC-3A. The format of a balance sheet is exhibited as per Exhibit 3.2 A. For the purpose of this book, the company's final statements are shown and presented as per detailed need in Chapter 13.

MARSHALLING OF A BALANCE SHEET

The marshalling of assets and liabilities refers to the order in which they are shown in the balance sheet. The term 'grouping' is also used for the same purpose. Grouping means putting together items of a similar nature under a common heading.

EXHIBIT 3.2 A (Revised as per GSR 191 (E) of MCA)

Name of the Company ....
Abridged Balance Sheet as at ....
(*As per permanency basis*)

(Rupees in ....)

Particulars	Notes No.	Figures at the End of Current Reporting Period (dd-mm-yy)	Figures at the End of Previous Reporting Period (dd-mm-yy)	Figures at the Beginning of the Previous Reporting Period (dd-mm-yy) (Note)
ASSETS OR USES OF FUNDS				
1 Non-current Assets				
(a) Property, plant and equipment				
(b) Capital work-in-progress				
(c) Investment property				
(d) Goodwill				
(e) Other intangible assets				
(f) Intangible assets under development				
(g) Biological assets other than bearer plants				
(h) Financial assets				
i. Investments				
ii. Trade receivables				
iii. Loans				
iv. Others (Specify)				
(i) Deferrred tax assets (Net)				
(j) Other non-current assets				
TOTAL NON-CURRENT ASSETS				
2 Current Assets				
(a) Inventories				
(b) Financial assets				
i. Investments				
ii. Trade receivables				
iii. Cash and cash equivalents				
iv. Bank balances other than (iii) above				
v. Loans				
vi. Others (to be specified)				
(c) Current tax assets (Net)				
(d) Other current assets				
TOTAL CURRENT ASSETS				
TOTAL ASSETS				
EQUITY AND LIABILITIES				
1 Equity				
(a) Equity share capital				
(b) Other equity				
TOTAL EQUITY				
LIABILITIES				
2 Non-current Liabilities				
(a) Financial liabilities				
i. Borrowings				
ii. Trade payables				
iii. Other financial liabilities (Other than those specified in item (b) to be specified)				
(b) Provisions				
(c) Deferred tax liabilities (Net)				
(d) Other non-current liabilities				
TOTAL NON-CURRENT LIABILITIES				
3 Current liabilities				
(a) Financial liabilities				
i. Borrowings				
ii. Trade payables				
iii. Other financial liabilities (other than those specified in item (c)				

(b)	Other current liabilities			
(c)	Provisions			
(d)	Current tax liabilities			
(e)	Other current liabilities			
	TOTAL CURRENT LIABILITIES			
	TOTAL EQUITY AND LIABILITIES			

Note: This column is applicable when an entity is required to present the opening balance sheet in accordance with the requirements of Ind AS.

B	**OTHER EQUITY**
(a)	Share application money pending allotment
(b)	Equity component of compound financial instruments
(c)	Reserves and Surplus:
	i. Capital reserve
	ii. Securities premium reserve
	iii. Other reserves (Specify nature)
	iv. Retained earnings
(d)	Debt instruments through other comprehensive income
(e)	Equity instruments through other comprehensive income
(f)	Effective portion of Cash Flow Hedge
(g)	Revaluation surplus
(h)	Exchange differences on translating the financial statements of a foreign operation
(i)	Other items of other comprehensive income (Specify nature)
(j)	Money received against share warrants
	TOTAL

The assets and liabilities can be shown either in the order of liquidity or in that of permanency.

Preparation of a Balance Sheet according to the Order of Permanency

In this method, long-lasting assets and liabilities are placed at the top and the most liquid assets or liabilities are placed at the bottom of the balance sheet. The assets that are to be put to use permanently, or for a longer period of time, and not meant for resale are written first. For example, goodwill, land, building, etc. are written first, followed by assets that are liquid or useful for a shorter period of time. Therefore, highly liquid assets, such as cash in hand, and liabilities would be the last items. For example, capital and long-term liabilities would be written first, and short-term liabilities such as income received in advance and outstanding expenses will be written in the end. This approach is also known as the fixity approach. A balance sheet based on the fixity order is shown in Exhibit 3.2.

The fixity or permanency base is recommended by law of the land, as per macro economical position, because use of non-current resources is important for the country's economy.

Preparation of Balance Sheet According to the Order of Liquidity

Liquidity refers to the convertibility of an asset into cash in a short period of time. In this method, the most liquid assets are placed at the top and the most permanent at the bottom of the balance sheet. Assets in the highest liquidity criterion or capacity will be written first, followed by the next highest, and so on: for example, cash on hand and cash at bank in the given sequence, with goodwill written in the end. The same concept is applicable for liabilities. Short-term liabilities will be written first, followed by long-term liabilities, such as bank loans, and finally the capital. A balance sheet in the order of liquidity is presented in Exhibit 3.1.

From the above two presentation tables, it is clear that the balance sheet is a statement of the financial status of a firm, an individual, or a legal entity, indicating the assets and liabilities as on the last day/date of the fiscal year followed. The firm, individual, or legal entity for whom the books of accounts are maintained and statement of financial status in the form of a balance sheet is prepared is referred to as the accounting entity. In other

IFRS Update

Differences in presentation style

The following table indicates the differences in the presentation style and format of balance sheet as per Indian Accounting Standards (Ind As), IFRS or International Accounting Standards (IAS), and US Generally Accepted Accounting Practices (GAAP).

Ind AS	IFRS/IAS	US GAAP
AS has prescribed certain items, which must be presented as part of the balance sheet. AS has not prescribed any format. The format is prescribed by Companies Act, 2013 for companies, and the banking Regulation Act, for banks.	IFRS has not prescribed any standard format. Certain items must be presented in the balance sheet. It has prescribed requirement to make separate presentation of total assets and total liabilities. A current and non-current presentation is recommended. A liquidity presentation of assets and liabilities is used, which will provide more relevant and reliable information.	Firms may present either a classified or non-classified balance sheet. The decreasing order of liquidity is to be used for presentation. Decreasing liquidity order means highly valued liquid assets or liabilities as first item, and valued fixed assets or liabilities as last item in the balance sheet.

words, a balance sheet is a statement of the assets (owned by an entity) and liabilities (owed by an entity) as on the last day/date of the fiscal year followed. It indicates the position of assets and liabilities, hence it is not the same as an account.

STATEMENT OF CHANGES IN OWNERS' EQUITY

A statement of changes in owners' equity specifically indicates information related to what happened to the owners' equity during the time period under study. The owners of a firm might want to identify and trace out the retained earnings of the firm during the period under consideration. The final result of this statement will be shown as part of the owners' equity in the balance sheet. The statement shows the starting amount of equity, added by new capital brought in and net profit of the period, and the decreased by net loss and withdrawal in the form of drawings or dividend payments to owners' of the business. Exhibit 3.3 indicates the format of a statement of changes in owners' equity.

CONTENTS OF BALANCE SHEET

The contents of the balance sheet may be grouped as (i) current assets, (ii) fixed assets, (iii) intangible assets, (iv) deferred expenditure, (v) other assets, (vi) current liabilities, (vii) non-current liabilities, (viii) net worth, and (ix) investments.

Current assets Current assets are assets acquired for reselling or converting during the course of business within an accounting period, for example, cash and bank balance, inventory, accounts receivable, etc.

Fixed/Non-current/Long-term assets Fixed assets are acquired for use in the conduct of business operations; they are not for reselling to earn profit. These assets are not readily convertible into cash in the normal course of business, for example, machinery, building, etc.

Intangible assets Intangible assets do not have physical existence. Their value depends upon the earning capacity of the business concern. One example of intangible assets is goodwill. It provides economic benefits through the rights and privileges associated with its possession. It may be classified as *identifiable* or *unidentifiable*. Identifiable intangible assets, such as patents, copyrights, trademarks, franchises, and licenses,

EXHIBIT 3.3 Statement of Changes in Owners' Equity

Name of an Entity

Particulars	Notes No.	Figures at the end of current reporting period (₹)
1. Equity Share Capital		
Beginning of the year balance		
Add: New equity shares issued		
Less: Buy back of equity shares		
Ending of the Year Balance		
2. Other Equity (Reserves and Surpluses)		
For Each Type of Reserves		
Beginning of the year balance of reserves (for each specific type of reserve)		
Add or Less: Changes in accounting policy		
Add or Less: Prior period errors		
Restated beginning of the year balance of reserves		
Add or Less: Pertains to current year		
Add or Less: Transfer to/from other reserves		
Less: Issuance of bonus shares		
Ending of the Year Balance of Reserves (a) (for each specific type of reserve)		
For Surplus (Profit and Loss Account Balance or Retained Earnings)		
Beginning of the year balance of retained earnings		
Add or Less: Changes in accounting policy		
Add or Less: Prior period errors		
Restated beginning of the year balance of reserves		
Add or Less: Pertains to current year		
Add or Less: Transfer to/from other reserves		
Less: Interim Dividend Paid		
Ending of the Year Balance of Retained Earnings (b)		
Ending Other Equity (Reserves and Surpluses) (a + b) (c)		

IFRS Update

Differences in presentation style

The following table indicates the differences in the presentation style and format of Statement of Changes in Owners' Equity per Indian Accounting Standards (Ind As), IFRS or International Accounting Standards (IAS), and US Generally Accepted Accounting Practices (GAAP).

Ind AS	IFRS/IAS	US GAAP
No separate statement to be prepared. In a schedule named as Reserves and Surplus in balance sheet, the changes in shareholders' equity are presented.	It is required to be presented as part of financial statements. It shows the capital transactions with owners; accumulated profits and its changes; and a reconciliation of each component of equity.	Securities Exchange Commission (SEC) allows certain items to be included in the notes to the accounts, and not in the statement.

EXHIBIT 3.4 Vertical Form of Balance Sheet
Coal India Limited

(₹ in Crore)

	Note No.	As at 31.03.2017	As at 31.03.2016 (Restated)	As at 01.04.2015 (Restated)
ASSETS				
Non-current Assets				
(a) Property, Plant & Equipments	3	306.13	317.35	99.52
(b) Capital Work in Progress	4	13.52	13.13	225.92
(c) Exploration and Evaluation Assets	5	14.89	14.89	13.68
(d) Intangible Assets	6	0.31	0.47	-
(e) Financial Assets				
(i) Investments	7	11,529.07	11,416.51	11,180.58
(ii) Loans	8	0.43	51.51	63.42
(iii) Other Financial Assets	9	3,301.23	3,083.43	2,595.68
(f) Other Non-current Assets	10	98.83	86.31	52.65
Total Non-current Assets (A)		**15,264.41**	**14,983.60**	**14,231.45**
Current Assets				
(a) Inventories	12	68.44	152.41	58.33
(b) Financial Assets				
(i) Investments	7	60.19	312.98	862.92
(ii) Trade Receivables	13	12.74	0.38	9.76
(iii) Cash & Cash equivalents	14	725.17	276.28	99.61
(iv) Other Bank Balances	15	196.92	4,188.29	5,695.38
(v) Loans	8	1,209.00	17.45	16.61
(vi) Other Financial Assets	9	503.40	712.18	800.86
(c) Current Tax Assets (Net)		795.77	630.95	378.38
(d) Other Current Assets	11	49.36	104.24	280.17
Total Current Assets (B)		**3,620.99**	**6,395.16**	**8,202.02**
Total Assets (A + B)		**18,885.40**	**21,378.76**	**22,433.47**
EQUITY AND LIABILITIES				
Equity				
(a) Equity Share Capital	16	6,207.41	6,316.36	6,316.36
(b) Other Equity	17	7,712.39	9,729.45	10,694.26
Total Equity (A)		**13,919.80**	**16,045.81**	**17,010.62**
Liabilities				
Non-current Liabilities				
(a) Financial Liabilities				
(i) Borrowings	18	-	-	-
(ii) Other Financial Liabilities	20	-	-	-
(b) Provisions	21	212.82	172.72	194.68
(c) Other Non-current Liabilities	22	3,449.67	3,177.66	2,904.44
Total Non-current Liabilities (B)		**3,662.49**	**3,350.38**	**3,099.12**
Current Liabilities				
(a) Financial Liabilities				
(i) Borrowings	18	-	-	-
(ii) Trade Payables	19	107.64	72.70	86.25
(iii) Other Financial Liabilities	20	775.14	1,470.78	1709.16
(b) Other Current Liabilities	23	279.09	233.00	319.61
(c) Provisions	21	141.24	206.09	208.71
Total Current Liabilities (C)		**1,303.11**	**1,982.57**	**2,323.73**
Total Equity and Liabilities (A + B + C)		**18,885.40**	**21,378.76**	**22,433.47**

Source: Coal India Limited Annual Report 2016–17, pp. 194–195.

EXHIBIT 3.5 Vertical Form of Balance Sheet
Balaji Telefilms Limited

Particulars	Note No.	As at March 31, 2017	As at March 31, 2016	As at April 1, 2015
ASSETS				
1. Non-current assets				
(a) Property, plant and equipment	4	3,060.44	2,886.33	2,295.50
(b) Capital work-in-progress	4	340.27	-	21.77
(c) Financial Assets				
(i) Investments	5	22,676.28	22,676.28	7,622.63
(ii) Other financial assets	6(i)	1,193.58	727.40	721.71
(d) Deferred tax assets (net)	7	358.77	136.03	-
(e) Current tax assets (net)	8	2,223.11	1,977.16	1,686.49
Total non-current assets		**29,852.45**	**28,403.20**	**12,348.10**
2. Current assets				
(a) Inventories	9	2,703.45	1,158.89	508.86
(b) Financial assets				
(i) Investments	10	5,141.01	4,598.42	16,169.40
(ii) Trade receivables	11	8,963.33	7,617.22	5,901.70
(iii) Cash and cash equivalents	12	617.02	398.16	646.05
(iv) Loans	13	23,111.81	23,238.44	10,997.24
(v) Other financial assets	6(ii)	-	241.00	41.37
(c) Other current assets	14	5,232.94	2,460.64	2,427.40
Total current assets		**45,769.56**	**39,712.77**	**36,692.02**
Total assets		**75,622.01**	**68,115.97**	**49,040.12**
EQUITY AND LIABILITIES				
Equity				
(a) Share capital	15	1,518.61	1,518.61	1,304.21
(b) Other equity	16	63,896.09	60,806.06	43,875.69
TOTAL EQUITY		**65,414.70**	**62,324.67**	**45,179.90**
Liabilities				
1. Non-current liabilities				
(a) Deferred tax liabilities (net)	7	-	-	338.83
Total non-current liabilities		**-**	**-**	**338.83**
2. Current liabilities				
(a) Financial liabilities				
(i) Trade payables	17	6,569.00	4,684.22	3,183.04
(ii) Other financial liabilities	18	982.83	12.96	5.65
(b) Other current liabilities	19	1,440.01	631.02	11.72
(c) Current tax liabilities (net)	20	1,215.47	463.10	320.98
Total current liabilities		**10,207.31**	**5,791.30**	**3,521.39**
Total Equity and Liabilities		**75,622.01**	**68,115.97**	**49,040.12**

Source: Balaji Telefilms Limited Annual Report 2016–17, p.102.

may be identified and separated from the rest of the entity's assets. Goodwill is an unidentifiable intangible asset because it is impossible to separate it from the rest of the enterprise. The cost of intangible assets is amortized (charged) against income over their useful life.

Investments Investments are business holdings of securities issued by governments or other businesses. Investments may appear as current assets and/or long-term investments.

Deferred expenditure Deferred expenditure, for example, preliminary and pre-operative expenses incurred for the establishment of an entity, contribute income or benefit in future but do not arise from the present operation or recur. This expenditure is written off over several years' operation. Each year's share in such expenditure is treated as a charge on profit for that year. The amount of such expenditure not written off at any time is treated as an asset in the balance sheet.

Other assets Other assets are tangible assets used in the operations of business, for example, investments in real assets, etc.

Current liabilities Current liabilities are all short-term obligationsdue and payable within, generally, one year, for example, bills payable, etc.

Non-current/Long-term liabilities Non-current liabilities are all long-term obligations due and payable over, generally, more than a year, for example, debentures, long-term loans, etc. It represents a contractual obligation to make periodic interest payments on the amount borrowed and to repay the principal upon maturity.

Net worth Net worth is the fund invested at the business owner's risk. It is calculated by deducting all outside liabilities—both current and non-current—from the total assets of the concern. Net worth equals the capital and retained earnings (reserves) as reduced by losses and miscellaneous expenses (if any) still not written off.

To make the readers and students aware about presentation of balance sheets, the annual reports of certain companies (listed below) in a few selected sectors are provided in the Online Resource Centre of the book.

Sector/Industry	Company Name
Energy	Suzlon (page no. 102)
Health-care sector	Apollo (page no. 88)
	HCG (page no. 112)
Hotel	IHCL (page no. 66)
Software	Infosys (page no. 145 and 146)
Air travel	Jet Airways (page no. 90)
	Spicejet (page no. 80)
Defence	Reliance Naval and Engineering (page no. 72)
Financial services	Vistaar Financial Services Pvt. Ltd (page no. 51)

Own funds Own funds (proprietor's funds) are owed by the firm to its owners.

Owed funds Owed funds (loan funds) are owed by the firm to its external creditors. Table 3.1 distinguishes their characteristics.

TABLE 3.1 Own Funds and Owed Funds

Own Funds	Owed Funds
Owner's investment in the firm	Firm's financial obligation to all other than owner's
Internal source of finance	External source of finance
Owner's claim on the firm's assets	Outsiders' claim on the firm's assets
Capital earns dividend	Loans earn interest
Dividend is paid out of profit (appropriations out of profit); the rate may vary	Interest is charged against profits (i.e., paid irrespective of profit or loss) at a fixed rate
In liquidation, own funds are returned last, and, therefore, called 'permanent funds'	In liquidation, owed funds are repaid before capital—even otherwise, loans have to be repaid according to the terms of the agreement—and, therefore, called 'semi-permanent funds'
Own funds are not secured by charge on assets	Loans may be secured by charge on fixed or current assets

Total owner's funds equal the sum of	Total owed funds equal to long-term loans and short-term loans
(a) capital plus reserves and (b) surplus less losses or fictitious assets	

Long-term Liabilities

Any liability, that is, obligations of a firm that arise on account of its operations, repayable after one year or twelve months from the date of balance sheet, is known as a long-term liability. For example, if a bank loan is taken on 1 May 2020 by Novel Fashion Ltd to purchase a machine, and according to the terms of contract with the bank, it is to be repaid after two years from the date of loan taken, then, for the purpose of the balance sheet dated 31 March 2021, it would be treated as a long-term liability of Novel Fashion Ltd.

> Owed funds means borrowed funds. Own funds means amount invested by owners.

Provisions

A provision is a charge against profit (reducing the profit available to owners) for all anticipated losses or expenses. The amounts set aside as provisions are worked out after considering the loss or liability likely to be incurred. The amount or the date on which they will arise may or may not be ascertained with reasonable accuracy. As a tentative list, it can be grouped under the following categories. Provisions can be created for

- liabilities and charges (e.g. provision for taxation, provision for sales tax, gratuity, etc.)
- fixed assets valuation adjustment (e.g. provision for depreciation)
- valuation adjustment for each and every component of current assets (e.g. provision for doubtful debts receivable from customers)

Provisions for liabilities and charges would directly reduce the retained earnings available for the owners, and will also be considered as a type of probable or anticipated liability, and hence is shown on the liabilities side of the balance sheet. Provision for valuation adjustments appears on the assets side of the balance sheet as a deduction from the concerned asset value (e.g. provisions for bad and doubtful debts are deducted from Accounts receivable/Sundry debtors or Provisions for depreciation are deducted from the asset account).

Reserves

A reserve is an amount of money that belongs to owners' equity on account of retention of profits, capital receipts, upward revaluation of asset, etc. Retention of profit means appropriation of profits. It is a sum of money set aside from distributable profits to meet some unforeseen requirements in future. Capital receipts arise on account of profit on the sale of a fixed asset or issue of shares at a premium, while upward revaluation of an asset indicates the current value of an asset as against the reported historical costs. The creation of a reserve is the result of an accounting entry. All reserves appear on the liabilities side of the balance sheet. By creation of a reserve, cash or other assets of the business are not set aside. If a firm

does set aside cash or other assets to achieve specific objectives (outside the firm,) then it is known as *reserve fund*.

Estimated Liabilities

In case the documentary proof for the amount of expense to be paid in the next period is not available at the time of preparing the financial statement, the amount may be estimated based on the period already completed. For example, suppose the telephone bill for the residence of the managing director is reimbursed by the firm as part of business expense. The telephone bill is available on a bi-monthly basis. Hence, for the year end, one month's bill amount (for the month of March) is estimated, and would be treated as the business expense and also as the estimated liability.

Contingent Liabilities

Contingent liability refers to the amount that is payable by a firm in case of certain unforeseen events. For example, a firm has undertaken a job that needs to be completed by a particular point of time. The agreement indicates that in case of failure of the firm in doing so, the firm has to pay a penalty. The penalty paid by the firm as a result of failure to fulfil its obligation is known as contingent liability.

IndAs 37, issued by ICAI and as approved by Ministry of Company Affairs, has described 'contingency' as a condition or situation of whose outcome in the form of gain or loss can be known or worked out only on the happening or non-happening of a certain event. If it is possible to work out the estimated value of loss, then it is to be provided as estimated liability in financial statements. In case it is not possible to estimate the amount, then the nature and approximate estimate on the financial position should be disclosed by way of notes to the accounts.

Contingent liability is the liability that may or may not arise depending on a contingent (uncertain) future event, for example, liability on partly paid shares (investments). A suit filed against a business for a claim not acknowledged as a debt is a contingent liability: whether the amount needs to be paid or not depends on the judgement of the court. This would not be reported as a liability in the balance sheet because of the uncertainty of the situation, but would be reported as part of notes to the accounts. The following is the extract of contingent liabilities reported by Star Cement Limited in its annual report of 2017–18.

Contingent Assets

Contingent asset refers to the amount that is receivable by a firm, in case of certain unforeseen events. For example, a firm has released a job that needs to be completed by a particular point of time by the supplier/vendor. The agreement indicates that in case of failure by the supplier/vendor to do so, the firm has the right to recover a penalty from the supplier/vendor. The penalty amount recovered from the supplier/vendor as a result of failure to fulfil the obligation is known as contingent asset.

EXHIBIT 3.6 Star Cement Limited

Notes to Standalone Financial Statements Contingent Liability and Commitments

(₹ in Lacs)

Sl. No	Particulars	31-Mar-18	31-Mar-17	01-Apr-16
1.	Estimated amount of contracts remaining to be executed on capital account and not provided for (net of advances)	–	236.26	125.23
2.	Claims against the Company not acknowledge as debts – excise VAT/income tax matters/royalty etc.	504.13	676.27	666.29
3.	Bill of exchange discounted with banks (Refer note c)	–	–	17.22
4.	Duty saved under EPCG scheme	46.65	46.65	46.65
5.	Letters of credit issued by bank	58.26	106.35	162.22
6.	Solvent surety furnished to excise department against differential excise duty refund	1,318.08	1,268.09	920.20

Note: Based on legal opinion/decisions in similar cases, the Management believes that the Company has a fair chance of favourable decisions in cases mentioned here-in-above and hence no provision is considered necessary.

(a) Against Company's claim in respect of its cement plant at Lumshnong for refund of differential excise duty, Hon'ble High Court at Guwahati (Shillong Bench) vide its order dated 12th September, 2012, has directed the Excise Department to release 50% of the disputed amount against furnishing of solvent surety. Based on the said judgment of the Hon'ble High Court in favour of the Company and legal opinion obtained by the Company, the differential excise duty refund of Nil (31 March 2017 - ₹127.80 Lac, 1 April 2016 - ₹223.19 Lacs) has been recognised the books of accounts.

(b) Against Company's claim in respect of its cement plant at Guwahati for refund of differential excise duty, Hon'ble High Court at Guwahati vide its order dated 1st December, 2016, in the matter of Raj Coke industries & others versus the Union of India has directed the Excise Department to release 50% of the disputed amount against furnishing of solvent surety. Based on the said judgment of the Hon'ble High Court and legal opinion obtained by the Company, the differential excise duty refund of Nil (31 March 2017 - ₹793.54 Lacs, 1 April 2016 - Nil) have been recognized as revenue in the books of accounts.

(c) Para B2 of Ind AS 101 states that except as permitted, a first time adopter shall apply the derecognition requirements in Ind AS 109 prospectively for transactions occurring on or after the date of transition to Ind ASs. As a result, no impact has been taken as on 1 April 2016.

Source: Star Cement Limited Annual Report 2017–18, p.114.

This type of expected gains will not be recorded in the books of accounts as per prudence norms of accounting.

Deferred Tax Liabilities and Assets

Generally, the amount with respect to profit used in calculating the income tax liability should be the same as per Generally Accepted Accounting Practices (GAAP) and as per the applicable Income Tax Act. The Income Tax Act permits revenue to be recognized at a later period or expense to be recognized at an earlier stage, as against the method used in financial accounting. This may give rise to a timing difference. If the income tax liability as per financial accounting is greater than that as per the Income Tax Act, then the amount pertaining to the timing difference will be recorded as deferred tax liabilities. If the income tax liability as per financial accounting is lower

than that as per the Income Tax Act, then the timing difference will be recorded as deferred tax assets.

Off Balance Sheet Financing

When a firm acquires an asset for use without resorting to capital or debt directly (i.e., the asset is acquired in such a way that neither asset nor liability appears in the balance sheet of the firm), such a financing of an asset is known as *off balance sheet financing*. An example is the acquiring of an asset for use through an operating lease.

Balance Sheet Formats

Exhibits 3.4 and 3.5 indicate the vertical format based on fixity used by corporates/companies in the presentation of balance sheet in their annual accounts and reports.

 # SUMMARY

- Accounting concepts are basic assumptions or conditions that form the basis of the science of accounting.
- Accountants develop accounting concepts, which are suggestions based on experience, reasoning, and observation, to ensure uniformity and understandability.
- For the accounting purpose, an enterprise exists in its own right, and is distinct from all categories of persons related to it.
- The 'going-concern' concept assumes that the entity is intended to continue indefinitely.
- The 'money measurement concept' is that all transactions need to be recorded and expressed in terms of money.
- All transactions are recorded at their money cost of acquisition.

- The accounts are prepared by 'playing safe' so that profit, or excess of income over expenses, is never overstated.
- The 'dual aspect' concept considers assets = liabilities + owner's equity, where owner's equity = contributed capital + retained net profit or – retained net loss.
- The dual concept is 'For every debit, there is a credit'. The adopted approach is, for every increase (or decrease) on one side of the equation, decrease (or increase) the other side of the equation correspondingly.
- The balance sheet may be written on the liquidity basis (arranged according to reliability and payment preference of assets and liabilities) or the fixity basis (arranged according to permanence of assets and liabilities).

 # KEYWORDS

Accounting concepts   They are basic assumptions or conditions that form the basis of the science of accounting.

Current assets   They are assets acquired for reselling or converting during the course of business within an accounting period, such as cash, bank balance, receivables, monetary claims against debtors of the firms, notes receivable (accepted and agreed claims by third parties), marketable securities (temporary investments made by the firm), inventory, pre-paid expenses, etc.

Current liabilities   They are all short-term obligations due and payable within, generally, one year, for example, accounts payable (debts owed to creditors by the firm), bills payable (notes payable,

evidenced by Negotiable Instruments Act), interest payable, salary and wages payable, current portion of long-term debt, and advance from customers.

Intangible assets   They are assets that have no physical existence. Their value depends upon the earning capacity of the business concern. Examples of intangible assets are goodwill, patents, copyrights, trademarks, franchises and licenses, knowhow costs, deferred charges, etc.

Owed funds   They are the financial obligations of an enterprise to all other than owners.

Own funds   They are owners' investment in an enterprise.

 # SOLVED PROBLEMS

■ **PROBLEM 3.1**   Marshal Company's profit and loss account for the year ended 31 December 2020 includes the following information.

Particulars	Amount (₹)
(i) Depreciation	57,500
(ii) Bad debts written off	21,000
(iii) Increase in provision for doubtful debts	18,000
(iv) Proposed dividend	15,000
(v) Retained profit for the year	20,000
(vi) Liability for tax	4,000

State which of the items (i) to (vi) is (a) a transfer to provisions, (b) a transfer to reserves, and (c) related neither to provisions nor to reserves.

Solution

(a) Transfer to provisions — (i), (iii) (vi)
(b) Transfer to reserves — (v)
(c) Neither related to provisions nor reserves — (ii), (iv).

■ **PROBLEM 3.2** Mr Amit wants to set up a new business. Before actually selling anything, he bought a motor vehicle for ₹4,00,000, premises for ₹10,00,000, and a stock of goods for ₹2,00,000. He did not pay in full for his stock of goods and still owes ₹80,000 in respect of them. He borrowed ₹6,00,000 from Dhavan. After the events described above, and before trading starts, he has ₹20,000 cash in hand and ₹1,40,000 cash at bank. Calculate the amount of his capital.

Solution

Balance Sheet of Mr Amit

ASSETS	
Motor	4,00,000
Premises	10,00,000
Stock	2,00,000
Bank	1,40,000
Cash	20,000
Total Assets	**17,60,000**
EQUITY AND LIABILITIES	
Loan from Dhavan	6,00,000
Creditors	80,000
Total Liabilities	6,80,000
Equity *(Balancing figure) i.e., Capital*	10,80,000
Total Equity and Liabilities	**17,60,000**

■ **PROBLEM 3.3** Draw up Mahindra's balance sheet from the following information as on 31 December 2019.

Particulars	Amount (₹)
Capital	4,75,000
Debtors	99,000
Motor vehicles	1,14,000
Creditors	49,000
Fixtures	1,10,000
Stock of goods	1,76,000
Cash at bank	25,000

Solution

Balance Sheet of Mahindra as at 31 December 2019

Particulars	Amount (₹)
I. EQUITY AND LIABILITIES	
1. Shareholders' Funds	
(a) Share capital	4,75,000
2. Current Liabilities	
(a) Creditors	49,000
Total Equity and Liabilities	**5,24,000**
II. ASSETS	
1. Non-current Assets	
(a) Fixed assets	
(i) Motor vehicles	1,14,000
(ii) Fixtures	1,10,000
2. Current Assets	
(a) Stock of goods	1,76,000
(b) Debtors	99,000
(c) Cash at bank	25,000
Total Assets	**5,24,000**

■ **PROBLEM 3.4** Mr Subram has the following items in his balance sheet as on 30 April 2019:

Capital ₹4,18,000; Creditors ₹32,000; Fixtures ₹70,000; Motor vehicle ₹84,000; Stock of goods ₹99,000; Debtors ₹65,600; Cash at bank ₹1,29,000; Cash in hand ₹2,400.

During the first week of May 2019,

(a) he bought extra stock of goods for ₹15,400 on credit;
(b) one of the debtors paid him ₹5,600 in cash;
(c) he bought extra fixtures for ₹20,000 by cheque.

You are to draw up a balance sheet as on 7 May 2019 after the above transactions have been completed.

Solution

Balance Sheet of Mr Subram as at 30 April 2019

Particulars	Amount (₹)
I. EQUITY AND LIABILITIES	
1. Shareholders' Funds	
(a) Share capital	4,18,000
2. Current Liabilities	
(a) Creditors	32,000
Total Equity and Liabilities	**4,50,000**
II. ASSETS	
1. Non-current Assets	
(a) Fixed assets	
(i) Motor vehicles	84,000
(ii) Fixtures	70,000
2. Current Assets	
(a) Stock of goods	99,000
(b) Debtors	65,600
(c) Cash at bank	1,29,000
(c) Cash in hand	2,400
Total Assets	**4,50,000**
Effect of Transactions on First Week of May 2019	
a. Increase in stock of goods	15,400
Increase in creditors	15,400
b. Increase in cash in hand	5,600
Decrease in debtors	5,600
c. Increase in fixtures	20,000
Decrease in cash at bank	20,000

Balance Sheet of Mr Subram as at 7 May 2019

Particulars	Amount (₹)
I. EQUITY AND LIABILITIES	
1. Shareholders' Funds	
(a) Share capital	4,18,000
2. Current Liabilities	
(a) Creditors	47,400
Total Equity and Liabilities	**4,65,400**
II. ASSETS	

1. Non-current Assets	
(a) Fixed assets	
(i) Motor vehicles	84,000
(ii) Fixtures	90,000
2. Current Assets	
(a) Stock of goods	1,14,400
(b) Debtors	60,000
(c) Cash at bank	1,09,000
(c) Cash in hand	8,000
Total Assets	**4,65,400**

■ **PROBLEM 3.5** Keyi is a realtor who operates in Nasik and owns a house there. She buys and sells properties and apartments on her own account, and also earns commissions as a real estate agent. She has incorporated her business as a sole proprietorship firm on 15 November 2020. Consider the following events as on 30 November 2020.

1. Keyi owes ₹1,80,000 as loan taken by her to acquire land worth ₹3,50,000 for business purpose.
2. She has spent ₹30,000 in cash for the development of a scheme named 'Trupti Enclave'.
3. She owes ₹2 lakh on a personal mortgage (it means asset given as security to the lender of funds) on her residence, which she acquired on 20 November 2020, for a total price of ₹3,60,000.
4. She owes ₹7,600 on a personal charge account with her HDFC Credit card.
5. On 28 November 2020 Keyi hired Gopi as her first employee. She was to begin work on 1 December 2020. Keyi was pleased because Gopi was one of the best real-estate salesperson in the area. On 29 November 2020 Gopi expressed her inability to join Keyi's company.
6. Keyi acquired business furniture for ₹17,000 on 25 November 2020 for which she paid ₹6,000 on open account plus cash of ₹11,000.
7. On 26 November 2020, Keyi sold a ₹2,000 business chair for ₹2,000 to her next-door neighbour for cash.
8. Keyi's balance in the bank account on 30 November 2020 was ₹18,000.

Prepare a balance sheet as at 30 November 2020, for Keyi Realtor.

Solution

Name of an Entity: Keyi Realtor
Balance Sheet as at 30 November 2019
(As per liquidity basis)

Particulars	Amount (₹)
LIABILITIES AND EQUITY OR SOURCES OF FUNDS	
1. Current Liabilities	
Accounts payable for furniture	6,000
TOTAL CURRENT LIABILITIES	**6,000**
2. Non-current Liabilities	
Bank loan	1,80,000
TOTAL NON-CURRENT LIABILITIES	**1,80,000**
3. Capital	
For land	1,70,000

For development of scheme 'Trupti Enclave'	30,000
For purchase of furniture	11,000
In the form of bank balance	18,000
TOTAL SHAREHOLDERS' FUNDS	**2,29,000**
TOTAL EQUITY AND LIABILITIES	**4,15,000**
ASSETS OR USES OF FUNDS	
1. Current Assets	
(a) Cash on hand	2,000
(b) Cash at bank	18,000
TOTAL CURRENT ASSETS	**20,000**
2. Non-current Assets	
(a) Furniture	
Purchase value	17,000
Less: Depreciation	2,000
Net Furniture Value	15,000
(b) Trupti Enclave Scheme	30,000
(c) Land	3,50,000
TOTAL NON-CURRENT ASSETS	**3,95,000**
TOTAL ASSETS	**4,15,000**

■ **PROBLEM 3.6** From the balances given below, prepare the balance sheet of M/s Bharat & Bros as on 31 December 2019, in (a) liquidity order and (b) permanency order.

Particulars	Amount (₹)	Particulars	Amount (₹)
Capital	50,000	Sundry debtors	24,000
Loan from bank	20,000	Bills payable	8,000
Cash in hand	2,500	Drawings	6,000
Cash at bank	12,800	Building	25,000
Closing stock	24,700	Furniture	4,500
Sundry creditor	15,000	Investments	15,000
Net profit	21,500		

Solution

A: Liquidity Order
Balance Sheet of M/s Bharat & Bros as at 31 December 2019

Particulars		Amount (₹)
EQUITY AND LIABILITIES		
Bills payable		8,000
Sundry creditors		15,000
Loan from bank		20,000
Capital:		
Opening	50,000	
Add: Net profit	21,500	
Less: Drawings	6,000	65,500
Total Equity and Liabilities		**1,08,500**
ASSETS		
Cash in hand		2,500
Cash at bank		12,800
Sundry debtors		24,000
Closing stock		24,700
Investments		15,000
Furnitures		4,500
Building		25,000
Total Assets		**1,08,500**

B: Permanency Order
Balance Sheet of M/s Bharat & Bros as at 31 December 2019

Particulars		Amount (₹)
EQUITY AND LIABILITIES		
Capital:		
Opening	50,000	
Add: Net Profit	21,500	
Less: Drawings	6,000	65,500
Loan from bank		20,000
Sundry creditors		15,000
Bills payable		8,000
Total Equity and Liabilities		**1,08,500**
ASSETS		
Building		25,000
Furniture		4,500
Investments		15,000
Closing stock		24,700
Sundry debtors		24,000
Cash at bank		12,800
Cash in hand		2,500
Total Assets		**1,08,500**

■ **PROBLEM 3.7** Prepare a statement indicating equity and liabilities of the balance sheet of Aiya Ltd as per the Companies Act, 2013 from the following balances:

Trade payables	₹30,000	Share capital	₹2,00,000
Long-term provisions	₹60,000	Short-term provisions	₹35,000
Reserves and surplus	₹80,000	Long-term borrowings	₹1,20,000
Other current liabilities	₹25,000	Other long-term liabilities	₹76,000
Short-term borrowing	₹24,000		

Solution

Name of Company: Aiya Ltd
Balance Sheet as at _____

Particulars	Notes No.	Figures at the end of current reporting period (₹)
EQUITY AND LIABILITIES		
1. **Shareholders' Funds**		
(a) Share Capital		2,00,000
(b) Reserves and Surplus		80,000
(c) Money received against share warrants		
TOTAL SHAREHOLDERS' FUNDS		**2,80,000**
2. **Share Application Money Pending Allotment**		
3. **Non-current Liabilities**		
(a) Long-term borrowings		1,20,000
(b) Deferred tax liabilities (Net)		
(c) Other long term liabilities		76,000
(d) Long-term provisions		60,000
TOTAL NON-CURRENT LIABILITIES		**2,56,000**
4. **Current Liabilities**		
(a) Short-term borrowings		24,000

(b) Trade payables	30,000
(c) Other current liabilities	25,000
(d) Short-term provisions	35,000
TOTAL CURRENT LIABILITIES	**1,14,000**
TOTAL EQUITY AND LIABILITIES	**6,50,000**

■ **PROBLEM 3.8** The following balances are taken from the books of Vijay Ltd as on 31 March 2019. Prepare a statement indicating the assets of balance sheet as on 31 March 2019 as per the Companies Act, 2013.

Balances	Amount (₹)
(1) Fixed assets – tangible	8,00,000
(2) Cash and cash equivalents	60,000
(3) Long-term loans and advances	34,000
(4) Inventory	43,000
(5) Other non-current assets	31,000
(6) Non-current investments	27,000
(7) Current investments	29,000
(8) Trade receivables	56,000
(9) Short-term loans and advances	40,000
(10) Other current assets	10,000
(11) Fixed assets – intangible	50,000

Solution

Name of Company: Vijay Ltd
Balance Sheet as at 31 March 2019

Particulars	Notes No.	Figures at the end of current reporting period (₹)
ASSETS		
1. **Non-current Assets**		
(a) Fixed assets		
(i) Tangible assets		8,00,000
(ii) Intangible assets		50,000
(iii) Capital work-in-progress		
(iv) Intangible assets under development		
(b) Non-current investments		27,000
(c) Deferred tax assets (Net)		
(d) Long-term loans and advances		34,000
(e) Other non-current assets		31,000
TOTAL NON-CURRENT ASSETS		**9,42,000**
2. **Current Assets**		
(a) Current investments		29,000
(b) Inventories		43,000
(c) Trade receivables		56,000
(d) Cash and cash equivalents		60,000
(e) Short-term loans and advances		40,000
(f) Other current assets		10,000
TOTAL NON-CURRENT ASSETS		**2,38,000**
TOTAL ASSETS		**11,80,000**

■ PROBLEM 3.9

The following balances are extracted from the books of Star Ltd. Prepare the balance sheet as per the Companies Act, 2013 as on 31 March 2020.

Balances	Amount (₹)
(1) Accrued commission	20,000
(2) Land-building	10,00,000
(3) Equity share capital	10,00,000
(4) Bank balance	45,000
(5) General reserve	20,000
(6) Closing stock	1,80,000
(7) Creditors	4,00,000
(8) Debtors	2,30,000
(9) 10% debentures	1,30,000
(10) Debentures redemption fund investments	30,000
(11) Custom deposits	1,25,000
(12) Gratuity fund	20,000
(13) Provision for taxation	60,000

Solution

Name of Company: Star Ltd
Balance Sheet of Star Ltd as at 31 March 2020

Particulars	Notes No.	Figures at the end of current reporting period (₹)
EQUITY AND LIABILITIES		
1. Shareholders' Funds		
(a) Share capital (Equity share capital)		10,00,000
(b) Reserves and surplus (General reserve)		20,000
(c) Money received against share warrants		
TOTAL SHAREHOLDERS' FUNDS		**10,20,000**
2. Share application money pending allotment		
3. Non-current liabilities		
(a) Long-term borrowings (10% debentures)		1,30,000
(b) Deferred tax liabilities (Net)		
(c) Other long term liabilities		
(d) Long-term provisions (Gratuity fund)		20,000
TOTAL NON-CURRENT LIABILITIES		**1,50,000**
4. Current liabilities		
(a) Short-term borrowings		
(b) Trade payables (Creditors)		4,00,000
(c) Other current liabilities		
(d) Short-term provisions (Provision for tax)		60,000
TOTAL CURRENT LIABILITIES		**4,60,000**
TOTAL EQUITY AND LIABILITIES		**16,30,000**
ASSETS		
1. Non-current assets		
(a) Fixed assets		
(i) Tangible assets (Land-building)		10,00,000
(ii) Intangible assets		
(iii) Capital work-in-progress		
(iv) Intangible assets under development		
(b) Non-current investments (Debentures redemption fund investments)		30,000
(c) Deferred tax assets (Net)		
(d) Long-term loans and advances (Custom deposit)		1,25,000
(e) Other non-current assets		
TOTAL NON-CURRENT ASSETS		**11,55,000**
2. Current assets		
(a) Current investments		
(b) Inventories (Closing stock)		1,80,000
(c) Trade receivables (Debtors)		2,30,000
(d) Cash and cash equivalents (Bank balance)		45,000
(e) Short-term loans and advances		
(f) Other current assets (Accrued Comission)		20,000
TOTAL NON-CURRENT ASSETS		**4,75,000**
TOTAL ASSETS		**16,30,000**

QUESTIONS

I. Choose the correct option.

1. Which of the following is not a fixed asset?
   (a) Building
   (b) Bank balance
   (c) Plant
   (d) Patents
   (e) Goodwill

2. Recording of capital contributed by the owner as liability ensures adherence to the principle of
   (a) Double-entry
   (b) Going concern
   (c) Separate entity
   (d) Materiality
   (e) Consistency

3. The basic concepts related to balance sheet are
   (a) Cost concept
   (b) Business entity concept
   (c) Accounting period concept
   (d) Both (a) and (b)
   (e) All of the above

4. The double-entry concept is that
   (a) Assets + Liabilities = Capital
   (b) Capital = Assets – Liabilities
   (c) Capital – Liabilities = Assets
   (d) Capital + Assets = Liabilities
   (e) None of the above

5. Only the events that affect the business must be recorded, as per the principle of
   (a) Separate entity
   (b) Accrual
   (c) Materiality
   (d) Going concern
   (e) None of the above

6. If the going concern concept were no longer valid, which of the following would be true?
   (a) All prepaid assets would be written off immediately and completely
   (b) Total contributed capital and retained earnings would be the same

(c) The allowance for uncollectible accounts would be eliminated

(d) Intangible assets would continue to be carried at net amortized historical cost

(e) Land held as investment would be valued at its realizable value

7. Under which of the following concepts are shareholders treated as creditors for the amount they paid on the shares they subscribed?
   (a) Cost
   (b) Duality
   (c) Business entity
   (d) Going concern
   (e) None; since the shareholders own the business, they are not treated as creditors

8. The accounting measurement that is not consistent with the going-concern concept is
   (a) Historical cost
   (b) Realization
   (c) Transaction approach
   (d) Liquidation value
   (e) Continuity

9. Recording of fixed assets at cost ensures adherence to the concept of
   (a) Conservatism
   (b) Going concern
   (c) Cost
   (d) Both (a) and (b) above
   (e) Both (b) and (c) above

10. The principles of accounting relate to how assets, liabilities, revenues, and expenses are to be identified, measured, recorded, and reported. An item that is not a basic principle of accounting is
    (a) Materiality
    (b) Historical cost
    (c) Revenue recognition
    (d) Matching
    (e) Full disclosure

11. Which of the following statement(s) is/are true?
    (i) The entity concept of accounting is not applicable to sole trading concerns and partnership concerns
    (ii) Assets are to be shown in the balance sheet at the value realizable on liquidation
    (iii) Money measurement concept takes into account changes in the value of the monetary unit
    (iv) When a creditor is paid, one asset is diminished and another asset is increased
    (a) Both i and iii above
    (b) Both i and ii above
    (c) Both iii and iv above
    (d) Both ii and iv above
    (e) None of the above statements is true

12. Accounting does not record non-financial transactions because of the concept of
    (a) Entity concept
    (b) Accrual concept
    (c) Cost concept
    (d) Measurement concept
    (e) Continuity concept

13. Mr Rohit, owner of Rohit Furniture Ltd, owns a house that cost ₹6,00,000, but has a market value of ₹9,00,000. The financial statement for the business ignored the value of the property. The concept followed was
    (a) Business entity
    (b) Cost principle
    (c) Going concern
    (d) Duality
    (e) Realization

14. Fixed assets and current assets are categorized as per concept of
    (a) Separate entity
    (b) Going concern
    (c) Contingency
    (d) Consistency
    (e) Time period

15. Capital is shown under liabilities because of the
    (a) Conservatism concept
    (b) Accrual concept

(c) Entity concept
(d) Revenue recognition concept
(e) Matching concept

16. If the opening capital of a trader is ₹50,000, the closing capital is ₹52,000, and net profit for the year is ₹5,000, her drawings, if any, are
    (a) ₹5,000
    (b) ₹3,000
    (c) ₹1,000
    (d) ₹6,000

17. If the total assets of the firm are ₹50,000, outside liabilities are ₹30,000, the capital contributed by the owner is
    (a) ₹50,000
    (b) ₹30,000
    (c) ₹20,000
    (d) ₹10,000
    (e) ₹80,000

18. If the opening capital of a trader is ₹80,000, the closing capital is ₹120,000, and net profit for the year is ₹20,000, the trader has
    (a) Drawings of ₹20,000
    (b) Brought additional capital of ₹20,000
    (c) Brought additional capital of ₹40,000
    (d) Drawings of ₹40,000
    (e) Both (a) and (c) above

19. If the opening balance of debtors is ₹50,000, the closing balance of debtors is ₹1,00,000, and receipt from debtors is ₹20,000, credit sale for the year is
    (a) ₹50,000
    (b) ₹70,000
    (c) ₹80,000
    (d) ₹50,000
    (e) ₹70,000

20. If the opening balance of creditors is ₹25,000, purchase is ₹30,000, and payment made is ₹15,000, the closing balance of creditors is
    (a) ₹15,000
    (b) ₹40,000
    (c) ₹45,000
    (d) ₹55,000
    (e) ₹70,000

21. A business owes money to
    (a) Debtors
    (b) Investors
    (c) Creditors
    (d) Shareholders
    (e) None of the above

II. Solve the following problems.

1. Complete the gaps in the following table.

Particulars	Assets (₹)	Liabilities (₹)	Capital (₹)
(a)	12,500	1,800	?
(b)	28,000	4,900	?
(c)	16,800	?	12,500
(d)	19,600	?	16,450
(e)	?	6,300	19,200
(f)	?	11,650	39,750

2. Complete the gaps in the following table.

Particulars	Assets (₹)	Liabilities (₹)	Capital (₹)
(a)	55,000	16,900	?
(b)	?	17,200	34,400
(c)	36,100	?	28,500
(d)	1,19,500	15,400	?
(e)	88,000	?	62,000
(f)	?	49,000	1,10,000

3. State which of the following are wrongly classified.

Assets	Liabilities
Loan from C Mahindra	Stock of goods
Cash in hand	Debtors
Machinery	Money owing to bank
Creditors	
Premises	
Motor vehicles	

4. Information as on 31 December 2019 of an NGO called Ever Green working for the preservation of forests is given below. Work out the balance sheet as on 31 December 2019 from the given information.

Particulars	Amount (₹)
Cash in hand	1,400
Cash at bank	21,800
Books	78,000
Furniture	16,000
Computer	24,000
Subscription outstanding	2,600
Fixed deposit with bank	1,00,000
Subscription received for 2020	3,800
Rent outstanding	4,000
Publicity fund	35,000
Building fund	80,000
Capital	?

5. Here is a list of balances as on 30 November of Aiya Ltd. Arrange them in the balance sheet.

Particulars	Amount (₹)
Cash	21,500
Bank balance	9,600
Capital	25,000
Computer	3,000
Furniture	2,300
Creditors	
Bhaskar	13,000
Geeta	18,600
David	6,400
Debtors	
Damu	12,900
Cashi	2,600
Building	45,900
Long-term debt	34,800

6. The following balances are extracted from the books of Shaan Ltd as on 31 March 2019. From these balances, prepare a statement indicating equity and liabilities of the balance sheet as per the Companies Act, 2013.

Particulars	Amount (₹)
26,000 equity shares of ₹10 each	2,60,000
9% loan from Bank of Baroda	50,000
Proposed dividend	18,000
Bills payable	10,000
Surplus as per statement of profit and loss statement	50,000
Provident fund provisions	70,000
Bank overdraft	17,000
Outstanding salary	30,000

7. The following balances are extracted from the books of Gujarat Ltd as on 31 March 2020. Prepare a statement indicating the assets of balance sheet as per the Companies Act, 2013.

Balances	Amount (₹)
Interest accrued	3,000
Plant – machinery	6,00,000
Cash on hand	37,000
Trademark	20,000
Debtors	42,000
10% Narmada bond	70,000
Loose tools	18,000
Telephone deposit	30,000
Investments in units of mutual fund (Temporary)	10,000

8. The following balances are taken from the books of Seema Limited as on 31 March 2020. Prepare a statement indicating the assets of balance sheet as at 31 March 2020 as per the Companies Act, 2013.

Balance	Amount (₹)
Current investments	12,000
Short-term loans and advances	16,000
Other current assets	7,200
Fixed assets – tangible	5,60,000
Cash and cash equivalents	14,000
Inventory	46,000
Trade receivables	15,800
Other non-current assets	18,000
Non-current investments	26,000
Fixed assets – intangible	1,20,000
Long-term loans and advances	22,000

9. The following balances are taken from the books of Yuva Ltd as on 31 March 2020. Prepare a statement indicating equity and liabilities of balance sheet as on 31 March 2020 as per the Companies Act, 2013.

Balance	Amount (₹)
1. 1,30,000 equity shares of ₹5 each	6,50,000
2. General reserve	70,000
3. Provident fund	3,60,000
4. Creditors	86,000
5. Public deposit	3,26,000
6. Outstanding rent	13,000
7. Provision for tax	68,000
8. Other long-term liabilities	15,000
9. Temporary loan (Credit balance)	12,000

10. The following balances are taken from the books of Moon Ltd. Prepare the balance sheet as at 31 March 2020 as per the Companies Act, 2013.

Balance	Amount (₹)
1. Interest accrued	30,000
2. Plant – machinery	15,00,000
3. Equity share capital	15,00,000
4. Bank balance and cash	67,500
5. General reserve	30,000
6. Closing stock	2,70,000
7. Creditors	6,00,000
8. Debtors	3,45,000
9. Provision for tax	90,000
10. 12% bank loan	1,95,000
11. Non-current investments	45,000
12. Electricity deposit	1,87,500
13. Provident fund	30,000

CASES

Conceptual Application Case

Eurasia Enterprise   Eurasia Enterprise was incorporated by three friends, Vardhman, Gautam, and Aseem, on 1 April 2018. To commence the activities, each friend introduced ₹2,00,000 in cash. In addition, Eurasia borrowed ₹4,00,000 from the Maharashtra Cooperative Bank, giving a three-year note payable. The note was dated 1 April 2018, and indicated an interest payable half yearly at the rate of 8% per annum.

As the necessary funds were available, Vardhman made arrangements for a place of work. The shop premise was taken on a rent of ₹20,000 per month.

As on 31 March 2019, the net profit of the firm was determined to be ₹2,00,000 after providing for rent and all other administrative and selling expenses and one payment of interest. Each friend even withdrew ₹40,000 in cash to meet their day-to-day expenses.

Questions

1. What were the different sources of cash and amounts to start Eurasia Enterprise?
2. Prepare a capital account of each friend individually, and in total for the firm as a whole, as on 31 March 2019.

Business Application Cases

1. Formation   Two sisters formed a corporation on 1 January 2018, each of them investing ₹1,00,000 and receiving 1,000 shares of the corporation's capital stock in exchange. The corporation issued no more shares of capital stock during the next three years. On 1 January 2021, the company had total assets of ₹12,00,000 and total liabilities of ₹6,40,000.

During 2021, the corporation issued 100 additional shares of its capital stock to a friend of the two sisters, receiving in exchange ₹60,000 in cash. Cash dividends amounting to ₹2,40,000 were declared and paid during the year. On 31 December 2021, the company had assets amounting to ₹14,00,000 and liabilities of ₹6,80,000.

Questions

1. Calculate the net income for 2021.
2. Present the owner's equity section of the company's balance sheet on 31 December 2021.

2. Christopher Department Shop   Vivaan runs a department store called Christopher Department Shop in Chamba town of Jammu and Kashmir. The business was handed over to him by his father Francis after deciding to retire.

Vivaan is a young and energetic graduate in commerce, and also holds a business degree in managing small and medium enterprises. Within two years of his joining the firm, Christopher Department Shop registered an annual growth of 20%. With this business success, he decided to purchase 15,000 square feet space in the nearby building. For this purpose, he approached the J&K Bank. The Bank Manager, Rashida Ahmed, asked him to furnish a statement of financial position. As part of the expansion plan, Vivaan arranged interviews for filling up the position of an accountant. Sushma Koshy had applied for the position of accountant, and on recruitment, Vivaan handed over the following information to Sushma, requesting her to do the needful.

Description	Amount (₹)
Accounts payable	1,02,000
Accounts receivable	76,000
Deposits payable	1,20,000
Cash	62,400
Trademark registered	12,400
Inventory	80,000
Investment in J&K Government securities (withdrawable)	32,800
Past years' accumulated profit	1,76,400
Loan from Mrs. Vivaan	1,00,000
Accumulated depreciation – Building	28,000
Accumulated depreciation – Equipment	34,000
Building	1,40,000
Share capital	2,00,000
Equipment	3,04,000
Investment in shares of Colgate Palmolive	40,000
Small shop measuring 230 square feet	16,000
Prepaid rent	2,400
Revenue received in advance	5,600

Question

Imagine you are Sushma and prepare a statement of financial position.

REFERENCES

'Indian Accounting Standards', announced by Institute of Chartered Accountants of India.

'Guidance Notes', issued by Institute of Chartered Accountants of India.

Pronouncements by Ministry of Company Affairs, Government of India.

Income Statement

After studying this chapter, you will understand

- the application of accounting concepts for presenting income statements
- the relationship between balance sheet and income statement
- the contents of income statements

INTRODUCTION

The income statement, also known as the profit and loss account, summarizes the financial results of a company during a particular period of time. The time period, known as the accounting period, is usually one year and this is indicated as the income statement for the period ended 2019–2020 or the income statement for the year ended 2020.

An income statement is a type of flow report, as compared to the balance sheet, which is a status report. Financial flows in firms are continuous. The essential nature of financial flows in a business is indicated in Fig. 4.1.

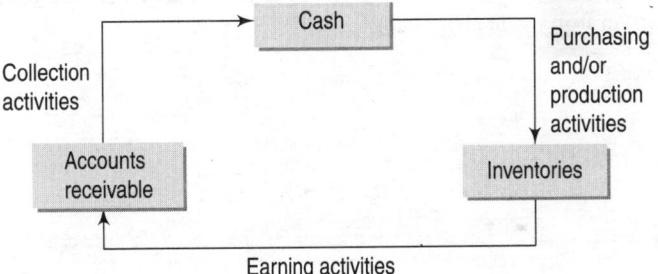

FIG. 4.1 Financial flows

An income statement enables the users to ascertain whether the business operations have been profitable or not during an accounting period. An income statement helps in the analysis of a company's bottom-line. It is a financial statement that summarizes the financial operations for a given period by disclosing the revenues earned and the expenses incurred.

The income statement focuses on the following elements:

- Inflows (or creation) of assets, cash, or accounts receivables that result from the sale of goods and services to customers or clients known as revenues
- Outflows (or consumption) of resources that are required in order to generate revenues known as expenses

Profit, net income, or net earnings is the amount by which revenues exceed expenses. If expenses exceed revenue, the amount of difference is known as *loss* or *net loss*.

CASH CONVERSION CYCLE/OPERATING CYCLE

The term 'operating' indicates the average time period taken from the purchase of merchandise and the conversion of the same in cash by the business firm. The word 'cycle' suggests a circular flow of capital from cash to inventory to receivables and back to cash again.

For the fast moving merchandise activities like supermall, the operating cycle may be completed in a few weeks. Generally, the operating cycle requires several months, but less than one year. The operating cycle period for retailers is usually shorter than that of manufacturers because retailers purchase goods in the form ready for sale or delivery to customers. The operating cycle time period also depends on the nature of products firms deal in. For example, a jewellery shop or an automobile dealer has a long operating cycle period in comparison to the consumer electronics stores dealer or grocery stores.

A manufacturing firm uses cash to acquire goods and services. These in turn pass through the production processes (cash is needed to pay off expenses including consumables and fuel) and are converted into finished goods. The finished goods are sold to wholesalers or retailers. These customers in turn pay for their purchases with cash, which brings the cash back to begin the next cycle. This is also known as the cash conversion cycle (Fig. 4.2).

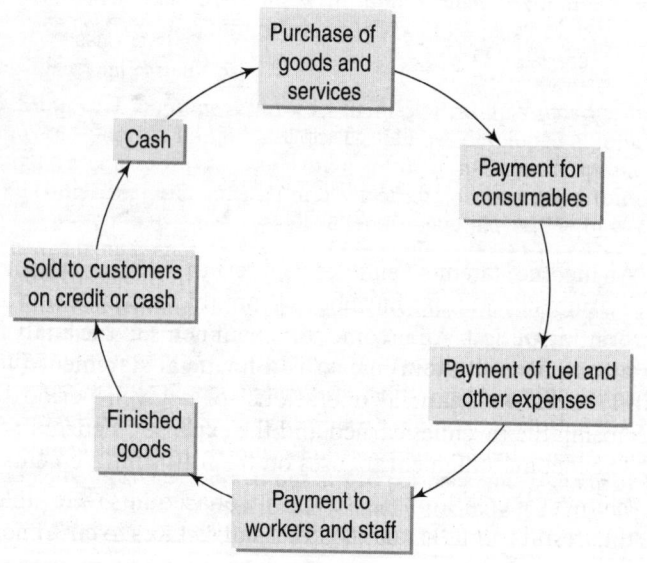

FIG. 4.2 Cash conversion cycle or operating cycle

ACCOUNTING CONCEPTS

Accounting concepts consist of rules, procedures, and techniques which are used in the preparation of financial statements. The accounting concepts related to income statements are explained in this section.

Periodicity

The life of the entity is considered to be indefinite. The measurement of income and studying the financial position of an entity after a very long period would not be helpful. Hence, it is necessary for business managers to analyse the performance of the enterprise regularly.

> *Accounting period is an artificial time period for measuring performance.*

The periodicity concept assumes that the activities of an enterprise are divided into artificial time periods, usually as long as a year, but sometimes as short as a month or a quarter. It is a concept under which each accounting period has an economic activity associated with it, and the activity can be accounted for, measured, and reported upon.

The standard time period over which the income or profits of a firm are evaluated is termed as a fiscal year. It generally spans a period of twelve complete months. In India, a fiscal year covers the period from April of one year to March end of the next year. The fiscal year concept has been developed and put to use purely for accounting purpose. While some Indian firms use Diwali as their financial year end, others follow the standard calendar year. Companies may adopt any other month as their financial year end: for example, AGC Network Limited considers September as their financial year end, while Balaji Telefilms follows a March ending.

Revenue Realization

The revenue realization concept revolves around the determination of the point of time when revenues are realized. According to this concept, revenue is realized when goods and services produced by a business enterprise are transferred to a customer based on a promise to pay cash or other assets in future. There must be a reasonable expectation that the revenue is realizable. In each period of revenue realization, all related expenses should be matched to revenue. This concept is also known as revenue recognition concept.

> *Revenue is the amount received or receivable.*

Exhibit 4.1 indicates the empirical practices for revenue recognition and realization adopted by various Indian companies.

The general guidelines mention that revenue is earned when a sales transaction is made through transfer of the property right of goods or when services are rendered. Some firms collect the revenue in advance for sale of their goods or for rendering their services; in such instances, revenue must be apportioned to the period in which the services are rendered or the merchandise sold is consummated. This concept is also known as revenue recognition.

EXHIBIT 4.1 Revenue Recognition

Following are the practices adopted by some Indian corporates for revenue recognition.

Balaji Telefilms Limited

Revenue Recognition

Revenue is recognized as and when the relevant episodes of the programmes (television serials) are telecast on broadcasting channels. Revenue (income) is recognized when no significant uncertainty as to its determination or realization exists.

(a) In respect of commission programmes, revenue is recognized as and when the relevant episodes of the programmes (television serials) are telecast on broadcasting channels.

(b) In respect of films produced/co-produced/acquired/distributed, revenue is recognized in accordance with the terms and conditions of the agreements on or after the first theatrical release of the films.

(c) In respect of events, revenue is recognized as and when the relevant event is delivered and technical clearance is received from the broadcasting channels. Revenue (income) is recognized when no significant uncertainty as to its determination or realization exists.

Star Cement Limited

Revenue Recognition

Revenue is measured at the fair value of the consideration received or receivable. Amounts disclosed as revenue are inclusive of excise duty and net of returns, trade allowances, rebates, value added taxes and amounts collected on behalf of third parties.

The Company recognizes revenue when the amount of revenue can be reliably measured, it is probable that future economic benefits will flow to the entity. The Company bases its estimates on historical results, taking into consideration the type of customer, the type of transaction and the specifics of each arrangement.

Sales are recognized when substantial risk and rewards of ownership are transferred to customer. Generally, sales take place when goods are dispatched or delivery is handed over to transporter.

Interest income is recognized using the effective interest rate (EIR) method. Dividend income on investments is recognized when the right to receive dividend is established.

Standards Issued but Not Yet Effective

Ind AS 115: Revenue from contracts with customers
The Company is in the process of assessing the detailed impact of Ind AS 115. Presently, the Company is not able to reasonably estimate the impact

that application of Ind AS 115 is expected to have on its financial statements, except that adoption of Ind AS 115 is not expected to significantly change the timing of the Company's revenue recognition for product sales. Consistent with the current practice, recognition of revenue will continue to occur at a point in time when products are dispatched to customers, which is also when the control of the asset is transferred to the customer under Ind AS 115. The Company intends to adopt the standard using the modified retrospective approach which means that the cumulative impact of the adoption will be recognized in retained earnings as of 1 April 2018 and that comparatives will not be restated.

Vistaar Financial Services Private Limited

Revenue Recognition

Revenue is recognized to the extent that it is probable that the economic benefits will flow to the Company and the revenue can be reliably measured.

i. Interest income on loans are charged and accounted on diminishing balance method.

However, interest income on non-performing assets ('NPA') is recognized only when it is realized. On an advance account turning into NPA, interest already charged on accrual basis and not collected, is reversed.

ii. Loan processing fee and documentation fee received upfront are considered to be accrued at the time of entering into a binding agreement upon its receipt and are recognized accordingly.

iii. Pre-closure charges are levied and accounted at the time of actual pre-closure.

iv. Commission income is accrued on the effective commencement of the policies basis confirmation obtained from the insurance company.

v. Interest income on deposits with banks is recognized on an accrual basis taking into account the amount of outstanding deposit and the applicable interest rate.

vi. Cash profit arising at the time of securitization/assignment of loan portfolio (Premium loan transfer transactions) is amortized over the life of the underlying loan portfolio and the unamortized amount is disclosed as 'Cash profit on loan transfer transactions pending recognition' within 'Other liabilities' on the balance sheet. Cash loss arising on premium loan transfer transactions are accounted for immediately in the Statement of profit and loss.

Sources: Balaji Telefilms Ltd Annual Report 2016–17, pp. 110 and 156; Star Cement Limited Annual Report 2017–18, pp. 98–99; and Vistaar Financial Services Private Limited Annual Report 2018, p. 103.

For example, if a Chartered accountant renders audit services to a client during the month of December, he/she must report the audit fees as revenue or income in the income statement of the month of December, irrespective of the fact that the amount is not yet received from the client.

A grocery shopkeeper records the shop's revenue at the time the goods are sold on credit and a bill is given to the customer.

Accrual

The accrual concept recognizes revenues and expenses as they are earned or incurred, without taking into account the date

of receipt or payment. The revenue earned and the expense incurred can be time specific, but the receipt and payments may not correspond to the period under consideration.

> Recognition of revenue or expenses as they are earned or incurred.

It recognizes that the buying, producing, selling, and other operations of an entity during a period often do not coincide with the cash receipts and payments of that period.

The accrual basis recognizes the impact of transactions in a financial statement for the time period when the revenue or expense occurred. It means that an accountant records

revenue and expenses as and when the firm incurs them. In the cash basis, the impact of transactions will be recorded only when a firm receives or pays cash for the same. In a nutshell, on accrual basis the revenue may be incurred before or after the cash transaction is completed, and so accounting is to be done based on the occurrence rather than on receipt of funds.

> Match revenue with expenses.

For example, Explorer Refrigeration has availed the services of a plumber for repairing the sewage line of the factory building in the month of March, and the charges are payable to the plumber after two months. In this case, Explorer Refrigeration would recognize this expense for the month of March, and not in the month of May when the cash payment will actually be made.

In some circumstance, a firm may make a payment before the expense is incurred, and such expenses are known as prepaid expenses. A prepaid expense would be considered as an expense based on time period lapse, and the amount for the uncovered period (future period) will be treated as an asset in the balance sheet. For example, Azalea Associates has chosen to pay in advance a three-year fire insurance policy premium for the office building. Assume that on 1 April 2019, a premium of ₹9,000 was paid for the period effective up to 31 March 2022. For the year ended as on 31 March 2020, ₹30,000 would be considered as an expense and ₹6,000 would be shown in the Balance sheet as an asset as advances/prepaid expenses. Exhibit 4.2 explains the contemporary practices for adoption of accrual concepts.

Matching

It is the process of matching revenue (as measured by the sale of goods and delivery of services) with efforts or expenses (as measured by the cost of goods and services rendered) to a particular period for which the income is being determined. The income of an enterprise is recognized when the revenue earned during a period is compared to the expenditure incurred for earning that revenue. For example, a sale of ₹20,000 generates revenue for the business. To determine the profit earned by a company, we need to know the cost of goods sold. In the above mentioned example, if the cost of goods sold is ₹16,000, the gross income will be ₹4000. The relationship between profit, expenses, and cost of goods is summarized below.

EXHIBIT 4.2   Basis of Accounting

Following are the practices adopted by Indian corporates for adoption accounting practices.

The Indian Hotels Company Limited

These financial statements have been prepared in accordance with IndAs as prescribed under section 133 of the Companies Act, 2013 read with Companies (Indian Accounting Standard) Rules, 2015 and other provisions of the Companies Act, 2013 as amended from time to time.

These financial statements have been prepared on a historical cost basis, except for certain financial instruments which are measured at fair value at the end of each reporting period.

All assets and liabilities are classified as current and non-current as per company's normal operating cycle of 12 months which is based on the nature of business of the company. Current assets do not include elements which are not expected to be realized within a 1 year and current liabilities do not include items which are due after 1 year, the period of 1 year being reckoned from the reporting date.

Apollo Hospitals Enterprise Limited

The financial statements have been prepared on the historical basis except for certain financial instruments that are measured at fair value at the end of reporting period. Historical cost is generally based on fair value of consideration given in exchange of goods and services. Fair value is the price that would be received to sell an asset or a paid to transfer a liability in an orderly transaction between market participants at measurement date, regardless whether that price is directly observable or estimated using another valuation technique.

Vinyl Chemicals (India) Limited*

Basis of Accounting & Preparation of Financial Statements

The financial statements of the Company have been prepared in accordance with the Indian Accounting Standards (Ind AS) prescribed under Section 133 of the Companies Act, 2013 ('Act') read with Rule 3 of the Companies (Indian Accounting Standards) Rules, 2015 and the Companies (Indian Accounting Standards) Amendment Rules, 2016.

For all periods upto and including the year ended March 31, 2016, the Company prepared its financial statements in accordance with the requirements of Indian GAAP to comply with Accounting Standards specified under Section 133 of the Companies Act, 2013, read with applicable rules and the relevant provisions of the Companies Act, 2013. These financial statements for the year ended 31st March, 2017 are the Company's first financial statements under Ind AS and the same are prepared in accordance with Ind AS 101 on "First-time Adoption of Indian Accounting Standards" - Refer to Note 2.12 for details of adoption of Ind AS.

The financial statements have been prepared on the historical cost basis except for certain Financial Assets/Liabilities (including derivative instruments) which have been measured at fair values.

Note 2.12 The Company has prepared the opening balance sheet as per Ind AS as of April 1, 2015 (the transition date) by recognizing all assets and liabilities whose recognition is required by Ind AS, not recognizing items of assets or liabilities which are not permitted by Ind AS, by reclassifying items from previous GAAP to Ind AS as required under Ind AS, and applying Ind AS in measurement of recognized assets and liabilities.

Sources: Indian Hotels Annual Report 2017–18, p. 132; Apollo Hospitals Enterprise Limited Annual Report 2016–17, pp. 175–176; and Vinyl Chemical (India) Limited Annual Report 2016–17, p. 31. Used by permission.

> Gross Income or Profit = Revenue – Expenses or Net Cost of Goods Sold
>
> Cost of Goods Sold = Beginning Inventory or Stock + Purchases + Direct Labour Charges + Direct Expenses + Chargeable Factory Expenses – Ending Inventory or Stock

Assume that Zep Enterprises has paid on 1 March 2020 rent of ₹30,000 for office space based on ₹10,000 per month for the quarter commencing from 1 March. For the year ended as on 31 March 2020, ₹10,000 for the month of March will be considered as an expense, and ₹20,000 would be considered as prepaid rental expenses, and would be treated as an asset because the use of the office space constitutes a future benefit.

The reasons for the need to match expenses with revenue for a given time period are mentioned in the following text in brief.

1. Certain fixed expenses such as rent of office building would be considered as a period expense and not as a product or service expense; hence, an adjustment may be needed for the unexpired periods and their respective costs.
2. Accountants may ignore instances where the adjustment amount is negligible or immaterial (in accounting terminology). For example, an amount of ₹300 paid to a tea supplier as on 31 March for providing tea/coffee to staff members on 1st April of the year may not be of material value for a firm having a total turnover of ₹10 lakh or more per annum.
3. When an expense is incurred for the acquisition of fixed assets that are useful for earning revenue over a long period of time (say 5 years), this may require appropriate allocation of the capital expenditure over the expected life period on a systematic basis, such as in the form of depreciation of the asset.

Disclosure

This accounting concept requires a business enterprise to provide all relevant information to the external users for the purpose of sound investment and credit decisions. The disclosure concept implies that no information of substance or of interest to the average investor will be omitted or concealed from an entity's financial statements.

Disclose material and significant information.

Accounting reports should be honestly prepared and sufficiently disclose information, which is of material interest to owners, (or equity shareholders, in case of a company), present and potential creditors, and investors. The practice of appending notes to accounting statements (such as notes to the accounts, contingent liabilities, market value of investment, etc.) is pursuant to the convention of disclosure. It should be the sincere effort of the accountant to present facts keeping in view the various accounting assumptions and principles.

Basis of preparation of financial statements

The financial statements are prepared under the historical cost convention on accrual basis of accounting and in accordance with generally accepted accounting principles in India, the Accounting Standard notified under the Companies (Indian Accounting Standard) Rules, 2015, and relevant provisions of the Companies Act, 2013.

Materiality

This concept implies that accounting transactions and events, which do not have material or significant effects on the business, should not be reported in the financial statements. It is for the accountant to interpret what is material or significant. There can be materiality of information and/or materiality of amount. Materiality depends on the amounts involved and the accounts affected. The American Accounting Association (AAA) defines the concept of materiality as, 'an item should be regarded as material if there is reason to believe that knowledge of it influences the decision of informed investors.'

Significant amount or information should be reported.

The basic idea of the materiality concept is that the requirements of accounting principles may be ignored if the effect on the financial statements is unimportant to the users of the accounting statement. In a way, it can be concluded that failure to follow the requirements of an accounting principle or concept is acceptable when the failure does not produce an error or mis-statement large enough to influence the judgment of users of the financial statement.

For example, purchase of a calculator costing ₹500 for staff members will be material amount for a small business, such as a small provision store. However, the same would not be a material amount for a big company such as Tata Chemicals Limited. Thus, the materiality concept differs from business to business.

Consistency

According to this concept, once an entity follows a particular method of accounting, it should use the same method for all subsequent transactions and events of the same nature. The entity should have a sound reason to change its accounting methods. If accounting methods are changed frequently, the comparison of financial statements from one period to another period would be difficult, for both internal users and external users. Accurate comparisons can be made, if the methods and practices of recording and presentation of accounts remain constant.

The consistency concept is applicable to inventory pricing methods, depreciation methods, and in the recognition of any other revenue or expense as capital expense or revenue expense. This concept helps users of the accounting information make meaningful comparisons over a given period of time. This concept does not imply that a firm can never make changes. A firm may change from one accounting method to

> Use same method of accounting consistently.

another as long as it justifies the change as an improvement in the preparation and presentation of financial statements.

OTHER CLASSIFICATIONS

In addition to the above concepts of income statement, in day-to-day life, the following additional classifications need to be worked out to present the true picture of the financial position and performance of a firm. The classification mentioned in the following text supports the managers of a firm to implement the accurate recording of transactions for better decision-making.

Revenue Receipts and Capital Receipts

Revenue receipts arise in the ordinary course of business transactions and normally appear on the credit side of an income statement, for example, commission, discount, interest, rent, fees, dividend on investment received, bad debts recovered etc. Capital receipts, on the other hand, do not arise in the ordinary course of business and such receipts are related to assets (sale of a fixed asset and sale of investment), capital brought into the business, issue of shares and debentures, bank loans, etc.

Revenue Loss and Capital Loss

Revenue losses arise during the normal course of business, whereas a capital loss arises when an asset is sold at a loss, or is destroyed by fire or in an accident. Bad debts, reduction in the market value of goods, etc. constitute revenue losses. Bad debts refer to non-recovery of amounts from the credit customers from whom an amount is receivable. However, when investments costing ₹9,000 are sold at ₹7,000, it would represent a capital loss of ₹2,000. Similarly, furniture costing ₹6,000 destroyed by fire should be treated as a capital loss.

Revenue Profit and Capital Profit

Revenue profits are the profits earned in the ordinary course of business and appear on the credit side of an income statement. Such profits are distributed among the members as dividend. On the other hand, capital profits are normally earned on account of sale of fixed assets. For example, if a machinery costing ₹50,000 is sold for ₹62,000, it results in a capital profit of ₹12,000. Similarly, share premium account is also a capital profit. Such profits are not available for distribution among the shareholders, but are transferred to a special account known as *capital reserve account*, from the management view, while from the legal view it is taken to the income statement.

CONTENTS OF INCOME STATEMENT

The various items of an income statement are discussed in this section.

Sales revenue   It is the principal activity or activities of an entity. In other words, sales revenue is the amount of money a

business earns during a particular accounting period. It results from the sale of goods or services by a business. A business can earn revenue by the following methods:

- Sales resulting from products and/or services
- Money generated from rents, interest, dividends, royalties, commissions, and licensing fees
- Sale of assets of the firm other than those held as stock-in-trade (such as plant and machinery, land and building, or investments).

The revenue generated from selling goods and providing services to customers is calculated as follows:

$$\text{Net Sales Revenue} = \text{Sales} - \text{Sales Return}$$

The three methods of revenue generation described above can be titled sales revenue, other revenue, and capital income, respectively.

Cost of goods sold   It is the cost a company incurs to manufacture, create, or sell its products during an accounting period. For a merchandiser, the cost of goods sold includes the manufacturing costs and the cost of preparing the goods for sale (such as the transportation cost). For a manufacturing company, the cost of goods sold includes the costs of raw material and packaging, and the cost of preparing the goods for sale.

$$\text{Cost of Goods Sold} = \text{Beginning Inventory or Stock} + \text{Purchases} + \text{Direct Labour Charges} + \text{Direct Expenses} + \text{Chargeable Factory Expenses} - \text{Ending Inventory or Stock}$$

The cost of goods sold includes items purchased in the year plus stock held at the start of the year, but stock at the end of the year is excluded. The cost of goods sold can be worked out as per Table 4.1.

TABLE 4.1   Calculation of Cost of Goods Sold

Particulars		Amount (₹)
Beginning of the year – Stock value or inventory value		xxxx
Add: Cost of purchases		
Purchase value	xxx	
Inward taxes related to purchases	xxx	
Carriage inward	xxx	
Loading and unloading expenses	xxx	
Other directly identifiable expenses	xxx	
Total cost of purchases		xxxx
Add: Manufacturing or directly operating expenses		
Direct labour charges	xxx	
Other direct expenses for manufacturing or operating activities	xxx	
Factory expenses	xxx	
Total manufacturing or directly operating expenses		xxxx
Less: Ending of the year – Stock value or inventory value		xxxx
Cost of goods sold		**xxxx**

In the given formula, some words are defined as follows:

- *Carriage* refers to the cost of transportation of goods from the supplier to the premises of the firm that has purchased them. When the purchaser pays the transportation charges, it is known as *carriage inward*, and it would be part of the cost of purchases. When the seller pays the transportation charges, it is known as *carriage outward*, and it would be part of the selling and distribution expenses. Carriage charges are also known as transportation charges.
- *Loading and unloading expenses*, paid by the purchaser, refer to the expenses that occur in bringing the goods purchased to the place of storage. It includes all charges paid during transit and agreed to be borne by the purchaser.

Goods written off or written down A firm may be unable to sell its goods because of any of the following events.

- Goods might be lost or stolen.
- Goods might be damaged, and hence their value lost.
- Goods might be stale or obsolete.

In a few cases, an insignificant value may be realized. When goods are lost, stolen, or thrown away, the firm suffers a loss on those goods. The amount of loss would be charged directly against the gross profit of the firm. When the cost of goods sold is deducted from the sales, it yields the gross profit or gross loss.

Gross profit and gross margin Gross profit is the first important subtotal on the classified income statement. Gross profit is the difference between the sales revenues and the cost of goods sold.

$$\text{Gross Profit} = \text{Net Sale Revenue} - \text{Cost of Goods Sold}$$

The *gross profit margin* is the measurement of a company's manufacturing and distribution efficiency during production and distribution processes. It is calculated as

$$\text{Gross Profit Margin} = \text{Gross Profit}/\text{Net Sales Revenue} \times 100$$

Operating expenses These are the expenses a business incurs in selling goods or providing services, and in managing the business. Operating expenses are usually separated from both cost of goods sold and income tax expenses, and are subtracted from the gross margin. Operating expenses are related to the main operations or business of the firm. It includes administrative expenses, depreciation, and selling and distribution expenses.

$$\text{Operating Expenses} = \text{Administrative Expenses} + \text{Depreciation} + \text{Selling and Distribution Expenses}$$

Non-operating income Revenues that are incidental or indirect to the main business of the firm constitute non-operating income. For example, the gross proceeds from the sale of old equipments and machinery, interests and dividends, income from temporary investments, etc. contribute towards the non-operating income of an enterprise.

Non-operating expenses The expenses that are incidental or indirect to the main operations of the firm are non-operating expenses. Non-operating expenses are non-recurring in nature. These include loss resulting from the sale of buildings, securities, machinery, or equipment.

Operating profit It is the difference between an entity's gross profit and operating expenses. It consists of general and administrative expenses, selling expenses, and depreciation. It is also known as earnings before interest and tax (EBIT).

$$\text{Operating Profit} = \text{Gross Profit} - \text{Operating Expenses}$$

Interest It is a charge made for the use of money. A borrower incurs interest expense. A lender earns interest revenue. When debt documents are payable in a firm's financial statements, the firm should work out interest expense paid or payable. When investments are made by a firm and indicated in the firm's financial statements, the firm should work out the interest income receivable or received. The borrower is bound to pay the interest irrespective of whether the funds are used or kept idle by him/her. The following formula is used in the computation of interest expense or income:

$$\text{Interest} = \text{Principal Amount} \times \text{Rate of Interest} \times \text{Time Period}$$

Income before tax It is the profit generated from a company's business operations before tax and after interest payments. Income before tax is also known as profit before tax (PBT). It is the operating profit plus or minus non-operating income or expenses respectively, minus interest charges.

$$\text{Profit before Taxes} = \text{Operating Profit} + \text{Non-operating Income} - \text{Non-operating Expenses} - \text{Interest charges}$$

Income tax expenses These relate to the income tax paid or owed to the government.

Profit after tax It is the difference between profit before tax and tax expenses. Profit after tax is also known as net income or net profit.

$$\text{Profit after Tax} = \text{Profit before Tax} - \text{Tax Expenses}$$

PRESENTATION OF INCOME STATEMENTS

The income statement may be presented in any one of the following forms—the step form or the accounts form. The step-form income statement may be single-step or multi-step. The single-step records all the revenues followed by the expenses items and the net profit. The multi-step income statement gives more useful information. It divides the income statement into separate sections, and is used to calculate different levels of profitability. The income statement can also be prepared in the accounts form. The accounts form divides the income statement into two sides; the expenses items are recorded on the left side and the revenue items are recorded on the right side (In today's culture, it is irrelevant).

Vertical Presentation of Income Statement

The vertical presentation of an income statement aids decision-makers in understanding and interpreting the financial performance of a firm. This can be performed in two ways: the single-step method and the multi-step method.

In the single-step income statement, all types of revenue are grouped together, and all expenses are then deducted without drawing any intermediate subtotals. Exhibit 4.3 presents a single-step income statement.

In a multi-step income statement, the revenues and expenses are combined and grouped in such a way that it highlights the significant relationships between these sets of data. The net profit or net loss represented by a single-step or a multi-step method would be the same. Exhibit 4.4 indicates a multi-step income statement for a non-corporate entity.

EXHIBIT 4.3   Single-step Income Statement

*Single-step income statement of M/s _____
for the period ended _____*

Particulars		Amount (₹)
Income		
Sales	XXX	
Rent revenue	XXX	
Interest revenue	XXX	
Other income	XXX	
Total sales and other revenue (a)		XXXX
Expenses		
Costs of goods sold	XXX	
Wages	XXX	
Rent	XXX	
Depreciation	XXX	
Interest	XXX	
Income tax	XXX	
Total expenses (b)		XXXX
Net profit or (loss) (c)		XXX

EXHIBIT 4.4   Multi-step Income Statement

*Multi-step income statement of M/s _____
for the period ended _____*

Particulars		Amount (₹)
Sales (a)	XXXX	
Less: Costs of goods sold (b)	XXXX	
Gross Profit (c) (a – b)		XXXX
Less: Operating Expenses		
Administrative and office expenses		
Salaries of office staff	XXX	
Office rental expenses	XXX	
Stationery and printing	XXX	
Communication expenses	XXX	
Travelling (Administrative staff)	XXX	
Office expenses	XXX	
Conveyance, etc.	XXX	
Total administrative and office expenses (d)	XXXX	
Selling and distribution expenses		
Salaries of marketing staff	XXX	
Warehouse rental expenses	XXX	
Sales commission	XXX	
Discount	XXX	
Advertisements	XXX	
Carriage outwards	XXX	
Travelling expenses (Sales staff)	XXX	
Distribution expenses	XXX	
Bad debts	XXX	
Bad debts provisions	XXX	
Total selling and distribution expenses (e)	XXXX	
Total Operating Expenses (d + e) (f)		XXXX
Cash Operating Income (Earnings before depreciation, interest, other income and expenses and tax) (c – f) (g)		XXXX
Depreciation (h)		XXX
Operating Income (Earnings before interest, other income and expenses and tax) (g – h) (i)		XXXX
Interest and financial charges (j)		XXX
Earnings before other income and expenses and tax (i – j) (k)		XXXX
Other Revenue		
Rental income	XXX	
Interest income	XXX	
Other income	XXX	
Prior period income	XXX	
Total Other Revenue (l)	XXXX	
Other Expenses	XXX	
Rental expenses	XXX	
Other expenses	XXX	
Prior period expenses	XXX	
Total Other Expenses (m)	XXXX	
Earnings before tax or profit before tax (k + l – m) (n)		XXXX
Income tax provisions (o)		XXX
Earnings after tax or profit after tax (n – o) (p)		XXX

Exhibit 4.5 indicates the multi-step income statement (Statement of Profit and Loss) which needs to be followed by corporate entities as per Section 123 of the Companies Act, 2013

EXHIBIT 4.5 Format of Multi-step Income Statement

Schedule III
(See Section 129)

PART II – STATEMENT OF PROFIT AND LOSS
Name of the Company ....
Profit and loss statement for the year ended ....
(Rupees in ....)

	Particulars	Note No.	Figures as at the End of Current Reporting Period	Figures as at the End of the Previous Reporting Period
	1	**2**	**3**	**4**
I	Revenue from operations			
II	Other income			
III	**Total Revenue (I + II)**			
IV	**Expenses:**			
	Cost of materials consumed			
	Purchases of stock-in-trade			
	Changes in inventories of finished goods work-in-progress and stock-in-trade			
	Employee benefits expense			
	Finance costs			
	Depreciation and amortization expense			
	Other expenses			
	Total expenses			
V	**Profit before exceptional and extraordinary items and tax (III – IV)**			
VI	Exceptional items			
VII	**Profit before extraordinary items and tax (V – VI)**			
VIII	Extraordinary items			
IX	**Profit before tax (VII – VIII)**			
X	Tax expense			
	(1) Current			
	(2) Deferred tax			
XI	Profit (Loss) for the period from continuing operations (VII – VIII)			
XII	Profit/(loss) from discontinuing operations			
XIII	Tax expense of discontinuing operations			
XIV	Profit/(loss) from discontinuing operations (after tax) (XII – XIII)			
XV	**Profit (Loss) for the period (XI + XIV)**			
XVI	**Earnings per equity share: (for continuing operation)**			
	(1) Basic			
	(2) Diluted			
XVII	**Earnings per equity share: (for discontinued operation)**			
	(1) Basic			
	(2) Diluted			
XVIII	**Earnings per equity share: (for discontinued and continuing operations)**			
	(1) Basic			
	(2) Diluted			

RELATIONSHIP BETWEEN BALANCE SHEET AND INCOME STATEMENT

The balance sheet and the income statement are not two separate and independent statements but are related to each other. The income statement is a link between the balance sheet at the the beginning of an accounting period and the balance sheet at the end of the period.

Generally, the income statement is prepared to compute net profit. Net profit can also be computed by comparing the balance sheet at the beginning and at the end of the period. This fact emphasizes the role of the income statement as a link between two consecutive statements of financial position.

The income statement provides a *historical* review of the account of the past transactions. The balance sheet gives a static picture of the financial position as on the last accounting period.

An income statement is an account, whereas a balance sheet is a statement of assets and liabilities. An income statement is prepared for the accounting period ended, whereas a balance sheet is prepared on the last day of the accounting period. The accounts cease to exist after transfer to the income statement. However, the accounts that are

Income statement is appendix to the balance sheet.

IFRS Update

The following table indicates the differences in the presentation style and format of Income Statement as per Indian Accounting Standards (Ind AS), IFRS, or International Accounting Standards (IAS) and US Generally Accepted Accounting Practices (GAAP).

Ind AS	IFRS/IAS	US GAAP
No standard format prescribed. Industry specific formats are prescribed by specific industry regulations. Present certain specific items in the income statement explicitly.	No standard format prescribed. An entity can present its expenses either by nature or by function. Present certain specific items in the income statement explicitly.	Income statement to be presented either in the format of single-step or in the format of multi-step. Expenditures are to be presented by functions only.

transferred to the balance sheet do not lose their identity and become the opening balances for the next accounting period.

The first statement prepared is the income statement. The income statement reports a business' performance for the period. And the second statement, which is the statement of retained earnings, reports how net, which income and dividends affect a company's financial position during the period. Income statement is prepared before the statement of retained earnings in order to see the effect of dividend payments on net income. The balance sheet must be prepared after the statement of retained earnings in order to calculate the ending balance of retained earnings.

Linkage between Balance Sheet and Income Statement

Figure 4.3 shows the relationship between a balance sheet and an income statement.

Income statement   A summary of the revenue and expenses for *a specific period of time* is an income statement.

Statement of retained earnings   A summary of the changes in the retained earnings that have occurred *during a specific period of time* is a statement of retained earnings.

Balance sheet   A list of the assets, liabilities, and owner's equity *as at a specific date* is a balance sheet.

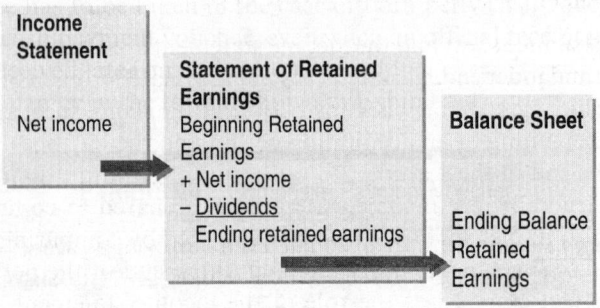

FIG. 4.3   Relationship between balance sheet and income statement

Table 4.2 indicates the methodology to work out the value of retained earnings at the end of an accounting period.

TABLE 4.2   Statement of Retained Earnings

Particulars	Working note	Amount (₹)
Beginning value of the retained earnings at the start of the year		xxxx
Add: Net Profit		xxx
Less: Net Loss		xxx
Less: Dividend or Drawings or Withdrawals		xxx
Ending value of the retained earnings at the end of the year		xxx

■ **ILLUSTRATION 4.1**   Deckers Scooters is in the business of selling Zebra scooters. The following information describes the business activities of Deckers Scooters during the year 2020.

(a) At the beginning of the year 2020, the company had 28 scooters in its inventory. Each scooter costs ₹1,20,000. During 2020, Deckers Scooters purchased 156 additional scooters from Zebra at ₹1,20,000, and sold 147 scooters at ₹1,40,000.

(b) At the beginning of 2020, the company owed money to Zebra for 24 scooters purchased during 2019. During 2020, it paid for 24 scooters and for 140 of the scooters purchased in 2020.

(c) At the beginning of 2020, customers owed money to Deckers Scooters for 23 scooters purchased during 2019. During 2020, Deckers Scooters collected payment for 23 scooters sold in 2019 and for 145 scooters sold in 2020.

(d) The operating and interest expenses of Deckers Scooters in 2020 were ₹42,80,000 and ₹3,70,000 respectively.

Answer the following questions:

1. Calculate Deckers Scooters' income before taxes in 2020.
2. Calculate the amount of Deckers Scooters' accounts receivables, amount payable, and inventory as on 31 December 2020.

Solution

1. The income calculation of Deckers Scooters for the period ended 2013 is as follows:

Particulars	Qty	Amount (₹)
Sales value (147 × 1,40,000)	147	2,05,80,000
Cost of goods sold		1,76,40,000
Gross profit		29,40,000
Less: Operating expenses		42,80,000
Operating profit		(–) 13,40,000
Less: Interest expenses		13,70,000
Net profit (+) or Net loss (–)		(–) 27,10,000

Working Note: Calculation of cost of goods sold = Opening Stock + Purchases – Closing Stock

2. Accounts receivable are computed as follows:

Particulars	Qty	Amount (₹)
Openings	23	32,20,000
Add: Sold	147	2,05,80,000
	170	2,38,00,000
Less: Payment received	168	2,35,20,000
Closing as on 31/12/2020	2	2,80,000

3. Accounts payable are calculated as follows:

Particulars	Qty	Amount (₹)
Openings	24	28,80,000
Add: Purchased	156	1,87,20,000
	180	2,16,00,000
Less: Paid for	164	1,76,80,000
Closing as on 31/12/2020	16	19,20,000

4. Inventory as on 31 December 2020 is calculated as follows:

Opening + Purchase – Consumption = Closing
28   +   156   –   147   =   37

■ **ILLUSTRATION 4.2**   Lopez Shoes uses paper bags to pack each pair of Hassan Shoes sold by them. The paper bag has the store name and Hassan's logo imprinted on it. Lopez

Shoes purchased 15,000 of these bags in October 2018 for ₹30,000. The bags were delivered in November 2018 and paid for in December 2018. Lopez Shoes began to use the bags in February 2019. By the end of 2019, 5000 of these bags remained in inventory and were subsequently used in 2020. Assume that the accounting period of Lopez Shoes is a calendar year.

Calculate the cost of goods sold which should be recorded in 2018, 2019, and 2020 to properly match with revenues.

Solution

The cost of goods sold for Lopez Shoes is as follows:

Calendar year	2018		2019		2020	
	Qty	Amount (₹)	Qty	Amount (₹)	Qty	Amount (₹)
Opening stock (a)	—	—	15,000	30,000	5,000	10,000
Purchases (b)	15,000	30,000	—	—	—	—
Closing stock (c)	15,000	30,000	5,000	10,000	—	—
Cost of goods sold (d) = (a + b − c)	Nil	Nil	10,000	20,000	5,000	10,000

■ ILLUSTRATION 4.3 Nakshatra Grah is a retailer of jewellery and gift items in Chennai. Some actual financial data from its annual reports ended 30 September 2019 are given in the following text. Nakshatra Grah does not pay dividends to its shareholders. Prepare the income statement for Nakshatra Grah.

Particulars	Amount (₹)
Net sales	4,73,172
Gross profit	1,88,766
Income from operations	15,436
Selling, general, and administrative expenses	?
Cost of sales	?
Other net income	170
Retained earnings at the beginning of the year	49,873
Retained earnings at the end of the year	?
Provision for income taxes	6,249

Solution

1. The income statement of Nakshatra Grah for the year ended 2019 is as follows:

Particulars	Amount (₹)
Sales	4,73,172
Less: Cost of goods sold (a)	2,84,406
Gross profit	1,88,766
Less: Selling, general, and administrative expenses (b)	1,73,330
Income from operations	15,436
Add: Other net income	170
Profit before tax	15,606
Less: Income tax	6,249
Profit after tax/Net profit	9,357

2. The statement of retained earnings for Nakshatra Grah is as follows:

Particulars	Amount (₹)
Profit after tax/Net profit	9,357
Add: Retained earnings at the beginning of year	49,873
Ending retained earnings	59,230

Working Notes:

(a) Sales – Cost of goods sold = Gross profit
⇒ Cost of goods sold = Sales – Gross profit
= 4,73,172 – 1,88,766
= 2,84,406

(b) Gross profit – Selling, general, = Income from
operations
and administrative expenses
⇒ Selling, general, and = Gross profit – Income from
administrative expenses   operations
= 1,88,766 – 15,436
= 1,73,330

■ ILLUSTRATION 4.4 Prepare a trading account from the following particulars for the year ended 31 March 2019.

Particulars	Amount (₹)
Opening stock	37,500
Purchases	1,05,000
Sales	2,70,000
Wages	30,000

Solution

Trading Account for the Year Ended 31 March 2019

Particulars	Amount (₹)
Income:	
Sales	2,70,000
Total Income	2,70,000
Expenses:	
Opening stock	37,500
Purchases	1,05,000
Wages	30,000
Total Expenses	1,72,500
Gross Profit	**97,500**

ILLUSTRATION 4.5 From the following information for the year ending 31 March 2020 furnished by Mr Vikram, a trader, calculate the cost of goods sold and also the gross profit or gross loss of business.

Particulars	Amount (₹)
Sales	1,20,000
Purchases	80,000
Octroi	1,600
Carriage on purchases	4,500
Purchase returns	2,400
Opening stock	27,600
Closing stock	32,400

Solution

Trading Account of Mr Vikram for the Year Ended 31 March 2020

Particulars		Amount (₹)
Income:		
Sales		1,20,000
Less: Sales return		0
Net sales		1,20,000

Particulars		Amount (₹)
Income:		
Total Income		1,20,000
Expenses:		
Opening stock	27,600	
Add: Purchases	80,000	
Less: Purchase return	2,400	
Less: Closing stock	32.400	
= Cost of materials consumed		72,800
Octroi		1,600
Carriage on purchase		4,500
Total Expenses		78,900
Gross Profit		41,100
Cost of Goods Sold		
Sales		1,20,000
Less gross profit		41,100
= Cost of Goods Sold		78,900

■ ILLUSTRATION 4.6 Prepare the income and expenditure account from the following information of Rajoji Club, Ahmedabad for the year ending 31 December 2019.

Particulars	Amount (₹)
Cash balance as on 1.1.2019	70,000
Subscriptions	3,00,000
Interest received	25,000
Sports material	2,40,000
Match fund	1,50,000
Donations	20,000
Sale of grass	3,000
Newspaper expenses	6,000
Investments purchased	1,00,000
Salaries paid	1,60,000
Rent paid	54,000
Miscellaneous receipts	6,000
Telephone charges	12,000
Cash balance as on 31.12.2019	2,000

Solution

Income Statement of Rajoji Club for the year ended 31 December 2019

Particulars	Amount (₹)
Income:	
Subscription	3,00,000
Interest Received	25,000
Sale of Grass	3,000
Miscellaneous Receipts	6,000
Donations (Assumed Regular)	20,000
Total Income	3,54,000
Expenses:	
Salaries	1,60,000
Rent	54,000
Newspaper Expense	6,000
Telephone charges	12,000
Total Expenses	2,32,000
Excess of Income over Expenses	1,22,000

■ ILLUSTRATION 4.7 From the following information, prepare a profit and loss account for the year ending 31 March 2020.

Particulars	Amount (₹)
Gross profit	6,00,000
Rent	50,000
Salary	1,50,000
Commission paid	70,000
Interest paid on loan	50,000
Advertising	40,000
Discount received	30,000
Printing and stationery	20,000
Legal charges	50,000
Bad debts	10,000
Depreciation	20,000
Interest received	40,000
Loss by fire	30,000

Solution

Profit and Loss Account (Income Statement)
for the year ending on March 31, 2020

Particulars	Amount (₹)
Income:	
Gross Profit C/f from trading account	6,00,000
Discount received	30,000
Interest received	40,000
Total Income	6,70,000
Expenses:	
Rent	50,000
Salary	1,50,000
Commission	70,000
Interest paid on loans	50,000
Advertising	40,000
Printing and stationery	20,000
Legal charges	50,000
Bad debts	10,000
Depreciation	20,000
Loss by fire	30,000
Total Expenses	4,90,000
Net Profit	1,80,000
(Transferred to the Capital Account)	

■ ILLUSTRATION 4.8 From the following balances obtained from a few accounts of Mr Hardik Nagar, prepare the trading account and the profit and loss account.

	Amount (₹)		Amount (₹)
Stock on 1.4.2019	8,000	Bad debts	1,200
Purchases for the year	22,000	Rent	1,200
Sales for the year	42,000	Discount allowed	600
Purchase expenses	2,500	Commission paid	1,100
Salaries and wages	3,500	Sales expenses	600
Advertisement	1,000	Repairs	600

Closing stock on 31 March 2020 is ₹4,500.

Solution

Trading Account (Part of Income Statement) of Mr Hardik Nagar for the Year Ending 31 March 2020

Particulars		Amount (₹)
Income:		
Sales		42,000
Less: Sales return		0
Net sales		42,000
Total Income		42,000
Expenses:		
Opening stock	8,000	
Add: Purchases	22,000	
Less: Purchase return	0	
Less: Closing stock	4,500	
= Cost of materials consumed		25,500
Octroi		0
Purchases expense		2,500
Total Expenses		28,000
Gross Profit C/f to Profit and Loss Account		**14,000**

Profit and Loss Account (Part of Income Statement)

Particulars	Amount (₹)
Income:	
Gross Profit b/f from Trading Account	14,000
Total Income	**14,000**
Expenses:	
Salaries and wages	3,500
Rent	1,200
Advertisement	1,000
Commission	1,100
Discount allowed	600
Bad debts	1,200
Sales expenses	600
Repairs	600
Total Expenses	9,800
Net Profit	**4,200**
(Transferred to the Capital Account)	

■ **ILLUSTRATION 4.9** From the following information of M/s Krishna & Bros. for the year ending 31 March 2020, prepare the trading account and the profit and loss account for the year ended 31 March 2020.

	Amount (₹)		Amount (₹)
Stock on 1.4.2019	5,800	Sales	72,000
Purchases - cash	42,000	Return inward	2,000
Purchases - credit	18,000	Interest on investment	1,500
Freight inward	1,800	Discount received	1,200
Wages	4,500	Closing stock	7,200
Carriage on sales	800	Telephone charges	1,600
Electricity expenses	1,200	Office rent paid	6,000
Salaries	8,000	Depreciation	1,400

Solution

Trading Account (Part of Income Statement) of M/s Krishna & Bros. for the Year Ending 31 March 2020

Particulars		Amount (₹)
Income:		
Sales		72,000
Less: Sales return (Return inward)		2,000
Net Sales		70,000
Total Income		70,000
Expenses:		
Opening stock	5,800	
Add: Purchases - Cash	42,000	
Add: Purchases - Credit	18,000	
Less: Closing stock	7,200	
= Cost of materials consumed		58,600
Freight inward		1,800
Wages		4,500
Total Expenses		64,900
Gross Profit C/f to Profit and Loss Account		**5,100**

Profit and Loss Account (Part of Income Statement)

Particulars	Amount (₹)
Income:	
Gross Profit b/f from Trading Account	5,100
Discount received	1,200
Total Income	**6,300**
Expenses:	
Salaries	8,000
Telephone charges	1,600
Electricity expenses	1,200
Office rent	6,000
Carriage on sale	800
Depreciation	1,400
Total Operating Expenses	19,000
Operating Profit	**(12,700)**
Add: Interest on investments	1,500
Net Profit or (Net Loss)	**(11,200)**
(Transferred to the Capital Account)	
Answer is negative, which means Net Loss	

SUMMARY

- Basic business financial flows consist of earning activities. The income statement focuses on creation and consumption of resources.
- To study the financial performance of the firm, the activities of an enterprise are divided into artificial time periods. The revenue recognition concept revolves around the determination of the point of time when revenue is realized. The accrual concept recognizes revenues and expenses as they are earned or incurred without regard to the date of receipt or payment.

- The matching concept is the process of matching accomplishments or revenues with efforts or expenses, to a particular period for which the income is being determined.

> Gross Income or Profit = Revenue – Cost of Goods Sold
> Cost of Goods Sold = Opening Stock + Purchase + Direct Expense – Closing Stock

- Business enterprise should provide all relevant information to external users for the purpose of sound economic decisions. The transactions and events that have material and significant effects should be reported in financial statements.
- According to the consistency concept, once an entity has decided on the method of accounting, it should use the same method for all subsequent transactions and events of the same nature, unless it has sound reason to change methods.

> Net Sales Revenue = Sales – Sales Return
> Operating Expenses = Administrative Expenses + Depreciation + Selling and Distribution Expenses
> Operating Profit = Gross Profit – Operating Expenses
> Profit Before Tax = Operating Profit + Non-Operating Income – Non-Operating Expenses – Interest Expenses
> Profit After Tax = Profit Before Tax – Tax Expenses

- The income statement is a link between the balance sheet at the beginning of the period and balance sheet at the end of the period.
- The income statement is an account of an entity's performance, whereas a balance sheet is a statement of its assets and liabilities.

KEYWORDS

Income statement It summarizes the results of an entity's operations over a period of time.

Loss It is the amount by which expenses exceed revenues.

Materiality concept An item should be regarded as material if there is reason to believe that its knowledge influences the decision of informed investors.

Profit It is the amount by which revenues exceed expenses.

Revenue It is the amount received or receivable from the sale of goods or services.

QUESTIONS

I. Choose the correct option.

1. The tabulation of balances of all the ledger accounts as a summary statement is known as
   - (a) Trial balance
   - (b) Balance sheet
   - (c) Reconciliation statement
   - (d) Financial statement

2. Purchase of equipment for cash
   - (a) Decreases total assets
   - (b) Increases total assets
   - (c) Leaves total assets unchanged
   - (d) Increases liabilities

3. Journal is
   - (a) Book of original entry
   - (b) Book of final entry
   - (c) Permanent record
   - (d) Incomplete record

4. Very small businesses may not keep complete records because
   - (a) The law requires them not to maintain it compulsorily
   - (b) They mainly deal in cash
   - (c) They mainly deal in credit
   - (d) They rarely make gross profit

5. The principle of accounting which recognizes the double aspect of a business transaction is
   - (a) Single-entry
   - (b) Dual aspect concept
   - (c) Cost concept
   - (d) Matching concept

6. The method used to find the profit of a petty trader is
   - (a) The straight line method
   - (b) The reducing balance method
   - (c) Measuring changes in opening and closing net worth

7. Dual aspect concept results in the accounting equation
   - (a) Capital + Liabilities = Assets
   - (b) Capital = Assets
   - (c) Revenue = Expenses
   - (d) Capital + Profit = Assets + Expenses

8. Which of the following is a personal account
   - (a) Creditor's account
   - (b) Rent account
   - (c) Motor vehicle account
   - (d) Cash account

9. In double-entry system of bookkeeping, every business transaction affects
   - (a) Two sides of the same account
   - (b) The same account on two different dates
   - (c) Two accounts
   - (d) One account

10. Classified summary of all transactions is called
    - (a) Cash book
    - (b) Ledger
    - (c) Journal
    - (d) Trial balance

11. Double-entry means
    - (a) Entry made at two sides
    - (b) Entry made in two sides of books
    - (c) Entry of two aspects of the transaction
    - (d) Entry of one aspect of the transaction

12. Sale of goods on credit to Goodwill Motors was recorded by
    - (a) Debiting sales account and crediting the company's account
    - (b) Debiting Goodwill's account and crediting the sales account
    - (c) Debiting cash account and crediting sales account
    - (d) Debiting cash account and crediting the company's account

13. Financial analysis of accounting data is not usually carried out from the view point of
    - (a) Financial institutions
    - (b) Shareholders
    - (c) Customers
    - (d) Statutory agencies

14. Withdrawal of goods from stock by the owner of the business for personal use is recorded by
    (a) Debiting stock account and crediting capital account
    (b) Debiting capital account and crediting drawings account
    (c) Debiting drawings account and crediting stock account
15. Purchase of goods for cash from Pallu is to be recorded by
    (a) Debiting purchases account and crediting Pallu's account
    (b) Debiting cash account and crediting Pallu's account
    (c) Debiting purchases account and crediting cash account
    (d) Debiting Pallu's account and crediting cash account
16. Purchases account, rent received account, and capital account will normally show
    (a) Debit, credit balance, and debit balance respectively
    (b) Debit, debit balance, and credit balance respectively
    (c) Debit, credit balance, and credit balance respectively
    (d) Credit, credit balance, and debit balance respectively
17. Payment of wages is recorded by
    (a) Debiting employees account and crediting wages account
    (b) Debiting employees account and crediting cash account
    (c) Debiting cash account and crediting wages account
    (d) Debiting wages account and crediting cash account

Answer questions 18 to 21 based on the following information:
A trader had a debtor's balance of ₹880 on 1 January 2013, and ₹910 on 31 December 2013; and creditor's balance of ₹660 on 1 January 2013 and ₹570 on 31 December 2013. During the year, customers to whom goods were sold on credit paid ₹2,450; ₹820 was received in respect of cash sales. Payments to suppliers amounted to ₹840.

18. The total net sales figure for the year was
    (a) ₹3,300   (b) ₹3,270
    (c) ₹1,460   (d) ₹1,430
19. Total credit sales for the year was
    (a) ₹2,480   (b) ₹2,450
    (c) ₹640   (d) ₹610
20. Total credit purchases amounted to
    (a) ₹2,450   (b) ₹1,840
    (c) ₹750   (d) ₹610
21. Total cash sales for the year was
    (a) ₹1,630   (b) ₹1,540
    (c) ₹910   (d) ₹820
22. Goods returned by customers is entered by
    (a) Debiting the purchase account and crediting the customers account
    (b) Debiting the customers account and crediting the sales account
    (c) Debiting the sales returns account and crediting the customers account
    (d) Debiting the customers account and crediting the goods account
23. Cash brought in by the proprietor as capital is recorded by
    (a) Debiting the cash account and crediting the capital account
    (b) Debiting the cash account and crediting the bank account
    (c) Debiting the capital account and crediting the cash account
    (d) Debiting the capital account and crediting the bank account
24. Salaries account, furniture account, and debtors account will normally show
    (a) Credit, debit, and, debit balance respectively
    (b) Debit, credit, and, debit balance respectively
    (c) Debit, debit, and debit balance respectively
    (d) Debit, debit, and credit balance respectively

Answer question 25–29 using the following information:
A statement of affairs (a rough form of a balance sheet) of a trader on 1 January 2013 revealed fixed assets of ₹1,800 and current assets of ₹2,000. As at 1 January 2014, the fixed assets totaled ₹10,150 and the current assets totaled ₹6,640. The trader had a current liability of ₹3,500 on 1 January 2014.

25. The trader's net worth on 1 January 2013 was
    (a) ₹3,800   (b) ₹1,800
    (c) ₹200   (d) Nil
26. The trader's total worth on 1 January 2013 was
    (a) ₹3,800   (b) ₹2,000
    (c) ₹1,800   (d) ₹200
27. The trader's net worth on 1 January 2014 was
    (a) ₹16,790   (b) ₹13,290
    (c) ₹10,150   (d) ₹3,500
28. The trader's total worth on 1 January 2014 was
    (a) ₹16,790   (b) ₹13,290
    (c) ₹10,150   (d) ₹6,640
29. The trader's increase in net worth was
    (a) ₹13,290   (b) ₹12,990
    (c) ₹9,490   (d) ₹3,800

Questions 30–32 are based on Shruti's statement of affairs. Her drawings are ₹20 per week.

Statement of Affairs

Particulars	As at 1 January 2020 Amount (₹)	As at 31 December 2020 Amount (₹)
Capital	7,000	12,000
Current liabilities	8,000	9,000
Assets	15,000	21,000

30. Shruti's total drawings were
    (a) ₹17,000   (b) ₹15,000
    (c) ₹9,000   (d) ₹1,040
31. Net profit for the year was
    (a) ₹6,040   (b) ₹5,000
    (c) ₹4,040   (d) ₹1,860
32. The increase in Shruti's net worth was
    (a) ₹21,000   (b) ₹15,000
    (c) ₹6,000   (d) ₹5,000
33. A trader has an opening capital of ₹45,000 and a closing capital of ₹47,000. Her drawings during the year amount to ₹5,000. What is the net profit?
    (a) ₹9,000   (b) ₹7,000
    (c) ₹3,000   (d) ₹2,000
34. On sale of old furniture, owners equity will
    (a) Increase   (b) Decrease
    (c) Remain unchanged   (d) May or may not change
35. A trader has an opening capital of ₹2,00,000 and a closing capital of ₹2,03,000. Her net profit is ₹5,000. Her drawings for the year are
    (a) ₹8,000   (b) ₹3,000
    (c) ₹2,000   (d) ₹1,000
36. On a particular date, the assets of a business are worth ₹2,00,000 and its capital is ₹70,000. Its liabilities on that date will be
    (a) ₹2,70,000   (b) ₹1,30,000
    (c) ₹70,000   (d) ₹1,10,000
37. Withdrawals by the proprietor will
    (a) Reduce assets and owner's equity
    (b) Reduce assets and increase liabilities
    (c) Reduce owner's equity and increase liabilities
    (d) Does not affect the balance sheet

38. A firm has liabilities worth ₹16,000. The claims of the proprietor are ₹24,000. The total assets are
    (a) ₹24,000   (b) ₹8,000
    (c) ₹40,000   (d) ₹16,000
39. Balance sheet discloses the
    (a) Cash position of the business
    (b) Financial position of the business
    (c) Profit earning capacity of the business
    (d) Income position of the business

II. Fill in the following blanks with appropriate word(s).

1. The principle of accounting, which recognizes the double aspect of a business transaction, is known as the _____ concept.
2. If a business has liabilities worth ₹2,00,000 and owner's equity worth ₹50,000, the total assets are _____.
3. The going-concern concept assumes that business will be carried out for _____ period.
4. If the assets of a business total ₹45,000 and the owner's equity is ₹35,000, the outside liabilities total _____.
5. Consideration of an event as material or otherwise depends on _____.
6. If a business has assets worth ₹80,000 and liabilities worth ₹20,000, the owner's equity is _____.
7. If a business is owned by one person, it is called a _____.
8. A decrease in the owner's capital (assuming that there are no drawings) will mean _____.
9. Contribution of capital by owners is shown as a liability according to the _____.
10. A withdrawal of cash by the proprietor reduces cash and _____.
11. Calculation of _____ or _____ and ascertainment of _____ of the business are the main objectives of maintaining accounts.
12. Withdrawal of money by the owner is not considered as an expense but leads to a reduction of _____.
13. In every transaction at least _____ parties are involved.
14. _____ the receiver; and _____ the giver.
15. The journal is a book of _____ entry.
16. Debit what _____, credit what _____.
17. The proprietor of a business is an _____ to it according to the entity concept.
18. Trial balance is _____.
19. Increase in the value of the asset could increase the _____.
20. Assets, which are to remain in a business for continuous use and for conversion into cash, are _____ assets.
21. Increase in the value of the assets could reduce the value of _____.
22. Liabilities + _____ = Assets
23. Decrease in the value of the assets could decrease the value of _____.
24. A balance sheet discloses the financial position of a business _____.
25. Decrease in the value of a liability could increase the value of _____.
26. Trial balance establishes the _____ of the accounting records.
27. _____ is a book where all business transactions find their place.
28. From the trial balance two separate accounting documents are produced—the income statement and the _____.
29. _____ is the excess of assets over liabilities.
30. The net result of an income statement is taken to _____.

31. Every business transaction has _____ effect.
32. All assets and _____ are taken to the balance sheet.
33. A person who owes something is called a _____.
34. All income and _____ are taken to the income statement.
35. The obligation of a business is a _____.
36. The idea that expenses and revenues can be identified and matched in a period that is shorter than the life of the business is known as _____.
37. _____ is a recording device used for sorting accounting information into similar groups.
38. Excess of expenses over revenues for a given period is _____.
39. A thing of value owned by an economic enterprise is _____.
40. A business transaction essentially involves _____ of money or money's worth.
41. The expired cost is _____.
42. All those to whom the business owed money are _____.
43. Following an adopted accounting method in a future period in the same way is _____.
44. Choosing the acceptable alternative that produces the least favourable immediate result is called _____.

III. Indicate whether the following statements are True or False.

1. Future profits may be recognized in the accounting process.
2. The balance sheet represents the equation, Assets = Liabilities + Capital.
3. A regular and systematic accounting system helps in ascertaining the financial position of a firm.
4. There cannot be more than two parties in a financial transaction.
5. Deepti has assets worth ₹10,000 and liabilities worth ₹2,000. Her capital, therefore, will be ₹12,000.
6. Accounting records are subject to the personal judgment of the accountant.
7. In the double-entry system of bookkeeping, every business transaction affects at least two accounts.
8. When a creditor is paid; the value of one asset diminishes and the value of another asset increases.
9. Books of accounts can be produced as evidence in court of law in case of disputes.
10. The entity concept of accounting is not applicable to sole trading concerns and partnership firms.
11. Sale of furniture for cash will increase one asset and reduce another.
12. All business decisions are made only on the basis of market information.
13. The dual aspect of accounting results in the accounting equation, Capital + Liabilities = Assets.
14. Cash purchase of goods increases the total number of creditors of an enterprise.
15. Every debit has an equal and corresponding credit.
16. Assets are shown in the balance sheet at the values realizable on liquidation.
17. Capital is diminished by drawings and increased by profits.
18. Maintenance of accounts enables calculation of tax liabilities.
19. The convention of conservatism has usually the effect of overstating losses and understating income.
20. Financial statements are prepared at the end of each business transaction.
21. Bookkeeping is an art of scientifically recording financial transactions.
22. The money measurement concept takes into account changes in the value of the monetary unit.

23. Net income is determined by subtracting expenses from revenues.
24. Business transactions essentially involve the transfer of money or money's worth.
25. The principle of consistency is particularly valuable when all alternative accounting methods are equally acceptable.
26. A transaction, which increases capital, is known as income.
27. Trade unions can make appropriate demands once they know the company's financial position through its books of accounts.
28. A balance sheet based on the cost concept is of no use to a potential investor.
29. Assets of a balance sheet will be equal to the liabilities.
30. If a company regularly maintains its books of accounts, its owners need not play any role in its day-to-day management.
31. The going-concern concept assumes that a business will continue its operations indefinitely.
32. Ownership in a joint stock company is evident by shares.
33. All business transactions are always recorded in the books of accounts.
34. The balance sheet is a statement of valuation.
35. The business entity is separate from the owner but the business and its owner are not separate entities as per law.
36. A business transaction is always recorded by both the parties involved in the transaction.
37. The double-entry system is not a complete system of bookkeeping.
38. Profit or loss can be calculated at periodic intervals.
39. The double-entry system is a complete system of accounting.
40. Ledger is the principal book of accounts.

IV. Solve the following problems.

1. Calculate the cost of goods sold and gross profit gained from the following information.

Particulars	Amount (₹)
Sales	62,500
Sales returns	500
Opening stock	6,400
Purchases	32,000
Direct expenses	4,200
Closing stock	7,200

2. Prepare a trading account of M/s Prime Products from the following particulars pertaining to the year 2019–20.

Particulars	Amount (₹)
Opening stock	50,000
Purchases	1,10,000
Return inwards	5,000
Sales	3,00,000
Return outwards	7,000
Factory rent	30,000
Wages	40,000

3. Prepare a trading account of M/s Anjali from the following information related to 2019–2020.

Particulars	Amount (₹)
Opening stock	60,000
Purchases	3,00,000
Sales	7,50,000
Purchases return	18,000

	Amount (₹)
Sales return	30,000
Carriage on purchases	12,000
Carriage on sales	15,000
Factory rent	18,000
Office rent	18,000
Dock and clearing charges	48,000
Freight and Octroi	6,500
Coal, Gas, and Water	10,000

4. The following balance is extracted from the books of a trader. Ascertain the gross profit, operating profit, and net profit for the year ended 31 March 2020.

Particulars	Amount (₹)
Sales	75,250
Purchases	32,250
Opening stock	7,600
Sales return	1,250
Purchases return	250
Rent	300
Stationary and printing	250
Salaries	3,000
Misc. expenses	200
Travelling expenses	500
Advertisement	1,800
Commission paid	150
Office expenses	1,600
Wages	2,600
Profit on sale of investment	500
Depreciation	800
Dividend on investment	2,500
Loss on sale of old furniture	300
Closing stock (31 March 2020) valued at ₹8,000	

5. Prepare the trading account and profit and loss account of M/s Loman Irani from the following balances for the year ending 31 March 2020.

Particulars	Amount (₹)
Opening stock	14,600
Purchases	68,700
Sales	85,300
Return outward	2,200
Carriage inward	2,100
Capital	50,000
Drawings	12,000
Advertisement	2,400
Trading expenses	1,450
Discount allowed	1,250
Discount received	800
Bill receivables	4,500
Debtors	16,800
Closing stock	28,700
Insurance	1,600
Salesmen's salaries	5,200

 # CASES

Conceptual Application Case

1. Sandstrom Company The following information pertains to Sandstrom Company. The total assets amounted to ₹2,20,000 as on 1 April 2019 and ₹2,48,000 as on 31 March 2019. During the year 2019–2020, the sales were worth ₹6,08,000, cash dividend was ₹10,000, and operating expenses (excluding the cost of goods sold) were ₹4,00,000. Total liabilities were ₹1,10,000 as on 31 March 2020, and ₹1,00,000 as on 1 April 2019. There was no additional capital brought in by Sandstrom during the year.

Compute the following:

(a) The capital of Sandstrom Company as on 1 April 2020 and as on 31 March 2020.

(b) Net income of the year 2019–2020.

(c) Cost of goods sold for the year 2019–2020.

2. Anil Garg Varun Zarivala and Anil Garg operate as estate agents in Mumbai. When their bookkeeper retired, Varun decided to take over the financial aspect of the business. While updating records, Varun was unsure about the treatment of a number of transactions.

(a) One month before the end of the financial year April 2019–March 2020, Varun sent a cheque for ₹60,000 to the landlord. This was to cover the payment of rent for the next 12 months. Varun decided not to record this payment because most of it was for the next financial year.

(b) The company purchased a new notebook computer for ₹14,000. However, two months after the purchase, Anil noticed that the same notebook computer was available in the market for ₹6,500. Now Varun is not sure which value to record.

(c) One of their clients sent a cheque for ₹32,000, while the amount due was ₹23,000. Varun is not sure which figure to enter in the financial records.

Questions

1. Explain how Varun should treat each of the above transactions according to the appropriate accounting concepts.

2. As Varun's accountant, write him a memo explaining why accounting concepts are integral to bookkeeping.

Business Application Cases

1. Supriya Language Courses Sriman Prabhu owns a small concern, 'Supriya Language Courses'. He has developed a popular language course in Gujarati language for non-Gujarati speakers. The course material consists of a set of audio cassettes, a tutorial book, a dictionary, and a small stereo cassette player. He buys the package from a manufacturer and sells it by mail order in response to advertisements in select journals.

Last year (ending 31 December 2019) Sriman sold 29,000 packs at ₹890 each. He started the year with 350 packs, valued at ₹1,92,500 and ended the year with a stock of 600 packs. During the year, he received 3,150 packs from his manufacturer, who charged him ₹590 per pack. This is the price Sriman uses to value the company's closing stock.

Sriman employs part-time staff whose salaries and wages totalled ₹1,45,000. Postages worked out at ₹20 per pack and packing at ₹5 per pack were sold. Sriman rented a small warehouse for ₹10,000 per month. Advertising bills totalled ₹1,50,000 and an invoice for a further ₹5,000 is still awaited. Insurance premiums paid were ₹35,000, but out of this amount, ₹6,500 refers to the current year (2020). Electricity bills worth ₹29,000 have to be paid by the company, with a further bill for the last quarter of 2019 expected to be of approximately ₹5,000.

Sriman uses a notebook computer for administrative purposes, and this, together with the word-processing equipment, cost ₹40,000 in 2017. Sriman reckons this equipment will last about five years, so he allows ₹8,000 per annum in his accounts for depreciation. In addition to this, his stationery bill totalled ₹13,500.

During 2019, he received four telephone bills, totalling ₹35,000, of which ₹2,000 relates to rental in advance for 2020. In the previous year (2018) rental in advance of ₹1,500 (relating to first quarter of 2019) had been deducted from the bills for 2018 for arriving at the expenses for 2018.

Sriman also spent ₹51,000 on the research and development of his product, which resulted in minor improvements to his language pack. The work on a new edition of the pack is to be completed by 2021. Sriman's policy on research and development is to write off all expenditures in the year in which they incur. He feels this is prudent, since research work may not prove to be productive.

Sriman's accountants are very busy and are not expected to produce figures for 2019 until next month.

Question

Give Sriman an idea of the company's profit for 2019.

2. Ashok Transport Company Ashok Transport Company (ATC) began trucking operations on 1 January 2019. The company's bank account showed a balance of ₹90,000 on 31 December 2019, which was in agreement with the bank statement received on the same date. The company had ₹6,000 as cash in office and ₹4,000 worth cheques received from customers.

On 31 December 2019, the receivables outstanding amounted to ₹3,00,000. The company had promissory notes worth ₹30,000. Employees had drawn their festival advance amounting to ₹6,000. The company owed ₹3,60,000 to Popular Service Station as on 31 December 2019.

During the year, ATC purchased stationery and office supplies worth ₹11,000 from Kumar & Co. The use of stationery and supplies during the year was estimated at ₹8,000.

The company purchased eight trucks each costing ₹4,00,000 during the year. It owed ₹20,00,000 to Popular Sales and Finance at the end of the year on account of trucks bought. The obligation was supported by a hire purchase agreement for payment at the rate of ₹50,000 per month. The depreciation amount was ₹80,000 for each truck for the year. Spare parts and tyres inventory amounted to ₹13,000.

The company had rented a garage, office space, and parking space on a 30 year lease at ₹1,00,000 a year. Due to the real estate boom, ATC could easily sublet the premises for ₹1,50,000 a year. On 1 January 2019, when ATC started operations, it had to pay the rent for the first two years in advance.

On 31 December 2019, ATC purchased an air-conditioned car costing ₹1,00,000 for office use. Insurance and registration costs amounted to ₹8,000.

The company had a bulk storage tank for diesel needed for its trucks. The tank was filled four times with 50,000 litres every time. On 31 December, the meter reading indicated that 1,80,000 litres had been used during the year. The average cost per litre of diesel was ₹3.

The company pays salary to its employees on the last day of each month. The bonus due for the year 2019 amounted to ₹2,12,000 and will be paid along with the salary in January 2021.

The owners of ATC originally invested ₹6,00,000. Net income for 2019 was ₹2,08,000. Drawings by the owners during the year amounted to ₹1,00,000.

Questions

Prepare the balance sheet of ATC as at 31 December 2019.

3. Subhadra Ventures Subhadra Ventures was established in the beginning of the year 2016 by two friends, Shruti and Sujata. They both individually contributed ₹1,00,000 in cash to start the venture.

Since then, the company has been more successful than expected by them. However, they have not spent money on the establishment of an internal control and a strong accounting system, and hence, sound accounting practices have not been followed by Subhadra Ventures. The accounts are prepared and maintained for the given accounting year, specifically with regard to income tax return submission to the Indian income tax department, as required by the Income Tax Act.

As a consequence of this practice, the financial performance of the firm was only vaguely known to them.

Recently, the income tax department sent a notice, asking for a detailed explanation about the working of the income statement, which indicated that the profit of Subhadra Ventures for the year ended 31 March 2020 is ₹34,200. Sujata approached her friend Jeevan, a chartered accountant, who discovered that the reported profit is wrong. He found that the interest expenses for the amount of ₹10,000 borrowed at the rate of 9 % interest in January 2016 from Aziz Latif, a neighboring shopkeeper, was not reported in the income statement. The depreciation on the notebook computer purchased for ₹20,000, with an estimated useful life of five years, had also not been recognized. Sujata gave Jeevan a photocopy of the income statement for the year ended as on 31 March 2020 submitted to the income tax department. The details as exhibited by the income statement are mentioned in the following text.

Particulars	Amount (₹)
Commission earned and collected	1,66,000
Property advising services fees collected (excluded ₹2,000 still not received)	8,000
Total income reported	1,74,000
Salaries paid (11 months; March, 2019 still not paid)	27,500
Commission paid	38,000
Service tax deposited	13,800
Office stationery and cleaning expenses paid	1,500
Rent paid in the beginning of the month	24,000
Office electricity bill paid (10 months paid)	2,000
Advertisement charges paid (₹1,000 paid in advance)	11,000
General expenses such as courier charges, telephone charges, etc.	22,000
Total expenses	1,39,800
Profit for the year 2019–2020	34,200

Question

Work out the correct taxable profit for the year 2019–2020, and also work out the tax liability by assuming an income tax rate of 20%.

REFERENCES

'Guidance Notes', issued by Institute of Chartered Accountants of India.

'Indian Accounting Standards', announced by Institute of Chartered Accountants of India.

'Pronouncements', by Ministry of Company Affairs, Government of India.

Recognition and Types of Transactions

Objectively Verifiable Evidence

Learning Objectives

After studying this chapter, you will understand

- concepts of receipt and capital maintenance
- different types of vouchers and their use in recording business events
- how business transactions can be done through electronic banking

INTRODUCTION

The assumption of objectively verifiable evidence is that every business record must be based on and supported by documentary evidence. Every entry made in the subsidiary books must be supported by a voucher. Receipts, bills, invoices, cash memos, salary bills, and deeds are some of the vouchers used for recording business transactions. *Objectivity* of the documents, that is, vouchers, means that these vouchers need to present facts without bias to any party. *Verifiability* refers to the capability of checking documents of transactions before they are recorded in the books of accounts. After the transaction has been recorded in the books of accounts, auditors check entries and postings against their corresponding vouchers. Accounting is not accepted as true or accurate if there is no documentary proof for every record in the books of accounts. Accounting should be definite, verifiable, and free from manipulation and personal bias.

Transactions or events are recorded in the books of accounts on the basis of documentary evidences. These documentary evidences should be objectively verifiable for truthfulness of the events or transactions. They are also known as source documents.

Source documents are basically written documents related to the external and internal activities of a firm, such as receipts, bills, proof of cash expenses, invoices, and pay in slip for deposits of cheques or funds in the bank account of the firm. These documents certify the actual happening of a transaction or an event, the amount involved, parties taking part in the transaction, nature of the transaction, etc. Accounting effects are described in the books of accounts of the firm based on these documents.

Vouchers may be classified broadly into two categories: supporting vouchers and accounting vouchers. Supporting vouchers are the documents providing evidence about a transaction having taken place. For example, payment of rent to the landlord would be duly supported by the rent receipt issued by the landlord. Accounting vouchers are prepared on the basis of supporting vouchers. Generally, supporting vouchers are clipped along with the accounting vouchers.

Vouchers may also be classified into two categories—based on the parties who draw the vouchers—as internal vouchers and external vouchers. An internal voucher is prepared by the firm itself to record all transactions that occurred. For example, conveyance charges, postage, normal canteen expenses in the form of tea payment, etc. Such vouchers are prepared by the firm's employees, and are sanctioned by the higher authority of the employee concerned. The employee who receives the money as reimbursement of expenses made by him/her has to sign the vouchers. Such vouchers are properly numbered and filed. An external voucher is prepared by an external party. Such vouchers support transactions with outsiders, for example, telephone bill, electricity bill, travelling expenses, etc. The original voucher is received from the outside source, and then properly numbered and placed in the concerned file of the firm.

CAPITAL MAINTENANCE

Capital is linked to the net assets or owners' equity (shareholders' net worth) of the firm. As per the modern approach of accounting, capital equals to assets of the firm less external liabilities. The success of any firm is measured through either an increase in capital or maintaining the capital base of the firm. If the capital of the firm deteriorates, then it is considered as a declining firm.

Capital is linked to the tangible and intangible plant, property, and equipment (PPE). A higher declaration of the PPE value in comparison to its intrinsic or realistic value indicates an untrue and unfair presentation of capital (derived value of capital is greater than reality) in the balance sheet of the firm. In other words, it indicates that the firm has not properly maintained the capital, and erosion in the value of capital happens. The modern approach indicates that owners' equity is the sum total of the capital contributed by owners in the firm and the profit retained in the firm. If the PPE value is greater than the realistic value, it should be understood that the firm has not provided a realistic reduction in the value of PPE on account of usage, passage of time, change in technology, etc. This results in lesser booking of expenses in the income statement, which leads to more profit.

In the same way, if a firm wrongly books less expenses (like manufacturing expenses, administration expenses, etc.) or more income, then also more profit is displayed. Maintenance of the firm's capital at the beginning of the period is known as capital maintenance. A proper measurement and evaluation can be done through objectively verifiable evidences. This shows the importance of these evidences.

RECEIPT

Receipt acknowledges receipt of money.

A receipt is a document acknowledging the fact that the recipient has received a certain sum of money. A receipt is signed by or on behalf of the party receiving money. It shows the

- amount received;
- mode of receipt, that is, cash, cheque, demand draft;

- name of the person from whom the amount is received;
- date on which the amount is received;
- purpose for which the amount is received; and
- signature of the person receiving the amount.

A business receives money mainly in respect of

- sale of goods or rendering of services;
- advance against future sale of goods, or rendering of services in future;
- loan from proprietor or any other party; and
- receipt towards capital.

The amount may be received in cash, by cheque, or by a bank draft; however, it is known, generally, as cash receipt. On receipt of the amount, the receiver issues a receipt to the payer. Such receipt is known as cash receipt. All receipts are recorded on the debit side or receipt side of the cash book and bank book. For the payer, the receipt serves as an acknowledgement of the

- amount given;
- purpose for which the amount is given; and
- date on which the amount is given.
- For the receiver, the counterfoil or the carbon copy of the receipt is evidence and the basis for the entry in the cash book or bank book of the receiver for the
- amount received;
- name of the party from whom the amount is received; and
- purpose for which the amount is received.

The original receipt is given to the payer. The carbon copy or the counterfoil is retained by the receiver. It is advisable to keep the receipt book with the carbon copy because

1. a carbon copy is the only exact and authentic replica of the copy of the receipt issued to the party making the payment and eliminates the chance of error and fraud; and
2. a carbon copy saves duplication of work, and time involved in writing the receipt twice—if the counterfoil is to be prepared separately, the receipt needs to be written twice.
   To facilitate control over issue of receipts, each receipt book is numbered serially. Each receipt in each receipt book is also numbered serially. The management must inquire into the missing receipt numbers, if any.

Cash Memo

Cash (or cheque) is received against the sale of goods in this transaction. When a sale is against cash, a cash memo is prepared (see a sample in Exhibit 5.1). A cash memo serves the purpose of (a) a receipt and (b) a sales invoice. Therefore, a cash memo is an evidence of receipt of cash as well as of sale of goods; the two aspects occur simultaneously. Hence, for cash sales only a cash memo is prepared. No separate receipt needs to be issued. However, when the money is received against credit sale, a receipt is prepared and is issued to the customer.

Cash memo indicates receipt of money against sale of goods.

In case a receipt is issued, reference of receipt number is mentioned in the cash book. In case of cash memo, the reference of cash memo number is given.

EXHIBIT 5.1   Cash Memo

Suparshwa[1] Pvt Ltd

[1]Registered Office:
9 Ambedkar Road Allahabad

No:[2] _____   Date:[3] _____

Received with thanks from[4] _____

_____ in cash/by cheque no.[5] _____ on

_____ Bank _____ Branch, Rupees[6] _____

_____ only as advance/on

account/in full/part payment of bill no[7] _____ dated _____

₹[8] _____

[9]Revenue Stamp

(Signature of receiver)

*Subject to realization of cheque

Notes

1. **Name and address**   This reveals the identity of the receiver and his/her address.
2. **Number**   The receipts should be pre-numbered and should be in a serial order.
3. **Date**   This is the date of receipt. Normally, the receipt number, date, and amount are referred to together, for example, 'Your receipt no _____ dated _____ for ₹ _____'.
4. **Party**   Here the name of the party giving the payment is written in full.

5. **Identification**   If the payment is received in cash, the words 'by cheque' are deleted. Where the amount is received by cheque, the words 'in cash' are struck out and the information is filled regarding cheque number and the bank on which the cheque is drawn. If the amount is received by bank draft, it is mentioned.
6. **Amount**   In the body of the receipt, after the word 'Rupees' the amount received is entered in words, for example, five thousand and five hundred rupees only.
7. **Purpose**   The amount may be received as an advance or on accounts or towards the total (or full) payment, or it may be in a part payment of the bill. Applicable words would be retained and the details not applicable would be struck out.
8. **Rupees**   Here, the amount received is entered in figures. The amount written in words must tally exactly with the amount written in figures, or else the receipt is defective.
9. **Signature**   Here, the person authorized by the management to issue the receipt puts his/her signature. The name of the company/firm receiving the money should also be pre-printed or affixed by a rubber stamp. If the amount received is rupees five thousand or more, a revenue stamp of one rupee is affixed. However, no revenue stamp is needed on the cash memo (irrespective of the amount).

When the payment is received by cheque, the amount is considered to be effectively received when the cheque is cleared or realized. This is the reason for mentioning the words 'subject to realization of cheque' as a footnote. If the cheque is dishonoured, the receipt is invalid.

Cash discount and trade discount should be shown separately in cash memo.
E. & O.E. means errors and omissions excepted.

■ **ILLUSTRATION 5.1**   Nehal and Co. sold 20 articles to Sheoran Bros on 30 April 2019 as mentioned in the following text at 10% cash discount.

1. 5 gold rings @ ₹10,000 each
2. 12 silver plates @ ₹30,000 each
3. 3 rings with American diamonds @ ₹1,30,000 each

Prepare a cash memo.

Solution

CASH MEMO

Nehal and Co.
1, Main Market, Ahmedabad

M/s Sheoran Bros
Cash Memo No. 1141
Date: 30-4-2019

No.	Description	Qty	Rate	Amount (₹)
1	Gold rings	5	10,000	50,000
2	Silver plates	12	30,000	3,60,000
3	Rings with American diamonds	3	1,30,000	3,90,000
				8,00,000
	Less: Cash discount @ 10%			80,000
			Total	7,20,000

E. & O.E.

Bank Receipt

A bank receipt is an acknowledgement of cheque from a certain party or a person. The original bank receipt is given to the person who pays the cheque. A carbon copy of the same is maintained in a file for office records. Each receipt is numbered and filed appropriately. A revenue stamp of ₹1 is affixed when the amount exceeds ₹5,000. This is prescribed as per Section 2 (23) and Section 30 of the Indian Stamp Act, 1899. It is generally kept in the safe custody of the account staff or the cashier. The content of the bank receipt book is the same as that of a cash receipt or cash memo discussed in an earlier paragraph.

Special Purpose Receipt

The specimen discussed above is of a general purpose receipt. Such receipts can be used for various purposes. A special receipt can be printed with the appropriate description if a company receives money recurrently on account of

- refund from supplier (being the refund received);
- receipt of a loan (being the amount of loan received @ 12% interest payable after one year);
- receipt of a deposit (being the deposit towards contract no. ___ dated ___ for ___); or
- repayment received against the loan given by firm to other firms.

Money may be received for a number of purposes. Hence, the description in the receipt showing the reason of the receipt will depend on the purpose of the receipt.

PAYMENT VOUCHERS

As receipts are evidence to support entries on the receipt side of the cash book, payment vouchers are the evidence of the payments made. Payments are made either in cash or by cheque. There may be cash payment vouchers or cheque payment vouchers. Normally, paper of different colours is used to identify cash payment voucher and cheque payment voucher easily. Alternatively, there may be general-purpose payment vouchers that can be used for both modes of payments.

Payment vouchers indicate payments of money.

Petty Cash Voucher

When a petty cash book is maintained, *petty cash vouchers* are maintained (see a sample in Exhibit 5.2). Such petty cash vouchers might be of a colour different from that of a cash payment voucher or a cheque payment voucher. A petty cash voucher is a cash payment voucher used for petty payments that are subsequently recorded in the petty cash book. All payment vouchers must be supported by documents and evidence, for example, cash paid for purchase of stationery must be supported by cash memo from the stationery supplier.

Cash Payment Vouchers

Cash payment voucher is almost identical to the petty cash voucher. The title of the voucher, which was petty cash voucher, is changed to cash payment voucher. Alternatively, it can be in the format as in Exhibit 5.3.

EXHIBIT 5.3 Cash Payment Voucher

Kalauny Bros
Classic Avenue, Nashik
Cash Payment Voucher

CBF Follio: _____
Cash voucher No. _____ Date: _____
Account _____ ₹ _____
Paid cash to _____
on account of _____
Rupees (in words) _____
Prepared by *Authorized by* *Receiver's Sign*

Bank Payment Vouchers

Due to the expansion of banking facilities, most payments are made by cheque. The business concern opens an account with the bank, deposits money in that account, and makes payment from the balance lying with the bank. The bank may also allow the business concern to overdraw the balance. For making payments, the bank gives the cheque book that contains cheques. The concern makes the payment by a cheque instead of giving cash. Hence, there are certain differences between cash payment voucher and cheque payment voucher.

■**ILLUSTRATION 5.2** Koshi and Co. makes a payment on 14 January 2019 by cheque no. 612228 of Dena Bank, Navrangpura Branch to Lopez and Co. towards full payment of their invoice no. 414 dated 4 January 2019 for ₹42,400. Prepare a payment voucher.

EXHIBIT 5.2 Petty Cash Voucher

[1]Narayan Bros
Classic Avenue, Mangalore
Petty Cash Voucher

PCB – Folio[2] _____ V.No.[3] _____
Date[4] _____
Debit[7] _____ A/c

Particulars[5]	₹[6]	P.

₹ _____ only[9]
Total[8]

Received by[10] *Prepared by*[11] *Authorized by*[12]

Notes

1. **Name** Name and address of the organization is always printed.
2. **PCB folio** The folio (page no.) of the petty cash book in which the voucher is entered.
3. **Voucher number** Voucher number should always be given. Its counter reference should be given in the petty cash book. Hence, the petty cash vouchers are also serially numbered and arranged with supporting evidence.
4. **Date** The date of payment is written here. The voucher is recorded in the petty cash book on this date only. This is an important control.
5. **Particulars** This is for general information in respect of a particular transaction. If the payment is as per cash memo, or as per a bill, reference of cash memo or bill is made. These details are written below 'Account'.
6. **Amount** Amount is written in figures.
7. **Account** Account to be debited in respect of the payment is entered here so that the amount can be entered in the appropriate column in the petty cash book.
8. **Total amount** If the items of expenditure are two or more, or if accounts affected are two or more, they are entered separately in 'Particulars' column with amount extended against each item. Total amount is mentioned at the end in figures.
9. **Amount** Here, the amount should be in words and should be the same as the amount in figures. There cannot be any difference.
10. **Received by** The person receiving the amount signs at this place.
11. **Prepared by** The voucher may not be prepared by the recipient only; the petty cashier may prepare the voucher. He/she puts his/her signature under this item.
12. **Authorized by** All payments must be authorized by a responsible person. Different persons have different authorities. A junior person may be authorized to sanction or pass payment up to, say, ₹1,000 only. Larger amounts may be sanctioned by a senior person.

Solution

```
                          Koshi & Co.
                          4, Ishwar Road
                          Faridabad
CBF Folio: 12
Bank Voucher No. 123                        Date  14.01.2019
Particulars                                            ₹
Paid to M/s Lopez & Co. in full payment of their
Invoice no. 414 dated 04.01.2020 by Cheque No. 612228
Dated 14.01.2019 on Dena Bank, Navarangpura Branch   42,400.00
Rupees   Four thousand two hundred and forty only   Total Rs 42,400.00
Prepared by          Authorized by          Receiver's Signature
```

Composite Payment Vouchers

At times, instead of keeping cash payment vouchers and bank vouchers separately, a trader may keep a common voucher combining the features of both and striking out items that are not necessary. Hence, there is only one series of vouchers and there is no need for paper of different colours. It is usual to take the signature of the receiver of the cheque on the payment voucher itself. This receiver may be the messenger or representative of the supplier. The (official) receipt from the payee may be received later on. This receipt should be attached with the voucher as an evidence for the payment. The signature of the payee has to be taken in the case of both petty cash voucher and cash payment voucher, even when an official receipt may be received later on.

It can be in the format shown in Exhibit 5.4.

EXHIBIT 5.4 Composite Payment Voucher

```
Payment Voucher No. 123              Date 14.1.2019
CBF Folio: 12
                    Koshi & Co.
                4, Ishwar Road, Faridabad
                                          ₹ 42,400
Debit : Lopez & Co.                   A/c.
Paid to Lopez & Co.
On account of full payment of their bill no. 414 dated 04.01.2020 of
Rupees (in words) Four thousand two hundred and forty only.
By Cheque No. 912228 dated 14.01.2019 drawn on Dena Bank, Navrangpura
Branch, or by cash.
Prepared by          Authorized by          Receiver's Signature
```

BUSINESS TRANSACTIONS THROUGH ELECTRONIC BANKING

Promptness of banks' operations depends on electronic banking. Electronic instruments are used by banks to provide quick and secure services to their customers. Banks provide various services to their customers, of which fund transfer is one of the most important. As per the traditional method, drafts and cheques are used to transfer funds. In this system, fund transfer from one account to another account usually takes more time.

These days, for fund transfer, four types of prompt services are provided by banks, as explained hereunder:

- NEFT (National Electronic Funds Transfer)
- RTGS (Real Time Gross Settlement)
- Debit card and Credit card
- Net banking, ECS, and Payment through Payment Gateway

NEFT (National Electronic Funds Transfer)

This service is available nationwide. Individuals, firms, and corporate units can benefit from this service. This service is provided to the customers by participating banks in this service. It is not necessary to have a bank account of the sender to get the benefit of this scheme. For NEFT service, it is necessary to have a bank account of the beneficiaries in such a bank which provides this service. There is no limit on the amount to be transferred. Banks charge nominal amount for this service. Reserve Bank of India (RBI) has determined a maximum charge for this service. Therefore, banks can give this service even free of cost. But it cannot charge more than the maximum charge prescribed by RBI. There is no charge levied on beneficiaries by the banks. The sender of the funds has to pay charges to the bank. Thus, the charges become expenses for the funds sender and have to be recorded in the cash and bank book. As per the present rule, NEFT services are available from 8 am to 7 pm, Monday to Friday. On Saturdays, this service is available as per the norms of respective period, i.e., 8 am to 1 pm. Generally, the amount transferred through NEFT is deposited within two hours in the account of the receiver. Although there is no minimum limit, the maximum limit of the amount for funds transfer under this service is ₹50,000.

RTGS (Real Time Gross Settlement)

This service is also provided by banks to their customers' through electronic mode. This service is provided to customers of the participating banks. This service is used to transfer large amounts. As per the present norms, the minimum amount to be remitted is ₹2,00,000 to get the benefit of this service. There is no upper limit for this service. RTGS charges are paid to the bank by the sender of funds, i.e., remitter. Therefore, this charge becomes an expense for the remitter. The RTGS service window is available from 9 am to 4.30 pm, Monday to Friday. On Saturdays, this service is available as per norms of the respective period, i.e., 9 am to 2 pm. However, banks themselves decide the time duration for this service for their customers. This service is on real-time basis. The amount is transferred immediately or in maximum 30 minutes from the sender's account to the receiver's account.

Debit Card and Credit Card

In present times, volumes of cash transactions are decreased remarkably with the help of various services provided by the banks. Debit card, credit card, and Internet services in the form of net banking are the various kinds of services provided by banks. For example, payments at restaurants or for hotel rooms can be made by the customers through debit card or

credit card or through net banking or through payment gateway instead of cash.

Debit card   A card is issued by the bank to an individual or a firm to withdraw an amount or to make payment from the available bank balance. This card is called debit card, for example, SBI debit card.

Credit card   A card is issued by the bank to an individual or a firm to withdraw an amount or to make payment up to a certain limit. This card is called credit card. This type of card may be issued to an account holder or non-account holder by a particular bank based on its rules and regulations, for example, SBI credit card.

Net Banking, ECS, and Payment through Payment Gateway

Internet banking transactions/e-banking/online banking/virtual banking

Internet banking, also known as online banking, e-banking, or virtual banking, is an electronic payment system that enables customers of a bank or other financial institutions to conduct a range of financial transactions through the financial institution's or bank's website. Under this service, the purchase or usage amount is debited in the remitter's account by the remitter's bank and sales or income amount is credited to the fund receiver's account by the fund receiver's bank. There is no charge debited by the payment making bank but the receiving bank charges some amount as commission and the balance amount is credited in the bank account of the receiver's account.

Electronic clearing system (ECS)

ECS is an alternative method of effecting payment transactions in respect of the utility bill payments such as telephone bills, electricity bills, insurance premiums, card payments, and loan payments, which would obviate the need for issuing and handling paper instruments and thereby facilitate improved customer service for banks, companies, corporations, or government departments, etc., for collecting or receiving payments.

Payment gateway

A payment gateway is a merchant service provided by an e-commerce application service provider that authorizes credit cards or debit cards or directs payments processing for e-businesses, online retailers, bricks and clicks, or traditional brick and mortar.

These gateways draw funds directly from the customers' bank accounts or credit cards, validate them, and then deposit them in the receivers' accounts. With a modern payment gateway, receivers do not need a merchant account to accept credit card payments—they just need a valid bank account, for example, Paytm account.

DEBIT NOTE

A debit note is issued to inform a person that the account has been debited to reduce the liabilities towards him/her, or to recover an amount due from him/her. For example, in case a firm wants to return the business goods purchased by it, a debit note is issued along with the goods returned by the firm to the supplier. Suppose a product is sold to a customer and it is subsequently realized that certain charges recoverable have not been included in the invoice raised to the customer, a debit note may be issued by the firm to indicate the increase in the receivable from the concerned customer. Such transactions are recorded in the sales return journal, purchase return journal, or a journal proper book as an additional supporting voucher.

CREDIT NOTE

A credit note is issued to inform a person that his/her account has been credited by the firm to increase the liability by the firm in favour of the party to whom it is issued. It also indicates that the receivable from the customer has been reduced by the firm. For example, if a higher amount has been charged in invoice due to an error during a sales transaction, the firm may later issue a credit note in favour of the customer to indicate that the amount receivable from the customer has been reduced by that extent. A credit note may also be issued by the supplier in case of purchase of goods when some extra charges such as transport charges are payable by the firm to the supplier. Such transactions are recorded in the sales return journal, purchase return journal, or journal proper book as an additional supporting voucher.

CUSTODY OF RECEIPT BOOKS

Each receipt page in a receipt book should be numbered serially. For the sake of convenience of printing and reducing the cost of printing, it is usual to print more than one receipt book at a time. Each receipt book is also serially numbered so that there is no misuse of any receipt book. All the receipt books should be in the custody of a responsible person in the office. At a time, only one receipt book in serial order is taken out for issuing receipts. After this receipt book is completely used, the next receipt book starting with the consecutive receipt number is taken for use.

JOURNAL VOUCHER

In a business house, the accounts department maintains cash book, bank book, petty cash book, sales book, purchase book, and other books of prime entry. All the transactions are recorded in appropriate books of account. Only those transactions that cannot be entered in these books are entered in the journal. The journal records entries relating to (i) opening, (ii) closing, (iii) adjustment, (iv) rectification, and (v) transactions for which a separate book of prime entry is not opened, such as consignment activities, acceptance of a bill of exchange, and endorsement of a bill of exchange are some examples. These entries are evidenced by journal vouchers and other related supporting documents. A journal voucher is a replica of a journal entry except for one

difference. A journal entry as recorded in the journal has a column for 'ledger folio'. A journal voucher does not have this column. Posting in the ledger is always made from the journal entry. In a journal voucher, there may be one or more debit accounts and one or more credit accounts. However, the total of debits and credits must always be equal. If this care is not taken, the trial balance will not tally. See a sample of a journal voucher in Exhibit 5.5.

EXHIBIT 5.5   Journal Voucher

Koshi and Co.
4, Ishwar Road, Faridabad
Journal Voucher
J.V.No. : _____
Date : _____
J.F.No. : _____

Date	Particulars		Debit (₹)	Credit (₹)
		Dr.		
	Total			
Authorized by			**Accountant**	

■ **ILLUSTRATION 5.3**   Prepare journal vouchers for the following transactions during April 2019 in the books of A. Narayan (the proprietor being Sahil).

1. April 1: A. Narayan started business with cash ₹1,00,000, machinery ₹2,50,000, goods ₹50,000, and loan from bank ₹1,00,000.
2. April 10: Goods worth ₹5,000 were withdrawn by Sahil, goods worth ₹15,000 were distributed as free samples, and goods worth ₹5,000 were stolen.

Solution

A. Narayan
10, Girdhar Mall, Noida – 9
Journal Voucher
J.V.No. : _____1_____
Date : _____01.04.2019_____
J.F.No. : _____1_____

Date	Particulars		Debit (₹)	Credit (₹)
2019 April 1	Cash	Dr.	1,00,000	
	Machinery	Dr.	2,50,000	
	Goods	Dr.	50,000	
	To Loan from bank			1,00,000
	To A's capital			3,00,000
	(Being entry recording the assets and liabilities brought in business on 1 April 2019)			
		₹	4,00,000	4,00,000
Authorized by			**Accountant**	

A. Narayan
10, Girdhar Mall, Noida – 9
Journal Voucher
J.V.No. : _____2_____
Date : _____10.04.2019_____
J.F.No. : _____2_____

Date	Particulars		Debit (₹)	Credit (₹)
2019 April 10	Goods withdrawn from personal A/c	Dr.	5,000	
	Goods distributed as free samples A/c	Dr.	15,000	
	Goods stolen A/c	Dr.	5,000	
	To Trading A/c			20,000
	(Being the above items as recorded in Trading A/c)			
		₹	20,000	20,000
Authorized by			**Accountant**	

■ **ILLUSTRATION 5.4**   On 31 March 2020, Travis Electro Works, Goel Estate, Sector-18 Noida is required to provide ₹32,000 as depreciation on machinery for the year 2019–20. Calculate depreciation @ 25% p.a. on the opening written down value of ₹1,28,000 under reducing balance method. There was no addition to or sale of machinery during 2019–20. Prepare the journal voucher.

Solution

Travis Electro Works
Goel Estate, Sector-18, Noida
Journal Voucher
J.V.No. : _____1_____   Date : _____31.03.2020_____
J.F.No. : _____

Date	Particulars		Debit (₹)	Credit (₹)
2020 March 31	Depreciation A/c	Dr.	32,000	
	To Machinery A/c			32,000
	(Being depreciation on machinery @ 25% p.a. on opening written down value of ₹1,28,000)			
		₹	32,000	32,000
Authorized by			**Accountant**	

■ **ILLUSTRATION 5.5**   Prepare necessary journal vouchers in the books of M/s Rana and Co., 23, Raj Flats, Gurgaon, for the following transactions as on 19 April 2020.

1. Goods withdrawn for personal use—₹8,000
2. Goods distributed as free samples—₹10,000
3. Goods lost due to theft—₹5,000

Solution

M/s Rana and Co.
23, Raj Flats,
Gurgaon
Journal Voucher
J.V.No. : _____102_____   Date : _____19.04.2020_____
J.F.No. : _____20_____

Date	Particulars		Debit (₹)	Credit (₹)
2020 April 19	Drawings A/c	Dr.	8,000	
	To Purchases A/c			8,000
	(Being goods withdrawn by proprietor for personal use)			
		₹	8,000	8,000
	Authorized by	Prepared by		Accountant

M/s Rana and Co.
23, Raj Flats,
Gurgaon
Journal Voucher
J.V.No. : _____ 103 _____   Date : _____ 19.04.2020 _____
J.F.No. : _____ 20 _____

Date	Particulars		Debit (₹)	Credit (₹)
2020 April 19	Sales promotion A/c	Dr.	10,000	
	To Purchases A/c			10,000
	(Being goods distributed as free samples)			
		₹	10,000	10,000
	Authorized by	Prepared by		Accountant

M/s Rana and Co.
23, Raj Flats,
Gurgaon
Journal Voucher
J.V.No. : _____ 104 _____
Date : _____ 19.04.2020 _____
J.F.No. : _____ 20 _____

Date	Particulars		Debit (₹)	Credit (₹)
2020 April 19	Loss due to theft A/c	Dr.	5,000	
	To Purchases A/c			5,000
	(Being goods lost due to theft)			
		₹	5,000	5,000
	Authorized by	Prepared by		Accountant

Exhibit 5.6 indicates the basic documents and the respective books of prime entry in which the transactions are entered.

From the original entries in the above-mentioned books, the respective posting is entered into the ledger accounts, and through the balancing of each ledger account, a trial balance is prepared. This aspect is discussed in detail in Chapter 7 on analysing transactions.

EXHIBIT 5.6   Linkages Between Document Name and its Books of Original Entry

Basic Document or Voucher Name	Name of Books of Original Entry
Cash receipt	Cash book
Bank receipt	Bank book
Special purpose receipt	Cash book (if hard cash received) or Bank book (if banking transactions in the form of cheque involved)
Petty cash voucher	Petty cash book
Cash payment	Cash book
Bank payment	Bank book
Composite payment vouchers	Cash book (if hard cash paid) or Bank book (if banking transactions in the form of cheque involved)
Purchase Invoice (received)	Purchase journal
Sales invoice (copy)	Sales journal
Sales credit notes	Sales returns journal
Purchase credit notes	Purchase returns journal
Other than above transactions such as invoice of purchase of fixed assets, investments on credit, sales of fixed assets, rectification entries, etc.	Journal proper book

 SUMMARY

- Source documents are basically written documents related to the external and internal activities of a firm. The source documents may be in the form of receipts, bills, proof of cash expenses, invoices, pay in slip for deposit of cheques or funds in the bank account of the firm, etc. These documents certify the actual happening of a transactions or an event, its amount, parties involved in the transactions, nature of the transactions, etc.

- Transactions or events are recorded in the books of accounts on the basis of documentary evidences.
- Supporting vouchers are the documents providing evidence about the transactions having taken place. Accounting vouchers are prepared on the basis of supporting vouchers.
- Every business event or record must be based on and supported by documentary evidence. These records are known as vouchers.

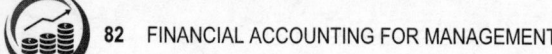
- Vouchers must present facts in an unbiased way. They should be scrutinized before they are recorded in the books of accounts.
- The receipts and payments vouchers are needed by all firms irrespective of their size.

- Internal vouchers are prepared by the firm itself to record the transactions that occur. External vouchers are prepared by an external party. Such vouchers support transactions with an outsider.
- For irregular transactions, a firm can use a journal voucher, in addition to the sales voucher, purchase voucher, and expense voucher.

KEYWORDS

Journal vouchers   They record accounting entries.
Payment vouchers   They indicate payments of money.

Verifiability   Examination or the scrutiny of documents of transactions before they are recorded in the books of accounts.

QUESTIONS

I. Answer the following questions in detail.

1. What is a cash receipt?
2. For what purpose is a receipt issued?
3. What is a bank payment voucher?
4. Explain the components of a voucher.
5. Explain the importance of a journal voucher. What is its format?
6. What are the different types of vouchers from the view of the party who raised it?
7. Elaborate the significance of debit and credit notes, as a supporting voucher for recording transactions in the books of accounts.

II. Solve the following problems.

1. Anjali and Co. received ₹4,000 from Bela and Co. by cheque in full and final settlement of invoice no. 425 dated 02/02/2020. Prepare a receipt that Anjali and Co. will pass over to Bela and Co. on 15/03/2020.
2. Dhruv and Co. Solicitors received on 01/03/2020 an advance of ₹10,000 by cheque from A Ltd for a suit to be filed against X on behalf of A Ltd. Draft a receipt that Dhruv and Co. will issue to A Ltd.
3. Ronak Ltd received a deposit from a shareholder on 01/01/2020 for ₹50,000. Prepare the receipt assuming the other necessary information.
4. Bharat and Co. sent to Minaxi and Co. a cheque for ₹25,000 in part payment of invoice no. 222 dated 02/02/2020 for ₹75,000. Prepare a receipt to be sent to Bharat and Co. by Minaxi and Co.
5. Sunil Bros deposited ₹50,000 with Kant and Co. This amount was refunded by Kant and Co. to Sunil Bros. Assuming the required information, prepare the receipt to be issued.
6. Ajay Bros sent ₹75,000 as advance to Maharaj Traders for supply of goods. On 1 March 2020, Maharaj Traders supplied goods worth ₹50,000, allowing 10% trade discount, and remitted the balance by cheque. Ajay Bros received the goods and the remittance on the same day. Prepare the receipt that Ajay Bros will issue for the amount received.

7. Mrs Damini Goel gave a loan of ₹25,000 to Patel and Co. on 15 March 2020 to be kept for one year at 15% interest per annum. Draft the receipt that Mrs Damini will get from Patel and Co.
8. Merchant Bros, a trader from Mumbai, received by bank draft an 'on account' payment of ₹15,000 from M/s Phadke and Co. of Pune against the pending invoices. Draft the receipt to be issued to Phadke and Co.
9. X & Y Co. purchased the following in cash on 20 February 2020.
   (a) 4 ink bottles @ ₹100 each
   (b) 1 dozen pencils for ₹120
   (c) 3 registers @ ₹150 each
   Prepare the petty cash voucher.
10. A firm paid ₹395 in cash to a newspaper vendor towards a bill for newspapers and magazines delivered during December 2019 on 2 February 2020. Prepare the cash payment voucher.
11. A and Co. debited its wages A/c by ₹500 after paying labour charges for installation of machinery. Prepare a journal voucher to rectify this error.
12. Advertisement expenses of ₹450 paid by PQ to XY on 25 May 2020 were debited to XY A/c. Prepare a journal voucher to rectify this error.
13. Sawant withdrew ₹24,000 during the year ended 31 March 2020 from his business. It was decided to transfer the drawings to his capital account. Prepare the journal voucher.
14. Prepare the required document for receipt of ₹4,000 in cash for sale of goods.
15. Agrawal Bros sold to Goel Bros on 10 April 2020 the articles mentioned here:
    (a) 5 gold rings at ₹5,000 each
    (b) 12 silver spoons at ₹1,000 each
    (c) 2 rings with American diamonds at ₹10,000 each
    Agrawal Bros allowed 10% cash discount on the total amount of the bill. Prepare a cash memo.
16. Prepare necessary journal vouchers in the books of Megha and Co. for the following transactions as on 30 April 2020.
    (a) Goods withdrawn for personal use ₹20,000
    (b) Goods distributed as free samples ₹15,000
    (c) Goods lost in fire ₹25,000

Revenue and Expense Recognition

Learning Objectives

After studying this chapter, you will understand

- the concept and recognition of revenue
- the concept and measurement of receipt
- the concept, classification, and measurement of expenses
- the relationship between assets and expenses

INTRODUCTION

Income increases the resources of an entity. In other words, income is the net increase in the owners' equity resulting from the operations of an entity and not from the capital contributed by the owner.

Income consists of the revenue generated less losses and less expenses that have been incurred to generate the revenue. Evaluation of an entity's operating performance requires the definition, measurement, and recognition of revenues and expenses.

CAPITAL AND REVENUE

The concepts of capital and revenue are of fundamental importance for correct determination of accounting profit and recognition of business assets at the end of a particular period. The distinction affects the measurement of profit in a number of accounting periods.

Capital has been defined by economists as those assets which are used in the production of goods and services for further production of assets. In accounting, on the other hand, the capital of a business is increased by that portion of the periodic net income (net profit) which has not been consumed by the owner.

The relationship between capital and revenue can be compared to the one between a tree and its fruits. It is the tree which produces the fruits, and it is the fruit that can be consumed. If the tree is tendered with care, it will produce more fruits; conversely, if the tree is destroyed, there will be no more fruits. Likewise, revenue comes out of capital and capital is the source of revenue. Capital is invested by an owner or group of owners' or group of promoters or group of shareholders, in a business so that it may produce revenue. Moreover, as a fruit may give birth to another new tree, different revenues may further produce new capital.

Capital can be brought in by a person into a business in different forms—cash or kind. When capital is brought in the form of cash, it is spent away on various items of assets that make the firm a running concern.

Capital of a business can be increased in two ways:

1. When the owner brings in more capital to the business; and/or
2. When the owner does not consume the entire periodic income.

When the owner brings in further capital to his business, the amount is added to the Capital Account. Likewise, the net income for a period is added to the Capital Account, and if drawings or withdrawals or dividends are less than that income, the capital is increased by the difference. Net income is also known as Net Gain.

The difference between the two terms 'revenue' and 'receipt' should be carefully distinguished. A receipt is the inflow of money into business, whereas revenue is the aggregate exchange value received for goods and services provided to the customers.

REVENUES

Assets and capital increase with increasing revenues.

Increased revenues lead to an increase in the value of assets and capital of an entity. A firm can generate revenues by the following methods:

1. Sale of products or services to customers
2. Supply of the firm's resources to other firms for use, such as rent from properties and interest from dividends
3. Sale of assets or investments of the entity

Operating revenue is the revenue generated from the sale of products or services. *Non-operating revenues* are incidental or indirect to the main operations of the entity. *Capital receipts* are receipts of an entity from shareholders, sale of fixed assets, or loans.

Receipt acknowledges receipt of money.

Revenue receipts are generated from— (a) the sales of goods; and/or (b) interests, commissions, etc.

Types of Revenues

Revenue or receipts of an entity can be classified into two types, capital receipts and revenue receipts.

Capital receipts or capital income

These consist of payments made to the entity by shareholders, proprietors, or owners of the business. An entity can generate capital receipts by selling fixed assets or by raising loans. In other words, a capital receipt is not the result of a firm's operating cycle. Capital receipt is different from capital gain or capital profit. Capital gain refers to the entity's profit over and above the cost of its fixed assets. For example, if machinery worth ₹30,000 is sold for ₹32,000, there is a capital receipt of ₹32,000 but the capital profit is worth only ₹2,000. If the same machine is sold for ₹25,000, there is capital receipt of ₹25,000 and a capital loss of ₹5,000.

It may be noted that capital profit is transferred to the 'capital reserve', whereas capital loss is charged to the income statement of the same year or over a few years, in case of a substantial amount.

Revenue receipts or revenue income

These receipts arise in the course of an entity's regular operating transactions. Revenue receipts comprise amounts received from the sale of goods, interest and commission received, etc. Revenue profit or revenue loss is included in the income statement in the same year in which they occur.

Revenue Recognition

An entity generates revenue at all stages of an operating cycle. It is, therefore, very important to decide at what time the revenue should be considered as realized. The various types of revenue recognition are explained in this section.

Point of sale

The objective of manufacturing or purchasing goods is achieved when the goods are sold by the entity. Thus, revenue is realized, when a sales transaction takes place in the ordinary course of business and goods are exchanged for cash or claims to cash.

Under this method, revenue is not recognized when a firm receives sales orders. A key point in recognizing revenue from a transaction is that the seller transfers the property rights of the goods to the buyer for a consideration in the form of cash or cash-in-kind.

Exhibit 6.1 indicates the revenue recognition practices adopted by a steel company, a coal company, and an FMCG company.

Providing services

In transactions that involve rendering of services, revenue is recognized usually as the services are performed, and it is immaterial whether the revenue amount is collected in advance or later by the service-providing firm.

The following example indicates an instance where a firm receives the revenue in advance of rendering a service. Passengers of the Indian Railways book their tickets by paying the necessary fare charges well in advance. However, this would be treated as a pre-received income or revenue by the railways, and would be recognized as revenue by the Indian Railways only from the date of journey by the passenger.

The following is an example of an instance where a firm receives revenue from the customer after the service has been rendered, but revenue will be booked at the point of time when the service was provided. True Sence Maintenance Ltd repaired the air conditioner plant of the factory of a reputed and long-standing customer in the month of June 2020; the repairing and maintenance work was worth ₹50,000, and the customer agreed to pay in the month of August 2020. In this situation, however, True Sense Maintenance Ltd will book the revenue in the month of June 2020, when the service was rendered, as against August 2020, when the payment was actually received.

Subscribers pay for magazine and journal subscriptions in advance. Such companies receive cash before providing services. If the subscription amount received this year is towards the magazines to be delivered next year, the revenue is entered the next year. Rent on property is often paid in advance. In this case, revenue is recognized in the period in which the services of rented property were provided, and not the period in which the rent payment was received. Revenues from hotel rooms are recognized each day the room is rented. Revenues from maintenance contracts are recognized each month.

Exhibit 6.2 indicates the revenue recognition practices adopted in entertainment and media, financial service, airlines, hotel, consultancy, education, and advertising sectors.

EXHIBIT 6.1   Revenue Recognition Practices of Companies

Let us look at the revenue recognition practices of some of the companies from different industries and sectors:

Steel Industry: Tata Steel Limited

Revenue is measured at the fair value of consideration received or receivable net of discounts, taking into account contractually defined terms and excluding taxes and duties collected on behalf of the government.

Sale of Goods

Revenue from sale of goods is recognised when the Company has transferred to the buyer the significant risks and rewards of ownership, no longer retains control over the goods sold, the amount of revenue can be measured reliably, it is probable that the economic benefits associated with the transaction will flow to the Company and the costs incurred or to be incurred in respect of the transaction can be measured reliably. Depending on the contractual terms, risks and rewards of ownership is transferred when the delivery is completed. In case of exports sale delivery is completed on issuance of bill of lading.

Coal Industry: Coal India Limited

Revenue from Sale of Goods

Revenue from the sale of goods is recognised when all the following conditions have been satisfied:

(a) the Company has transferred to the buyer the significant risks and rewards of ownership of the goods;

(b) the Company retains neither continuing managerial involvement to the degree usually associated with ownership nor effective control over the goods sold;

(c) the amount of revenue can be measured reliably;

(d) it is probable that the economic benefits associated with the transaction will flow to the Company; and

(e) the costs incurred or to be incurred in respect of the transaction can be measured reliably.

Revenue is measured at the fair value of the consideration received or receivable, taking into account contractually defined terms of payment and excluding taxes, levies or duties collected on behalf of the government/ other statutory bodies.

Advances received from the customers are reported as customer's deposits unless the above conditions for revenue recognition are met.

FMCG Sector: Future Retail Limited

Revenue Recognition

Revenue is recognised on a fair value basis to the extent that it is probable that the economic benefits will flow to the company and the revenue can be reliably measured.

Sale of Products

Revenue from sale of products is recognised, when significant risks and rewards of ownership have been transferred to the buyer and no significant uncertainty exists regarding the amount of the consideration that will be derived from the sale of products. It also includes excise duty and excludes value added tax / sales tax and GST (Goods and Service Tax). It is measured at fair value of consideration received or receivable, net of returns and allowances.

Rendering of Services

Revenue from services are recognised as they are rendered based on arrangements with the customers.

Interest Income

For all financial instruments measured at amortised cost, interest income is recorded using the effective interest rate (EIR), which is the rate that exactly discounts the estimated future cash payments or receipts over the expected life of the financial instrument or a shorter period, where appropriate, to the net carrying amount of the financial asset.

Dividend Income

Dividend income is recognised when the Company's right to receive such dividend is established.

Sources: Tata Steel Ltd Annual Report 2017–18, p. 209; Coal India Ltd Annual Report 2016–17, p. 210; Future Retail Limited Annual Report 2017–18, p. 93.

EXHIBIT 6.2   Revenue Recognition Practices Adopted by Services

Let us look at the revenue recognition practices adopted by financial services:

Entertainment and Media Industry: Sun TV Networks Limited

Revenue is recognized to the extent that it is probable that the economic benefits will flow to the Company and the revenue can be reliably measured. Revenue is measured at the fair value of the consideration received or receivable, taking into account contractually defined terms of payment and excluding taxes or duties collected on behalf of the government. The Company has concluded that it is the principal in all of its revenue arrangements since it is the primary obligor in all the revenue arrangements as it has pricing latitude and is also exposed to credit risks.

- Advertising income and income from sales of broadcast slots are recognised when the related commercial or programme is telecast.
- International subscription income represents income from the export of program software content, and is recognised as and when the services are rendered in accordance with the terms of agreements with customers.
- Subscription income represents subscription fees billed to cable operators and Direct to Home ('DTH') service providers towards pay-channels operated by the Company, and are recognised in the period during which the service is provided. Subscription fees billed to cable operators are determined based on number of subscription points to which the service is provided based on relevant agreements with such cable operators (along

with management's best estimates of such subscription points wherever applicable), at contractually agreed rates with the Company's authorised distributor. Subscription income from DTH customers is recognised as and when services are rendered to the customer in accordance with the terms of agreements entered into with the service providers.

- Revenues from sale of movie distribution rights are recognised in accordance with the terms of agreements with customers.
- Income from content trading represent revenue earned from mobile service providers and DTH service providers through exploitation of content owned by the Company. Income is recognised as per the terms of contract with the respective service providers and based on the services being rendered to the service provider.
- Income from Indian Premier League represents following:
  - Income from franchisee rights is recognised when the rights to receive the payments is established as per the terms of the agreement entered with The Board of Control for Cricket in India ("BCCI"). Revenue is recognised as per the information provided by BCCI or as per Management's estimate in case the information is not received.
  - The revenue is allocated on a pro-rata basis to number of matches played during the year as against the total number of matches for the season.
  - Income from sponsorship fees is recognised on completion of terms of the sponsorship agreement.
  - Income from sale of tickets is recognised on the dates of the respective matches. The Company reports revenues net of discounts offered on sale of tickets.
  - Prize money is recognised when right to receive payment is established.
- Revenues from barter transactions, and the related costs, are recorded at fair values of the services received or if the same cannot be measured reliably, then the fair value of the services rendered, as estimated by management.

Financial Services Industry: Dena Bank

(i) Commission on Letters of Credit/Bank Guarantees/Government Business/Distribution of Insurance Policies/Mutual Fund Products/ASBA; Locker Rent, Interest on Refund of Taxes, Dividend, Income on Units of Mutual Funds, Rental Income, and Service Charges on various Deposit Accounts are recognized on realization basis.

(ii) Interest/ Discount on Non-Performing Loans & Advances/Investments is recognized to the extent realized as per the prudential guidelines of RBI.

(iii) Recoveries in Written Off Advances/Investments are being accounted for as 'Miscellaneous Income'.

Airline Industry: SpiceJet Limited

Revenue is recognised to the extent that it is probable that the economic benefits will flow to the Company and the revenue can be reliably measured, regardless of when the payment is being made. Revenue is measured at the fair value of the consideration received or receivable, taking into account contractually defined terms of payment and excluding taxes or duties collected on behalf of the government. The revenue is recognized net of VAT/ Service tax (if any). The specific recognition criteria described below must also be met before revenue is recognised.

Rendering of Services

Passenger revenues and cargo revenues are recognised as and when transportation is provided, i.e., when the service is rendered. Amounts received in advance towards travel bookings/reservations are shown under current liabilities as unearned revenue. Fees charged for cancellations or any changes to flight tickets and towards special service requests are recognized as revenue on rendering of related services. The unutilized

balances in unearned revenue is recognized as income based on past statistics, trends and management estimates, after considering the Company's refund policy.

Revenue from wet lease of aircraft is recognised as follows:

(a) The fixed rentals under the agreements are recognised on a straight line basis over the lease period.

(b) The variable rentals in excess of the minimum guarantee hours are recognised based on actual utilisation of the aircraft during the period.

Income in respect of hiring/renting out of equipment and spare parts is recognised at rates agreed with the lessee, as and when related services are rendered.

Sale of Food and Beverages

Revenue from sale of food and beverages is recognised when the products are delivered or served to the customer. Revenue from such sale is measured at the fair value of the consideration received or receivable, net of returns and allowances, trade discounts and volume rebates. Amounts received in advance towards food and beverages are shown undercurrent liabilities as unearned revenue.

Training Income

Revenue from training income is recognized proportionately with the degree of completion of services, based on management estimates of the relative efforts as well as the period over which related training activities are rendered for individual employees by the Company.

Hotel Industry: Indian Hotels Company Limited (Taj)

Income from Operation

Revenue is measured at the fair value of the consideration received or receivable. Revenue comprises sale of rooms, food and beverages and allied services relating to hotel operations, including management fees for the management of the hotels.

Revenue is recognised upon rendering of the service, provided pervasive evidence of an arrangement exists, tariff/rates are fixed or are determinable and collectability is reasonably certain. Revenue from sale of goods or rendering of services is net of Indirect taxes, returns and discounts.

The Group operates loyalty programme, which allows its eligible customers to earn points based on their spending at the hotels. The points so earned by such customers are accumulated. The revenue related to award points is deferred and on redemption of the award points, the revenue is recognised. Membership fees received from the loyalty program is recognized as revenue on time-proportion basis.

Management fees earned from hotels managed by the Group are usually under long-term contracts with the hotel owner and is recognised when earned in accordance with the terms of the contract.

Consultancy Industry: Tata Consultancy Services

The Group earns revenue primarily from providing information technology, business solutions and consultancy services through development and maintenance of IT applications and infrastructure, implementation of enterprise solutions, business process services, assurance services, engineering and industrial services using its own products, framework of solutions and third party products.

The Group recognises revenue as follows:

- Contracts are unbundled into separately identifiable components and the consideration is allocated to those identifiable components on the basis of their relative fair values. Revenue is recognised for respective components either at the point in time or over time, as applicable.
- Revenue from contracts priced on a time and material basis is recognised as services are rendered and as related costs are incurred.

- Revenue from software development contracts, which are generally time bound fixed price contracts, is recognised over the life of the contract using the percentage-of-completion method, with contract costs determining the degree of completion. Losses on such contracts are recognised when probable.
- Revenue in excess of billings is recognised as unbilled revenue in the balance sheet; to the extent billings are in excess of revenue recognised, the excess is reported as unearned and deferred revenue in the balance sheet.
- Revenue from Business Process Services contracts priced on the basis of time and material or unit of delivery is recognised as services are rendered or the related obligation is performed.
- Revenue from the sale of internally developed and manufactured systems and third party products which do not require significant modification is recognised upon delivery, which is when the absolute right to use passes to the customer and the Group does not have any material remaining service obligations.
- Revenue from maintenance contracts is recognised on a pro-rata basis over the period of the contract.
- Revenue is recognised only when evidence of an arrangement is obtained and the other criteria to support revenue recognition are met, including the price is fixed or determinable, services have been rendered and collectability of the resulting receivables is reasonably assured.
- Revenue is reported net of discounts and indirect taxes.

Education Industry: MT Educare Limited

Revenue is recognized to the extent that it is probable that economic benefits will flow to the Company and revenue can be reliably ascertained.

Revenue from Gross fees (inclusive of Robomate + CRF)received is recognized equally over the period of service rendered (course duration) except CRF & Robomate. At the time of admission, fees received from students are booked at gross amount and shown as 'advance fees'. Discounts and concessions are accounted for separately in a similar manner. The Course Registration Fees (CRF)is part of total fees and is non-refundable. The Company receives CRF as part of the initial payment made by a student and recognises the same on admission. Revenue from Gross Fees include fees from classroom coaching and government projects.

The Company has entered into agreements/arrangements with PU Colleges on revenue sharing basis where the same is recognised on mutually agreed terms and accounted as Management Fees. The Company sells "Robomate", digitized content (recorded lectures of expert faculty, notes, high-end animation and question/answers) online and/or offline through home installations/pen drive/SD card/Tablet. Sales price is inclusive of Robomate and all hardware cost. Royalty income is accounted on accrual basis.

Advertising and Marketing Industry: Pressman Advertising Limited

Revenue is recognized to the extent that it is probable that the economic benefit will flow to the company and the revenue can be reasonably measured, regardless of when the payment is being made.

Income from services: Revenue from advertising, public relations and allied services are recognized when the services are rendered and the same becomes chargeable. GST and other statutory dues are collected on behalf of government and are excluded from revenue.

Sources: Sun TV Network Limited Annual Report 2016–17, p. 82; Dena Bank Annual Report 2017–18, p. 204; SpiceJet Limited Annual Report 2016–17, pp. 87–88; Indian Hotels Company Limited Annual Report 2017–18, p. 206; Tata Consultancy Services Annual Report 2017–18, pp. 115–116; MT Educare Limited Annual Report 2015–16, p. 87; Pressman Advertising Limited Annual Report 2017–18, pp. 30–31. Used by permission.

CONSTRUCTION

Construction contract is a contract specifically negotiated for the construction of an asset or combination of assets closely interrelated or interdependent, for example, contract for construction of bridge, building, dam, pipeline road, etc. [As per Ind AS 11 entitled Construction Contracts (revised)].

As per Ind AS 11, the construction contract also includes the following:

(i) Contracts for rendering of services which are directly related to the construction of assets, for example, service of architect

(ii) Contract for destruction or restoration of asset and the restoration of the environment following the demolition of asset

Construction activities Long-term construction projects, which may extend over several years, involve financial transactions based on contracts. For example, the construction of dams, bridges, ships, aircrafts, residential and commercial complexes is based on contract.

As per Ind AS 11, the allocation of contract revenue and contract cost is to be performed in the accounting period in which the construction work is performed. This standard is applicable only to the contractor and not to the firm that undertakes the project on its own account.

Contract revenue includes the initial amount of the revenue agreed upon, variations in the contract as the work proceeds, contract claims such as the reimbursement of specific expenses,

IFRS Update

Differences in recognition style

The following table indicates the differences in the revenue recognition style as per Indian Accounting Standards (Ind AS), IFRS or International Accounting Standards (IAS), and US Generally Accepted Accounting Practices (GAAP).

Ind AS	IFRS/IAS	US GAAP
Does not provide any guidance on revenue measurement.	The revenue to be recognized only when risks and rewards have been transferred and the revenue can be measured reliably.	Detailed guidelines exist for specific types of transactions.
Revenue from services is to be recognized only on the completion of the service.	Revenue from services is to be recognized in proportion to the state of completion of the transaction at the balance sheet date.	It lays emphasis on persuasive evidence that an arrangement exists, and delivery has occurred or services have been rendered.

and any additional financial incentive offered by the contractee to the contractor.

The composition of contract costs include the (a) specific cost to contract such as material, labor, hire of plant, and design costs, (b) cost attributable to contract such as insurance costs and borrowing costs, and (c) cost specifically chargeable to the contractee (customer) such as general administrative costs and development costs. Selling costs, depreciation of idle plant and machinery etc., cannot be the part of the contract cost.

As per Ind AS 11, when the outcome of a construction contract can be estimated reliably, contract revenue and contract costs associated with the construction contract should be recognized as revenue and expense respectively with reference to the stage of completion of the contract activity on the last date of the reporting period. An expected loss on the construction contract is to be considered as an expense, and charged in the income statement by the contractor immediately. It cannot be carried forward to the next period.

The amount of revenue for the work completed till the date of reporting is to be recognized in the books of account of the contractor according to the percentage-of-completion method as the turnover of the period. The percentage (stage) of completion can be determined by (a) the cost-to-cost method, (b) a survey of work performed (certified by an independent engineer or valuer), or (c) the physical proportion of the contract work.

The contractor books the contract revenue, while the contractee has to make the piecemeal payment to the contractor as work progresses. Hence, the contractee needs to recognize the contract expense in their books of accounts. The contractee considers the expense incurred for contract work undertaken by self/firm or through the contractor as Capital Work-in-Progress in the books of account. Once the contracted work is completed and constructed property or asset is put into use, it is recognized as fixed asset.

The contract revenue recognition criteria adopted by Indian construction companies and the expense recognition criteria used by contractee companies are presented in Exhibit 6.3.

Under such transaction contracts, revenue is recognized on the basis of work completion and certification. The work certification is an approval by the entity awarding the contract. Some of the basic accepted norms for work completion and certification are explained in the following text.

Less than one-fourth When less than one-fourth of the work is completed, no profits should be taken to the income statement.

One-fourth or more but less than one-half When one-fourth or more but less than one-half of the work is complete, one-third of the profit made as of date should be taken to the income statement.

$$\text{Profit} = \text{Notional Profit} \times 1/3(\text{Cash Received/Work Certified})$$

Less than 90% When one-half or more but less than 90% of the work is complete, two-third of the profit as of date should be transferred to the income statement.

$$\text{Profit} = \text{Notional Profit} \times 2/3(\text{Cash Received/Work Certified})$$

More than 90% If 90% or more of the work is complete, then estimate the profit as if work is fully completed. The profit is then transferred to the income statement by applying following formula:

$$\text{Profit} = \text{Estimated Profit} \times \text{Cash Received/Contract Price}$$

This method has four characteristics:

1. Costs are accumulated separately for each distinct work project, contract, or job order. Each of these may be referred to as a job.
2. The ratio of the work done on each job to the total amount of job is measured by the ratio of the work done to the total work required.
3. Revenue from each job is recognized in proportion to progress on the job. The progress of each job is measured by the ratio of the work done to the total work required.
4. When revenues are recognized, job costs are recognized as expenses. This method recognizes revenues prior to realization. It allows entities involved in long-term projects to report profits on a yearly basis.

■ **ILLUSTRATION 6.1** On 1 December 2019, Shraddha Construction undertook a contract to construct a corporate building for ₹170 lakh. On 31 March 2020, Shraddha Construction found that it had already spent ₹129.98 lakh on the construction. Prudent estimates of additional costs for completion were ₹64.02 lakh. What amount should be treated as income in the income statement for the year ended 31 March 2020?

Solution

Amounts treated as income in the income statement for the year ended 31 March 2020 are as follows:

	Amount (₹) in lakh
Cost incurred till 31 March 2020	129.98
Prudent estimates of additional costs	64.02
Total cost of construction	194.00
Less: Contract price	170.00
Total foreseeable loss	24.00

According to Ind AS 11, an amount of ₹24 lakh is required to be recognized as an expense.

$$\text{Contract work in progress} = \frac{₹129.98 \times 100}{₹194.00} = 67\%$$

Proportion of total contract value to be recognized as turnover as per Ind AS 11

67% of ₹170 lakh	= ₹113.90 lakh
Less: Actual cost incurred	= ₹129.98 lakh
Net Loss	₹16.08 lakh

Provision of foreseeable loss = ₹24 lakh less ₹16.08 lakh

= ₹7.92 lakh.

The revenue recognition criteria adopted by Indian construction companies are as follows:

Hindustan Construction Company Limited

Revenue from Construction Contracts

The Company follows the percentage completion method, based on the stage of completion at the Balance Sheet date, taking into account the contractual price and revision thereto by estimating total revenue including claims/variations as per Ind AS 11, Construction Contracts, and total cost till completion of the contract and the profit so determined proportionate to the percentage of the actual work done. Revenue is recognised as follows:

- In case of item rate contracts on the basis of physical measurement of work actually completed, at the Balance Sheet date.
- In case of Lump sum contracts, revenue is recognised on the completion of milestones as specified in the contract or as identified by the management. Foreseeable losses are accounted for as and when they are determined except to the extent they are expected to be recovered through claims presented or to be presented to the customer or in arbitration.

Advance payments received from contractee for which no services are rendered are presented as 'Advance from contractee'.

Larsen and Tourbo Limited

Revenue from construction/project related activity and contracts for supply/ commissioning of complex plant and equipment is recognised as follows:

1. Cost plus contracts: Revenue from cost plus contracts is determined with reference to the recoverable costs incurred during the period plus the margin as agreed with the customer.
2. Fixed price contracts: Contract revenue is recognised only to the extent of cost incurred till such time the outcome of the job cannot be ascertained reliably subject to the condition that it is probable such cost will be recoverable.

When the outcome of the contract is ascertained reliably, contract revenue is recognised at cost of work performed on the contract plus proportionate margin, using the percentage of completion method. Percentage of completion is the proportion of cost of work performed to-date, to the total estimated contract costs.

The estimated outcome of a contract is considered reliable when all the following conditions are satisfied:

(i) the amount of revenue can be measured reliably;
(ii) it is probable that the economic benefits associated with the contract will flow to the Company;
(iii) the stage of completion of the contract at the end of the reporting period can be measured reliably; and
(iv) the costs incurred or to be incurred in respect of the contract can be measured reliably.

Expected loss, if any, on a contract is recognised as expense in the period in which it is foreseen, irrespective of the stage of completion of the contract.

For contracts where the aggregate of contract cost incurred to date plus recognised profits (or minus recognised losses as the case may be) exceeds the progress billing, the surplus is shown as due from customers. For contracts where progress billing exceeds the aggregate of contract costs incurred to-date plus recognised profits (or minus recognised losses, as the case may be), the surplus is shown as the amount due to customers. Amounts received before the related work is performed are disclosed in the Balance Sheet as a liability towards advance received. Amounts billed for work performed but yet to be paid by the customer are disclosed in the Balance Sheet as trade receivables. The amount of retention money held by the customers is disclosed as part of other current assets and is reclassified as trade receivables when it becomes due for payment.

The expense recognition criteria adopted by Indian companies are as follows:

Star Cements Limited

Capital Work In Progress

Capital work in progress is carried at cost and includes any directly attributable cost incurred during construction period.

Expenditure during Construction Period

In case of new projects and substantial expansion of existing units, expenditure incurred including trial production expenses net of revenue earned, and attributable interest and financing costs, prior to commencement of commercial production/completion of project are capitalised.

The Indian Hotels Company Limited (Taj)

All property, plant and equipment are initially recorded at cost. Cost includes the acquisition cost or the cost of construction, including duties and non-refundable taxes, expenses directly related to bringing the asset to the location and condition necessary for making them operational for their intended use and, in the case of qualifying assets, the attributable borrowing costs (refer note no. 2(o), Page 117). Initial estimate of costs of dismantling and removing the item and restoring the site on which it is located is also included if there is an obligation to restore it. First time issues of operating supplies for a new hotel property, consisting of linen and chinaware, glassware and silverware (CGS) are capitalised and depreciated over their estimated useful life.

Subsequent expenditure relating to property, plant and equipment is capitalised only when it is probable that future economic benefits associated with these will flow to the Company and the cost of the item can be measured reliably.

Capital work in progress represents projects under which the property, plant and equipment are not yet ready for their intended use and are carried at cost determined as aforesaid.

Sources: Hindustan Construction Company Limited Annual Report 2017–18, p. 87, Used by permission; L&T Ltd Annual Report 2017–18, p. 250; Star Cements Ltd Annual Report 2017–18, p. 93; Indian Hotels Company Limited Annual Report 2016–17, pp. 113–114.

IFRS Update

Differences in construction contracts recognition style

The following table indicates the differences in the construction contracts recognition style as per Indian Accounting Standards (Ind AS), IFRS or International Accounting Standards (IAS), and US Generally Accepted Accounting Practices (GAAP).

Ind AS	IFRS/IAS	US GAAP
Expected losses to be recognized as an expense immediately.	Completed contract method is not allowed.	Similar to IFRS.
If the outcome is reasonably measurable then percentage of completion method is recommended.	The percentage of completion method is recommended.	Completed contract method is permitted in rare circumstances when the extent of progress of work cannot be measured reliably.

OTHER CATEGORIZATION OF SALES OF GOODS AND SERVICES

In addition to the normal way of sales by firms, to achieve higher levels of growth of firms, firms are adopting different ways of sales and services. These are discussed hereunder.

Goods on Sale or Return

In commercial activities, goods are sometimes supplied by a manufacturer or a wholesaler to a retailer or a prospective customer on the basis of 'sale or return'. This indicates that if the retailer or prospective customer sells or retains the goods, he/she will incur the liability towards the manufacturer or wholesaler with respect to future payment in cash.

If the retailer or prospective customer is unable to sell or reject the goods, then he/she will return the goods to the manufacturer or wholesaler, having incurred no liability for the goods. It is possible that part of the goods are sold or retained, in which case only that portion for the goods which was sold or retained is payable to the manufacturer or wholesaler.

Only on confirmation from the retailer or the prospective customer about the goods sold or retained does the manufacturer or wholesaler increase the sales figures. Goods still unsold and lying with the retailer or the prospective customer would be recorded as part of the manufacturer's or wholesaler's stock lying with a third party at cost.

From the view of a retailer, goods on sale or return are not purchases until he/she actually incurs liability for them, that is, the goods are sold. Neither do they constitute part of his stock as they belong to the manufacturer.

The revenue recognition criteria adopted by Indian FMCG companies are explained in Exhibit 6.4.

■ **ILLUSTRATION 6.2**   The year end for LeBlanc & Co. is 31 December 2020. When the firm sends goods on sale or return to retailers, it charges them out as ordinary sales. The following details are relevant to its end-of-year position.

	₹
Stock (at factory) at cost as on 31 December 2020	10,400
Sales (including goods on sale or return ₹15,000)	60,000
Unsold goods by retailer	3,000
Debtors as on 31 December 2020 (including goods booked out on sale or return basis)	8,800

The goods sent on sale or return were at cost price plus 25% for profit. Compute the value of reportable debtors and reportable stock for LeBlanc & Co.

Solution

The following figures will be reported in the financial statement for the year ended 31 December 2020.

Particulars	Amount (₹)
Sales	60,000
Less: Goods on sale or return still unsold	3,000
Reportable sales	57,000
Debtors	8,800
Less: Charges for goods on sale or return in respect of goods not sold	3,000
Reportable debtors	5,800

Particulars	Amount (₹)	
Stock at the factory at cost		10,400
Add: Goods in customers' hand at third party place on sale or return basis at the selling price	3,000	
Less: Profit content (25 % on cost price means 20% on selling price)	600	
		2,400
Reportable stock		12,800

EXHIBIT 6.4   Revenue Recognition Criteria Adopted by Indian FMCG Companies

The revenue recognition criteria adopted by Indian FMCG companies are as follows:

Future Retail Limited

Revenue is recognised on a fair value basis to the extent that it is probable that the economic benefits will flow to the company and the revenue can be reliably measured.

Sale of Products

Revenue from sale of products is recognised, when significant risks and rewards of ownership have been transferred to the buyer and no significant uncertainty exists regarding the amount of the consideration that will be derived from the sale of products. It also includes excise duty and excludes value added tax/sales tax and GST (Goods and Service Tax). It is measured at fair value of consideration received or receivable, net of returns and allowances.

Rendering of Services

Revenue from services are recognised as they are rendered based on arrangements with the customers.

Marico Limited

Revenue Recognition

Revenue is measured at the fair value of the consideration received or receivable. Amounts disclosed as revenue are inclusive of excise duty and

net of returns, trade allowances, rebates, value added taxes and amounts collected on behalf of third parties.

The Group recognizes revenue when the amount can be reliably measured, it is probable that future economic benefits will flow to the entity and specific criteria have been met for each of the Group's activities as described below. The Group bases its estimates on historical results, taking into consideration the type of customer, the type of transaction and the specifics of each arrangement.

(i) Sale of goods

   Timing of recognition: Sale of goods is recognized when substantial risks and rewards of ownership are passed to the customers, depending on individual terms, and are stated net of trade discounts, rebates, incentives, subsidy, sales tax and value added tax except excise duty.

   Measurement of revenue: Accumulated experience is used to estimate and provide for discounts, rebates, incentives & subsidies. No element of financing is deemed present as the sales are made with credit terms, which is consistent with market practice.

(ii) Revenue from services is recognized in the accounting period in which the services are rendered.

Sources: Future Retail Limited Annual Report 2017–18, p. 93; Marico Limited Annual Report 2017–18, p. 152. Used by permission.

Instalment Credit Sales

Many merchandising firms sell goods on an instalment basis. The customer pays a certain amount as instalment on the payment due date. In such cases, revenue attributable to the sale price exclusive of interest should be recognized on the date of sale. The interest element should be recognized as revenue proportionate to the unpaid balance due to the seller. If collection is not reasonably assured, revenue can be recognized by the instalment method as and when cash instalments are received.

When goods are sold on instalment credit basis, the buyer does not have a clear title until the instalment payments have been completed. If, however, there is a reasonable certainty that these payments will be made, revenue is recognized at the time of delivery. In case of consignment shipment, the supplier or consignor ships goods to the consignee, who attempts to sell them. The consignor retains title to the goods until they are sold. The consignee can return any unsold goods to the consignor. In these circumstances, performance has not been substantially completed until the goods are sold by the consignee. Thus, the consignor does not recognize revenue until that time.

Production Process

It is generally accepted that income is accrued only at the time of sale and it should not be anticipated by considering assets at their current market price. However, in case of certain industries, where products have an immediate marketability, the revenue may be recognized as soon as the production process is complete. The amount of income earned is the excess of the estimated sales price of the completed products over the cost of their production or extraction. Expenses incurred in the shipping of these products should be charged to such income and should be disclosed fully in the financial statements. This is particularly true in case of companies dealing in precious metals (such as gold and silver), extractive industries (such as oil), and agriculture. In the case of these industries, the inventories are calculated at realizable sales prices.

The revenue recognition criteria adopted by gold and mineral mines are explained in Exhibit 6.5.

Franchise

A franchise provides an exclusive right to use a formula, design, technique, or territory. This right is provided to the *franchisee* (user of the right) by the *franchisor* (owner of the right). For the franchisee, it is considered as an intangible asset. The right period or quantum of works or activities would be specified in the terms of agreement between the franchisor and the franchisee. An example of franchise is the right to operate the McDonald's chain of restaurants in India by the parent company, McDonald's.

If the value of a franchise is small or very nominal, it may charge directly to the expense, whereas if the value of the franchise is significant, it could be amortized over the period for which the exclusive right is available with the franchisee. The amount paid or agreed to be paid will be considered as the franchise or license fee and would be amortized over an agreed period of time or quantum of work or activities undertaken during a given period of time. Hence, during the lifetime or estimated lifetime, a proportionate amount would be considered as an

---

EXHIBIT 6.5 Revenue Recognition Criteria Adopted by Production Process-oriented Companies

The revenue recognition criteria adopted by production process-oriented companies are as follows:

Deccan Gold Mines Limited

Revenue is recognized to the extent it is probable that the economic benefits will flow to the Company and the revenue can be reliably measured.

(i) Exploration Income is recognized when services are rendered.
(ii) Interest Income is recognized on accrual basis
(iii) Dividend Income is accounted on accrual basis when the right to receive the dividend is established
(iv) Consultancy Income is recognized as and when services are rendered.

Revenue Recognition

1. Sales revenues and Contract Receipts are accounted on accrual basis goods.
2. All incomes to the extent they are ascertained are accounted on accrual basis.

Gujarat Mineral Development Corporation Ltd
Revenue Recognition

Revenue is measured at fair value of the consideration received or receivable. Amounts disclosed as revenue are net of the amounts collected on behalf of third parties. The Company recognises revenue when the amount of revenue can be reliably measured, it is probable that future economic benefits will flow to the Company and specific criteria have been met for each of the Company's activities. The Company bases its estimates on historical results, taking into consideration the type of customer, the type of transaction and the specifics of each arrangement.

Sales are recognized at the time of dispatch of finished goods. Sales include amounts in respect of excise duty (on the basis of payments made in respect of goods cleared), royalty, transportation, packing charges, generation based incentives, clean energy cess, mine closure charges wherever applicable and other taxes or duties, if any, but excludes VAT/GST. Sales are reduced to the extent of the amount of cash discount.

The liquidated damage/penalty, if any, on capital contracts are generally determined on completion of contract and the same is recognised in the Statement of Profit and Loss. Liquidated damages/penalty on long term revenue contracts are determined at the end of one year from the date of award of contracts and the same is recognised in the Statement of Profit and Loss.

In respect of power plants, Unscheduled Interchange (UI) Charges and Generation Based Incentives (GBI) are recognized as and when the same are received / incurred by the Company.

Sources: Deccan Gold Mines Limited Annual Report 2017, pp. 101 & 132, Used by permission; Gujarat Mineral Development Corporation Ltd Annual Report, 2017–18, p. 80.

expense every year and would be charged against the income of the firm. This in turn reduces the profit of the firm. The balance amount will be treated as an asset, and carried forward in the balance sheet as on date.

In the same way, the owner of the franchise, who handed over the right to use to another party, would receive the income in the beginning of the contract period, and would amortize a proportionate amount as an income in the income statement for the year, and the balance amount would be treated as unearned revenue, and will be carried forward for a future period on the liability and capital side of the balance sheet.

Lease

Leasing is an integral part of today's commercial world. It is one of the popular methods of acquiring and financing operating capital assets. Leasing for operating assets may, in many cases, be considered as a financing tool. It implies that rather than borrow the funds from a bank, it is financed through a leasing arrangement.

A lease is a contract where one firm gains the right to use assets owned by another firm for a specific period of time at a specified periodic cost. A lease is generally similar in nature to a rent.

When the *lessor* (owner of the asset) gives the *lessee* (user of the asset) the right to use an asset for a limited period of time, but retains the risks and rewards of ownership of the asset, then it is known as an *operating lease*. For example, consider a contract of leasing office space in an office building by the lessor to the lessee: the risks and rewards with respect to decrease or increase in the price of the office building belong to the lessor only.

The lessor permits the lessee to use the asset for a specified payment but retains the title to the property. The lease agreement sets forth the period covered by the lease, provisions for payment of taxes, insurance, maintenance expenses and the like, provisions for renewal of the lease or purchase of the asset at the expiration, and the timing and amounts of periodic rental payments during the lease period. The income received by the lessor is known as either *lease rental income* or *rental income*.

A *capital lease* contract is intended to provide financing to the lessee for the eventual purchase of an asset or to provide the lessee with the right to use an asset over the majority of the useful life of the asset. In the case of capital lease transactions, the majority of the risk and reward of ownership is transferred from the lessor to the lessee. For example, Kotak Mahindra Finance leases a car for a period of three years to Mr Rao, and as per the agreement, the title of the car transfers to Mr Rao at no additional cost at the end of the lease period. Hence, it can be considered as a lease agreement that aids in financing the purchase of the car by Mr. Rao. Capital lease is also known as *financing lease*, and is very popular for the purchase of computers, medical equipments, plant and equipment by firms, etc.

Under the operating lease arrangement, the lease equipment or asset is not listed among the assets, and the obligation to make the lease payment is not listed as part of the liabilities of the lessee. Hence, it is also known as *off-balance-sheet*

financing from the view of the lessee (Meigs and Meigs 1989). The lessee would not recognize the leased asset or leased liability, but will report only a periodic lease rental as an expense equal to the annual lease payment. The lessor would not recognize it as sale on the lease signing date, but would consider the same as lease rental revenue as and when received or receivable.

Capital lease is regarded as an equivalent to the sale of the leased asset, with the original owner of the asset allowing the lessee (user of the leased property) to pay for the asset over a period of time with a series of lease payments. Even though the property right of the asset is not transferred from the lessor to the lessee, the lessor would record the transaction as a sale of asset and the lessee as purchase of the asset. In a capital lease agreement, an appropriate interest charge is added to the regular sales price to work out the amount of lease payment instalment. The lease payments are nearly equivalent to the equated annual instalment payment for bank loan.

Under the capital lease arrangement, the equipment or asset is actually recorded as an asset and the required lease payments as a liability in the books of the lessee. The asset and liability would be recorded at the present value of the required lease payments over the time period of lease agreement, at an appropriate interest rate. The present value of the required lease payments calculated is also known as the fair value of the lease asset. Lease payments made by the lessee are allocated between the interest expense and a reduction in the liability of lease payment. The leased asset would be depreciated over the life of the asset rather than the period of the lease.

Exhibit 6.6 elaborates the method of accounting adopted by lessor companies and by lessee companies.

The lessor would consider the amount receivable from the lessee as an asset, which shows an increase in the revenue or sale of the year. Generally, the present value of future lease payments is equal to the regular sale price or revenue amount for the lessor. When the lease payments are received, the lessor should recognize an appropriate portion of the payment as representing interest revenue and the remainder as a reduction in lease payments.

Sale and Lease Back

Sale and lease back is nearly equivalent to a lease transaction. In a sale and lease back agreement, also known as a *sale and repurchase agreement*, the seller of an asset shall buy the asset back at a higher price specified in the agreement. The difference between the sale price and the purchase price would be treated as the lease revenue income for the period of lease by the lessor and as the lease revenue expense by the lessee. This arrangement is generally made in the nature of capital lease, and it supports the original owner of an asset to overcome liquidity issues.

Factoring

A factoring arrangement is made with an intention to accelerate the receipt of cash by the seller of the goods and commodities from the credit sale made by him/her. In this situation, the seller receives the funds before the due date

---

EXHIBIT 6.6 Lease Income Treated by Lessor and Lessee Company

Let us look how lease income is treated by a lessor company:

DLF Limited

Rental Income

Rental income is recognized on a straight-line basis over the terms of the lease, except for contingent rental income which is recognized when it arises and where scheduled increase in rent compensates the lessor for expected inflationary costs. Parking income and fit out rental income is recognized in statement of profit and loss on accrual basis.

Marico Limited

As a Lessor

Lease income from operating leases where the company is a lessor is recognised in income on a straight-line basis over the lease term unless the receipts are structured to increase in line with expected general inflation to compensate for the expected inflationary cost increases. The respective leased assets are included in the balance sheet based on their nature.

Let us look how lease expense is treated by a lessee company:

Marico Limited

As a Lessee

Leases of property, plant and equipment where the company, as lessee, has substantially all the risks and rewards of ownership are classified as finance leases at the fair value of the leased property or, if lower, the present value of the minimum lease payments. The corresponding rental obligations, net of finance charges, are included in borrowings or other financial liabilities as appropriate. Each lease payment is allocated between the liability and finance cost. The finance cost is charged to the profit or loss over the lease period so as to produce a constant periodic rate of interest on the remaining balance of the liability for each period.

Leases in which a significant portion of the risks and rewards of ownership are not transferred to the company as lessee are classified as operating leases. Payments made under operating leases (net of any incentives received from the lessor) are charged to profit or loss on a straight-line basis over the period of the lease unless the payments are structured to increase in line with expected general inflation to compensate for the lessor's expected inflationary increase.

Dhanuka Agritech Limited

Leases

Lease arrangements where the risk and rewards incidental to ownership of an asset substantially vests with the lessor, are recognized as operating lease. Lease rentals under operating leases are recognized as expense in the statement of profit and loss account on a straight-line basis over the lease term.

Sources: DLF Annual Report 2016–17, p. 92; Marico Limited Annual Report 2016–17, p. 244, Used by permission; Dhanuka Agritech Limited Annual Report 2016–17, pp. 98–99. Used by permission.

---

from the *factor* (the financier) for the credit sale transaction made. This method supports business, and also helps the seller overcome liquidity issues. The party who finances the seller is known as the factor.

For example, Daisy Traders has sold goods worth ₹5 lakh to Sunset Company with a credit period of three months. Daisy Traders, in order to overcome its liquidity problem, wishes to sell or transfer the accounts receivable from Sunset Co to Rashi Finance. In this case, Rashi Finance would provide immediate finance against the purchase of receivables from Daisy Traders, and hence would be known as the factor, and the arrangement is known as factoring.

Rashi Finance can provide the factoring facility with recourse or without recourse. Factoring with recourse implies that the seller of the receivables (Daisy Traders) is liable to the factor (Rashi Finance) if the receivable is not collected from the buyer of the goods (Sunset Co), while factoring without recourse implies that the factor bears the loss of non-collection of funds from the buyer of the goods.

A fee income is charged as factoring service income by the factor for the period under consideration. The fee for factoring without recourse is normally greater than that for factoring with recourse. The factoring fees paid by the seller of the goods would be treated by him/her as the financing expense for the period under consideration. The seller of the goods availing the factoring arrangement with recourse would treat the amount yet to be collected by the factor from the buyer of the goods as contingent liability.

Goods on Consignment

In a consignment arrangement, the owner (the *consignor*, main firm, or supplier) will ship merchandise goods and commodities to a dealer (*consignee*, agent, or seller) with the agreement that payment is expected only when the merchandise is sold by the consignee. The consignee has a right to return the unsold merchandise to the consignor. In effect, the consignee is offering to sell the consigned merchandise on behalf of the consignor. This arrangement is applicable when the agent does not wish to block a significant amount in an inventory that may be slow moving or sale of merchandise is uncertain. The title of the consigned merchandise remains with the consignor. Hence, at the end of the year, the consigned merchandise should be reported as inventory lying at third place by the consignor. Such consignment merchandises would not be reported as inventory or stock by the consignee.

Once the goods are sold, the consignee will remit the amount to the consignor after deducting his/her service charges, commission, and other expenses as per the agreement. The service charge revenue and commission earned would be treated as revenue in the income statement of the consignee. The deducted amount, as explained above, would be treated as consignment business expenses by the consignor in the income statement.

Interest, Royalties, and Dividends

A firm receives revenue when it allows other entities to use resources and thereby receives interest, royalties, and dividends.

Interest   The amount charged for the use of cash resources or amounts due to an entity is referred to as interest. The interest accrual is based on the principal outstanding and the applicable interest rates. Usually the discount or premium on debt securities is accrued over the period of maturity.

Royalty   The charges for the use of assets such as technical knowledge, patents, trademarks, and copyrights constitute royalties. Royalties accrue in accordance with the terms of the relevant agreement and are usually recognized when the holder becomes legally entitled to benefit from them.

Dividends   Companies make dividend payments out of their current or retained earnings. Dividends from investments in shares are recognized in the statement when a right to receive payment is established.

Exhibit 6.7 indicates the income recognition criteria adopted by companies of certain sectors.

Interest, royalties, and dividends from foreign countries require foreign exchange permission. When uncertainty in remittance is anticipated, revenue recognition is done at the time of receiving permission or remittance.

Amount Paid in Advance

Sometimes, money is received or amount is billed before delivering goods or rendering services. Rent and magazine subscriptions are examples of such transactions. Such items are rightly not treated as revenue in the period they are received. Revenue received or billed should be different and recognized either on a straight-line basis over time or on the value of the items if the items shipped vary in value. In other words, revenue should be based on the sales value of the item shipped.

Unearned revenue is the amount received as revenue of a future period. Such revenues are treated as liabilities until the earning process is complete. In the future, when these amounts are recognized as revenues, it results in a decrease in liabilities rather than an increase in assets.

REVENUE MEASUREMENT

Revenue is measured in terms of the estimated amount of revenue to be received from the customer. This is the amount that the customer is reasonably certain to pay (after providing for the trade discounts).

If a sales transaction involves a non-cash transaction or non-cash asset, like the exchange of an old television for a new one, the amount of revenue to be recorded will be the cash equivalent of the goods received or given up, whichever is more clearly determinable.

The realization concept states that the amount recognized as revenue is the amount that is equal to or reasonably certain to be realized.

The amount of revenue recognition under this concept is generally less than the actual selling price of goods or services provided. If the sale of goods or services is made on credit, the amount of revenue recognized is the total value of sale less the estimated amount of unrealized receivables, that is, bad debts. Such an estimate can be made by previous records/experience. However, in practice, the entire amount of sale is taken as income, and bad debts, if any, are shown separately on bad debt expenses in the income statement.

EXPENSES

Expenses are the outflows of assets by an entity in order to produce goods and provide services. Expenses are measured in terms of the cost of goods or services sold to customers. Expenses can occur through—(a) the transfer of assets to customers; and/or (b) use of assets in a business operation. An expense may also represent the cost of using a plant or building that was purchased to be used in the entity's operating cycle. For example, the depreciation amount on plant and machinery is considered a cash-less expense.

According to the matching concept, the expenses of a particular accounting period are the costs of the assets used

---

EXHIBIT 6.7   Interest Income, Royalty Income, and Dividend Income Treated by Indian Corporates

Let us look how interest income, royalty income, and dividend income are treated by Indian corporates:

DLF Limited

Interest Income

Interest income is recorded on accrual basis using the effective interest rate (EIR) method.

Dividend Income

Dividend income is recognized at the time when the right to receive is established by the reporting date.

Future Retail Limited

Interest Income

For all financial instruments measured at amortised cost, interest income is recorded using the effective interest rate (EIR), which is the rate that exactly discounts the estimated future cash payments or receipts over the expected life of the financial instrument or a shorter period, where appropriate, to the net carrying amount of the financial asset.

Dividend Income

Dividend income is recognised when the Company's right to receive such dividend is established.

Sources: DLF Annual Report 2016–17, pp. 92–93; Future Retail Limited Annual Report 2017–18, pp. 93.

to earn the revenue that is recognized in that period. Let us assume that goods costing ₹8000 were sold for ₹10,000. As per the matching concept, ₹8000 will be booked as an expense when ₹10,000 is booked as an income.

Expenses and unexpired costs Expenses are incurred costs associated with the revenue of the period often directly or indirectly through association with the period to which the revenue has been recognized. Costs associated with future revenues or with a future accounting period are known as *unexpired costs*. Costs associated with past revenues or prior periods are adjusted with the expenses of those prior periods. The expenses of a period are listed in the following text.

- Costs directly associated with the revenue of the period
- Costs directly associated with an accounting period
- Costs that cannot be associated with any other period

Classification of Expenditure

Expenditure of an enterprise can be classified into three categories, capital, revenue, and deferred revenue expenditure.

Capital expenditure

It refers to an expenditure which has been incurred for the purpose of obtaining a long-term advantage for an entity. In other words, such expenses do not pertain to the running of the operating cycle. Some examples of the capital expenses relate to

- purchasing additional quantity of fixed assets;
- increasing the capacity of fixed assets;
- replacing of old machine or assets with new equipment or assets;
- acquisition of new plant and machinery; and
- expenses paid for acquiring patents, rights, licenses, copyrights, trademarks, etc.

Determining capital expenditure Expenditure can be recognizedas of a capital nature if it is incurred for the following purposes:

Purchasing long-term assets Expenditure incurred for the purpose of acquiring long-term assets can be classified as capital expenditure. The useful life of these assets should be more than at least one accounting period. When expenditure is incurred for improving the present condition of a machine, putting an old asset into working condition, or paying installing charges for machines, it is treated as capital expenditure in the books of accounts.

Capacity expansion If the expenditure is incurred to increase the earning capacity of a business, it will be considered to be of capital nature. For example, expenditure incurred for shifting the location of the factory for easier availability of raw materials is treated as capital expenditure.

Deferred benefit When expenditure, though incurred in one accounting year, provides benefit in a number of accounting years, it is referred to as deferred benefit. For example, a huge amount spent on advertisement is considered as deferred expenditure.

Initial expenses The preliminary expenses incurred before the commencement of business are considered as capital expenditure. For example, legal charges paid for drafting the memorandum and articles of association is treated as capital expenditure.

Revenue expenditure

Expenses which arise in the course of a firm's operating activities are termed as revenue expenditure. Costs of stock consumed, money spent on repairing existing fixed assets, depreciation on fixed assets, interest on loans, costs of goods purchased for resale or production, etc. constitute a firm's revenue expenditure.

Determining revenue expenditure Revenue expenditure temporarily influences only the profit-earning capacity of the business. Expenditure is recognized as revenue when it is incurred for the following purposes:

- Expenditure for day-to-day conduct of the business; the benefit of which will last for less than one year such as wages of workers, rent, selling expenses, etc
- Expenditure on consumable items, or goods and services for resale either in the original or improved form such as purchase of raw materials, office stationery, etc
- Expenditure incurred for maintaining fixed assets in proper working condition such as repair work commissioned for assets

Table 6.1 indicates the points of distinction between capital expenditure and revenue expenditure.

TABLE 6.1 Distinction between Capital Expenditure and Revenue Expenditure

Sl. No.	Capital Expenditure	Sl. No.	Revenue Expenditure
1	Capital expenditures are incurred for more than one accounting period.	1	Revenue expenditures are incurred for a particular accounting period.
2	Capital expenditures are of non-recurring nature.	2	Revenue expenditures are of recurring nature.
3	All capital expenditures eventually become revenue expenditures.	3	Revenue expenditures are not generally capital expenditures.
4	Capital expenditures are not matched with capital receipts.	4	All revenue expenditures are matched with revenue receipts.
5	Capital expenditures are incurred before or after the commencement of the business.	5	Revenue expenditures are incurred always after the commencement of the business.

Deferred revenue expenditure

Deferred revenue expenditure comprises of the expenditure incurred during an accounting period but the benefit of which is receivable in a future period. For example, development costs in mines, market research, etc. constitute a firm's deferred revenue expenditure.

Exhibit 6.8 indicates the accounting treatment for the same, adopted by agricultural and logistic sectors.

EXPENSE MEASUREMENT

A significant concern in business is the measurement and management of expenses. This section discusses the most common methods of measuring expense.

Historical Costs

This concept states that the value of an asset should be recorded at the original amount paid to acquire it. According to this concept, an asset's market value is not recorded in the financial statements. Historical costs are considered to be fair and verifiable when compared to other methods of measuring expenses.

Current Measurement

It is the cost of replacing an asset at current market prices. This method is applicable and useful when a company plans to replace an obsolete asset.

Revenues are generally measured in terms of the current market price received against products sold. Therefore, the expenses matched should also be measured in terms of the current price of goods or services used. The measurement of expenses in terms of current price has advantages between the income from transactions and the gains and losses, that arise from the holding of assets before the use.

Opportunity Costs

Opportunity costs include the best economic benefits foregone as a result of choosing a particular action from a number of available options. While determining opportunity costs, one has to note the fact that there are no exchanges of economic resources. For example, System Tools Roofing Limited has ₹20 lakh available for investment. System Tools may choose to buy machinery or can invest in a bank's fixed deposit. If it decides to purchase the machinery by paying ₹20 lakh, then the company has to forgo its interest income on the bank's fixed deposit of say ₹3 lakh; thus, the opportunity cost of the machine is ₹3 lakh.

The economic resources, that is, interest income from fixed deposit in this case, foregone due to the choice of an action from several alternatives, are termed as the opportunity cost. The opportunity cost concept is very important for decision making by the management.

In the same way, the current price of an asset may be taken either from the recent liquidation value (amount that can be realized if immediately sold in the market) or the replacement costs (the price to be paid if an asset of same and equal characteristics is to be purchased) of an asset, whichever is higher. This concept is to be used when the firm has alternative uses of resources or funds.

REVENUE EXPENSE AS CAPITAL EXPENSE

Revenue expenses may be taken as capital expenses in the books of accounts under the following situations:

- Expenses incurred for immediate repairing of an acquired second-hand asset
- Transaction, unloading, and installation charges paid for installing a new asset such as plant and machinery
- Legal charges paid or incurred to confirm the legal status of an acquired asset
- Interest paid to financial institutions and the administrative expenses incurred during the installation (pre-production) stage of an entity, that is, preliminary and pre-operative expenses

ASSETS AS EXPENSES

Examination of some specific cases of assets that become expenses will enable us to understand the concept.

EXHIBIT 6.8 Expenses Treated by Indian Agricultural and Logistic Companies

Let us look how expenses are treated by Indian companies operating in the area of agricultural and logistic activities:

Dhanuka Agritech Limited

Property, Plant, and Equipment (Tangible Assets) & Intangible Assets

Property, Plant & Equipment are stated at Cost of Acquisition (Net of recoverable taxes, wherever applicable), less accumulated depreciation and impairment loss, if any. Cost is inclusive of freight, duties, levies, installation expenses and any directly attributable cost of bringing the assets to their working condition for intended use which is capitalized till the assets are ready to be put to use. Subsequent expenditures related to an item of property, plant & equipment are added to their book value only if they increase the future benefits from the existing asset beyond its previously assessed standard of performance. Projects/ Units under which assets are not ready for their intended use are disclosed under Capital Work-In-Progress.

ASIS Logistics Limited

Fixed assets are stated at cost less accumulated depreciation and impairment losses if any. Cost comprises the purchase price and any attributable cost of bringing the asset to its working condition for its intended use. Borrowing costs relating to acquisition of fixed assets which takes substantial period of time to get ready for its intended use are also included to the extent they relate to the period till such assets are ready to be put to use.

In respect of accounting periods commencing on or after 7th December, 2006, exchange differences arising on reporting of the long-term foreign currency monetary items at rates different from those at which they were initially recorded during the period, or reported in the previous financial statements are added to or deducted from the cost of the asset and are depreciated over the balance life of the asset, if these monetary items pertain to the acquisition of a depreciable fixed asset.

Sources: Dhanuka Agritech Limited Annual Report 2016–17, p. 97, Used by permission; ASIS Logistics Limited Annual Report 2015–16, p.43.

Inventories or stocks The inventory of merchandise becomes expenses when it is sold. In case of manufacturing firms, all the costs incurred on the transaction of raw materials add value to the inventory. These costs are treated as expenses only when the inventory is sold.

Prepaid expenses These expenses represent services or assets paid for prior to their actual use. Prepaid expenses represent unexpired costs. They become expenses after the services and assets are used.

Long-lived assets Fixed assets have a limited useful life. Most assets lose their value over time as a result of wear and tear, age, or obsolescence. Depreciation is a non-cash expense that reduces the value of an asset.

Expenditure as Expense

Expenditures take place when an entity acquires goods and services. An expenditure can be incurred by paying cash, incurring a liability (such as an account payable), or exchanging other assets (such as trade-in-item). Over the life of an entity, all expenditures become expenses.

For example, an entity purchased fuel oil for ₹5,00,000 in late 2019. An expenditure of ₹5,00,000 was made in acquiring an asset in exchange of cash. No expense was recorded in 2019 since the fuel oil was not completely consumed that year. Rather, the fuel oil was an asset at the end of 2019. An expense of ₹5,00,000 was recorded in 2020 as the fuel oil was completely consumed in the same year.

The different types of transactions needed to be considered for distinguishing between amounts that are properly considered as expenses of a given accounting period made in connection with these items are listed in the following text. Figure 6.1 illustrates the concept further.

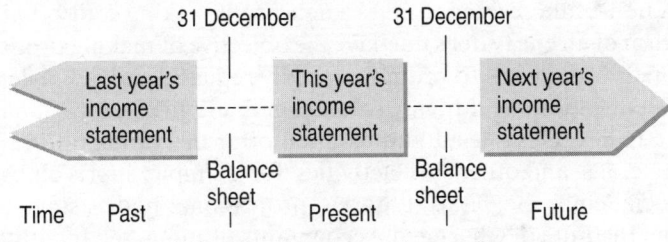

FIG. 6.1 Expenses and expenditures

1. Expenditures made this year are expenses of this year.
2. Expenditures made prior to the current year become expenses during the current year. These expenses appear as assets on the balance sheet at the beginning of the current year.
3. Expenditures made in the current year become expenses in future years. These expenses appear as assets on the balance sheet at the end of the current year.
4. Expenses made in the current year that will be paid for in a future year. On the balance sheet at the end of the current year, these expenses appear as liabilities.

Figure 6.2 presents a decision diagram illustrating the proper classification of expenditures as either assets or expenses.

Decreases in retained earnings (except on account of appropriated profits such as dividends) for reasons not associated with an entity's operations are referred to as *losses*. Losses are different from expenses. For example, loss of assets by fire, theft, or sale of marketable securities at an amount less than was paid for, is recorded as a loss in financial statements.

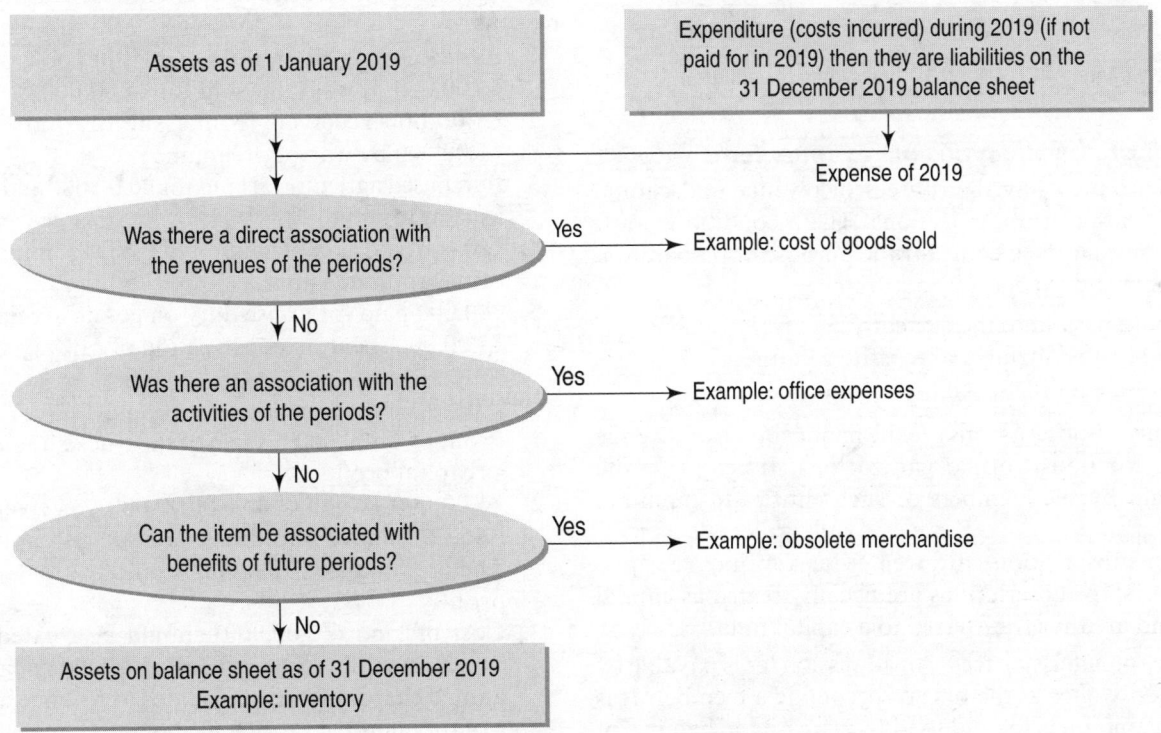

FIG. 6.2 Decision diagram—assets and expenses

Non-profit Organization or Non-government Organization

A non-trade-seeking entity is a non-profit-seeking entity. This form of an entity does not have the objective of making profit. Their objective is to promote socially required activities such as education, health care, old age homes, girls' educational activities. This is in addition to promotion of artistic, cultural, religious, and other such activities: for example, sports clubs, social clubs, hospitals, libraries, professional bodies such as the Institute of Chartered Accountants of India, the Institute of Cost Accountants of India, etc. It prohibits the payment of any dividend to its members. Such entities may or may not have trading activities. If trading activities are carried out by such entities, then the profit arising from there is used for the purpose of promoting the objectives for which such entities are formed. Since such organizations do not function to earn profit, the excess of income over expense is named as surplus of the year. The income and expenditure account of these organizations is prepared in the same way as an income statement.

The website of CRY, an NGO that works for children

Treatment of specific types of revenue items

Following are normally the sources of revenue and capital income of non-profit organizations. These conditions must be met to consider the income for the purpose of preparation of the income and expenditure account.

1. It should pertain to the current year.
2. It can be of recurring and repetitive nature.
3. It is not meant for specific use.

Subscriptions Subscriptions are the major source of revenue or income for non-profit organizations. It refers to the amount paid by the members of such entities to maintain their membership.

Periodic subscriptions are treated as revenue receipts. Life membership subscriptions are usually treated as capital receipts, and are thus transferred to a capital fund.

Entrance fee or admission fee An admission fee is payable by a member only once at the time of becoming a member. It is treated as capital receipt and used to increase the balance of the capital fund account.

Where the amount is small even to cover the expenses of admission, it should be treated as revenue receipt and considered as an income of the period in which it is received, and in turn taken to the income and expenditure account.

Donations Donations refer to the amounts donated by members or outsiders to an entity for a general or a specific purpose. If the amount of donation is large and non-recurring, then it should be added directly to the capital fund. Small amounts of general donations and recurring donations collected or received should be considered as an income for the period in which it is received, and taken to the income and expenditure account of the period concerned. Specific donations are treated as capital receipts, and are thus transferred to a 'special fund account' maintained for that purpose. Any income or revenue expenses related to such funds should be added or deducted from the respective fund's account balance.

Legacies Legacies represent the donations that are given under a will on the death of the donor. Legacies received are directly added to capital fund, deducting any tax payable under the law for the time being in force. Legacies are never to be considered as an income irrespective of the amount received.

Aid (from government and other institutions) General aids are treated as revenue receipts, and are thus transferred to the credit of the income and expenditure account. Specific grants are considered as capital receipts and specific fund accounts are prepared for the same. The said account balance is increased later on.

■ **ILLUSTRATION 6.3** Classify the following items relating to Cama Limited as capital or revenue expenditure. Give reasons.

1. A truck costing ₹10,00,000 stands in the books of accounts at ₹6,00,000. It was later sold for ₹7,00,000.
2. ₹5,00,000 received from issue of shares including ₹1,00,000 by way of premium.
3. Purchased agricultural land for ₹6,00,000 and paid ₹5,000 as land revenue.
4. ₹50,000 paid as contribution to PWD for improving roads of the approach area.
5. ₹40,000 paid for excise duty on goods manufactured.
6. ₹7,00,000 spent on construction of railway siding.

Solution

1. Profit of ₹1,00,000 on sale of the truck should be treated as capital profit.
2. ₹4,00,000 (₹5,00,000 – ₹1,00,000) received from the issue of shares should be treated as capital receipt. The premium of ₹1,00,000 should be treated as capital profit.
3. Cost of land (₹6,00,000) should be treated as capital expenditure and the payment of ₹5,000 as land revenue annual charges should be treated as revenue expenditure.
4. Contribution paid to PWD should be treated as revenue expenditure.

5. Excise duty of ₹40,000 should be treated as revenue expenditure.

6. ₹7,00,000 spent for constructing railway siding should be treated as capital expenditure.

■ **ILLUSTRATION 6.4** State with reasons whether the following items can be classified as capital expenditure or revenue expenditure.

1. An amount of ₹1,00,000 was incurred as expense to obtain a license for starting the factory.

2. ₹10,000 was paid for removal of the stock to a new site.

3. Rings and pistons of an engine were changed at a cost of ₹50,000.

4. ₹20,000 was spent as lawyer's fees to defend a suit claiming that the firm's factory site belonged to the plaintiff. The suit was not successful.

5. ₹1,00,000 was spent on advertising a new product in the market, the benefit on which will be effective for four years.

6. A factory shed was constructed at a cost of ₹10,00,000. A sum of ₹50,000 was incurred for the construction of the temporary huts to store building materials.

Solution

1. ₹1,00,000 incurred in connection with obtaining a license for starting a factory is capital expenditure. It was incurred for acquiring a right to carry on business for a long period.

2. ₹10,000 incurred for removal of stock to a new site is treated as revenue expenditure. Removal of the stock does not enhance the value of the assets. It is required to start the operations on the new site.

3. ₹50,000 incurred for changing rings and pistons of an engine is revenue expenditure. Changing rings and pistons will restore only the efficiency of engine and will not add anything to engine capacity.

4. ₹20,000 incurred for defending the title to the firm's asset is revenue expenditure (as the suit was unsuccessful). However, any expenditure rectifying the title will be considered as capital expenditure.

5. ₹1,00,000 incurred on advertising shall be treated as deferred revenue expenditure because the benefit of advertisement is available for four years. ₹25,000 is to be written off every year.

6. ₹10,00,000 used for constructing a factory shed shall be considered as capital expenditure. Similarly, the cost of constructing small huts to store building material should also be considered as capital expenditure.

■ **ILLUSTRATION 6.5** State clearly how you would deal with the following in the books of Ajitnath Co.

1. Redecoration expenses of ₹60,000.

2. Installation of a new wine bar for ₹1,00,000.

3. Building an extension to the club dressing room for ₹1,50,000.

4. Purchase of wines and spirits for ₹20,000.

5. The purchase of VCR and TV for use in the club lounge for 1,50,000.

Solution

1. Redecoration expenses of ₹60,000 shall be treated as deferred revenue expenditure.

2. Installation of a new wine bar is a capital expenditure because it is the acquisition of an asset.

3. ₹1,50,000 spent for the extension of the club dressing room is a capital expenditure because it creates an asset of a permanent nature.

4. The purchase of wines and spirits for ₹20,000 is revenue expenditure.

5. The purchase of VCR and TV for ₹1,50,000 is a capital expen-diture because it is an acquisition of assets.

■ **ILLUSTRATION 6.6** Would you consider the following items chargeable to capital expenditure or capital revenue?

1. Accrued dividend or interest including the cost price of an investment.

2. Lawyer's fees for drafting an agreement of lease for an immovable property.

Solution

1. Cost of investment less accrued dividend or interest should be treated as capital expenditure.

2. Lawyer's fees for drafting an agreement of lease should be treated as deferred expenditure, and it should be written off throughout the life of the lease.

■ **ILLUSTRATION 6.7** The building account of Fenil High School is ₹7,50,000 in the financial records. The following expenses were incurred on the building during the year. You are required to state how these items are to be treated in the books.

1. Construction of a common room for students amounted to ₹20,000.

2. Repairing cost of school benches and the tables amounted to ₹1,500.

3. Whitewashing cost amounted to ₹15,000.

4. Demolition cost of an old structure amounted to ₹7,500 and rebuilding cost amounted to ₹1,05,000.

Solution

1. Cost of constructing common room for students (₹20,000) is capitalized and added with the cost of building.

2. Repairing of student benches and tables is to be treated as revenue expenditure.

3. Whitewashing of building is to be treated as revenue expenditure.

4. Demolition cost of ₹7,500 is to be capitalized as a part of the cost of sight, rebuilding cost of ₹1,05,000 should also be treated as capital expenditure.

■ **ILLUSTRATION 6.8** State the nature (capital or revenue) of the following expenditures, which were incurred by M/s Moon Brothers during the year ended 31 March 2020.

1. ₹21,000 was spent on repairing a used machine purchased on 8 April 2019. ₹5,000 was paid on carriage and freight in connection with the machine's acquisition.

2. A sum of ₹30,000 was paid as compensation to two employees who were retrenched.
3. ₹2,000 was paid in connection with carriage on goods purchased.
4. ₹1,50,000 was paid as custom duty while importing machinery for modernizing the factory production during the current year. ₹50,000 was paid as import duty for the purchase of raw materials.
5. ₹1,20,000 was the interest accrued during the year on the term loan. This loan was obtained and utilized for the construction of a factory building and purchase of machinery. However, the production has not commenced till the last date of the accounting year.

Solution

1. ₹21,000 spent on repairing and ₹5,000 spent as carriage and freight charges should be treated as capital expenditure. These expenses were incurred to transform the old asset in a proper working condition.
2. ₹30,000 paid as retrenchment compensation should be treated as revenue expenditure. This expenditure does not bring any enduring benefits nor does it increase the value of any asset.
3. ₹2,000 paid as carriage on goods purchased should be treated as revenue expenditure as it is a business expenditure incurred for earning revenue.
4. ₹1,50,000 paid as custom duty on the import of machinery for modernizing the production capacity should be treated as a capital expenditure as it will improve the business and enhance its earning capacity. ₹50,000 paid as an import duty for purchase of raw material should be treated as revenue expenditure. This amount was not used to purchase a new asset but was incurred to produce goods and generate revenue.
5. ₹1,20,000 as interest accrued on term loan obtained should be treated as capital expenditure because commercial production has not started till the last day of the accounting year.

■ **ILLUSTRATION 6.9** State whether the following expenses are capital expenditures or revenue expenditures. Give reasons for your answers.

1. Purchased old machinery for ₹5,000 and paid ₹500 as wages to labourers for installing the said machinery.
2. Labour welfare expenses ₹500.
3. Expenses for air-conditioning of office ₹10,000.
4. Loss on sale of investments ₹1,500.
5. Research expenses ₹2,000.
6. Commission on sale ₹1,000.
7. General repairing charges of machinery ₹500.
8. Whitewashing expenses of building ₹3,000.
9. Cost of installation of lights and fans in the office ₹3,000.
10. Travelling expenses ₹1,200.

Solution

1. Purchase of old machinery for ₹5,000 is a capital expenditure because it results in bringing into existence an asset, having a future utility value. The wages paid for installation of machinery is also capital expenditure and would be part of capital expense of machinery. Installation charges are not a recurring expenditure. It is to be incurred only once at the time of installation.
2. Labour welfare expenses are revenue expenditure because they are of a recurring nature and are general administrative expenditure of a business and non-business firm.
3. Expenses incurred for air-conditioning of an office are capital expenditure because they result into acquisition of a fixed asset and increase in efficiency of the office staff.
4. Loss on sale of investments may be capital loss or revenue loss which depends on the nature of the business. In case of a business which is trading in investments, the loss on sale of investments will be a revenue loss, but where investments are purchased for specific purposes and not for sale, then the loss on sale of investments will be a capital loss.
5. Research expenses of ₹2,000 will be considered as revenue expenditure as per the latest accounting standard. Logically, research expenses should be treated as deferred revenue expenditure because such expenses will benefit the business for many years if the research becomes successful and commercially viable.
6. Commission on sale is a revenue expenditure because it is of recurring nature.
7. Expenditure for repairs to machinery of ₹500 is revenue expenditure because such expenditure will be incurred to maintain the machinery in good working condition.
8. Whitewashing expenses of building of ₹3,000 is deferred revenue expenditure because the benefit of such expenditure last for 3 to 5 years.
9. Cost of installation of lights and fans in office ₹3,000 is a capital expenditure because it results into acquisition of an asset of a lasting value and the business will be benefitted for a long time because of it.
10. Travelling expense of ₹1,200 is revenue expenditure because it is of a recurring nature.

CONCEPT OF GST AND ITS IMPACT ■

The **Goods and Services Tax (GST)** is an indirect tax (or consumption tax) levied in India on the supply of goods and services. GST is levied at every step in the production process, but is refunded to all parties in the chain of production other than the final consumer. France was the first country to introduce GST system in 1954. The tax came into effect in India from July 2017. GST is a destination-supply-based tax system. Rules and regulations are governed by the GST Council which comprises finance ministers of the centre and all the states.

Central taxes such as central excise duty, additional excise duty, service tax, additional custom duty, and special additional duty, as well as state-level taxes such as Value-added Tax or sales tax, central sales tax, entertainment tax, entry tax, purchase

tax, luxury tax, and octroi are subsumed in GST, hence making it centralized and avoiding the cascading effect of taxation.

The states will have the right to levy GST on intra-state (within state) transactions, including on services. The central government levies Integrated GST (IGST) on inter-state (between states) supply of goods and services. Import of goods is subject to basic customs duty and IGST.

Types of GST

The following four types of GST rates are applicable in India:

1. **Central GST (CGST):** This is applicable on supplies of goods and services within the state. The tax collected has to be shared with the central government of India.
2. **State GST (SGST):** This is applicable on supplies of goods and services within the state. The tax collected has to be shared with the concerned state of India.
3. **Integrated GST (IGST):** This is applicable on inter-state import and export transactions related to supplies of goods and services. The tax collected is shared between the central government and the concerned state of India.
4. **Union Territory GST (UTGST):** This is applicable on supplies of goods and services within the union territory. The tax collected is to be shared with the concerned union territory.

Scenario under GST

Under the GST regime, the tax will be levied at every point of sale. In case of intra-state sales, both central and state GST are charged. In case of inter-state sales, integrated GST is charged.

The definition of GST is 'a comprehensive, **multi-stage, destination-based tax** that will be levied on every **value addition**'.

Multi-stage tax

There are multiple change-of-hands in GST as an item goes through along its supply chain: from manufacture to final sale to the consumer. For example, consider the following sequence of events that take place, starting from buying of raw materials by the manufacturer and finally reaching to the end consumer.

1. Purchase of raw materials
2. Production or manufacture
3. Warehousing of finished goods
4. Sale of the product to wholesaler
5. Sale to the retailer
6. Sale to the end consumer

Destination-based GST

Consider some goods manufactured in Maharashtra but sold to the final consumer in Karnataka. Since GST is levied at the point of consumption (in this case, Karnataka), the entire tax revenue will go to Karnataka and not to Maharashtra.

■ **ILLUSTRATION 6.10** The following diagram indicates the process involved in making and selling of biscuits by a biscuit manufacturer.

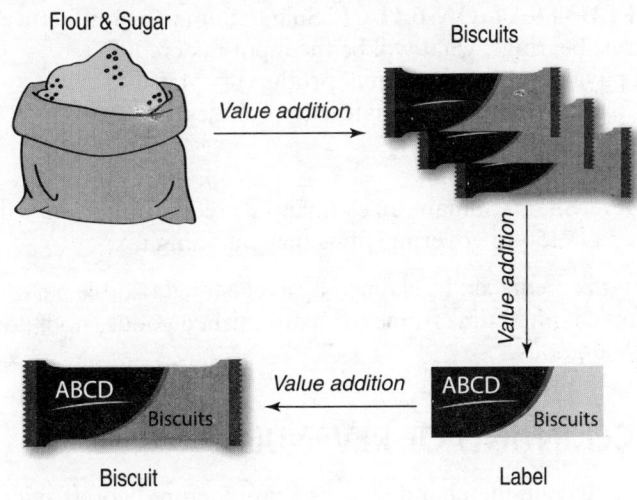

The manufacturer who makes biscuits buys flour, sugar, and other material. The value of the inputs increases when the sugar and flour are mixed and baked into biscuits.

The manufacturer then sells the biscuits to the warehousing agent who packs large quantities of biscuits and labels them. That is another addition of value, after which the warehouse sells them to the retailer.

The retailer packages the biscuits in smaller quantities and invests in the marketing of the biscuits, thus further increasing their value.

GST will be levied on these value additions, that is, the monetary worth added at each stage, to achieve the final sale to the end customer.

Input Tax Credit (ITC)

The basic objective of ITC is to avoid the cascading effect of duty.

Input It means any goods other than capital goods used or intended to be used by a supplier in the course or furtherance of business.

Capital goods It means goods, the value of which is capitalized in the books of account of the person claiming the input tax credit and which are used or intended to be used in the course or furtherance of business.

Input service It means any service used or intended to be used by a supplier in the course or furtherance of business.

Input tax In relation to a registered person, it means the central tax, state tax, integrated tax, or union territory tax charged on any supply of goods or services or both made to him. It includes (a) the integrated goods and services tax charged on import of goods; (b) the tax payable under the provisions of CGST Act 2017, IGST Act 2017, SGST Act 2017 (i.e., person liable to pay GST under Reverse Charge Mechanism (RCM)) and under UTGST Act 2017 (i.e., person liable to pay GST under RCM).

Input tax credit It means the credit of input tax. Input credit means at the time of paying tax on output, the supplier can reduce the tax that has already been paid on the input.

■ **ILLUSTRATION 6.11** If Shanti Suman manufactures various bearings, what will be the input tax credit?

Tax payable on output (Final product) = ₹450

Tax paid on input (Raw material purchases) = ₹300

Solution

Here, Shanit Suman can claim input credit of ₹300 and will only pay ₹150 to government as the remaining tax.

Input tax credit can be claimed by a registered taxable person within a limited time frame for semi-finished goods, stock, or finished goods.

ACCOUNTING OF REVENUE

Revenue from merchandise sales, manufactured goods sales, semi-finished goods sales, etc. are usually identified as *sales*. Sometimes, a firm may use more exact title, such as Sales of particular or Group of product.

When goods are sold on credit or cash basis, both parties should understand the amount and timing of payment as well as other terms of purchase, such as who pays delivery charges and what warranties or rights of return apply. Sellers quote prices in different ways.

The following journals are maintained by firms to have proper accounting of sales of goods and services transactions.

Sales Journal

A sales journal is meant for recording all sales of goods on credit. Cash sales are recorded in cash book and sales of articles other than goods on credit is to be recorded in general journal, that is, journal proper. At the end of the period, each entry is posted to the debit side of the appropriate individual account in the debtor's ledger and on the credit side of the sales account (at the value equal to gross amount less trade discount), excise duty account, and sales tax account.

Sales book or sales journal can be maintained in two ways: (a) Simple sales book (refer to Illustration 6.12); (b) Columnar sales book or sales journal according to the types of goods (refer to Illustration 6.13); and (c) Columnar sales book with columns for goods and expenses (refer to Illustration 6.14).

■ **ILLUSTRATION 6.12** From the following transactions, prepare the sales book for the year 2020 in the books of Shri Prabhat Hardware Store who is an iron trader.

June 1: Sold goods of ₹20,000 to Neha on a credit of 3 months and bill No.80 was sent.

June 8: Sold goods of ₹10,000 to Vidhi Store at 5% trade discount and sent bill No. 85 with carriage of ₹400.

June 12: Sold goods ₹15,000.

June 18: Sold machinery of ₹10,000 for ₹3,000 to Krima.

June 23: Sold goods of ₹15,000 to Shimoli at 10% trade discount and half of the amount was immediately paid by Shimoli. Bill No. 90 was sent.

June 28: Sold goods of ₹20,000 on cash to Riddhi at 10% cash discount.

June 29: Meet placed an order for supply of goods of ₹15,000.

June 30: Sold goods of ₹30,000 to Vraj at 10% trade discount. Bill No. 95 was sent.

Solution

Sales Book of Shri Prabhat Hardware Store

Date 2020	Name of Customer	Outward Invoice No.	L.F. No.	Total Amount (₹)
1 June	Neha A/c	80		20,000
8 June	Vidhi Store A/c (Amount of Goods ₹9,500 + Wages of ₹400)	85		9,900
23 June	Shimoli A/c	90		13,500
30 June	Vraj A/c	95		27,000
	Total Credit Sales			**70,400**

Note:

Date 12: Cash sales is recorded in sales book.

Date 18: Credit Sale of machine in journal proper.

Date 28: Cash Sale of goods will be recorded in cash book.

Date 29: Non-economic transaction will not be recorded.

■ **ILLUSTRATION 6.13** From the following transactions, prepare the columnar sales book for the year 2020 in the books of Nitin Store. Nitin Store deals in three types of clothes, namely cotton, khadi, and silk.

May 1: Sold Janki Store 100 meters of cotton cloth at ₹40 per meter, 200 meters of khadi at ₹20 per meter, and 50 meters of silk at ₹200 per meter with 10% trade discount. Bill No. 125 was sent. Credit period was 3 months.

May 8: Sold to Gopi Traders 200 meters of cotton cloth at ₹60 per meter and 80 meters of silk at ₹190 per meter at 10% trade discount. Goods sold on 2 month credit. Bill No. 126 sent. Gopi Traders paid half of the amount immediately in cash.

May 15: Sold to Nisarg Trading Company 100 meters of khadi and 50 meters of silk at ₹40 and ₹200 per meter, respectively. Nisarg Trading Company paid the amount immediately by cheque at 10% trade discount and 10% cash discount. Bill No. 127 was sent.

May 20: Preeti Store placed an order for the supply of 40 meters of khadi, 60 meters of cotton, and 100 meters of silk cloth.

May 22: Supplied goods to Preeti Store as per order under Bill No. 128 at ₹30 per meter. ₹50 per meter and ₹220 per meter at 10% trade discount was allowed.

May 26: Sold to Desai & Company cotton cloth of ₹15,000 at 10% trade discount under Bill No. 129.

May 30: Sold to DCM Store cotton cloth goods of ₹20,000 at 5% trade discount. Sent Bill No. 130 after adding 13% GST.

Solution

Sales Book of Nitin Store

Date 2020	Name of Customer	Outward Invoice No.	L.F. No.	Cotton	Khadi	Silk	Total Amount (₹)
1 May	Janki Store A/c	125		3,600	3,600	9,000	16,200
8 May	Gopi Traders A/c	126		10,800		13,680	24,480
22 May	Priti Store A/c	128		2,700	1,080	19,800	23,580
26 May	Desai and Company A/c	129		13,500			13,500
30 May	DCM Store A/c	130			21,470		21,470
	Total Credit Sales			**70,400**	**26,150**	**42,480**	**99,230**

Note:

Date 15: Cash sales will be recorded in cash book.

Date 20: Non-economic transaction will not be recorded.

■ **ILLUSTRATION 6.14** From the following transactions, prepare the sales book for the year 2020 with expenses columns in the book of Sachin Store. Sachin Store maintains record for GST, railway freight, and carriage.

Dec. 1: Sold goods of ₹60,000 to Dhoni Store at 10% trade discount. 5% GST and ₹2,000 for railway freight were applied. Bill No. 101 was given.

Dec. 10: Sold goods of ₹40,000 on cash to Virat Store at 10% trade discount. 5% GST and ₹200 for carriage were charged.

Dec. 16: Sold goods of ₹30,000 to Raina at 5% trade discount with a credit of 1 month. 5% value added tax on behalf of Raina, ₹500 for carriage, and ₹1,000 for railway freight were paid. Bill No. 110 was sent after charging carriage and railway.

Dec. 20: One machinery was sold for ₹35,000 to Jadeja Store. Paid ₹700 for carriage. 15 days credit was allowed to Jadeja Store.

Dec. 25: Sold goods of ₹25,000 to Rohit at 5% trade discount on 1 month credit. 5% GST and ₹1,000 for railway freight were applied. Half of the amount was paid immediately by Rohit. Bill No. 115 was sent.

Dec. 30: Sold goods of ₹15,000 to Umesh at 10% trade discount on one month credit. Bill No. 118 was sent after charging 5% GST and ₹1,000 for railway freight.

Dec. 31: Yuvraj placed an order for supply of goods of ₹70,000.

Solution

Sales Book of Shri Sachin Store

Date 2020	Name of Customer	Outward Invoice No.	L.F. No.	Net Amount of Goods	GST	Railway Freight	Wages	Total Amount (₹)
1 Dec	Dhoni Store A/c	101		54,000	2,700	2,000		58,700
16 Dec	Raina A/c	110		28,500	1,425	1,000	500	31,425
25 Dec	Rohit A/c	115		23,750	1,188	1,000		25,938
30 Dec	Umesh A/c	118		13,500	675	1,000		15,175
	Total Credit Sales			**1,19,750**	**5,988**	**5,000**	**500**	**1,31,238**

Note:

Date 10: Cash sales is recorded in cash book.

Date 20: Credit sale of machine is recorded in journal proper.

Date 31: Non-economic transaction will not be recorded.

Sales Returns Journal

A sales returns journal is meant to record transactions relating to goods sold on credit and received back from customers as not conforming to the specification or for any other reason. The customer who returns the goods gets credit for the value of the goods returned and a credit note stating that his/her account has been credited, that is, dues from him/her are reduced, by the value of the goods returned. At the end of the agreed period, each entry is posted to the credit side of the individual account in the debtor's ledger, and the total of the amount column is posted into the sales returns account.

■ **ILLUSTRATION 6.15** From the following transactions, prepare the sales book and sales returns book for the year 2020 in the books of Pratibha Furniture Mart.

Sept. 1: Sold goods of ₹10,000 to Rajesh Furniture Mart at 10% cash discount. Rajesh paid half of the amount immediately.

Sept. 5: Sold goods of ₹8,000 at 10% trade discount and 5% cash discount to Pushpa. Credit period was 1 month. Sent Bill No. 130 after charging ₹100 for carriage.

Sept. 12: Sold goods of ₹4,000 at 10% trade discount and 5% cash discount.

Sept. 15: Rajesh returned goods of ₹5,000. Pratibha sent Credit Note No. 16 after receipt of the returned goods.

Sept. 20: One old machine was sold to Manju for ₹3,000. Credit period was 1 month.

Sept. 22: Sold goods of ₹30,000 to Harish at 5% trade discount. Bill No. 136 was sent after charging 5% GST and ₹200 for carriage.

Sept. 23: Sold goods of ₹20,000 to Nita on a credit of one month, with trade discount 10% and cash discount 10%.

Sept. 30: Mukesh placed an order for supply of goods for ₹15,000.

Solution

Sales Book of Pratibha Furniture Mart

Date 2020	Name of Customer	Outward Invoice No.	L.F. No.	Total Amount (₹)
1 Sept	Rajesh Furniture Mart A/c			10,000
5 Sept	Pushpa A/c	130		7,300
22 Sept	Harish A/c	136		30,125
23 Sept	Neeta A/c			18,000
	Total Credit Sales			**65,425**

Sales Return Book of Pratibha Furniture Mart

Date 2020	Name of Customer	Outward Invoice No.	L.F. No.	Total Amount (₹)
15 Sept	Rajesh Furniture Mart A/c	16		5,000
	Total Credit Sales Return			**5,000**

Note:

Date 12: Cash sales are recorded in cash book.
Date 20: Credit sale of machine will be recorded in journal proper.
Date 30: Non-economic transaction will not be recorded.

Bills Receivable Book

The bills receivable book of an entity consists of all promissory notes given or bills of exchange accepted by customers in respect of amounts due from them. The bills receivable book is used to record all promissory notes given or bills of exchange accepted by customers or debtors.

Cash Sales Journal

A cash sales journal records the transactions with respect to the sale of goods and services, and in turn receipts of cash, or bank cheque, or payment through net banking, etc. The recording procedures are discussed in detail in Chapter 7 on Analysing Transactions.

ACCOUNTING OF EXPENSES

An expenditure takes place when assets or services are acquired in exchange of cash or other assets or by incurring a liability. For example, payment of wages is an expenditure and purchase of an insurance policy is also an expenditure. The assets or services acquired by incurring expenditure may yield benefit either only during the current accounting year or the benefits could be spread over several accounting years. When the benefits are received during the current accounting period, it is known as an expense. Thus, expenditure represents an outflow of resources or assets consumed during an accounting period. Expenditures can be assets, but expenses can only be costs. Hence, accounting of the same plays a significant role.

Exhibit 6.9 indicates the fundamentals of accounting treatment for the same, adopted by mines, agriculture, and telecommunication sectors.

Purchase Journal

A purchase journal is meant for recording the credit purchases of goods. It is also known as the *purchase day book or bought day book*. It has columns for date of purchase, invoice number, name of the party, ledger folio number, and the amount of purchases. It should be noted that the book records only purchase of goods on credit. The term *goods* covers only those items procured by the business for resale or for conversion into finished goods. Purchase of items other than goods is recorded in the general journal, that is, journal proper. Similarly, cash purchases are recorded in the cash book. The purchase journal shows the names of the parties from whom goods have been purchased on credit, and they are known as creditors. Their accounts have to be credited for the respective accounts shown in the purchase journal. The total of the amount column is debited to purchase account to indicate the receipt of the goods.

Purchase book or purchase journal can be maintained in two ways: (a) Simple purchase book (refer to Illustration 6.16); (b) Columnar purchase book or purchase journal according to the types of goods (refer to Illustration 6.17); and (c) Columnar purchase book with columns for goods and expenses (refer to Illustration 6.18).

EXHIBIT 6.9 Recognition of Expenses

Let us look at the recognition of expenses in different industries:

Mines: Deccan Gold Mines Limited

The financial statements have been prepared on an accrual basis and under the historical cost convention. The accounting policies adopted in the preparation of financial statement are consistent with those of previous year.

Agriculture: Dhanuka Agritech Limited

These financial statements are prepared in accordance with Indian Generally Accepted Accounting Principles (IGAAP) under the historical cost convention on the accrual basis. IGAAP comprises mandatory Accounting Standards as prescribed under section 133 of the Companies Act,2013 ('The Act') read with rule 7 of the Companies (Accounts) Rules, 2014, the provisions of the The Act (to the extent notified) and guidelines issued by the Securities and Exchange Board of India (SEBI). Accounting Policies have been consistently applied except where a newly issued accounting standard is initially adopted or a revision to an existing accounting standard requires a change in the accounting policy hitherto in use.

- Inventories of Raw Materials and Packing Materials are valued at Cost (net of CENVAT) on first-in first-out basis.

- Inventory of Work-in-Progress is valued at cost of Raw Material plus conversion cost wherever applicable.
- Finished Goods are valued at the lower of Cost (including overheads and excise duty) or Net Realizable Value.
- Excise duty in respect of closing inventory of Finished goods is included as a part of inventory.

Telecommunication: Bharti Airtel Limited

The financial statements have been prepared on the accrual and going concern basis, and the historical cost convention except where the Ind AS requires a different accounting treatment. The principal variations from the historical cost convention relate to financial instruments classified as fair value through profit or loss or through other comprehensive income (refer Note 2.11 b), liability for cash-settled awards (refer Note 2.18), the component of carrying values of recognised liabilities that are designated in fair value hedges (refer Note 2.11 d) - which are measured at fair value.

Sources: Deccan Gold Mines Limited Annual Report 2016–17, p. 101; Dhanuka Agritech Limited Annual Report 2016–17, p. 98, Used by permission; Bharti Airtel Limited Annual Report 2016–17, p. 192.

■ ILLUSTRATION 6.16 Prepare the purchase book for the year 2020 in the books of Shri Suresh.

Oct. 1:   Purchased goods of ₹10,000 from Dipak on a credit of 1 month.

Oct. 3:   Purchased goods of ₹20,000 from Sardar Store at 10% trade discount. Invoice No. was 116.

Oct. 7:   Purchased goods of ₹18,000 from Pankaj on cash.

Oct. 15:   Placed order with Rajesh for supply of goods of ₹20,000 at 10% trade discount.

Oct. 20:   Purchased furniture of ₹16,000 from Vyas Furniture Mart on a credit of 1 month.

Oct. 21:   Rajesh has sent goods as per order and sent invoice No. 350 after adding ₹1,000 for railway freight.

Oct. 24:   Purchased goods of ₹14,000 at 5% discount.

Oct. 25:   Purchased goods of ₹30,000 from Nilesh at 10% trade discount and half of the amount was paid immediately by cheque.

Oct. 26:   Purchased goods of ₹15,000 from Chirag at 10% trade discount and 5% cash discount. Amount was paid immediately.

Oct. 30:   Purchased goods of ₹40,000 from Nitin. Invoice No. was 151.

Solution

Purchase Book of Shri Suresh

Date 2020	Name of Supplier	Inward Invoice No.	L.F. No.	Total Amount (₹)
1 Oct	Dipak A/c			10,000
3 Oct	Sardar Store A/c	116		18,000
21 Oct	Rajesh A/c (goods of ₹18000 + Railway freight ₹1000)	350		19,000
25 Oct	Nilesh A/c			27,000
30 Oct	Nitin A/c	151		40,000
	Total Credit Purchases			**1,14,000**

Note:

Date 7:   Cash purchase is recorded in cash book.

Date 15:   Non-economic transaction will not be recorded.

Date 20:   Credit purchase of furniture will be recorded in journal proper.

Date 24:   Cash purchase is recorded in cash book.

Date 25:   Total purchase is considered on credit and recorded in purchase book.

Date 26:   It is a cash purchase; so recorded in cash book.

■ ILLUSTRATION 6.17 From the following transactions of Shri Gadda Electronics Store, prepare the columnar purchase book for the year 2020. Shri Gadda Electronics deals in TV, refrigerator, and washing machine.

May 1:   Purchased 10 TV sets at ₹30,000 per set, 5 refrigerators at ₹15,000 per piece, and 2 washing machines at ₹8,000 per piece from Shri Daya Electronics store. Credit period was 1 month and Invoice No. 100.

May 7:   Purchased from Shri Tarak Electronic Store 5 pieces of TV at ₹25,000 per piece and 10 refrigerators at ₹16,000 per piece at 10% trade discount. Received invoice No. 151. Half of the amount was paid immediately.

May 12:   Purchased cycle of ₹5,000 from Shree Ambey Cycle Store.

May 20:   Purchased 5 refrigerators at ₹20,000 per piece and 10 washing machines at ₹15,000 per piece at 10% trade discount and 5% cash discount from Shree Atmaram Electronic Store and the amount was paid immediately.

May 25:   Placed an order to Smt. Babita for supplying 20 pieces of TV sets at ₹28,000 per piece and 6 pieces of washing machines at ₹21,000 per piece.

May 31:   From Shree Gokuldham Electronic store purchased 5 TV sets at ₹30,000 per piece and 5 washing machines at ₹23,000 per piece, with 10% trade discount and Invoice No. 123.

Solution

Purchase Book of Shri Gadda Electronics

Date 2020	Name of Supplier	Inward Invoice No.	L.F. No.	Amount (₹) T.V.	Fridge	Washing Machine	Total Amount (₹)
1 May	Shri Daya Electronics Store A/c	100		3,00,000	75,000	36,000	4,11,000
7 May	Shri Tarak Electronics Store A/c	151		1,12,500	1,44,000		2,56,500
31 May	Shri Gokuldham Electronics Store A/c	123		1,35,000		1,03,500	2,38,000
	Total Credit Purchases			**5,47,500**	**2,19,000**	**1,39,500**	**9,06,000**

Note:

Date 12:   Credit purchase of asset will be recorded in journal proper.

Date 20:   Cash purchase will be recorded in cash book.

Date 25:   Non-economic transaction will not be recorded.

■ ILLUSTRATION 6.18 Abhishek Store deals in iron. Prepare the columnar purchase book with expense columns in the books of Abhishek Store for the year 2020. Abhishek Store maintains record of expenses like value added tax, carriage, and railway freight.

April 1:   Puchased goods of ₹50,000 from Shahrukh Store at 10% trade discount, 5% GST, ₹2,000 for carriage, and ₹5,000 for railway freight under Invoice No. 51.

April 5:   Purchased goods of ₹30,000 from Dipika at 5% trade discount. Total amount with carriage of ₹500 and railway freight ₹600 was paid in cash immediately.

April 20:   Purchased goods of ₹40,000 from Amitabh at 10% trade discount, 5% GST, ₹1,000 for carriage, and ₹2,500 for railway freight. Invoice No. was 251. Amitabh paid half of the amount immediately.

April 25:   Purchased machinery of ₹35,000 from Pooja on a credit of 1 month. Carriage of ₹2,000 for machinery was paid in cash.

April 30: Purchased goods of ₹25,000 from Anushka at 10% trade discount and 5% cash discount. Bill No. 44 was received with 5% GST and ₹500 for railway freight.

Solution

Purchase Book of Shri Abhishek Store

Date 2020	Name of Customer	Inward Invoice No.	L.F. No.	Amount (₹) Net Amount of Goods	GST	Railway Freight	Carriage	Total Amount (₹)
1 Apr	Shahrukh Store A/c	51		45,000	2,250	5,000	2,000	54,250
20 Apr	Amitabh A/c	251		36,000	1,800	2,500	1,000	41,300
30 Apr	Anushka	44		22,500	1,125	500		24,125
	Total Credit Purchases			**1,03,500**	**5,175**	**8,000**	**3,000**	**1,19,675**

Note:

Date 5: Cash purchase is recorded in cash book.

Date 25: Credit purchase of machinery will be recorded in journal proper.

Purchase Returns Journal

A purchase returns journal is used to record goods purchased on credit and sent back to a supplier if they are found not conforming to specifications or for any other reason. When the goods are returned to a supplier, a debit note is sent to him/her along with the goods returned indicating that its account has been debited with the amount mentioned in the debit note. The supplier, in turn, will prepare a credit note. Entries in the purchase returns journal are made on the basis of the original credit note received from the supplier. At the end of the agreed period, each entry is posted to the debit side of the appropriate individual account in the creditors' ledger, and total of the amount column is posted to the credit side of the purchase returns account.

■ **ILLUSTRATION 6.19** From the following transactions, prepare the purchase book and purchase returns book for the year 2020 in the books of Gujarat Store.

Jan. 1: Purchased goods of ₹1,00,000 from Punjab Store at 5% trade discount.

Jan. 3: Purchased goods of ₹60,000 from Maharashtra Store. Credit period was 1 month. Trade discount 10% in Bill No. 330.

Jan. 10: Purchased goods of ₹50,000 from Kerala Store on credit. 50% of the amount was paid immediately.

Jan. 17: Returned 1/3rd of goods purchased from Maharashtra Store. Sent Debit Note No. 43 for the amount thereof.

Jan. 21: Purchased goods of ₹40,000 from Rajasthan Store at 10% trade discount. Rajasthan Store sent Bill No. 160 after charging 5% GST and ₹400 for carriage.

Jan. 25: Purchased goods of ₹50,000 from Uttar Pradesh Store on credit. Credit period was 2 months. Trade discount was 10%. Bill No. 380 was sent.

Jan. 29: Returned 30% of the goods purchased from Uttar Pradesh Store and sent Debit Note No. 44 with goods.

Jan. 30: Placed an order with Madhya Pradesh for supply of goods of ₹80,000 at 10% trade discount.

Jan. 31: Purchased goods of ₹30,000 from Haryana Store at 10% trade discount and 5% cash discount on cash.

Solution

Purchase Book of Gujarat Store

Date 2020	Name of Supplier	Inward Invoice No.	L.F. No.	Total Amount (₹)
1 Jan	Punjab Store A/c			95,000
3 Jan	Maharashtra Store A/c	330		54,000
10 Jan	Kerala Store A/c			50,000
21 Jan	Rajasthan Store A/c (36,000 + 1800 + 400)	160		38,200
25 Jan	Uttar Pradesh Store A/c	380		45,000
	Total Credit Purchase			**2,82,200**

Purchase Return Book of Gujarat Store

Date 2020	Name of Supplier	Debit Note No.	L.F. No.	Total Amount (₹)
17 Jan	Maharashtra Store A/c	43		18,000
29 Jan	Uttar Pradesh Store A/c	44		13,500
	Total Credit Purchase Return			**31,500**

Note:

Date 30: Non-economic transaction will not be recorded.

Date 31: Cash purchase will be recorded in cash book.

Bills Payable Book

The bills payable book consists of all promissory notes given or bills of exchange accepted by business or entity in respect of amounts owing to its suppliers. The bills payable book is used to record all such promissory notes given or bills of exchange accepted by the entity.

Cash Purchase Journal

A cash purchase journal records the transactions with respect to purchase of goods and services, and in turn payment by cash, or bank cheque, or payment through net banking, etc. The recording procedures are discussed in detail in Chapter 7 on Analysing Transactions.

■ **ILLUSTRATION 6.20** Prepare the purchase book, sales book, purchase returns book, and sales returns book for the year 2020 in the books of P.K. Store from the following transactions:

Nov. 1: Purchased goods of ₹30,000 from Ramanuj at 10% trade discount. Bill No. was 120.

Nov. 4: Purchased goods of ₹12,000 from Nirmi at 10% cash discount. Credit period was 1 month. Bill No. was 130.

Nov. 6: Sold goods of ₹15,000 to Suresh at 5% trade discount and 3% cash discount under Bill No. 350.

Nov. 11: Purchased goods of ₹10,000. Cash memo No. was 58.

Nov. 15: Suresh returned goods of ₹3,000. Credit Note No. 20 was sent to Manoj.

Nov. 17: 40% goods returned to Nirmi and Debit Note No. 17 was sent.

Nov. 19: Purchased furniture of ₹7,000 from Shree Saraswati Furniture Mart.

Nov. 20: Purchased goods of ₹90,000 from Aunti. Half of the amount was paid immediately.

Nov. 21: All the goods purchased from Aunti were sold to Bala for ₹1,08,000. Credit was 1 month, trade discount 10%, and Bill No. 360.

Nov. 23: Bala returned half of the goods which was sent to Aunti.

Nov. 24: Karan placed an order for ₹30,000 at 10% trade discount for supply of goods.

Nov. 25: Goods sent to Karan as per order. ₹500 added for carriage under Bill No. 365.

Nov. 26: Cash purchase ₹16,000 and cash sales ₹20,000.

Nov. 27: Returned goods of ₹10,000 to Sweety, which was purchased in October and Debit Note No. 20 was sent.

Nov. 30: Karan returned half of the goods, and a proportionate amount of carriage was given credit.

Solution

Purchase Book of Shri P.K. Store

Date 2020	Name of Supplier	Inward Invoice No.	L.F. No.	Total Amount (₹)
1 Nov	Ramanuj A/c	120		27,000
4 Nov	Nirmi A/c	130		12,000
20 Nov	Aunti A/c			90,000
	Total Credit Purchases			**1,29,000**

Sales Book of Shri P.K. Store

Date 2020	Name of Customer	Onward Invoice No.	L.F. No.	Total Amount (₹)
6 Nov	Suresh A/c	350		14,250
21 Nov	Bala A/c	360		97,200
25 Nov	Karan A/c	365		27,500
	Total Credit Sales			**1,38,950**

Purchase Return Book of Shri P.K. Store

Date 2020	Name of Supplier	Debit Note Number	L.F. No.	Total Amount (₹)
17 Nov	Nirmi A/c	17		4,800
23 Nov	Aunti A/c			45,000
27 Nov	Sweety A/c	20		10,000
	Total Credit Purchase Return			**59,800**

Sales Return Book of Shri P.K. Store

Date 2020	Name of Supplier	Credit Note Number	L.F. No.	Total Amount (₹)
15 Nov	Suresh A/c	20		3,000
23 Nov	Bala A/c			48,600
30 Nov	Karan A/c			13,750
	Total Credit Sales Return			**65,350**

Note:

Date 11: Cash purchase of goods is recorded.

Date 19: Credit purchase of furniture is recorded in journal proper.

Date 24: Non-economic transactions will not be recorded.

Date 26: Cash purchase and cash sales are recorded in cash book.

Date 30: According to trasaction, if propotionate wages are recorded, then answer of sales return book will come to ₹65,350.

■ **ILLUSTRATION 6.21** The following are some of the transactions of M/s Kishore and Sons. Prepare their sales book.

Sold to M/s Gupta and Verma on credit
   30 shirts at ₹8 per shirt
   20 trousers at ₹10 per trouser
   Less Trade discount at 10%
Sold furniture to M/s Sehgal and Co. on credit ₹80.
Sold 50 shirts to M/s Jain and Sons at ₹8 per shirt.
Sold 13 shirts to Smart Store at ₹7.50 each for cash.
Sold on credit to M/s Mathur and Jain:
   100 shirts at ₹7.50 per shirt
   10 overcoats at ₹50 per overcoat
   Less Trade discount at 10%

Solution

Sales Book of M/s Kishore and Sons

Date 2019	Particulars	L.F.	Details (₹)	Amount (₹)
	M/s Gupta and Verma 30 shirts @ ₹8	240.00		
	20 Trousers @ ₹10	240.00		
		440.00		
	Less: 10% Discount (Sales as per invoice no. dated)	440.00		396.00
	M/s Jain and Sons 50 shirts @ ₹8 (Sales as per invoice no. dated)			400.00
	M/s Mathur and Jain			
	100 shirts @ ₹7.50	750.00		
	10 overcoats @ ₹50	500.00		
	Less: 10% Discount (sales as per invoice No. dated)	1,250.00		1,125.00
		125.00		
	Total (Sales account to be credited)			**1,921,00**

Individual party account to be debited and the total of this book to be credited in sales account.

Note: Cash sales and sale of furniture are not entered in sales book, as sales book records only the events relating to goods sold on credit.

SUMMARY

- Income is the increase in the resources of an entity, which results from the operations of an entity.
- Revenue generated from the sale of products or services is known as operating revenue, while others are known as non-operating revenue.
- Income consists of revenue generated less losses and expenses incurred to generate the revenue.
- Income is of two types—capital income and revenue income.
- Expenses are the outflow or other use of assets by an entity to produce goods and provide services.
- Expenditures can be classified into three categories—capital expenditure, revenue expenditure, and deferred revenue expenditure.
- Decreases in retained earnings for reasons not associated with operations are referred to as losses.
- In transactions that involve rendering of services, revenue is usually recognized as the service is performed, and it is immaterial whether the revenue amount is collected in advance or later by the service-providing firm.
- Long-term construction projects, which may extend over several years, involve financial transactions based on contracts. For example, the construction of dams, bridges, ships, aircrafts, residential and commercial complexes, etc. is based on contract.
- The amount of revenue for the work completed till the date of reporting is to be recognized in the books of account of the contractor according to the percentage of completion method as the turnover of the period.
- In commercial activities, goods are sometime supplied by a manufacturer or a wholesaler to a retailer or a prospective customer on the basis of 'sale or return'. This indicates that if the retailer or prospective customer sells or retains the goods, he/she will incur the liability towards the manufacturer or wholesaler with respect to future payment in cash.
- Franchise provides an exclusive right to use a formula, design, technique, or territory. This right is provided to the franchisee (user of the right) by the franchisor (owner of the right). For the franchisee, it is considered as an intangible asset.

- A lease is a contract where one firm gains the right to use assets owned by another firm for a specific period of time at a specified periodic cost. A lease is generally similar in nature to a rent.
- When the lessor (owner of the asset) gives the lessee (user of the asset) the right to use an asset for a limited period of time, but retains the risks and rewards of ownership of the asset, then it is known as an operating lease.
- A capital lease contract is intended to provide financing to the lessee for the eventual purchase of an asset or to provide the lessee with the right to use an asset over the majority of the useful life of the asset.
- In a consignment arrangement, the owner (consignor, main firm, or supplier) will ship merchandise goods and commodities to a dealer (consignee, agent, or seller) with the agreement that payment is expected only when the merchandise is sold by the consignee. The consignee has a right to return the unsold merchandise to the consignor.
- Factoring arrangement is made with an intention to accelerate the receipt of cash by the seller of the goods and commodities from the credit sale made by him/her. In this situation, the seller receives the funds before the due date from the factor, for the credit sale transaction made.
- Opportunity costs include the best economic benefits foregone as a result of choosing a particular action from a number of available options. While determining opportunity costs, one has to note the fact that there are no exchanges of economic resources.
- A non-trade-seeking entity is a non-profit-seeking entity. This form of entity does not have the objective of making profit. Their objective is to promote socially required activities.
- All credit sales of business goods and services are recorded in sales journal.
- When all goods from customers to whom goods were originally sold on credit are returned, they are recorded in sales return journal.
- All credit purchases of business goods and services are recorded in purchase journal.
- When all returns of goods to suppliers from whom goods were originally bought on credit are returned, they are recorded in purchase return journal.

KEYWORDS

Capital expenditure It refers to an expenditure which has been incurred for the purpose of obtaining a long-term advantage for an entity.

Capital receipt It is a receipt that does not pertain to the running of the operating cycle.

Current measurement It refers to the cost of replacing an asset at current market price.

Deferred revenue expense It is that class of revenue expenditure which is incurred during an accounting period but the benefit of which is available either wholly or in part in a future period.

Expense It is the outflow or other use of assets by an entity in order to produce and sell goods or services.

Historical cost It is actually the cash or cash-in-kind outlay for goods and services actually received.

Income It is the increase in the resources of an entity that results from the operations of an entity.

Loss It refers to a decrease in retained earning for reason not associated with operations.

Opportunity cost It refers to the concept where the current price may be taken either from current liquidation of sale price or from a replacement cost.

Revenue expenditure It is an expense that arises out of and in the course of a firm's operating activities.

Revenue receipt It is an income that arises out of the regular operating transactions of an entity.

 **QUESTIONS**

I. Answer the following questions.

1. Explain the basic principles which would guide you in allocating capital or revenue expenditure.

2. Define capital expenditure, revenue expenditure, and deferred revenue expenditure.

3. Explain the different types of lease and their accounting methods.

4. What do you mean by factoring? How are the factoring charges to be registered in the books of accounts?

5. Explain the concept of percentage of completion as used in case of long-term construction activities.

6. Do you feel that the accounting of non-profit organizations is different from that of the commercial organizations? If yes, describe the differences.

7. What is the difference between a legacy and a donation?

8. How is the admission fee received by a club recorded?

9. State which of the following items would be charged to capital expenditure and which to revenue expenditure.
   (a) A second-hand truck was purchased for ₹50,000 and ₹12,000 was spent on overhauling and painting it.
   (b) An amount of ₹10,000 was spent on whitewashing the factory building.
   (c) An old machine which stood in the books at ₹50,000 was sold for ₹30,000.
   (d) An amount of ₹10,000 was paid to workers as wages for installing new machinery.
   (e) Legal expenses amounting to ₹5,000 were incurred for purchasing land.

10. The Swadeshi Industries removed their works to more suitable premises. State which items would be charged to capital expenditure and which to revenue expenditure.
    (a) A sum of ₹4,750 was expended on dismantling, removing, and reinstalling plant and machinery.
    (b) The removal of stock from the old works to the new one amounted to ₹500.
    (c) Plant and machinery, which stood in the books at ₹75,000, included an obsolete machine at a book value of ₹1,700. This machine was sold off for ₹450 and was replaced by a new one costing ₹2,400.
    (d) The freight and carriage on the new machine amounted to ₹150 and the installation charges amounted to ₹275.
    (e) The fixtures and furniture appeared in the books at ₹76,500. Out of this, some furniture valued at ₹1,500 was discarded and sold at ₹600. New furniture worth ₹1,200 was acquired.
    (f) A sum of ₹1,100 was spent on painting the new factory.

11. An old building, which originally costs and stands in the books at ₹2,62,500, is pulled down and a new one is being built in its place. ₹4,250 worth of material out of the demolished building is sold. Material costing ₹5,000 is used in the new building. In addition to this, ₹5,56,250 is spent under a contract for its construction. ₹2,15,000 had been set aside by the firm for the deprecation on the old building and is now being appropriated. What additions to the building account will legitimately arise out of the rebuilding?

12. Explain with reasons whether the below mentioned items appearing in the books of a manufacturing concern constitute capital expenditure or revenue expenditure.
    (a) Legal expenses incurred in raising a debenture loan.
    (b) Legal expenses incurred in an action for infringement of its trade mark.

(c) Profit realized on the sale of investment.
(d) Labour welfare expenses.
(e) Subsidy received from state government.

13. A newly set up manufacturing firm has incurred various expenses during the construction period. The factory is still under construction. The company desires to capitalize the following expenses. Justify the reasons.
    (a) Travelling expenses of directors for a trip abroad for purchasing capital goods.
    (b) Salaries and wages paid to technical staff for installation of machinery.
    (c) Salaries and wages paid to non-technical staff.
    (d) Miscellaneous expenses such as rent, stationery, postage, telegram, etc.

II. State whether the following statements are True or False.

(a) Any expenditure which is unreasonably large is capital expenditure.
(b) Any expenditure intended to benefit the current period is revenue expenditure.
(c) Sale of stock in trade is a capital receipt.
(d) Capital expenditure is any expenditure benefitting a future period.
(e) Amount obtained on sale of fixed assets is an example of revenue receipt.
(f) Revenue expenditure is not intended to benefit future period.
(g) Premium received on issue of shares is a revenue receipt.
(h) Amount paid for acquiring goodwill is capital expenditure.
(i) Carriage paid on the purchase of new machinery is an example of revenue expenditure.
(j) Wages paid for installing new machinery are usually debited to wages account.

III. Classify the following into capital or revenue expenditure.

(a) ₹4,000 spent towards additions to the machinery in order to double production.
(b) ₹2,400 incurred for repairing machinery, necessitated by the negligence of employees.
(c) ₹1,600 incurred towards replacing the worn-out parts of the machinery.
(d) ₹1,000 was paid for painting the factory premises.

IV. Solve the following problems.

1. State with reasons whether the following are capital or revenue expenditure.
   (a) Freight and carriage charges on the new machine amounted to ₹150, and installation charges ₹200.
   (b) Fixtures of the book value of ₹1,500 were sold off at ₹600 and new fixtures of the value of ₹1,000 were acquired; cartage on purchase amounted to ₹5.
   (c) A sum of ₹1,000 was spent on painting the factory.
   (d) ₹5,150 was spent on repairs before using a second-hand car purchased recently.

2. Explain clearly the circumstances under which the following revenue expenses may be treated as capital expenditure.
   (a) repairs
   (b) carriage and freight
   (c) advertisement
   (d) wages
   (e) raw materials and stock

3. Do you consider the following to be capital or revenue items? Give reasons.
   (a) A gain of ₹5,000 from the sale of a motor car for ₹15,000. The book value of the car was ₹10,000.
   (b) Legal expenses incurred in raising a debenture loan.
   (c) ₹15,000 paid as compensation to a discharged employee.
   (d) The removal of stock from old works to new works costing ₹5,000.

4. Classify the following expenses as capital and revenue, stating reasons in each case.
   (a) The petrol engine of a passenger bus was replaced by a diesel engine.
   (b) Expenses incurred on research for a particular product which ultima-tely did not result in success.
   (c) A sum of ₹30,000 expended by a large factory for overhauling its entire machinery which resulted in adding three years to its working life.
   (d) Legal expenses incurred to raise a loan.
   (e) ₹3,000 embezzled by the accountant and ₹1,00,000 embezzled by the managing director.
   (f) Cost of repainting the factory shed.
   (g) ₹40,000 received as premium received on the issue of shares.
   (h) ₹1,60,000 used for constructing a school building meant for the children of employees for whom ₹50,000 was received from government as grant-in-aid.
   (i) Brokerage and stamp duty paid on purchase of investment.

5. Ketan & Co. incurred expenditure on the following items. How would you treat them while preparing the accounts of the concern?
   (a) Machinery standing in the books of the concern at ₹25,000 was sold for ₹23,500
   (b) Stock of ₹10,000 was destroyed by fire and ₹8,500 was received from the insurance company.
   (c) Investments costing ₹5,000 were sold for ₹6,200.
   (d) During the year, the concern undertook heavy advertising campaign and spent ₹60,000 for it.
   (e) An expenditure of ₹6,500 was incurred for pulling down an old factory preparatory to build a new one.
   (f) ₹9,000 spent on repairs to machinery necessitated by negligence of a worker.
   (g) Carriage inward and freight for bringing machinery from the dealer together amounted to ₹2,200.

6. Discuss briefly whether the following are capital or revenue items. Give reasons.
   (a) The firm's motor van was damaged in an accident. An amount of ₹6,000 was spent towards the repairs while only ₹4,800 could be recovered from the insurance company.
   (b) Old premises were renovated and remodeled at a cost of ₹46,500, resulting in enhanced income.
   (c) Cost of labour ₹1,500 and materials costing ₹2,300 were consumed to manufacture loose tools in the factory.
   (d) The firm spent ₹300 as payment of association fee for the next two years.
   (e) On the first day of the business, the firm had spent ₹1,800 as opening ceremony' expenses and distributed sweets worth ₹700 among the employees.
   (f) ₹14,000 were spent on air-conditioning the office of the manager.
   (g) A sum of ₹800 was received as dividend on investments.
   (h) A sum of ₹2,250 previously written off as bad debts is now recovered.
   (i) A sum of ₹850 was received as sales tax refund.
   (j) A sum of ₹700 was realized from the sale of old furniture.

   (k) A cash award of ₹6,000 was received from the government for outstanding export performance.

7. State the nature (capital or revenue) of the following expenditures which were incurred by M/s Suraj Brothers during the year ended 30 June 2012.
   1. ₹210 were spent on repairing a second-hand machine which was purchased on 8 July 2011 and ₹100 were paid on carriage and freight in connection with its acquisition.
   2. Sum of ₹300 was paid as compensation to the two employees who were retrenched.
   3. ₹50 were paid in connection with carriage on goods purchased.
   4. ₹10,000 customs duty paid on import of machinery for modernization of the factory and in turn to increase the production capacity during the current year and ₹5,000 paid on import duty for purchase of raw materials.
   5. ₹12,000 interest had accrued during the year on term loan obtained and utilized for the construction of factory building and purchase of machineries, however the production has not commenced till the last date of the accounting year.

8. Classify the following as capital and revenue giving reasons for the same.
   1. ₹5,000 spent towards additions to the machinery.
   2. Repairs for ₹1,000 necessitated by negligence.
   3. ₹500 spent to remove worn-out part and replace it with a new one.
   4. ₹100 wages paid in connection with the erection of new machinery.
   5. Old machinery of book value of ₹7,500 worn-out and dismantled at a cost of ₹1,000 and scrap realized at ₹200.
   6. Second-hand car purchased for ₹10,000 and spent ₹1,000 for repairs immediately.
   7. Employees' state insurance premium ₹600 paid.
   8. Insurance claim of ₹5,000 received from the insurance company for loss of goods by fire of ₹6,000.

9. State whether the following statements are 'True' or 'False'.
   1. Any expenditure which is unreasonably large is capital expenditure.
   2. Any expenditure intended to benefit the current period is revenue expenditure.
   3. A sale of stock-in-trade is capital receipt.
   4. Amount obtained on sale of fixed assets is an example of revenue receipt.
   5. Capital expenditure is any expenditure benefitting a future period.
   6. Revenue expenditure is not intended to benefit future period.
   7. Premium received on issue of shares is a revenue receipt.
   8. Amount paid for acquiring goodwill is capital expenditure.
   9. Carriage paid on the purchase of new machinery is an example of revenue expenditure.
   10. Wages paid for erection of new machinery are usually debited to wages account.

10. Classify the following into capital/revenue expenditure.
    1. Spent towards additions to the machinery in order to double the production ₹4,000.
    2. Incurred for repairs to the machinery necessitated by the negligence of the employees ₹2,400.
    3. Expended ₹1,600 towards replacement of worn-out parts of the machinery.
    4. Paid for painting the factory premises ₹1,000.

11. From the following transactions, prepare various subsidiary books with columns of expense for the year 2020 in the books of Sajan Traders:

Aug. 1: Purchased goods of ₹20,000 from Viramgam Store at 10% trade discount. 5% GST and ₹1,000 railway freight were added. Invoice No. was 171.

Aug. 5: Purchased goods of ₹30,000 from Manisha. 5% GST, 5% railway freight of ₹1,200, and ₹400 for carriage were applied. Invoice No. was 204.

Aug. 11: Sold goods of ₹15,000 to Dattu Corporation at 10% trade discount. 10% GST, ₹450 for carriage, and ₹900 for railway freight were added. Invoice No. was 231.

Aug. 16: Entire goods purchased from Manisha was sold to Alia after adding 20% profit on cost. 5% GST at ₹1,200 for railway freight and ₹300 for carriage were added. Credit period was 1 month. Invoice No. was 232.

Aug. 18: Alia returned 50% of the goods sold to her. Proportionate amount of GST, railway freight, and carriage were given credit. Credit Note No. 15 was given. These goods were immediately returned to Manisha. Received proportionate amount credit for GST, railway freight, and carriage. Debit Note No. 30 was given.

Aug. 20: Sold goods of ₹30,000 to Shresth Corporation. 5% GST, ₹250 for carriage, and ₹600 for railway freight were added. Invoice No. was 240.

Aug. 25: Purchased furniture of ₹18,000 from Gandhi Furniture Mart. Invoice No. 120 was received with 5% GST.

Aug. 27: Dattu Corporation returned 50% of the goods sold. Only a proportionate amount of GST was given credit. Credit Note No. 16 was given.

Aug. 28: Purchased goods of ₹10,000 from Raju on cash.

Aug. 30: Sold goods of ₹15,000 on cash to Kanu at 5% cash discount.

12. Prepare columnar subsidiary books, namely purchase book, sales book, purchase return book, and sales returns book for the year 2015 in the book of Nirmi Sports Stores.

May 1: Purchased the following goods from Sania at 10% trade discount and 5% cash discount with a credit of 1 month:
Balls 200 Nos. at ₹150 per piece Bats 100 Nos. at ₹800 per piece Stump pair (Nos.) 50 at ₹300 per pair

May 5: Sold the following goods to Malik at 5% trade discount:
Balls 60 Nos. at ₹250 per piece
Bats 30 Nos. at ₹1,000 per piece
Stump pair (Nos.) 10 at ₹500 per pair

May 10: Purchased the following goods from Kapil at 10% trade discount:
Balls 30 Nos. at ₹160 per piece
Bats 20 Nos. at ₹1,200 per piece
Stump pair (Nos.) 6 at ₹400 per pair

May 13: The following goods were sold to Yusuf at 5% trade discount:
Balls 40 Nos. at ₹200 per piece
Bat 30 Nos. at ₹1,300 per piece
Stump pair (Nos.) 10 at ₹700 per pair

May 15: Yusuf returned half of the goods. Credit Note No. 21 was sent to him.

May 20: The following goods were returned to Sania:
Balls 10 Nos.
Bats 5 Nos.
Stumps pair 3 Nos.

May 25: Half of the goods purchased from Kapil were sold to Sehwag after adding 20% profit on cost.

May 27: Sehwag returned all of the goods which were returned to Kapil.

May 30: *Cash purchases:*
Balls 60 Nos. at ₹120 each
Bats 50 Nos. at ₹400 each
Stump pair 10 Nos at ₹200 each
Cash sales:
Balls 40 Nos. at ₹200 each
Bat 30 Nos. at ₹800 each

 # CASES

Conceptual Application Cases

1. **Saswat Kalyani** Saswat Kalyani runs a printing business. He specializes in printing greetings cards for birthdays and festivals. His firm operates from a rented premise in Delhi. There are three employees under Saswat. He used to employ a bookkeeper, but in order to cut costs he has decided to record all business transactions himself. Now he records all the financial transactions at the end of the week. Saswat's accountant has suggested that regular maintenance of the firm's books of accounts can lead to lower accountancy fees. Saswat uses a manual system that consists of day books, a cash book, a purchases ledger, a sales ledger, and a nominal ledger. When he first started, Saswat was uncertain how to record the transactions listed in the following text.

(a) Payment of annual rent amounting to ₹50,000.
(b) Purchase of printing paper from a supplier for ₹4,000.
(c) Payment of wages to staff amounted to ₹6,000.
(d) Sale of wedding cards resulted in sales of ₹1,000.

Questions

1. In which ledgers should the transactions be recorded? Explain your answer.
2. Suggest why accountancy fees might be lower if Saswat maintains careful records.

3. What might be the consequences if Saswat makes a mistake when recording transactions?

2. **Suketu Sharma** Suketu Sharma runs a property development firm in Calcutta. He owns a number of cottages and holiday homes. Most of these cottages are let out on a short-term basis to holiday-makers. However, he does have some properties that are occupied by permanent residents. In January 2020 he purchased a large property in Delhi for ₹100 lakh. The property was in need of restoration and modernization. Suketu decided to split the property into two luxury holiday apartments and invested ₹60 lakh to develop it. By June the apartments were complete. Almost immediately, Suketu was offered ₹130 lakh for both the apartments. He accepted one of the offers but decided to let out the other apartment.

Questions

1. What valuation should be placed on the unsold apartment in Suketu's balance sheet? Explain your answer with reference to the relevant accounting concepts.
2. One of Suketu's long-term tenants failed to give the rent on time. At the end of April, she owed the rent of two months, amounting to a total of ₹60,000. Suketu was not sure how to record the situation. Since he had not received any money, he decided that

he should not enter the rent due from for that tenant as revenue. Applying the accrual concept, explain how Suketu should deal with the unpaid rent.

3. If Suketu decides to evict the tenant and there is no prospect of receiving any more rent, how should be the unpaid rent treated?

Business Application Cases

1. **Furniture Sales**   A furniture store commenced its business on 1 January 2017. The store's transactions in 2019, its third year of operations, included the following:

   (a) The company purchased office furniture for ₹42,000 on 1 July 2019. The supplier was paid on 1 October 2019. The office furniture of this company has a useful life of 12 years.

   (b) The management hired a sales representative on 1 October 2019 at a salary of ₹7,000 a month. The representative started work immediately and remained in the company's employment until 31 January 2020. The salary for each month is paid on the 15th of the next month.

   (c) The company sold merchandise worth ₹30 lakh. This merchandise was placed in the inventory in 2018. The cost of inventory in 2018 was ₹22 lakh.

   (d) The company paid a supplier ₹2,40,000 for merchandise received in 2018.

   (e) The company paid ₹2,25,000 on 1 November 2019 for store rental covering the period from 1 October 2019 to 31 March 2020.

Questions

1. How much expense should have been recognized in the income statement of the company in 2019?

2. Identify the effects of each of the events in 2019 on the company's assets, liabilities, and owners' equity.

2. **Reliance Company**   Reliance Company recognizes revenues at the time it delivers its products to customers. Customer defaults average 1% of gross sales. You have the following information for the month of June 2020.

   (a) Opening balances
       Accounts receivable: ₹9,50,000
       Allowance for uncollectible accounts: ₹25,000

   (b) Gross sales: ₹5,00,000

   (c) Collections from customers: ₹5,10,000

   (d) Specific uncollectibles written off: ₹8,000

Questions

1. Analyse the effects of items (2), (3), and (4) on the company's assets, liabilities, and owners' equity. (Use +/– notation).

2. Prepare journal entries to reflect your analyses.

3. What amount should be reported to the shareholders as the amount of the accounts receivable at the end of June?

4. What amount should be shown as customer defaults on the income statement for the month of June?

3. **Nakshatra Company**   Nakshatra Company purchased 20 radios on 12 February 2020 from JK Company. The radios were priced at ₹500 each. The terms of the sale were—2 %, 10 days; net 30 days. On 14 February, Nakshatra sold ten of these radios to Raj Electrics Company for ₹600 each. The terms of the sale were—2 %, 10 days; net 30 days. Raj Electrics Company sold five of these radios during February at a price of ₹1,000 each. The terms of the sale were—net 30 days. It returned the other five radios to Nakshatra on 16 February because of some defect in the units. Nakshatra Company gave Raj Electrics full credit for the radios it returned. It appraised the returned radios at a wholesale value of ₹300 each and offered them for sale at a price of ₹360 each. On 21 February, JK Company agreed to deduct the difference between the original gross price and the appraised wholesale value from the gross amount due from Nakshatra. Nakshatra Company sold none of the returned radios in February.

Nakshatra Company follows the perpetual inventory method. Under this method, Nakshatra Company maintains, for all types of goods stocked, a detailed record that shows (a) units and cost of each purchase, (b) units and cost of the goods for each sale, and (c) units and cost of the item on hand. This record is maintained continuously on a transaction-to-transaction basis throughout the period under consideration. It provides an ending inventory and cost of goods sold for the period.

Nakshatra Company paid JK Company ₹8,820 on 21 February. Raj Electrics paid Nakshatra Company ₹3,000 on 13 March.

Questions

1. Calculate the following amounts:
   (a) Net cost of the goods sold by Nakshatra
   (b) Nakshatra Company's net revenue from sales to Raj Electrics
   (c) Nakshatra Company's income from discounts lost by Raj Electrics

2. Analyse each of the transactions that took place during February and prepare appropriate journal entries for Nakshatra Company and Raj Electrics. Each company accounts for its inventories by the perpetual inventory method.

3. In what way would the methods used by these two companies to record these transactions provide misleading income statement for February or incorrect balance sheets as of 28 February?

 **REFERENCES**

'GST Act and Explanatory Notes', issued by Institute of Chartered Accountants of India and Institute of Cost Accountants of India.

Meigs, Robert, F. and Meigs Walter, B. 1989, *Financial Accounting*, 6th edition, McGraw-Hill International Edition, pp. 441–443.

Shah, Paresh 2009, *Financial Management*, 2nd edition, Biztantra-Wiley, pp. 621–625.

Analysing Transactions

Learning Objectives

After studying this chapter, you will understand

- mechanics of an accounting system
- recording of transactions in the books of accounts
- errors in accounting
- objectives and importance of a trial balance

INTRODUCTION

The double entry accounting system is a system of recording transactions, which is based on recording increases and decreases in accounts so that the accounting equation is tallied, as per modern approach of accounting. Account is a form used to record additions and deductions for each individual asset, liability, capital, income, and expense. The double entry accounting system is a very powerful tool in analysing the effects of a transaction. The process of this system is summarized here:

1. Determine whether an asset, a liability, capital, income, or expense account is affected by the transaction.
2. For each account affected by the transaction, determine whether the account increases or decreases.
3. Determine whether each increase or decrease should be recorded as a debit or a credit column item.

Financial statements are the result of a firm's accounting process. These statements are presented in condensed (highly summarized) form and cannot be prepared until the financial transactions of the business entity have been recorded, classified, and summarized. The spectrum of business transactions is so wide and varied that it is not possible to formulate a generalized model to determine the impact such transactions will have on these statements, unless they are analysed and recorded individually, since business enterprises, particularly large ones, are likely to have numerous transactions everyday. It is not feasible to analyse each transaction individually for its effect on the financial statements.

Accounting records can be prepared under any one of the following systems—(a) single-entry system, or (b) double-entry system. Under the single-entry system, all transactions relating to the proprietor's personal use are recorded in the books of accounts. All the transaction not related to the proprietor's personal use is excluded from the books of accounts. This system is partially based on the dual aspect concept, and is incomplete and inaccurate. The single-entry system is primarily used by small traders. The concept has been explained further in Chapter 14.

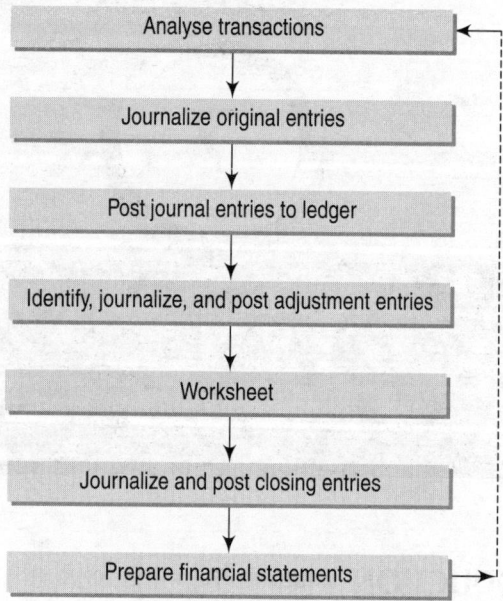

Analyse transactions

Journalize original entries

Post journal entries to ledger

Identify, journalize, and post adjustment entries

Worksheet

Journalize and post closing entries

Prepare financial statements

FIG. 7.1 The accounting cycle

As mentioned in Chapter 1, the double-entry system was introduced by Luca Pacioli in 1494. According to this system, every transaction has two aspects. Both the aspects are recorded in the books of accounts. The effect of each transaction is recorded in both the aspects. The double-entry system is generally used by partnership firms, companies, government organizations, non-profit organizations, etc.

Accounting mechanics help us in arriving at the 'output' in the form of the financial statements. Accounting mechanics recognize and depict the flows of accounting data in the design and preparation of actual financial statements. Figure 7.1 depicts the accounting cycle (Hawkins 2004).

MECHANICS OF ACCOUNTING

In sequential order, the steps involved are as follows:

Day books and journal proper are known as books of original entry.

1. Business transactions take place.
2. The transactions are recorded in a document (usually called a voucher) with all the necessary details.
3. The transactions recorded in the voucher are then analysed to decide the effect of transactions in an accounting equation.
4. The transaction is then recorded in one of the special journals such as the cash book (for cash transactions), the sales day book (for credit sales transactions), the purchase day book (for credit purchase transactions), or in the journal proper (for residual transactions). Depending on the volume of transactions and particular needs of the business, other special journals, such as the purchase return day book, sales return day book, bills receivable book, and petty cash book are used. These are also known as *books of original entry*.
5. From the books of original entry or the journal, the related accounts are posted to the left or right column of the related columnar account in ledger.

6. The ledger balances are transferred to the appropriate columns of the trial balance.
7. If any part of the transaction has to be adjusted or reversed later, appropriate entries are made in the journal proper, and postings are made to the relative columnar accounts of the ledger. These are known as *adjustment entries*.
8. Worksheet is a working paper that accountants use to summarize adjusting entries and account balances for financial statements. It is a useful device of accounting data from the unadjusted trial balance to the financial statements.
9. If any of the columnar accounts has to be adjusted after the trial balance has been closed, it is done as *closing entries*.
10. Next, the ledger balance, as amended by the closing entries, is transferred to the appropriate financial statement.
    (a) If they represent expenses or revenues, the ledger balance is transferred to the profit and loss account or income statement.
    (b) If they represent assets, liabilities, or owner's equity, the ledger balance is transferred to the balance sheet.
11. The profit or loss for the period is then adjusted in the owner's equity account in the balance sheet presented as on the last date of the accounting period.

VOUCHER SYSTEM

The transaction is recorded in a document known as the *prime document*, *voucher*, or *source document*. It may be a cash receipt voucher, cash payment voucher, bank receipt voucher, bank payment voucher, purchase order, supplier's invoice, entity's invoice, etc. In the voucher, normally all details of the transaction are recorded. Source documents are the source of all the information recorded by a business.

During the course of its business, a company sends and receives many source documents. The details on these source documents need to be recorded, otherwise the business might forget to ask for some money, forget to pay, or even accidentally pay twice.

JOURNAL PROPER OR BOOKS OF ORIGINAL ENTRY

The books of prime entry document and record all the transactions of the business. The transactions are then recorded in either one of the special journals or in the journal proper in sequential or chronological order. The vouchers are used to record the entries in the books of original entry with the objective of use for future internal reference, for example, to know when a payment was made to creditors, or to know when an account was receiving from the debtors, or for external purpose such as providing data to income tax authorities, etc. These records serve the purpose of a permanent accounting record entered in the chronological

order in which transactions take place. A business organization maintains a number of books for recording original entries based on its needs.

A journal is a chronological record of transactions, because the journal is where the transactions are first recorded in the accounting system. It is often called the book of original entry. Entries recorded in the journal are called Journal Entries.

The logical extension of the accounting system is to maintain several special journals. Each special journal is designed to be used for recording a single and similar kind of transaction that occurs frequently. An illustrative list of books of original entry with chapter number in which details are provided is elaborated in Table 7.1.

TABLE 7.1 Name of special journal and its related chapter number and name

Name of Special Journal and Its Different Types	Covered in Chapter No.	Covered in Chapter Name
Cash and Bank Books	Chapter 9	Current Assets: Cash and Bank
Purchase Journal	Chapter 6	Revenue and Expense Recognition
Sales Journal	Chapter 6	Revenue and Expense Recognition
Bills Receivables	Chapter 6	Revenue and Expense Recognition
Bills Payable	Chapter 6	Revenue and Expense Recognition

JOURNAL PROPER BOOK

A journal proper book is used to record all transactions that cannot be included in any of the books discussed earlier. The transactions that are recorded in the journal proper are purchase or sale of fixed assets, investments on credit, adjusting entries, rectification entries, etc. The journal proper is meant for recording transactions that do not occur frequently in the business and, therefore, do not warrant setting up of special books. The journal records all the daily transactions of an entity in the order in which they occur. A journal may, therefore, be defined as a book containing a chronological record of transactions. It is the

book in which the transactions are recorded first of all under the double-entry system. A journal is the book of original record. A journal does not replace but precedes the ledger. The process of recording transactions in a journal is termed as journalizing.

Before journalizing transactions, an accountant must think on the basis of the rules of debit and credit and on the basis of the effect of the transactions on assets, liabilities, and owner's equity of the firm. In accordance with the effects, the account to be debited or credited will be determined. The papers or documents supporting the transactions and establishing its validity (normally known as voucher) should be filed in proper order, together with necessary references, for reference. The entry needs to show the particular account head that needs to be added or reduced, along with the traditional concept of accounting for debit and credit. Exhibit 7.1 depicts a typical journal entry.

EXHIBIT 7.1 Journal Entry

Date	Particulars	L.F. No.	Cr. (₹)	Cr. (₹)
	Particular account (Add/Less) Dr....			
	To Particular account (Add/Less)			
	(Being...................)			

In the bracket, the narration of the transaction should be written in brief starting with the word 'being'.

Usually, the transactions of an entity are so numerous that to record the transactions for a particular period, that is, a month, will require many pages in a book of original entry. At the bottom of one page the total of the columns are written together with the words 'carried forward' in the particular column. The next page is started with the respective total in the column with the words 'brought forward' in the particular column.

Table 7.2 indicates the different types of books of original entry and the respective category of business transactions recorded in them.

TABLE 7.2 Books of original entry and business transactions recorded

Name of Book of Original Entry	Category of Business Transactions Recorded
Cash book	All cash transactions
Double column cash book	All cash and bank transactions
Petty cash book	All petty cash transactions
Purchase journal	Credit purchases of business goods only
Sales journal	Credit sales of business goods only
Sales returns journal (Return inward journal)	All return of business goods sold by a firm to customers on credit
Purchase returns journal (Return outward journal)	All return of business goods purchased by a firm from suppliers on credit
Bills receivable book	All bills of exchanges received by a firm
Bills payable book	All bills of exchanges accepted by a firm
Journal proper book	All such transactions that cannot be entered in any of the above-mentioned books or journals

TABLE 7.3 Subsidiary books and source of entry

Subsidiary Books	Source of Entry	Posting to Account	
		Debit	Credit
Purchase book	Inward invoice	Purchase A/c (Total)	Each supplier's A/c (Respective amount)
Sales book	Outward invoice	Each customer's A/c (Respective amount)	Sales A/c (Total)
Returned outwards book	Debit note	Each supplier's A/c (Respective amount)	Returned outward A/c (Total)
Returned inward book	Credit note	Returns inwards A/c (Total)	Each customer's A/c (Respective amount)

Table 7.3 indicates the main subsidiary books and their respective source of entry, that is, voucher and also the place of an accounting entry.

FUNDAMENTALS OF THE ACCOUNT

According to the modern approach of accounting system, the impact of debit entry (left hand side of T account and debit column in columnar ledger account) and credit entry (right hand side of T account and credit column in columnar ledger account) is explained in Table 7.4. Table 7.4 also explains the normal balance concept, which is based on the positive balance of the concerned account.

TABLE 7.4 Impact of debit and credit column of columnar ledger account and normal balance

Account Type	Increase	Decrease	Normal Balance
Asset	Debit column	Credit column	Debit
Liabilities	Credit column	Debit column	Credit
Capital	Credit column	Debit column	Credit
Income	Credit column	Debit column	Credit
Expenses	Debit column	Credit column	Debit

We need to remember that as per modern approach of accounting, every transaction gives rise to a minimum of two effects on the accounting equation: one entry on debit column of the account and another on credit column of the account. Table 7.5 explains with an illustration how to have debit and credit.

TABLE 7.5 Having debit and credit

Account Type	Having Debit	Having Credit
Asset	Purchase of new office furniture	Payment of cash to supplier of service provider
Liability	Repayment of borrowed funds	Purchase of business goods on credit
Capital	Buyback of own equity shares	Issue of new equity shares
Income	Sales returns by customer	Sales of business goods to customer
Expense	Incurrence of an advertisement expense	Receiving the refund from suppliers of service, whose services are defective; hence, returned to supplier
Impact on Columnar Account		
Shown on Columnar Account	Debit column	Credit column

The format of account to be used is as per either Exhibit 2.1 or Exhibit 2.2.

LEDGER

Accounting systems typically contain many accounts. Collectively, these individual accounts are contained in a record known as ledger. A ledger is simply a grouping of the accounts that are used to prepare financial statements for a business or an entity. A ledger account is a summary device and its simplest traditional form is shaped like the letter 'T' and is referred to as a T account. In today's computerized structure, the traditional form is unsuitable and has been widely replaced by the columnar ledger account format, as explained earlier in this chapter. Still in day-to-day language, majority of people call the columnar ledger a T account.

Ledger is a group of accounts.

A ledger is a principal book of the entity although it is not an independent record. The ledger is the accounting record that summarizes the financial affairs of a business. It contains details of assets, liabilities and capital, income and expenditure, and, therefore, profit and loss. It consists of many different ledger accounts, each account having its own purpose or 'name' and an identity or code. Other names for the main ledger are *nominal ledger* or *general ledger*.

Classification

Ledger accounts are classified into five categories as per the modern approach of accounting equation. These categories are—(i) asset account; (ii) liabilities account; (iii) capital account; (iv) revenue account; and (v) expenses account. These ledger accounts may be grouped as—(a) permanent ledger account; and (b) temporary ledger account. Permanent ledger accounts show closing balances at the end of accounting year, and these balances are carried forward to the next accounting year. Temporary ledger accounts do not have any opening and closing balance. These accounts are closed at the end of the accounting year by transferring them to the trading account or the profit and loss account. Purchases, sales, and direct expenses accounts are closed by transfer to the trading account. While the accounts relating to selling and distribution expenses, indirect expenses, and losses are transferred to the debit side of the income statement, the accounts related to income and gains are transferred to the credit side of the profit and loss account.

Advantages

Ledger accounts record all the important business transactions of an entity. Every business transaction whether it is recorded in a journal, a cash book, or any subsidiary book must be

posted into the ledger account. The advantages of maintaining a ledger account are explained in this section.

Separate accounts

There are separate ledger accounts for different items such as cash, accounts receivable, and accounts payable. For example, if we prepare John's A/c, information regarding John's purchases, sales, payments, bills drawn, and bills accepted will be brought to John's A/c from the purchase book, sales book, cash book, bills payable book, and bills receivable book.

Information at a glance

The correct position and status of every account can be ascertained at a glance by going through the general ledger of an enterprise. Information regarding purchases, sales, and returns are easily available from the respective ledger accounts.

Trial balance

Ledger accounts facilitate the preparation of a trial balance. A trial balance is prepared by carrying forward the balance of ledger accounts.

Preparation of financial statements

Ledger accounts supply information for the preparation of trading account, profit and loss account, and balance sheet. Ledger accounts also help in identifying adjustments that are incorporated in a company's final accounts.

POSTING

Posting is the process of transferring debits and credits from the journal and other books of original entry to their respective accounts in the ledger. The aim of posting is to make a classified and summarized record of business transactions in appropriate accounts. The following rules are observed while posting or transferring the transactions in the ledger.

> Posting is the process of transferring debit and credit to account from entry.

1. Separate account should be opened in the ledger by using the same name of accounts as used in the journal for posting the transactions recorded in the books of original entry.
2. The account that has been debited in the journal should also be debited in the ledger account. However, a reference should be made of the other account that has been credited in the journal.
3. The account that has been credited in the journal should also be credited in the ledger and reference should be given of the account that has been debited in the journal.

> Prefix 'To' to the left side of an account and 'By' to the right side of an account as a prefix.

It is generally accepted practice to use the words 'To' and 'By' while making posting in the ledger. The word 'To' is used with the accounts, which appears on the debit column of a ledger account. Similarly, the word 'By' is used with accounts that appears on the credit column of a ledger account.

BALANCING AN ACCOUNT

At the end of an accounting period, an owner or a business manager is interested to know the position of a particular account. In other words, he needs to total the debits and credits of the account separately and find out the net balance. The process of finding out the net balance of an account after considering the totals of both debit and credit appearing in the account is known as balancing the account. The balance is put on the side of the account that is smaller in total and a reference is given that it has been carried forward (c/f) or carried down (c/d) to the next period. In the next period, a reference is given

> If the sum of the debit side is more than the sum of the credit side, the balance is known as debit balance. If the sum of the debit side is less than the sum of the credit side, the balance is known as credit balance.

that the opening balance, which has been brought forward (b/f) or brought down (b/d) from the previous period, on the heavier side in the total of the past period. The balance of an account will be termed 'debit balance' if the total of debit column is greater than the total of credit column. If the credit column total is greater than the debit column total, the balance will be known as credit balance.

It should be noted that revenue, that is, income and expenses accounts are not balanced, and that the final residual amount is transferred to the income statement or profit and loss account. Only assets, liabilities, and capital accounts ultimately show balances, which are transferred to the balance sheet.

If the debit column total is equal to the credit column total, there is no balance. The balance is nil. The accounts stand automatically balanced or closed and are known as *tallied*.

TRIAL BALANCE

The various debit balances and credit balances are taken down in a statement. The statement so prepared is termed *trial balance*. A trial balance is a listing of all the accounts and their respective balances. It is a statement of debit balances and credit balances extracted from the ledger account on a par-

> Trial balance is a listing of all accounts with their respective balances.

ticular date. The two sides of trial balance tally. It means the books or account are arithmetically accurate. The format of a trial balance is shown in Exhibit 7.2.

EXHIBIT 7.2 Trial Balance

Sr. No.	Ledger Accounts Name	L.F. No.	Dr. (₹)	Cr. (₹)
Total				

Objectives of a Trial Balance

A trial balance (a) confirms arithmetical accuracy; (b) forms the basis of financial statements; and (c) summarizes the ledger.

Arithmetical Accuracy

When the trial balance tallies, it is an indication of the fact that ledger accounts are arithmetically accurate. It also indicates that (a) for each transaction, the debits and credits recorded were of equal amounts; (b) the balance for each account was calculated correctly; and (c) the balances of the various debit and credit amounts were correctly added.

Basis for Financial Statements

The trial balance forms the basis of the preparation of financial statements and of the balance sheet.

Summarized Ledger

Trial balance serves as a summary of all ledger accounts and provides a balance of each account in the ledger. The ledger may be also seen only when details regarding the account are required.

Preparing a Trial Balance

There are three methods of preparing a trial balance. The total of both the debit and credit columns of the trial balance must be equal under all the methods. The following methods can be used for preparing trial balance—(a) balance method; (b) total method; or (c) total and balance method.

Balance method

A trial balance is prepared with the balance of ledger accounts. Every ledger account has a debit column amount and a credit column amount. At the end of a certain period, ledger accounts are balanced. An excess of the total of the debit column of an account over its credit column is known as debit balance and written in the debit column of the trial balance. In the same way, excess of credit column of an account over its debit column shows credit balance and will be written at the credit column of the trial balance. The total of both the debit and credit columns must always be equal.

Total method

According to this method, the total of the debit and credit side of every account is separately written in the debit and credit columns of the trial balance. The total of both the debit and credit must be equal. If the total of both columns is not equal, there are definitely certain errors that should be located and rectified.

Total and balance method

This method presents both the balance and the total in the same trial balance. The amount column is divided between the total and balance methods. Each method has further two columns of debit and credit. The total of the debit and credit under each method must be equal. There will be different totals according to the different methods but the total of debit and credit of each method will be equal.

■ **ILLUSTRATION 7.1** Vimal Shah has started a new business in the name of Mahavir Electronics on 1 March 2020 with a capital of ₹2,00,000. The vouchers for all the transactions are given below. Prepare subsidiary books, do the posting, and prepare a trial balance of Mahavir Electronics.

(1)

Dena Bank		
Current Account No: 101		Date
M/s Mahavir Electronics (Account credited)		1/3/2020
Particulars	**Amount (₹)**	
(₹100 × 800 Notes)	80,000	
Total	80,000	
Cashier		Bank Stamp
Helly Shah		

(2)

Credit Memo				Date
Maheshwari Electronics, Ahmedabad				1/3/2020
Mahavir Electronics				
Gandhinagar				

Sr. No.	Particulars	Qty	Rate (₹)	Amount (₹)
(1)	Radio	25	400	10,000
(2)	Tape Recorder	20	500	10,000
(3)	Television	10	10,000	1,00,000
				1,20,000
				12,000
	Less: 10% Trade Discount			1,08,000

Note: If payment is made within 10 days, 5% cash discount allowed.

Jaya Mehta
(Manager)

(3)

Credit Memo				Date
Mahavir Electronics, Gandhinagar				8/3/2020
M/s Rupali Music Centre, Pant Nagar				

Sr. No.	Particulars	Qty	Rate (₹)	Amount (₹)
(1)	Radio	10	500	5,000
(2)	Tape Recorder	10	600	6,000
(3)	Television	5	11,000	55,000
				66,000
	Less: 10% Cash Discount			6,600
				59,400
	Add: Freight paid on your behalf			100
				59,500

Vimal Shah
(Proprietor)
(Signatory)

(4)

Credit Note No.11   Maheshwari Electronics Ahmedabad   Date: 9/3/2020
To,
Mahavir Electronics, Gandhinagar.
Received back one TV, being defective, from you and towards that ₹9,000 has been credited to your account.

Jaya Mehta
(Manager)

(5)

Maheshwari Electronics Ahmedabad   Date: 11/3/2020
Received with thanks from Mahavir Electronics, Gandhinagar ₹16,050 by cash and ₹78,000 by cheque No.12753 dated 9-3-2020 drawn on Dena Bank towards full and final settlement of your account.

Jaya Mehta
(Manager)

(6)

Cash Memo	Date
Mahavir Electronics	21/3/2020
Gandhinagar	
M/s Rupali Music Centre, Pant Nagar	

Sr. No.	Particulars	Qty	Rate (₹)	Amount (₹)
(1)	Television	1	10,000	10,000
(2)	Radio	1	600	600
				10,600
	Less: 10% Cash Discount			600
				10,000
				Harsh Shah (Signatory)

(7)

Mahavir Electronics Gandhinagar	Date: 26/3/2020

Voucher No. : 1
Account : Salary Account
Rupees : Rupees five hundred only
Particulars : Amount paid to Rupa towards salary for the month of March.

Vimal Shah
(Proprietor)
Sanctioned by

(8)

Credit Note No.1   Mahavir Electronics Gandhinagar   Date: 28/3/2020

To,
Rupali Music Centre,
Radio No. 2 being defective, are received back and towards that ₹900 has been credited to your account.

Vimal Shah
(Proprietor)

Solution

Purchase Books of M/s Mahavir Electronics

Date	Names of the Suppliers	Inward Invoice No.	L.F.	Amount (₹)
3/3/2020	Maheshwari Electronics			1,08,000
	Total credit purchases			1,08,000

Sales Books of M/s Mahavir Electronics

Date	Names of the Customers	Outward Invoice No.	L.F.	Amount (₹)
8/3/2020	Rupali Music Centre, Pant Nagar			59,400
	Total credit sales			59,400

Purchase Returns Book of M/s Mahavir Electronics

Date	Names of the Suppliers	Debit Note	L.F.	Amount (₹)
9/3/2020	Maheshwari Electronics			9,000
	Total purchase returns			9,000

Sales Returns Book of M/s Mahavir Electronics

Date	Names of the Customers	Credit Note	L.F.	Amount (₹)
28/3/2020	Rupali Music Centre, Pant Nagar			900
	Total sales returns			900

Name of Account: Maheshwari Electronics Ahmedabad

Type of Account: Liability   Normal Balance: Credit

Date	Reference Account	Voucher Type	Post Ref No.	Dr. (Less)	Cr. (Add)
	By Purchase A/c				1,08,000
	To Purchase return A/c			9,000	
	To Cash discount A/c			4,950	
	To Cash A/c			16,050	
	To Dena Bank A/c			78,000	
	Total			1,08,000	1,08,000
	Account Tallied				

Name of Account: Rupali Music Centre, Pant Nagar

Type of Account: Asset   Normal Balance: Dedit

Date	Reference Account	Voucher Type	Post Ref No.	Dr. (Add)	Cr. (Less)
	To Sales A/c			59,400	
	To Cash A/c (Freight paid)			100	
	By Sales return A/c				900
	By Balance c/f or c/d				58,600
	Total			59,500	900
	To Balance b/f or b/d			58,600	

Three Columnar Cash Book of M/s Mahavir Electronics

Date	Reference Account	Voucher Type and No.	Post Ref. No.	Discount Allowed	Debit (₹)		Discount Received	Credit ₹		Balance (₹) Dr. (Normal)	
					Cash	Bank		Cash	Bank	Cash	Bank
2020											
1 Mar	To Capital A/c				2,00,000					2,00,000	0
1 Mar	By Bank A/c		C					80,000		1,20,000	0
1 Mar	To Cash A/c		C			80,000				1,20,000	80,000
8 Mar	By Rupali Music Centre A/c							100		1,19,900	80,000
11 Mar	By Maheshwari Electronics A/c						4,950	16,050	78,000	1,03,850	2,000
21 Mar	To Sales A/c			600	10,000					1,13,850	2,000
26 Mar	By Salary A/c							500		1,13,350	2,000
31 Mar	By Balance c/f							1,13,350	2,000	0	0
	Total			600	2,10,000	80,000	4,950	2,10,000	80,000		
1 Apr	To Balance b/f				1,13,350	2,000					

Trial Balance of Mahavir Electronics as on 31 March 2020

Particulars	L.F. No.	Debit (₹)	Credit (₹)
Purchase A/c		1,08,000	
Sales A/c			70,000
Purchase return A/c			9,000
Sales return A/c		900	
Capital A/c			2,00,000
Salary A/c		500	
Cash A/c		1,13,350	
Bank A/c		2,000	
Cash discount A/c (given)		600	
Cash discount A/c (received)			4,950
Rupali Music Centre, Pant Nagar		58,600	
Total		2,83,950	2,83,950

■ **ILLUSTRATION 7.2** Pass journal entries for the following information. Also prepare ledger accounts and trial balance as on January 2020, by using (a) balance method, (b) total method, (c) total and balance method.

Date and Particulars		Amount (₹)
1 Jan	Pradhan started business with cash	20,000
3 Jan	He opened a current account in the bank	5,000
7 Jan	Purchased goods on credit from Suparsh	4,000
10 Jan	Paid to Suparsh in full settlement	3,900
13 Jan	Machinery purchased	2,000
16 Jan	Goods sold to Twinkle	3,000
18 Jan	Amount received from Twinkle	1,000
20 Jan	Salaries paid	700
23 Jan	Rent received	300
28 Jan	Goods purchased from Sahil	4,000
31 Jan	Interest on capital @ 10% for the month	167
31 Jan	Depreciation on machinery	100

Solution

Journal Book Entries

Date	Particulars	L.F.	Dr. (₹)	Cr. (₹)
2020 1 Jan	Cash A/c (Add)　　　　　Dr.		20,000	
	To Capital A/c (Add)			20,000
	(Being Pradhan started business with cash)			
3 Jan	Bank A/c (Add)　　　　　Dr.		5,000	
	To Cash A/c (Less)			5,000
	(Being amount paid to bank)			
7 Jan	Purchase A/c (Add)　　　Dr.		4,000	
	To Suparsh's A/c (Add)			4,000
	(Being goods purchased from Suparsh)			
10 Jan	Suparsh's A/c (Less)　　Dr.		4,000	
	To Cash A/c (Less)			3,900
	To Discount received A/c (Add)			100
	(Being amount paid to Suparsh who allowed discount)			

Date	Particulars	L.F.	Dr. (₹)	Cr. (₹)
13 Jan	Machinery A/c (Add)　　　Dr.		2,000	
	To Cash A/c (Less)			2,000
	(Being purchase of machinery)			
16 Jan	Twinkle's A/c (Add)　　　Dr.		3,000	
	To Sales A/c (Add)			3,000
	(Being sales of goods to Twinkle)			
18 Jan	Cash A/c (Add)　　　　　Dr.		1,000	
	To Twinkle's A/c (Less)			1,000
	(Being amount received from Twinkle)			
20 Jan	Salaries A/c (Add)　　　Dr.		700	
	To Cash A/c (Less)			700
	(Being payment of salaries)			
23 Jan	Cash A/c (Add)　　　　　Dr.		300	
	To Rental Income A/c (Add)			300
	(Being rent received)			
28 Jan	Purchase A/c (Add)　　　Dr.		4,000	
	To Sahil's A/c (Add)			4,000
	(Being goods purchased from Sahil)			
31 Jan	Interest on capital A/c (Add)　Dr.		167	
	To Capital A/c (Add)			167
	(Being interest on capital)			
31 Jan	Depreciation A/c (Add)　Dr.		100	
	To Machinery A/c (Less)			100
	(Being depreciation on machinery)			
	Total		44,267	44,267

Name of Account: Bank Account
Type of Account: Asset　　　　　**Normal Balance: Debit**

Date	Reference Account	Voucher Type	Post Ref No.	Dr. (Add)	Cr. (Less)
3 Jan	To Cash A/c			5,000	
31 Jan	By Balance c/f				5,000
	Total			5,000	5,000
1 Feb	To Balance b/f			5,000	

Name of Account: Cash Account
Type of Account: Asset　　　　　**Normal Balance: Debit**

Date	Reference Account	Voucher Type	Post Ref No.	Dr. (Add)	Cr. (Less)
1 Jan	To Capital A/c			20,000	
3 Jan	By Bank A/c				5,000
10 Jan	By Suparsh's A/c				3,900
13 Jan	By Machinery A/c				2,000
18 Jan	To Twinkle's A/c			1,000	
20 Jan	By Salaries A/c				700
23 Jan	To Rent A/c			300	
31 Jan	By Balance c/d				9,700
	Total			21,300	21,300
1 Feb	To Balance b/f			9,700	

Name of Account: Purchase Account
Type of Account: Asset　　　　　**Normal Balance: Debit**

Date	Reference Account	Voucher Type	Post Ref No.	Dr. (Add)	Cr. (Less)
7 Jan	To Suparsh's A/c			4,000	
28 Jan	To Sahil's A/c			4,000	
31 Jan	By Balance c/f				8,000
	Total			8,000	0
1 Feb	To Balance b/f			8,000	

Name of Account: Machinery Account

Type of Account: Asset — Normal Balance: Debit

Date	Reference Account	Voucher Type	Post Ref No.	Dr. (Add)	Cr. (Less)
13 Jan	To Cash A/c			2,000	
31 Jan	By Depreciation A/c				100
31 Jan	By Balance c/f				1,900
	Total			**2,000**	**2,000**
1 Feb	To Balance b/f			1,900	

Name of Account: Twinkle Account

Type of Account: Asset — Normal Balance: Debit

Date	Reference Account	Voucher Type	Post Ref No.	Dr. (Add)	Cr. (Less)
16 Jan	To Sales A/c			3,000	
18 Jan	By Cash A/c				1,000
31 Jan	By Balance c/f				2,000
	Total			**3,000**	**3,000**
1 Feb	To Balance b/f			1,900	

Name of Account: Salaries Account

Type of Account: Expense — Normal Balance: Debit

Date	Reference Account	Voucher Type	Post Ref No.	Dr. (Add)	Cr. (Less)
20 Jan	To Cash A/c			700	
31 Jan	By Balance c/f				700
	Total			**700**	**700**
1 Feb	To Balance b/f			700	

Name of Account: Interest on Capital Account

Type of Account: Expense — Normal Balance: Debit

Date	Reference Account	Voucher Type	Post Ref No.	Dr. (Add)	Cr. (Less)
31 Jan	To Capital A/c			167	
31 Jan	By Balance c/f				167
	Total			**167**	**167**
1 Feb	To Balance b/f			167	

Name of Account: Depreciation Account

Type of Account: Expense — Normal Balance: Debit

Date	Reference Account	Voucher Type	Post Ref No.	Dr. (Add)	Cr. (Less)
31 Jan	To Machinery A/c			100	
31 Jan	By Balance c/f				100
	Total			**100**	**100**
1 Feb	To Balance b/f			100	

Name of Account: Sahil's Account

Type of Account: Liability — Normal Balance: Credit

Date	Reference Account	Voucher Type	Post Ref No.	Dr. (Less)	Cr. (Add)
31 Jan	By Purchase A/c				4,000
31 Jan	To Balance c/f			4,000	
	Total			**4,000**	**4,000**
1 Feb	By Balance b/f				4,000

Name of Account: Suparsh's Account

Type of Account: Liability — Normal Balance: Credit

Date	Reference Account	Voucher Type	Post Ref No.	Dr. (Less)	Cr. (Add)
7 Jan	By Purchase A/c				4,000
10 Jan	To Cash A/c			3,900	
10 Jan	To Discount A/c			100	
	Total			**4,000**	**4,000**
	Account Tallied				

Name of Account: Capital A/c

Type of Account: Capital — Normal Balance: Credit

Date	Reference Account	Voucher Type	Post Ref No.	Dr. (Less)	Cr. (Add)
1 Jan	By Cash A/c				20,000
31 Jan	By Interest on Capital A/c				167
31 Jan	To Balance c/f			20,167	
	Total			**20,167**	**20,167**
1 Feb	By Balance b/f				20,167

Name of Account: Discount Received Account

Type of Account: Income — Normal Balance: Credit

Date	Reference Account	Voucher Type	Post Ref No.	Dr. (Less)	Cr. (Add)
10 Jan	By Suparsh's A/c				100
31 Jan	To Balance c/f			100	
	Total			**100**	**100**
1 Feb	By Balance b/f				100

Name of Account: Sales Account

Type of Account: Income — Normal Balance: Credit

Date	Reference Account	Voucher Type	Post Ref No.	Dr. (Less)	Cr. (Add)
16 Jan	By Twinkle's A/c				3,000
31 Jan	To Balance c/f			3,000	
	Total			**3,000**	**3,000**
1 Feb	By Balance b/f				3,000

Name of Account: Rental Income Account

Type of Account: Income — Normal Balance: Credit

Date	Reference Account	Voucher Type	Post Ref No.	Dr. (Less)	Cr. (Add)
23 Jan	By Cash A/c				300
31 Jan	To Balance c/f			300	
	Total			**300**	**300**
1 Feb	By Balance b/f				300

(A) The preparation of trial balance under the balance method is given in the following text.

Trial Balance as on 31 January 2020

Particulars	L.F.	Amount Dr. (₹)	Amount Cr. (₹)
Cash A/c		9,700	—
Capital A/c		—	20,167
Bank A/c		5,000	—
Purchase A/c		8,000	—
Discount A/c		—	100
Machinery A/c		1,900	—
Twinkle's A/c		2,000	—
Salaries A/c		700	—
Sales A/c		—	3,000
Rent A/c		—	300
Depreciation A/c		100	—
Sahil's A/c		—	4,000
Interest on capital A/c		167	—
Total		**27,567**	**27,567**

Notes:

1. The trial balance, prepared as above contains the list of all ledger accounts except Suparsh's account which is closed and does not show any balance (the totals of the debit and credit of Suparsh's account are equal).

2. Cash account, bank account, purchase account, machinery account, Twinkle's account, salaries account, depreciation account, and interest on capital account show debit balance (excess of debit over credit). Hence, the balance has been shown in the debit column. In the same way, capital account, discount account, sales account, rent account, and Sahil's account show credit balance, so the amount has been written in the credit column.

3. The total of the debit and credit side each is ₹27,567 and is equal.

(B) The preparation of trial balance under the total method is given in the following text.

Trial Balance as on 31 January 2020

Particulars	L.F.	Amount Dr. (₹)	Amount Cr. (₹)
Cash A/c		21,300	11,600
Capital A/c		—	20,167
Bank A/c		5,000	—
Purchase A/c		8,000	—
Suparsh's A/c		4,000	4,000
Discount A/c		—	100
Machinery A/c		2,000	100
Twinkle's A/c		3,000	1,000
Salaries A/c		700	—
Sales A/c		—	3,000
Rent A/c		—	300
Depreciation A/c		100	—
Sahil's A/c		—	4,000
Interest on capital A/c		167	—
Total		**44,267**	**44,267**

Notes:

1. Trial balance has the list of all the ledger accounts including Suparsh's account which was dropped in the balance method. Cash account, Suparsh's account, machinery account, and Twinkle's account have posting at the debit and the credit side, so the total of their debit side is written in the debit column and the total of the credit side is written in the credit column. Bank account, purchase account, salaries account, depreciation account, and interest on capital account have posting only at their debit side so their totals have been written only at the debit side. In the same way, capital account, discount account, sales account, rent account, and Sahil's account have posting only at the credit side, so the amount has been written in the credit column.

2. The total of debit and credit columns according to this method is also equal.

(C) The preparation of trial balance under the total and balance method is given in the following text.

Trial Balance as on 31 January 2020

Particulars	L.F.	Amount Dr. (₹)	Amount Cr. (₹)	Amount Dr. (₹)	Amount Cr. (₹)
Cash A/c		21,300	11,600	9,700	—
Capital A/c		—	20,167	—	20,167
Bank A/c		5,000	—	5,000	—
Purchase A/c		8,000	—	8,000	—
Suparsh's A/c		4,000	4,000	—	—
Discount A/c		—	100	—	100
Machinery A/c		2,000	100	1,900	—
Twinkle's A/c		3,000	1,000	2,000	—
Salaries A/c		700	—	700	—
Sales A/c		—	3,000	—	3,000
Rent A/c		—	300	—	300
Depreciation A/c		100	—	100	—
Sahil's A/c		—	4,000	—	4,000
Interest on capital A/c		167	—	167	—
Total		**44,267**	**44,267**	**27,567**	**27,567**

Notes:

1. The amount column is divided between total and balance methods. Each method has got its own debit and credit column. Names of all ledger accounts are enlisted. The debit and credit total of every account is posted in the total method. The balances of accounts have been written in the balance method. The total of the total method is ₹44,267 as per both the debit and credit side. The total of the debit and credit columns under balance method is ₹27,567 and is also equal.

■ **ILLUSTRATION 7.3** The following trial balance was drawn from the books of Jasmine Traders. Even though the debit and credit sides agree, the trial balance contains certain mistakes. You are required to redraft the trial balance.

Trial Balance of Jasmine Traders

Debit	Amount (₹)	Credit	Amount (₹)
Building	60,000	Capital	73,600
Machinery	17,000	Fixtures	5,600
Returns outward	2,600	Sales	1,04,000
Bad debts	2,800	Debtors	60,000
Cash	400	Interest received	2,600
Discount received	3,000		
Bank overdraft	10,000		
Creditors	50,000		
Purchase	1,00,000		
	2,45,800		**2,45,800**

Solution

Trial Balance of Jasmine Traders

Particulars	Types of Accounts	Normal Balance	L.F.	Amount Dr. (₹)	Amount Cr. (₹)
Building A/c	Asset	Debit		60,000	
Machinery A/c	Asset	Debit		17,000	
Returns outward A/c	Asset (Reduction)	Credit			2,600
Bad debts A/c	Expense	Debit		2,800	
Cash A/c	Asset	Debit		400	
Discount received A/c	Revenue	Credit			3,000
Bank overdraft A/c	Liability	Credit			10,000
Creditors A/c	Liability	Credit			50,000
Purchase A/c	Asset	Debit		1,00,000	
Capital A/c	Capital	Credit			73,000
Fixtures A/c	Asset	Debit		5,600	
Sales A/c	Revenue	Credit			1,04,000
Debtors A/c	Asset	Debit		60,000	
Interest received A/c	Revenue	Credit			2,600
Total				**2,45,800**	**2,45,800**

■ **ILLUSTRATION 7.4** From the following transactions, pass the journal entries in the books of Dharmendra Traders and post them in ledger. Find out the balance of cash account and decide which account has which balance:

2020

1 July: Commenced a business by bringing in cash of ₹80,000 and furniture of ₹20,000.

2 July: A bank account was opened by depositing ₹30,000.

3 July: Goods of ₹12,000 purchased from Mahendra at 6% trade discount and paid cash of ₹4,000.

5 July: Goods of ₹7,500 sold to Narendra at 10% trade discount and he paid ₹2,000.

6 July: Paid ₹3,000 in cash for shop board and ₹4,000 for advertisement in a newspaper.

7 July: Paid life insurance premium of ₹6,000 and ₹2,200 for son's school fees from the shop.

8 July: Gave a cheque of ₹7,200 to Mahendra and settled his account.

10 July: Received a cheque of ₹4,700 from Narendra in full settlement.

11 July: Purchased furniture of ₹5,000 from Surendra Hardware. Against this was given ₹3,000 by cheque and ₹2,000 in cash.

Solution

Journal of Shri Dharmendra Traders

Date	Reference Account	Post Ref No.	Debit (Add)	Credit (Less)
2020				
1 Jul	Cash A/c (Add) Dr.		80,000	
	Furniture A/c (Add) Dr.		20,000	
	To Capital A/c (Add)			1,00,000
	[Being started business with cash and furniture.]			
2 Jul	Bank A/c (Add) Dr.		30,000	
	To Cash A/c (Less)			30,000
	[Being ₹30,000 deposited in bank to open an account.]			
3 Jul	Purchase A/c (Add) Dr.		11,280	
	To Cash A/c (Less)			4,000
	To Mahendra A/c (Add)			7,280
	[Being goods of ₹12,000 purchased from Mahendra at 6% trade discount and paid ₹4,000 by cash.]			
5 Jul	Cash A/c (Add) Dr.		2,000	
	Narendra A/c (Add) Dr.		4,750	
	To Sales A/c (Add)			6,750
	[Being goods of ₹7,500 sold to Narendra at 10% trade discount ane received ₹2,000 by cash.]			
6 Jul	Shop Expense A/c (Add) Dr.		3,000	
	Advertisement Expenses A/c (Add) Dr.		4,000	
	To Cash A/c (Less)			7,000
	[Being cash paid for board of shop and Advertisement Expense.]			
7 Jul	Drawings A/c (Add) Dr.		8,200	

Date	Reference Account	Post Ref No.	Debit (Add)	Credit (Less)
	To Cash A/c (Less)			8,200
	[Being Life Insurance Premium ₹6,000 and ₹2,200 school fees of son are paid from shop.]			
8 Jul	Mahendra A/c (Less) Dr.		7,280	
	To Bank A/c (Less)			7,200
	To discount received A/c (Add)			80
	[Being cheque of ₹7,200 given to Mahendra to settle his account.]			
10 Jul	Bank A/c (Add) Dr.		4,700	
	Discount allowed A/c (Add) Dr.		50	
	To Narendra A/c (Less)			4,750
	[Being cheque ₹4,700 received from Narendra to settle his account.]			
11 Jul	Furniture A/c (Add) Dr.		5,000	
	To Bank A/c (Less)			3,000
	To Cash A/c (Less)			2,000
	[Being purchased furniture from Surendra hardware and paid ₹3,000 by cheque and ₹2,000 by cash.]			
	Total		**1,80,260**	**1,80,260**

Ledger of Dharmendra Traders

Cash Account

Account No:

Normal Balance: Debit   Account Type: Asset

Date	Reference Account	Voucher Type	Post Ref No.	Debit (Add)	Credit (Less)	Balance (₹)
2020						
1 Jul	To Capital A/c			80,000		80,000
2 Jul	By Bank A/c				30,000	50,000
3 Jul	By Purchase A/c				4,000	46,000
5 Jul	To Sales A/c			2,000		48,000
6 Jul	By Shop Expense A/c				3,000	45,000
6 Jul	By Advertisment Exp. A/c				4,000	41,000
7 Jul	By Drawings A/c				8,200	32,800
11 Jul	By Furniture A/c				2,000	30,800
15 Jul	By Balance c/f				30,800	0
	Total			**82,000**	**82,000**	
16 Jul	To Balance b/f			30,800		30,800

Answer: Cash account shows debit balance of ₹30,800.

Furniture Account

Account No:

Normal Balance: Debit   Account Type: Asset

Date	Reference Account	Voucher Type	Post Ref No.	Debit (Add)	Credit (Less)	Balance (₹)
2020						
1 Jul	To Capital A/c			20,000		20,000
11 Jul	To Bank A/c			3,000		23,000
11 Jul	To Cash A/c			2,000		25,000
15 Jul	By Balance c/f				25,000	0
	Total			**25,000**	**25,000**	
16 Jul	To Balance b/f			25,000		25,000

Answer: Furniture account shows debit balance of ₹25,000

Capital Account
Account No:
Normal Balance: Credit   Account Type: Liability

Date	Reference Account	Voucher Type	Post Ref No.	Debit (Less)	Credit (Add)	Balance (₹)
2020						
1 Jul	By Cash A/c				80,000	80,000
1 Jul	By Furniture A/c				20,000	1,00,000
15 Jul	To Balance c/f			1,00,000		0
	Total			1,00,000	1,00,000	
16 Jul	By Balance b/f				1,00,000	1,00,000

Answer: Capital account shows credit balance of ₹1,00,000

Bank Account
Account No:
Normal Balance: Debit   Account Type: Asset

Date	Reference Account	Voucher Type	Post Ref No.	Debit (Add)	Credit (Less)	Balance (₹)
2020						
2 Jul	To Cash A/c			30,000		30,000
8 Jul	By Mahendra A/c				7,200	22,800
10 Jul	To Narendra A/c			4,700		27,500
11 Jul	By Furniture A/c				3,000	24,500
15 Jul	By Balance c/f				24,500	0
	Total			34,700	34,700	
16 Jul	To Balance b/f			24,500		24,500

Answer: Bank account shows debit balance of ₹24,500.

Purchase Account
Account No:
Normal Balance: Debit   Account Type: Asset

Date	Reference Account	Voucher Type	Post Ref No.	Debit (Add)	Credit (Less)	Balance (₹)
2020						
3 Jul	To Cash A/c			4,000		4,000
3 Jul	To Mahendra A/c			7,280		11,280
15 Jul	By Balance c/f				11,280	0
	Total			11,280	11,280	
16 Jul	To Balance b/f			11,280		11,280

Answer: Purchase account shows debit balance of ₹11,280

Mahendra's Account
Account No:
Normal Balance: Credit   Account Type: Liability

Date	Reference Account	Voucher Type	Post Ref No.	Debit (Less)	Credit (Add)	Balance (₹)
2020						
3 Jul	By Purchase A/c				7,280	7,280
8 Jul	To Bank A/c			7,200		80
8 Jul	To Discount received A/c			80		0
	Total			7,280	7,280	
	Account Tallied					

Answer: As total of both the sides of Mahendra's account are equal, it is called account squared up.

Narendra's Account
Account No:
Normal Balance: Debit   Account Type: Asset

Date	Reference Account	Voucher Type	Post Ref No.	Debit (Add)	Credit (Less)	Balance (₹)
2020						
5 Jul	To Sales A/c			4,750		4,750
10 Jul	By Bank A/c				4,700	50
10 Jul	By Discount allowed A/c				50	0
	Account Tallied					
	Total			4,750	4,750	

Answer: As total of both the sides of Narendra's account are equal, it is called account squared up.

Sales Account
Account No:
Normal Balance: Credit   Account Type: Income

Date	Reference Account	Voucher Type	Post Ref No.	Debit (Less)	Credit (Add)	Balance (₹)
2020						
5 Jul	By Cash A/c				2,000	2,000
5 Jul	By Narendra A/c				4,750	6,750
15 Jul	To Balance c/f			6,750		0
	Total			6,750	6,750	
16 Jul	By Balance b/f				6,750	6,750

Answer: Sales account shows credit balance of ₹6,750

Shop Expense Account
Account No:
Normal Balance: Debit   Account Type: Expense

Date	Reference Account	Voucher Type	Post Ref No.	Debit (Add)	Credit (Less)	Balance (₹)
2020						
6 Jul	To Cash A/c			3,000		3,000
15 Jul	By Balance c/f				3,000	0
	Total			3,000	3,000	
16 Jul	To Balance b/f			3,000		3,000

Answer: Shop expense account shows debit balance of ₹3,000.

Advertisment Expense Account
Account No:
Normal Balance: Debit   Account Type: Expense

Date	Reference Account	Voucher Type	Post Ref No.	Debit (Add)	Credit (Less)	Balance (₹)
2020						
6 Jul	To Cash A/c			4,000		4,000
15 Jul	By Balance c/f				4,000	0
	Total			4,000	4,000	
16 Jul	By Balance b/f			4,000		4,000

Answer: Advertisement expense shows debit balance of ₹4,000

Drawings Account
Account No:
Normal Balance: Debit   Account Type: Implied Expense or Negative Capital

Date	Reference Account	Voucher Type	Post Ref No.	Debit (Add)	Credit (Less)	Balance (₹)
2020						
7 Jul	To Cash A/c			8,200		8,200
15 Jul	By Balance c/f				8,200	0
	Total			**8,200**	**8,200**	
16 Jul	To Balance b/f			8,200		8,200

Answer: Drawings account shows debit balance of ₹8,200.

Discount Received Account
Account No:
Normal Balance: Credit   Account Type: Income

Date	Reference Account	Voucher Type	Post Ref No.	Debit (Less)	Credit (Add)	Balance (₹)
2020						
8 Jul	By Mahendra A/c				80	80
15 Jul	To Balance c/f			80		0
	Total			**80**	**80**	
16 Jul	To Balance b/f				80	80

Answer: Discount received account shows credit balance of ₹80.

Discount Allowed Account
Account No:
Normal Balance: Debit   Account Type: Asset

Date	Reference Account	Voucher Type	Post Ref No.	Debit (Add)	Credit (Less)	Balance (₹)
2020						
10 Jul	To Narendra A/c			50		50
15 Jul	By Balance c/f				50	0
	Total			**50**	**50**	
16 Jul	To Balance b/f			50		50

Answer: Discount allowed account shows debit balance of ₹50.

■ **ILLUSTRATION 7.5**   Record the following transactions in the three columnar cash book of Mohan Trading Company. Post them in necessary accounts. Find out the balance of each account and show the amount and type of balance.

2020

1 Aug: Opening cash balance ₹24,000 and bank balance ₹20,000.

2 Aug: Cash deposited in bank ₹14,000.

3 Aug: Goods of ₹20,000 sold to Sureshbhai, for which cash of ₹8,000 was received and for the balance a cheque which has been deposited in the bank was received.

5 Aug: Paid rent of ₹1,500 to a shop by cheque and salary of ₹2,500 to employees in cash.

7 Aug: Goods of ₹8,700 purchased from Dineshbhai, for which ₹700 was paid in cash.

9 Aug: Paid electricity bill of ₹1,870 and telephone bill of ₹530 by cheque.

11 Aug: Goods of ₹9,000 sold to Kanji at 10% trade discount, for which ₹1,900 was received in cash.

13 Aug: Jayantibhai has paid ₹4,800 for his dues of ₹5,000 and settled his account.

16 Aug: Gave a cheque of ₹7,600 to Dineshbhai and settled his account.

17 Aug: Paid ₹1,800 in cash from business for gift towards Shital's marriage function.

20 Aug: Goods of ₹11,000 sold to Pandya Brothers and he paid the full amount at 2% cash discount.

22 Aug: Received a cheque of ₹6,000 from Kanji in full settlement against his dues of ₹6,200.

24 Aug: Received a cheque of ₹1,600 for commission, which was deposited in the bank.

Solution

Cash and Bank Account of Mohan Trading Company

Date 2020	Reference Account	Voucher Type and No.	Post Ref No.	Discount Allowed	Debit (₹) (Add) Cash	Debit (₹) (Add) Bank	Discount Received	Credit (₹) (Less) Cash	Credit (₹) (Less) Bank	Balance (₹) Dr. (Normal) Cash	Balance (₹) Dr. (Normal) Bank
1 Aug	To Balance b/f				24,000	20,000				24,000	20,000
2 Aug	To Cash A/c		C			14,000				24,000	34,000
2 Aug	By Bank A/c		C					14,000		10,000	34,000
3 Aug	To Sales A/c				8,000	12,000				18,000	46,000
5 Aug	By Shop rent A/c								1,500	18,000	44,500
5 Aug	By Salary A/c							2,500		15,500	44,500
7 Aug	By Purchase A/c							700		14,800	44,500
9 Aug	By Electricity exp. A/c								1,870	14,800	42,630
9 Aug	By Telephone exp. A/c								530	14,800	42,100
11 Aug	To Sales A/c				1,900					16,700	42,100
13 Aug	To Jayantibhai A/c			200	4,800					21,500	42,100
16 Aug	By Dineshbhai A/c						400		7,600	21,500	34,500

Date	Reference Account								
17 Aug	By Drawings A/c					1,800		19,700	34,500
20 Aug	To Sales A/c	220	10,780					30,480	34,500
22 Aug	To Kanji A/c	200		6,000				30,480	40,500
24 Aug	To Commission A/c			1,600				30,480	42,100
31 Aug	By Balance c/f					30,480	42,100	0	0
	Total	620	49,480	53,600	400			49,480	53,600
1 Sep	**To Balance b/f**		30,480	42,100					

Ledger of Mohan Trading Company
Sales Account
Account No:

Normal Balance: Credit   Account Type: Income

Date	Reference Account	Voucher Type	Post Ref No.	Debit (Less)	Credit (Add)	Balance (₹)
2020						
3 Aug	By Cash A/c (As per cash book)				8,000	8,000
3 Aug	By Bank A/c (As per cash book)				12,000	20,000
11 Aug	By Cash A/c (As per cash book)				1,900	21,900
11 Aug	By Kanji A/c (Credit sales -amount receivables)				6,200	28,100
20 Aug	By Discount allowed (As per cash book)				220	28,320
20 Aug	By Cash A/c (As per cash book)				10,780	39,100
31 Aug	To Balance c/f			39,100		
	Total			**39,100**	**39,100**	
2020						
1 Sep	By Balance b/f				39,100	

Answer: Sales account shows credit balance of ₹39,100.

Shop Rent Account
Account No:

Normal Balance: Debit   Account Type: Expense

Date	Reference Account	Voucher Type	Post Ref No.	Debit (Add)	Credit (Less)	Balance (₹)
2020						
5 Aug	To Bank A/c (As per cash book)			1,500		1,500
31 Aug	By Balance c/f				1,500	0
	Total			**1,500**	**1,500**	
1 Sep	To Balance b/f			1,500		

Answer: Shop rent account shows debit balance of ₹1,500.

Salary Account
Account No:

Normal Balance: Debit   Account Type: Expense

Date	Reference Account	Voucher Type	Post Ref No.	Debit (Add)	Credit (Less)	Balance (₹)
2020						
5 Aug	To Cash A/c (As per cash book)			2,500		2,500
31 Aug	By Balance c/f				2,500	0
	Total			**2,500**	**2,500**	
2020						
1 Sep	To Balance b/f			2,500		

Answer: Salary account shows debit balance of ₹2,500.

Purchase Account
Account No:

Normal Balance: Debit   Account Type: Asset

Date	Reference Account	Voucher Type	Post Ref No.	Debit (Add)	Credit (Less)	Balance (₹)
2020						
7 Aug	To Cash A/c (As per cash book)			700		700
7 Aug	To Dineshbhai A/c (as per credit purchase—still payable)			8,000		8,700
31 Aug	By Balance c/f				8,700	0
	Total			**8,700**	**8,700**	
2020						
1 Sep	To Balance b/f			8,700		

Answer: Purchase account shows debit balance of ₹8,700.

Electricity Expense Account
Account No:

Normal Balance: Debit   Account Type: Expense

Date	Reference Account	Voucher Type	Post Ref No.	Debit (Add)	Credit (Less)	Balance (₹)
2020						
9 Aug	To Bank A/c (As per cash book)			1,870		1,870
31 Aug	By Balance c/f				1,870	0
	Total			**1,870**	**1,870**	
2020						
1 Sep	To Balance b/f			1,870		

Answer: Electricity expense account shows debit balance of ₹1,870.

Telephone Expense Account
Account No:

Normal Balance: Debit   Account Type: Expense

Date	Reference Account	Voucher Type	Post Ref No.	Debit (Add)	Credit (Less)	Balance (₹)
2020						
9 Aug	To Bank A/c			530		530
31 Aug	By Balance c/f				530	0
	Total			**530**	**530**	
2020						
1 Sep	To Balance b/f			530		

Answer: Telephone expense shows debit balance of ₹530.

Jayantibhai's Account

Account No:

Normal Balance: Debit Account Type: Asset

Date	Reference Account	Voucher Type	Post Ref No.	Debit (Add)	Credit (Less)	Balance (₹)
2020						
13 Aug	By Discount allowed A/c (As per cash book)				200	–200
13 Aug	By Bank A/c (As per cash book)				4,800	–5,000
31 Aug	To Balance c/f			5,000		0
	Total			**5,000**	**5,000**	
2020						
1 Sep	By Balance b/f					5,000

Answer: Jayantibhai's account shows credit balance of ₹5,000.

Dineshbhai's Account

Account No:

Normal Balance: Credit Account Type: Liability

Date	Reference Account	Voucher Type	Post Ref No.	Debit (Less)	Credit (Add)	Balance (₹)
2020						
7 Aug	By Purchase A/c (Part credit purchase)				8,000	8,000
16 Aug	To Discount received A/c (As per cash book)			400		7,600
16 Aug	To Bank A/c (As per cash book)			7,600		0
	Total			**8,000**	**8,000**	
	Account Tallied					

Answer: Dineshbhai's account squared up.

Drawings Account

Account No:

Normal Balance: Debit Account Type: Implied Expense or Negative Capital

Date	Reference Account	Voucher Type	Post Ref No.	Debit (Add)	Credit (Less)	Balance ₹
2020						
17 Aug	To Cash A/c (As per cash book)			1,800		1,800
31 Aug	By Balance c/f				1,800	0
	Total			**1,800**	**1,800**	
2020						
1 Sep	To Balance b/f			1,800		

Answer: Drawings account shows debit balance of ₹1,800.

Kanji's Account

Account No:

Normal Balance: Debit Account Type: Asset

Date	Reference Account	Voucher Type	Post Ref No.	Debit (Add)	Credit (Less)	Balance (₹)
2020						
11 Aug	To Sales A/c (Credit sales)			6,200		
22 Aug	By Discounnt allowed A/c (As per cash book)				200	6,000
22 Aug	By Bank A/c (As per cash book)				6,000	0
	Total			**6,200**	**6,200**	
	Account Tallied					

Answer: Dineshbhai's account squared up.

Commission Received Account

Account No:

Normal Balance: Credit Account Type: Income

Date	Reference Account	Voucher Type	Post Ref No.	Debit (Less)	Credit (Add)	Balance (₹)
2020						
24 Aug	By Bank A/c (As per cash book)				1,600	1,600
31 Aug	To Balance c/f			1,600		0
	Total			**1,600**	**1,600**	
2020						
1 Sep	By Balance b/f					1,600

Answer: Commission received shows credit balance of ₹1,600.

Discount Allowed Account

Account No:

Normal Balance: Debit Account Type: Expense

Date	Reference Account	Voucher Type	Post Ref No.	Debit (Add)	Credit (Less)	Balance (₹)
2020						
24 Aug	To Total discount allowed A/c (As per cash book)			620		620
31 Aug	By Balance c/f				620	0
	Total			**620**	**620**	
2020						
1 Sep	To Balance b/f			620		

Answer: Discount allowed account shows debit balance of ₹620.

Discount Received Account

Account No:

Normal Balance: Credit Account Type: Income

Date	Reference Account	Voucher Type	Post Ref No.	Debit (Less)	Credit (Add)	Balance ₹
2020						
24 Aug	By Total discount received A/c (As per cash book)				400	400
31 Aug	To Balance c/f			400		0
	Total			**400**	**400**	
2020						
1 Sep	By Balance b/f					400

Answer: Discount received account shows credit balance of ₹400.

■ **ILLUSTRATION 7.6** In the books of Shri Katara & Sons, write journal entries for the transactions mentioned below, draw necessary accounts in the ledger, and post them accordingly.

1 May: Brought ₹3,30,000 in business. From this ₹2,30,000 deposited in a bank.

2 May: Cash purchase of ₹85,000 done.

3 May: From Ajmal Furniture Mart, furniture of ₹11,500 purchased for office use.

4 May: A cheque of ₹8,000 given to Kanubhai against dues.

5 May: Against the receivables of ₹7,800 from Rajubhai, a cheque of ₹7,500 was received for full and final payment.

6 May: Cash sales of ₹15,000 done.

7 May: Credit sales of ₹75,000 done to Rameshbhai.

8 May: Salary paid for ₹6,200.

Solution

Journal of Shri Katara & Sons

Date	Reference Account	Post Ref No.	Debit (₹)	Credit (₹)
1 May	(a) Cash A/c (Add) Dr.		3,30,000	
	To Capital A/c (Add)			3,30,000
	[Being cash intoduced into the business.]			
	(b) Bank A/c (Add) Dr.		2,30,000	
	To Cash A/c (Less)			2,30,000
	[Being cash deposited in bank.]			
2 May	Purchase A/c (Add) Dr.		85,000	
	To Cash A/c (Less)			85,000
	[Being goods purchased for cash.]			
3 May	Furniture A/c (Add) Dr.		11,500	
	To Ajmal Furniture Mart A/c (Add)			11,500
	[Being furniture purchased for office from Ajmal Furniture Mart.]			
4 May	Kanubhai A/c (Less) Dr.		8,000	
	To Bank A/c (Less)			8,000
	[Being against dues of Kanubhai cheque is given.]			
5 May	Bank A/c (Add) Dr.		7,500	
	Discount A/c (Add) Dr.		300	
	To Rajubhai A/c (Less)			7,800
	[Being cheque received from Rajubhai in full settlement of his account.]			
6 May	Cash A/c (Add) Dr.		15,000	
	To Sales A/c (Add)			15,000
	[Being goods sold for cash.]			
7 May	Rameshbhai A/c (Add) Dr.		75,000	
	To Sales A/c (Add)			75,000
	[Being goods sold to Rameshbhai on credit.]			
8 May	Salary A/c (Add) Dr.		6,200	
	To Cash A/c (Less)			6,200
	[Being salary paid.]			
	Total		7,68,500	7,68,500

Ledger of Katara & Sons
Cash Account
Account No:
Normal Balance: Debit

Account Type: Asset

Date	Reference Account	Voucher Type	Post Ref No.	Debit (Add)	Credit (Less)	Balance (₹)
1 May	To Capital A/c			3,30,000		3,30,000
1 May	By Bank A/c				2,30,000	1,00,000
2 May	By Purchase A/c				85,000	15,000
6 May	To Sales A/c			15,000		30,000
8 May	By Salary A/c				6,200	23,800
9 May	By Balance c/f				23,800	
	Total			3,45,000	3,45,000	

Capital Account
Account No:
Normal Balance: Credit

Account Type: Capital

Date	Reference Account	Voucher Type	Post Ref No.	Debit (Less)	Credit (Add)	Balance (₹)
1 May	By Cash A/c				3,30,000	3,30,000
9 May	To Balance c/f			3,30,000		
	Total			3,30,000	3,30,000	

Bank Account
Account No:
Normal Balance: Debit

Account Type: Asset

Date	Reference Account	Voucher Type	Post Ref No.	Debit (Add)	Credit (Less)	Balance (₹)
1 May	To Cash A/c			2,30,000		2,30,000
4 May	By Kanubhai A/c				8,000	2,22,000
5 May	To Rajubhai A/c			7,500		2,29,500
9 May	By Balance c/f				2,29,500	
	Total			2,37,500	2,37,500	

Purchase Account
Account No:
Normal Balance: Debit

Account Type: Asset

Date	Reference Account	Voucher Type	Post Ref No.	Debit (Add)	Credit (Less)	Balance (₹)
2 May	Cash A/c			85,000		85,000
9 May	By Balance c/f				85,000	
	Total			85,000	85,000	

Furniture Account
Account No:
Normal Balance: Debit

Account Type: Asset

Date	Reference Account	Voucher Type	Post Ref No.	Debit (Add)	Credit (Less)	Balance (₹)
3 May	To Ajmal Furniture Mart A/c			11,500		11,500
9 May	By Balance c/f				11,500	
	Total			11,500	11,500	

Ajmal Furniture Mart Account
Account No:
Normal Balance: Credit

Account Type: Liability

Date	Reference Account	Voucher Type	Post Ref No.	Debit (Less)	Credit (Add)	Balance (₹)
3 May	By Furniture A/c				11,500	11,500
9 May	To Balance c/f			11,500		
	Total			11,500	11,500	

Kanubhai's Account

Account No:

Normal Balance: Credit   Account Type: Liability

Date	Reference Account	Voucher Type	Post Ref No.	Debit (Less)	Credit (Add)	Balance (₹)
4 May	To Bank A/c			8,000		−8,000
9 May	By Balance c/f				8,000	
	Total			8,000	8,000	

Discount Account

Account No:

Normal Balance: Debit   Account Type: Expense

Date	Reference Account	Voucher Type	Post Ref No.	Debit (Add)	Credit (Less)	Balance (₹)
5 May	To Rajubhai A/c			300		300
9 May	By Balance c/f				300	
	Total			300	300	

Rajubhai's Account

Account No:

Normal Balance: Debit   Account Type: Asset

Date	Reference Account	Voucher Type	Post Ref No.	Debit (Add)	Credit (Less)	Balance (₹)
5 May	By Bank A/c				7,500	−7,500
5 May	By Discount A/c				300	−7,800
9 May	To Balance c/f			7,800		
	Total			7,800	7,800	

Sales Account

Account No:

Normal Balance: Credit   Account Type: Income

Date	Reference Account	Voucher Type	Post Ref No.	Debit (Less)	Credit (Add)	Balance (₹)
6 May	By Cash A/c				15,000	15,000
7 May	By Rameshbhai A/c				75,000	90,000
9 May	To Balance c/f			90,000		
	Total			90,000	90,000	

Rameshbhai Account

Account No:

Normal Balance: Debit   Account Type: Asset

Date	Reference Account	Voucher Type	Post Ref No.	Debit (Add)	Credit (Less)	Balance (₹)
7 May	To Sales A/c			75,000		75,000
9 May	By Balance c/f				75,000	
	Total			75,000	75,000	

Salary Account

Account No:

Normal Balance: Debit   Account Type: Expense

Date	Reference Account	Voucher Type	Post Ref No.	Debit (Add)	Credit (Less)	Balance (₹)
8 May	To Cash A/c			6,200		6,200
9 May	By Balance c/f				6,200	
	Total			6,200	6,200	

ERRORS IN ACCOUNTING

The total of the debit column should always tally with the total of the credit column.

The trial balance is prepared to ensure the arithmetical accuracy of the ledger and to ensure that for every debit entry a credit of an equal amount has been recorded. If in the trial balance, the total of debits does not equal total of credits, it shows the existence of some errors in the records. However, some errors do not affect the trial balances. So, trial balance tallies.

Errors may be (a) errors of omission; (b) errors of commission; (c) errors of principle; or (d) compensating errors.

Errors of Omission

An error of omission occurs when a transaction is completely omitted from the books of accounts and not recorded in the books of original entry. The two sides of the trial balance will not at all be affected on account of this error. Such errors cannot be located easily.

Errors of Commission

Such errors include errors on account of wrong balancing of an account, wrong posting, wrong carry forwards, wrong totaling, etc. Errors of commission affect the agreement of the trial balance and, therefore, their location is easier.

Errors of Principle

Errors of principle are committed when proper distinction between revenue and capital items is not made. Such errors do not affect the trial balance and are difficult to locate.

Compensating Errors

These compensate each other and are also difficult to locate.

Nature of Errors

Errors in accounts may be discovered in various ways:

  (a) Through audit procedures,
  (b) By chance, or
  (c) By looking at the trial balance.

With computerized accounting systems being followed by majority of firms, manual errors in posting on wrong side, wrong totalling, same erroneous amount for both debit and credit sides, posting a part of transaction, etc. are less likely to occur. Hence, the important errors in accounting that may occur today are error of omission and error of principle.

Errors of trial balance

The various errors disclosed by a trial balance can be classified as—(a) errors committed in casting the subsidiary books; (b) errors committed in carrying forward the total amount from one page to another; (c) errors committed during posting from the books of journal or subsidiary books to ledger; (d) errors committed in balancing the ledger accounts; (e) errors committed during preparation of debtors' and creditors' list of accounts; and (f) errors committed due to ignorance in carrying forward a balance of an account to the trial balance.

Methods of Rectification of Accounting Errors

A rectification entry is passed to nullify the effect of errors that occurred at the time of original recording of an event or transaction in the books of accounts.

Generally, an accountant can rectify the errors at two stages: before the trial balance is prepared and after the trial balance is prepared.

Error rectification before preparation of trial balance

Before preparing the trial balance, rectification can be done in either of the following ways:

(a) Instant correction: If the error is traced out by the accountant immediately on passing of an accounting entry, it may be corrected by crossing out the wrong entry neatly and writing the correct entry. In such cases, it is important, from the view of internal control, for the accountant to sign his or her initials at the respective place in the books of account. Suppose ₹3,735 is written as ₹3,375, this can be corrected to ₹3,735 after crossing out the amount written as ₹3,375, with the accountant's initials signed on the correction.

(b) Correction in the affected accounts: When the error in an accounting is detected after recording the transaction, but before preparation of the trial balance, then the necessary rectification can be made for correction of the error, before proceeding for finalization of accounting statements, that is, preparation of financial statements.

For example,

1. The purchase book is overcast for the month of June 2020 by ₹16,000, and hence the purchase book total is posted to the debit of purchase account. As a result, the purchase account is now affected. To rectify this, one can credit the purchase account by ₹16,000 to nullify the ₹16,000 debited due to an error, giving the explanation 'Purchase book overcast'.

2. A sum of ₹2,400 paid to Anushka has been credited to her account because of an error. Anushka's account has thus been credited instead of being debited. In this case, one may debit ₹4,800 from the account, ₹2,400 to nullify the error and ₹2,400 for the actual debit.

3. Let us assume that on purchase of furniture worth ₹10,000, the purchase account was debited by ₹10,000 and the furniture account was not debited because of an accounting error. In this case, the purchase account has to be credited by ₹10,000 and simultaneously the furniture account to be debited by ₹10,000 in order to nullify the error caused in the account.

Error rectification after preparation of trial balance

When a rectification entry is to be passed and the accountant has insufficient time to find out the error, a temporary suspense account is created to tally the total of debit and credit in the account. Any difference that appears on either side of the trial balance will be taken to the suspense account, which in turn helps tally the trial balance and rectify the error while preparing financial statements. Suspense accounts are generally created to rectify one-sided errors.

Errors that affect two different accounts on the same side or different sides are called two-sided errors.

For example,

1. Gautam's account was debited short by ₹135. The error is rectified by debiting the account by ₹135, and crediting the same amount in a suspense account.

2. Sales book for the month of June 2020 is undercast by ₹2,350. The rectification can be carried out by crediting the sales account by ₹2,350, and simultaneously debiting the suspense account by ₹2,350.

SUSPENSE ACCOUNT

When a combination of the various errors have been committed, the mismatch in the totals of the trial balance will be totally different for the amounts of the individual transactions. Only a thorough scrutiny and checking of the books of accounts will help in detecting the errors. Sometimes, when trial balance disagrees and sufficient time is not available to scrutinize the books, the accountant will include a *suspense account* in the trial balance to make it agree and proceed with the preparation of financial statements. Later, the books may be scrutinized to detect the errors and the rectification entries passed to clear the balance in the suspense account. However, it should be noted that the existence of suspense account creates doubt about the authenticity of the books of the accounts. The books of accounts may not be trusted by the proprietor, tax officials, or other government authorities. This may create complications for the business.

Procedures to Correct Errors

The procedures used to correct an error in journalizing or posting vary according to the nature of error and time of discovery of the error. These procedures are summarized in Table 7.6.

TABLE 7.6   Procedures to correct an error

Error	Correction Procedures
Journal entry is incorrect but not posted. (System bug at the time of processing ledger posting)	Draw the line through the error and insert correct entry with amount.
Journal entry is correct but posted inaccurately. (System bug at the time of processing ledger posting)	Draw a line through the error and post correctly.
Journal entry is incorrect and posted.	Journalize and post correct entry. Correct entry working as explained hereunder.

Methods to Work Out Correct Entry

The following three steps need to be followed to work out a correct entry:

1. Write down the incorrect entry.
2. Write down the correct entry.
3. Reverse the wrong entry and work out the correction needed.

The following illustration explains the method correctly by way of an example.

■ **ILLUSTRATION 7.7**   Assume that as on 5 May, a firm has purchased a computer for ₹55,000 on credit from M/s. Computech Ltd.

1. Incorrect entry passed as under:
   Purchases A/c (Add) Dr.... ₹55,000
   To Computech Ltd A/c (Add) ₹55,000

2. Correct entry would be as under:
   Computer A/c (Add) Dr.... ₹55,000
   To Computech Ltd A/c (Add) ₹55,000
3. Entry to correct the error:
   Computer A/c (Add) Dr.... ₹55,000
   To Purchases A/c (Less) ₹55,000

DISTINCTION BETWEEN SUBSIDIARY AND PRINCIPAL BOOKS

The books in which transactions or events are first recorded are called subsidiary books. Those books which furnish information for preparation of trial balance and financial statements are called principal books. Figure 7.2 depicts an illustrative list of these books.

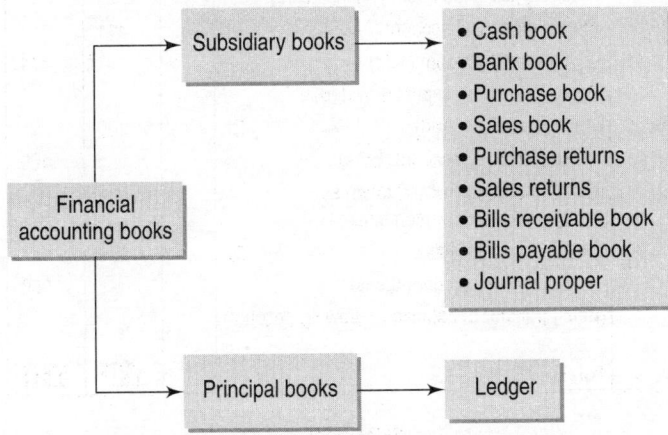

FIG. 7.2 Subsidiary and principal books of accounts

■ **ILLUSTRATION 7.8** From the following transactions, find out the nature of account and also state which account should be debited and which account should be credited along with (+) and (–) sign by using the modern approach of accounting equation.

(a) Rent paid
(b) Salaries paid
(c) Interest received
(d) Dividend received
(e) Furniture purchase for cash
(f) Machinery sold
(g) Outstanding for salary
(h) Telephone charges paid
(i) Paid to Trupti
(j) Received from Nutan (the proprietor)
(k) Lighting

Solution

Transactions	Accounts Involved	Type of Account	Rules of Debit and Credit
(a) Rent paid	Rent A/c	Capital	(–)Debit
	Cash A/c	Assets	(–)Credit
(b) Salaries paid	Salaries A/c	Capital	(–)Debit
	Cash A/c	Assets	(–)Credit
(c) Interest received	Cash A/c	Assets	(+)Debit
	Interest A/c	Capital	(+)Credit

(d) Dividend received	Cash A/c	Assets	(+)Debit
	Dividend A/c	Capital	(+)Credit
(e) Furniture purchased for cash	Furniture A/c	Assets	(+)Debit
	Cash A/c	Assets	(–)Credit
(f) Machinery sold	Cash A/c	Assets	(+)Debit
	Machinery A/c	Assets	(–)Credit
(g) Outstanding for salary	Salaries A/c	Capital	(–)Debit
	Outstanding salaries A/c	Liabilities	(+)Credit
(h) Telephone charges paid	Telephone charges A/c	Capital	(–)Debit
	Cash A/c	Assets	(–)Credit
(i) Paid to Trupti	Trupti A/c	Assets	(+)Debit
	Cash A/c	Assets	(–)Credit
(j) Receive From Nutan (The proprietor)	Cash A/c	Asses	(+)Debit
	Capital A/c	O/E	(+)Credit
(k) Lighting	Lighting A/c	O/E	(–)Debit
	Cash A/c	Assets	(–)Credit

Note: Capital account refers to an owner's equity (O/E) account. O/E account consists of capital, income, and expense. In the traditional method, capital account is considered as personal account, while income and expense account is considered as nominal type account.

■ **ILLUSTRATION 7.9** Prepare a trial balance of Mr Vimal as on 31 March 2020.

Particulars	Amount (₹)	Particulars	Amount (₹)
Capital	9,20,000	Cash at bank	1,45,340
Creditors	1,88,520	Bills receivable	58,440
Bills payable	69,300	Purchases	8,55,220
Sales	12,18,500	Carriage inwards	12,910
Provision for doubtful debts	13,200	Carriage outwards	8,000
Interest (Cr)	3,400	General expenses	60,850
Buildings	7,00,000	Insurance	7,830
Machinery	1,20,000	Bad debts	6,130
Furniture	16,400	Audit fees	4,000
Debtors	1,56,000	Travelling	3,250
Opening stock	1,50,400	Discount (Dr)	6,200
Cash in hand	9,880	Sales returns	2,850
		Investments	89,220

Solution

Trial Balance of Mr Vimal
as on 31 March 2020

Particulars	Types of Accounts	Normal Balance	Dr. (₹)	Cr. (₹)
Capital	Capital	Credit		9,20,000
Creditors	Liability	Credit		1,88,520
Bills payable	Liability	Credit		69,300
Sales	Income	Credit		12,18,500
Provision for doubtful debts	Capital	Credit		13,200
Interest (credit)	Income	Credit		3,400
Buildings	Asset	Debit	7,00,000	
Machinery	Asset	Debit	1,20,000	
Furniture	Asset	Debit	16,400	
Debtors	Asset	Debit	1,56,000	

Opening stock	Asset	Debit	1,50,400	
Cash in hand	Asset	Debit	9,880	
Cash at bank	Asset	Debit	1,45,340	
Bills receivable	Asset	Debit	58,440	
Purchases	Asset	Debit	8,55,220	
Carriage inwards	Expense	Debit	12,910	
Carriage outwards	Expense	Debit	8,000	
General expenses	Expense	Debit	60,850	
Insurance	Expense	Debit	7,830	
Bad debts	Expense	Debit	6,130	
Audit fees	Expense	Debit	4,000	
Travelling	Expense	Debit	3,250	
Discount allowed	Expense	Debit	6,200	
Sales returns	Income (Reduction)	Debit	2,850	
Investments	Asset	Debit	89,220	
Total			**24,12,920**	**24,12,920**

The total of the debit side should always equal the total of the credit side.

Note: Carriage inward is the transportation expense occurred for input materials while carriage outward occurred for goods sold to customers.

■ **ILLUSTRATION 7.10**   Record the following transactions in various subsidiary books and post them into ledger and prepare a trial balance of M/s Dowling Traders for the period ending June 2020.

1 June: Cash in hand ₹15,700, cash at bank ₹25,400, and capital account ₹41,100.

3 June: Bought goods for cash ₹4,000.

4 June: Purchased goods from Mahesh and Co. for ₹5,800 less 10% Trade discount.

7 June: Sold goods to Bindia and Co. for cash ₹8,900 less 20% Trade discount.

9 June: Withdrew ₹500 from bank for private use.

12 June: Sold goods to Amjad for ₹6,400.

15 June: ₹5,000 paid to Mahesh and Co. in full settlement of their account.

18 June: Goods worth ₹400 returned by Amjad.

20 June: Received ₹4,000 from Amjad.

21 June: Purchased furniture for ₹800 from Subject Furniture House on credit.

21 June: Purchased goods from Shiv and Company ₹8,700

23 June: Paid ₹6,000 to Shiv and Company by cheque, and received ₹300 discount.

26 June: Paid into bank ₹2,200.

28 June: Amjad declared insolvent, a first and final dividend of 50 paise on a rupee is received from him.

29 June: Goods worth ₹600 returned to Shiv and Co.

30 June: Interest on capital provided ₹411.

30 June: Goods worth ₹400 taken by the proprietors for their personal use.

30 June: Paid salaries to staff ₹1,800.

30 June: Cash sales ₹21,800.

30 June: Paid into bank ₹20,000.

30 June: Bought 100 shares in Hindmills Ltd at ₹11 per share. Brokerage paid ₹25.

The total of debit and credit column should tally.

June 30:   Received ₹5,900 from Bindia and Co. Discount allowed ₹100.

Solution

Journal Proper of M/s Dowling Traders

Date	Particulars	L.F.	Dr. (₹)	Cr. (₹)
2020 June 24	Furniture account (Add) Dr.		800	
	To Subject Furniture House (Add) account			800
	(Being Furniture purchased on credit)			
June 28	Bad debts account (Add) Dr.		1,000	
	To Amjad's account (Add)			1,000
	(Being 50% amount due written of as bad debts as Amjad becoming insolvent)			
June 30	Interest on capital account (Add) Dr.		411	
	To capital account (Add)			411
	(Being Interest an capital provided)			
June 30	Drawing account (Add) Dr.		400	
	To Purchase account (Less)			400
	(Being goods worth ₹400 taken by proprietors for personal use)			
June 30	Capital account (Less) Dr.		900	
	To Drawing account (Less)			900
	(Being transfer of balance of drawing account)			
	Total		**3,511**	**3,511**

Sales Book

Date	Particulars	L.F.	Amount (₹)	Amount (₹)
2020 June 7	Bindia and Co. goods sold Less 20% Trade discount		8,900 1,780	7,120
June 12	Amjad's account			6,400
June 30	Sales account (Add) Cr.			13,520

Purchase Book

Date	Particulars	L.F.	Amount (₹)	Amount (₹)
2020 June 4	Mahesh and Co. goods purchased Less 10% Trade discount		5,800 580	5,220
June 21	Shiv and Co.'s account			8,700
June 30	Purchase account (Add) Dr.			13,920

Sales Return Book

Date	Particulars	L.F.	Amount (₹)	Amount (₹)
2020 June 28	Amjad's account			400
June 30	Sales return account (Less) Dr.			400

Note:
Individual party account to be credited and the sum of sales return book to be debited in the sales return account.

Three Columnar Cash Book of M/s Dowling Traders

Date	Particulars	L.F.	Discount (₹) (Add)	Cash (₹) (Add)	Bank (₹) (Add)	Date	Particulars	L.F.	Discount (₹) (Add)	Cash (₹) (Add)	Bank (₹) (Add)
2020						2020					
1 June	To Balance b/d			15,700	25,400	3 June	By Purchase A/c			4,100	500
20 June	To Amjad's A/c			4,000		9 June	By Drawing A/c				
26 June	To Cash's A/c	C			2,200	15 June	By Mahesh and Co. A/c		220	5,000	
28 June	To Amjad's A/c			1,000		23 June	By Shiv and Co. A/c		300		
30 June	To Sales A/c			21,800		26 June	By Bank A/c	C		2,200	
30 June	To Cash A/c	C			20,000	30 June	By Advertisement A/c				500
30 June	To Bindia and Co. b/d		100	5,900		30 June	By Salaries A/c			1,800	
						30 June	By Bank A/c	C		20,000	
						30 June	By Investment in Shares A/c			1,125	
						30 June	By Balance c/d			14,175	40,600
			100	48,400	47,600		Total		520	48,400	47,600
10 June	To Balance b/d			14,175	40,600						

Note: 'C' refers to 'contra entry'. The netting of the balance of discount columns of the left hand side and the right hand side need not be done. It is to be directly charged to the income statement. The closing difference on credit side indicates normal balance, otherwise it is known as overdraft.

Purchase Return Book

Date	Particulars	L.F.	Amount (₹)	Amount (₹)
2020				
29 June	Shiv and Co.'s account			600
30 June	Purchase return account (*Less*)	Cr.		600

General Notes:

1. J.F. indicates journal folio number, that is, page number of books of original entry for cross-referencing. Balance c/d or c/f refers to balance taken to next accounting period.

2. Balance b/d or b/f refers to balance brought forward from earlier accounting period to current accounting period.

Name of Account: Furniture Account

Type of Account: Asset   **Normal Balance: Debit**

Date	Reference Account	Voucher Type	Post Ref No.	Dr. (Add)	Cr. (Less)
24 Jun	To Subject Furniture House A/c			800	
30 Jun	By Balance c/f				800
	Total			800	800
1 Jul	To Balance b/f			800	

Name of Account: Purchase Account

Type of Account: Asset   **Normal Balance: Debit**

Date	Reference Account	Voucher Type	Post Ref No.	Dr. (Add)	Cr. (Less)
4 Jun	To Cash A/c			4,100	
30 Jun	To Sundries A/c (amount as per purchase book)			13,920	
30 Jun	By Drawing A/c				400

				17,620
30 Jun	By Balance c/f			17,620
	Total		18,020	18,020
1 Jul	To Balance b/f		17,620	

Name of Account: Bindia and Co. Account

Type of Account: Asset   **Normal Balance: Debit**

Date	Reference Account	Voucher Type	Post Ref No.	Dr. (Add)	Cr. (Less)
9 Jun	To Sales A/c			7,120	
30 Jun	By Cash A/c				5,900
30 Jun	By Discount A/c				100
30 Jun	By Balance c/f				1,120
	Total			7,120	7,120
1 Jul	To Balance b/f			1,120	

Name of Account: Purchase Return Account

Type of Account: Asset   **Normal Balance: Debit**

Date	Reference Account	Voucher Type	Post Ref No.	Dr. (Add)	Cr. (Less)
30 Jun	By Sundries A/c (Amount as per purchase return book)				600
30 Jun	To Balance c/f			600	
	Total			600	600
1 Jul	By Balance b/f				600

Name of Account: Investment in Shares Account

Type of Account: Asset   **Normal Balance: Debit**

Date	Reference Account	Voucher Type	Post Ref No.	Dr. (Add)	Cr. (Less)
30 Jun	To Cash A/c			1,125	
30 Jun	By Balance c/f				1,125
	Total			1,125	1,125
1 Jul	To Balance b/f			1,125	

Name of Accout: Amjad's Account
Type of Account: Asset   Normal Balance: Debit

Date	Reference Account	Voucher Type	Post Ref No.	Dr. (Add)	Cr. (Less)
12 Jun	To Sales A/c			6,400	
18 Jun	By Sales return A/c				400
20 Jun	By Cash A/c				4,000
28 Jun	By Cash A/c				1,000
28 Jun	By Bad debt A/c				1,000
	Total			6,400	6,400
	Account Tallied				

Name of Account: Subject Furniture Account
Type of Account: Liability   Normal Balance: Credit

Date	Reference Account	Voucher Type	Post Ref No.	Dr. (Less)	Cr. (Add)
24 Jun	To Furniture A/c			800	
30 Jun	To Balance c/f				800
	Total			800	800
1 Jul	By Balance b/f				800

Name of Account: Mahesh and Co. Account
Type of Account: Liability   Normal Balance: Credit

Date	Reference Account	Voucher Type	Post Ref No.	Dr. (Less)	Cr. (Add)
1 Jun	By Purchase A/c				5,220
15 Jun	To Cash A/c			5,000	
15 Jun	To Discount A/c			220	
	Total			5,220	5,220
	Account Tallied				

Name of Account: Shiv and Co. Account
Type of Account: Liability   Normal Balance: Credit

Date	Reference Account	Voucher Type	Post Ref No.	Dr. (Less)	Cr. (Add)
21 Jun	By Purchase A/c				8,700
23 Jun	To Bank A/c			6,000	
23 Jun	To Discount A/c			300	
29 Jun	To Purchase return A/c			600	
30 Jun	To Balance c/f			1,800	
	Total			8,700	8,700
1 Jul	By Balance b/f				1,800

Name of Account: Capital Account
Type of Account: Owner's Equity Account   Normal Balance: Credit

Date	Reference Account	Voucher Type	Post Ref No.	Dr. (Less)	Cr. (Add)
1 Jun	By Balance b/d				41,100
30 Jun	To Drawing A/c			900	
30 Jun	By Interest on capital A/c				411

Date	Reference Account	Voucher Type	Post Ref No.	Dr. (Less)	Cr. (Add)
30 Jun	To Balance c/f			40,611	
	Total			41,511	41,511
1 Jul	By Balance b/f				40,611

Name of Account: Drawing Account
Type of Account: Owner's Equity Account   Normal Balance: Credit

Date	Reference Account	Voucher Type	Post Ref No.	Dr. (Less)	Cr. (Add)
9 Jun	To Bank A/c			500	
30 Jun	To Purchase A/c			400	
30 Jun	By Capital A/c				900
	Total			900	900
	Account Tallied				

Name of Account: Sales Account
Type of Account: Income   Normal Balance: Credit

Date	Reference Account	Voucher Type	Post Ref No.	Dr. (Less)	Cr. (Add)
30 Jun	By Sundries A/c (Amount as per sales book)				13,520
30 Jun	By Cash A/c				21,800
30 Jun	To Balance c/f			35,320	
	Total			35,320	35,320
1 Jul	By Balance b/f				35,320

Name of Account: Sales Return Account
Type of Account: Income   Normal Balance: Credit

Date	Reference Account	Voucher Type	Post Ref No.	Dr. (Less)	Cr. (Add)
30 Jun	To Sundries A/c (Amount as per sales return book)			400	
30 Jun	By Balance c/f				400
	Total			400	400
1 Jul	To Balance b/f			400	

Name of Account: Discount Account
Type of Account: Income   Normal Balance: Credit

Date	Reference Account	Voucher Type	Post Ref No.	Dr. (Less)	Cr. (Add)
30 Jun	To Sundries A/c (Amount as per cash book)			100	
30 Jun	By Balance c/f				100
	Total			100	100
1 Jul	To Balance b/f			100	

Name of Account: Bad Debt Account
Type of Account: Expense   Normal Balance: Credit

Date	Reference Account	Voucher Type	Post Ref No.	Dr. (Add)	Cr. (Less)
28 Jun	To Amjad's A/c			1,000	
30 Jun	By Balance c/f				1,000
	Total			1,000	1,000
1 Jul	To Balance b/f			1,000	

Name of Account: Interest on Capital Account

Type of Account: Expense   Normal Balance: Credit

Date	Reference Account	Voucher Type	Post Ref No.	Dr. (Add)	Cr. (Less)
30 Jun	To Capital A/c			411	
30 Jun	By Balance c/f				411
	Total			411	411
1 Jul	To Balance b/f			411	

Name of Account: Advertisement Account

Type of Account: Expense   Normal Balance: Credit

Date	Reference Account	Voucher Type	Post Ref No.	Dr. (Add)	Cr. (Less)
30 Jun	To Bank A/c			500	
30 Jun	By Balance c/f				500
	Total			500	500
1 Jul	To Balance b/f			500	

Name of Account: Salaries Account

Type of Account: Expense   Normal Balance: Credit

Date	Reference Account	Voucher Type	Post Ref No.	Dr. (Add)	Cr. (Less)
30 Jun	To Cash A/c			1,800	
30 Jun	By Balance c/f				1,800
	Total			1,800	1,800
1 Jul	To Balance b/f			1,800	

Trial Balance of M/s Dowling Traders
as on 30 June 2020

Sr. No.	Name of the Account	L.F.	Debit Balance (₹)	Credit Balance (₹)
1.	Capital account			40,611
2.	Furniture account		800	
3.	Subject Furniture House account			800
4.	Bad debts account		1,000	
5.	Interest on capital account		411	
6.	Purchase account		17,620	
7.	Bindia and Co. account		1,120	
8.	Sales account			35,320
9.	Shiv and Co. account			1,800
10.	Sales returns account		400	
11.	Purchase return account			600
12.	Advertisement account		500	
13.	Salaries account		1,800	
14.	Investment in shares account		1,125	
15.	Discount account			420
16.	Cash in hand as per cash book		14,175	
17.	Cash at bank as per cash book		40,600	
	Total		79,551	79,551

■ **ILLUSTRATION 7.11** State whether the balance of the following accounts should be placed in debit column or credit column of the trial balance.

1. Plant and machinery
2. Furniture
3. Salary
4. Discount allowed
5. Bank overdraft
6. Cash in hand
7. Creditors
8. Sundry debtors
9. Carriage inward
10. Carriage outward
11. Sales
12. Purchases
13. Discount received
14. Interest paid

Solution

Trial Balance as on ....

Sr. No.	Name of the Account	Modern Approach	Add or Less	Debit Balance	Credit Balance
1.	Plant and machinery	Assets	(Add)	✓	
2.	Furniture	Assets	(Add)	✓	
3.	Salary	Expenses	(Add)	✓	
4.	Discount allowed	Expenses	(Add)	✓	
5.	Bank overdraft	Liabilities	(Add)		✓
6.	Cash in hand	Assets	(Add)	✓	
7.	Creditors	Liabilities	(Add)		✓
8.	Sundry debtors	Assets	(Add)	✓	
9.	Carriage inward	Expenses	(Add)	✓	
10.	Carriage outward	Expenses	(Add)	✓	
11.	Sales	Revenues	(Add)		✓
12.	Purchases	Asset	(Add)	✓	
13.	Discount received	Revenues	(Add)		✓
14.	Interest paid	Expenses	(Add)	✓	

■ **ILLUSTRATION 7.12** Enter the following transactions in the three columnar cash book of Surendra Ram & Traders and post them to ledger accounts.

1 June 2020: Surendra Ram & Traders brought cash ₹7,500 and started business.

2 June 2020: Opened a bank account with ₹6,700.

3 June 2020: Purchased goods of ₹500 from B. Basu at a trade discount of 20% and cash discount of 5%; paid half the amount in cash and half the amount by cheque.

4 June 2020: Purchased furniture from Kishore ₹150, paid ₹50 in cash and a cheque for the balance.

5 June 2020: Sold goods ₹500 to Chaman Singh, paid by a crossed cheque of ₹490.

7 June 2020: Withdrew from bank ₹500 for office use and ₹100 for household expenses.

8 June 2020: Paid ₹400 for salary by cheque and ₹100 for rent in cash.

9 June 2020: Sold goods of ₹500 to Mohan Lal at a trade discount of 10% and received a crossed cheque for the amount.

10 June 2020: Cheque given to Kishore was returned by bank on account of signature difference.

11 June 2020: Paid cash to Kishore against dishonoured cheque.

Solution

Dr. (Add)   **Three Columnar Cash Book of Surendra Ram & Traders**   *Cr. (Less)*

Date 2020	Receipts	L.F.	Receipt No.	Discount	Cash	Bank	Date 2020	Payments	L.F.	Vou. No.	Discount	Cash	Bank
1 June	To Capital A/c				7,500		2 June	By Bank A/c	(C)			6,700	
2 June	To Cash A/c	(C)				6,700	3 June	By Purchase A/c			20	190	190
5 June	To Sales A/c			10		490	4 June	By Furniture A/c				50	100
7 June	To Bank A/c	(C)			500		7 June	By Cash A/c					500
9 June	To Sales A/c					450	7 June	By Drawings A/c					100
10 June	To Kishore's A/c					100	8 June	By Salary A/c	(C)				400
	(Cheque						8 June	By Rent A/c				100	
	dishonoured)						8 June	By Kishore's A/c				100	
							8 June	Balance c/d				860	6,450
			Total	**10**	**8,000**	**7,740**				**Total**	**20**	**8,000**	**7,740**
12 June	To Balance b/d				860	6,450							

Name of Account: Furniture A/c
Type of Account: Asset   **Normal Balance: Debit**

Date	Reference Account	Voucher Type	Post Ref No.	Dr. (Add)	Cr. (Less)
4 Jun	To Cash A/c			50	
4 Jun	To Bank A/c			100	
30 Jun	By Balance c/f				150
	Total			**100**	**150**
1 Jul	To Balance b/f			150	

Name of Account: Purchase A/c
Type of Account: Asset   **Normal Balance: Debit**

Date	Reference Account	Voucher Type	Post Ref No.	Dr. (Add)	Cr. (Less)
3 Jun	To Bank A/c			190	
3 Jun	To Cash A/c			190	
3 Jun	To Discount A/c			20	
30 Jun	By Balance c/f				400
	Total			**400**	**400**
1 Jul	To Balance b/f			400	

Name of Account: Salary A/c
Type of Account: Expense   **Normal Balance: Debit**

Date	Reference Account	Voucher Type	Post Ref No.	Dr. (Add)	Cr. (Less)
8 Jun	To Bank A/c			400	
30 Jun	By Balance c/f				400
	Total			**400**	**400**
1 Jul	To Balance b/f			400	

Name of Account: Rent A/c
Type of Account: Expense   **Normal Balance: Debit**

Date	Reference Account	Voucher Type	Post Ref No.	Dr. (Add)	Cr. (Less)
8 Jun	To Cash A/c			100	
30 Jun	By Balance c/f				100
	Total			**100**	**100**
1 Jul	To Balance b/f			100	

Name of Account: Kishore's A/c
Type of Account: Liability   **Normal Balance: Credit**

Date	Reference Account	Voucher Type	Post Ref No.	Dr. (Less)	Cr. (Add)
10 Jun	By Bank A/c				100
11 Jun	To Cash A/c			100	
	Total			**100**	**100**
	Account Tallied				

Name of Account: Drawing A/c
Type of Account: Expense A/c   **Normal Balance: Debit**

Date	Reference Account	Voucher Type	Post Ref No.	Dr. (Add)	Cr. (Less)
7 Jun	To Bank A/c			100	
30 Jun	By Balance c/f				100
	Total			**100**	**100**
1 Jul	To Balance b/f			100	

Name of Account: Capital A/c
Type of Account: Capital   **Normal Balance: Credit**

Date	Reference Account	Voucher Type	Post Ref No.	Dr. (Less)	Cr. (Add)
1 Jun	By Cash A/c				7,500
30 Jun	To Balance c/f			7,500	
	Total			**7,500**	**7,500**
1 Jul	By Balance b/f				7,500

Name of Account: Sales A/c
Type of Account: Income   **Normal Balance: Credit**

Date	Reference Account	Voucher Type	Post Ref No.	Dr. (Less)	Cr. (Add)
5 Jun	By Cash A/c				490
5 Jun	By Discount A/c				10
9 Jun	By Bank A/c				450
30 Jun	To Balance c/f			950	
	Total			**950**	**950**
1 Jul	By Balance b/f				950

Name of Account: Discount A/c

Type of Account: Income   **Normal Balance: Credit**

Date	Reference Account	Voucher Type	Post Ref No.	Dr. (Less)	Cr. (Add)
11 Jun	To Sundry Debtors A/c			10	
11 Jun	By Sundry Creditors A/c				20
30 Jun	To Balance c/f			10	
	Total			**20**	**20**
1 Jul	By Balance b/f				10

■ **ILLUSTRATION 7.13** Some of the transactions of Sujata's business for the year 2020 are given in the following text. Enter them in the journal proper:

Jan. 1: Opening balances of assets and liabilities: machinery ₹5,000; furniture ₹3,000, stock of goods ₹4,000; debtors ₹3,000; and creditors ₹5,000.

Feb. 3: Goods worth ₹200 was given as charity to an orphanage.

Mar. 5: Purchased a machine costing ₹1,200 in exchange of goods of ₹1,000.

April 10: Goods of ₹1,500 was burnt by fire for which the insurance company accepted a claim of ₹1,000 and the damaged goods was sold to Mahendra for ₹100.

May 9: Goods worth ₹300 was taken away for personal use.

June 16: Goods of ₹100 was distributed as free samples.

June 30: A fixed deposit of ₹2,000 made in 2010 with Arvind Mills matured and was renewed with interest of ₹400.

July 20: ₹200 payable to Dipen was now accepted by Prabhat as his debt.

July 25: A cupboard was purchased for household use in exchange of goods ₹400.

Aug. 11: ₹100 due from Atul is now accepted as payable by Mehul.

Sept. 13: A machine of ₹1,000 was purchased from Hina Stores and ₹100 for railway freight was added in the invoice.

Oct. 16: Old furniture sold to Paresh ₹100.

Nov. 24: ₹200 due from Samir was written off as he was declared insolvent.

Dec. 31: ₹200 has become payable for interest to Mohit.

Solution

Sujata's Journal

Date 2020	Particulars		L.F.	Dr. (₹)	Cr. (₹)
1 Jan	Machinery A/c (Add)	Dr.		5,000	
	Furniture A/c (Add)	Dr.		3,000	
	Stock A/c (Add)	Dr.		4,000	
	Debtors A/c (Add)	Dr.		3,000	
	To Creditors A/c (Add)				5,000
	To Capital A/c (Add)				10,000
	(Opening balances of assets and liabilities brought into books)				
3 Feb	Charity A/c (Add)	Dr.		200	
	To Goods given in charity A/c (Less)				200
	(Goods given as charity to an orphanage)				
5 March	Machinery A/c (Add)	Dr.		1,200	
	To Sales A/c (Add)				1,200
	(Machinery costing ₹1,200 was purchased in exchange of goods worth ₹1,000)				
10 April	Insurance Co.'s A/c (Add)	Dr.		1,000	
	Mahendra's A/c (Add)	Dr.		100	
	Loss by Fire A/c (Add)	Dr.		400	
	To Goods destroyed by fire A/c (Less)				1,500
	(Goods worth ₹1,500 destroyed by fire against which Insurance Co. accepted a claim of ₹1,000 and damaged goods sold for ₹100)				
9 May	Drawings A/c (Add)	Dr.		300	
	To Goods taken for personal use A/c (Less)				300
	(Goods withdrawn from business for personal use)				
16 June	Advertisement A/c (Add)	Dr.		100	
	To Goods given for advertisement A/c (Less)				100
	(Goods of ₹100 given as free samples)				
30 June	Fixed Deposit (Arvind Mills)(2020) A/c (Add)	Dr.		2,400	
	To Interest A/c (Add)				400
	To Fixed deposit (Arvind Mills) (2010) A/c (Less)				2,000
	(Fixed Deposit with Arvind Mills matured and was renewed along with interest due)				
20 July	Dipen's A/c (Less)	Dr.		200	
	To Prabhat's A/c (Less)				200
	(Amount payable to Dipen now accepted as debt by Prabhat)				
25 July	Drawings A/c (Add)	Dr.		400	
	To Sales A/c (Add)				400
	(Purchased a cupboard for private use in exchange of goods)				
11 Aug	Mehul's A/c (Less)	Dr.		100	
	To Atul's A/c (Less)				100
	(Amount due from Atul now accepted by Mehul as payable by him)				

13 Sept	Machinery A/c (Add)	Dr.	1,100	
	To Hina Stores A/c (Add)			1,100
	(Machine costing ₹1,000 purchased from Hina stores and ₹100 was paid by them for railway freight)			
16 Oct	Paresh's A/c (Add)	Dr.	100	
	To Furniture A/c (Less)			100
	(Old furniture sold to Paresh)			
24 Nov	Bad debts A/c (Add)	Dr.	200	
	To Samir's A/c (Less)			200
	(Amount due from Samir now written off as he is declared insolvent)			
31 Dec	Interest A/c (Add)	Dr.	200	
	To Mohit's A/c (Add)			200
	(Amount of interest became due to Mohit)			
	Total		**20,600**	**20,600**

■ **ILLUSTRATION 7.14** Journalize the transactions given as under in the books of Nandan.

Date 2020	Particulars
1 January	Nandan starts business with ₹20,000.
2 January	Nandan purchases furniture for ₹850 and typewriter for ₹1,500. Payment is made by cheque.
3 January	Goods purchased on credit from Yogi ₹5,000.
4 January	Goods purchased for cash from Namita ₹1,000.
5 January	Goods sold on credit to Mallika ₹2,000.
6 January	Goods sold for cash to Lila ₹1,000.
7 January	Paid rent for January ₹200.
8 January	Paid for postage stamps, ₹100.
9 January	Received cash from Mallika ₹1,900.
10 January	Issued cheque to Yogi ₹5,000.
11 January	Deposited ₹1,000 in a bank.
12 January	Paid insurance premium ₹450 by cheque.

Solution

Journal Entries in the Books of Nandan for the Month of January 2020

Date	Particulars		L.F.	Dr. (₹)	Cr (₹)
1 January	Cash A/c (Add)	Dr.		20,000	
	To Capital A/c (Add)				20,000
2 January	Furniture A/c (Add)	Dr.		850	
	Typewriter A/c (Add)	Dr.		1,500	
	To Bank A/c (Less)				2,350
3 January	Purchase A/c (Add)	Dr.		5,000	
	To Yogi's A/c (Add)				5,000
4 January	Purchase A/c (Add)	Dr.		1,000	
	To Cash A/c (Less)				1,000
5 January	Mallika's A/c (Add)	Dr.		2,000	
	To Sales A/c (Add)				2,000
6 January	Cash A/c (Add)	Dr.		1,000	
	To Sales A/c (Add)				1,000
7 January	Rent A/c (Add)	Dr.		200	
	To Cash A/c (Less)				200
8 January	Postage stamps A/c (Add)	Dr.		100	
	To Cash A/c (Less)				100
9 January	Cash A/c (Add)	Dr.		1,900	
	Discount allowed A/c (Add)	Dr.		100	
	To Mallika's A/c (Less)				5,000
10 January	Yogi's A/c (Less)	Dr.		5,000	
	To Bank A/c (Less)				5,000
11 January	Bank A/c (Add)	Dr.		1,000	
	To Cash A/c (Less)				1,000
12 January	Insurance premium A/c (Add)	Dr.		450	
	To Bank A/c (Less)				450

■ **ILLUSTRATION 7.15** There was an error in the trial balance of Mr Arora on 31 December 2020 and the difference in books was carried to a suspense account. On going through the books you find that

1. ₹5,400 received from Rajiv were posted to the debit of his account.
2. ₹1,000 being purchase returns were posted to the debit of purchase account.
3. Discount of ₹2,000 received were posted to the debit of discount account.
4. ₹2,740 paid for repairs to car were debited to motor car account as ₹1,740.
5. ₹4,000 paid to Sanjai were debited to Sanjiv's account.

Answer the following questions:

(a) Give journal entries to rectify the above errors and ascertain the amount transferred to suspense account on 31 December 2020 by showing the suspense account, assuming that the suspense account is balanced after the above corrections.

(b) How will you rectify the errors, if no suspense account is to be opened?

Solution

(a) When suspense account is opened

	Particulars		L.F.	Dr. (₹)	Cr. (₹)
(1)	Suspense A/c (Add)	Dr.		10,800	
	To Rajiv's A/c (Less)				10,800
	(Posting on wrong side of Rajiv's account now corrected by writing double amount on correct side)				
(2)	Suspense A/c (Add)	Dr.		2,000	
	To Purchase A/c (Less)				1,000
	To Purchase return A/c (Add)				1,000
	(Wrong posting of purchase return to purchase account now corrected)				
(3)	Suspense A/c (Add)	Dr.		4,000	
	To Discount A/c (Add)				4,000
	(Posting of discount received to the wrong side of discount account now rectified)				
(4)	Repairs A/c (Add)	Dr.		2,740	
	To Motor car A/c (Less)				1,740
	To Suspense A/c (Less)				1,000
	(Wrong debit given to Motor car account for repairs, now rectified)				
(5)	Sanjai's A/c (Less)	Dr.		4,000	
	To Sanjiv's A/c (Add)				4,000
	(Wrong debit given to Sanjiv's for cash paid by us to Sanjai now rectified)				

Note:

As the suspense account is now closed, it must have been credited with ₹15,800 (10,800 + 4,000 – 1,000), previously when the mistakes could not be located, as can be seen from the following suspense account. Hence, it is treated as opening balance before starting of rectification entries, as balancing amount.

Name of Account: Suspense A/c

Type of Account: Asset   **Normal Balance: Debit**

Date	Reference Account	Voucher Type	Post Ref No.	Dr. (Add)	Cr. (Less)
	By Balance b/f (Opening Balance)				15,800
	To Rajiv's A/c			10,800	
	To Purchase A/c			1,000	
	To Purchase return A/c			1,000	
	To Discount A/c			4,000	
	By Repairs A/c				1,000
	Total			**16,800**	**16,800**

(b) If no suspense account has been opened, the errors would have been rectified as follows:

1. ₹5,400 received from Rajiv have been posted to his debit instead of to his credit. Hence, ₹5,400 should be credited to his account for cancelling the wrong debit and ₹5,400 again should be credited to him for giving correct credit. Thus, Rajiv's account will be credited with ₹10,800 as 'By wrong debit given'. No journal entry will be made.

2. As purchase account has been wrongly debited, it should now be credited with ₹1,000. The correct credit should be given to purchase returns account as wrong debit given to purchases A/c. Thus, both accounts are credited and no journal entry is made.

3. Discount is received, which should be credited to discount account. It has been wrongly debited to that account. Hence double the amount will be credited to discount account as 'By wrong debit given.'

4. ₹2,740 will now be debited to repairs account and ₹1,740 will be credited to motor car account.

5. Sanjiv's account has been wrongly debited instead of debiting the account of. Sanjai. So, now debit Sanjai's account by ₹4,000; and with same amount credit Sanjiv's account.

■ **ILLUSTRATION 7.16** A ledger keeper of Acharya and Co. could not tally the trial balance. He transferred the amount of ₹296, being excess of the debit side total, to the suspense account. The following errors were subsequently discovered:

1. Sales book was overcast by ₹300.

2. Purchase of furniture worth ₹615 was passed through the purchase book.

3. An amount of ₹55 received from M/s Agarwal and Co. was posted to their account as ₹550.

4. A cash sale of ₹1,235 though duly entered in the cash book was posted to the sales account as ₹235.

5. Purchase returns book total on a folio was carried forward as ₹221 instead of ₹112.

6. Rest of the difference was due to a wrong total in the salaries account in the ledger. Pass the necessary journal entries and prepare suspense account in the books of Acharya and Co.

Solution

Understanding the Errors

Before we make rectification entries let us understand how errors occur or are made:

1. Sales account is credited with ₹300 more, because total of sales book was more by ₹300 than the correct one. Now sales account should be debited with ₹300 and as there is no mistake in any other account, suspense account must be credited.

2. Purchase of furniture is not a purchase of goods and therefore cannot be entered in purchase book. Hence, purchase account should be credited to cancel the wrong debit given to it and correct debit should be given to furniture account. No suspense account is involved here because the error is two-sided and affects two accounts.

3. Agarwal & Co. got an excess credit of ₹495 (550 – 55). Hence, their account should be debited with ₹495 and suspense account should be credited with the same amount, as no other account is involved.

4. In this case, sales account got less credit of ₹1,000. Hence sales account should be credited with ₹1,000 and similar debit must be given to suspense account, because there is no mistake in any other account.

5. The total of purchase return book is credited to purchase returns account, because goods are sent out. Here, the total is more by ₹109 (₹221 – ₹112) than the correct one. Consequently purchase returns account got an excess credit. Hence, purchase returns account must be debited.

6. In order to close the suspense account there is a shortage of ₹200 on the debit side. It means that the error relating to salaries account is for ₹200. To rectify this error, suspense account is debited with ₹200 and salaries account must be credited with that amount.

The rectification entries are as follows:

Journal Entries of Acharya and Co. for Rectification of Errors

	Particulars		L.F.	Dr. (₹)	Cr. (₹)
(1)	Sales A/c (Less)	Dr.		300	
	To Suspense A/c (Less)				300
	(Entry to rectify an error of overcasting sales book)				
(2)	Furniture A/c (Add)	Dr.		615	
	To Purchase A/c (Less)				615
	(Entry to rectify an error of recording purchase of furniture in the purchase book)				
(3)	Agarwal & Co's A/c (Less)	Dr.		495	
	To Suspense A/c (Less)				495
	(Entry to rectify an error of crediting Agarwal & Co. with ₹550 instead of with ₹55)				

(4)	Suspense A/c (Add) To Sales A/c (Add) (Entry to rectify an error of crediting Sales A/c with ₹1000 less)	Dr.	1,000	1,000
(5)	Purchase returns A/c (Less) To Suspense A/c (Less) (Entry to rectify an error of carrying forward ₹112 instead of ₹221)	Dr.	109	109
(6)	Suspense A/c (Add) To Salaries A/c (Less) (Entry to rectify an error in the salaries account)	Dr.	200	200

■ **ILLUSTRATION 7.17** The following errors were traced while preparing the final accounts of a firm. How will they be rectified?

1. ₹3,000 paid for the purchase of machinery has been entered in purchase book.
2. Goods worth ₹838 sold to K. Kapoor on credit is recorded as purchase of ₹983 in the purchase book.
3. Goods valued at ₹240 is sold to A. Ahuja on credit, for which an entry was made correctly in the sales book, but while posting it, A. Ahuja's Account has been credited with ₹420.
4. The monthly total of purchase book for December 2020 has been overcast by ₹250 through an error.
5. Repairing charges of ₹180 paid for repairing a machine have been debited to the machinery account.
6. ₹400 paid to Bhagwandas Misra, the owner of the shop, for rent has been debited to his personal account.
7. ₹320 received in cash from Pravin Kumar are entered in the discount column of cash book through an error.
8. Goods worth ₹550 were distributed as free samples. But no entry is made in the books.
9. ₹220 received from K. Krishnakumar which were written off last year as bad debts was received in cash, which has been credited to his personal account.
10. The balance of ₹300 of the salaries account has been shown in the credit balance column in the trial balance.

Solution

Understanding the Errors

1. The purchase of machinery cannot be entered in the purchase book. Wrong debit is given to purchase account. Hence purchase account should be credited. Correct debit should be given to machinery account.
2. The sale of ₹838 made to K. Kapoor has been entered as ₹983 in the purchase book through an error. In order to cancel this error, ₹983 will be debited to K. Kapoor's account and credited to the purchase account. Besides, the correct entry must be made for sale. For that, ₹838 will be debited to K. Kapoor's account and credited to the sales account. Here both the entries have Kapoor's account and credited to the sales account. Here both the entries have been combined.
3. While posting from the sales book to A. Ahuja's account, his account should have been debited with ₹240 but, instead, ₹420 is credited. Thus in order to cancel the wrong credit ₹420 should be debited to his account, and

the correct amount of ₹240 should also be debited. Thus, a total of ₹660 should be debited to Ahuja's account.

4. No journal entry should be made to rectify this entry. As the total of purchase book is more by ₹250 the purchase account has got an excess debit of ₹250. This should be rectified by writing ₹250 on the credit side of purchase account.
5. Repairing charges are revenue expenses and should always be debited to repairing charges account, whereas here it has been treated as capital expenditure and wrongly debited to machinery account. Hence, machinery account must be credited and repairing charges account must be debited with ₹180 to rectify this mistake.
6. The amount paid for rent cannot be debited to the personal account of the owner. So the amount which has been wrongly debited to Bhagwandas Misra should be credited to his account.
7. The amount received from Pravin Kumar has been entered in the discount column on the debit side in the cash book; so it was incorrectly debited to the discount account from there. To rectify the error, the amount should be credited to the discount account. Besides, since cash comes in the amount has to be debited to the cash account.
   In Pravin Kumar's account, the posting on the credit side would have been made correctly. But in the particulars column it might have been written in discount account, whereas it should be written in cash account.
8. Goods worth ₹550 were distributed as free samples for which advertisement account should be debited and goods distributed as samples account should be credited. As no entry is made so far, a fresh journal entry as above should now be made.
9. The amount written off as bad debts last year has been received from K. Krishnakumar. When bad debts were written off, his account must have been closed by crediting his account with the same amount. When such amount is received back, it should not be credited to K. Krishnakumar's account, but it should be credited to the bad debts recovered account.
10. The salaries account shows a debit balance and should therefore, be put in the debit side column, instead it has been shown on the credit side column. Hence double the amount (i.e., ₹600) should now be shown on the debit side column.

The rectification entries are as follows:

Journal Entries for Rectification of Errors

	Particulars	L.F.	Dr. (₹)	Cr. (₹)
(1)	Machinery A/c (Add) .... Dr.		3,000	
	To Purchase A/c (Less)			3,000
	(Entry to rectify an error of entering purchase of machinery in the purchase book)			
(2)	K. Kapoor's A/c (Add) .... Dr.		1,821	
	To Purchase A/c (Less)			983
	To Sales A/c (Add)			838
	(Entry to rectify an error of recording credit sale in the purchase book)			
(3)	No journal entry will be made. But ₹660 should be written on the debit side of A. Ahuja's Account.			
(4)	No journal entry will be made, But ₹250 will be written on the credit side of Purchases A/c to cancel excess debit.			
(5)	Repairing charges A/c (Add) .... Dr.		180	
	To Machinery A/c (Less)			180
	(Entry to rectify an error of debiting Machinery A/c for repairing charges)			
(6)	Rent A/c (Add) .... Dr.		400	
	To Bhagwandas Misra's A/c (Less)			400
	(Entry to rectify an error of debiting Personal A/c of the owner for the rent paid)			
(7)	Cash A/c (Add) .... Dr.		320	
	To Discount A/c (Add)			320
	(Entry to rectify an error of entering cash received from Pravin Kumar into discount column)			
(8)	Advertisement A/c (Add) .... Dr.		550	
	To goods distributed as free samples A/c (Less)			550
	(Entry to record the distribution of free samples omitted to be recorded)			
(9)	K. Krishnakumar's A/c (Add) .... Dr.		220	
	To Bad debts recovered A/c (Add)			220
	(Entry to rectify an error of wrongly crediting Krishnakumar's A/c with amount received against bad debts written off)			
(10)	No journal entry is necessary. Only ₹600 should be shown in the debit side column of the trial balance			

■ **ILLUSTRATION 7.18** In the following trial balance, there are some errors. Correct them and prepare a correct trial balance as on 31 December 2020.

Solution

Trial Balance as on 31 December 2020

Name of Account	L.F.	Dr. (₹)	Cr. (₹)
Cash		540	
Cash at bank		2,630	
Purchase			40,675
Sales		98,780	
Wages		10,480	
Lighting and fuel		4,730	
Carriage inward			3,200
Carriage outward		2,040	
Opening stock of goods			5,760
Building			30,000
Land		10,000	
Goods returned (Customer)			680
Goods returned (Supplier)		500	
Salary		15,000	
Machinery and Tools		27,500	
Postages, telegrams and stationery		1,300	
Railway freight		800	
Trade expenses		200	
Office expenses		700	
Discount (Received)			500
Insurance		600	
Drawings			5,245
Capital			71,000
Sundry debtors		15,000	
Sundry creditors			6,300
Total		**1,90,800**	**1,90,800**

Trial Balance as on 31 December 2020

Name of Account	L.F.	Dr. (₹)	Cr. (₹)
Cash on hand		540	
Cash at bank		2,630	
Purchase		40,675	
Sales			98,780
Wages		10,480	
Lighting and fuel		4,730	
Carriage inward		3,200	
Carriage outward		2,040	
Opening stock of goods		5,760	
Building		30,000	
Land		10,000	
Goods returned (Customer)		680	
Goods returned (Supplier)			500
Salary		15,000	
Machinery and tools		27,500	
Postages, telegrams, and stationery		1,300	
Railway freight		800	
Trade expenses		200	
Office expenses		700	
Discount (Received)			500
Insurance		600	
Drawings		5,245	
Capital			61,000
Sundry debtors		15,000	
Sundry creditors			6,300
Total		**1,77,080**	**1,77,080**

 # SUMMARY

- Financial statements are the result of the accounting process for a firm.
- Accounting mechanics help the accounting process.
- Special journals are maintained by firms based on specific needs such as purchase journal, sales journal, cash and bank journal, etc. These are known as books of original entry. Any entry made to adjust or reverse a part of the transaction is known as adjustment entry.
- Any entry made to close an account after the trial balance has been closed is known as closing entry.
- Books of prime entry form the record of all transactions made and documented by the business.
- The transactions are recorded in chronological order.
- A ledger is the grouping of accounts that are used to prepare financial statements for a business or an entity.
- A ledger is the principal book of entry.
- An account is a standardized format used to record information on individual transactions to facilitate the preparation of periodical financial statements and to provide a continuous check on the accuracy of the recording of the transactions.
- For any given account, the difference between debit and credit amounts is known as account balance.
- The modern approach of accounting equation classifies accounts into five types and uses the following method.

Account type	Debit side	Credit side
1. Assets	Add	Less
2. Liabilities	Less	Add
3. Capital	Less	Add
4. Revenue	Less	Add
5. Expenses	Add	Less

- Posting is the process of transferring debits and credits from the journal and other books of original entry to their respective accounts in the ledger.
- The process of finding out the net balance of account after considering the totals of both debit and credit appearing in the account is termed balancing of account.
- A trial balance is the listing of all the accounts, and their respective balances. The two sides of a trial balance must tally.
- A rectification entry is passed to nullify the effect of errors that occurred at the time of original recording of an event or transaction in the books of accounts.
- Generally, an accountant can rectify the errors at two stages: before the trial balance is prepared and after the trial balance is prepared.
- When an accountant has insufficient time to find out the error, a temporary suspense account is created to tally the trial balance. The difference in trial balance will be taken to the suspense account, which in turn helps tally the trial balance and in turn prepare financial statements.

 # KEYWORDS

Account An account is a standardized format used to record information on individual transactions to facilitate the preparation of periodical financial statements and to provide a continuous check on the accuracy of the recording of the transactions.

Account balance It is the difference between the debit and credit amounts of any given account.

Credit It is an entry on the right side of an account.

Credit balance It is the excess of the credit side of an account over the debit side.

Debit It is an entry on the left side of an account.

Debit balance It is the excess of the debit side of an account over the credit side.

Journal It is a book that contains a chronological record of transactions.

Journalizing It is the process of recording transactions in a journal.

Ledger A ledger is the grouping of accounts that are used to prepare financial statements for a business or an entity. A ledger is a principal book of entry although not an independent record.

Normal balance It is the positive balance of an account.

Posting It is the process of transferring debits and credits from the journal and other books of original entry to the ledger.

Prime document It is the document in which transactions are recorded; it is also called voucher document or source document.

Purchase journal It records credit purchases of business goods.

Sales journal It records credit sales of business goods.

Tallied It means that the total of the debit side of an account is equal to the total of the credit side.

Trial balance A trial balance is a listing of all the accounts and of their balances.

 # QUESTIONS

I. Choose the correct option.

1. The adjustment to be made for depreciation is
   (a) Credit profit and loss account and deduct depreciation from fixed assets.
   (b) Credit profit and loss account and add depreciation to fixed assets.
   (c) Debit profit and loss account and add depreciation to fixed assets.
   (d) Debit profit and loss account and deduct depreciation from fixed assets.

2. The adjustment to be made for income received in advance is
   (a) Add income received in advance to respective income and show it as a liability.
   (b) Deduct income received in advance from respective income and show it as a liability.
   (c) Add income received in advance to respective income and show it as an asset.
   (d) Deduct income received in advance from respective income and show it as a liability.

3. Net profit is equal to
   (a) Gross profit minus expenses.
   (b) Net sales plus purchases minus gross profit.
   (c) Expenses minus gross profit.
   (d) Gross profit minus net sales plus purchases.

4. Which of the following is/are incorrect?
   (a) Gross Profit + Salary + Direct Expenses + Purchases + Closing Stock = Opening Stock
   (b) Gross Profit + Direct Expenses + Purchases – Closing Stock + Opening Stock = Sales
   (c) Gross Profit + Direct Expenses + Purchases – Opening Stock + Closing Stock = Sales
   (d) Gross Profit + Direct Expenses + Purchases + Opening Stock + Closing Stock = Sales

5. The cost of sales is equal to
   (a) Opening stock minus purchases.
   (b) Opening stock plus purchases.
   (c) Opening stock minus purchases plus closing stock.
   (d) Opening stock plus purchases minus closing stock.

6. The adjustment to be made for interest on capital is
   (a) Debit profit and loss account and deduct interest from capital.
   (b) Credit profit and loss account and deduct interest from capital.
   (c) Debit profit and loss account and add interest to capital.
   (d) Credit profit and loss account and deduct interest from capital.

7. The adjustment to be made for interest on drawing is
   (a) Debit profit and loss account and add interest to drawings.
   (b) Credit profit and loss account and add interest to drawings.
   (c) Debit profit and loss account and deduct interest from drawings.
   (d) Credit profit and loss account and deduct interest from drawings.

8. Which one of the following is correct?
   (a) Gross Profit + Purchases + Sales = Net Profit
   (b) Gross Profit + Purchases + Administrative and Other Expenses = Net Profit
   (c) Gross Profit + Sales + Administrative and Other Expenses = Net Profit
   (d) Gross Profit – Administrative and Selling Expenses = Net Profit

9. If the gross profit of a trader is ₹10,000 and the net profit is 75% of the gross profit, her expenses total
   (a) ₹7,500   (b) ₹2,500
   (c) ₹750   (d) ₹250

10. The adjustment to be made for provision for doubtful debts is
    (a) Credit profit and loss account and deduct the provision from debtors.
    (b) Debit profit and loss account and deduct the provision from debtors.
    (c) Credit profit and loss account and add the provision to debtors.
    (d) Debit profit and loss account and add the provision to debtors.

11. The adjustment to be made for outstanding expenses is
    (a) Add outstanding expenses to respective expenses and show it as asset.
    (b) Deduct outstanding expenses from respective expenses and show it as liability.
    (c) Add outstanding expenses to respective expenses and show it as liability.
    (d) Deduct outstanding expenses from respective expenses and show it as asset.

12. Depreciation is to be calculated on
    (a) Fixed assets   (b) Outward charges
    (c) Current assets   (d) Intangible assets

13. If a trader's net sales amount to ₹18,000, gross profit is 60% of sales, and net profit is 40% of sales, her expenses are
    (a) ₹10,800   (b) ₹7,200
    (c) ₹3,600   (d) ₹1,800

14. The adjustment to be made for period expenses is
    (a) Deduct prepaid expenses from respective expenses and show it as liability.
    (b) Add prepaid expenses to respective expenses and show it as asset.
    (c) Deduct prepaid expenses from respective expenses and show it as asset.
    (d) Add prepaid expenses to respective expenses and show it as liability.

15. Gross profit is equal to
    (a) Gross profit minus expenses.
    (b) Purchases plus stock minus net sales.
    (c) Net sales plus selling price of stock minus purchases.
    (d) Net sales minus cost price of sales.

16. Which one of the following statements is correct
    (a) Gross profit on trading is entered on the right side of the trading account and carried down to the left side of the profit and loss account.
    (b) Gross profit on trading is entered on the left side of the trading account and carried down to the right side of the profit and loss account.
    (c) Net profit on trading is entered on the right side of the trading account and carried down to the left side of the profit and loss account.
    (d) Net profit on trading is entered on the left side of the trading account and carried down to the right side of the profit and loss account.

17. A trader buys goods worth ₹2,000 and pays carriage worth ₹65. She sells the goods for ₹3,500 incurring expenses totalling ₹725.
    (i) The trader's gross profit is
        (a) ₹1,500   (b) ₹1,435
        (c) ₹1,345   (d) ₹710
    (ii) The trader's net profit is
        (e) ₹1,500   (f) ₹1,435
        (g) ₹1,345   (h) ₹710

II. Fill in the blanks.

1. _____ is a special term indicating the recording of entries in the ledger.
2. Cash purchases are entered in the _____.
3. Suppliers' account will usually be _____ when goods are received on credit.
4. Withdrawal of goods by the proprietor are generally recorded in the _____.
5. The _____ of the sales returns book is posted to the side of the sales returns account.
6. The goods account is divided into _____.
7. The main book of account is _____.
8. If there are 51 credit purchases during a given month, then there will be _____ postings from the purchase book at the end of the month.
9. Subsidiary journals are all books of _____ entry.
10. The ledger is a book of _____ entry.
11. The bank statement is sent by _____ to _____.
12. Entries that occur _____ are each allotted a subsidiary journal.
13. The _____ column in a ledger account shows the location of each entry in the journal.

14. A _____ balance in the cash book will reflect in a credit balance in the pass book.
15. Every prime entry must have a _____ appended to it.
16. Purchase account will always have a balance.
17. For purpose of reconciliation only the _____ columns of the cash are to be considered.
18. An allowance of ₹300 given to Mr Tanus for prompt payment will be debited to the _____ account.
19. Cash discount allowed will appear on the _____ side of the purchaser's account in the books of the seller.
20. Payment from petty cash is used for _____.
21. The value of goods rejected for poor quality and returned by a customer is entered in the _____ initially.
22. Bank charges decrease _____ balance.
23. The receiver of goods returned will send a _____ note to the returner.
24. Accounts of _____ items always show a debit balance.
25. The pass book is .
26. The document from which the returns to suppliers are recorded is known as_____ .
27. A bank reconciliation statement is prepared to ____ _____.
28. The entries in the purchase returns book are based on _____ issued by the concern.
29. An aspect that is debited in the journal entry will be given a _____ in the ledger account.
30. A credit sale of a non-trading asset will be recorded in the _____.
31. Cash receipts and payments are recorded in _____ book.
32. Non-cash transactions are normally recorded through _____.
33. The receiver of a benefit is to be _____.
34. _____ and _____ are the two aspects of every business transaction.
35. Motor vehicles account is _____ (personal/real/nominal) account.
36. The double-entry _____ of bookkeeping records the aspect of a transaction in two _____.
37. Summary of balances of ledger account is called _____.
38. The cash transactions and credit transactions are entered in _____ and _____ respectively.

III. Indicate whether the following statements are True or False.

1. In case of overdraft, the bank account will show a credit balance.
2. A trial balance is a list of the balances in the ledger.
3. Drawing account will appear on the credit side of a trial balance.
4. A credit note must not be sent for returns inward of a non-trading asset.
5. Undercasting of the receipts side increases the overdraft balance in the cash book.
6. Capital account will always have a credit balance.
7. If a trial balance tallies, it always means that none of the transactions has been completely omitted.
8. A trial balance will not tally if a transaction is omitted.
9. A credit balance in the pass book indicates excess of deposits over withdrawals.
10. A dishonoured cheque should be recorded on both the debit and credit sides of the cash book.
11. Any account can have only a debit or a credit balance.
12. Debit note is a note informing the seller that buyer owes some money in addition to invoice.
13. The balance of the goods account shows the value of stock in hand.
14. In case of overdraft (i.e., excess of withdrawals over deposits) both the pass book and the cash book will have credit balances.

15. Entries of goods in trade must be made first in the main journal and then in the subsidiary books.
16. Suppliers' accounts in the cash book will be reflected as a credit balance in the pass book.
17. A debit balance in the cash book will be reflected as a credit balance in the pass book.
18. A debit note is normally received by the seller of the goods.
19. A customer to whom goods have been sold on credit cannot avail a cash discount.
20. A suspense account is opened when the cash book and bank statement differ.
21. If cheques deposited but not cleared is an 'add' item, their cheques issued but not presented will have to be 'less'.
22. A rebate allowed to a customer on the bill value because of a complaint from him about quality subsequent to the transaction will be recorded in the return inward book.
23. In drawing of a trial balance, sundry creditors balance will appear on the credit side.
24. Balancing of all accounts must be done at the end of each day.
25. A bank reconciliation statement as on 31 December 2012 can be made by comparing the cash book of December 2012 with the pass book of January 2013.
26. The purchase account in the ledger is debited individually by the value of each transaction in the purchase book.
27. A debit note is sent usually on receipt of a credit note.

IV. Solve the following problems.

1. In the books of Shri Panchal Stores, write journal entries for the following transactions, draw necessary account in the ledger, and post them accordingly.

2020

1 April: Cash ₹40,000 and furniture of ₹20,000 brought into the business.
2 April: Goods of ₹36,000 sold to Dhaval Stores at 10% trade discount. For this, Dhaval Stores paid a cash of ₹15,000.
3 April: ₹18,000 deposited in a bank.
4 April: Goods of ₹20,000 purchased at 12% trade discount from Dhara Stores. For this a cheque of ₹8,000 was given.
5 April: Withdrew ₹5,000 from the bank for office expenses and ₹4,000 for household expenses.
7 April: ₹2,200 paid for office expenses .
8 April: Against the dues of ₹4,830, paid ₹4,800 in cash for final settlement to Jayeshbhai.
9 April: Due to a fire in godown, goods of ₹3,200 burnt by fire and insurance company accepted a claim of ₹2,600 for the same.
10 April: Goods of ₹6,600 purchased from Anil Traders and towards this, payment of ₹2,600 made in cash.
12 April: Paid ₹4,800 for shop rent and ₹6,000 for house rent.
13 April: Paid ₹4,000 to Anil Traders by cheque.

2. From the following transactions, pass journal entries in the books of Badshah, post them in the ledger, find out the balance of each account and state whether it is a debit balance or a credit balance. Also mention the amount.

2020

1 Nov: Brought cash of ₹75,000 and goods of ₹15,000 into the business.
2 Nov: Deposited ₹40,000 in the bank.
3 Nov: Goods of ₹15,000 purchased from Aunti at 10% trade discount and ₹3,000 cash paid.
5 Nov: Goods of ₹20,000 sold at 30% profit to Govind at 10% trade discount. Govind gave a cheque of ₹5,000, which has been deposited in the bank.

7 Nov: Paid salary of ₹4,500 and cartage of ₹450.

8 Nov: Fire insurance premium of ₹2,000 paid by cheque.

10 Nov: Paid ₹3,500 by cheque to Shah Agency for an advertisement in newspaper.

12 Nov: Goods of ₹24,000 purchased from Chakan at 10% trade discount and ₹9,600 cash paid to Chakan.

14 Nov: Paid ₹10,000 by cheque to Aunti and the balance amount in cash.

15 Nov: A cheque of ₹18,400 sent by Govind, which has been deposited in the bank.

16 Nov: Paid ₹4,000 from the business for school fees of daughter Urja.

3. Given below are a few transactions of Mr Kovid for the month of January 2020. Record the transactions in the journal and prepare a trial balance.

1 January 2020: Commenced business with cash ₹8,00,000.

2 January 2020: Taken bank loan for ₹1,00,000 @ 5 %.

7 January 2020: Purchased land and fixtures worth ₹3,00,000.

8 January 2020: Purchased machine worth ₹2,00,000.

15 January 2020: Purchased raw material on credit for ₹1,00,000 from Ram.

17 January 2020: Sold goods worth ₹1,55,000 to Ranjan on credit.

18 January 2020: Paid ₹95,000 to Ram in full settlement.

20 January 2020: Purchased raw material worth ₹1,40,000 from Gaurav.

23 January 2020: Goods sold worth ₹2,00,000 in cash.

26 January 2020: Ranjan was declared insolvent and only ₹1,40,000 could be recovered from his account.

30 January 2020: Paid office expenses ₹20,000 of which ₹5,000 is due for the next month.

31 January 2020: Paid interest on bank loan, ₹5,000.

31 January 2020: Depreciation provided on machine @ 10 % per month.

31 January 2020: Wages outstanding at the end of the month ₹10,000.

4. Ruksana started business as a cloth dealer. On 1 July 2020, her assets were: furniture and office equipment, ₹2,500; stock, ₹25,000; cash in hand, ₹600; bank balance, ₹8,500; and amount due from Rahat Ali, ₹1,200. On that date she owed ₹2,000 to Mallika and ₹1,450 to Namita. Her transactions during the month of July 2020 were as follows:

Date 2020	Particulars	Amount (₹)
2 July	Sold cloth on credit to Sam	500
3 July	Purchased cloth on credit from Yogi	2,000
4 July	Paid rent for July by cheque	800
5 July	Purchase of cloth (paid by cheque)	2,000
7 July	Cash sales	450
8 July	Received cheque from Rahat, allowed him discount	1,180 20
9 July	Paid for stationery and postage	50
10 July	Drawn cash for personal use	250
11 July	Purchased goods on credit from Mallika	2,500
12 July	Sent cheque to Mallika in full settlement (for 1 July position)	1,950
13 July	Sold goods on credit to Ganesh	1,800
14 July	Paid telephone charges	80
15 July	Cash sales	300
18 July	Paid for advertising	350
19 July	Cash purchases	600
30 July	Paid salaries for the month	800

Record the transactions in the books of Ruksana.

5. Rajan started the Touch Wood Company. The transactions of the business for December 2020 are as follows:

Date 2020	Particulars
1 December	Rajan started business by depositing ₹50,000 in cash in the company by issuing 5,000 equity shares of ₹10 each.
5 December	Paid rent for office premises ₹4,000.
6 December	Purchased equipment for cash ₹2,000.
8 December	Purchased supplies on credit ₹800.
10 December	Received ₹10,000 for services performed.
15 December	Paid cash for telephone charges ₹5,000.
17 December	Received ₹2,30,000 for doing the interiors of an office.
26 December	Paid salaries to workers ₹3,500.
27 December	Bought a printer ₹10,000.
28 December	Accounts receivable for work done from customers ₹12,500.
30 December	Received part payment of 28 December transaction ₹8,000.
31 December	Paid dividends ₹4,000.

Record the transactions in the journal, explaining briefly each transaction.

6. Give journal entries to rectify the following errors:
   1. ₹500 paid for erecting a machine is debited to the wages account.
   2. Goods worth ₹2,000 were destroyed by fire, which was not insured. This has not been recorded in the books.
   3. ₹400 paid to Shantibhai have been recorded in Kantibhai's account.
   4. A bill payable of ₹850 was drawn by Jitendra Bhatia but has been entered in the bills receivable book.
   5. Purchase of ₹425 made from Vinayak More has been entered as ₹452 in the purchase book.
   6. The sale of ₹125 made to V. Raman has been entered as ₹152 in the sales book.
   7. Goods worth ₹750 were sold to Badal Brothers which has been written in the purchase book.
   8. Salaries ₹400 paid to Vimal Jain is debited to his personal account.

7. The following balances are taken from the books of Madhu Joshi as on 31 March 2020. Classify them into debit and credit and prepare a trial balance.

Name of Account	Amount (₹)	Name of Account	Amount (₹)
Capital	12,000	Jyoti Printers (Creditor)	260
Drawings	500	Bank balance	3,500
Loan taken	300	Cash balance	1,200
Provident fund	250	Stock of goods	5,000
Provident fund contribution	80	Rent	150
Discount allowed	100	Interest received	50
Discount received	70	Ramakant Dave (Creditor)	500
Purchase	7,000	Prem Parikh (Debtor)	3,110
Sales	9,200	Salary	200
Purchase return	350	Machinery	1,800
Sales return	550	Ms. Sharma Stores (Debtors)	400
Furniture	450	Travelling expenses	120
Stationery expenses	100	Nirmal Company Ltd (Creditors)	1,400
Advertisement expenses	120		

8. Record the following transactions of Jagdish Joshi in his journal, post them to ledger accounts, find out the balances, and say whether they are debit or credit balances:

1 May 2020: Jagdish started business with cash ₹25,000.

3 May 2020: Purchased goods worth ₹8,000 at a trade discount of 10% from Pravin.

5 May 2020: Paid to Pravin ₹5,200 on account.

7 May 2020: Sold goods worth ₹4,600 to Vimal for ₹4,200 for cash and opened a bank account with that amount.

9 May 2020: Purchased a typewriter for ₹2,600.

12 May 2020: Sold goods worth ₹6,400 at a trade discount of 10% to Jitendra.

14 May 2020: Sold goods worth ₹2,400 purchased from Pravin to Chetan Gupta at a profit of 12.5%.

18 May 2020: Chetan returned goods worth ₹360, which Joshi returned to Pravin.

24 May 2020: Received ₹1,400 by a crossed cheque from Chetan Gupta.

31 May 2020: Paid ₹500 for rent by a cheque.

9. Present the following transactions in the books of Murli of Chennai for the month of January 2020 in the form of an accounting equation.
   1. Started business with Cash ₹12,000, Furniture of ₹5,000, and Building ₹53,000.
   2. Goods of ₹6,000 purchased for cash.
   3. Cash sales of ₹2,700.
   4. Goods of ₹500 distributed as free samples.
   5. Goods of ₹10,000 purchased from Polly.
   6. Goods of ₹5,000 sold to Suresh of which ₹3500 received immediately.
   7. Paid ₹550 as printing charges.
   8. Paid ₹2,000 to Polly on her account.
   9. Salary paid ₹1,000.

10. You are required to record the following transactions in the book of Priya for the month of April 2020 in the form of an accounting equation.
    1. Opening cash balance ₹3000.
    2. Goods sold for cash ₹1500.
    3. Received ₹520 from Trupti.
    4. Paid ₹850 to Aamir.
    5. Cash sales ₹1800.
    6. Cash purchases ₹2200.
    7. Paid ₹750 to Akash.
    8. ₹1000 deposited in the bank.
    9. Received ₹500 from Deepa.
    10. Withdrawn for personal purpose by Priya ₹250.
    11. Paid salary ₹500.

11. The following are the transactions of Ambika Stores in the month of January 2020.

1	Amba Lal started a new business with cash ₹2,40,000.
2	Opened a bank account with SBI and deposited ₹1,50,000.
6	Purchased machinery for ₹10,000 and furniture for ₹5,00,000. The machinery was purchased from Delhi Machines & Tools Ltd and furniture from Durga Furniture Mart.
8	Purchased goods of ₹1,50,000 at 10% trade discount from Ganga Stores.
13	Goods of ₹72,000 were sold to Jeevan.
17	Cash sales ₹36,000. Purchased goods of ₹30,000 from Deepali and issued a cheque for the amount.
20	Jeevan returned goods of ₹18,000 as they were defective, which were in turn returned to Ganga Stores with a debit note of ₹15,000.
26	Jeevan settled his account by paying a crossed cheque of ₹51,300 in full settlement.
31	Salary paid by cheque ₹7,500 and miscellaneous expenses of ₹4,500 by cash.

From the given transactions, prepare a purchase book, a sales book, a return book, a three-columnar cash book, and a journal proper in the books of Ambika Stores.

12. Pass journal entries in the books of Shraddha Corporation for the following transactions.
    1. Purchase of goods costing ₹2,000 from Kumar on credit.
    2. Sales of goods to Roshni on credit costing ₹3,000.
    3. Cash purchase worth ₹4000.
    4. Cash sales worth ₹6,000.
    5. Paid cash to Kumar ₹2,000.
    6. Received cash from Roshni ₹3,000.

13. The following are the transactions of Satish Bros & Co for the month of March 2020:

1	Mr Satish commenced business with cash of ₹60,000.
2	Opened a current account with the bank by depositing cash of ₹50,000.
4	Purchased furniture of ₹5,000 on credit from Tip-Top Furniture Mart.
5	Purchased from Ravi Stores goods of ₹25,000 at 20% trade discount.
7	Half the goods purchased from Ravi Stores were sold to Kapil Stores at 20% profit on cost price.
10	Kapil Stores returned goods of ₹1,200 as they were defective and the same were returned to Ravi Stores.
15	Cash sales of ₹1,000 at 2% cash discount.
17	Purchased from Sagar Stores goods of ₹20,000 at 20% trade discount and paid carriage charges ₹100.
20	Received from Kapil Stores a crossed degree of ₹10,584 in full settlement of their account.
25	Paid on account to Ravi Stores ₹9,800 by cheque after deducting ₹200 as cash discount.
31	Paid a rent of ₹500 by cheque and salary of ₹1,000 by cash.

From the information, prepare subsidiary books of Satish Bros & Co., including a purchase book, a sales book, a returns book, a cash book with three columns, and a journal.

14. Prepare subsidiary books of Lindsay Furniture Mart with the help of the following vouchers, post the transactions therefrom to respective ledger accounts, and also prepare a trial balance. On 1 January 2020, cash and bank balances were ₹6,000 and ₹5,200 respectively. On the same date, the capital was ₹11,200. The vouchers of all the transactions are as follows:

(i)

CREDIT MEMO

Bill No.505   Date: 2/1/2020

Style Furniture Mart
Station Road, Surat

Lindsay Furniture Mart

Sr. No.	Particulars	No.	Rate	Amount (₹)
1.	Tables	20	50	1,000
2.	Sofa Set	4	700	2,800
3.	Chairs	4	150	600
				4,400
	Less: Trade Discount @ 10%			440
				3,960

Saumya Singh
(Signatory)

(ii)

CREDIT MEMO

Bill No.59   Date: 3/1/2020

Lindsay Furniture Mart
Satellite Road, Ahmedabad.

Shri Patel & Sons, Rajkot

Sr. No.	Particulars	No.	Rate	Amount (₹)
1.	Sofa Set	2	900	1,800
2.	Tables	8	60	480
3.	Chairs	2	200	400
				2,680
	Less: Trade Discount @ 10%			268
				2,412

Sanjay Lindsay
(Signatory)

(iii)

DEBIT NOTE NO.9

Date 4/1/2020

PATEL & SONS
Rajkot

Lindsay Furniture Mart A/c Debit.
Received from you two damaged tables for which ₹120 are credited to your account.

P.P. Patel
(Signatory)

(iv)

DEBIT NOTE NO.5

Date 6/1/2020

Style Furniture Mart
Station Road, Surat

Lindsay Furniture Mart A/c Debit
Received from you two damaged tables for which ₹100 are credited to your account.

Saumya Singh
(Signatory)

(v)

RECEIPT NO.30

Date 10/1/2020

Style Furniture Mart
Station Road, Surat

Received from Lindsay Furniture Mart, Ahmedabad ₹2,000 cash and a crossed cheque ₹1,800. Discount ₹60 deducted.

Saumya Singh
(Signatory)

(vi)

VOUCHER NO.52

Date 26/1/2020

Lindsay Furniture Mart

Account : Charity
Amount : ₹ 51/-
Particulars: Paid ₹51/- in cash to Secretary of Little Angels orphanage.

Sanjay Lindsay
(Signatory)

(vii)

CREDIT MEMO

No.101   Date: 20/1/2020

Lindsay Furniture Mart
Satellite Road, Ahmedabad.

Shah & Sons, Valsad

Sr. No.	Particulars	No.	Rate	Amount (₹)
1.	Sofa Set	2	850	1,700
2.	Tables	8	55	440
3.	Chairs	2	175	350
				2,490
	Less: Cash Discount @ 10%			249
				2,241

Sanjay Lindsay
(Signatory)

15. From the following information of Ace Corporation, prepare the trial balance for the year ended 31 December 2020 by the balance method and the total amounts method.

Account Head	Dr. (₹)	Cr. (₹)
Cash	59,900	45,600
Bank	56,000	48,000
Furniture	12,000	
Account Head	**Dr. (₹)**	**Cr. (₹)**
Capital		50,000
Purchases	35,000	
Sales		30,000
Vaidyanathan	12,000	15,000
Rashi	14,000	10,000
Freight	200	
Salary	3,000	
Rent	2,400	
Drawings	4,000	
Discount	100	

16. Prepare a trial balance of Manav & Company as on 31 March 2020 from the following information.

Accounts head	Amount (₹)	Accounts head	Amount (₹)
Cash in hand	2,500	Debtors	18,200
Cash at bank	14,500	Creditors	16,600
Capital	70,000	Opening stock	8,700
Drawings	9,000	Wages	6,700
Purchase	60,000	Rent	5,000
Sales	82,000	Salary	8,400
Machine	35,000	Bills payable	11,400
Furniture	12,000		

17. Following are some accounting errors. Rectify them in the books of Kat Enterprises.
   (a) A sale of ₹20,000 made to Malika was not entered in the sales book.
   (b) Salary of ₹5,000 paid to Mr Tushar was debited to his personal account.
   (c) Old furniture sold for ₹2,830 was entered in the sales book.
   (d) Carriage paid for purchase of computer was debited to the carriage account as ₹500.
   (e) Cash ₹5,000 paid to the creditor Poonam was debited to Poorvi's account.

18. Following are the some of the accounting errors traced out in the books of Modern Garments Ltd after the trial balance was prepared. Rectify the same with the help of a suspense account.

    (a) The purchase book has been overcast by ₹400.

    (b) Goods purchased from Moon Enterprises for ₹5,000 have been posted to the debit of the account.

    (c) Cash of ₹9,000 paid to Priyadarshini was credited to Priyanka.

    (d) Discount of ₹200 allowed to Polly was not debited to the discount account.

REFERENCES

Anthony, Robert, N., David Hawkins, and Kenneth Merchant (2003), *Accounting Text and Cases*, 11th edn, p. 87.

Hawkins, David, F. (2004), *The Mechanics of Financial Accounting*, Harvard Business School, p. 3.

Non-current Assets

Learning Objectives

After studying this chapter, you will understand

- nature of fixed assets and methods to determine their costs
- tangible and intangible assets and their valuation
- importance of depreciation expenses
- importance of write-offs of intangible assets
- methodology for valuation of goodwill
- treatment of research and development costs
- different accounting methods available and their impact

INTRODUCTION

Non-current assets are widely known as fixed assets.

Fixed assets are long-term assets owned and used by an enterprise. The use of fixed assets in the operations of the firm is likely to extend beyond one accounting period. Fixed assets include furniture, equipment, buildings, property intangible assets, and natural resources. The expenditure, which results in the acquisition of a fixed asset, must be capitalized (i.e., they should be recorded as part of the asset's cost) in the books of accounts. Any expenditure incurred for improvement of a fixed asset must also be capitalized. In other words, expenditure on assets is not written off completely against income in the accounting period in which it is incurred. The expenditure need not be a payment made to another entity in cash. The payment may be made by cheque, by exchanging another asset, or by incurring a liability. Capital expenditure is treated in the books of accounts by adding the financial outlay to an asset account. Non-current assets are both tangible and intangible valuable things owned by a firm with the intention of carrying on business operations over a long period of time. Thus, non-current assets are durable. The usefulness of an asset to a firm is always on the grounds of either technology or economic benefits.

Fixed assets are long-term assets.

Generally, all the fixed assets are grouped together at the original cost value to represent the *gross block*, from which the accumulated depreciation (for tangible asset) or accumulated amortization (for intangible asset) or accumulated depletion (for natural asset) on all the assets till date is subtracted to arrive at the *net block*.

ACQUISITION COST OF FIXED ASSETS

The gross book value of an asset is the historical cost, that is, the cost at which the asset was originally acquired. The cost of an asset comprises the purchase price (including import duties, other taxes, or levies) and any directly attributable cost of bringing the asset to a working condition. Any trade discounts and rebates offered by the supplier should be deducted. The directly attributable costs, such as expenses incurred for site preparation, initial delivery and handling, installation and/or foundation of plant, professional fees of engineers and architects, etc. should be added to the acquisition cost of the asset. Exhibit 8.1 depicts a statement showing the cost determination of a procured fixed asset.

EXHIBIT 8.1 Cost Determination of a Fixed Asset

Particulars	Amount (₹)
Purchase price of the asset	
Add: Import duties	
Ineligible input credit of GST	
Loading and unloading expenses	
Installation and commissioning expenses	
Installation expenses	
Technical consultancy fees	
Less: Trade discount	
Cost of a procured fixed asset	

The possibility of ineligible input credit of GST from output, if any, may need to be added, as it will increase the effective cost of procured asset.

The cost of a self-constructed asset consists of all expenses that relate directly to the asset. The costs attributable to the construction activity in general can be allocated to specific assets. If several assets are purchased for a consolidated amount, the cost so paid must be apportioned or distributed to the various assets on a fair basis as determined by competent valuers.

CAPITALIZATION OF BORROWING COSTS

The cost of an asset can be determined easily if it is purchased with cash. The cost is the cash outlay, including directly attributable expenses such as freight, in-transit insurance, installation expenses, and any other expense incurred to make the asset utilizable.

If the asset is purchased by issuance of debt instrument, by borrowing from banks or financial institutions, or under instalment, the interest expense is recorded as of recurring nature (it means charged against operating income of the period) and not as part of the cost of the asset.

If a firm constructs an asset or acquires an asset by paying an advance amount to the supplier of the asset, then the interest cost incurred during the construction period or waiting period before the asset is put to use can be viewed as part of the cost of the asset.

Exhibit 8.2 shows how different companies from mining, logistic, media and entertainment, and airline industries treat their borrowing costs.

COMPONENT ACCOUNTING

According to Ind AS 16 and Ind AS 23, in certain circumstances, the accounting for an item of fixed asset may be carried out on the basis of its separable components, if

- they are separable in practice; and
- their useful lives are different.

For example, the metal body of a motor car has a shorter life than the engine of the car. Hence, it is better to record the

---

EXHIBIT 8.2 Borrowing Costs

Let us see how various companies treat their borrowing costs:

Mining Industry: Western Coalfields Limited

Borrowing costs are expensed as and when incurred except where they are directly attributable to the acquisition, construction or production of qualifying assets i.e. the assets that necessarily takes substantial period of time to get ready for its intended use, in which case they are capitalised as part of the cost of those asset up to the date when the qualifying asset is ready for its intended use.

Logistic Industry: VRL Logistic Limited

General and specific borrowing costs directly attributable to the acquisition/construction of qualifying assets, which are assets that necessarily take a substantial period of time to get ready for their intended use, are added to the cost of those assets, until such time the assets are substantially ready for their intended use. All other borrowing costs are recognised as an expense in Statement of Profit and Loss in the period in which they are incurred.

Media and Entertainment Industry: Sun TV Network

Property, plant and equipment are stated at cost less accumulated depreciation and impairment losses, if any. Cost comprises the purchase price (including all duties and taxes after deducting trade discounts and rebates if

any) and any attributable cost of bringing the asset to its working condition for its intended use. Such cost includes the cost of replacing part of the plant and equipment and borrowing costs for long-term construction projects if the recognition criteria are met. Likewise, when a major expenditure is incurred, its cost is recognised in the carrying amount of the plant and equipment, if it increases the future benefits from the existing asset. All other expenses on existing fixed assets, including day-to-day repair and maintenance expenditure, are charged to the statement of profit and loss for the period during which such expenses are incurred.

Airline Industry: SpiceJet Limited

Borrowing costs directly attributable to the acquisition, construction or production of an asset that necessarily takes a substantial period of time to get ready for its intended use or sale are capitalised as part of the cost of the asset. All other borrowing costs are expensed in the period in which they occur. Borrowing costs consist of interest and other costs that an entity incurs in connection with the borrowing of funds. Borrowing cost also includes exchange differences to the extent regarded as an adjustment to the borrowing costs.

Sources: Western Coalfields Limited Annual Report 2017–18, p. 136; VRL Logistic Limited Annual Report 2017–18, p. 100, Used by permission; Sun TV Network Limited Annual Report 2016–2017, p. 78; SpiceJet Limited Annual Report 2016–2017, pp. 87–88.

costs of the metal body and the engine of the motor car as two separate assets. This would support a better estimation and recovery of depreciation from the income in a particular year. This practice is difficult to implement, and hence is rarely put to use by firms. It is used only in case of a wide difference in the value or lifespan of the asset's components.

SPARE PARTS

Regularly used spare parts are usually carried as inventory at the end of the year, and are charged as an expense as and when put to use.

If the spare parts can be used only in connection with an item of fixed asset and their use is expected to be irregular, then they are treated as fixed assets. They are depreciated on a systematic basis over the useful life of the principal fixed assets.

BASKET PURCHASES OR GROUP PURCHASES

Firms sometimes purchase a group of assets for a lump sum value agreed upon. The value paid or agreed to be paid is apportioned among the assets using the fair value approach, that is, as per the fair market value. This allows an equitable and fair allocation of the lump sum purchase price among individual components of the single purchase.

Fair market value is the price that would be agreed to in an open and unrestricted market between knowledgeable and willing parties who are fully informed and not under any compulsion to transact. In case the open market price of an asset is not available for part of the basket purchase, then the fair basis can be determined through the support of competent values.

■ **ILLUSTRATION 8.1** Enjoyment Resort Ltd purchased a running lodging and boarding in the hill station of Mount Abu. They have made a payment of ₹12 lakh for the purchase of land, hotel building, and furniture. The fair value of the three individual assets is estimated as follows: (A) land ₹5 lakh; (B) hotel building ₹8 lakh; and (C) furniture ₹5 lakh. Work out the identifiable value for each and every individual asset.

Solution

The statement showing the allocation of the lump sum purchase price among individual assets is as follows:

Individual Assets	Fair Value as Estimated Amount in lakh (₹)	Proportion of Fair Value	Allocated Cost of Lump Sum Purchase (₹ in lakh) to be Capitalized
Land	5.00	0.2778	0.2778 × 12 = 3.33
Hotel Building	8.00	0.4444	0.4444 × 12 = 5.33
Furniture	5.00	0.2778	0.2778 × 12 = 3.34
Total	**18.00**	**1.0000**	**12.00**

ECONOMICAL AND PHYSICAL LIFE

With the exception of land, all fixed assets have a limited useful economic life, that is, fixed assets are of use to the firm for a limited number of accounting years. As the benefit is accrued over a number of years, a part of the cost of fixed assets should be charged as an expense in each of the accounting years. This process of charging is known as *allocation* or *amortization* or *depreciation* of the cost of usage of fixed assets.

For computing the depreciation expense of an accounting period, the following judgements of estimates should be made for each fixed asset:

1. Its useful economic life
2. The salvage or scrap value at the end of a useful economic life.
3. The method of depreciation

The useful economic life of an asset should not be confused with technical or operational life of that asset. An asset may be fully operational but may not be economically useful for generating profits. The operational life of an asset is its physical life. The economical life of an asset is either equal to or less than its physical life.

TANGIBLE ASSETS

Tangible assets are things that are valuable to the business or firm as assets. Plant assets, also called property, plant and equipment, or fixed assets, are tangible resources that are used in the operations of the business or firm and are not intended for sale to customers. These assets are generally long-lived and are expected to provide services to the firm for a number of years. Except for land, other plant assets experience a decline in service potential over their useful life (economical life).

Land

The cost of land includes (a) cash purchase price, (b) legal costs such as title and lawyers' fees, etc., (c) real estate brokers' commission, and (d) accrued property taxes and other liens on the land assumed by the purchaser. The cost of land improvements includes all expenditures necessary to make the improvements ready for their intended use. For example, the cost of fencing, etc.

Land will not get depreciated, but the land improvements will be depreciated over their useful life.

Building

All necessary expenditures related to the purchase or construction of a building should be charged to the building value. When a building is purchased, its costs include the purchase price, legal expenses, and brokers' commission. Costs to make the building ready for intended use consist of expenditure incurred for remodelling rooms and offices and replacing or repairing the roof, floors, electric wiring, plumbing, etc.

Plant, Property, and Equipment

Plant, property, and equipment are the assets which have physical existence, that is, they can be seen and touched. Examples are machinery, furniture and fixtures, computers, vehicles, office equipment, etc. The calculation of cost of an asset is explained in Exhibit 8.1.

According to Ind AS 16: 'Property, Plant and Equipment', the gross book value of a self-constructed fixed asset includes the costs of construction that relate directly to the specific asset and the costs that are attributable to the construction activity in general can be allocated to the specific asset. If there is any internal profit, it should be eliminated.

Natural Resources

The non-current assets of a firm include timber, metal ores, minerals, or other natural resources. The firm involves in plantation, mineral activities, etc. and expends funds for land development, site development, etc. The expenses incurred for development of site and/or land must be considered as part of acquisition cost of the asset. The process of transferring the cost of natural resources as charges against the revenue of the period is known as *depletion*.

Assets with Lower Economic Life than Physical Life

The economical or useful life of an asset is limited for two reasons:

1. *Deterioration:* It is the process of wearing out of an asset on account of usage.

2. *Obsolescence:* It occurs on account of improved technologies, resulting in bringing out inefficiency in the operating cycle of the firm.

On account of technological developments and improvements these days, majority of plants, machineries, etc. are facing a lower economical life for their assets.

REGENERATIVE ASSETS

Regenerative assets and their use in agricultural activities and in the pharmaceutical sector are important points of concern for accountants. Agricultural activities use the services of regenerative assets such as livestock, while pharmaceutical firms use regenerative assets such as forests, plantations, and animals for testing. The productive capacity of regenerative assets is a gift of nature and a few assets may be lost as a result of death. Thus, the valuation of assets at the end of the year is performed with the assessment and advice of a special valuer, and the balancing figure would be charged in the profit and loss account of the period or would be treated as an income in the profit and loss account of the period. Exhibit 8.3 helps compile the statistics for regenerative assets.

EXHIBIT 8.3 Cost Determination of a Fixed Asset

Particulars	Nos	Amount (₹)
Opening stock of livestock		
Add: Purchases		
Add: Newborn livestock		
Less: Sale of livestock		
Less: Sale of slaughtered livestock		
Less: Sale of carcasses		
Less: Death of livestock (and no value realized)		
Less: Closing stock (as valued by a valuer)		
Difference		

■ **ILLUSTRATION 8.2** From the following data, prepare the livestock account in the books of M/s Matthew Agriculture Farm.

Particulars	Nos	Amount (₹)
Cattle (opening value of live stock)	100	3,00,000
Purchases of cattle	200	5,85,000
Sale of cattle	150	62,500
Sale of slaughtered cattle	40	30,000
Sale of carcasses	5	750
Cattle (closing value as certified by a valuer)	115	5,85,000

Solution

The statement showing the allocation of the lump sum purchase price

Livestock Account in the Books of M/s Matthew Agriculture Farm

Particulars	Nos	Amount (₹)
Opening stock of Cattle	100	3,00,000
Add: Purchases	200	5,85,000
Add: Newborn	?? (a)	NIL
Less: Sale of cattle	150	62,500
Less: Sale of slaughtered livestock	40	30,000
Less: Sale of carcasses	5	750
Less: Death of livestock (and no value realized)	?? (b)	
Less: Closing Stock (as valued by the valuer)	115	5,85,000
Difference		??? (c)

Note: Either *a* or *b* would have a value.

Ans:
$$100 + 200 + a - 150 - 40 - 5 = 115$$
$$300 + a - 195 = 115$$
$$a = 310 - 300$$
$$\Rightarrow \quad a = 10$$
$$a = 10; \ b = \text{nil}; \ c = ₹2,06,750$$

An amount of ₹2,06,750 would be debited in the profit and loss account of the year.

INTANGIBLE ASSETS

Intangible assets are those assets that do not have physical existence. They cannot be seen or touched, for example, goodwill. Such assets may have a fixed term of existence by law, regulation, or agreement, for example, patents, copyrights, and leases. Difficulties may arise in ascertaining the existence and quantum of future benefits from such assets. Therefore, it is usually recommended that expenditures made by the firm in developing these assets should not be recognized. Only if an intangible asset is acquired through purchase from another firm, then should it be recognized as an asset.

GOODWILL

Goodwill is the advantage that arises from the good reputation and connections of business. An established business earns more than normal profits because of its reputation for quality products, punctuality in delivery, social consciousness, integrity, honesty, harmonious relation with employees,

IFRS Update

The following table indicates the differences in the recognition of acquired intangible assets like goodwill as per Indian Accounting Standards (Ind AS), IFRS or International Accounting Standards (IAS), and US Generally Accepted Accounting Practices (GAAP).

Acquired Intangible Asset

Ind AS	IFRS/IAS	US GAAP
To be amortized over useful life with a rebuttable presumption of not more than 10 years.	To be amortized over the useful life.	Similar to IFRS.
	If intangible asset is assigned an indefinite life, then amortization not allowed, but reviewed at least annually for impairment.	
Revaluations are not permitted.	Revaluations are permitted in few circumstances only.	Revaluations are not permitted.

customers, dealers, etc. Therefore, goodwill is an asset that ensures the prosperity of the business. It is an asset with marketable money value. Goodwill can be identified only with the business as a whole.

Goodwill recognition, as an asset without any exchange transaction in the form of cash or cash in kind, is always subject to personal estimation of the evaluator or assessor, which can be challenged for objectivity. The recording of goodwill on a subjective basis leads to the financial statements presenting an unfair position. Goodwill is to be recorded only when there is an exchange transaction involving the purchase of business, name, or reputation of a business, etc.

When an entire firm is purchased, then the excess of cost over the fair market value of net assets taken over is known as goodwill. The fair market value of net assets includes the assessed or agreed value of assets taken over minus the agreed value of liabilities taken over by the purchaser of the firm.

In recording the purchase of a firm, net assets are shown at their agreed fair market value, goodwill is recorded as cost, and any cash is shown as reduction in the cash balance of the purchaser (for the balancing amount of purchase price). The different methods for valuation of goodwill have been explained hereunder. Exhibit 8.4 indicates the emergence of the value of goodwill in case of purchases of other firms by pharmaceutical and telecommunication industries.

The accepted accounting practice requires the purchased goodwill to be reported as a separate line item in the balance sheet and to be reviewed regularly for impairment. If the fair value of goodwill is less than the carrying amount (book value), then the goodwill is considered to be impaired. The impairment charges are to be reported in the profit and loss account as an expense, and the value of goodwill is reduced by the same amount.

Valuation of Goodwill

Goodwill is the advantage that arises from the good name, reputation, and connections in business. An established business earns more than normal profits because of its reputation for quality products, punctuality in delivery, social consciousness, integrity, honesty, harmonious relationship with employees, customers, and dealers, etc. Therefore, goodwill is an asset originating from the future maintainable profit of a firm. It is an asset with marketable money value.

The need for valuation of goodwill depends on the form of business organization. In the case of a sole trader, it is usually valued at the time of selling the business so as to determine the amount payable by the buyer towards goodwill. In the case of partnership, there are several circumstances when goodwill has to be valued, such as in case of admission of a new partner, retirement or death of an existing partner, a change in the profit-sharing ratio, dissolution of a firm, or sale of a firm. In the case of a company, goodwill needs to be estimated in instances such as when two or more companies decide to amalgamate, when one company takes over another company completely, etc.

EXHIBIT 8.4 Goodwill

Let us look how various companies treat goodwill in their books of accounts:

Pharmaceutical Industry: RPG Life Sciences Ltd

The Company measures goodwill as of the applicable acquisition date at the fair value of the consideration transferred, including the recognized amount of any non-controlling interest in the acquiree, less the net recognized amount of the identifiable assets acquired and liabilities (including contingent liabilities in case such a liability represents a present obligation and arises from a past event, and its fair value can be measured reliably) assumed. When the fair value of the net identifiable assets acquired and liabilities assumed exceeds the consideration transferred, a bargain purchase gain is recognized as capital reserve. Consideration transferred includes the fair values of the assets transferred, liabilities incurred by the Company to the previous owners of the acquiree, and equity interests issued by the Company.

Telecommunication Industry: Bharti Airtel Limited

The Group's investments in its joint ventures and associates are accounted for using the equity method. Accordingly, the investments are carried at cost as adjusted for post-acquisition changes in the Group's share of the net assets of investees. Any excess of the cost over the Group's share of net assets in its joint ventures/associates at the date of acquisition is recognised as goodwill. The goodwill is included within the carrying amount of the investment. The un-realised gains/losses resulting from transactions (including sale of business) with joint ventures and associates are eliminated against the investment to the extent of the Group's interest in the investee. However, un-realised losses are eliminated only to the extent that there is no evidence of impairment.

Sources: RPG Life Sciences Limited Annual Report 2017–18, p. 64; Bharti Airtel Limited Annual Report 2016–17, p. 193.

Future Maintainable Profit

Future maintainable profit (FMP) refers to the future maintainable operating profit. It is the amount of profit likely to be earned on account of usual operations under normal business circumstances. It is decided on the basis of the average profit of the last four or five years after adjusting the future possibilities regarding expenses, losses, incomes, and gains. The FMP can be worked out by following the sequences of calculations given in this section.

Average profit   When there are no fluctuations in the profit from year to year, the profits of the previous years can be expected to be maintained in future also. If there are fluctuations in profits, the past profits should be averaged. Such an average profit may be simple or weighted.

Simple average   When the fluctuations are normal, the average may be a simple average.

> Simple Average = Normal Profits/Number of Years

Weighted average   When the profits show a trend of increase or decrease in profits, the weighted average profit may be calculated by utilizing weights for the first year, for the second year, for the third year, and so on.

The profits of each year are multiplied by the weight of the respective year. The weighted average profit is calculated as follows:

> Weighted Average = Total Weighted Profits/Total of Weights

Adjusted average profits   After determining the average profit, adjustments are to be made to obtain the adjusted average profit. The following points should be remembered when determining the adjusted average profit, that is, the future maintainable profit.

1. Adjust any non-recurring and extraordinary items from the profits of the relevant years.
2. Adjust past expenses and incomes not likely to arise in future.
3. Adjust any expenses likely to be incurred in the future or incomes likely to arise in the future, and decide the adjusted average profit.
4. Deduct any non-trading income from the adjusted average.
5. Calculate the average adjusted past profits.
6. Finally, deduct the income tax from the above profit to obtain the adjusted average profit after tax or FMP.

Specific notes for FMP

1. Adjust abnormal losses and losses of any isolated transactions that are not concerned with the business of the company.
2. Eliminate profits or losses from investments that are not considered as part of the main business activity.
3. Eliminate capital profit or loss or receipt of expenses that have been considered while calculating profit or loss.
4. Adjust any interest, remuneration, commission, etc., forgone by the directors of the company.

5. Provide for bad and doubtful debts.
6. Ensure that depreciation is provided adequately on a consistent basis.
7. Ensure that the basis of valuation of stock is consistent.
8. Calculate the past average profit after deducting tax at current rates.
9. Exclude non-recurring items from the past average profit.
10. If the profits show a regular trend (upward or downward), weighted average may be calculated.
11. In the case of sole trading concerns or partnership firms, it is better to make a provision for reasonable remuneration to the proprietor or partners in the average normal operating profits.

The following statement illustrates the calculation of FMP.

Particulars	Amount (₹)	Amount (₹)
Average profit		XX
Add: Expenses and losses incurred so far, but not likely to be incurred in the future		XX
Add: Income and gains not earned so far, but likely to be earned in the future		XX
Less: Expenses or losses not incurred so far, but likely to be incurred in the future	XX	
Less: Incomes and gains earned so far, but not likely to be earned in the future.	XX	XXX
FMP		XXX

Methods of Valuation of Goodwill

Following are the different methods used for the valuation of goodwill of a firm.

Simple profit method

In this method, goodwill can be worked out by the average profit or the number of years' purchase method.

1. Average profit method
   In this method, the goodwill is equal to the average profit, that is, FMP as calculated earlier.

> Goodwill = Average Profit

2. Number of years' purchase of average profit method:
   Under this method, the goodwill is equal to the average profit of the year multiplied by the number of years' purchase of FMP.

> Goodwill = Average Profit × Number of Year's Purchase

Annuity of average profit method

The average adjusted profit is taken as the annuity, and the average adjusted profit is multiplied by the present value of a rupee. The resulting amount is the total value of the business. From the total value, the net tangible value of assets of the firm is deducted to arrive at the value of goodwill. The steps mentioned in this section need to be followed in this method.

1. Determine the adjusted average profit.

2. Decide the present value of a rupee from the annuity table by considering the number of future years for which the FMP is expected to be earned.
3. Multiply the present value of a rupee and the adjusted average profit.
4. Deduct the net tangible assets from the present value of the adjusted annual profit. The value thus derived is known as goodwill.

Super profit method

Super profit is the excess of profit earned by the proprietor over the average profit earned by similar concerns in the industry (normal profit). It is an excess of FMP over the normal profit.

$$\text{Super Profit} = \text{FMP} - \text{Normal Profit}$$

Normal profit is the average profit earned by similar concerns in the industry, decided on the basis of the normal rate of return (NRR) and the average capital employed during the year.

$$\text{Normal Profit} = \text{NRR}/100 \times \text{Average Capital Employed}$$

Normal rate of return (NRR) NRR is the average return expected from an investment in particular business activities, such as the nature of business and the risk involved. In general, the average return on the equities of similar concerns should be taken as the normal return. NRR can be calculated using the following formula.

$$\text{NRR} = \frac{\text{Dividend per Share in Similar Companies}}{\text{Market Value per Share in Similar Companies}} \times 100$$

Average capital employed The term *capital employed* refers to the present value of tangible trading assets minus all liabilities. Non-trading assets such as investments outside the business are to be omitted. Investments that are made on account of surplus funds are to be omitted, whereas investments that are made by the firm to acquire certain business benefits are considered as part of the tangible trading assets. While calculating the capital employed on the basis of total assets, intangibles such as goodwill, useless patents, and trademark are to be excluded. Investments in government securities made outside the business are excluded as they are non-trading assets. Fictitious assets should be excluded.

Capital employed as decided from the balance sheet pertains to a certain date only. For this purpose, it is advisable to have the fair value of capital employed during the year. Hence, it is better to arrive at the average capital employed (ACE). ACE is determined as follows:

(a) When information about the opening capital employed and closing capital employed is given:

$$\text{ACE} = \frac{\text{Opening Capital Employed} + \text{Closing Capital Employed}}{2}$$

(b) When information about the opening capital employed is given:

$$\text{ACE} = \text{Opening Capital Employed} + \tfrac{1}{2} \text{ of the Profit Earned}$$

(c) When information about the closing capital employed is given:

$$\text{ACE} = \text{Closing Capital Employed} - \tfrac{1}{2} \text{ of the Profit Earned}$$

In short, ACE can be calculated by adopting the following tabular method with respect to the asset side of the balance sheet and the liabilities side of the balance sheet.

1. Asset-side approach:

Particulars	Amount (₹)
Tangible trading assets at the received value (all assets except goodwill, deferred revenue expenditure, fictitious assets, and investments)	XX
Less: Liabilities payable (third party's liabilities or outsider's liabilities) (e.g., Creditors, bills payable, outstanding expenses, debentures, loans, etc.)	XX
Tangible trading capital employed at the end of the year	XXX
Less: ½ of the profit earned during the year	XX
ACE	XXX

2. Liability-side approach:

Particulars		Amount (₹)
Paid-up share capital		XX
Add: Various reserves		XX
Add: Profit and loss account balance		XX
Add: Revaluation profit		XX
Less: Revaluation loss	XX	
Less: Fictitious assets	XX	
Less: Non-trading assets	XX	XX
ACE		XXX

There is a difference of opinion about the deduction of half of the profit while determining the ACE during the year. If it is assumed that the entire profit is withdrawn by the proprietor from the business, half of the current year's profit should not be deducted. If it is assumed that the profit is not withdrawn from the business, half of the current year's profit has to be deducted while determining the ACE.

Different methods to value goodwill by the super profit method

Under the super profit method, there are three methods of valuation of goodwill.

Number of years' purchase of super profit method

$$\text{Goodwill} = \text{Super Profit} \times \text{Number of Years' Purchases}$$

Annuity of super profit method Under this method, goodwill is the discounted value of the total amount calculated as per the FMP method. According to this method, goodwill is equal to the present value of the future returns for the expected years of future. Steps to be taken are as follows:

1. First, determine the super profit of the business.
2. Second, ascertain the present value of a rupee from the annuity tables.
3. Finally, multiply the super profit by the present value of a rupee. The resulting figure is the value of goodwill.

$$\text{Goodwill} = \text{Super Profit} \times \text{Annuity Value}$$

$$\text{Annuity Value} = \frac{(1+i)^n}{i(1+i)^n} \text{ where } i = \frac{r}{100}$$

Capitalization of the super profit method Under this method, goodwill is equal to the capitalized value of super profit at the normal rate of return. The method attempts to decide the amount of capital required to earn super profit.

$$\text{Goodwill} = \frac{100}{\text{NRR}} \times \text{Super Profit}$$

Capitalization of FMP method Under this method, goodwill is considered to be equal to the excess of the capitalized value of FMP at the normal rate of return over the net tangible trading assets.

Following are the steps to be taken to decide the value of goodwill.

1. Determine the FMP.
2. Work out the capitalized value of FMP at the normal rate of return as follows:

$$\frac{100}{\text{NRR}} \times \text{FMP}$$

3. Decide net tangible trading assets, which are equal to the total tangible trading assets less the liabilities payable to outsiders.
4. Determine the value of goodwill as follows:

$$\text{Goodwill} = \text{Capitalized Value of FMP} - \text{Net Tangible Trading Assets}$$

Valuation based on turnover (gross receipts)

Under this method, goodwill is calculated on the basis of the turnover and not the net profit. The buyer pays for goodwill, which may be one or more year's purchase of the gross receipts or turnover. This method is suitable for the valuation of goodwill of professionals such as chartered accountants, advocates, etc. Valuation of goodwill is based on the recurring fees income. After estimating the expenses, the worth of the practice can be decided, and accordingly, the value of goodwill determined. In the case of a medical professional, goodwill may be calculated on the basis of a few years' purchase of the average of the gross fees of the last few years.

■ **ILLUSTRATION 8.3** Trupti and Company purchased a division from PeaPack Company on 30 June 2020. Profits earned by PeaPack Company for the preceding years ending on 31 December each year were as follows: 2017, ₹41000; 2018, ₹40,000; and 2019, ₹42,000.

It was ascertained that the profit of 2018 included a non-recurring profit item of ₹1,500 and the profit of 2019 was reduced by ₹2,000 due to an extraordinary loss on account of theft. The properties were not insured, and it was thought prudent to insure the business in future. The premium was estimated at ₹2,000 p.a. Trupti at the time was employed with Hari Bros Ltd and was getting ₹5,000 p.a. She intends to replace the manager of the business who at present is getting ₹3,500 p.a. The goodwill is estimated at two years' purchase of the average profit. You are required to calculate the goodwill of the business.

Solution

Particulars		Amount (₹)
Profits 2017		41,000
Profits 2018	40,000	
Less: Non-recurring profit	1,500	38,500
Profit 2019	42,000	
Add extraordinary loss	2,000	44,000
Total profit		1,23,500
Average profits (i.e., `1,23,500/3)		41,167
Less: Expenses to be paid in the future:		
Insurance premium	2,000	
Salary of Trupti	5,000	7,000
		34,167
Add expenses not to be paid in the future		
Salary of a manager		3,500
Net average profit to come in the future		37,667

$$\text{Goodwill} = 2 \text{ years} \times ₹37,667 = 75,334$$

■ **ILLUSTRATION 8.4** Druv Ltd proposed to purchase the business of Shri Lila. Goodwill for this purpose is agreed to be valued at three years' purchase of the weighted average profits of the past four years. The appropriate weights to be used are as follows: 2017, 1; 2018, 2; 2019, 3; and 2020, 4.

The profits for these years are as follows: 2017, ₹10,000; 2018, ₹12,400; 2019, ₹10,000; and 2020, ₹15,000.

On a scrutiny of the accounts, the following details are revealed: (a) on 11 September 2018, the plant incurred an expense of ₹3,000 on account of a major repair, which was charged to the revenue. The firm follows the method of charging depreciation of 10% p.a. on reducing balance methods. (b) The closing stock for the year 2018 was overvalued by ₹1,200. (c) To cover the management cost, an annual charge of ₹2,400 is to be made for the purpose of goodwill valuation. Compute the value of the goodwill of the firm.

Solution

Particulars	Amount (₹)			
	2017	2018	2019	2020
Profit as per the profit and loss account	10,000	12,400	10,000	15,000
Adjustments				
Add:				
(a) Repair transfer to plant	--	+ 3,000	--	
(b) Stock adjustments	--	- 1,200	+ 1,200	--
(c) Management expenses	- 2,400	- 2,400	- 2,400	- 2,400
(d) Depreciation on `3,000	--	--	- 300	- 290
Adjusted profit (1)	7,600	11,800	8,500	12,310
Weightage (2)	1	2	3	4
Product (3) (1 x 2)	7,600	23,600	25,500	49,240
Cumulative total	7,600	31,200	56,700	1,05,940
Average profit (Weightage)	1,05,940/10 = 10,594			
Goodwill:	10,594 × 3 = 31,782			

RESEARCH AND DEVELOPMENT COSTS ■

Research and development activities are carried out by a firm for the development of new products, testing of existing and proposed products, and development of scientific or technical knowledge related to the business.

Exhibit 8.5 shows how pharmaceutical and agricultural companies treat their research and development costs.

The Financial Accounting Standard Board (in association with the American Institute of Certified Public Accountants, USA) requires that all research and development costs be treated as revenue expenditure and charged to expense in the period in which they are incurred (Ind AS 38).

As per Ind AS 38 of ICAI, entitled *intangible assets*, expense incurred in the research phase are termed as research costs, while expenditure incurred in development phase are treated as development costs.

Research phase costs are included if the research is original and based on a planned investigation, and it would be undertaken with the prospect of gaining new scientific or technical knowledge and understanding. All costs occurred in this phase should be recognized as an expense for the period when it occurred.

The development phase constitutes application of research findings or other knowledge to a plan or design for the production of new or substantially new or improved materials, products, processes, systems, etc. This phase precedes the commencement of regular commercial production or use. The cost incurred during development phase is recognized as an asset if the following conditions are satisfied.

- A technical feasibility study supporting the completion of development of the intangible asset
- Ability to use or sell the created intangible asset
- Existence of market for output of the intangible asset or internal use of the intangible asset
- Availability of adequate technical, financial, and other resources to complete the development and to use or sell the intangible asset
- Ability to measure the expenditure on the intangible asset reliably and fairly

The development cost is to be amortized over the estimated physical life of the asset or productive capacity of the intangible asset.

EXHIBIT 8.5   Research and Development Costs

Let us look how various companies treat their research and development costs:

Pharmaceutical Industry: RPG Life Sciences Ltd

Internally Generated: Research and Development

Expenditure on research activities is recognised in profit or loss as incurred. Development expenditure is capitalised as part of the cost of the resulting intangible assets only if the expenditure can be measured reliably, the product or process is technically and commercially feasible, future economic benefits are probable, and the Company intends to and has sufficient resources to complete development and use or sell the assets. Otherwise, it is recognised on profit or loss as incurred. Subsequent to initial recognition, the asset is measured at cost less accumulated amortization and any accumulated impairment losses.

Pharmaceutical Industry: Cadila Healthcare Limited

(A) Expenditure on research and development is charged to the Statement of Profit and Loss of the year in which it is incurred.
(B) Capital expenditure on research and development is given the same treatment as Property, Plant and Equipment.

Agriculture Industry: Dhanuka Agritech Limited

Research and Development Expenses

Research and Development Expenses of revenue nature are charged to Profit and Loss Account.

Sources: RPG Life Sciences Limited Annual Report 2017–18, p. 57; Cadila Healthcare Limited Annual Report 2016–17, p. 106; Dhanuka Agritech Limited Annual Report, 2016–17, p. 99. Used by permission.

■ **ILLUSTRATION 8.5**   Supreme Tech Ltd had spent ₹35 lakh on researching one of its new products known as Raymin during the period of 2014–16. The development of the product was based on a market feasibility study undertaken during the period 2016–18, and ₹32 lakh was incurred as development cost. Raymin put it to commercial use during the year 2018–19, with an estimated life of 5 years. In the year 2019–20, a legal restriction on sale and production of the product Raymin was imposed by statute. Discuss the treatment of various costs incurred during the period of research and development.

Solution

(a) The research cost of ₹35 lakh would be considered by Supreme Tech as an expense in the year in which they occurred, that is, from 2014 to 2016.
(b) The development cost for the period of 2016 to 2018 would be considered as an asset in the respective year it occurred.
(c) Raymin was put to commercial use during 2018–19; hence, the amount would be amortized as ₹6.40 lakh (₹32 lakh divided by 5) each year starting from 2018 to 2019.
(d) From the year 2019 to 2020, Raymin is considered an as illegal product, and hence further future benefits from the

---

IFRS Update

Differences in recognition style

The following table indicates the differences in the recognition of research costs and development costs as internally generated tangible assets as per Indian Accounting Standards (Ind AS), IFRS or International Accounting Standards (IAS), and US Generally Accepted Accounting Practices (GAAP).

Internally Generated Intangible Asset

Ind AS	IFRS/IAS	US GAAP
Research costs are treated as an expense incurred.	Similar to Indian AS.	Research and development costs are expensed as incurred.
Development costs are capitalized and amortized only if specific criterions are met.		As an exception, software and web site development expenses are allowed to be capitalized.

sale of the product would not be available. Therefore, the carrying amount of ₹25.60 lakh (₹32 lakh less ₹6.40) as on 1/4/2019 would be recognized as non-beneficial value. Hence, during the year 2019–20, ₹25.60 lakh would be expensed in the profit and loss account, and the asset value will be nullified in the books of accounts. Hence, the balance sheet as at 31 March 2020 would not indicate any value of the said asset, that is, Raymin.

SOFTWARE COSTS

Firms normally have either customized software (developed internally or through a software development firm) or buy the readymade software. The expense recognition happens throughout the estimated useful life in a number of years or in a number of transactions, etc. If it is purchased, it is recorded as its acquisition cost. If the software is developed by the firm itself, its costs include the cost of the consumed resource, cost of legal fees, and other associated costs of securing it.

These expenses are amortized over the useful life based on either passage of time or utilization level or a combination of both.

PATENTS

Patents are granted to inventors of products, machines, or processes, with a view to protect the rights of the inventors from infringement by others. Patents could be acquired by a firm in two ways: firstly, by purchase from a patent holder, and secondly by developing the product or process. If it is purchased, it is recorded as its acquisition cost. If the patent is developed by the firm itself, its costs include the cost of legal fees and other associated costs of securing it. It may be noted that the cost of research and development of the product or process are not included in the cost of patents. Such costs are treated separately.

COPYRIGHTS

The holder of copyright has the exclusive right to publish, produce, and sell artistic, musical, or literary works. Copyrights may be sold by authors or publishers to other parties interested in the copyrighted material. The accounting treatment of copyright is similar to that of patents.

LEASEHOLD AND LEASEHOLD IMPROVEMENTS

Leasehold refers to the rights transferred to the lessee (user of an asset) by the lessor (owner of an asset) for the period of lease. At the beginning of the lease period, the lessee may require to make payment of a substantial amount in order to hold the lease. This amount would be an asset for the firm because it represents the exclusive right to use the leased property. The annual rent payments made by the firm after the commencement of the lease are recorded as rent expenses. The permanent improvements made by the lessee to the leased property are termed as leasehold improvements. The leasehold improvements become the property of the landlord if they are still in use at the expiration of the lease. It may be noted that leasehold improvements are classified as intangible assets, even though, they are usually physical in nature. This is because the lessee does not own the tangible asset to which improvements are made. Lessee right is restricted to the use of a tangible asset for the lease period.

The accounting treatment of leaseholds and leasehold improvements is to amortize the cost over the estimated useful life, which is specified in the lease agreement. The amortization period is generally the lease term. However, it may include any anticipated renewal periods, if renewal is fairly certain.

TRADEMARK AND TRADEMARK NAMES

A firm uses trademarks and trade names to distinguish their products and processes from those of other producers. Trademarks and trade names are indicators of quality, e.g., Amul. Trademark and trade names are registered with the government, so as to prevent another party from producing and selling goods under the same name.

OTHER INTANGIBLE ASSETS

The assets that are result of specific transactions on the part of the owner firm, such as preliminary expenses, heavy corporate advertisements, and deferred revenue expenditures, are considered as *other intangible assets*.

Other intangible assets also include the expenditure incurred for development of software for providing the ease in operations of the firm, trademarks, etc.

Capitalized costs of computer programs developed for sale, lease, or internal use would be recognized as an intangible asset. The cost includes the production costs, and would be amortized over the useful life or estimated economic life of the product. The accounting practices of recording and treatment of intangible assets are explained in Exhibit 8.6.

Trademark or brand name is a recognized symbol or name that can be used only by its owner to identify a product or service. The cost of a trademark or brand name would be amortized over its reasonable life.

OTHER SITUATIONS

Self-constructed Assets

When a fixed asset is constructed by a firm for its own use, the cost includes materials costs, labour costs, and a reasonable amount of indirect overhead costs such as heat, lights, power, and depreciation of machinery used to construct the asset. This cost also includes the design fees, building permits fees, building use fees, insurance, and interest charges that occur during the construction period. The insurance and interest charges for coverage after the asset has been placed in use come under operating expenses, and the said amount would not be capitalized as it is not appropriate to record profit on its own construction.

For example, Buildwell Construction Limited was involved in the construction of a parking area adjoining their office building for the staff members. The self-constructed cost amounts to ₹5 lakh, while the lowest price quotation available from an outside contractor is ₹5,60,000. The amount to be recorded as the parking area costs should be ₹5 lakh only.

EXHIBIT 8.6 Other Intangible Assets

Let us look how various companies treat and recognize other intangible assets in their books of accounts:

Pharmaceutical Industry: Dabur India Ltd

Intangible Assets

Intangible assets acquired separately are measured on initial recognition at cost of acquisition. The cost comprises of purchase price and directly attributable costs of bringing the assets to its working condition for intended use. Intangible assets arising on acquisition of business are measured at fair value as at date of acquisition. In case of internally generated assets, measured at development cost subject to satisfaction of recognition criteria (identifiability, control and future economic benefit) in accordance with Ind AS 38 'Intangible Assets'.

Following initial recognition, intangible assets are carried at cost less accumulated amortization and accumulated impairment loss, if any.

Intangible Assets with finite lives are amortized on a straight-line basis over the estimated useful economic life. The amortization expense on intangible assets with finite lives is recognized in the Standalone Statement of Profit and Loss.

Amortization of intangible assets such as softwares is computed on a straight-line basis, at the rates representing estimated useful life of up to 5 years. The brands and trademarks acquired as part of business combinations normally have a remaining legal life of not exceeding ten years but is renewable every ten years at little cost and is well established.

Media and Entertainment Industry: Sun TV Network Ltd

The company has elected to continue with the carrying value for all of its Intangible assets as recognised in its Indian GAAP financial statements as deemed cost at the transition date, viz., April 1, 2015. Intangible assets acquired are measured on initial recognition at cost. Following initial recognition, Intangible assets are carried at cost less accumulated amortisation and accumulated impairment losses, if any. Intangible assets with finite lives are amortised over the useful economic life and assessed for impairment whenever there is an indication that the intangible asset may be impaired. The amortisation period and the amortisation method for an intangible asset with a finite useful life are reviewed at least at the end of each reporting period. Changes in the expected useful life or the expected pattern of consumption of future economic benefits embodied in the asset are considered to modify the amortisation period or method, as appropriate, and are treated as changes in accounting estimates. The amortisation expense on intangible assets with finite lives is recognised in the statement of profit and loss unless such expenditure forms part of carrying value of another asset.

Computer Software

Costs incurred towards purchase of computer software are depreciated using the straight-line method over a period based on management's estimate of useful lives of such software being 3 years, or over the license period of the software, whichever is shorter.

Film and Program Broadcasting Rights ('Satellite Rights')

Acquired Satellite Rights for the broadcast of feature films and other long-form programming such as multiepisode television serials are initially stated at cost. Future revenues from use of these Satellite Rights cannot be estimated with any reasonable accuracy as these are susceptible to a variety of factors, such as the level of market acceptance of television products, programming viewership, advertising rates etc., and accordingly cost related to film is fully expensed on the date of first telecast of the film and the cost related to program broadcasting rights/multi episodes series are amortized based on the telecasted episodes.

Film Production Costs, Distribution and Related Rights

The cost of production/acquisition of all the rights related to each movie is amortised upon the theatrical release of the movie.

Licenses

Licenses represent one time entry fees paid to Ministry of Information and Broadcasting ('MIB') under the applicable licensing policy for Frequency Modulation ('FM') Radio broadcasting. Cost of licenses are amortised over the license period, being 15 years.

Sources: Dabur India Ltd Annual Report 2017–18, p. 150; Sun TV Network Limited Annual Report 2016–17, pp. 80–81.

To record the parking area at ₹5,60,000 and recognize a gain of ₹60,000 would be a violation of the cost concept.

Repairs and Improvements

After an asset has been put to use, costs may be incurred for ordinary maintenance and repairs. Such costs are recorded as an expense of the period under study. These expenses are termed as revenue expenses, and are directly charged against the income of the year under *repairs and maintenance expense*.

Sometimes, an expense may be incurred to improve the efficiency or productivity, to enhance the life of an asset, or to implement cost saving. Such expenses would be treated as an *asset improvement expense*. It is a type of capital expenditure, and is recorded as an increase in the value of an asset. Subsequently, as the value of the asset increases, the depreciation claim would also increase proportionately per annum.

Discarded Assets

If a fixed asset is no longer used or useful and has no residual value or scrap value, such assets are discarded. In such cases, if the fixed asset is not fully depreciated, then the depreciation should be recorded before removal of the asset from the accounting records. The book value as on the date of discarding the fixed asset should be charged as 'loss on discard of fixed asset account'. At the end of the year, the same should be written off against the profit of the firm, by debiting the profit and loss account of the firm. Losses on the discarding of fixed assets are considered as non-operating expenses and reported separately in the income statement.

Donated Assets

Firms may sometimes receive an asset as a gift. For example, to increase the local employment, a particular government may give a piece of land to a firm to build their plants or factories. When a firm receives such gifts, both the total assets and the total capital funds of the firm increase by the fair market value of the assets received.

No profit is recognized when a gift is received; the increase in capital funds is regarded as an increase in the owners' capital. The receipt of a gift is recorded by debiting the appropriate asset account and crediting an account named as donated capital account.

Impairment of Assets

When the carrying value of an asset is higher than its fair value, then it is termed as impairment in the value of the asset. The carrying value of an asset refers to the book value of the asset as appearing on the date of balance sheet in the books of accounts of a firm.

Fair value refers to the amount for which the asset could be bought or sold in the current period or as on a particular date. The fair value can also be determined by working out the present value of future cash flow.

Exhibit 8.7 explains the contemporary practices followed by Balaji Telefilms Limited.

For example, if the sum of present value of expected cash flows from an asset is lower than the carrying value of the asset, then the asset would be impaired. Reducing the carrying value of an asset to the fair value is an application of the concept of conservatism. The impaired value of an asset is termed as an impairment loss and would be debited in the profit and loss account of the period in which the impairment has been noted.

EXHIBIT 8.7 Other Impairments of Assets

Let us look how Balaji Telefilms Ltd treats and recognizes other impairments of assets in its books of accounts:

Media and Entertainment Industry: Balaji Telefilms Ltd

Impairment of Tangible

At the end of each reporting period, the Company reviews the carrying amounts of its tangible to determine whether there is any indication that those assets have suffered an impairment loss. If any such indication exists, the recoverable amount of the asset is estimated in order to determine the extent of the impairment loss (if any). When it is not possible to estimate the recoverable amount of an individual asset, the Company estimates the recoverable amount of the cash-generating unit to which the asset belongs. If the recoverable amount of an asset (or cash enerating unit) is estimated to be less than its carrying amount, the carrying amount of the asset (or cash-generating unit) is reduced to its recoverable amount. An impairment loss is recognised immediately in the statement of profit or loss.

When an impairment loss subsequently reverses, the carrying amount of the asset (or a cash-generating unit) is increased to the revised estimate of its recoverable amount, but so that the increased carrying amount does not exceed the carrying amount that would have been determined had no impairment loss been recognised for the asset (or cash generating unit) in prior years. A reversal of an impairment loss is recognised immediately in the Statement of profit or loss.

Source: Balaji Telefilms Ltd Annual Report 2016–17, p. 108.

IFRS Update

The following table indicates the differences in the recognition of impairment of an asset, and its accounting treatment in the financial statements as per as per Indian Accounting Standards (Ind AS), IFRS or International Accounting Standards (IAS), and US Generally Accepted Accounting Practices (GAAP).

Impairment of Asset

Ind AS	IFRS/IAS	US GAAP
Asset is impaired, at higher of either fair value less costs to sale or value in use based on discounted cash flows. Impairment test is to be conducted every year and if upward revaluation seen later on then reversal of impairment losses are required in certain situations only.	Similar to Indian AS.	Impairment loss to be measured when the carrying amount is greater than the market value or discounted cash flow value. Impairment loss cannot be reversed later on.

Disposal of Asset by Cash

In the sale of an asset, the cash may be realized immediately or in future. The proceeds received from the disposal of an asset are compared with the book value of the asset. If the proceeds is greater than the book value, then the difference is known as profit or gain on sale of the asset. If the proceeds is less than the book value, then the difference is known as loss on sale of the asset.

For example, Kainaz Ltd has sold a computer with a book value of ₹13,000 for ₹15,000. Here, the difference between the sale value and book value, that is, ₹2,000, would be recorded as profit on sale of the asset.

If the computer had been sold for ₹10,000, then the difference of ₹3,000 would be treated as loss on sale of the asset. The impact of this transaction would be a reduction in the value of the asset (i.e., the computer) by ₹13,000, an increase in asset in the form of cash by ₹10,000 and booking of an expense, that is, loss on sale of computer, ₹3,000.

Exchange of Assets

This section discusses the implication of trading in used assets for new.

Assets such as automobiles, computer equipments, and office furniture, are customarily traded in for new assets of the same kind. The trade-in-allowance (commonly known as exchange value) granted by the dealer or manufacturer differs from the book value of the old asset. If the dealer grants an exchange value greater than the book value, then a gain

is realized on exchange of the asset. If the dealer grants an exchange value lesser than the book value, then a loss is realized on exchange of the asset. As per prudent and accepted accounting practices, the loss will be taken to the profit and loss account of the year concerned, and profit on exchange will be deducted from the value of the new asset. If the exchange involved dissimilar assets (for example computer exchanged for chairs), then the profit or loss incurred on account of difference between the agreed exchange value and the book value of the computer would be charged directly in the profit and loss account for the period concerned (Shankaranarayana and Ramanath 2011).

Para No. 22 of AS-10 prescribes that the cost of the new asset acquired would be equal to the additional amount paid or to be paid plus the fair market value or at the net book value of the assets given up. For this purpose, the fair market value may be determined by reference either to the assets given up or to the assets acquired, whichever is more clearly evident. Fixed assets acquired in exchange for shares or other securities in the enterprise should be recorded at its fair market value, or the fair market value of the securities issued, whichever is more clearly evident.

■ **ILLUSTRATION 8.6** Assume that Marigold Company purchased machinery for ₹5,20,000 on 1 April 2016, with an estimated life of six years and estimated scrap value of ₹40,000. They charged the depreciation as per the straight-line method. The firm followed the fiscal year as the accounting year. The machinery was exchanged for a new machinery costing ₹6,40,000, and the agreed exchange value was ₹1,80,000 as on 30 September 2020. Also assume that the agreed value is ₹1,40,000. Calculate the cost of new machinery.

Solution

The book value of the present machine as on 30 September 2020 is ₹1,60,000 as calculated here.

Purchase value of present machine as on 1 April 2016	₹5,20,000
Depreciation as per SLM per year ((5,20,000 – 40,000)/6)	₹80,000
Depreciation provided till the date of exchange (₹80,000 × 4 ½ years)	₹3,60,000
Book value on the date of exchange (₹5,20,000 – ₹3,60,000)	₹1,60,000

If the agreed exchange value is ₹1,80,000, then the new machinery cost can be calculate as under:

Agreed exchange value	₹1,80,000
Profit on exchange of machinery (₹1,80,000 – ₹1,60,000)	₹20,000
New machinery cost (₹6,40,000 – ₹20,000)	₹6,20,000

If the agreed exchange value is ₹1,40,000, then the new machinery cost can be calculate as follows:

Agreed exchange value	₹1,40,000
Loss on exchange of machinery (₹1,40,000 – ₹1,60,000)	₹20,000
Charge against the income of the year, through debit to profit and loss account of the year 2020–21.	₹20,000
New machinery cost	₹6,40,000

Revaluation of Assets

Fixed assets may be restated in value with the help of appraisal undertaken by competent and approved valuers. Such a change in the value of the assets is termed as *revaluation*. When an asset or group of assets is revalued upwards, the accumulated depreciation for the asset(s) cannot be credited to the profit and loss account. When an asset is revalued upwards, the asset account, and owner's fund will be increased to the extent of increase in the value of the concern asset.

The value of fixed assets is presented in financial statements, either by restating both the gross book value and adjusted accumulated depreciation, so as to give a net book value equal to the net revalued amount, or by restating the net book value by adding the net increase on account, of revaluation. After revaluation, the provision for depreciation should be based on the revalued amount and on the revised estimated balance useful life of the assets.

To determine the periodic net income, the cost relating to the use of long-term assets should be properly calculated and matched against the revenue earned. These use cost or expenses or periodic write-offs and are known by different names for different category of assets as shown in Table 8.1.

TABLE 8.1 Terms of write-offs for long-term assets

Long-term Assets	Term of Expenses for Write-offs
1. Tangible assets	
(a) Land (free hold)	None
(b) Lease hold land	Write off or amortization
(c) Plant, building, equipment, tools, furniture, fixtures, vehicles, etc.	Depreciation
(d) Natural resources such as oil, timber, coal, and mineral deposits	Depletion
2. Intangible assets such as patents, copyrights, trademarks, goodwill, etc.	Amortization

Land is a tangible asset and has an indefinite or unlimited useful life. Hence, it is not subject to depreciation and is not written-off periodically.

REDUCTION IN VALUE OR WRITE OFF ■

Recording of the reduction in value of an asset or writing off the value of an asset, during the accounting period, is a system of accounting which aims to distribute the cost or other basic value of tangible, intangible, and natural capital asset over the estimated useful life of the asset in a systematic and rational way. It is the process of *allocation not of valuation*. Hence, writing off the value for the year is the portion of that charge under such a system that is allocated to the accounting period under consideration. The reduction in value of an asset is recorded as depletion cost, amortization cost, or depreciation expense, as explained hereunder.

DEPLETION COST

Depletion is the portion of the cost of natural resources that is allocated to extraction or production of resources over time. The first step in calculating the depletion value of an asset is to determine its depletion rate. *Depletion rate* is the acquisition and development cost less residual value at the end of the estimated life divided by the total estimated recoverable units of the natural resources during the expected life of the asset. Usually natural resources do not have residual values, however, any associated equipment may have residual value.

> Depletion Rate = (Acquisition and Development Costs – Residual Value)/Estimated Recoverable Units

Depletion amount is calculated by multiplying the depletion rate by the number of units of the resources recovered during the concerned accounting period. Depletion amount should be taken as an expense only when the resources are sold. If a portion of the current production remains in inventory, then a corresponding portion of depletion amount should be recorded in the inventory as depletion expense.

> Depletion Cost = Depletion × Number of Units

■ **ILLUSTRATION 8.7** M/s NewTee took a mine on lease on 1 January 2018 for ₹50,00,000. As per the technical estimate, the total quantity of mineral deposits is 1,00,000 tonnes. Depreciation is charged on the basis of depletion method. The actual output in 2018 was 5,000 tonnes, in 2019, it was 12,000 tonnes; and in 2020, it was 20,000 tonnes. Prepare the mine lease account for the above years.

Solution

Rate of depreciation = Cost of mine/Estimated quantity to be raised
= ₹50,00,000/1,00,000 tonnes

Rate of depreciation = ₹50 per ton

The depreciation for year 2018, 2019, and 2020 is calculated as follows:

Depreciation for 2018 = 5,000 tonnes × ₹50 = ₹2,50,000
Depreciation for 2019 = 12,000 tonnes × ₹50 = ₹6,00,000
Depreciation for 2020 = 20,000 tonnes × ₹50 = ₹10,00,000

Name of Account: Mine Lease Account
Type of Account: Asset   **Normal Balance: Debit**

Date	Reference Account	Voucher Type	Post Ref No.	Dr. (Add)	Cr. (Less)
1.1.2018	To Bank A/c			50,00,000	
31.12.2018	By Depreciation A/c				2,50,000
	By Balance c/d				47,50,000

	Total			50,00,000	50,00,000
1.1.2019	To Balance b/d			47,50,000	
31.12.2019	By Depreciation A/c				6,00,000
	By Balance c/d				41,50,000
	Total			47,50,000	47,50,000
1.1.2020	To Balance b/d			41,50,000	
31.12.2020	By Depreciation A/c				10,00,000
	By Balance c/d				31,50,000
	Total			41,50,000	41,50,000
1.1.2021	**To Balance b/d**			**31,50,000**	

Note: b/d refers to the amount brought down.
c/d refers to the amount carried down.

AMORTIZATION COST

The cost of acquiring intangible long-term operating assets is allocated over the life of the asset to reflect the decline in its service potential. The allocated cost of services given up at each period of the asset's life is known as *amortization*. The expected life of an intangible asset is determined either by the end of the economic advantage it offers or by the expiry of its legal life. Therefore, the cost of any intangible asset should be amortized over its economic or legal life (whichever is shorter). Since the residual value of an intangible asset is nearly always zero by the end of its expected life, the entire cost of an intangible asset is usually subject to amortization.

> Amortization per Period = Cost of an Intangible Asset/Expected Life in Periods

DEPRECIATION EXPENSES

Firms use long-term operating assets to provide a variety of services extending over periods ranging from 1 to 40 years or more. Factory buildings used for 30 years or more and automated manufacturing equipments used over periods ranging from 5 to 10 years are examples of long-term assets.

The cost of using long-term operating assets, also known as depreciation, is recorded gradually as the assets are used. Depreciation is an allocation of the cost that is calculated using an asset's acquisition cost, it's expected life, and expected residual value.

The expected life of an asset is the period of time over which the business anticipates using the asset. The expected life can be estimated in terms of measurement units (e.g., tonnes of mineral oil) or units of time (e.g., number of years). The expected residual value of a depreciable asset is the estimated amount of cash or trade-in-value that the business expects to recover at the end of an asset's expected life. The residual value is also known as salvage or scrap value. The depreciable cost is the difference between the acquisition cost and the estimated residual value. The accumulated depreciation is the amount of

depreciation that has been recorded for an asset at any given time. An asset's net book value is the difference between the acquisition cost and accumulated depreciation.

The Institute of Chartered Accountants of India (ICAI) defines depreciation in the accounting standard Ind AS 16 on depreciation accounting as, 'Depreciation is a measure of wearing out, consumption or other loss of value of depreciable asset arising from use, time, or obsolescence due to technology and market changes. Depreciation is allocated so as to charge a fair proportion of the depreciable amount in each accounting period during the expected useful life of the asset. Depreciation includes amortization of assets whose useful life is pre-determined.' In other words, depreciation is the allocated cost of services given up by a tangible long-term operating asset (other than land) over a period of time.

Depreciation accounting becomes necessary as assets (except land) lose their economic utility, significance, or potential over time. Many factors such as wear and tear, passage of time, obsolescence, technological change, physical deterioration, etc. cause decline in the utility of an asset. To determine the amount of depreciation, factors such as actual acquisition cost, estimated net residual value, and estimated useful life are considered. Hence, the amount of depreciation recorded in books of accounts is only an estimate.

Causes of Depreciation

As mentioned in the earlier section, assets decline in value due to various reasons. The causes of decline in the value of an asset are explained in the following text.

Wear and tear   Assets get worn out on account of constant use in a firm's business activities.

Obsolescence   Some assets are discarded before they are worn out because of changed business conditions. For example, an old machine, which is still workable, may have to be replaced by a new machine because the latter is more efficient and economical. Such a loss on account of new invention or change in technology is termed as loss on account of obsolescence.

Time   Certain assets decrease in their value with the passage of time. This is applicable to assets such as leasehold premises, patents, and copyrights.

Accidents   Due to an accident, an asset may depreciate in value.

Objectives of Depreciation

The various objectives of providing depreciation are explained in this section.

Correct income measurement   Depreciation is used to calculate the net profit or loss in an accounting period. It is the portion of the cost of the fixed asset that has expired during the period.

True position statements   To present a true and fair view of the state of affairs of an entity, assets must be valued correctly on the balance sheet. If the depreciation is not charged, the assets may be overstated in the balance sheet. Hence, an asset will be shown in the balance sheet at its net book value or written down value (i.e., its original cost less the amount charged as depreciation).

Funds for replacement   Depreciation is used to calculate the amount of funds required to replace an asset at the end of its useful life.

Effects of Not Providing for Depreciation

If depreciation is not provided, then the income statement and the balance sheet will not exhibit a true and fair view of the business. The following problems may arise if depreciation is not provided.

- Periodic expenses will be understated
- Profits will be overstated
- Asset valuation will be overstated
- Capital depletion will take place
- Cost of production will be understated
- Price determination will be inappropriate
- Net worth will be overstated

Allocation of Depreciation

Accumulated depreciation is that part of the cost of a fixed asset that is not recoverable when the asset is finally put out of use. Depreciation is the value of the benefit the asset has provided during a given accounting period. The benefit is valued at the portion of the cost of the asset. It does not provide funds for the replacement of a depreciable asset. Depreciation provides funds for the replacement of an asset, if the entity has invested that amount in outside securities.

Depreciation accounting attempts to allocate the acquisition costs and estimated residual value (salvage value) over the useful life of the asset. Depreciation is simply the allocation of the cost of an asset to the periods that benefit from the services of the assets, with the intention to allocate the same as an expense and to be matched with revenues in each period. It is related to the income statement which shows the net income after accounting for depreciation.

Depreciation accounting is helpful to ascertain the true profit and the real financial position of the entity. Accumulated depreciation is deducted from the related asset account on the balance sheet to compute the asset's book value. We shall briefly discuss some methods. However, in order to understand the methods, we should be clear about certain commonly used terms.

Original cost of the asset   This is the cost incurred in making the asset available for use in the first instance.

Salvage value   This is the expected recovery of the sales value of an asset at the end of its useful life.

Useful life   The expected time period for which the asset provides economic services, that is, the period in which the asset could be used for an entity's production or operational activities.

Depreciable cost   This is the original cost less expected salvage value. This is the amount of expenses the enterprise will be incurring on amount of expired costs of the machine over its useful or economic life.

Written down value   The written down value of an asset at any point of time is original cost less depreciation to date (i.e., accumulated depreciation). It is also referred to as book value.

LIFE OF AN ASSET

The service life or productive life of an asset is the length of time for which it can be used in the operations of the firm. The service life may not be as long as the asset's potential or physical life. The physical life period is termed as the *physical life period*, while the productive life period is termed as the *economic life period.*

For example, the potential life of computer equipment is six to eight years; a firm may plan to exchange its old computers with new computer equipment every three years. Here, the physical life period of the computer equipment is six to eight years, while the economic life period is three years. Therefore, the firm should charge the cost of computers as reduced by expected trade in allowance (exchange) value (at the end of three years' period) over the three-year period.

The economic life is often difficult to predict because of several factors such as wear and tear, inadequacy, obsolescence of technology, etc. Inadequacy occurs with respect to the productive capacity of an asset, when the firm's business grows more rapidly than expected at the time of purchase of a fixed asset. Obsolescence is difficult to anticipate because the exact occurrence of new inventions and improvements cannot be normally predicted. To predict the economic life of an asset with reasonable accuracy, a firm's decisions must be based on its own and others' past experiences, or engineering studies and judgment.

DEPRECIATION METHODS

The different depreciation methods aim to allocate the cost of an asset to different accounting periods in a systematic and rational manner. Each method produces a different pattern of expenses over time.

As per Ind AS 16, *depreciable asset*s are assets which

1. are expected to be used during more than one accounting period;
2. have a limited useful life;
3. are held by an enterprise for use in the production or supply of goods and services, for rental to others or for administrative purpose and not for the purpose of sale in the ordinary course of business.

Land is not depreciated as per accounting standard, because it does not fulfil all conditions needed to be claimed as a depreciable asset. The main condition for being a depreciable asset would be its limited life. Land has unlimited life, its supply is inelastic (cannot be increased), and its productivity never deteriorates; hence, land does not qualify as a depreciable asset. The depreciation methods are categorized into four types as explained hereunder:

1. Based on life in terms of time phenomenon
2. Based on life in terms of capacity phenomenon
3. Based on precautionary phenomenon
4. Based on funds management phenomenon

DEPRECIATION METHODS BASED ON LIFE IN TERMS OF TIME PHENOMENON

Depreciation based on time phenomenon takes into consideration the passage of time, as considered wear and tear. The decrease in the value of an asset is recorded based on passage of time.

Straight-line Method

The straight-line method (SLM), also known as the fixed instalment method, allocates an equal amount of an asset's cost to each year of its expected useful life. This allocation assumes that an equal amount of an asset's potential is consumed in each period of its life. However, this may not be true under all circumstances. The repairs and maintenance cost will be lower in earlier years of use but will gradually be higher as the asset becomes old. Moreover, the asset might have different capacities over different years of its life.

The amount of depreciation for each period is computed by deducting the asset's expected residual value from its acquisition cost, and dividing the result by the asset's expected economical and useful life.

The rate of depreciation is the reciprocal of the estimated useful life. This may be presented as under:

$$\text{Annual Depreciation} = (\text{Cost of the Asset} - \text{Residual Value})/\text{Estimated Economic Life}$$

or,

$$\text{Annual Depreciation} = \text{Depreciation per Unit of Output} \times \text{Number of Units Produced during an Accounting Period}$$

$$\text{Depreciation per Unit Output} = (\text{Cost of Asset} - \text{Residual Value})/\text{Estimated Output during Economic Life}$$

For example, a machine costing ₹20,000 on 1 January 2020 has a residual value of ₹1,000 and a useful life of 10 years. Assuming the accounting year ends on 31 December 2020, the depreciation per annum (p.a.) will be calculated as

$$\text{Depreciation} = (20,000 - 1,000)/10 = ₹1,900$$

Instead of assuming the life of 10 years, let us assume that machine will produce 1,00,000 units. The depreciation per unit will be

$$\text{Depreciation per Unit} = (20,000 - 1,000)/1,00,000 = ₹0.19$$

In a particular year, if 10,000 units will be produced, then depreciation charged will be ₹0.19 × 10,000 = ₹1,900

This method is simple, logical, consistent, and stable. It can be applied to an asset with relatively uniform periodic usage and low obsolescence factor.

Under the straight-line method, the depreciable cost of the asset is proportionately allocated as an expense against the revenues during each year of its useful life. Assume that a company acquires a machine at the beginning of operations at ₹1,000. It is expected that the machine will last 10 years and will have no salvage value at that time.

The depreciation for the machine every year under SLM will be ₹100 (1,000/10). The written down value at the end of first year will be ₹900 (1,000 – 100), at the end of second year will be ₹800 [1,000 – (100 + 100) or (900 – 100)], and so on. It becomes zero at the end of 10 years. The straight-line method is depicted graphically in Fig. 8.1.

If we draw a graph showing the annual depreciation, it will be a straight line parallel to the base line. The accumulated depreciation increases annually at a uniform rate and becomes

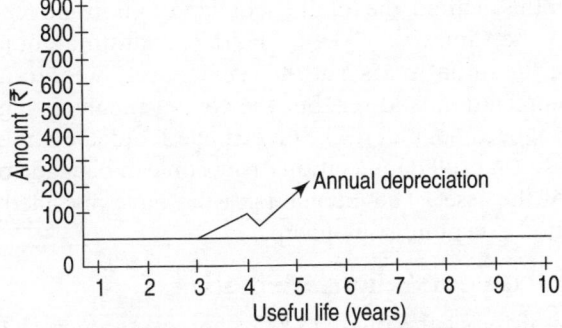

FIG. 8.1 SLM—annual depreciation charge

equal to the depreciable cost of the asset at the end of its useful life. As shown in Fig. 8.2, it is a straight line sloping upward to the right from the origin, whereas the written down value steadily declines to become zero at the end of useful life of the asset. Hence, a downward sloping straight line reaches origin at the end of the asset's useful life (Fig. 8.3).

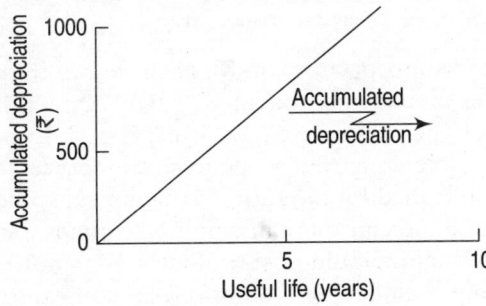

FIG. 8.2 SLM—accumulated depreciation

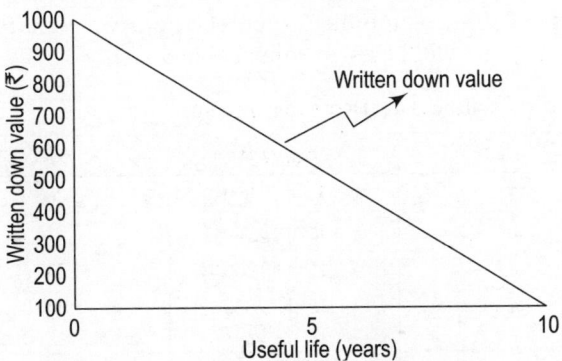

FIG. 8.3 SLM—accumulated depreciation

Written Down Value Method

Under the written down value (WDV) method of calculating depreciation, the amount charged for depreciation declines over the asset's expected life. This method is suitable in cases where (a) the receipts are expected to decline, as the asset gets older; and (b) it is believed that the allocation of depreciation should be related to the pattern of asset's expected receipts. The WDV method is also known as the reducing, diminishing, or declining balance method.

The depreciation charge is calculated by multiplying the net book value of the asset (acquisition cost less accumulated depreciation) at the start of each period by a fixed rate. Under the WDV method, it is impossible to reduce the asset value to zero, because there is always some balance to reduce the asset value even further. When the asset is sold, abandoned, or retired from use, the WDV appearing in books is written off as depreciation for the final period. Under this method, the fixed depreciation rate used charges the acquisition cost less salvage or residual value of the asset over its service life. The formula is given as

$$r = 1 - \sqrt[n]{s/c}$$

where r = Rate of depreciation or a fixed percentage
n = Number of years of asset's useful life
s = Salvage value or residual value
c = Acquisition cost of the asset

Depreciation at a certain rate is applied to the WDV of the asset as at the beginning on each year. The effect of this method is that the depreciation amount charged every year is an amount less than the previous year. In other words, larger amounts are charged to depreciation during the initial years of an asset's useful life.

Let us assume that a company buys an asset at a cost of ₹1,000. It decides to depreciate the asset at the cost of 20% per annum based on the WDV method. The annual book values, depreciation charge, and accumulated depreciation are provided in Table 8.2.

TABLE 8.2 WDV depreciation, Amount (₹)

Year	WDV at the End of the Year	Annual Depreciation	Accumulated Depreciation
0	1,000	—	—
1	800	200	200
2	640	160	360
3	512	128	488
4	410	102	590
5	328	82	672
6	262	66	738
7	210	52	790
8	168	42	832
9	134	34	866
10	107	27	893

Annual depreciation under the WDV method is the highest during the first year and keeps on reducing over the subsequent years. This is shown by a rapidly declining curve in Fig. 8.4. However, the declining rate reduces as the number of years approach the end of an asset's life. Similarly, accumulated depreciation increases at a rapid rate during initial years and

the rate of increase declines in later years (Fig. 8.5). The 'written down' value of the asset is a declining curve (Fig. 8.6). The unallocated portion of the cost is usually charged as depreciation in the last year of the life of the asset.

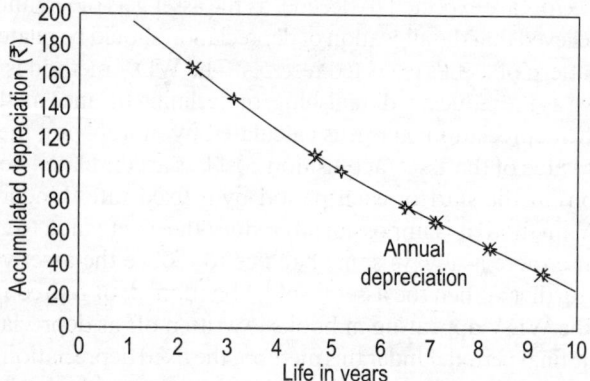

FIG. 8.4   SLM—annual depreciation

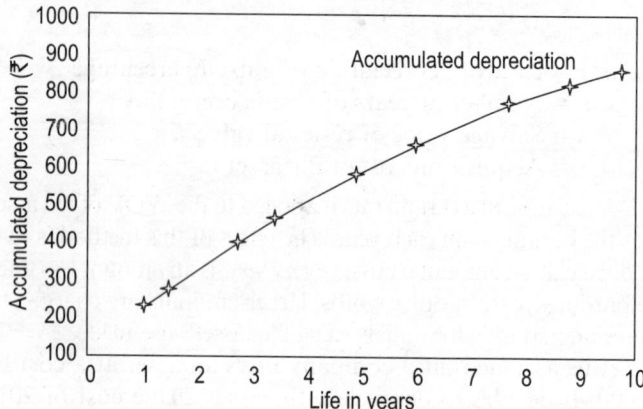

FIG. 8.5   WDV method—accumulated depreciation charge

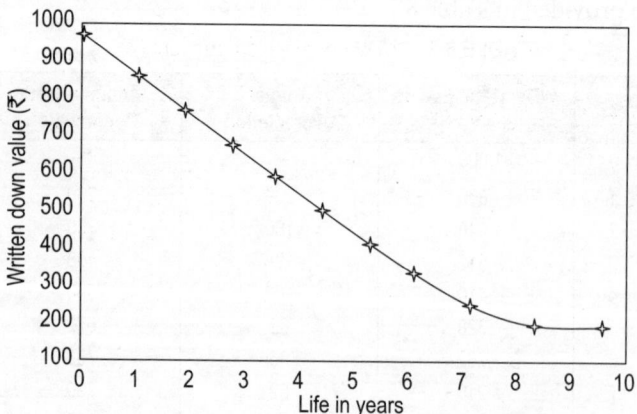

FIG. 8.6   WDV method—accumulated depreciation

For example, if the cost of a machine is ₹10,000 and its scrap value after four years is ₹2,000, the rate of depreciation (R) is calculated as

$$R = 1 - \sqrt[4]{2,000/10,000} = 33.33\%$$

The calculation of depreciation for each of the four years is illustrated in Table 8.3.

TABLE 8.3   Calculation of depreciation using WDV method, Amount (₹)

Year (1)	Cost of Machine (2)	Annual Depreciation (33.33%) (3)	Accumulated Depreciation (4)	WDV (5) = (2) – (3)
1	10,000	3333	3,333	6,667
2	6,667	2222	5,555	4,445
3	4,445	1482	7,037	2,963
4	2,963	963*	8,000	2,000

*In the last year, the depreciation is adjusted to ₹24 (987 – 963) to bring the carrying value of the asset to its estimated scrap value.

Under this method, the total cost of depreciation and repairs is almost the same every year. The depreciation amount is higher in the initial years but the repairs are lower. In later years, depreciation is lower, but the cost of repairs is higher as the asset becomes older. The percentage should be carefully adopted so that full depreciation provision can be made over the life of the asset. The income tax rules have provided for this method except in case of ships.

Sum-of-the-years'-digits Method

The sum-of-the-years'-digits (SYD) method of depreciation charges larger amount of asset costs to expenses in the early years of life, and lesser amount in later years. The depreciation is calculated by multiplying an asset's depreciable cost by a declining ratio derived from the sum of the number of years in the asset's expected life. To calculate the appropriate SYD ratio, first find the sum of the digits in the expected life. For example, the SYD for an asset with a life of 5 years is calculated as

$$5 + 4 + 3 + 2 + 1 = 15$$

Next, the appropriate ratio for each year of the expected life is determined. Each balance year is divided figure by the sum of the digits (e.g., 5/15, 4/15, ...,1/15). Finally, the depreciable cost, that is, acquisition cost less residual value is multiplied by the ratio for each year to determine the annual depreciation. This method applies a changing rate to the depreciable cost which is constant, whereas the declining balance method applies a constant rate to a changing book value.

If the cost of machine is ₹10,000 and scrap value after 5 years is ₹200, the amount of depreciation to be charged in different years will be as given in Table 8.4.

TABLE 8.4   Depreciation charged over years

Year	Computation	Amount (₹)
1	5/15 of ₹9,800	3,266
2	4/15 of ₹9,800	2,614
3	3/15 of ₹9,800	1,960
4	2/15 of ₹9,800	1,306
5	1/15 of ₹9,800	654
	Total	9,800

Double-declining Method

This method charges larger amounts of depreciation to the early years of an asset's life. Under this method, a constant rate is applied to the asset balance, that is, acquisition cost less accumulated depreciation. The rate used for a new asset is twice the rate under the straight-line method of depreciation. In double-declining method, the book value of an asset never reaches zero. Thus, the depreciation in the final year should be calculated as the difference between the book value at the beginning of the year and the residual value.

DEPRECIATION METHODS BASED ON LIFE IN TERMS OF CAPACITY PHENOMENON

Depreciation based on capacity phenomenon takes into consideration the firm's business activities. The decrease in the value of an asset is recorded based on usage of an asset for productive or operational purposes.

Usage Method

The usage method of depreciation allocates the cost of an asset over its expected life in direct proportion to the actual use made of the asset, for example, the miles travelled by a delivery truck. Usage depreciation is computed by multiplying an asset's depreciable cost by a usage ratio, as in the following equation.

$$\text{Usage Depreciation} = \text{Usage Ratio} \times \text{Acquisition Cost Less Residual Value}$$

The usage ratio is the actual usage of the asset during the accounting period divided by the total expected usage of the asset over its expected life.

$$\text{Usage Ratio} = \text{Actual Usage During the Period}/\text{Total Expected Usage}$$

Depending on the use of an asset over its life, this formula can produce a depreciation schedule that is accelerated, decelerated, or erratic. In the last year of an asset's useful life, depreciation is calculated as the remaining depreciable cost (net book value less residual value).

Machine Hour Method

Where it is practical to keep a record of the actual running hours of each machine, depreciation may be calculated on the basis of hours that the concerned machine has worked. The machine hour rate of depreciation is calculated after estimating the total number of hours that machine would work during its whole life. However, it may vary from time to time due to change in economic and technological conditions. The machine hour method is only a slight variation of the straight-line method, under which depreciation is calculated per year. Under this method, depreciation is calculated for each hour the machine works.

$$\text{Depreciation for the Period} = \text{Depreciable Amount} \times (\text{Number of Hours a Machine Works}/\text{Estimated Total Machine Hours})$$

Production Units Method

Under this method, depreciation of the asset is determined by comparing the annual production with the estimated total production. The amount of depreciation is computed by using the following method.

$$\text{Depreciation} = \text{Depreciable Amount} \times (\text{Production during the Period}/\text{Estimated Total Production})$$

This method is applicable to machines manufacturing products of uniform specifications.

DEPRECIATION METHODS BASED ON PRECAUTIONARY PHENOMENON

Under this method, the precautionary expenses over the life of an asset are added to the original cost of the asset, with an intention to keep aside the amount from every year's revenue. Thus, wrong presentation of profit or loss can be omitted. Although this method is highly useful from management view, legal regulations do not permit it.

Repair Provision Method

Under this method, repairs and maintenance costs over the life of an asset is added to the original cost of the asset. It is used to calculate the total capital outlay and is apportioned over the life of the asset. A combined rate is calculated to account for depreciation as well as maintenance costs of the asset.

$$\text{Depreciation Charge per Year} = [(\text{Original Cost} - \text{Residual Value}) + \text{Maintenance Charges})]/\text{Number of Years of an Asset's Life}$$

The repair provision method is applied in conjunction with other methods of calculating depreciation such as straight-line, diminishing balance, etc. Fluctuations of cost due to abnormal and huge maintenance in a particular period can be avoided by using this method since cost of maintenance is evenly spread throughout the life of the asset. The drawback of this method is that it is almost impossible to accurately forecast the maintenance cost of an asset. The amount of repairing expenses during the life of an asset is estimated and then the annual amount is calculated. The annual amount is charged to the product cost each year and kept in the repair provision account. Actual repair expenses incurred in the lifetime of the asset is charged to the repair provision account. The balance amount at the end of the life of the asset is transferred to the profit and loss account.

■ILLUSTRATION 8.8 A combined provision for depreciation and repairs was made every year at 15% of the original cost of the machine purchased for ₹50,000. The provision for depreciation and maintenance account was opened for the purpose and was debited with the actual cost of repairs and renewals as given in the following text:

Cost of Repairs and Renewals

Year	Amount (₹)
1	1,500
2	1,600
3	2,100
4	3,000
5	4,200

At the end of fifth year, the machine was sold at ₹20,000 after utilizing a few of its minor parts valued at ₹4,000. A new machine, costing ₹75,000, was installed in its place. The resulting loss in the disposal of the machine was debited to the revenue account. Prepare a provision for depreciation and maintenance account, old machinery account, and new machinery account for five years.

Solution

Name of Account: Provision for Depreciation and Maintenance Account
Type of Account: Reduction in Asset   Normal Balance: Credit

Date	Reference Account	Voucher Type	Post Ref No.	Dr. (Less)	Cr. (Add)
Year 1	To Repairs and renewals A/c			1,500	
	By Profit and loss A/c				7,500
	Total			**1,500**	**7,500**
	By Balance c/d			6,000	
Year 2	By Balance b/d				6,000
	To Repairs and renewals A/c			1,600	
	By Profit and loss A/c				7,500
	Total			**1,600**	**13,500**
	By Balance c/d			11,900	
Year 3	By Balance b/d				11,900
	To Repairs and renewals A/c			2,100	
	By Profit and loss A/c				7,500
	Total			**2,100**	**19,400**
	By Balance c/d			17,300	
Year 4	By Balance b/d				17,300
	To Repairs and renewals A/c			3,000	
	By Profit and loss A/c				7,500
	Total			**3,000**	**24,800**
	By Balance c/d				21,800
Year 5	By Balance b/d				21,800
	To Repairs and renewals A/c			4,200	
	By Profit and loss A/c				7,500
	To Old Machines A/c (transfer)			25,100	
	Total			**29,300**	**29,300**

Name of Account: Old Machine A/c
Type of Account: Asset   Normal Balance: Debit

Date	Reference Account	Voucher Type	Post Ref No.	Dr. (Add)	Cr. (Less)
Year 5	To Balance b/d			50,000	
	By Bank A/c				20,000
	By New machine A/c (Parts used in new machine)				4,000
	By Provision for depreciation and machine A/c				25,100
	By Profit and loss A/c (Balance figure)				900
	Total			**50,000**	**50,000**

Name of Account: New Machine Account
Type of Account: Asset   Normal Balance: Debit

Date	Reference Account	Voucher Type	Post Ref No.	Dr. (Add)	Cr. (Less)
Year 5	To Bank A/c			75,000	
	To Old machine A/c (old parts used)			4,000	
	Total			**79,000**	–
	By Balance c/d				79,000
Year 6	By Balance b/d			79,000	

Note: b/d refers to brought down.
     c/d refers to carried down.

DEPRECIATION METHODS BASED ON LIFE IN TERMS OF FUNDS MANAGEMENT PHENOMENON

These methods keep aside the amount of depreciation to enable availability of funds in case of a replacement in asset in future. This will help the firm in receiving an easy replacement of an asset without any loss of time, to manage the funds. Depreciation is a non-cash expense; hence this method is highly suitable and advisable for majority of firms in today's state-of-the-art technology advancements.

Annuity Method

This is a method of depreciation that also takes into account the element of interest on capital outlay and seeks to write off value of the asset as interest cost over the life of the asset. It assumes that the amount laid down in acquiring an asset, if invested elsewhere could have earned interest. This interest must also be reckoned as part of the cost of the assets. On that basis, the amount of depreciation to be provided annually in the account is ascertained from the annuity tables. These tables are used to write off each year's interest on the capital outlay as well as part of the capital sum at a rate that the whole amount could be written off over the life of the asset. Although the amount written off annually is constant, the proportion of the interest written off is greater than the capital written off. This proportion is recovered with the passage of time.

This method is eminently suitable for writing off amounts paid for long leases which involve a considerable capital outlay. This method is not used for writing off depreciation on plant and machinery because of frequent changes in the value of such assets. These changes necessitate the recalculation of the amount of depreciation to be written off annually. Relevant journal entries are as given in the following text:

1. For charging interest on asset account
   Assets account Dr. (Add)
      To Interest account (Add)
2. For charging depreciation on asset
   Depreciation account Dr. (Add)
      To Asset account (Less)
3. For transferring depreciation to profit and loss account
   Profit and loss account Dr. (Add)
      To Depreciation account (Less)
4. For transferring interest to profit and loss account
   Interest account Dr. (Less)
      To Profit and loss account (Add)

Sinking Fund Method

If a large sum of money is required for the replacement of an asset at the end of its effective life, the amount of depreciation set apart annually for it may or may not be available in the form of readily realizable assets when needed. To safeguard this position, the amount provided annually for depreciation may be placed to the credit of the sinking fund account and at the same time an equivalent amount may be invested in government securities. The interest on those securities when received would be reinvested, and the amount would be credited to the sinking fund account. The amount of the annual provision for depreciation in such cases is calculated by taking into account the interest that the amount annually invested shall be earning over the investment period.

When the asset is due for replacement, securities are sold and new assets are purchased with the proceeds of the sale. The book value of the old asset at the time is transferred to the sinking fund account. Any amount realized on sale of the old asset and the profit or loss on sale of securities, is transferred to the sinking fund account. This account is closed off by transfer of the balance to the profit and loss account or general reserve. Relevant journal entries are as given in this section:

1. For transfer of depreciation to sinking fund
   Depreciation account Dr. (Add)
      To Sinking fund account (Add)
2. For charging depreciation to profit and loss account
   Profit and loss account Dr. (Less)
      To Depreciation account (Less)
3. For investment of amount of depreciation
   Sinking fund investment account Dr. (Add)
      To Bank account (Less)
4. In subsequent years, for interest earned on sinking fund investment
   Bank account Dr. (Add)
      To Interest on sinking fund investment account (Add)
   Interest on sinking fund investment account Dr. (Less)
      To Sinking fund account (Add)

5. For sale of sinking fund investment at the end of useful life of the asset
   Bank account Dr. (Add)
      To Sinking fund investment account (Less)
   If sale is at a profit,
   Sinking fund investment account Dr. (Add)
      To Sinking fund account (Add)
   If sale is at loss,
   Sinking fund account Dr. (Less)
      To Sinking fund investment account (Less)
6. For transfer of the amount to the extent of book value of the asset from asset account to sinking fund account
   Sinking fund account Dr. (Less)
      To Asset account (Less)
7. Any surplus in sinking fund account may be transferred to general reserve account, and any deficit may be transferred to the profit and loss account
   Sinking fund account Dr. (Less)
      To General reserve account (Add)
   or
   Profit and loss account Dr. (Less)
      To Sinking fund account (Add)

Insurance Policy Method

This method is similar to the depreciation fund method. The insurance policy method ensures the supply of desired cash on the expiry of an asset's useful life in return of periodic contribution (known as premium) to the insurance company. Under this method, a firm takes an insurance policy from the insurance company for an amount equal to the cost of replacing the asset. The annual premium paid by the firm is treated as depreciation expense and charged to the profit and loss account. The asset account is shown in the books at its original cost. The following journal entries are passed under this method:

First and subsequent years

(i) For payment of premium at the beginning of the year
   Depreciation insurance policy A/c (Add) Dr.
      To Bank A/c (Less)
(ii) For providing the charge of depreciation expense (equal to periodic premium) at the end of the year out of the profit and loss account
   Profit and loss A/c (Less) Dr.
      To Depreciation fund (for Reserve) A/c (Add)

Last year

(i) For the receipt of amount of policy on maturity
   Bank A/c (Add) Dr.
      To Depreciation insurance policy A/c (Less)
(ii) For the transfer of the excess of the received money over the premium contributions so as to close the insurance policy A/c
   Depreciation insurance policy A/c (Add) Dr.
      To Depreciation fund A/c (Add)
(iii) For transferring the balance of Depreciation fund to Asset A/c

Depreciation fund A/c (Less) Dr.
　　To Asset A/c (Less)

(iv) For sale of old asset as scrap
　　Bank A/c (Add) Dr.
　　　　To Asset A/c (Less)

(v) For transfer of the old asset's credit or debit balance depicting over or under estimate of depreciation to Profit and loss A/c
　　Asset A/c (Add) Dr.
　　　　To Profit and loss A/c (Add)

The distinction between sinking fund method and insurance policy method are explained in Table 8.5.

TABLE 8.5　Distinction between sinking fund method and insurance policy method

Sinking Fund Method	Insurance Policy Method
1. This method endeavors to provide a certain sum at a given date since there is no guarantee of realization of the security at cost. It depends on ruling prices which may vary according to market conditions.	1. This method provides a certain sum at a given date since the insurer undertakes to do so in consideration of regular periodic premiums.
2. Investment in marketable securities is made at the end of each year as this method is closely associated with the provision for depreciation.	2. Premium on insurance policy is paid at the beginning of each year as this method is associated with purchase of assets.
3. Interest at a higher rate is annually received and reinvested in securities.	3. Interest at a lower rate is received at the maturity of the policy.
4. Usually, marginal loss or profit occurs on sale of the security prior to the asset's retirement.	4. Heavy loss occurs on surrender of policy prior to asset's retirement.
5. The interest is received every year on the investments made.	5. Interest is accumulated and realized at the time of surrender/maturity of the policy.

Exhibit 8.8 explains the practices adopted by companies in India to treat depreciation in their books of accounts.

REVALUATION METHOD

Under this method, assets are revalued periodically and the decline in their values is considered as depreciation. Thus, the difference between the values assigned to the assets at the beginning and end of a period is equal to the depreciation. This method is generally used for depreciation of loose tools, livestock, patents, patterns, plant on contract sites, etc.

The amount of decrease in an asset's value shows the amount by which the asset is deemed to have depreciated. This method is used in case of livestock, corks, packages, bottles, trade marks, etc.

According to the revised accounting standard AS-6, when depreciable assets are revalued, the provision for depreciation should be based on the revalued amount and on the estimate of the remaining useful life of such asset. In case the revaluation has a material effect on the amount of depreciation, the same should be disclosed separately in the year in which it was carried out.

■ **ILLUSTRATION 8.9**　A company manufactures loose tools for its own use. At the end of each year, depreciation is charged using the revaluation method. From the following particulars, show the loose tools account.

Year Ended	Loose Tools Manufactured	Revalued at
31/12/2017	₹5,000	₹4,100 (31/12/2017)
31/12/2018	₹2,700	₹5,700 (31/12/2018)
31/12/2019	₹1,000	₹6,000 (31/12/2019)
31/12/2020	₹1,500	₹5,100 (31/12/2020)

The value as on 31/12/2020 is after considering the sale of old asset with the book value of ₹1200 for ₹950.

Name of Account: Loose Tools Account
Type of Account: Asset　　　　　　　　　**Normal Balance: Debit**

Date	Reference Account	Voucher Type	Post Ref No.	Dr. (Add)	Cr. (Less)
2017	To Cost of production			5,000	
	By Depreciation A/c				900
	Total			**5,000**	**900**
	By Balance c/f				4,100
2018	To Balance b/d			4,100	
	To Cost of production			2,700	
	By Depreciation A/c (Balance figure)				1,100
	Total			**6,800**	**1,100**
	By Balance c/f				5,700
2019	To Balance b/d			5,700	
	To Cost of production			1,000	
	By Depreciation A/c (Balance figure)				700
	Total			**6,700**	**700**
	By Balance c/f				6,000
2020	To Balance b/d			6,000	
	To Cost of production			1,500	
	By Bank A/c (Sale)				950
	By Profit and loss A/c (Loss)				250
	By Depreciation A/c (Balance figure)				1,200
	Total			**7,500**	**2,400**
	By Balance c/f (Balance figure)				5,100
2021	To Balance b/d			5,100	

INFLATION AND DEPRECIATION

The valuation of an asset on a cost basis and providing the depreciation in terms of cost will work successfully

EXHIBIT 8.8 Corporate Practices of Treating Depreciation on Assets

Let us look how various companies treat and recognize depreciation on assets in their books of accounts:

Media and Entertainment Industry: Balaji Telefilms Ltd

Depreciation and Amortisation

Depreciation on Property, Plant and Equipment has been provided on the straight-line method as per the useful life prescribed in Schedule II to the Companies Act, 2013 except for the following assets which are depreciated as per management estimates of their useful life which are as under:

- Studios and sets – 3 years
- Leasehold improvements – on a straight line basis over the period of lease

Retail Market Industry: Future Retail Ltd

The company depreciates property, plant and equipment over their estimated useful lives using the straight-line method. The estimated useful lives of assets are as follows:

Building:	30 years
Plant and Equipment:	15 years
Office Equipment*:	3 to 6 years
Furniture and Fixture:	10 years
Leasehold Improvement*:	Lease term or 15 years, whichever is lower
Vehicle:	8 years

*Based on technical evaluation, the management believes that the useful lives as given above best represent the period over which management expects to use these assets. Hence, the useful lives for these assets is different from the useful lives as prescribed under Part C of Schedule II of the Companies Act 2013.

The residual values, useful lives and methods of depreciation of property, plant and equipment are reviewed at each financial year end and adjusted prospectively, if appropriate.

Leasehold lands are amortised over the period of lease. Buildings constructed on leasehold land are depreciated based on the useful life specified in Schedule II to the Companies Act, 2013, where the lease period of land is beyond the life of the building.

In other cases, buildings constructed on leasehold lands are amortised over the primary lease period of the lands.

Steel Industry: Tata Steel Ltd

Depreciation or amortisation is provided so as to write off, on a straight line basis, the cost/deemed cost of property, plant and equipment and intangible assets, including those held under finance leases to their residual value. These charges are commenced from the dates the assets are available for their intended use and are spread over their estimated useful economic lives or, in the case of leased assets, over the lease period, if shorter. The estimated useful lives of assets and residual values are reviewed regularly and, when necessary, revised. No further charge is provided in respect of assets that are fully written down but are still in use.

Depreciation on assets under construction commences only when the assets are ready for their intended use. The estimated useful lives for main categories of property, plant and equipment and intangible assets are:

	Estimated Useful Life (Years)
Buildings upto	60 years*
Roads	5 years
Plant and Machinery upto	40 years*
Railway Sidings upto	35 years*
Vehicles and Aircraft	5 to 20 years
Furniture, Fixtures and Office Equipments	4 to 6 years
Computer Software	5 years
Assets covered under Electricity Act (life as prescribed under the Electricity Act)	3 to 34 years

Mining assets are amortised over the useful life of the mine or lease period whichever is lower. Major furnace relining expenses are depreciated over a period of 10 years (average expected life). Freehold land is not depreciated. Assets value upto ₹25,000 are fully depreciated in the year of acquisition.

*For these class of assets, based on internal assessment and independent technical evaluation carried out by chartered engineers, the Company believes that the useful lives as given above best represents the period over which the Company expects to use these assets. Hence the useful lives for these assets are different from the useful lives as prescribed under Part C of Schedule II of the Companies Act, 2013.

Sources: Balaji Telefilms Ltd Annual Report 2016–17, p. 154; Future Retail Limited Annual Report 2017–18, p. 94; Tata Steel Ltd Annual Report 2017–18, pp. 202–203.

---

at stable price levels in the economy. However, in reality, the price levels are rising constantly, and so there is a need to provide for depreciation on the *estimated current replacement cost*.

For example, Modern Cements purchased machinery in the year 2018 at a cost of ₹10 lakh. The estimated useful life of the machinery was 10 years, and Modern Cements used the straight-line method of depreciation. For the year ended December 2020, the firm would provide for the depreciation of ₹1 lakh [(₹10 lakh less expected salvage value (nil))/10 years] as per the accepted accounting practices.

Mr Gautam, owner of Modern Cements, realized that the new machinery is not significantly different from the old one, which would now cost ₹12 lakh. Hence, he would provide for additional depreciation proportionately to take care of future needs. He thus decided to provide the per year depreciation based on the current replacement cost ₹1.20 lakh. He has provided only ₹3 lakh in the last three years by way of depreciation. Hence, he should provide for an additional ₹60,000 (₹20,000 short provided in each year × 3 years completed life of machine) in the profit and loss account of the year 2020. Mr Gautam knows that this additional charge is his discretionary charge; the income tax department as well as accepted practices will not accept it. However, this will provide him the necessary cushion to run the firm successfully over the period. As he provides a higher amount apart from the year's profit, he will not face dire consequences with respect to liquidity in future when there is a need to replace the machinery.

■ **ILLUSTRATION 8.10** On 1 January 2016, a lease of premises is purchased for four years for ₹5,00,000 and it is decided to make provision for the replacement of the lease by means of an insurance policy purchased for an annual premium of ₹1,20,000.

Show the necessary ledger accounts for four years assuming that the renewal of the lease costs ₹5,50,000 on 1/1/2020.

Solution

Name of Account: Lease Account
Type of Account: Asset   **Normal Balance: Debit**

Date	Reference Account	Voucher Type	Post Ref No.	Dr. (Add)	Cr. (Less)
1.1.2016	To Bank A/c			5,00,000	
31.12.2016	By Balance c/d				5,00,000
1.1.2017	To Balance b/d			5,00,000	
31.12.2017	By Balance c/d				5,00,000
1.1.2018	To Balance b/d			5,00,000	
31.12.2018	To Balance c/d				5,00,000
1.1.2019	To Balance b/d			5,00,000	
31.12.2019	By Depreciation fund A/c (Transfer)				5,00,000

Name of Account: Depreciation Fund Account
Type of Account: Reduction in Asset   **Normal Balance: Credit**

Date	Reference Account	Voucher Type	Post Ref No.	Dr. (Less)	Cr. (Add)
1.1.2016	By Profit and loss A/c				1,20,000
31.12.2016	To Balance c/d			1,20,000	
	Total			1,20,000	1,20,000
1.1.2017	By Balance b/d				1,20,000
1.1.2017	By Profit and loss A/c				1,20,000
31.12.2017	To Balance c/d			2,40,000	
	Total			2,40,000	2,40,000
1.1.2018	By Balance b/d				2,40,000
1.1.2018	By Profit and loss A/c				1,20,000
31.12.2018	To Balance c/d			3,60,000	
	Total			3,60,000	3,60,000
1.1.2019	By Balance b/d				3,60,000
31.12.2019	By Profit and loss A/c				1,20,000

				20,000	
By Depreciation insurance policy A/c (Profit on realization)				20,000	
To Lease A/c					5,00,000
Total				5,00,000	5,00,000

Name of Account: Depreciation Insurance Policy Accont
Type of Account: Asset   **Normal Balance: Debit**

Date	Reference Account	Voucher Type	Post Ref No.	Dr. (Add)	Cr. (Less)
1.1.2016	To Bank A/c			1,20,000	
31.12.2016	To Balance c/d				1,20,000
	Total			1,20,000	1,20,000
1.1.2017	To Balance b/d			1,20,000	
31.12.2017	To Bank A/c			1,20,000	
31.1.2017	By Balance c/d				2,40,000
	Total			2,40,000	2,40,000
1.1.2018	To Balance b/d			2,40,000	
31.12.2018	To Bank A/c			1,20,000	
31.12.2018	By Balance c/d				3,60,000
	Total			3,60,000	3,60,000
1.1.2019	To Balance b/d			3,60,000	
31.12.2019	To Bank A/c			1,20,000	
31.12.2019	To Depreciation fund A/c (Profit on realization policy)			20,000	
31.12.2019	By Bank A/c (Insurance policy matured)				5,00,000
	Total			5,00,000	5,00,000

Name of Account: New Lease Account
Type of Account: Asset   **Normal Balance: Debit**

Date	Reference Account	Voucher Type	Post Ref No.	Dr. (Add)	Cr. (Less)
1.1.2020	To Bank A/c			5,50,000	

SELECTION OF DEPRECIATION METHOD

Depreciation determines the financial position and operational efficiency of an entity by calculating the net income and the deduction from taxable income. The quantum of depreciation to be provided in an accounting period involves the exercise of judgement in the light of technical, commercial, accounting, and legal requirements. The methods used for depreciation may need periodical review. The management selects the most appropriate method based on various factors such as type of asset, the nature of the use of such asset, prevailing business environment, etc. A combination of more than one method can also be used. In the case of fixed assets which do not have material value, depreciation is often allocated fully in the accounting period in which they are acquired.

Disclosure   Ind AS 16, issued by ICAI has provided that if the depreciation rate used is different from the principal rate specified in the statute governing the entity, this information should also be disclosed in the financial statements along with the disclosure of other accounting policies. A change in the method of depreciation is treated as a change in the accounting policy and is to be disclosed accordingly.

RECORDING DEPRECIATION

There are two ways of recording depreciation in the books of accounts—(a) when no provision for depreciation account is maintained; and (b) when provision for depreciation account is maintained.

When no provision for depreciation account is maintained   Under this method, depreciation is directly charged to an asset account. In the balance sheet, the asset is shown at its written down value (acquisition cost less depreciation provided till date). At the end of the accounting period, the depreciation account is closed by transferring it to the company's profit and loss account. This is done by passing the following entries in the books of accounts as given in the following text:

1. Depreciation account Dr. (Add)
       To Asset account (Less)
    (Being the depreciation provided for the accounting year)
2. Profit and loss account Dr. (Less)
       To Depreciation account (Less)
    (Being depreciation transferred to the profit and loss account)

When the asset appears in the balance sheet at its written down value, on disposal, the written-down value of such assets (at the beginning of the year of the disposal) is transferred to asset disposal account and profit or loss on sale of assets are ascertained with the help of that account. The detailed entries for the said purpose are given in this section:

1. Assets disposal A/c Dr. (Add)
    (At WDV of asset)
       To Asset A/c (Less)
    (Value at the beginning of the year)
    (Being the amount transferred to assets disposal account)
2. Depreciation account Dr. (Add)
       To Assets disposal A/c (Less)
    (Being the depreciation of current year on disposal of the asset)
3. Bank A/c Dr. (Add)
       To Assets disposal A/c (Less)
    (Being sale proceeds of asset for cash)
4. Assets disposal A/c Dr. (Add)
       To Profit and loss A/c (Add)
    (Being the credit side of the assets disposal account greater than debit side, that is, the profit on disposed asset transferred to the profit and loss account)
    or
    Profit and loss account Dr. (Less)
       To Assets disposal A/c (Less)

(Being the loss on disposed asset transferred to profit and loss account)

When provision for depreciation account is maintained   Under this method, depreciation is not directly charged to the asset account, but credited to accumulated depreciation account, provision for depreciation account, depreciation fund account, or accumulated depreciation account. Depreciation account is closed by transferring it to the profit and loss account. The detailed entries are as under:

1. Depreciation A/c Dr. (Add)
       To Accumulated depreciation A/c (Add)
    (Being the depreciation provided for the accounting period)
2. Profit and loss A/c Dr. (Less)
       To Depreciation A/c (Less)
    (Being the depreciation for the period charged to profit and loss account).

In the balance sheet, asset appears at its original cost and the accumulated depreciation is shown as a deduction from the asset account. As per the Companies Act, 2013, this way of presentation is obligatory on the part of a company.

If the asset account is maintained at cost price, on disposal, the original cost of such asset is transferred to the asset disposal account along with the accumulated depreciation on such asset. The entries are as follows:

1. Asset disposal account Dr. (at original cost) (Add)
       To Asset account (Less)
    (Being the original cost of the disposed asset transferred to asset disposal account)
2. Accumulated depreciation account Dr. (value at the beginning of the year) (Less)
       To Asset disposal account (Less)
    (Being the accumulated depreciation on disposed asset transferred to asset disposal account)
3. Depreciation account Dr. (Add)
       To Asset disposal account (Less)
    (Being current year's depreciation on disposed asset)
4. Bank account Dr. (Add)
       To Asset disposal account (Less)
    (Being sale proceeds of asset for cash)
5. Asset disposal account Dr. (Add)
       To Profit and loss account (Add)
    (Being profit on sale of asset transferred to profit and loss account)
    or
    Profit and loss account Dr. (Less)
       To Asset disposal account (Less)
    (Being loss on sale of asset transferred to profit and loss account)

Exchange of used asset with new asset   When a new fixed asset is acquired in exchange for another old asset (already used and depreciated) of the same kind or other, the entity is to pay only the difference, that is, the difference between the cost of a new asset and the value of the old asset granted by the seller. This value of old asset is known as trade-in-allowance which becomes a part of the cost of the new asset. If the trade-in-allowance is less than WDV, it is termed as a loss.

The following entries are to be passed in the books of accounts. The details are given in this section:

1. Asset disposal account Dr. (Add)
   (At WDV)
   To Asset account (Less)
   (Being transfer of WDV of the old asset)
2. Asset account Dr. (Add)
   To Vendor account or seller account (Add)
   (Being ascertainment of the value of the new asset, that is, the sum total of trade-in-allowance and cash payment to the seller)
3. Vendor account Dr. (Less)
   To Bank account (Less)
   (Cash payment)
   To Asset disposal account (Less)
   (Trade-in-allowance)
   (Being settlement of account with the vendor)
4. Depreciation account Dr. (Add)
   (Depreciation of the year of disposal)
   To Asset disposal account (Less)
   (Being ascertainment of the amount of current year's depreciation on old asset)

Note: The depreciation on new asset will be charged in the usual manner as discussed earlier. The balance of disposal account should be transferred to the profit and loss account to close the disposal account.

Exhibit 8.8 given earlier indicates the corporate practices adopted by Indian companies with respect to recognition of depreciation expenses in their books of accounts.

DEPRECIATION IMPACT ON PROFIT MEASUREMENT

Depending on the method used, there is a difference in the amount charged for annual depreciation. It may also be noticed that over the entire life of an asset, the total amount of depreciation charge cannot be different. Thus, the difference is only in terms of annual apportionment. The net effect to the methods is in terms of showing less or more profit in any particular year. This could be explained using an example.

Suppose a company acquires a machine at the beginning of a year at ₹1,000. The expected life of the machine is 10 years and salvage value is zero. The WDV rate is 20%. The company earns ₹500 per annum before depreciation. The difference in annual measurement of profit under straight-line and WDV methods is as follows (Table 8.6).

TABLE 8.6 Profit under WDV and SLM depreciation

(1) Year	(2) Profit before Depreciation Amount (₹)	(3) Straight-Line Depreciation Amount (₹)	(4) New Profit under Straight-Line Method of Depreciation (2) – (3) Amount (₹)	(5) Written Down Value 20% Depreciation Amount (₹)	(6) Net Profit under Written Down Value Method of Depreciation (2) – (5) Amount (₹)
1	500	100	400	200	300
2	500	100	400	160	340
3	500	100	400	128	372
4	500	100	400	102	398
5	500	100	400	82	418
6	500	100	400	66	434
7	500	100	400	52	448
8	500	100	400	42	458
9	500	100	400	34	466
10	500	100	400	134*	366
Total	5000	1000	4000	1000	4000

*Includes the unallocated depreciation, since there is no salvage value for the asset. Under this method, there will always be a terminal unabsorbed depreciation. Figures are rounded off.

IFRS Update

The following table indicates the differences in the recognition of property, plant, and equipment in the books of accounts, its revaluation and later on its presentation in the financial statements as per Indian Accounting Standards (Ind AS), IFRS or International Accounting Standards (IAS), and US Generally Accepted Accounting Practices (GAAP).

Property, Plant, and Equipment

Ind AS	IFRS/IAS	US GAAP
Historical cost is used. Revaluations are permitted, but the frequency of the revaluations has not been mentioned.	Historical cost or revalued amounts are used.	Historical cost is used.
Entire class of assets or systematically selected assets is to be revalued.	Entire class of assets is to be revalued.	Revaluations are not permitted.

■ **ILLUSTRATION 8.11** X Ltd purchased a machine for ₹60,000 on 1 January 2017. Depreciation is provided @ 10% p.a. using diminishing balance method.

Prepare the machinery account for the year 2019 in each of the following alternative cases:

1. If this machine is sold on 1 July 2019 for ₹28,000.
2. If a new machine costing ₹60,000 is purchased on 1/7/2019 after surrendering the old one and paying ₹35,000 cash.
3. If this machine was destroyed by fire on 1 July 2019 and its setup was sold for ₹600, and the insurance company paid ₹28,000 only.

Solution

A: If this machine is sold on 1 July 2019 for ₹28,600

Name of Account: Machine A/c

Type of Account: Asset   Normal Balance: Debit

Date	Reference Account	Voucher Type	Post Ref No.	Dr. (Add)	Cr. (Less)
1.1.2019	To Balance b/d			48,600	
1.7.2019	By Depreciation A/c				2,430
1.7.2019	By Bank A/c				28,600
1.7.2017	By Profit and loss A/c (Loss)				17,570
	Total			48,600	48,600

B: If this machine is exchanged

Name of Account: Machine A/c

Type of Account: Asset   Normal Balance: Debit

Date	Reference Account	Voucher Type	Post Ref No.	Dr. (Add)	Cr. (Less)
1.1.2019	To Balance b/d			48,600	
1.7.2019	By Depreciation A/c				2,430
1.7.2019	By Vendor A/c				25,000
1.7.2019	By Profit and loss A/c (Loss)				21,170
1.7.2019	To Vendor A/c			60,000	
31.12.2019	By Depreciation A/c				3,000
31.12.2019	By Balance c/d				57,000
	Total			1,08,600	1,08,600
1.1.2020	To Balance b/d			57,000	

C: If this machine is destroyed

Name of Account: Machine A/c

Type of Account: Asset   Normal Balance: Debit

Date	Reference Account	Voucher Type	Post Ref No.	Dr. (Add)	Cr. (Less)
1.1.2019	To Balance b/d			48,600	
1.7.2019	By Depreciation A/c				2,430
1.7.2019	By Bank A/c (Scrap)				600
1.7.2019	By Bank A/c (Claim)				28,000
1.7.2019	By Profit and loss A/c (Loss)				17,570
	Total			48,600	48,600

Working notes:

I. Calculation of book value as on 1/7/2019		Amount (₹)
(a) Original cost as on 1/1/2017		60,000
(b) Less: Depreciation for 2017		6,000
(c) Book value as on 1/1/2018	54,000	
(d) Less: Depreciation for 2018		5,400
(e) Book value as on 1/1/2019	48,600	
(f) Less: Depreciation up to 1/7/2019	2,430	
(g) Book value as on 1/7/2019	46,170	

II. Loss on sales = Book value as on date of sale – Proceeds
   = 46,170 – 28,600

   Loss on sales   = ₹17,570

III. Loss on exchange = Book value as on date of exchange – Trade-in-allowance
   = 46,170 – (60,000 – 35,000)
   = 46,170 – 25,000

   Loss on exchange = 21,170

IV. Loss by fire = Book value as on date of fire – (Scrap proceeds + Claim received)
   = ₹46,170 – (₹600 + ₹28,000)

   Loss by fire = ₹17,570

■ **ILLUSTRATION 8.12** On 1/4/2017 a machine was acquired for ₹4,00,000. The machine was expected to have a useful life of 10 years. The residual value was estimated at 10% of the original cost. At the end of the third year, an attachment was made to the machine at a cost of ₹1,80,000 to enhance its capacity. The attachment was expected to have a useful life of 10 years and zero terminal value. During the same time the original machine was revalued upwards by ₹90,000 and remaining useful life was reassessed at 9 years and residual value was reassessed at NIL.

Find the depreciation for the year if

i. the attachment retains its separate identity.
ii. the attachment becomes integral part of the machine.

Solution

i. If attachment retains its separate identity:

Cost of machine on 1/4/2017	= 4,00,000
Less: Residual value 10%	= 40,000
Depreciable value	= 3,60,000
Estimated useful life	= 10 years
Dep. p.a.	= 3,60,000 ÷ 10 = ₹36,000
Total dep. in 3 years	= 36,000 × 3 = ₹1,08,000
WDV for 4th year	= 4,00,000 – 1,08,000 = 2,92,000
Upward revaluation of original machine = 90,000	
WDV for 4th year after revaluation = 2,92,000 + 90,000 = 3,82,000	
Remaining useful life	= 9 years
Dep. in 4th year	= 3,82,000 ÷ 9 = ₹42,444
Dep. on attachment	= 1,80,000 ÷ 10 = ₹18,000
Total depreciation	= 42,444 + 18,000 = ₹60,444

Notes:

1. Since upward revaluation of the machine and reassessment of remaining useful life had been made at the end of the 3rd year, it is implied that depreciation for the 3rd year has been charged on the basis of old calculations and

remaining useful life of 9 years is to be calculated from the beginning of the 4th year onwards.

2. Depreciation for the 4th year, i.e., 2020–21 is given in the solution.

ii. If attachment becomes integral part of machine:

In this case, the cost of attachment will be added to the value or cost of the machine, and revised value or cost of the machine will be depreciated over the life of the machine.

Value of machine after revaluation = 3,82,000
Add: Cost of attachment = 1,80,000
Total value = 5,62,000
Life = 9 years
Depreciation = 5,62,000 ÷ 9 = ₹62,444

■ **ILLUSTRATION 8.13** M/s Versatile Limited purchased machinery for ₹4,80,000 (inclusive of GST of ₹40,000). GST input tax credit is available for 50% of the GST paid. The company incurred the following other expenses for installation.

	Amount (₹)
Cost of preparation of site for installation	21,000
Total labour charges	66,000
(200 out of the total of 600 men hours worked, spent for installation of the machinery)	
Spare parts and tools consumed in installation	6,000
Total salary of supervisor	24,000
(Time spent for installation was 25% of the total time worked)	
Total administrative expenses	32,000
(1/10 relates to the plant installation)	
Test run and experimental production expenses	23,000
Consultancy charges to architect for plant set-up	9,000
Depreciation on assets used for the installation	12,000

The machine was ready for use on 15/1/2020 but was used from 1/2/2020. Due to this delay further expenses of ₹19,000 were incurred. Calculate the value at which the plant should be capitalized in the books of M/s Versatile Limited.

Solution

Calculation of Value of Plant & Machinery Capitalized in the Books of M/s Versatile Limited as done on date

Particulars	Amount (₹)
Purchase price	4,80,000
(−) GST @ 50% not recoverable	(20,000)
(+) Cost of preparation of site for installation	21,000
(+) Labour charges	22,000
(Only 200 hours work to be considered)	
(+) Spare parts and tools consumed	6,000
(+) Salary of supervisor	6,000
(25% of total salary)	
(+) Administrative expenses (1/10)	3,200
(+) Test run and experimental production expenses	23,000
(+) Consultancy charges	9,000
(+) Depreciation of asset	
(Only from put to use)	12,000
Value capitalized in the books	**5,62,200**

Further expense occurred is not allowed to be capitalized, as it is the expense occurred after the machine is ready to put to use.

■ **ILLUSTRATION 8.14** The machinery account of a factory showed a balance of ₹1,90,000 on 1 January 2020. Its accounts were made on 31 December each year and depreciation is written off at 10% p.a. under the diminishing balance method. On 1 June 2020, new machinery was acquired at a cost of ₹28,000 and installation charges incurred in erecting the machine work out to ₹892 on the same date. On 1 June 2020 a machine which had cost ₹6,000 on 1 January 2015 was sold for ₹750. Another machine, which had cost ₹600 on 1 January 2016, was scrapped on the same date, and it realized nothing.

Prepare a plant and machinery account for the year 2020, allowing the same rate of depreciation as in the past. Calculate depreciation to the nearest multiple of a rupee.

Solution

Name of Account: Plant and Machinery A/c
Type of Account: Asset
Normal Balance: Debit

Date	Reference Account	Voucher Type	Post Ref No.	Dr. (Add)	Cr. (Less)
1.1.2020	To Balance b/d			1,90,000	
1.1.2020	To Balance (28,000 + 892)			28,892	
1.6.2020	By Bank A/c (Sale)				750
	By Depreciation (On sold machine)				148
	By Profit and loss A/c (Loss on sale)				2,645
	By Profit and loss A/c (Loss on scrapped machine)				377
	By Depreciation (on scrapped machinery)				16
31.12.2020	By Depreciation (see Note II)				20,291
	By Balance c/d				1,94,665
	Total			**2,18,892**	**2,18,892**
1.1.2021	By Balance c/d			1,94,665	

Working notes:

I. Calculation of profit/loss on machine sold and scrapped

	Particulars	Machine Sold Amount (₹)	Machine Scrapped Amount (₹)
1.	Cost on 1/1/2015	6,000	—
2.	Less: Depreciation @ 10% for 2015	600	—
3.	WDV on 31/12/2015	5,400	600
4.	Less: Depreciation @10% for 2016	540	60
5.	WDV on 31/12/2016	4,860	540
6.	Less: Depreciation @10% for 2017	486	54
7.	WDV on 31/12/2017	4,374	486
8.	Less: Depreciation @10% for 2018	4 37	49
9.	WDV on 31/12/2018	3,937	437
10.	Less: Depreciation @10% for 2019	394	44
11.	WDV on 31/12/2019	3,543	393
12.	Less: Depreciation @10% up to date of sale/scrapped (For 5 months)	148	16

13.	Book values as on date of sale/scrapped	3,395	377
14.	Sale proceeds	750	NIL
15.	Loss (13 – 14)	2,645	377

II. Calculation of depreciation for current year is as follows:

Particulars		Amount (₹)
Balance on machinery 1/1/2020		1,90,000
Less: WDV of machinery sold	3,453	
Less: WDV of machinery scrapped	393	3,936
WDV of other old machinery on 1/1/2020		1,86,064
Depreciation @ 10% of ₹1,86,064 for 12 months		18,606
Depreciation @ 10% on ₹28,892 (28,000 + 892) new machine for 7 months		1,685
Total depreciation for current year (d + e)		20,291

■ **ILLUSTRATION 8.15** A machine was purchased at the cost of ₹2,00,000. Its residual value is ₹8,000 and expected useful life is 10 years. Calculate the rate of depreciation using the diminishing method.

Solution

The rate of depreciation using the diminishing method is as follows:

$$\text{Rate} = 1 - \sqrt[10]{8,000/2,00,000} \times 100$$

$$= (0.275) \times 100$$

$$= 27.5\%$$

■ **ILLUSTRATION 8.16** A company purchased a machine on 1 January 2017 for ₹38,000 and paid the amount by cheque. Installation charges of ₹2,000 were incurred, and were paid in cash. The useful life of the machine is estimated to be 10 years and its scrap value is estimated at ₹4,000. The accounts are closed each year on 31 December.

Prepare the machinery account and depreciation account for first three years and show how machinery account will appear in the balance sheet for the three years. The company follows the straight-line method of depreciation. Also give the journal entries at the end of the first year.

Solution

The amount of annual depreciation on machinery will be ascertained as follows:

$$\text{Annual Depreciation} = \frac{\text{Original Cost} - \text{Estiamted Scrap Value}}{\text{Useful Life}}$$

$$= \frac{40,000\,(38,000 + 2,000) - 4,000}{10}$$

$$= \frac{36,000}{10}$$

Annual Depreciation = ₹3,600.

Name of Account: Machinery Account

Type of Account: Asset **Normal Balance: Debit**

Date	Reference Account	Voucher Type	Post Ref No.	Dr. (Add)	Cr. (Less)
1.1.2017	To Bank A/c			38,000	
	To Cash A/c			2,000	
31.12.2017	By Depreciation A/c				3,600
	By Balance c/d				36,400
	Total			**40,000**	**40,000**
1.1.2018	To Balance b/d			36,400	
31.12.2018	By Depreciation A/c				3,600
	By Balance c/d				32,800
	Total			**36,400**	**36,400**
1.1.2019	To Balance b/d			32,800	
31.12.2019	By Depreciation A/c				3,600
31.12.2019	By Balance c/d				29,200
	Total			**32,800**	**32,800**
1.1.2020	To Balance b/d			29,200	

Name of Account: Depreciation Account

Type of Account: Expense **Normal Balance: Debit**

Date	Reference Account	Voucher Type	Post Ref No.	Dr. (Add)	Cr. (Less)
31.12.2017	To Machinery A/c			3,600	
31.12.2017	By Profit and loss A/c				3,600
	Total			**3,600**	**3,600**
31.12.2018	To Machinery A/c			3,600	
31.12.2018	By Profit and loss A/c				3,600
	Total			**3,600**	**3,600**
31.12.2019	To Machinery A/c			3,600	
31.12.2019	By Profit and loss A/c				3,600
	Total			**3,600**	**3,600**

Balance Sheet as at 31 December 2017

Assets:				
Machinery			40,000	
Less: Depreciation			3,600	
Net Value of Machinery				36,400

Balance Sheet as at 31 December 2018

Assets:				
Machinery			36,400	
Less: Depreciation			3,600	
Net Value of Machinery				32,800

Balance Sheet as at 31 December 2019

Assets:				
Machinery			32,800	
Less: Depreciation			3,600	
Net Value of Machinery				29,200

Journal Entries

Date	Particulars	L.F.	Debit (₹)	Credit (₹)
31 Dec. 2019	Depreciation A/c (Add) Dr.		3,600	
	To Machinery A/c (Less)			3,600
	(Provision of annual depreciation on machinery)			
31 Dec. 2019	Profit and Loss A/c (Less) Dr.		3,600	
	To Depreciation A/c (Less)			3,600
	(Transfer of the depreciation to Profit and Loss A/c)			

If an entry is made in the beginning of the year when the machinery was purchased, it would be as under:

Date	Particulars	L.F.	Debit (₹)	Credit (₹)
1 Jan 2017	Machinery A/c (Add) Dr.		40,000	
	To Bank A/c (Less)			38,000
	To Cash A/c (Less)			2,000
	(Machinery purchased for ₹38,000 by cheque and installation charges ₹2,000 paid in cash)			

■ **ILLUSTRATION 8.17** On 1 January 2019 in the books of Kavita Pumps, the machinery account showed a debit balance of ₹37,250. On 1 July 2019, a machine worth ₹11,000 was purchased. A machine was sold for ₹5,000 on 1 October 2019. The original cost of the machine sold was ₹15,000 on 1 July 2016.

Depreciation on machinery is charged at 10% p.a. on the reducing balance method. Assuming that the books are closed on 31 December, prepare machinery account for the year 2019.

Solution

Name of Account: Machinery Account
Type of Account: Asset   Normal Balance: Debit

Date 2019	Reference Account	Voucher Type	Post Ref No.	Dr. (Add)	Cr. (Less)
1 Jan 19	To Balance b/d			37,250	
1 Jan 19	To Bank A/c (Machinery purchased)			11,000	
1 Oct 19	To Bank A/c (Sale of machinery)				5,000
1 Oct 19	To Profit and loss A/c (Loss on sale of machinery)				5,677
31 Dec 19	To Depreciation on machinery				
	Sale 865				
	Old machinery 2571				
	New machinery 550				3,986
31 Dec 19	By Balance c/d				33,587
	Total			**48,250**	**48,250**
1 Jan 20	To Balance b/d			33,587	

Working Notes:

1. Calculation of loss on sale of machinery

	₹
Cost on 1/7/2016	15,000
Less: Depreciation for six months for 2016 at 10%	750
Value on 1/1/2017	14,250
Less: Depreciation for 2017 at 10%	1,425
Value on 1/1/2018	12,825
Less: Depreciation for 2018 at 10%	1,283
Value on 1/1/2019	11,542

Now let us find out its depreciated value on date of sale, that is, on 1/10/2019

	₹
Value on 1/1/2019 (from 1/1/2019 to 1/10/2019)	11,542
Less: Depreciation for nine months at 10%	865
Depreciated value on 1/10/2019	10,677
Less: Sale price	5,000
Loss on sale of machinery	5,677

2. Total Depreciation for 2019

Total value on 1/1/2019	37,250
Less: Value on date on sale	11,542
	25,708

1. Depreciation on ₹25,708 for one year   2,571
2. *Add:* Depreciation on new machinery of ₹11,000 for six months at 10%   550

■ **ILLUSTRATION 8.18** On 1 April 2016, a new plant was purchased for ₹40,000 and a further sum of ₹2,000 was spent on its installation.

On 1 October 2018, another plant was acquired for ₹25,000. Due to an accident on 3 January 2019, the first plant was totally destroyed and the scrap was sold for ₹1,000 only. On 21 January 2020, a second hand plant was purchased for ₹30,000 and a further sum of ₹5,000 was spent for bringing the same to use on and from 15 March 2020.

Depreciation has been provided at 10% on straight-line basis. It was a practice to provide depreciation for five years on all acquisitions made at any time during any year and to ignore depreciation of any item sold or disposed off during any year. None of the assets are insured. The accounts are closed annually on 31 March.

It was decided to follow the rate of 15% on diminishing balance method with retrospective effect in respect of the existing items of plant and to make the necessary adjustment entry on 1 April 2020.

Show the journal entries to be passed for the purpose and the plant account and the depreciation provision account for all the years.

Solution

Name of Account: Plant Account
Type of Account: Asset   Normal Balance: Debit

Date	Reference Account	Voucher Type	Post Ref No.	Dr. (Add)	Cr. (Less)
1.4.2016	To Bank (Cost and installation)			42,000	
31.3.2017	By Balance c/d				42,000
	Total			**42,000**	**42,000**
1.4.2017	To Balance b/d			42,000	
31.3.2018	By Balance c/d				42,000
	Total			**42,000**	**42,000**
1.4.2018	To Balance b/d			42,000	
1.10.2018	To Bank			25,000	
3.1.2019	By Bank				1,000
31.3.2019	By Depreciation provision A/c				8,400
	By Profit and loss A/c				32,600
31.3.2019	By Balance c/d				25,000
	Total			**67,000**	**67,000**
1.4.2019	To Balance b/d			25,000	
21.1.2020	To Bank			30,000	
	To Bank			5,000	

Date	Reference	Voucher	Post Ref	Dr.	Cr.
31.3.2020	By Balance c/d				60,000
	Total			60,000	60,000
1.4.2020	To Balance b/d			60,000	

Date	Reference	Voucher	Post Ref	Dr.	Cr.
31.3.2020	To Balance c/d			8,500	
	Total			8,500	8,500
1.4.2020	By Balance b/d				8,500
	By Depreciation (Additional)				3,687

Name of Account: Provision for Depreciation Account
Type of Account: Liabilities   **Normal Balance: Credit**

Date	Reference Account	Voucher Type	Post Ref No.	Dr. (Less)	Cr. (Add)
31.3.2017	By Depreciation A/c				4,200
31.3.2017	To Balance c/d			4,200	
	Total			4,200	4,200
1.4.2017	By Balance b/d				4,200
31.3.2018	By Depreciation A/c				4,200
31.3.2018	To Balance c/d			8,400	
	Total			8,400	8,400
1.4.2018	By Balance b/d				8,400
3.1.2019	To Plant A/c			8,400	
31.3.2019	By Depreciation A/c				2,500
31.3.2019	To Balance c/d			2,500	
	Total			10,900	10,900
1.4.2019	By Balance b/d				2,500
31.3.2020	By Depreciation A/c				6,000

Journal Entries

Date	Particulars	L.F.	Dr. (₹)	Cr. (₹)
1/4/2020	Depreciation A/c (Add) Dr.		3,687	
	To Provision for depreciation A/c (Add)			3,687
	(Being the provision made for depreciation for additional depreciation required due to change in the method of depreciation with retrospective effect)			

Working Notes:

Depreciation @ 15 % on diminishing balance method:

Plant Purchased in	Cost ₹	Depreciation 2018–2019 ₹	Depreciation 2019–2020 ₹	Total ₹
2018–2019	25,000	3,750	3,187	6,937
2019–2020	35,000	-	5,250	5,250
				12,187

Less: Provision already made (as per provision for depreciation A/c)	8,500
Additional depreciation required	3,687

SUMMARY

- Non-current assets are tangible and intangible valuable things owned by a firm with the intention of carrying on business operations over a long period of time.
- Fixed assets are long-term assets whose usefulness in the operation of the firm is likely to extend for more years.
- The gross book value of an asset is the historical cost of the cost at which the asset is actually acquired. Fixed assets may be restated in value, with the help of appraisal undertaken by competent and approved valuers.
- Fixed assets are grouped together at the original cost value to represent the *gross block*. From this accumulated depreciation (for tangible asset) or accumulated amortization (for intangible asset) or accumulated depletion (for natural asset) on all the assets till date is subtracted to arrive at the *net block*.
- The use cost, expenses, or periodic write offs for tangible assets (viz., plant and building) are known as depreciation. The cost of intangible long-term operating assets (such as patent, goodwill, etc) is allocated over the life of the asset known as amortization.
- Tangible assets are those that are valuable to the business or firm. Plant assets, also called property, plant and equipment, or fixed assets, are tangible resources that are used in the operations of the business or firm and are not intended for sale to customers.
- Intangible assets are the assets that do not have physical existence; therefore, they cannot be seen or touched. For example, goodwill is an intangible asset. Such an asset may have a fixed term of existence by law, regulation, or agreement, for example, patents, copyrights, and lease.

- Goodwill is the advantage that arises from the reputation of a business. An established business earns more than normal profits because of its reputation for quality products, punctuality in delivery, social consciousness, integrity, honesty, harmonious relation with employees, customers, dealers, etc. Therefore, goodwill is an asset that reflects success of the business.
- Other intangible assets also include the expenditure incurred for development of software for providing the ease in operations of the firm, trademarks, etc.
- Regenerative assets and their use in agricultural activities and pharmaceutical sectors are important points of concern for accountants. Agricultural activities use the services of regenerative assets, such as livestock while pharmaceutical firms use regenerative assets such as animals for medical tests.
- The valuation of an asset on a cost basis and providing the depreciation in terms of cost will work successfully at stable price levels in the economy. However, in reality, the price levels are rising constantly, and therefore there is a need to provide for depreciation on the estimated current replacement cost.
- Firms sometimes purchase a group of assets for a lump sum value agreed upon. The value paid or agreed to be paid is apportioned among the assets using the fair value approach, that is, as per the fair market value.
- When a fixed asset is constructed by a firm for its own use, the cost includes materials costs, labour costs, and a reasonable amount of indirect overhead costs such as heat, lights, power, and depreciation of machinery used to construct the asset.

- The service life or productive life of an asset is the length of time for which it can be used in the operations of the firm. The service life may not be as long as the asset's potential or physical life. The physical life period is termed as the physical life period, while the productive life period is termed as the economic life period.
- When the carrying value of an asset is higher than its fair value, then it is termed as impairment in the value of the asset. The carrying value of an asset refers to the book value of the asset as appearing on the date of balance sheet in the books of accounts of a firm.
- Fair value refers to the amount for which the asset could be bought or sold in the current period or as on a particular date.
- Depreciation is an allocation of cost of services given up by a tangible long-term operating asset (other than land) during a period of time. Depreciation recorded in the books of account is only an estimate.
- Depreciation occurs on account of wear and tear, obsolescence, time, or accidents. By providing the depreciation, the financial statements indicate correct income and true position. There are different methods for providing depreciation such as straight-line method, reducing balancing method, and usage method.
- The depreciation supports to provide funds for replacement of assets in future. Through accounting mechanisms, funds are kept aside by using annuity method and sinking fund method.
- Firms can do the accounting by maintaining or not maintaining the provision for depreciation account.

KEYWORDS

Amortization cost The allocated costs of services given up by intangible long-term operating assets during each period of the asset's life are called amortization costs.

Depletion cost It is the portion of the cost of natural resources that is allocated to extraction or production of the resource over time.

Depreciable cost It is the original cost less expected salvage value.

Depreciation It is the allocated cost of services given up by a tangible long-term operating asset (other than land) during a period of time.

Development cost It refers to the cost incurred in the application of research findings or other knowledge to a plan or design for the production of new or substantially new or improved materials, products, processes, systems, etc.

Fixed assets Fixed assets are long-term assets whose usefulness in the operation of the firm is likely to extend beyond one accounting period. It is an expenditure that is not written off completely against income in the accounting period in which it is incurred.

Goodwill It is the advantage that arises from the reputation and connections of a business. An established business earns more than normal profits because of its reputation for quality products, punctuality in delivery, social consciousness, integrity, honesty, harmonious relation with employees, customers, dealers, etc.

Leasehold The rights transferred to the lessee (user of an asset) by the lessor (owner of an asset) for the period of lease.

Original cost of the asset This is the cost incurred in making the asset available for use.

Patents These are granted to the inventors of products, machines, or processes, with a view to protect the rights of an inventor from infringement by others.

Research cost It can be determined if the research is original and based on planned investigation, and it is undertaken with the prospect of gaining new scientific or technical knowledge and understanding.

Revaluation of asset Change in the value of asset by competent and approved valuer.

Salvage value The expected recovery of sales value of the asset at the end of the useful life.

Straight-line method It allocates an equal amount of an asset's cost to each year of its expected useful life.

Useful life of the asset The period for which asset could be used for production or operation.

Written down value It is the original cost less depreciation to date.

QUESTIONS

I. Answer the following questions in detail.

1. Define depreciation. Distinguish it from
   (a) Depletion (b) Amortization
2. Why it is necessary to calculate depreciation? Discuss various factors which are considered for calculating depreciation.
3. What causes depreciation? Discuss the reasons.
4. Enumerate the methods of calculating depreciation? Discuss briefly the merits and limitations of these methods.

II. Answer the following questions in one sentence.

1. What is depreciation?
2. What are the different causes of depreciation?
3. What are the features of depreciation?
4. Why is depreciation charged to an asset?
5. How does physical wear and tear result in depreciation?
6. Why is depreciation charged by business which makes losses?

7. Why is depreciation charged even in the year of loss?
8. What do you mean by exhaustion of an asset?
9. In case of which assets depletion takes place?
10. What do you mean by obsolescence?
11. What is the main cause of depreciation in case of intangible assets?
12. Is depreciation charging compulsory or voluntary as per the Companies Act, 1956?
13. Why fixed instalment method is also called as straight-line method?
14. How is cost of an asset determined?
15. What is scrap value?
16. Give equation for calculating depreciation under straight-line method.
17. Give equation for calculating depreciation under reducing balance method.
18. What is prospective change in depreciation method?
19. What is retrospective change in depreciation method?

20. Give journal entry for adjusting profit made due to change in method of depreciation.
21. Is depreciation charged to reduce profits or to reduce the value of asset during a financial year?
22. Which account is credited when a profit is made on sale of an asset?
23. Where is depreciation transferred at the close of the year?
24. What do you understand by reducing balance method?
25. Which method of depreciation would you suggest for depreciating a five year lease?
26. Explain purpose of providing depreciation.
27. What journal entry will be passed when expenses are paid for installation of machinery?
28. How depreciation per year is fixed under fixed instalment method?
29. What is fixed instalment method of depreciation?

III. Choose the right answer for the following options.

1. The cost of self-constructed assets is taken as
   (a) Prime cost + Indirect cost
   (b) Construction cost + Interest cost on funds borrowed for construction till all the inputs are acquired
   (c) Construction cost + Interest cost on funds borrowed for construction till the asset is ready for its intended use
   (d) Construction costs + Interest on borrowing – Losses due to strikes
   (e) Total construction cost or market value whichever is less.
2. Which of the following enhances the earning capacity of an asset?
   (a) Increase in working capacity of an asset
   (b) Reduction in operating costs
   (c) Replacing damaged parts of an asset
   (d) Both (a) and (c) above
   (e) (a), (b), and (c) above
3. Assets bought for non-monetary consideration can recorded at
   (a) Their fair value
   (b) The book value of the asset given up
   (c) Market value of shares (if exchanged for shares)
   (d) All of the above
   (e) Both (a) and (b) above
   Answer questions 4 to 6 based on the following information:
   Z Ltd purchased a machine for ₹3,00,000 on 1 April 2006. Depreciation is provided on straight-line method. The estimated life of machine is 9 years and the scrap value is ₹30,000.
4. The amount of depreciation charged is
   (a) ₹33,333   (b) ₹30,000
   (c) ₹27,000   (d) ₹35,000
   (e) ₹41,111
5. The rate of depreciation in the above case is
   (a) 10%   (b) 9%
   (c) 15%   (d) 8%
   (e) 7%
6. If the asset is disposed of on 31 March 2012 for ₹2,00,000 the profit/loss in such case is
   (a) ₹40,000 (profit)   (b) ₹40,000 (loss)
   (c) ₹70,000 (profit)   (d) ₹70,000 (loss)
   (e) ₹30,000 (profit)
7. An asset was purchased for ₹10,000 on which depreciation was provided @ 5% on SLM method, the WDV of the asset at the end of two years is
   (a) ₹7,500   (b) ₹8,000
   (c) ₹8,500   (d) ₹9,000
   (e) ₹9,500
8. Star Ltd purchased a machine for ₹10,000 on 1 April 2011. Depreciation is provided @ 10% on written down value method.

The depreciation provided on the machine in financial year 2012–13 is
   (a) ₹750   (b) ₹900
   (c) ₹1,000   (d) ₹1,900
   (e) ₹2,000
9. The written down value of the machine as on 31 March 2012 is (based on the information given in question 8)
   (a) ₹10,000   (b) ₹9,000
   (c) ₹8,100   (d) ₹8,000
   (e) ₹7,000
10. If the machine (given in the previous question) is sold for ₹8,000 on 1 December 2012 the profit/loss on sale of machine is
   (a) Profit of ₹400   (b) Loss of ₹400
   (c) Profit of ₹1,000   (d) Loss of ₹2,000
   (e) Profit of ₹2,000
11. When a fixed asset is obtained as a gift, the account to be credited is
   (a) Asset A/c   (b) Goodwill A/c
   (c) Capital reserve A/c   (d) Donor's A/c
   (e) General reserve A/c
12. As per the accounting standard AS-10, fixed assets that have been retired from active use and held for disposal should be stated in balance sheet at
   (a) Realizable value
   (b) Net book value
   (c) Original cost
   (d) Higher of net book value or realizable value
   (e) Lower of net book value or realizable value
13. In the books of ACB Ltd, the machinery A/c shows a debit balance of ₹50,000 as on 1 April 2011. The machinery was sold on 30 September 2011 for ₹30,000. If the company charges depreciation @ 20% p.a. on diminishing balance method, the final accounts of the company at the end of the year will show as
   (a) Depreciation of ₹20,000
   (b) Depreciation of ₹10,000
   (c) Depreciation of ₹5,000
   (d) Depreciation of ₹5,000 and loss on sale of machinery ₹15,000
   (e) Loss on sale of machinery ₹20,000
14. Property and plant and equipment are conventionally presented in the balance sheet at
   (a) Replacement cost less accumulated depreciation
   (b) Historical cost less salvage value
   (c) Historical cost less depreciation portion thereof
   (d) Original cost adjusted for general price level changes
   (e) Market value less depreciation.
15. ABC Ltd purchased a machine for ₹5,00,000 on 1 October 2010. The salvage value of the machine after 6 years is ₹80,000. The straight-line rate of depreciation on the machine is _____ %
   (a) 16.66   (b) 16.00
   (c) 15.00   (d) 14.00
   (e) 12.00
16. If a machine costing ₹18,000 is sold after 2 years for ₹16,000 and the depreciation rate is 15% per annum on straight-line method, then the profit or loss from the sale of machine is
   (a) ₹3,400 (loss)   (b) ₹2,995 (loss)
   (c) ₹2,995 (profit)   (d) ₹3,000 (profit)
   (e) ₹3,400 (profit)
17. A machine was purchased for ₹50,000. The machine was depreciated @ 20% p.a. on WDV basis for 3 years. If the machine is sold at

a value of ₹25,000, the profit and loss account will be debited/credited by

(a) ₹25,000 (credit)   (b) ₹1,000 (credit)

(c) ₹1,000 (debit)   (d) ₹600 (credit)

(e) ₹600 (debit)

18. The book value of a machine is ₹4,000. Two years later the book value is expected to be ₹2,000. The rate of depreciation according to diminishing balance method is

(a) 50%   (b) 33.33%

(c) 29.29%   (d) 25%

(e) 20%

19. The main objective of providing depreciation is to

(a) Calculate the true profit

(b) Show the true financial position in the balance sheet

(c) Reduce tax burden

(d) Provide funds for replacement of fixed assets

(e) Comply with the legal requirements

20. Depreciation is a process of

(a) Valuation   (b) Valuation and allocation

(c) Allocation   (d) Appropriation

(e) Segregation

21. Chauhan Company acquired equipment for ₹40,000 with an expected useful life of five years and of ₹2,000 expected residual value. Straight-line method of depreciation was used. The equipment was sold at the end of fourth year for ₹15,000. The gain or loss on sale will be

(a) ₹7,400 (gain)   (b) ₹5,400 (gain)

(c) ₹7,600 (gain)   (d) ₹13,000 (loss)

(e) ₹5,400 (loss)

22. An asset was purchased for ₹20,000 on which depreciation is provided @ 10% on reducing balance method. The WDV of the asset at the end of 4 years is

(a) ₹12,000   (b) ₹12,400

(c) ₹13,122   (d) ₹14,400

(e) ₹16,200

23. An asset was purchased for ₹10,000 on which depreciation is provided @ 10% on reducing balance method. The WDV of the asset at the end of 4 years is

(a) ₹6,000   (b) ₹7,200

(c) ₹6,561   (d) ₹8,100

(e) ₹6,200

24. On 1 October 2010, XYZ Ltd purchased an asset at a cost of ₹50,000. The company provides depreciation at 12% p.a. on written down value method. On 31 December 2011, the asset was sold for ₹45,000. For the financial year ended 31 March 2012, the profit on sale of the asset is recorded at

(a) ₹6,280   (b) ₹5,230

(c) ₹5,000   (d) ₹3,640

(e) ₹2,230

25. Dito Ltd sold a depreciable asset for ₹30,000 payable in cash. The accumulated depreciation amounted to ₹50,000 and a loss of ₹10,000 was recognized on sale. The original cost of the asset was

(a) ₹90,000   (b) ₹70,000

(c) ₹60,000   (d) ₹40,000

(e) ₹30,000

26. A fixed asset has a life of 4 years. If it is depreciated by the WDV method, its book value at the end of 4 years is 24% of its original cost. Hence the rate of depreciation applied is (choose nearest answer).

(a) 24%   (b) 28%

(c) 30%   (d) 32%

(e) 34%

27. Another name for the straight-line method is

(a) The equal instalment method

(b) The reducing balance method

(c) The diminishing balance method

(d) The revaluation method

28. Generally accepted practice require that

(a) Assets are shown at cost

(b) Assets are shown at cost less total depreciation to date

(c) Assets are shown at cost less previous year's depreciation

(d) Assets are shown at current net value

29. Which of the following is/are the advantages of the equal instalment method?

(i) Easy to understand; calculations simple

(ii) Decreasing depreciation charges cancel out increasing repairs

(iii) No recalculation necessary when further asset are purchased

(a) (i), (ii), and (iii)   (b) (i) and (ii) only

(c) (i) only   (d) (iii) only

30. Which of the following is/are the disadvantages of the reducing balance method?

(i) Percentage figure to be deducted annually is too difficult to calculate

(ii) The charge against the profit and loss account increases over the years

(iii) If a further asset is purchased, the amount now required to be written off needs to be recalculated

(a) (i), (ii), and (iii)   (b) (i) and (ii) only

(c) (i) only   (d) (ii) only

31. Depreciation results from

(i) Wear and tear

(ii) Obsolescence

(iii) The passage of time

(a) (i), (ii), and (iii)   (b) (i) and (ii) only

(c) (i) only   (d) (iii) only

32. Using the equal instalment method for depreciation, the relevant formula is

(a) Annual Charge Against Profits = Original Cost – Residual Value/No. of Years of Active Life

(b) Annual Charge Against Profits = Number of Years of Active Life/Original Cost – Residual Value

(c) Annual Charge Against Profits = Original Cost – Residual Value/Estimated No. of Remaining Years

(d) Annual Charge Against Profits = Estimated Number of Remaining Years/Original Cost – Residual Value

33. The book of prime entry necessary to introduce the annual depreciation is

(a) The cash book   (b) The purchase book

(c) The ledger   (d) The journal

34. Consider a piece of machinery costing ₹30,000 with an estimated life of 10 years. At the end of this time it can be sold for ₹3,000. Using the equal instalment method the annual charge against profits would be

(a) ₹3,000   (b) ₹3,300

(c) ₹2,700   (d) None of above

35. At cost a firm's assets were valued at ₹18,000. Three years later their book value is ₹10,000. The depreciation charge for the three years is

(a) ₹12,000   (b) ₹10,000

(c) ₹8,000   (d) ₹6,000

36. An asset was purchased for ₹12,500 and, under reducing balance method 20% of the reducing value of the asset is written off each year. What is the value of the asset at the end of three years?
    (a) ₹8,000
    (b) ₹7,500
    (c) ₹6,400
    (d) ₹5,000

37. A machine is purchased for ₹200. To achieve a residual value of ₹128 at the end of the second year (assuming the depreciation is calculated at the end of the year), the percentage of depreciation using the reducing balance method must be
    (a) 12%
    (b) 36%
    (c) 20%
    (d) 12%

38. Which of the following is/are methods of depreciation?
    (i) Straight-line
    (ii) Reducing balance
    (iii) Revaluation
    (a) (i), (ii), and (iii)
    (b) (i) and (ii) only
    (c) (i) only
    (d) (iii) only

39. The book value of a machine is ₹2,000. Two years later the book value is ₹1,000. The straight-line percentage depreciation is
    (a) 50%
    (b) 33.33%
    (c) 25%
    (d) 20%

IV. Fill in the blanks.

1. Under _____ system, amount of depreciation changes every year.
2. Depreciation amount remains _____ under fixed instalment method.
3. The amount of depreciation goes on decreasing every year under the _____ method of depreciation.
4. At the end of every year the balance of depreciation account is transferred to _____ account.
5. Under the _____ system of depreciation, the amount of depreciation does not change from year to year.
6. Under _____ method, the cost of asset cannot be reduced to zero.
7. Amount spent on installation of machinery is a _____ expenditure.
8. Depreciation = Cost of an Asset less _____/Estimated Life of an Asset.
9. Under the _____ system the amount of depreciation remains constant every year.
10. Depreciation = Cost of the Asset – Estimated Scrap Value/_____.
11. Wages paid for installation of machinery should be debited to _____ account.
12. Under _____ method, depreciation is calculated on written down value.
13. Balance of depreciation A/c is transferred to _____ A/c.
14. Under the straight-line method, the asset is reduced to its _____ by the end of its estimated economical life.
15. Gradual and permanent decrease in the value of asset is known as _____.
16. Depreciation is charged on _____ asset.

V. Giving reasons to state whether the following statements are True or False.

1. Profit cannot be computed properly unless depreciation is provided.
2. It is not necessary to depreciate a building if it is not in use.
3. Depreciation increases the value of asset as well as increases the profit of the year.
4. Repairs to machinery are revenue expenditure.
5. Installation charges incurred on machinery are capital expenditure.
6. Under reducing balance method, value of fixed asset is reduced to zero.
7. Depreciation is not charged by loss making business.
8. Freehold land never depreciates.
9. Under fixed instalment method, amount of depreciation remains constant.
10. The profit or loss on sale of fixed asset can be ascertained only after the depreciation is calculated.

VI. Write the word/term/phrase which can substitute each of the following statements.

1. The method of depreciation in which depreciation amount remains constant every year.
2. The method of depreciation in which depreciation amount charged to an asset decrease every year.
3. Formula used for calculating depreciation under straight-line method.
4. The type of asset on which depreciation is charged and written off.
5. Fixed asset which never depreciates.
6. Two reasons due to which fixed assets depreciate.
7. Price expected to be fetched on disposal of an asset at the end of its useful life.
8. The process due to which the value of an asset decreases every year.
9. The account to which balance remaining under depreciation account is transferred at the end of each financial year.
10. The method of depreciation under which the fixed asset is reduced to zero in the books at the end of its expected useful life.
11. The gradual and permanent decrease in the value of fixed asset due to any cause.

VII. Match the following pairs.

A	B
1. Residual value	(a) Depreciable
2. Fixed assets	(b) SLM to WDV or vice versa
3. Fixed instalment method	(c) Expected realizable value of used assets at end of its life
4. Cost of assets	(d) Total useful working period of asset
5. Reducing balance method	(e) Depreciation charged on original cost
6. Current assets	(f) Purchase price plus installation charges
7. Depreciation	(g) Reduction in the value of asset due to its use
8. Life period	(h) Liquid/quick assets
9. Change of depreciation method	(i) Depreciation charged on opening balance of asset
10. Machinery	(j) Tangible assets

VIII. Solve the following problems.

1. On 1 April 2017, Rajul Ltd purchased a machine for ₹4,00,000. The company incurred ₹28,000 towards freight and insurance, and ₹12,000 towards installation charges. The estimated useful life of machinery is four years. The estimated scrap value of machinery on the expiry of its useful life is ₹40,000. On 1 April 2020, the company spent ₹10,000 towards the machine's repair. You are required to calculate the depreciation amount and the rate of depreciation.

   Also, prepare the machinery account for the first four financial years ending 31 March year according to straight-line method under the following conditions—(a) If no provision for depreciation account is maintained; and (b) If provision for depreciation account is maintained.

2. A firm purchased a machine on 1 January 2018 for ₹2,00,000. A new machine was purchased for ₹80,000 on 1 July 2019. It is decided to write off depreciation on machinery at 10% p.a. according to the reducing balance method. Accounts are closed every year on 31 December. Prepare the machinery account for three years.

3. The cost of an asset is ₹4,50,000 and its useful life is 5 years. Calculate depreciation according to SYD method.

4. A lease was purchased on 1 April 2015 for a five year period at a cost of ₹50,000. It is proposed to depreciate the lease by annuity method by charging 5% interest. Show the lease account for five years and also the relevant entries in the profit and loss account. The reference to the annuity table shows that to depreciate ₹1 by annuity method over 5 years by charging interest 5%, one must write off a sum of ₹0.230975 every year.

5. On 1 July 2016, ABC Ltd purchased a machine for ₹1,10,000 and spent ₹6,000 on its installation. The expected life of the machine is four years at the end of which the estimated scrap value of the machine will be ₹16,000. Desiring to replace the machine on the expiry of its life, the company establishes a sinking fund. Investments are expected to realize 5% interest per annum. Investments were realized at 5% less than the book value. The machine realized ₹18,000 at the end of its useful life. On 1 July 2020, a new machine is installed at a cost of ₹1,25,000. The sinking fund table shows that ₹0.2320 invested each year will produce ₹1 at the end of four years at 5%.

   Show the necessary ledger accounts in the books of ABC Ltd for all the years.

6. A machine was purchased for ₹7,50,000 having an estimated 60,000 total working hours. The scrap value is expected to be ₹50,000. The machine actually worked for the following number of hours during the first three years of its life: 2010 – 4,000 hours; 2011 – 3,400 hours; 2012 – 3,000 hours.

   Determine annual depreciation for each year.

7. A company purchased some machines at a cost of ₹60,000 on 1 April 2015. The company provides depreciation on machines at 10% p.a. on straight-line method. On 30 June 2019, one machine, which cost ₹20,000 on 1 April 2015, was destroyed by accident. It was sold as scrap for ₹1,000. The machine was insured and the insurance company paid ₹8,000 in full settlement of the claim.

   Prepare machine account for 2019 and show the necessary calculations as part of your answer.

8. A firm purchased certain machineries on 1/1/2016 for ₹1,80,000 for which the cost of carriage was ₹10,000 and cost of installation was ₹10,000. Depreciation on machinery is charged at 10% per annum on reducing balance method. The accounting year of the firm ends on 31st December.

   On 1/7/2018, one-fourth of the machinery was sold at 20% more than the book value and another machine costing ₹80,000 was purchased on the same date.

   On 1/1/2019 one-fourth of the machinery installed on 1/1/2016 was sold at 10% less than its depreciated value. Another machine was purchased on 1/1/2019 for ₹1,00,000.

   Prepare the machinery account for four years from 2016 to 2019.

9. Pritam Corporation purchased machinery of ₹50,000 on 1 January 2015 and it was decided to write off depreciation by the fixed instalment system by charging ₹5,000 a year. After writing off depreciation for two years, it was decided to change the system to that of diminishing balance method at the rate of 20% right from the beginning and to adjust the difference due to this change of method by writing off this difference to profit and loss account of the third year.

   Prepare the machinery account for the five years.

10. The valuation of a group of assets (plant and machinery), on 1 January 2017 was ₹32,000 and the estimated life was 8 years.

    The following purchases and sales took place up to 31 December 2019:

    Purchases:
    31 March 2017: Cost ₹15,000 estimated life 10 years
    30 September 2018: Cost ₹12,000 estimated life 6 years
    30 April 2019: Cost ₹20,000, estimated life 8 years

    Sales: Out of the initial group of assets, a machine (whose valuation on 1 January 2017 was ₹5,000) was sold for ₹4,700 on 30 June 2019.

    Assuming the break-up value of each asset to be 10 % of the initial valuation or original cost, prepare the asset account for the first three years.

 # CASES

Conceptual Application Case

Fixed Assets An automobile manufacturer bought six heavy stamping machines at a price of ₹1,62,500 each. When they were delivered, the purchaser paid freight charges of ₹42,000 and handling fees of ₹12,000. Four employees, each earning ₹100 an hour, worked for three 40-hour weeks setting up and testing the machines. Special wiring and other materials applicable to the new machines cost ₹6,000.

Questions

How much of these costs should be capitalized as costs of these machines?

Business Application Case

1. **Dairy Farm** Danny Mahanta owns a small dairy farm in Ahmedabad. He purchased the farm for ₹24 lakh in 2011. ₹10 lakh was paid for the land and ₹14 lakh for the farm buildings. In 2016, the farm was revalued. According to a local firm of estate valuers, the land was worth ₹16 lakh and the buildings were valued at ₹22 lakh. When the farm was purchased, the straight-line method was used to depreciate the buildings. A residual value of zero was assumed and the useful life of the buildings was expected to be 25 years. It was decided that no depreciation charge would be made on the land. Two years ago Danny also owned a tractor which he bought for ₹3 lakh. The reducing balance method is used to calculate depreciation on this asset.

Questions

1. Calculate the annual depreciation charge for the farm buildings: (1) between 2011 and 2015 (2) between 2016 and 2020.

2. Draw up a table to show the historical cost/revaluation, annual depreciation charge, and the asset book value of the buildings from 2011 to 2020.

3. Why are fixed assets such as land and property sometimes revalued?

4. Calculate the current net book value of the tractor. Write off the tractor at a rate of 30% each year.

5. Suggest two other assets that the farm will depreciate in its accounts.

2. **Laurence Kell** (This case study discusses the impact on financial position on account of change in accounting policy). Laurence Kell is not happy with her depreciation policy for fixtures and fittings and her estate car. She feels that the fixtures and fittings (purchased on 1 April 2017 for ₹4 lakh) will not last the ten years as originally planned, because a new look to her shop may become essential within a shorter period of time. However, she considers that the original items will still have a good resale value when she decides to replace them. Also, concerning the estate car (valued at ₹1,80,000 on 1 April 2017), she feels that a period of five years is the time after which she will need to replace the car, but that it will have some resale value.

Make theoretical calculations that will show the figures that would have resulted if the following depreciation policies had been followed from the beginning, in April 2020.

Fixtures and fittings: 20% per annum on a reducing balance basis (instead of 10% on a straight-line basis)

Estate car: 20% per annum on a reducing balance basis (instead of 20% on a straight-line basis)

Questions

1. Prepare a table that compares the original (straight-line) and suggested (reducing balance) calculations for depreciation of Laurence's fixtures and fittings, and (separately) her estate car, for the three separate years ending 31 March 2020. The table should show the depreciation charge against profits for each year and also the reduced balance or written down value at the end of each year.

2. Calculate how much more (or less) depreciation the suggested revised policy would have been charged against profit in the first two years, the years ending 31 March 2018 and 2019.

3. Calculate the revised figure for Laurence's opening capital on 1 April 2020 (which at present is ₹20,17,900), assuming the revised policy had been applied from April 2018.

4. Calculate the revised figure for net profit for the year ended 31 March 2021 (₹2,02,400), again assuming the revised policy had been applied from April 2018.

5. Calculate the revised figure for owner's worth (₹18,29,100 as on 1 April 2020) at 31 March 2021, again assuming the revised policy had been applied from April 2018.

6. Which depreciation policy would you have recommended to Laurence in April 2018?

7. What would you advise now on the accounts for the third year ended 31 March 2021, assuming that the accounts for the first two years cannot now be altered?

3. **Book Publishers** Book publishers spend substantial sums to edit textbook manuscripts and to prepare the photographic plates from which the books themselves are printed. Textbook A is expected to remain in print for about five years. Up-to-date competing textbooks will be published each year by other publishing companies. The longer a textbook has been in print, the more out of date it is likely to be, making it more and more difficult to compete with the newer textbooks in the market.

Questions

1. What depreciation method should be adopted for textbook A?

2. What effects would your choice have on the publisher's financial statements?

4. **Morarji Mills Ltd** In January 2004, Morarji Mills Ltd bought and placed in service a new paper machine costing ₹5 lakh. Its estimated useful life was 20 years, with no major overhauls planned for that period. Depreciation was to be calculated on a straight-line basis, with a zero estimated salvage value.

In December 2007, certain improvements were added to this machine at a cost of ₹60,000. Twelve years later, in the fall of 2019, the machine was thoroughly overhauled and rebuilt at a cost of ₹1,20,000. It was estimated that the overhaul would extend the machine's useful life by five years, or until the end of 2018. Depreciation charges for 2019 were unaffected by the overhaul.

Questions

1. Calculate the machine's book value at the end of 2007, after depreciation for the year was recorded but before the improvements were accounted for.

2. Show the journal entry requirement to record the improvements added in December 2007.

3. Compute depreciation for 2008 on a straight-line basis.

4. Show the journal entry required to record the overhauling of the machine in the fall of 2019.

5. Compute depreciation for 2020 on a straight-line basis.

REFERENCES

Shankaranarayana, H.V. and H.R. Ramanath (2011), *Financial Accounting for Management*, Cengage Learning, Delhi, pp. 205–212.

Statement of Financial Accounting Standards No. 2, (1974), 'Accounting for Research and Development Costs', para 12.

Current Assets—Cash and Bank

Learning Objectives

After studying this chapter, you will understand

- meaning of voucher system
- cash book, bank book, and their types
- how transactions with banks are recorded
- different types of cash books
- meaning and types of petty cash books

INTRODUCTION

The management of current assets, that is, cash, receivables, and inventory is critical to maintain adequate liquidity. These assets are important components of the operating cycle, which also includes accounts payable.

Cash usually consists of currency and coins on hand, cheques and money orders from customers, and deposits in chequing, current, and savings accounts. Cash is the most liquid of all assets and is readily available to pay debts. It is central to the operating cycle because all operating transactions eventually use or generate cash. Money deposited in a bank or any other financial institution that is available for withdrawal is also considered cash. A firm may have several bank accounts. Cash is the asset most likely to be stolen or used improperly in a firm. For this reason, the firm must carefully control all cash and cash transactions.

Like cash, accounts receivables and notes receivables are major types of short-term financial assets. Both kinds of receivables result from extending credit to individual customers or to other companies. They are classified as current assets, which we shall discuss in Chapter 10.

For any firm that makes and sells merchandise, inventory is an extremely important asset. Managing this asset is a challenging task. It requires not only protecting goods from theft or loss, but also ensuring that operations are highly efficient. Proper accounting of inventory is essential because misstatements may affect the calculation of the cost of goods sold and in turn affect the net income or net profit of the firm. The primary objective of inventory accounting is to determine income properly by matching the costs of the period against revenue for that period. The management of any firm must use proper valuation method to work out the cost of goods sold, etc. This will be discussed in Chapter 10.

VOUCHER SYSTEM

Voucher system is a method of providing internal control over the function of purchasing goods or services, paying for them, and ensuring that the correct account balances are added or reduced. The elements of a voucher system include the voucher, voucher register, cheque register, unpaid voucher file, and paid voucher file. A voucher is a document used to summarize a transaction and approve payments and recordings. A voucher system is a set of procedures for authorizing and recording assets, liabilities, and cash payments.

A voucher is any document that serves as a proof of authority to receive or pay cash, or for issuing inventory item to the user department, or for allowing the dispatch of merchandise to the customers, etc. An invoice that has been approved for payment could be considered a voucher. In many firms, however, a voucher is a special form used to record data about an asset and liability, and the details of the payment. For purchase of goods, a voucher is supported by the supplier's invoice, a purchase order, and a receiving report. After a voucher is prepared, it is submitted for approval. Once approved, the voucher is recorded in the accounts and filed by the due date. Upon payment, the voucher is recorded in the same manner as the payment of an account payable.

CASH BOOK, BANK BOOK, AND THEIR TYPES

Cash book, bank book, and petty cash book are important types of subsidiary books. Generally, in any manufacturing, business, trade, or service firm, two types of transactions take place:

1. Cash transactions
2. Credit transactions

Credit transactions also get converted into cash transactions in future. For example, if goods or services are delivered by a firm on credit, it is initially treated as a credit transaction, but in the future, at a fixed time, the cash is received and at that time the transaction which took place on credit gets converted into a cash transaction. Cash book is a type of subsidiary book in which cash transactions are only recorded.

Meaning of Cash Book

In the language of a layperson, cash book means 'a subsidiary book that is prepared to keep record of cash transactions'.

Cash transactions are recorded in the cash book. Cash receipts and payments are recorded in the cash book. At the end of a given period (may be shift of a day, week, month, etc.), the cash balance can be known from the cash book.

Cash book serves the purpose of journal entry and cash account both, as cash book is prepared in the form of a ledger account. The debit side of cash book is known as the income or receipt side. The credit side of cash book is known as the expense side or payment side.

Utility or importance of cash book

The following points indicate illustratively the utility or importance of cash book for any firm engaged in business, manufacturing, trading, or service profession (commonly used as firm):

1. *Saving of time and labour:* Cash transactions are directly recorded in a cash book without being recording in a journal. Therefore, a separate cash account is not needed. Cash book serves the purpose of both a journal and a ledger, which results in saving time and labour.

2. *Benefit of division of labour:* Cash book is maintained separately from the journal. Therefore, responsibility of preparing it can be strictly allotted to a different person and the benefit of division of labour can be obtained.

3. *Cash balance can be known:* Cash balance can be known at the end of each shift on a daily basis or daily or at the end of the given period by maintaining a cash book.

4. *Cash embezzlement:* The balance of cash book is worked out daily or at the end of the given period. Therefore, the physical cash balance can be compared with it and if there is any error or cash embezzlement, then it can be known immediately.

5. *Inclusion of bank account:* As per the requirement of the firm and the nature and volume of transactions, the cash book can be prepared in different types. If two-columnar cash book is prepared, then the transactions of cash and bank can be recorded in the same journal. If three-columnar cash book is prepared, then the transactions of cash, bank, and discount can be recorded in the same journal. In such a circumstance, a separate bank account need not be prepared.

Meaning of Bank Book

When the trader or firm or hotelier keeps more than one account in a bank or keeps accounts in more than one bank, a bank book is maintained to record the bank transactions easily. For example, a firm might keep both savings and current account in Bank of Baroda or might keep one account in Bank of Baroda, second in State Bank of India, and third in Bank of India.

In such a situation, a bank book is maintained to facilitate easy recording of the transactions with the bank(s). Various columns are kept in the bank book, same as the accounts in the banks. If various accounts are kept in one bank, then separate columns for such accounts are maintained and if accounts are kept in various banks, then bank-wise separate columns are maintained in the bank book. The form and structure of the bank book is exactly like the cash book, as explained in detail in this chapter.

Advantages of bank book

The following are the advantages gained from a bank book when maintained separately:

1. The transactions with banks can be easily recorded, especially, when the volume of transactions through the banks is more.

2. At any given point of time, the bank balance of various bank accounts can be known.

3. Reconciliation of bank book and bank pass book or bank statement can be easily made and if there is any error, it can be rectified immediately.

4. Constant check on the transactions with the bank can be kept, so that while issuing the cheque for making any payment or withdrawing money from the bank, the position of the bank balance (extent of balance or overdraft utilised) can be known.

TRANSACTIONS WITH BANK

This section will show how the transactions between traders, manufactures, service providers (generally known as firm), and banks are recorded in the cash and bank books.

A. Transactions Relating to Cash and Cheque

When any firm or individual opens an account with a bank, the bank gives to the concerned party (1) pay-in-slip book, (2) cheque book, and (3) pass book or an account statement for smooth banking transactions.

Pay-in-slip is used to deposit cash or cheque in the bank. Cheque book is used to withdraw cash from the bank or to make payment by cheque. Pass book or account statement is an abstract of the firm's ledger account in the books of the bank.

Presently, use of cheque for payments in any business is very common. Cheque is a negotiable instrument under the provision of Negotiable Instrument Act, 1881 in India. There are three parties involved in chequing transactions: (1) drawer of the cheque, (2) drawee of the cheque (bank), and (3) receiver of money. For example, Gaurang has given a cheque of his account in State Bank of India amounting to ₹1,500 to Preeti towards amount payable. Here, Gaurang is the drawer, State Bank of India is the drawee, and Preeti is the receiver of money.

When the customer or debtor gives a cheque towards the amount payable by him, the firm deposits the cheque in the bank account. There are two types of cheques: (1) simple or bearer cheque and (2) crossed cheque.

1. *Simple or bearer cheque:* In a bearer cheque, the bank makes payment to the person who holds and presents the cheque to the bank for receipt of payment. A bearer cheque is worded: 'Pay……….. or Bearer' and would be paid to the person presenting the cheque. Bearer cheques are not as safe as order cheques and are, therefore, used infrequently.

2. *Crossed cheque:* In a crossed cheque, the amount is credited in the bank account of the firm or person whose name is written in the cheque as payee by drawer and in a such case, the physical cash is not paid to the presenter of cheque. An order cheque is worded: 'Pay………… or Order' and is payable to a specified person or to such a person as the payee may order to receive the money.

A cheque which is not crossed is known as an open cheque, and cash may be obtained for it from the banker on whom it is drawn. In practice, in order to secure a measure of protection against fraud, nearly all cheques are crossed cheques. A crossed cheque has two parallel lines drawn across the face of it. Sometimes, the words 'and Co' are written between the lines, but they are not essential to the crossing. When a cheque is crossed, the banker does not pay cash over the counter. The payee must hand over the cheque to his own banker who will collect it for him and credit his account.

When the customer or debtor gives a cheque to the firm towards the amount payable, it will be recorded in the bank column of cash book on debit or receipt side assuming that it is deposited in the bank. The name of the customer who has given the cheque is written in particulars column.

Generally, when a crossed cheque is received, it is recorded on the receipt side, that is, debit side of the cash book in the bank column, because the amount of crossed cheque is not received in cash but is credited in the bank account.

When a firm makes the payment of amount payable to any person by cheque, it is recorded on the credit or payment side of the cash book in the bank column. It is recorded on the date on which such a cheque is issued for payment irrespective of the date on which it is given to the payee or receiver of money.

B. Endorsement

'When the cheque is received from the customers or debtors, the name of the creditors or traders written on the backside of the cheque (overleaf of cheque) and the payment is made directly to the firm by bank whose name is written on the back-side of cheque, then it is called endorsement.' This transaction is recorded in journal proper.

If the cheque received is recorded in the cash book as cheque deposited in the bank and if such a cheque is endorsed, it is recorded on the payment side of the cash book in the bank column. If any cheque is dishonoured, the entry, which was made at the time of receipt or payment of the cheque, will be reversed.

C. Dishonour

Cheques are sometimes 'dishonoured' (returned by the banker unpaid) for various reasons, for example, in the event of the drawer's death or bankruptcy, or where there are insufficient funds to pay the cheque. The bank will attach a slip to the cheque so returned. This is usually marked 'R/D' (refer to drawer) and means that there are insufficient funds to pay the cheque. When a cheque is returned for some technical reason, the bank usually indicates this by means of an appropriate wording, for example, 'words and figures differ' or 'another signature required' or 'signature differs' or 'endorsement irregular', etc.

Banks refuse to cash a cheque that is more than three months old. Such a cheque is then said to be a 'stale cheque'.

D. Bank Charges, Commission, Interest, etc.

When a bank provides any service to a firm, it collects charges for that. Similarly, if a bill is discounted with the bank or is sent for collection with the bank, the bank charges commission from the firm. If the firm takes overdraft facility from a bank, the bank charges interest for overdraft facility use. Similarly, the bank pays interest on the bank balance.

Bank charges commission and interest on overdraft, which are expenses for the firm; hence these are shown on the payment side that is credit side of the cash book in the bank column. On the other hand, the interest received on the bank balance is an income for the firm; therefore, it is shown on the receipt side, that is, debit side of the cash book in the bank column.

TREATMENT OF DISCOUNTS

Many suppliers offer cash discounts. A cash discount is a deduction allowed from the amount due to the supplier, provided the payment is made within a specified time. Thus, if a firm owes to supplier M/s Veg Traders ₹1,000, and the latter

allows a discount of 5%, provided the payment is made within the specified time, ₹50 may be deducted from the amount due and only ₹950 need to be paid. It may be seen, therefore, that the main objective of cash discounts is to encourage prompt payment.

In order to facilitate the recording of cash discount received, firms add a discount received column on the payment side of their cash book.

TYPES OF CASH BOOK

According to the necessity of firms, cash books can be prepared. Following are three types of cash books that can be maintained by firms.

(1) Simple cash book
(2) Two columnar cash book. It can be of three types:
   (a) Cash and discount columnar
   (b) Cash and bank columnar
   (c) Bank and discount columnar
(3) Three columnar cash book: Cash, discount, and bank columnar cash book

Simple Cash Book

Only cash transactions are recorded in a simple cash book. Cash receipts and payments are recorded in a simple cash book. As the format of a cash book is similar to the structure of an account, it is divided into two parts. The left side of the cash book is known as debit side or receipt side or income side and the right side of the cash book is known as credit side or payment side or expense side.

Cash payment is never more than cash receipts; therefore, balance of cash account is always debit. Therefore, in the beginning of the period, cash balance is shown as 'balance brought forward' (Balance b/f) or 'opening balance' on the left hand side of cash book. At the end of the period, the closing cash balance is worked out and is shown as 'balance carried forward' (Balance c/f) or 'closing balance' on the right hand side of cash book.

In short, in the cash book, on the left hand side, the opening cash balance and cash receipts are recorded, whereas, on the right hand side of the cash book, cash payments and closing cash balance are recorded. The format of a simple cash book is as per Format 9.1.

FORMAT 9.1   Format (Specimen) of Simple Cash Book

Dr. (Add)   Cr. (Less)

Date	Particular (Receipts)	Rec. No.	L.F.	Amount (₹)	Date	Particulars (Payments)	Vou. No.	L.F.	Amount (₹)
	To Opening balance (Balance b/f)								
	Receipts					Payments By closing balance (Balance c/f)			

Explanation of cash book

Receipt side or debit side   When cash is received, it is recorded on the receipt side of cash book and the following particulars are mentioned on it:

1. **Date:** In this column, the date on which cash is received is chronologically recorded.
2. **Particulars (Receipts):** In this column, the ledger account name or description of transactions, other than cash account of the transaction due to which the cash is received, is shown. It means, as per the journal entry, the account which is to be affected is shown here. Many times, a brief explanation about the transaction is also written within brackets.
3. **Receipt No.:** When cash is received in any business, a receipt is given to the payer against it. If cash is received on account of cash services or provision items, then cash memo is given. The number of the receipt or cash memo is written in this column. It is recorded on the basis of the copy of receipt or cash memo retained by the firm.
4. **L.F. (Ledger Folio No.):** The page number of the ledger folio, where the account is maintained for the second part

of transaction, is recorded. It means that in case of sale of provision items, the ledger folio number of the Sale of Provision Items Account is written in this column.
5. **Amount:** In this column, the amount received is recorded.

Payment side or credit side   The following particulars are mentioned on the payment side of cash book.

1. **Date:** In this column, the date on which the cash is paid is chronologically recorded.
2. **Particulars (Payment):** In this column, the ledger account, other than cash account of the transactions, due to which the cash goes out is shown. It means that as per the journal entry, the account which is affected is shown here. Many times, brief particulars about the transaction are also written within brackets.
3. **Voucher No.:** When cash is paid, the payee issues a receipt of cash received or cash memo of cash purchase or internally document is created to record the transactions by the firm itself. The number of such a receipt or cash memo or the number given by the firm is written in this column.
4. **L.F. (Ledger Folio No.):** The page number of the ledger folio, where the account is maintained for the second

part of transaction, is recorded. It means that in case of purchase of provision items, the ledger folio number of the Purchase of Provision Items Account is written in this column.

5. **Amount:** In this column, the amount paid or the amount of cash given away is recorded.

Closing cash balance   In a simple cash book, on the receipt side, opening cash balance and cash receipts are recorded, whereas on the payment side, cash payments are recorded. Regularly at the end of shift of the day or at the end of day or at the end of the pre-decided time period, cash book is closed and closing cash balance is worked out. The total of the payment side of such a cash book is deducted from the total of the cash receipt side; and the amount of difference, known as the closing cash balance, is placed on the credit side of cash book.

Here, the important point is that the total of receipt side of cash book can never be less than the total of payment side, as more cash cannot be paid than what is received. Therefore, the total of receipt side is always more than or equal to the total of payment side in a simple cash book.

As the total of receipt side is more than the total of payment side in a cash book, the closing balance is treated as debit balance. It is quite obvious that non-cash transactions are not recorded in cash books.

■ **ILLUSTRATION 9.1**   Prepare a simple cash book from the following transactions of Rajesh Hotel for February, 2020.

1 Feb: Cash on hand ₹5,000.

3 Feb: Received ₹3,000 from Mrs Gita in cash for one single bedroom.

5 Feb: Purchased wheat of worth ₹2,000 from Amit Traders for cash.

7 Feb: Cash of ₹5,000 brought into the hotel, because more funds are required in the hotel as capital by owner Rajesh.

9 Feb: Insurance premium ₹800 paid.

10 Feb: Dining table of ₹4,000 purchased from Ganesh Furniture Mart for cash.

12 Feb: ₹1,500 received towards commission from City Tour and Travels for directing visitors for sightseeing in the last month, and ₹1,200 paid towards brokerage for agent who directed visitors to Rajesh Hotel.

14 Feb: ₹3,000 received from Mahesh towards receivable for room service provided in the last week.

16 Feb: Salary of ₹1,000 and freight on furniture of ₹200 paid.

18 Feb: ₹3,000 paid to Prakruti Traders towards an old account with respect to purchases of cereals.

20 Feb: Hot Kitneys kettles are purchased for the benefit of visitors by paying cash of ₹2,000.

23 Feb: As more funds are required for hotel renovation, ₹10,000 borrowed as loan bearing 10% rate of interest from Raja Bank.

26 Feb: Cash purchase of different types of dry fruits for ₹7,000.

28 Feb: ₹3,000 deposited in current account maintained with Prime Co-operative Bank.

Solution

Simple Cash Book of Rajesh Hotel for February 2020

Dr. (Add)   Cr. (Less)

Date 2020	Particulars (Receipts)	Vou. No.	L.F.	Amount (₹)	Date 2019	Particulars (Payments)	Vou. No.	L.F.	Amount (₹)
1 Feb	To Balance b/f (Opening balance)			5,000	5 Feb	By Grains purchase A/c			2,000
3 Feb	To Room Sales A/c			3,000	9 Feb	By Insur. Premum A/c			800
					10 Feb	By Furniture A/c			4,000
7 Feb	To Capital A/c			5,000	12 Feb	By Brokerage A/c			1,200
12 Feb	To Commission A/c			1,500	16 Feb	By Salary A/c			1,000
14 Feb	To Mahesh A/c			3,000	16 Feb	By Furniture A/c			200
23 Feb	To Raja Bank's				18 Feb	By Prakruti A/c			3,000
	10% loan A/c			10,000	20 Feb	By Electrical Equipment A/c			2,000
					26 Feb	By Dry fruits purchase A/c			7,000
					28 Feb	By Bank (Prime Co. Bank) A/c			3,000
					28 Feb	By Balance c/f			**3,300**
	Total			**27,500**					**27,500**
2019									
1 Mar	To Balance b/f			3,300					

Two Columnar Cash Book

Following are the three types of two columnar cash book: (A) Cash and Discount Columnar Cash Book, (B) Cash and Bank Columnar Cash Book, (C) Bank and Discount Columnar Cash Book.

Cash and discount columnar cash book

In this type of cash book (Format 9.2) one additional column of discount is added, which results in two columns—cash and discount. Trade discount is not recorded in the cash book. The discount column is kept to record only the cash

FORMAT 9.2   Format of Cash and Discount Columnar Cash Book

Dr. (Add)   Cr. (Less)

Date	Particulars (Receipts)	Rec. No.	L.F.	Discount Allowed	Cash Amount (₹)	Date	Particulars (Payments)	Vou. No.	L.F.	Discount Received	Cash Amount (₹)

discount. For cash column, the cash account is an 'Asset Account'; hence asset account rule is applied. For discount column, discount is an expense account; hence rule of expense account is applied.

The 'discount received' column is described as a memorandum column. It is convenient and does not count for double entry purposes. Double entry in respect of discount received is completed as follows:

Reduce the cash balance by cash paid and note the discount received as reduction in the balance of account of the supplier. Consider the total of the discount received account in the ledger as an income periodically (usually weekly, fortnightly, or monthly).

The purpose of the detail column on the debit and credit side of the cash book is twofold: to indicate the sources of any cash banked or disbursed and to facilitate an easy cross-reference to the ledger account concerned.

Cash discount is an expense for businesses, manufacturers, traders, service providing firms, etc. Therefore, discount (discount allowed) is debited or considered as an expense for the firm. This indicates the reduction in receivable from the customers; hence credited in the customers' account (reduction in asset). Cash discount is income for the trader who is receiving the benefit. Therefore, discount (discount received) account is credited.

Let us understand with the help of an example. Debtor Parth makes payment of ₹3,000 as against his debt of ₹3,080 and if the firm accepts it towards full settlement of account, then ₹80 (3,080 – 3,000) is said to be the discount allowed. As per the rules, the transaction results in increase in cash balance to the extent of cash received, and the discount allowed is recorded on the receipt side of the cash book. The discount allowed will indicate the expense in the nature of discount.

Similarly, when cash purchase is made or payment is made to any creditor, and if less amount is paid than the amount payable, then the difference amount is known as cash discount. The 'discount received' is the gain. Therefore, as per rule, the discount received is credited. For example, suppose a person purchases goods of ₹2,040 from Ashok for cash. ₹2,000 is paid for the final settlement. Here, cash goes out from the person but the discount received is his gain, both of which are recorded on the payment side of the cash book.

Here, the important point is that, in two columnar cash book, the balance of cash book is worked out but the balance of discount column is not worked out. Here, the total of discount column on debit side is made and the total amount is debited to the discount allowed account. On the other hand, the discount received column on credit side is totalled and the total amount is credited in the discount received account.

■ **ILLUSTRATION 9.2**   Prepare a two columnar cash book (with cash and discount columns) for Well Care Hotel from the following transactions:

2020

1 March:	Opening cash balance ₹8,000.
4 March:	Dates and dried figs of ₹6,000 purchased at 10% trade discount.
7 March:	Raisins of ₹3,000 sold to Pravin for cash at 5% cash discount.
10 March:	Dates of ₹4,000 sold for cash at 10% discount and 5% cash discount.
12 March:	Furniture of ₹5,000 purchased from Gopal Furniture Mart.
15 March:	₹1,000 paid to Vishnu towards full settlement of ₹1,020 for old purchases of grains.
16 March:	₹900 paid for commission to travel agent who recommended Well Care Hotel to tourists and visitors.
18 March:	₹1,500 received from Kamlesh towards full settlement of ₹1,560, for providing the banquet hall for their use.
20 March:	Paid ₹2,000 for salary and ₹400 for wages.
23 March:	Saffrons of ₹2,000 purchased from Vishwa for cash at 10% trade discount and 10% cash discount.
26 March:	Cash of ₹4,000 brought in to the business by the owner Rajaram.
28 March:	A microwave oven of ₹8,000 is purchased from Maheshwari Engineering, for which ₹5,000 is paid and the balance amount is agreed to be paid after one month.

Solution

Two Columnar Cash Book of Well Care Hotel for March 2020

Dr. (Add)   Cr. (Less)

Date 2020	Particulars (Receipts)	Rec. No.	L.F.	Disc. Allowed	Amount (₹)	Date 2020	Particulars (Payments)	Rec. No.	L.F.	Disc. Received	Amount (₹)
1 Mar	To Balance b/f (Cash balance)				8,000	1 Mar	By Dry fruits purchase A/c (Cash purchase)				5,400
7 Mar	To Dry fruits sales A/c (Cash sales)			150	2,850	15 Mar	By Vishnu A/c			20	1,000
10 Mar	To Dry fruits sales A/c			180	3,420	16 Mar	By Commission A/c				900
18 Mar	To Kamlesh A/c			60	1,500	20 Mar	By Salary A/c				2,000
26 Mar	To Capital A/c				4,000	20 Mar	By Wages A/c				400
						23 Mar	By Dry fruits purchase A/c			180	1,620
						28 Mar	By Machinery A/c (Partial amount is paid for the purchase of machine of ₹8,000)				5,000
						31 Mar	Balance c/f (Closing balance)				3,450
	Total			**390**	**19,770**		**Total**			**200**	**19,770**
1 April	To balance b/f				3,450						

Notes:

1. Trade discount allowed given in the transaction of cash purchase dated March 4 will not be recorded as it is trade discount.
2. Credit purchase of furniture dated March 12 will not be recorded in cash book.
3. Here, the total of discount allowed column is ₹390 which will be posted on the debit side of discount account in the ledger.
4. The total of discount received column is ₹200 which will be posted on the credit side of discount received account in the ledger.

Cash and bank columnar cash book

The single column cash book indicates that it is inadequate in some respects. First, majority of firms keep most of their cash in a bank account and some amount of cash is maintained in the premises. Second, considering the legal and safety aspect, firms usually like to make and receive payments through bank cheques or through direct debit or credit in firms' bank accounts in lieu of cash dealings. Hence, it is necessary to have a cash book which will distinguish between the two separate forms of cash (that is, bank account and an office cash account), and thus differentiate between receipts and payments in the form of cheque and cash.

In this type of cash book (Format 9.3), an additional column (bank) is inserted on both the sides of the simple cash book. This column is kept to record the transaction with the bank. The double columnar cash book has two columns for amount, headed as 'cash' and 'bank' on the debit or receipt side, and two columns for amount, also headed as 'cash' and 'bank' on the credit or payment side.

When (1) cash is deposited, (2) cheque is deposited, (3) draft is deposited, (4) any debtor, that is, customer to whom credit goods or services provided in the past deposit money directly in the bank, (5) bank credits interest or various incomes after collecting the same on the firm account, then the firm's bank balance is increased. In a cash book, the above mentioned transactions are recorded on the debit side in the bank column.

When (1) cash is withdrawn from the bank, (2) amount is paid by cheque, (3) bank debits bank commission, charges, bank overdraft interest, (4) bank pays expenses (like electricity bill, insurance premium, telephone bill, etc.) on firm's behalf, then the firm's bank balance is reduced. The above mentioned

FORMAT 9.3   Cash and Bank Columnar Cash Book

Dr. (Add)   Cr. (Less)

Date	Particulars (Receipts)	Rec. No.	L.F.	Cash Amt (₹)	Bank Amt (₹)	Date	Particulars (Payments)	Vou. No.	L.F.	Cash Amt (₹)	Bank Amt (₹)

transactions are recorded on the credit side of the cash book in the bank column.

In a simple cash book, cash payment can never be more than cash receipt. Therefore, the closing balance of cash account in a cash book is always debit balance.

In a two columnar cash book, 'bank column' is prepared differently. If the total of receipt column is more than the total of payment column, bank column will also have a debit balance, which will be treated as closing bank balance. In the bank column, if the total of payment column is more than the total of receipt column, the difference is called bank overdraft, which is explained hereunder.

Bank overdraft (BOD)   When a trader or business or service provider makes an agreement with the bank to withdraw more than the available balance in the firm's account upto a fixed agreed amount (as per credit granted to the firm by the banker based on financial performance and growth parameters of the firm), such a facility is known as bank overdraft.

When a firm or trader gets the bank overdraft facility, the bank balance can be debit or credit. If the bank column has a credit balance, it shows more withdrawal (overdraft). Interest is payable at a fixed rate on such bank overdraft amount. Thus, if the total of receipt side of bank column in the cash book is more than the total of payment side, it is known as 'closing bank balance'. But if the total of payment side in the bank column is more than the total of receipt side, it is known as 'closing bank overdraft'.

If the opening balance with the bank is 'bank balance', it is shown on the debit or receipt side of cash book in the bank column as 'balance brought down' or 'balance brought forward' and if the opening balance with the bank is 'bank overdraft', it is shown on the payment or credit side of cash book in the bank column as 'balance brought down' or 'balance brought forward'.

Similarly, if the closing balance of bank column in the cash book is 'bank balance', it is shown on the payment side as 'balance carried down' or 'balance carried forward' (Balance c/f) and if the closing balance of bank column is 'bank overdraft', it is shown on the debit side as 'balance carried down' or 'balance carried forward' (overdraft).

Contra transaction   'Contra transaction' is a financial transaction in which cash and bank both get affected. For example, cash withdrawn from a bank or cash deposited in a bank. This type of transaction is recorded on both sides of the cash book, when the cash and bank columnar cash book is kept.

Such a cash and bank columnar cash book serves the purpose of both cash account and bank account. Thus, when such a cash book is maintained, 'cash' and 'bank' accounts are not required to be opened separately. Any amount of cash transferred from the bank to the office cash should be credited in the bank column (bank balance reduced) and debited in the cash column (cash balance increased). Any transfer of cash from the office to the bank should be credited in the cash column and debited in the bank column. Any transfer of cash from the bank to the office, or vice versa, is shown in the cash book by means of a 'contra entry'. The term contra entry means that both the debit and the credit entries are to be found in the same two columnar cash book. Contra entries are denoted by the sign 'C'. 'Contra transaction' affects only 'cash' and 'bank' account, hence the posting is not required, but 'C' (Contra) will be written in the Ledger Folio No. (L.F.) column.

Generally, contra transaction is of two types: (1) cash deposited in the bank and (2) cash withdrawn from the bank.

1. *Cash deposited in the bank from business:*
   When cash is deposited in a bank, cash balance is reduced on one hand and bank balance is increased on the other hand. Suppose cash of ₹2,000 is deposited in a bank.
   ₹2,000 will be recorded on the receipt side, which means debit side of cash book in the bank column and 'cash account' will be written in the Particulars column. On the other hand, ₹2,000 will also be recorded on the payment side, which means credit side of cash book in the cash column and 'bank account' will be written in the Particulars column.
   Further 'C' (Contra) will be written in the L.F. No. column of cash book on both the sides. As contra transactions are not required to be posted, L.F. No. is not required, but in order to know the nature of transactions, 'C' is shown in that column.

2. *Cash withdrawn from the bank for business:*
   When cash is withdrawn from a bank, cash balance is increased and bank balance is reduced. Suppose cash of ₹3,000 is withdrawn from a bank. ₹3,000 will be recorded on the receipt side, meaning debit side of cash book in the cash column. ₹3,000 and 'bank account' will be written in the Particulars column. ₹3,000 will also be recorded on the payment side, meaning credit side of cash book in the bank column. ₹3,000 and 'cash account' will be written in the Particulars column.
   Further 'C' will be written in the L.F. No. column of cash book when the above transaction is recorded in cash and bank columnar cash book.

■ **ILLUSTRATION 9.3**   From the following transactions, prepare a cash and bank columnar cash book in the books of M/s Saviour Resort.

1 April: Opening cash balance ₹6,000. Opening bank balance ₹5,000.

3 April: Meal dishes of ₹10,000 sold to Pankaj Associates for their staff members for cash at 10% trade discount.

5 April: Vegetables of ₹3,000 purchased for cash from Janki Bros.

7 April: Cash of ₹1,500 deposited in the bank account maintained with Dena Bank.

9 April: Stationery expenses of ₹1,000 and salary of ₹3,000 paid by cheque.

11 April: ₹1,100 paid towards parking area rent.

14 April: Cheque of ₹3,000 received from visitor Mr Yogesh, which is immediately deposited in the bank.

17 April: ₹1,000 withdrawn from the bank to pay fire insurance premium in cash in future.

21 April: Furniture of ₹800 purchased for household need of Mr Yogi (owner), and cheque for the necessary amount is issued from the bank account of Savior Resort.

23 April: Fire insurance premium paid in cash of ₹1,000.

27 April: Placed an order with Akbarbhai for supply of cereals of ₹5,000.

Solution

Two Columnar Cash Book of Savior Resort for April 2019

Dr. (Add)   Cr. (Less)

Date 2019	Particulars (Receipts)	Vou. No.	L.F.	Cash Amt (₹)	Bank Amt (₹)	Date 2019	Particulars (Payments)	Vou. No.	L.F.	Cash Amt (₹)	Bank Amt (₹)
1 Apr	To Balance b/d			6,000	5,000	1 Apr	By Vegetables			3,000	
3 Apr	To Meals sales A/c			9,000			purchase A/c				
	(Cash)					7 Apr	By Bank A/c		C	1,500	
7 Apr	To Cash A/c	C			1,500	9 Apr	By Stationery				1,000
14 Apr	To Yogesh A/c				3,000		expense A/c				
17 Apr	To Bank A/c	C		1,000		9 Apr	By Salary A/c				3,000
						11 Apr	By Rent A/c			1,100	
						17 Apr	By Cash A/c				1,000
						21 Apr	By Drawings A/c				800
						23 Apr	By Fire insurance premium A/c			1,000	
						30 Apr	By Balance c/f			9,400	3,700
	Total			16,000	9,500		Total			16,000	9,500
1 May	To Balance b/d			9,400	3,700						

Notes:

1. Transaction dated 7 is a contra transaction.
2. In the transaction dated 17, ₹1,000 has been withdrawn from the bank for the payment of fire insurance premium of the business. Therefore, first it will be recorded as contra transaction. It means that bank balance will be reduced and cash balance will be increased by ₹1,000.
3. On 23rd, fire insurance premium has been actually paid by cash. Therefore on that date, ₹1,000 will be recorded in the cash book on the payment side in the cash column.
4. Transaction dated 27 is a non-economic transaction; only an order is placed, hence it will not be recorded.

Bank and discount columnar cash book

In this type of cash book, bank column and discount column are only kept. This is specifically prepared and maintained by a firm that does not involve in cash transaction with either customers or suppliers. When the payment is made through cheque and the discount is received or when the amount is received by cheque and the discount is allowed, to record such discount and bank transactions, a bank and discount columnar cash book is prepared.

This type of cash book (Format 9.4) is normally prepared when most of the transactions are made through cheque. At the end of the given period the cash book is closed and the closing bank balance or overdraft is worked out. On the receipt or debit side of the cash book 'discount allowed' and on the payment or credit side 'discount received' are recorded.

Transaction of cheques issued and received, bank charges, bank commissions, bank interests, etc. are recorded in the same manner as are recorded in a cash and bank columnar cash book. Here, the cash column is not maintained; hence, when the cheque is deposited in the bank, on that date, it is recorded on the debit side of the cash book in the bank column. Similarly, the date on which the cheque is issued, it is recorded on the credit side of the cash book in the bank column.

FORMAT 9.4 Bank and Discount Columnar Cash Book

Cash Book of M/s Krishna

Dr. (Add)   Cr. (Less)

Date	Particulars (Receipts)	Rec. No.	L.F.	Disc. Allowed (₹)	Bank Amt (₹)	Date	Particulars (Payments)	Vou. No.	L.F.	Disc. Rece. (₹)	Bank Amt (₹)

In this type of cash book, in bank column balancing amount may be either the closing bank balance or overdraft. The total of discount allowed account is debited or added to the discount given account in the ledger, whereas the total of discount received column is credited or added to the discount received account in the ledger.

This type of cash book is not very popular because cash transactions do take place to some extent in any firm along with bank transactions. Here, cash column is not maintained to record cash transactions. To remove such a limitation, a three columnar cash book is maintained, in which three columns for cash, bank, and discount are maintained on both the sides of cash book.

■ **ILLUSTRATION 9.4**   From the following transactions, prepare a bank and discount columnar cash book in the books of Suresh Restaurant.

1 June: Bank overdraft ₹12,000.
7 June: Food dishes of ₹9,000 sold to Nila at 10% trade discount. Nila gave a cheque after deducting discount, which is deposited in the bank.
14 June: Cheque of ₹5,000 issued to Nayana in full settlement of account of ₹5,050.
16 June: Commission of ₹1,100 to travel agent paid by cheque.
20 June: Vipul Ltd has given a cheque of ₹11,000 towards amount payable of ₹11,125 in full settlement of account.
23 June: Milk of ₹4,000 sold to Chandulal at 10% trade discount and 10% cash discount. Chandulal made the payment immediately by cheque. Cheque is deposited in the bank.
26 June: ₹1,800 paid to Devanshi by cheque.
28 June: Cheque issued by Vipul Ltd is dishonoured.

Solution

Two Columnar Bank Book of Suresh Restaurant for June 2019

Dr. (Add) Cr. (Less)

Date 2019	Particulars (Receipts)	Rec. No.	L.F.	Disc. Allowed	Amount (₹)	Date 2019	Particulars (Payments)	Rec. No.	L.F.	Disc. Received	Amount (₹)
7 Jun	To Sales (Food dishes) A/c				8,100	1 Jun	By Balance b/f				12,000
						14 Jun	By Nayana A/c			50	5,000
20 Jun	To Vipul Ltd A/c			125	11,000	16 Jun	By Commission account				1,100
24 Jun	To Sales (Milk) A/c			360	3,240						
30 Jun	To Balance c/f				8,560	26 Jun	By Devanshi A/c				1,800
						28 Jun	By Vipul Ltd A/c				11,000
	Total			**485**	**30,900**		**Total**			**50**	**30,900**
						1 Jul	By balance b/f				8,560

Notes:

1. Here, total of discount allowed column is ₹485, which will be recorded or posted on the debit side of discount allowed account in the ledger.
2. Here, total of discount received column is ₹50, which will be recorded on the credit side of the discount received account in the ledger.
3. Total of payment side is more; therefore it shows bank overdraft at the end of June.
4. Cheque of ₹11,000 has been received from Vipul Ltd on 20th towards amount payable of ₹11,125 in full settlement of account, which is deposited in the bank and dishonoured on 28th. Generally, in such cases, if the cheque given by the customer is dishonoured, then discount allowed is also cancelled. Here, cash discount of ₹125 has been given to Vipul Ltd, which is required to be cancelled due to the dishonour of cheque on 28th. The journal entry for cancellation of discount is as under:

Vipul Ltd account	Dr.	125
To Discount Allowed A/c		125

From the above journal entry, it can be seen that ₹125 will be recorded on the credit side of discount allowed account. Therefore, discount has not been recorded on the credit side where the entry for cheque dishonoured has been made. If the bank balance is reduced by ₹11,000 only and if the effect of discount is given, the amount of discount received and discount allowed would be incorrectly reflected more. Hence, it is required to be cancelled and thereby it is reduced.

Three columnar cash book

In this type of cash book (Format 9.5), three columns are kept on both sides: discount column, cash column, and bank column. Presently, this type of cash book is more useful because cash and bank transactions, discount received and allowed are recorded in the same structure. For the discount column, discount is the income or expense; therefore rule of income and expense account is applicable. For cash column, cash is an asset; therefore, rule of asset account is applicable. At last, for bank column, bank is an asset account (in case of savings account) or a liability account (in case of overdraft or cash credit account) and so the rule of asset account or liability account is applicable respectively.

On the receipt side of the cash book, the transactions increasing the cash or bank balance and discount allowed are recorded, whereas on the payment side of the cash book, the

FORMAT 9.5 Three Columnar Cash Book: Cash, Bank, and Discount Columnar Cash Book

Dr. (Add) | | | | | | | | | | | | Cr. (Less)

Date	Particulars (Receipts)	Rec. No.	L.F.	Disc. Allowed (₹)	Cash Amt (₹)	Bank Amt (₹)	Date	Particulars (Payments)	Vou. No.	L.F.	Disc. Recd. (₹)	Cash Amt (₹)	Bank Amt (₹)

transactions reducing the cash or bank balance (or increase in bank overdraft) and discount received are recorded.

Points to be considered at the time of preparing three columnar cash book:

A. Opening balance of cash balance and bank balance are recorded on the debit side, that is, receipt side of cash book as Balance b/f, whereas the bank overdraft is recorded in the credit side, that is, payment side of cash book as Balance b/f in bank column.

B. All types of cash receipt transactions are recorded on the debit side, that is, receipt side of the cash book and all types of cash payment transactions are recorded on the credit side, that is, payment side of the cash book.

C. All types of cash transactions increasing bank balance or decreasing overdraft are recorded on debit side, that is, receipt side in the bank column and all types of transactions decreasing bank balance or increasing overdraft are recorded on the credit side, that is, payment side in the bank column of the cash book.

D. Contra transactions are recorded on both the sides of cash book.

E. Discount allowed is recorded on debit side and discount received is recorded on credit side of the cash book.

■ **ILLUSTRATION 9.5** From the following transactions, prepare a three columnar cash book of M/s Manisha Guesthouse.

1 July: Opening cash balance ₹10,000, bank overdraft ₹4,000.

Solution

3 July: Apricot of ₹3,000 purchased from Iyer Dry Fruits Brothers at 10% cash discount and issued cheque of the necessary amount.

5 July: Salary of ₹800 and stationery of ₹700 paid by cheque.

7 July: Cinnamon of ₹6,000 purchased from Babita Spices at 10% trade discount. Half of the amount paid by cash and the balance amount is paid by cheque.

9 July: ₹4,000 deposited in the bank.

10 July: Cheque of ₹6,000 issued to Prima Traders towards full settlement of the account of ₹6,050.

12 July: Atmaram has given ₹6,000 cash and cheque of ₹4,000 which is deposited in the bank towards the amount payable for occupied room for two days ₹10,070.

14 July: Cheque of ₹5,000 received from Sundar towards payment of an old debt, which is deposited in the bank.

19 July: ₹3,000 cash paid towards Income Tax of M/s Manisha (owner of guesthouse).

20 July: Cheque of Sundar is dishonoured.

22 July: 50 paisa dividend per rupee received from receiver of Sundar.

28 July: Room services of ₹10,000 sold to Tipendra at 10% cash discount. For 60% of the amount cheque received which is deposited and the remaining amount is received in cash.

31 July: After keeping cash on hand of ₹2,000, remaining amount is deposited in the bank.

Three Columnar Cash Book of Manisha Guesthouse for July 2019

Dr. (Add) | | | | | | | | | | | | Cr. (Less)

Date 2019	Particulars (Receipts)	Rec. No.	L.F.	Disc. Allowed (₹)	Cash Amt (₹)	Bank Amt (₹)	Date 2019	Particulars (Payments)	Vou. No.	L.F.	Disc. Recd. (₹)	Cash Amt (₹)	Bank Amt (₹)
1 Jul	To Balance b/f				10,000		1 Jul	By Balance b/f					4,000
9 Jul	To Cash A/c		C			4,000	3 Jul	By Dry fruits purchase A/c			300		2,700
12 Jul	To Atmaram A/c			70	6000	4,000	5 Jul	By Salary A/c					800
14 Jul	To Sundar A/c					5,000	5 Jul	By Stationery A/c					700
22 Jul	To Sundar A/c					2,500	7 Jul	By Spices purchase A/c				2,700	2,700
28 Jul	To Sales A/c			1,000	3,600	5,400	9 Jul	By Bank A/c		C		4,000	
31 Jul	To Cash A/c		C			7,900	10 Jul	By Prima Traders A/c			50		6,000
							19 Jul	By Drawing A/c				3,000	

					Cash	Bank	Date		C		Cash	Bank
							20 Jul	By Sundar A/c (cheque dishonour)				5,000
							31 Jul	By Bank A/c	C		7,900	
							31 Jul	By Balance c/f			2,000	6,900
	Total			1,070	19,600	28,800		Total		350	19,600	28,800
2019												
1 Aug	To Balance b/f				2,000	6,900						

Notes:

1. Dt. 1 Bank overdraft: Recorded on the credit side in the bank column as balance b/f.
2. Dt. 9 and 31: Transaction involving both cash and bank (contra transactions).
3. In the transaction dated 22, 50% dividend received from Sundarlal's receiver. Dividend (Recovery) is always received in crossed cheque. Therefore, it is recorded in the bank account.
4. Here, for the transaction dated 31, we need to find out the amount deposited in the bank. Amount deposited in the bank = Total receipts ₹24,600 − (Total payment ₹14,700 + Cash on hand ₹2,000) = ₹7,900
5. Here, discount allowed is ₹1,070 and discount received is ₹350.

■ **ILLUSTRATION 9.6**   From the following transactions, prepare a three columnar cash book of Rangapa Resort and Hotel for the first fortnight of April 2020.

1 April: Opening cash balance ₹30,000, bank balance ₹8,00,000.

3 April: Cereals of ₹3,00,000 purchased from Nilesh Cereals at 2% cash discount and amount paid by RTGS. RTGS charge is ₹30. Bank has debited the amount.

5 April: Services of five suites for one week used for ₹1,00,000 by Rajesh. Rajesh has sent amount through NEFT. Bank has credited the amount.

6 April: Banqueting sales of ₹4,00,000 made to Mahesh Ltd at 2% cash discount. Mahesh Ltd has sent the amount through RTGS. Bank has credited the amount.

7 April: Insurance premium of ₹10,000 paid through NEFT and NEFT charges incurred ₹3. Bank has debited the amount in their account.

9 April: Salary of ₹15,000 paid in cash.

10 April: Restaurant sales amount to ₹30,000.

11 April: ₹10,000 withdrawn from bank for personal expenses by Manager Mrs Agnihotri.

12 April: ₹12,000 paid to Ramesh towards payable amount.

13 April: Raman has paid ₹22,000 through NEFT towards receivable amount. Bank has credited the amount.

14 April: Rent of ₹5,000 paid.

15 April: Bank has credited ₹3,000 of dividend for investments made by Rangapa Resort and Hotel in LTC shares.

Solution

Three Columnar Cash Book of Rangapa Resort and Hotel for April 2019

Dr. (Add) — Cr. (Less)

Date 2019	Receipts	Rec. No.	L.F.	Disc. (₹)	Cash (₹)	Bank (₹)	Date 2019	Payments	Vou. No.	L.F.	Disc. (₹)	Cash (₹)	Bank (₹)
1 Apr	To Balance b/f				30,000	8,00,000	1 Apr	By Cereals purchase A/c			6,000		294,000
							3 Apr	By RTGS charge A/c					30
5 Apr	To Suites sales A/c					1,00,000							
							7 Apr	By Ins. Pre. A/c					10,000
6 Apr	To Banqueting sales A/c			8,000		3,92,000	7 Apr	By NEFT charge A/c					3
10 Apr	To Restaurant sales A/c				30,000		9 Apr	By Salary A/c				15,000	
							11 Apr	By Mrs. Agnihotri A/c					10,000
13 Apr	To Raman A/c					22,000	12 Apr	By Ramesh A/c				12,000	
							14 Apr	By Rent A/c				5,000	
15 Apr	To Dividend A/c					3000	15 Apr	By Balance c/f				28,000	10,02,967
	Total			8,000	60,000	13,17,000		Total			6,000	60,000	13,17,000
16 Apr	To Balance b/f				28,000	10,02,967							

PETTY CASH BOOK ■■■■

Firms are often required to make numerous payments of small amounts for various expenses. Although small, such payments may occur often enough to total a significant amount. Thus, it is desirable to control such payments. Where this is so, it may be convenient to have a main cash book and a separate petty cash book. The main cash book would be in the charge of a senior clerk or the head cashier, whereas the responsibility for maintaining the petty cash book would be delegated to a relatively junior clerk. Hence, a special cash fund, called a petty cash fund or Cash Imprest System, is used.

Petty cash books are usually analysed and kept on what is known as the Imprest System or Petty Cash Fund. This operates as follows: At the beginning of a period, a fixed amount of cash, say ₹2,000, is advanced to the petty cashier. At the end of the period, the petty cashier balances his petty cash book, and the total amount expended by him (and represented by appropriate vouchers) is refunded to him by the person in charge of the main cash book. Thus, at the beginning of each period, the petty cashier will start with the same fixed float of cash. The book kept for keeping a record for the payment of small expenses is known as Petty Cash Book.

For example:

	Amount (₹)
Petty cashier's cash float on 1 January 2020	2,000
Petty cashier's weekly expenditure (total vouchers)	1,600
Petty cashier's balance of cash on 7 January 2020	400
Therefore, (1) cash refunded to him on 7 January 2020	1,600
(2) his cash float on 8 January 2020	2,000

When the volume of cash transactions are more in respect of any firm, trader, concern, or unit, then generally, to help main (chief) cashier and to keep him free from making payment and recording petty or small expenses, an assistant (petty) cashier is employed. The main job of a petty cashier is to pay and keep a detailed record of the petty expenses. The petty cashier is given the responsibility for the same by the main cashier and the required amount for the same is received from the main cashier. Normally a petty cashier is given the responsibility of the payment and the recording of expenses like normal small amount of expenses need to be paid to buy on spot, postage expenses, tea and refreshment expenses, stationery expenses, freight, wages to temporary workers, etc. The book (cash book) kept by a petty cashier for keeping a record for the payment of each expense is known as petty cash book.

A petty cashier prepares the petty cash book and pays the specific expenses. So, the information of various types of expenses (and total amount) paid by the petty cashier is available. This facilitates work division and control on the cash transactions.

It should be noted that every petty cash payment is recorded twice, once in the total column and once in one of the analysis columns. Consequently, the sum of the analysed totals should be equal to that of the total column. In the folio column the numbers of the petty cash vouchers are recorded. These would be numbered consecutively and presented to the head cashier when requesting a refund in respect of payments made.

Double entry in respect of petty cash items is completed as follows:

(a) Any amounts drawn by the petty cashier are recorded on payment side of the main cash book and in turn increase the balance in the petty cash book.

(b) Petty cash payments are credited (individually) or they reduce the balance in the petty cash book and are debited (added as particular expense account) in total in the appropriate account in the ledger. Thus, the total of the, say, postage column, ₹400, would be debited or shown as an increase in expense account maintained in the name of postage account in the main ledger.

The petty cash book, though physically separated from the ledger, is a ledger account. As a result, every entry made in it counts for double entry purposes. It is also a subsidiary book where it collects and analyses detailed transactions and enables totals to be posted to the ledger.

Types of Petty Cash Book

A petty cash book can be prepared in two ways: (1) Simple or columnar cash book (2) Petty cash book on imprest system.

Simple petty cash book

In this type of petty cash books, the petty cashier is given a fixed amount in the beginning. At the end of a given period, the main cashier gives more cash, if required. As and when the expenses are paid, they are recorded in the petty cash book. Suppose, in the beginning, ₹1,000 is given to the petty cashier and various payments are made by the petty cashier. He has the balance of ₹50 and more cash is required to pay other expenses. At this time, the required amount is given by the main cashier on the estimated basis.

When any such expense is paid, it is recorded in the petty cash book in a specific column for different expenses, which can be seen in the following specimen (Format 9.6) of a petty cash book.

Particulars of simple petty cash book

Receipt In this column, the opening cash balance and the amount received from the main cashier are recorded.

FORMAT 9.6 Petty Cash Book

Receipts	Date	Particulars	Voucher No.	Total Amt Paid	Particulars of Various Expenses					L.F.	Personal Account in the Ledger
					Carriage (₹)	Postage Exp (₹)	Stationery (₹)	Tea & Refreshments (₹)	Other misc. (₹)		

Date   The date on which cash is received or expense is paid is recorded here.

Particulars   The particulars of expense paid are recorded here and if the amount is received from the main cashier, it is credited to the main cashier account.

Voucher no.   The number of the voucher prepared while making payment of expense or the number of receipt received is recorded here.

Total amount   If more than one expense is paid, then the total of expenses paid on a particular date is recorded in this total amount column.

Particular of various expenses   Separate columns are kept for various specified expenses to be paid by the petty cashier. As seen in the above form of petty cash book, separate columns are kept for carriage, postage, stationery, tea and refreshments, and other misc. expenses. When the given expenses are paid, it is recorded in the respective column at that time in the petty cash book.

L.F. no.   The page number on which the ledger account of the expense paid is opened in the ledger is shown here. If required, the ledger folio number of the personal ledger account is also shown here.

Personal account in the ledger   When the transaction takes place with any person, it is recorded in this column. For example, if some amount is given as advance for business working to any employee, it is recorded in this column of the petty cash book.

Petty cash book on imprest system or petty cash fund

In this type of petty cash book, a fixed amount is given at the beginning of the fixed period (for example, every week or fortnight or month) by the chief cashier to the petty cashier. The petty cashier makes the payment for various expenses from the amount so received and keeps the record of such expenses. At the end of the fixed period, the petty cashier gives the details of expenses made by him to the main cashier. The main cashier provides cash equal to the amount spent by the petty cashier at the beginning of the next period, so that again the pre-decided fixed balance remains with the petty cashier at the beginning of the next period. In this type of a system, a fixed amount is maintained at the beginning of each period and so it is known as imprest system of petty cash book.

For example, if the petty cash book is maintained as per imprest petty cash book system, then it means that a cash imprest of ₹5,000 is required to be maintained. Suppose on 1 September, the petty cash balance is ₹3,500 and in such a position, ₹1,500 is to be given to the petty cashier by the chief cashier.

■ **ILLUSTRATION 9.7**   From the following transactions, prepare a petty cash book for Bhumoosha Restaurant.

2020

1 Sept: Opening cash balance (with petty cashier) ₹3,500.

1 Sept: Amount received from main cashier ₹1,500.

3 Sept: ₹1,200 paid for purchase of spring onion.

4 Sept: ₹800 paid for purchase of potato.

5 Sept: ₹100 paid to carriage for bringing spring onion and potato from market.

7 Sept: ₹200 paid for purchase of garlic.

8 Sept: ₹250 paid for purchase of corriander.

10 Sept: ₹1,200 paid to Tushar, who is working as waiter at restaurant, towards advance salary.

11 Sept: ₹150 paid to carriage for bringing garlic and corriander from market.

12 Sept: ₹180 paid for potato and ₹170 paid for corriander.

13 Sept: ₹150 paid for purchase of garlic.

14 Sept: ₹150 paid to carriage for bringing garlic from market to restaurant.

15 Sept: Other misc. expenses paid for purchase of few common ingredients amounted to ₹100.

Solution

Petty Cash Book of Bhumoosha Restaurant

Receipts (₹)	Date 2020	Particulars	Vou. No.	Total Amt Paid (₹)	Potatoes (₹)	Garlic (₹)	Spring Onion (₹)	Corriander (₹)	Carriage (₹)	Other Misc. Exp. (₹)	L.F.	Personal A/c in the Ledger
3,500	1 Sep	To Opening balance										
1,500	1 Sep	To Chief cashier A/c										
	3 Sep	By Spring onion purchase A/c		1,200			1,200					
	4 Sep	By Potatoes purchase A/c		800	800							
	5 Sep	By Carriage expense A/c		100					100			
	7 Sep	By Garlic purchase A/c		200		200						
	8 Sep	By Corriander purchase A/c		250				250				
	10 Sep	By Tushar A/c		1,200								1,200
	11 Sep	By Carriage expense A/c		150					150			
	12 Sep	By Potatoes purchase A/c		350	180			170				
	13 Sep	By Garlic purchase A/c		150		150						
	14 Sep	By Carriage expense A/c		150					150			

5,000	15 Sep	By Miscellaneous expenses A/c	100						100		
		Sub-total	**4,650**	**980**	**350**	**1,200**	**420**	**400**	**100**	**0**	**1,200**
5,000	15 Sep	By Balance c/f	350								
		Total	**5,000**								
	2019										
350	16 Sep	To Balance b/f									

■ **ILLUSTRATION 9.8** The following information has been obtained in respect of the petty cash book maintained as per petty cash book on imprest system for the month ending on 31.3.2019.

Imagining yourself as the chief cashier, pass the journal entries from this information:

Carriage ₹100; Misc. expenses ₹50; Yam purchases ₹50; Tomato purchases ₹90; and Cucumber purchases ₹60.

Solution

Date	Particulars		L.F.	Debit (₹)	Credit (₹)
31/3/19	Carriage A/c	Dr.		100	
	Misc. expenses	Dr.		50	
	Yam purchases A/c	Dr.		50	
	Tomato purchases A/c	Dr.		90	
	Cucumber purchases A/c	Dr.		60	
	To Petty cashier A/c				350
	(Being the particulars of expenses paid as per petty cash book)				
1/4/19	Petty cashier A/c	Dr.		350	
	To Cash A/c				350
	(Being cash given to petty cashier.)				

SUMMARY

- The management of current assets, that is, cash, receivables, and inventory is critical to maintain adequate liquidity. These assets are important components of the operating cycle, which also includes accounts payable.
- Cash usually consists of currency and coins on hand, cheques and money orders from customers, and deposits in chequing, current, and savings accounts. Cash is the most liquid of all assets and is quite readily available to pay debts.
- A voucher system is a method of providing internal control over the function of purchasing goods or services, paying for them, and ensuring that the correct account balances are added or reduced.
- Cash book means a subsidiary book that is prepared to keep record of cash transactions. A cash book serves the purpose of journal entry and cash account both, as a cash book is prepared in the form of a ledger account. The debit side of cash book is known as income or receipt side. The credit side of cash book is known as expense or payment side.

KEYWORD

Cash discount It is a deduction allowed from the amount due to the supplier, provided that the payment is made within a specified time.

QUESTIONS

I. Answer the following questions.
1. Explain the meaning of cash book.
2. What is a bank overdraft?
3. What does balance of a bank account indicate?
4. Explain the meaning of petty cash book.
5. Briefly explain the importance of cash books.
6. Explain what contra transactions are.
7. Explain a bank book with illustrations.
8. Explain the meaning of petty cash book on imprest system.

II. Solve the following problems.
1. On 1 April 2020, Darshini Mehta, the petty cashier of M/s Leisure Travels has received ₹4,000 from the chief accountant, who manages the main cash book of firm. Leisure follows the imprest system of petty cash. According to this system, the petty payments during the month has been made by Darshini.

   You are required to prepare the petty cash book of M/s Leisure Travels for the month of April 2020.

Date	Particulars	Amount (₹)
2 April	Auto fare	400
3 April	Courier charges	100
4 April	Postages and telegram	190
5 April	Pencils and other stationery items	130
6 April	Speed post expenses	80
8 April	Taxi charges	590
9 April	Refreshments	620
11 April	Auto rickshaw fare	120
13 April	Telegram and fax expenses	128
16 April	Computer stationery	330
19 April	Bus fare	80
21 April	International STD charges	410
23 April	Refreshment	160
25 April	Photocopy charges	90
28 April	Courier charges	80
30 April	Bus fare	80

2. From the following transaction of Ramesh Kohli, prepare his three columnar cash book:

   1 June 2020: Cash on hand ₹450 and bank balance ₹2,500.

   1 June 2020: ₹100 paid to petty cashier.

   1 June 2020: Cash sales ₹1,500 and cash purchases ₹300.

   2 June 2020: Received a crossed cheque of ₹1,000 on the date of maturity of a bill receivable.

   3 June 2020: A creditor Lalit was paid ₹500 at a cash discount of 2% by a cheque.

   3 June 2020: A hundred rupee note was exchanged for change from which a five rupee note was found to be counterfeit.

   4 June 2020: A cheque of ₹750 deposited in the bank was received from Dinesh for full settlement of his account. His account showed a debit balance of ₹760.

   4 June 2020: Purchased a machine of ₹1,300 and paid ₹50 for installation charges and sold old furniture of ₹150.

   5 June 2020: Withdrew from the bank ₹200 for office expenses and ₹150 for personal use.

   6 June 2020: Paid salary for clerk ₹150 cash and paid daughter's college fees ₹220 by a cheque.

   7 June 2020: A cheque received from Dinesh and deposited in the bank was dishonoured. In return, cash was received immediately.

   7 June 2020: Interest credited by bank ₹10.

   7 June 2020: ₹450 cash on hand was carried forward and the remaining amount was deposited in the bank.

3. From the following particulars of the first week of March, 2020, write out petty cash book on imprest system in analytical form:

   1. Drew a cheque for petty cash ₹100.
   2. Purchased postal stamps for ₹20 and paid for carriage on goods sold ₹8.
   3. Paid for a telegram ₹7 and for stationery ₹13.
   4. Paid for refills and paper ₹3.
   5. Paid to office cleaner ₹4.
   6. Paid for bus charges ₹3 and for pencils for the office ₹5.
   7. Paid for repairs to typewriter ₹5.

4. From the following transactions, prepare a cash and bank columnar cash book in the books of Hotel Dharmistha:

   1 May: Cash balance ₹7,000, bank overdraft ₹2,500.

2 May: Food dishes of ₹7,000 sold to Urvashi and crossed cheque is received from her, which is deposited in the bank.

4 May: Food dishes of ₹2,000 sold to Ashok at 10% trade discount, 50% amount received in cash and for the balance amount cheque is received, which is deposited in the bank.

5 May: ₹2,000 cash deposited in the bank.

7 May: Refrigerator of ₹5,000 purchased. Cheque of necessary amount is issued.

9 May: Cheque of ₹6,000 is received from Mansi Ltd for hiring of banquet hall towards receivable which is immediately deposited in the bank.

11 May: Wages ₹500; telephone bill ₹500, and electricity bill ₹1200 paid by cheque.

13 May: ₹2,000 withdrawn from the bank for the payment of insurance premium.

15 May: Insurance premium is paid for ₹1,600.

21 May: Bank debited ₹150 to their account for interest on overdraft and ₹100 for bank charges and it is informed to them through bank advice.

23 May: Milk dishes of ₹3,000 sold to Dharti. Crossed cheque is received.

24 May: Cheque of ₹3,000 received from Tejal, which is endorsed to Sejal.

26 May: Bank informed about the dishonour of cheque issued by Dharti.

28 May: ₹1,500 paid to Vibodh for settlement of account. ₹2,000 withdrawn for personal use of Ms Dharmistha from the bank.

29 May: Cheque of ₹3,000 received from the customer Virendra Bakery.

30 May: Cheque of ₹3,000 received from the customer Virendra Bakery, which is endorsed in favour of Surendra Milk Stores.

5. From the following transactions, prepare the State Bank of India (SBI) and Bank of India (BOI) columnar bank book in the books of Kumbhalgarh Hotel.

   2019

   1 August: Opening bank overdraft (SBI) ₹6,000; bank balance (BOI) ₹4,000.

   4 August: Single occupancy room of ₹4,000 provided, against which a cheque is received, which is deposited in SBI account.

   5 August: Tapioca and beaten rice, each of lot of 50 kgs. purchased worth ₹6,000, against which a cheque of ₹2,000 of BOI is issued and SBI cheque of ₹4,000 is issued.

   7 August: SBI cheque of ₹1,400 issued for salary.

   11 August: Bank interest ₹500 and dividend ₹2,500 collected by SBI and credited in the account.

   13 August: A cheque of ₹7,000 received from Anuj towards the payment of an old debt which was deposited in BOI.

   18 August: Cheque of ₹3,000 issued from BOI and deposited in the SBI account.

   23 August: Cashew nuts of ₹2,500 purchased, for which a cheque of full amount is issued from BOI account.

   26 August: Electrical geyser of ₹6,000 purchased, for which a cheque of 50% amount from SBI account for the remaining amount cheque is issued from BOI account.

6. From the following transactions, prepare a three columnar cash book of Jiyu Hotel.

   2019

   1 July: Opening cash balance ₹7,000. Bank overdraft ₹4,000.

   2 July: Single room occupancy for two days provided for ₹4,000 to Khushali. A cheque is received from her which is deposited in the bank.

4 July: Apartment occupancy for two nights provided for ₹8,000 to Yesha at 10% cash discount. Half of the amount is received in cash and remaining amount is received by cheque which is deposited in the bank.

6 July: Food and beverages of ₹3,000 purchased in cash from Dipen at 10% cash discount.

7 July: ₹1,000 deposited in the bank.

9 July: ₹800 paid to Gopi for salary by cheque.

11 July: Stationery of ₹300 purchased from Suresh Stationery Mart and the amount is paid by cheque.

14 July: Dipak paid ₹5,900 by cash towards total debt of ₹6,005.

17 July: Cheque of ₹8,000 issued to Preity towards full settlement of account of ₹8000.

20 July: GST of ₹3,000 paid by cash.

24 July: ₹2,000 withdrawn from the business for personal use by Axay, Chef.

28 July: Postage expenses of ₹200 paid by cash.

29 July: Paid cash of ₹600 for wages.

31 July: After keeping cash on hand of ₹2,000, remaining amount is deposited in the bank.

7. From the following transactions, prepare a three columnar cash book in the book of Krunal Restaurant.

2019

1 Aug: Opening cash balance ₹3,000. Bank balance ₹6,000.

2 Aug: Deluxe Suite occupancy provided for ₹10,000 sold to Nilesh at 10% trade discount. Amount is received by cheque, which is deposited in the bank.

7 Aug: Cheque issued by Nilesh is dishonoured.

9 Aug: Receiver of Nilesh paid the dividend of 50 paisa against one rupee by cheque.

10 Aug: Beer and liquor of ₹6,000 sold to Bhikhubhai for cash at 10% cash discount.

13 Aug: Beer and liquor of ₹5,000 purchased from Chetna at 10% cash discount. Half of the amount is paid by cheque and remaining amount is paid in cash.

15 Aug: Bank has collected a dividend of ₹1,000 and credited in their account for investments made in equity shares of Xinga Fags.

17 Aug: Bank has credited ₹100 towards bank interest in their account.

24 Aug: Advertisement expense of ₹3,000 paid by cheque.

26 Aug: ₹1,000 paid from business for 'Satyanarayan Katha' at restaurant premises.

27 Aug: Chairs of ₹3,000 purchased for home. The amount is paid by cheque.

28 Aug: A cheque of ₹3,000 is issued to Girish in full settlement of account of ₹3,090.

29 Aug: Pravin has paid by cheque ₹2,500 in full settlement of ₹2,575.

31 Aug: After keeping cash on hand of ₹500, remaining amount is deposited in the bank.

Current Assets—Receivables and Inventory

Learning Objectives

After studying this chapter, you will understand

- meaning of inventory
- methods to account for uncollectible receivables
- objectives of measuring and maintaining inventory
- importance and ways of stock verification
- different types of inventory system
- different methods of costing of inventories
- importance of freight costs and reverse charge under GST
- non-historical cost methods of costing of inventories

INTRODUCTION

The most common transaction creating a receivable is selling merchandise or services on credit, that is, on account. The receivable is recorded as an increase in asset of the firm in the form of accounts receivable. Such accounts receivables are normally collected within a short period, such as 30 or 60 days. They are known as accounts receivables and notes receivables. Notes receivables are the amounts that customers owe for which a formal, written instrument of credit has been issued. If notes receivables are expected to be collected within a year, they are classified as current assets. Notes may also be used to settle the customer's accounts receivable. Notes and accounts receivables that result from sale transactions are sometimes called trade receivables. Other receivables include interest receivables, tax receivables, and receivables from officers or employees. Other receivables are normally reported separately on the balance sheet.

Inventories are composed of thousands of different products or materials and millions of individual units that are stored in hundreds of different locations. These vast and varied inventories are at the heart of an entity or a firm and must be carefully controlled and accounted for. Controlling invento-

> *Inventory means tangible property held for sale or to use for processing.*

ries requires accurate record-keeping and appropriate security to prevent theft and fraud. Inventory includes tangible property that (a) is held for sale in the normal course of business or (b) will be used in providing goods or services for sale.

Thus, the term inventory includes stock of

- finished goods—goods produced, completed, and ready for sale;
- work-in-progress—goods in the process of being produced but not yet completed as finished goods (when completed, work-in-progress inventory becomes finished goods inventory); and
- raw material and components—items purchased or acquired for using in making finished goods (such items are known as raw materials inventory until issued on the production floor for in turn process).

In the case of a trading concern or merchandising firm, inventory consists, primarily, of finished goods. In the case of a manufacturing concern, inventory consists of raw material and components, stores, work-in-process, and finished goods. Inventory is not purchased as an investment to hold or to realize a gain from possession, but to sell and realize a gain. Inventory is considered an investment and a current asset, and is reported on the balance sheet. As a current asset, it can be used or converted into cash within one year or within the next operating cycle of the firm. Inventory assures the firm that it will not have to close down due to shortage of saleable goods, etc.

The semi-finished goods, or goods under process, are called work-in-progress for construction-related activities, while they are known as work-in-process for manufacturing activities.

RECEIVABLES

After deciding the point of recognizing the revenue, the amount of revenue needs to be recorded in the books of accounts.

Recording of Sales

A cash sale increases the sales revenue in the income statement and increases the cash or bank balance in the balance sheet. In case of credit sales or on account sales, like cash sales, receivables accounts in the balance sheet increase instead of cash or bank balance.

■ **ILLUSTRATION 10.1**   Sales of ₹10,000 would be recorded as under:

Situation 1: Cash Sales

Cash A/c (Asset type) (Add)	Dr. 10,000	
To Sales A/c (Income type) (Add)		10,000

Situation 2: Credit Sales

Accounts Receivable A/c (Asset type) (Add)	Dr. 10,000	
To Sales A/c (Income type) (Add)		10,000

Sales Returns

A firm recognizes the revenue for a given sale at the point of sale, but suppose later on the customer returns the merchandise or goods. This may happen due to various reasons—the purchaser firm could be unhappy with the product's colour, size, style or quality, or may simply have a change of decision. Such returns are treated as sales return by the seller firm and purchase returns by the customer.

■ **ILLUSTRATION 10.2**   *Situation 1:* A merchandise has been received back from a customer to whom originally a cash sale was made. In this situation, the firm may return the cash immediately or agree to pay it later on. Let us assume the value of sales return is ₹5,000.

In such a situation, the following entry would be passed:

Sales Returns A/c (Income type) (Less)	Dr. 5,000	
To Cash A/c (Asset type) (Less)		5,000
Or		
To Customer's A/c (Liability type) (Add)		5,000

Situation 2: A merchandise has been received back from a customer to whom originally a credit sale was made. In this situation, the firm may provide the due reduction in receivable from the customer. Let us assume the value of sales return is ₹5,000.

In such a situation, the following entry would be passed:

Sales Returns A/c (Income type) (Less)	Dr. 5,000	
To Accounts Receivable A/c (Asset type) (Less)		5,000

Sales Allowances or Discounts

Sometimes, instead of returning the merchandise, the customer demands a reduction in the selling price. The seller firm often settles such complaints by granting a sales allowance, which is essentially a reduction in the original selling price (for the purchaser or buyer, it is purchase allowance). Sales allowance is also called sales discount, while purchase allowance is also known as purchase discount. Sales discount is an expense for the seller firm, while purchase discount is a gain for the buyer firm.

■ **ILLUSTRATION 10.3**   *Situation 1:* Suppose a merchandise is found to be faulty. And the customer to whom originally a cash sale was made has demanded a sales allowance of ₹1,000. In this situation, the firm may return the cash immediately or agree to pay it later on. Let us assume the value of sales allowance is ₹1,000.

In such a situation, the following entry would be passed:

Sales Allowance A/c (Expense type) (Add)	Dr. 1,000	
To Cash A/c (Asset type) (Less)		1,000
Or		
To Customer's A/c (Liability type) (Add)		1,000

Situation 2: Suppose a merchandise is found to be faulty. And the customer to whom originally a credit sale was made has demanded a sales allowance of ₹1,000. In this situation, the firm may provide the due reduction in receivable from the customer. Let us assume the value of sales return is ₹1,000.

In such a situation, the following entry would be passed:

Sales Allowance A/c (Expense type) (Add)	Dr. 1,000	
To Accounts Receivable A/c (Asset type) (Less)		1,000

UNCOLLECTIBLE AMOUNTS OF RECEIVABLES

Sometimes a firm may not be able to collect all its accounts receivables from the customers or clients on account of insolvency of the buyer firm, or any other reasons. Losses from the inability to collect the receivables are recorded in the accounting system as bad debt expenses. The uncollectible amounts from buyers are a normal part of commercial activities, hence bad debt is considered as an operating expense. There are two methods to account for bad debt expenses, that is, direct write off and provision method.

Direct Write-off Method or Bad Debts

The sales revenue recorded in the books of account of an entity represents the amount received or to be received from the sale of goods or/and services. When goods or services sold on credit turn out to be bad or non-receivable, then logically, the entry of this transaction at the time of sale should be reversed as the situation is similar to the sale not having taken place. In practice, however, instead of reversing the previous entry, the amount which cannot be recovered is considered as a loss, and termed as bad debts. A bad debt is a loss to the entity and gain to the debtors. The expense is increased by debiting the bad debts account. The receivables will be reduced by crediting the concerned party or customer account.

Provision Method or Provisions for Bad and Doubtful Debts

Based on past experience, most entities are able to make reasonably good estimates of the amounts which are likely to turn bad before they are required to be written off. Bad debts reduce the profit and prevent an estimated portion of profits from being distributed to the owners. Any one of the following methods may be used to estimate the amount of possible bad debts:

- As a percentage of total sales
- As a percentage of credit sales during the period
- As a percentage of receivable outstanding at the end of the accounting period

The percentage used is based on the management's judgment and past experience with regard to bad debts. The provision in this context refers to any amount retained by providing for any known diminution in value of assets. Provision for bad and doubtful debts decreases the operating profit and reduces the accounts receivable (debtors) amount in the balance sheet.

Writing off bad debts

Bad debts, which are to be written off during the current accounting period, are usually adjusted against the provision for bad and doubtful debts. The debtor's account (i.e., the concerned customer's account) is scaled down for that amount. This is done by debiting the provision for bad debts account and crediting the concerned customer's account.

However, if no provision for bad debts account is in existence, bad debts have to be written off as an expense, by setting off the amount against the debtor's balance. If the actual bad debts expense is more than the provision for bad debts, the difference will be treated as an expense by debiting to the bad debts, and the receivables will be reduced by crediting the concerned customer's account. The bad debts (expense not provided for) account will be debited, and will decrease the operating profit.

Recovery of bad debts written off

Sometimes, an account written off as bad debts may be subsequently recovered. Any such recovery is treated as windfall income and transferred to the income statement as a gain.

PROVISION FOR SALES ALLOWANCE OR DISCOUNT

It is a normally accepted commercial practice to offer attractive cash discounts to debtors (customers to whom credit sale is made) to encourage them to make an early and immediate payment, resulting in the firm receiving a smaller amount from the debtors. This is an expense for the firm, and the profit of the firm would reduce by that extent. The period for which the cash discount is available is pre-decided; hence, there is always a possibility that a few customers to whom goods have been sold on credit in an earlier accounting period would be entitled to claim the cash discount in the next year by making payments according to the terms. Thus, through the application of the conservatism concept, it is prudent to provide for the discount on debtors at the end of the accounting period, to work out the profit of the firm. The provision for sales allowance is also widely known as provision for discount on debtors.

The provision for discount on debtors will be calculated after deducting the following items from the debtors balance indicated in the trial balance: (i) bad debts as provided by additional information, and (ii) provision for bad and doubtful debts.

■ **ILLUSTRATION 10.4** The books of Taranga Carpets Co. show the following information in their trial balance as on 31 March 2020:

1. Total debtors balance ₹40,300
   Provision for doubtful debts ₹2,000
   Bad debts ₹700
2. Additional information:
   (a) There was a further bad debt of ₹300
   (b) Make a provision for doubtful debts @ 5% of debtors
   (c) Create discount on debtors @ 2%.
   Calculate the net expense and the debtors balance

Solution

1. Net expense as accounted in the income statement:
   Bad and doubtful debts:

	Amount (₹)
Bad debts as per trial balance	700
Add: Further bad debts (as per information – provided earlier)	300
Add: Provision for doubtful debts (Working Note 1 below)	2,000
Add: Discount on debtors (Working Note 2 below)	760
Less: Provision for doubtful debts (as per the formula Trial Balance – Old provisions available)	2,000
Net expense as bad and doubtful debts	1,760

2. Debtors balance as indicated in the balance sheet on 31 March 2020:
   Debtors:

	Amount (₹)
Balance as per trial balance	40,300
Less: Further bad debts	300
Less: Provision for doubtful debts	2,000
Less: Discount on debtors	760
Balance as per balance sheet	37,240

Working Notes:

1. Calculation of provision for doubtful debts:
   Amount on which provision is to be made
   (₹40,300 – 300) ₹40,000

Percentage of provision	5%
Provision amount (40,000 × 5%)	₹2,000

2. Calculation of discount on debtors:

Amount on which discount provision is to be made [40300 – (300 + 2000)]	₹38,000
Percentage of provision	2%
Provision amount (38,000 × 2%)	₹760

INVENTORY

Inventory cost refers to the cost associated with a firm's inventory in hand at the end of an accounting period. Inventories owned by a manufacturing firm typically include raw materials, work-in-process, and finished goods. Inventory valuation is recorded as a current asset in the firm's balance sheet.

Ind AS 2

Ind AS 2 (Indian Accounting Standard AS 2) specified the following terms with respect to inventories:

Inventories are assets:

(a) held for sale in the ordinary course of business;

(b) in the process of production for such sale; or

(c) in the form of materials or supplies to be consumed in the production process or in the rendering of services.

Inventories involve goods purchased and held for resale, for example, merchandise purchased by a retailer and held for resale, computer software held for resale, or land and other property held for resale. Inventories also comprise finished goods produced, or work-in-progress (for construction activities) or work-in-process (for manufacturing activities) being produced by the firm and include materials, maintenance supplies, consumables, and loose tools awaiting for use in the production process. Inventories do not include machinery spares which can be used only in connection with an item of fixed asset and whose use is expected to be irregular. Such machinery spares are accounted for in accordance with Ind AS 16: Property, Plant and Equipment.

OBJECTIVES OF INVENTORY MEASUREMENT

The measurement of inventory or the value of inventory has a significant effect on the income determination and the financial position of an entity. It can be defined as 'A major objective of accounting for inventories is the proper determination of income through the process of matching appropriate costs against revenue' (American Institute of Certified Public Accountants, USA).

A direct relationship exists between cost of goods sold and closing inventory. Cost of goods sold is measured by deducting closing inventory from cost of goods available for sale. In this way, measurement of closing inventory influences the income statement (by influencing cost of goods sold and not income) and the balance sheet, because inventory appears as a current asset on the balance sheet. The closing inventory also influences the net income of the next accounting period because it becomes the opening inventory and part of goods sold. The cost of goods sold equals the opening inventory plus purchases less closing inventory.

Cost of Goods Sold = Opening Inventory + Purchases – Closing Inventory

The other objective of inventory measurement is to state the fair value of inventory, which appears as a current asset on the balance sheet. In addition, the value of inventory helps investors and other users to predict the future cash flow of the firm.

MATERIAL VALUATION

Inventory or material accounting helps in determining two parameters: the value of materials stored and the value of materials consumed for the operating cycle of the firm. Material consumption costs constitute a very significant proportion of total costs or expenses of a firm. To work out the profit or loss incurred during the period under consideration, a firm should work out the cost of goods sold. Calculation of cost of goods sold is discussed in detail in Chapter 4 'Income Statement'.

To work out the cost of goods sold, one has to determine the cost of material receipts and closing stock value on a regular basis.

Valuation of Material Receipts

The landed cost of materials purchased during a given period is known as the value of material receipts. The costs incurred up to the receipt of materials at the factory and all associated costs till the material can be issued to production or sold to the customer (in case of a trading firm) constitute the landed costs of material receipts.

Landed cost of materials can be computed as per Exhibit 10.1. Based on the location of the firm and tax rules, other factors may need to be effected by the firm during the time of actual compilation of costs of material purchase.

EXHIBIT 10.1 Calculation of Costs of Material Purchases

Item code: Item description:
Unit of measurement:
Purchase order no:
Name and address of supplier:
Goods receipt no: Goods receipt date:
Quantity received and accepted:

Particulars	Amount (₹)
Gross invoice price	
Less: Trade discount	
Add: Custom duty	
Add: Cost of containers and packing charges	
Add: Freight	
Add: Delivery charges, i.e., loading of materials and unloading of materials	

Add: Transit insurance	
Add: Goods and Services Tax (GST)	
Add: Any specific taxes applicable and non-refundable	
Less: Any input tax credit, if available	
Add: Any specific charges, such as inspection charges	
Total landed costs (A)	
Total quantity received and accepted (B)	
Landed costs per unit of quantity received (C) = (A/B)	

Normally, custom duty is charged on the invoice value of the supplier/exporter, and on that arrived value, GST is applicable.

Other charges such as freight, delivery charges, and inspection charges depend on the quantity involved. The transit insurance is based on the value of goods involved.

■ **ILLUSTRATION 10.5** A consignment received by Mach Tech Ltd, Surat, consists of Chemical A and Chemical B. The invoice received from the supplier, Ashoka Ltd, Mumbai, indicates the following information.

(a) Chemical A: 10,000 kg at ₹10 per kg   ₹1,00,000
(b) Chemical B: 8,000 kg at ₹13 per kg   ₹1,04,000
(c) GST @ 10%   ₹20,400
(d) Railway freight from Mumbai to Surat   ₹3,840

Following is an additional information with respect to the transaction received from the books of accounts.

(a) ₹1,920 was paid to workers for loading and unloading of materials at the Surat station and then at the factory of Mach Tech Ltd.

(b) ₹860 was paid to Surat Municipality as special tax.

You are required to work out the cost of materials purchased, in total as well as for each chemical.

Solution

Particulars	Amount (₹)	Basis for Apportionment	Chemical A	Chemical B
Quantity received and accepted kg (B)		kg Given	10,000	8,000
Gross value of goods	2,04,000	Given	1,00,000	1,04,000
Add: GST	20,400	@ 10% of gross value	10,000	10,400
Add: Railway freight	3,840	Based on weight @ ₹0. 2133 per kg.	2,133	1,707
Add: Loading and unloading expenses	1,920	Based on weight @ ₹0. 10667 per kg.	1,067	853
Add: Special tax	860	Based on Gross value of goods @ 0.4216%	422	438
Total landed costs of materials (A)	2,31,020		1,13,622	1,17,398
Landed costs per unit of quantity received (C) = (A/B)			11.3622	14.6748

STOCK VERIFICATION ■■■■

Good inventory control procedures require a physical count of items held in inventory at least annually in both periodic and perpetual inventory systems. This counting is an imposing, time consuming and expensive procedure. To simplify the counting and valuation, firms often choose financial accounting year so that the year ends when inventories are generally low.

The physical inventory is so important for profit determination that external auditors usually observe the client's physical count and confirm the accuracy of the subsequent valuation.

PHYSICAL INVENTORY OF STOCK ■■■■

The quantity of inventory items lying with a firm has to be known in order to determine the value of closing stock on the date of preparation of the financial statement. This task consists of two stages: physical verification of stock at the workplace (workshop, factory premises, or godown of the firm) and determining whether the goods in transit belong to the firm.

Physical Verification of Stock or Inventory at Workplace

Physical verification involves the actual counting, weighing, or measuring of each kind of inventory on hand. A year-end inventory counting is generally more accurate when goods are not being sold or received during the period of counting. A majority of firms adapt to the practice of taking an inventory when the business is closed or is slow. It is statutorily required to disclose the value of inventory lying with the firm at the end of the period. This information is required to work out the taxable profit of the firm, in addition to submission of statistics to bankers and financial institutions to avail of funds or borrowings for the purpose of working capital.

The following types of internal steps are normally undertaken by a firm to achieve the accurate level of working and in turn proper calculation of profit or loss for the period under consideration.

1. The counting of physical stock should be carried out by employees who are not custodians of the goods in question.
2. Each counter is expected to establish the authenticity of each inventory item, such as standardize the size of one count, for example, resistor in the batch of 25 units.
3. The second verification is a second count performed by an independent outsider, such as an internal auditor or statutory auditor.
4. For proper monitoring, prenumbered tags should be used, and all inventory tags should be accounted for.
5. A designated supervisor, generally a member of the finance and accounts department, should ascertain at the conclusion of the count that all inventory items are tagged and no items have more than one count or are left out.

Goods in Transit

Goods are considered to be in transit when they are lying with the transporter on the date of preparation of financial statements. Goods in transit include the inventory of the firm for which the legal title of the goods is not transferred to the buyer or a third party. Legal title deeds of the goods are based on the terms of sale of business goods and merchandise as follows.

1. Free on board at shipping point or factory (FOB-SP) means that the title of the goods is transferred to the buyer when the goods are acknowledged and received by the transporter to be conveyed to the buyer. Such goods will not be covered as goods in transit for stock purpose by the firm.

2. Free on board at destination point or buyer's place (FOB-DP) means that it is the duty of the seller to deliver the goods at the buyer's place. In other words, the title of the goods is with the seller until the goods are delivered to the buyer by the transporter. Such goods will be covered as goods in transit for stock purpose by the firm.

After the physical inventory is taken and goods in transit have been ascertained, the quantity of each item along with the item code and item description will be recorded in the *inventory summary sheet*. Later, the inventory summary sheet will be used by the finance and accounts department for valuing the same to ascertain the value of the inventory.

Stock Lying at Third-party's Place

In normal commercial business activities, the firm sends goods to the prospective customer for sale on approval basis. But during the accounting period it may not be possible for the customer to convey the acceptance of goods received by him. In other words, it is the goods lying at the prospective customer's place, that is, third-party place, and this needs to be covered as stock of the firm, in reporting for financial statement purpose.

The stock lying at the place of third party is always quoted at the value as per invoice price of the goods sent on approval basis. Necessary adjustments are required to be made for the removal of profit elements from the said value, as the stock is always to be valued at cost price, that is, margin on such goods needs to be adjusted.

Perpetual Inventory System

This method provides a continuous record of the goods in hand. It requires a continuous record of additions to or reductions in the goods on a day-to-day basis. Under this system,

a trading concern keeps a merchandise account and records the purchases by debiting the purchase account and crediting the cash or creditors account.

Manufacturing concerns usually keep an account of inflows and outflows of materials in the stores ledger. Stores ledger indicate the quantity of a particular product in stock. It may also specify the minimum and maximum amount of each item so as to avoid the oversupply or undersupply of inventory. Perpetual inventory system, thus, not only indicates the quantity and amount of inventory in hand at any time, but also aids in controlling the investment needed to replenish the stock. The perpetual inventory system clearly indicates the quantity of stock to be replenished at any point of time

> *Perpetual inventory system means continuous updating of records and continuous verification of stock.*

to maintain the safety stock and reorder level. Under this method, discrepancies and errors are promptly discovered, and remedial actions can be taken to avoid their occurrence in the future.

Periodic Inventory System

> *Periodic inventory system verification is done at the end of the specified period.*

Under this method, physical inventory is usually taken at the end of the accounting year or at regular intervals. At each accounting date, it involves actual counting of units, weighing, and measuring in quintals or meters each product in stock at that date. Under this system, cost of sales is obtained as

$$\text{Cost of Sales} = (\text{Opening Inventory} + \text{Current Purchases}) - \text{Closing Inventory}$$

It must be ensured that (a) all items have been counted accurately; (b) counting procedures usually involve teams of people; and (c) larger items are counted individually, while small items are weight-counted. Counted items are tagged to prevent double counting, and information from the tags concerning each item's description and quantity is recorded on the inventory sheet.

The periodic inventory system is suitable for enterprises having a large quantity of low cost items. For example, an enterprise manufacturing nuts and bolts can use the periodic inventory system for maintaining stocks. Table 10.1 provides a comparison of the perpetual inventory system and the periodic inventory system.

TABLE 10.1 Perpetual inventory system and periodic inventory system

Perpetual Inventory	Periodic Inventory
1. It provides a running record of cost of sales and inventory balance.	1. It provides periodic data of inventory and cost of sales.
2. It directly determines cost of sales from the book record.	2. It directly determines ending inventory by physical stock-taking.
3. It derives closing inventory by adding opening inventory to purchases and deducting the cost of sales.	3. It derives cost of sales by adding opening inventory to purchases and deducting closing inventory.
4. It involves innumerable entries and cost calculations throughout the year. Hence, it is prohibitively expensive and usually confined to high cost items.	4. This system entails fewer entries and cost calculations as these are required usually once a year. Hence, it is relatively less expensive and commonly applied to all the terms.
5. Better inventory control is possible due to availability of stock position at any point of time.	5. It indicates the stock position only at specified dates of physical stock-taking. Hence, during the period date, the exact position of inventory is not known.
6. It can be performed without affecting the operation of business.	6. It requires the closure of operations for a few days and employment of staff for counting of stock.

COSTING INVENTORIES OR INVENTORIES PRICING

All entities, that is, merchandise and manufacturing, have inventories that are used on a regular basis for operations or processes, which in turn result in sale to customers. The need arises to allocate the cost between ending or closing inventory and goods or materials transferred out. If the prices paid for goods are constant over time, then the cost of the ending inventory is computed by multiplying the unit cost with the number of units on hand at period-end. On the other hand, if the price paid for the goods changes over time, then the cost of goods available for sale is based on different unit costs. In such cases, two questions arise—(a) which price should be assigned to the units sold?; and (b) which price should be assigned to the units in closing inventory? It is not possible to trace the respective costs for goods sold and/or closing inventory units. Instead of tracking the specific units sold and in inventory, firms usually make simple assumptions about cost flow by using any one or more of the methods as described in this section. Each of these methods involves a procedure for allocating the cost of goods available for sale between inventory and cost of goods sold. The methods discussed are based on the flow-of-cost principle and not on the flow-of-goods principle. An accounting entity discloses its choice of inventory methods in a note in the financial statement.

Cost of Inventories

The basis of inventory accounting is the cost of the merchandise a firm purchases and then sells it or consumes it by converting it to finished goods. The cost includes all or part of the following: invoice price, transportation charges, trade and cash discounts, cost of handling and placing a stock, storage, purchasing department, receiving department, and other indirect charges. The following are the detailed explanation with respect to cost of inventories.

Components of cost to include

1. **Cost of purchase:** Cost of purchase includes purchase price plus taxes and duties (which are not subsequently recoverable) plus other expenditure directly attributable to acquisition (like freight inward). It also excludes trade discount, rebates, duty drawbacks, subsidiaries, and taxes (which are subsequently recoverable).
2. **Cost of conversion:** Cost of conversion includes direct labour, direct expenses, sub-contracted work, and production overheads absorbed on the basis of normal capacity.
3. **Other costs:** Costs incurred in bringing the inventories to their present location and condition, e.g., cost incurred in designing products for specific customers.

Components of cost to exclude

Ind AS 2: Valuation on Inventories lists down the following specific costs which are to be excluded from cost of inventories:

1. **Abnormal amounts** of wasted materials, labour, and other production cost.
2. **Storage costs** unless they are necessary in the production process prior to the further production stage.
3. **Administrative overheads** that do not contribute towards bringing the inventories to their present location and condition.
4. **Selling and distribution costs**
5. **Interest and other borrowing costs** which are usually considered not related to bringing the inventories to their present location and condition and are therefore usually not included in the cost of inventory.

FREIGHT COSTS

When a merchandise is shipped by a firm through a transport agency, the transport agency prepares a freight bill in accordance with the instructions of the seller (goods giver) party who makes the transportation arrangements. The freight bill designates which party (giver or receiver) bears the shipping costs and whether the shipment is freight prepaid (freight paid before the shipment) or freight collect (freight paid after the shipment.)

Freight bills usually show shipping terms like FOB shipping point or FOB destination. FOB is an abbreviation for 'free on board'. When the freight terms are FOB shipping point, the purchaser bears the shipping costs; when the terms are FOB destination, the seller bears the shipping costs. Often, the party bearing the freight cost pays the transport agency. Thus, goods are typically shipped as freight collect when the terms are FOB shipping point and freight prepaid when the terms are FOB destination. Sometimes, as a matter of convenience, the firm not bearing the freight cost pays the transport agency. When this situation occurs, the seller and the buyer simply adjust the amount of the payment for the merchandise.

Table 10.2 shows which party—the buyer or the seller—pays the shipper and bears the freight cost for various freight terms.

Table 10.2   Treatment of freight costs

Freight Terms	Pays Shipper	Bears Freight Cost
FOB Shipping Point, Freight Collect	Buyer	Buyer
FOB Destination, Freight Prepaid	Seller	Seller
FOB Shipping Point, Freight Prepaid	Seller	Buyer
FOB Destination, Freight Collect	Buyer	Seller

■ **ILLUSTRATION 10.6**   Sony Pharma ordered 12,000 kg of a certain material at ₹80 per unit. The purchase price includes GST of ₹4 per kg in respect of which full input tax credit is admissible. Freight incurred amounted to ₹77,400. Normal transit loss is 3%. The company actually received 11,600 kg and consumed 10,100 kg of material. Compute the cost of inventory as per Ind AS 2 and abnormal loss.

Solution

Computation of Cost of Inventory

Particulars	Working Notes	Amount (₹)
Purchase price	12,000 kgs × ₹80	9,60,000
Less: GST Input tax credit	12,000 kgs × ₹4	48,000
		9,12,000
Add: Freight		77,400
Total material cost		9,89,400
Number of units after normal loss	97% of 12,000 kg	11,640
Average or normal cost per kg	9,89,400/11,640	85
Value of closing stock	(11,600 kg–10,100 kg) × ₹85	1,27,500
Abnormal loss	(11,640 kg–11,600 kg) × ₹4	3,400

ACCOUNTING STANDARD (IND AS 2)— VALUATION OF INVENTORIES

According to Ind AS 2, inventories includes merchandise, goods, and commodities held for the following purposes:

- Sale in the ordinary course of business activities
- Use in the process of production of saleable goods
- In the form of materials or supplies to be consumed in the process of production or in the process of rendering of services

The inventories are to be valued at the lower of the cost price and the market price. Here, the market price refers to the net realizable value. The cost comprises of the cost of purchase, the cost of conversion, and other costs directly attributable to bringing the inventory to the present location and condition.

The net realizable value is determined as the estimated selling price reduced by the estimated cost of further completion and additional selling expenses, if any to be incurred.

According to Ind AS 2, any one of the following methods can be used by a firm for the determination of cost. The firm may also use different methods for different groups of inventory items. It is not necessary for all items to be covered by the same method of inventory costing. However, a method once adopted should be consistently applied over the period of time. A change in the method is allowed only if it would bring equitability and a fair position. The methods allowed for cost formulae are mentioned in the following text:

- Specific identification method
- First in first out (FIFO) method
- Weighted average method
- Standard cost method (can be used conveniently if results are approximately equal to the actual cost)
- Retail price method (can be used conveniently if results are approximately equal to the actual cost)

GOODS AND SERVICES TAX (GST)

The input tax credit with respect to GST has been discussed in Chapter 6 on Revenue and Expense Recognition. The additional point provided in the GST Act is Reverse Charge.

Reverse Charge

Normally, the supplier of goods or services pays the tax on supply. In the case of Reverse Charge, the receiver becomes liable to pay the tax, that is, the chargeability gets reversed.

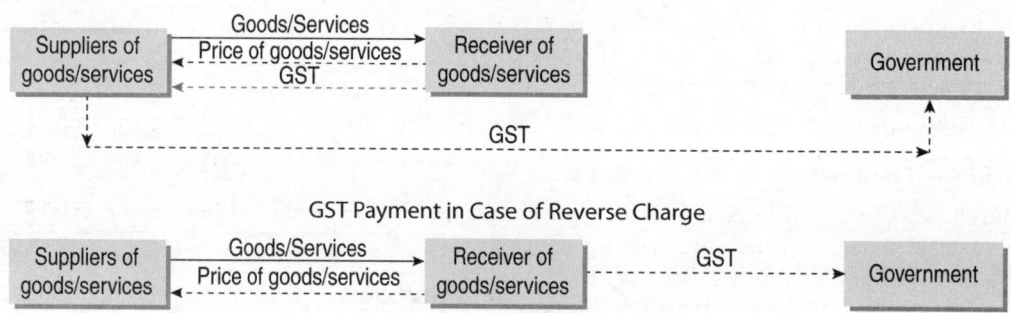

FIG. 10.1   GST payment process

Time of supply under reverse charge

The GST Act has mentioned the time of supply under the reverse charge provision. The following are the two distinct features:

Time of supply in case of goods   In case of reverse charge, the time of supply shall be the earliest of the following dates:

1. The date of receipt of goods
2. The date of payment
3. The date immediately after 30 days from the date of issue of an invoice by the supplier

If it is not possible to determine the time of supply, the time of supply shall be the date of entry in the books of account of the recipient.

■ **ILLUSTRATION 10.7**   Suppose,

1. the date of receipt of goods is 15 May 2018;
2. the date of invoice is 1 June 2018; and
3. the date of entry in the books of receiver is 18 May 2018.

The time of supply of service, in this case, will then be 15 May 2018.

Time of supply in case of services   In case of reverse charge, the time of supply shall be the earliest of the following dates:

1. The date of payment
2. The date immediately after 60 days from the date of issue of invoice by the supplier

If it is not possible to determine the time of supply, the time of supply shall be the date of entry in the books of account of the recipient.

■ **ILLUSTRATION 10.8**   Suppose,

1. the date of payment is 15 July 2018;
2. the date of invoice is 15 May 2018; and
3. the date of entry in the books of receiver is 18 July 2018.

The time of supply of service, in this case, will then be 15 May 2018.

Self-invoicing

Self-invoicing is done when a firm purchases goods or services from an unregistered supplier and such a purchase falls under reverse charge. This happens because the firm's supplier cannot issue a GST-compliant invoice to the firm, and thus the firm becomes liable to pay taxes on behalf of the supplier. Hence, self-invoicing, in this case, becomes necessary.

INVENTORY METHODS

Inventory methods are based on the flow-of-cost principle and not on the flow-of-goods principle. The accounting practices adopted by corporates are discussed in Exhibit 10.2. The following are the significant methods for valuation of inventories.

First In First Out (FIFO) Method

This method is based on the assumption that costs move through an inventory in an unbroken stream, with costs entering and leaving the inventory in the same order. In other words, the earliest purchased item (the first in) is assumed to be first sold or consumed (the first out). Under this method, the most recent purchases are allocated to the closing inventory. It is possible to calculate the FIFO costs of goods sold directly by adding the cost of the beginning inventory to the purchases of which it is composed and by subtracting the cost of the closing inventory. The advantages of the FIFO method are as given in the following text.

EXHIBIT 10.2   Practices Adopted by Indian Corporates for Reporting and Presentation of Inventories in Financial Statements

Cadila Healthcare Limited

Inventories are valued at the lower of cost and net realisable value. Costs incurred in bringing each product to its present location and condition are accounted for as follows:

A. Raw Materials, Stores & Spare Parts, Packing Materials, Finished Goods, Stock-in-Trade and Works-in-Progress are valued at lower of cost and net realisable value.
B. Cost [Net of CENVAT and Input tax credit availed] of Raw Materials, Stores & Spare Parts, Packing Materials, Finished Goods & Stock-in-Trade is determined on Moving Average Method.
C. Costs of Finished Goods and Works-in-Progress are determined by taking material cost [Net of CENVAT and Input tax credit availed], labour and relevant appropriate overheads based on the normal operating capacity, but excluding borrowing costs.

Net realisable value is the estimated selling price in the ordinary course of business, less estimated costs of completion and the estimated costs necessary to make the sale.

Write down of inventories to net realisable value is recognised as an expense and included in 'Changes in Inventories of Finished goods, Work-in-progress and Stock-in-Trade' and 'Cost of Material Consumed' in the relevant note in the Statement of Profit and Loss.

Future Retail Limited

Inventories are valued at lower of cost or net realizable value. Inventories of traded goods are valued at lower of cost or net realizable value. Finished Goods and Work-in-Progress include cost of purchase, cost of conversion and other costs incurred in bringing the inventories to their present location and condition. Costs of inventories are computed on weighted average basis.

Balaji Telefilms Limited

Inventory comprise of television serials which are at lower of cost and net realizable value.

Cost is determined on the basis of average cost. Net realisable value represents the estimated selling price for inventories less all estimated costs of completion and costs necessary to make the sale.

Items of Inventory are valued at lower of cost and net realisable value. Cost is determined on the following basis.

Television Serials: At average cost

Films/Events: Actual Cost

Unamortised cost of films: The cost of film is amortised in the ratio of current revenue to expected total revenue. At the end of each accounting period, balance unamortised cost is compared with net expected revenue. If net expected revenue is less than unamortised cost, the same is written down to net expected revenue. Net realisable value represents the estimated selling price for inventories less all estimated costs of completion and costs necessary to make the sale.

SpiceJet Limited

Inventories are comprised of expendable aircraft spares and miscellaneous stores. Inventories have been valued at cost or net realizable value, whichever is lower after providing for obsolescence and other losses, where considered necessary. Cost includes cost of purchase and other costs incurred in bringing the inventories to their present location and condition and is determined on a weighted average basis.

Tara Jewels Limited

Inventories are valued at cost or net realizable value, whichever is less. Cost of raw materials and stores, consumables and packing material are determined on weighted average basis. Cost of Work in progress and finished goods comprises of raw material cost & appropriate overheads incurred for bringing them to their present condition.

Traded goods are valued at the cost or net realizable value whichever is less and cost is determined on first-in-first-out basis.

Sources: Cadila Healthcare Limited Annual Report 2016–17, pp. 106–107; Future Retail Limited Annual Report 2017–18, p. 97; Balaji Telefilms Ltd Annual Report 2016–17, pp. 153–154; SpiceJet Limited Annual Report 2016–17, p. 170; Tara Jewels Limited Annual Report 2015–16, p. 108.

1. The value of inventory is near the current market price, as the value of the stock is based on the prices of the latest purchases.
2. This method is considered logical as firms like to sell the goods in order of the purchase to avoid deterioration in stock.
3. There is no question of unrealized profit or loss, as it strictly adheres to the cost principle.
4. The method is simple to operate, provided that there is no major price fluctuation.

The disadvantages of the FIFO method are given in the following text.

1. If the prices fluctuate violently, the method involves complicated calculations and more clerical work.
2. The application of this system may prove unjust in the sense that one job executed earlier may be charged a price different from a job executed a little later, because the stock from the earlier lot may have exhausted.
3. In a period of rising prices, this method may report a larger profit. This will entail higher income tax.

In case of a manufacturing unit, the charge to production will be unduly low in a period of rising prices.

Last In First Out (LIFO) Method

The LIFO method allocates the cost of the goods available for sale between closing inventory and cost of goods sold based on the assumption that the most recent purchases (the last in) are the first to be sold or consumed (the first out). Under this method, the most recent purchase (newest cost) is allotted to the cost of goods sold and the earliest purchase (oldest cost) is allotted to closing inventory. The LIFO cost of goods sold is calculated by adding the cost of beginning inventory to purchases and subtracting the cost of closing inventory.

As the sales are charged at the latest purchase price, the current revenue is matched with current costs, which will result in profit reflecting the current condition. The advantages of the LIFO method are as given in the following text.

1. In a period of rising prices, the profit ascertained under this method would be lower, resulting in lower tax liability.
2. As the stock is valued strictly at cost, there is no question of unrealized profit in stock.
3. The method is more suitable in case of manufacturing firms as the raw materials issued to the production department are charged at the rates near to market rates and, hence, it is easier to determine the selling price based on the cost of production.

The disadvantages of the LIFO method are as given in the following text.

1. The method seems to be unrealistic, as the physical flow of goods does not follow the assumption of last in first out.
2. The value of closing stock does not resemble the current market price, as inventory is valued at prior purchases.

Weighted Average Method

This method allocates the cost of goods available for sale between closing inventory and the cost of goods sold based on a single weighted average cost per unit. The weighted average cost per unit is calculated by dividing the cost of goods available for sale by the number of units available for sale. The weighted average cost per unit is then multiplied by the number of units sold to calculate cost of goods sold, and by the number of units in closing inventory to calculate the cost of closing inventory.

Highest In First Out Method (HIFO)

This method calculates the price of issues at the highest rates of materials in stock irrespective of their date of purchase. The purpose of this method is to charge with the highest rate of materials to the current cost of production. The impact of this method is that cost of production is overstated.

Next In First Out Method (NIFO)

This method calculates the price of issues at the purchased rates of materials that are yet to arrive. In simple words, the material rates that have been agreed upon by the supplier is used for issue purpose, though materials have not physically arrived. In this method, materials are issued at the price at which a new order has been placed, and this price is considered good for all future issues until a new order is placed.

Specific Price Method

This method is used for materials purchased for a particular job, order, or process. These are generally non-standardized materials and the actual cost is charged to a particular job, order, or process.

Base Stock Method

In this method, a minimum quantity of material, that is, base stock is always held at original cost. Any issue of materials above the base stock quantity is priced using one of the conventional methods, that is, FIFO or LIFO, at actual cost. This method is suitable for tanning, smelting, brass, copper, mining, and lead industries where

- raw materials being manufactured are basic and homogeneous;
- cost of finished product comprises of some basic raw materials, for example, hides, crude oils, non-ferrous metals, etc.; and
- processing time is longer, and it is required to maintain a fixed stock of raw materials in process.

Replacement Price Method

In this method, materials issues are valued at the replacement price prevailing in the market on the date of issue. Replacement price means the price at which an identical material can be purchased from the market.

Standard Price Method

It is a pre-determined price fixed on the basis of factors, such as probable trend of prices, market conditions, discounts, etc., for a certain period. Standard prices are fixed for each type of material and all the issues are valued at the standard price.

The difference between the actual and standard prices is the material price variance. All receipts are posted in the stores ledger account at actual cost if such variance is calculated at the point of issues to production.

Inflated Price Method

This method is applied when materials are subject to some inevitable losses that may arise due to evaporation, breaking the bulk, etc. The issue price is slightly inflated to cover all losses. This price not only includes the cost involved in bringing the material to the buyer's premises, but also losses due to the earlier mentioned costs as well as inventory carrying costs. If a liquid is purchased at ₹8 per litre and a loss of 8% is expected, then to recover the losses the inflated issue price will be ₹100/92 × 8 = ₹8.7 per litre.

Reuse Price Method

This method is used to value a material for reuse. This method is used when rejected or surplus materials are returned to the store or are reissued to other departments for alternative use. The reissue price is more than scrap value but less than actual price.

■ **ILLUSTRATION 10.9** HP is the leading distributor of petrol. A detail inventory of petrol in hand is taken when the books are closed at the end of each month. At the end of the month, the following information is available:

Sales	₹2,47,25,000
General overhead costs	₹11,25,000
Inventory of beginning	1,00,000 litres @ ₹75 per litre
Purchases	
June 1: 2 lakh litres @ ₹74.25	
June 30: 1 lakh litres @ ₹75.15	
Closing inventory: 1.30 lakh litres	

Compute the following by FIFO method as per Ind AS 2:

1. Value of inventory on June 30
2. Amount of cost of goods sold for June
3. Profit/Loss for the month of June

Solution

1. Cost of Closing Inventory for 1,30,000 litres as on 30 June

Particulars	Amount (₹)
1,00,000 litres @ ₹75.15	75,15,000
30,000 litres @ ₹74.25	22,27,500
Total	97,42,500

2. Computation of Cost of Goods Sold

Particulars	Amount (₹)
Opening inventories (1,00,000 litres @ ₹75)	75,00,000
Purchases: 1 June (2,00,000 litres @ ₹74.25)	1,48,50,000
30 June (1,00,000 litres @ 75.15)	75,15,000
	2,98,65,000
Less: Closing inventories	(97,42,500)
Cost of goods sold	2,01,22,500

3. Computation of Profit

Particulars	Amount (₹)
Sales (Given) (A)	2,47,25,000
Cost of goods sold	2,01,22,500
Add: General overheads	11,25,000
Total Cost (B)	2,12,47,500
Profit (A – B)	34,77,500

■ **ILLUSTRATION 10.10** Inventory cost data for calculators is as follows:

Particulars	Qty (in nos)	Cost per No.	Total Cost (₹)
Opening inventory	10	60	600
Purchase 1	50	100	5,000
Purchase 2	60	120	7,200
Purchase 3	40	150	6,000
Goods available for sale	160		18,800
Less: Closing inventory	20		
Quantity sold	140		

Calculate the cost of goods sold (for 140 calculators).

Solution

1. FIFO Method—Cost of Closing Inventory

Particulars	Qty	Amount (₹)
Opening inventory	(10)	600
Purchase 1	(50)	5,000
Purchase 2	(60)	7,200
Purchase 3	(20)	3,000
FIFO cost of goods sold		15,800

FIFO cost of closing inventory part of purchase 3 (20) ₹3,000

2. LIFO Method—Cost of Closing Inventory

Particulars	Qty	Amount (₹)
Opening inventory	(10)	600
Part of purchase 1	(10)	1,000
Total		1,600
Cost of goods sold		₹
Beginning inventory	(10)	600
Add purchase	(150)	18,200
Cost of goods available for sale	(160)	18,800
Less: Closing inventory	(20)	1,600
LIFO cost of goods sold	(140)	17,200

3. Weighted Average Method
   Weighted average cost per unit = Cost of goods available for sale/Units available for sale
   = 18,800/160
   = ₹117.50

   Weighted average of goods sold = ₹117.50 × 140 = ₹16,450
   Weighted average cost of closing inventory = ₹117.50 × 20
   = ₹2,350

DEPARTURES FROM THE COST CONCEPT ■

The inventory costing procedures described earlier follow the cost concept, that is, inventory is recorded in the firm's records at cost. Now, we turn to departures from the cost concept that are permitted by accounting principles, that is, the lower of cost or market price and non-cost methods.

Lower of Cost or Market Price

The price for which the inventory can be sold (i.e., its market value) may decline because the goods have become obsolete, shopworn, or have otherwise diminished in value. The decline in the value of inventory below cost can be due to different causes such as physical deterioration, obsolescence, and drop in price level. This reduction of carrying amount of inventory when market value is lower than cost is considered a prudent reaction to the uncertainty about the amount of income to be realized from inventory. In these situations, inventory is reported at market value. The difference in value (i.e., cost less market value) is recognized as a loss during the current period.

It should be understood that the market value of inventory needs to be estimated, as the inventory has not, in fact, been sold. As a rule, the market value of the item is what it will cost currently to purchase or manufacture the item. Thus, this rule recognizes a holding loss in the period in which the replacement or procurement cost of an item drops rather than in the period in which the item is actually sold. This principle or rule is an example of the conservatism principle.

Non-cost Methods

The following are the methods that support to value the closing inventory without confirming or verifying the actual cost incurred for the procurement of the same. These methods, not widely used in practical life, serve as indicators of the financial health of the firm.

Base stock method

It is essential to carry a certain minimum quantity of stock of material in order to carry on production. The investment involved in such minimum stock is like that in fixed assets. So, it is suggested to value the base stock at its original cost. This method recognizes, thus, that the value assigned to the minimum stock originally acquired (though it may have been used up and replaced by fresh supplies) is equal to the amount originally spent. If the actual stock on hand exceeds the minimum figure, the excess is valued by using any of the cost methods.

Specific identification method

This method attributes specific costs to identified goods that have been purchased or manufactured and are segregated for a specific purpose. The historical cost of such specific purpose inventory may be determined on the basis of their specific purchase price or production cost.

Standard cost method

This method is often used to arrive at historical cost for the purpose of inventory valuation. The use of standard cost requires that the standards are realistic; reviewed regularly; revised in the light of current conditions where necessary; and

that there is a proper system of pro-rating significant variances between the cost of sales and inventories.

Adjusted selling price method

This method is also called inventory method. It is used widely in the retail business and in businesses in which it is difficult to ascertain the individual costs of the items of the inventory. The historical cost of inventory is estimated by deducting the estimated gross margin of profit from the selling price of inventory. Such estimation may be made for individual items or group of items or by departments as may be appropriate to the circumstances.

Latest purchase price method

Under this method, inventory is valued at the latest purchase price; however, the quantity of closing inventory may be higher than the latest purchase quantity. This formula uses cost that might not have been incurred for the specific item in inventory, and is, therefore, not based on historical cost. So, it is good to avoid the use of this method.

■ **ILLUSTRATION 10.11** The raw materials inventory of a company includes certain materials purchased at ₹100 per kg. The price of the materials is on decline and replacement cost of the inventory at the year end is ₹75 per kg. It is possible to convert the materials into a finished product at a conversion cost of ₹125.

Decide whether to make the product or not to make the product, if selling price is

i. ₹175
ii. ₹225

Also find out the value of inventory in each case.

Solution

In the circumstances given above, the replacement cost of the materials may be the best available measure of their net realizable value.

i. **When the selling price is ₹175,**
Incremental profit = ₹175 – ₹125 = ₹50
Current price of the materials = ₹75
Therefore, it is better not to make the product. Raw materials inventory would be valued at net realizable value, that is, ₹75 because the selling price of the finished product is less than ₹225 (100 + 125) per kg.

ii. **When the selling price is ₹225,**
Incremental profit = ₹225 – ₹125 = ₹100
Current price of the raw materials = ₹75
Therefore, it is better to make the product. Raw materials inventory would be valued at ₹100 per kg because the selling price of the finished product is not less than ₹225.

■ **ILLUSTRATION 10.12** Best Ltd deals in five products P, Q, R, S, and T, which are neither similar nor interchangeable. At the time of closing of its accounts for the year ending 31 March 2020, the historical cost and net realizable value of the items of the closing stock are determind as follows:

Items	Historical Cost (₹)	Net Realizable Value (₹)
P	5,70,000	4,75,000

Q	9,80,000	10,32,000
R	3,16,000	2,89,000
S	4,25,000	4,25,000
T	1,60,000	2,15,000

What will be the value of closing stock for the year ending 31 March 2020 as per Ind AS 2: Valuation of Inventories?

Solution

According to In AS 2: Valuation of Inventories, inventories should be valued at the lower of cost and net realizable value. Inventories should be written down to net realizable value on an item-by-item basis.

Valuation of Inventory (Item-wise) for the Year Ending 31 March 2020

Item	Historical Cost (₹)	Net Realizable Value (₹)	Valuation of Closing Stock (₹)
P	5,70,000	4,75,000	4,75,000
Q	9,80,000	10,32,000	9,80,000
R	3,16,000	2,89,000	2,89,000
S	4,25,000	4,25,000	4,25,000
T	1,60,000	2,15,000	1,60,000
			23,29,000

The value of inventory for the year ending 31 March 2011 = ₹23,29,000

NON-HISTORICAL COST METHODS

In case of non-implementation of a periodical inventory system on account of impracticability, size of business, impossibility, expensiveness, or time limitations, non-historical cost methods are to be used.

Gross Profit Method

The gross profit method is widely used in case of single-product companies for valuing the finished closing stock and when physical stock verification is not performed. In this method, a firm first determines the gross profit of the firm. The gross profit is worked out by deducting the cost of goods sold from the sales revenue. This is accomplished through the following steps:

Step 1: Compute net sales less estimated gross profit.
Step 2: The resultant value of Step 1 is known as the estimated cost of goods sold.

Step 3: The amount obtained in Step 2 would be deducted from the cost of goods available for sale.
Step 4: The resultant value is known as the value of closing stock or inventory.

■ **ILLUSTRATION 10.13** Green Grocers Company wishes to prepare an income statement for the year ended Diwali 2020. The net sales recorded for the period of Diwali 2019 to Diwali 2020 is ₹2 lakh; the inventory in hand as on Diwali 2019 was ₹40,000; and the cost of goods purchased during the year amounts to ₹1,20,000. In the preceding year, Green Grocers had realized a gross profit of 30%, and expects the same in the current year. Work out the cost of closing inventory as on Diwali 2020.

Solution

The statement showing calculation of closing stock value of Green Grocers Company as on Diwali 2020 is as follows.

Particulars	Amount (₹)
Net sales revenue	2,00,000
Estimated gross profit (30% of net sales revenue)	60,000
Estimated costs of goods sold	1,40,000
Estimation of closing stock value	
Opening stock	40,000
Costs of goods purchased	1,20,000
Costs of goods available for sale	1,60,000
Less: Estimated costs of goods sold	1,40,000
Estimated costs of closing stock or inventory	20,000

The gross profit method has the following negative factors: it assumes that the gross profit rate remains constant over the period; it also assumes that the gross profit rate estimated by the management of the firm is acceptable and not disputable.

Retail Inventory Method

Retail stores, such as grocery and convenience stores, have thousands of different types of merchandise of low cost or value. In such circumstances, application of the physical flow of work and physical counting of stock becomes very cumbersome. Hence, words like *adjusted selling price method* are used in a few cases.

This method is easy to apply and does not require detailed record maintenance. It is also used by the income tax department to justify the value of the closing stock reported by the firm.

IFRS Update

Differences in recognition of inventory valuation in accounting standards

The following table indicates the differences in the recognition of inventories valuation as per Indian Accounting Standards (Ind AS), IFRS or International Accounting Standards (IAS), and US Generally Accepted Accounting Practices (GAAP).

Ind AS	IFRS/IAS	US GAAP
Inventories to be carried at lower cost and net realizable value. FIFO or weighted average method is used to determine the cost. LIFO method is prohibited.	Same as Indian AS. Reversal is needed in the financial statements if later on value is increased for previous write downs.	Similar to IFRS; however use of LIFO is permitted. Reversal of write downs is prohibited.

The information required for this process is mentioned in the following text:

(a) Rupee value of opening stock (no need to mention the quantity) – both at cost and at retail price
(b) Sales value
(c) Purchases during the period—both at cost and at retail price
(d) Adjustments to original retail price such as additional discount, etc.
(e) Data regarding return, damage, breakage of goods, etc.

The following steps are used by the firm to implement this method.

Step 1: Deduct the goods available for sale at retail price from the net sales value.
Step 2: The value from Step 1 is known as the closing inventory at retail price.
Step 3: Divide the goods available for sale at cost by goods available for sale at retail price.
Step 4: The resultant quotient is known as the cost to retail ratio.
Step 5: Multiply the cost to retail ratio on the closing stock value at retail price.
Step 6: The resultant value is known as the estimated cost of closing inventory.

■ **ILLUSTRATION 10.14** Find the closing stock value at cost and at retail price of Continental Groceries Shop, for the year ended March 2020.

	At cost	At retail price
(a) Opening stock as on 1 April 2019	₹25,000	₹40,000
(b) Purchase during the year	₹3,00,000	₹4,23,000
(c) Sales revenue		₹4,00,000

Solution

Statement Showing the Calculation of Closing Stock Value

Particulars	At Cost (₹)	At Retail Price (₹)
Opening stock	25,000	40,000
Purchases	3,00,000	4,23,000
Total stock available for sale	3,25,000	4,63,000
Deduct : Retail sale		4,00,000
Closing stock at retail value		63,000

Average cost ratio = (Total stock available at cost price/Total stock available at retail price) × 100
= (3,25,000/4,63,000) × 100
= 70%

Closing stock at Cost = ₹63,000 × 70%
= ₹44,100

VALUATION OF STOCK AND FINAL ACCOUNTS

While preparing the final accounts of an enterprise, if the physical stock-taking is done at the end of the year, it is referred to as periodic inventory. Usually, the physical stock-taking and stock valuation is done on the last day of the financial year.

However, if the stock-taking is done on any date other than the date of preparation of final accounts, then adjustments will have to be made with respect to transactions that took place between the date of stock-taking and the date of preparation of final accounts.

For example, if the financial year of a firm ends of 30 June 2020 and stock-taking is done on 25 June 2020, then in order to find out the value of stock on 30 June 2020, the adjustment will have to be made with respect to the transactions which took place between 25 June 2020 and 30 June 2020. The treatment of the various transactions when the stock-taking is done prior to the date of financial year is provided in the following text:

Amount (₹)

Value of stock on (date of stock-taking)	—
Add: Purchases (from the date of stock-taking to the date of final accounts)	—
Less: Purchase returns (for above-mentioned period)	—
Less: Sales at cost price (from the date of stock-taking to the date of final accounts)	
Add: Sales returns (for above-mentioned period)	—
Value of closing stock on the date of final accounts	—

Similarly, when the stock-taking is done on a date which is subsequent to the last date of the final accounts, adjustments will have to be made taking into consideration, the transactions that took place between the last date of final accounts and the date of stock-taking. Let us assume that the financial year of a firm ends on 30 June 2020 and stock-taking is done on 3 July 2020. The transactions that took place between 1 July 2020 to 3 July 2020, and the necessary adjustment should be made to the value of the stock on 3 July 2020.

■ **ILLUSTRATION 10.15** A firm started its business on 1 April 2019, and purchased the following raw materials during 2019–2020:

Date	Units	Cost per unit (₹)
1 April	1,600	60
20 May	2,400	62
28 June	4,000	65
30 August	6,000	70
18 October	3,000	74
15 December	2,000	80
20 February	3,000	75
24 March	5,000	82

While preparing its final accounts on 31 March 2020, the firm had 4,000 units of raw material in stock. Calculate the value of closing stock of raw materials according to (a) FIFO basis; (b) LIFO basis; and (c) weighted average price basis.

Solution

(a) The value of stock according to FIFO basis is as follows: Under this method closing inventory will consist of the recently purchased. Thus, 4,000 units in stock will be considered from the stock purchased on March 24.
Value of closing inventory = 4,000 × 82
= ₹3,28,000

(b) The value of stock according to LIFO basis is as follows:
Under this method closing inventory will consist of the units purchased at earlier dates. Thus, stock will comprise of 1,600 units purchased on 1 April and 2,400 units purchased on May 20.

Value of closing inventory = 1,600 units × ₹60 = ₹   96,000
2,400 units × ₹62 = ₹ 1,48,800
= ₹ 2,44,800

The value of stock according to the weighted average price basis is as follows:

Calculation of Weighted Average Price

Units bought	Cost per unit (₹)	Amount (₹)
1,600	60	96,000
2,400	62	1,48,800
4,000	65	2,60,000
6,000	70	4,20,000
3,000	74	2,22,000
2,000	80	1,60,000
3,000	75	2,25,000
5,000	82	4,10,000
27,000		19,41,800

Cost per unit = ₹19,41,800/27,000 units = ₹71.92 (approx.)
Value of stock = 4,000 units × ₹71.92
= ₹2,87,680

ERRORS IN INVENTORY

Errors in the merchandise inventory will significantly affect the income statement and the balance sheet of the firm. Some causes of errors are mentioned in the following text.

(a) Error in counting the physical stock of an item.

(b) Incorrect assignment of costs at the time of valuation of material receipts.

(c) Incorrect assignment of costs for issue of materials for production purpose or for delivery to the customer. For instance, valuation performed as per LIFO method instead of the FIFO method may result in an error.

(d) Incorrect inclusion or exclusion of inventory in transit in the inventory list.

(e) Incorrect inclusion or exclusion of a consigned inventory in the inventory list.

Effect on Income Statement

Inventory errors will affect both the determination of cost of goods sold and the net profit or net loss reported by the firm. The closing stock or inventory value of one particular accounting period would be carried forward as opening stock or inventory value for the next accounting period. The effects of inventory errors on the current period's profit and loss account, that is, income statement, are tabulated in Exhibit 10.3.

EXHIBIT 10.3 Impact of Inventory Errors on the Income Statement

Inventory Errors	Cost of Goods Sold	Net Profit
Opening inventory under valued	Understated	Overstated
Opening inventory over valued	Overstated	Understated
Closing inventory under valued	Overstated	Understated
Closing inventory over valued	Understated	Overstated

It should also be noted that if the effect of an error in closing is not corrected immediately before the end of the next accounting period, it will have a reverse effect on the net profit of that accounting period. This is because the opening inventory of the next accounting period is exactly the same as the closing inventory of the current accounting period. In case of such errors, carry forward of the error would not affect the total reported profit or loss of the two years combined together, because the reduced profit reported in one year would result in a higher profit being reported in the next accounting period.

Effect on Balance Sheet

The effect of closing stock errors on the balance sheet can be determined using the modern approach of accounting equation as discussed in Chapter 2. Exhibit 10.4 shows the effect of errors in inventory valuation of stock on the components of a balance sheet.

EXHIBIT 10.4 Impact of Inventory Errors on the Balance Sheet

Closing Inventory or Stock—Error type	Assets	Liabilities	Owners' Equity
Over valued	Overstated	No effect	Overstated
Under valued	Understated	No effect	Understated

The impact of such errors is nullified at the end of the subsequent year following the occurrence of the error because the balance sheet will indicate the position of the firm on a particular date, and not for the period. As the combined profit value of the two periods would be the same (lower profit reported in one year is offset by the higher amount of profit for the next year), the financial position of the firm at the end of the second year would remain intact.

OBSOLETE AND DAMAGED ITEMS

Loss due to damage or obsolescence of items is measured by the difference between the cost of the unit and its expected net realizable value. The net realizable value is the expected sales value less the expected cost involved in disposing the said unit.

■ **ILLUSTRATION 10.16** Assume that 10 units of Softel mobile phones bought by Central Stores have been damaged

as a result of a minor fire in the store. Each unit costs ₹5,000 and is expected to realize ₹2,000 after the necessary repairs worth ₹500 and a special discount of ₹100 to the middlemen. Find out the loss on writing down the value of damaged units.

Solution

The calculation of net realizable value is as follows:

Particulars	Amount (₹)
Expected sales price	₹2,000
Less: Disposal costs:	
Special commission to pay	₹100
Repairs	₹500
Net realizable value	₹1,400
The inventory value (1400 × 10)	₹14,000
The actual costs of goods (5,000 × 10)	₹50,000
Loss on writing down the value of damaged units	₹36,000

The loss on writing down the value of damaged units will be charged in the profit and loss account of the year.

ACCOUNTING FOR CHANGING PRICES

In periods of rapidly changing prices, the matching concept should be extended to use the current cost (cost of replacement of an item) for the cost of goods sold. In other words, the current cost price should match against current sales price. In this way, firms will exclude from their income the amount required to replace the goods that have been sold.

Although the generally accepted accounting principles (GAAP) do not permit use of current cost accounting in the preparation of financial statements, they do permit companies to disclose the current cost of their inventory in a footnote to the financial statement.

Accounting standards do not currently allow inflation-adjusted accounting. Changing prices represent a broader concept than the concept of inflation. It consists of two types of price changes that affect any economy: general price level changes and specific price level changes.

General price level changes are changes in the general price level that affect the ability of the currency to purchase a variety of commodities, goods, merchandise, and services. In the case of inflation, the purchasing power of the currency declines over a period of time, as being represented by increases in the price of commodities. Inversely, deflation occurs when prices of commodities decline, in turn increasing the purchasing power of the currency.

Specific price level changes indicate changes in the value of specific goods, commodities, merchandise, and services. It reflects an adjustment in the price of a particular item, such as a litre of petrol, a kilogram of wheat, etc.

Inflation accounting is explained in detail in the chapter on contemporary accounting.

■ **ILLUSTRATION 10.17** A firm had to take complete stock on 21 June 2019 because of a deal to sell its business, which failed at the last stage. Consequently, it decided not to carry out stock-taking on 30 June 2019, when accounts were closed for the year.

The stock on 21 June 2019 was ₹67,460. The following transactions in stock occurred between 21 June 2019 and 30 June 2019.

(a) Goods purchased between 21 June 2019 to 30 June 2019 amounted to ₹4,820, of which goods worth ₹1,900 were received on 2 July 2019.

(b) Sales during the period between 21 June 2019 to 30 June 2019 amounted to ₹16,800, including ₹3,600 for goods sent of approval, half of which were still returnable on 30 June 2019. The firm sells goods at cost plus 25%, but there was one lot of damaged goods that had cost ₹2,800 that had to be sold for ₹1,200. The stock as on 21 June 2019 included these goods at cost.

(c) Unsold goods in the hand of a consignee on 30 June 2019 were revalued at ₹3,200.

Prepare a statement showing the actual value of stock as on 30 June 2019.

Solution

The statement of actual value of stock as on 30 June 2019 is as follows:

Particulars	Amount (₹)	Amount (₹)
Stock as on 21/06/2019		67,460
Add: Goods purchased between 21/06/2019 and 30/06/2019	4,820	
Less: Goods not received	1,900	2,920
Add: Unsold goods in hands of consignee		3,200
Less: Cost of goods sold: sales	16,800	73,580
Less: Goods still returnable by customers	1,800	
	15,000	
Less: Special sales	1,200	
	13,800	
Less: Gross profit @ 20%	2,760	11,040
		62,540
Less: Cost of goods included in stock on 21/06/2019 since sold stock on 30 June 2019		2,800
Actual value of stock		59,740

■ **ILLUSTRATION 10.18** Mr Sharma's financial year ends on 30 June 2019, but actual stock is not taken until the following 8 July 2019, when it is ascertained at ₹7,425. You find information as follows:

1. Sales are entered in the sales book on the same day as dispatched and returns inward are entered in the returns inward book the day they are received;

2. Purchases are entered in the purchases day book as the invoices are received;

3. Sales between 30 June 2019 and 8 July 2019 as per the sales day book and cash book are ₹8,600;

4. Purchases between 30 June 2019 and 8 July 2019 as per the purchase day book are ₹660 but of these goods amounting to ₹60 were not received until after the stock was taken;

5. Goods invoiced before 30 June but not received until 30 June amounted to ₹500, of which goods received worth ₹350 were received between 30 June 2019 and 9 July 2019;

6. Gross profit is 33.33% of cost.

Ascertain the value of stock on 30 June 2019.

Solution

Computation of Stock Value in Books of Mr Sharma
as on 30 June 2019

Particulars	Amount (₹)	Amount (₹)
Stock as on 8 July 2019		7,425
Add: Cost of goods sold:		
Cost of goods sales	8,600	
Less: Gross profit @ 33.33% on cost, that is, 25% on sales	2,150	6,450
		13,875
Less: purchases: (30 June to 8 July)	660	
Less: received after 8 July	60	600
		13,275
Add: Purchases invoiced before 30 June, not received up to 8 July 2019 (500 – 350)		150
Stock on 30 June 2019		13,425

■ **ILLUSTRATION 10.19** Diamond Chemicals Ltd takes a periodic inventory of their stock of chemical X at the end of each month. The physical inventory taken on 30 June shows a balance of 1,000 litres of chemical X in hand @ ₹2.28 per litre.

The following purchases were made during July.

1 July	14,000 litres @ ₹2.30 per litre
7 July	10,000 litres @ ₹2.32 per litre
9 July	20,000 litres @ ₹2.33 per litre
25 July	5,000 litres @ ₹2.35 per litre

A physical inventory taken on 31 July discloses that there is a stock of 10,000 litres.

You are required to compute the inventory value on 31 July by each of the following methods.

(a) FIFO
(b) LIFO
(c) Weighted average cost

Solution

(a) FIFO

			Amount (₹)
25 July	5,000 litres @ ₹2.35	=	11,750
9 July	5,000 litres @ ₹2.33	=	11,650
Closing inventory on July 31			
1,000 litres			23,400

(b) LIFO

			Amount (₹)
30 June	1,000 litres @ ₹2.28	=	2,280
1 July	9,000 litres @ ₹2.30	=	20,700
Closing inventory on 31 July			
1,000 litres			22,980

(c) Weighted Average Cost

			Amount (₹)
30 June	1,000 litres @ ₹2.28	=	2,280
1 July	14,000 litres @ ₹2.30	=	32,200
7 July	10,000 litres @ ₹2.32	=	23,200
9 July	20,000 litres @ ₹2.33	=	46,600
25 July	5,000 litres @ ₹2.35	= 11,750	
Total 50,000 litres		1,16,030	

Average cost per litre = 1,16,030/50,000
= 2.3206

Total value of inventory on 31 July = 10,000 × 2.3206
= ₹23,206

■ **ILLUSTRATION 10.20** Following are the details regarding the receipts and issue of material Cappa in respect of a firm.

Receipts:
1 Jan Balance 50 units @ ₹4 per unit
5 Jan Purchase order (P.O.) no. 10, 40 units @ ₹3 per unit
8 Jan Purchase order no. 19, 30 units @ ₹4 per unit
15 Jan Purchase order no. 11, 20 units @ ₹5 per unit
26 Jan Purchase order no. 13, 40 units @ ₹3 per unit

Issues:
10 Jan Material requisition (M.R.) no. 4, 70 units
12 Jan Material requisition no. 5, 10 units
20 Jan Material requisition no. 6, 20 units
31 Jan Shortage 5 units

The firm follows the perpetual inventory system for maintaining its stores records. You are required to calculate the value of inventory on 31 January according to

(a) FIFO
(b) LIFO
(c) HIFO
(d) Weighted average price

Solution

(a) Stores ledger card (FIFO)
Material Cappa

Date (Jan.)	Receipts Reference	Quantity	Rate (₹)	Amount (₹)	Issues Reference	Quantity	Rate (₹)	Amount (₹)	Balance Quantity	Amount (₹)
1	Balance	50	4	200	—	—	—	—	50	200
5	P.O. No. 10	40	3	120	—	—	—	—	90	320
8	P.O. No. 12	30	4	120	—	—	—	—	120	440
10	—	—	—	—	M.R. No. 4	50	4	200 }	50	180
						20	3	60 }		
12	—	—	—	—	M.R. No. 5	10	3	30 }	40	150
15	P.O. No. 11	20	5	100	—	—	—	—	60	250
20	—	—	—	—	M.R. No. 6	10	3	30 }	40	180
						10	4	40 }		
24	—	—	—	—	M.R. No. 7	10	4	40	30	140
26	P.O. No. 13	40	3	120	—	—	—	—	70	260
31	—	—	—	—	Shortage	5	4	20	65	240

The stock consists of
40 units purchased on 26 Jan @ ₹3 per unit = ₹120
20 units purchased on 15 Jan @ ₹5 per unit = ₹100
5 units purchased on 9 Jan @ ₹4 per unit =₹20
Total = ₹240

(b) Stores Ledger Card (LIFO)
Material Cappa
The stock consists of:
30 units of the balance on 1 Jan. @ ₹4 = ₹120
35 units of the balance on 26 Jan. @ ₹3 = ₹105
Total = ₹225

Date (Jan.)	Receipts Reference	Quantity	Rate (₹)	Amount (₹)	Issues Reference	Quantity	Rate (₹)	Amount (₹)	Balance Quantity	Amount (₹)
1	Balance	50	4	200	—	—	—	—	50	200
5	P.O. No. 10	40	3	120	—	—	—	—	90	320
8	P.O. No. 12	30	4	120	—	—	—	—	120	440
10	—	—	—	—	M.R. No. 4	30	4	120 }	50	200
						40	3	120 }		
12	—	—	—	—	M.R. No. 5	10	4	40	40	160
15	P.O. No. 11	20	5	100	—	—	—	—	60	260
20	—	—	—	—	M.R. No. 6	20	5	100	40	160
24	—	—	—	—	M.R. No. 7	10	4	40	30	120
26	P.O. No. 13	40	3	120	—	—	—	—	70	260
31	—	—	—	—	Shortage	5	3	15	65	225

(c) Stores ledger card (HIFO)
Material Cappa

Date (Jan.)	Receipts Reference	Quantity	Rate (₹)	Amount (₹)	Issues Reference	Quantity	Rate (₹)	Amount (₹)	Balance Quantity	Amount (₹)
1	Balance	50	4	200	—	—	—	—	50	200
5	P.O. No. 10	40	3	120	—	—	—	—	90	320
8	P.O. No. 12	30	4	120	—	—	—	—	120	440
10	—	—	—	—	M.R. No. 4	70	4	280	50	160
12	—	—	—	—	M.R. No. 5	10	4	40	40	120
15	P.O. No. 11	20	5	100	—	—	—	—	60	220
20	—	—	—	—	M.R. No. 6	20	5	100	40	120
24	—	—	—	—	M.R. No. 7	10	3	30	30	90
26	P.O. No. 13	40	3	120	—	—	—	—	70	210
31	—	—	—	—	Shortage	5	3	15	65	195*

*This consists of purchase on 5 Jan. and 26 Jan. This stock has been valued at the lowest price.

(d) Stores Ledger Card (Weighted Average Price)
Material Cappa

Date (Jan.)	Receipts Reference	Quantity	Rate (₹)	Amount (₹)	Issues Reference	Quantity	Rate (₹)	Amount (₹)	Balance Quantity	Amount (₹)	Weighted Average Price (₹)
1	Balance	50	4	200	—	—	—	—	50	200	4
5	P.O. No. 10	40	3	120	—	—	—	—	90	320	3.56
8	P.O. No. 12	30	4	120	—	—	—	—	120	440	3.67
10	—	—	—	—	M.R. No. 4	70	3.67	256.90	50	183.10	—
12	—	—	—	—	M.R. No. 5	10	3.67	36.70	40	146.40	—
15	P.O. No. 11	20	5	100	—	—	—	—	60	246.40	4.16
20	—	—	—	—	M.R. No. 6	20	4.16	183.20	40	164.40	—
24	—	—	—	—	M.R. No. 7	10	4.16	41.60	30	123.40	—
26	P.O. No. 13	40	3	120	—	—	—	—	70	243.40	3.48
31	—	—	—	—	Shortage	5	3.48	17.40	65	226	—

■ **ILLUSTRATION 10.21** Supriya closed her books of accounts on 31 March 2020, but due to certain difficulties, it was not possible for her to conduct physical stock-taking on that date. Physical stock was taken on 7 April when it was valued at ₹45,000. An examination of the record of inventories from 1 to 7 April revealed the following:

(a) Net sales during the period were ₹10,200. These goods were sold at the usual rate of gross profit of 25% on cost except goods, which realized ₹1,200 on the basis of 20% profit on cost.

(b) Purchases during the period were ₹8,000 of which ₹1,000 worth of goods were delivered only on 9 April.

(c) Sales returns during the period were ₹1,200 of which 50% were out of sales at 20% gross profit mentioned earlier.

(d) On 5 April, Supriya received certain goods costing ₹5,000 to be sold by her on consignment basis.

Prepare a statement showing the value of stock to be shown in final accounts for the year ended 31/3/2020.

Solution

**Statement Showing the Value of Stock
as on 31 March 2020**

		Amount (₹)
Stock as on 7/4/2020		45,000
Add: Cost of goods sold between 1 April		
and 7 April		
₹9,000 × 4/5 = ₹7,200		
₹1,200 × 5/6 = ₹1,000	8,200	53,200
Less: Purchases during the period	₹7,000	
Sales returns at cost		
(₹600 × 5/6) ₹500		
(₹600 × 4/5) ₹480	₹980	
Goods received on consignment on		
5 April	₹5,000	12,980
Value of closing stock on 31/3/2020		40,220
(To be shown in final accounts)		

■ **ILLUSTRATION 10.22** The following information is available from the books of accounts of Ajit and Co. for the year 2019–2020:

Particulars	Amount (₹)
Purchases during the year	28,200
Stock on 1/4/2019	5,960
Sales during the year	31,610

At the time of valuation of stock for the period 2018–2019, a part of the stock costing ₹1,800 was recorded in the books for ₹1,560. One-third of these goods were sold during the year for ₹610.

Find out the value of the stock as on 31 March 2020 assuming that firm makes 25% profit on cost.

Solution

**Statement Showing the Value of Stock
as on 31 March 2020**

	Amount (₹)	Amount (₹)
Stock of goods on 1/4/2019	5,960	
Less: Stock of abnormal items	1,560	4,400
Add: Purchases		28,200
		32,600
Less: Cost of goods sold:		
Sales	31,610	
Less: Sale of abnormal item	610	
	31,000	
Less: Gross profit @ 20% on sales		
which is equal to 25% on cost	6,200	24,800
Value of stock (Normal on 31/3/2020)		7,800
Add: Stock of abnormal item (1800 × 2/3)		1,200
Total stock value		9,000

SUMMARY

- Inventory includes tangible property used for sale in the normal course of business or used for providing goods or services for sale.
- A major objective of accounting for inventory is the proper determination of income through the process of matching appropriate costs against revenue.
- Inventory or material accounting helps determining two parameters: the value of materials stored and the value of materials consumed for the operating cycle of the firm. Material consumption costs constitute a very significant proportion of total costs or expenses of a firm.
- Perpetual inventory system is such in which a continuous record of addition to or reduction in each category and item of inventory is maintained.
- In the periodic inventory system, the entire book inventory is verified at a particular date by actual count of materials on hand.
- Costing inventory or inventory pricing is needed to allocate the cost between ending or closing inventory and goods or materials transferred out. Different methods such as FIFO, LIFO, average, weighted average, etc., are available for the same purpose.
- The generally accepted accounting principles (GAAP) permit a departure from the cost concept in certain cases.
- The landed cost of material purchases during a given period is known as the value of material receipts. The costs incurred up to the receipt of materials at the factory, and all associated costs till the material can be issued to production or sold to the customer

(in case of trading firms) constitute the landed cost of material receipts.
- The quantity of inventory items lying with a firm has to be known in order to determine the value of closing stock on the date of preparation of the financial statement.
- Physical verification involves the actual counting, weighing, or measuring of each kind of inventory on hand. A year-end inventory counting is generally more accurate when goods are not being sold or received during the period of counting.
- Goods are considered as in transit, when they are lying with the transporter on the date of preparation of financial statements. Goods in transit include the inventory of the firm for which legal title of the goods are not transferred to the buyer or a third party.
- Free on board at shipping point or factory (FOB-SP) means that the title of the goods is transferred to the buyer when the goods are delivered to the transporter to be carried to the buyer.
- Free on board at destination point or buyer's place (FOB-DP) means that it is the duty of the seller to deliver the goods at the buyer's place.
- Errors in the merchandise inventory will affect the income statement and the balance sheet of the firm significantly.
- Inventory errors will affect both the determination of cost of goods sold and the net profit or net loss reported by the firm. It should also be noted that the effect of an error in closing is not corrected immediately before the end of the next accounting period; it will

have a reverse effect on the net profit of that accounting period. In case of such errors, carry forward of the error would not affect the total reported profit or loss of the two years combined together.

- According to Ind AS 2, any one of the following methods can be used by a firm for the determination of cost. The firm may also use different methods for different groups of inventory items. The methods allowed for cost formulae include (a) the specific identification method, (b) the first in first out (FIFO) method, (c) the weighted average method, (d) the standard cost method, and (e) the retail price method.

KEYWORDS

Free on board at destination point or buyer's place It means that it is the duty of the seller to deliver the goods at the buyer's place.

Free on board at shipping point or factory It means that the title of the goods is transferred to the buyer when the goods are delivered to the transporter to be carried to the buyer.

Inventory It is tangible property that (a) is held for sale in the normal course of business; or (b) will be used to provide service for sales.

Landed costs of material purchases It includes the costs incurred till the receipt of materials at the factory, and associated costs in bringing the material to the stores.

Periodic inventory system It verifies the entire book inventory on a particular date by an actual count of materials on hand.

Perpetual inventory system It maintains a continuous record of addition to or reduction in each category and item of inventory.

Physical verification It involves the actual counting, weighing, or measuring of each kind of inventory on hand.

QUESTIONS

I. Choose the right answer from the given options.

1. Which of the following statements is/are true?
   (a) Perpetual inventory system implies continuous stock-taking.
   (b) Perpetual inventory system is costly.
   (c) In case of unusual circumstances, periodic inventory system can be more costly in the long run.
   (d) Both (a) and (b) above.
   (e) All of (a), (b), and (c) above.

2. Which of the following methods for stock valuation for normal inventory is recommended by Ind AS 2?
   (a) FIFO method
   (b) LIFO method
   (c) Weighted average method
   (d) Both (b) and (c) above
   (e) All of (a), (b), and (c) above

3. Unique Ltd uses a periodic inventory system. The purchases of a particular product for the year are as given in the following text.

Jan.	1	Opening inventory	500 units @	₹5	2,500
May	5	Purchases	500 units @	₹10	5,000
Aug.	8	Purchases	1,000 units @	₹8	8,000
Dec.	5	Purchases	500 units @	₹5	2,500

On 31 December, the ending inventory consisted of 1,000 units.
   (i) The cost of ending inventory based on the LIFO method of inventory valuation is
       (a) ₹5,000 (b) ₹6,500
       (c) ₹7,500 (d) ₹8,000
       (e) ₹10,000
   (ii) The cost of goods sold during the year based on the LIFO method of inventory valuation is
       (a) ₹7,500 (b) ₹8,000
       (c) ₹10,000 (d) ₹10,500
       (e) ₹12,500
   (iii) The cost of ending inventory based on the FIFO method of inventory valuation is
       (a) ₹5,000 (b) ₹6,500
       (c) ₹8,000 (d) ₹10,000
       (e) ₹10,500
   (iv) The cost of goods sold for the year based on the FIFO method of inventory valuation is
       (a) ₹6,500 (b) ₹8,000
       (c) ₹10,000 (d) ₹10,500
       (e) ₹11,500

4. The appropriate attribute used to measure damaged inventory is
   (a) Historical cost (b) Current cost
   (c) Current market value (d) Net realizable value
   (e) Present value of future cash flows

5. Closing stock is generally valued at
   (a) Cost price
   (b) Market price
   (c) Cost price or market price, whichever is higher
   (d) Cost price or market price, whichever is lower
   (e) Net realizable value

6. DB Company's accounting records indicated the following information:

Particulars	Amount (₹)
Opening inventory	5,00,000
Purchases during 2019–2020	25,00,000
Sales during 2019–2020	32,00,000

A physical inventory taken on 31 March 2013 resulted in an ending inventory of ₹5,75,000. Company's gross profit on sales has remained constant at 25%. The management of the company suspects some inventory may have been taken by a new employee. What is the estimated cost of missing inventory on the last day of the financial year?
   (a) ₹2,25,000 (b) ₹2,00,000
   (c) ₹1,75,000 (d) ₹1,00,000
   (e) ₹25,000

7. At the beginning of the year, AB Ltd had an inventory of ₹1,50,000. During the year, the company purchased goods costing ₹9,75,000. Net sales for the year totaled ₹15,00,000 and gross profit rate was 40%. The cost of goods sold and the ending inventory, respectively, were
   (a) ₹10,50,000 and ₹75,000
   (b) ₹6,00,000 and ₹5,25,000
   (c) ₹6,00,000 and ₹1,00,000
   (d) ₹9,00,000 and ₹2,25,000
   (e) ₹9,00,000 and ₹2,00,000

8. Polo Ltd uses a periodic inventory system. The beginning inventory was ₹50,000 and year-end inventory was ₹60,000. Purchase of goods and sales during the year were ₹2,00,000 and ₹3,00,000 respectively. The company's cost of goods sold during the year is
   (a) ₹2,00,000
   (b) ₹1,90,000
   (c) ₹1,50,000
   (d) ₹1,40,000
   (e) ₹1,10,000

9. During a period of steadily rising prices, which of the following methods of measuring the cost of goods sold is likely to result in the lowest possible taxable income?
   (a) Average cost
   (b) Weighted average cost
   (c) First in first out
   (d) Last in first out
   (e) Next in first out

10. The cost of goods sold is equal to
   (a) Total purchases minus total sales
   (b) Opening stock plus total purchases
   (c) Closing stock plus total purchases
   (d) Opening stock minus total purchases plus closing stock
   (e) Opening stock plus total purchases minus closing stock

11. The following information is available for Miracle Co. Ltd for 2019–2020.

Particulars	Amount (₹)
Net sales	₹12,00,000
Gross profit on sales	30%
Purchase discounts @1%	₹9,000
Ending inventory	₹1,60,000
Freight in	₹20,000

   The beginning inventory is
   (a) ₹1,00,000
   (b) ₹90,000
   (c) ₹80,000
   (d) ₹75,000
   (e) ₹70,000

12. Bluetech Software Ltd uses a periodic inventory system. The purchases of a particular product during the year are shown in the following text.

1 January	Beginning inventory	1,500 units	@ ₹9.00	₹13,500
18 April	Purchases	1,250 units	@ ₹9.50	₹11,875
11 August	Purchases	1,750 units	@ ₹10.00	₹17,500
23 October	Purchases	500 units	@ ₹10.25	₹5,125
				₹48,000

   At 31 December, the ending inventory consisted of 1,750 units.
   (i) The cost of ending inventory based on the LIFO method of inventory valuation is
      (a) ₹32,125
      (b) ₹15,875
      (c) ₹17,625
      (d) ₹30,375
      (e) ₹31,200
   (ii) The cost of goods sold for the current year based on the LIFO method of inventory valuation is
      (a) ₹32,125
      (b) ₹15,875
      (c) ₹17,625
      (d) ₹30,375
      (e) ₹31,200

   (iii) The cost of ending inventory based on the FIFO method of inventory valuation is
      (a) ₹32,125
      (b) ₹15,875
      (c) ₹17,625
      (d) ₹30,375
      (e) ₹31,200
   (iv) The cost of goods sold for the current year based on the FIFO method of inventory valuation is
      (a) ₹32,125
      (b) ₹15,875
      (c) ₹17,625
      (d) ₹30,375
      (e) ₹31,200

13. The method of pricing inventory where all items are assigned the same unit cost is
   (a) LIFO
   (b) FIFO
   (c) Average cost
   (d) Specific identification
   (e) Base stock

14. Under inflationary conditions, FIFO method will lead to
   (a) Lower profits
   (b) Higher sales
   (c) Lower sales
   (d) Higher profits
   (e) No change in sales

15. ABC Ltd uses a periodic inventory system. The purchases of a particular product during the year are shown in the following text.

1 January	Opening inventory	100 units @ ₹5	500
3 March	Purchases	100 units @ ₹10	1,000
6 March	Sales	100 units @ ₹15	1,500

   The cost of goods sold, based on the LIFO method of inventory valuation is
   (a) ₹500
   (b) ₹1,000
   (c) ₹1,500
   (d) ₹2,000
   (e) ₹3,000

16. In a perpetual inventory system, an inventory flow assumption (i.e., LIFO or FIFO) is used primarily for determining costs that are used in
   (a) Forecasts of future sale
   (b) Recording purchases of inventory
   (c) Recording the cost of goods sold
   (d) Recording sales revenue
   (e) Forecasts of future operating results

17. Saahil Inc. uses a periodic inventory system. The purchase of a particular product for the year are as given in the following text:

1 January	Opening inventory	500 units @ ₹5	2,500
1 May	Purchases	500 units @ ₹10	5,000
8 August	Purchases	1,000 units @ ₹8	8,000
5 December	Purchases	500 units @ ₹5	2,500

   On 31 December, the ending inventory consisted of 1,000 units.
   (i) The cost of ending inventory based on the LIFO method of inventory valuation is
      (a) ₹5,000
      (b) ₹6,500
      (c) ₹7,500
      (d) ₹8,000
      (e) ₹10,000
   (ii) The cost of goods sold for the year based on the FIFO method of inventory valuation is
      (a) ₹6,500
      (b) ₹8,000
      (c) ₹10,000
      (d) ₹10,500
      (e) ₹11,500

II. Solve the following problems.

1. Neha Yadav prepares accounts annually on 31 December, but the stock-taking takes place on the following weekend.

   The stock-taking for the year ended 31 December 2019 was made on 6 January 2020 on which date the value of stock found in the premises was ₹35,970.

   Ascertain the following further particulars:
   1. Sales during the period from 1 January to 6 January 2020, ₹3,000 and goods sent on approval at selling price ₹2,000.
   2. Purchases during the same period as per purchase day book ₹6,000.
   3. Included in the above purchases were goods worth ₹2,000, which were not actually delivered but the invoice was received and accordingly entries were made in the purchase day book.
   4. The average ratio of gross profit to turnover is 30%.

   Ascertain the value of stock on 31 December 2019.

2. Determine the value of stock to be taken for balance sheet as at 31 March 2020 from the following information:

   The stock was physically verified on 23 March, 2020 and was valued at ₹6,00,000. Between 23 March 2020 and 31 March 2020 the following transactions had taken place:
   1. Purchases were of ₹50,000; of this, goods worth ₹20,000 were delivered on 5 April 2020.
   2. Out of goods sent on consignment, goods worth ₹30,000 (at cost) were unsold.
   3. Sales were of ₹1,70,000. This included goods worth ₹40,000 sent on approval. Half of these were returned before 31 March. As regards remaining, no intimation is received.
   4. Normally, a firm sells goods on cost plus 25%. However, a lot of goods costing ₹30,000 was sold for ₹15,000.

3. Fast Track Ltd prepares accounts to 31 March each year. On 31 March 2020 its stock-taking expert was ill and the preparation of the physical inventory was delayed until 3 April 2020 on which date the stock valued at cost amounted to ₹2,40,000.

   An examination of inventories and related financial record disclosed that between 1 and 3 April 2020, the following events took place.
   1. Sales totalled ₹40,000 including (i) ₹2,000 in respect of goods which left the warehouse on 29 March 2020. And (ii) ₹4,000 in respect of goods not dispatched until 12 April 2020. The rate of gross profit to sales was 30%.
   2. Returns from customers totalled ₹6,000.
   3. Purchases totalled ₹18,000 which included (i) ₹6,000 for goods received in March 2020 and (ii) ₹3,000 for goods received on 10 April 2020.
   4. Returns to suppliers totalled ₹4,000.
   5. There were arithmetical errors in the stock sheets on 3 April 2020 resulting in an over valuation of ₹4,600.

   Prepare a statement showing the correct amount of the company's stock at cost on 31 March 2020.

4. Moonbucks Ltd conducts physical stocks taking every year at the end of the accounting year. Owing to certain difficulties, it was not possible for it to conduct physical stock-taking at the end of the accounting year ending 30 June 2020. Physical stock was taken on 8 July 2020, when it was valued at ₹34,500.

   The following transactions took place during 1 and 8 July 2020:
   1. Net sales during the period were ₹9,340. These goods were sold at the usual rate of gross profit of 25% on cost, except goods which realized ₹840 on the basis of 20% profit on cost.
   2. Purchases during the period were ₹7,500 of which ₹800 worth of goods were delivered to the company only on 10 July 2020.
   3. Sales returns during the period were ₹1,500 of which 50% were out of the sales at 20% gross profit mentioned earlier.
   4. On 5 July 2020, goods worth ₹4,000 were received which were to be sold on consignment basis.

   You are required to prepare a statement showing clearly the value of the stock to be taken into account in Moonbucks Ltd's final accounts for the year ended 30 June 2020.

5. The movement of inventory in a company was as follows:

	Qty	Cost per unit (₹)
Opening balance of inventory purchases:	6,000	50
On 15/5/2020	1,000	60
On 30/9/2020	2,500	75
On 31/1/2021	2,000	80
Issues:		
On 20/5/2020	1,500	
On 10/10/2020	2,000	
On 2/2/2021	2,500	

   Calculate the value of inventory by FIFO and LIFO methods.

6. On the basis of the following information, calculate the amount of raw materials used in production by Moon-Light Company for the year ended 31 March 2020.

Date	Amount (₹)
Stock of raw materials on 1 April 2019	10,000
Stock of raw materials on 31 March 2020	13,000
Total amount paid for raw materials during the year ended 31 March 2020 (inclusive of advance payment of ₹2,000 to raw material supplier)	41,000
Creditors for raw material as on 1 April 2019	12,500
Creditors for raw material as on 31 March 2020	15,000

7. A firm started its business on 1 April 2019 and purchased the following raw materials during 2019–2020.

1 April	:	1,600 units @ ₹60 each
20 May	:	2,400 units @ ₹62 each
28 June	:	4,000 units @ ₹65 each
30 August	:	6,000 units @ ₹70 each
18 October	:	3,000 units @ ₹74 each
15 December	:	2,000 units @ ₹80 each
20 February	:	3,000 units @ ₹75 each
24 March	:	5,000 units @ ₹82 each.

   While preparing its final accounts on 31 March 2020, the firm had 4,000 units of raw material in the godown. Calculate the value of closing stock of raw materials according to
   (a) First in first out basis
   (b) Last in first out basis and
   (c) Weighted average price basis

8. XY Ltd has purchased and issued the material 'M' in the following order.

2019			Units	Unit Cost (₹)
1	Dec.	Purchased	300	3
4	Dec.	Purchased	600	4
6	Dec.	Issued	400	
10	Dec.	Purchased	600	4
15	Dec.	Issued	1,000	
20	Dec.	Purchased	400	5
23	Dec.	Issued	200	

Which of the methods of pricing issue of materials would you recommend in the above case? Ascertain the quantity of closing stock as on 31 December and state the value if issues are made under the method recommended by you.

9. The Fairdeal Granary was not maintaining a perpetual inventory system for its stock until recently. Only physical inventory was taken at the end of each month. The physical inventory at the end of December 2019 showed 200 bags of fine rice at ₹212.25 per bag. The following purchases were made in January 2020.

   3 : 400 bags at ₹218 per bag
  10 : 900 bags at ₹223.50 per bag
  15 : 400 bags at ₹220 per bag
  28 : 700 bags at ₹213 per bag
  30 : 300 bags at ₹224 per bag

On 31 January 2020 the physical stock was 1,200 bags. Calculate the value of stock on 31 January 2020 according to
  (a) First in first out,
  (b) Last in first out; and
  (c) Average price method.

10. The annual accounts of a trading company are to be made till 31 December but it was not possible to carry out a stock-taking until 5 January at which date the stock was valued at cost at ₹68,567. The following transactions took place between 1 January and 5 January.

                            Amount (₹)

	Amount (₹)
Goods received	4,600
Goods returned	200
Sales	10,500
Returns by customers	625

The rate of gross profit is 25% of cost.

Prepare a statement to show the valuation of stock as on 31 December.

III. Answer the following questions briefly.

1. What are the objectives of inventory valuation?
2. Compare and contrast LIFO and FIFO systems of valuation of inventories.
3. Discuss in detail the components needed to determine the valuation of material receipts.
4. What do you understand by the term 'landed costs of material purchase'?
5. What does physical verification of stock mean?
6. Discuss in detail the components to be considered in the physical verification of stock.
7. Discuss in detail the importance of goods in transit.
8. Differentiate between free on board at destination and shipping point.
9. How should obsolete materials be valued for the purpose of the financial statement?
10. Describe the non-historical cost methods, and their utility.

 CASE

Business Application Case

High Aluminium Company High Aluminium Company adopted LIFO on 1 January 2018. Its 15,000 ton inventory was costed at its FIFO cost of ₹125 a ton on that date at ₹18,75,000. During 2018, the company purchased 1,00,000 tonnes at an average price of ₹130 a ton, and sold 95,000 tonnes. The last 20,000 tonnes purchased during December 2018 cost ₹135 a ton. Sale in 2019 amounted to 1,05,000 tonnes, but purchases totalled only 90,000 tonnes at an average cost of ₹140 a ton. (The last 5,000 tonnes purchased during 2019 also cost ₹140 a ton.) The inventory was down to 5,000 tonnes at the end of 2019 because a steel strike had cut off supplies. The company expected to rebuild its inventories to 15,000 tonnes as soon as steel became available again in 2020. High Aluminium Company measures the annual increments to its LIFO inventory at the average of all purchase prices paid during the year.

Questions

1. Provide the figures necessary to complete the following table, showing inventories and cost of goods sold on both FIFO and LIFO basis.

	Inventory Cost		Costs of Goods Sold	
	FIFO	LIFO	FIFO	LIFO
1 January 2018	₹18,75,000	₹18,75,000		
31 December 2018	_____	_____	2018 _____	_____
31 December 2019	_____	_____	2019 _____	_____

2. Assuming that 15,000 tonnes is the normal inventory quantity and that the company intended to rebuild its inventories to this level as soon as possible, what was the effect of the 'involuntary liquidation' of inventory on income before taxes for 2019?

3. Assuming that inventories were increased to 15,000 tonnes by the end of 2020, with 2020 purchases at a cost of ₹145 a ton, what was the net effect of the 2019 involuntary liquidation on LIFO inventory cost as on 31 December 2020?

4. Assuming an income tax rate of 50%, calculate the effect of the choice between FIFO and LIFO on the company's cash flows in 2018, 2019, and 2020. The company purchased 1,00,000 tonnes of steel in 2020.

Capital and Liabilities

Learning Objectives

After studying this chapter, you will understand

- liabilities and capital from the view of balance sheet
- characteristics of the company form of organization
- different types of shares and the accounting procedures
- different types of debentures and the accounting techniques
- presentation of a company's true financial position

INTRODUCTION

The liabilities of a firm represent what a firm as a distinct entity owes to various parties, namely to shareholders for share capital and retained earnings, and to other parties, for loans to a firm or entity either against some specific securities for either a longer or a shorter period of time. In other words, the liabilities of a firm includes two components: owners' equity and liabilities. Owners' equity is the sum of contributed capital plus retained earnings, as already discussed in Chapter 2.

Liabilities that are due within a short time period (usually one year or less) and that are to be paid out of current assets are called current liabilities. The most common liabilities in this group are bills payable, notes payable, and accounts payable. Other current liabilities that accounts comprise commonly are wages payable, interest payable, taxes payable, expenses payable, etc.

Liabilities that are not due for a long period of time (usually more than one year) are called long-term liabilities. As long-term liabilities are due to be paid within one year, they are classified as current liabilities. If they are renewed rather than paid, they will continue to be classified as long-term liabilities. When an asset is pledged as security for a liability, the obligation may be called a *mortgage note payable* or *mortgage payable*.

So, the content of total liabilities of a firm is studied under three heads: owner's equity, non-current liabilities (long-term liabilities), and current liabilities. Additionally, it also includes the contingent liabilities of the firm.

CLASSIFICATION OF LIABILITIES

Liabilities are obligations to outside parties arising from events that have already happened. In simpler terms, liabilities are claims against the entity's assets. They are broadly classified into four major categories: a) Long-term liabilities, b) Short-term liabilities (current liabilities) c) Estimated liabilities, and d) Contingent liabilities.

Long-term liabilities Long-term liabilities are those obligations which are going to be met after one year or more.

Examples are term loans from banks and financial institutions, debentures, mortgage loans, etc.

Short-term liabilities   Obligations which are going to be met in a short span of time (within one year of the date of balance sheet) are called short-term liabilities. Examples of such liabilities are bank overdrafts, bill payable, unearned revenues, and outstanding expenses. Such short-term liabilities are widely known as current liabilities.

Estimated liabilities   There are certain liabilities with respect to goods delivered or services provided, where the amount of liability is not known precisely, as in the case of electricity charges, repairs, etc. These liabilities are certain and are not contingent. However, precise determination of such amounts is not possible at the time of preparing the final financial statements. Only approximate, estimated values of these liabilities are made in setting up the financial statements; hence they are known as estimated liabilities.

Contingent liabilities   A contingency is an occurrence that might arise in future. These liabilities are repayable only on the occurrence of such an event, otherwise not. Since these liabilities are uncertain, they don't appear in the balance sheet. However, they are shown as a footnote at the bottom of the balance sheet. Examples are as follows:

Liability against a suit pending in a court of law   This will become a liability when a firm loses a case in the court of law.

Liability in respect of guarantee given   In case the person/firm for whom guarantee is given by a firm fails to meet its obligations, the firm will be liable for such a guarantee.

Liability for bill discounts   In case the acceptor dishonours a bill discounted on the due date, the firm will become liable to the bank.

CURRENT LIABILITIES

Current liabilities represent short-term debts and obligations recognized in the books of accounts and are payable within one year. They include bank borrowings for short period, sundry creditors, bills payable, accrued employee benefits, income tax, dividend payable, long-term debts that are due for payment in the next year, etc.

A precise calculation of these liabilities can be made by using accounting information based on accounting events provided in accounts payable, bills payable, taxes, accrued liabilities with respect to payroll dues, etc. These are recognized in the books of account and are shown in the liabilities portion of the balance sheet. Current liabilities are discussed across various chapters. In this chapter discussions on owners' equity (i.e., share capital, reserve funds, and others funds) and long-term liabilities are covered.

OWNERS' EQUITY

The owners' equity or equity section of the balance sheet shows the amount the owners or shareholders have invested in the firm. Equity is the liability towards the firm's shareholders and is termed as shareholders' fund or shareholders' equity or just equity. The following three categories come under owners' equity:

1. Capital or share capital
2. Reserves and surplus
3. Money received against share warrants

Capital or Share Capital

In case of a sole proprietorship firm or partnership firm or limited liability partnership firm, this category of owners' equity shows the stated value of capital contributed by owners or partners to start the business and later on to run the firm's activities without any interruption, with an intention not to withdraw in the normal course of activities.

In case of a corporate firm, this category of owners' equity shows the stated value of the share certificates issued (issued share capital) and the value contributed by the shareholders to the share pool of the company (paid-up share capital).

Reserves and Surplus

This section of owners' equity represents the earnings foregone by the shareholders in the previous year(s) and retained with the firm or ploughed back into the operating activities of the firm. The net profit is apportioned to various reserves. Some of these are investment allowance reserve, rehabilitation reserve, dividend distribution reserve, contingency reserve, capital reserve, capital redemption reserve, securities premium reserve, debenture redemption reserve, etc.

The surplus, that is, balance in the statement of profit and loss is shown as a separate item under Reserves and Surplus. It is the accumulated balance of profits of the past years and also for the remaining part of the current year after all appropriations towards reserves and dividends are made. It may have a credit balance or debit balance. The current year's profit or loss is added to the balance of earlier years brought forward, from which appropriations towards other reserves and dividends are made.

The difference between statement of profit and loss and surplus (balance in statement of profit and loss statement) is that profit and loss is a statement which shows the profit earned or loss incurred during the accounting year. On the other hand, surplus is an item of Reserves and Surplus.

Money Received against Share Warrants

Share warrants are the financial instruments which give the holder the right to acquire equity shares at a specific date and at a specific rate. These are financial instruments which are converted into equity shares, and are classified or shown as shareholders' funds.

In between shareholders' funds and non-current liabilities, 'Share Application Money Pending Allotment' is shown.

Share Application Money Pending Allotment

The amount received by a company towards share application and against which it will certainly allot shares is shown against share application money pending allotment.

COMPANY

The human need to grow without bounds has given rise to the expansion of business activities, which in turn has necessitated the increase of the scale of operations in order to provide goods and services to the ever-increasing needs of the growing population of consumers. This requires money, modern technology, and large human contribution, which are not possible to arrange under partnership or proprietorship. The human mind has given rise to a concept of organizational form known as *joint stock company*, or simply a *company* or *corporation*. The company form of organization is one of the creations of the human mind that has enabled the business to carry on its wealth creation activities throughout the world. In course of time, the joint stock company has become the most important form of business enterprise.

In law, a *company* is defined as an entity which is formed and registered under the Companies Act, 1956 or an existing company formed and registered under any of the previous laws (an Act or Acts relating to companies before the Indian Companies Act, 1956). As per this definition of law, there must be a group of persons who agree to form a company under the law and once so formed, it becomes a separate legal entity with a distinct name of its own. Its existence is not affected by changes in the composition of its members. Generally, the capital of the company consists of transferable shares, and members have limited liabilities.

According to Justice Marshall, 'A corporation is an artificial being, invisible, intangible, and existing only in the contemplation of law'. Lord Justice Hanay has defined a company as 'an artificial person created by law with a perpetual succession and a common seal'.

> A corporation or company is an artificial entity.

CHARACTERISTICS OF A COMPANY

The characteristics of a company are discussed in this section.

Incorporated Association

A company comes into existence through the operation of law. Therefore, its incorporation under the Companies Act is imperative. Without such registration, no company can come into existence. Being created by law, it is regarded as an artificial legal person. Also, the registration provides the status of domicile to the company.

Separate Legal Entity

A company has a separate legal entity, which is not affected by changes in its membership. Mathematically, the separation of entity of company and that of members can be expressed as $(n + 1)$, where n is the number of members and 1 refers to the identity of the company. Therefore, a company, being a separate entity, can contract, sue, and be sued in its corporate name and capacity.

Perpetual Existence

Since a company has existence independent of its members, it continues to be in existence despite the death, insolvency, or change in the composition of its members.

Limited Liability

The liability of every shareholder of a company is limited to the amount he/she has agreed to pay to the company on the shares allotted to him/her. If such shares are fully paid up, he/she is subject to no further liability.

Divorce between Ownership and Management

The control and management of company's affairs are entrusted to the directors who are vested with the overall responsibility of management and operational control, even though the shareholders have contributed to the capital. Thus, the managers (directors) of the company carry on the business of the company on the basis of fiduciary relationship with the shareholders.

Common Seal

A company is not a natural person; hence, it cannot sign the documents in the same manner as a natural person. In order to enable the company to sign its document, it is provided with a legal arm known as *common seal*. The common seal is affixed on all documents by the person authorized to do so; he/she signs for and on behalf of the company.

Right of Access to Information

The right of the shareholders of a company to inspect its books of accounts, with the exception of books open for inspection under the Statute, is governed by the Articles of Association. The shareholders have a right to seek information from the directors by participating in the meetings of the company and through periodic reports.

Maintenance of Books

> A limited company is required to maintain books of accounts as prescribed by law.

A limited company is required by law to keep a prescribed set of account books and any failure in this regard attracts penalties.

Periodic Audit

A company has to get its accounts periodically audited through the chartered accountants appointed for the purpose by the shareholders on the recommendation of the board of directors.

Not a Citizen

A company is not a citizen in the same sense as a natural person is, though it is created through the process of law. It has a legal existence but does not enjoy the citizenship rights and duties as are enjoyed by the natural citizens.

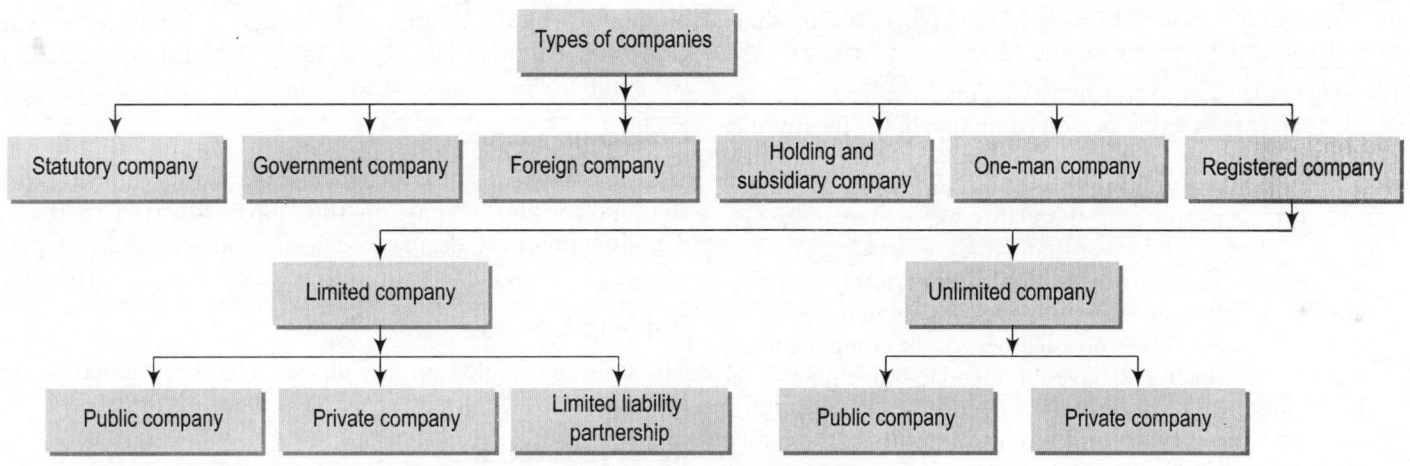

FIG. 11.1 Types of companies

TYPES OF COMPANIES

The different types of companies are detailed in this section (Fig. 11.1).

Statutory Company

All companies that operate under a special Act passed by the state legislature or parliament, such as the Reserve Bank of India, are known as statutory companies. Such companies are not required to use the word 'limited' as part of their name.

Government Company

Under Section 2(45) of the Companies Act, 2013, a government company is defined as 'any company in which not less than 51% of the paid-up share capital is held by the Central Government, or by any State Government or Governments, or partly by the Central Government and partly by one or more State Governments, and includes a company which is a subsidiary company of such a Government company'.

Thus, the important feature of a government company is not less than 51% ownership by central/state government, either individually or jointly. This definition includes what is generally known as public sector undertakings/enterprises in India.

A 'subsidiary company' or 'subsidiary' of a government company is actually a government company which (i) controls the composition of the Board of Directors; or (ii) exercises or controls more than one-half of the total share capital either at its own or together with one or more of its other subsidiary companies.

Foreign Company

As per Section 2(42) of the Companies Act, 2013, a foreign company is a body corporate incorporated outside India (a) with a place of business in India whether by itself or through an agent, physically or through electronic mode and (b) which conducts any business activity in India in any other manner.

Holding Company

As per Section 2(46) of the Companies Act, 2013, a holding company holds/owns at least 50% of other companies and has the authority to make management decisions, and influences and controls the company's board of directors. A holding company may even exist for the primary purpose of managing and controlling its subsidiary companies.

Subsidiary Company

Section 2(87) of the Companies Act, 2013 defines subsidiary company as the company that is controlled by the holding or parent company. It is a company/body corporate where the holding company controls the composition of the board of directors. As per the Companies Amendment Act, 2017, Section 2(87)(ii), if the holding company has control over more than one-half of the voting power of another company, that particular company will be identified as a subsidiary company.

Note: If a holding company owns 100% of the stock of another company, then the other company would be known as a whole-owned subsidiary of the holding company.

Incorporated or Registered Company

A company which is formed and registered under the Companies Act, 2013 is called an incorporated or registered company. It includes the companies which have earlier been registered under any of the previous Companies Act.

Public Company

Unser Section 2(71) of the Companies Act, 2013, a public company has been defined as a company which (a) is not a private company and (b) has a minimum paid-up share capital of five lakh rupees or such higher paid-up capital, as may be prescribed; provided that a company which is a subsidiary of a company and not a private company shall be deemed to be public company for the purposes of this Act even where such a subsidiary company continues to be a private company in its Articles. It is nowhere mentioned regarding the minimum number of members for a public company (i.e., seven).

Private Company

As per Section 2(68) of the Companies Act, 2013, a private company means a company which has a minimum paid-up share capital of one lakh rupees or such higher paid-up share capital as may be prescribed, and which by its Articles,

- restricts the right to transfer its shares;
- except in case of a one-person company, limits the number of its members to 200; provided that where two or more persons hold one or more shares in a company jointly, they shall, for the purposes of this clause, be treated as a single member: Provided further that—

(A) persons who are in the employment of the company; and (B) persons who, having been formerly in the employment of the company, were members of the company while in that employment and have continued to be members after the employment ceased, shall not be included in the number of members; and (iii) prohibits any invitation to the public to subscribe for any securities of the company.

This definition clearly states that a maximum number of members that a private limited company can accommodate is 200 which previously was just 50. Also, the same Act mentions that the financial year for balance sheet will be 31st of March for all the companies.

One-man Company

As per provision of Section 2(62) of the Companies Act, 2013, a one-man company is defined as a company which has only one person as its member.

Limited Liability Partnership

As per the Limited Liability Partnership Act, 2008, a limited liability partnership is a corporate business vehicle that enables professional expertise and entrepreneurial initiative to combine and operate in flexible, innovative, and efficient manner, providing benefits of limited liability while allowing its members the flexibility for organizing their internal structure as a partnership.

SHARE CAPITAL OF A COMPANY

Share capital is the amount of money contributed by shareholders for the furtherance of the objectives of the company for which it was created. It is divided into six categories.

Authorized, Registered, or Nominal Capital

This is the amount stated in the 'capital clause' of the Memorandum of Association, with which the company is registered. On registration, an ad valorem duty is paid on the amount of authorized capital. Since the company is registered with a given amount of share capital, on incorporation, it becomes entitled to issue shares of that much amount and number. Hence, it is also referred to as authorized capital.

Issued Capital

It is the part of authorized capital, which is offered to the public for subscription, including shares offered to the vendors for subscription other than cash.

Subscribed Capital

It is that part of issued capital that represents the face or nominal value of shares subscribed for by persons, that is,

applied for by prospective shareholders and allotted by the company. This also includes the face value of shares issued by the company for consideration other than cash.

Called-up Capital

It is the portion of subscribed capital that the directors require the shareholder to pay on the shares allotted to them. The directors may decide to call the entire amount or part of the amount of the face value of the shares as the need may be.

Paid-up Capital

The amount of called-up capital, which has been actually paid by the shareholders, is referred to as paid-up capital.

Reserve Capital

A company may decide by special resolution that a certain portion of its uncalled capital shall not be available for being called up except in the event, and for the purpose, of liquidation. Such a portion is called reserve capital.

■ **ILLUSTRATION 11.1** A limited company has been incorporated with an authorized capital of ₹10,00,000 divided into 1,00,000 shares of ₹10 each. It offered 90,000 shares for subscription by the public and, out of these, 85,000 shares were subscribed for. The directors called for an amount of ₹6 per share and received the entire amount except a call for ₹2 per share on 500 shares. Calculate the amount of different categories of share capital.

Solution

Types of Share Capital

Particulars	No. of Shares	Price Per Share (₹)	Amount (₹)
(a) Authorized capital	1,00,000	10	10,00,000
(b) Issued capital	90,000	10	9,00,000
(c) Unissued capital (a – b)	10,000	10	1,00,000
(d) Subscribed capital	85,000	10	8,50,000
(e) Unsubscribed capital (b – d)	5,000	10	50,000
(f) Called-up capital	85,000	6	5,10,000
(g) Uncalled capital (d – f)	85,000	4	3,40,000
(h) Paid-up capital	85,000	6 – 500 × 2	5,09,000
(i) Calls-in-arrears (f – h)	500	2	1,000

Note:

Calls-in-arrears is the difference between the called-up capital and paid-up capital.

SHARES OF A COMPANY

According to Justice Farwel, 'A share is the interest of a shareholder in the company measured by a sum of money, for the purpose of liability in the first place and of interest in the second, but also consisting of mutual covenants entered into by all the shareholders in terms of the Act and the Articles'. Therefore, a share is a fractional part of the share capital and

forms the basis of ownership interest in a company. The persons who contribute money through shares are referred to as shareholders. Any company can have two types of shares—(a) preference shares; and (b) equity shares.

Equity Shares

According to Section 43 of the Companies Act, 2013, equity share capital means all share capital which is not preference share capital. Equity share capital may be divided into (i) Equity share capital with voting right; or (ii) Equity share capital with differential rights.

This 'differential rights' may have difference related to dividend, voting, or otherwise in accordance with rules. The term 'otherwise' brings scope for innovation within the limit of rules. It may be difference related to managing control, power to appoint director, or power to appoint proxy and so on.

Preference Shares

According to Section 85 of the Companies Act, 1956, a preference share fulfils the following conditions:

1. It carries a preferential right to dividend to be paid either as a fixed amount or an amount calculated by a fixed rate which may be either free of or subject to income tax
2. With respect to capital it carries or will carry, on the winding up of the company, the right to the repayment of capital before anything is paid to equity shareholders.

However, notwithstanding the two conditions, a holder of a preference share may have a right to share fully or to a limited extent in the surpluses of the company as specified in the Memorandum or Articles of the company. Preference shares can be of various types.

Cumulative preference shares

A cumulative preference share is one that carries the right to a fixed amount of dividend or dividend at a fixed rate. Such a dividend is payable even out of future profits if the current year's profits are insufficient for the purpose. This means that dividend on these shares accumulates unless it is paid in full and, therefore, the shares are known as cumulative preference shares. The arrears of dividend are then shown in the balance sheet as a contingent liability.

Non-cumulative preference shares

A non-cumulative preference share carries with it the right to a fixed amount of dividend. In case no dividend is declared in a year due to any reason, the right to receive such dividend for that year expires. It implies that the holder of such a share is not entitled to arrears of dividend in future.

Participating preference shares

Notwithstanding the right to a fixed dividend, this category of preference share confers on the holder the right to participate in the surplus profits, if any, after the equity shareholders have been paid dividend at a stipulated rate. Similarly, in the event of winding up of the company, this type of share carries the right to receive a pre-determined proportion of surplus as well, once the equity shareholders have been paid.

Non-participating preference shares

Shares on which only a fixed rate of dividend is paid every year, without any accompanying additional rights in profits and in the surplus on winding up, are known as non-participating preference shares.

Redeemable preference shares

These are shares that a company may issue on the condition that the company will repay after the fixed period or even earlier at the company's discretion. The repayment on these shares is called redemption and is governed by Section 80 of the Companies Act, 1956.

Non-redeemable preference shares

Preference shares that do not carry with them the arrangement regarding redemption are known as non-redeemable preference shares.

Convertible preference shares

These shares give the right to the holder to get them converted into equity shares at their option according to the terms and conditions of their issue.

Non-convertible preference shares

A non-convertible preference share is a preference share that may not be converted into an equity share.

According to Section 43 of the Companies Act, 2013, preference share capital of the issued share capital of the company which carries or would carry a preference right with respect to (a) payment of dividend, either as a fixed amount or an amount calculated at a fixed rate; which may be either free of or subject to income tax; and (b) repayment of amount of share capital or share capital deemed to be paid up, whether or not, there is preferential right specified in the memorandum or article of the company.

This Act does not interfere in the rights of preference shareholders who are entitled to participate in the proceeds of winding up before commencement of this Act.

Sweat Equity Shares

As per Section 2(88) of the Companies Act, 2013, sweat equity shares are such equity shares which are issued by a company to its directors or employees at a discount or for consideration, other than cash, for providing their know-how or making available rights in the nature of intellectual property rights or value additions, by whatever name called.

Employee

As per Explanation (i) of Rule 8(1) of the Companies (Share Capital and Debentures) Rules, 2014, employee means (a) a permanent employee of a company who has been working in India or outside India, for at least last one year; or (b) a director of the company, whether a whole time director or not; or (c) an employee or a director as defined in sub-clauses (a) or

(b) above of a subsidiary, in India or outside India, or of a holding company of the company;

Value additions

As per Explanation (ii) of Rule 8(1) of the Companies (Share Capital and Debentures) Rules, 2014, employee means actual or anticipated economic benefits derived or to be derived by the company from an expert or a professional for providing know-how or making available rights in the nature of intellectual property rights, by such person to whom sweat equity is being issued for which the consideration is not paid or included in the normal remuneration payable under the contract of employment, in the case of an employee.

Employee Stock Option

The idea that employees should have an ownership stake in the company led to the emergence of the concept of Employee Stock Option Plan (ESOP). The concept of ESOP is believed to belong to an American lawyer, economist, and philosopher, Louis Kelso, who convinced a Senator from Louisiana to support legislation legalizing ESOPs. The definition of 'Employee Stock Option' was first incorporated by way of a clause (15A) in Section 2 of the Companies Act, 1956, based on the recommendations of the Working Group. Section 62 of the Companies Act, 2013 further incorporates enabling provision for the issue of ESOPs subject to the sanction of special resolution and compliance with Rules (in case of unlisted public company) and SEBI Regulations (in case of listed companies).

ISSUE OF SHARES

The shares of a company can be issued (a) for cash, or (b) for consideration other than cash.

Issue of Shares for Cash

A salient characteristic of the capital of a company is that the amount on its shares can be gradually collected in easy instalments spread over time depending upon its growing financial requirements. However, this in no way prevents a company from calling for the full amount on shares right at the time of application. Shares may be issued either at par, or at premium, or at a discount. Shares are said to have been issued at par when their issue price is exactly equal to their nominal/face value according to the terms and conditions of the issue. When the issue price is more than the par value, the difference is known as premium, and the issue is said to have been made at a premium. In contrast to this, the issue price may be less than the par value, then the issue is said to have been made at a discount.

Application for shares

The starting point for the issue of share capital is the application for shares by prospective investors. When applications for shares along with the money have been received, the journal entry is as follows:

Bank A/c (*Add*) Dr.(Total amount received on application)
       To Share application A/c (*Add*)
(Amount received on applications for _____ shares @ ₹ per share)

Allotment of shares

The allotment of shares means acceptance by the company of the offer made by the applicants to take up the shares applied for. In this way, a contract is made between the company and the applicants who now become the allottees and get the status of shareholders or members.

Accounting Entries

1. *Transfer of application money*
   Share application A/c (*Less*)   Dr.
   (Number of shares allotted × Application money per share)
        To Share capital A/c (*Add*)
   (Application money on _____ shares allotted/transferred to share capital)
   Note:
   In case all the shares applied for have been allotted, share application account would be automatically closed after this entry.

2. *Money refunded on regretted applications*
   Share application A/c (*Less*)   Dr.
   (Number of shares regretted × Application money per share)
        To Bank A/c (*Less*)
   (Application money returned on rejected application for _____ shares)

3. *Amount due on allotment*
   Share allotment A/c (*Add*)   Dr.
   (Number of shares allotted × Allotment amount per share)
        To Share capital A/c (*Add*)
   (Amount due on the allotment of _____ shares @ ₹ _____ per share)

4. *Adjustment of excess application money*
   Share application A/c (*Less*)   Dr.
   (Application amount received – (Application money transferred to share capital + Money refunded))
        To Share allotment A/c (*Less*)
   (Application amount of _____ shares @ ₹ _____ per share adjusted to the amount due on allotment)

5. *Receipt of allotment amount*
   Bank A/c (*Add*)   Dr.
        To Share allotment A/c (*Less*)
   (Allotment money received on _____ shares @ ₹ _____ per share)

Call on shares

In the event of shares not being fully called up until the completion of allotment, the directors have the authority to call for the

remaining amount on shares as and when they decide about the same. It is also possible that the timing of the payment of calls by the shareholders is determined by the terms and conditions of share issue, that is, fixed in the prospectus itself. Any number of calls—first call, second call, third call, and final call—may be made to get the full face value of the shares in cash.

Accounting Treatment

When a call is made on the shares and the amount of the same is received, the journal entries are as given in the following text.

1. *Call amount due*
   Share call A/c (*Add*)   Dr.
   (Number of Shares × Call amount per share)
       To Share capital A/c (*Add*)
   (Call money due on _____ shares @ ₹ _____ per share)
2. *Receipt of call amount*
   Bank A/c (*Add*)   Dr.

    To Share call A/c (*Less*)
(Call money received)

Note:
The name of the call, namely, first, second, and final, is added between the words 'share' and 'call' in the entry depending upon the identity of the call made, such as, share first call, share second call, share third call, etc.

■ **ILLUSTRATION 11.2** Zankara Tele Systems Ltd has offered to the public 20,000 shares of ₹100 each for subscription, payable as ₹30 per share on application, ₹30 per share on allotment, and the balance on call. Applications were received for 30,000 shares. Applications for 5000 shares were rejected altogether and the application money was returned. The remaining applicants were allotted the offered shares.

The excess application money was adjusted towards the sum due on allotment. Calls were made and duly received. Make journal entries in the books of the company.

Solution

Journal Entries in the Books of Zankara Tele Systems Ltd

Sr. No.	Particulars		L.F.	Dr. (₹)	Cr. (₹)
1	Bank A/c (*Add*)	Dr.		9,00,000	
	To Share application A/c (*Add*)				9,00,000
	(Application money received for 30,000 shares @ ₹30 per share)				
2	Share application A/c (*Less*)	Dr.		9,00,000	
	To Share capital A/c (*Add*)				6,00,000
	To Bank A/c (*Less*)				1,50,000
	To Share allotment A/c (*Less*)				1,50,000
	(Application money of 20,000 shares was transferred to the share capital A/c on their allotment. The application money of 5,000 shares was returned, and that of 5,000 shares was adjusted towards the sum due on allotment.)				
3	Share allotment A/c (*Add*)	Dr.		6,00,000	
	To Share capital A/c (*Add*)				6,00,000
	(Allotment money due)				
4	Bank A/c (*Add*)	Dr.		4,50,000	
	To Share allotment A/c (*Less*)				4,50,000
	(Allotment money received)				
5	Share first and final call A/c (*Add*)			8,00,000	
	To Share capital A/c (*Add*)				8,00,000
	(Call money due)				
6	Bank A/c (*Add*)	Dr.		8,00,000	
	To Share first and final call A/c (*Less*)				8,00,000
	(Call money received)				

■ **ILLUSTRATION 11.3** On 1 January 2020, a limited company was incorporated with an authorized capital of ₹4,00,000 divided into shares of ₹100 each.

It offered to the public for subscription 3,000 shares payable thus.

On application	₹30 per share
On allotment	₹20 per share
On first call (One month after allotment)	₹25 per share

On second call (Three months after allotment) ₹25 per share

The shares were fully subscribed for by the public and application money duly received on 15 January 2020. The directors made the allotment on 1 February 2020.

Record journal entries in the books of the company to record these share capital transactions, assuming that amount due have been received within 15 days of making the allotment and calls.

Solution

Separate Accounts for Application and Allotment Books of Company Journal

Date 2020	Particulars		L.F.	Dr. (₹)	Cr. (₹)
15 Jan.	Bank A/c (*Add*)	Dr.		90,000	
	To Equity share application A/c (*Add*)				90,000
	(Money received on applications for 3,000 shares @ ₹30 per share)				
1 Feb.	Equity share application A/c (*Less*)	Dr.		90,000	
	To Equity share capital A/c (*Add*)				90,000
	(Transfer of application money on 3,000 shares to share capital)				

1 Feb.	Equity share allotment A/c (*Add*) To Equity share capital A/c (*Add*) (Amount due on the allotment of 3,000 shares @ ₹20 per share)	Dr.	60,000		60,000
15 Feb.	Bank A/c (*Add*) To Equity share allotment A/c (*Less*) (Allotment money received)	Dr.	60,000		60,000
1 Mar.	Equity share first call A/c (*Add*) To Equity share capital A/c (*Add*) (First call money due on 3,000 shares @ ₹25 per share)	Dr.	75,000		75,000
15 Mar.	Bank A/c (*Add*) To Equity share first call A/c (*Less*) (First call money received)	Dr.	75,000		75,000
1 May	Equity share second and final call A/c (*Add*) To Equity share capital A/c (*Add*) (Final call money due on 3,000 shares @ ₹25 per share)	Dr.	75,000		75,000
15 May	Bank A/c (*Add*) To Equity share second and final call A/c (*Less*) (Final call money received)	Dr.	75,000		75,000

Note:

In case nothing is mentioned regarding the class of shares issued, they are always taken to be equity shares.

Calls-in-arrears

Sometimes, shareholders fail to pay the amount due on allotment or calls. The total unpaid amount on one or more instalments is known as calls-in-arrears or unpaid calls.

For recording calls-in-arrears, the following journal entry is recorded.

    Calls-in-arrears A/c (*Add*) Dr.   (Amount of unpaid calls)
        To Share allotment A/c (*Less*)
        To Share call A/c (*Less*)

The Articles of Association of a company usually empower the directors to charge interest at a stipulated rate on calls-in-arrears. According to Table F of the Companies Act, 2013, interest at the rate of 10% p.a. is to be charged on unpaid calls for the period intervening between the due date of the call and the time of actual payment.

The journal entries for calls-in-arrears are as follows:

1. *For interest receivable on calls-in-arrears*
    Sundry members (shareholders') A/c (*Add*)   Dr.
        To Interest on calls-in-arrears A/c (*Add*)
2. *For receipt of interest*
    Bank A/c (*Add*)   Dr.
        To Sundry members (shareholders') A/c (*Less*)

■ **ILLUSTRATION 11.4** Solar Ltd made its first call of ₹20 per share on 1 July 2020. Rakesh, holding 200 shares, failed to pay the call money. He could pay the money only on 31 December 2020. The company charged interest @12% per month. Make the necessary journal entry for the interest charged by the company.

Solution

$$\text{Amount of interest due} = 4000 \times \frac{2}{100} \times \frac{6}{12} = 240$$

Journal Entries

Sr. No.	Particulars		L.F.	Dr. (₹)	Cr. (₹)
1	Bank A/c	Dr.		240	
	To Interest on calls-in-arrears A/c				240
	(Receipt of interest on calls-in-arrears)				

Calls-in-advance

Some shareholders may sometimes pay a part, or whole of the amount not yet called up, such amount is known as calls-in-advance. According to Table F, interest at the rate of 12% is to be paid on such advance call money. This amount is credited in the calls-in-advance account.

    Bank A/c (*Add*)   Dr.
        To Calls-in-advance A/c (*Add*)

When calls become actually due, calls-in-advance account is adjusted at the time of the call. For this, the following journal entry is recorded:

    Calls-in-advance A/c (*Less*)   Dr.
    (Call amount due)
        To Particular call A/c (*Less*)

The accounting treatment of interest on Calls-in-advance is as follows:

1. *Interest Due*
    Interest on calls-in-advance A/c (*Add*)   Dr.
    (Amount of interest due for payment)
        To Sundry members (shareholders') A/c (*Add*)
2. *Payment of Interest*
Sundry members (shareholders') A/c
        (*Less*)   Dr.
    (Amount of interest paid)
        To Bank A/c (*Less*)
    (Interest paid on calls-in-advance)

> The shareholders pay in advance the uncalled amount known as calls-in-advance.

■ **ILLUSTRATION 11.5** Vivaan Retailers Ltd offered 50,000 shares of ₹10 each to the public, payable as ₹2 on application, ₹3 on allotment, ₹2 on the first call, and the balance as and when required.

All the shares were applied for and duly allotted, but Mehmood, a shareholder holding 200 shares, paid the entire balance on allotment. Make the necessary journal entries.

Solution

Journal Entries in the Books of Vivaan Retailers Ltd

Sr. No.	Particulars	L.F.	Dr. (₹)	Cr. (₹)
1	Bank A/c (*Add*) Dr. To Share application A/c (*Add*) (Application received for 50,000 shares @ ₹2 per share)		1,00,000	1,00,000
2	Share application A/c (*Less*) Dr. To Share capital A/c (*Add*) (Application money transferred to the share capital A/c on allotment)		1,00,000	1,00,000
3	Share allotment A/c (*Add*) Dr. To Share capital A/c (*Add*) (Share allotment money due on 50000 shares @ ₹3 per share)		1,50,000	1,50,000

6	Bank A/c (*Add*) Dr.
	    To Share allotment A/c (*Less*)
	    To Calls-in-advance A/c (*Add*)
	(Allotment money received)
			1,51,000	1,50,000
				1,000

7	Share first and final call A/c (*Add*) To Share capital A/c (*Add*) (Share call money due on 50,000 shares @ ₹2 per share.)		1,00,000	1,00,000
8	Bank A/c (*Add*) Dr. Calls-in-advance A/c (*Less*) Dr. To Share first and final cal A/c (*Less*) (First call money is received on 49,800 shares, and call-in-advance is adjusted on 200 shares)		99,600 400	1,00,000

Over-subscription and pro-rata allotment

The offer response from the investors' community would be considered as encouraging if the number of applications received from the public is more than the issue size (number of shares offered by the company for public subscription); this is known as over-subscription.

In any case, if a company has offered a specific number of shares to the public, it cannot allot more shares. The Securities and Exchange Board of India (SEBI) has provided guidelines to ensure that allotments are made among the applicants on a proportional basis in case of over-subscription; this is widely known as pro-rata allotment.

According to the SEBI guidelines, and the generally adopted practices by companies in India, the directors of a company have three alternatives to deal with over-subscription:

- Rejection of share applications: a few applicants may not be allotted any shares
- Pro-rata allotment: some applicants may be allotted a fewer number of shares than they applied for
- Full allotment: a few applicants may be allotted all the shares they applied for

Pro-rata allotment In these situations, the applicants may be allotted a fewer number of shares than they applied for. The excess money received along with the application will be adjusted on account of the money due on allotment. Generally, companies do not return the excess application money and ask for it later, in order to save the transaction costs. The following accounting entry is passed in the books of accounts with respect to the adjustment of the excess application money against the allotment money due.

Share application A/c   Dr
(Excess application money received)
To Share allotment A/c
(Excess application money transferred to share capital A/c)
(Excess application money received on shares @ ₹ transferred to allotment)

■ **ILLUSTRATION 11.6** Jeeyansh Ltd issued 50,000 shares of ₹10 each, payable as ₹3 on application, ₹4 on allotment, and the balance on call. Applications for 70,000 shares had been received. Applications for 8000 shares were rejected and the remaining applicants were allotted the 50,000 shares on a pro-rata basis. The excess amount on application was adjusted towards the amount due on allotment. All the shareholders paid the amount due. Journalize the transactions.

Solution

Over-subscription—Pro-rata allotment:

Particulars	Number of Shares (₹)	Amount (₹)
Number of applications received	70,000 × 3	2,10,000
Less: Transferred to share capital	50,000 × 3	1,50,000
Excess application money	20,000 × 3	60,000
Less: Refunded	8,000 × 3	24.000
Excess money to be adjusted towards allotment money	12,000 × 3	36,000

Calculation of allotment money to be received:

	Amount (₹)
50,000 shares of ₹4 each	2,00,000
Less: Excess Application money adjusted towards allotment money (12,000 × 3)	36,000
Money to be received	1,64,000

Journal Entries in the Books of Jeeyansh Ltd

Sr. No.	Particulars	L.F.	Dr. (₹)	Cr. (₹)
1	Bank A/c (*Add*) Dr. To Share application A/c (*Add*) (Application received for 70,000 shares)		2,10,000	2,10,000
2	Share application A/c (*Less*) Dr. To Share capital A/c (*Add*) (Application money received on 50,000 shares @ ₹3 per share transferred to share capital)		1,50,000	1,50,000
3	Share application A/c (*Less*) Dr. To Bank A/c (*Less*) (Application money on 8,000 shares @ ₹3 per share refunded)		24,000	24,000
4	Share application A/c (*Less*) Dr. To Share allotment A/c (*Less*) (Surplus application money on 12,000 shares @ ₹3 per share adjusted towards allotment)		36,000	36,000
5	Share allotment A/c (*Add*) Dr. To Share capital A/c (*Add*) (Allotment money due on 50,000 shares @ ₹4 per share)		2,00,000	2,00,000
6	Bank A/c (*Add*) Dr. To Share allotment A/c (*Less*) (Allotment money received)		1,64,000	1,64,000
7	Share first and final call A/c (*Add*) To Share capital A/c (*Add*) (Share call money made due on 50,000 shares @ ₹3 per share.)		1,50,000	1,50,000
8	Bank A/c (*Add*) Dr. To Share first and final call A/c (*Less*) (Being call money received)		1,50,000	1,50,000

■ **ILLUSTRATION 11.7** A limited company, with an authorized capital of ₹2,00,000 divided into shares of ₹100 each, issued for subscription 1,000 shares payable at ₹25 per share on application, ₹30 per share on allotment, ₹20 per share on first call three months after allotment, and the balance as and when required. The subscription list closed on 31 January 2020 when application money on 1,000 shares was duly received and allotment was made on 1 March 2020. The allotment amount was received in full but, when the first call was made, one shareholder failed to pay the amount on 100 shares held by him and another shareholder with 50 shares paid the entire amount on her shares. Give journal entries in the books of the company to record these share capital transactions assuming that all amounts due were received within one month of the date they were called.

Solution

Journal Entries in the Books of the Company

Date 2020	Particulars	L.F.	Dr. (₹)	Cr. (₹)
31 Jan.	Bank A/c (*Add*) Dr. To Equity share application A/c (*Add*) (Money received on applications for 1,000 shares @ ₹25 per share)		25,000	25,000
1 March	Equity share application A/c (*Less*) Dr. To Equity share capital A/c (*Add*) (Transfer of application money on 1,000 shares to share capital)		25,000	25,000
1 March	Equity share allotment A/c (*Add*) Dr. To Equity share capital A/c (*Add*) (Amount due on the allotment of 1,000 shares @ ₹30 per share)		30,000	30,000
1 April	Bank A/c (*Add*) Dr. To Equity share allotment A/c (*Less*) (Allotment money received)		30,000	30,000
1 June	Equity share first call A/c (*Add*) Dr. To Equity share capital A/c (*Add*) (First call money due on 1,000 shares @ ₹20 per share)		20,000	20,000

1 July	Bank A/c (*Add*) Dr.
	 Calls-in-arrears A/c (*Add*) Dr.
	      To Equity share first call A/c (*Less*)
	      To Calls-in-advance A/c (*Add*)
	 (First call money received on 900 shares and calls-in-advance on 50 shares @ ₹25 per share)
			19,250
			 2,000
				20,000
				 1,250

Issue of shares at a premium

When a company issues its securities at a price that exceeds the face value, it is said to be an issue at a premium. Premium is the excess of issue price over face value of the security. It is quite common for the financially strong and well-managed companies to issue their shares at a premium, that is, at an amount more than the nominal or par value of shares. Thus, where a share of the nominal value of ₹100 is issued at ₹105, it is said to have been issued at a premium of 5%. When shares are issued at a premium, the journal entries are as follows:

1. *Premium amount called with application money*
    1. Bank A/c (*Add*)   Dr.
        (Total application money + Premium amount)
        To Share application A/c (*Add*)(Amount received)
        (Money received on applications for _____ shares @ ₹ _____ per share including premium)
    2. Share application A/c (*Less*)   Dr.
        (Number of shares applied for × Application amount per share)
        To Securities premium A/c (*Add*)
        (Number of shares allotted × Premium amount per share)
        To Share capital A/c (*Add*)
        (Number of shares allotted × Per share for capital)
2. *Premium amount called with allotment money*
    1. Share allotment A/c (*Add*)   Dr.
        (Number of shares allotted × Allotment and premium money per share)
        To Share capital A/c (*Add*)
        (Number of shares allotted × Allotment amount per share)
        To Securities premium A/c (*Add*)
        (Number of shares Allotted × Premium amount per share)

(Amount due on allotment of shares @ ₹ _____ per share including premium)

2. Bank A/c (*Add*)   Dr.
    To Share allotment A/c (*Less*)
    (Money received including premium consequent upon allotment)

According to Section 52 of the Companies Act, 2013, the amount of share premium can be utilized

(a) towards the issue of unissued shares of the company to the members of the company as fully paid bonus shares;

(b) in writing off the preliminary expenses of the company;

(c) in writing off the expenses of, or the commission paid or discount allowed on, any issue of shares or debentures of the company;

(d) in providing for the premium payable on the redemption of any redeemable preference shares or of any debentures of the company; or

(e) for the purchase of its own shares or other securities under Section 68.

Further, the company may demand the total amount of premium in more than one instalment. In case the company does not specify the particular call with which the security premium is to be paid, it is supposed to be called at the time of allotment.

■ **ILLUSTRATION 11.8** Electro Cars Ltd issued 1,00,000 shares of ₹10 each at a premium of ₹5 per share, payable as follows:

On application	₹4 (including ₹2 premium) per share
On allotment	₹8 (including ₹3 premium) per share
On call	₹3 per share

Applications were received for 1,00,000 shares and allotment was made to all. Make journal entries.

Solution

Journal Entries in the Books of Electro Cars Ltd

Sr. No.	Particulars	L.F.	Dr. (₹)	Cr. (₹)
1	Bank A/c (*Add*) Dr.		4,00,000	
	To Share application A/c (*Add*)			4,00,000
	(Application received for 1,00,000 shares)			
2	Share application A/c (*Less*) Dr.		4,00,000	
	To Share capital A/c (*Add*)			2,00,000
	To Securities premium A/c (*Add*)			2,00,000
	(Share application money transferred to share capital A/c and Securities Premium A/c)			
3	Bank A/c (*Add*) Dr.		8,00,000	
	To Share allotment A/c (*Less*)			8,00,000
	(Allotment money is received on 1,00,000 shares @ ₹8 per share)			
4	Share allotment A/c (*Add*) Dr.		8,00,000	
	To Share capital A/c (*Add*)			5,00,000
	To Securities premium A/c (*Add*)			3,00,000
	(Share allotment money made due)			
5	Share first and final call A/c (*Add*)		3,00,000	
	To Share capital A/c (*Add*)			3,00,000
	(Share call money due on 1,00,000 shares @ ₹3 per share.)			
6	Bank A/c (*Add*) Dr.		3,00,000	
	To Share first and final call A/c (*Less*)			3,00,000
	(Share call money received on 1,00,000 shares @ ₹3 per share.)			

Issue of shares at discount

There are instances when the shares of a company can also be issued at a discount, that is, at an amount less than the nominal or par value of shares. The excess of the nominal value over the issue price represents discount on the issue of shares. For example, when a share of the nominal value of ₹100 is issued at ₹98, it is said to have been issued at a discount of 2%. The journal entry to record discount on the issue of shares is given in the following text.

Share allotment A/c (Add)	Dr.
Discount on the issue of shares A/c (Add)	Dr.
To Share capital A/c (Add)	

(Amount due on allotment of _____ shares @ ₹ _____ per share and discount on issue brought into account)

Discount on the issue of shares account, showing a debit balance, denotes a loss to the company, which is in the nature of a capital loss. Therefore, the account is presented on the asset side of the company's balance sheet under miscellaneous expenditure. It is written off by charging it to the securities premium account if any, and, in its absence, by charging to the profit and loss account over a period of time.

The amount of discount offered on shares is a loss to the company. Section 53 of the Companies Act, 2013 has laid down certain conditions subject to which a company can issue its shares at a discount.

These conditions are as follows:

(a) The shares must belong to a class already issued.
(b) Discount rate should not be more than 10%.
(c) One year must have passed since the date at which the company was allowed to commence business.
(d) The issue of such shares must take place within two months after the date of court's sanction or within such extended time as the court may allow.
(e) The issue must be authorised by a resolution passed by the company in general meeting and sanctioned by the Company Law Board.

■ **ILLUSTRATION 11.9** Sri Raja Agritech Ltd was registered with a capital of ₹50,00,000, divided into 50,000 shares of ₹100 each. It issued 10,000 shares at a discount of ₹10 per share, payable as follows:

₹40 per share on application
₹30 per share on allotment
₹20 per share on call

The company received applications for 15,000 shares. Applicants for 12,000 shares were allotted 10,000 shares and the applicants of the remaining shares were sent letters of regret and their application money was returned. Calls were made. Allotment and call money were duly received. Make journal entries in the books of the company.

Solution

Journal Entries in the Books of Sri Raja Agritech Ltd

Sr. No.	Particulars		L.F.	Dr. (₹)	Cr. (₹)
1	Bank A/c (Add)	Dr.		6,00,000	
	To Share application A/c (Add)				6,00,000
	(Application money received for 15,000 shares @ ₹40 per share)				
2	Share application A/c (Less)	Dr.		4,00,000	
	To Share capital A/c (Add)				4,00,000
	(Application money of 10,000 shares transferred to share capital A/c on their allotment.)				
3	Share allotment A/c (Add)	Dr.		2,00,000	
	To Share capital A/c (Add)				80,000
	To Bank A/c (Less)				1,20,000
	(Application money of 3,000 shares returned and of 2,000 shares adjusted towards sum due on allotment)				
4	Shares allotment A/c (Add)	Dr.		3,00,000	
	Share discount A/c (Add)	Dr.		1,00,000	
	To Share capital A/c (Add)				4,00,000
	(Allotment money due)				
5	Bank A/c (Add)	Dr.		2,20,000	
	To Share allotment A/c (Less)				2,20,000
	(Allotment money received)				
6	Share first and final call A/c (Add)			2,00,000	
	To Share capital A/c (Add)				2,00,000
	(Call money due)				
7	Bank A/c (Add)	Dr.		2,00,000	
	To Share first and final call A/c (Less)				2,00,000
	(Call money received)				

FORFEITURE OF SHARES

It may happen that certain shareholders fail to pay one or more instalments, namely allotment money and/or call money. In such circumstances, the company can forfeit their shares by giving due notice and following the procedure specified in the Articles of Association on this behalf. To forfeit a share means

Forfeit means cancelling the name of the defaulting shareholder from the register of members.

to cancel the allotment of the defaulting shareholders and to treat the amount already received thereon as forfeited to the company within the framework of provisions embodied in the Articles of Association.

1. *Forfeiture of shares issued at par*

   When the shares issued at par are forfeited, the journal entry required to record the forfeiture is as follows:

   Share capital A/c (*Less*)   Dr.
   (Amount called-up)
       To Share forfeited A/c (*Add*)
   (Amount received)
       To Share allotment A/c (*Less*)
   (Amount called-up but unpaid)
       To Share call/calls A/c (*Less*)

   Note: In case calls-in-arrears account is maintained by the company, 'Calls-in-arrears' account would be credited in the entry discussed earlier instead of share allotment and/or share call/calls accounts.

2. *Forfeiture of shares issued at a premium*

   1. When premium is received: Where shares originally issued at a premium, on which premium amount has been fully realized, are later on forfeited due to non-payment of allotment or call money, accounting treatment of forfeiture would be on the same pattern as in the case of shares issued at par. Thus, securities premium account is not to be debited at the time of forfeiture. Following is the journal entry:

      Share capital A/c (*Less*)   Dr.
      (Amount called-up)
          To Share forfeited A/c (*Add*)
      (Amount received on capital account)
          To Share allotment A/c (*Less*)
      (Amount called-up but unpaid)
          To Share call/calls A/c (*Less*)

   2. When premium is not received: However, if shares originally issued at a premium on which the premium amount has not been received either wholly or partially, are subsequently forfeited, securities premium account is debited, with the full amount of premium along with the share capital account at the time of forfeiture.

      Share capital A/c (*Less*)   Dr.
      (Amount called-up)
      Securities premium A/c (*Less*)   Dr.
      (Amount of premium not received)
          To Share forfeited A/c (*Add*)
      (Amount received on capital account)

    To Share allotment A/c (*Less*)
(Amount unpaid)
    To Share call/calls A/c (*Less*)

3. *Forfeiture of shares issued at a discount*

   When shares forfeited were originally issued at a discount, the discount applicable to such shares must be cancelled or written back. In view of the fact that the discount on the issue of shares is a loss debited at the time of issue, it should be credited at the time of forfeiture in order that the balance on discount on issue of shares account relates only to the remaining shares forming part of the share capital amount.

   When the shares issued at a discount are forfeited, the journal entry to record the forfeiture is as thus:

   Share capital A/c (*Less*)   Dr.
   (Amount called up)
       To Forfeited shares A/c (*Add*)
   (Amount received)
       To Discount on issue of shares A/c (*Less*)
   (Discount on forfeited shared)
       To Calls-in-arrears A/c (*Less*)
   (Amount unpaid)

■ **ILLUSTRATION 11.10** Mushkara Ltd issued 5,000 shares of ₹10 each at par payable as ₹3 per share on application, ₹3 per share on allotment, ₹2 per share on first call, and ₹2 on final call. Reema was allotted 50 shares. Give the necessary journal entries relating to forfeiture of shares in each of the following alternative cases.

1. If Reema failed to pay the first call money, and his shares were forfeited
2. If Reema failed to pay both the calls, and his shares were forfeited

Solution

Journal Entries in the Books of March Ltd

Sr. No.	Particulars	L.F.	Dr. (₹)	Cr. (₹)
1	Case (1):			
	Share capital A/c (*Less*) Dr.		400	
	To Forfeited shares A/c (50 × 6) (*Add*)			300
	To Share first call A/c (50 × 2) (*Less*)			100
	(50 shares forfeited for non-payment of first call money)			
2	Case (2):			
	Share capital A/c (50 × 10) (*Less*) Dr.		500	
	To Forfeited shares A/c (50 × 6) (*Add*)			300
	To Share first call A/c (*Less*)			100
	To Share final call A/c (*Less*)			100
	(50 shares forfeited for non-payment of first and final call)			

■ **ILLUSTRATION 11.11** Kumar Ltd issued 1,000 shares of ₹10 each at ₹12 per share. The amount is payable as ₹3 on application, ₹5 on allotment (including premium), ₹2 on first call, and ₹2 on final call. The company did not make the final call; Mr Mani was allotted 25 shares. Give journal entries for forfeiture in the following cases.

1. If Mr Mani failed to pay first call money, and his shares were forfeited
2. If Mr Mani failed to pay first and final call money, and his shares were forfeited

Solution

Journal Entries in the Books of Kumar Ltd

Sr. No.	Particulars	L.F.	Dr. (₹)	Cr. (₹)
1	Case (1):			
	Share capital A/c (25 × 8) (Less) Dr.		200	
	To Forfeited shares A/c (25 × 6) (Add)			150
	To Share first call A/c (25 × 2) (Less)			50
	(25 shares forfeited for non-payment of first call money)			
2	Case (2):			
	Share capital A/c (25 × 10) (Less) Dr.		250	
	To Forfeited shares A/c (25 × 6) (Add)			150
	To Share first call A/c (Less)			50
	To Share final call A/c (Less)			50
	(25 shares forfeited for non-payment of call money)			

■ **ILLUSTRATION 11.12** Nitin Ltd issued 10,000 shares of ₹10 each to the public at a discount of 10%, payable as follows:

On application, ₹2.50;

On allotment, ₹3.00;

On first and final call, ₹3.50.

All money due were received except from one shareholder, Mr Uday, who has been allotted 100 shares and failed to pay the final call money. The directors forfeited the shares after giving due notice. Pass the journal entries for forfeiture.

Solution

Journal Entries in the Books of Nitin Ltd

Sr. No.	Particulars	L.F.	Dr. (₹)	Cr. (₹)
1	Share capital A/c (100 × 10) (Less) Dr.		1,000	
	To Forfeited shares A/c (100 × 5.5) (Add)			550
	To Discount on issue of shares A/c			100
	(100 × 1) (Less)			
	To Final call A/c (100 × 3.5) (Less)			350
	(Forfeiture of 100 shares for non-payment of final call money)			

Reissue of forfeited shares

The directors of a company have the authority to reissue the shares once forfeited by them due to non-payment of calls. They can reissue the forfeited shares even at a discount provided the discount on reissue does not exceed the amount paid on such shares by the original holder.

For example, a share of ₹10, on which ₹6 has been received till its forfeiture, can be reissued as fully paid-up at an amount not less than ₹4 (10 – 6); in case the share is reissued as ₹8 paid-up, an amount of not less than ₹2 (8 – 6) should be received from the person to whom the reissue is sought to be made.

When forfeited shares are reissued at a discount, the journal entry is as given in the following text:

Bank A/c (Add)   Dr. (Amount received)
Shares forfeited A/c (Less)   Dr. (Discount allowed)
    To Share capital A/c (Add)   (Amount called up)
(Reissue of _____ forfeited shares at ₹ _____ per share and discount on reissue debited to forfeited shares)

In case shares originally issued at a discount are reissued after forfeiture, the discount on the issue of such shares is brought back into account by debiting discount on the issue of shares account with the amount proportionate to the number of shares reissued. This helps in maintaining a proportionate relationship between the discount on issue shares account and the share capital account.

Closure of forfeited shares account

After all forfeited shares have been reissued, the credit balance left on the forfeited shares account is transferred to the capital reserve account, the entry being:

Share forfeited A/c (Less)   Dr.
    To Capital reserve A/c (Add)

If all forfeited shares have not been reissued, the balance on the forfeited share account relating to shares not reissued

> Unutilized portion of the share forfeiture account is treated as capital reserve.

is carried forward, and only the balance left thereafter on the forfeited shares account is transferred to the capital reserve account.

■ **ILLUSTRATION 11.13** The directors of a company after due notice forfeited 100 shares of ₹10 each on which the final call money of ₹3 was not paid. Later, these shares were reissued at ₹8 per share. Pass the entries.

Solution

Journal Entries in the Books of the Company

Sr. No.	Particulars	L.F.	Dr. (₹)	Cr. (₹)
1	Share capital A/c (100 × 10) (Less) Dr.		1,000	
	To Forfeited shares A/c (100 × 7) (Add)			700
	To Final call A/c (100 × 3) (Less)			300
	(100 shares forfeited for non-payment of final call money)			
2	Bank A/c (100 × 8) (Add) Dr.		800	
	Forfeited shares A/c (100 × 2) (Less) Dr.		200	
	To Share capital A/c (Add)			1,000
3	Forfeited shares A/c (Less) Dr.		500	
	To Capital reserve A/c (Add)			500
	(Profit on reissue of forfeited shares transferred to capital reserve)			

Note:

Calculation of profit on reissue.

Amount received on forfeiture	100 shares × ₹7 =	₹700
Less: Loss on reissue	100 shares × ₹2 =	₹200
Profit on reissue (capital reserve)	100 shares × ₹5 =	₹500

■ **ILLUSTRATION 11.14** Corrtech Company Ltd issued 1,000 shares of ₹10 each at a discount of ₹1, payable as follows:

₹3 on application

₹3 on allotment (along with discount)

₹3 on first and final calls

All shares were duly subscribed and the money was received, except from a shareholder who failed to pay the final call amount on 100 shares. The directors forfeited the shares after giving due notice. Later, these shares were reissued for ₹8 fully paid. Pass entries to record the forfeiture and the reissue.

Solution

Journal Entries in the Books of Corrtech Company Ltd

Sr. No.	Particulars		L.F.	Dr. (₹)	Cr. (₹)
1	Share capital A/c (*Less*)	Dr.		1,000	
	To Forfeited shares A/c (*Add*)				600
	To Discount on issue of shares A/c (*Less*)				100
	To Final call A/c (*Less*)				300
	(Forfeiture of 100 shares for non-payment of call money)				
2	Bank A/c (*Add*)	Dr.		800	
	Discount on issue of shares A/c (*Add*)	Dr.		100	
	Forfeited shares A/c (100 × 1) (*Less*)	Dr.		100	
	To Share capital A/c (*Add*)				1,000
3	Forfeited shares A/c (*Less*)	Dr.		500	
	To Capital reserve A/c (*Add*)				500
	(Profit on reissue of transferred to capital reserve)				

ISSUE OF SHARES FOR CONSIDERATION OTHER THAN CASH

There are instances where a company enters into an arrangement with the vendors, from whom it has purchased assets, whereby the latter has agreed to accept payment in the form of fully paid shares of the company issued to them.

In such a case, the following journal entries are required.

(i) Purchase of assets
   Assets A/c (*Add*) (Purchase Price)   Dr.
      To Vendor A/c (*Add*)
   (Record of assets purchased)
(ii) Issue of shares
   Vendor A/c (*Less*)   Dr.
      To Share capital A/c (*Add*)
   (Issue of _____ fully paid shares of ₹ _____ each to the vendors for consideration other than cash)

PREFERENTIAL ALLOTMENT

Preferential allotment is the process by which allotment of securities/shares is done on a preferential basis to a select group of investors. In this, the company makes bulk allotment of shares/securities to individuals, companies, venture capitalists, or any other person through a fresh issue of shares.

SURRENDER OF SHARES

The voluntary return of shares by shareholders to the company for cancellation of their shares and removal of their name from the register of members of the company is known as surrender of shares. The company, however, can accept these shares only if they are likely to be forfeited for non-payment of calls.

The discretionary powers to reissue the surrendered shares are with the company, as such shares become the property of the company once the surrender is accepted by the company.

However, some compensation may be paid by the company on the shares surrendered.

The accounting entries on the surrender of shares are made in the same pattern as in the case of forfeiture of shares.

PREFERENCE SHARES

Preference shares allow an investor to own a stake at the issuing company with a condition that whenever the company decides to pay dividends, the holders of the preference shares will be the first to be paid.

Preference shares are considered as quasi-debt instruments since they combine the features of equity as well as debt. On one side, they carry a preferential right over the ordinary shares to receive dividend at a fixed rate and on the other, they carry an equity risk of not being secured, except to the preferential right of repayment in case of winding-up of the company. Preference shares have proved beneficial for investors, since such quasi-debt instrument provides protection to their investment by possessing voting rights on matters affecting their interest, more so with the fixed rate of dividend. For the promoters, issue of preference shares to investors ensures access to capital without a need to provide any security, with a continued control.

Important Condition on Preference Shares

As per Section 55 of the Companies Act, 2013, a company can issue only redeemable preference shares, that is, a company is not allowed to issue irredeemable preference shares.

It is mandatory for every company issuing preference shares to redeem it within a period of 20 years from the date of issue.

As per Rule 10 of The Companies (Share Capital and Debentures) Rules, 2014, a company may issue preference shares for a period exceeding 20 years for infrastructure projects; subject to redemption of a minimum 10% of such preference shares per year from the 21st year onward or earlier, on proportionate basis, at the option of preference shareholder.

Methods of Redemption

Redemption means repayment of the principal capital amount to the preference shareholders by the company. The redemption amount is decided as per issue arrangement in the beginning, or in case of any further resolution passed later in the meeting of preference shareholders. The company is not allowed to redeem the partly paid-up preference shares. In such circumstances, the company has to make the call for balance amount from the present preference shareholders', and only after receipt of call money, the fully paid-up preference shares can be redeemed.

The company can redeem the preference shares by any of the following ways.

From past accumulated funds

When a company redeems the preference share out of past accumulated profits, then the amount of capital repaid from accumulated profits is to be transferred to the capital redemption reserve account.

From new issue of any share

A company can make any new fresh issue of shares for the purpose of redemption of preference shares. The proceeds from the new issue of debentures cannot be used for the purpose of redemption of preference shares. The new issue can be made for the total or part requirement of the amount of redemption. The Companies Act allows premium on redemption of preference shares to be adjusted against the share premium account but the redemption itself cannot be financed out of the share premium account.

When the new shares are issued at a discount to arrange the funds, the number of shares to be issued at a discount should be manipulated to ensure that at least the face value of the shares to be redeemed has been procured. Out of the proceeds of the fresh issue at a discount, redemption of shares can be done. For example, a share of ₹100 (face value) is issued at a discount of 10%; money available from the proceeds of a fresh issue is ₹90 and not ₹100. Hence, the company can redeem only ₹90 from the fresh issue.

Capital Redemption Reserve Account

Capital redemption reserve account (CRR) is created with an intention to protect the interest of the creditors and to maintain the working capital. CRR can be used by the company for issuance of bonus shares. CRR is not available for payment to shareholders in the form of dividend.

Accounting entries

1. When new shares are issued at par
   Bank A/c (*Add*)   Dr.
       To Share capital A/c (*Add*)
   (Being the issue of .... shares of ₹ .... each for the purpose of redemption of preference shares, as per board's resolution number dated ....)
2. When new shares are issued at a premium
   Bank account (*Add*)   Dr.
       To Share capital A/c (*Add*)

   To Securities premium A/c (*Add*)
   (Being the issue of .... shares of ₹ .... each at a premium of ₹ .... each for the purpose of redemption of preference shares as per board's resolution number dated ....)
3. When new shares are issued at a discount
   Bank A/c (*Add*)   Dr.
   Discount on issue of shares A/c (*Add*)   Dr.
       To Share capital A/c (*Add*)
   (Being the issue of .... shares of ₹ .... each at a discount of ₹ .... each for the purpose of redemption of preference shares, as per board's resolution number dated ....)
4. When preference shares are redeemed at par
   Redeemable preference share capital A/c (*Less*)   Dr.
       To Preference shareholders A/c (*Add*)
5. When preference shares are redeemed at a premium
   Redeemable preference share capital A/c (*Less*)   Dr.
   Premium on redemption of preference shares A/c (*Add*) Dr.
       To Preference shareholders A/c (*Add*)
6. When payment is made to preference shareholders
   Preference shareholders A/c (*Less*)   Dr.
       To Bank A/c (*Less*)
   For adjustment of premium on redemption
   Profit and loss A/c (*Add*)   Dr.
   Share premium A/c (*Less*)   Dr.
       To Premium on redemption of preference
          shares A/c (*Less*)

Calculation of Minimum Fresh Issue of Shares

Section 55 of the Companies Act, 2013, requires a minimum number of shares to be issued. This is done in four steps as given in this section:

1. The maximum amount of reserves and surplus available for redemption is ascertained taking into account the balances appearing in the balance sheet before redemption and the additional information available from the financial records of the company.
2. After ascertaining the maximum amount of reserves and surplus available for redemption, adjustment for premium on redemption payable out of profits is made, and then it is compared with the nominal value of the shares to be redeemed. By comparison, one gets the minimum proceeds of fresh issue as Section 55 permits redemption either out of proceeds of fresh issue or out of divisible profits. Thus, Minimum proceeds of fresh issue of shares:
   Nominal value of preference shares to be redeemed – Maximum amount of reserve and surplus available for redemption.
3. After computation of minimum proceeds, the minimum numbers of shares to be issued are determined by dividing the minimum proceeds by the proceeds of one share. This is done as follows:

$$\text{Minimum Number of Shares} = \frac{\text{Minimum Proceeds to Comply with Section 55}}{\text{Proceeds of One Share}}$$

Proceeds of one share means the par value of a share issued, if it is issued at par or premium. However, in case of issue of a share at a discount, it refers to the discounted value.

4. Minimum number of shares calculated as per (3) earlier, needs to be adjusted due to various reasons. Firstly, shares as fractions cannot be issued. Thus, if the minimum number of shares as per (3) includes a fraction, it must be approximated to the next higher figure to ensure that provisions of Section 55 are not violated. Secondly, if the company's policy states that the proceeds/number of shares should be a multiple of say, 10 or 50 or 100, then again the next higher multiple should be considered.

■ **ILLUSTRATION 11.15** The board of directors of a company decide to issue minimum number of equity shares of ₹10 each at 10% discount to redeem ₹5,00,000 preference shares. The maximum amount of divisible profits available for redemption is ₹3,00,000. Calculate the number of shares to be issued by the company to ensure that provisions of Section 55 are not violated. Also determine the number of shares if the company decides to issue shares in multiples of ₹50 only.

Solution

Nominal value of preference shares ₹5,00,000
Maximum redemption possible out of profits ₹3,00,000
Minimum proceeds of fresh issue ₹5,00,000 – 3,00,000 = ₹2,00,000
Proceeds of one share = Nominal value – Discount = 10 – 1 = ₹9

$$\text{Minimum number of shares} = \frac{2,00,000}{9} = 22,222.22 \text{ shares}$$

As fractional shares are not permitted, the minimum number of shares to be issued is 22,223 shares.

If shares are to be issued in multiples of 50, then the next higher figure which is a multiple of 50 is 22,250.

Hence, minimum number of shares to be issued in such a case is 22,250 shares.

■ **ILLUSTRATION 11.16** Sunset Ltd has the following balance sheet as at 31/03/2020.

Balance Sheet of Sunset Ltd
as at 31 March 2020

Particulars	Amount (₹)
ASSETS	
Fixed assets	22,00,000
Current assets	8,00,000
Total Assets	**30,00,000**
EQUITY AND LIABILITIES	
Share capital	
Issued, subscribed and fully paid up	
10,000 Equity shares of ₹100 each	10,00,000
5,000 Preference shares of ₹100 each	5,00,000
Capital reserve	1,00,000
Security premium account	2,00,000
General reserve	1,00,000
Profit and loss account	1,00,000
Current liabilities	10,00,000
Total Equity and Liabilities	**30,00,000**

The preference shares are to be redeemed at 10% premium. Fresh issue of equity shares is to be made to the extent it is required under the Companies Act for the purpose of this redemption. The shortfall in funds for the purpose of the redemption after utilizing the proceeds of the fresh issue is to be met by taking a bank loan. Make the necessary journal entries.

Solution

Journal Entries in the Books of Sunset Ltd

Date	Particulars	L.F.	Dr. (₹)	Cr. (₹)
1	Bank A/c (*Add*) Dr.		2,00,000	
	To Equity share application A/c (*Add*)			2,00,000
	(Being the issue of 2,000 equity shares of ₹100 each for redemption of preference shares, as per board's resolution number dated)			
2	General reserve A/c (*Less*) Dr.		2,00,000	
	Profit and loss account (*Less*) Dr.		1,00,000	
	To Capital redemption reserve A/c (*Add*)			3,00,000
	(Being the amount trasferred to capital redemption reserve)			
3	Preference share capital A/c (*Less*) Dr.		5,00,000	
	Premium on redemption of preference share A/c (*Less*) Dr.		50,000	
	To Preference shareholders A/c (*Add*)			5,50,000
	(Being the amount payable on redemption of preference shares transferred to shareholders' A/c)			
4	Bank A/c (*Add*) Dr.		3,50,000	
	To Bank loan A/c (*Add*)			3,50,000
	(Being the necessary amount taken from bank as loan for redeeming the preference shares)			
5	Preference shareholders A/c (*Less*) Dr.		5,50,000	
	To Bank A/c (*Less*)			5,50,000
	(Being the preference shareholders paid-off on redemption)			
6	Securities premium A/c (*Less*) Dr.		50,000	
	To Premium on redemption of preference shares A/c (*Add*)			50,000
	(Being the premium payable on redemption transferred to securities premium A/c)			

Working Notes:

1. Calculation of number of shares to be issued

Face value of shares redeemed	₹5,00,000
Less: Profits available for dividend	₹3,00,000
	2,00,000

Therefore, number of shares to be issued ₹2,00,000/100 = 2,000

2. Amount required for payment to preference shareholders = ₹5,50,000.
Amount received by issuing equity shares is ₹2,00,000.
Therefore, ₹3,50,000 is to be taken from the bank (₹5,50,000 less ₹2,00,000).

Redemption of Preference Shares by Capitalization of Undistributed Profits

When a company uses the distributable retained profit for redemption of preference shares, an amount equal to the face value of shares redeemed is transferred to the capital redemption reserve account by debiting the distributable profit. Section 55 of the Companies Act states that

'When any such shares are redeemed otherwise than out of the proceeds of a fresh issue, there shall, out of profits which would otherwise have been available for dividend, be transferred to a reserve fund to be called the Capital Redemption Reserve Account sum equal to the nominal amount of the shares redeemed'.

Accounting entries

1. When shares are redeemed at par
   Redeemable preference share capital A/c (*Less*)   Dr.
   To Preference shareholders A/c (*Add*)
   (Being the amount payable on redemption of preference shares transferred to preference shareholders account)
2. When shares are redeemed at a premium
   Redeemable preference share capital A/c (*Less*)   Dr.
   Premium on redemption of preference shares A/c (*Add*) Dr.
   To Preference shareholders A/c (*Add*)
   (Being the amount payable on redemption transferred to preference shareholders account)
3. When payment is made to preference shareholders
   Preference shareholders A/c (*Less*)   Dr.
   To Bank A/c (*Less*)
   (Being the payment to preference shareholders as per the terms)

4. For adjustment of premium of redemption
   Profit and loss account   Dr.
   Securities premium A/c (*Less*)   Dr.
   To Premium on redemption of preference shares account (*Less*)
   (Being the premium on redemption adjusted against profit and loss account and securities premium account)
5. For transferring nominal amount of shares redeemed to capital redemption reserve account
   General reserve account (*Less*)   Dr.
   Profit and loss account (*Less*)   Dr.
   To Capital redemption reserve account (*Add*)
   (Being the amount transferred to capital redemption reserve account as per the requirement of the Act).

■**ILLUSTRATION 11.17**   The following are the extracts from the balance sheet of Aishwarya Ltd as at 31 December 2020.
Share capital:
40,000 Equity shares of ₹10 each fully paid = ₹4,00,000;
1,000 10% Redeemable preference shares of ₹100 each fully paid = ₹1,00,000.
Reserve and surplus:
Capital reserve = ₹50,000;
Securities premium = ₹50,000;
General reserve = ₹75,000;
Profit and loss account = ₹35,000
On 1st January 2021, the board of directors decided to redeem the preference shares at par by utilization of reserve. Make necessary journal entries including cash transactions in the books of the company.

Solution

Journal Entries in the Books of Aishwarya Limited

Sr. No.	Particulars	L.F.	Dr. (₹)	Cr. (₹)
1 Jan. 2021	10% Redeemable preference share capital A/c (*Less*) Dr.			
	To Preference shareholders A/c (*Add*)		1,00,000	
	(Being the amount payable on redemption transferred to preference shareholders account)			1,00,000
	Preference shareholders A/c (*Less*) Dr.		1,00,000	
	To Bank A/c (*Less*)			1,00,000
	(Being the amount paid on redemption of preference shares)			
	General reserve A/c (*Less*) Dr.		75,000	
	Profit and loss account (*Less*) Dr.		25,000	
	To Capital redemption reserve A/c (*Add*)			1,00,000
	(Being the amount transferred to capital redemption reserve account as per the requirement of the Act)			

Note:
Securities premium cannot be utilized for transfer to capital redemption reserve because dividend cannot be paid out of the securities premium account.

■ **ILLUSTRATION 11.18**   The balance sheet of Swing Ltd as at 31 March 2020 is given alongside. In order to facilitate the redemption of preference shares at a premium of 10% the company decided on the following:

1. Sell all the investments for ₹15,000
2. Part finance the redemption from company funds, subject to, leaving a bank balance of ₹12,000
3. Issue minimum equity share of ₹50 each at a premium of ₹10 per share to raise the balance of funds required

Balance Sheet of Swing Ltd
as at 31 March 2020

Particulars	Note No.	Amount (₹)	Amount (₹)
I. EQUITY AND LIABILITIES			
Share capital:			
Preference shares of ₹100 each fully paid up		65,000	
Equiy shares of ₹50 each fully paid up		2,25,000	2,90,000
Profit and loss A/c			48,000
Creditors			56,500
Total Equity and Liabilities			**3,94,500**
II. ASSETS			
Fixed Assets			3,45,000
Investments			18,500
Balance at bank			31,000
Total Assets			**3,94,500**

Solution

Journal Entries in the Books of Swing Ltd

Sr. No.	Particulars	L.F.	Dr. (₹)	Cr. (₹)
1	Bank A/c (*Add*) Dr.		37,500	
	To Share application A/c (*Add*)			37,500
	(For application money received for 625 shares @ ₹60 per share)			
2	Share application A/c (*Less*) Dr.		37,500	
	To Equity share capital A/c (*Add*)			31,250
	To Securities premium A/c (*Add*)			6,250
	(For disposition of application money received)			
3	Preference share capital A/c (*Less*) Dr.		65,000	
	Premium on redemption of preference shares A/c (*Less*) Dr.			
	To Preference shareholders A/c (*Add*)		6,500	
				71,500
	(For amount payable on redemption of preference shares)			
4	Securities premium A/c (*Less*) Dr.		6,250	
	Profit and loss account (*Less*) Dr.		250	
	To Premium on redemption of			6,500
	Preference shares A/c (*Add*)			
	(For writing off premium on redemption firstly out of securities premium and balance out of profits)			
5	Bank A/c (*Add*) Dr.		15,000	
	Profit and loss account (loss on sale) A/c (*Less*) Dr.		3,500	
	To Investment A/c (*Less*)			18,500
	(For sale of investment at a loss of ₹3,500)			
6	Profit and loss account (*Less*) Dr.		33,750	
	To Capital redemption reserve A/c (*Add*)			33,750
	(For transfer to CRR out of divisible profits an amount equivalent to excess of nominal value over proceeds from new equity issue, ₹65,000 – ₹31,250)			
7	Preference shareholders A/c (*Less*) Dr.		71,500	
	To Bank A/c (*Less*)			71,500
	(For payment of preference shareholders)			
8	Capital redemption reserve A/c (*Less*) Dr.		25,000	
	To Bonus to shareholders A/c (*Add*)			25,000
	(For making provision for issue of 500 bonus shares			
9	Bonus to shareholders A/c (*Less*) Dr.		25,000	
	To Equity share capital A/c (*Add*)			25,000
	(For issue of bonus shares)			

Balance Sheet of Swing Ltd as at 31 March 2020 (After Redemption)

Particulars	Note No.	Amount (₹)	Amount (₹)
I. EQUITY AND LIABILITIES			
Share capital:			
Equiy shares of ₹50 each fully paid up			2,81,250
Capital redemption reserve			8,750
Profit and loss A/c			10,500
Creditors			56,500
Total equity and liabilities			3,57,000
II. ASSETS			
Fixed assets			3,45,000
Balance at bank			12,000
Total Assets			**3,57,000**

Working Note:

Calculation of number of shares:	Amount (₹)
Amount payable on redemption	71,500
Less: Sale price of investment	15,000
	56,500
Less: Available bank balance (31,000 – 12,000)	19,000
Funds from fresh issue	37,500

∴ Number of shares = 37,500/60 = 625 shares

LONG-TERM BORROWED FUNDS

Generally, long-term liabilities, that is, non-current liabilities, are the firm's obligations for money obtained for a relatively long period, generally more than a year. These liabilities are incurred to finance the operations of the firm. Hence, this represents the claims against assets of the firm. These liabilities are more often against the securities or documentations by hypothecation or mortgage of the assets, through the creation of a pledge or lien on assets of the firm. The firm obtains the long-term funds from different sources like

a) debentures or public deposits and
b) loans from banking and financial service sectors.

DEBENTURES

According to Section 2(30) of the Companies Act, 2013, debenture includes 'debenture stock, bonds, and any other securities of a company, whether constituting a charge on the assets of the company or not'. Debenture is an instrument of debt owed by a company. As an acknowledgement of debt, such instruments are issued under the seal of a company and duly signed by the authorized signatory. The debenture

> *Debenture is an instrument of debt owed by a company.*

instrument specifies nominal/par value, the rate of interest, periodicity of payment, the tenure of the debentures, and terms of redemption.

Types of Debentures

Debentures may be classified from the following standpoints.

1. Security
2. Tenure
3. Mode of redemption
4. Coupon rate

Security

Debentures may be secured or unsecured. Secured debentures may be fully secured or unsecured. Fully secured debenture holders are given a fixed charge on specific assets.

Tenure

Debentures may be redeemable debentures or perpetual debentures from the tenure point of view. *Redeemable debentures* are to be redeemed on the expiry of a fixed period of time specified in the debenture trust deed. The debentures can be redeemed in its entirety after the expiry of the tenure or before the expiry of the entire tenure in instalments by draw of lots. *Perpetual debentures* are those debentures which are redeemable only on the happening of a contingency, however remote, or on the expiration of a period, however long.

Mode of redemption

Debentures can be convertible or non-convertible keeping in view the mode of redemption.

Convertible debentures Those debentures are convertible into equity shares or other securities either at the option of debenture holders or at the option of the company, as the case may be. Convertible debentures (CD) are of two types—*fully convertible debentures (FCD)* and *partly convertible debentures (PCD)*. Fully convertible debentures are those debentures where the full amount is to be converted into equity shares of the company at agreed terms and conditions. Partly convertible debentures are those debentures where only a portion of the amount of the debentures is convertible into shares or other securities at a specified time and the remaining part of the debentures is redeemable on agreed terms.

Non-convertible debentures The debentures that cannot be converted into shares or any other securities are called non-convertible debentures.

Coupon rate

Usually, the debentures are issued with a specified rate of interest, which is called coupon rate. The specified rate may either be *fixed* or *floating*. The floating interest rate is usually tagged with the bank rate and the yield on treasury bonds plus a reward for risk. Since the bank rate and yield on treasury securities fluctuate, any change is compensated in the risk premium. The rate of interest in such a case is quoted as Prime Landing Rate plus 50 basis points (PLR + 50 basis points). In this case, if we assume a PLR of 9%, the rate of interest would be 9.5%. The '+ basis points' is determined in relation to the risk involved.

A *zero coupon bond* is one that does not carry a specified rate of interest. In order to compensate the investors, such bonds are then issued at a substantial discount. The difference between the face value and issue price is the total amount of interest related to the duration of the bond.

Issue of Debentures for Cash

Debentures may be issued with or without a coupon rate. Debentures issued with a coupon rate may be categorized as given in the following text.

1. Debentures issued at par and redeemable at par
2. Debentures issued at a discount and redeemable at par
3. Debentures issued at a premium and redeemable at par
4. Debentures issued at par and redeemable at premium
5. Debentures issued at a discount and redeemable at premium

Journal entries in each of the cases discussed earlier are discussed in this section.

Debentures issued at par and redeemable at par When debentures are issued at par, the issue price is equal to the par value. In this regard, the following entries are recorded.

(a) For receipt of application money:
Bank A/c (*Add*)   Dr.
    To Debenture application A/c (*Add*)

(b) For transfer of application money to debentures account:
Debenture application A/c (*Less*)   Dr.
    To X% debenture A/c (*Add*)

(c) Call made consequent upon allotment:
Debenture allotment A/c (*Add*)   Dr.
    To X% debenture A/c (*Add*)

Debentures issued at discount and redeemable at par When debentures are issued at discount, issue price will be less than par value. The difference between the two is considered as loss on issue of debentures and is to be written off over the life of the debentures. The entries with regards to issue are given in the following text.

1. For receipt of application money:
Bank A/c (*Add*)   Dr.
    To Debenture application A/c (*Add*)

2. At the time of making allotment
1. Transfer of application money to debenture account
Debenture application A/c (*Less*)   Dr.
    To X% Debenture A/c (*Add*)

2. Call made consequent upon allotment
Debenture allotment A/c (*Add*)   Dr.
Discount on issue of debenture A/c (*Add*)   Dr.
    To X% sebenture A/c (*Add*)

3. For receipt of call made consequent upon allotment
Bank A/c (*Add*)   Dr.
    To Debenture allotment A/c (*Less*)

Debentures issued at a premium and redeemable at par When debentures are issued at a premium, the issue price is more than the par value. The premium is transferred to the securities premium account. In this regard, the following journal entries are recorded:

(A) When premium amount is received at the time of application

1. For receipt of application money
Bank A/c (*Add*) Dr.
To Debenture application A/c (*Add*)
2. At the time of making allotment
    1. Transfer of application money to debenture account
    Debenture application A/c (*Less*) Dr.
    To X% debenture A/c (*Add*)
    To Securities premium A/c (*Add*)
    2. Call made on consequent upon allotment
    Debenture allotment A/c (*Add*) Dr.
    To X% debenture A/c (*Add*)
3. For receipt of call made consequent upon allotment
Bank A/c (*Add*) Dr.
To Debenture allotment A/c (*Less*)

(B) When premium amount is received at the time of allotment
1. For the receipt of application money
    1. Bank A/c (*Add*) Dr.
    To Debenture application A/c (*Add*)
2. At the time of making allotment
    1. Transfer of application money to debenture account
    Debenture application A/c (*Less*) Dr.
    To X% debenture A/c (*Add*)
    2. Call made consequent upon allotment
    Debenture allotment A/c (*Add*) Dr.
    To X% debenture A/c (*Add*)
    To Securities premium A/c (*Add*)
3. For receipt of call made consequent upon allotment
Bank A/c (*Add*) Dr.
To Debenture allotment A/c (*Less*)

Debentures issued at par and redeemable at premium In this case, the issue price is same as the par value but the redemption value is more than the par value. Therefore, redemption premium is recorded as a loss on issue of debentures at the time of allotment of the debentures. The following journal entries are recorded in this regard.

1. For receipt of application money
Bank A/c (*Add*) Dr.
To Debenture application A/c (*Add*)
2. At the time of making allotment
    1. Transfer of application money to debenture account
    Debenture application A/c (*Less*) Dr.
    To X% debenture A/c (*Add*)
    2. Call made consequent upon allotment
    Debenture allotment A/c (*Add*) Dr.
    Loss on issue of debenture A/c (*Add*) Dr.
        (Equal to debenture redemption premium)
    To X% debenture A/c (*Add*)
    To Debenture redemption premium A/c (*Add*)
3. For receipt of allotment money
Bank A/c (*Add*) Dr.
To Debenture allotment A/c (*Less*)

Debentures issued at a discount and redeemable at premium In this situation, the issue price is less than the par value and redemption value is more than the par value. The difference between the redemption price and the issue price is treated as discount or loss on issue of debentures. If a 10% debenture of ₹1,000 is issued at a discount of ₹100 and redeemable at a premium of ₹5

per debenture, the amount of loss will be equal to ₹105 (1,005 – 900). This is to be treated as loss on issue. It is to be noted that premium on redemption of debentures is also credited by ₹5.

1. For the receipt of application money
Bank A/c (*Add*) Dr.
To Debenture application A/c (*Add*)
2. At the time of making allotment
    1. Transfer of application money to debenture account
    Debenture application A/c (*Less*) Dr.
    To X% debenture A/c (*Add*)
    2. Call made consequent upon allotment of debenture at discount and redeemable at premium
    Debenture allotment A/c (*Add*) Dr.
    Discount or loss on issue of debenture (*Add*) Dr.
        (Amount equal to the discount on issue of debenture plus premium on redemption)
    To X% debenture A/c (*Add*)
    To Debenture redemption premium A/c (*Add*)
3. For receipt of call made on allotment
Bank A/c (*Add*) Dr.
To Debenture allotment A/c (*Less*)

Issue of Debentures for Consideration Other than Cash

Sometimes, debentures can be issued to the vendors or suppliers of patents, copyrights, and transfer of intellectual property rights, on a preferential basis, without receiving the money in cash. Such issue of debentures is termed as issue for consideration other than cash. When debentures are issued to the vendors in satisfaction of the purchase consideration, the following entries are made.

1. For acquiring the assets and liabilities
Assets A/c (*Add*) Dr. (Value of assets acquired)
To Liabilities A/c (*Add*) (Liabilities taken over)
To Vendor's A/c (Add) (Purchase consideration)
2. For issue of debentures in satisfaction of purchase consideration
    1. Debenture issued at par:
    Vendor's A/c (by name) (*Less*) Dr.
    To X% debenture A/c (*Add*)
        Or
    2. Debenture issued at premium
    Vendor's A/c (*Less*) Dr.
    To X% Debenture A/c (*Add*)
    To Securities premium A/c (*Add*)
        Or
    3. Debenture issued at discount
    Vendor's A/c (*Less*) Dr.
    Discount on issue of debenture A/c (*Add*) Dr.
    To X% debenture A/c (*Add*)

Purchase consideration

Purchase consideration is the amount paid by the purchasing company in consideration for purchase of assets or business from another enterprise. Purchase consideration is arrived at by using the following formula.

Purchase Consideration = Value of Assets – Liabilities Assumed

For example, XYZ Ltd has acquired from ABC Ltd assets worth ₹10,00,000 and liabilities of ₹4,00,000. In this case, purchase consideration is ₹6,00,000 (10,00,000 – 4,00,000).

Issue of Debentures as Collateral Security

It implies standby or additional security to obtain a secured loan. When the lender is of the view that the primary security is not enough to cover the risk, the lender may ask for further security. The borrower may issue bonds or debentures by way of additional security in favour of the latter, known as collateral security. In this case, the lender will simply be the custodian of these debentures or bonds. He/she will not be entitled to any interest on these debentures or bonds.

Accounting treatment

For pledging debentures as collateral security, no immediate liability is created by the company, therefore, no liability entries are recorded. On the part of the company, the liability arises only when the lender invokes his right vested in the collateral security. It is important that collateral security creates a contingent liability which has to be disclosed in the published accounts.

The following entry is passed:

Loan A/c (*Less*)	Dr.

(Principal and interest outstanding on loan)

Outstanding interest A/c (*Less*)	Dr.

(Outstanding interest for the period intervening the date of default on the loan to the date of invoking security by the lender)

    To X% debenture A/c (*Add*)

Debenture interest

Interest payable on coupon debentures is treated as a charge against the profits of the company. Interest on debentures is paid periodically and is calculated at coupon rate on the nominal value of the debentures. The company will pay interest net of tax to the debenture holders because the company is under obligation to deduct tax at source at the rates applicable under tax rules from time to time. The companies will deposit the tax so deducted with income tax authorities. Following accounting entries are to be recorded in this regard.

1. For making interest due
Interest A/c (*Add*)	Dr.
       To Debenture holders' A/c (*Add*)
2. For making payment of interest and deduction of tax at source (TDS)
Debenture holders' A/c (*Less*)	Dr.
       To TDS payable A/c (*Add*)
       To Bank A/c (*Less*)
3. For making payment of tax deducted at source
TDS payable A/c (*Less*)	Dr.
       To Bank A/c (*Less*)
4. For transferring interest to profit and loss account
Profit and loss account (*Less*)	Dr.
       To Interest A/c (*Less*)

Without coupon rate

When debentures are issued without the specific prefix of interest rate and issue price is heavily discounted, the issue of debenture is said to have been made as a deep discount bond. The difference between issue price and the redemption price is the total amount of notional discount representing the interest amount to be spread over the duration of the bond. From the accounting point of view, this amount is recorded in the deferred interest expense account at the time of issue of debentures and a proportionate amount is written off as interest expense every year over the life of the debentures. Accounting entries in this regard are as follows:

1. Receipt of application money:
Bank A/c (*Add*)	Dr.
       To Debenture application A/c (*Add*)
2. Application money and deferred interest expense transferred to debenture account consequent upon allotment:
Debenture application A/c (*Less*)	Dr.
Deferred interest expenses A/c (*Add*)	Dr.
       To X% debenture A/c (*Add*)

Writing off Discount or Loss on Issue of Debentures

Discount or loss on issue of debentures must be written off before such debentures are redeemed. Section 52 of the Companies Act, 2013, permits the utilization of securities premium for writing off the discount or loss on issue of debentures.

1. The entry to write off the discount out of securities premium account is as follows
Securities premium A/c (*Less*)	Dr.
       To Discount or loss on issue of debenture A/c (*Less*)
2. The company may decide to write off certain portion of unwritten part of discount or loss on issue of debenture from accumulated past years or current year profits. The following entry is to be recorded:
Profit and loss A/c (*Less*)	Dr.
       To Discount/loss on issue of debenture A/c (*Less*)

Redemption of Debenture

The term redemption implies the discharge of an obligation arising out of the contractual obligations created through the debenture trust deed. The redemption of debentures can take place either out of profits or through conversion of convertible debentures into shares, or by issuing a new series of debentures/bonds. In case of convertible debentures, there is no cash outflow but only issue of shares in discharge of the obligation. Redemption of debentures out of profit implies payment in the form of cash to non-convertible debenture holders. Following accounting entries are to be recorded in this regard.

1. Accounting entry for creation of debenture redemption reserve
Profit and loss appropriation A/c (*Less*)	Dr.
       To Debenture redemption reserve A/c (*Add*)

   In the year of redemption, the debenture holders will be credited with the amount due according to the terms of redemption.

2. If the debentures are redeemable at par, the par value of the debenture to be redeemed will be transferred to the debenture holders' account by recording the following entries.

Debenture A/c (*Less*)   Dr.
   To Debenture holders' A/c (*Add*)

3. In case the debentures are redeemable at a premium, the amount of premium will also be transferred to the debenture holders' account by recording the following entry.

X% debenture (*Less*) A/c   Dr.
Debenture redemption premium A/c (*Less*)   Dr.
   To Debenture holders' A/c (*Add*)

4. For payment to debenture holders

Debenture holders' A/c (*Less*)
   To Bank A/c (*Less*)

■ **ILLUSTRATION 11.19** Trupti Ltd issued 5,00,000 debentures @ 12% of ₹100 each on 1 April 2020 redeemable at par on 1 July 2021. The company received applications for 6,00,000 debentures and the allotment was made to all the applicants on pro-rata basis. The debentures were redeemed on the due date. How much debenture redemption reserve is to be created before the redemption is carried out? Also record necessary journal entries regarding issue and redemption of debenture.

Solution

Journal Entries in the Books of Trupti Ltd

Date 2020	Particulars	L.F.	Dr. (₹)	Cr. (₹)
1 April	Bank A/c (*Add*) Dr.		6,00,00,000	
	To Debenture application A/c (*Add*)			6,00,00,000
	(For receiving application money)			
1 April	Debentures application A/c (*Less*) Dr.		6,00,00,000	
	To 12% Debenture A/c (*Add*)			5,00,00,000
	To Bank A/c (*Less*)			1,00,00,000
	(Debenture application money transferred to debenture account consequent upon allotment of debenture)			
2021 31 Mar.	Interest A/c (*Add*) Dr.		60,00,000	
	To Debenture holders' A/c (*Add*)			60,00,000
	(For interest due)			
31 Mar.	Debenture holders' A/c (*Less*) Dr.		60,00,000	
	To Bank A/c (*Less*)			60,00,000
	(For payment of interest)			
31 Mar.	Profit and loss A/c (*Less*) Dr.		60,00,000	
	To Interest A/c (*Less*)			60,00,000
	(For writing off interest)			
31 Mar.	Profit and loss account (*Less*) Dr.		2,50,00,000	
	To Debenture redemption reserve A/c (*Add*)			2,50,00,000
	(Appropriation of profit to debenture redemption reserve as per Section 17C(I) of the Companies Act, 1956)			
30 June	Interest A/c (*Add*) Dr.		10,00,000	
	To Debenture holders' A/c (*Add*)			10,00,000
	(Interest due for two months)			
1 July	12% Debentures A/c (*Less*) Dr.		5,00,00,000	
	To Debenture holders' A/c (*Add*)			5,00,00,000
	(Payment on redemption of debentures due to debenture holders)			
1 July	Debenture holders' A/c (*Less*) Dr.		5,10,00,000	
	To Bank A/c (*Less*)			5,10,00,000
	(Payment due to debenture holders discharged)			
2022 31 Mar.	Profit and loss account (*Less*) Dr.		10,00,000	
	To Interest A/c (*Less*)			10,00,000
	(Transfer of interest)			
31 Mar.	Debenture redemption reserve A/c (*Less*) Dr.		2,50,00,000	
	To General reserve A/c (*Add*)			2,50,00,000
	(For transfer of debenture redemption reserve to general reserve)			

Financing of Redemption of Debentures

The redemption of debentures requires a huge amount of cash whenever non-convertible debentures are to be paid off. To meet this requirement, the board of directors may decide, at their own discretion, to invest money appropriately and judiciously in securities or bonds of other business entities. In this situation, funds allocated are invested periodically outside the business. For this purpose, an appropriate amount may be transferred to the debenture redemption sinking fund account. An appropriate amount will be calculated by referring to the sinking fund factor, depending upon the interest rate on investments and the number of years for which investments are to be made.

The journal entries in this regard can be categorized into three groups.

Entries at the end of the first year Entries relating to issue of debenture, payment of interest, and amortization of discount or loss on issue of debenture have already been discussed in the earlier sections. The other related entries at the end of the first year are as given in this section:

1. For transfer of profits to debenture redemption reserve
   Profit and loss appropriation A/c (*Less*)   Dr.
      To Debenture redemption reserve A/c (*Add*)
2. For purchase of debenture redemption sinking fund investments with the amount of debenture redemption reserve set aside as discussed before.
   Debenture redemption sinking fund
      Investment A/c (*Add*)   Dr.
        To Bank A/c (*Less*)

Entries at the end of the second and subsequent years In the second and subsequent years, the company will start receiving interest on the previous years' investments which will be transferred to the debenture redemption reserve. The company will purchase investments with the amount of debenture redemption reserve kept aside and interest received on debenture redemption sinking fund investments in the respective years. The journal entries are as given in the following text.

1. For receiving of interest on debenture redemption sinking fund investments
   Bank A/c (*Add*)   Dr.
      To Interest on debenture redemption sinking fund
        investment A/c (*Add*)
2. For interest received transferred to debenture redemption reserve
   Interest on debenture redemption sinking
      fund investment A/c (*Less*)   Dr.
      To Debenture redemption reserve (*Add*)
3. For transfer of profits to debenture redemption reserve
   Profit and loss appropriation A/c (*Less*)   Dr.
      To Debenture redemption reserve (*Add*)
4. For purchase of investments with the amount of debenture redemption reserve and interest received
   Debenture redemption sinking fund
      investment A/c (*Add*)   Dr.
      To Bank A/c (*Less*)

Year of redemption The entries for receipt of interest, the transfer to debenture redemption reserve, and setting aside the profits for debenture redemption reserve will be recorded as usual during the year in which the redemption of debentures is due. However, instead of purchase of investments, all investments purchased in previous years will be sold out to provide liquidity for redemption of debentures. After all the debentures are redeemed on maturity, the debenture redemption reserve account will be closed by transferring its balance to the general reserve account. In case of redemption of debentures by the draw of lots, withdrawal from the debenture redemption reserve can be made after redemption of 10% of the debentures. The following entries are to be recorded.

1. For receipt of interest on debenture redemption sinking fund investments
   Bank A/c (*Add*)   Dr.
      To Interest on debenture redemption sinking fund
        investment A/c (*Add*)
2. For transfer of interest to debenture redemption reserve interest on debenture redemption
   Sinking fund investment A/c (*Less*)   Dr.
      To Debenture redemption reserve (*Add*)
3. For transfer of profits to debenture redemption reserve
   Profit and loss appropriation A/c (*Less*)   Dr.
      To Debenture redemption reserve (*Add*)
4. 1. For sale of debenture redemption sinking fund investments (it is to be noted that gain or loss on sale of debenture redemption sinking fund investments, if any, will be transferred to the debenture redemption reserve account)
   2. Investment sold at book value
      Bank A/c (*Add*)   Dr.
      (Sale price of investment)
         To Debenture redemption sinking fund
           investment A/c (*Less*)
      (Investment sold at cost price)
           Or
   3. Investment sold at less than book value
      Bank A/c (*Add*)   Dr.
      Debenture redemption reserve (*Less*)   Dr.
      (Loss on sale of investments)
         To Debenture redemption sinking fund
           investment A/c (*Less*)
           Or
   4. Investment sold at more than book value
      Bank A/c (*Add*)   Dr.
         To Debenture redemption sinking fund
           investment A/c (*Add*)
         To Debenture redemption reserve A/c
      (Gain on sale of investment) (*Add*)
5. On redemption of debentures at par, amount due to debenture holders
   X% debenture A/c (*Less*)   Dr.
      To debenture holders' A/c (*Add*)
        Or
   In case the debentures are redeemed at a premium, the following entry will be recorded.
   X% debenture A/c (*Less*)   Dr.
   Debenture redemption premium A/c (*Less*)   Dr.
      To Debenture holders' A/c (*Add*)
6. Amount due to debentureholders paid
   Debenture holders' A/c (*Less*)   Dr.
      To Bank A/c (*Less*)
7. After the debentures are redeemed, debenture redemption reserve account is transferred to the general reserve account by recording the following entry.
   Debenture redemption reserve (*Less*)   Dr.
      To General reserve A/c (*Add*)

■ ILLUSTRATION 11.20 Pooja Detergents Ltd issued 2,00,000 debentures @ 10% of ₹10 each on 1 January 2016 redeemable after 4 years. For this purpose, the company established a debenture redemption sinking fund investment account. The investments are expected to earn interest @ 4% p.a. The sinking fund factor table shows that ₹0.2355 invested annually @ 4% will accumulate to ₹1 at the end of the 4th year. On 31 December 2019, the investments realized ₹15,00,000. The debentures were paid off as per terms of issue of the debentures.

Give journal entries to record transaction relating to the issue and investment of reserve and redemption of debentures.

Solution

Journal Entries in the Books of Pooja Detergents Ltd

Date	Particulars		L.F.	Dr. (₹)	Cr. (₹)
1 Jan. 2016	Bank A/c (*Add*)	Dr.		20,00,000	
	To Debenture application A/c (*Add*)				20,00,000
	(Debenture application money received)				
1 Jan.	Debenture application A/c (*Less*)	Dr.		20,00,000	
	To 10% Debenture A/c (*Add*)				20,00,000
	(Application money transferred to 10% debentures consequent upon allotment)				
31 Dec.	Profit and loss appropriation A/c (*Less*)	Dr.		4,71,000	
	To Debenture redemption reserve A/c (*Add*)				4,71,000
	(Profits transferred to debenture redemption reserve)				
31 Dec.	Debenture redemption sinking fund investments A/c (*Add*)	Dr.		4,71,000	
	To Bank A/c (*Less*)				4,71,000
	(Investments purchased)				
31 Dec. 2017	Bank A/c (*Add*)	Dr.		18,840	
	To Interest on debenture sinking fund Investments A/c (*Add*)				18,840
	(Interest received on investment)				
31 Dec.	Interest on sinking fund investments A/c (*Less*)	Dr.		18,840	
	To Debenture redemption reserve (*Add*)				18,840
	(Interest transferred to sinking fund)				
31 Dec.	Profit and loss appropriation A/c (*Less*)	Dr.		4,71,000	
	To Debenture redemption reserve (*Add*)				4,71,000
	(Profits transferred to debenture redemption reserve)				
31 Dec.	Debenture sinking fund investments A/c (*Add*)	Dr.		4,89,840	
	To Bank A/c (*Less*)				4,89,840
	(₹4,71,000 + 18,840 = 4,89,840 investments purchased)				
31 Dec. 2018	Bank A/c (*Add*)	Dr.		38,433.60	
	To Interest on debenture sinking fund investments A/c (*Add*)				38,433.60
	(Interest received on investment)				
31 Dec.	Interest on sinking fund investments A/c (*Less*)	Dr.		38,433.60	
	To Debenture redemption reserve (*Add*)				38,433.60
	(Interest transferred to sinking fund)				
31 Dec.	Profit and loss appropriation A/c (*Less*)	Dr.		4,71,000	
	To Debenture redemption reserve (*Add*)				4,71,000
	(Profits transferred to debenture redemption reserve)				
31 Dec.	Debenture sinking fund investments A/c (*Add*)	Dr.		5,09,433.60	
	To Bank A/c (*Less*)				5,09,433.60
	(₹4,71,000 + 38,433.60 = 5,09,433.60 investments purchased)				
31 Dec. 2019	Bank A/c (*Add*)	Dr.		58,810.94	
	To Interest on debenture sinking fund Investments A/c (*Add*)				58,810.94
	(4% of ₹4,71,000 + ₹4,89,840 + ₹5,09,433.60, interest received)				
31 Dec.	Interest on sinking fund investments A/c (*Less*)	Dr.		58,810.94	
	To Debenture redemption reserve (*Add*)				58,810.94
	(Interest transferred to sinking fund)				
31 Dec.	Profit and loss appropriation A/c (*Less*)	Dr.		4,70,915.46	
	To Debenture redemption reserve (*Add*)				4,70,915.46
	(Profits transferred to debenture redemption reserve)				
31 Dec.	Bank A/c (*Add*)	Dr.		15,00,000	
	To Debenture sinking fund investments A/c (*Less*)				14,70,273.60
	To Debenture redemption reserve (*Add*)				29,726.40
	(Investment sold at profit)				
31 Dec.	10% Debenture A/c (*Less*)	Dr.		20,00,000	
	To Debenture holders' A/c (*Add*)				20,00,000
	(Payment to debenture holders due on redemption)				
31 Dec.	Debenture holders' A/c (*Less*)	Dr.		20,00,000	
	To Bank A/c (*Less*)				20,00,000
	(Payment made to debenture holders)				
31 Dec.	Debenture redemption reserve (*Less*)	Dr.		20,29,726.40	
	To General reserve account (*Add*)				20,29,726.40
	(After redemption, debenture redemption reserve account closed by transferring to general reserve)				

Note:

Annual amount to be transferred from profits to debenture redemption reserve

0.2355 × ₹20,00,000 = ₹4,71,000

Redemption of Convertible Debentures

The debentures may be redeemed by conversion into equity shares as per the terms of their issue.

Accounting treatment

Following are the journal entries to be recorded for discharging obligation in respect of convertible debentures:

(A) Redemption of debentures at par through conversion into shares:

    1. For amount due to debenture holders

        X% debenture A/c (*Less*)   Dr.

          To Debenture holders' A/c (*Add*)

    2. For discharging debenture holders by issue of equity shares at par:

        Debenture holders' A/c (*Less*)   Dr.

          To Equity share capital A/c (*Add*)

              Or

    3. For discharging debenture holders by issue of equity share at premium:

        Debenture holders' A/c (*Less*)   Dr.

          To Equity share capital A/c (*Add*)

          To Security premium A/c (*Add*)

Since shares are issued at a premium, the number of shares to be issued will be equal to the amount of debentures to be redeemed divided by the issue price.

(B) Redemption of debentures (at premium) through conversion into shares:

    1. For amount due to debenture holders

        X% debenture A/c (*Less*)   Dr.

        Debenture redemption premium (*Less*)   Dr.

          To Debenture holders' A/c (*Add*)

    2. For discharging debenture holders by issue of shares at par:

        Debenture holders' A/c (*Less*)   Dr.

          To Equity share capital A/c (*Add*)

    3. For discharging debenture holders by issuing shares at premium:

        Debenture holders' A/c (*Less*)   Dr.

          To Equity share capital A/c (*Add*)

          To Securities premium A/c (*Add*)

Redemption of Debentures through Open Market Operations

The Companies Act, 2013, permits the issuer company to purchase and hold or cancel the debentures through open market purchases, obviously at favourable prices, provided the Articles of Association provide for this.

A company may also purchase the debentures with an intention to cancel them. It is assumed that the company has sufficient amount in the debenture redemption reserve before initiating the purchase of debentures for cancellation. The debentures may either be purchased

(a) on the date(s) when interest on these debenture is due, or
(b) on the date(s) between the two interest dates.

Therefore, the accounting treatment for purchase of debentures in the two situations discussed earlier will be different due to accrual and non-accrual of interest.

(A) When purchase of debentures is on due date

    1. When debentures are purchased for investment purpose, the following journal entry is recorded

        Investment in own debenture A/c (*Add*)   Dr.

          To Bank A/c (*Less*)

    2. When own debentures are subsequently sold in the market, the following entry is recorded

        Bank A/c (*Add*)   Dr.

          To Investment in own debenture A/c (*Less*)

              Or

When investment is sold at a price below its purchase price

    Bank A/c (*Add*)   Dr.

    Loss on sale of investment (*Add*)   Dr.

      To Investment in own debenture A/c (*Less*)

          Or

When investment is sold at a price above its purchase price

    Bank A/c (*Add*)   Dr.

      To Investment in own debenture A/c (*Less*)

      To Gain on sale of investments A/c (*Add*)

It is to be noted that gain or loss on sale of investments is transferred to the profit and loss account.

On cancellation of own debentures

Debentures purchased from the open market will be cancelled only after passing the resolution by board of directors to this effect. The following journal entries are to be recorded for the cancellation of debentures:

When debentures are purchased at nominal value of debentures

    X% debenture A/c (*Less*)   Dr.

      To Investment in own debenture A/c (*Less*)

          Or

When own debentures are purchased at price below nominal value of debentures

    X% debenture A/c (*Less*)   Dr.

      To Own debenture A/c (*Less*)

      To Profit on cancellation A/c (*Add*)

Balance in profit on cancellation of debentures will be transferred to the capital reserve or may be utilized to write off discount or loss on issue of debentures. In this regard, the following journal entry is recorded:

    Gain on cancellation A/c (*Less*)   Dr.

    To Capital reserve   (*Add*)

          Or

    Gain on cancellation A/c (*Less*)   Dr.

    To Discount or loss A/c   (*Less*)

■ **ILLUSTRATION 11.21** Daisy India Ltd has outstanding 11,00,000 debentures @ 10% of ₹200 each on 1 April 2018. The board of directors have decided to purchase 20% of their own debentures for cancellation at ₹200 each. Record the necessary entries for the same.

Solution

Journal Entries in the Books of Daisy India Ltd

Date	Particulars	L.F.	Dr. (₹)	Cr. (₹)
	Own debenture A/c (*Add*) Dr.		4,40,00,000	
	To Bank A/c (*Less*)			4,40,00,000
	(Purchased its own debentures @ ₹200 each)			
	10% debenture A/c (*Less*) Dr.		4,40,00,000	
	To Own debenture A/c (*Less*)			4,40,00,000
	(Own debentures purchased are cancelled)			

LOANS FROM BANKING AND FINANCIAL SERVICE SECTORS

A loan comprises the money, property, or other material goods that are given to another party in exchange for future repayment of the loan value amount along with interest or other finance charges. Loans are in the form of borrowed funds for the borrower firm. Loans from banking and/or financial service sectors are sum of the money borrowed by a firm from a bank or financial service sector for a specific purpose, such as buying a machinery. A loan is to be repaid over the agreed periods in piece-meal way or as bullet repayment. A bank loan is the most common form of loan funds for a firm. It provides the medium for long-term finance. The bank sets a fixed period over which the loan is provided (for 5 years, 10 years, 20 years, etc.), the rate of interest, and the timing and amount of repayments.

Interest Paid or Payable on Loan or Borrowed Funds

Loans are generally borrowed by a firm from persons, other firms, corporates, banks, and financial institutions. Interest on borrowed funds would be an expense, and so it would be charged against the income of the firm during that period. Interest on loan is to be paid to the lender according to the loan agreement. The interest is normally payable by the firm on a quarterly basis (three-month basis).

When the interest on a loan is paid, the appropriate accounting is carried out during that year under the interest expenses account in the trial balance of the firm.

Often the interest on loan accrues but is not due for payment on account of the terms of the loan agreement. In such circumstances, at the end of the accounting period, the interest expense accrued needs to be recorded as an adjustment entry. In such cases, the interest expense of the firm will be increased by the accrued amount (interest expense account to be debited) and the liability account in the name of interest expense payable will be increased (liability account to be credited).

■ **ILLUSTRATION 11.22** Odeon & Co. has availed a loan of ₹2,00,000 from Dena Bank, Ashram Road, Ahmedabad, on 1 October 2018 for a longer period at an interest rate of 10% p.a., and the interest is payable on a quarterly basis. At the end of the accounting year as on 31 March 2020, the interest is accrued for the period from 1 January 2020 to 31 March 2020, but would be due for payment on 1 April 2020. Thus, interest

of ₹5,000 is due (2,00,000 × 10% × 3/12). Analyse the effect of these transactions on the accounting equation.

Solution

Assets = Liabilities + Contributed + Revenue – Expenses
                          Capital

In the books of Odeon:

As on 31 March 2020

⬆ Liability increased by ₹5,000 Interest expense payable account credit

⬆ Expense increased by ₹5,000 Interest expense account debit

As on 1 April 2020

The firm has to pay the interest on the loan of ₹5,000 borrowed from the bank. Thus, the bank balance in the form of asset account would be decreased by ₹5,000 and the interest expense payable as a liability would be reduced by ₹5,000.

⬇ Asset decreased Bank account credit ₹5,000

⬇ Liabilities decreased Interest expense payable account debit ₹5,000

REPAYMENT OF BORROWED FUNDS

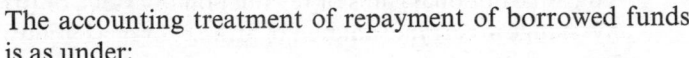

The accounting treatment of repayment of borrowed funds is as under:

Bank Loan Account or Borrowed Funds Account Dr.
      (Liability type-Less)
        To Bank account...........
      (Asset type-Less)

DIVISIBLE PROFIT

The net profit after tax available for distribution to shareholders as dividend is called divisible profits. The guidelines of the ICAI and the Companies Act, 2013 have not provided any clear definition of divisible profit. Generally, it is taken to mean profit after tax and after deduction of the dividend among the preference shareholders. It is also known as profit available for distribution among the equity shareholders of the company.

Section 123 of the Companies Act specifies the sources from which dividends can be paid. It also makes it compulsory for a company to provide for depreciation before declaration of dividend. The different provisions of Section 123 of the Companies Act are as follows:

Dividend Declaration

Following are the important dividend declarations:

1. No dividend shall be declared or paid by a company for any financial year except
   (a) out of the profits of the company for that year arrived at after providing for depreciation in accordance with the provisions of sub-section.
   (b) out of the profits of the company for any previous financial year or years arrived at after providing for depreciation in accordance with the provisions of

that sub-section and remaining undistributed, or out of both; or (b) out of money provided by the central government or a state government for the payment of dividend by the company in pursuance of a guarantee given by that government.

Conditions to be Fulfilled for Declaration of Dividend

Following are the conditions that need to be met for declaration of dividend:

1. Provided that a company may, before the declaration of any dividend in any financial year, transfer such percentage of its profits for that financial year as it may consider appropriate to the reserves of the company:

   Provided further that where, owing to inadequacy or absence of profits in any financial year, any company proposes to declare dividend out of the accumulated profits earned by it in previous years and transferred by the company to the reserves, such declaration of dividend shall not be made except in accordance with such rules as may be prescribed in this behalf:

   Provided also that no dividend shall be declared or paid by a company from its reserves other than free reserves.

2. Proviso to S. 2. (43) (i) any amount representing unrealized gains, notional gains or revaluation of assets, or (ii) any change in carrying amount of an asset or of a liability recognized in equity, including surplus in profit and loss account on measurement of the asset or the liability at fair value, shall not be treated as free reserves;

3. For the purposes of clause (a) of sub-section (1), depreciation shall be provided in accordance with the provisions of Schedule II.

   (Power of the Central Government in public interest to allow company to declare dividend for any financial year out of profits of the company for that year or any previous financial year or years without providing for depreciation, has been dispensed with).

Interim Dividend

1. The Board of Directors of a company may declare interim dividend during any financial year out of the surplus in the profit and loss account and out of profits of the financial year in which such interim dividend is sought to be declared:

   Provided that in case the company has incurred loss during the current financial year up to the end of the quarter immediately preceding the date of declaration of interim dividend, such interim dividend shall not be declared at a rate higher than the average dividends declared by the company during the immediately preceding three financial years.

2. The amount of the dividend, including interim dividend, shall be deposited in a scheduled bank in a separate account within five days from the date of declaration of such dividend.

Payment of Dividend

(1) No dividend shall be paid by a company in respect of any share therein except to the registered shareholder of such share or to his order or to his banker (erstwhile S. 206) and shall not be payable except in cash:

Provided that nothing in this sub-section shall be deemed to prohibit the capitalization of profits or reserves of a company for the purpose of issuing fully paid-up bonus shares or paying up any amount for the time being unpaid on any shares held by the members of the company:

Provided further that any dividend payable in cash may be paid by cheque or warrant or in any electronic mode to the shareholder entitled to the payment of the dividend.

(2) A company which fails to comply with the provisions of Sections 73 and 74 shall not, so long as such failure continues, declare any dividend on its equity shares.

Unpaid Dividend Account (S. 124)

1. Where a dividend has been declared by a company but has not been paid or claimed within thirty days from the date of the declaration to any shareholder entitled to the payment of the dividend the company shall, within seven days from the date of expiry of the said period of thirty days, transfer the total amount of dividend which remains unpaid or unclaimed to a special account to be opened by the company in that behalf in any scheduled bank to be called the Unpaid Dividend Account.

2. The company shall, within a period of ninety days of making any transfer of an amount under sub-section (1) to the Unpaid Dividend Account, prepare a statement containing the names, their last known addresses and the unpaid dividend to be paid to each person and place it on the website of the company, if any, and also on any other website approved by the Central Government for this purpose, in such form, manner and other particulars as may be prescribed.

3. If any default is made in transferring the total amount referred to in sub-section (1) or any part thereof to the Unpaid Dividend Account of the company, it shall pay, from the date of such default, interest on so much of the amount as has not been transferred to the said account, at the rate of twelve per cent. per annum and the interest accruing on such amount shall accrue to the benefit of the members of the company in proportion to the amount remaining unpaid to them.

4. Any person claiming to be entitled to any money transferred under sub-section (1) to the Unpaid Dividend Account of the company may apply to the company for payment of the money claimed. (S. 205B)

5. Any money transferred to the Unpaid Dividend Account of a company in pursuance of this section which remains unpaid or unclaimed for a period of seven years from the date of such transfer shall be transferred by the company along with interest accrued, if any, thereon to the Fund established under sub-section (1) of section 125 and the company shall send a statement in the prescribed form of the details of such transfer to the authority which administers the said Fund and that authority shall issue a receipt to the company as evidence of such transfer.

6. All shares in respect of which unpaid or unclaimed dividend has been transferred under sub-section (5) shall also be transferred by the company in the name of Investor

Education and Protection Fund (IEPF) along with a statement containing such details as may be prescribed:

7. Provided that any claimant of shares transferred above shall be entitled to claim the transfer of shares from Investor Education and Protection Fund in accordance with such procedure and on submission of such documents as may be prescribed.

8. If a company fails to comply with any of the requirements of this section, the company shall be punishable with fine which shall not be less than five lakh rupees but which may extend to twenty-five lakh rupees and every officer of the company who is in default shall be punishable with fine which shall not be less than one lakh rupees but which may extend to five lakh rupees.

(The above text has been sourced from www.mca.gov.in/SearchableActs/Section123.htm; www.rna-cs.com/note-on-dividend/; https://taxguru.in/company.../complete-analysis-section-123-companies-act-2013.html)

Accounting Entries of Dividend

Dividends are declared from the profit after tax, as decided by the Board of Directors, subject to rules, regulations, or restrictions if any. Once the amount of divided is decided, a provision for the proposed dividend is created by way of closing entries.

1. Proposal of Dividend by Board of Directors:
   Profit and Loss Appropriation A/c or Retained Statement Account Dr.
   (Income type-Less)
      To Provision for proposed dividend account...........
      (Liability type-Add)
2. When the payment of dividend is made:
   Provision for proposed dividend account...........Dr.
   (Liability type-Less)
      To Bank account ....
      (Asset type-Less)

STATEMENT OF RETAINED EARNINGS ■■

The statement of retained earnings was previously known as profit and loss appropriation account, as per the Companies Act, 1956. Now, as per the Companies Act, 2013, it is known as the Statement of Retained Earnings. The net profit of a company is disclosed by the profit and loss account. When the profit and loss account is prepared (without dividing into trading account, profit and loss account, and profit and loss appropriation account), the net profit or loss is transferred to the opposite side of the profit and loss account 'below the line'. All entries, relating to (i) disposal or distribution of profit; and (ii) adjustment relating to previous years, etc. are made in that section.

When the profit and loss account is prepared by dividing into (a) trading account, (b) profit and loss account, and (c) profit and loss appropriation account, all 'below the line' entries are made in the profit and loss appropriation account. The entries appear as follows:

Statement of Retained Earnings

Particulars	Amount (₹)
By Balance b/d (1)	Xxx
By Net profit (Current year) (2)	Xxxx
By Provision of taxation (excess of previous year) (3)	Xx
Total availability (4)	**Xxxx**
To General reserve (5)	Xxx
To Interim dividend (6)	Xxx
To Preference dividend (7)	Xx
To Proposed dividend (8)	Xx
To Corporate dividend tax (9)	Xx
Total utilization (10)	**Xxx**
To Balance c/d (to next year) (11) (4–10)	Xxx

The positive closing balance of statement of retained earnings is shown in the balance sheet under the head 'Reserve and Surpluses'. The negative closing balance of statement of retained earnings is shown in the balance sheet under the head 'Reserve and Surpluses', as reduction in the value of Reserve and Surpluses in the balance sheet.

■ **ILLUSTRATION 11.23** A limited company has a paid-up equity share capital of ₹15,00,000 divided into 1,50,000 shares of ₹10 each and 11% preference share capital of ₹5,00,000 divided into 5,000 shares of ₹100 each. The balance of profit brought forward from the previous balance sheet was ₹38,000.

The profit for the year ended on 31 March 2020 amounted to ₹5,80,000 after tax. The directors proposed a dividend of 24% on equity share capital, after the following provisions:

1. Statutory minimum transfer to general reserve
2. Provision for dividend on preference shares
3. Prepare profit and loss appropriation account

Solution

Statement of Retained Earnings for the year ended.......

Particulars	Amount (₹)
By Balance b/d (1)	38,000
By Net profit (Current year) (2)	5,80,000
Total availability (3)	**6,18,000**
To General reserve (4) (Note 1)	58,000
To Preference dividend (5) (11% of ₹5 lakh)	55,000
To Proposed dividend on equity shares (6) (note 2)	3,60,000
To Corporate dividend tax (7) (note 3)	70,550
Total utilization (8)	**5,43,550**
To Balance c/d (to next year)	**74,450**

Working Notes:

1. When the proposed dividend exceeds 20% of the paid-up capital, the amount to be transferred to reserves should not be less than 10% of the current profits. Here, proposed dividend is 24%. Therefore, the minimum amount to be transferred to general reserve = 10% of ₹5,80,000 = ₹58,000.
2. Proposed dividend on equity shares = 24% of ₹15,00,000 = ₹3,60,000.
3. Corporate dividend tax has been calculated @ 17% on (₹55,000 + ₹3,60,000) = ₹70,550.

INTEREST ON CAPITAL

Capital is a liability of a firm towards its owners. Normally, no interest is paid on the owners' capital. The owner is entitled to receive a share in the profit of the firm. Sometimes, a firm may decide to pay an interest on the capital. For this purpose, an adjustment entry is passed in the books of accounts at the end of the accounting period for interest on capital. Such an entry increases the owner's equity in the form of capital (capital account would be credited) and decreases the retained profit. A reduction in the retained profit means that the interest on capital is considered as an expense of the firm (the net income account would be debited).

■ **ILLUSTRATION 11.24** Kisco Gears started its business from 1 April 2019 with a capital of ₹2,00,000. It was decided by the firm to pay interest on its capital at the rate of 10% p.a. Therefore, the interest on capital would be ₹20,000 for the year ended as on 31 March 2020. Analyse the effect of these transactions on the accounting equation.

Solution

Kisco will increase its expense by ₹20,000 by charging it against the income of the year, and the capital of firm will be increased by the same amount.

Assets	=	Liabilities	+	Contributed Capital	+	Revenue	−	Expenses

In the books of Kisco Gears:

As on 31 March 2020

⬆ Capital increased by ₹20,000
Capital account credit account

⬆ Expense increased by ₹20,000
Interest on capital debit

INTEREST ON DRAWINGS

The owner of a business may withdraw cash to meet personal or household expenses. Drawing is a type of advance provided by the firm to the owner. If the firm pays interest on its capital, then the firm is normally justified to charge interest on the amount or goods withdrawn by the owner. Thus, interest on drawings would be considered as an increase in the income of the firm (credit income account) and a reduction in the capital of the owner (debit capital account).

■ **ILLUSTRATION 11.25** Anuraj Systems started its business on 1 April 2019 with a capital of ₹2,00,000. Its owner Ms Anu used to withdraw ₹5,000 per month. It was decided by the firm to charge interest at a rate of 10% p.a. on the drawings. Therefore, the interest on drawings would be ₹3,000 [(5000 × 12 × ½) × 10%] for the year ended as on 31 March 2020. As the amount is withdrawn every month constantly and evenly, the interest on drawings would be charged on a half yearly basis. Analyse the effect of these transactions on the accounting equation.

Solution

Assets	=	Liabilities	+	Contributed Capital	+	Revenue	−	Expenses

In the books of Anuraj Systems:

As on 31 March 2020

⬇ Capital decreased by ₹3,000
Capital account debit

⬆ Income increased by ₹3,000
Interest on drawings account credit

Thus, the income of Anuraj Systems will increase by ₹3,000 and the capital of the firm will decrease by the same amount.

BONUS ISSUE OF SHARES

A company may capitalize profits by issuing fully paid-up shares to the members, thereby transferring the sums capitalized from the profits and loss account or reserve account to the share capital. Such shares are known as bonus shares and are issued to the existing members of the company free of charge. A issue of a bonus share is a sort of dividend without actual cash payout like in the case of actual dividend.

Cash dividend bonus is paid by the company when it has large accumulated profits and cash to pay the dividend, whereas bonus shares are issued by a company when it wants to capitalize the accumulated profits by issuing shares. The issue of bonus shares increases the number of outstanding shares of a firm. The shares are distributed proportionately. Thus, a shareholder retains his proportionate ownership of the firm. For instance, if a shareholder owns 200 shares at the time when a 10% (i.e., 1: 0.10) bonus issue is made, he will receive 20 additional shares.

The declaration of the bonus shares will enhance the paid-up share capital and reduce the reserve and surplus (retained earnings) of the firm. The total net worth is not affected by the bonus issue. In fact, bonus issue is merely an accounting entry through which funds are transferred from the reserves and surplus to the paid-up capital. As per the Companies Act, a company cannot issue bonus shares in lieu of a cash dividend.

In accordance with the Capital Issue (Control) Act, 1974 (effective from August, 1981), a company can issue bonus shares out of the following:

- Capital redemption reserve account
- Share premium account
- General reserves
- Credit balance in the profit and loss account
- Capital profit (i.e., profit before incorporation, profit on purchase of business, and profit on sale of fixed assets)
- Any other reserves accumulated out of profits

Circumstances of Issuing Bonus Shares

The circumstances in which a company may decide to issue bonus shares to the existing equity shareholders are as follows:

1. A company has accumulated large reserves.
2. The value of fixed assets far exceeds the amount of capital.

3. The market value of shares far exceeds the paid-up value of shares.
4. The higher rate of dividend is not advisable for the distribution of accumulated reserves.

Guidelines on Bonus Issue

A company shall, while issuing bonus shares, ensure the following guidelines issued by the SEBI on 11 June 1992:

1. The bonus issue is made out of the free reserves built out of the genuine profits or share premium collected in cash only.
2. Reserves created by revaluation of fixed assets are not capitalized.
3. The development rebate reserve or the investment allowance reserve is considered as a free reserve in order to calculate the residual reserve test.
4. The residual reserves after the proposed capitalization shall not be less than 40% of the increased paid-up capital.
5. All contingent liabilities disclosed in the audited accounts, which have a bearing on the net profits, shall be considered for computing the residual reserves.
6. The bonus issue is not declared in lieu of dividend.
7. The bonus issue is not made unless the partly paid shares, if any, are fully paid up.
8. No bonus issue shall be made within 12 months of any public/rights issue.
9. No bonus issue shall be made that will dilute the value or rights of the debenture holders.
10. Consequent to the issue of bonus shares, if the subscribed and paid-up capital exceeds the authorized share capital, a resolution shall be passed by the company at its general body meeting for enhancing the authorized capital.
11. There should be a provision in the Articles of Association of the company for the capitalization of reserves. If no such provision is made, the company shall pass a resolution at its general body meeting for making provisions in the Articles for capitalization.
12. A company that announces its issue after the approval of the board of directors should implement the proposals within a period of six months from the date of such approval.

Advantages of Bonus Shares Issue

The advantages of a bonus issue are as follows:

1. It conserves the company's liquidity as no cash leaves the company.
2. The shareholder who receives a dividend can convert it into cash as and when he wants, through selling the additional shares.
3. It broadens the capital base and enhances the image of the company.
4. It helps in reducing the market price of the shares, rendering them more marketable.
5. It is an indication to the prospective investors about the financial soundness of the company.

6. It is one of the best ways of bringing the paid-up capital of the company in line with the actual capital used in the business.
7. It absolves the liability of the shareholders when bonus is applied for converting partly paid-up shares into fully paid-up shares.

Disadvantages of Bonus Shares Issue

The following are the major drawbacks of a bonus issue:

1. After bonus issue, there is a sharp decrease in the future market price of the share.
2. The rate of dividend in future will come down.
3. Lengthy legal procedures and approvals are involved in the issue of bonus shares.
4. When the conversion of partly paid-up shares into fully paid-up shares is made, the company foregoes cash equivalent to the amount of bonus applied for this purpose.

Accounting Entries in the Books of a Company for Bonus Issue of Shares

1. If the bonus is utilized in making partly paid-up shares fully paid-up
   1. For the profits utilized (partly paid-up bonus shares)

Profit and loss A/c (*Less*)	Dr.
General reserve A/c (*Less*)	Dr.
Dividend equalization fund A/c (*Less*)	Dr.
To Bonus to shareholders A/c (*Add*)	

   2. For marking shares fully called-up

Share final call A/c (*Add*)	Dr.
To Share capital A/c (*Add*)	

   3. For making shares fully paid-up

Bonus to shareholders A/c (*Less*)	Dr.
To Share final call A/c (*Less*)	

2. For issuing fully paid-up bonus shares
   1. For profit utilized

Capital redemption reserve A/c (*Less*)	Dr.
Securities premium A/c (*Less*)	Dr.
General reserve A/c (*Less*)	Dr.
Dividend equalization fund A/c (*Less*)	Dr.
Profit and loss account (*Less*)	Dr.
To Bonus to shareholders A/c (*Add*)	

   2. For shares issued

Bonus to shareholders A/c (*Less*)	Dr.
To Share capital A/c (*Add*)	
To Securities premium A/c (*Add*)	

■ **ILLUSTRATION 11.26** Anu Ltd has 50,000 equity shares of ₹10 each, with ₹8 paid-up. It resolves to make the shares fully paid-up by bonus issue. It also resolves to issue fully paid-up bonus shares in the ratio of one share for every two shares held. The company has general reserves of ₹1,50,000 and a share premium balance of ₹2,75,000.

Pass journal entries in connection with the bonus issue.

Solution

Journal Entries in the Books of Anu Ltd

Date	Particulars		L.F.	Dr. (₹)	Cr (₹)
	General reserve A/c (*Less*) To Bonus to shareholders' A/c (*Add*) (The amount used for bonus issue as per shareholders' resolution number... dated....)	Dr.		1,00,000	1,00,000
	Equity share final call A/c (*Add*) To Equity share capital A/c (*Add*) (Shares made fully called-up)	Dr.		1,00,000	1,00,000
	Bonus to shareholders' A/c (*Less*) To Equity share final call A/c (*Less*) (The shares made fully paid-up as per resolution number....)	Dr.		1,00,000	1,00,000
	Securities premium A/c (*Less*) To Bonus to shareholders' A/c (*Add*) (Utilized share premium for bonus issue)	Dr.		2,50,000	2,50,000
	Bonus to shareholders' A/c (*Less*) To Equity share capital A/c (*Add*) (Issued 25,000 shares as fully paid bonus shares)	Dr.		2,50,000	2,50,000

■**ILLUSTRATION 11.27** Techno Services Ltd has ₹2,80,000 in equity share capital, comprising 20,000 shares of ₹10 each, fully paid, and 10,000 shares of ₹10 each, with ₹8 paid-up per share. It has ₹10,000 in the capital reserve, ₹10,000 in the share premium account, ₹35,000 in the capital redemption reserve account, and ₹75,000 in the general reserve. By way of bonus dividend, the partly paid-up shares are converted into fully paid-up shares, and the holder of the fully paid-up shares is allotted a fully paid-up bonus share in the same ratio.

Give journal entries showing the two types of bonus issues stated earlier separately. It is desired that there should be a minimum reduction in the general reserves.

Solution

Journal Entries in the Books of Techno Services Ltd

Date	Particulars		L.F.	Dr. (₹)	Cr (₹)
	Equity share final call A/c (*Add*) To Equity share capital A/c (*Add*) (Final call money of 10,000 shares at ₹2 each due as per board's resolution number dated ....)	Dr.		20,000	20,000
	General reserve A/c (*Less*) To Bonus to shareholders' A/c (*Add*) (Bonus payable @ ₹2 on 10,000 partly called-up shares as per shareholders' resolution number dated....)	Dr.		20,000	20,000
	Bonus to shareholders' A/c (*Less*) To Equity share final call A/c (*Less*) (Utilized bonus towards final call)	Dr.		20,000	20,000
	Capital redemption reserve A/c (*Less*) Securities premium A/c (*Less*) General reserve A/c (*Less*) To Bonus to shareholder's A/c (*Add*) (Bonus share payable to fully paid-up shareholders' in the ratio of 4:1 as per shareholders' resoltuion number dated....)	Dr. Dr. Dr.		35,000 10,000 5,000	50,000
	Bonus to shareholders' A/c (*Less*) To Equity share capital A/c (*Add*) (Issued 5,000 shares of ₹10 each as per shareholders' resolution number dated....)	Dr.		50,000	50,000

Note:

Capital redemption and share premium cannot be utilized for partly paid-up bonus shares.

Further, it is noted that capital reserve arising out of revaluation of assets and/or without the accrual of cash resources are not available for bonus dividend. Here, it is assumed that no cash resources are accrued and hence, not considered.

For ₹8 paid-up, bonus paid is ₹2. Hence, the ratio of bonus issue is 4:1. As such, the fully paid-up shareholders will get ₹50,000 as bonus.

Exhibit 11.1 indicates the treatment and presentation of bonus shares done by Lancer Container Lines Ltd.

EXHIBIT 11.1   Bonus Shares of Lancer Container Lines Ltd

Note 3: SHARE CAPITAL

Particulars	As at 31st March 2018 (₹)	As at 31st March 2017 (₹)
(a) Authorized		
1,50,00,000 (1,10,00,000) Equity shares of ₹10 each	15,00,00,000	11,00,00,000
(b) Issued		
1,00,47,040 (57,09,400) Equity shares of ₹10 each	10,04,70,400	5,70,94,000
(c) Subscribed and fully paid up		
1,00,47,040 (57,09,400) Equity shares of ₹10 each	10,04,70,400	5,70,94,000
TOTAL	10,04,70,400	5,70,94,000

Note 3.1: The Reconciliation of the number of the shares outstandinig is set out below

Particulars	As at 31st March 2018	As at 31st March 2017
	(No of Shares)	(No of Shares)
Equity shares at the beginning of the year	57,09,400	41,69,400
Shares issued during the year	5,70,000	15,40,000
Bonus shares allotted during the year in the ratio of 3:5	37,67,640	-
Equity shares at the end of the year	1,00,47,040	57,09,400

Note 3.2: Terms/Rights attached to Equity Shares
The Company has only one class of Equity Shares having a par value of ₹10/- per share. Each holder of the Equity shares is entitled to one vote per share. The Company declares and pays dividends in Indian rupees and every equity share is entitled to the same rate of dividend.
In the event of liquidation of the company, the holders of the equity shares will be entitled to receive the remaining assets of the company after distribution of all preferential amounts, in proportion to their shareholding.

Source: Lancer Container Lines Ltd Annual Report 2017–18, p. 52. Used by permission.

RIGHTS ISSUE

The issue of shares by an existing company to the existing shareholders as a first right to acquire the shares of the company is known as rights issue. It is the exclusive right of the shareholder to decide whether to accept the offer or not. Normally, if the offered right price is lesser than the prevailing market price, then shareholders will accept it, because, through the exercise of the right shares, shareholders can gain profit by selling the shares in the open, market. Sometimes, instead of exercising the right, shareholders may sell their entitlement in the open market, and book the profits. The entitlement price is normally close to the value of the right. The right can be valued in terms of money as given in this section:

1. Calculate the market value of the shares that an existing shareholder is required to have in order to obtain fresh right shares.
2. Add to the derived price, the amount paid to the company for the fresh right shares.
3. Determine the average price of the existing shares and the fresh shares.
4. The average price of the share should be deducted from the market price, and the difference thus ascertained is the value of the right.

$$\text{Average Price of the Share} = \frac{\text{Market Price of the Existing Shares} + \text{Issue Price of Proportionate Right Shares}}{\text{Existing Shares} + \text{Right Shares}}$$

There are some basic differences between rights issue and public issue as shown in Table 11.1.

Table 11.1   Rights Issue vs Public Issue

Rights Issue	Public Issue
It is made to the existing shareholders.	It is made to the public at large.
Low floatation cost as there is no chance of over-subscription of shares.	High floatation cost as there is a chance of over-subscription and pro-rata allotment of shares.
Its price is much lesser than the existing market price.	Its price is generally lower than the expected market price.

■ **ILLUSTRATION 11.28**   A company offers to its existing shareholders the right to buy one share of ₹100 each at ₹120 for every three shares held. The cum rights quotations in the market for the company's shares are ₹180. Compute the value of the rights.

Solution

1. Cum rights market price of three shares is ₹180 × 3 = ₹540
2. Add the issue price of one new share   = ₹120

   Total price of four shares after the rights are availed = ₹660

3. Average price = 660/4 = ₹165
4. Market price – Average Price = Value of Rights
₹180 – ₹165 = ₹15
Therefore, the value of the right = ₹15

EMPLOYEE STOCK OPTION PLAN

In order to retain high-calibre employees or to give them a sense of belonging, companies may offer them equity shares to be purchased at their will. Such a scheme is known as employee stock option plan (ESOP). An ESOP implies the right, but not an obligation, granted to an employee to purchase shares of the company at a pre-determined price, in pursuance of the ESOP.

Accounting Treatment

The value of options granted to the employees is to be treated as another form of employee compensation. In other words, it will be treated as an expense of the company and hence has to be written off over the vesting period. When the option is granted, the value of the option is the difference between exercised price and closing market price of the share multiplied by the number of options. In other words, accounting value of an option is equal to the number of options multiplied by the difference of the market price and exercise price.

Option Value = Number of Options × (Market Price – Exercise Price)

If a company grants 200 options to its employees at the rate of ₹30 per option, and on that date the market price of the share is ₹160, the value of options will be

= 200 × (160 – 30) = ₹26,000

This is also known as option discount, which can also be determined by using the Black Scholes formula or any other similar valuation method.

1. When option is granted
Deferred employee compensation expense A/c (*Add*)Dr.
To Employee stock option outstanding A/c (*Add*)
2. When employees exercise the option
Cash/bank A/c (*Add*)   Dr.
Employee stock option outstanding A/c (*Less*)   Dr.
To Equity share capital A/c (*Add*)
To Securities premium A/c (*Add*)

3. For amortizing the expense
Employee compensation expense A/c (*Add*)   Dr.
To Deferred employee compensation expense A/c (*Less*)
4. When the options lapse

When the options lapse, the value of such options is divided into two parts, namely, the amortized portion of the value of options and the unamortized portion of the value of options.

Amortized Value of Options Lapsed = Number of Options Lapsed × Discount × Time Interval between the Offer Date and Date of Lapse/Vesting Period

Unamortized Value of Options Lapsed = Number of Options Lapsed × Discount × Time Interval between the Date of Lapse and Vesting Period/Vesting Period

Entry for this will be as follows:
Employee stock options outstanding A/c (*Less*)   Dr.
To Employee compensation expense (amortized value) A/c (*Less*)
To Deferred employee compensation expense (unamortized value) A/c (*Less*)

In the balance sheet, employee stock options outstanding will appear as part of shareholders' equity and deferred employee compensation will appear as a negative item forming a part of shareholders' equity. This implies that liability will be treated as issued capital and expense as debit to equity capital.

■ **ILLUSTRATION 11.29** Cauvery Software Limited granted 2,000 options on 1 April 2018 at ₹50, when the market price was ₹150. The vesting period is two years.

You are required to

- calculate the value of options;
- calculate the amount to be amortized every year; and
- make the necessary journal entries for the years 2018/19 and 2019/20.

Solution

1. Value of Opitons = Number of Options Granted × (Market Price - Exercise Price) = 2000 × (150 – 50) = ₹2,00,000
2. Vesting period is two years. This value of options shall be amortized on a straight-line basis over the vesting period. Therefore, the amount to be amorized every year = ₹2,00,000/2 = ₹1,00,000

Journal Entries in the Books of Cauvery Software Limited

Date	Particulars		L.F.	Dr. (₹)	Cr (₹)
1/4/2018	Deferred employee compensation expense A/c (*Add*)	Dr.		2,00,000	
	To Employee stock options outstanding A/c (*Add*)				2,00,000
	(Being the grant of 2,000 options at a discount of ₹100 each)				
1/4/2019	Employee compensation expense A/c (*Add*)	Dr.		1,00,000	
	To Deferred employee compensation expense A/c (*Less*)				
	(Being the amortization of the deferred compensation over two years on straight-line basis)				1,00,000
1/4/2020	Employee compensation expense A/c (*Add*)	Dr.		1,00,000	
	To Deferred employee compensation expense A/c (*Less*)				
	(Being the amortization of the deferred compensation over two years on straight-line basis)				1,00,000

■ **ILLUSTRATION 11.30** PWC Limited granted 1,500 options on 1 April 2015 at ₹80, when the market price was ₹160. The vesting period was 3 years. The maximum exercise period was 1 year. All the 1,500 options were exercised by the employees on 30 October 2018. Make the necessary journal entries recording the transactions.

Solution

Value of Options = Number of Options Granted × (Market Price – Exercise Price)

= 1500 × (160 – 80) = ₹1,20,000

Amount to be amortized = ₹1,20,000/3 = ₹40,000 each year.

Journal Entries In the Books PWC Limited

Date	Particulars	L.F.	Dr. (₹)	Cr (₹)
1/4/2015	Deferred employee compensation expense A/c (*Add*)	Dr.	1,20,000	
	To Employee stock options outstanding A/c (*Add*)			1,20,000
	(Being the grant of 1,500 options at a discount of ₹80 each)			
31/3/2016	Employee compensation expense A/c (*Add*)	Dr.	40,000	
	To Deferred employee compensation expense A/c (*Less*)			
	(Being the amortization of the deferred compensation over 3 years on straight-line basis)			40,000
31/3/2017	Employee compensation expense A/c (*Add*)	Dr.	40,000	
	To Deferred employee compensation expense A/c (*Less*)			
	(Being the amortization of the deferred compensation over 3 years on straight-line basis)			40,000
31/3/2018	Employee compensation expense A/c (*Add*)	Dr.	40,000	
	To Deferred employee compensation expense A/c (*Less*)			
	(Being the amortization of the deferred compensation over 3 years on straight-line basis)			40,000
30/10/2018	Bank A/c (1,500 × ₹80) (*Add*)	Dr.	1,20,000	
	Employee stock options outstanding A/c (*Less*)		1,20,000	
	To Equity share capital A/c (*Add*)			15,000
	To Securities premium A/c (*Add*)			2,25,000
	(Being the exercise of 1,500 options)			

Working Note:
Security Premium is ₹150 per option (₹160 – ₹10). Total options are 1,500. Hence, ₹2,25,000 (150 × 1,500)

Exhibit 11.2 indicates the presentation of ESOP and its scheme, as explained by Future Retail Ltd.

EXHIBIT 11.2   ESOP of Future Retail Ltd

ANNEXURE III

Future Retail Limited Employees Stock Option Plan – 2016 (FRL ESOP – 2016) of the Company as at March 31, 2018.

To encourage ownership of Company's equity by its employees on an ongoing basis and also in order to reward the employees for their contribution to the successful operation of the Company and to provide an incentive to continue contributing to the success of the Company, it was proposed to create, grant and offer options to the Eligible Employees of the Company under Future Retail Limited Employees Stock Option Plan – 2016 (FRL ESOP – 2016) as recommended by the People Office.

SI. No.	Particulars	FRL ESOP-2016
A.	Disclosures in terms of the Guidance note on accounting for employee share based payments issued by ICAI or any other relevant accounting standards as prescribed from time to time	Refer Note No. 39 in Notes to Financial Statements
B.	Diluted Earnings Per Share (EPS) on issue of shares pursuant to all the schemes covered under the regulations shall be disclosed in accordance with Accounting Standard 20 – Earnings Per Share issued by ICAI or any other relevant accounting standards as prescribed from time to time	Refer Note No. 38 in Notes to Financial Statements

C. Description of ESOS that existed at any time during the year including the general terms and conditions

I.	Date of Shareholders' approval	The Shareholders of the Company had passed necessary resolutions through Postal Ballot dated November 07, 2016 and approved the FRL ESOP - 2016 which *inter-alia* provides to offer, issue and allot at any time or to acquire by way of Secondary Acquisition (through Trust Route), to or for the benefit of Eligible Employees of the Company and/or to the Eligible Employees of the Subsidiary Company(ies) of the Company, if any.
II.	Total number of options approved under FRL ESOP-2016	90,00,000 (Ninety Lakh only) Equity Shares of face value of ₹2/- each

III.	Vesting requirements	Option -1*	Option - II^
		Options in respect of employees transferred from FEL pursuant to the Scheme of Arrangement were vested effective December 15, 2016.	Options granted under FRL ESOP 2016 plan would vest not less than 1 year and not more than 3 years from the Grant of such options.
IV.	Exercise price or pricing formula	Exercise price for Options granted during the year was ₹10/-	Exercise price for Options granted during the year was ₹10/-
V.	Maximum term of options granted	3 years from the respective date of option granted	3 years from the respective date of option granted
VI.	Source of shares (primary, secondary or combination)	Primary	Primary
VII.	Variation in terms of options	None	None
VIII.	Method used to account for ESOS	Black Scholes Method	Black Scholes Method

D. The stock-based compensation cost was calculated as per the fair value method, the total cost to be recognised in the financial statements for the year 2017-18 would be ₹5.13 Crore.

E. Option movement during the year ended on March 31, 2018

Sl. No.	Particulars	Details	
		Option -1*	Option - II^
I.	Details Number of options outstanding at the beginning of the year	1,73,421	6,56,710
II.	Number of options granted during the year	NIL	NIL
II.	Number of options forfeited/Cancelled/lapsed during the year	8,392	NIL
IV.	Number of options vested during the year	NIL	3,28,355
V.	Number of options exercised during the year	1,51,622	NIL
VI.	Number of shares arising as a result of exercise of options	1,51,622	NA
VII.	Exercise Price	₹10/- per share	NA
VIII.	Money realized by exercise of options, if scheme is implemented directly by the Company	₹15,16,220/-	NA
IX.	Loan repaid by the Trust during the year from exercise price received	NA	NA
X.	Total number of options outstanding (in force) at the end of the year	13,407	6,56,710
XI.	Number of options exercisable at the end of the year	13,407	3,28,355

F. Weighted average Share Price of options granted during the year:

The Company has not granted any options during the year under review. However, the details pertaining to the options granted during the financial year 2016-17 are as follows:

		Option -1*	Option - II^	
		Grant on December 15, 2016	Grant on December 06, 2016	Grant on December 15, 2016
I.	Exercise price equals market price (₹)	-	-	-
II.	Exercise price is greater than market price (₹)	-	-	-
III.	Exercise price is less than market price (₹)	10	10	10

Weighted average Fair Value of options (Black Scholes) granted during the year whose:

		Option -1*	Option - II^	
		Grant on December 15, 2016	Grant on December 06, 2016	Grant on December 15, 2016
I.	Exercise price equals market price (₹)	-	-	-
II.	Exercise price is greater than market price (₹)	-	-	-
III.	Exercise price is less than market price (₹)	119.03	116.82	119.02

G. Employee-wise details of options granted during the year on March 31, 2018
Employee-wise details of options granted during the year on March 31, 2018

Source: Future Retail Limited Annual Report 2017–18, pp. 35–36.

EMPLOYEE STOCK PURCHASE SCHEME

Under the *employee stock purchase scheme* (ESPS), a company can issue shares to its employees at a price lesser than the market value. The journal entry will be as follows:

Cash or Bank A/c (*Add*)	Dr. (Issue price × Number of shares)
Employee compensation expense A/c (*Add*)	Dr. (Accounting value of options)
To Share capital A/c (*Add*)	(Number of shares × Face value)
To Securities premium A/c (*Add*)	(Number of shares) × (Market price – Face value)

Note:

Accounting Value of Options = Number of Options (Shares) × (Market Price – Exercise Price)

■ ILLUSTRATION 11.31 Krishnan & Company Ltd issued 5,000 shares on 1 January 2020 under ESPS at ₹50 per share when the market price was ₹100 per share. The nominal value of one share is ₹10. Make the journal entry.

Solution

Accounting value of shares = 5,000 × (100 – 50) = ₹2,50,000
Share Premium = Number of Options Exercised × (Market Price – Face Value)
= 5,000 × (100 – 10) = ₹4,50,000

Journal Entries in the Books of Krishnan and Co. Ltd

Date	Particulars		L.F.	Dr. (₹)	Cr. (₹)
1 Jan. 2020	Bank A/c (*Add*)	Dr.		2,50,000	
	Employee's compensation expense (*Add*)	Dr.		2,50,000	
	To Equity share capital A/c (*Add*)				50,000
	To Share premium A/c (*Add*)				4,50,000
	(Issued 5,000 shares under ESPS at a price of ₹50 each when the market price is ₹100)				

PRIVATE PLACEMENT OF SHARES

According to Section 42 of the Companies Act, 2013, private placement of shares implies issue and allotment of shares to a selected group of persons. In other words, an issue, which is not a public issue but offered to a select group of persons, is referred to as 'private placement of shares'. All SEBI guidelines concerning preferential issue are applicable to private placement of shares as well. In order to make issue of shares through the private placement route, a company should pass a special resolution to this effect. Where no such resolution is passed, but the number of votes cast in favour exceeds the number of votes cast against the proposal, the board of directors of such company can make an application to the central government for obtaining consent by stating that the proposal is required by the company.

Accounting Treatment

Accounting entries relating to the private placement of securities will be similar to those discussed earlier at the time of applications and allotments as also the accounting entries stated under the caption 'Issue of shares for a consideration other than cash'. If shares are issued for redeeming the convertible portion of debentures or the time of surrender of warrants, the following entries will be made:

1. For transferring amount convertible debentures
   Convertible debentures A/c (*Add*)   Dr.
   To Debenture holders A/c (*Add*)
2. For receiving applications:
   Debenture holders A/c (*Less*)   Dr.
   To Equity share application A/c (*Add*)
3. For making allotment
   Equity share application A/c (*Less*)   Dr.
   To Equity share capital A/c (*Add*)
   To Securities premium (If any) (*Add*)

When warrants are surrendered, the warrants are cancelled and the shares are issued.

BUYBACK OF SHARES

The term *buyback of shares* implies the act of purchasing its own shares by a company either from free reserve, securities premium, or proceeds of any shares or securities. According to

Section 68 to 70 of the Companies Act, 2013, a company can buy its own shares either from the (a) existing equity shareholders on a proportionate basis, (b) open market, (c) odd lot shareholders, or (d) employee of the company pursuant to a scheme of stock option or sweat equity. Following are the procedural rules:

1. The buyback should be authorized by the Articles.
2. The special resolution is to be passed at the general meeting of shareholders.
3. The buyback of the shares cannot exceed 25% of the paid-up capital and free reserves in a financial year.
4. The debt–equity ratio should not be more than 2:1 after such buyback.
5. All the shares for buyback should be fully paid-up.
6. The buyback should be completed within 12 months from the date of passing the special resolution.
7. The company must file a solvency declaration with the registrar and SEBI in the form of an affidavit signed by at least two directors of the company. The affidavit must state that the board has made full inquiry into the affairs of the company as a result of which they have formed an opinion that the company is capable of meeting its liabilities and will not render insolvent within a period of one year from the date of declaration adopted by the board.

Extinguishment of Certificates

A company that buys back its own shares shall extinguish and physically destroy such shares within seven days of the last date of completion of buyback in the presence of merchant bankers or registrar or statutory auditor.

No Future Issue

Where a company completes the buyback of its shares, it shall not make further issue of shares within a period of 24 months except by way of bonus issue or in the discharge of some obligation such as conversion of warrants, stock option schemes, sweat equity, or conversion of preference shares and debentures into equity shares.

■ **ILLUSTRATION 11.32** ABC Limited furnished the following balance sheet as at 31 March 2020.

Balance Sheet of ABC Limited
as at 31 March 2020

(in crore)

Particulars		Amount (₹)
Sources of Funds		
Share capital		
Authorized		100
Issued : 12% Redeemable preference shares of ₹100 each	75	
Equity shares of ₹10 each	25	100
Reserves and surplus		
Revenue reserves	260	
Capital reserves	15	
	25	300
Securities premium		
Total sources		400
Uses of Funds		
Fixed assets	100	
Less: Provision for depreciation	100	NIL
Investments at cost (Market value ₹400 crores)		100
Current Assets:	340	
Less: Current Liabilities	40	300
Total uses		400

The company bought back 50 lakhs equity shares of ₹10 each at ₹50 per share. The payment for this was made out of the bank balance, which appears as part of current assets. Pass journal entries to record these transactions.

Solution

Journal Entries in the Books of ABC Limited
(in crore)

Date	Particulars		L.F.	Dr. (₹)	Cr (₹)
	Equity share capital A/c (*Less*)	Dr.		5	
	Securities premium A/c (*Less*)	Dr.		20	
	To Equity shareholders A/c (*Add*)				25
	(Being the amount payable to equity shareholders on buyback of equity shares as per special resolution number dated...)				
	Equity shareholders A/c (*Less*)	Dr.		25	
	To Bank A/c (*Less*)				25
	(Being the equity shareholders paid-off against buyback of shares)				
	Securities premium A/c (*Less*)	Dr.		5	
	To Capital redemption reserve A/c (*Add*)				5
	(Being the creation of capital redemption reserve as per requirement of the Act)				

DISCLOSURE OF SHARE CAPITAL IN CORPORATE BALANCE SHEET ▬▬

The disclosure of share capital in the balance sheet is presented in Exhibit 11.3. Exhibit 11.3 shows the presentation of the annual report of Pressman Advertising Ltd (Annual Report, p. 37).

EXHIBIT 11.3   Share Capital in Balance Sheet: Pressman Advertising Ltd

Notes to financial statements for the year ended 31st March, 2018

₹ in lakh

	As at 31st March 2018	As at 31st March 2017	As at 1st April 2016
13) EQUITY SHARE CAPITAL			
Authorised Share Capital			
12,50,00,000 (31st March 2017:12,50,00,000,1st April 2016:12,50,00,000)			
equity shares of ₹2/- each	2,500.00	2,500.00	2,500.00
2,50,00,00 (31st March 2017: 2,50,00,000,1st April 2016: 2,50,00,000)			
redeemable cumulative preference shares of ₹10/- each	2.500.00	2,500.00	2,500.00
	5,000.00	5,000.00	5,000.00
Issued, subscribed and fully paid-up			
2,34,82,843 (31st March 2017:2,34,82,843,1st April 2016: 2,34,82,843)			
equity shares of ₹2/- each fully paid-up	469.66	469.66	469.66

(a) Reconciliation of shares outstanding at the beginning and at the end of the reporting period

	31st March 2018		31st March 2017		1st April 2016	
Equity Shares	No.	₹ in lakh	No.	₹ in lakh	No.	₹ in lakh
At the beginning and end of the year	23,482,843	469.66	23,482,843	469.66	2,348,283	469.66

(b) Terms/rights attached to equity shares

The Company has issued equity shares having par value of ₹2 per share. Each holder of an equity share is entitled to one vote per share. The Company declares and pays dividends in Indian rupees.

In the event of liquidation of the Company, after distribution of all preferential amounts, the remaining assets of the company will be distributed to equity shareholders in proportion to their shareholding.

(c) Details of shareholders holding more than 5% Equity Shares of ₹2 each fully paid up in the Company

Name of the shareholder	31st March 2018		31st March 2017		1st April 2016	
	No. of Equity Shares	% holding	No. of Equity Shares	% holding	No. of Equity Shares	% holding
Equity shares of ₹2 each fully paid up						
Dr Niren Suchanti	5,297,714	22.56%	5,297,714	22.56%	5,312,216	22.62%
Mr Navin Suchanti	4,445,800	18.93%	4,445,800	18.93%	5,060,902	21.55%
Mrs Sujata Suchanti	795,353	3.38%	795,353	3.38%	1,706,338	7.27%
Mrs Pramina Suchanti	541,713	2.31%	541,714	2.31%	1,940,729	8.26%

As per records of the Company and information provided by its registrar, the above shareholding represents both legal and beneficial ownership of shares.

Source: Pressman Advertising Ltd Annual Report 2017–18, pp. 30–31. Used by permission.

SUMMARY

- A company is an artificial person created by law with a perpetual succession and a common seal.
- A company comes into existence through the operation of law and has a separate legal entity.
- Share capital is the amount of money contributed by shareholders for the furtherance of objectives of the company for which it was created. There are different classes of shares such as equity shares and preference shares.
- Groups of individuals, companies, venture capitalists, or other association of persons, want to have control over the management of the company. In such circumstances, the equity shares of the company are allotted by company to such members on preferential basis at pre-determined price.
- The voluntary return of the shares by shareholders with an intention to cancel their shares, and in turn remove their name from the register of members of the company, is known as surrender of shares.
- The issue of shares by an existing company to the existing shareholders as a first right to acquire the shares of the company is known as rights issue. It in the exclusive right of the shareholder whether to accept the offer or not.
- Bonus implies an extra dividend to the shareholders of a company.

- It may be distributed by way of cash bonus or bonus share. Cash bonus is paid by the company when it has large accumulated profits and cash to pay dividend, whereas bonus shares are issued by a company when it wants to pay dividend by issuing shares. Thus, issuing bonus shares, without charging any amount from the existing shareholders, is called bonus issue.
- Redemption means repayment of the principal capital amount to the preference shareholders by the company. The redemption amount is decided as per issue arrangement in the beginning, or in any further resolution passed later in the meeting of preference shareholders. The company is not allowed to redeem the partly paid-up preference shares.
- When a company uses the distributable retained profit, an amount equal to the face value of shares redeemed is transferred to capital redemption reserve account by debiting the distributable profit.
- The net profit after tax available for distribution to shareholders as dividend is called divisible profits. The divisible profit means profit after tax and after deducting the dividend among the preference shareholders. It is also known as profit available for distribution among the equity shareholders of the company.
- Company can also raise the funds through debentures, which is one type of liability for the firm.

KEYWORDS

Calls-in-advance It is the amount that is paid but not yet called up.

Calls-in-arrears or unpaid call The total unpaid amount on one or more instalments is known as calls-in-arrears.

Charge It is an encumbrance to meet the obligation under trust deed, whereby the company agrees to mortgage a specific portion either by way of a first or second charge.

Company It is an artificial entity created by law with perpetual succession and a common seal.

Corporation A corporation is an artificial entity that is invisible and intangible and that exists only in the contemplation of law.

Debenture It is an instrument of a company's debt.

Employee stock option value It is the product of the number of options multiplied by the difference in the market price and the

exercise price of the stock.

Forfeiture of share It is the cancellation of allotment to defaulting shareholders and to treat the amount already received thereon as forfeited to the company.

Share A share is the interest of a shareholder in the company measured by a sum of money, for the purpose of liability in the first place and of interest in the second, but also consisting of mutual covenants entered into by all the shareholders in terms of the Act and the Articles.

Share capital It is the amount of money contributed by shareholders for furthering the objectives of the company.

Share premium It is the excess of the issue price over the face value of the security.

QUESTIONS

I. Solve the following problems.

1. A company issued 10,000 equity shares of ₹10 each at a premium of ₹3 per share, payable as follows:

On application	₹4 per share
On allotment	₹5 per share (including premium)
On first and final calls	₹4 per share

Subscriptions were received for 13,000 shares. The excess money was refunded, and the allotment money was received in full. The first and final calls were made in due course, and the amount due was received with the exception for 100 shares. These shares were forfeited and subsequently reissued as fully paid for ₹8 per share. Pass journal entries recording the transactions discussed earlier.

2. Neon Limited issued a prospectus offering 2,00,000 equity shares of ₹10 each, at a premium of ₹2 per share, payable as follows:

On application	₹2.50 per share
On allotment (including premium)	₹4.50 per share
On first call (three months from allotment)	₹2.50 per share
On second call (three months after call)	₹2.50 per share

Subscriptions were received for 3,17,000 shares on 23 April 2020, and the allotment made on 30 April was as given in the following text:

Shares allotted

- Allotment in full (two applicants paid in full on allotment in respect of 4,000 shares each)   38,000

- Allotment of two shares for every three shares applied for   1,60,000
- Allotment of one share for every four shares applied for   2,000

Cash amounting to ₹77,500 (being application money received with applications on 31,000 shares upon which no allotments were made) was returned to applicants on 6 May 2020. The amounts called from the allottees were received on the due dates with the exception of the final call on 100 shares. These shares were forfeited on 15 November 2020 and reissued to A on 16 November for payment of ₹9 per share. The Company adopted Table F as its Article of Association. Record journal entries other than those relating to cash, in the books of Neon Limited, and also show how the transactions would appear in the balance sheet, assuming that the company paid interest due from it on 31 October 2020.

3. Zeta Limited had 3,000, redeemable preference shares of ₹100 each at 12%, fully paid-up. The company had to redeem these shares at a premium of 10%. It was decided by the company to issue the following:
   1. 25,000 equity shares of ₹10 each at par
   2. 1,000 14% debentures of ₹100 each

The issue was fully subscribed and all amounts were received in full. The payment was duly made. The company had sufficient profits. Make journal entries in the books of the company.

4. The balance sheet of Sarovar Ltd as at 31 March 2020 is as follows:

Balance Sheet of Sarovar Ltd
as at 31 March 2020

Particulars	Amount (₹)
ASSETS	
Sundry assets	2,20,000
Cash at bank	50,000
Total Assets	**2,70,000**
EQUITY AND LIABILITIES	
Issued and Paid up Share Capital	
10,000 equity shares of ₹10 each fully paid up	1,00,000
8,000 equity shares of ₹10 each, with ₹8 per share called up	40,000
General reserves	1,10,000
Sundry creditors	20,000
Total Equity and Liabilities	**2,70,000**

The company declares bonus shares out of the general reserve and decides to capitalize the shares of ₹10 each by

- issuing one equity share of ₹10 against four existing fully paid equity shares of ₹10 each, and
- making partly paid-up equity shares into fully paid-up shares.

Pass journal entries for the transactions, and also show the balance sheet.

5. National Textiles Ltd have an issued capital of ₹20,000 equity shares of ₹10 each, of which ₹8.75 per share is paid. The following decisions are taken by the company:

- To forfeit 100 shares on which only ₹5 per share has been paid-up, and to reissue these at ₹15 per share (paid-up value ₹8.75)
- To make shares fully paid-up through capitalization of the reserve
- To issue right shares in the ratio of one fully paid-up share for every four existing shares held at ₹15 per share

Assuming that the company has sufficient general reserve, record the events discussed through a journal.

6. Hindustan Lever Limited granted 500 options on 1 April 2017 at ₹40 (nominal value ₹10 each) when the market price was ₹160, the vesting period was two-and-a-half years. The maximum exercise period was three years. On 1 May 2019, 150 unvested options lapsed and 300 options were exercised on 30 June 2020, and the remaining 50 options lapsed at the end of the exercise period. Record the necessary journal entries.

7. On 31 March 2018, following was the balance sheet of New Era Ltd (figures in rupees lakhs).

Balance Sheet of New Era Ltd
as at 31 March 2018

Particulars	Amount (₹)
ASSETS	
Machinery	3,600
Furniture	452
Investments	148
Stock	1,200
Debtors	520
Cash at bank	740
Total Assets	**6,660**
EQUITY AND LIABILITIES	
Equity share capital (Fully paid up of ₹10 each)	2,400
Share premium	350
General reserves	930
Profit and loss account	340
12% Debentures	1,500
Sundry creditors	750
Sundry provisions	390
Total Equity and Liabilities	**6,660**

On 1 April 2018, the company announced the buyback of 25% of its equity shares @ ₹15 per share. For this purpose, it sold all of its investments for ₹150 lakhs and issued 2,00,000, 14% preference shares of ₹100 each at par—the entire amount being payable with application.

The issue was fully subscribed. The company achieved the target of the buyback. Later, the company issued one fully paid-up equity share of ₹10 by way of bonus shares for every four equity shares held by the equity shareholders.

Make journal entries for all the transactions including cash transactions.

8. The balance sheet of Modern Marbles Ltd as at 31 March 2018 is as follows:

On 31 March 2018, the shareholders adopted the following resolution:

Balance Sheet of Modern Marbles Ltd
as at 31 March 2018

Particulars	Amount (₹)
ASSETS	
Fixed assets	66,00,000
Investments	18,00,000
Stock	11,87,000
Sundry debtors	9,60,000
Cash and bank balance	7,10,000
Total Assets	**1,12,57,000**
EQUITY AND LIABILITIES	

Share capital of ₹10 each	50,00,000
Securities premium	5,40,000
General reserves	6,50,000
Profit and loss account	3,75,000
12% Debentures	25,00,000
Term loan	13,25,000
Current liabilities and provisions	8,67,000
Total Equity and Liabilities	**1,12,57,000**

1. Buyback 20% of the paid-up capital @ ₹15 each.
2. Issue 5,000, 13% debentures of ₹100 each at a premium of 10% to finance the buyback of shares
3. Maintain a balance of ₹3,00,000 in general reserve account
4. Sell investments worth ₹8,00,000 for ₹6,50,000.

Make the necessary journal entries to record the transactions and prepare the balance sheet immediately after the buyback.

REFERENCES

ICAI's various guidelines.
Companies Act, 2013.
The Gazette of India.

ICSI's study notes.
Legal documents of SEBI.

Financial Statements

Bank Reconciliation Statement

Learning Objectives

After studying this chapter, you will understand

- meaning of bank reconciliation statement and its objectives
- reasons for differences in balances and their implications
- how to prepare a bank reconciliation statement

INTRODUCTION

A firm's cash balance is a very important indicator of its financial condition. In the context of accounting, *cash* means any item that is customarily accepted by the public at large, that is, physical unit for exchange of value (e.g., rupees in India) and bank cheque. A firm mentions transactions through the bank in the bank column of the cash book or in the bank book for the purpose of accounting and to fulfil the requirement of accounting mechanics. Such transactions are recorded in the bank book or in the bank columns of the cash book and can be verified through an external record, namely, the bank statement received periodically from the banker.

To keep control over cash transactions and to prevent the misuse of or misappropriation of cash, a firm may keep an account with one or more banks. It is not necessary for the firm to keep large amounts of cash in the office or at the workplace, which is risky; receipts and payments through banks reduce the chance of fraud and misappropriation and the accounting work of the firm to some extent.

Every firm keeps a cash book to record its cash and bank transactions. The bank also keeps a record of customer's account showing the deposits, withdrawals, service charges, and other transactions of the customer. When any individual or firm opens an account in any bank, the bank issues a pass book to its customers or periodically sends a statement of account to show the bank transactions. This pass book is nothing but a copy of the ledger account of the customer in the books of the bank. The form of bank pass book (or Statement of Account) is produced in Exhibit 12.1.

EXHIBIT 12.1 Bank Pass Book or Statement of Account

State Bank of India, Kamala Nagar, Delhi-110007

Name of the Customer   Account No.

Date	Particulars	Cheque No.	Amount Withdrawn (Dr.)	Amount Deposited (Cr.)	Balance Dr. or Cr.

Cash book has already been discussed in an earlier chapter. Here in the context of the bank reconciliation statement, cash book means bank column in the columnar cash book or bank account in the books of the firm. The balance shown by the bank pass book on a particular date should show the same balance as shown by the bank balance in the cash book of the firm. However, in actual practice, both pass book and cash book balances may not agree.

A bank book is a copy of the bank account in the books of the customer. A pass book or bank statement is a copy of the customer's account in the ledger books of the bank.

The banker acts as a custodian of the spendable funds of the firm. The customer may deposit cash or cheque with the aid of a *paying-in-slip*, and can withdraw money by means of a *cheque* or *withdrawal slip*. Since the banker is the trustee of the customer, the bank provides to its customer a *bank statement* (for current or cash credit account) or updates *the pass book* (for savings bank account) at regular intervals, which summarizes payments as well as deposits, other charges levied by bank for the period, etc. In other words, a bank statement is a copy of the customer's account in the bank's ledger.

Overdraft is a facility with a bank enabling a customer to overdraw an account up to a specified limit.

Therefore, the bank balance as per the bank book of a firm and the balance as per bank statement or pass book should be equal and *opposite* on a stated date; opposite meaning that as per the firm's book it is deposit or receivable from bank, while as per the bank statement it is payable.

However, in practice, these two balances may not agree. The main reason for the difference in balance is that one party does not intimate the other every time that a transaction takes place. Many of the transactions of the customer are intimated to a banker by a third party (e.g., when a cheque is presented). Disagreement in balances may arise owing to a mistake or mistakes in the cash book or bank book. When all the facts are traced and brought together, it is possible for the firm to reconcile the differences in balance by noting down the reasons in one statement, which is known as *bank reconciliation statement*.

The difference between the balance as per bank book and bank pass book is known as the bank reconciliation statement.

By reconciliation, the bank book balance can be verified by a comparison with the bank statement. Bank reconciliation is an important part of an internal control system, and as a prudent policy, is carried out by a person who is not in charge of the banking transactions of the firm.

MEANING AND OBJECTIVE OF A BANK RECONCILIATION STATEMENT

A bank reconciliation statement is a statement reconciling the balance as shown by the bank statement (or bank pass book) and the balance shown by the bank book. The objective of preparing such a statement is to know the causes of difference between the two balances, and pass necessary correcting or adjusting entries in the books of the firm if required. The preparation of a bank reconciliation statement is not part of the double-entry bookkeeping system or accounting mechanics. It is just a procedure to prove the bank book balance.

A bank reconciliation statement is prepared with the view to find out the causes responsible for the difference between the balance of cash book and pass book, and to reconcile the balance. The cash book is maintained and possessed by the firm but the pass book or statement of customer's account is prepared by the bank and sent to the customer for information. In this way, both the books are with the customer and he/she can compare them and verify records at his/her own convenience. Bank reconciliation statements are prepared by the firm at regular intervals. It may be prepared every month, every week, or even daily, depending on the number of transactions and the size of the firm. While preparing a bank reconciliation statement, the first step is to identify the transactions that cause a difference between the balance of the cash book and that of the pass book.

NEED FOR A BANK RECONCILIATION STATEMENT

A bank reconciliation statement is needed for the following reasons:

1. It reflects the actual bank balance position.
2. It helps to detect any mistake in the bank book or the bank column of the cash book and in the pass book or the bank statement.
3. It prevents fraud in recording banking transactions.
4. It explains any delay in the collection of cheques.
5. It presents misappropriation of cheques, bank drafts, and other transactions with the book.

CAUSES OF DIFFERENCE

The difference in the two balances arises due to (a) timing, (b) transactions, and (c) errors.

Timing

There may be a delay between the recording of transactions in the customer's book and the recording of transactions in the bank book, for example, when a cheque is issued to a party, it is recorded immediately in the customer's book (i.e., an accounting entity's book). However, the bank will record it only when it makes payment against that cheque.

Transactions

Some difference may arise from the bank's action that has not been intimated to the customer; for example, the entries of bank charges.

Errors

Some difference in the balance may arise owing to errors committed by the bank or by the person responsible for preparing the bank book. A wrong credit or debit may be made by the firm or by the bank. The two balances, therefore, may not tally. For the first two reasons, discussed earlier, neither of the parties is wrong nor is there a mistake to correct. However, for the third reason, the books of an entity are to be properly rectified. The following are examples of errors:

1. Cheques issued by the firm to its suppliers or third parties may not have been presented for the payment.
2. Cheques received from customers and deposited in bank may not have been collected by the banker.
3. Deposits may have been directly made by the customers in the bank account of the entity.
4. Collection charges, service charges, and interest on overdraft (on excess drawings) charged by the banker are not recorded by the firm. The entity or firm ascertains the exact amount of charges from bank statement and records them in the cash book.
5. Interest credited or given by the bank for the balance maintained with it and any other income such as interest on securities, dividend, etc. collected by the bank on behalf of the firm can be ascertained only from the bank statement.
6. Wrong entries made by the firm in the bank column of the cash book or in the bank book or errors committed by the bank in its records.
7. Omission of entries in the bank book.
8. Dishonour of customers' cheques deposited in the bank account.
9. Dishonour of a bill discounted with the bank.
10. Bills collected by the bank on behalf of the customer.

UTILITY OF BANK RECONCILIATION STATEMENT

The utility of a bank reconciliation statement can be judged on the basis of the following points:

1. *Detection of errors:* Reconciliation helps to detect errors, like wrong totalling or balancing or/and entering wrong amount, in recording transactions either by the firm or by the bank. It may also be due to omission of a transaction in either of the books. A bank reconciliation statement usually highlights these anomalies, which can be set right by rectification.
2. *Reduction in chances of frauds:* Periodic comparison of cash book and pass book reduces the chances of fraud by the office staff who are handling cash and bank transactions. Reconciliation points out if the cash is not deposited in the bank in time even though an entry has been made in the cash book.
3. *Highlighting the causes of difference:* Reconciliation highlights the reason for the difference in cash book balance and pass book balance.
4. *Completion of cash book:* In the process of reconciliation, information about dishonoured cheques, bank charges, direct deposit by customer, etc. is gathered from bank

pass book and entries for the same are made in the cash book so as to complete the cash book and find out the true cash balance.

PREPARING A BANK RECONCILIATION STATEMENT

On receipt of the bank statement, a comparison of the entries in the bank book with those appearing in the bank statement or pass book will help in identifying reasons of the items or events or transactions. While the difference due to reasons of errors (1) and (2) can be eliminated in the near future (e.g., creditors or third parties will soon present their cheques for payment), the difference due to reasons of errors (3) to (5) can be eliminated only if such items are recorded in the bank book. In addition, the firm must rectify any errors in the bank book, including any transactions omitted and record the dishonour, if any, and can take up the matter with bank for item (6). The bank reconciliation statement is prepared usually at the end of the period, that is, a month, a quarter, a half-year, or a year, as may be found convenient and necessary by the firm taking into account the number of transactions involved. The following are the steps to be taken for preparing the bank reconciliation statement.

1. The bank column of the cash book, or the bank book, should be completed and the balance as per the bank column on a particular date should be found out covering the period for which the bank reconciliation statement has to be prepared.
2. The bank should be requested to complete the bank statement and send it to the firm or update the bank pass book up to the date as mentioned in point (1) before.
3. The balance shown by any book (i.e., the bank book or the bank pass book) should be taken as the base or the starting point for determining the balance as shown by the other book after making suitable adjustments based on the causes of difference.
4. The effect of the particular cause of difference on the balance shown by the other book should be studied.
5. In case the cause has resulted in an increase in the balance shown by the other book, the amount of such increase should be added to the balance as per the former book that has been taken as the base.
6. In case the cause has resulted in a decrease in balance shown by the other book, the amount of such decrease should be subtracted from the balance as per the former book that has been taken as the base.

This can be summarized as under:

'Do what the other party has done; undo what the other party has not done'.

The bank reconciliation statement can be prepared by the following two methods:

- Accounting method, that is, debit-credit columns method or plus and minus sign columns method.
- Arithmetical method, that is, add and subtract method.

Determining the Effect of the Transaction

The statement can be prepared either from the balance of the cash book or from the balance of the pass book. If it is prepared from the balance of the cash book, the effect of the transaction will be studied on the pass book as compared to the cash book. The item will be added if the bank balance as per the pass book increases. The item will be deducted if the bank balance as per pass book decreases. For example, a cheque not presented for payment will decrease the balance of the cash book, but, as the bank has not passed any entry, the bank balance as per pass book will not decrease. In other words, the balance as per the pass book will be more than the balance as per the cash book. Therefore, the transaction needs to be accounted for to bring the balance of the cash book at par with that of the pass book.

In case the statement is being prepared from the balance of the pass book, the effect of the transaction on the cash book needs to be studied. In the above example—a cheque has been issued but not presented by the firm to the bank—the balance of the cash book has gone down but the balance of the pass book remains the same. As the statement is being prepared from the pass book, its effect will be studied on the cash book, whose balance has decreased, so the item will be deducted.

To illustrate it further, take the example of bank charges. The balance as per the pass book will be less than that of the cash book, because while the bank balance has already been reduced by the bank charges, the cash book balance has not been affected. In this case, the item is deducted, if statement is prepared with the balance of cash book, because the balance as per pass book is less than the balance of the cash book. The item will be added if the statement is prepared from the pass book, because the balance of the reverse book, that is, cash book is more than the pass book.

If the statement is prepared from the balance of cash book,

- add those items that have increased the balance of the pass book; and
- deduct those items that have decreased the balance of the pass book.

If the statement is prepared from the balance of pass book,

- add those items that have increased the bank balance as per the cash book; and
- deduct those items that have decreased the balance as per the cash book.

In case the books show an adverse balance (i.e., overdraft) the amount of the overdraft should be prefixed with a minus sign. The bank reconciliation statement should then be prepared on the same pattern as if there is a favourable (positive) balance instead of an overdraft. This is the simplest and easiest method.

Considering the Date of Preparing the Statement

Only those transactions that are entered in one of the books, that is, cash book or pass book, but not entered in the other, by the date of preparing the bank reconciliation statement are identified as transactions to be accounted for. If the date of preparing the bank reconciliation statement is 30 June 2020, all transactions that have been recorded in the cash book but not in the pass book or recorded in the pass book but not in the cash book by 30 June 2020 will be entered in the bank reconciliation statement. If the transactions have been recorded in both the cash book and the pass book correctly, the balances of both the books will either increase or decrease simultaneously by the same amount by 30 June 2020. Such transactions will be ignored at the time of preparing the bank reconciliation statement.

Balancing the Statement

The final step is to balance the plus and minus columns. If the statement is to be prepared based on the balance of the cash book, the balance of the pass book will have to be ascertained. If the statement is to be prepared based on the balance of the pass book, the balance of the cash book will have to be ascertained. If the total of the plus items exceeds the total of the minus items, the balance ascertained will be plus. In the same way, if the total of the minus items exceeds the total of the plus items, the balance ascertained will be minus.

The preparation of the bank reconciliation statement may be summarized as shown in Exhibit 12.2.

EXHIBIT 12.2 Bank Reconciliation Statement—What to 'Add' and What to 'Less'

Reason Number	Reason for Difference between Cash Book and Pass Book Balances	Starting Point is Cash Book Balance		Starting Point is Pass Book Balance or Bank Statement	
		Favourable Balance (Dr.)	Overdraft Balance (Cr.)	Overdraft Balance (Dr.)	Favourable Balance (Cr.)
1	Cheques issued or drawn but not yet presented for payment or encashed by payee or not debited in pass book	Add	Less	Add	Less
2	Cheque deposited in bank but not yet collected	Less	Add	Less	Add
3	Direct deposit by a customer in the bank, not entered in cash book	Add	Less	Add	Less
4	Direct collection by bank, not entered in cash book	Add	Less	Add	Less
5	Direct payment from bank, not entered in cash book	Less	Add	Less	Add
6	Dishonour of a cheque deposited (or bill discounted)	Less	Add	Less	Add
7	Cheque paid into the bank but omitted to be entered in cash book	Less	Add	Add	Less
8	Interest income allowed by bank but not entered in cash book	Add	Less	Add	Less
9	Bank charges not entered in cash book	Less	Add	Less	Add

There are two techniques of preparing a bank reconciliation statement—one if the bank balance is normal, and another if the bank balance is overdrawn.

Normal Bank Balance

A normal bank balance indicates the positive balance from the view of the party who submits the balance as per bank book or cash book (i.e., firm) or as per bank statement or pass book (i.e., banker).

The debit balance as per cash book or bank book indicates the positive balance of a firm in bank account as receipts are more than payments. It also indicates that the firm has not overdrawn (excess withdrawal) the amount from the bank account maintained with a specific banker.

The credit balance as per pass book or banker's statement indicates the positive balance of the customer in the books of the banker. It indicates that the customer's deposits in the bank are greater than their withdrawal from the bank.

> Debit balance as per cash or bank book means positive balance.

The example in the following text explains this technique.

■ **ILLUSTRATION 12.1** From the following particulars, prepare bank reconciliation statement as on 31 March 2020.

1. Balance as per bank book ₹12,300.
2. Cheques sent for collection but not collected ₹3,300.
3. Cheques issued but not presented for payment ₹2,300.
4. The bank had debited the firm's account by ₹70 on account of bank charges.
5. Balance as per bank statement ₹11,230.

Solution

Bank Reconciliation Statement
As on 31 March 2020 of M/s...

(Amount in ₹)

Particulars	Dr. (₹) Add	Cr. (₹) Minus
1. Balance as per bank book	12,300	
2. Cheques sent for collection but not collected		3,300
3. Cheques issued but not presented for payment	2,300	
4. Bank charges debited by bank		70
	14,600	3,370
Balance as per bank statement	11,230	

Notes:

1. The cheques sent for collection but not collected until the date of reconciliation, that is, 31 March 2020 must have been entered in the bank book but have not been credited by the bank to the firm's account since they have not yet been collected. The balance in the bank statement should, therefore, be less than the bank book. So, the amount of ₹2,300 is deducted from the balance.
2. The cheques issued but not presented for payment have not been recorded in the bank statement. The bank has not yet passed the entry for the payment of these cheques, since they have not been presented for payment. The balance, therefore, in the bank statement should be more.

So, the amount of ₹3,300 will be added to the balance as shown by the bank book.

3. The bank has debited the firm's account by bank charges. This has reduced the balance as per the bank statement. So, the amount of ₹70 should be deducted from the balance shown as per the bank book.

Alternatively, the bank reconciliation statement can be prepared in the vertical form, by separately adding and subtracting the items from the base balance. See the following example.

Particulars	Amount (₹)
Balance as per bank book	12,300
Add:	
Cheques issued but not presented for payment	2,300
	14,600
Less:	
Cheques sent for collection but not collected	3,300
Bank charges debited by bank	70
Balance as per bank statement	17,230

Overdrawn Bank Balance

In the case discussed earlier, a favourable balance as per bank book or bank column of cash book is given. In case of an unfavourable bank balance (i.e., overdraft) as per bank book, the simplest and easiest way is to show the balance in the positive column by using minus sign in the beginning of the bank reconciliation statement or show such balance with negative sign in the vertical format of the bank reconciliation statement. The following example explains this technique.

■ **ILLUSTRATION 12.2** From the following particulars, prepare a bank reconciliation statement as on 31 March.

1. The balance as per bank book shows an overdraft of ₹12,300.
2. Cheques sent for collection but not collected ₹3,300.
3. Cheques issued but not presented for payment ₹2,300.
4. The bank had debited the firm's account by ₹70.
5. Balance as per bank pass book ₹13,370 (overdrawn).

Solution

Bank Reconciliation Statement
As on 31 March of M/s ...

Particulars	Dr. (₹) Add	Cr. (₹) Minus
1. Overdraft as per bank book	(–)12,300	
2. Cheques sent for collection but not collected		3,300
3. Cheques issued but not presented	2,300	
4. Bank charges debited by book		70
	(–)10,000	3,370
Overdraft as per bank statement	(–)13,370	

Note:

The summation or total of the positive column is (–) ₹10,000. The summation of the negative column is ₹3,370. So, mathematically it is represented as:

$$(-)10,000 - 3,370 = (-)13,370$$

The minus sign shows the overdrawing, that is, overdraft.

Alternatively, in the vertical format it can be presented as given in the following text:

Particulars	Amount (₹)
Balance as per bank book	(–)12,300
Add:	
Cheques issued but not presented for payment	2,300
	(–)10,000
Less:	
Cheques sent for collection but not collected	3,300
Bank charges debited by bank	70
Balance as per bank statement	(–)13,370
The negative sign shows the overdraft	

■ **ILLUSTRATION 12.3** Prepare a bank reconciliation statement from the following particulars on 31 March 2019:

	₹
(1) Debit balance as per cash book	3,70,000
(2) Credit balance as per pass book	4,33,980
(3) Cheque issued to creditors, but not yet presented to bank for payment	74,000
(4) Dividend received by bank, but not entered in cash book	5,000
(5) Interest given by bank	1,250
(6) Cheque deposited in bank for collection, but not collected by bank up to this date	13,400
(7) Bank charges	200
(8) A cheque deposited into bank was dishonoured, but no intimation received	1,320
(9) Bank paid house tax on our behalf, but no information received from bank in this connection	1,350

Solution

(When Balance as per Cash Book is the Starting Point)

Bank Reconciliation Statement (in Add-Less Form)
As on 31st March 2019

Particulars	Details	Total
Debit Balance as per Cash Book (Deposit)		3,70,000
Add: 1. Cheque issued but not yet presented to bank for payment	74,000	
2. Dividend received by bank not entered in cash book	5,000	
3. Interest given by bank	1,250	80,250
		4,50,250
Less: 1. Cheques depostied into bank but not yet collected	13,400	
2. Bank charges	200	
3. A cheque deposited into bank was dishonoured	1,320	
4. House tax paid by bank	1,350	16,270
Credit Balance as per Pass Book (Deposit)		4,33,980

Alternative Presentation (When Balance as per Pass Book is the Starting Point)

Bank Reconciliation Statement (in Add-Less Form)

Particulars	Details	Total
Balance as per Pass Book (Deposit)		4,33,980
Add: 1. Cheques deposited into bank but not yet collected	13,400	

2. Bank charges		200
3. A cheque deposited into bank was dishonoured		1,320
4. House tax paid by bank	1,350	16,270
		4,50,250
Less: 1. Cheque issued but not yet presented to bank for payment	74,000	
2. Dividend received by bank not entered in cash book	5,000	
3. Interest given by bank	1,250	80,250
Debit Balances as per Cash Book (Deposit)		3,70,000

Alternative Form: As stated earlier, a bank reconciliation statement may be presented in Debit-Credit form instead of Add-Less form. An alternative presentation of Illustration 12.3 is produced below in Debit-Credit form:

Bank Reconciliation Statement (in Debit-Credit Form)
as on 31.3.2019

Particulars	Dr. (₹) Add	Cr. (₹) Less
Balance as per Cash Book (Deposit)	3,70,000	
Cheque issued but not yet cleared by bank	74,000	
Dividend directly collected by bank	5,000	
Interest credited by bank	1,250	
Cheque deposited but not yet collceted by bank		13,400
Bank charges charged by bank		200
Cheque deposited and dishonoured but not yet intimated		1,320
House tax paid by bank		1,350
Balance as per Pass Book (Deposit)		4,33,980
Total	**4,50,250**	**4,50,250**

EXTRACTS FROM CASH BOOK AND PASS BOOK

Sometimes, in a question the reasons for a difference between cash book and bank pass book are not given. Instead, relevant extracts from the cash book and the pass book are given. In such a case, comparison of cash book entries with pass book entries reveals the reasons of the difference. The accountant should pay special attention to the period for which cash book and pass book are given. There may be two types of situations:

1. When extracts from cash book and pass book relate to the same period: In this case, the reason of difference will be the transactions which are not common in both cash book and pass book. (refer to Illustration 12.4)

2. When pass book relates to the succeeding period: In this case, the reasons of difference will be those transactions which are common in both cash book and pass book. (refer to Illustration 12.5)

■ **ILLUSTRATION 12.4** Prepare a bank reconciliation statement as on 30 September 2019 from the following extracts from the bank pass book and the cash book (bank columns):

276   FINANCIAL ACCOUNTING FOR MANAGEMENT

Date 2019	Particulars	Withdrawals	Deposit	Dr. or Cr.	Balance
1 Sept	By Balance b/d			Cr.	9,810
3 Sept	To Mahesh Chander	740		Cr.	9,070
7 Sept	To Balwant	580		Cr.	8,490
8 Sept	By Salaria		200	Cr.	8,690
12 Sept	By Cash		1,000	Cr.	9,690
18 Sept	By Santosh Arora		500	Cr.	10,190
21 Sept	To Rameswar Vohra	440		Cr.	9,750
26 Sept	To Insurance premium	400		Cr.	9,350
30 Sept	To Bank charges	20		Cr.	9,330
30 Sept	To Cash	3,000		Cr.	6,330
30 Sept	By Interest		70	Cr.	6,400
30 Sept	By Interest on investment		600	Cr.	7,000

Cash Book (Bank Columns Only)

Date September 2019	Particulars	Dr. (₹) Add	Cr. (₹) Less
1	To Balance b/d	9,810	
2	By Mahesh Chander		740
6	To S.P. Jain	300	
6	By Balawant Garg		580
10	To Salaries	200	
10	By Nath		470
12	To Cash	1,000	
14	To Santosh Arora	500	
15	By Ashok		350
18	By Rameshwar		440
19	To Baljeet	460	
24	By Kamal		630
26	To Bharat	780	
30	By Cash		3,000
30	By Balance c/d		6,840
Total		13,050	13,050

Solution

As both balances as per cash book and pass book are given, reconciliation statement may be prepared by starting with either of the balances and arrive at the other balance. Here we are starting with balance as per pass book.

Bank Reconciliation Statement as on 30.9.2019

	Amount (₹)	Amount (₹)
Balance as per pass book		7,000
Add: 1. Cheques deposited and not credited in pass book		
(S.P. Jain 300 + Baljeet 460 + Bharat 780)	1,540	
2. Insurance premium not appearing in cash book	400	
3. Bank charges not shown in cash book	20	1,960
		8,960
Less: 1. Cheques issued but not presented for payment	1,450	
(Nath 470 + Ashok 350 + Kamal 630)		
2. Interest not credited in cash book	70	

3. Interest on investments not credited in cash book	600	2,120
Balance as per cash book		6,840

■ **ILLUSTRATION 12.5** A copy of the Bank of Baroda account maintained in the ledger of Jariwala and Co. for January 2020 and the summary of the pass book relating to the transactions of February 2020 are given. You are required to prepare the bank reconciliation statement therefrom.

Ledger of Jariwala and Co.

Date 2020 January	Particulars	Dr. (₹) Add	Cr. (₹) Less
1	To Balance b/d	2,000	
3	To Bank interest A/c	10	
3	By Bank commission A/c		5
4	By Girish A/c		100
7	To Cash A/c	100	
8	By Chetan's A/c		180
12	To Sanghavi Bros's A/c	150	
15	To Lavsi Bros's A/c	200	
17	By Dayaram's A/c		200
20	By Inamdar's A/c		90
22	To Modi Bros's A/c	40	
27	By Fakir Chand's A/c		150
29	To Patel Bros's A/c	160	
30	By Ganpat's A/c		220
31	By Balance c/d		1,715
Total		2,660	2,660

Ledger of Bank of Baroda
Jariwala and Co. Account

Date 2020	Particulars	Dr. (₹) Minus	Cr. (₹) Add	Balance (₹)
1 Feb	By Balance b/d			1,925
2 Feb	To Fakirchand's A/c	150		1,775
4 Feb	By Patel Bros's A/c		160	1,935
5 Feb	To Hiralal's A/c	100		1,835
6 Feb	To Ganpat's A/c	220		1615
10 Feb	To Cash A/c	205		1,410
15 Feb	By Sheth Bros's A/c		350	1,760
20 Feb	To Iswarlal's A/c	180		1,580
25 Feb	To Jaisingh's A/c	290		1,290
28 Feb	To Bank charges A/c	10		1,280
29 Feb	By Balance c/d			1,280

Solution

1. The transactions in the cash book are for the month of January while the pass book shows transactions for the month of February. Thus, there are transactions for different months. Transactions that are common in both the books should first be identified and shown in the bank reconciliation statement.
2. Begin with the bank balance of the cash book on 31/1/2021.
3. On comparison of the credit side of the pass book with the debit side of the cash book, there appears only one common item, which is ₹160 in the name of Patel Bros.

The entry on the debit side of the cash book means that the amount must have been paid into the bank. Thus, the cheque received from Patel Bros was paid to the bank in January, which was entered in the cash book. But this item has been entered in the pass book in February. Thus, the cheque has not been credited in the pass book up to 31 January. As the balance in the pass book is less, it must be deducted by ₹160.

4. Comparing the credit side of the cash book and the debit side of the pass book, the amounts in the name of Fakirchand and Ganpat appear in both the books. Since the amounts are on the credit side of the cash book, it means that the two merchants might have drawn both these cheques in January. They were cashed in February and therefore, they have not been debited in the pass book up to 31 January. The balance in the other book, that is, pass book is more, so it must be added.

5. The effects of bank interest entered on the debit side of the cash book and of bank commission entered on the credit side must have been given in the bank reconciliation statement for last December. They would not be shown in this bank reconciliation statement. In the same way the effect of the bank charges of ₹10 entered in the pass book will be on the bank reconciliation statement of the last day of February. Hence, no effect has been given for that in the bank reconciliation statement for January that we are preparing.

Bank Reconciliation Statement
as on 31 January 2021

Particulars	Amount (₹)	Amount (₹)
Bank balance as per cash book		1,715
Add: Cheques paid into the bank but not credited		
Fakirchand	150	
Ganpat	220	370
		2,085
Less: Cheques paid into the bank but not credited		
Patel Bros		160
Bank balance as per cash book		1,925

■ **ILLUSTRATION 12.6** Prepare a bank reconciliation statement as on 30th September 2019 from the following particulars:

1. Bank balance as per pass book   10,000
2. Cheque deposited into bank but no entry was passed in cash book   500
3. Cheque received but not sent to bank   1,200
4. Credit side of bank column cast short   200
5. Insurance premium paid directly by bank under standing advice   600
6. Bank charges entered twice in cash book   120
7. Cheque issued but not presented to bank for payment   400
8. Cheque received entered twice in the cash book   1,000
9. Bills discounted dishonoured not recorded in cash book   5,000

Solution

Bank Reconciliation Statement as on 30th September 2019

Particulars	Amount (₹)	Amount (₹)
Bank Balance as per Pass Book		10,000
Add: 1. Cheque received but not sent to bank	1,200	
2. Credit side of bank column cast short	200	
3. Insurance premium paid directly, not recorded in cash book	600	
4. Cheque received entered twice in cash book	1,000	
5. Bills dishonoured not recorded in cash book	5,000	8,000
		18,000
Less: 1. Cheque deposited into bank but no entry passed in cash book	500	
2. Bank charges recorded twice in cash book	120	
3. Cheque issued but not presented to bank	400	1,020
Bank Balance as per Cash Book		16,980

■ **ILLUSTRATION 12.7** On 31st March, Ram compared his pass book with his cash book and found the following differences:

1. Cheques amounting to ₹2,500 were paid on 27th March, out of which cheques of the value of ₹800 were credited in the pass book on 4th April.
2. Cheques totalling ₹4,000 were issued during the month of March, out of which cheques of the value of ₹900 were debited in the pass book after 31st March.
3. There was a debit of ₹20 for bank charges in the pass book.
4. There was a credit of ₹50 in the pass book for interest on customer account.
5. An entry of ₹100 of a payment by a customer directly into the bank appears in the pass book.
6. Bank column on the payment side of the cash book was found to be overcast by ₹1,000.
7. Interest on investment amounting to ₹200 collected by the bank appears in the pass book.
8. Insurance premium of ₹300 paid by the bank on behalf of the merchant appeared in the pass book.

The merchant's cash book disclosed a debit balance of ₹7,579 on 31st March. Prepare the bank reconciliation statement as on 31 March 2019.

Solution

Bank Reconciliation Statement

Particulars	Amount (₹)	Amount (₹)
Balance as per Cash Book		7,579
Add: 1. Cheques issued but not debited in pass book	900	
2. Interest on bank account not shown in cash book	50	
3. Direct payment by a customer in bank not shown such in cash book	100	
4. Bank column on the payment side of cash book overcast	1,000	
5. Interest on investments not shown in cash book	200	2,250
		9,829
Less: 1. Cheques paid into bank, not credited in pass book	800	

2. Bank charges not shown in cash book		20	
3. Insurance premium paid directly by bank not appearing in cash book		300	1,120
Balance as per Pass Book			**8,709**

■ **ILLUSTRATION 12.8** On 31 January 2019, the cash book showed a credit balance of ₹12,300. Prepare a bank reconciliation statement with the following details:

1. Cheques amounting to ₹4,680 were drawn on 25 January 2019, out of which cheques for ₹3,300 were cashed up to 31 January 2019.
2. A wrong debit of ₹240 has been given by the bank in the pass book.
3. A cheque of ₹60 was credited in the pass book but was not recorded in the cash book.
4. Cheques amounting to ₹6,300 were deposited for collection. But cheques for ₹2,200 have been credited in the pass book on 5 February 2019.
5. A cheque for ₹300 returned dishonoured and was debited in the pass book.
6. Interest and bank charges amounted to ₹30 were not accounted in cash book.
7. A cheque of ₹150 that was received has been entered in cash book but not sent to the bank for collection.

Solution

Bank Reconciliation Statement

Particulars		Amount (₹)	Amount (₹)
Bank overdraft (Cr. Bal.) as per Cash Book			**12,300**
Add:	1. Wrong debit in pass book	240	
	2. Cheques deposited but not credited (₹6,300 – ₹2,220)	4,080	
	3. Dishonoured cheque not recorded in cash book	300	
	4. Interest and bank charges not entered in cash book	30	
	5. A cheque received but not sent to bank for collection	150	4,800
			17,100
Less:	1. Cheques issued but not presented for payment (₹4,680 – ₹3,300)	1,380	
	2. Cheque credited only in pass book	60	1,440
Bank Overdraft as per Pass Book			**15,660**

■ **ILLUSTRATION 12.9** Prepare a bank reconciliation statement as on 31 December 2019 from the following information.

1. Bank balance as per the cash book (debit) on 31 December was ₹10,000.
2. Cheques worth ₹10,000 were deposited for collection on 29 December and 30 December. Out of those, cheques worth ₹2,500 were credited by bank up to 31 December.
3. Incidental charges of ₹50 were debited but no advice was issued to the company.
4. Cheques worth ₹6,000 were issued but cheques worth only ₹2,000 were presented before 31 December.
5. Two entries of ₹590 and ₹950 were wrongly debited in the pass book. The entry for ₹590 was reversed by the bank

before 31 December. It was found that the entry for ₹950 relates to the subsidiary of this company.
6. The bank transferred ₹2,500 to another account of the company but did not issue an advice.

Solution

Bank Reconciliation Statement
as on 31 December 2019

Particulars	Amount (₹)	Amount (₹)
Bank balance as per the cash book (Dr.)		10,000
Add: cheques issued but not presented for payment (₹6,000 – ₹2,000)	4,000	4,000
		14,000
Less: Cheque deposited but not collected by bank within December (₹10,000 – ₹2,500)	7,500	
Incidental charges not recorded in the cash book	50	
Wrong debit by bank relating to subsidiary	950	
Transfer by bank to another account of the company not recorded in cash book	2,500	11,000
Bank balance as per the pass book		3,000

■ **ILLUSTRATION 12.10** The bank account of Mukesh was balanced on 31 March 2020. It showed an overdraft of ₹5,000. The bank statement of Mukesh showed a credit balance of ₹76,750. Prepare a bank reconciliation statement considering the following.

1. Cheques issued but not presented for payment until 31 March—₹12,000.
2. Cheques deposited but not collected by bank until 31 March—₹20,000.
3. Interest on term loan worth ₹10,000 debited by bank on 31 March but not accounted in Mukesh's books.
4. Bank charge ₹250 was debited by bank during March 2020, but accounted in Mukesh's books on 4 April.
5. An amount of ₹1,00,000 representing collection of Mukesh's cheque was wrongly credited to the account of Mukesh by the bank in their bank statement.

Solution

Bank Reconciliation Statement
as on 31 March 2020

Particulars	Amount (₹)	Amount (₹)
Overdraft as per cash book		(5,000)
Less: Cheques deposited in bank but not collected and credited by bank until 31 March	20,000	
Interest on term loan not accounted in books	10,000	
Bank charge not accounted in books	250	(30,250)
Add : Cheques issued but not presented for payment till 31 March	12,000	
Erroneous credit by bank pertaining to Mukesh credited to Mukesh's account	1,00,000	
Total		**1,12,000**
Balance as per bank statement		76,750

Note:
Credit balance as per cash or bank book is overdraft.

■ ILLUSTRATION 12.11 Ranganath has two accounts with Hanuman Bank Ltd, styled Account no. 1 and Account no. 2. On 31 December 2020, his cash book showed balances of ₹5,400 and ₹2,70,400 in the two accounts respectively. On an examination of the bank's statements, the following were noticed.

1. ₹27,000 has been transferred from Account No. 2 to Account No. 1 by the bank without advice to Ranganath.
2. ₹10 has been the bank's incidental charges in respect of each account, which has also not been advised.
3. Cheques for ₹5,421 issued on Account No. 1 late in December have not yet been presented to the bank.
4. A cheque for ₹4,272 deposited by Ranganath into Account No. 2 has been credited by the bank into Account No. 1.

You are required to prepare bank reconciliation statement showing the balance as per bank statement.

Solution

Bank Reconciliation Statement of Ranganath (A/c No. 1)
as on 31 December 2020

Particulars	Amount (₹)	Amount (₹)
Bank balance as per cash book		5,400
Add: Transfer from Account No. 2 without advice	27,000	
Cheques issued but not yet presented to the bank	5,421	
Cheque deposited into Account No. 2 wrongly credited to Account No. 1	4,272	36,693
		42,093
Less: Incidental charges debited in the pass book not recorded in cash book.	10	10
Bank balance as per the bank statement		42,083

Bank Reconciliation Statement of Ranganath (A/c No. 2)
as on 31 December 2020

Particulars	Amount (₹)	Amount (₹)
Bank balance as per the cash book (Dr.)		2,70,400
Less: Transfer to Account No. 1 without advice	27,000	

Incidental charges debited in the pass book not recorded in the cash book	10	
Cheque deposited into Account No. 2 wrongly credited to Account No. 1	4,272	31,282
Bank balance as per bank statement		2,39,118

■ ILLUSTRATION 12.12 The treasurer of the Calcutta Club is attempting to reconcile the balance shown in the cash book with that appearing on the bank statement. According to the cash book, the balance at the bank as on 31 May 2020 was ₹1,900 whilst the bank statement disclosed an overdraft amount of ₹470. Upon investigation, the treasurer discovers the following errors.

1. A cheque paid to S Ltd for ₹340 was entered in the cash book as ₹430.
2. Cash paid to the bank for ₹100 was entered on the cash book as ₹90.
3. A transfer of ₹1,500 to the bank savings account was not entered in the cash book.
4. A receipt of ₹10 shown on the bank statement was not entered in the cash book.
5. Cheque drawn amounting to ₹40 was not presented to the bank.
6. The cash book balance had been incorrectly brought down at 1 June 2020 as a debit balance of ₹1,200 instead of a debit balance of ₹1,100.
7. Bank charges of ₹20 did not appear in the cash book.
8. Receipt of ₹900 paid into the bank on 31 May 2020 did not appear on the bank statement until 1 June 2020.
9. A standing order of payment of ₹30 had not been entered in the cash book.
10. A cheque for ₹50 previously received and paid into the bank had been returned by the bank marked 'account closed'.
11. The bank received a direct deposit of ₹100 from an anonymous member.
12. Cheques paid into the bank had been incorrectly totalled. The total amount should have been ₹170 instead of ₹150.

Draw up a bank reconciliation statement as on 31 May 2020.

Solution

Bank Reconciliation Statement of Calcutta Club
as on 31 May 2020

Particulars	Amount (₹)	Amount (₹)
Bank balance as per the cash book (Dr.)		1,900
Add:		
Cheques paid for ₹340 had been entered in the cash book as ₹430.	90	
Cash paid to the bank ₹100 had been entered in the cash book as ₹90.	10	
A receipt of ₹10 shown in the bank statement not recorded in the cash book.	10	
Cheque drawn but not presented to the bank.	40	
Direct deposit by a member into the bank not recorded in cash book.	100	250
		2,150
Less:		
Transfer to saving bank had not been recorded in the cash book.	1,500	
A debit balance of the cash book of ₹1,100 brought forward as ₹1,200.	100	

Bank charges not recorded in the cash book.	20	
Receipt of ₹900 paid into the bank on 31 May 2020 did not appear in the bank statement until 1/6/2020.	900	
A payment made by bank as per standing order not recorded in the cash book.	30	
Cheque dishonoured but not entered in the cash book.	50	
Cheque deposited ₹170 wrongly totalled as ₹150.	20	2,620
Bank balance as per pass book (Dr.)		(–)470

Note:

Debit balance as per pass book is overdraft. It means negative balance.

■ **ILLUSTRATION 12.13** On a certain date the cash book showed a bank balance of ₹1,200, which did not tally with the balance in the pass book. On comparing the cash book with the pass book, it was found that

1. A cheque of ₹500 was deposited in the bank but was not collected by the bank.
2. A cheque of ₹200 was issued but not presented.
3. The bank had debited ₹50 as commission.

You are required to prepare the bank reconciliation statement.

Solution

In the problem, the bank balance as per cash book is given, that is, a debit balance. The entry will be made in the debit column of the bank reconciliation statement. Thereafter, the reconciliation will be as follows:

1. The cheque of ₹500 deposited in the bank is not credited by the bank. Since it is a debit item, the actual entry is made on the debit side in the cash book. Hence, for reconciliation purposes it will be shown in the credit column of the bank reconciliation statement.
2. Cheque of ₹200 issued is credited to the bank account in the cash book. Thus, it is a credit item. Since the cheque has not been presented it will be shown in the debit column of the bank reconciliation statement.
3. The bank has debited ₹50 to the bank account. The actual entry made is on the debit side in the pass book. It is a debit item and will be shown in the credit column of the bank reconciliation statement.

Now the bank reconciliation statement will be prepared as follows:

Bank Reconciliation Statement

Particulars	Dr. (₹) Add	Cr. (₹) Minus
Bank balance as per cash book	1,200	
1. Cheques deposited but not credited		500
2. Cheques issued but not paid	200	
3. Bank commission debited		50
Balance as per pass book (credit)		850
	1,400	1,400

■ **ILLUSTRATION 12.14** The pass book of Mohinder Rathi shows a credit balance of ₹7,500 on 31 December 2020. The balance of the cash book does not tally. On examination, the following differences are noticed:

1. Cheques for ₹4,000 were issued before this date, of which cheques for ₹2,500 only were presented for payment till 31 December 2020.

2. Cheque for ₹500 had been deposited in the bank on 30 December for collection. The amount had not been credited till 31 December.
3. Cheque for ₹160 had been received, which was entered in the bank column in the cash book, but the same had not yet been sent to the bank for collection.
4. Cheque for ₹400 was received on 21st December and deposited in the bank, but through oversight it was not entered in the cash book.
5. In the pass book, ₹45 was credited for interest on the current account, and ₹10 was debited for bank charges. These had not been entered in the cash book.
6. Cheque of ₹250 favouring Kishore was entered in the cash column in the cash book.
7. Cheque of ₹110 received from Rajesh and returned dishonored was debited by the bank. No entry for the dishonored cheque was found in the cash book.
8. The total of the bank column on the receipt side of the cash book was understated by ₹100 through oversight.
9. Dividend of ₹450 of Mohinder's son was paid into the account of his son in the same bank, which was credited by the bank into the account of Mohinder through oversight.
10. The bank collected dividend of ₹500 on his shares and credited the same in the pass book, but it had not been entered in the cash book.

Prepare a bank reconciliation statement.

Solution

The problem starts with credit balance as per pass book (i.e., bank balance; means positive balance for Mohinder) and will be entered in the credit column (from banker's view it is positive balance).

1. Out of cheques of ₹4,000 issued, cheques of ₹2,500 have already been presented to the bank. They are thus recorded in both the books and will not appear in the bank reconciliation statement.

   But the remaining cheques of ₹1,500 issued will create difference in the two books. These cheques have not been presented to the bank and have not been recorded by the bank. The actual entry for these cheques has, however, been made in the cash book. They are credited to the bank account, that is, it is a credit item and will, therefore, be shown in the debit column.

2. The cheque of ₹500 deposited into the bank has not been recorded in the pass book, but its actual entry is made in the cash book on the debit side of the bank account. It is thus a debit item and will be put in the credit column.

3. The cheque of ₹160 is recorded on the debit side of the bank column in the cash book. It is a debit item and will therefore, be shown in the credit column of the statement.

4. The cheque of ₹400 is deposited in the bank which has been credited by the bank in the pass book. It is a credit item and will be shown in the debit column.

5. The bank has credited ₹45 for bank interest. It is a credit item and will put in the debit column. Conversely, the bank charges of ₹10 which are debited in the pass book, which is a debit item. Hence, it will be put in the credit column.

6. The cheque of ₹250 issued to Kishore has not been recorded in the cash book in the bank column. But as the bank has paid the amount, it is debited to Mohinder's account by the bank in the pass book. It is a debit item and will therefore be put in the credit column.

7. The cheque of ₹110 which is dishonored must be debited by the bank to Mohinder's account in the pass book. It is a debit item and will therefore be shown in the credit column.

8. The total of the receipt side of cash book is less by ₹100. It has the same effect as if an item of ₹100 is written on the credit side. Thus it is a credit item and will, therefore, appear in the debit column.

9. The bank has wrongly credited ₹450 for dividend to Mohinder's account. It is a credit item. It will appear in the debit column.

10. The bank has collected ₹500 for dividend and credited it to Mohinder's account. It is a credit item and will appear in the debit column.

The bank reconciliation statement will appear as follows:

Bank Reconciliation Statement of Mohinder
as on 31 December 2020

Particulars	Dr. (₹) Minus	Cr. (₹) Add
Bank balance as per pass book (from banker's view)		7,500
1. Cheques issued but not presented for payment	1,500	
2. Cheques paid in the bank but not credited		500
3. Cheques entered in cash book but not paid in bank		160
4. Cheque paid into the bank, but not recorded in the cash book	400	
5. Bank interest	45	
6. Bank charges		10
7. Cheque entered in the cash column		250
8. Cheque dishonoured		110
9. Total of the receipt side of the cash book understated	100	
10. Dividend wrongly credited in the pass book	450	
11. Dividend collected by bank	500	
Bank balance as cash book	5,535	
	8,530	8,530

■ **ILLUSTRATION 12.15** A copy of the Bank of Baroda account maintained in the ledger of Jariwala and Co. for January 2019 and the summary of the pass book relating to the transactions of February 2019 are given. You are required to prepare the bank reconciliation statement therefrom.

Cash Book of Jariwala and Co.
Bank of Baroda Account

Date 2019	Receipts	Bank (₹)	Date 2020	Payments	Bank (₹)
1 Jan	To Balance b/d	2,000	3 Jan	By Bank commission A/c	5
3 Jan	To Bank interest A/c	10	4 Jan	By Girish's A/c	100
7 Jan	To Cash A/c	100	8 Jan	By Chetan's A/c	180
12 Jan	To Sanghavi Bros's A/c	150	17 Jan	By Dayaram's A/c	200
15 Jan	To Lavsi Bros's A/c	200	20 Jan	By Inamdar's A/c	90
22 Jan	To Modi Bros's A/c	40	27 Jan	By Fakir Chand's A/c	150
29 Jan	To Patel Bros's A/c	160	30 Jan	By Ganpat's A/c	220
			31 Jan	By Balance c/d	1,715
		2,660			2,660

Ledger of Bank of Baroda
Jariwala and Co. Account

Date 2019	Particulars	Dr. (₹) Minus	Cr. (₹) Add	Balance (₹)
1 Feb	By Balance b/d			1,925
2 Feb	To Fakirchand's A/c	150		1,775
4 Feb	By Patel Bros's A/c		160	1,935
5 Feb	To Hiralal 's A/c	100		1,835
6 Feb	To Ganpat 's A/c	220		1615
10 Feb	To Cash A/c	205		1,410
15 Feb	By Sheth Bros's A/c		350	1,760
20 Feb	To Iswarlal 's A/c	180		1,580
25 Feb	To Jaisingh 's A/c	290		1,290
28 Feb	To Bank charges A/c	10		1,280
29 Feb	By Balance c/d			1,280

Solution

1. The transactions in the cash book are for the month of January while the pass book shows transactions for the month of February. Thus, there are transactions for different months. Transactions that are common in both the books should first be identified and shown in the bank reconciliation statement.

2. Begin with the bank balance of the cash book on 31/1/2020.

3. On comparison of the credit side of the pass book with the debit side of the cash book, there appears only one common item, which is ₹160 in the name of Patel Bros. The entry on the debit side of the cash book means that the amount must have been paid into the bank. Thus, the cheque received from Patel Bros was paid to the bank in January, which was entered in the cash book. But this item has been entered in the pass book in February. Thus, the cheque has not been credited in the pass book up to 31 January. As the balance in the pass book is less, it must be deducted by ₹160.

4. Comparing the credit side of the cash book and the debit side of the pass book, the amounts in the name of Fakirchand and Ganpat appear in both the books. Since

the amounts are on the credit side of the cash book, it means that the two merchants might have drawn both these cheques in January. They were cashed in February and therefore, they have not been debited in the pass book up to 31 January. The balance in the other book, that is, pass book is more, so it must be added.

5. The effects of bank interest entered on the debit side of the cash book and of bank commission entered on the credit side must have been given in the bank reconciliation statement for last December. They would not be shown in this bank reconciliation statement. In the same way the effect of the bank charges of ₹10 entered in the pass book will be on the bank reconciliation statement of the last day of February. Hence, no effect has been given for

that in the bank reconciliation statement for January that we are preparing.

Bank Reconciliation Statement
as on 31 January 2020

Particulars	Amount (₹)	
Bank balance as per cash book		1,715
Add: Cheques paid into the bank but not credited		
Fakirchand	150	
Ganpat	220	370
		2,085
Less: Cheques paid into the bank but not credited		
Patel Bros		160
Bank balance as per cash book		1,925

SUMMARY

- A bank statement is a copy of the customer's account in the bank's ledger.
- The bank reconciliation statement can be prepared by either the accounting method or the arithmetical method.
- The basic principle for the preparation of bank reconciliation statement is 'Do what the other party has done, undo what the other party has not done'.

- Disagreement in balances between bank book and statement may arise owing to a mistake or mistakes in the cash book or the bank statement. When all the facts are traced and brought together, it is possible for the firm to reconcile the differences in balances, by noting down the reasons in the bank reconciliation statement. It is an important part of a firm's internal control system.
- The difference in the two balances arises due to (a) timing gap, (b) nature of transaction, and (c) errors in recording.

KEYWORDS

Bank reconciliation statement   It is a statement reconciling the balance as shown by the bank statement or bank pass book and the balance shown by the bank book.

Bank statement   It is a copy of the customer's account in the bank's ledger.

QUESTIONS

I. Fill in the blanks.

(a) The _____ balance of the bank column of the cash book means the balance in the bank and the debit balance of the pass book means an _____.

(b) If an amount is written on the payment side of the cash book, the bank balance is _____.

(c) If transactions of the same month are given in the cash book and the pass book _____ transactions will be shown in the bank reconciliation statement.

(d) The bank balance _____ in the cash book by a cheque drawn and it _____ by a cheque paid into the bank.

(e) The amount of overdraft is _____ by the dividend collected by the bank.

(f) Bank overdraft is _____ balance as per cash book.

(g) The _____ balance of the bank column of the cash book means bank overdraft.

(h) _____ balance as per pass book means bank overdraft.

II. Choose the correct answer from the given options.

1. A bank reconciliation statement may be prepared with the balance of _____.
   (a) Cash book
   (b) Pass book
   (c) Either cash book or pass book
   (d) Neither cash book nor pass book

2. The debit balance of pass book is _____.
   (a) Plus balance

(b) Minus balance

(c) Either plus or minus

(d) Neither plus nor minus

3. Pass book is _____.

(a) The copy of banking transactions entered in the cash book.

(b) The copy of the customers' ledger account maintained by the bank.

(c) The record of all cash transactions.

(d) The copy of the firm's receipts and payments.

4. If the statement is prepared from the balance of the cash book, we shall finally find out the balance of _____.

(a) Cheque book

(b) Pay-in-slip book

(c) Cash book

(d) Pass book

5. Overdraft facilities are available only in _____.

(a) Current account

(b) Savings bank account

(c) Recurring deposit account

(d) Fixed deposit account

6. Bank reconciliation statement is prepared by _____.

(a) Customers of the bank

(b) Bank

(c) Proprietor of the business

(d) Tax authorities

7. The bank balance is treated as plus balance if it is a balance of _____.

(a) Cash book

(b) Credit balance of pass book

(c) Debit balance of cash book

(d) In all the above cases

III. Point out whether the following statements are True or False.

1. Bank column of the cash book always shows a debit balance.

2. Pass book and statement of account is the same thing, because both are the copy of a customer's ledger account maintained by the bank.

3. The debit balance of the cash book and the credit balance of the pass book carry the same meaning.

4. The balance of the pass book is always plus.

5. The debit balance of the pass book means minus balance.

6. If deposits exceed the withdrawals from the bank, cash book will show plus balance.

7. Bank reconciliation statement can be prepared with either the balance of the cash book or the balance of the pass book.

IV. While preparing bank reconciliation statement from the balance of the cash book, indicate whether the following items will be added or deducted:

1. Cheques debited in the cash book but not credited in the pass book.

2. Cheques credited in the cash book but not debited in the pass book.

3. Payment by debtors direct into the bank but not debited in the cash book.

4. Payment of the firm's factory rent by the bank has been entered in the pass book but not in the cash book.

5. Debiting a cheque twice into the bank column of the cash book.

6. Cheque deposited into the bank but not entered in the cash book.

7. Cheques entered in the cash book but omitted to be banked.

V. Answer the following questions.

1. What is a bank reconciliation statement? How is it prepared?

2. Discuss at least five causes of disagreement between the balance shown by a cash book and the balance shown by a pass book.

3. Discuss the usefulness of a bank reconciliation statement.

4. Explain how a correct bank balance can be ascertained with the help of a bank reconciliation statement.

5. 'Bank reconciliation statement means the statement for resolving the difference between the balance of cash book and that of the pass book'. Discuss.

VI. Solve the following problems.

1. From the following particulars, prepare a bank reconciliation statement as on 30 September 2019:

		₹
1.	Bank overdraft as per pass book	21,494
2.	A cheque deposited as per pass book, but not recorded in cash book	600
3.	Debit side of bank column undercast	200
4.	A cheque of ₹5,000 deposited, but credited to pass book as	4,996
5.	A party's cheque returned dishonoured as per pass book only	530
6.	Bills collected directly by bank	3,500
7.	Bank charges recorded twice in the cash book	25
8.	A bill of ₹8,000 discounted for ₹7,960 returned dishonoured by the bank. No charges being charged	15
9.	Cheque deposited, but not yet collected by the bank	2,320
10.	Cheque issued, but not yet presented to the bank for payment	1,250

2. Draw up a reconciliation statement from the following details:

1. On 31 March 2019, a bank pass book showed a balance of ₹26,000 to his credit.

2. Before that date, he had issued cheques amounting to ₹1,80,000, out of which cheques amounting to ₹1,32,000 have so far been presented for payment.

3. A cheque of ₹22,000 paid by him to the bank on 26 March is not yet credited in the pass book.

4. He had also received a cheque for ₹5,000, which although entered by him in the bank column of the cash book was omitted to be paid to the bank.

5. On 30 March a cheque for ₹1,570 received by him was paid to the bank but the same was omitted to be entered in the cash book.

6. There was a credit of ₹150 for interest on current account and a debit of ₹25 for bank charges.

3. From the following particulars, prepare the bank reconciliation statement as on 30.11.2019.

		₹
1.	Balance as per pass book (overdraft)	5,000
2.	Cheque of Ajay Ltd deposited but not presented	7,160
3.	Cheque issued to Bijay Ltd but not presented	290
4.	Bank charges and commission not entered in cash book	120
5.	Amount directly credited by the bank against transfer of fund	500
6.	Dividend credited by bank but not entered in cash book	1,000

4. From the following particulars, prepare the bank reconciliation statement.

1. Bank overdraft as per bank column of cash book ₹16,200.

2. A cheque deposited as per bank statement, but not recorded in the cash book ₹700.

3. Debit side bank column of the cash book cast short ₹100.

4. A cheque for ₹5,000 deposited, but collection as per bank statement ₹4,996.

5. Dividends collected directly by bank ₹3,500.

6. A party's cheque returned dishonoured only as per bank statement ₹530.

5. The overdraft as per cash book of Mr X was ₹7,640 as on 31.3.2019. As per the bank statement, Mr Vivek ascertained the following information:

1. Cheque deposited but not credited by the bank ₹10,000.
2. Interest on securities collected by the bank but not recorded in cash book ₹1,080.
3. Credit transfer not recorded in the cash book ₹200.
4. Dividend collected by the bank directly but not recorded in the cash book ₹1,000.
5. Cheque issued but not presented for payment ₹37,400.
6. Interest debited by the bank but not recorded in the cash book ₹1,000.
7. Bank charges not recorded in the cash book ₹340.

   From the above information you are asked to prepare a bank reconciliation statement to ascertain the balance as per the bank statement.

6. From the following information, prepare a bank reconciliation statement as on 31 December 2020 for M/s Mahavir Ltd.

Particulars	Amount (₹)
1. Bank overdraft as per the cash book	2,45,900
2. Interest debited by the bank on 26 December 2020 but advice not received.	27,870
3. Cheques issued before 31 December 2020 but not presented to bank.	66,000
4. Transport subsidy received from State Government directly by the bank but not advised to the company.	42,500
5. Draft deposited in the bank, but not credited until 31/12/2020.	13,500
6. Bills for collection credited by the bank until 31 December 2020 but no advice received by the company.	83,600
7. Amount wrongly debited to the company account by the bank for which no details are available.	7,400

 # CASES

Business Application Cases

1. **Anant Mansawala**   Data 1 is a market research agency run by Anant Mansawala. At the end of August 2020, Anant prepared his regular bank reconciliation statement. After matching the entries on the statement with those in the cash book, there were four un-ticked items remaining in the cash book. Details of these items were as follows:

   - Unpresented cheque no. 000991 ₹43.90
   - Unpresented cheque no. 000995 ₹1,528.00
   - Unpresented cheque no. 000999 ₹269.07
   - Uncleared lodgement for ₹670.00

After updating the cash book, there was a (debit) balance b/d of ₹1,990.30. The end of the month balance in the bank statement was ₹3,071.27.

Questions

1. Using the balance in the cash book as the opening balance, draw up a bank reconciliation statement for Data 1.
2. Redraw the bank reconciliation statement using the balance in the bank statement as the opening balance.
3. How might drawing up a bank reconciliation statement help Anant avoid cash flow problems when running Data 1?

2. **M/s Gupta and Siddiqui**   The following are extracts from the cash book and from the pass book of M/s Gupta and Siddiqui.

Extracts of Cash Book
(Bank Column Only)

Date	Receipts	L.F.	Amount (₹)	Date	Payments	L.F.	Amount (₹)
2020				2020			
1 Mar	To Balance b/d		40,000	2 Mar.	By Wages A/c		10,000
3 Mar	To Kiran's A/c		20,000	4 Mar.	By Bir Bahadur's A/c		20,000
8 Mar	To Swati's A/c		15,000	6 Mar.	By Rent A/c		1,000
10 Mar	To Ramanujam's A/c		16,000	9 Mar.	By Hira Lal's A/c		14,000
16 Mar	To Kamini's A/c		3,000	11 Mar.	By Manohar Lal's A/c		30,000
20 Mar	To Charu's A/c		2,700	18 Mar.	By Saurabh's A/c		5,000
28 Mar	To Dividend A/c		1,000	20 Mar.	By Ranjan's A/c		2,000
31 Mar	To Sikander's A/c		1,700	26 Mar.	By Tarun's A/c		1,500
				30 Mar.	By Kaushal's A/c		1,000
				31 Mar.	By Balance c/d		14,900
			99,400				99,400

Extracts of the Pass Book

Date	Particulars	Withdrawals	Deposits	Dr. or Cr.	Balance
2020					
1 Mar	By Balance b/d			Cr.	40,000
2 Mar	To Cheque A/c	10,000	—	Dr.	30,000
8 Mar	To Cheque A/c	1,000	—	Dr.	29,000
10 Mar	By Swati's A/c	—	15,000	Cr.	44,000
20 Mar	To Saurabh's A/c	5,000	—	Dr.	39,000
25 Mar	By Charu's A/c	—	2,700	Cr.	41,700
28 Mar	To Bir Bahadur's A/c	20,000	—	Dr.	21,700
30 Mar	To Insurance Premium A/c	1,000	—	Dr.	20,700
30 Mar	To Electricity A/c	500	—	Dr.	20,200
31 Mar	By Interest A/c	—	2,000	Cr.	22,200
31 Mar	By Dividend A/c	—	7,000	Cr.	29,200

Question
Prepare the bank reconciliation statement as on 31 March 2020.

Preparation of Financial Statements

Learning Objectives

After studying this chapter, you will understand

- different types of entries used to prepare financial statements
- uses of balance sheet and the linkage between income statement and balance sheet
- how to work out and finalize financial statements
- concept of worksheet
- closing entries for sustainability of books of accounts
- statement of retained earnings
- GST accounting
- financial statements of non-profit-seeking organizations
- presentation of company's true financial position and performance

INTRODUCTION

After the trial balance has been prepared, several adjustments relating to the accounting period have to be made in order to finalize the financial statements. In a manufacturing business, products are first manufactured and then sold, whereas in a trading business, finished goods are purchased and sold. A manufacturing business, therefore, involves the process of converting raw materials into finished goods before they can be sold in the market.

Thus, the two main activities, namely, manufacturing and trading, are separately evaluated by the preparation of a manufacturing account and a trading account. The manufacturing account discloses the cost of manufacture of finished goods, which is transferred to the trading account. The trading account discloses the gross trading results. The income statement reveals the final net profit or loss made by the firm during the year from all its activities. The profit and loss appropriation account is next created, which shows the appropriation of the company's funds/profits, for example, interest on capital and drawings, salary to proprietors and partners, etc. The balance sheet shows the position of the business with respect to all its assets and liabilities for a particular period. The balance sheet, income statement, cash flow statement, and the statement of changes in owners' equity have been discussed in the earlier chapters.

OBJECTIVES OF PREPARATION OF FINANCIAL STATEMENTS

The main aim of preparing a final account in the form of a financial statement is given in the following text:

1. Determine the result of the activities of a firm with regard to the profit or loss earned during the period under consideration.
2. Determine the state of affairs of a firm, in terms of its assets and liabilities.
3. Use the information contained in the final accounts to formulate the necessary rules, regulations, and policies for

the smooth functioning of the firm, for example, decisions pertaining to reduction of cost, selling price of products or services, replacement of machineries, the sources of finance for long-term survival of the firm, etc.

4. Use the final accounts as a basis to prepare future budgets and to have a better control over the activities of the business.
5. Determine the financial strength and stability of a business.
6. Determine the legal liability of a firm with respect to its tax position.

PROCEDURAL ASPECTS FOR PREPARATION OF FINANCIAL STATEMENTS

Broadly, the financial statement for a given period, including the accounting procedure for the preparation of the final accounts, is as follows:

Preparation of the initial trial balance Financial transactions recorded in the sales register, purchase register, etc. are posted in the general ledger. The balance of each ledger account is called a trial balance.

Adjustment entries Outstanding financial transactions as well as transactions connected with the previous year or subsequent year (including rectifications) are required to be adjusted in the final accounts to determine the net profit or loss during the accounting year. The adjustment entries are incorporated into the worksheet.

Worksheet It is a multicolumn schedule showing the relationship among the current account balances (a trial balance), proposed or actual adjusting entries or transactions, and the financial statements that would result if theses adjusting entries or transactions were recorded. It is used at the end of the period as an aid to preparing financial statements and for planning purposes.

Preparation of the final trial balance After posting the adjustment entries in a worksheet, the final trial balance (adjusted trial balance) is prepared.

Closing entries Nominal accounts as per the traditional approach or expense, loss, income, and gain accounts as per the modern approach are transferred to the manufacturing account, trading account, or income statement. No closing entries are passed for the real accounts, such as fixed assets, cash, etc. Neither are the entries passed for the personal accounts, such as debtors, creditors, etc., as per the traditional approach. Such accounts are known as assets, liabilities, and capital account as per the modern approach.

The cost of production (balancing figure) from the manufacturing account is transferred to the trading account. The gross profit (or loss) is transferred from the trading account to the income statement. The net profit (or loss) from the income statement is transferred to the capital account. Entries of all such transfers (i.e., closing entries) are passed to prepare the final accounts.

Preparation of the manufacturing account, the trading account, and the income statement for the year On the basis of the procedures discussed earlier, the manufacturing account, the trading account, and the income statement are prepared to determine the cost of production, the gross profit or loss, and the net profit or loss, respectively.

Preparation of the balance sheet at the end of the year Real accounts and personal accounts as per the traditional approach or assets, liabilities, and capital accounts as per the modern approach are transferred from the adjusted trial balance to the balance sheet. The net profit or loss is also transferred to the capital account from the income statement.

A flow chart for the preparation of a financial statement is shown in Fig. 13.1.

ADJUSTMENT ENTRIES

For most firms, revenue is neither always earned as cash is received nor an expense necessarily incurred as cash is disbursed. The timing differences between cash flows and the recognition of revenue and expenses are referred to as *accruals* and *deferrals*.

There is more to the measurement of profit or loss than merely recording simple revenue and expense transactions that affect only a single accounting period. Certain transactions affect the revenue or expenses of two or more accounting periods. The purpose of adjustment entries is to assign appropriate amount of revenue and expense to respective accounting periods. For example, Music Telefilms Ltd purchased the cosmetic items that will be used for several months. Thus, an accounting entry is required to record the expense associated with the cosmetic items that Music Telefilms uses each month.

Need for Adjustment Entries

For purposes of measuring income and preparing financial statements, the life of a firm is divided into a series of *accounting periods*. This practice supports the decision-makers to compare the financial statements of successive periods and to identify significant trends, which is very useful for financial analysis.

But measuring the net income for a relatively short accounting period, such as a month or even a year, poses a problem because some firms' activities affect the revenue and expenses of multiple accounting periods. Therefore, adjusting entries are needed at the end of each accounting period to make certain that appropriate amounts of revenue and expense are reported in the firm's income statement.

In theory, a firm could make adjustment entries on a daily basis. But as a practical matter, these entries are made *only at the end of each accounting period*. In most of the firms, adjusting entries are made on a monthly basis.

Nature of Adjustment Entries

The number of adjustments needed at the end of each accounting period depends entirely upon the nature of the firm's business activities. However, most adjusting entries fall into one of the following five general natures.

Converting assets to expenses

A cash expenditure (or cost) will benefit more than one accounting period usually recorded by increasing the value of an asset

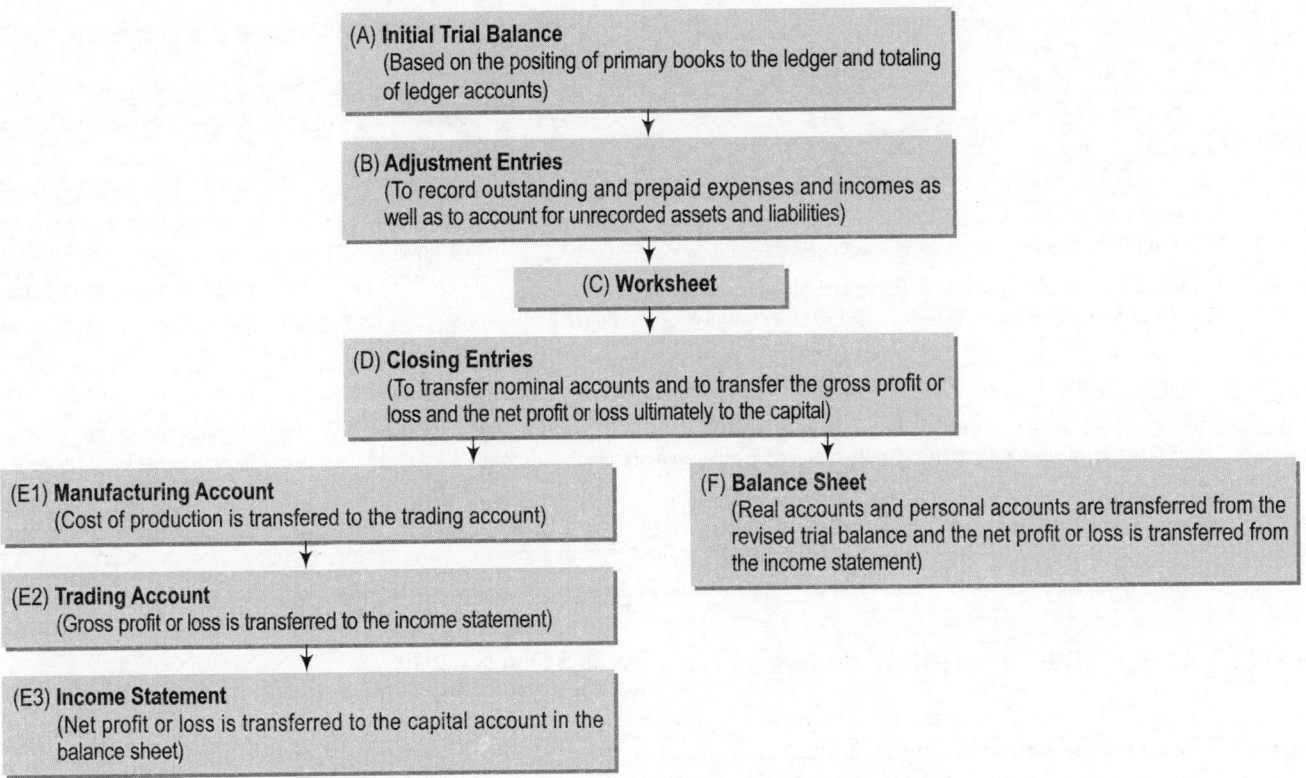

FIG. 13.1 Flow chart for the preparation of a financial statement

(for example, cosmetic items by Music Telefilms Ltd) and by reducing the cash balance. The asset account created actually represents the *deferral (or postponement)* of an expense. In each future period that benefits from the use of this asset, an adjusting entry is made to allocate a portion of the asset's cost from the balance sheet to the income statement as an expense account. This is also known as *deferred expense*.

Converting liabilities to revenues

A firm may collect cash in advance for services or goods to be rendered or provided respectively, in future accounting periods. Transactions of this nature are usually recorded by increasing the cash balance and also by increasing the unearned revenue (typically, liability). Here, the liability account created represents the *deferral (or postponement)* of the revenue. In the period that services are actually rendered or goods are delivered, an adjusting entry is made to allocate a portion of the liability from the balance sheet to the income statement to recognize the revenue earned during the period. The adjusting entry is recorded by reducing the liability (unearned revenue) and increasing the revenue or income (service income account or sales account) for the value involved. This is also known as *deferred revenue*.

Accruing unpaid expenses

An expense may be incurred in the current accounting period even though no cash payment will occur until a future period. These *accrued expenses* are recorded by an adjusting entry made at the end of each accounting period. The adjusting entry is recorded by increasing the appropriate expense account (for example, wages expense or interest expense) and by increasing

the related liability account (for example, wages payable or interest payable).

Accruing uncollected revenues

The revenue may be earned or *accrued* during the current period, even though the collection of cash will not occur until a future period. Unrecorded earned revenue, for which no cash has been received, requires an adjusting entry at the end of the accounting period. The adjusting entry is recorded by increasing the appropriate asset (for example, accounts receivable or interest receivable) and by increasing the appropriate revenue account (for example, service revenue earned or interest earned). This is also known as *accrued revenue*.

Adjustment related to valuation of assets

In the balance sheet, long-term assets (for example, plant, property and equipment, office equipment, furniture and fixtures), current assets (for example, inventory items), and financial assets (financial investments made by the firm to outside of the firm) are recorded at the historical value. Such a historical value needs to be brought to the current value (net realizable value) in the balance sheet. The conservatism concept of accounting advocates that *Provide for all expected losses and expenses, but do not provide for expected gains or income.* Hence, it is needed to bring the correct or realistic value into the books of account, by reducing the asset value and considering the same as a loss in the income statement, in case of reduction in the value of an asset. This is known as *assets valuation*.

A summary of the nature of adjustments, the adjusting entry and its effect of omitting an adjustment on the financial statement is shown in Exhibit 13.1.

EXHIBIT 13.1 Summary of Nature of Adjustments

Nature of Adjustment	Adjusting Entry	Effect of Omitting Adjusting Entry on the Balance Sheet and Income Statement	
		Effect on the Balance Sheet	**Effect on the Income Statement**
Deferred Expense	Increase the Expense Account (Dr. Particular Expense Account) Decrease the Asset Account (Cr. Particular Asset Account)	Assets Overstated and Owners' Equity Overstated	Expenses Understated and Net Income or Net Profit Overstated
Deferred Revenue	Decrease the Liability Account (Dr. Particular Liability Account) Increase the Revenue Account (Cr. Particular Revenue Account or Income Account)	Liability Overstated and Owners' Equity Understated	Revenue Understated and Net Income or Net Profit Understated
Accrued Expense	Increase the Expense Account (Dr. Particular Expense Account) Increase the Liability Account (Cr. Particular Liability Account)	Liability Understated and Owners' Equity Overstated	Expenses Understated and Net Income or Net Profit Overstated
Accrued Revenue	Increase the Asset Account (Dr. Particular Asset Account) Increase the Revenue Account (Cr. Particular Revenue or Income Account)	Asset Understated and Owners' Equity Understated	Revenue Understated and Net Income or Net Profit Understated
Asset Valuation	Increase the Expense Account (Dr. Particular Expense Account) Decrease the Asset Account (Cr. Particular Asset Account)	Asset Overstated and Owners' Equity Overstated	Expenses Understated and Net Income or Net Profit Overstated

TYPES OF ADJUSTING ENTRIES

This section explains the various types of adjusting entries such as accrued expenses, outstanding income, outstanding expenses, revenue received in advance, expenses paid in advance, closing entries, etc.

Outstanding Expenses

Any expenditure, which solely benefits the current accounting period, becomes an expense for the period. All expenses which are due for payment but have not been paid during the accounting period are also brought into the books to help in matching revenues and expenses.

The amount of expenses taken from the trial balance is increased by the outstanding amount and shown in the income statement. The actual outstanding amount is shown as a liability in the balance sheet. In the subsequent accounting period, the liability of the outstanding expense is set off by the entry of actual payment, when it is made. Outstanding expenses are also known as accrued expenses.

Note: 'Revenue' and 'income' can be at times used interchangeably.

■ **ILLUSTRATION 13.1** M/s Kanika Traders pays a salary of ₹5,000 per month to its account assistant. The current salary is payable on the 5th of the next month. The firm follows October to September as accounting year. For the month of September 2020, the salary would be payable on 5 October 2020. Analyse the effect of these transactions on the accounting equation.

Solution

Assets = Liabilities + Contributed Capital + Revenue − Expenses

In the books of M/s Kanika Traders

As on 30 September 2020

⇧ Liability increase ₹5,000 Salary payable account credit   ⇧ Expense increase ₹5,000 Salary expense account debit

As on 5 October 2020

When the payment is made to the account assistant

⇩ Asset reduction ₹5,000 Bank account credit   ⇩ Liability reduction ₹5,000 Salary payable account debit

Outstanding Income or Accrued Income

There will be cases where an entity has earned revenue but has not received the amount during the current accounting period. For example, interest earned on deposits or investment made with outside agencies are examples of outstanding income. It is also known as accrued income or accrued revenue. The steps to be followed in relation to outstanding income are as follows:

1. Estimate the amount of revenue earned.
2. Debit the asset account, that is, accrued income account or outstanding income account, and credit the revenue account.

Outstanding revenue refers to the income that has become due during the accounting period or year, but has not been received by the firm. The income earned will increase by the amount earned and shown in the income statement, and the outstanding income account will be listed as an asset in the balance sheet. In the subsequent accounting period, the outstanding income account will be set off by entering the actual receipt of income when it is received by crediting the accrued income account, and debiting the cash or bank account.

Accrued income or outstanding income is the income of the current year that has not yet been received. However, (following the accrual method of accounting), it will be treated as income since it has accrued in the current year.

■ **ILLUSTRATION 13.2** M/s Berner has rented part of its office situated in Nariman Point of Mumbai to M/s Carrello for a monthly rent of ₹1,00,000 payable in the beginning of the next month. M/s Berner adopts an accounting year from July to June. Prepare the final account for the year ended as on 30 June 2020.

Solution

Assets = Liabilities + Contributed + Revenue – Expenses
Capital

In the books of M/s Berner

As on 30 June 2020

⬆ Asset increase ₹1,00,000
Rent receivable account
debit

⬆ Income increase ₹1,00,000
Rental income account
credit

As on 1 July 2020

⬇ Asset decrease ₹1,00,000
Rent receivable account
credit

⬆ Asset increase ₹1,00,000
Bank account debit

Revenue Received in Advance

The revenue or income received in advance during the current accounting period in respect of the period of services to be rendered or goods to be delivered in future, that is, in the subsequent accounting period, will have to be recorded as revenue only in the subsequent accounting period.

The first step in such a situation consists of estimating the account of revenue for the current and the subsequent accounting periods. The income received in advance will be shown as deferred revenue and income taken from the trial balance will be decreased by the said amount. The actual income received in advance will be shown as a liability in the balance sheet. In the subsequent accounting period, it will be adjusted against the revenue of the subsequent period for services rendered or goods delivered in that period.

Revenue received in advance of the accounting period would be treated as an increase in liabilities (credit) and entitled as unearned revenue or revenue collected in advance, or income received in advance. The subscription received in advance by journal or magazine publishers is a typical example of unearned revenue for journal publishing firms. Similarly, the Indian Railways and Air India earn their revenue in advance from passengers as they book their tickets in advance of a journey.

Unearned revenue becomes the revenue of the firm when the services are rendered to the customer from whom the advance amount has been received. A liability–revenue account relationship comes into existence on the event of unearned revenue by the firm. The adjustment entry has to book the revenue when the services are provided by the firm. This would result in a decrease in the liability in the form of unearned revenue (debit) and an increase in the revenue or income of the firm (credit).

■ **ILLUSTRATION 13.3** On 2 March 2020, Airly India received an advance amount of ₹12,000 from Mr Jamal for a journey from Ahmedabad to Delhi on 25 April 2020. Airly India will record (this advance received on 2 March 2020) as receipt of cash; that is, increase the asset account in the form of cash (debit) and simultaneously record the liability as unearned revenue (credit). Mr Jamal travelled from Ahmedabad to Delhi on 25 April 2020. Hence, on 25 April

2020, Airly India will reduce its liability (debit) in the form of unearned revenue and increase the revenue income (credit). Analyse the effect of these transactions on the accounting equation.

Solution

Assets = Liabilities + Contributed + Revenue – Expenses
Capital

In the books of Airly India:

As on 2 March 2020

⬆ Cash received ₹12,000
Cash A/c debit

⬆ Unearned revenue ₹12,000
Unearned revenue A/c
credit

₹12,000 ⟨ ₹0 Current accounting period income
(Transferred to income statement)

₹12,000 Succeeding accounting period income
(Carried forward as a liability in balance sheet)

As on 25 April 2020

⬇ Unearned revenue ₹12,000
Unearned revenue A/c
debit

⬆ Revenue income ₹12,000
Revenue income A/c
credit

Expenses Paid in Advance or Prepaid Expenses

The expenses paid in advance during the current accounting period for the services or benefits to be received in the subsequent period is recorded as an expense in the subsequent accounting period. The expenses paid in advance are also known as prepaid expenses.

The rules to be followed in case of prepaid expenses are as follows:

1. Estimate the amount of prepaid expenses.
2. Debit the prepaid expenses account and credit the concerned expenses account.

The expenses incurred decreases by the amount of expenses paid in advance and is shown in the income statement. The prepaid expenses will be listed as an asset in the balance sheet. In the subsequent accounting period, prepaid expenses will be transferred to the concerned expenses account.

When a firm makes a payment that covers expenses for more than one accounting period or year, the portion of expense for which the benefit will be available in the next accounting period would be known as prepaid expenses or prepayments.

When a cost is incurred in the form of payment of funds, the asset account is increased (debited) to indicate that the services or benefits will be received in future. Prepayments are generally incurred with respect to insurance premium, advance payment of rent, advertising agreements, etc.

The benefits of prepaid expenses will expire either with the passage of time or as the services are utilized. Eventually, the asset will convert into an expense. The expiry of the benefits of prepaid expenses does not result in a daily recurring transaction or entry; hence, it has to be recorded properly to

determine the correct financial performance and position of the firm. For this purpose, an increase (debit) in expenses is recorded in the adjustment entry along with a decrease (credit) in the asset account. If the adjustment entries are not passed, it will result in the assets being overstated and the expenses being understated.

■ **ILLUSTRATION 13.4**   Aiiya & Co. has paid a fire insurance premium of ₹12,000 on 1 October 2019 for a 12-month period. The current accounting period ends on 31 March 2020. In the accounting year 2019–2020, expenditure of ₹6000 will be booked as current expense, and balance ₹6,000 will be shown as an asset in the form of prepaid expense as on 31 March 2020, as the benefit of fire insurance premium is available for the next six months. Subsequently, in the accounting year 2020–2021, an expense of ₹6,000 and a reduction the assets in the form of prepaid expense would be recorded. Analyse the effect of these transections on the accounting equation.

Solution

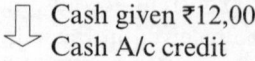

Assets = Liabilities + Contributed + Revenue – Expenses
                          Capital

In the books of Aiiya & Co.

As on 1 October 2019

⬇ Cash given ₹12,000   ⬆ Insurance premium ₹12,000
   Cash A/c credit   Insurance premium A/c
                               debit

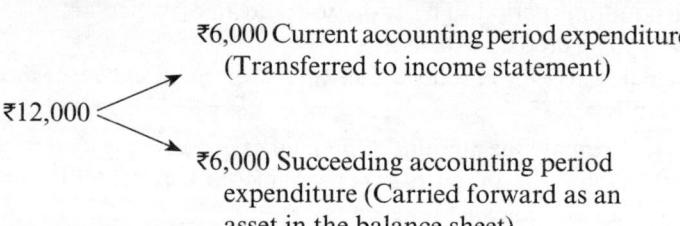

₹12,000 ➡ ₹6,000 Current accounting period expenditure (Transferred to income statement)

₹6,000 Succeeding accounting period expenditure (Carried forward as an asset in the balance sheet)

As on 31 March 2020

⬆ Prepaid insurance ₹6,000   ⬇ Insurance premium ₹6,000
   Prepaid insurance A/c   Insurance premium A/c
   debit   credit

As on 1 April 2020

⬇ Prepaid insurance ₹6,000   ⬆ Insurance premium ₹6,000
   Prepaid insurance A/c   Insurance premium A/c
   credit   debit

Closing Inventory

The closing inventory of every item is arrived at by physically counting the inventory available and assigning a value to the stock. The value of the closing inventory is brought to the books of accounts by debiting the closing inventory account and crediting the trading account.

The stock at the end appears in the balance sheet at the end of the accounting year and is carried forward to the next year. The closing inventory appears on the credit side of the income statement to reduce the cost of goods sold or to increase the operating profit. The closing inventory appears as an asset in the balance sheet.

Opening Inventory

The closing inventory of the immediately preceding accounting period is the opening inventory of the next accounting period. The opening inventory is brought to the books of account by debiting the trading account, and crediting the opening inventory account (i.e., last period's closing inventory account).

The opening inventory appears on the debit side of the trading account to increase the cost of goods sold, while the opening inventory will be closed. Hence, no second effect will appear in financial statements.

Provision or Reserve for Discount from Creditors

This provision or reserve is the amount of discount expected to be received from the creditors on settling their account within the prescribed time. Such discounts receivable from the suppliers or creditors are an income for the firm, and the profit of the firm would increase by that extent. The period for which the cash discount is available is pre-determined, and hence, there is always a possibility that a firm having surplus cash flow can make their payment on time and avail the benefit of the cash discount offered by the supplier. In such cases, the firm would be entitled to claim the cash discount in the next year by making payments according to the terms for the credit purchases made in the previous year. Hence, it is normally an accepted practice to provide for the discount on creditors at the end of an accounting period, to work out the profit of the firm.

In the adjustment entry, the income of the year would be increased (discount income account would be credited) and the said amount will be considered as future benefits receivable as an increase in the asset value (provision for discount on creditor account would be debited).

The provision for discount on creditors will be calculated from net creditors as provided in the trial balance duly adjusted based on additional information.

■ **ILLUSTRATION 13.5**   The trial balance of Merry Moon Stores indicates ₹71,000 as sundry creditors, ₹1,300 as the opening balance of provision of discount from creditors, and ₹3,250 as discount income earned during the year.

₹1,000 is payable to Ideal Fab; the owner of Ideal Fab has agreed to write off the recovery of ₹1,000 to maintain their long-term relationship. Merry Moon always makes the payments to the majority of creditors before the due date and avail the cash discount benefit. Hence, Mrs Padma, the owner of Merry Moon Stores, has decided to provide for a 3% cash discount available from creditors in future.

Calculate the net income and creditors balance.

Solution

1. Net income as accounted in the income statement:
   Discount income:

	Amount (₹)
Discount income as per trial balance	3,250

Add: Provision for discount from creditors
(Working Note 1 below) 2,100
Less: Provision for discount from creditors
(as per the formula
Trial Balance – Old Provisions Available) 1,300
Net income as discount from creditors 4,050

2. Creditors balance as indicated in the balance sheet as at 31 March 2020:

Creditors:

	Amount (₹)
Balance as per trial balance	71,000
Less: Not payable to Ideal Fab as given	1,000
Less: Provision for discount from creditors	2,100
Balance as per balance sheet	67,900

Working Note:

1. Calculation of provision for discount from creditors:
Amount on which provision is to be made
(₹71,000 – 1,000) ₹70,000
Percentage of provision 3%
Provision amount (70,000 × 3%) ₹2,100

Amortizing Assets Held for Certain Specific Purpose

Certain assets such as patents, leasehold land, technical know-how, etc. are owned by an entity on the condition that the use or benefits will be restricted to a pre-determined period. At the end of the each accounting period, the value of such assets is written down by—(a) increasing the expense or reducing the operating profit (i.e., by debiting the income statement); (b) reducing the value of such asset (i.e., by crediting the asset account); and (c) depicting the asset at reduced value in the balance sheet.

Providing for Depreciation

Depreciation expense is the amortization of a fixed asset during the course of its useful economic and technological life. This is done by charging a pro-rata amount in the current accounting period. There are two methods for the recording of depreciation. Under the first method, the asset value is directly reduced by crediting the asset account by the depreciation amount.

Under the second method, the depreciation charge is credited to a depreciation provision, also known as a depreciation fund or accumulated depreciation account, and not to the asset directly. The written down value of the asset is shown in the balance sheet by deducting the depreciation provision from the original cost of the asset. The depreciation amount is transferred to the income statement as a charge against income.

■ **ILLUSTRATION 13.6** Rainbow & Co. purchased furniture worth ₹2 lakh on 1 April 2019. It was put to use during the year 2019–2020. Its utility and leisure benefits in later years will not be the same as during 2019–2020. As part of the cost and utility of the furniture, Rainbow & Co has decided to write off the value by 10% p.a. Analyse the effect of these transactions on the accounting equation.

Solution

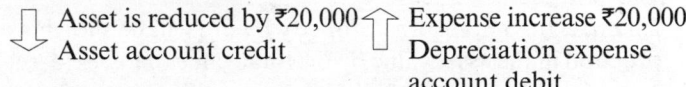

In the books of Rainbow & Co.
Depreciation ₹1,000 (₹2 lakh × 10%)

As on 31 March 2020

⬇ Asset is reduced by ₹20,000   ⬆ Expense increase ₹20,000
Asset account credit   Depreciation expense
account debit

Or provision for depreciation account credit

Goods Withdrawal for Office Use

All Books Stationery Mart, a trader in stationery items, uses part of its stock of papers, pencils, and pens for its own office use as stationery. Here, the effective purchases of the firm would be reduced (purchase account would be credited) and the expenses in the stationery and printing expenses account would be increased (stationery and printing account would be debited). If the drawings of stationery for personal use are not accounted in the year when withdrawn, then during the finalization of the financial performance of the firm, that is, while preparing the income statement, the trading account would be credited instead of the purchase account.

Drawings in Kind

Cash may be withdrawn by the owner of a firm or the partners of a partnership firm to meet their household expenses in addition to a few personal investments. For example, the owner of a grocery shop, instead of buying the grains from other shops, draws food grains for personal use from the shop stock. In such circumstances, the effective purchases of the firm would be reduced (purchase account would be credited) and drawings account would be increased (drawing account would be debited). If the drawings are not accounted in the year when withdrawn, during the finalization of the financial performance of the firm, that is, while preparing the income statement, the trading account would be credited instead of the purchase account.

Accidental Loss

Firms may have to bear extraordinary losses on account of unexpected accidental events caused by damage, accidents, earthquakes, flood, storm, fire, etc. Such events may lead to the loss of goods or other property such as machinery, building etc.

Losses incurred on account of accidental events will be recorded under two categories: uninsured or insured.

Loss of *uninsured goods* by fire will be shown as a reduction in the purchase value (purchase account would be credited). The loss thus incurred will be reported in a separate account titled 'Loss of goods by accident (name of accidental event)' and expenses would be increased.

Loss of *insured goods* by fire will be shown as a reduction in the purchase value by the total value of losses (purchase account would be credited). The amount of claim accepted by the insurance company would be treated as future benefits

receivable, and a new asset type account named 'Insurance company account' would be created and its balance would be increased (insurance company account will be debited). The difference between the total value of loss and the amount of claim accepted by the insurance company would be treated as a loss for the firm. A separate account titled 'Loss of goods by accident (name of accidental event)' would be created and expenses would be increased.

Likewise, loss of insured property by fire will be shown as a reduction in the asset value by the total value of losses (asset account would be credited). The amount of claim accepted by the insurance company would be treated as future benefits receivable, and a new asset type account named 'Insurance company account' would be created and its balance would be increased (insurance company account will be debited). The difference between the total value of loss and the amount of claim accepted by the insurance company would be treated as a loss for the firm. A separate account titled 'Loss of asset by accident (name of accidental event)' and expenses would be increased.

If, during a financial year, the transactions discussed earlier are not properly recorded, then the trading account would be credited instead of the purchase account in the year end.

■ **ILLUSTRATION 13.7**   M/s Smartphone reported to New India Assurance Company on 25 March 2019 a fire accident that happened at their factory on the previous day, that is, 24 March 2019. In the first week of April 2019, the final estimates of losses incurred by the company was made and submitted to New India Assurance Company. In the last week of April 2019, before the finalization of the annual reports for the year ended 31 March 2019, the insurance company intimated the status of acceptance of the claim with the respective amounts. The management of M/s Smartphone has accepted the decision of New India Assurance Company (NIAC).

Particulars	Claim Amount (₹)	Acceptance of Claim Amount (₹)
Passive devices	23,000	14,000
Electrical cables	12,000	Nil
Furniture	7,000	7,000

Analyse the effect of these transactions on the accounting equation.

Solution

Assets = Liabilities + Contributed + Revenue − Expenses
                              Capital

In the books of M/s Smartphone

As on 31 March 2019

1. Passive Devices:
   NIAC has accepted the partial claim amount, leading to the following effects as on 31 March 2019:

   Asset decreased by ₹23,000
   Stock of passive devices ₹23,000

   Expense increased by ₹9,000
   Loss on account of fire (Passive devices reduced by ₹9,000)

   Asset increased by ₹14,000
   Insurance company account debit ₹14,000

2. Electrical Cables:
   NIAC has not accepted the claim amount, leading to the following effects as on 31 March 2019:

   Asset decreased by ₹12,000
   Stock of electrical cables ₹12,000

   Expense increased by ₹12,000
   Loss on account of fire (Electrical cables reduced by ₹12,000)

3. Furniture:
   NIAC has accepted the full claim amount, leading to the following effects:

   Asset decreased by ₹7,000
   Stock of furniture reduced by ₹7,000

   Expense increased by ₹NIL

   Asset increased by ₹7,000
   Insurance company account debit by ₹7,000

In the year 2019–2020, when the total claim amount of ₹21,000 is received from the Insurance company, the asset in the name of the insurance company would be reduced and that in the name of bank balance would be increased by ₹21,000. The net effect on gross asset will be zero.

Asset decreased by ₹21,000
Insurance company credit by ₹21,000
Asset increased by ₹21,000
Bank balance debit by ₹21,000

Goods Distributed as Free Samples

To encourage middlemen to provide business, or sometimes to maintain a cordial long-term relationship with the existing customers, it is normal practice to distribute business goods among the parties concerned as free samples. For example, pharmaceutical companies provide free samples of medicines to general medical practitioners. The value of the free samples would be considered as an advertisement expense, and the advertisement expense account would be increased (debit advertisement expense account), whereas the value of goods available would be reduced by crediting the trading account. Another effect will be a reduction in the value of goods available; the trading account would be credited instead of the purchase account. The value of purchases will not be reduced because samples are not in the form of raw materials.

Goods Received but Purchase Bill Not Received

Suppose the firm has received goods in the month of March 2019, but the corresponding purchase bill is received in the month of April 2019, and the year ends as on 31 March 2019. Such goods either form part of the closing stock or are sold immediately for which the sales entry is recorded in the month

of March 2019 itself. In such circumstance, the purchase is recorded in March even though the purchase bill is not yet received. Otherwise, the trading account will give a distorted picture of purchases and gross profit. Therefore, the entry should be passed in the month of March 2019 as an increase in the purchase account (debit purchase account) as well as an increase in the liability in the name of creditors (credit the creditors account).

In the subsequent year, when the purchase invoice or bill is received from the supplier, no entry will be passed, and a note will be written on the said purchase invoice about entry already passed in the year 2018–2019 with the specific journal voucher number.

Goods Despatched but Sale Bill Not Prepared

A firm may sell and deliver the goods to a customer during the final days of the current accounting year. However, the sales invoice is prepared only in the first week of the next accounting period. The sales entry is thus omitted inappropriately. Hence, at the year end, an adjustment entry has to be passed, through which the asset account in the name of debtors will be increased (debit debtor's account) and the income account in the name of sales will be increased (debit the sales account).

In the subsequent year, when the sales bill is prepared and sent to the customer, no entry will be passed, and a note will be written on the said sales bill about the entry already passed in the year 2018–2019, with the specific journal voucher number.

Purchase Bill Received but Goods Not Received

If the purchase bill is received before the goods are received, the accounting treatment depends on the legal position under the Sales of Goods Act, 1931. If the firm becomes the owner of the goods during the accounting period, the purchase entry should be recorded in the purchase book when the title of the goods has been received by the firm based on receipt of purchase bill (no consideration for physical receipt of goods). Simultaneously, the closing stock should be increased by the same amount.

If the title of the goods is received only when the goods are physically received, no entry should be made in the purchase book and in the closing stock value till the firm becomes the owner of the goods.

Sales Bill Prepared but Goods Not Sent

If the ownership of the goods has passed from the firm to its customer during the accounting period, then the sales bill is entered in the sales book, ensuring that the stock covered by this bill is not included in the value of the closing stock. The physical custody of the stock lying with the firm should be noted in a separate sheet rather than in the inventory sheet, as the property rights of goods have been transferred by the firm to the customer. It is recorded in a separate sheet as reminder of goods with the firm.

If, however, the ownership of the goods has not passed from the business to its customers, then the sales bill is not entered in the sales book of the current year, and the closing stock includes the goods covered under the said invoice in the inventory sheet. The stock should be valued at its cost price and not at the invoice price.

Interest and Dividend Income on Investment

Firms having surplus funds normally make investments such as in shares, debentures, and other securities of other companies or firms, mutual funds, or banks. The firm will receive the interest and dividend income on such investments, which would be considered as 'other' income of the firm. If the investment income (in the form of dividend and interest) is received during the year, then it is accounted appropriately during that year in an investment income account in the trial balance of the firm.

It may often happen that interest on investment has accrued but is not due for receipt on account of terms of the investment. In such circumstances, at the end of the accounting period, the investment income accrued needs to be recorded as an adjustment entry. In such a case, the income of the firm will increase by the accrued amount (investment income account to be credited) and the asset account in the name of investment income receivable will be increased (asset account debit).

■ **ILLUSTRATION 13.8** Sharky Traders has made a fixed deposit of ₹2,00,000 with Dena Bank, Ashram Road, Ahmedabad, on 1 October 2019 for a period of one year at the interest rate of 10% p.a. At the end of the accounting year as on 31 March 2020, the interest has accrued for the period from 1 October 2019 to 31 March 2020, but would be due for receipt on 30 September 2020. Thus, the interest due amounts to ₹10,000 (2,00,000 × 10% × 6/12). Analyse the effect of these transactions on the accounting equation.

Solution

Assets = Liabilities + Contributed Capital + Revenue – Expenses

In the books of Sharky Traders:

As on 31 March 2020

⬆ Asset Increased by ₹10,000 Investment income receivable account debit

⬆ Income increased by ₹10,000 Investment income account credit

As on 30 September 2020

The fixed deposit matured. Hence, the firm will receive ₹2,20,000 [2,00,000 + (2,00,000 × 10%)] from the bank. The bank balance in the form of asset account would increase by ₹2,20,000; the investment in the form of fixed deposit as an asset would reduce by ₹2,00,000; the investment in the form of investment income receivable account as an asset would reduce by ₹10,000; and the income of the firm in the form of investment income would increase by ₹10,000.

⬆ Bank balance increased by ₹2,20,000
⬇ Fixed deposit reduced by ₹2,00,000

⬆ Investment income increased by ₹10,000
⬇ Investment income receivable reduced by ₹10,000

Commission Based on Sale, Purchase, or Profit

Business practice prescribes commission to be paid to commission agents for the work done by them to promote the firm's business. The commission payable is recorded as adjustment entries. Commission may be payable to sales agents who promote the sale of the firm's goods, commodities, and merchandise or to middlemen who interact with the suppliers of raw materials for the firm. Commission may also be payable to the manager or partners of a firm as a percentage of the profit earned by the firm.

At the year end, an adjustment entry is passed to record the commission expense incurred in that accounting year. If an amount of commission is payable in the next accounting period, the commission payable is recorded as liabilities.

■ **ILLUSTRATION 13.9**   VLS Enterpises paid a commission of 2% on the net profit of the year to Mr Dharm, the manager of the firm. For the year ended as on 31 March 2020, the chief accountant of the firm informed that the profit of the year 2019–2020 amounts to ₹2,00,000. Analyse the effect of these transactions on the accounting equation.

Solution

The commission payable to Mr Dharm is ₹4,000 (2,00,000 × 2%).

Assets	=	Liabilities	+	Contributed Capital	+	Revenue	–	Expenses

In the books of VLS Enterpises:

As on 31 March 2020

⬆ Increase in liability ₹4,000 Commission payable account credit

⬆ Expense increase ₹4,000 Commission expense account debit

In the financial year 2020–2021

when the commission will be paid to Mr Dharm

⬇ Asset reduced by ₹4000 Bank account credit

⬇ Liability reduced by ₹4,000 Commission payable account debit

Royalty

Royalty is payable by a firm to the inventor of a manufacturing process or the collaborators who have allowed the firm to use the knowledge provided by them. The royalty payable to a collaborator, inventor, author, or artist is worked out at the time of finalization of the financial performance of the accounting period. The royalty payable may depend on the quantity produced or the quantity sold. If the royalty payable depends on the quantity produced, then it would be directly related to the expense, and hence would be treated as a trading expense. If it depends on thequantity sold, then it would be considered as a selling expense of the firm, and hence would be charged against the income of the year by debiting to the profit and loss account or income statement of the year. The amount would be treated as a liability of the firm, and liability in the name of royalty payable will be increased. In short, the royalty expense account will be debited and the royalty payable account will be credited.

Providing for Income Tax

After the profit for the current accounting period has been determined, an estimate is made of the income tax payable in the context of prevailing tax laws and regulations. The income tax expense is charged to the income statement and the payable amount is shown as a liability in the balance sheet. In the subsequent accounting period, when the tax is paid, it is set off by an entry in the tax payable account.

Income tax is not an expense incurred by a firm in order to earn any revenue or income. It is a charge against the profit of the firm. It reduces the profit available to the owner of the firm and reduces the final net profit available to the firm, and would be treated as a liability as income tax payable.

If the income tax is payable as a personal expense of the owner of the firm, then the profit of the firm will not be reduced, but the amount would be treated as drawings by the owner.

Appreciation in the Value of Assets

The value of certain assets such as land and building may often increase with time. This increase in the value of an asset is a gain, and so it needs to be credited in a separate account. This would result in an increase in the value of the respective asset. This gain is actually not realized in cash by the firm, but is considered as a paper gain. Such gains cannot be recorded as profit or gain in the books of account, since there are no real or actual gains.

However, firms often need to record such gains in order to show a higher value or to make major changes in the constitution of the firm, such as adding a new partner, etc. In such circumstances, the difference between the revised value of the asset and the book value of the asset will be named as an increase in the value of the asset. The asset account balance will be increased by the said amount (asset account debit) and the revaluation reserve or appreciation account will be increased as part of retained earnings account (revaluation reserve account will be credited).

■ **ILLUSTRATION 13.10**   Vardhman Engineers Ltd purchased office space for ₹10,00,000 on 1 April 2019. It was put to use during the year 2019–2020. As on 31 March 2020, the company decided to include Mr Krishna as a partner in the firm. As on 31 March 2020, the estimated market value of the office space is ₹11,20,000. As a part of the cost and utility of the office, Vardhman Engineers Ltd has decided to write off the cost by 10% p.a. Analyse the effect of these transactions on the accounting equation.

Solution

Assets	=	Liabilities	+	Contributed Capital	+	Revenue	–	Expenses

In the books of Vardhman Engineers Ltd:
The book value of the office is ₹9,00,000 {₹10,00,000 less depreciation ₹1,00,000 (₹10,00,000 × 10%)}. Now the revised value is ₹11,20,000, which means that the increase in the value of the office is ₹2,20,000 (₹11,20,000 – ₹9,00,000).

As on 31 March 2020

⬆ Asset is increased by ₹2,20,000

Asset account credit

⬆ Retained earnings in the form of capital increased by ₹2,20,000

Revaluation reserve account credit

WORKSHEET

Accountants often use Working Papers for collecting and summarizing data that they need for preparing various analyses and reports. The worksheet is a working paper that accountants may use to summarize adjusting entries and account balances for the financial statements. In small firms with few accounts and adjustments, a worksheet may not be necessary. In a computerized accounting system, a worksheet may not be necessary because the software program automatically posts entries in the accounts and prepares the financial statements.

Worksheet is a useful device for understanding the flow of accounting data from the unadjusted trial balance to the financial statements. The flow of data is the same in both manual and computerized accounting systems.

A worksheet serves several purposes. It allows accountants to *see the effects* of *adjusting entries* without actually entering these adjustments in the accounting records. This makes it relatively easy for accountants to correct errors or make changes in the estimated amounts. It also enables the accountants and management to preview the financial statements before the final drafts are developed.

A worksheet is started by first listing at the top of the firm the type of working papers (worksheet) and the period of time, as shown in Exhibit 13.2. Next, the unadjusted trial balance is entered directly into the worksheet. The adjustments explained and illustrated in this chapter are entered in the adjustment columns. Cross referencing (by letters) the debit and credit of each adjustment is useful in reviewing the worksheet. It is also helpful for identifying the adjustment entries that need to be recorded in the journal. Then the total of the columns of the adjusted trial balance has to be calculated to verify the equality of debits and credits.

Worksheet is completed by extending the adjusted trial balance amounts to the income statement and balance sheet columns. The amounts of revenue and expenses are extended to the income statement columns. The amounts of assets, liabilities, and owner's equity are extended to the balance sheet columns. A sample worksheet is presented in Exhibit 13.2.

CLOSING ENTRIES

The next stage in the preparation of financial statements is the recording of closing journal entries for drawing up the income statement. While the balance sheet is a mere listing of the assets and liabilities, the income statement is prepared in the form of a ledger account. The postings can be made into such accounts only if they have been entered in the books of prime entry, that is, the journal proper. The expenses are shown on the debit side by debiting the income statement, and crediting the concerned expense account. The revenues are shown on the credit side of the income statement by crediting the income statement, and debiting the concerned income account. Manufacturing account, trading account, and income statement can be treated under the category of revenue accounts.

Manufacturing A/c Dr. (*Less*)
Trading A/c Dr. (*Less*)
Profit and Loss A/c Dr. (*Less*)
    To Concerned expenses A/c (*Less*)
(Being the expense account of nominal in nature, it is transferred to calculate the operating results.)
Concerned income A/c Dr. (*Less*)
    To Manufacturing A/c (*Add*)
    To Trading A/c (*Add*)
    To Income statement (*Add*)
(Being the income account, it is transferred to calculate the operating results.)

The purchase returns and sales returns are transferred to purchase and sales account respectively, and purchases and sales are reduced accordingly. The credit balance in the income statement represents the net profit earned and belongs to the proprietors or owners. The net profit is transferred to the capital account by debiting the income statement and crediting the capital account. In case of a loss, it is transferred to the capital account by crediting the income statement and debiting the capital account.

Income statement Dr. (*Less*)
    To Capital A/c (*Add*)
(Being transfer of net profit to proprietor's capital account)
    Or
Capital A/c Dr. (*Less*)
    To Income statement (*Add*)
(Being transfer of net loss to the proprietor's capital account)

The capital account is debited by drawings (withdrawals) and interest on drawings by crediting the cash or bank account and interest received account respectively. The capital account is credited by the salary payment made to the proprietor and owners, and the interest on capital is debited by the salary expenses account and interest expenses account. In case the retained earnings account is maintained, the owner's capital consists of the capital account and the retained earnings account. The retained earnings are commonly referred to

EXHIBIT 13.2 Worksheet

M/s. PARSHWA LIMITED
Worksheet
For the year ended as on...

Sr. No.	Name of Account	Trial Balance		Adjustments		Adjusted Trial Balance		Income Statement		Balance Sheet	
		Dr. (₹)	Cr. (₹)	Dr. (₹)	Cr. (₹)	Dr. (₹)	Cr. (₹)	Dr. (₹)	Cr. (₹)	Dr. (₹)	Cr. (₹)

as reserves and surplus. Retained earnings comprise of the residual amount after income tax and dividends are provided in income statements.

Provision for dividend Dividends are declared from the profits after deduction of income tax. The dividend amount is set as a provision by credit to the 'Dividend payable account' and charged to the dividend account through debit. The dividend account is in turn debited to the income statement. In the accounting period in which the dividend is actually paid, the dividend payable account is set off by an entry in the dividend payable account.

The balance will be carried forward to the next accounting period at the beginning of the subsequent period, when a new general ledger is brought into use. The opening assets, liabilities, and owner's equity account will be brought into the ledger through an opening journal entry, which is as given in the following text:

Assets A/c Dr. (*Add*)
  To Liabilities A/c (*Add*)
  To Owner's equity A/c (*Add*)

The closing entries in detail is as follows:

(A) **Closing entries to prepare manufacturing account**

1. For ascertaining raw materials consumed

(i) Raw materials consumed account (*Add*)Dr. x
  To Opening stock of raw materials (*Less*)   x
  To Purchase of raw material (*Less*)   x
(ii) Closing stock of raw materials
  account (*Add*)   Dr. x
  To Raw materials consumed account (*Less*)   x

2. For grouping the items of factory expenses in one head

Factory overheads account (*Add*)   Dr. x
  To Power, fuel, and water charges (*Less*)   x
  To Rent, rates, and taxes (factory) (*Less*)   x
  To Stores and spares (indirect material) (*Less*)   x
  To Insurance (factory and machinery) (*Less*)   x
  To Repairs to plant and machinery (*Less*)   x
  To Depreciation (on factory building and
    machinery) (*Less*)   x

3. For transferring the elements of cost of production to manufacturing account

Manufacturing account (*Less*)   Dr. x
  To Raw materials consumed account (*Less*)   x
  To Direct wages account (*Less*)   x
  To Factory overhead account (*Less*)   x

4. For closing 'work-in-progress accounts'

(a) Manufacturing account (*Less*)   Dr. x
  To Opening work-in-progress account (*Less*) x
(b) Closing work-in-progress account (*Add*)Dr. x
  To Manufacturing account (*Add*)   x

5. For sale of scrap

Sale of scrap account (*Less*)   Dr. x
  To Manufacturing account (*Add*)   x

6. For transfer of cost of production to trading account

Trading account (*Less*)   Dr. x
  To Manufacturing account (*Add*)   x

(B) **Closing entries to prepare trading account**

1. For closing purchase returns account

Purchase return/returns outwards account (*Add*)Dr. x
  To Purchase account (*Less*)   x

2. For closing sales returns account

Sales account (*Less*)   Dr. x
  To Sales return/return inward account (*Add*)   x

3. For closing the following accounts
  (a) opening stock, (b) purchases, (c) wages
  (d) trading expenses, or direct expenses

Trading account (*Less*)   Dr. x
  To Opening stock account (*Less*)   x
  To Purchases account (*Less*)   x
  To Wages account (*Less*)   x
  To Direct expenses/trading expenses
    account (*Less*)   x

4. For closing sales and closing stock

Sales account (*Less*)   Dr. x
Closing stock account (*Add*)   Dr. x
  To Trading account (*Add*)   x

5. For transfer of gross profit to income statement

Trading account (*Less*)   Dr. x
  To Income statement (*Add*)   x

6. For transfer of gross loss to income statement

Income statement (*Less*)   Dr. x
  To Trading account (*Add*)   x

(C) **Closing entries to prepare income statement**

1. For closing expenses/losses accounts

Income statement (*Less*)   Dr. x
  To Expense/loss accounts (*Less*)   x

2. For closing income/gains accounts

Income/gain accounts (*Less*)   Dr. x
  To Income statement (*Add*)   x

3. For transfer of profit to capital account

Income statement (*Less*)   Dr. x
  To Capital account (*Add*)   x

4. For transfer of loss to capital account

Capital account (*Less*)   Dr. x
  To Income statement (*Add*)   x

(D) **Closing entries to prepare balance sheet:** There cannot be any closing entry to prepare a balance sheet, because *a balance sheet is not an account*. It is just the statement of assets and liabilities on a particular date, arranged in a particular way.

However, the real accounts and personal accounts can be closed by passing the following entry at the end of an accounting period.

Liabilities account (*Less*)	Dr. x	
Capital account (*Less*)	x	
To Asset account (*Less*)		x

In the beginning of the next accounting period, the following entry is passed to bring the assets, liabilities, and capital in the books of accounts.

Assets account (*Add*)	Dr. x	
To Capital account (*Add*)		x
To Liabilities account (*Add*)		x

COST OF GOODS SOLD

It is necessary to ascertain the cost of producing the goods in the case of an entity manufacturing goods and selling them at a profit. In such a situation, the profit or loss made by an entity can be ascertained by preparing the following three accounts—(a) manufacturing account; (b) trading account; and (c) income statement.

Manufacturing Account

This account provides the cost of the goods produced by a manufacturer during a particular period. The manufacturing account shows in detail, with appropriate classifications, the constituent elements of such costs. It provides details of the factory cost and facilitates reconciliation of financial books with cost records. It also serves as a basis of comparison of manufacturing operations from one accounting period to another. This account is debited with the cost of material consumed, wages, and other expenses incurred directly or indirectly on manufacturing. Exhibit 13.3 presents a sample manufacturing account.

EXHIBIT 13.3 Manufacturing Account

Name of Account: Manufacturing Account of (Firm's Name)
for the year ended (date)

Reference Account	Post Ref No.	Dr. (Less)	Cr. (Add)
By Sale of scrap			X
By Sale of by-product			X
By Closing stock of work-in-process			X
By Cost of production of the finished goods transferred to the Trading Account			X
TO RAW MATERIAL CONSUMED			
Opening stock of raw materials		X	
Purchases		X	
Carriage inward or inward freight		X	
Dock charges		X	
Less: Purchase returns		(X)	
Less: Closing stock of raw materials		(X)	
= RAW MATERIALS CONSL'MED		**XX**	
To Opening stock of work-in-process		X	
To Factory expenses		X	
To Consumable stores		X	
To Power and fuel		X	
To Wages		X	
To Depreciation on factory building		X	
To Depreciation on plant, property, and equipment		X	
To Repairs of factory building		X	
To Repairs of the plant, property, and equipment		X	
To Factory rent		X	
To Gas, water, coal, woods, etc.		X	
To Insurance of factory		X	
To Royalty (based on production)		X	
TOTAL		**XX**	**XX**

TRADING ACCOUNT

This account gives the information about the gross profit or gross loss made by a manufacturer in selling the manufactured products. In cases where the manufacturer also functions as a trader, he/she will be a manufacturer–trader. Gross profit is the difference between the selling price and the cost of goods sold. The trading account can be prepared as shown in Exhibit 13.4.

The definition of gross profit can be put up in the form of an equation as given in this section.

Gross Profit = Sales – Cost of Goods Sold

Cost of Goods Sold = Stock in the Beginning + Purchases + Direct Expenses – Stock at the End

The key features of a manufacturing account and a trading account are as follows:

Cost of each item It would be useful to have a column for percentage in the manufacturing account showing the cost of each item as a percentage of the total.

Carriage inwards The expenses incurred for bringing the raw materials to the factory, the octroi, or the custom duty paid by the manufacturer on the raw material purchased or imported is also charged to the manufacturing account.

Stock It refers to the inventory of an entity. There can be three types of the stock:

Stock of raw materials It includes stock of raw materials and components purchased by the manufacturer for the products to be produced, but still lying unused (i.e., remain in the form in which it was purchased).

Stock of work in process It includes goods in the semi-finished form on the production floor or in the intermediate stores.

EXHIBIT 13.4 Trading Account

Trading Account of (Firm's Name)
for the year or period ending (Date)...

Particulars	Amount (₹)	Amount (₹)
REVENUE		
By Sales	XX	
Less: Sales returns or sales inwards	X	XX
Total Revenue		**XX**
EXPENSES		
COST OF GOODS SOLD		
To Opening stock of finished goods	X	
To Cost of production of finished goods		
b/d from Manufacturing account	X	
To Trade purchases	X	
To Direct expenses	X	
for example, freight and carriage, etc.	X	
To Customs duty	X	
To Wages	X	
To Royalty (based on sales)	X	
To Packing materials	X	
Less: Closing stock of finished goods	(X)	
= COST OF GOODS SOLD or Total Expenses		**XX**

Gross Profit (Total Revenue – Total Expenses)
Brought down to Profit and Loss Account or Income Statement

Stock of finished goods It includes stock of those goods which have been completely processed and are lying unsold at the end of the period with the manufacturer. This will be shown in the trading account.

Sale of scrap Certain scrap is unavoidable in manufacturing operations. The scrap may or may not have any sales value. In order to calculate the cost of production of finished goods, it is necessary to consider the sale value and/or realizable value of the unsold scrap.

Sale of products In processing industries, the production of the main product is accompanied by the production of a saleable subsidiary product. For example, the production of hydrogenated vegetable oil is accompanied by the production of oxygen gas. The subsidiary product is termed as a by-product because its production is not consciously undertaken but it is a result of the production of the main product. It is usually very difficult to ascertain the cost of such a product. Moreover, its value usually forms a very small percentage of the sales revenue. In such cases, the correct treatment is to credit the sale value of the by-product to the manufacturing account.

Dock charges These are charges levied on ships and cargo when entering or leaving docks. Dock charges paid on goods purchased are entered on the debit side of the manufacturing account.

Royalty These are payments made by the entity to the technology supplier, franchiser, etc. for using rights, trademarks,

or patents. They are productive expenses and if charged or payable on quantity produced, should be charged to the manufacturing account. If the royalty payment is based on the sale price of the goods sold, it should be charged to the trading account.

Consumable stores It includes engine oil, grease, cotton waste, etc. Consumable stores are required to keep the plant and machinery in a proper working condition. They are essential for production and are debited to the manufacturing account.

Packing materials and charges Primary packing refers to the packing necessary to bring the goods in a saleable state. It is debited to the manufacturing account. Packing made for the sale of goods (i.e., attractive packing or packing for easy movement of goods) is known as *secondary packing*, and is debited to the trading account.

Trade discount Usually, trade discount does not appear in the trial balance because it is deducted at the time of making the invoice. The entries for purchases and sales are made with the net amounts. If, however, they appear in the trial balance, then it is by deduction from the purchase or sales in the manufacturing account.

Purchases It includes both cash and credit purchases. It includes purchases of only such goods which are used in the manufacturing process. Purchase of assets such as car, furniture, computers, plant and machinery, etc. are not included in the manufacturing account.

If the goods purchased are in-transit, it is better to record them by debiting the goods-in-transit account and show them as an asset in the balance sheet. The corresponding credit should be given to the supplier's account, and should be shown as a liability in the balance sheet. Goods withdrawn by proprietors, managers, or employees for their personal use should be deducted from the total purchases on the debit side of the manufacturing or trading account. Correspondingly, that amount should be shown as amount recoverable or due from them on the asset side of the balance sheet.

Sometimes, invoices of the goods are received in advance before the receipt of goods. In such cases, it is better not to record the goods as received. This amount will neither be added to the purchase account on the debit side nor added to 'stock at the end' on the credit side of the trading or manufacturing account.

The important features of a manufacturing account are equally applicable at the time of preparing the trading account for the trader or the wholesaler, and for the trading activities of the manufacturer. The main business of trading consists of buying and selling the same goods. In addition to the amount of opening stock, the expenses are incurred in bringing the goods to the godown of the firm and making them ready for sale. For example, freight paid on purchases, cartage, custom duty, etc. will also be debited to the trading account. In addition, all expenses for bringing the goods to their present location and condition are also debited.

Sales Both cash and credit sales are included in a trading account. Sales will include only the sale of goods. Goods refer to the products and/or commodities sold by an entity. Proper care should be taken in recording the sale of those goods, which have been sold at the end of the financial year, but have not yet been delivered. The sales value of such goods should be included in the sales account, but care should be taken that the sales value should not be included in the closing stock at the end of the accounting period. Sale of assets such as plant and machinery should not be included in the sales figures.

INCOME STATEMENT

The manufacturing account and the trading account do not take into account the other operating expenses incurred by an entity during the course of an entity's business operations. For example, an entity has to maintain an office for getting and executing orders, taking and implementing policy decisions, etc. All such expenses are charged to the income statement. Besides this, an entity may have other sources of income. For example, an entity may receive rent from some of the entity's properties.

In order to ascertain the true profit or loss made by an entity in an accounting period, it is necessary that all expenses and incomes should be considered. The income statement considers all expenses and revenues and shows the net profit made or net loss suffered by an entity during a particular accounting period. Exhibit 13.5 illustrates a trading and profit and loss account.

EXHIBIT 13.5 Income Statement or Profit and Loss Account

Income Statement of (Firm's Name)
for the year or period ending (Date)…

Particulars	₹	Amount (₹)
REVENUE		
By Gross Profit brought from Trading Account		**XX**
Other Income		
By Discount received	X	
By Commission received	X	X
Non-trading Income		
By Bank interest	X	
By Rent of property let out	X	
By Dividend from shares	X	
By Interest from investments	X	X
Abnormal Gain		
By Profit on sale of assets	X	
By Profit on sale of investment	X	
By Miscellaneous income		X
Total Revenue		**XXX**
EXPENSES		
Office and Administrative Expenses		
To Salaries	X	
To Office rent	X	
To Rates and taxes	X	
To Electricity charges	X	
To Telephone or communication expenses	X	
To Fax and internet expenses	X	
To Postage and courier charges	X	
To Insurance	X	
To Legal charges	X	
To Conveyance (local travelling expenses)	X	
To Audit fees	X	
= Office and Administrative Expenses		**X**
Maintenance Expenses		
To Repairs	X	
To Annual maintenance charges	X	
= Maintenance Expenses		**X**
Selling and Distribution Expenses		
To Advertisment	X	
To Godown rent	X	
To Carriage outward or outward freight	X	
To Selling commission	X	
To Sales staff salaries	X	
To Delivery van expenses	X	
To Goods and Services Tax	X	
To Customs duty on export	X	
Bad and Doubtful debts	X	
Bad debts (as per before adjusted trial balance)	X	
Add: Bad debts (as per adjustment entries)	X	
Add: Provision for bad and doubtful debts (as per adjustment entries)	X	
Less: Provision for bad and doubtful debts (as per before adjusted trial balance)	(X)	
= Bad and Doubtful debts	X	
To Discount on debtors	X	
= Selling and Distribution Expenses		**X**
Depreciation		
To Office building	X	
To Office equipment	X	
To Office furniture	X	
To Office vehicles	X	
To Office electric fittings	X	
= Depreciation		**X**
Financial Expenses or Charges		
To Bank charges	X	
To Interest on loans	X	
To Discount on bills of exchanges	X	
To Discount allowed to others	X	
To Foreign transactions charges (not considered as specific part)	X	
= Financial Expenses or Charges		**X**
Abnormal Losses		
To Loss on sale of assets	X	
To Loss on sale of investments	X	
To Loss by fire	X	
To Loss by theft, etc.	X	
= Abnormal Losses		**X**
Total Expenses		**XXX**

Net Profit (Total Revenue – Total Expenses)
Transferred to Statement of Retained Earnings or Capital Account

Gross profit or gross loss This figure is carried forward from the trading account. There will be only one figure, that is, gross profit or gross loss.

Salaries Employees are paid salaries for the services rendered by them. If the salaries relate to office and administrative activities, it will be shown under the subheading of office and administrative expenses.

Annual maintenance contract charges Normally, these type of charges are paid by an entity to the service provider for preventive and corrective maintenance of all equipments.

Advertisements The advertising expenses are incurred for attracting customers to buy a product. Therefore, these are considered as selling expenses. The advertisement expenses incurred for purchasing goods are charged to the trading account, while advertisement expenses incurred for purchase of capital assets should be taken as capital expenditure and debited to the concerned asset account.

Commission The commission paid or received may be treated as an item of income as well as an item of expense. Commission on business brought by agents, field staff, and salespersons is treated as an item of expense, while commission earned by an entity for giving business to others is treated as an item of income.

Bad debts It refers to the amount not realized from debtors to whom the goods were sold on credit. It is a loss and, therefore, should be debited to the income statement. An entity needs to make provision at the end of the accounting period for likely bad debts which may happen during the course of the next accounting period on account of sales made in the current accounting period. The provision can be charged against the income of the period. Bad debts and provision for bad debts (as per net adjustment entries) should be deducted from the balance of amount to be shown in the balance sheet on the assets side.

DEFERRED TAX LIABILITIES AND ASSETS

Ind As 12, as issued by ICAI, and duly approved by Ministry of Corporate Affairs, explains the treatment of income tax expenses and its deferment in the books of accounts.

Tax expense (tax income) is the aggregate amount included in the determination of profit or loss for the period in respect of current tax and deferred tax.

Current tax is the amount of income taxes payable (recoverable) in respect of the taxable profit (tax loss) for a period.

Deferred tax liabilities are the amounts of income taxes payable in future periods in respect of taxable temporary differences.

Deferred tax assets are the amounts of income taxes recoverable in future periods in respect of

(a) deductible temporary differences;
(b) the carry forward of unused tax losses; and
(c) the carry forward of unused tax credits.

Temporary differences are differences between the carrying amount of an asset or liability in the balance sheet and its tax base. Temporary differences may be either:

(a) *taxable temporary differences*, which are temporary differences that will result in taxable amounts in determining taxable profit (tax loss) of future periods when the carrying amount of the asset or liability is recovered or settled; or

(b) *deductible temporary differences*, which are temporary differences that will result in amounts that are deductible in determining taxable profit (tax loss) of future periods when the carrying amount of the asset or liability is recovered or settled.

Deferred tax accounting seeks to deal with this mismatch. It is based on the temporary differences between the tax base of an asset or liability and its carrying amount in the financial statements. For example, if an asset is revalued upwards but not sold, the revaluation creates a temporary difference (if the carrying amount of the asset in the financial statements is greater than the tax base of the asset), and the tax consequence is a deferred tax liability.

Deferred tax is provided in full for all temporary differences arising between the tax bases of assets and liabilities and their carrying amounts in the financial statements, except when the temporary difference arises from the following:

1. Initial recognition of goodwill (for deferred tax liabilities only)
2. Initial recognition of an asset or liability in a transaction which is not a business combination and which affects neither accounting profit nor taxable profit
3. Investments in subsidiaries, branches, associates and joint ventures, but only when certain criteria apply

Deferred tax assets and liabilities are measured at the tax rates that are expected to apply to the period when the asset is realized or the liability is settled based on tax rates (and tax laws) that have been enacted or substantively enacted by the balance sheet date. The discounting of deferred tax assets and liabilities is not permitted.

Generally, the measurement of deferred tax liabilities and deferred tax assets reflects the tax consequences that would follow based on what the entity expects, at the balance sheet date, to recover or settle the carrying amount of its assets and liabilities. The expected manner of recovery of land with an unlimited life is always through sale. For other assets, the manner in which management expects to recover the asset (that is, through use or through sale or through a combination of both) is considered at each balance sheet date.

■ **ILLUSTRATION 13.11** Due to temporary differences, in 2018 a company reported ₹10 lakh pretax income to its shareholders and an income tax expense of ₹4 lakh but only ₹8 lakh taxable income to the income tax department. Thus, its income tax expense was ₹4 lakh, but its actual income tax were only ₹3,20,000 (₹8 lakh x 40%). Assume that these taxes have been paid (i.e., the taxes have been credited to cash; none is still a credit in tax payable account).

Is the missing ₹80,000 (₹4 lakh – ₹3,20,000) credit entry a further reduction in assets or is it in a liability account or an owner's equity account?

Solution

The answer is that the credit entry is an increase in an asset account, in the name of 'Deferred Tax Asset Account'.

■ **ILLUSTRATION 13.12** On 1 April 2017, Aspects Limited purchased an equipment, the relevant details of which are as under:

Cost: ₹24,00,000   Useful life: 4 years

Expected salvage value: Nil

Depreciation allowable for tax purposes: 100% in first year

Depreciation method for accounting purpose: Straight line method

The profit before depreciation and tax of aspects for next years are as under:

Year Ended	Amount (₹)	Tax Rate %
31.3.2017	50 lakh	30
31.3.2018	50 lakh	30
31.3.2019	50 lakh	30
31.3.2020	50 lakh	30

Compute the deferred tax assets or liability and also the tax expense at the end of each of the years.

Solution

Calculation of deferred tax liability (DTL) and tax expense of a year is as follows:

Year Ended	Opening Book Value (₹)	Depreciation of Year (₹)	Closing Book Value (₹)	Calculation of DTL	DTL Amount (₹)	Tax Expense (₹)
31.3.2017	24,00,000	6,00,000	18,00,000	18,00,000 × 30%	5,40,000	1,80,000
31.3.2018	18,00,000	6,00,000	12,00,000	12,00,000 × 30%	3,60,000	1,80,000
31.3.2019	12,00,000	6,00,000	6,00,000	6,00,000 × 30%	1,80,000	1,80,000
31.3.2020	6,00,000	6,00,000	NIL	NIL	NIL	1,80,000

The treatment of deferred tax liability and deferred tax asset in the financial statements provided by Indian corporates are shown in Exhibit 13.6.

EXHIBIT 13.6   Deferred Tax Assets and Liabilities Disclosure

Steel Industry: Tata Steel Ltd

Income taxes

Tax expense for the period comprises current and deferred tax. The tax currently payable is based on taxable profit for the period. Taxable profit differs from net profit as reported in the statement of profit and loss because it excludes items of income or expense that are taxable or deductible in other years and it further excludes items that are never taxable or deductible. The Company's liability for current tax is calculated using tax rates and tax laws that have been enacted or substantively enacted by the end of the reporting period.

Deferred tax is the tax expected to be payable or recoverable on differences between the carrying values of assets and liabilities in the financial statements and the corresponding tax bases used in the computation of taxable profit and is accounted for using the balance sheet liability method. Deferred tax liabilities are generally recognised for all taxable temporary differences. In contrast, deferred tax assets are only recognised to the extent that it is probable that future taxable profits will be available against which the temporary differences can be utilised. The carrying value of deferred tax assets is reviewed at the end of each reporting period and reduced to the extent that it is no longer probable that sufficient taxable profits will be available to allow all or part of the asset to be recovered.

Deferred tax is calculated at the tax rates that are expected to apply in the period when the liability is settled or the asset is realised based on the tax rates and tax laws that have been enacted or substantially enacted by the end of the reporting period. The measurement of deferred tax liabilities and assets reflects the tax consequences that would follow from the manner in which the Company expects, at the end of the reporting period, to recover or settle the carrying value of its assets and liabilities.

Deferred tax assets and liabilities are offset to the extent that they relate to taxes levied by the same tax authority and there are legally enforceable rights to set off current tax assets and current tax liabilities within that jurisdiction.

Airline Industry: Spice Jet Ltd

Deferred tax

Deferred tax is recognised on temporary differences between the carrying amounts of assets and liabilities in the financial statements and the corresponding tax bases used in the computation of taxable profit.

Deferred tax liabilities are generally recognised for all taxable temporary differences, except: (a) When the deferred tax liability arises from the initial recognition of goodwill or an asset or liability in a transaction that is not a business combination and, at the time of the transaction, affects neither the accounting profit nor taxable profit or loss (b) In respect of taxable temporary differences associated with investments in subsidiaries, associates and interests in joint ventures, when the timing of the reversal of the temporary differences can be controlled and it is probable that the temporary differences will not reverse in the foreseeable future. Deferred tax assets are generally recognised for all deductible temporary differences to the extent that it is probable that taxable profits will be available against which those deductible temporary differences can be utilised. Such deferred tax assets and liabilities are not recognised if the temporary difference arises from the initial recognition (other than in a business combination) of assets and liabilities in a transaction that affects neither the taxable profit nor the accounting profit.

Deferred tax asset is recognised for the carry forward of unused tax losses and unused tax credits to the extent that it is probable that future taxable profit will be available against which the unused tax losses and unused tax credits can be utilised.

Minimum alternate tax (MAT) paid in a year is charged to the statement of profit and loss as current tax. The Company recognizes MAT credit available as an asset only to the extent that there is convincing evidence that the Company will pay normal income tax during the specified period, i.e., the period for which MAT credit is allowed to be carried forward. In the year in which the Company recognizes MAT credit as a deferred tax asset.

The carrying amount of deferred tax assets is reviewed at the end of each reporting period and reduced to the extent that it is no longer probable that sufficient taxable profits will be available to allow all or part of the asset to be recovered.

Deferred tax assets and liabilities are measured at the tax rates that are expected to apply in the year when the asset is realised or the liability is settled, based on tax rates (and tax laws) that have been enacted or substantively enacted at the reporting date.

Deferred tax relating to items recognised outside profit or loss is recognised outside profit or loss (either in other comprehensive income or in equity).

Deferred tax assets and deferred tax liabilities are offset if a legally enforceable right exists to set off current tax assets against current tax liabilities and the deferred taxes relate to the same taxable entity and the same taxation authority.

Sources: Tata Steel Ltd Annual Report 2017–18, p. 208; SpiceJet Limited Annual Report 2016–17, pp. 89–90.

GST ACCOUNTING

In spite of initial transition challenges, GST is bringing in clarity in many areas of business including accounting and bookkeeping.

While apparently the number of accounts is more under GST, it brings the clarity for record keeping. One of the biggest advantage a firm or trader will have is that the firm can set off input tax on service with his output tax on the sale.

■ **ILLUSTRATION 13.13** Consider the following accounting events that took place at Ubuntu India Ltd intrastate (within state).

1. Ubuntu India purchased bearings worth ₹1,00,000 from a local trader (intrastate).
2. Next, Ubuntu India sold them for ₹1,50,000 in the same state.
3. It paid a legal consultation fees of ₹5,000.
4. The company purchased assets (laptop) for the office for ₹12,000.

Assume CGST @ 8% and SGST @ 8%.

Solution

The accounting entries will be as under:

Sr. No.	Particulars	Amount (₹)
1	Purchase A/c (Asset type) (Add) Dr.	1,00,000
	Input CGST A/c (Asset type) (Add) Dr.	8,000
	Input SGST A/c (Asset type) (Add) Dr.	8,000
	To Creditors A/c (Liability type) (Add)	1,16,000
2	Debtors A/c (Asset type) (Add) Dr.	1,74,000
	To Sales A/c (Income type) (Add)	1,50,000
	To Output CGST A/c (Liability type) (Add)	12,000
	To Output SGST A/c (Liability type) (Add)	12,000
3	Legal fees A/c (Expense type) (Add)	5,000
	Input CGST A/c (Asset type) (Add)	400
	Input SGST A/c (Asset type) (Add)	400
	To Bank A/c (Asset type) (Less)	5,800
4	Laptop A/c (Asset type) (Add)	12,000
	Input CGST A/c (Asset type) (Add)	960
	Input SGST A/c (Asset type) (Add)	960
	To XYZ Electronics shop A/c (Liability type) (Add)	13,920
5	Output CGST A/c (Liability type) (Less)	9,360
	To Input CGST A/c (Asset type) (Less)	9,360
6	Output SGST A/c (Liability type) (Less)	9,360
	To Input SGST A/c (Asset type) (Less)	9,360
7	Output CGST A/c (Liability type) (Less)	2,640
	To CGST Payable A/c (Liability type) (Add)	2,640
8	Output SGST A/c (Liability type) (Less)	2,640
	To SGST Payable A/c (Liability type) (Add)	2,640

Working Notes:

Total Input CGST = 8,000 + 400 + 960 = ₹9,360
Total Input SGST = 8,000 + 400 + 960 = ₹9,360

Total output CGST = 12,000
Total output SGST = 12,000
Net CGST payable = 12,000 – 9,360 = 2,640
Net SGST payable = 12,000 – 9,360 = 2,640

Thus, due to input tax credit, the liability of ₹24,000 is reduced to ₹5,280. Also, GST on legal fees comes under reverse charge mechanism which is included.

■ **ILLUSTRATION 13.14** Consider the following accounting events that took place at Ubuntu India Ltd within interstate (between states).

1. Ubuntu India purchased bearings worth ₹1,50,000 from outside the state.
2. Ubuntu India sells to ZF Limited locally for ₹1,50,000.
3. Ubuntu India later sold it to ARB Bearings located outside the state for ₹1,00,000.
4. Ubuntu India paid telephone bill ₹5,000.
5. Ubuntu India purchased an air cooler worth ₹12,000 for the office.

Solution

Assuming CGST @ 8% and SGST @ 8%:

Sr. No.	Particulars	Amount (₹)
1	Purchase A/c (Asset type) (Add) Dr.	1,50,000
	Input IGST A/c (Asset type) (Add) Dr.	24,000
	To Creditors A/c (Liability type) (Add)	1,74,000
2	Debtors A/c (Asset type) (Add) Dr.	1,74,000
	To Sales A/c (Income type) (Add)	1,50,000
	To Output CGST A/c (Liability type) (Add)	12,000
	To Output SGST A/c (Liability type) (Add)	12,000
3	Debtors A/c (Asset type) (Add)	1,16,000
	To Sales A/c (Income type) (Add)	1,00,000
	To Output IGST A/c (Liability type) (Add)	16,000
4	Telephone bill expenses A/c (Expense type) (Add) Dr.	5,000
	Input CGST A/c (Asset type) (Add) Dr.	400
	Input SGST A/c (Asset type) (Add) Dr.	400
	To Bank A/c (Asset type) (Less)	5,800
5	Office Equipment A/c (Asset type) (Add) Dr.	12,000
	Input CGST A/c (Asset type) (Add) Dr.	960
	Input SGST A/c (Asset type) (Add) Dr.	960
	To XYZ Electronics shop A/c (Liability type) (Add)	13,920

	Setoff against output GST	Amount (₹)
1	Output CGST (Liability type) (Less) Dr.	9,360
	To Input CGST A/c (Asset type) (Less)	1,360
	To Input IGST A/c (Asset type) (Less)	8,000
2	**Setoff against SGST output**	
	Output SGST (Liability type) (Less) Dr.	1,360
	To Input SGST A/c (Asset type) (Less)	1,360
3	**Setoff against IGST output**	
	Output IGST (Liability type) (Less) Dr.	16,000

	Particulars	Debit (₹)	Credit (₹)
4	To Input IGST A/c (Asset type) (Less)		16,000
	Output CGST A/c (Liability type) (Less)	2,640	
	To CGST Payable A/c (Liability type) (Add)		2,640
	Output SGST A/c (Liability type) (Less)	10,640	
	To SGST Payable A/c (Liability type) (Add)		10,640

Working Notes:

Total CGST input = 400 + 960 = 1,360
Total CGST output = 12,000
Total SGST input = 400 + 960 = 1,360
Total SGST output = 12,000
Total IGST input = 24,000
Total IGST output = 16,000

Particulars	CGST	SGST	IGST
Output liability	12,000	12,000	16,000
Less: **Input tax credit**			
CGST	1,360		
SGST		1,360	
IGST	8,000		16,000
Amount payable	2,640	10,640	NIL

Any IGST credit will first be applied to set off IGST and then CGST.

Balance, if any, will be applied to set off SGST. So out of the total input IGST of ₹24,000, firstly it will be completely set off against IGST. Then balance ₹8,000 against CGST. From the total ₹40,000, only ₹13,280 is payable.

Set off entries will be as above.

■ **ILLUSTRATION 13.15** This is a consolidated example of sales, purchases, purchases under Reverse charge mechanism and using of input tax credit for payment of GST (set off).

Godwin India sold bearings worth ₹1,00,000 to Premier India Limited situated locally in Gujarat and simultaneously sold goods to ZF India Limited worth ₹2,00,000 situated in Maharashtra. Assume IGST @ 18%, SGST @ 8%, and CGST @ 8%. (Being a bearing manufacturing company, it deals exclusively in goods and not in services).

Particulars	Debit (₹)	Credit (₹)
Premier India Limited (Asset type) (Add) Dr.	1,16,000	
To CGST Payable (Liability type) (Add)		8,000
To SGST Payable (Liability type) (Add)		8,000
To Sales A/c (Income type) (Add)		1,00,000
ZF India Limited (Asset type) (Add) Dr.	2,36,000	
To IGST Payable (Liability type) (Add)		36,000
To Sales A/c (Income type) (Add)		2,00,000

Godwin India purchased bearings worth ₹1,50,000 from Automotive Engineering located locally in Gujarat and worth ₹3,00,000 from Rollman Bearings located in Tamil Nadu. Assume IGST @ 18%, SGST @ 8%, and CGST @ 8%.

Particulars	Debit (₹)	Credit (₹)
Purchase A/c (Asset type) (Add) Dr.	1,50,000	
Input CGST (Asset type) (Add) Dr.	12,000	

Input SGST Receivable (Asset type) (Add) Dr.	12,000	
To Cash A/c (Asset type) (Less)		1,74,000
Purchase A/c (Asset type) (Add) Dr.	3,00,000	
Input IGST (Asset type) (Add) Dr.	54,000	
To Cash A/c (Asset type) (Less)		3,54,000

Godwin India opts for services from a lawyer (services from a lawyer come under reverse charge mechanism) of ABC Limited. The GST rate applicable is 5% for the month of July 2017.

CASE 1: Payment to be made within 30 days or 60 days from the date of issue of invoice. Invoice is received on 3.7.2017. Payment for the same is done on 29.7.2017.

	Particulars	Debit	Credit
3.7.2017	Lawyer's fees A/c (Expense type) (Add) Dr.	20,000	
	To ABC Limited A/c (Liability type) (Add)		20,000
29.7.2017	ABC Limited A/c (Liability type) (Less) Dr.	20,000	
	To Bank A/c (Asset type) (Less)		20,000

Adjustment Entry:

	Particulars	Debit	Credit
31.7.2017	Reverse Charge A/c (Liability type) (Less) Dr.	1,000	
	To Output CGST A/c (Liability type) (Add)		500
	To Output SGST A/c (Liability type) (Add)		500

GST Payment:

	Particulars	Debit	Credit
31.7.2017	Output CGST A/c (Liability type) (Less) Dr.	500	
	Output SGST A/c (Liability type) (Less) Dr.	500	
	To Bank A/c (Asset type) (Less)		1,000

Entry for transfer of Reverse Charge A/c to Input Tax Credit:

	Particulars	Debit	Credit
31.7.2017	Input CGST A/c (Asset type) (Add) Dr.	500	
	Input SGST A/c (Asset type) (Add) Dr.	500	
	To Reverse Charge A/c (Liability type) (Add)		1,000

CASE 2: Payment not made within 30 days or 60 days from the date of issue of invoice. Invoice received on 3.7.2017, payment for the same is yet to be made.

	Particulars	Debit	Credit
3.7.2017	Lawyer's fees A/c (Expense type) (Add) Dr.	20,000	
	To ABC Limited A/c (Liability type) (Add)		20,000

Adjustment entry (assuming 60 days lapsed):

	Particulars	Debit	Credit
30.9.2017	Reverse charge A/c (Liability type) (Add) Dr.	1,000	
	To Output CGST A/c (Liability type) (Add)		500
	To Output SGST A/c (Liability type) (Add)		500

GST Payment:

	Particulars	Debit	Credit
30.9.2017	Output CGST A/c (Liability type) (Less) Dr.	500	
	Output SGST A/c (Liability type) (Less) Dr.	500	
	To Bank A/c (Asset type) (Less)		1,000

Entry for transfer of Reverse Charge A/c to Input Tax Credit:

	Particulars	Debit	Credit
30.9.2017	Input CGST A/c (Asset type) (Add) Dr.	500	
	Input SGST A/c (Asset type) (Add) Dr.	500	
	To Reverse Charge A/c (Liability type) (Add)		1,000

CASE 3: In case of Advance Payment done. Paid on 3.7.2017. Bill for the same received on 20.8.2017.

3.7.2017	ABC Limited A/c (Liability type) (Less) Dr.	20,000	
	To Bank A/c (Asset type) (Less)		20,000

Adjustment Entry:

31.7.2017	Reverse charge A/c (Liability type) (Less) Dr.	1,000	
	To Output CGST A/c (Liability type) (Add)		500
	To Output SGST A/c (Liability type) (Add)		500

GST Payment:

31.7.2017	Output CGST A/c (Liability type) (Less) Dr.	500	
	Output SGST A/c (Liability type) (Less) Dr.	500	
	To Bank A/c (Asset type) (Less)		1,000

Entry for transfer of Reverse Charge A/c to Input Tax Credit:

31.7.2017	Input CGST A/c (Asset type) (Add) Dr.	500	
	Input SGST A/c (Asset type) (Add) Dr.	500	
	To Reverse Charge A/c (Liability type) (Add)		1,000

20.8.2017	Lawyer's fee A/c (Expense type) (Add) Dr.	20,000	
	To ABC Limited A/c (Liability type) (Add)		20,000

■**ILLUSTRATION 13.16** Saniya India purchased 3 machineries in April 2017 to be used for various purposes as per the table given below. Total aggregate supplies = ₹18 crore; Value of exempt supplies = ₹3 crore. Calculate ITC for the month of April 2017.

Details	Machine 1	Machine 2	Machine 3
	Exclusively for exempt supply	Exclusively for taxable supply	For both exempt and taxable supply
Purchase price	4,00,000	5,00,000	6,00,000
IGST @ 12%	48,000	60,000	72,000
Invoice value	4,48,000	5,60,000	6,72,000
ITC – eligibility	Ineligible	Eligible	*Note
Amount of ITC	0	60,000	72,000

Note: Here the total supplies are of ₹18 crore, which includes exempted ₹3 crore, hence taxable is ₹15 crore, pertains to Machine 3.

Tax credit for a tax period for Machine 3 = 72,000/18 crore × 15 crore = ₹60,000 available as ITC.

ITC attributable to exempted supplies = 72,000/18 crore × 3 crore = ₹12,000, which is not available as ITC.

STATEMENT OF RETAINED EARNINGS OR PROFIT AND LOSS APPROPRIATION ACCOUNT

In the case of a sole proprietorship, the net profit is credited to the capital account of the owner, that is, the proprietor. Some entities may wish to transfer a portion of the net profit to a specific reserve for achieving specific business objectives.

For computing and demonstrating the division of net profits, a new section known as profit and loss appropriation account is added to the income statement. This account shows how the net income or profit of the entity is being apportioned among multiple owners and how much amount is earmarked for the business. The format of statement of retained earnings is explained in Chapter 4, Table 4.2.

■**ILLUSTRATION 13.17** The following is a partial list of account balances of Clean Eye Opticals for the year ended 30 June 2020.

Particulars	Amount (₹)
Sales	7,10,000
Sales returns and allowances	20,000
Sales discounts	21,000
Purchases	5,83,000
Purchase returns and allowances	68,000
Purchase discounts	3,000
Office staff salaries	48,000
Sales staff salaries	96,000
Office rent	12,000
Freight expense (in)	43,000
Freight expense (out)	18,000

The beginning and closing merchandise inventories were ₹47,000 and ₹69,000 respectively.

Prepare a multiple-step income statement (in vertical form) of Clean Eye Opticals for the year ended 30 June 2020.

Solution

Income Statement of Clean Eye Opticals
for the Year Ended 30 June 2020

Sales (I)		6,69,000
Less: Cost of goods sold (II)		5,33,000
Gross profit		**1,36,000**
Less: Operating expenses		1,74,000
Freight expenses (outward)	18,000	
Office salaries	48,000	
Office rent	12,000	
Sales salaries	96,000	
Operating Loss		**38,000**

Working Notes:

1.	Sales	Amount (₹)	
	Gross sales	7,10,000	
	Less: Sales returns and allow	20,000	
	Less: Sales discounts	21,000	
	Net sales		**6,69,000**

II	Cast of Goods Sold	Amount (₹)	
	Inventory on 1 July 2019		47,000
	Add: Purchase	5,83,000	
	Less: Returns and allowance	68,00	
	Less: Purchase discount	3,000	
	Net purchase		**5,12,000**
	Add: Freight inward expenses	43,000	
	Goods available for sale		**6,02,000**
	Less: Inventory on 30 June 2020	69,000	
	Cost of goods sold		**5,33,000**

BALANCE SHEET

One of the basic objectives of accounting is to convey information. This is achieved by different accounting reports prepared by an entity. One of the most important reports is the balance sheet. The preparation of the balance sheet is related to the reporting of the financial position of an entity at a particular point of time. This position is conveyed in terms of listing all the things of value owned by the entity and the claims against these things of value. The position as reflected by the balance sheet is valid only until another transaction is carried out by the entity.

The American Institute of Certified Public Accountants (AICPA) defines the balance sheet as a tabular statement of summary of balances (debit and credit) carried forward after an actual and constructive closing of books of accounts and maintained according to the principles of accounting. The purpose of preparing a balance sheet is to know the true and fair view of the status of the business as a going concern during a particular period. The balance sheet is one of the important statements used by owners or investors to evaluate the financial position of a concern. It shows the list of liabilities and capital of credit balances of the business on the left-hand side, and the list of assets and other debit balances are recorded on the right-hand side.

The balance sheet is also described as a statement showing the sources and application of capital or funds. In other words, the liability side shows the sources of capital and the assets side shows how the capital was utilized in the business. Accordingly, a balance sheet gives a description of all the assets owned by a concern and all the liabilities and claims of owners and outsiders.

The outsider's claim has priority over the owner's claim on the assets and hence, the net worth or owner's equity is a residual claim against assets. In other words, owner's equity and liabilities for any accounting entity will be equal to the assets owned by that entity. This idea is fundamental to accounting and could be expressed in the form of the following equations:

$$\text{Assets} = \text{Liabilities} + \text{Owner's Equity}$$
$$\text{Owner's Equity} = \text{Assets} - \text{Liabilities}$$

A balance sheet shows the duality represented by benefit and sacrifice from the point of view of an entity. In other words, assets of an entity are always equal to the claims of outsiders and owners. This equality enables us to reduce the impact of all transactions in terms of the following possibilities.

1. An increase in assets is followed by an increase in liabilities and equity and vice versa.
2. An increase in an asset is followed by a decrease in another asset.
3. An increase in a liability is followed by a decrease in another liability.

The increase in the owner's equity is equal to the profit earned out of business activities. Normally, profitable operations increase the owner's equity. Thus, owner's equity comprises of two parts—contributed capital and retained earnings. Retained earnings are the profits earned but not withdrawn by the owners. This relationship is expressed in the following equation:

$$\text{Owner's Equity} = \text{Contributed Capital} + \text{Retained Earnings}$$

The dual aspect principle is particularly relevant to the balance sheet. This is shown by the relationship of assets with liabilities and owner's equity. All the transactions reflected are concerned with the principal operations of an entity. The valuations are based on the assumption of a going concern and not on the breakup value. The asset cost is determined on the basis of valuation.

Specimen form of balance sheet

The Companies Act, 2013 has prescribed a particular format for showing assets and liabilities in the balance sheet for companies registered under the Act.

There is no prescribed format of balance sheet for a sole trader or partnership firm. The assets and liabilities can be arranged in the balance sheet in the order of liquidity or performance.

In the order of liquidity   When assets and liabilities are arranged according to their order of liquidity and ability to meet its short-term obligations, the balance sheet follows the order of liquidity. The specimen of a balance sheet arranged in the order of liquidity is presented in Exhibit 3.1 (in Chapter 3 titled Balance Sheet).

In the order of performance   When assets and liabilities are arranged according to their order of fixity, the balance sheet follows the order of performance or fixity. This method is commonly used by the companies. The specimen of a balance sheet arranged in the order of fixity is given in Exhibit 3.2 (in Chapter 3 titled Balance Sheet).

Uses of Balance Sheet

The balance sheet is a summary of a firm's assets and liabilities including the share capital and reserves at a defined moment of time. That is why it has been described as a snapshot of the financial position of a business entity. The balance sheet is also known as the position statement.

In the addition to income statement, the various groups interested in the company can also draw useful inferences from an analysis of the information contained in the balance sheet. Shareholders usually have twin interests—(a) regular income; and (b) appreciation of their investments. The market worth of their shares depends not only on the dividends they receive, but also on the extent of retained earnings, which the firm has accumulated over the years. The bonus shares awarded to shareholders also depend on the retained earnings of the firm. Investment decisions of prospective investors and disinvestments decisions of the existing investors are influenced by the composition of assets and liabilities as shown in the balance sheet.

The main interest of trade creditors centres on the liquidity position of the company. The credit decisions assess whether the company will be able to meet its obligations. Creditors are, therefore, concerned about the working capital and cash resources available with the entity. All this information can be gained from the balance sheet. The interests of long-term creditors lie in—(a) regular servicing of their debts (that is payment of periodic interest); and (b) repayment of their loans after the expiry of the stipulated period. They are interested in not only the profitability of the enterprise, but also in its long-term solvency and financial viability. A study of the balance sheet of the firm over the past several years can yield a lot of useful information to such long-term investors.

Similarly, other interested parties such as regulatory and developmental agencies of the government, consumers, and welfare organizations can derive useful conclusions by analysing the balance sheet of a company. It should be emphasized here that the income statement and the balance sheet in conjunction with each other can yield a harvest of information for the interested parties or analysts.

INCOME STATEMENT AND BALANCE SHEET—THE LINKAGE

The measurement of the net income is achieved by comparing the revenue from sales against the cost of materials consumed for earning that revenue. The net difference of this comparison represents the net income or profit. The importance of profit and its measurement in accounting leads to the significance of the income statement. However, it will be interesting to see how this document is related to the balance sheet. The link between trial balance, income statement, and balance sheet is illustrated in Fig. 13.2. As mentioned earlier, an increase in revenues increases the owner's equity.

$$\text{Assets} = \text{Liabilities} + \text{Owner's Equity} \qquad (1)$$

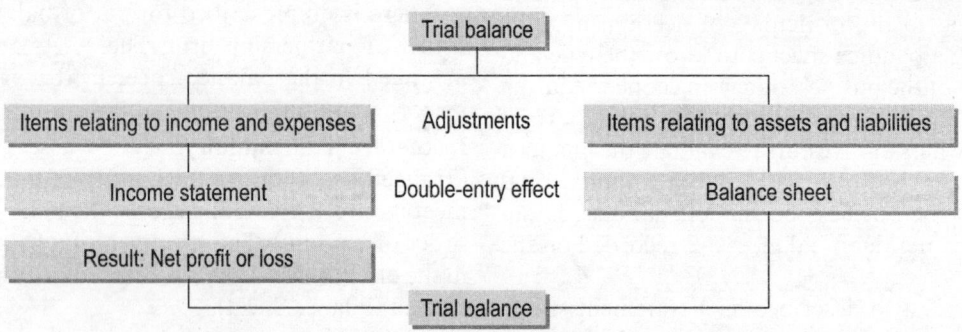

FIG. 13.2 Trial balance, income statement, and balance sheet

The owner's equity at any point of time is represented by the following equation:

$$\text{Owner's Equity} = \text{Assets} - \text{Liabilities} \qquad (2)$$

This implies that except in the case of the first balance sheet, owner's equity needs not be equal to contributed capital. The owner's equity changes with sale transactions in the following ways— (a) the amount of sales revenue realized increases the owner's equity; and (b) the amount of goods parted with decreases the owner's equity. Thus, an increase in the owner's equity is equal to the net increase in assets.

$$\text{Owner's Equity} = \text{Contributed Capital} + \text{Retained Earnings} \quad (3)$$

Assuming no withdrawals took place, retained earnings are nothing but revenues less expenses.

$$\text{Retained earnings} = \text{Revenue} - \text{Expenses} \qquad (4)$$

Now, substituting the right hand side of the first equation, we derive the following equation:

$$\text{Assets} = \text{Liabilities} + \text{Contributed Capital} + \text{Revenue} - \text{Expenses} \qquad (5)$$

The last two terms of the fifth equation are referred to as profit and loss account or income statement. Thus, income statement is an integral part of any balance sheet as it is an expansion of one of the terms of the balance sheet.

Table 13.1 indicates the difference between an income statement and a balance sheet.

TABLE 13.1   Difference between income statement and balance sheet

Income Statement	Balance Sheet
It is prepared with the debit or credit balances of income and expense accounts.	It shows the assets and liabilities on a particular date.
It reveals the net profit or loss of an entity during a particular period.	It is a statement of a firm's financial position on a particular date.
The difference between the two sides of income statement—net profit or net loss—is transferred to equity and liability portion of the balance sheet.	There is no difference between two sides of balance sheet.
The debit or credit balances of income and expense accounts are closed by transferring to the income statement.	The accounts are not closed.

Table 13.2 indicates the points of differences between trial balance and balance sheet.

TABLE 13.2   Differences between trial balance and balance sheet

Trial Balance	Balance Sheet
Statement showing the debit column and credit column balance of accounts is called trial balance.	Statement showing financial position of the firm on a particular date is called balance sheet.
Trial balance has two additional columns: debit balance and credit balance.	Balance sheet has two vertical portions: Equity and Liability, and Assets.
It is not compulsory to prepare a trial balance.	It is compulsory to prepare balance sheet.
To know arithmetical accuracy of accounts and to have overview of all accounts' position, firms prepare trial balance.	To know the financial position of the business, firms prepare balance sheet.

Trial balance can be prepared without incorporating the items of adjustment entries.	Balance sheet cannot be prepared without incorporating the items of adjustments.
In trial balance, balances of assets, liabilities, capital, income and expense accounts are shown.	In balance sheet the balances of assets, liabilities, and capital accounts are shown, including retained earnings.

■ ILLUSTRATION 13.18 Neeti started her own delivery service. The following transactions took place in the month of June 2020.

1 Neeti as a stockholder has invested ₹25,000 cash in the business.

2 Neeti purchased for ₹13,000 a used van for deliveries. She paid ₹2,000 cash and signed a note payable for the remaining balance.

3 She paid ₹900 for office rent for the month.

5 Services worth ₹3,000 were performed on account.

9 The concern (firm) paid ₹200 in cash dividends.

12 Purchased supplies for ₹400 on account.

15 Received a cash payment of ₹750 for services provided on June 5.

17 Purchased gasoline for ₹350 on account.

20 Received a cash payment of ₹350 on account.

23 Made cash payment of ₹1, 900 for services provided.

26 Paid ₹450 for utilities.

29 Paid for the gasoline purchased on account on June 17.

30 Paid ₹600 for employee salaries.

Prepare the following:

(a) An income statement for the month of June
(b) A balance sheet as at 30 June 2020

Solution

Income Statement of Neeti
for the Month of June 2020

Particulars	Amount (₹)
Sales	3,000
Cost of goods sold	(1,200)
Office and administration expense	(1,500)
Cash dividend	(200)
Income before taxes	100
Income tax	-
Net income	100

Solution

(a)

Balance Sheet of Neeti
as at 30 June 2020

Particulars	Amount (₹)
Assets	22,250
Cash	350
Debtors (all receivable)	
Current assets	22,600
Fixed assets	
Van	13,000
Less: Depreciation	-
Net fixed assets	13,000
Total assets	35,600
Liabilities and equity	
Accounts payable	10,500
Common stock	25,000
Net income – retained earnings	100
Total liabilites	35,600

■ ILLUSTRATION 13.19 From the following trial balance of Silicon Pumps on 31 March 2020 and additional information, (a) pass adjustment entries, (b) prepare final trial balance, (c) pass closing entries, (d) prepare manufacturing account, trading account, and income statement for the year ended 31 March 2020, and (e) prepare a balance sheet as at the same date.

Trial balance of Silicon Pumps
as on 31 March 2020

Particulars	Dr. (₹)	Cr. (₹)
Opening stock (1/4/2019) – Raw materials	60,000	-
Work-in-progress	10,000	-
Finished goods	40,000	-
Purchases and sales	2,00,000	4,00,000
Wages	25,000	-
Sale of scrap	-	5,000
Salaries	30,000	-
Insurance	20,000	-
Miscellaneous expenses and income	50,000	15,000
Drawings and capital	10,000	2,00,000
Debtors and creditors	1,00,000	60,000
Plant and machinery	1,00,000	
Cash and bank	35,000	-
Total ₹	6,80,000	6,80,000

Additional Information: (1) Closing stock as 31 March 2020 (a) raw materials ₹70,000; (b) work-in-progress ₹20,000; (c) finished goods ₹30,000. (2) Outstanding salary ₹5,000. (3) Prepaid insurance ₹2,000. (4) Provide 10% p.a. depreciation on plant and machinery.

Solution

(a)

Journal (Adjustment Entries) in the Books of Silicon Pumps

Date 2020	Particulars	LF	Dr. (₹)	Cr. (₹)
March 31	Closing stock (raw materials) account (*Add*)	Dr.	70,000	-
	Closing stock (work-in-progress) account (*Add*)	Dr.	20,000	-
	Closing stock (finished goods) account (*Add*)	Dr.	30,000	-
	To Manufacturing account (*Add*)			90,000
	To Trading account (*Add*)			30,000
	(Being closing stock on 31/3/2020 accounted)			
				5,000

March 31	Salary account (*Add*)	Dr.	5,000	
	To Outstanding salary account (*Add*)			
	(Being outstanding salary on 31/3/2020 accounted)			2,000
March 31	Prepaid insurance account (*Add*)	Dr.	2,000	
	To Insurance account (*Less*)			
	(Being prepaid insurance on 31/3/2020 accounted)			10,000
March 31	Depreciation on plant and machinery account (*Add*)	Dr.	10,000	
	To Plant and machinery account (*Less*)			
	(Being depreciation on plant and machinery for the year at 10% p.a.)			

(b)

Final (Adjusted) Trial Balance of Silicon Pumps
as on 31 March 2020

Particulars	Dr. (₹)	Cr. (₹)
Opening stock (1/4/2019) – Raw materials	60,000	-
Work-in-progress	10,000	-
Finished goods	40,000	-
Closing stock (31/3/2020) – Raw materials	70,000	-
Work-in-progress	20,000	-
Finished goods	30,000	-
Manufacturing account (for closing stock) raw material and work-in-progress)		
Trading account (for closing stock of finished goods)	-	90,000
Purchases and sales	-	30,000
Wages	2,00,000	4,00,000
Sale of scrap	25,000	-
Salaries (30,000 + 5,000)	-	5,000
Outstanding salary	35,000	-
Insurance (20,000 – 2,000)	-	5,000
Prepaid insurance	18,000	-
Miscellaneous expenses and incomes	2,000	
Drawings and capital	50,000	15,000
Debtors and creditors	10,000	2,00,000
Plant and machinery (1,00,000 – 10,000)	1,00,000	60,000
Depreciation on plant and machinery	90,000	-
Cash and bank	10,000	-
	35,000	-
Total ₹	**8,05,000**	**8,05,000**

(c)

Journal (Closing Entries) In the Books of Silicon Pumps

Date 2020	Particulars	LF	Dr. (₹)	Cr. (₹)
March 31	Manufacturing account (*Less*)	Dr.	3,05,000	-
	To Opening stock of raw materials account (*Less*)			60,000
	To Opening stock of work-in-progress account (*Less*)			10,000
	To Purchase account (*Less*)			2,00,000
	To Wages account (*Less*)			25,000
	To Depreciation on plant and machinery account. (*Less*)			10,000
March 31	Sale of scrap account (*Less*)	Dr.	5,000	
	To Manufacturing account (*Add*)			5,000
	(Being sale of scrap account closed)			
March 31	Trading account (*Less*)	Dr.	2,10,000	
	To Manufacturing account (*Add*)			2,10,000
	(Being cost of production transferred)			
March 31	Trading account (*Less*)	Dr.	40,000	
	To Opening stock of finished goods account (*Less*)			40,000
	(Being opening stock account closed)			
March 31	Sales account (*Less*)	Dr.	4,00,000	
	To Trading account (*Add*)			4,00,000
	(Being sales account closed)			

		Dr.	1,80,000	
March 31	Trading account (Less)			
	To Income statement (Add)			1,80,000
	(Being gross profit transferred)			
March 31	Income statement (Less)	Dr.	1,03,000	
	To Salaries account (Less)			35,000
	To Insurance account (Less)			18,000
	To Miscellaneous expenses account (Less)			50,000
	(Being expenses transferred)			
March 31	Miscellaneous income (Less)	Dr.	15,000	
	To Income statement (Add)			15,000
	(Being income transferred)			
March 31	Income statement (Less)	Dr.	92,000	
	To Capital account (Add)			92,000
	(Being net profit transferred)			
	Capital account (Less)		10,000	
	To Drawings account (Less)			10,000
	(Being drawings transferred)			

(d) Name of Account: Manufacturing Account of Silicon Pumps
for the year ended 31 March 2020

Reference Account	Dr. (Less)	Cr. (Add)
By Sale of scrap		5,000
By Closing stock of work-in-process		20,000
BY Cost of production of the finished goods transferrred to the Trading Account		2,10,000
TO RAW MATERIAL CONSUMED		
Opening stock of raw materials	60,000	
Purchases	2,00,000	
Less: Closing stock of raw materials	70,000	
= **RAW MATERIALS CONSUMED**	1,90,000	
To Opening stock of work in process	10,000	
To Wages	25,000	
To Depreciation on plant and machinery	10,000	
TOTAL	**2,35,000**	**2,35,000**

Solution

Trading Account of Silicon Pumps
for the year ended 31 March 2020

Particulars	Amount (₹)	Amount (₹)
REVENUE		
By Sales		4,00,000
Total Revenue		**4,00,000**
EXPENSES		
To Opening stock of finished goods		40,000
To Cost of production transferred from Manufacturing account		2,10,000
Less: Closing stock of finished goods		30,000
Total Expenses		**2,20,000**
Gross Profit (Total Revenue – Total Expenses)		**1,80,000**
Brought down to Profit and Loss Account or Income Statement		

Income Statement of Silicon Pumps
for the year ended 31 March 2020

Particulars	Amount (₹)	Amount (₹)
REVENUE		
Gross Profit brought from Trading Account		1,80,000
By Miscellaneous income		15,000
Total Revenue		**1,95,000**
EXPENSES		
To Salaries		35,000
To Insurance		18,000
To Miscellaneous expenses		50,000
Total Expenses		**1,03,000**
Net Profit (Total Revenue – Total Expenses)		**92,000**
Transferred to Statement of Retained Earnings or Capital Account		

Balance Sheet of Silicon Pumps
as at 31 March 2020

Particulars	Note	Amount (₹)	Amount (₹)
I. EQUITY AND LIABILITIES			
Capital		2,00,000	
Add: Net profit		92,000	
		2,92,000	
Less: Drawings		10,000	2,82,000
Outstanding salary			5,000
Creditors			60,000
Total Equity and Liabilities			**3,47,000**
II. ASSETS			
Stock - Raw material		70,000	
- Work in progress		20,000	
- Finished goods		30,000	1,20,000
Prepaid insurance			2,000
Debtors			1,00,000
Plant and Machinery			90,000
Cash and Bank			35,000
Total Assets			**3,47,000**

■ **ILLUSTRATION 13.20** A firm maintains its provision for bad debts @ 5% and a provision for discount on debtors @ 2%. You are given the following details:

Particulars	2019	2020
Bad debts	800	1,500
Discount allowed	1,200	500
Recovery of bad debts written off in earlier years	500	300

Sundry debtors (before writing off bad debts and discount) amount to ₹60,000 on 31 December 2019 and ₹42,000 on 31 December 2020. On 1 January 2019, provision for bad debts and provision for discount on debtors had a balance of ₹4,550 and ₹800 respectively. Show the provision for bad debts account and provision for discount on debtors account for 2019 and 2020.

Solution

Name of Account: Provision for Doubtful Debts
Type of Account: Retained Earnings

Date	Reference Account	Voucher Type	Post Ref No.	Dr. (Less)	Cr. (Add)
1-Jan-19	By Balance b/d				4,550
31-Dec-19	To Bad debts			800	
31-Dec-19	To Income statement (balancing figure)			850	
31-Dec-19	To Balance c/d (working note 1)			2,900	
	Total			**4,550**	**4,550**
1-Jan-20	By Balance b/d				2,900
31-Dec-20	To Bad debts			1,500	
31-Dec-20	To Balance c/d (working note 2)			2,000	
31-Dec-20	By Income statement (balancing figure)				600
	Total			**3,500**	**3,500**
1-Jan-21	By Balance b/d				2,000

Name of Account: Provision for Discount on Debtors Account
Type of Account: Retained Earnings

Date	Reference Account	Voucher Type	Post Ref No.	Dr. (Less)	Cr. (Add)
1-Jan-19	By Balance b/d				800
31-Dec-19	To Discount allowed			1,200	
31-Dec-19	To Balance c/d (working note 1)			1,102	
31-Dec-19	By Income statement (balancing figure)				1,502
	Total			**2,302**	**2,302**
1-Jan-20	By Balance b/d				1,102
31-Dec-20	To Discount allowed			500	
31-Dec-20	To Balance c/d (working note 2)			760	
31-Dec-20	By Income statement (balancing figure)				158
	Total			**1,260**	**1,260**
1-Jan-21	By Balance b/d				760

Working Notes:

1. Balance of debtors as on 31/12/2019   ₹60,000
   Less: Bad debts   ₹800
   Discount allowed   1,200   2,000
       58,000
   ∴ Provision for bad debts @ 5% on ₹58,000 = ₹2,900
   Provision for discount on debtors @ 2% on (₹58,000 – ₹2,900) = ₹1,102

2. Balance of debtors as on 31/12/2020   ₹42,000
   Less: Bad debts   ₹1,500
   Discount allowed   500   2,000
       40,000
   ∴ Provision for bad debts @ 5% on ₹40,000 = ₹2,000
   Provision for discount on debtors @ 2% on (₹40,000 – ₹2,000) = ₹760

■ **ILLUSTRATION 13.21** The following trial balance was extracted from the books of Ms Aarohi as on 31 December 2019:

Balances	Amount (₹)	Balances	Amount (₹)
Plant and machinery	20,000	Purchases	1,02,000
Wages	34,500	Sales returns	3,100
Salaries	15,850	Bad debts	1,400
Furniture	10,000	Interest and bank charges	400
Freight on purchases	1,860	Cash at bank	4,200
Freight on sales	2,140	Cash in hand	1,120
Building	24,000	Credit Balances:	
Manufacturing expenses	9,500	Capital	80,000
Insurance and tax	4,250	Sundry creditors	44,560
Goodwill	25,000	Bank loan	15,000
General expenses	8,200	Purchases returns	1,740
Fuel and power	1,280	Sales	2,50,850
Sundry debtors	78,200	Provision for bad debts	2,000
Factory lighting	950		
Opening stock	34,200		
Motor car	12,000		

Additional Information:

1. Stock in hand on 31 December 2019 was valued at ₹30,500.
2. Depreciate plant and machinery by 10% p.a., furniture by 5% p.a., and motor car by ₹1,000.
3. Bring provision for bad debts to 5% on debtors.
4. A commission of 1% on the gross profit is to be provided to the works manager.
5. A commission of 2% on the net profit (after charging the works manager's commission) is to be credited to the general manager.

Prepare the trading and profit and loss account for the year ended 31/12/2019, and a balance sheet as at that date.

Solution

Trading and Profit and Loss Account of Ms Aarohi
for the year ended 31 December 2019

Particulars	Amount (₹)	Amount (₹)
REVENUE		
By Sales	2,50,850	

Less: Returns	3,100	
		2,47,750
Total Revenue		**2,47,750**
EXPENSES		
To Opening stock		34,200
To Purchases	1,02,000	
Less: Returns	1,740	1,00,260
Less Closing stock		30,500
= Cost of Goods Sold		1,03,960
To Freight on purchases		1,860
To Wages		34,500
To Fuel and power		1,280
To Factory lighting		950
To Manufacturing expenses		9,500
Total Expenses		**1,52,050**
Gross Profit (Total Revenue – Total Expenses)		**95,700**
Brought down to Profit and Loss Account or Income Statement		

Income Statement

REVENUE		
By Gross profit b/d		95,700
Total Revenue		**95,700**
EXPENSES		
To Salaries		15,850
To Freight on sales		2,140
To Insurance and tax		4,250
To General expenses		8,200
To Bad debts	1,400	
Add: New provision	3,910	
	5,310	
Less: Old provision	2,000	
		3,310
To Interest and bank charges		400
To Depreciation:		
Plant and machinery		2,000
Furniture		500
Motorcar		1,000
To Work manager's commission		957
To General manager's commission		1,142
(2% on 57100)		
Total Expenses		**39,749**
Net Profit (Total Revenue – Total Expenses)		**55,951**
Transferred to Statement of Retained Earnings or Capital Account		

Balance Sheet of Ms Aarohi
as at 31 December 2019

Particulars	Note	Amount (₹)	Amount (₹)
I. EQUITY AND LIABILITIES			
Capital		80,000	
Add: Net profit		55,951	
			1,35,951
Outstanding commission:			
Works manager			957
General manager			1,142
Bank loan			15,000
Sundry creditors			44,560
Total Equity and Liabilities			**1,97,610**
II. ASSETS			
Goodwill			25,000
Building			24,000
Plant and machinery		20,000	
Less: Depreciation		2,000	
			18,000
Furniture		10,000	
Less: Depreciation		500	
			9,500
Motor car		12,000	
Less: Depreciation		1,000	
			11,000
Closing stock			30,500
Sundry debtors		78,200	
Less: Provision		3,910	
			74,290
Cash at bank			4,200
Cash in hand			1,120
Total Assets			**1,97,610**

■ **ILLUSTRATION 13.22** The following is the trial balance of Vivaan Ltd as on 31 March 2020. Prepare the trading and profit and loss account for the year ended 31 March 2020, and balance sheet as at that date after making the necessary adjustments.

Particulars	Dr. (₹)	Cr. (₹)
Debtors and creditors	5,00,000	2,00,000
Outstanding liability for expenses	55,000	
Wages	1,00,000	
Carriage outwards	1,10,000	
Carriage inwards	50,000	
General expenses	70,000	
Cash discount	20,000	
Bad debts	10,000	
Motor car	2,40,000	
Printing and stationery	15,000	
Furniture and fittings	1,10,000	
Advertisement	85,000	
Insurance	45,000	
Salesperson's commission	87,500	
Postage and telephone	57,500	
Salaries	1,60,000	
Rates and taxes	25,000	
Drawings	20,000	
Capital		14,43,000
Purchases and sales	15,50,000	19,87,500
Stock on 1/4/2019	2,50,000	
Cash in hand and at bank	70,500	
	36,30,500	36,30,500

Adjustments:

1. Stock on 31 March 2020 was valued at ₹7,25,000.
2. A provision for bad and doubtful debts is to be created to the extent of 5% on debtors.
3. Depreciate furniture and fittings by 10% p.a. and motor car by 20% p.a.
4. Vivaan Ltd had withdrawn goods worth ₹25,000 during the year.
5. Sales include goods worth ₹75,000 sent out to Shanti & Co. on approval and remaining unsold on 31 March 2020. The cost of the goods was ₹50,000.
6. Salespersons are entitled to a commission of 5% on total sales.
7. Debtors include ₹25,000 bad debts.
8. A printing and stationery expense of ₹55,000 relating to 2018–19 had not been provided in that year but was paid in this year by debiting outstanding liabilities.
9. Purchases include purchase of furniture worth ₹50,000.

Solution

Trading and Profit and Loss Account of Vivaan Ltd
for the year ended 31 March 2020

Particulars	Amount (₹)	Amount (₹)
REVENUE		
By Sales	19,87,500	
Less: Sale on approval	75,000	
		19,12,500
Total Revenue		**19,12,500**
EXPENSES		
To Opening stock		2,50,000
To Purchases	15,50,000	
Less: Drawings	25,000	
Less: Closing stock	7,25,000	
Less: Stock with customers (at cost)	50,000	
Less: To Furniture	50,000	7,00,000
= Cost of Goods Sold		9,50,000
To Wages		1,00,000
To Carriage inwards		50,000
Total Expenses		**11,00,000**
Gross Profit (Total Revenue – Total Expenses)		**8,12,500**
Brought down to Profit and Loss Account or Income Statement		

Income Statement

REVENUE	Amount (₹)	Amount (₹)
REVENUE		
By Gross profit b/d		8,12,500
Total Revenue		**8,12,500**
EXPENSES		
To Carriage outwards		1,10,000
To General expenses		70,000
To Discount		20,000
To Bad debts	10,000	
Add: Further b/d	25,000	
	35,000	
Add: New provision	20,000	

		Amount
		55,000
To Printing and stationery		15,000
To Advertisement		85,000
To Insurance		45,000
To Salesperson's commission	87,500	
Add: Outstanding	8,125	
		95,625
To Postage and telephone		57,500
To Salaries		1,60,000
To Rates and taxes		25,000
To Depreciation:		
Furniture		16,000
Motor car		48,000
Total Expenses		**8,02,125**
Net Profit (Total Revenue – Total Expenses)		**10,375**
Transferred to Capital Account		

Balance Sheet of Vivaan Ltd
as at 31 March 2020

Particulars	Note	Amount (₹)	Amount (₹)
I. EQUITY AND LIABILITIES			
Capital		14,43,000	
Add: Net profit		10,375	
		14,53,375	
Less: Drawings			
(20,000 + 25,000)		45,000	
		14,08,375	
Less: Printing and stationery of last year		55,000	
			13,53,375
Salesperson's commission outstnding			8,125
Sundry creditors			2,00,000
Total Equity and Liabilities			**15,61,500**
II. ASSETS			
Furniture		1,10,000	
Add: Addition		50,000	
		1,60,000	
Less: Depreciation		16,000	
			1,44,000
Motor car		2,40,000	
Less: Depreciation		48,000	
			1,92,000
Closing stock			7,75,000
Cash in hand			10,500
Cash at bank			60,000
Debtors		5,00,000	
Less: Sale on approval		75,000	
		4,25,000	
Less: Further b/d		25,000	
		4,00,000	
Less: Provision for doubtful debts		20,000	
			3,80,000
Total Assets			**15,61,500**

COMPANY FINAL ACCOUNTS

The final accounts of a company consist of (a) a balance sheet disclosing the financial position as at the end of a financial year, and (b) profit and loss account (or an income and expenditure account in the case of a company not carrying on business for profit) disclosing the results of the operations of the company for the period covered by the financial year.

The financial year of a company is the period for which the profit and loss account of a company is prepared. Such a financial year may be more or less than a calendar year but it shall not exceed 15 months unless the registrar grants a special permission in which case it may extend up to 18 months.

A COMPANY'S BALANCE SHEET AND A FIRM'S BALANCE SHEET

A company's balance sheet is different from a firm's balance sheet in the following respects:

A company's balance sheet is prepared in the order of permanence whereas a partnership firm's balance sheet is usually prepared in the order of liquidity.

For a company's balance sheet, there are two standard forms prescribed under the Companies Act, 2013, whereas there is no standard form prescribed under the Indian Partnership Act, 1932 for a partnership firm's balance sheet.

In the case of a company's balance sheet, the previous year's figures are required to be given, whereas it is not so in the case of a partnership firm's balance sheet.

FORM OF INCOME STATEMENT

No standard form has been prescribed under the Companies Act, 1956 for the profit and loss account of a company. However, the income statement or profit and loss account is required to comply with the requirements of Schedule III to the Companies Act. It may be noted that the income statement must be annexed to the balance sheet.

FORMS OF PREPARING BALANCE SHEET AND INCOME STATEMENT

Schedule III of the Companies Act, 2013 prescribes vertical format of balance sheet and income statement (i.e., profit and

loss account). The formats of balance sheet as per Exhibit 3.2 (Chapter 3) and that of income statement as per Exhibit 4.5 (Chapter 4) have been provided in earlier chapters.

■ ILLUSTRATION 13.23 The following is the trial balance of Shakti Ltd as on 31.3.2020.

Debit Balance	₹	Credit Balance	₹
Debenture interest paid	15,000	Share capital	10,00,000
Calls in arrears	50,000	General reserve	60,000
Purchases	5,00,000	Debenture red. reserve	40,000
Opening stock	80,000	10% Debentures	2,00,000
Debtors	2,00,000	Public deposits	80,000
Prepaid insurance	30,000	Purchase return	20,000
10% Government loan	1,00,000	Sales	12,00,000
Land & building	14,00,000	Creditors	30,000
Plant & machinery	2,30,000	Unclaimed dividend	10,000
Sales return	25,000	Bad debt reserve	18,000
Salary and office exp.	70,000	Profit & Loss A/c (1.4.2019)	42,000
Total	**27,00,000**	**Total**	**27,00,000**

Additional Information:

(i) Closing stock ₹40,000.
(ii) Make provision for taxation at 50% of profit.
(iii) Make provision for bad debt at 10% on debtors.
(iv) Proposed dividend 10% on share capital, after transferring ₹20,000 to General Reserve.

Prepare the final accounts as per Schedule III of Companies Act, 2013.

Solution

Balance Sheet of Shakti Ltd
as at 31.3.2020

Particulars	Note	₹
I. EQUITY AND LIABILITIES		
(1) Shareholder's Funds:		
(A) Share capital	1	9,50,000
(B) Reserves and Surplus	2	3,28,500
(2) Non-current Liabilities:		
Long-term borrowings	3	2,80,000
(3) Current Liabilities:		
(A) Trade payables - Creditors		30,000
(B) Other current liabilities		
Unclaimed dividend		10,000

IFRS Update

Differences in presentation of dividends on equity shares

The following table indicates the differences in the presentation of dividends on equity shares as per Indian Accounting Standards, IFRS or International Accounting Standards, and US Generally Accepted Accounting Practices.

Ind AS	IFRS/IAS	US GAAP
To be shown as an appropriation of profit in the income statement. Dividends to be accounted in the year for which it is proposed.	To be shown as a deduction in the statement of changes in shareholders' equity in the period in which it is authorized by the shareholders.	Similar to IFRS.

(C) Short-term provisions	4	3,91,500
Total Equity and Liabilities		**19,90,000**
II. ASSETS		
(1) (A) Non-current Assets:		
Fixed assets - Tangible assets	5	16,30,000
(B) Non-current Investments:		1,00,000
10% Govt. loan		
(2) Current Assets:		
(A) Inventories		40,000
(B) Trade receivables		1,80,000
(2,00,000 – BDR 20,000)		
(C) Short-term loan and advances		30,000
Prepaid insurance		
(D) Other current assets:		
Interest due on govt. loans		10,000
Total Assets		**19,90,000**

Profit and Loss Statement of Shakti Ltd
for the year ending on 31.3.2020

Particulars	Note	₹
I. REVENUE FROM OPERATIONS		
(Sales 12,00,000 - Sales Return 25,000)		11,75,000
II. OTHER INCOME		
(Int. due on Govt. loan)		10,000
III. TOTAL REVENUE (I + II)		**11,85,000**
IV. EXPENSES:		
(A) Purchases (5,00,000 – Purchase returns 20,000)		4,80,000
(B) Changes in inventories of furnished goods/WIP and stock in trade (80,000 – 40,000)		40,000
(C) Employee benefits expense		70,000
(D) Finance costs (Debenture interest) (15,000 + 5,000)		20,000
(E) Other expenses – B.D. Reserve (20,000 – 18,000)		2,000
Total Expenses		**6,12,000**
V. PROFIT BEFORE TAX (III – IV)		5,73,000
VI. INCOME TAX EXP.		2,86,500
(50% of Profit ₹5,73,000)		
Profit after tax		2,86,500
Profit for the Period		**2,86,500**

Note 1: Share Capital

Particulars		₹
Share capital	10,00,000	
Less: Calls in arrears	50,000	**9,50,000**

Note 2: Reserves and Surplus

Particulars	Op. Bal.	Additions	Deductions	Cl. Bal.
Gen. reserve	60,000	20,000	-	80,000
De. Red. Res.	40,000	-	-	40,000
Surplus			Gen Res. A/c	
(P&L A/c)	42,000	2,86,500	20,000	
			Prop. Dividend	2,08,500
			1,00,000	
	1,42,000	**3,06,500**	**1,20,000**	**3,28,500**

Note 3: Long-term Borrowings

Particulars	₹
(A) 10% debentures (Secured)	2,00,000
(B) Public deposits (Unsecured)	80,000
	2,80,000

Note 4: Short-term Provision

Particulars	₹
Provision for taxation	2,86,500
Prop. dividend	1,00,000
Outstanding interest on debentures	5,000
	3,91,500

Note 5: Tangible Fixed Assets

Items	Cost			Depreciation			Net Block/ WDV	
Column	Op. Bal. (1)	Add. Ded. (2)	Cl. Bal. (3)=1+2	Op. Bal (4)	Add. Ded. (5)	Cl. Bal (6)=4+5	As at year beginning (7)=1-4	As at year end (8)=3-6
Land & buildings	-	-	14,00,000	-	-	-	-	14,00,000
Plant & machinery	-	-	2,30,000	-	-	-	-	2,30,000
			16,30,000					**16,30,000**

■ **ILLUSTRATION 13.24** You are required to prepare the profit and loss statement for the year ending 31.3.2020 and a balance sheet (Schedule III) as on that date from the following balances taken out from the books of Aaram Industries Ltd as on 31.3.2020.

Particulars	₹	Particulars	₹
6% Debentures		Rent	1,230
(Redeemable on 31.3.2029)	45,000	Share transfer fees	60
Commercial Bank Ltd		Debentute redemption fund	37,500
Cash credit A/c		Interest on A'bad muni. cor.	
Credit balance	450	Debentures	450
Securities premium	2,200	Interest on debenture redemption	
Capital reserves	4,940	Fund investments	1,200
Dena Bank Ltd	2,660	Debenture redemption fund	
6% A'bad muni. loan	15,000	Investments	37,500
(1.10.2019)		Stationery stock (31.3.2020)	90
Bad debts reserves	1,500	Creditors for goods supplied	30,050

Sales	146,820	Depreciation-machinery	8,250
Profit & loss A/c		Loose tools	210
(Previous year credit balance)	1,440	Debtors	37,500
Depreciation fund		Machinery	156,400
(31.3.2020)	30,360	Office expenses	4,980
Bills payable	1,400	Stores	420
Unclaimed dividend	250	Depreciation-building	2,250
Director's fees	300	Paid up share capital	187,500
Insurance	450	Building	90,060
Stationery, postage, etc.	330	Productive wages	14,400
Bad debts	510	Purchases	101,850
Debenture interest	1350	Stock (31.3.2019)	14,630
Discount on issue of debentures	750		

Consider the following at the time of preparing the final accounts:

(1) Insurance premium accounting to ₹300 is paid for the year ending on 30.6.2020.
(2) Provide ₹1,500 for debenture redemption fund.
(3) Increase bad debt reserve by ₹375.
(4) Authorized capital consists of 11,250 shares of ₹20 each.
(5) Closing stock ₹37,200. This includes defective stock which requires estimated repairing charges of ₹1,275.

Solution

Balance Sheet of Aaram Industries Ltd
as at 31-3-2020

Particulars	Notes	₹
I. EQUITY AND LIABILITIES		
(1) Shareholder's Funds:		
(A) Share capital	1	1,87,500
(B) Reserves and surplus	2	78,280
(2) Non-current Liabilities:		
Long-term borrowings	3	45,450
(3) Current Liabilities:		
(a) Trade payables - Creditors		30,050
(b) Other current liabilities	4	3,000
Total Equity and Liabilties		**3,44,280**
II. ASSETS		
(1) (A) Non-current Assets:		
Fixed assets - Tangible assets	5	2,16,100
(B) (i) Non-current investments:		
A'bad muni. loan		15,000
(ii) Deb. red fund investments		37,500
(2) Current Assets:		
(A) Inventories	6	35,925
(B) Trade receivables - Debtors	7	35,625
(C) Other current assets	8	1,395
(D) Cash and cash equivalants		2,660
(E) Short-terms loans and advances	9	75
Total Assets		**3,44,280**

Profit and Loss Statement of Aaram Industries Ltd
for the year ending 31.3.2020

Particulars	Note	₹
I. REVENUE FROM OPERATIONS		1,46,820
II. OTHER INCOME		
(a) Share transfer fees	60	
(b) Int on A'bad muni. loan	450	510
III. TOTAL REVENUE (I + II)		**1,47,330**
IV. EXPENSES		
(A) Purchases		1,01,850
(B) Charges in inventories of finished goods/WIP/Stock in trade [14,630 – 35,925 (37,200 – 12,75 Repairing)]		21,295
(C) Employee benefits expense		
(D) Finance costs: Deb. int.	1,350	
(+) Outstanding	1,350	2,700
(E) Depriciation: Machinery	8,250	
Building	2,250	10,500
(F) Other expenses	10	22,575
Total Expenses		**1,16,330**
Profit for the Period		**31,000**

Notes to Accounts:

Note 1: Share Capital

Particulars	₹
Authorized:	
11,250 Equity shares of ₹20 each	2,25,000
Issued subscribed and paid up:	
9,375 Equity shares of ₹20 each fully paid	1,87,500
	1,87,500

Note 2: Reserves and Surplus

Particulars	Op. Bal.	Additions	Deductions	Cl. Bal.
Capital reserve	4,940			4,940
Securities premium	2,200			2,200
Deb. red. fund	37,500	1,500		40,200
Surplus		Int 1,200		
(P & L A/c)	1,440	31,000	Deb. Red. Fund 1,500	30,940
	46,080	33,700	1,500	78,280

Note 3: Long-term Borrowings

Particulars	₹
Debenture	45,000
Commercial bank	450
	45,450

Note 4: Other Current Liabilities

Particulars	₹
Unclaimed dividend	250
Bills payable	1,400
Interest accrued on debentures	1,350
	3,000

Note 5: Tangible Fixed Assets

Item	Cost			Depriciation			Net Block/ WDV
Column	Op. Bal. (1)	Add./ Ded (2)	Cl. Bal. (3)=1+2	Op. Bal. (4)	Add./ Ded (5)	Cl. Bal. (6)=4+5	As at year end (8)=3–6
Machinery	1,56,400	-	1,56,400	-	-	-	1,56,400
Building	90,060	-	90,060	30,360	-	30,360	59,700
	2,46,460		2,46,460	30,360		30,360	21,6,100

Note 6: Inventories

Particulars		₹
Stock of goods	37,200	
Less: Repair charges	1,275	35,925
		35,925

Note 7: Trade receivables (Debtors)

Particulars		₹
Sundry debtors	37,500	
Less: Bad debts reserve	1,875	35,625
		35,625

Note 8: Other Current Assets

Particulars		₹
Prepaid insurance	75	
Stores	420	
Loose tools	210	
Stationery stock	90	
Debenture discount (750 – 75)	675	1,395
		1,395

Note 9: Short Terms Loan & Advances

Particulars		₹
Prepaid insurance		75
		75

Note 10: Other Expenses

	Particulars	₹
(A)	Productive wages	14,400
(B)	Insurance (450 – Prepaid 75)	375
(C)	Stationery postage, etc.	330
(D)	Other expenses	4,980
(E)	Rent	1,230
(F)	Bad debts	570
(G)	Discount on debenture (1/10)	75
(H)	Director's fees	300
(I)	Bad debt reserve (1,875 – 1,500)	375
		22,575

Notes:

1. As depreciation on assets is provided by the depreciation fund method, depreciation will be debited to the profit and loss account and credited to the depreciation fund account. Assets will be shown at cost price.
2. Interest on debenture redemption fund should be credited to the debenture redemption fund account.
3. The stock is defective and will require repairing charges of ₹1,275. Hence, the value of stock should be reduced by that amount. Alternatively, a reserve for repairs of stock may be created by debiting the profit and loss account.

4. Debenture interest is paid for 6 months only and as such there is an implied adjustment that debenture interest for 6 months is unpaid, and it has to be provided for.
5. As debentures are to be redeemed in 10 years, 1/10th of the discount on issue of such debentures would be written off this year.

■ **ILLUSTRATION 13.25** The trial balance of Gautam Ltd as on 31.3.2020 was as under:

Particulars	Debit (₹)	Credit (₹)
Equity share capital	-	12,00,000
12% Preference share capital	-	3,00,000
10% Redeemable debentures	-	3,00,000
Opening stock	1,40,000	-
Purchases and sales	18,60,000	32,00,000
Goods returned	80,000	60,000
Land and building	8,00,000	-
Plant and machinery	6,00,000	
Debtors and creditors	4,00,000	2,00,000
Octroi	1,80,000	-
Selling and distribution expenses	40,000	-
Carriage outward	16,000	-
Wages	6,80,000	-
Administrative expenses	1,70,000	-
Vehicles	1,20,000	-
Directors' fees	20,000	-
Loan of director	-	40,000
Interest on debentures	12,000	-
Interest of investments	-	16,000
Staff pension fund	-	16,000
Investments	3,00,000	
Discount on debentures	80,000	-
Bills	72,000	20,000
Fixed deposits	-	48,000
General reserve	-	1,40,000
Share forfeiture account		20,000
Cash and bank	50,000	-
Profit and loss account (1.4.2019)	-	60,000
Total	**56,20,000**	**56,20,000**

Additional Information:

1. Authorized capital of the company is as under: 15,000 equity shares of ₹100 each and 3,000, 12% preference shares of ₹100 each.
2. Closing stock is valued at ₹2,80,000.
3. Depreciate land and building by 5%, plant and machinery by 10%, and vehicles by 20%.
4. Interest receivable on investments is ₹14,000.
5. Provide bad debts reserve on debtors by 5%.
6. Transfer ₹40,000 to general reserve.
7. The directors have proposed 10% dividend on equity share capital.
8. 10% redeemable debentures are to be redeemed on 31.3.2021.

Prepare the final accounts of the company as per Schedule III of the Companies Act, 2013.

Solution

Gautam Limited
Balance Sheet as on 31 March 2020

Particulars	Notes	₹
I. EQUITY AND LIABILITIES		
(1) Shareholder's Funds:		
(A) Share capital	1	15,20,000
(B) Reserves and surplus	2	2,44,000
(2) Non-current liabilities:		
Long-term borrowings	3	3,88,000
(3) Current Liabilities:		
(A) Trade payables - Creditors		2,00,000
(B) Other current liabilities	4	54,000
(C) Short-term provisions	5	1,56,000
Total Equity and Liabilities		**25,62,000**
II. ASSETS		
(1) Non-current Assets:		
(A) Fixed assets - Tangible assets	6	13,96,000
(B) Non-current investments		3,00,000
(2) Current Assets:		
(A) Inventories - Stock	7	2,80,000
(B) Trade receivables - Debtors		4,52,000
(C) Cash and cash equivelants		50,000
(D) Other current assets	8	84,000
Total Assets		**25,62,000**

Profit and Loss Statement of Gautam Ltd
for the year ending on 31.3.2020

Particulars		Notes	₹
I.	**REVENUE FROM OPERATIONS**		
	(Sales 32,00,000 – Return 80,000)		31,20,000
II.	**OTHER INCOME**		
	Int. on investments	16,000	
	(+) Int. due on investments	14,000	30,000
	Total Revenue	(I + II)	**31,50,000**
III.	**EXPENSES**		
(A)	Purchases of raw materials		
	(18,60,000 – Return 60,000)		18,00,000
(B)	Changes in inventories of finished goods/WIP/Stock in trade		
	(1,40,000 – 28,03,000)		1,40,000
(C)	Finance costs: Db int.	12,000	
	(+)Outstanding	18,000	30,000
(D)	Depreciation	1,24,000	
	Deb. discount	10,000	1,34,000
(E)	Other expenses	9	11,26,000
	Total Expenses		**29,50,000**
	Profit for the period		**2,00,000**

Notes to Accounts:

Note 1: Share Capital

Particulars	₹
Authorized:	
15,000 equity shares of ₹100 each	15,00,000
3,000 12% pref. shares of ₹100 each	3,00,000
Issued Subscribed and Paid up:	**18,00,000**
12,000 equity shares of ₹100 each	12,00,000
(+) Forfieted shares A/c	20,000	12,20,000
3,000 12% pref. shares of ₹100 each	3,00,000
	1,87,500

Note 2: Reserves and Surplus

Particulars	Op. Bal.	Additions	Deductions	Cl. Bal.
General reserve	1,40,000	40,000	-	1,80,000
Surplus			Gen. Res. ₹40,000	
(P&L A/c)	6,0,000	2,00,000	Eq. Divi. 1,20,000	
			Pref. Divi. 36,000	64,000
	2,00,000	**2,40,000**	**196,000**	**2,44,000**

Note 3: Long-term Borrowing

Particulars	₹
Debentures	3,00,000
Fixed deposits	48,000
Loans from directors	40,000
	3,88,000

Note 4: Other Current Liabilities

Particulars	₹
Bills payable	20,000
Staff pension fund	16,000
Outstanding debenture interest	18,000
	54,000

Note 5: Short-term Provisions

Particulars	₹
Pref. dividend	36,000
Equity dividend	1,20,000
	1,56,000

Note 6: Tengible Fixed Assets

Item	Gross Balance Cost			Depreciation			Net Block/WDV	
Column	Op. Bal. (1)	Add, Ded. (2)	Cl. Bal. (3)=1+2	Op. Bal. (4)	Add, Ded. (5)	Cl. Bal. (6)=4+5	As at year beginning (7)1–4	As at year end (8)=3–6
Land-Building	8,00,000	-	8,00,000	-	40,000	40,000	8,00,000	7,60,000
Plant & machineries	6,00,000	-	6,00,000	-	60,000	60,000	6,00,000	5,40,000
Vehicles	1,20,000	-	1,20,000	-	24,000	24,000	120,000	96,000
	15,20,000	-	15,20,000	-	1,24,000	1,24,000	15,20,000	13,96,000

Note 7: Trade Receivables

Particulars		₹
Sundry debtors	4,00,000	
Less: B.D. reserve	20,000	3,80,000
Bills receivable		72,000
		4,52,000

Note 8: Other Current Assets

Particulars	₹
Outstanding int. on investments	14,000
Debenture discount	70,000
	84,000

Note 9: Other Expenses

Particulars	₹
(A) Wages	680,000
(B) Octroi	180,000
(C) Admini. expenses	170,000
(D) Selling & dist. expenses	40,000
(E) Carriage outward	16,000
(F) Director's fees	20,000
(G) Bad debts reserve	20,000
	1,126,000

LIMITATIONS OF FINANCIAL ACCOUNTING

Accounting is an information system that helps compile, generate, and report information in a refined way. It supports the users of accounting for/in decision making. The information generated and reported should be complete, unbiased, honest, and based on sound data and recording as it helps in long-term decision making by users. The practical limitations are mentioned in this section.

Lack of qualitative factors Qualitative factors such as loyalty of employees and skill and efficiency of operating managers and team members is difficult to quantify. These factors which constitute valuable assets of the firm are not reported in the financial statements.

Judgmental and personal factors The outcomes of financial accounting statements are largely affected by the personal judgment of the accountant with respect to the accounting policy to be adopted, such as depreciation policy, accounting of inventory valuation, etc.

The timelines of submission and availability of information Financial reports should be prepared on a timely basis for planning and decision making. Internal users such as managers have better access to accounting data that are normally maintained in the computerized environment. External users such as stock market analysts, investors, equity shareholders, etc. lack access to these data. The time taken to prepare the financial statement and for it to reach the external users may dilute the significance of the information presented. Over a period of time, such data become historical and is not significant for decision making.

Historical valuation convention Financial statements are prepared and reported based on the historical cost concept, wherein assets used in the firm for operating purposes are reported at their historical costs less till date reduction in the value of an asset on account of wear and tear, etc. The realistic valuation should be based on replacement value, net sales realizable value, economical value, or inflation adjusted value to determine the clear position of the firm. The accounting system does not account or provide for it.

Window dressing Window dressing is the process of accounting information that helps manipulate the state of affairs of a firm, that is, the information disclosed is not the actual data. Firms may do this by overestimation or underestimation of their figures of profits, assets, and liabilities.

ACCOUNTING FOR NON-PROFIT-SEEKING OR NOT-FOR-PROFIT ORGANIZATIONS

A non-profit-seeking entity or firm (NPE) does not have the objective of making profit. A NPE is generally incorporated with the intention to promote socially beneficial activities such as education, health care, art, charity, religious activities, etc. Examples of such entities include sports clubs, social clubs, educational institutions, hospitals, libraries, professional bodies such as the Institute of Chartered Accountants of India, the Institute of Cost and Works Accountants of India, etc. NPEs prohibit the payment of any dividend to its members out of surplus earned

---

IFRS Update

Differences in constituents of financial statements

The following table indicates the differences in the constituents of financial statements as per Indian Accounting Standards, IFRS or International Accounting Standards, and US Generally Accepted Accounting Practices.

Ind AS	IFRS/IAS	US GAAP
Company's stand-alone – two years' income statement, balance sheet, cash flow statement, and accounting policies and notes.	Company's consolidated two years' income statement, change in equity, balance sheet, cash flow statement, and accounting policies and notes. Voluntarily company may present the same data for stand-alone company also.	For US companies and Securities Exchange Commission (SEC) registered companies two years' balance sheet and three years' income statement, cash flow statement, changes in equity statement, and accounting policies and notes. For non-US companies with registered securities in US have an option to adopt US GAAPs or IFRS, and also to submit reconciliation of net income and equity to US GAAPs as part of notes.

during the period of operations or activities. The excess of income over expenses during the period is termed as the surplus. If the expenses are greater than the income, it is termed as a deficit.

If a NPE is involved in trading activities, then the profit arising from the trading activities would be used for the purpose of promoting the objectives of the NPE.

NPEs prepare annual accounts in the form of financial statements to reflect their financial affairs. The financial statement prepared at the end of the accounting period, as in normal accounting, consists of the following three statements:

1. Receipts and payments account
2. Income and expenditure account
3. Balance sheet

Receipts and Payments Account

A receipts and payments account is a summary of the cash book. It is similar in form and nature to a cash book. It incorporates the opening cash and bank balance, receipts and payment by cash or by cheque, and the resultant balance of cash and bank balance at the end of the accounting period. All receipts are shown on the left-hand side (indicating an increase in asset value) and all payments are shown on the right-hand side (indicating a decrease in asset value). Exhibit 13.7 indicates the format of a receipts and payments account.

Income and Expenditure Account

The income and expenditure (IE) account of a NPE is equivalent to the income statement of a business entity. It is prepared by matching the revenues against the expenses for an accounting period, usually a year. This account shows surplus or deficit of income over expenses.

The IE is prepared for the period based on the normally accepted accounting principle of the merchandise system of accounting, that is, accrual accounting system. IE takes into consideration the revenue receipts and revenue expenses

---

EXHIBIT 13.7 Name of Account: Receipts and Payments Account

Name of Entity _____

Receipts and Payments Account for the period ending on _____

Type of Account: Asset

Date	Reference Account	Post Ref No.	Dr. (Add)	Cr. (Less)
	To Balance b/d			
	Cash		x	
	Bank		x	
	Fixed deposits		x	
	By Balance b/d			
	Bank overdraft			x
	To Subscriptions			
	For previous year		x	
	For current year		x	
	For next year		x	
	To Entrance fees		x	
	To Donations for building		x	
	To General donations		x	
	To Life membership fees		x	
	To Legacy		x	
	To Grant from government		x	
	To Contribution for annual functions		x	
	To Dividend		x	
	To Interest		x	
	To Rent		x	
	To Receipt on annual sports		x	
	To Sale of old sports materials		x	
	To Sale of old magazines		x	

Reference Account		Dr.	Cr.
To Affiliation fees		x	
To Sundry receipts		x	
By Annual sports expenses			x
By Salaries and wages			x
By Rent, rates, and taxes			x
By Insurance			x
By Purchase of fixed assets			x
By Annual function expenses			x
By Purchase of sports equipment			x
By Books and periodicals			x
By Magazines			x
By Audit fees			x
By Printing and stationery			x
By Honorarium			x
By Bank charges			x
By Postage and courier expenses			x
By Communication expenses			x
By Water and electricity			x
By Conveyance			x
By Travelling			x
By Repairs and maitenance			x
By Sundry expenses			x
By Investment on fixed deposits			x
By Balance c/d			
Cash			x
Bank			x
Fixed deposits			
To Balance c/d			
Bank overdraft		x	
Total		**0**	**0**

only, while the capital expenditure or receipt is not taken into consideration. All incomes are shown on the right-hand side (income side) and all expenses are shown on the left-hand side (expenses side) of an income and expenditure account (It is the reverse of the receipt and payment account). Exhibit 13.8 indicates the format of an income and expenditure account.

EXHIBIT 13.8   Name of Account: Income and Expenditure Account

Name of Entity: _____

Income and Expenditure Account for the period ending on _____

Type of Account: Income

Date	Reference Account	Post Ref No.	Dr. (Less)	Cr. (Add)
	By Subscription			
	Received			x
	Add: Receivable or outstanding at the end			x
	Less: Advance at the end			x

Add: Advance at the beginning			x
Less: Receivable or outstanding in the beginning			x
By Entrance fees (only the portion that is to be treated as revenue)			x
By Life membership fees (only the portion that is to be treated as revenue)			x
By Profit from annual functions			
Contribution			x
Less: Expenses			x
By Profit from annual sports			
Contribution			x
Less: Expenses			x
By Profit from sale of provisions			
Sales			x
Add: Closing stock			x
Less: Purchases			x
Less: Opening stock			x
By Rent of hall or other infrastructure			x
By Sundry receipts			x
To Salaries and wages			
Paid		x	
Add: Payable at the end, i.e., outstanding		x	
Less: Prepaid at the end		x	
Add: Prepaid in the beginning		x	
To Salaries and wages		x	
To Rent, rates, and taxes		x	
To Insurance		x	
To Depreciation			
On Furniture		x	
On Sports equipment		x	
On Building		x	
To Books or periodicals		x	
To Audit fees		x	
To Printing and stationery		x	
To Honorarium		x	
To Bank charges		x	
To Postage and courier expenses		x	
To Communication expenses		x	
To Water and electricity		x	
To Conveyance		x	
To Travelling		x	
To Repairs and maitenance		x	
To Sundry expenses		x	
To Surplus (Excess of income over expenditure)		x	
OR			
By Deficit (Excess of expenditure over income)			x
Total		**0**	**0**

Balance Sheet

A NPE prepares the balance sheet on the same lines as a trading and manufacturing concern. The balance sheet may be prepared either in the order of liquidity or in the order of permanence. Exhibit 13.9 elaborates the format of a balance sheet of a NPE.

EXHIBIT 13.9 Balance Sheet

Name of Entity: _____

Balance Sheet of _____ as on _____

Particulars	Note	Amount (₹)	Amount (₹)
I. EQUITY AND LIABILITIES			
Funds:			
Capital Fund			
Opening balance		x	
Add: Surplus		x	
Less: Deficit		x	
Add: Entrance fees (to the extent capitalized)		x	
Add: Life membership fees (to the extent capitalized)		x	
Add: Amount of capital transfer from a specific fund			
(for example Building fund)		x	xx
Prize Fund			
Opening balance		x	
Add: Donations for prizes		x	
Add: Income		x	
Less: Expenses		x	xx
Building Fund			
Opening balance		x	
Add: Donations for building		x	
Add: Income		x	
Less: Transfer to capital fund		x	xx
Liabilities:			
Long-term Liabilities			
Borrowing from social or other organizations			xx
Current Liabilities			
Subscription received in advance		x	
Outstanding expenses		x	
Bank overdraft		x	
Creditors for purchases of supplies, etc.		x	xx
Total Equity and Liabilities			xxx
II. ASSETS			
Fixed Assets:			
Building			
Opening balance		x	
Add: Additions		x	
Less: Depreciation		x	xx
Furniture			
Opening balance		x	
Add: Additions		x	
Less: Depreciation		x	
Less: Sales		x	xx
Sports Equipments			
Opening balance		x	
Add: Additions		x	
Less: Depreciation		x	

				X	XX
Investments:					
	Prize funds investments in government securities			X	
	Fixed deposits			X	XX
Current Assets:					
	Sports materials			X	
	Accured interest			X	
	Accrued rent			X	
	Cash at hand			X	
	Cash at bank			X	XX
Total Assets					**XXX**

The capital of a NPE is known as the capital fund. It represents the surplus of assets over liabilities. A capital fund is made up in part by special donations or by capitalizing admission fees, special grants from the government, etc. The surplus on the income and expenditure account results in an increase in the capital fund. It is decreased by any deficit on the income and expenditure account. It is also known as the general fund or the accumulated fund.

■ **ILLUSTRATION 13.26** The receipts and payment account of Kalisto Football Club for the year ended 31 March 2020 was as follows:

Name of Account: Receipt and Payment Account
Type of Account: Asset

Date	Reference Account	Voucher Type	Post Ref No.	Dr. (Add)	Cr. (Less)
	To Balance b/d			48,000	
	Subscription received			2,46,000	
	Interest			2,000	
	Sale of furniture			10,000	
	Donation for club building			60,000	
	By Purchase of balls				80,000
	Tournament fees				10,000
	Affiliation fees				2,000
	Rent of playground				5,000
	Refreshment expenses				4,000
	Travelling expenses				30,000
	Instruments purchased at face value				1,00,000
	Office expenses				8,000
	Salary				12,000
	Balance c/d				1,15,000
	Total			**3,66,000**	**3,66,000**

Prepare the club's income and expenditure account for the year ended 31 March 2020, and the balance sheet as at that date taking the following information into account.

1. The subscriptions received include ₹10,000, of the year 2018–19. Subscriptions for the year 2019–2020 amounting to ₹16,000 is still outstanding from members. Some members have paid subscriptions for the year 2020–2021 amounting to ₹8,000, which is included in the subscriptions received.

2. Interest accrued but not received was ₹500.
3. The book value of the furniture sold was ₹14,000.
4. The rent of the playground of ₹6,000 and a salary of ₹5000 for the year 2019–20 are still outstanding, and a rent of ₹1000 for the playground for the year 2018–19 has been paid during this year.
5. There is a stock of balls with the club worth ₹4000 as on 31 March 2020.

Solution

Income and Expenditure Account of Kalisto Football Club
for the year ended 31 March 2020
Name of Account: Income and Expenditure Account
Type of Account: Income

Date	Reference Account	Post Ref No.	Dr. (Less)	Cr. (Add)
	To Tournament fees		10,000	
	To Affiliation fees		2,000	
	To Balls consumed			
	Purchase	80,000		
	Less: Closing stock	4,000	76,000	
	To Rent of playground	5,000		
	Add: Outstanding for last year	6,000		
		11,000		
	Less: Outstanding for last year	1,000	10,000	
	To Refreshment to players		4,000	
	To Players' travelling expenses		30,000	
	To Salary	12,000		
	Add: Outstanding for current year	5,000	17,000	
	To Office expenses		8,000	
	To Loss on sale of furniture			
	(14,000 – 10,000)		4,000	
	To Surplus			
	(excess of income over expenditure)		85,500	
	By Subscriptions:			
	Received	2,46,000		
	Add: Outstanding for current year	16,000		
	Less: Outstanding for current year	10,000		
	Less: Received in advance for next year	8,000		2,44,000
	By Interest	2,000		
	Add: Interest due but not received	500		2,500
	Total		**2,46,500**	**2,46,500**

Balance Sheet of Kalisto Football Club
as at 31 March 2020

Particulars	Note	Amount (₹)	Amount (₹)
I. EQUITY AND LIABILITIES			
Subscription received in advance			8,000
Outstanding expenses:			
Rent		6,000	
Salary		5,000	
			11,000
Donation for building			60,000
Capital fund:			
Opening balance			
(As per balance sheet as at 1 April 2019)		71,000	
Add: Surplus		85,500	
			1,56,500
Total Equity and Liabilities			**2,35,500**
II. ASSETS			
Cash in hand			1,15,000
Instruments			1,00,000
Interest accrued			500
Subscription outstanding			16,000
Stock of balls			4,000
Total Assets			**2,35,500**

Balance Sheet of Kalisto Football Club
as at 1 April 2019

Particulars	Note	Amount (₹)	Amount (₹)
I. EQUITY AND LIABILITIES			
Outstanding rent for 2018–2019			1,000
Capital fund (balance figure)			71,000
Total Equity and Liabilities			**72,000**
II. ASSETS			
Cash			48,000
Outstanding subscription for 2018–2019			10,000
Furniture			14,000
Total Assets			**72,000**

ACCOUNTING OF EDUCATIONAL INSTITUTIONS

Let us discuss two concepts that come under accounting of educational institutions.

Receipts

A ledger may be maintained for every student separately, and all collections such as tuition fees, admission fees, fine, and annual charges should be credited to the respective student. In addition, details of free studentship concessions and irrecoverable fees should also be noted separately in a columnar form. Periodic reconciliation should be made between fees collected and fees outstanding at the beginning and end of the period. Fees written off, or fee concessions offered to students, such as registers for grant from UGC and other bodies, should be maintained separately. All these are to be brought to the cash book, where the data is maintained in a columnar form.

Payments

In addition to the salary book, separate books and registers must be maintained to show the disbursements, for example, scholarships, stipends, etc. The cash book may be ruled with columns for each head, and collections and payment for each head may be posted in the appropriate column. The monthly total on the cash side should be transferred to a ledger or a monthly abstract account. There may be income from legacies, and dividends and interests from investments.

On the basis of the above records, the receipts and payments account, the income and expenditure account, and the balance sheet are compiled in the usual manner as applicable for a NPE.

ACCOUNTING OF HOSPITALS

Hospitals receive their income from subscriptions, donations, amounts for trusts, patient fees, charges for operations, special treatments and medicines, etc. Separate registers should be maintained for each of these incomes, and the daily total should be taken into account. Adequate control should be exercised over the purchase of food stuff, medicines, and equipments, and on the number and nature of meals and snacks served to the patients. Special control is required over purchase, usage, and storage of surgical equipment, medicines, blood banks, etc. For each and every category of item of income and expense, a separate record should be maintained in such a way that it can be qualitatively controlled. If a college is attached to the hospital, its records should be maintained separately.

ACCOUNTING FOR SERVICE ORGANIZATION

The accounting scheme of a firm will depend on its size and requirements, but the principles of accounting remain the same across all hotels. Hotels may provide a wide range of services such as serving refreshment only or lunch, dinner, and/or lodging in addition to the special catering facilities in or outside for weddings and other special occasions or events. In such cases, all purchases made will have to be recorded separately to ensure adequate control. Expenses may be recorded in a purchase book or a cash book in the appropriate columns with suitable headings. The receipts side will reflect the details of sales, and a detailed visitor's ledger would indicate the details of receipts and payments for each visitor separately. Final accounts are prepared at the end of the period on the basis of the information derived from the records discussed earlier.

FARM ACCOUNTING

In recent years, commercial farming has gained considerable importance, and hence the need for farm accounting. Most of the farms are engaged in composite farming activities. The following illustrative activities are generally covered under farming:

1. Poultry farming
2. Animal husbandry (rearing of live stock)

3. Sericulture (silk worm breeding)
4. Pisciculture (rearing of fish)

As these multifaceted activities are covered under farming, it is necessary to establish a proper and effective accounting. It is essential to record the transactions, compile the final accounts, and analyse the data for farm management.

The transactions are to be recorded either on a single-entry system or a double-entry system. To establish proper control over the activities, analytical columnar records are to be maintained for each activity undertaken. Periodical schedules of inventories of crops, sheep, and poultry supplied seeds, feeds, etc. should be maintained properly. If livestock is kept by the firm for trading purpose, then it is treated as a current asset, otherwise it would be treated as a fixed asset. Livestock may be classified as calves, cows, and bulls.

Depreciation must be provided on all farm machinery, equipment, and buildings. No depreciations are to be provided on land. Land development expenses are treated as cost of land and are capitalized. Land development expenses may include clearing of land, leveling, fencing, and banding to provide irrigation facilities. Drawings apart from cash may comprise dairy products, crops consumed by the family of the farmer, etc.

If inadequate records are maintained, the single-entry method will be followed, wherein an increase or decrease in the net worth is assumed to work out the profit or loss after adjusting drawing and addition of fresh capital. Valuation of assets is usually on a market price basis, whereas land may be valued at the net realizable value. The valuation of farm machinery, equipment, wells, etc. is performed at the original cost less depreciation.

If double-entry accounting is followed, then a single income statement and balance sheet is compiled for the activities in the usual manner with appropriate headings for the various items. The other salient features of farm accounting are as follows:

1. The family provides the labour for the farm in addition to management.
2. Part of the products of the farm is consumed by the family and the livestock.
3. Usually, a family type business and a single-bank account is operated for business and family purposes.
4. There are several divisions on the farm: crops, dairy, cattle rearing poultry, etc. The output of one division may become the input for another division.
5. The business is subject to the vagaries of the monsoons, pests, floods, and other natural calamities.
6. The market price of inputs and outputs are to a large extent controlled by the government.
7. Inventory valuation of crops, cattle, and poultry is difficult due to their short life, susceptibility to disease, and capacity to reproduce. However, the accuracy of the final statement will to a large extent depend on the exactness in the inventory's valuation procedures.

ACCOUNT OF PROFESSIONAL PERSONS

The transactions of most of the professionals such as solicitors, lawyers, doctors, chartered accountants, etc. consist of cash receipts and payments only. They normally do not maintain elaborate accounts as in ordinary commercial concerns as most of their transactions are cash transactions.

It is important for professionals to maintain books of accounts in view of the following points:

1. There must be an accurate record of all money received and paid. The money received on account of clients and the payments on their behalf out of the money so received should be recorded separately from the funds of the firm.
2. There must be a systematic record of the work performed on behalf of clients, from which the bills of costs for claim of reimbursement can be prepared.
3. There must be an equally systematic and reliable record of all expenditure paid or incurred on behalf of the clients or on behalf of the firm.
4. There must be a ledger account of clients, showing the position of the firm with regard to each client separately.

The following types of different books of accounts must be maintained by professionals:

1. Books for recording fees and expenses on behalf of clients:
    1. Bills delivered book
    2. Client's ledger
2. Book for recording disbursements:
    1. Petty cash book (petty disbursements books)
    2. Client's disbursements ledger
    3. Disbursements journals
3. General books:
    1. General cash books
    2. General ledger or nominal ledger

Most professionals maintain their accounts for receipt on cash basis and treat only the actual fees received as income. The logic behind this treatment is that unrealized profit cannot be divided. As per Indian Income Tax Act, 1961, it is provided that professionals are assessed for tax on cash basis also.

■ **ILLUSTRATION 13.27** Following are some of the balances taken from the trial balance of Hassan Traders for the year ended 31 March 2020. Prepare his trading and profit and loss account and also give closing entries.

Particulars	Amount (₹)	Particulars	Amount (₹)
Purchases	12,140	Stock (1/4/2019)	1,420
Sales	29,580	Salaries	3,800
Purchases return	120	Miscellaneous expenses	800
Sales return	170	Insurance	160
Carriage inward	480	Office expenses	390
Carriage outward	790	Discount	280
Railway freight and GST	1,140	Commission received	1,400
Wages	2,620	Goods burnt by fire	1,540
Trade expenses	690	Loss by fire	540

Closing stock on 31 March 2020 is valued at cost price ₹2,300, while its market price is ₹2,100.

Solution

Trading Account of Hassan Traders
for the year ended 31 March 2020

Particulars	Amount (₹)	Amount (₹)
REVENUE		
By Sales	29,580	
Less: Returns	170	
		29,410
Total Revenue		**29,410**
EXPENSES		
To Opening stock		1,420
To Purchases	12,140	
Less: Returns	120	
Less: Goods burnt by fire	1,540	
Less: Closing stock	2,100	8,380
= Cost of Goods Sold		9,800
To Carriage inward		480
To Railway freight and GST		1,140
To Wages		2,620
To Trade expenses		690
Total Expenses		**14,730**
Gross Profit (Total Revenue – Total Expenses)		**14,680**
(Transferred to Profit and Loss A/c)		

Note: The cost price of closing stock is ₹2,300 but its market value is ₹2,100, which is less.

Hence, closing stock is valued at ₹2,100 on the principle of cost or market price, whichever is lower.

Profit and Loss Account of Hassan Traders
for the year ended 31 March 2020

Particulars	Amount (₹)	Amount (₹)
REVENUE		
By Gross profit		14,680
(Transferred from Trading A/c)		
By Commission received		1,400
Total Revenue		**16,080**
EXPENSES		
To Salaries		3,800
To Insurance		160
To Miscellaneous expenses		800
To Discount		280
To Loss by fire		540
To Carriage outward		790
To Office expenses		390
Total Expenses		**6,760**
Net Profit (Total Revenue – Total Expenses)		**9,320**
Transferred to Statement of Retained Earnings		

Closing Entries of Hassan Traders

Date 31 March 2020	Particulars		L.F.	Dr. (₹)	Cr. (₹)
1.	Trading A/c (*Less*)	Dr.		18,660	
	To Opening Stock A/c (*Less*)				1,420
	To Purchase A/c (*Less*)				12,140
	To Sales returns A/c (*Less*)				170
	To Carriage inward A/c (*Less*)				480
	To Trade expenses A/c (*Less*)				690
	To Railway freight and octroi A/c (*Less*)				1,140
	To Wages A/c (*Less*)				2,620
	(Various direct expenses accounts closed and carried to trading A/c at the end of the year.)				
2.	Sales A/c (*Less*)	Dr.		29,580	
	Purchases return A/c (*Less*)	Dr.		120	
	Goods Burnt by fire A/c (*Less*)	Dr.		1,540	
	To Trading A/c (*Add*)				31,240
	(Entry for closing various goods accounts and transferring them to trading A/c)				
3.	Closing Stock A/c (*Add*)	Dr.		2,100	
	To Trading A/c (*Add*)				2,100
	(Closing stock brought into the books of account)				
4.	Trading A/c (*Less*)	Dr.		14,680	
	To Income statement (*Add*)				14,680
	(Gross profit transferred to income statement)				
5.	Income statement (*Less*)	Dr.		6,760	
	To Salaries A/c (*Less*)				3,800
	To Insurance A/c (*Less*)				160
	To Miscellaneous expenses A/c (*Less*)				800
	To Discount A/c (*Less*)				280
	To Loss by fire A/c (*Less*)				540
	To Carriage outward A/c (*Less*)				790
	To Office expenses A/c (*Less*)				390

	(Various expenses accounts closed and carried to income statement)			
6.	Commission A/c (Less)	Dr.	1,400	
	To Income statement (Add)			1,400
	(Commission A/c closed and transferred to income statement)			
7.	Income statement (Less)	Dr.	9,320	
	To Capital A/c (Add)			9,320
	(Net profit carried to capital A/c)			

■ **ILLUSTRATION 13.28** From the following trial balance of Teton Equipment Co., prepare the trading and profit and loss account for the year ended 31 December 2020 and balance sheet as at that date.

Particulars	Dr. (₹)	Particulars	Cr. (₹)
Opening stock (1/1/2020)	17,000	Capital	1,00,000
Purchases	96,100	Creditors	55,600
Wages	7,400	Sales	1,72,000
Carriage inward	5,400	Rent	2,400
Carriage outward	2,000		
Salary	6,000		
Building	80,000		
Furniture	4,600		
Depreciation on furniture	500		
Debtors	81,000		
Insurance premium	1,600		
Printing and stationery	2,500		
Sundry expenses	4,400		
Repairs	1,000		
Cash on hand	12,500		
Drawings	8,000		
	3,30,000		3,30,000

Adjustments:

1. Value of closing stock was ₹7,600.
2. ₹1,200 was outstanding for salaries.
3. Depreciate building by 5% p.a.
4. Insurance paid in advance ₹100.
5. Buildings rent received in advance amounted to ₹300.

Solution

Trading Account of Teton Equipment Co.
for the year ended 31 March 2020

Particulars	Amount (₹)	Amount (₹)
REVENUE		
By Sales		1,72,000
Total Revenue		**1,72,000**
EXPENSES		
To Opening stock (1/1/2020)		17,000
To Purchases	96,100	
Less: Closing stock	7,600	88,500
= Cost of Goods Sold		1,05,500
To Wages		7,400
To Carriage inward		5,400
Total Expenses		**1,18,300**
Gross Profit (Total Revenue – Total Expenses)		**53,700**
(Transferred to Profit and Loss A/c)		

Profit and Loss Account of Teton Equipment Co.
for the year ended 31 December 2020

Particulars	Amount (₹)	Amount (₹)
REVENUE		
By Gross profit		
(Bought from Trading A/c)		53,700
By Rent	2,400	
Less: Received in advance	300	
		2,100
Total Revenue		**55,800**
EXPENSES		
To Salaries	6,000	
Add: Unpaid	1,200	
		7,200
To Carriage outward		2,000
To Depreciation on furniture		500
To Depreciation on building		4,000
To Insurance premium	1,600	
Less: Prepaid	100	
		1,500
To Printing and stationery		2,500
To Sundry expenses		4,400
To Repairs		1,000
Total Expenses		**23,100**
Net Profit (Total Revenue – Total Expenses)		**32,700**
Transferred to Capital Account		

Balance Sheet of Teton Equipment Co.
as at 31 December 2020

Particulars	Note	Amount (₹)	Amount (₹)
I. EQUITY AND LIABILITIES			
Capital		1,00,000	
Add: Net profit		32,700	
		1,32,700	
Less: Drawings		8,000	
			1,24,700
Creditors			55,600
Unpaid salary			1,200
Rent received in advance			300
Total Equity and Liability			**1,81,800**
II. ASSETS			
Building		80,000	
Less: Depreciation at 5% p.a.		4,000	
			76,000

Furniture			4,600
Closing stock			7,600
Sundry debtors			81,000
Cash on hand			12,500
Prepaid insurance premium			100
Total Assets			**1,81,800**

Notes:

1. Depreciation on furniture is given in the trial balance, which suggests that depreciation has already been written off the asset. Hence, it has not been deducted from furniture in the balance sheet. Only one effect of depreciation is given on the debit side of the income statement.

2. Depreciation on building will have two effects in final accounts, as it is given in the adjustments.

■ **ILLUSTRATION 13.29** From the following transactions of The O'Seven Club, prepare its receipts and payments account for the year ended 31 March 2020.

Cash on hand (1/4/2019) ₹1,500; cash at bank (1/4/2019) ₹16,000; Receipts: Subscription ₹75,000; entrance fees ₹4,000; donation for prizes ₹6,500; ground rent ₹15,000; sale of old newspapers ₹1,000, sale of furniture ₹4,250.

Payments: Expenses of 2018–2019 ₹5,000; 2019–2020 ₹20,000; Rate and taxes ₹1,500; billiard table purchases ₹16,000; books purchased ₹14,000; repairs ₹3,000; new telephone connection deposit ₹12,000; salaries ₹14,250. Cash at bank (31/3/2020) ₹35,000.

Solution

Name of Account: Receipt and Payments Account of The O'Seven Club
Type of Account: Asset

Date	Reference Account	Voucher Type	Post Ref No.	Dr. (Add)	Cr. (Less)
	To Cash on hand b/d			1,500	
	To Cash at bank b/d			16,000	
	To Subscriptions			75,000	
	To Donations			6,500	
	To Entrance fees			4,000	
	To Ground rent			15,000	
	To Sale of old newspapers			1,000	
	To Sale of furniture			4,250	
	By Expenses:				
	2018–2019	5,000			
	2019–2020	20,000			
					25,000
	By Rates and taxes				1,500
	By Purchases of billiard table				16,000
	By Books purchased				14,000
	By Repairs				3,000
	By New telephone connection deposit				12,000
	By Salaries				14,250
	By Cash at bank c/d				35,000
	By Cash on hand c/d				2,500
	Total			1,23,250	1,23,250

■ **ILLUSTRATION 13.30** From the receipts and payments account of Sudhanshu Gymkhana for the year 2020, prepare income and expenditure account for the year ended 31 December 2020.

Name of Account: Receipt and Payments Account of Sudhanshu Gymkhana
Type of Account: Income

Date	Reference Account	Voucher Type	Post Ref No.	Dr. (Add)	Cr. (Less)
	To Balance			2,416	
	To Interest			624	
	To Subscription			8,740	
	To Rent			540	
	To Entrance fees			2,400	
	To Sale of old newspapers			128	
	To Sale of old furniture			420	
	To Receipts from lectures			732	
	By Purchase of a bicycle				424
	By Rates and taxes				496
	By Printing and stationery				1,508
	By Subscription on newspapers				2,694
	By Expenses				1,882
	By Salaries				2,400
	By Investments				4,770
	By Payment to creditors of the previous year				1,508
	By Balance				318
	Total			16,000	16,000

Subscription for newspapers paid in 2020 includes ₹250 for 2019. ₹464 is outstanding for salaries. Subscription received includes ₹500 for 2021 and ₹200 for 2019.

Provide depreciation of ₹300 on books and ₹250 on building. Half of the entrance fees is to be capitalized.

Solution

Name of Account: Income and Expenditure Account of Sudhanshu Gymkhana
for the year ended 31 December 2020

Date	Reference Account	Voucher Type	Post Ref No.	Dr. (Less)	Cr. (Add)
	To Rates and taxes			496	
	To Printing and stationery			1,508	
	To Subscription for newspapers	2,694			
	Less: For 2019	250			
				2,444	
	To Expenses			1,882	
	To Salaries	2,400			
	Add: Outstanding	464			
				2,864	
	To Depreciation				
	Books	300			
	Building	250			
				550	
	By Interest				624
	By Subscription	8,740			
	Less: For 2021	500			

Particulars		Amount	Amount
For 2019	200		
			8,040
By Rent			540
By Entrence fees (1/2)			1,200
By Sale of old newspapers			128
By Receipts from lectures			732
To Excess of income over expenditure		1,520	
Total		**11,264**	**11,264**

Notes:

1. Opening and closing balances of cash will not be shown in the income and expenditure account.
2. Sale of old furniture is a capital receipt and has not been shown in this account. Half the entrance fees is capitalized, hence only half the amount has been credited to the income and expenditure account.
3. Purchase of a bicycle and investments are capital expenses and hence have been excluded from this account. They will be shown in the balance sheet.
4. Payment made to creditors of last year will not be shown in the income and expenditure account of the current year.

■ **ILLUSTRATION 13.31** Mr Suketu, a solicitor, has furnished to you the following particulars regarding his practice for the financial year ended 30 September 2020.

	Amount (₹)
Fees (profit costs) charged to clients	36,000
Office: Rent	3,000
Office: Salaries	9,000
Own capital	20,000
Drawing for household expenses	8,000
Advance received from clients on account of pending matters	6,000
Office expenses	9,100
Furniture and library	9,000
Due from clients in respect of profit costs	8,000
Disbursements made on behalf of clients	3,000
Sundry creditors	350
Bank balance (clients' account)	5,000
Bank balance (office account)	8,250

Prepare his trading and profit and loss account and balance sheet after considering the following points:

1. An amount of ₹100 being sundry petty expenses incurred on behalf of clients is included in 'Office expenses'.
2. A sum of ₹50 which was received from a client against disbursement made on his behalf has been included in 'Advance received from clients'.

Solution

Trading and Profit and Loss Account of Mr Suketu
for the year ended 30 September 2020

Particulars	Amount (₹)	Amount (₹)
REVENUE		
By Fees (profit cost) charged to clients received	28,000	
Add: Not received	8,000	
		36,000
Total Revenue		**36,000**
EXPENSES		
To Office rent		3,000
To Office salaries		9,000
To Office expenses	9,100	
Less: Disbursement on behalf of clients	100	
		9,000
To Reserve for fees not received		8,000
Total Expenses		**29,000**
Net Profit (Total Revenue – Total Expenses)		**7,000**
Transferred to Capital Account		

Balance Sheet of Mr Suketu
as at 30 September 2020

Particulars	Note	Amount (₹)	Amount (₹)
I. EQUITY AND LIABILITIES			
Capital:		20,000	
Add: Profit		7,000	
		27,000	
Less: Drawings		8,000	
			19,000
Reserve for fees not received			8,000
Sundry creditors			350
Advance received from clients		6,000	
Less: Transferred to disbursement		50	
			5,950
Total Equity and Liabilities			**33,300**
II. ASSETS			
Furniture and library			9,000
Due from clients			8,000
Sundry disbursements made on behalf of clients		3,000	
Add: Additional		100	
		3,100	
Less: Received for sundry expenses		50	
			3,050
Bank balance: Clients			5,000
Bank balance: Office			8,250
Total Assets			**33,300**

Notes:

1. Solicitors prepare their accounts on cash basis. Hence, the problem has been worked out accordingly. Credit is taken only for fees received. When they credit fees not received to their income statement, they create a reserve of equal amount. Therefore, a reserve of ₹8,000 has been created here as the amount it still not received from clients.
2. Disbursements made on behalf of clients are receivable from them and so they appear on the asset side.

3. As sundry expenses incurred on behalf of clients are included in office expenses, they have been deducted from office expenses and added to 'Disbursement on behalf of clients'.

4. Similarly, ₹50 received from a client against disbursements has been wrongly included in 'Advances received from clients'. The same should be deducted from amount receivable from clients' on account of disbursements made on their behalf because the dues from clients on account of disbursements are reduced to that extent. Similarly, it should be deducted from 'Advances from clients' as it is wrongly included in it.

Summary

- The two main activities, namely manufacturing and trading are evaluated separately by the preparation of a manufacturing account and a trading account. The manufacturing account discloses the cost of manufacturing the finished goods from the raw materials, which is transferred to the trading account. The trading account discloses the gross trading results. The income statement reveals the final net profit or loss made by the firm during the year from all its activities.

- Revenue received in advance of the accounting period would be treated as an increase in liabilities (credit) and entitled as unearned revenue, revenue collected in advance, or income received in advance.

- When the payment made by a firm for expenses would benefit more than one accounting period or year, then the portion of the expense for which the benefit will be available in future, that is, in the next accounting period, is known as prepaid expenses or prepayments.

- Goods or cash withdrawn by the owner of a firm or the partners in a partnership firm for their personal use or household expenses meet up in addition to a few personal investment purposes.

- Losses incurred on account of accidental events will be recorded under two categories: goods or property not insured and goods or property insured. Loss of uninsured goods by fire will be shown as a reduction in the purchase value. The amount of claim accepted by the insurance company would be treated as future benefits receivable; hence, a new asset type account named as 'Insurance company account' would be created, and its balance would be increased (insurance company account will be debited). The difference between the total value of loss and the amount of claim accepted by the insurance company would be treated as a loss for the firm.

- To encourage middlemen to garner more business, or sometimes to maintain a cordial and long-term relationship with the present customers, it is a normal practice to distribute business goods among the parties in the form of free samples.

- Adjustment entries are passed for the commission payable to commission agents for the support provided to smoothen the firm's activities as per the agreement entered into with them. Commission agents for the sales are affected through their business or sale of the firm's goods, commodities, and merchandise.

- Four types of adjustments are needed at the end of the accounting period, prior to the preparation of financial statements.

- Closing journal entries are needed for preparing the income statement.

- In order to prevent errors and to facilitate the preparation of the financial statement, a worksheet is prepared. It incorporates all balances of the trial balance, the necessary adjustments to be made therein, and shows separately the items relating to the income statement and the balance sheet.

- Manufacturers prepare a manufacturing account in addition to a trading and profit and loss account.

- The manufacturing account indicates the cost of production; the trading account indicates the gross profit; and the income statement indicates the net profit of the firm.

- The preparation of the balance sheet is related to the reporting of the financial position of an entity at particular point of time. It is the snapshot of the financial position of a business entity.

Keywords

Balance sheet It relates to the reporting of the financial position of an entity at a particular point of time. It is also known as the position statement.

Retained earnings The residual amount, after income tax and dividends, provided in the income statement.

Worksheet It is large columnar statement specially designed to organize and arrange accounting data required at the end of the accounting period.

Questions

I. Choose the right answer from the following options.

1. The balance sheet gives information regarding
   (a) Results of operations for a particular period
   (b) The financial position as on a particular date
   (c) The operating efficiency of the firm
   (d) Financial position during a particular period

2. The item 'closing inventory' is shown in balance sheet as
   (a) Fixed assets   (b) Current assets
   (c) Current liabilities   (d) Miscellaneous expenditure

3. Net assets are
   (a) Total assets minus total liabilities
   (b) Total assets minus current liabilities
   (c) Total assets minus capital
   (d) Fixed assets plus current assets

4. Sundry debtors are
   (a) Parties who owe money to the firm
   (b) Parties to whom the firm owns money
   (c) Parties who have supplied goods to the firm

(d) Parties who have failed to pay the money owed by them to the firm

5. Capital is shown under liabilities because of the
   (a) Entity concept
   (b) Accrual concept
   (c) Dual aspect
   (d) Going-concern concept

6. A bad debt is
   (a) A large sum of money owed
   (b) A debt incurred by employees
   (c) A debt owed by one trader to another
   (d) Amount unrealized from debtors

7. Which of the following is true
   (a) Assets + Equity = Liabilities
   (b) Assets – Liability = Owner's Fund
   (c) Liabilities to Outsiders + Reserve = Equity
   (d) Assets + Reserve = Equity

8. Bad debts are written off by
   (a) Debiting the debtor's account and crediting bad debts account
   (b) Crediting the debtor's account and debiting bad debts account
   (c) Debiting the provision for bad debts account and crediting the debtor's account

9. Fixed assets are held for the purpose of
   (a) Use in the operation of the business
   (b) Resale
   (c) Conversion into cash
   (d) Getting loan by mortgage

10. At the end of a financial year, the entries made regarding bad debts are
    (a) Debit the debtor's account, credit provision for bad debts account
    (b) Credit the debtor's account, debit provision for bad debts account
    (c) Debit the income statement, credit bad debts account
    (d) Credit the income statement, debit the bad debts account

11. The various amounts owned by an enterprise are called
    (a) Assets
    (b) Liabilities
    (c) Income
    (d) Expenses

12. Provision for bad debts is made to
    (a) Prevent debts arising
    (b) Obtain a debtor's figure for the balance sheet
    (c) Even out actual bad debts incurring
    (d) Encourage prompt payment of debts by debtors

13. Accounting policies may differ from one firm to another firm with respect to one of the following
    (a) Deciding credit and debit assets of transactions
    (b) Classification of assets and liabilities
    (c) Classification of revenue and expense
    (d) Classification of revenue and capital expenditure

14. The provision for bad debts account represents
    (a) Some of the profit
    (b) Some of the credit withheld
    (c) The total of actual bad debts
    (d) The total amount owing to the business

15. A balance sheet is
    (a) A trial balance
    (b) A trading account
    (c) A statement showing the distribution of profit
    (d) A statement of assets and liabilities as on a particular date

16. In the balance sheet, provision for bad debts is shown as
    (a) Deduction from debtors
    (b) Deduction from capital
    (c) Addition to current liabilities
    (d) Deduction from fixed assets

17. Which one of the following is a fixed asset
    (a) Stock
    (b) Motor vehicles
    (c) Capital
    (d) Creditors

18. Provision for bad debts is made by
    (a) Debiting the provision for the bad debts account, crediting the debtor's account
    (b) Crediting the provision for the bad debts account, debiting the debtor's account
    (c) Debiting the provision for the bad debts account, crediting the income statement
    (d) Crediting the provision for the bad debts account, debiting the income statement

19. On a balance sheet, the fixed assets are included at
    (a) Cost price less depreciation
    (b) Book value
    (c) Selling price
    (d) Replacement value

20. Which one of the following statements is not correct
    (a) The provision for bad debts account is owned to the proprietor
    (b) Bad debts could exceed the provision for bad debts
    (c) Bad debts could be less than the provision for bad debts
    (d) Provision for bad debts appears as a liability on the balance sheet

21. If actual bad debts are less than the sum set aside then
    (a) There will be a credit balance on the provision for bad debts account
    (b) There will be a debit balance on the provision for bad debts account
    (c) There will be a credit balance on the bad debts account
    (d) There will be a debit balance on the bad debts account

22. Sumati has a capital of ₹6,000 on 31 December 2020. During the year, she has made a profit of ₹2,400. If her drawings had amounted to ₹1,800, her capital on 1 January 2020 was
    (a) ₹7,200
    (b) ₹5,400
    (c) ₹3,600
    (d) ₹1,800

23. Which one of the following is a current liability
    (a) Sundry debtors
    (b) Sundry creditors
    (c) Five years bank loan
    (d) Rent prepayment

II. Fill in the blanks with appropriate word(s).

1. _____ account shows money or money's worth contributed by the proprietor to the business.

2. What is owned by a business to another is known as its _____.

3. The balance sheet is _____ and not _____.

4. All expenses incurred by the proprietor which are not related to business are treated as _____.

5. Excess debit over credit in the trading account represents a _____.

6. The liability of a business _____ when it makes a profit.

7. The balance sheet is a _____ of the assets, liabilities, and capital of a concern as on a particular date.

8. Properties and possessions of a business are termed as _____ of the business.

9. Carriage inwards account is transferred to the _____ account, whereas carriage outwards account is transferred to the _____ account.

10. Amounts irrecoverable are _____ by transferring them from the respective receivables account to the _____ account.

11. An expenses payable account will show a _____ balance and will be shown on the _____ side of the balance sheet.

12. Prepaid expenses appearing in the trial balance will appear in _____.

13. A gross profit is transferred to the _____ side of the income statement.

14. An estimate of future bad debts is known as a _____.
15. A debit balance in the suspense account will appear on the _____ side of the balance sheet.
16. Bills payable are classified as _____.
17. If the opening and closing stock is ₹20,000 each, purchases are ₹50,000, manufacturing expenses are ₹10,000, and sales ₹90,000, the gross profit will be _____.
18. Bad debts written off during the year are transferred at the end of the year to the _____ account or in the absence of it to the _____ account.
19. Capital is the excess of _____ over _____.
20. Changing the accounting policy to show a rosy picture is called _____.
21. If the gross profit is ₹11,000, administrative expenses are ₹3,000, and miscellaneous income is ₹700, the net profit will be _____.
22. The provision for bad debts as well as the provision for discount on debtors are _____ from accounts receivable in the balance sheet.
23. The capital of a firm whose assets are ₹53,000 and liabilities are ₹19,000 is ₹_____.
24. A balance sheet is a statement of what an enterprise _____ and what it _____ at a particular date.
25. An income received in advance will be _____ the respective income's account, whereas an income receivable is _____.
26. At the end of the year, the discount allowed account is transferred to the _____ account, whereas the discount earned account is transferred to the _____ account, when provisions are maintained.
27. Amount of _____ is deducted from the value of respective assets in the balance sheet.
28. _____ include cash and assets which can be normally converted into cash during the operating cycle of the business.
29. Excess credit over debit in the income statement indicates _____.
30. In the absence of provision regarding future discounts allowed and earned, the discounts allowed account and discounts earned account at the end of the current year are to be transferred to the _____ and _____ sides respectively of the _____ account.
31. The assets are ₹49,000 and the liabilities are ₹18,000. The total of the liabilities side of the balance sheet will be _____.
32. Fixed assets represent the employment of money on a _____ basis.
33. Net profit/loss is transferred to the _____ account.
34. If the total of discounts allowed during the year plus the new provision for discount on debtors exceeds the old provision for discounts and debtors, then the difference between the two will appear on the _____ side of the income statement.
35. The capital of a proprietor _____ when it makes a profit.
36. Assets are usually listed on a balance sheet under two main groups namely _____ and _____.

III. Giving reasons, state whether the following statements are True or False.

1. Profit on sale of a machine will appear on the credit side of the machinery account.
2. All accounts are closed by transferring them either to the trading account or to the income statement.
3. Reducing balance method of depreciation is best suited for assets with a long working life.
4. Provision for doubtful debts represents the amount that cannot be collected.
5. The opening entry is posted on the respective account as 'To/By balance b/d'.
6. Reserve for doubtful debts account always has a credit balance.
7. Adjustment entries are made at the time of closing the business everyday.
8. All rectification entries are passed through the journal proper.
9. Provision for future bad debts and discounts reduce the correctness of profit or loss, as they are only estimates.
10. Drawings by the proprietor should be debited to the income statement.
11. Depreciation is a measure of the exact loss in the intrinsic value of an asset.
12. Provision for discount to debtors can be estimated only after computing the provision for doubtful debts.
13. Carriage inwards is an expense and carriage outwards is an income.
14. A well-maintained asset need not be depreciated.
15. Each partner's liabilities are limited to the extent of his/her capital contribution.
16. Return outwards are nothing but sales return.
17. All assets must be depreciated at the end of the year.
18. Partners' salaries are debited to the income statement and credited to their respective personal account.
19. The income statement summarizes the company's operations, and profit or loss.
20. Goodwill is never depreciated.
21. Interest on drawing charged to the partners increases the profit available for distribution to the partner.
22. Cash balance in hand shows whether the business has earned profit or loss.
23. Appreciation of the market value of assets must be taken into account if the correct profit of the year is to be determined.
24. The current account is maintained only on the fixed system of capital account.
25. Free samples received are business gains.
26. The amount of depreciation remains constant over the years in the original cost method of depreciation.
27. The distinction between capital and revenue items is important because it is of fundamental importance to the determination of profit.
28. If trading assets are exchanged for non-trading assets, then the entry will be recorded in the journal proper.
29. The written down value of an asset calculated using the reducing balance method can never become zero.
30. Interest paid on borrowings is a capital expenditure.
31. When a bad debt is written off, the loss from it is equal to the profit expected from the particular business transaction with the debtors.
32. The value of an asset reduces faster in the reducing balance method than in other methods.
33. Capital expenditure should be shown in the books by debiting the assets account and crediting the supplier or cash account.
34. Goods lost due to fire need not be accounted for since they have not been sold.
35. If a motor car is given for repair for three months in a year, depreciation should be charged for only nine months at the end of the year.
36. Furniture and fittings are classified as capital expenditure.
37. Adjusting entries are necessary only when the mercantile system of accounting is followed.
38. Depreciation should be charged in the first year on the landed cost of the asset.
39. A forklift truck purchased by a business is considered as a capital expenditure.
40. In the cash system of accounting, all pre-received revenues are current gains.
41. Nominal accounts fall within the category of impersonal accounts.
42. Depreciation appears in the income statement.
43. Petty cash is an expense.

44. The double-entry rules for nominal account is—debit all expenses and gains, and credit all incomes and losses.
45. Gross profit is transferred to the income statement.
46. Provision for doubtful debts is added to sundry debtor's balance in the balance sheet.
47. Bad receivables appearing in the trial balance must be deducted from accounts receivable in the balance sheet.
48. A narration may not be written for entries that occur frequently.
49. Closing stock given in the trial balance is to be credited to the trading account.
50. Some adjustments made to the final accounts may only have a single effect.
51. Any number of entries can be combined, provided only that they occur on the same day.
52. Balance sheet is a position statement.
53. If capital account is debited with ₹300 as drawings over the year and reflects a net credit increase of ₹500, the net profit of the concern for the year transferred to the capital account is ₹1,800.
54. The purchase of goods-in-trade and its subsequent resale (for profit) on the same day can be conveniently combined.
55. Assets that are meant to be converted into cash as soon as possible are termed as current assets.
56. Final account can be prepared only after the suspense account becomes nil.
57. The capital account is a record of the proprietor's investment in his/her business including amounts borrowed as a business loan for supplementing the investment.
58. Withdrawal of money or money's worth by the proprietor is reflected in the drawings account.
59. A capital expenditure, though it involves an outgo of cash, does not appear in the income statement.
60. Preparation of the trading account precedes the drawing up of the income statement.
61. Capital expenditure means expenditure incurred for the owners of the business.
62. Amounts due from customers are shown collectively in the balance sheet.
63. Carriage outwards account does not appear in the trading account.
64. The profit made by the assets and liabilities, and the debtors and creditors of the business can be fairly determined.
65. A net profit is a liability to the concern.
66. The expenses incurred in carriage for transporting the raw materials to the factory for production and finally delivering the finished goods to the buyers are transferred to the trading account.
67. The giver of a benefit must be debited.

IV. Elaborate the effect as required.

Explain the following adjustments with an entry for each of them.
1. Outstanding income (income receivable).
2. Outstanding expenses (expenses payable).
3. Income received in advance.
4. Expenses paid in advance (prepaid expenses).
5. Bad debts and provision for doubtful debts.
6. Reserve for discount on debtors and creditors.
7. Depreciation.
8. Closing stock.
9. Goods withdrawn by proprietor/partner.
10. Goods distributed as free samples.
11. Goods destroyed by fire/accident/flood/theft, etc.
12. Goods sent on 'sale or return basis.'
13. Sale of assets considered as sale of goods.
14. Interest, salary to proprietor/partner.
15. Interest on drawings.

V. Solve the following problems.

1. From the following balance extracted from the books of M/s Shruti & Trupti Co., prepare the necessary closing entries, a trading and profit loss account, and a balance sheet.

Particulars	Amount (₹)	Particulars	Amount (₹)
Opening stock	1,250	Plant and machinery	6,230
Sales	11,800	Return outwards	1,380
Depreciation	667	Cash in hand	835
Commission Cr.	211	Salaries	750
Insurance	380	Debtors	1,905
Carriage inwards	300	Discount Dr.	328
Furniture	670	Bills receivable	2,730
Printing charges	481	Wages	1,589
Carriage outwards	200	Return inwards	1,659
Capital	9,228	Bank overdraft	4,000
Creditors	1,780	Purchases	8,679
Bills payable	541	Petty cash in hand	47
		Bad debts	180

The value of stock on 31 December 2020 was ₹3,700.

2. From the following trial balance, prepare the manufacturing account, the trading and profit and loss account for the year ended 31 March 2020, and the balance sheet as at that date.

Particulars	Dr. (₹)	Cr. (₹)
Capital account		41,000
Drawing account	6,100	
Loan account		4,000
Sundry creditors		45,000
Cash in hand	250	
Cash at bank	4,000	
Sundry debtors	40,500	
Patents	2,000	
Plant and machinery	20,000	
Land and buildings	26,000	
Purchases of raw materials	35,000	
Raw materials 1/4/2012	3,500	
Work in process 1/4/2012	2,000	
Finished stock 1/4/2012	18,000	
Carriage inwards	1,100	
Wages	27,000	
Salary of works manager	5,600	
Factory expenses	3,400	
Factory rent and taxes	2,500	
Royalties (Paid on sales)	1,200	
Sales (*Less*: Returns)		1,23,400
Advertising	3,000	
Office rent and insurance	4,800	
Printing and stationery	1,000	
Office expenses	5,800	
Carriage outwards	600	
Discounts	1,400	2,100
Bad debts	750	
Total	**2,15,500**	**2,15,500**

The stock on 31 March 2020 was as follows—raw materials worth ₹4,000; work-in-progress amounted to ₹4,500; and finished goods amounted to ₹28,000.

3. The following balances were extracted from the books of Mr Ash on 31 March 2020. Prepare the trading account for the year ended 31 March 2020.

Particulars	Amount (₹)	Particulars	Amount (₹)
Opening stock	40,000	Power and fuel	6,000
Purchases	1,80,000	Octroi	11,000
Carriage	4,000	Freight	8,000
Wages	42,000	Sales	3,20,000
Returns outwards	7,000	Sales returns	10,000

Additional Information:

Closing stock on 31 March 2020 amounted to ₹60,000.

4. From the following figures, prepare the trading and profit and loss account of Mr Aamir for the year ended 31 March 2020.

Particulars	Dr. (₹)	Particulars	Cr. (₹)
Salaries and wages	10,000	Income tax paid	5,000
Commission paid	1,000	Advertising	11,000
Postage and telegram	500	Discount allowed	500
Fire insurance premium	2,000	Rent received	3,000
Life insurance premium	4,000	Interest on investments	4,000
Interest paid	1,000	Depreciation on assets	9,000
Carriage outwards	3,000	Bad debts	2,000

The gross profit was 40% of sales, which amounted to ₹1,80,000.

5. The following is the trial balance of Jiyansh Ltd as on 31 March 2020.

Particulars	Dr. (₹)	Particulars	Cr. (₹)
Cash in hand	540	Patents	7,500
Cash at bank	2,630	Salaries	15,000
Purchases	40,675	Sundry expenses	3,000
Return inwards	680	Insurance	600
Wages	10,480	Drawings	5,245
Fuel and power	4,730	Debtors	14,500
Carriage outwards	3,200	Credit balances:	
Carriage inwards	2,040	Sales	98,780
Opening stock	5,760	Return outward	500
Premises	30,000	Ashok's capital	71,000
Land	10,000	Creditors	6,300
Machinery	20,000		

Taking into consideration the following adjustments, prepare trading and profit and loss account, and a balance sheet as at 31 March 2020.

1. Closing stock as on 31 March 2020, ₹5,800.
2. Depreciate machinery and patents by 10% p.a. and 20% p.a. respectively.
3. Salaries due for the month of March amounted to ₹1,500.
4. The insurance policy expired on 30 September 2020.
5. ₹2,000 spent on installation of a shed were included in the wages account.
6. Provide 5% for doubtful debts.
7. A fire occurred on 25 March 2020 in the godown and stock valued at ₹1,000 was destroyed. It was fully insured and the insurance company admitted the claim in full.
8. ₹2,000 is to be transferred to reserve fund out of profits, if any.

6. From the following particulars, prepare the trading and profit and loss account of Lila Ltd for the year ended 31 March 2020, and a balance sheet as at that date.

Particulars	Dr. (₹)	Cr. (₹)
Building	5,00,000	
Machineries	2,00,000	
Furniture	1,00,000	
Cash at bank	90,000	
Cash in hand	10,000	
18% p.a. loan obtained by Lila Ltd on 1/6/2019 on mortgage of his building		3,00,000
Lila Ltd's capital		5,20,000
Sundry debtors/sundry creditors	5,00,000	4,00,000
Stock on 1/4/2019	1,20,000	
Purchases/sales	25,00,000	32,20,000
Sales returns/purchases returns	1,20,000	1,00,000
Rent	60,000	
Establishment expenses	1,80,000	
Electricity charges	15,000	
Telephone charges	10,000	
Commission on sales	30,000	
Insurance premium	10,000	
Bad debts	20,000	
Bills receivable	75,000	
	45,40,000	45,40,000

1. You are required to provide for depreciation on building at 5% p.a.; on machineries at 25% p.a.; and on furniture at 10% p.a.
2. Provision for bad and doubtful debts is to be made at 5% on sundry debtors.
3. Lila Ltd's manager is entitled to a commission of 10% on the net profit after charging his commission.
4. Closing stock was not taken on 31/3/2020 but on 7/4/2020.
5. Following transactions had taken place during the period from 1/4/2020 to 7/4/2020—Sales ₹2,50,000, purchases ₹1,50,000, stock on 7/4/2020 was ₹1,80,000, and the rate of gross profit on sales was 20%.
6. Insurance premium mentioned in the trial balance was for building and machineries.
7. Interest on mortgage loan is to be provided up to 31/3/2020.

7. From the following particulars furnished by Ajatashatru Limited, prepare the balance sheet as at 31 March 2020 as required by Schedule III of the Companies Act, 2013.

Particulars			Debit (₹)	Credit (₹)
Equity capital (Face value of ₹100)			-	10,00,000
Calls in arrears			1,000	
Land			2,00,000	
Building			3,50,000	
Plant and machinery			5,25,000	
Furniture			50,000	
General reserve				2,10,000
Loan fron State Financial Corporation				1,50,000
Stock:	Finished Goods	2,00,000		
	Raw Materials	50,000	2,50,000	
Provision for taxation				68,000
Sundry debtors			2,00,000	
Advances (Short term)			42,700	
Proposed dividend				60,000
Profit & loss account				1,00,000
Cash balance			30,000	
Cash at bank			2,47,000	
Preliminary expenses			13,300	
Loans (Unsecured)				1,21,000

	Debit	Credit
Sundry creditors (For goods and expenses)		2,00,000
Total	**19,09,000**	**19,09,000**

The following additional information is also provided:
1. 2,000 equity shares were issued for consideration other than cash.
2. Debtors of ₹52,000 are due for more than six months.
3. Cost of assets were as under:
   a) Building ₹4,00,000
   b) Plant and machinery ₹7,00,000 and
   c) Furniture ₹62,500
4. The balance of ₹1,50,000 in the loan account with State Finance Corporation, which is secured by Hypothecation of Plant & Machinery, includes ₹7,500 interest accrued.
5. Bills receivable for ₹2,75,000 maturing on 30th June 2020 have been discounted.
6. The company had contract for the erection of machinery of ₹1,50,000, which is still incomplete.
8. The authorised capital of Xiomaa Ltd is ₹5,00,000 consisting of 2,000 6% preference shares and 30,000 equity shares of ₹10 each. The following was the trial balance of the company as on 31 March 2020:

Particulars	Debit (₹)	Credit (₹)
Investment in share at cost	50,000	
Purchases	4,90,500	
Selling expenses	79,100	
Stock as at the beginning of the year	1,45,200	
Salaries and wages	52,000	
Cash on hand	12,000	
Interim preference dividend for the half year to 30 September 2019	6,000	
Discount on issue of debentures	2,000	
Preliminary expenses	1,000	
Bills receivable	41,500	
Interest on bank overdraft	7,800	
Interest on debentures upto 30.9.2019	3,750	
Sundry debtors and creditors	50,100	87,850
Freehold property at cost	3,50,000	
Furniture at cost less depreciation of ₹15,000	35,000	
6% Preference share capital		2,00,000
Equity share capital fully paid up		2,00,000
5% Mortgage debenture secured on freehold properties		1,50,000
Income tax paid in advance for the current year	10,000	
Dividends		4,250
Profit and loss A/c (Opening balance)		28,500
Sales (Net)		6,70,350
Bank overdraft secured by hypothecation of stock and receivables		1,50,000
Technical knowhow fees at cost paid during the year	150,000	
Audit fees	5,000	
Total	**14,90,950**	**14,90,950**

You are required to prepare the profit and loss statement for the year ended 31 March 2020 and balance sheet (as per Schedule III) as on that date after taking into account the following:
1. Closing stock was valued at ₹1,42,500.
2. Purchases include ₹5,000 worth of goods and articles distributed among valued customer.
3. Salaries and wages include ₹2,000 being wages incurred for installation of electrical fitting which were recorded in furniture.
4. Bills receivable include ₹1,500 being dishonoured bills, 50% of which had been considered irrecoverable.
5. Bills receivable of ₹2,000 maturing after 31st March were discounted.
6. Depreciation on furniture to be charged at 10% on written down value.
7. ₹1,000 of discount on issue of debenture is to be written off.
8. Interest on debentures for the half year ending on 31st March was due on that date.
9. Make provision for taxation of ₹4,000.
10. Technical knowhow fees is to be written off over a period of 10 years. Preliminary expenses are to be written off.
11. Salaries and wages include ₹10,000 being director's remuneration.
12. Sundry debtors include ₹6,000 debts due for more than six months.

9. From the following balances extracted from the ledger of Krishna Lal, prepare his trading account for the year ended 31 March 2020.

Particulars	Dr. (₹)	Particulars	Cr. (₹)
Stock (1/4/2019)	12,000	Purchases returns	260
Purchases	28,000	Sales returns	1,200
Sales	42,000	Carriage inward	540
Railway freight	400	Wages	860
GST	760		

Closing stock on 31 March 2020 is valued at ₹8,250.

10. From the following balances of Laxmi Engineering Works, prepare manufacturing account and trading account for the year ended 31 December 2020.

Particulars	Amount (₹)	Particulars	Amount (₹)
Opening Stock:		Wages	6,400
Raw Materials	17,000	Factory rent	3,800
Work-in-progress	8,000	Factory insurance	900
Finished goods	12,000	Coal and electricity	1,600
Purchases:		Manufacturing packing expenses	500
Raw materials	50,000	Repairs to machinery	
Finished goods	25,000	Depreciation on machinery	450
Carriage:		Royalty	750
Raw materials	700	Consumable stores	1,000
Finished goods	300	Sales	200
Railway freight and GST:		Sales return	1,20,000
Raw materials	1,400	Closing stock:	1,100
Finished goods	600	Raw materials	8,000
Purchases return:		Work-in-progress	5,200
Raw materials	700	Finished goods	25,000
Finished goods	800		

11. From the following balances taken from the ledger of NMC Constructions, prepare a combined manufacturing and trading account for the year ended 31 March 2020.

Particulars	Amount (₹)	Particulars	Amount (₹)
Opening Stock :		Carriage inwards	450
Raw materials	7,200	Railway freight and octroi	200
Work-in-progress	5,800	Repairs to machinery	650
Finished goods	7,400	Royalty	400
Purchases of raw materials	22,000	Purchases return	200
Productive wages	13,000	Sales returns	600
Coal, power etc.	1,600	Factory rent, tax, and	7,500
Sales	60,500	Insurance	

The closing stock was as follows: Raw materials ₹4,500; work-in-progress ₹7,500; finished goods ₹4,200.

12. From the following balances of Sanjay Kumar, prepare the trading and profit and loss account for the year ended 31st March, 2020.

Particulars	Amount (₹)	Particulars	Amount (₹)
Gross profit	15,000	Salesmen's remuneration and	
Salaries	5,000	travelling expenses	2,600
Advertisement expenses	400	Packing expenses	200
Postage and telegrams	250	Rates and taxes	900
Printing and stationery	180	Insurance premium	750
Rent	2,500	Commission received	1,800
Interest on loan taken	400	Dividend on investment	1,700
Discount allowed	600	Donation	350
Discount received	750	Carriage outward	480
Interest on bank overdraft	250	Apprentice premium received as per state government policy	160

13. Prepare the income and expenditure account for the year ended 31 March 2020 and balance sheet as at that date from the following particulars supplied to you by the Bollywood Sports Club.

Balance Sheet of Bollywood Sports Club
as on 31 March 2019

Particulars	Note	Amount (₹)	Amount (₹)
I. EQUITY AND LIABILITIES			
Subscription received in advance			1,200
Outstanding expenses			2,800
6% loan			10,000
Income and expenditure A/c			3,240
Capital fund			64,000
Total Equity and Liability			**81,240**

II. ASSETS			
Land and building			60,000
Cash on hand			20,000
Outstanding debtors			
For subscription			760
For lockers sent			480
Total Assets			**81,240**

Name of Account: Receipt and Payments Account of Bollywood Sports Club
for the period ended 31 March 2020

Type of Account: Asset

Date	Reference Account		Voucher Type	Post Ref No.	Dr. (Add)	Cr. (Less)
	To Balance (1/4/2019) b/d				20,000	
	To Subscriptions					
	2018–2019	400				
	2019–2020	4,200				
	2020–2021	300				
					4,900	
	To Entrance fees				1,600	
	To Lockers' rent				1,400	
	To Income from refreshments				8,000	
	By Expenses:					
	2018–2019	2,400				
	2019–2020	4,000				
						6,400
	By Furniture (1/10/2019)					8,000
	By Interest on loan					300
	By Refreshment expenses					4,500
	By Balance c/d					16,700
	Total				35,900	35,900

Adjustments:

1. Subscriptions due but not received for the year 2019–2020 ₹1,600.
2. Expenses due but not paid for the year 2019–2020 ₹500.
3. Salary due but not paid ₹1,000.
4. Depreciate land and building at 5% p.a. and furniture at 10% p.a.
5. One-half of the entrance fees is to be capitalized.
6. Lockers' rent due but not received for the year 2019–2020 ₹180.

CASES

Conceptual Application Cases

1. **Saumya House Company** On 15 September, Saumya House Company borrowed ₹6,000 from the bank, promising to pay the bank the principal plus accrued interest at 8%, 60 days from the date of the note. On 14 November, the company paid the accrued interest and renewed the note for an additional 30 days. At the second maturity, on 15 December, Saumya paid ₹4,000 in cash and gave a new 30 day, 8% note for the remaining due amount. This last note was paid in full when due.

Questions

1. Calculate Saumya's interest expense for the year that ended on 31 December.
2. Prepare a journal entry to record the 31 December accrual.
3. Assuming that no additional entry was made between the accrual entry and the repayment date in January, prepare a journal entry to record the January payment.

2. **Astha Manufacturing Co.** Astha Manufacturing Co. has just been formed to produce a new product at a cost of ₹12 a unit.

The amount will be paid in cash at the time of production. It will cost ₹6 per unit to sell the product and this amount will be paid for at the time of shipment. The sale price is decided at ₹25 per unit. All sales will be on credit and no collection costs will be incurred. The following results are expected during the first two years of the company's operations:

Year	Units Produced	Units Shipped	Cash Collected from Customers
First year	1,00,000	70,000	₹15,00,000
Second year	80,000	90,000	₹18,75,000

Questions

1. State the effect on the assets and the owner's equity by producing, shipping, and collecting money per unit. Assume that revenue is recognized at the time of production.
2. What total income should the company report each year if revenue is recognized at the time that cash is collected from the customer? Assume that general administrative expenses amount to ₹2,00,000 a year and that income taxes are zero.

Business Application Cases

1. **May Department** May Department is a mail order company which specializes in the manufacture and distribution of women's clothes. Its owner is Rashid Mohammad. The end of the trading year extracts from the ledgers is listed in the following text.

Particulars	Amount (₹)
Sales	3,41,998
Purchases	2,23,990
Purchase returns	21,001
Postage and packaging	23,776
Advertising	65,990
Wages	87,990
Rent and rates	12,900
Trade debtors	54,000
Trade creditors	32,771
Interest paid	4,553
Sundry expenses	2,991
Bank overdraft	13,330
Bank loan	1,19,000
Director's salary	40,000
Motor car	10,000
Taxation paid	12,000
Capital	10,000

Questions

1. Prepare a trial balance for May Department as on 31 January 2020.
2. Describe the initial checks that an accountant might make if the above trial balance fails to balance.
3. After some routine checking of the Farzana books, it was discovered that sundry expenses should have been ₹3,991 and sales should have been ₹3,42,998. Explain why these errors might not have been detected when the trial balance was drawn.
4. What will be the effect on the trial balance when the corrections are made?

2. **Macys Company** Macys Company was established on 1 January 2014 for the purpose of manufacturing pianos. Mr Suresh, the managing director, has 20 years of experience in manufacturing musical instruments and is an acknowledged technical expert in this field. He had invested his savings of ₹1,50,000 in the company. His decision to launch the company reflected his desire for complete financial independence. Nevertheless, his commitment to the company represented a considerable financial gamble. Mr Suresh did not pay close attention to the management of the company's financial affairs and has not submitted an income tax return till date. On 18 January 2020, he received an income tax notice, asking him to immediately submit the return on income for the year ended March 2019. He contacted his part-time accountant Mr Mani. The part-time accountant has provided the following ledger balances as on 31 March 2019. Mr Suresh is confused by the statements and wants to know whether the accounts are in order.

Particulars	Amount (₹ in '000)
Capital	100
General reserve	360
Income statement	20
Loans	100
Provision for bad debts	40
Provision for tax	80
Creditors	200
Outstanding expenses	20
Sales	2900
Purchase return	20
Income from investments	100
Opening stock	100
Purchases	1100
Sales return	20
Salaries	300
Excise duties	200
Sales tax	200
Audit fees	20
Office expenses	100
Selling expenses	100
Advertisement	200
Land and building	200
Plant and machinery	1100
Investments	500
Accumulated depreciation	200

3. **Manav Shah** Mr Manav Shah is the general manager in the plant of Mahavir Fasteners Limited. It is a large manufacturing company headquartered in Chennai. Mr Shah had been called to his head office for the purpose of immediately submitting the details of his plant's performance. Mr Ashwin, the accountant, met with an accident a week ago before Mr Shah's scheduled trip. Hence, Mr Shah checked Mr Ashwin's cabin and found a single list which consists of different accounts and the respective balance amounts. Mr Shah felt that these figures must be pertaining to 31 June 2019. You are supposed to check whether the accounts are in order and explain to Mr Shah the nature of accounts.

Particulars	Amount (₹ in '000)
Capital	400
General reserve	2200
Income statement	10
Loans	1200
Provision for bad debts	20
Provision for tax	60
Provision for warranty	25
Creditors	200
Outstanding expenses	50
Sales	4900

Purchase return	70
Income from investments	120
Opening stock	400
Purchases	2600
Sales return	40
Salaries	600
Excise duties	500
Sales tax	500
Audit fees	40
Office expenses	500
Selling expenses	400
Advertisement	400
Land and building	320
Furniture	25
Plant and machinery	2100
Investments	700
Accumulated depreciation	300
Advances to employees	290
Debtors	640

Questions

1. What do you observe? How do you treat the difference in the credit balance?
2. Should the difference be accounted for as suspense account?
3. What will be the nature of the suspense account?

4. **Comptronix Soaps Ltd**   Mr Sachin Shah, a young chartered accountant, was appointed as an accountant in Comptronix Soaps Ltd on 29 September 2020. Mr Atul Mehta, the accounts officer, working with company since the last seven years, was expecting to be promoted as an accountant. He was very unhappy with the decision of the management. The board meeting was scheduled on 1 October 2020. To convey his unhappiness, Mr Mehta went on a leave without notice. Mr Shah had seen the following statements dated 31 August 2020, which were available on Mr Mehta's table. You are required to help Mr Shah to prepare the trial balance before the board meeting.

Particulars	Amount (₹ in '000)
Capital	400
General reserve	2200
Income statement	10
Loans	1200
Provision for bad debts	20
Provision for tax	60
Provision for warranty	25
Creditors	200
Outstanding expenses	50
Sales	5900
Purchase return	70
Income from investments	120
Opening stock	400
Purchases	2600
Sales return	40
Salaries	600
Excise duties	500
Sales tax	500
Audit fees	40
Office expenses	500
Selling expenses	400
Advertisement	400
Land and building	320
Furniture	25
Plant and machinery	1900
Investments	1200

Accumulated depreciation	300
Advances to employees	290
Debtors	640
Cash	200

It was found subsequently that the following five transactions were not recorded:

(a) Credit sales amounting to ₹2,00,000
(b) Bad debts amounting to ₹20,000
(c) Commission paid was ₹10,000
(d) The insurance claim agreed upon by the insurance company was ₹20,000 against loss of plant and machinery.
(e) Tax refund amounted to ₹10,000

Questions

1. How do you adjust these omitted transactions?
2. What is the unadjusted total of the trial balance? What is the total of the adjusted trial balance? Should the total increase by the total value of omitted transactions?
3. Can you adjust the value of closing stock at ₹1,20,000 in the trial balance?
4. How do you record outstanding expenses which are not included in the expenses balance in the trial balance?
5. How do you record accrued income in the income account which is not yet incorporated?

5. **Angel Ltd**   Rajesh Selvan, who owns Angel Ltd, started the business on 1 January 2020, which related to buying and selling sports equipment. Prepare some accounts for him for the year till 31 December 2020. He has left the following message on your answering machine:

'Aunt Chakreshwari lent me ₹5 lakh in her will, and this formed my initial capital in my Angel account. A friend also loaned me ₹2 lakh at 10% p.a. interest. He gave me a cheque, which I encashed. I bought an estate car to help with my collection and delivery stock, and I made ₹50,000 profit on this car deal. The salesman wanted ₹1,70,000 for the car but I beat him down to ₹1,20,000, and I paid him by cheque. I reckon the car is good for four years before it goes to the scrap yard.

I rent a garage to keep my stock in, and this cost me ₹40,000 p.a. I have paid ₹50,000 so far (by cheque) as the owner insists on quarterly payments in advance.

My first bit of trading was to buy 3,000 pairs of trainers for ₹9 lakh. I have paid a cheque to the supplier for ₹6 lakh, and shall have to pay the balance soon. I've sold 2,500 pairs so far for ₹9.50 lakh cash, and I am yet to receive ₹50,000. 20% of this is doubtful, but the rest should be collectable.

Then I bought 200 golf clubs for ₹4 lakh (by cheque). I've sold 180 of these for ₹5,40,000 in cash, but the remaining are faulty, and I've found someone who says he can repair them, and will take them off my hands for ₹10,000.

I also do a good business in track-suits. Three hundred pairs of cost me only ₹1,50,000. I haven't paid for them yet, since a number of them appear to have faulty stitching. I've complained to the supplier who says he will reduce the price to ₹90,000. I think I'll accept, since I know someone who will look them all over and repair as necessary for ₹200 a garment. I can sell them for ₹10 each and make a profit of ₹1,50,000.

The cash I got from the golf clubs has been used to pay some bills: petrol for the estate car came to ₹50,000, and electricity for the garage ₹20,000. I've spent ₹4,50,000 on myself.

I also had a holiday in August, which cost ₹70,000, but I paid for that by cheque from the Angel account. I must also pay the first year's interest on the loan soon, I suppose.'

Questions

1. You are required to prepare a trading account and income statement for Angel Ltd for the year ended 31 December 2020, and a balance sheet as at that date.

2. Show the cash and bank balances separately on the balance sheet and present the figures in the vertical format.

6. **Diamond Stone Ltd** Diamond Stone Ltd, a manufacturer of stone ornaments for temples, has supplied you with the following financial information of the business as on 1 January 2020.

Particulars	Amount (₹)
Premises	30,000
Machinery	15,000
Stock	15,000
Debtors	10,000
Insurance prepaid	500
Creditors	7,000
Cash	2,000
Accrual for maintenance charge	400

During the course of 2020, Diamond Stone Ltd received ₹85,000 from customers and at the end of the year it was yet to receive ₹5,000. Suppliers were paid ₹62,000, but ₹10,000 remained to be paid on 31 December 2020. The following cash payments were also made during the year:

Wages ₹6,000
Motor expenses ₹1,900
Insurance ₹850

₹250 paid for insurance was with respect to the period 1 January 2021 to 30 June 2021. You also discover at the end of 2020 that there is still an unpaid bill for maintenance charges of ₹250. Further investigation reveals that the value of stock on 31 December 2020 is ₹25,000. The owner of Diamond Stone Ltd informs you that ₹5,000 had been drawn out in cash during 2020 for her own use. After consideration you decide that the machinery should be depreciated by ₹2,000 for the year.

Question

You are required to draw up a trading account and income statement for the year ended 31 December 2020, and a balance sheet as at that date.

7. **Corning Co.** The trial balance of Corning Co. as on 31 December 2020 is given here.

Trial Balance of Corning Co.
as on 31 December 2020

Particulars	Dr. (₹)	Cr. (₹)
Cash	28,800	
Notes receivable	17,700	
Accounts receivable	91,600	
Allowance for uncollectible accounts		1,500
Inventory of merchandise, 1 January 2020	89,000	
Prepaid insurance	1,900	
Other prepayments	1,340	
Land	16,000	
Building and equipment	45,800	
Allowance for depreciation		8,100
Accounts payable		18,800
Mortgage payable		45,000
Capital stock		1,50,000
Retained earnings		53,720
Sales revenues		4,12,000
Sales discounts, returns, and allowances	12,000	
Customer defaults	2,100	
Interest income		480
Purchases	3,44,500	
Advertising expenses	1,200	
Salaries and wages expenses	16,400	
Miscellaneous selling expenses	5,800	
Property tax expense	3,300	
Insurance expense	525	
Miscellaneous general expenses	8,435	
Interest expense	3,200	
Total	**6,89,600**	**6,89,600**

The following information had not yet been recorded in the accounts when the trial balance was prepared:

(a) A customer's account amounting to ₹165 was 18 months overdue with little chance of it ever being collected. The management decides to write it off.

(b) Outstanding of the accounts receivable remaining in the books after the write-off indicated that receivables amounted to ₹89,315.

(c) The cost of the merchandise in the inventory on 31 December 2020 was ₹86,440.

(d) Merchandise costing ₹975 was received on 31 December 2020, but was still in the receiving room and therefore was not included in the inventory count [item (c)]. The invoice covering this shipment was not reflected in the trial balance.

(e) ₹1,725 of the insurance premiums paid before 31 December 2020 was for insurance coverage in 2021.

(f) Depreciation for the year was ₹1,240.

(g) Unrecorded interest accruing on the mortgage payable since the last interest payment amounted to ₹400.

(h) Unrecorded wages earned by employees between the end of the last payroll period of 2020 and the end of the year amounted to ₹240.

(i) Cash discounts still available to customers on 31 December 2020 on credit sales made to them in 2020 amounted to ₹890. (Use an allowance for sales discount account.)

(j) The income tax rate was 40% in 2020.

Questions

1. Set up a columnar worksheet to enter the figures from the trial balance and make the necessary adjusting entries.

2. Prepare a balance sheet as at 31 December 2020, and an income statement for the year ended 31 December 2020.

3. Prepare a journal entry or entries to close the accounts for 2020 and prepare the ledger for 2021. You should assume that the adjusting entries have been posted.

8. **Cadilla Ltd** Cadilla Ltd recognizes revenue at the time of production and classifies selling costs as expenses as and when they are incurred. You have the following information about the operations of Cadilla in the year 2021.

(a) The company produced 1,00,000 units of the product in 2021 at a total production cost of ₹3,50,000. It sold and delivered 90,000 units at a price of ₹5 per unit.

(b) Payments to factory employees, raw material suppliers, and service providers amounted to ₹3,30,000.

(c) Factory depreciation (included in production costs) amounted to ₹10,000.

(d) Customer defaults were expected to average 2% of gross sales.

(e) Selling costs for the year, all paid in cash, totalled ₹80,000.

(f) Administrative costs for the year, including collection costs, amounted to ₹50,000. These expenses were paid in cash.

(g) Collections from customers totalled ₹4,20,000; write-offs of specific accounts as uncollectible totalled ₹8,500.

(h) The company's liability under its product warranties was negligible.

Questions

1. Prepare an income statement for Cadilla Ltd for the year 2021. (Ignore income taxes.)

2. The company had no inventories at the beginning of 2021. At what amount was finished goods inventory reported in the company's balance sheet as at 31 December 2021?

3. Calculate the net income on the assumption that the company recognizes revenue at the time of delivery.

4. What effect, if any, would changing to a delivery basis of revenue recognition have on the reported finished goods inventory figure?

Accounting from Incomplete Records

Learning Objectives

After studying this chapter, you will understand

- the characteristics of the single-entry system
- the method of preparing financial statements from incomplete accounting records

INTRODUCTION

Single entries refer to incomplete records, not single-entry accounting. The term 'single-entry' does not mean that there is only one entry for each transaction; it denotes an incomplete, inaccurate, unscientific, and unsystematic system of bookkeeping.

Under the single-entry system,

1. certain transactions are recorded just like the double-entry system, for example, cash collected from debtors is recorded in the debtors' account as well as in the cash account, etc.;
2. certain transactions are recorded partially, for example, cash sales, etc.; and
3. certain transactions are not recorded at all, for example, bad debts, depreciation, etc.

Kohler defines the single-entry system as 'a system of book-keeping in which, as a rule, only records of cash and personal accounts are maintained; it is always incomplete double-entry, varying with circumstances'.

The system makes use of the double-entry system partially. Only personal accounts are prepared. Real and nominal accounts are not prepared, so the single-entry system, essentially, is a defective and an unscientific double-entry system manipulated to meet the needs of small trading concerns and the convenience of the proprietor.

Carter defines the single-entry system as 'a method or a variety of methods employed for recording of transactions, which ignores the two-fold aspect, and consequently fails to provide the businessman with the information necessary for him to be able to ascertain the position'.

Single-entry means incomplete double-entry.

The characteristics of the single-entry system are as follows:

1. There is a mixture of double-entry, single-entry, and of no entry in respect of certain transactions. The system varies from transaction to transaction.

2. Generally, personal accounts are kept but real and nominal accounts are ignored.

3. Since no nominal accounts are maintained, the manufacturing, trading, and profit and loss account cannot be prepared. Therefore, to collect the necessary information, one has to depend on original vouchers.

4. The system may differ from firm to firm as per their individual requirements and conveniences. This invites fraud and misappropriation.

5. The system is suitable for small proprietary and partnership firms. No limited company can keep accounts under this system, because of legal restrictions.

6. This system is not governed by any definite rules of operation.

7. Since no trial balance can be prepared, the arithmetical accuracy of the books of account cannot be checked.

8. Owing to the incompleteness of records, proper appraisal of the financial position of the firm is not possible, and the composition of profit or loss will not be available.

9. The profit under the system is only an estimate. True net income cannot be calculated.

10. The true financial position cannot be ascertained, as the balance sheet is not prepared.

DIFFERENCE BETWEEN DOUBLE-ENTRY SYSTEM AND SINGLE-ENTRY SYSTEM

Table 14.1 presents the differences between the double-entry and single-entry systems.

ADVANTAGES OF SINGLE-ENTRY SYSTEM

A single-entry system has the following advantages.

Simple method It is an easy and simple method of recording transactions. It does not require any special knowledge of accounting unlike the double-entry system. This method is very useful for those who do not know the double-entry system.

Economical The single-entry system requires fewer books of accounts, that is, only cash book and ledger accounts, and fewer staff to maintain them, and is, therefore, cheaper.

Economy of time The single-entry system is quicker because both transactions and books of accounts are fewer.

Useful for small firms This method is most suitable for firms of small means, because it is not very costly. This method is also useful for those concerns that have cash transactions and many personal accounts.

Tax evasion The system is incomplete; so the actual income may be concealed. The firm has to pay tax on its net income. Taxes usually reduce with the reduction of income.

DISADVANTAGES OF SINGLE-ENTRY SYSTEM

Single-entry system suffers from the following weaknesses.

Incomplete and unscientific methods The system is incomplete, because real and nominal accounts are not prepared, and the debit and credit aspects of all transactions are not recorded.

Trial balance is not prepared The trial balance, prepared to check the arithmetical accuracy of accounting, cannot be prepared, because accounting is incomplete.

No knowledge of financial position It is very difficult to prepare the balance sheet, the mirror of the financial position of the enterprise; therefore, its true financial position cannot be ascertained.

Comparison with previous years' performance is not possible Due to incomplete information and non-availability of the previous years' information, comparison between the current and previous years' performance cannot be made. Comparison is required to identify the areas of weakness and to rectify them.

Control over assets is not possible Balance sheet is not prepared, so the value of assets cannot be accurately ascertained, and control over assets is not possible.

Unacceptable to tax authorities Tax authorities (income tax and sales tax) do not accept accounts prepared according to the single-entry system for computation of taxes.

TABLE 14.1 Differences between double-entry and single-entry systems

Double-entry System	Single-entry System
1. Both aspects of each transaction are recorded.	1. Neither aspect of a transaction is recorded.
2. Real and nominal accounts are kept fully.	2. Only personal accounts are kept and real and nominal accounts are ignored. (However, in some cases cash account is maintained.)
3. In this system, the cash book, general ledger, debtors' ledger, and creditors' ledger are maintained.	3. In this system, only the debtors' and creditors' ledgers are kept. Cash book is also kept but personal transactions are mixed up with business transactions.
4. Arithmetical accuracy can be checked by preparing the trial balance at any moment of time.	4. Arithmetical accuracy cannot be checked because no trial balance can be prepared.
5. Trading account, profit and loss account, and balance sheet can be prepared.	5. Trading account, profit and loss account, and balance sheet cannot be prepared.
6. For interpretation of financial statements, we can compute different ratios.	6. Vital ratios (gross profit ratio, net profit ratio, etc.) cannot be computed.
7. This system is scientific and follows certain rules.	7. This system is unscientific and does not follow any concrete rules.
8. There are few chances of tax evasion.	8. There are more chances of avoiding and evading tax.
9. It is suitable for all business firms.	9. It is suitable for the sole trader, who has few transactions and that too mostly in cash.

Difficulty in obtaining loan Accounts prepared according to this system are not accepted by banks and other money-lending institutions, so it is very difficult to obtain loan.

COMPUTATION OF PROFIT OR LOSS

There are two approaches for computation of profit or loss, which are, (a) balance sheet approach or statement of affairs method and (b) conversion approach.

Balance Sheet Approach or Statement of Affairs Method

It is not possible to determine the profit or loss as full information regarding all transactions is not available. However, this problem can be solved within the context of the accounting equations, as discussed in Chapter 3.

> Assets = Liabilities + Capital
> or, Assets − Liabilities = Capital

Under this method, two statements of affairs (normally known as balance sheet) are prepared—one at the beginning of the period for ascertaining the opening capital and other at the end of the period for ascertaining the closing capital. If the closing capital is more than the opening capital, the balance sheet shows an increase in capital, or profit. Conversely, if the closing capital is less than the opening capital, the balance sheet shows a decrease in capital, or loss.

Closing capital less opening capital = Profit or Loss

Mathematically,

If Closing Capital > Opening Capital,
Then Closing Capital Less Opening Capital = Profit
If Closing Capital < Opening Capital, Then
Opening Capital Less Closing Capital = Loss
So, this method is also known as *net worth method*.

■ **ILLUSTRATION 14.1** Mr Hanuman does not keep adequate records. The firm was set up on 1 January 2020 with capital of ₹5,00,000 in cash. At the end of the year, the following assets and liabilities were revealed. Prepare a statement of net profit/lost in the context of the accounting equation.

Assets:	Building at cost	₹3,00,000
	Stock	₹1,00,000
	Trade debtors	₹2,00,000
	Cash	₹1,50,000
Liabilities:	Trade creditors	₹50,000

Solution

From this, it appears that the changes for the year are as follows:

	Assets	=	Liabilities	+	Capital
Closing position (₹)	7,50,000	=	50,000	+	7,00,000
Opening position (₹)	5,00,000	=	Nil	+	5,00,000
Net profit (₹)	2,50,000		50,000		2,00,000

Assets have increased by ₹2,50,000. Out of this increase, ₹50,000 owes to increase in liabilities; and ₹2,00,000 is owing to increase in capital and it is nothing but profit earned during the year 2020. The information given earlier is only the initial figures for income. Any fresh capital introduced during the period by the owner or any withdrawal by him/her will definitely affect the size of the profit calculated. The ascertainment of profit by the above process needs to be adjusted for the introduction or withdrawal of capital or other adjustments such as depreciation, etc. In such cases, the profit or loss should be calculated as explained hereunder and supported by Exhibit 14.1.

The important considerations for preparing a statement of affairs are detailed in the following text.

1. Actual cash balance should be verified with the cash balance shown by the cash book.
2. The bank balance shown by the cash book should be verified with the balance of the pass book.
3. A list of debtors and of creditors should be prepared.
4. Assets such as building, machinery, and furniture should be valued and depreciation should be deducted from their values.
5. Closing stock should be properly valued.
6. Expenses should be correctly ascertained on actual basis—outstanding expenses should be added and prepaid expenses should be deducted.
7. Accrued income, if any, should be added and unearned income should be deducted.

EXHIBIT 14.1 Statement of Profit or Loss

Statement of Profit or Loss
for the Year Ended...

Particulars	Amount (₹)
Closing capital (before adjustment)	...
Add: Drawings for the period	...
Less: Opening capital	...
New capital introduced	...
Profit before adjustments	...
Less: Adjustments: (i) Depreciation	...
(ii) Provision for bad debts, etc.	...
Net profit for the period:	...
Less: Appropriations: (i) Salary to owners, etc.	...
Profit transferred to capital account	...

After ascertaining profit by following the procedures discussed earlier, a final statement of affairs is prepared at the end of the period after incorporating adjustments for depreciation, provision for bad debts, etc. Exhibit 14.2 exhibits the format of a statement of affairs.

EXHIBIT 14.2 Format of Statement of Affairs

Statement of Affairs
as at......

Particulars	Note No.	Amount (₹)	Amount (₹)
I. EQUITY AND LIABILITIES			
Opening		X	
Add: New Capital introduced		X	
Add: Profit for the period		X	

Less: Drawings	<u>x</u>	xx
Long-term loans		x
Bank overheads		x
Creditors		x
Total		**xx**
II. ASSETS		
Land and building	x	
Less: Depreciation	x	x
Plant and machinery	x	
Less: Depreciation	x	x
Furniture		
Less: Depreciation		
Debtors	x	
Less: Provision for bad debts	x	x
Stock		x
Cash at bank		x
Cash in hand		x
Total		**xx**

To study the financial position of a firm on a particular date, information pertaining to the available assets and liabilities is gathered and a statement is prepared by setting in its assets and liabilities on the date. This statement is called a statement of affairs. The assets and liabilities are recorded in the form of a balance sheet. That is why this approach is known as the balance sheet approach. Although a 'statement of affairs' has a format similar to a balance sheet, there are certain differences between them (Table 14.2).

TABLE 14.2 Differences between statement of affairs and balance sheet

Statement of Affairs	Balance Sheet
1. It is a statement of assets, liabilities, and capital recorded under the single-entry system.	1. It is a statement of assets, liabilities, and capital recorded under the double-entry system.
2. It is prepared partly from the trader's books and partly from other sources of information.	2. It is prepared with the available data extracted from ledger balances maintained under the double-entry accounting system.
3. It is compiled from incomplete books and information, the accuracy of which cannot be relied upon.	3. It is prepared from a set of books kept according to the double-entry system, the arithmetical accuracy of which can be proved.
4. Assets are recorded at their estimated realized value and liabilities are recorded at their payable value.	4. Assets and liabilities are recorded at their book value.

A statement of affairs is a statement of assets, liabilities, and capital prepared from incomplete records, whereas a balance sheet is a statement of assets, liabilities, and capital extracted from ledger balances maintained under the double-entry accounting system.

The steps for preparing a statement of affairs are given in the following text:

1. In most cases in the single-entry system, a cash book is maintained. In case, this has been done, the cash and the bank balance can be taken from the cash book. However, if the cash book is not maintained, cash balance can be found out by preparing the receipts and payment accounts or the balance can be physically verified.
2. A list of sundry debtors and sundry creditors should be prepared.
3. The value of fixed assets such as land and building, plant, etc. should be ascertained from vouchers or other documents available with the entity.
4. A physical verification of the stock should be taken and the value of the stock should be ascertained based on the different invoices received from suppliers from time to time.
5. The amount of outstanding expenses and the accrued income should also be determined.

Conversion Approach

The calculation of profit according to the balance sheet approach is only an estimate. It cannot be said to be a true indication of profit. In order to make accounts prepared according to the single-entry system more scientific, accurate, trustworthy, and meaningful, we convert these accounts into the double-entry system.

Under the single-entry system, adequate accounting information is not available and the profit disclosed by the system is not accepted by the revenue authority, for example, income tax department, sales tax department, etc. So, the firm is required to adopt the double-entry system and give up the single-entry system. It will, therefore, be better to collect all such information from the books of accounts and all other sources, which are necessary for preparing the trial balance of an entity. This is done by adopting the following generally accepted steps, through the support of which missing figures are to be found out, and the trial balance can be drawn.

1. A statement of affairs of an entity is prepared at the beginning of the accounting period from which the change is to be effected.
2. If no cash account or bank account is maintained properly, a careful scrutiny of the bank statement or pass book is made and enquiry is done in respect of the amount of cash that has been used by the trader for meeting personal expenses, business expenses, for cash purchases, etc. From the information gathered, a cash book (with cash and bank column) should be prepared.
3. The total debtors' account, total creditors' account, bills receivable account, bills payable account, total sales account, and total purchase account is prepared.
4. The statement of affairs at the beginning of the accounting period is prepared by incorporating the opening information, if found.
5. The appropriate opening entry is passed in the journal in respect of assets and liabilities included in the opening statement of affairs.
6. The real and nominal accounts are prepared from the information contained in the cash book and other accounts.
7. Every account is carefully scrutinized and the double-entry effect of every transaction is given by passing

corresponding debit and credit entries in the appropriate ledger accounts, which are opened, if necessary.

8. The accounts are balanced and the trial balance is prepared in the usual manner.

CALCULATION OF MISSING FIGURES

This section illustrates the various methods of calculating missing figures such as ascertaining the credit sales in the beginning or at the end of the accounting period, or the amount to be received from debtors; calculating credit purchases or creditors; and calculating stock.

Calculation of Credit Sales or Debtors

In order to calculate the amount of credit sales or the amount to be recovered from debtors, an entity prepares debtors' accounts. Out of these four items—opening balance, closing balance, credit sales, and receipt of payment—three items are given. Then the amount of the fourth item is the balancing figure. All these items are required for preparing final accounts according to the conversion method, that is, double-entry system. Credit sales is required for preparing the trading account, and opening and closing balance of debtors are required to prepare the opening and closing balance sheets. The opening balance sheet is prepared to ascertain the capital in the beginning of the year. Sometimes, the amount received from debtors is required to be posted to the cash book in order to ascertain the closing balance of cash. The debtors' account contains the following items (see Exhibit 14.3).

EXHIBIT 14.3 Debtor's Account

Name of Account: Debtor's Account
Type of Account: Asset

Date	Reference Account	Note No.	Dr. (Add)	Cr. (Less)
	To Balance b/d		x	
	(Opening balance of debtors—may be balancing figure)			
	To Bills dishonoured		x	
	To Interest and expenses		x	
	By Cash A/c			x
	(Amount received from debtors—may be balancing figure)			
	By Bills receivable A/c			x
	(Bills drawn during the year or bills receivable received during the year)			
	By Return inward (Goods returned by debtors)			x
	By Discount allowed			x
	By bad debts			x
	By Shortage/leakage or wastage			x
	By Transfer (if any)			x
	By Balance c/d (closing balance of debtors—may be a balancing figure)			x
	Total		xx	xx

The debtors' account displayed in this section shows four question marks, which show that one of the four items may be a balancing figure. Bills drawn during the year at the credit side of the debtors' account are starred, which shows that the amount may not be specifically given. In such a case, we may be required to prepare a bills receivable account to ascertain the amount of bills drawn. The bills receivable account is prepared to find the amount of bills drawn as shown in Exhibit 14.4.

EXHIBIT 14.4 Bills Receivable Account

Name of Account: Bills Receivable Account
Type of Account: Asset

Date	Reference Account	Note No.	Dr. (Add)	Cr. (Less)
	To Balance b/d		x	
	(Opening balance of bills receivables)			
	To Bills drawn during the year or bills receivable received during the year		x	
	By Cash A/c			x
	(Amount received against bills receivable)			
	By Bills dishonoured			
	By Bills endorsed A/c			
	(if the bills are endorsed)			x
	By Bank A/c (if the bill is discounted)			x
	By Balance c/d			x
	(Closing balance of bills receivable)			
	Total		xx	xx

Bills receivable account, like the debtors' account, is an asset and thus shows a debit balance. This is why opening balance has been shown at the debit side as 'To balance b/d'. If the amount of bills drawn or bills receivable received during the year is not given, bills receivable account as prepared according to the discussion will be prepared first to find out the amount of bills drawn. This amount will be transferred to the credit side of debtors' accounts.

Special mention must be made here to show the item of bills dishonoured. The item appears at two places, that is, at the debit side of debtors' account and at the credit side of bills receivable account. This is because in the case of dishonour, both the items are involved. It can be verified from the following journal entry in case of dishonour of the bill.

Debtor's A/c (Add)   Dr.
    To Bills receivable (Less) A/c

The displayed entry supports the fact that the posting will be made at the debit side of the debtors' account and the credit side of the bills receivable account. The bills receivable account may also be prepared to find out the opening or the closing balance of bills receivable to be posted at the assets side of the opening and closing balance sheet.

Calculation of Credit Purchases or Creditors

In order to calculate these items we prepare creditor's accounts. We require credit purchases to prepare the trading account.

Opening and closing balance of creditors are required to complete the opening and closing balance sheet respectively. Creditors constitute liabilities which are posted at the liabilities side of balance sheet. Creditor's account contains the items shown in Exhibit 14.5.

EXHIBIT 14.5   Creditor's Account

Name of Account: Creditor's Account
Type of Account: Liability

Date	Reference Account	Note No.	Dr. (Less)	Cr. (Add)
	To Cash A/c (Amount paid to creditors—may be a balancing figure)		x	
	To Bills accepted during the year		x	
	To Discount received		x	
	To Returns outward		x	
	To Transfer (if any)		x	
	To Balance c/d (Closing balance—may be a balancing figure)		x	
	By Balance b/d (Opening balance of creditors—may be a balancing figure)			x
	By Bills payable dishonored			x
	By Interest and expenses			x
	By Credit purchases (May be a balancing figure)			x
	Total		**xx**	**xx**

The creditor's account given in this section shows four question marks. It means that one of the four items may be missing out of the four items; three items are given so the fourth item is the balancing figure.

Bills accepted marked 'star' in the account might not be given. If it is not given, we will have to prepare the bills payable account. It is also a liability, so it will also be prepared as a creditor's account. The specimen of the bills payable account is given in Exhibit 14.6.

EXHIBIT 14.6   Bills Payable Account

Name of Account: Bills Payable Account
Type of Account: Liability

Date	Reference Account	Note No.	Dr. (Less)	Cr. (Add)
	To Cash A/c (Amount paid against bills payable)		x	
	To Bills payable dishonoured		x	
	To Balance c/d		x	
	By Balance b/d (Opening balance of bills payable)			x
	By Bills accepted (Transferred to creditor's account)			x
	Total		**xx**	**xx**

Bills accepted marked * in the account discussed earlier will be transferred to the creditor's account. While accepting bills payable, the following journal entry is passed:

Creditor's A/c (Less)   Dr.
　　To Bills payable A/c (Add)

This entry shows that the posting will be made at the debit side of the creditor's account and at the credit side of bills payable account.

Calculation of Stock

While calculating profit according to the conversion method, we have to prepare a trading account. Opening stock is shown at the debit side of the trading account and closing stock is shown at the credit side. Sometimes, opening stock and closing stock are not given, so we have to find them out. The amount of stock can be ascertained as under.

Calculation of opening stock

We are given sales and percentage of profit either on cost of goods sold or on sales.

(i) If profit on cost of sales is given   In this case, we calculate the cost of sales based on the following formula.

$$\text{Cost of Sales} = \frac{\text{Sales} \times 100}{(100 + \text{Profit }\%)}$$

For example, if the firm has sales worth ₹1,00,000, profit is 25% on cost, purchases are ₹60,000, and closing stock is ₹10,000, the opening stock will be calculated as under.

$$\text{Cost of Sales} = \frac{1,00,000 \times 100}{(100 + 25)} = \frac{1,00,000 \times 100}{125} = 80,000$$

$$\text{Opening Stock} = \text{Cost of Sales} + \text{Closing Stock} - \text{Purchases}$$
$$= 80,000 + 10,000 - 60,000$$
$$= 30,000$$

Alternatively, we may ascertain the opening stock by preparing a memorandum trading account (see Exhibit 14.7).

EXHIBIT 14.7   Memorandum Trading Account

Name of Account: Memorandum Trading Account
Type of Account: Income

Date	Reference Account	Note No.	Dr. (Less)	Cr. (Add)
	To Opening stock (Balancing figure)		30,000	
	To Purchase		60,000	
	To Gross profit		20,000	
	By Sales			1,00,000
	By Closing stock			10,000
	Total		**1,10,000**	**1,10,000**

$$\text{Gross Profit} = \text{Sales} - \text{Cost of Sales}$$
$$= 1,00,000 - 80,000$$
$$= 20,000$$

(ii) If rate of gross profit on sales is given, then we calculate the cost of sales as under:

$$\text{Cost of Sales} = \frac{\text{Sales} \times (100 - \text{Rate }\%)}{100}$$

In the example discussed earlier, if rate of gross profit on sales is 25%, cost of sales and opening stock will be calculated as given in the following text (see Exhibit 14.8).

$$\text{Cost of Sales} = \frac{\text{Sales} \times (100 - \text{Rate }\%)}{100}$$
$$= \frac{1,00,000 \times 75}{100}$$
$$= 75,000$$
$$\text{Gross Profit} = \text{Sales} - \text{Cost of Sales}$$

$$= 1,00,000 - 75,000$$
$$= 25,000$$
$$\text{Opening Stock} = \text{Cost of Sales} + \text{Closing Stock} - \text{Purchases}$$
$$= 75,000 + 10,000 - 60,000$$
$$= 25,000$$

EXHIBIT 14.8 Memorandum Trading Accounting (Alternative Calculation)

Name of Account: Memorandum Trading Account (Alternative Calculation)
Type of Account: Income

Date	Reference Account	Note No.	Dr. (Less)	Cr. (Add)
	To Opening stock (Balancing figure)		25,000	
	To Purchases		60,000	
	To Gross profit		25,000	
	By Sales A/c			1,00,000
	By Closing stock			10,000
	Total		1,10,000	1,10,000

Calculation of closing stock

We use the following formula for calculating closing stock:

Closing Stock = (Opening Stock + Purchases – Cost of Sales)

Closing stock may also be calculated by preparing a memorandum trading account. For preparing a memorandum trading account, we need gross profit. Calculation of gross profit may be summarized as:

Gross Profit @ 25% or 1/4 th of cost = 1/5 th of sales
Gross Profit @ 20% or 1/5 th of cost = 1/6 th of sales
Gross Profit @ 33.33% or 1/3 rd of cost = 1/4 th of sales

■ **ILLUSTRATION 14.2** Calculate the closing stock on the basis of the following information.

Particulars	Amount (₹)
Stock in the beginning	10,000
Cash sales	30,000
Credit sales	20,000
Purchases	35,000
Rate of gross profit on cost	1/3

Solution

Name of Account: Memorandum Trading Account
Type of Account: Income

Date	Reference Account	Note No.	Dr. (Less)	Cr. (Add)
	To Opening account		10,000	
	To Purchases		35,000	
	To Gross profit		12,500	
	By Sales			
	Cash 30,000			
	Credit 20,000			50,000
	By Closing stock			7,500
	(Balancing figure)			
	Total		57,500	57,500

Notes:
(i) Gross Profit is 1/3rd of Cost = 1/4th of Sales
   Gross Profit = $50,000 \times 1/4 = 12,500$
(ii) Closing stock will be the balancing figure.

Calculation of Closing Balance of Cash

The preparation of a balance sheet requires the closing balance of cash. If the closing balance of cash is not given, we shall prepare the cash account or bank account. The opening balance of the cash account is written at the debit side of the cash account. The opening balance of the bank account may be written at either the debit side or credit side. If bank account shows a debit balance, it will be written at the debit side of bank account as 'To Balance b/d'. If it is a credit or overdraft balance, it will be written at the credit side as 'By Balance b/d'. If nothing is specified, it will be supposed to be a debit balance.

All the receipts during the year will be posted at the debit side. All payments will be posted at the credit side. Excess of the debit side over the credit side will be the closing balance of cash or bank account and will be written at the assets side of the balance sheet. If it is a bank account, its credit side may exceed the debit side. It will be an overdraft balance and will be written at the liabilities side.

If closing balance is given and the opening balance is not given, it will be the balancing figure.

Calculation of Capital

Generally, the amount of capital is not given. We need capital at the beginning of the year, so the balance sheet of the previous year or the beginning of the current year is prepared. The excess of assets over liabilities is known as capital. It is the balancing figure. All the assets relating to the previous year are recorded at the assets side, whereas liabilities are posted at the liabilities side. Outstanding expenses and income received in advance is written at the liabilities side. Prepaid expenses and accrued income, if any, are recorded at the assets side. It should be noted that these adjustments relate to the previous year.

■ **ILLUSTRATION 14.3** Mr Chaney, a trader, does not keep a complete set of books. On 1 May 2019, his debts were ₹49,000 and credits were ₹15,000. A summary of his cash book for the year ended 30 April 2020 showed the following totals.

Particulars	Cash (₹)	Bank (₹)
Credits—Payments to creditors for purchases	2,700	22,500
Debits—Receipts from debtors for sales	—	42,500
Sale of machinery	26,000	—
Rent of warehouse	780	—
Cash sales	10,000	7,500
Cash capital introduced on 1 Nov. 2019	—	5,000

On 30 April 2020, the debts and credits respectively amounted to ₹88,000 and ₹19,500; cash discounts allowed to debtors were ₹460 and those received from creditors were ₹1,620.

Ascertain the total sales and total purchases for the year.

Solution

Name of Account: Total Debtors Account
Type of Account: Asset

Date	Reference Account	Note No.	Dr. (Add)	Cr. (Less)
1-May-19	To Balance b/d		49,000	
30-Apr-20	To Credit sales (Balancing figure)		81,960	
30-Apr-20	By Bank			42,500
30-Apr-20	By Discount allowed			460
30-Apr-20	By Balance c/d			88,000
	Total		1,30,960	1,30,960

Name of Account: Total Creditors Account
Type of Account: Liability

Date	Reference Account	Note No.	Dr. (Less)	Cr. (Add)
1-May-19	By Balance b/d			15,000
30-Apr-20	To Cash		2,700	
30-Apr-20	To Bank		22,500	
30-Apr-20	To Discount received		1,620	
30-Apr-20	To Balance c/d		19,500	
30-Apr-20	By Credit purchases (Balancing figure)			31,320
	Total		46,320	46,320

■ **ILLUSTRATION 14.4** Prepare a trading account, and profit and loss account for the year ended 31 December 2019 and the balance sheet as at that date from the following information available from the books of a trader.

1. Liabilities and assets

Particulars	31/12/2018 Amount (₹)	31/12/2019 Amount (₹)
Bank balance	20,000	9,400
Cash in hand	3,000	2,000
Prepaid expenses	5,000	7,000
Stock	70,000	60,000
Debtors for sales	2,30,000	?
Bills receivable	—	?
Furniture at written down value	70,000	82,000
Creditors for purchases	2,20,000	2,60,000
Outstanding liabilities	30,000	15,000

2. Receipts and payments during 2019 are given as under:

Particulars	Amount (₹)
Collection from debtors (after allowing 2.5% discount)	5,85,000
Proprietor's drawings	50,000
Capital introduced by proprietor	95,150
Purchase of furniture at the middle of the year	20,000
4% government securities purchased at 96% on 1/7/2019	96,000
Expenses	2,00,000
Sale of scrap	5,000
Payment of creditors (after receiving 2% discount)	3,92,000
Proceeds of bills receivable discounting at 2%	61,250

3. Sales are made to realize 33.33% on sales proceeds.
4. Goods worth ₹5,000 were taken by the proprietor.
5. During the year, bills receivable worth ₹1,50,000 were drawn on debtors. Of these, bills amounting to ₹30,000 were endorsed in favour of the creditors. Out of this later amount, a bill for ₹5,000 was dishonoured by the debtors.
6. Sales and purchases are made on credit.

Solution

Trading and Profit and Loss A/c
for the year ended 31 December 2019

Particulars	Amount (₹)	Amount (₹)
REVENUE		
By Sales		7,05,000
Total Revenue		**7,65,000**
EXPENSES		
To Opening Stock		70,000
To Purchases	4,65,000	
Less: Drawings by proprietor	5,000	
Less: Closing stock	60,000	4,00,000
= Cost of goods sold		
Total Expenses		**4,70,000**
Gross Profit (Total Revenue – Total Expenses)		
Brought down to Profit and Loss Account or Income Statement		2,35,000

Income Statement

	Amount (₹)	Amount (₹)
REVENUE		
Gross Profit brought from Trading Account		2,35,000
By Interest on security		2,000
By Discount		8,000
By Sale of scrap		5,000
Total Revenue		**2,50,000**
EXPENSES		
To Expenses		1,83,000
To Depreciation		8,000
To Discount on debtors		15,000

		Amount
To Discount on biils receivables		1,250
Total Expenses		**2,07,250**
Net Profit (Total Revenue – Total Expenses)		**42,750**
Transferred to Statement of Retained Earnings or Capital Account		

Balance Sheet
as at 31 December 2019

Particulars	Note No.	Amount (₹)	Amount (₹)
I. EQUITY AND LIABILITIES			
Capital:			
Capital Balance at the beginning of the year		1,48,000	
Add: Introduced during the year		95,150	
Add: Profit for the year		42,750	2,85,900
Less: Drawings			55,000
= Capital balance at the end of the year			**2,30,900**
Sundry Creditors			2,60,000
Outstanding Expenses			15,000
Total Equity and Liabilites			**5,05,900**
II. ASSETS			
Fixed Assets			
Furniture		90,000	
Less: Depreciation		8,000	
			82,000
Investment 4% Govt. securities			
(Nominal value ₹1,00,000)			96,000
Current Assets			
Stock in trade			60,000
Sundry debtors			1,90,000
Bills receivable			57,500
Interest accrued			2,000
Prepaid expenditure			7,000
Cash in hand			2,000
Cash in bank			9,400
Total Assets			**5,05,900**

Working Notes:

(i)
Balance Sheet
as at 31 December 2018

Particulars	Note No.	Amount (₹)	Amount (₹)
I. EQUITY AND LIABILITIES			
Sundry creditors			2,20,000
Outstanding expenses			30,000
Capital (balancing figure)			1,48,000
Total Equity and Liabilites			**3,98,000**
II. ASSETS			
Furniture			70,000
Stock in trade			70,000
Sundry debtors			2,30,000
Prepaid expenses			5,000
Cash at bank			20,000
Cash in hand			3,000
Total Assets			**3,98,000**

(ii)
Name of Account: Total Creditors Account
Type of Account: Liability

Reference Account	Note No.	Dr. (Less)	Cr. (Add)
By Balance b/d			2,20,000
To Cash/Bank		3,92,000	
To Discount		8,000	
To Bills receivable		30,000	
To Balance c/d		2,60,000	
By Sundry debtors			
(Bills dishonoured)			5,000
By Purchase (Balancing figure)			4,65,000
Total		**6,90,000**	**6,90,000**

(iii) Sales during the Year

Particulars	Amount (₹)
Stock on 1 January 2019	70,000
Purchases	4,65,000
	5,35,000
Less: Closing stock plus goods withdrawn	65,000
Cost of goods sold	4,70,000
Add: Profit margin @ 33.33% on selling price, that is, 50% on cost	2,35,000
Sales (₹)	7,05,000

(iv)
Name of Account: Total Debtors Account
Type of Account: Asset

Reference Account	Note No.	Dr. (Add)	Cr. (Less)
To Balance b/d		2,30,000	
To Sales		7,05,000	
To Sundry creditors			
(Bills endorsed dishonoured)		5,000	
By Cash/Bank			5,85,000
By Discount			15,000
By Bills receivable			1,50,000
By Balance c/d			
(Balancing figure)			1,90,000
Total		**9,40,000**	**9,40,000**

(v)
Name of Account: Bills Receivable Account
Type of Account: Asset

Reference Account	Note No.	Dr. (Add)	Cr. (Less)
To Sundry debtors		1,50,000	
By Sundry creditors			30,000
By Cash/Bank			61,250
By Discount			1,250
By Balance c/d			57,500
Total		**1,50,000**	**1,50,000**

(vi)

Name of Account: Furniture Account
Type of Account: Asset

Reference Account	Note No.	Dr. (Add)	Cr. (Less)
To Balance b/d		70,000	
To Cash/Bank		20,000	
By Depreciation (Balancing figure)			8,000
By Balance c/d			82,000
Total		**90,000**	**90,000**

(vii)

Name of Account: Cash/Bank Account
Type of Account: Asset

Reference Account	Note No.	Dr. (Add)	Cr. (Less)
To Balance b/d		23,000	
To Sundry debtors		5,85,000	
To Bills receivable		61,250	
To Sale of scrap		5,000	
To Capital A/c (Capital introduced)		95,150	
By Sundry creditors			3,92,000
By Furniture			20,000
By 4% Govt securities			96,000
By Expenses			2,00,000
By Drawings			50,000
By Balance c/d			11,400
Total		**7,69,400**	**7,69,400**

(viii) **Expenses Charged to Profit and Loss Account**

Particulars	Amount (₹)
	2,00,000
Add: Outstanding expenses on 31/12/2019	15,000
	2,15,000
Less: Outstanding expenses on 31/12/2018	30,000
	1,85,000
Add: Prepaid expenses as on 31/12/2018	5,000
	1,90,000
Less: Prepaid expenses as on 31/12/2019	7,000
	1,83,000

■ **ILLUSTRATION 14.5** Purva does not maintain her books in the double-entry system and bank accounts. From the following information, prepare the trading and profit and loss account and balance sheet as at 31 March 2020.

1.

Particulars	31/3/2019 Amount (₹)	31/3/2020 Amount (₹)
Assets and Liabilities		
Stock	19,800	1,13,200
Creditors	31,000	14,500
Debtors	1,18,000	1,25,000
Premises	90,000	90,000
Furniture	11,000	11,500
Air conditioner	15,000	15,000

2. Creditors as on 31/3/2019 include ₹15,000 for purchase of air conditioner.

3.

Cash Transactions	Amount (₹)
Cash as on 1 April 2019	15,000
Collections from customers	1,60,800
Payments to creditors (trade)	1,44,000
Rent, rates, and taxes	11,500
Salaries	1,12,000
Sundry expenses	18,000
Sundry income	16,500
Drawings by Purva	30,000
Loan from Mrs Niranjana	23,000
Capital introduced	12,000
Cash sales	11,500
Cash purchases	15,000
Payments to creditors for air conditioner	15,000

4. Bad debts written off   ₹1,200

Solution

Trading and Profit and Loss Account in the books of Purva
for the year ended 31 March 2020

Particulars	Amount (₹)	Amount (₹)
REVENUE		
By Sales		
Cash	11,500	
Credit	1,69,000	1,80,500
Total Revenue		**1,80,500**
EXPENSES		
To Opening stock		19,800
To Purchases		
Cash	15,000	
Credit	1,42,500	1,57,500
Less: By Closing Stock		1,13,200
= Cost of Goods Sold		**64,100**
Total Expenses		**64,100**
Gross Profit (Total Revenue – Total Expenses)		**1,16,400**
Brought down to Profit and Loss Account or Income Statement		

Income Statement

REVENUE		
Gross profit brought from trading account		1,16,400
By Sundry income		16,500
Total Revenue		**1,32,900**
EXPENSES		
To Salaries		1,12,000
To Rent, rates, and taxes		11,500
To Sundry expenses		18,000
To Bad debts		1,200
Total Expenses		**1,42,700**
Net Loss (Total Expenses – Total Revenue)		**9,800**
transferred to Capital A/c		

Balance Sheet of Purva
as at 31 March 2020

Particulars	Note No.	Amount (₹)	Amount (₹)
I. EQUITY AND LIABILITIES			
Bank overdraft			1,07,200
Loan from Mrs Niranjana			23,000

Creditors				14,500
Capital Account:				
Balance		2,37,800		
Add: Capital introduced		12,000		
		2,49,800		
Less: Loss		9,800		
Less: Drawings		30,000		
		39,800		
				2,10,000
Total Equity and Liabilities				**3,54,700**
II. ASSETS				
Stock				1,13,200
Debtors				1,25,000
Air Conditioner				15,000
Furniture				11,500
Premises				90,000
Total Assets				**3,54,700**

Working Notes:

1. Calculation of Capital as on 1 April 2019

Balance Sheet of Purva
as at 1 April 2019

Particulars	Note No.	Amount (₹)	Amount (₹)
I. EQUITY AND LIABILITIES			
Creditors: For trade			
(31,000 – 15,000)		16,000	
For air conditioner		15,000	
			31,000
Capital (balancing figure)			**2,37,800**
Total Equity and Liabilities			**2,68,800**
II. ASSETS			
Cash			15,000
Stock			19,800
Debtors			1,18,000
Air conditioner			15,000
Furniture			11,000
Premises			90,000
Total Assets			**2,68,800**

2. Calculation of Bank Balance as on 31 March 2020

Name of Account: Bank Account
Type of Account: Asset

Date	Reference Account	Note No.	Dr. (Add)	Cr. (Less)
	To Balance b/d		15,000	
	To Collections from customers		1,60,800	
	To Sundry income		16,500	
	To Loan from Mrs Niranjana		23,000	
	To Capital		12,000	
	To Sales - Cash		11,500	
	To Balance c/d			
	[balancing figure (Bank overdraft)]		1,07,200	
	By Creditors (Trade)			1,44,000
	By Rent, rates, and taxes			11,500
	By Salaries			1,12,000

By Sundry expenses				18,000
By Drawings				30,000
By Purchases - Cash				15,000
By Furniture				500
By Creditors for air conditioner				15,000
Total			**3,46,000**	**3,46,000**

3. Calculation of Credit Sales

Name of Account: Debtors Account
Type of Account: Asset

Date	Reference Account	Note No.	Dr. (Add)	Cr. (Less)
	To Balance b/d		1,18,000	
	To Sales - Credit			
	(balancing figure)		1,69,000	
	By Bank/cash			1,60,800
	By Bad debts			1,200
	By Balance c/d			1,25,000
	Total		**2,87,000**	**2,87,000**

4. Computation of Credit Purchases

Name of Account: Total Creditors Account
Type of Account: Liability

Date	Reference Account	Note No.	Dr. (Less)	Cr. (Add)
	By Balance b/d - Trade			
	(31000 – 15000)			16,000
	To Bank/ cash		1,44,000	
	By Purchases – Credit			
	(balancing figure)			1,42,500
	By Balance c/d		14,500	
	Total		**1,58,500**	**1,58,500**

■ ILLUSTRATION 14.6 Ashish Walia commenced business on 1 January 2020 with ₹15,000 as capital. On 1 July 2020, he introduced a further capital of ₹8,000. During the year he withdrew ₹500 every month for domestic use. On 31 December 2020, his assets and liabilities were as given in the following table.

Particulars	Amount (₹)
Stock	21,000
Sundry debtors	10,000
Furniture	3,500
Cash at bank	2,100
Expenses unpaid	700
Sundry creditors	8,300

Calculate the profit for the year.

Solution

Staement of Affairs of Ashish Walia
as at 31 Dec 2020

Particulars	Note No.	Amount (₹)	Amount (₹)
I. EQUITY AND LIABILITIES			
Expenses unpaid			700
Sundry creditors			8,300

Capital (Balancing figure)		27,600
Total Equity and Liabilities		**36,600**
II. ASSETS		
Stock		21,000
Sundry debtors		10,000
Furniture		3,500
Cash at bank		2,100
Total Assets		**36,600**

Calculation of Profit or Loss of the Year

Particulars	Amount (₹)
Profit or Loss:	
Capital on 31 Dec 2020	27,600
Add: Drawings	6,000
	33,600
Less: Fresh capital introduced	8,000
	25,600
Less: Capital 1 January 2020	15,000
Profit of the year	10,600

■ **ILLUSTRATION 14.7** The balance sheet of Kim Jong as at 31/12/2019 and 2020 are set out in the following text. He does not understand as to what has happened to the profit of ₹1,20,000 as disclosed by 2020 balance sheet as he does not find it in his bank balance.

Solution

Increase in assets or decrease in liabilities = Profit
Decrease in assets or increase in liabilities = Loss

Draw up a statement which will explain to him as to how the profit may be accounted for:

Liabilities and Equity	Amount (₹)	
	2019	2020
Capital (31/12/2019)	2,30,000	2,30,000
Add: Profit for 2020		1,20,000
		3,50,000
Less: Drawings during 2020		24,000
		3,26,000
Mortgage on freehold property	1,60,000	1,20,000
Sundry creditors	2,00,000	1,80,000
	5,90,000	6,26,000

Assets	Amount (₹)	
	2019	2020
Cash at bank	10,000	10,000
Sundry debtors	1,40,000	1,60,000
Stock	60,000	1,00,000
Motor vehicles	20,000	16,000
Plant:	1,60,000	1,40,000
Less: Depreciation		
Freehold property	2,00,000	2,00,000
	5,90,000	6,26,000

Statement for Ascertaining Profit of Kim Jong

Particulars	Year	Amount (₹)	Amount (₹)	Amount (₹)
Increase in assets				
Sundry debtors	2020	1,60,000		
Less: Sundry debtors	2019	1,40,000	20,000	
Stock	2020	1,00,000		
Less: Stock	2019	60,000	40,000	60,000
Add: Decrease in liabilities:				
Mortgage freehold property	2019	1,60,000		
Less: Mortgage freehold property	2020	1,20,000	40,000	
Creditors	2019	2,00,000		
Less: Creditors	2020	1,80,000	20,000	60,000
				1,20,000
Less: Decrease in assets				
Motor vehicle	2019	20,000		
Less: Motor vehicle	2020	16,000	(4,000)	
Depreciation	2019	1,60,000		
Less: Depreciation	2020	1,40,000	(20,000)	24,000
Net Increase in net assets				96,000
Add: Drawings				24,000
Profit for the year 2020				1,20,000

■ **ILLUSTRATION 14.8** Sampat Rao does not keep complete records of his business but gives the following information:

His assets on 31 March 2020 consisted of machineries ₹1,50,000, furniture - ₹60,000; motor car - ₹40,000; stock-in-trade - ₹50,000; debtors - ₹80,000; cash in hand - ₹12,000 and cash at bank - ₹30,000; creditors on that date were ₹1,20,000.

On further information, you find that on 1 October 2019, he purchased a machine costing ₹50,000. Sales are made for cash as well as on credit. There is no cash purchase. He always sells his goods at cost plus 25%. Cash sales for the year 2019–20 were ₹80,000.

During the year 2019–20, collection from debtors amounted to ₹5,00,000 and creditors were paid ₹4,25,000.

A bank loan was obtained for ₹50,000 on 1 February 2019. The entire amount was repaid in February 2020 with interest worth ₹2,500.

In November 2019, his life insurance policy for ₹50,000 matured and the amount received was invested in the business. His drawings were ₹2,500 per month through the year.

On 1 April 2019, he had ₹1,500 as cash in hand and balance at bank was ₹40,000. Debtors and Creditors on that date amounted to ₹60,000 and ₹90,000 respectively.

Provide depreciation on machinery at 15% p.a; furniture and equipment at 10% p.a.; and motor car at 20% p.a.

Prepare a statement of profit and loss for the year ended 31 March 2020 for Sampat Rao.

Solution

In the Books of Sampat Rao

Name of Account: Total Debtors Account
Type of Account: Asset

Date	Reference Account	Note No.	Dr. (Add)	Cr. (Less)
	To Balance b/d		60,000	
	To Credit sales (Balancing figure)		5,20,000	
	By Bank			5,00,000
	By Balance c/d			80,000
	Total		**5,80,000**	**5,80,000**

Name of Account: Total Creditors Account
Type of Account: Liability

Date	Reference Account	Note No.	Dr. (Less)	Cr. (Add)
	By Balance b/d			90,000
	To Bank		4,25,000	
	By Credit purchases (Balancing figure)			4,55,000
	To Balance c/d		1,20,000	
	Total		**5,45,000**	**5,45,000**

Balance Sheet of Sampat Rao

Particulars	Note No.	Amount (₹) 1-Apr-19	Amount (₹) 31-Mar-20
I. EQUITY AND LIABILITIES			
Creditors		90,000	1,20,000
Bank loan		50,000	
Capital (Balancing figure)		2,36,500	2,69,250
Total Equity and Liabilities		**3,76,500**	**3,89,250**
II. ASSETS			
Machineries		1,00,000	1,31,250
Furniture		60,000	54,000
Motorcar		40,000	32,000
Stock		75,000	50,000
Debtors		60,000	80,000
Cash in hand		1,500	12,000
Cash at bank		40,000	30,000
Total Assets		**3,76,500**	**3,89,250**

Working Notes:
Values of fixed assets on 31 March 2019 have been taken after depreciation.

Cash Book (with Cash and Bank Columns)

Dr. (Add)   Cr. (Less)

Particulars	Cash (₹)	Bank (₹)	Particulars	Cash (₹)	Bank (₹)
To Balance b/d	1,500	40,000	By Creditors	-	4,25,000
To Debtors	-	5,00,000	By Machinery	-	50,000
To Sales	80,000	-	By Loan	-	50,000
To Capital (Life insurance policy)		50,000	By Interest on loan	-	2,500
			By Drawings	30,000	-
			By Expenses (balancing figure)	39,500	32,500
			By Balance c/d	12,000	30,000
	81,500	5,90,000		81,500	5,90,000

Credit Sales + Cash Sales = Total Sales
₹5,20,000 + ₹80,000 = ₹6,00,000
Cost of Goods Sold = ₹6,00,000 × 100/125 = ₹4,80,000

Particulars	Amount (₹)
Stock-in-trade as at 1st April 2019 Cost of Goods Sold	4,80,000
Add: Closing stock	50,000
	5,30,000
Less: Purchases	4,55,000
Opening stock as on 1st April, 2019	75,000

Statement of Profit and Loss Account of Sampat Rao
for the Year Ended 31/3/2020

Particulars	Amount (₹)	
Capital as on 31/3/2020	2,69,250	
Add: Drawings	30,000	
		2,99,250
Less: Capital as on 1/4/2019	2,36,500	
Additional capital	50,000	2,86,500
Net profit for the year		12,750

■ **ILLUSTRATION 14.9** The income tax officer, assuming the income of Moti Lal for the financial years 2018–2019 and 2019–2020, feels that the latter has not disclosed his full income. He gives you the following particulars of assets and liabilities of Moti Lal on 1 April 2018 and 1 April 2020.

Date		Particulars	Amount (₹)
1/4/2018	Assets	Cash in hand	25,500
		Stock	56,000
		Sundry debtors	41,500
		Land and building	1,99,000
		Wife's jewellery	75,000

1/4/2020	Liabilities	Loan from Moti's brother	40,000
		Sundry creditors	35,000
	Assets	Cash in hand	16,000
		Stock	91,500
		Sundry debtors	52,500
		Land and building	1,90,000
		Motor car	1,25,000
		Wife's jewellery	1,25,000
		Loan to Moti's brother	20,000
	Liabilities	Sundry creditors	55,000

During the two years, the domestic expenditure was ₹4,000 p.m. The declared income of the financial years were ₹1,05,000 for 2018–2019 and ₹1,23,000 for 2019–2020 respectively. State whether the income tax officer's contention is correct. Explain by providing notes.

Solution

Calculation of Capital of Moti Lal

Particulars	1/4/2018 Amount (₹)		1/4/2020 Amount (₹)	
Assets				
Cash in hand		25,500		16,000
Stock		56,000		91,500
Sundry debtors		41,500		52,500
Land and building		1,90,000		1,90,000
Wife's jewellery		75,000		1,25,000
Motor car		-		1,25,000
Loan to Moti's brother		-		20,000
		3,88,000		6,20,000
Liabilities				
Loan from Moti's brother	40,000		0	
Sundry creditors	35,000	75,000	55,000	55,000
		313,000		5,65,000

Income during the Two Years

Particulars	Amount (₹)
Capital as on 1/4/2020	5,65,000
Add: Drawings – Domestic expenses for the two years (₹4000 × 24)	96,000
	6,61,000
Less: Capital as on 1/4/2018	3,13,000
Income earned in 2018–2019 and 2019–2020	3,48,000
Income declared (₹1,05,000 + ₹1,23,000)	2,28,000
Suppressed income	1,20,000

The income tax officer's contention that Moti Lal has not declared his true income is correct. Moti Lal's true income is in excess of the disclosed income by ₹1,20,000

■ **ILLUSTRATION 14.10** Krishnan does not maintain proper books of accounts. However, he provides the following details:

(a) Sales and purchase policy: Total sales during 2020—₹6,00,000. Volume of sales during 2nd half of 2020 was 1/3 that of 1st half. Volume of credit sales was twice that of cash sales throughout the year.

(b) Credit policy: Closing debtors represent last two months sales whereas closing creditors represent last 3 months purchases.

(c) Price policy: Goods were sold at 10% profit on credit sales. Cash selling price was always at a profit of 5% of sales.

(d) Inventory policy: First 2 months requirement was held as opening stock whereas last month's requirement was held as closing stock.

From the given details, ascertain the following:

1. Opening stock as on 1/1/2020,
2. Closing stock as on 31/12/2020,
3. Total purchases during 2020, and
4. Closing debtors and creditors as on 31/12/2020

Solution

Basic Calculation

(i) Cash and Credit sales (1 : 2)
    Cash sales: 1/3rd of ₹6,00,000   = ₹2,00,000
    Credit sales: 2/3rd of ₹6,00,000   = ₹4,00,000

(ii) Sales in 1st Half and 2nd Half

	Total (₹)		1st Half		2nd Half
Cash	2,00,000	3/4 th	1,50,000	1/4 th	50,000
Credit	4,00,000	3/4 th	3,00,000	1/4 th	1,00,000
	6,00,000		4,50,000		1,50,000

1. **Opening stock as on 1/1/2020:**
    Total sales for 1st two months: 1/3rd ₹4,50,000 = ₹1,50,000 (i.e., January and February)

(a) Cash sales: 1/3rd of ₹1,50,000   ₹50,000
    Less: Profit margin @ 5% on sales   ₹2,500
    Cost of good sold   47,500
(b) Credit sales: 2/3 of ₹1,50,000   ₹1,00,000
    Less: Profit margin @ 10%   ₹10,000
    Cost of goods sold   90,000
    Total opening stock at cost as on 1/1/2020   1,37,500

2. **Closing stock as on 31/12/2020:**
    Total sales for last month = 1/6th of ₹1,50,000 = ₹25,000 (i.e., December, 2020)

(a) Cash sales : 1/3rd of ₹25,000   ₹8,333
    Less: Profit margin @ 5% on sales   ₹417   ₹7,916
(b) Credit sales: 2/3rd of ₹25,000   ₹16,667
    Less: Profit margin @ 10% on sales ₹1,667   ₹15,000
    Total closing stock at cost   ₹22,916

3. **Total Purchases during 2020:**
    Total sales during 2020   ₹6,00,000
    Less: Profit on goods sold:
    5% on ₹2,00,000 = ₹10,000
    10% on ₹4,00,000 = ₹40,000   ₹50,000   ₹5,50,000
    Add: Closing stock   ₹22,916
                                                                      ₹5,72,916
    Less: Opening stock   ₹1,37,500
    Total Purchases made during 2020   ₹4,35,416

4. **Closing debtors and creditors as on 31/12/2020:**
    (a) Closing Debtors:

Total credit sales for the late two months
(i.e., Nov. and Dec.)
= 1/3rd of ₹1,00,000   ₹33,333

(b) Closing Creditors:
Total purchases for the last three months
(i.e., Oct., Nov., and Dec.
= 1/4 of ₹4,35,416)   ₹1,08,854

■ **ILLUSTRATION 14.11** Arya Singh does not maintain proper books of accounts. However, he maintains a record of his bank transactions and also is able to give the following information. Prepare the final accounts for the year 2020.

Particulars	Amount (₹)	
	1/1/2020	31/12/2020
Debtors	1,02,500	-
Creditors	-	46,000
Stock	50,000	62,500
Bank balance	-	50,000
Fixed assets	7,500	9,000

Details of his bank transactions were as follows:

Particulars	Amount (₹)
Received from debtors	3,40,000
Additional capital brought in	5,000
Sale of fixed assets (book value ₹2,500)	1,750
Paid to creditors	2,80,000
Expenses paid	49,250
Personal drawings	25,000
Purchase of fixed assets	5,000

No cash transaction took place during the year. Goods are sold cost plus 25%. Cost of goods sold was ₹2,60,000.

Solution

Trading and Profit and Loss Account of Arya Singh
for the year ended 30 June 2020

Particulars	Amount (₹)	Amount (₹)
REVENUE		
By Sales:		
(2,60,000 x 125/100)		3,25,000
Total Revenue		**3,25,000**
EXPENSES		
To Opening stock	50,000	
To Purchases		
(Balancing figure)	2,72,500	
Less: By Closing stock	62,500	
= Cost of Goods Sold		2,60,000
Total Expenses		**2,60,000**
Gross Profit (Total Revenue – Total Expenses) (Working note 1)		65,000
Brought down to Profit and Loss Account or Income Statement		

Income Statement

REVENUE		
Gross Profit		65,000
EXPENSES		

	49,250	
To Expenses	49,250	
To Loss on sale of fixed assets	750	
To Depreciation on fixed assets	1,000	
Total Expenses		**51,000**
Net Profit (Total Revenue – Total Expenses)		**14,000**
Transferred to Statement of Retained Earnings or Capital Account		

Working Notes:
W.N. 1
Gross profit is calculated as under:
= [(₹2,60,000 × 25)/100] = ₹65,000

Balance Sheet of Arya Singh
at 31 December 2020

Particulars	Note No.	Amount (₹)	Amount (₹)
I. EQUITY AND LIABILITIES			
Capital		16,9000	
Add: Additional Capital		5,000	
Net Profit		14,000	
		1,88,000	
Less: Drawings		25,000	
			1,63,000
Creditors			46,000
Total Equity and Liabilities			**2,09,000**
II. ASSETS			
Fixed assets			9,000
Debtors			87,500
Stock			62,500
Bank balance			50,000
Total Assets			**2,09,000**

Working Notes:
W.N. 2
Name of Account: Fixed Assets Account
Type of Account: Asset

Reference Account	Note No.	Dr. (Add)	Cr. (Less)
To Balance b/d		7,500	
To Bank		5,000	
By Bank			1,750
(Sale)			
By Loss on sale of fixed assets			750
By Depreciation			1,000
(Balancing figure)			
By Balance c/d			9,000
Total		**12,500**	**12,500**

W.N. 3
Name of Account: Bank Account
Type of Account: Asset

Date	Reference Account	Note No.	Dr. (Add)	Cr. (Less)
	To Balance b/d		62,500	
	(Balancing figure)			
	To Debtors		3,40,000	
	To Capital		5,000	

To Sale of fixed assets	1,750	
By Creditors		2,80,000
By Expenses		49,250
By Drawings		25,000
By Fixed assets		5,000
By Balance c/d		50,000
Total	**4,09,250**	**4,09,250**

W.N. 4

Name of Account: Debtors Account
Type of Account: Asset

Date	Reference Account	Note No.	Dr. (Add)	Cr. (Less)
	To Balance b/d		1,02,500	
	To Sales (2,60,000 x 125/100)		3,25,000	
	By Bank			3,40,000
	By Balance c/d			
	(Balancing figure)			87,500
	Total		**4,27,500**	**4,27,500**

W.N. 5

Name of Account: Creditors Account
Type of Account: Liability

Date	Reference Account	Note No.	Dr. (Less)	Cr. (Add)
	By Balance b/d			
	(Balancing figure)			53,500

To Bank	2,80,000	
By Purchases		
(From trading account)		2,72,500
To Balance c/d	46,000	
Total	**3,26,000**	**3,26,000**

W.N. 6

Balance Sheet of Arya Singh
as at 1 January 2020

Particulars	Note No.	Amount (₹)	Amount (₹)
I. EQUITY AND LIABILITIES			
Creditors			53,500
Capital			
(Balancing figure)			1,69,000
Total Equity and Liabilities			**2,22,500**
II. ASSETS			
Fixed assets			7,500
Debtors			1,02,500
Stock			50,000
Bank balance			62,500
Total Assets			**2,22,500**

SUMMARY

- Under the single-entry system, (a) certain transactions are recorded just like the double-entry accounting system; (b) certain transactions are recorded partially; and (c) certain transaction are not recorded at all.
- Under the double-entry system, both aspects of each transaction are recorded, while under the single-entry system, both aspects of each transaction is not recorded.
- The profit calculated by the single-entry system is only an estimate and the true financial position cannot be ascertained as the balance sheet is not prepared.

- There are two approaches for computation of profit or loss, that is, the balance sheet approach and conversion approach.
- In the system of accounting from incomplete records, non-cash transactions or internal transactions of the firm, that is, depreciation, etc., are not recorded.
- Exact amount of profit or loss is not ascertained by the method of accounting from incomplete records.

KEYWORDS

Single-entry system It is a method or one of a variety of methods employed for recording transactions that ignores the two-fold aspect and consequently fails to provide the businessperson the information he/she needs to ascertain the business's true financial position.

QUESTIONS

I. Answer these questions in a few sentences.

1. What is a statement of affairs? Distinguish between a statement of affairs and a balance sheet.

2. State the steps that need to be taken to convert single-entry books into double-entry books when all the subsidiary books are maintained.

3. State the salient characteristics of single entry accounting system.

4. How can profit or loss of a firm be found out by capital comparison parameters?

5. What are the main disadvantages of single entry accounting system?

6. Which items are added or which items are deducted from closing capital in a statement showing profit or loss?

II. Choose the correct option.

1. Under the single-entry system only, accounts are maintained.
   - (a) Personal
   - (b) Impersonal
   - (c) Real
   - (d) Nominal

2. Statement of affairs is prepared to find out .
   - (a) Liability
   - (b) Assets
   - (c) Capital
   - (d) Fixed assets

3. While preparing statement of profit or loss, drawings made during the year is .
   - (a) Added
   - (b) Deducted
   - (c) Omitted
   - (d) Either added or deducted

4. Fresh capital introduced during the year is while preparing statement of profit or loss.
   - (a) Added
   - (b) Deducted
   - (c) Either added or deducted
   - (d) Omitted

5. Single-entry system of accounting shows .
   - (a) Only three type of accounts
   - (b) Financial position of business
   - (c) Only one aspect of the transaction
   - (d) Essentials of unscientific system of accounting

6. Credit purchases are calculated by preparing .
   - (a) Debtor's account
   - (b) Creditor's account
   - (c) Bills receivable account
   - (d) Bills payable account

7. Bills receivable endorsed is posted in the account.
   - (a) Bills payable
   - (b) Bills receivable
   - (c) Debtors
   - (d) Creditors

8. Closing balance of cash is obtained by preparing .
   - (a) Debtor's account
   - (b) Creditor's account
   - (c) Cash book
   - (d) Balance sheet

9. Bills dishonoured account is shown in .
   - (a) Debtors' account
   - (b) Bills receivable account
   - (c) Both debtor's and bills receivable account
   - (d) Creditors account

10. Single-entry system of bookkeeping is .
    - (a) Inaccurate
    - (b) Unscientific
    - (c) Unsystematic
    - (d) All the above

III. Solve the following problems.

1. From the following particulars, ascertain the amount of credit sales and credit purchases for the year ended 31 March 2020.

Particulars	Amount (₹)
Total creditors: 1/4/2019	4,00,000
Total debtors: 1/4/2019	7,00,000
Cash received from customers	14,50,000

Particulars	Amount (₹)
Received for bills receivable	80,000
Paid to sundry creditors	5,60,000
Bills payable met	1,20,000
Discount allowed to customers	20,000
Discount earned	10,000
Sales returns	60,000
Purchase returns	80,000

Particulars	Amount (₹)
Bad debts	30,000
Total creditors: 31/3/2020	9,20,000
Total debtors: 31/3/2020	8,80,000
Bills receivable: 1/4/2019	60,000
Bills payable: 1/4/2019	1,40,000
Bills receivable: 31/3/2020	1,80,000
Bills payable: 31/3/2020	1,00,000

2. Form the following information, prepare the profit and loss account for the year ended 31 March 2020 and the balance sheet as at that date.

Particulars	Amount (₹)	Amount (₹)
Assets and liabilities	31/3/2019	31/3/2020
Sundry assets	₹18,000	₹20,000
Stock	14,000	19,000
Cash in hand	8,200	4,800
Cash at bank	2,200	8,000
Debtors		26,000
Creditors	22,000	19,800
Miscellaneous expenses outstanding	1,000	600
Details relating to year's transactions are:		
Receipts in the year and discount credited to debtors accounts		2,45,000
Return from debtors		6,000
Sales—Cash and credit		3,00,000
Returns to creditors		3,000
Payments to creditors by cheque		2,36,200
Receipts from debtors deposited into bank		2,43,000

Particulars	Amount (₹)
Cash purchases	10,000
Salary and wages paid out of bank	18,000
Miscellaneous expenses paid by cash	5,000
Drawing by cash	9,400
Purchase of sundry assets by cheque	2,000
Cash withdrawals from bank	21,000
Cash sales deposited in bank	0
Discount allowed by creditors	4,000

3. Hardik Solanki had the following assets and liabilities.

Particulars	Amount (₹)	
	1/4/2019	31/3/2020
Cash in hand	5,000	6,000
Bank balance	12,000	29,000
Stock	25,000	24,000
Sundry debtors	10,000	18,000
Furniture	20,000	?
Equipments	30,000	?
Sundry creditors	15,000	12,000

During the year he introduced ₹7,000 as additional capital. He has withdrawn 75% of the profits earned. Depreciation on furniture and equipments is to be charged at 10% p.a Calculate the capital and prepare the statement of profit and loss for the year ended 31 March 2020.

4. A trader has not kept proper books of account. The following balances are placed before you.

Particulars	Dec. 31 2019	Dec. 31 2020	Particulars	Dec. 31 2019	Dec. 31 2020
Cash in hand	10,700	10,800	Bills receivable	21,200	20,400
Bank overdraft	22,500	20,000	Land and buildings	26,500	26,500
Stock-in-trade	27,000	28,400	Furniture and fittings	2,300	2,300
Sundry creditors	19,300	18,600	Bills payable	31,000	29,000
Sundry debtors	15,100	14,900			

Drawings during the year amounted to ₹3,000. Depreciation is to be calculated on land and buildings at 2% p.a. and on furniture and fittings at 10% p.a. Of the debtors worth ₹500 is bad, bad debt reserve is 5% of the debtors balance, and 2.5% on bills receivable. Calculate the net profit and gross profit for the year ended 31 December 2020.

5. Calculate the closing stock from the following data.

Particulars	Amount (₹)
Stock as on 1/4/2019	40,000
Purchases (1/4/2019 to 31/3/2020)	3,00,000
Sales (1/4/2019 to 31/3/2020)	4,00,000
Gross profit rate	30%

6. From the following details, you are required to calculate total gross and net sales.

Particulars	Amount (₹)
Bills receivable (Opening balance)	7,000
Sundry debtors (Opening balance)	35,000
Cash received against bills receivable	15,000
Cash received from debtors	80,000
Bad debts written off	2,000
Cash sales	40,000
Discount allowed	1,500
Sales returns	5,000
Bills receivable dishonoured	1,000
Bills receivable (Closing balance)	5,000
Sundry debtors (Closing balance)	25,000

7. From the following details, calculate the total purchases (gross as well as net).

Particulars	Amount (₹)	Particulars	Amount (₹)
Bills payable (opening balance)	5,000	Cash purchases	25,800
Sundry creditors (opening balance)	6,000	Cash paid to creditors	30,900
Bills payable (closing balance)	7,000	Bills payable paid during the year	8,800
Sundry creditors (closing balance)	4,000	Purchase returns	1,200
		Discounts received	1,000

8. Aleena John, a trader, does not keep her books of accounts in the double-entry method, and the following data is furnished by her from her rough records. It was also stated that the cost of goods sold excluding wages is 25% of sale value.

Balances in Rupees as at June 30

Particulars	Amount (₹) 2020	Amount (₹) 2019
Debtors	88,000	53,000
Creditors	19,500	15,000
Stock	19,000	?
Plant and machinery	20,000	20,000
Furniture and fittings	1,400	1,400

From the rough cash book, the following were available:

Particulars	Amount (₹)
Due to bank as at 1 July 2019	7,400
Creditors	25,000
General expenses	10,000
Wages	15,500
Drawings	3,000
Total payments	60,900
Receipts: Collection from customers	60,000
Loans from friends	5,000
Total receipts	**65,000**

Prepare the profit and loss account and balance sheet after providing depreciation on assets at 10%, and a provision of ₹3,000 for doubtful debts. The payment to creditors includes ₹5,000 as advance to a contractor for new premises.

9. The books of Zubair & Co. showed the following information:

Particulars	Amount (₹) 1/1/2020	Amount (₹) 31/12/2020
Bank balance	-	50,000
Debtors	-	87,500
Creditors	-	46,000
Stock	50,000	62,500
Fixed assets	7,500	9,000

The following are the details of the bank transactions:

Particulars	Amount (₹)	Amount (₹)
Receipt from customers	3,40,000	
Payment to creditors	2,80,000	
Capital and Drawings	5,000	25,000
Sale of fixed assets	1,750	
Expenses paid	49,250	
Drawings	-	
Purchase of fixed assets	5,000	

Other information:
1. Cost of goods sold ₹2,60,000.
2. Gross profit 25% on cost of goods sold.
3. Book value of assets sold ₹2,500.

Prepare the trading and profit and loss account for the year ended 31/12/2020 and balance sheet as at 31/12/2020.

CASES

Business Application Cases

1. Labdhi Donda Labdhi Donda runs a pub called College Arms in Mumbai. The pub is leased from a local brewery and was taken over by Labdhi in 2018. Although Labdhi built the trade and made the business profitable, she experienced staffing problems. At the end of the trading year, on 31 July 2020, she provided her accountant the information that is listed here. During the preparation of the final accounts, the accountant told Labdhi that some cash was missing.

(a) All sales are for cash. During the year ended 31 July 2020, takings (revenue is also known as takings in service industry) amounted to ₹1,26,000 of which ₹93,070 was banked.

(b) The total of payments to creditors by cheque was ₹63,000.

(c) Labdhi withdrew ₹10,400 cash for personal use.

(d) Wages paid in cash were ₹17,200.

(e) The leasing charge made by the brewery for premises was ₹15,000. It was paid by standing order through the bank.

(f) A vehicle that is owned by the business is depreciated using the straight-line method. The annual charge is ₹1,000.

(g) General expenses were a total of ₹5,830, of which ₹1,720 was paid in cash and the rest by cheque.

(h) The total paid for heat and light for the year by cheque was ₹3,220. However, ₹310 was still owed at the end of the year.

(i) Details of assets and liabilities are as follows.

Particulars	31/7/2020 Amount (₹)	1/8/2019 Amount (₹)
Vehicle (historical cost)	7,000	7,000
Stock	6,220	5,160
Bank	n/a	1,220
Cash	1,020	810
Trade creditors	3,140	2,460

Questions

1. Prepare a statement of affairs as at 1/8/2019 to determine the opening capital for Labdhi's business.

2. Prepare a cash book summary and determine the amount of missing cash and the closing bank balance.

3. Calculate the total purchases for the year.

4. Prepare a trading and profit and loss account for Labdhi's business and identify the missing cash.

5. Prepare a balance sheet for Labdhi's business.

2. Aadhishwar Shroff Aadhishwar Shroff is a wholesaler trader in railway spares. On 30 June 2020, he had a balance sheet that showed the following items.

Particulars	Amount (₹)
Capital	1,00,000
Long-term loan from S. Shaban	20,000
Overdraft at bank	2,000
Trade and other creditors	18,000
Debtors	17,000
Stocks	9,000
Delivery van (at book value)	12,000
Fixtures and fittings	8,000
Warehouse and offices	94,000

During the three months ending 30 September, the following transactions were recorded.

(a) Purchased ₹63,000 worth of stock on credit.

(b) Sold ₹55,000 worth of stock to his credit customers for ₹86,000.

(c) Received ₹83,000 from his credit customers, all of which he paid into the bank.

(d) Paid off ₹5,000 of his long-term loan from S. Shaban.

(e) Paid his trade creditors ₹59,000.

(f) Bought (and paid for) some new fixtures and fittings for ₹4,000.

(g) Traded in his old van for his book value and bought a new van for ₹15,000, paying the balance by cheque.

(h) Paid out ₹11,000 in expenses, all of which were chargeable against profits.

Question

Draw up the balance sheet for Aadhishwar Shroff's business as at 30 September 2020, after all the transactions have been taken into account.

Analytical Accounting

Average Due Date, Account Current, and Negotiable Instruments

Learning Objectives

After studying this chapter, you will understand

- importance of average due date and its application for commercial transactions
- preparation of account current and its use in commercial transactions
- the utility and accounting treatment of negotiable instruments

INTRODUCTION

In the present scenario, sale and purchase of goods is done both on cash basis and credit basis. In case of credit transactions, the buyer is under an obligation to pay the amount after a specified period. In such a case, the payment needs to be made by the buyer to the seller on the exact due date, or once in a particular time period (for example, once in a month), or in piecemeal way. The mode of payment is always based on the business and commercial relationships between the parties involved. If trust is not built between the buyer and the seller, or in cases of early need of funds, the seller may resort to bills of exchange or promissory note, as legal documents.

AVERAGE DUE DATE

In business enterprises, a large number of receipts and payments by and from a single party may occur at different points of time. The idea of average due date has been developed to simplify the calculation of interest involved in such transactions. The principle of determining average due date can be applied in cases where (a) the amount is lent in various instalments but repayment is made in a single instalment; (b) the amount is lent in one instalment but repayment is made in various instalments; and (c) the interest on drawings made by proprietors or partners of a firm at several points of time needs to be calculated.

An average due date is an equated date on several payments due on different dates which can be made in one lump sum without loss of interest to any party (i.e., debtor or creditor). It is a date on which a single payment can be done for all different bills maturing on different dates instead of setting the bill on their respective maturity dates. The debtor and the creditor can settle payment on the average due date, which when calculated, ensures that none of the parties to the bill loses or gains interest for late or early payments.

Determining Average Due Date

The following steps are used for calculating the average due date:

1. If the due date of bill drawn is not given, the due dates of each bill are calculated by taking the date of the bill drawn and period of the bill. Three days of grace is added while calculating the due date.
2. For easy calculations, arrange all the due dates in ascending or descending order.
3. Select the earliest date as zero date/base date.
4. Count the number of days from the base date up to the due date of each bill. In other words, calculate the period gap between base date and due date of each bill.
5. Derive product by multiplying the period calculated in step four with the corresponding amount in each bill.
6. Derive the total by adding all the products of each bill.
7. Add the amount of each bill and derive total amounts.
8. Divide the total of products by the total of amount of bills to get the equated period.

> Equated Period = Total of Products/Total Amount

9. Add the equated period to the base date so as to derive the average due date.

If the equated period is derived in decimals, and the decimal equal to or greater than 5, add one day to the equated period. If the decimal is less than 5, ignore it. For example, an equated period of 40.56 will be counted as 41 days, whereas 20.28 will be counted as 20 days.

■ **ILLUSTRATION 15.1**   Find the average due date of the following bills of exchange.

Date on Which Drawn	Amount (₹)	Period (in Months)
7 January 2019	₹300	4
15 February 2019	₹400	2
25 March 2019	₹500	3
8 April 2019	₹200	1

Solution

Step 1: Calculate the due date of each bill as follows:

7 1 (Jan)–2019	15–2–2019	25–3–2019	8–4–2019
+3 (grace days) 4 (period)	+3 + 2 ...	+3 + 3...	+3 + 1...
10–5–2019	18–4–2019	28–6–2019	11–5–2019

Hence the due dates are 10 May, 18 April, 28 June, and 11 May.

Step 2: Arrange the due dates in ascending order along with their respective amounts and take the earliest date as base date. Calculate the period gap of each bill from the base date as shown, then multiply the number of days from base date with corresponding amount of the bill to derive the product.

Amount (₹) (a)	Due Dates	No. of Days from Base Date (b)	Product c = (a × b) Amount (₹)
400	18 April 2019 Base (date)	0 (zero)	(400 × 0) = 0 (zero)
300	10 May 2019	12 days of April + 10 days of May — 22 days	(300 × 22) = 6,600
200	11 May 2019	12 days of April + 11 days of May — 23 days	(200 × 23) = 4,600
500	28 June 2019	12 days of April + 31 days of May + 28 days of June — 71 days	(500 × 71) = 35,500
1,400			**₹46,700**

Equated period = Total of product/Total amount

= 46,700/1400

= 33.35 days

33.35 days can be rounded off to 33 days.

Average due date = Base date + Equated period

= 18 April 2019 + 33 days

that is, 18 – 4 – 2019

+33 – –

51   4   2019

– 30+ 1   (i.e., minus days of April and adding one to the month)

21   5   2019

Therefore, the average due date is 21 May 2019.

■ **ILLUSTRATION 15.2**   Find the average due date from the following bills of exchange.

Bill No.	Date of Bill Drawn	Date of Acceptance	Amount (₹)	Tenure of the Bill
1	05/2/2019	07/2/2019	1,000	3 months after date
2	08/3/2019	10/3/2019	3,000	60 days after date
3	20/5/2019	24/5/2019	2,500	30 days after sight
4	10/6/2019	12/6/2019	1,500	2 months after sight

Solution

Amount (₹) (a)	Due Dates	No. of Days from Base Date (b)	Product (c) (c = a × b)
1,000	08/05/2019 (Base date)	0	0
3,000	10/5/2019	2 days of May	6,000
2,500	26/6/2019	23 days of May + 26 days of June — 49 days	1,22,500
1,500	15/8/2019	23 days of May + 30 days of June + 31 days of July + 15 days of August — 99 days	1,48,500
8,000			**2,77,000**

Equated period = Total of product/Total amount

= 2,77,000/8,000

= 34.63

34.63 can be rounded off to 35 days

Average due date = Base date + Equated period
= 5/2/2019 + 35 days

that is,

	5	2	2019
+ 35	–	–	
	40	2	2019
– 28 + 1			
	12	3	2019

Therefore, the average due date is on 12 March 2019.

■ **ILLUSTRATION 15.3** Padmavati has given details of the bills drawn by Laxmi and accepted by her. Padmavati requested Laxmi to accept payment on one single date so as to avoid loss of interest on either side. Calculate the average due date.

Bill No.	Date of Bill Drawn	Date of Acceptance	Amount of Bill (₹)	Period of Each Bill
1992	15/3/2019	16/3/2019	9,000	2 months after date
1993	28/4/2019	29/4/2019	10,000	90 days after sight
1994	30/6/2019	1/7/2019	1,000	Two weeks after sight
1995	3/7/2019	6/7/2019	5,000	45 days after date

Amount of Bill (a)	Date of Bill Drawn	Date of Acceptance	Period	Due Date	No. of Days (b)	Product (c) = (a) ¥ (b)
9,000	15/3/2019	16/3/2019	2 months after date	18/5/2019	0	0
10,000	28/4/2019	29/4/2019	90 days after sight	30/7/2019	13 days of May +30 days of June +30 days of July 73 days	7,30,000
1,000	30/6/2019	1/7/2019	2 weeks after sight	18/7/2019	13 days of May +30 days of June +18 days of July 61 days	61,000
5,000	3/7/2019	6/7/2019	45 days after date	23/8/2019	13 days of May +30 days of June +31 days of July +23 days of August 97 days	4,85,000
25,000						12,76,000

Points to Remember

1. February has 28 days in an ordinary year and 29 days in a leap year. A leap year is completely divisible by 4.
2. If the calculated average due date falls on a public holiday, the average due date is taken as one preceding the derived average due date. In India, public holidays fall on 26 January, 15 August, and 2 October.
3. While calculating the due date from the period of the bill, if the due date falls on public holidays, take it on the same date. It is to be noted that the final average due date must not fall on a public holiday.

Interest on drawings

When different amounts are due on different dates, but are ultimately settled on one day, the interest may be calculated using the principle of average due date. When the drawings and the interest chargeable on drawings fall on different dates, the interest may be calculated on the basis of average due date.

Solution

Average due date = Base date + (Total products/Total amounts)
= 18/5/19 + (12,76,000/25,000)
= 51.04

51.04 can be rounded off to 51 days.

Average due date = Base date + Equated period
= 18/5/2019 + 51.04
= 18/5/2019 + 51 days

that is,

	18	– 5	– 2019
+ 51	–	–	
	69	5	2019
– 31 + 1			
	38	6	2019
– 30 + 1			
	8	7	2019

Therefore, the average due date is 8 July 2019.

■ **ILLUSTRATION 15.4** Amit and Bimal are two partners of a firm. They have drawn the following amounts from the firm in the year ended 31 March.

Date	A (Amount in ₹)	Date	B (Amount in ₹)
1/7/2019	500	12/6/2019	1,000
30/9/2019	800	11/8/2019	500
1/11/2019	1,000	9/2/2019	400
28/2/2020	400	7/3/2020	900

Interest at 6% p.a. is charged on all drawings. You are required to calculate the interest chargeable.

Solution

1. Calculation of interest using the usual method
   The interest calculation on Amit's drawings are as follows:

500 for 9 months	= 4,500 for 1 month
800 for 6 months	= 4,800 for 1 month
1,000 for 5 months	= 5,000 for 1 month
400 for 1 month	= 400 for 1 month
	14,700 for 1 month

14,700 @ 6% for 1 month
$$= 1/2\% \text{ of } 14,700$$
$$= ₹73.50$$

The interest calculation on Bimal's drawings is as follows:
1,000 for 292 days = 2,92,000
500 for 232 days = 1,16,000
400 for 50 days   =   20,000
900 for 24 days   =   21,600
————————
4,49,600

$$4,49,600 \times (6/100) \times (1/365) = ₹73.91$$

2. Calculation of interest using the average due date system
Either: (a) Taking 1 July 2019 as zero day, the interest calculation on Amit's drawings is as follows:

Dates	Amount (₹)	Months from Zero Day	Products
1/7/2019	500	0	0
30/9/2019	800	3	2,400
1/11/2019	1,000	4	4,000
28/2/2020	400	8	3,200
	2,700		**9,600**

Average due date = 9,600/2,700 = 3.556
Hence the average due date is 17 October 2019. Interest is chargeable from 17 October to 31 March, that is, 5.444 months.
$$2,700 \times (6/100) \times (5.444/12) = ₹73.49$$

OR   (b) Taking 1 April 2019 as zero day, the interest calculation on Amit's drawings is as follows:

Dates	Amount (₹)	Months from Zero Day	Products
1/7/2019	500	3	1,500
30/9/2019	800	6	4,800
1/11/2019	1,000	7	7,000
28/2/2020	400	11	4,400
	2,700		**17,700**

Average due date = 17,700/2,700 = 6.556
Hence the average due date is 17 October. Interest is chargeable from 17 October to 31 March, that is, 5.444 months.
$$2,700 \times (6/100) \times (5.444/12) = 73.49$$
(c) Taking 12 June as zero day, the interest calculation on Bimal's drawings is as follows:

Dates	Amount (₹)	Months from Zero Day	Products
12/6/2019	1,000	0	0
11/8/2019	500	60	30,000
9/2/2020	400	242	96,800
7/3/2020	900	268	2,41,200
	2,800		**3,68,000**

Average due date = 3,68,000/2,800 days from 12.6, that is, 131 days.

June 18
July 31
Aug. 31
Sept. 30

131 – 110, that is, 21 October 110
So interest is chargeable from 21/10/2019 to 31/3/2020, that is, for 101 days
$$2,800 \times (6/100) \times (161/365) = ₹74.10$$
The differences in amounts in the two systems (a) and (b) are due to approximation.

Application of average due date

As mentioned earlier, the principle of average due date can be applied in cases where the amount is lent in one instalment but the repayment is made in several instalments.

The procedure for calculating average due date can be summarized as:

Step 1: Calculate number of days, months, or years from the date of lending money to the date of each repayment.
Step 2: Find the total of such days, months, or years.
Step 3: The number of days, months, or years by which average due date falls away from date of commencement of loan is divided by the number of instalments.

Thus, the formula for the average due date is as follows:

> Average Due Date = Date of Loan + Sum of Days, Months, or Years from the Date of Lending to the Date of Repayment of Each Instalment/Number of Instalments

■ ILLUSTRATION 15.5   M/s Jain Bros lent ₹10,000 to Shah & Sons on 1 January 2016. The amount was to be repaid in five equal annual instalments commencing from 1 January 2017. Find the average due date and the interest at 5% p.a. to be recovered by M/s Jain Bros from Shah & Sons.

Solution
Average due date = Date of loan + Sum of days, months, or years from the date of lending to the date of repayment of each instalment/Number of instalments
$$= 1 \text{ January } 2016 + (1+2+3+4+5)/5$$
$$= 1 \text{ January } 2016 + 3 \text{ years}$$
$$= 1 \text{ January } 2019$$

Notes:
Interest at a certain rate on the instalments paid from the date of payment to any fixed date will be the same as on ₹10,000 (if lent on 1 January 2019 to that fixed date). There will be no loss to either party. Assuming the rate of interest to be 5% p.a., and the date of settlement as 1 December 2019, the interest calculation using product method will be as follows:

Amount (₹)	Paid on	Money Used by Das Bros up to 31 December 2009	Product (₹)
2,000	1 January 2017	5 years	10,000
2,000	1 January 2018	4 years	8,000
2,000	1 January 2019	3 years	6,000
2,000	1 January 2020	2 years	4,000
2,000	1 January 2021	1 years	2,000
			30,000

Interest at 5% p.a. on ₹30,000 for one year

$$= (30,000 \times 5)/100$$
$$= ₹1,500$$

Jain Bros will receive interest (if given on 1 January 2019) on ₹10,000 to 31 December 2021, that is, for 3 years at 5% p.a.

$$= (5 \times 3 \times 10,000)/100$$
$$= ₹1,500$$

From the above calculations, it can be concluded that if the borrower pays ₹2,000 per year from 1 January 2017 for 5 years, and if the lender gives ₹10,000 on 1 January 2019, then both will charge the same interest from each other. There is no loss to any of the parties. However, if the lender gives ₹10,000 on 1 January 2016, he/she can charge interest on ₹10,000 for 3 years.

$$\text{Interest} = (10,000 \times 5 \times 3)/100 = 1,500$$

Therefore, ₹1,500 is the interest to be charged by Jain Bros.

ACCOUNT CURRENT

An account current is a running statement of transactions between parties for a given period of time and includes interest allowed or charged on various items. It takes the form of an account and is prepared when frequent transactions take place between two parties. For example, a manufacturer may sell goods frequently to a merchant on credit and receive payments from him/her. The payments may be made at different intervals and the interest charged on the amount remains outstanding. A consignee of goods can also prepare an account current. An account current is also prepared to record transactions between a bank and its customer.

> *Account current is a running statement of transactions between parties.*

An account current involves two parties—(a) one who renders the account; and (b) the other to whom the account is rendered. This is indicated in the heading of an account current, which states the following: 'A in account current with B'. It implies that A is the customer, and the account is being rendered to A by B.

Red Ink Interest

In cases where the due date of a bill falls after the date of closing the account, no interest is allowed on the amount. However, the interest from the closing date to the due date is written in red ink in the appropriate side of the account current. This interest is called red ink interest and is treated as negative interest. However, in actual practice, the product of such bills [value of bill × (due date – closing date)] is written in ordinary ink on the opposite side of the bill entry. This method is also known as *interest table method*.

Periodic Balance

The preparation of account current using product balance, also known as periodic balance method, is usually adopted in the cases where the account balance is recorded after every transaction. Under this method, the number of days written against each transaction is counted from the due date to the date of the transaction. In the case of the last transaction, the number of days is counted to the close of the period.

Each amount is multiplied with the number of days. If the amount represents a debit balance, the product is entered in the *Dr. product column;* and if it represents a credit balance, the product is written in the *Cr. product column.* The Dr. product and Cr. product columns are then totalled. Interest is calculated on each amount at the given rate of interest to ascertain the net interest. If net interest is payable to the customer, it will appear as 'By Interest A/c' and if it is due from the customer, it will appear as 'To Interest A/c'. This method is also known as the *product method.*

■ **ILLUSTRATION 15.6** On 2 January 2019, Vinod opened an account current with the Allahabad Bank Ltd and deposited a sum of ₹30,000. He further deposited the following amounts:

15 January	₹12,000
12 March	₹ 8,000
10 May	₹16,000

His withdrawals are as follows:

15 February	₹26,000
10 April	₹30,000
15 June	₹14,000

Show Vinod's A/c in the ledger of the Allahabad Bank. Interest is to be calculated at 5% p.a. on the debit balance and 2% p.a. on the credit balance. The account is to be prepared as on 30 June 2019. Calculation may be made correct to the nearest rupee.

Solution

Account Current of Vinod with Allahabad Bank Ltd

Date 2019	Particulars	Dr. Less	Cr. Add	Dr. or Cr.	Balance	Days	Dr. Product	Cr. Product
2 January	By Cash A/c	—	30,000	Cr.	30,000	13	—	3,90,000
15 January	By Cash A/c	—	12,000	Cr.	42,000	31	—	13,02,000
15 February	To Self A/c	26,000	—	Cr.	16,000	25	—	4,00,000
12 March	By Cash A/c	—	8,000	Cr.	24,000	29	—	6,96,000
10 April	To Self A/c	30,000	—	Dr.	6,000	30	1,80,000	—
10 May	By Cash A/c	—	16,000	Cr.	10,000	36	—	3,60,000
15 June	To Self A/c	14,000	—	Dr.	4,000	15	60,000	—
30 June	By Interest A/c	—	140	Dr.	3,860	—	—	—
30 June	By Balance c/d	—	3,860	—	—	—	—	—
		70,000	**70,000**				**2,40,000**	**31,48,000**
1 July	To Balance b/d	3,860						

Interest is calculated as follows:

On ₹31,48,000 @ 2% for 1 day = ₹172.49

On ₹2,40,000 @ 5% for 1 day = ₹32.87

Net interest = ₹139.62

NEGOTIABLE INSTRUMENTS

Often when goods are sold on credit, the seller would like the purchaser to give a definite promise in writing to pay the amount of the goods on a certain date. Commercial practice has developed to treat these written promises into valuable instruments of credit, so much so, that when a written promise is made in proper format and is properly stamped, it is assumed that the buyer has discharged his/her debt and that the seller has received payment. A negotiable instrument represents ownership of debts and obligations.

Negotiable instruments are often accepted by banks, and money is advanced against them. They can be passed on from person to person. The written promise is either in the form of a bill of exchange or a promissory note.

Bill of Exchange

According to the Negotiable Instrument Act 1881, a bill of exchange is defined as 'an instrument in writing containing an unconditional order, signed by the maker, directing a certain person, to pay on demand or at a future date a certain sum of money only, to the order of a certain person, or to the bearer of the instrument'. Kohler describes it as 'an unconditional order in writing addressed by one person to another, signed by the person giving it, requiring the person to whom it is addressed to pay on demand or at a fixed or pre-determinable future time, a certain sum in money to order or to bearer'.

A bill of exchange is an instrument (document) prepared as evidence to show that a particular amount is receivable from a debtor on account of sale of goods. For example, Sunil sells goods worth ₹15,000 to Amit. Since Amit is unable to pay on spot the value of the goods, Sunil prepares a draft of a bill of exchange (as shown in Exhibit 15.1) and sends it to Amit for signature.

Bills of exchange can be presented as evidence.

As soon as Amit signs the instrument with or without the words *accepted*, it becomes a legal document (Refer Exhibit 15.2). Here in this case, after signing, Amit undertakes to pay Sunil ₹15,000 after expiry of the period mentioned in the bill of exchange. In case Amit fails to pay by the expiry of the period, Sunil can present this bill as evidence of sale. This bill enables Sunil to file a suit in the court of law and recover the amount from Amit's personal property.

A bill of exchange is stamped as required by prevailing law.

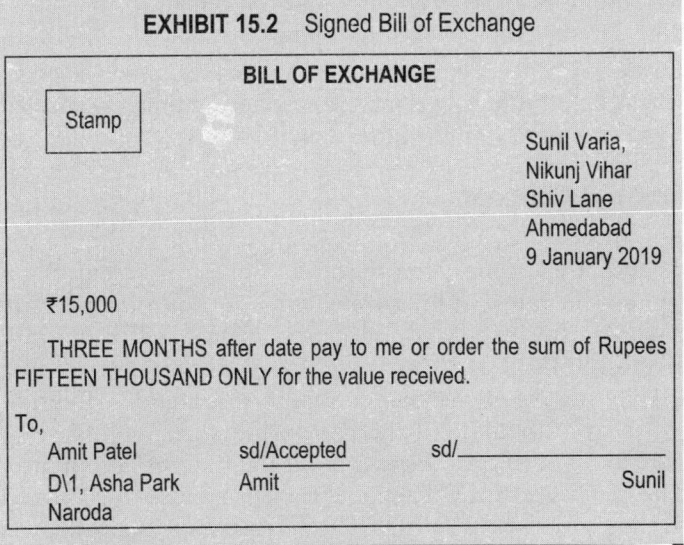

EXHIBIT 15.1   Bill of Exchange

Stamp

Sunil Varia,
Nikunj Vihar
Shiv Lane
Ahmedabad
9 January 2019

₹15,000

THREE MONTHS after date pay to me or order the sum of Rupees FIFTEEN THOUSAND ONLY for the value received.

To,
Amit Patel
D\1, Asha Park
Naroda

sd/_____
Sunil

EXHIBIT 15.2   Signed Bill of Exchange

BILL OF EXCHANGE

Stamp

Sunil Varia,
Nikunj Vihar
Shiv Lane
Ahmedabad
9 January 2019

₹15,000

THREE MONTHS after date pay to me or order the sum of Rupees FIFTEEN THOUSAND ONLY for the value received.

To,
Amit Patel
D\1, Asha Park
Naroda

sd/Accepted
Amit

sd/_____
Sunil

Parties to a bill of exchange

A bill of exchange involves the following five parties. This section provides a description of their roles.

Drawer   A drawer is the person who draws the bill of exchange. He/she is a creditor. He/she is ought to receive money on the bill.

Drawee   A drawee is the person who is liable to pay the amount of the bill. He/she is the person on whom the bill is drawn. He/she is a debtor and owes money to the drawer.

Payee   A payee is the person who is supposed to receive the money on maturity of the bill. He/she is the holder in due course who finally receives the amount of the bill on expiry of its period.

Endorser   An endorser is the person who transfers the title of the bill from his/her own name to another creditor to whom he/she owes the same amount.

Endorsee   An endorsee is a person in whose favour the title of the bill is transferred. He/she becomes the ultimate payee of the bill.

Promissory Note

A promissory note has been defined by the Negotiable Instrument Act 1881 under Section 4 as 'A promissory note is an instrument in writing (not being currency note or bank note) containing an unconditional undertaking signed by the maker to pay on demand or at a future date, a certain sum of money only to or to the order of a certain person'. Under the Reserve Bank of India regulations, a promissory note cannot be made payable to the bearer.

Parties to a promissory note

A promissory note involves the following two parties. This section provides a description of their roles.

Maker   A maker, also known as a promissor, is the person who promises to pay a certain amount on demand or at a future date. He/she prepares the note and is the debtor.

Payee   A payee, also known as a promisee, is the person in whose favour the note is made and who is ultimately entitled to receive money on the note.

Related Concepts

Bills drawn *on demand* or *at sight* are payable by the drawee or acceptor on presentation of the bill for payment or on sight of the bill. The bills drawn *after date* or *after sight* are payable after expiry of the period mentioned in the bill. Exhibit 15.3 illustrates the relevant journal entries. For calculating the expiry date in case of after date, the period starts from the date of the bill drawn, whereas in case of after sight, the period starts from the date of acceptance. The various features of negotiable instruments are explained in the section.

Due date

It is a date on which the bill becomes due for payment. This date is calculated by adding additional three days of grace to the period of the bill. Due date is also known as maturity date. Due date can be derived as follows:

If the bill is drawn after date, the calculation of the due date is calculated from the date of the bill drawn. If the bill is drawn after sight, the due date is calculated from the date of the acceptance.

	Day	Month	Year
Date of bill drawn/accepted	—	—	—
Add: Days of grace	+ 3		
Add: Period (if given in days then below days + or below month if given in months)	+ —	+ —	
Due date	xxx	xxx	xxx

■ **ILLUSTRATION 15.7**   Calculate the due date of a bill drawn on 2 March 2019 for two months.

Solution

	Day	Month	Year
Date of bill drawn	2	3 (March)	2019
Add: Days of grace	+3 (days)		
Add: Period		+2 (months)	
Due date	5	5 (May)	2019

■ **ILLUSTRATION 15.8**   Calculate the maturity date of a bill drawn after sight on 5 May 2019 for 60 days. The bill was accepted on 7 May 2019.

Solution

Since the bill is drawn after sight, the due date is calculated from the date of acceptance.

	Day	Month	Year
Date of acceptance	7	5 (May)	2019
Add: Days of grace	+ 3	—	—
Add: Period of the bill	+ 60	—	—
	70	5 (May)	2019

Since May does not have 70 days, deduct from the day column the number of days of May and add 1 to month column as follows:

	Day	Month	Year
	−31	+ 1	
	39	6	2019
Less: 30 days and add 1 to month	30	+ 1	
Due date	9	7	2019

Hence, the maturity date of this bill is 9 July 2019.

Due date of bill payable many months after date or sight   When the bill is made payable at a particular time period months after date, after sight, or after certain events, then the period stated shall be held to terminate on the date of month which corresponds with the day on which the instrument is dated. If the month in which the period would terminate has no corresponding day, the period shall be held to terminate on the last day of such month. For example, a bill dated 29 January 2019 is made payable one month after date. The due date of the instrument is the third day after 28 February. Therefore, the due date of the bill will be calculated as 3 March (since February has 28 days in 2019).

Due date when the day of maturity is a holiday   When the day on which a promissory note or bill of exchange is at maturity (after including days of grace) is a public holiday, the instrument shall be deemed to be due on the preceding business day. The expression public holiday includes Sundays and other days declared by the Central Government by notification in the official gazette. However, if the holiday is declared due to an emergency or unforeseen circumstance, the following day will be the due date.

Discounting of bill

It is a process whereby the holder in due course encashes the bill before its maturity by selling the bill to the bank. Banks charge a nominal amount for encashing the bill before due date. The amount deducted by the bank from the bill amount is termed as *discount*.

EXHIBIT 15.3 Journal Entries at a Glance

S No.	Transaction	In the Books of Drawer				In the Books of the Drawee
		Bills Retained	Bill Discounted	Bill Endorsed	Bill Sent to Bank for Collection	
1.	Sale of goods on credit by drawer to drawee	Debtor's A/c Dr. (Add) To Sales (Add)	Debtor's A/c Dr. (Add) To Sales (Add)	Debtor's A/c Dr. (Add) To Sales (Add)	Debtor's A/c Dr. (Add) To Sales (Add)	Purchase A/c Dr. (Add) To Creditor's A/c (Add)
2.	Drawing a draft B/E	No entry	No entry	No entry	No entry	No entry
3.	Acceptance of a B/E by the drawee	Bills receivable A/c Dr. (Add) To Drawee's A/c (Less) [Debtor's A/c]	Bills receivable A/c Dr. (Add) To Drawee's A/c (Less) [Debtor's A/c]	Bills receivable A/c Dr. (Add) To Drawee's A/c (Less) [Debtor's A/c]	Bills receivable A/c Dr. (Add) To Drawee's A/c (Add)	Drawer's A/c Dr. (Less) To Bills Payable A/c (Add)
4.	Treatment of bills by drawer	No entry	Bank A/c Dr. (Add) Discount A/c Dr. (Add) To Bills receivable A/c (Less)	Endorsee's A/c Dr. (Add) To Bills receivable A/c (Less)	Bill sent to bank for collection A/c Dr. (Add) To Bills receivable A/c (Less)	No entry
5.	Honour of a B/E on due date by drawee	Cash/bank A/c Dr. (Add) To Bills receivable A/c (Less)	No entry	No entry	Bank A/c Dr. (Add) To Bill sent to bank for collection A/c (Less)	Bills payable A/c Dr. (Less) To Cash balance A/c (Less)
6.	Dishonoured B/E on due date (a) If noting charges are not incurred	Drawee's A/c Dr. (Add) To Bills receivable A/c (Less)	Drawee's A/c Dr. (Add) To Bank (Less)	Drawee's A/c Dr. (Add) To Endorsee's A/c (Less)	Drawee's A/c Dr. (Add) To Bill sent to bank for collection A/c (Less)	Bills payable A/c Dr. (Less) To Drawer's A/c (Add)
	(b) If noting charges are incurred	Drawee's A/c Dr. (Add) To Bills receivable A/c (Less) (B/R) To Cash A/c (By NC)	Drawee's A/c Dr. (Add) (By B/R + NC)	Drawee's A/c Dr. (Add) (By B/R + NC)	Drawee's A/c Dr. (Add) To Bill sent to bank for collection A/c (By B/R) To Bank A/c (Less) By (NC)	Bills payable A/c Dr. (Less) Noting charges A/c Dr. (Add) To Drawer's A/c (Less)
7.	Retirement of a B/E at a rebate by drawee	Cash A/c or (Add) Discount A/c Dr. (Add) To Bills receivable A/c (Less)	No entry	No entry	Bank A/c Dr. (Add) Discount A/c Dr. (Add) To Bill sent for collection A/c (Less)	Bills payable A/c Dr. (Less) To Cash A/c (Less) To Discount A/c (Add)
8.	Renewal of a B/E (a) Cancellation of old B/E	Drawee's A/c Dr. (Add) To Bills receivable A/c (Less)	Drawee's A/c Dr. (Add) To Bank (Less)	Drawee's A/c Dr. (Add) To Endorsee's A/c (Less)	Drawee's A/c Dr. (Add) To Bill sent to bank for collection A/c (Less)	Bills payable A/c Dr. (Less) To Drawer's A/c (Add)
	(b) Part payment by the drawee	Cash A/c Dr. (Add) To Drawee's A/c (Less)	Cash A/c Dr. (Add) To Drawee's A/c (Less)	Cash A/c Dr. (Add) To Drawee's A/c (Less)	Cash A/c Dr. (Add) To Drawee's A/c (Less)	Drawer's A/c Dr. (Less) To Cash (Less)
	(c) Interest charged to drawee	Drawee's A/c Dr. (Add) To Interest A/c (Add)	Drawee's A/c Dr. (Add) To Interest A/c (Add)	Drawee's A/c Dr. (Add) To Interest A/c (Add)	Drawee's A/c Dr. (Add) To Interest A/c (Add)	Interest A/c Dr. (Add) To Drawer's A/c (Add)
	(d) Acceptance of a new B/E by drawee	Bills receivable A/c Dr. (Add) To Drawee's A/c (Less) [Debtor's A/c]	Bills receivable A/c Dr. (Add) To Drawee's A/c (Less) [Debtor's A/c]	Bills receivable A/c Dr. (Add) To Drawee's A/c (Less) [Debtor's A/c]	Bills receivable A/c Dr. (Add) To Drawee's A/c (Less)	Drawer's A/c Dr. (Less) To Bills payable A/c (Add)
9.	Treatment of a new bill by drawer	No entry	Bank A/c Dr. (Add) Discount A/c Dr. (Add) To Bills receivable A/c (Less)	Endorsee's A/c Dr. (Add) To Bills receivable A/c (Less)	Bill sent to bank for collection A/c Dr. (Add) To Bills receivable A/c (Less)	No entry
10.	Insolvency of the drawee (a) Dishonour of a B/E	Drawee's A/c Dr. (Add) To Bills receivable A/c (Less)	Drawee's A/c Dr. (Add) To Bank (Less)	Drawee's A/c Dr. (Add) To Endorsee's A/c (Less)	Drawee's A/c Dr. (Add) To Bill sent to bank for collection A/c (Less)	Bills payable A/c Dr. (Less) To Drawer's A/c (Add)
	(b) Receipt of amount from the drawee's estate as final dividend	Cash A/c Dr. (Add) Bad debts A/c Dr. (Add) To Drawee's A/c (Less)	Cash A/c Dr. (Add) Bad debts A/c Dr. (Add) To Drawee's A/c (Less)	Cash A/c Dr. (Add) Bad debts A/c Dr. (Add) To Drawee's A/c (Less)	Cash A/c Dr. (Add) Bad debts A/c Dr. (Add) To Drawee's A/c (Less)	Drawer's A/c Dr. (Less) To Cash A/c (Add) To Deficiency A/c (Add)

Notes: B/E denotes bills of exchange, B/R denotes bills receivable, and NC denotes noting charges.

Retirement of bill

Premature payment of a bill is known as the retirement of the bill. The drawee pays the amount due before the maturity date of the bill. The drawee earns a discount which is more popularly termed as *rebate*.

Dishonour of bill

On maturity when the drawee or acceptor of the bill refuses to make payment, the act is termed as *dishonour* of a bill.

Noting, protesting, and noting charges

If the bill is dishonoured by the drawee on presentation of payment, the fact must be legally established. When approached by the holder in due course, the public notary establishes the fact of dishonour on the bill and returns it to him/her. Such an act on the part of the public notary is known as *noting*. The certificate issued by the public notary stating the fact of dishonour with its causes is known as *protesting*. Noting charge is the amount charged by a public notary for his/her services. These noting charges are to be recovered from the drawee.

Renewal of bill

It is the drawing of a new bill in the place of an old bill with an extension of time as requested by the drawee. The new bill is drawn after maturity of the original bill. Interest at a nominal market rate is charged from the drawee. Sometimes the drawee pays some amount of the original bill with or without interest and accepts a new bill for the balance amount with or without interest. The steps taken on the renewal of a bill are as follows:

- Cancellation of the old bill
- Recording of interest due from the drawee
- Recording the receipt of cash from the drawee in part payment of the original bill with or without interest
- Drawing a new bill and accepting receipt from the drawee for the balance amount due with or without interest

Inland bill and foreign bill

According to Section 11 of the Negotiable Instrument Act, a promissory note, a bill of exchange, or a cheque drawn or made in India or made payable in or drawn upon any person who is a resident of India can be called an inland bill or inland negotiable instrument. For example:

- A bill drawn in Delhi on a trader in Aurangabad and accepted and payable in Shimla, Srinagar, or Singapore, is an inland bill or inland negotiable instrument.

- A bill drawn in Ahmedabad on a trader in New York accepted and payable in Delhi is an inland bill.

An instrument which is not an inland instrument is deemed to be a foreign bill or foreign negotiable instrument, as per Section 12 of the Negotiable Instrument Act. It means that foreign bills are

- bills drawn outside India and made payable or drawn upon any person resident of any country outside India.
- bills drawn outside India and made payable in India or drawn upon any resident in India.
- bills drawn in India upon persons resident outside India and made payable outside India.

For example,

- A bill of exchange drawn in London and payable to a person who is a resident of Auckland (New Zealand)
- A bill drawn in Sydney and payable in Delhi
- A bill drawn in favour of a person who is a resident of Tokya and payable in Tokyo or Paris

ACCOUNTING TREATEMENT

The accounting treatment is same in case of both bill of exchange and promissory note, that is, same accounting entries are passed in both the cases. For the purpose of accounting, bills are divided into two categories:

1. Bills receivable or B/R
2. Bills payable or B/P

The same bill is bills receivable from the point of view of the drawer who is entitled to receive its payment and is bills payable from the point of view of the drawee who has accepted it and is liable to make its payment. The drawer of bill will show B/R on the asset side and drawee will show B/P on the liabilities side of the balance sheet.

The accounting entries are depicted in Exhibit 15.3.

■ **ILLUSTRATION 15.9** Prepare a bill of exchange from the following details.

Drawer:	Pinky Bhatt, Ahmedabad
Drawee:	Dhruv Bhatt, Ahmedabad
Period:	2 months
Date of bill:	17 September 2020
Accepted on:	20 September 2020
Amount:	₹5000

Solution

```
                        BILL OF EXCHANGE

   ┌─────────┐
   │  Stamp  │                                      Pinky Bhatt,
   └─────────┘                                      Ahmedabad,
                                                    17 September 2020


   ₹15,000

   TWO MONTHS after date pay to me or my order, the sum of Rupees FIVE THOUSAND ONLY for the value received.

   To,                    Accepted sd/_____          sd/_____
   Dhruv Bhatt,           Dhruv Bhatt                 Pinky Bhatt
   Ahmedabad              20 September 2020
```

■ **ILLUSTRATION 15.10**   Draft a bill of exchange from the following details.

Drawer:	Dhaval Shah, Gandhinager
Drawee:	Milan Pandya, Baroda
Payee:	Dev Kumar, Ahmedabad
Amount:	₹10,000
Date of bill:	10 January 2020
Date of acceptance:	15 January 2020
Period of bill:	60 Days

Solution

BILL OF EXCHANGE

Stamp

Dhaval Shah,
Gandhinagar,
10 January 2020

₹10,000

SIXTY DAYS after date pay to Mr Dev Kumar, Ahmedabad or his order, the sum of Rupees TEN THOUSAND ONLY for the value received.

To,	Accepted sd/_____	sd/_____
Milan Pandya,	Milan Pandya	Dhaval Shah
Baroda	15 January 2020	

■ **ILLUSTRATION 15.11**   On 1 May 2020, Sunil purchased goods worth ₹8,000 from Anil. Two days later Sunil gave Amit the acceptance for four months. On 3 June 2020, Anil discounted the bill with a bank @ 12% p.a. On due date, when the bill was presented for payment, Sunil dishonoured the bill. Anil paid ₹50 as noting charges to a public notary. On 25 September 2020, Sunil was adjudged insolvent and only 30 paise per rupee could be recovered from his estate.

Prepare journal entries in the books of both the parties and show Sunil's A/c in the books of Anil.

Solution

Journal Entries in the Books of Anil (Drawer)

Date 2020	Particulars	L.F.	Dr. (₹)	Cr. (₹)
1 May	Sunil's A/c Dr. (Add)		8,000	
	To Sales A/c (Add)			8,000
	(Being credit sales made to Sunil)			
3 May	Bills receivable A/c Dr. (Add)		8,000	
	To Sunil's A/c (Less)			8,000
	(Being received acceptance on bill from Sunil)			
3 June	Cash/Bank A/c Dr. (Add)		7,760	
	Discount A/c Dr. (Add)		240	
	To Bills receivable A/c (Less)			8,000
	(Being Sunil's acceptance discounted with the bank @ 12% p.a.)			
4 September	Sunil's A/c Dr. (Add)		8,050	
	To Bank A/c (Less)			8,000
	To Cash A/c (Less)			50
	(Being Sunil dishonouring his acceptance and noting charges paid)			
25 September	Cash/Bank A/c Dr. (Add)		2,415	
	Bad debts A/c Dr. (Add)		5,635	
	To Sunil's A/c (Less)			8,050
	(30 paise per rupee recovered from Sunil's property due to insolvency)			
	Total		**40,100**	**40,100**

Ledger of Anil
Sunil's Account

Account No:

Account Type: Asset

Normal Balance: Debit

Date 2020	Reference Account	Voucher Type	Post Ref No.	Dr. (Add)	Cr. (Less)	Balance (₹)
1 May	To Sales A/c			8,000		8,000
3 May	By Bills receivable A/c				8,000	0

Date	Particulars			Dr. (₹)	Cr. (₹)	
4 September	To Bank A/c			8,000		8,000
4 September	To Cash A/c (Noting charges)			50		8,050
25 September	By Cash or bank A/c				2,415	5,635
25 September	By Bad debts A/c				5,635	0
	Total			16,050	16,050	

Journal Entries in the Books of Sunil (Drawee)

Date 2020	Particulars	L.F.	Dr. (₹)	Cr. (₹)
1 May	Purchase A/c Dr. (Add)		8,000	
	To Anil's A/c (Add)			8,000
	(Being credit purchase made from Anil)			
3 May	Anil's A/c Dr. (Less)		8,000	
	To Bills payable A/c (Add)			8,000
	(Being acceptance given for 4 months)			
4 September	Bills payable A/c Dr. (Less)		8,000	
	Noting charges A/c Dr. (Add)		50	
	To Anil's A/c (Add)			8,050
	(Being our acceptance to Anil dishonoured and noting charges payable)			
25 September	Anil's A/c Dr. (Less)		8,050	
	To Cash/bank A/c (Less)			2,415
	To Deficiency A/c (Add)			5,635
	(30 paise per rupee was paid to Anil from private estate)			

Working Notes:

Discount on a bill is calculated as follows:

Discount Amount = Bill amount × Rate of discount × (Unexpired period of bill/12 months or 365 days)

= 8000 × (12/100) × (3/12)

■ **ILLUSTRATION 15.12**   Shabnam owed Tina ₹8,000 as on 1 January 2020. Tina drew two bills amounting to ₹6,000 for two months and ₹2,000 for three months. Shabnam accepted the bills. Tina endorsed the first bill to Minu on 3 January 2020 on full settlement of her dues of ₹6,050, and sent the second bill to the bank for collection on the same date. On the due date of the first bill, Shabnam expressed her inability to meet the bill and requested Tina to accept ₹2,000 in cash and draw a new bill for the balance amount for one month with interest @ 18% p.a. and loss of discount previously earned from Minu. Tina settled Minu's A/c by paying ₹6,025 as cash and accepted Shabnam's offer. On the due date both the bills were dishonoured. Tina paid ₹50 each on both bills as noting charges. On 15 May 2020, Tina recovered 50 paise per rupee from Shabnam's private estate.

Prepare necessary journal entries in the books of Tina.

Solution

Journal Entries in the Books of Tina

Date 2020	Particulars	L.F.	Dr. (₹)	Cr. (₹)
1 January	Bills receivable–I A/c Dr. (Add)		6,000	
	Bills receivable–II A/c Dr. (Add)		2,000	
	To Shabnam's A/c (Less)			8,000
	(Being two bills drawn on Shabnam duly accepted by her for 2 and 3 months)			
3 January	Minu's A/c Dr. (Less)		6,050	
	To Bills receivable–I A/c (Less)			6,000
	To Discount earned A/c (Add)			50
	(Being endorsed first acceptance of Shabnam to Minu in full settlement of ₹6,050)			
3 January	Bills for collection A/c Dr. (Add)		2,000	
	To Bills receivable–II A/c (Less)			2,000
	(Being sent second acceptance of Shabnam to bank for collection)			
4 March	Shabnam's A/c Dr. (Add)		6,025	
	Discount earned A/c Dr. (Less)		25	
	To Minu's A/c (Add)			6,050
	(Being Shabnam's acceptance endorsed to Minu dishonoured and discount also disallowed)			

Date 2020	Particulars	L.F.	Dr. (₹)	Cr. (₹)
4 March	Shabnam's A/c Dr. (Add)		60	
	To Interest A/c (Add)			60
	(Being interest charged to Shabnam on balance amount due @ 18% p.a. for one month)			
4 March	Cash A/c Dr. (Add)		2,000	
	New bills receivable–I A/c Dr. (Add)		4,085	
	To Shabnam's A/c (Less)			6,085
	(Being original bill renewed for balance amount with interest and loss of discount for one month)			
4 March	Minu's A/c Dr. (Less)		6,050	
	To Cash A/c (Less)			6,025
	To Discount earned A/c (Add)			25
	(Being settlement of Minu's A/c by paying ₹6,025)			
4 April	Shabnam's A/c Dr. (Add)		2,050	
	To Bank for collection A/c (Less)			2,000
	To Cash A/c (Less)			50
	(Being second acceptance of Shabnam dishonoured and noting charges paid)			
7 April	Shabnam's A/c Dr. (Add)		4,135	
	To New bills receivable—I A/c (Less)			4,085
	To Cash A/c (Less)			50
	(Being third acceptance of Shabnam dishonoured and noting charges paid)			
15 May	Cash/Bank A/c Dr. (Add)		3,092.50	
	Bad debts A/c Dr. (Add)		3,092.50	
	To Shabnam's A/c (Less)			6,185
	(Being 50 paise per rupee recovered from private estate of Shabnam for amount due, on her becoming insolvent)			
	Total		**46,665**	**46,665**

Working notes:

The calculation of interest on renewal of first bill is as follows:

Interest = Balance amount + Loss of discount × Rate ×

(New bill period/12)

= 4,000 + (25 × 18/100 × 1/12)

= ₹60.38

ACCOMMODATION BILLS

Finance is one of the important elements of every business enterprise. There are different ways of raising funds for running a business. One of the easiest ways of raising quick short-term finance is by drawing *accommodation bills.* Accommodation bills are drawn by a business to meet its temporary financial problems. An accommodation bill is raised by drawing a non-trade bill of exchange by a drawer on the drawee who is willing to help him/her out during financial crises. Accordingly, the drawer approaches the drawee and requests him/her to accept a bill drawn for a stipulated amount and period. After the drawee gives acceptance on the bill, the same is discounted by the drawer with the bank.

On receiving the funds, the drawer and the drawee decide about using the amount. At times the full amount of the bill is used by the drawer for the period of the bill and just before the maturity date of the bill, he/she remits the bill amount to the drawee, so as to enable the drawee to honour the bill on being presented by the bank for payment.

At times, the drawer and the drawee decide to share the proceeds of the bill in a predetermined proportion. In this case, the drawer after discounting the bill remits a portion of the proceeds to the drawee. The drawee also bears

> Accommodation bill is a non-trade bill of exchange.

a part of the discount amount in the same proportion of the funds. Before maturity, the drawer has to remit the balance amount left with him/her or else the drawee can dishonour the bill.

Occasionally, the persons in need of money decide to draw two different bills on each other and use the proceeds amongst them in agreed proportion. The discount amount, which is the expense for raising money through the accommodation bill, is borne by the persons in the same proportion in which they use the funds of the bills. Accommodation bills raise short-term finance at a minimum cost. The features of accommodation bills are as follows:

1. They are drawn to raise short-term quick finances.
2. They are drawn by business persons to overcome mutual financial needs.
3. They are not based on any genuine trade transaction.
4. Both the drawer and the drawee can use the bill amount in pre-decided proportions.
5. The drawer must remit the amount of the bill before maturity to the acceptor to enable him/her to honour the bill.
6. Accommodation bills are always discounted with the bank. The drawer sells the bill to the bank for cash.
7. Three days of grace is not allowed on an accommodation bill as it is considered illegal in the eyes of law.

■ **ILLUSTRATION 15.13** For financing a business deal, Gautam draws a bill of ₹9,000 on Farid for 2 months on 10 June 2020. Farid returns the bill to Gautam after accepting it. Gautam discounts the bill with the bank on 13 June 2020 for ₹8,700 and remits one-third of the amount to Farid.

Gautam was unable to remit his share of the bill to Farid before the due date of the bill. Therefore, on 14 April 2020, Gautam accepted a bill for ₹12,000 for 1 month drawn on him by Farid. On the same day, Farid discounted the bill with his bank for ₹11,820 and honoured his acceptance. On 16 August 2020, Farid remitted ₹1,880 to Gautam. On 7 September 2020, Gautam became insolvent and on 7 October 2020, Farid received 50% in a rupee as first and final dividend from Gautam's estate. Prepare journal entries in the books of Gautam and show Farid's A/c in the books of Gautam.

Solution

Journal Entries in the Books of Gautam

Date 2020	Particulars	L.F.	Dr. (₹)	Cr. (₹)
10 June	Bills receivable A/c Dr. (Add)		9,000	
	To Farid's A/c (Less)			9,000
	(Being accommodation bill drawn on Farid duly accepted by him for two months)			
13 June	Bank A/c Dr. (Add)		8,700	
	Discount A/c Dr. (Add)		300	
	To Bills receivable A/c (Less)			9,000
	(Being Farid's acceptance discounted with the bank)			
13 June	Farid A/c Dr. (Add)		3,000	
	To Cash/bank A/c (Less)			2,900
	To Discount A/c (Less)			100
	(Being one-third of the bill proceeds remitted to Farid)			
14 August	Farid A/c Dr. (Add)		12,000	
	To Bills payable A/c (Add)			12,000
	(Being given acceptance on accommodation bill to Farid for one month)			
16 August	Cash/bank A/c Dr. (Add)		1,880	
	Discount A/c Dr. (Add)		120	
	To Farid's A/c (Less)			2,000
	(Being remittance received from Farid from the bill accepted by us)			
7 September	Bills payable A/c Dr. (Less)		12,000	
	To Farid's A/c (Less)			12,000
	(Being our acceptance dishonored)			
7 October	Farid's A/c Dr. (Add)		8,000	
	To Cash/bank A/c (Less)			4,000
	To Deficiency A/c (Add)			4,000
	(Being 50% in a rupee paid as first and final dividend from our estate)			
	Total		**55,000**	**55,000**

Ledger of Gautam
Farid's Account

Account No:

Account Type: Asset

Normal Balance: Debit

Date 2020	Reference Account	Voucher Type	Post Ref No.	Dr. (Add)	Cr. (Less)	Balance (₹)
10 June	By Bills receivable A/c				9,000	(9,000)
13 June	To Cash or bank A/c			2,900		(6,100)
13 June	To Discount A/c			100		(6,000)
14 August	To Bills payable A/c			12,000		6,000
16 August	By Cash or bank A/c				1,880	4,120
16 August	By Discount A/c				120	4,000
17 September	By Bills payable A/c				12,000	(8,000)
7 October	To Cash or bank A/c			4,000		(4,000)
7 October	To Deficiency A/c			4,000		
	Total			23,000	23,000	

Working Notes:

In this problem, both Gautam and Farid become drawer and drawee interchangeably in the first and the second bill. In case of an accommodation bill, each party must bear the proportional amount of discount depending upon the funds available at his disposal.

In the case of the first bill, Gautam used two-thirds of the bill proceeds and Farid utilized one-third of the amount. Therefore, the amount resulting from the discounting of the bill is also borne by them in the same proportion. Hence, when Gautam remitted one-third of the proceeds to Farid, he transferred one-third of the discount amount along with the cash amount to Farid (i.e., ₹100).

When the second bill is discounted, Farid remitted ₹1,880 to Gautam. Since Gautam receives a cash payment of ₹1,880, he is also liable to bear the proportionate discount of the second bill. The discount can be calculated using two methods.

Method I

	Gautam	Farid
Proportion of sharing bill proceeds	2/3	1/3
Division of discount ₹180 of second bill	₹120	₹60
Second bill in the same proportion	180(2/3)	180(1/3)

Method II

Total funds available with Gautam = Share in proceeds of the first bill + Share in proceeds of the second bill
= ₹6,000 + ₹2,000
= ₹8,000

Now, when the second bill is discounted, cash amounts to ₹11,820 and the discount amounts to ₹180. The total cash available with Gautam is ₹8,000

Discount = (8,000/11,820) × 180
= 120

■ **ILLUSTRATION 15.14** Virat has advanced the following amounts to Aman.

₹1,000 paid on 15/1/2020: credit period 1 month
₹2,000 paid on 10/2/2020: credit period 2 months
₹3,000 paid on 5/3/2020: credit period 3 months

Aman wants to pay all these debts in one lump sum. Find out the due date when he should make payment without loss of interest to either party.

Solution

1. First ascertain the due dates for making payment.
2. Next select the earliest due date as a zero date.

Date of Advance	Credit Period	Due Date	No. of Days from Zero Date to Due Date	Amount (₹)	Products (Days ¥ Amount)
15/1/2020	1 month	15/2/2020	0	1,000	0
10/2/2020	2 months	10/4/2020	55	2,000	1,10,000
5/3/2020	3 months	5/6/2020	111	3,000	3,33,000
				6,000	**4,43,000**

$$\text{Equated period} = \frac{\text{Sum of products}}{\text{Sum of amounts}}$$

$$= \frac{4,43,000}{6,000}$$

$$= 73\frac{5}{6}$$

$$= 74 \text{ days}$$

Average due date = Zero date + Equated period
= 15/2/2020 + 74 days = 29/4/2020
So average due date = 29 April 2020

Note:

1. There are no bills of exchange and hence, 3 days of grace are not added to arrive at due dates.
2. 2020 is a leap year and there are 29 days in February.

Working Note:

It is for the convenience of calculations that the first due date is selected as the starting date. However, any other date can also be selected as a zero date. But the difficulty is that, it will involve minus number of days and minus product.

■ **ILLUSTRATION 15.15** Abhinav sells goods to his customers on credit, the credit period being 1 month from the date of transaction. Interest at 6% p.a. is charged for late payment. His transactions with Babita for 2020 were as follows:

Date of Sale	Value of Goods Sold (₹)	Date of Amounts Received	Amount Received (₹)
1/8/2020	200	15/9/2020	100
15/9/2020	800	20/10/2020	600
25/10/2020	1,000	1/12/2020	900

Calculate the amount of interest charged to Babita for 2020.

Solution

Date of Sale	Credit Period	Due Date	No. of Days	Amount (₹)	Products
1/8/2020	1	1/9/2020	0	200	0
15/9/2020	1	15/10/2020	44	800	35,200
25/10/2020	1	25/11/2020	85	1,000	85,000
				2,000	**1,20,200**

Date of Payment	No. of Days	Amount Paid (₹)	Products
15/9/2020	14	100	1,400
20/10/2020	49	600	29,400
1/12/2020	91	900	81,900
		1,600	**1,12,700**

	₹	Product
Amount due and products	2,000	1,20,200
Less: Amount received and products	1,600	1,12,700
	400	7,500

$$\therefore \text{ Equated period} = \frac{7,500}{400}$$

$$= 18\frac{3}{4}$$

$$= 19 \text{ days}$$

∴ Average due date = 1/9/2020 + 19 days = 20/9/2020
Number of days from 20/9/2020 to 31/12/2020 = 102 days

$$\therefore \text{ Interest} = \frac{400}{1} \times \frac{6}{100} \times \frac{102}{365} = \frac{2448}{365} = ₹6.72$$

■ **ILLUSTRATION 15.16** From the following particulars, prepare the account current to be rendered by Ashwin to Zoya as on 31 December 2020. The rate of interest is 10% p.a. Use product method.

Date	Particulars	Amount (₹)
11/10/2020	Goods sent to Zoya	1,020
15/10/2020	Cash received from Zoya	500
20/10/2020	Goods sent to Zoya	650
7/11/2020	Goods sent to Zoya	700
8/11/2020	Cash received from Zoya	1,000

Solution

Let us prepare an account that will appear in the ledger, without interest calculations.

Ledger of Ashwin
Zoya's Account

Account No:
Account Type: Asset   Normal Balance: Debit

Date 2020	Reference Account	Voucher Type	Post Ref No.	Dr. (Add)	Cr. (Less)	Balance (₹)
11 October	To Sales A/c			1,020		1,020
15 October	By Cash or bank A/c				500	520
20 October	To Sales A/c			650		1,170
7 November	To Sales A/c			700		1,870
8 December	By Cash or bank A/c				1,000	870
31 December	By Balance c/d				870	
	Total			**2,370**	**2,370**	**(2,370)**
1 January	To Balance b/d			870		870

Let us prepare an account current, that is, the account with interest calculations.

1. First Method: (Interest table method):

Zoya in Account Current with Ashwin as on 31 December 2020

Date	Particulars	Amount (₹)	Days upto 31 Dec. 2020	Interest (₹)	Date	Particulars	Amount (₹)	Days up to 31 Dec. 2020	Interest (₹)
11/10/2020	To Sales A/c	1,020	81	22.64	15/10/2020	By Cash A/c	500	77	10.55
20/10/2020	To Sales A/c	650	72	12.82	08/12/2020	By Cash A/c	1,000	23	6.30
07/11/2020	To Sales A/c	700	54	10.36	31/12/2020	By Interest difference A/c			28.97
31/12/2020	To Interest A/c	29			31/12/2020	By balance c/d	899		
		2,399		45.82			2,399		45.82
01/01/2021	To Balance b/d	899							

2. Second Method (Product method)

Zoya in Account Current with Ashwin as on 31 December 2020

Date	Particulars	Amount (₹)	Days upto Dec. 31 2020	Product	Date	Particulars	Amount (₹)	Days up to Dec. 31 2020	Interest (₹)
11/10/2020	To Sales A/c	1,020	81	82,620	15/10/2020	By Cash A/c	500	77	38,500
20/10/2020	To Sales A/c	650	72	46,800	08/12/2020	By Cash A/c	1,000	23	23,000
07/11/2020	To Sales A/c	700	54	37,800	31/12/2020	By Balance of products			1,05,720
31/12/2020	To Interest (WN) A/c	29			31/12/2020	By balance c/d	899		
		2,399		1,67,220			2,399		1,67,220
01/01/2021	To Balance b/d	899							

Working Note:

Interest = Balance of product × rate of interest × 1/365
= 1,05,720 × 10/100 × 1/365
= ₹29

■**ILLUSTRATION 15.17** Anandi drew a bill on 1/3/2019 for ₹1,000 on Priya for 3 months. Before maturity, Priya requested Anandi to cancel the bill and accept ₹425 in cash including ₹25 for interest and drew another bill for the balance for 2 months. Anandi agreed to the proposal which was carried out. The bill was met on the due date.

Make entries in the books of both Anandi and Priya.

Solution

Journal Entries in the Books of Anandi

Date 2019	Particulars	L.F.	Dr. (₹)	Cr. (₹)
1 Mar	Bills receivable A/c (Add) Dr.		1,000	
	To Priya's A/c (Less)			1,000
	(Bill for 3 months received from Priya duly accepted)			
4 June	Priya's A/c (Add) Dr.		1,000	
	To Bills receivable A/c (Less)			1,000
	(Priya's acceptance cancelled on maturity at her request)			
4 June	Priya's A/c (Add) Dr.		25	
	To Interest A/c (Add)			25
	(Interest chargeable to Priya for the extension allowed)			
4 June	Cash A/c (Add) Dr.		425	
	To Priya's A/c (Less)			425
	(Cash received from Priya in part payment of her dues)			
4 June	Bills receivable A/c (Add) Dr.		600	
	To Priya's A/c (Less)			600
	(A new bill for 2 months received from Priya in full settlement of her dues)			
7 Aug	Cash A/c (Add) Dr.		600	
	To Bills receivable A/c (Less)			600
	(Priya's new acceptance met on due date)			

Journal Entries in the Books of Priya

Date 2019	Particulars	L.F.	Dr. (₹)	Cr. (₹)
1 Mar	Anandi's A/c (Less) Dr.		1,000	
	To Bills payable A/c (Add)			1,000
	(Bill drawn by Anandi for 3 months duly accepted)			
4 June	Bills payable A/c (Less) Dr.		1,000	
	To Anandi's A/c (Add)			1,000
	(Our acceptance cancelled at our request on due date)			
4 June	Interest A/c (Add) Dr.		25	
	To Anandi's A/c (Add)			25
	(Amount of interest agreed to be paid by us for extension)			
4 June	Anandi's A/c (Less) Dr.		425	
	To Cash A/c (Less)			425
	(Cash paid to Anandi in part payment of our dues to her)			
4 June	Anandi's A/c (Less) Dr.		600	
	To Bills payable A/c (Add)			600
	(A new bill drawn by Anandi for 2 months for the balance of her dues accepted by us)			
7 Aug	Bills payable A/c (Less) Dr.		600	
	To Cash A/c (Less)			600
	(Our new acceptance paid on maturity)			

■ **ILLUSTRATION 15.18** For his temporary accommodation, Ajit draws a bill of ₹2,000 for three months on his friend Chandran on 1 July 2020. Chandran accepts the bill and returns it to Ajit, who gets it discounted with the bank for ₹1,950. On due date, Ajit remits the amount to Chandran, who meets the bill.

Give journal entries in the books of both Ajit and Chandran.

Solution

Journal Entries in the Books of Ajit

Date 2020	Particulars	L.F.	Dr. (₹)	Cr. (₹)
1 July	Bills receivable A/c (Add) Dr.		2,000	
	To Chandran's A/c (Less)			2,000
	(Chandran's acceptance received)			
1 July	Cash A/c (Add) Dr.		1,950	
	Discount A/c (Add) Dr.		50	
	To Bills receivable A/c (Less)			2,000
	(Chandran's acceptance discounted for ₹1,950)			
4 Oct.	Chandran's A/c (Add) Dr.		2,000	
	To Cash A/c (Less)			2,000
	(Amount remitted to Chandran to enable him to meet the bill)			

Journal Entries in the Books of Chandran

Date 2020	Particulars	L.F.	Dr. (₹)	Cr. (₹)
1 July	Ajit's A/c (Less) Dr.		2,000	
	To Bills payable A/c (Add)			2,000
	(Acceptance of the bill drawn by Ajit for his accommodation)			
1 July	Cash A/c (Add) Dr.		2,000	
	To Ajit's A/c (Add)			2,000
	(Cash received from Ajit to meet the bill drawn by him)			
4 Oct	Bills payable A/c (Less) Dr.		2,000	
	To Cash A/c (Less)			2,000
	(Payment of bill drawn by Ajit)			

SUMMARY

- Average due date is an equated date on several payments due on different dates.
- An account current is a running statement of transactions between parties for a given period of time and includes interest allowed or charged on various items. It takes the form of an account.

KEYWORDS

Account current It is a running statement of transactions between parties for a given period of time and includes interest allowed or charged on various items.

Average due date It is an equated date on several payments due on different dates. The payment can be made in one lump sum without loss of interest to any party.

Bill of exchange An instrument in writing containing an unconditional order, signed by the maker, directing a certain person, to pay on demand or at a future date a certain sum of money only, to the order of a certain person or to the bearer of the instrument.

Drawee The person who is liable to pay the amount of the bill.

Drawer The person who draws a bill of exchange.

Endorsee The person in whose favour the title of the bill is transferred.

Endorser The person who transfers the title of the bill from his/her name to another creditor.

Payee The person who is supposed to receive money of the bill on maturity.

Promissory note It is an instrument in writing containing an unconditional undertaking signed by the maker to pay on demand or at a future date, a certain sum of money only to or to the order of a certain person.

QUESTIONS

I. Fill in the blanks.

1. _____ is an equated date on which a single payment is made instead of several payments on different dates.
2. The average due date is also called _____ date.
3. Average due date = Basic date + _____/Total amount.
4. When an amount of the bill is paid before maturity the bill is said to be _____.
5. The person who endorses a bill is called _____.
6. If a bill is drawn on 14 May, and its duration is 90 days, payment on it must be made on _____.
7. If the bill falls due for payment on 26 January, then the payment must be made on _____ January.
8. If a bill of exchange of 2 months duration is accepted on 15 September, its maturity date will be _____.
9. If a bill falls due for payment on 15 August, it will be paid on _____.
10. If a bill of exchange of one month duration is accepted on 23 December 2012, its due date will be _____.
11. If a bill of exchange of 2 months duration is accepted on 13 June 2012, its due date will be _____.
12. A bill drawn and accepted on 23 November 2012, and duration of a bill is two months, the date of the bill will be _____.
13. A bill is required to be _____ by the drawee.
14. A bill of exchange must be signed by _____.
15. Before accepting a bill it is called _____.
16. When the bill is dishonoured, _____ is held responsible for noting charges.
17. A person to whom the bill is endorsed is called _____.
18. The drawee becomes an _____ on acceptance of bill.
19. If the bill is drawn on 26 December 2013, and duration of a bill is two months, the due date of the bill will be _____.
20. The acceptor is allowed _____ days of grace to meet the bill in time.
21. There are _____ parties to a bill of exchange.
22. There are _____ parties to a promissory note.
23. A bill after sight drawn for 2 months on 18 December 2013 and accepted on 28 December 2013 will mature on _____.
24. Accommodation bill is a _____ bill.
25. Accommodation bill is drawn to raise _____ finance.

26. Businessmen draw _____ bill to overcome mutual financial needs.
27. Accommodation bill is _____ based on any trade transaction.
28. _____ bills are always _____ with the bank.
29. In case of accommodation bill, the drawer _____ the bill to the bank or cash.
30. Accommodation bills are drawn without any _____.

II. Giving reasons, state whether the following statements are True or False.

1. Average due date is a date on which payment of several amounts can be made in a lump sum.
2. Average due date is used by partnership firms for calculating interest on partners' drawings on different dates.
3. Average due date falls before or after base date.
4. The ownership of bills of exchange can be changed by endorsing it.
5. When the amount of a bill is paid on due date, it is said to be retired.
6. When a discounted bill is honoured by the drawee, no entry is passed in the books of the drawer.
7. A bill of exchange may be without a date.
8. A bill of exchange which arises out of a trading relationship of two persons is called a trade bill.
9. A promissory note can be made payable to the bearer.
10. A bill of exchange cannot be made payable to the bearer.
11. A bill falling due on 15 August must be paid for on 16 August.
12. A bill can be endorsed only once.
13. Accommodation bills are drawn to raise long-term finance.
14. In case of raising funds through an accommodation bill, one has to undergo long procedures at a bank.
15. Accommodation bills are not based on any genuine trade transaction.
16. An accommodation bill can either be discounted or sent to the bank for collection.
17. It is not possible for the drawee to retire the accommodation bill without the consent of the drawer.
18. After discounting, the proceeds of an accommodation bill are always shared by the drawer and drawee in pre-decided proportions.
19. An accommodation bill is a non-negotiable instrument.
20. Three days of grace are allowed in case of an accommodation bill.
21. Law considers an accommodation bill to be an illegal bill.
22. The drawer before maturity must remit the amount of accommodation bill retained by him to the drawee to enable the acceptor to honour the bill on maturity.

III. Write the word/term/phrase which can substitute each of the following statements.

1. An equated date on which several payments due on different dates can be made in one lump sum amount without loss of interest to any party.
2. The other name by which average due date is popularly known.
3. The date which is the starting point for calculating average due date.
4. The public holidays on which the payment of the bills cannot be made even if they are due, instead the payments are done one day prior to them.
5. The formula by which the equated period is derived.
6. Payment before the due date.
7. Officer appointed by the government for the noting of a dishonoured bill.
8. A person on whom the bill is drawn.

9. A bill drawn in India and payable in Japan.
10. A person who endorses a bill.
11. A bill drawn for valid consideration.
12. A written promise given for payment to be made on some future date for goods transacted.
13. The person to whom the amount of the bill is made payable.
14. The request by the acceptor of the bill to the drawer to extend the period of credit.

IV. Match the following pairs.

A	B
1. Foreign bill	(a) Drafting a new bill on cancellation of old bill.
2. Accommodation bill	(b) Bill drawn, accepted, and payable within the country.
3. Inland bill	(c) A person in whose favour the bill is transferred.
4. Renewal of the bill	(d) A person who endorses the bill.
5. Endorsee	(e) Bill drawn without consideration.
	(f) Bill drawn and/or accepted in one country and payable in other country.

V. Solve the following problems.

1. Pravin, for the mutual and temporary accommodation for his business and Dilip's business, draws upon Dilip a bill of exchange of three months for ₹15,000 dated 1 August 2020. Pravin discounted this bill immediately at his bank @ 6% p.a. on quarterly basis, and remits half the amount to Dilip.

   At the same time, Dilip for a mutual business need draws a bill at 3 months on Pravin for ₹8,000. Dilip discounts his bill at his bank @ 3% p.a. on quarterly basis, and remits half the proceeds to Pravin. On 31 November 2020, Dilip became bankrupt and the first and final dividend of 50 paise per rupee was paid from his estate on 31 December 2020.

   Prepare journal entries in the books of Pravin and prepare Pravin's A/c in the books of Dilip.

2. Kavita has drawn the following bills for 4 months on Asmita.

Date of Bill	Amount (₹)
7/1/2019	4,000
22/4/2019	3,000
16/6/2019	2,000
18/8/2019	1,000

   Find out the average due date of the above four bills.

3. Aditya borrowed ₹50,000 from a bank on 1 January 2018 repayable in 10 quarterly equal instalments commencing from 31 December 2019. Calculate the average due date and interest at 15% p.a.

4. Taking into account the following transactions between Vasant and Pravin, prepare an account current to be rendered to Pravin by Vasant, according to product method on 31 March 2019.

Date 2019	Particulars	Amount (₹)
1 Jan	Balance due by Pravin	4,000
15 Jan	Goods sold to Pravin (Credit : 1 month)	2,000
2 Feb	Pravin paid cash	500
20 Feb	Pravin accepted one month's bill	1,200
28 Feb	Purchased goods from Pravin (Credit period : 1 month)	1,000
15 Mar	Pravin paid cash	1,000

   Interest is to be reckoned at 10% p.a.

5. Asmita sells to Priya goods valued at ₹2,000 and draws on 1/4/2019 a 3 months' bill for the amount which Priya accepts. Asmita discounts the same with the bank for ₹1,950 on 4/4/2019. On maturity, Priya fails to honor the bill and requests Asmita to accept ₹1,000 in cash and to draw a new bill, payable after four months for the balance together with interest at 12% p.a. Asmita agrees to it, and draws a new bill on 4/7/2019. The new bill is met on the due date.

     Make necessary journal entries in the books of Asmita.

6. Rajan sold goods worth ₹2,000 to Sheeba on 1 January 2019 and drew a bill on Sheeba for two months which Sheeba accepted. Rajan discounted the bill on 4 January 2019 at 12% p.a. with his bank. Before maturity, Sheeba requested Rajan to renew the bill by accepting ₹320 in cash, including ₹20 for interest and for another bill of 3 months. Rajan accepted this proposal and drew a new bill on 4 March 2019. The bill was duly met on the due date.

     Make entries in the books of both parties.

7. Keshav drew a bill for ₹1,500 on 1 October 2018 on Reshma for 4 months. Reshma duly accepted it and returned it to Keshav, who endorsed the bill to Arnab on 4 October 2018. The bill was dishonoured on maturity and Arnab paid ₹20 as noting charges. Reshma paid ₹320 in cash to Keshav and accepted a fresh bill for the balance, including interest for 3 months at 10% p.a. On 7 May 2019, Reshma was declared insolvent and only 50 paise in a rupee was received from her receiver.

     Make entries in the books of Keshav.

8. Polly draws a bill of ₹3,000 on Sangeeta on 1 August 2020 for 3 months for the mutual accommodation, which Sangeeta duly accepts. Sangeeta, for a similar purpose, draws a bill of ₹3,000 on the same date on Polly which the latter duly accepts. Both the bills are discounted with the bank at 6% p.a. On due date, Polly meets her bill but Sangeeta fails to honour her acceptance. However, she paid ₹1,000 in cash to Polly and accepted another bill for two months for ₹2,040 including interest. The new bill was duly met by Sangeeta.

     Draft journal entries in the books of Polly and Sangeeta.

9. For mutual accommodation, Abhilash drew upon Bhavin a bill of three months' duration for ₹12,000 on 1 January 2020, which was duly accepted by Bhavin and returned to Abhilash on the same day. The bill was discounted by Abhilash at 5% p.a. on 4 January 2020, and half the proceeds were remitted to Bhavin.

     Abhilash remitted the balance due on his account to Bhavin on 3 April 2020. Abhilash had to pay the amount of the bills as Bhavin could not make the payment of the bill on maturity.

     On 4 April 2020, Abhilash drew another bill for three months' duration on Bhavin for the amount due together with the amount of interest of ₹120 thereon, which was duly accepted by Bhavin.

     Abhilash sent that bill for collection to his bank. Bhavin became bankrupt before the maturity of the bill and fifty paise in a rupee was received by Abhilash as first and final dividend from his estate.

     From the above particulars, draft the necessary journal entries in the books of Abhilash.

Analysis and Interpretation of Financial Statements

Learning Objectives

After studying this chapter, you will understand

- how to study and analyse financial statements
- the utility and critical evaluation of financial ratios
- different methods for analysis of financial statements

INTRODUCTION

Accounting is the recording and reporting of the business activities of an entity. It covers activities of—(a) the principal business (selling goods or services), (b) investment (purchasing assets), and (c) financing (raising money for investment).

Business

Business covers all the activities carried out by a firm to earn profits. It includes trading or purchase of goods to be sold later at profit. It also includes manufacturing of raw materials into finished goods (for example, conversion of cotton into cloth) with the help of machinery and labour. The business activities of a firm also include services such as transporting, warehousing, etc.

Business activities of trading, manufacturing, and services give rise to revenue receipts and revenue expenditure. Revenue receipts refer to the amount received by a firm from sale of goods, fees received for rendering services, interest received for loans given, etc. Revenue expenditure refers to the amount paid by a firm to purchase goods, salaries paid to employees for services rendered, travelling expenses, interest paid on loans taken from banks, etc. Income refers to the revenue earned during an accounting year. Expenses refer to revenue expenditure incurred during an accounting year. Profit is the excess of income over expenses and loss is the excess of expenses over income.

Investment

In order to produce goods, a manufacturer has to make investments in machinery, land, factory, etc. Such investments are called assets. These assets are used to produce goods, which are in turn, sold for a profit. Assets refer to property of any kind owned by a business. Assets such as building, machinery, and trucks, which remain in the business for a long time, are referred to as fixed assets. Fixed assets are not meant to be sold under normal business conditions.

Current assets refer to assets such as cash, goods, and debts receivable. These remain in the business for only a short

period. Current assets are constantly changed into cash. Thus, goods are sold and cash is received, debts are repaid and cash is received, and so on. Intangible assets are items such as goodwill, trade marks, and patents. Intangible assets do not physically exist but indicate valuable rights belonging to the business. The benefits of intangible assets are reaped by a business over a long period. Investment activities of purchase of assets and investments give rise to capital expenditure.

Financing

In order to purchase assets, a business must have the necessary finance. The money needed for such purposes may come from the owners of the business or from loans from outsiders. Capital refers to the money invested in the business by the owners (proprietors, partners, or shareholders). Capital also includes the goods or assets brought in the business by the owner. Loans which must be paid back sometime in future are known as liabilities. The financing activity of a business involves obtaining money through capital and loans.

TYPES OF FINANCIAL STATEMENTS

This section explains the nature of financial statements—the income statement and the balance sheet. Both these statements are together known as the final accounts or financial statements. Figure 16.1 provides a summary of the management activities of a firm.

Income Statement

At the end of the year, the balances of all revenue accounts, that is, income and expense accounts are summarized and reported in a statement called the income statement. This financial statement helps in ascertaining whether the business activity has helped to earn any profits. The income statement helps to match revenue receipts against revenue expenses. The difference between revenue receipts and expenses, known as

profit or loss, helps to judge the efficiency of a firm in carrying out its business activities.

Balance Sheet

The balances of all capital receipts and capital payments, that is, assets, liabilities, and capital accounts, at the end of the year, are summarized and reported in a statement called balance sheet. The balance sheet helps to match the capital receipts against the capital expenditure. The difference between the capital expenditure (assets and investments) and the capital receipts from outsiders (liabilities) indicates the proprietor's capital or the net worth of business. The balance sheet indicates the efficiency of the firm in carrying out its financing and investing activities. While the income statement helps to judge the financial performance of the business, the balance sheet helps to judge its financial position.

ANALYSIS AND INTERPRETATION OF FINANCIAL STATEMENTS

According to the American Institute of Certified Public Accountants (AICPA), financial statements are prepared for the purpose of presenting a periodical review or report on the progress by the management and deals with the (a) status of the investments in business; and (b) results achieved during the period under review.

Thus, the balance sheet shows the position of the assets and the liabilities of the business on a particular date and the income statement shows the profit or loss during a particular year.

The AICPA has summed up the nature of financial statements in the following words, 'financial statements reflect a combination of recorded facts, accounting principles, and personal judgment'.

A typical financial statement of a company may run into several pages. It normally contains a huge mass of data and figures. A common user would be at a loss to understand which figures are important and what is the exact significance of all

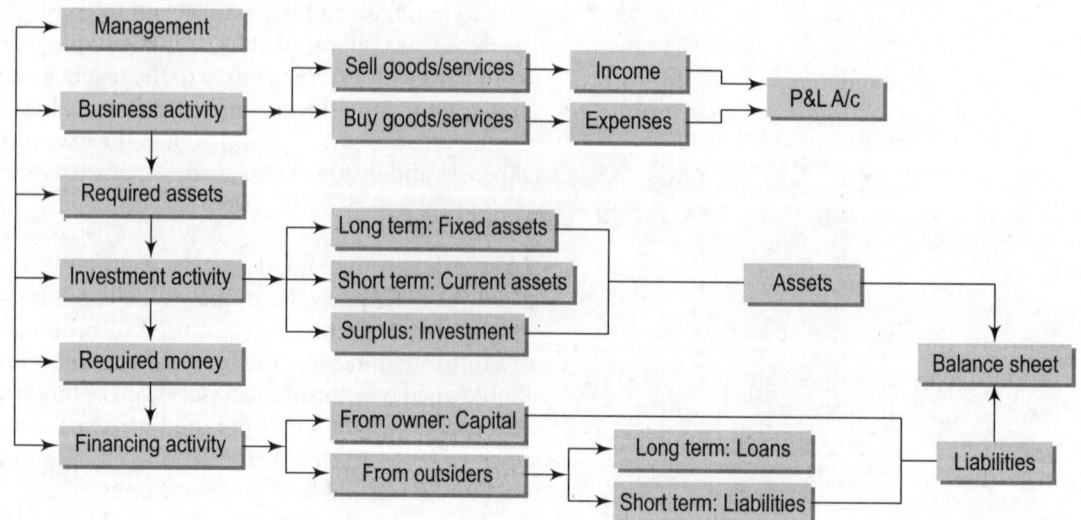

FIG. 16.1 Summary of management activities

these figures. Financial statements are basically prepared for the owners or managers of the business. Outsiders such as creditors, lenders, or researchers can use the figures appearing in the financial statements for their own specific needs.

For an outside user, the details in the financial statements signify only raw data. This data needs to be reorganized, processed, and converted into an easy to understand form. The process of breaking up a large mass of raw data into manageable form is referred to as analysis of the financial statements.

During analysis, the income statement is broken down into its various components or segments, that is, gross sales, net sales, cost of goods sold, operating profit, etc. This is done by converting an income statement in the T form into the vertical form. Analysis of a balance sheet refers to analysing the total funds available and employed. Total funds available with the business consists of owners' funds and loan funds. The total funds employed are broken down into fixed assets and working capital. This is done by converting a balance sheet in the T form into a vertical form.

Types of Analysis

The analysis of financial statements may be of two types—horizontal analysis and vertical analysis. Horizontal analysis involves the comparison of two firms or two years with respect to the same entries. Since horizontal analysis moves over a number of years or across many firms, it is also referred to as dynamic analysis. Trend percentage is an example of horizontal analysis. Vertical analysis, on the other hand, involves the comparison of two entries of the same firm and in the same year. Vertical analysis is, therefore, referred to as static analysis. Ratio analysis and cash flow statements are examples of vertical analysis. External analysis is done by outside users and internal analysis is done by the company.

Vertical balance sheet

The horizontal format of balance sheet is designed from the point of view of the owner of a firm. It enables the owner to know at a glance the amount of total funds owned (total assets) and the amount of total funds owed (total liabilities). It also enables the owner to know which assets will take time to sell (fixed assets) and which assets can be realized quickly (current assets). The order of payment of liabilities in the event of liquidation can also be ascertained from a balance sheet in the conventional form. However, the conventional form of balance sheet is not suitable for financial analysis because of the following factors:

1. It does not serve the purpose of the other users, such as potential investors or lenders.
2. The presentation and sequence or order of items is relevant only in the event of liquidation. It is unsuitable for financial analysis of a going firm.

Hence, a user or financial analyst generally converts the horizontal balance sheet into a vertical format, for the purpose of ratio analysis. The vertical format of a balance sheet is also allowed in the case of a limited company according to Schedule III of the Companies Act. The balance sheet in a vertical format appears as presented in Exhibit 3.2 (Chapter 3).

■ **ILLUSTRATION 16.1** The financial information of Shreyas Ltd as at 31 March 2020 was as follows:

Particulars	Amount (₹)	Particulars	Amount (₹)
Share capital	6,50,000	Goodwill	25,000
Capital reserve	2,500	Land	1,29,000
General reserve	1,20,410	Premises (leasehold)	1,50,000
Contingency reserve	42,500	Plant	2,34,395
Profit and loss account	18,777	Furniture	8,575
5% Debentures	1,57,500	MF liquid scheme units	71,400
Sundry creditors	73,900	Stock	1,96,770
Proposed dividend	75,000	Debtors	2,03,942
Provision for taxation	25,000	Cash and bank	1,21,280
		Advance tax	23,675
		Preliminary expenses	1,550

Rearrange the given balance sheet in a form suitable for analysis and calculate the following:

1. Current assets
2. Quick assets
3. Intangible assets
4. Fictitious assets
5. Fixed assets
6. Fixed liabilities
7. Proprietors' funds
8. Working capital
9. Total funds employed
10. Secured loans
11. Owed funds

Solution

Vertical Balance Sheet of Shreyas Ltd
as at 31 March 2020

No.	Particulars	Amount (₹)		
I	SOURCES OF FUNDS			
	1. Proprietors' funds			
	(A) *Capital*		6,50,000	
	(B) *Reserves and surplus*			
	(i) Capital reserve	2,500		
	(ii) General reserve	1,20,410		
	(iii) Contingency reserve	42,500		
	(iv) Profit and loss account	18,777		
	(C) *Less:* Fictitious assets	1,84,187		
	(Preliminary expenses)	1,550	1,82,637	
	Proprietors' funds			8,32,637
	2. Non-current liabilities (loan funds)			
	Secured loan/fixed liabilities/owed funds (5% debentures)			1,57,500
	Total funds available or capital employed (1 + 2)			9,90,137
II	APPLICATION OF FUNDS			
	1. Non-current assets (fixed assets)			
	Tangible assets			
	Land	1,29,000		
	Premises	1,50,000		
	Plant	2,34,395		
	Furniture	8,575	5,21,970	
	Intangible assets			
	Goodwill		25,000	

	(in lakh)	(in lakh)
Non-current assets (fixed assets)		5,46,970
2. Working capital		
Cash at bank	1,21,280	
Debtors	2,03,942	
MF units (liquid inventory)	71,400	
Quick assets	3,96,622	
Stock	1,96,770	
Advance tax	23,675	
Current assets (a)	6,17,067	
Sundry creditors	73,900	
Provision for tax	25,000	
Proposed dividends	75,000	
Current liabilities (b)	1,73,900	
Working capital (a – b)		4,43,167
Total funds employed (1 + 2)		9,90,137

■ **ILLUSTRATION 16.2** The following position statement has been prepared by a new employee. You are required to arrange it in the right order.

Condensed Balance Sheet of Sidhah & Co.
as at 31 March 2020

Particulars	Amount (₹) (in lakh)	(in lakh)
Current assets:		
Cash	13.8	
Short-term investment	17.4	
Inventories	159.3	
Accounts receivable (gross)	118.4	
Prepaid expenses	15.6	
Total current assets		324.5
Add: Non-current assets (gross) (Gross fixed assets)	1,109.5	
Investment in affiliated	28.0	
Long-term investments	6.7	1,144.2
Total of tangible assets		1,468.7
Less: Non-current liabilities (Long-term liabilities)		
Long-term mortgage debt	266.6	
Debenture debt	67.0	
Loan from IDBI	16.6	350.2
Net working capital		1,118.5
Less: Current liabilities		
Overdraft	5.3	
Notes payable	7.7	
Dividend payable	7.0	
Account payable	82.5	
Accrued taxes	8.5	111.00
		1,007.5
Preliminary expenses		9.4
Excess of assets over liabilities		1,016.9
Represented by		
Retained earnings	433.4	
Reserve for bad debts	2.2	
Depreciation	445.0	
Equity share capital	116.3	
Preference share capital	20.0	
		1,016.9

Solution

Vertical Balance Sheet of Sidhah & Co.
as at 31 March 2020

No.	Particulars	Amount (₹) (in lakh)		
I	SOURCES OF FUNDS			
	1. Owners' funds			
	(A) *Capital*			
	Equity share capital	116.3		
	Preference share capital	20.0	136.3	
	(B) *Reserves and surplus*			
	Retained income	433.4		
	(C) *Less:* Preliminary expenses	9.4	424.0	
	Shareholders' funds/net worth/own funds			560.3
	2. Loan funds			
	Non-current liabilities (Long-term loans)			
	(i) Long-term mortgage loan		266.6	
	(ii) Debentures		67.0	
	(iii) Loan from IDBI		16.6	
	Total loan funds/owed funds			350.2
	Total funds available (1 + 2)			910.5
II	APPLICATION OF FUNDS			
	1. Non-current assets (Fixed assets)			
	(i) Tangible fixed assets (gross)		1,109.5	
	Less: Depreciation		445.0	664.5
	2. Investments			
	(i) Investments in affiliated companies		28.0	
	(ii) Long-term investments		6.7	34.7
	3. Working capital			
	(a) Cash		13.8	
	(b) Accounts receivable (gross)	118.4		
	Less: Provision for bad debts	2.2	116.2	
	(c) Short-term investments		17.4	
	Quick or liquid assets (a + b + c)		147.4	
	(d) Inventories		159.3	
	(e) Prepaid expenses		15.6	
	Current assets (a + b + c + d + e)		322.3	
	Less:			
	(a) Notes payable	7.7		
	(b) Dividend payable	7.0		
	(c) Accounts payable	82.5		
	(d) Accrued taxes	8.5		
	Quick liabilities	105.7		
	(e) Overdraft	5.3		
	Current liabilities (a + b + c + d + e)		111.0	
	Working capital			211.3
	Total funds employed (1 + 2 + 3)			910.5

Vertical income statement

The conventional form of an income statement is not suitable for financial analysis because it does not show the gross profit. Hence, it is not possible to ascertain whether the goods are being sold above cost or not. The conventional income statement does not classify expenses. Financial analysis requires expenses to be classified into operating expenses, administrative expenses, etc. Such classification enables financial analysis to establish the relationship between expenses and sales. The T format does not separately reveal the net non-operating income.

Thus, a proper financial analysis is possible only if the profit is disclosed step by step, that is, gross profit, then net operating profit, followed by net profit before tax and after tax, and profits distributed and retained. This is useful in financial analysis, especially in ratio analysis. This is done through the vertical or multi-step form of an income statement, as shown in Exhibit 16.1.

■ **ILLUSTRATION 16.3** Rearrange the following figures in a form suitable for financial analysis.

Particulars	Amount (₹) (in '000)	Particulars	Amount (₹) (in '000)
Sales	16,000	Equity share capital	5,000
Raw materials consumed	7,800	Profit and loss account	1,500
Consumables	800	Bank loans	12,000
Direct labour	750	Short-term loans	1,500
Other direct expenses	480	Trade creditors	3,350
Administrative expenses	1,200	Trade investments	400
Selling expenses	260	Inventories	6,000
Interest	1,440	Receivables	3,700
Machinery	14,000	Cash in hand and at bank	100
Income tax 50%		Outstanding expenses	650
Depreciation	700	Other current liabilities	200

Solution

Vertical Income Statement

No.	Particulars		Amount (₹) (in '000)
1.	Sales		16,000
2.	*Less:* Cost of goods sold		
	Raw materials consumed	7,800	
	Consumables	800	
	Direct labour	750	
	Other direct expenses	480	9,830
3.	Gross profit (1 – 2)		6,170
4.	*Less:* Operating expenses		
	Administrative expenses	1,200	
	Selling expenses	260	
	Depreciation	700	2,160
5.	Profit before interest and tax (3 – 4)		4,010
6.	*Less:* Interest		1,440
7.	Net profit before tax (5 – 6)		2,570
8.	*Less:* Income tax @ 50%		1,285
9.	Net profit after tax (7 – 8)		1,285

EXHIBIT 16.1 Vertical Income Statement

No.	Particulars	Amount (₹)
1.	Gross sales	
2.	Less: Returns and allowances	
3.	Net sales (1 – 2)	
4.	*Less:* Cost of goods sold	
	(a) Opening stock	
	(b) Purchases	
	(c) Direct expenses	
	(d) Depreciation on machinery, factory, and building	
	Less: (e) Closing stock	
	Cost of goods sold (a + b + c + d – e)	
5.	Gross profit (3 – 4)	
6.	*Less:* Operating expenses	
	(a) Administration expenses	
	(b) Selling and distribution expenses	
	(c) Finance charges	
	Total operating expenses (except interest) (a + b + c)	
7.	Operating profit before interest	
8.	*Less:* Interest	
9.	Net profit after interest	
10.	Net non-operating income	
	(a) Non-operating income	
	Less: (b) Non-operating expenses	
	Net non-operating income (a – b)	
11.	Net profit before tax (9 + 10)	
12.	*Less:* Income tax	
13.	Net profit after tax (11 – 12)	
14.	*Less:* Proposed dividends	
15.	Retained profits (13 – 14)	

Vertical Balance Sheet

No.	Particulars		Amount (₹) (in '000)
1.	Share capital	5,000	
2.	Reserves and surplus	1,500	
3.	Own funds (1 + 2)		6,500
4.	Non-current loans (Long-term loans)	12,000	
5.	Short-term loans	1,500	
6.	Loan funds (4 + 5)		13,500
7.	Total funds available (3 + 6)		20,000
8.	Non-current assets (Fixed assets)		14,000
9.	Investments		400
10.	Current assets		
	Inventories	6,000	
	Receivables	3,700	
	Cash and banks	100	
		9,800	

11.	Less: Current Liabilities		
	Trade creditors	3,350	
	Provisions	650	
	Others	200	
		4,200	
12.	Working capital (10 – 11)		5,600
13.	Total funds employed (8 + 9 + 12)		20,000

■ ILLUSTRATION 16.4 The following is the information related to the operating cycle of Neminath Ltd, for the year ended 31 March 2020.

Particulars	Amount (₹)	Particulars	Amount (₹)
Opening stock	50,000	Sales	
Purchases	1,10,000	Cash	33,000

Wages	30,000	Credit	1,72,000
Factory expenses	20,000		2,05,000
Office salaries	4,000	Less: Returns	5,000	2,00,000
Office rent	2,400	Closing stock	60,000
Postage and telegram	500	Dividend on investments	1,000
Directors' fees	600	Profit on sale of plant	2,000
Salesperson's salaries	2,000	Depreciation:	
Advertising	1,000	Office furniture	1,000
Delivery expenses	2,000	Plant	3,000
Debenture interest	2,000	Cars	2,000
		Loss on sale of car	500
		Income tax	17,500
		Net profit	14,500

You are required to prepare a vertical income statement from the given information so as to facilitate analysis.

Solution

Income Statement of Neminath Ltd
for the Year Ended 31 March 2020

No.	Particulars	Amount (₹)		
	1. Gross sales			
	Cash	33,000		
	Credit	1,72,000		
			2,05,000	
	2. Less: Returns		5,000	
	3. Net sales (1 – 2)			2,00,000
	4. Cost of goods sold			
	(a) Opening stock		50,000	
	Add: (b) Purchase		1,10,000	
	(c) Direct expenses			
	(i) Wages	30,000		
	(ii) Factory expenses	20,000		
	(iii) Depreciation plant	3,000	53,000	2,13,000
	Less: (d) Closing stock			60,000
	Cost of goods sold (a + b + c – d)			1,53,000
	5. Gross profit (3 – 4) (or gross margin)			47,000
	6. Operating expenses			
I.	Administration expenses			
	(i) Office salaries	4,000		
	(ii) Office rent	2,400		
	(iii) Postage and telegrams	500		
	(iv) Directors' fees	600		
	(v) Depreciation			
	Office furniture	1,000		
	Cars	2,000	10,500	
II.	Selling and distribution expenses			
	(i) Salespersons' salaries	2,000		
	(ii) Advertising	1,000		
	(iii) Delivery expenses	2,000	5,000	15,500
	Operating profit before interest			31,500
III.	Interest charges			
	Debenture interest			2,000
	7. Net profit after interest (5 – 6)			29,500
	8. Non-operating income			
	(i) Dividends on investments	1,000		
	(ii) Profit on sale of plant	2,000	3,000	
	Less: Non-operating expenses			
	(iii) Loss on sale of car		500	
	Net non-operating income (i + ii – iii)			2,500
	9. Net profit before tax (7 + 8)			32,000
	10. Less: Income tax			17,500
	11. Net profit after tax (9 – 10)			14,500

COMPARATIVE FINANCIAL STATEMENTS ▪

A business firm does not exist in isolation. It coexists with other competing firms in the same industry. It has to, therefore, constantly compare its performance with these firms to analyse its position in the market. Such a comparison is known as inter-firm comparison. A company also needs to compare its own past performance with its current performance to ascertain the progress or decline in the market position over the years. This is known as inter-period comparison. Such statements prove that the accounts of one period are an instalment of the continuous history of a going concern. Comparative financial statements (balance sheet and income statement) are prepared for the purpose of inter-firm and inter-period comparisons. A common example of comparative financial statements is the final accounts of a limited company presented in the Schedule III format by giving the figures for the current year and the previous year.

The usual financial statements have to be presented in a different manner to facilitate such inter-firm and inter-period comparisons. The comparative financial statements are prepared as shown in Exhibit 16.2.

EXHIBIT 16.2 Comparative Financial Statements

Particulars	Inter-firm comparisons			
	Firm 1 (₹)	Firm 2 (₹)	Absolute Difference (₹)	Percentage Difference %
	(1)	(2)	(3) = (1) − (2)	(3)/(1) × 100

Particulars	Inter-period comparisons			
	Year 1 (₹)	Year 2 (₹)	Absolute Increase or Decrease (₹)	Percentage Increase or Decrease %
	(1)	(2)	(3) = (1) − (2)	(3)/(1) × 100

Limitations

Comparative statements have limitations such as inflation, common size comparisons, trend comparisons, and different accounting policies.

Inflation Inter-period comparison of several years in terms of currency may give absurd results because of the effect of inflation on the value of currency. Thus, the comparison of sales from 1970 to 2002 would be of little use as the value of rupee has fallen greatly during this period.

Common size comparisons Comparing financial statements is easier if all the figures are expressed in a common size. The

concept of common size statements is discussed in a later section of the chapter.

Trend comparisons Instead of comparing a year with its previous year, a specific year can be taken as a base year and all the other years can be compared with it. This will clearly reveal the trend. The concept of trend analysis is discussed in a later section of the chapter.

Horizontal comparisons Comparative statements may involve only horizontal comparisons. Comparative statements ignore the inter-relationship among the various items as presented in vertical analysis. For example, sales revenue is related to capital employed and expenses incurred. Such inter-relationship among many items in the financial statements can be determined with the help of ratio analysis.

Different accounting policies Inter-firm comparisons are misleading when different firms follow different accounting policies with respect to depreciation, valuation of closing stock, etc. Inter-period comparisons too can be misleading if the firm changes its accounting policies during the period under study.

▪ **ILLUSTRATION 16.5** Kumar and Jyothi have a partnership business. The position of their firm as on 31 March 2020 and 2019 is given in the financial statements given in the following text. You are required to prepare a comparative statement and provide comments.

Summarized Balance Sheet of Kumar and Jyothi

Particulars	Amount (₹)	
	2020	2019
ASSETS		
Fixed assets	52,500	43,750
Investments	3,500	1,750
Stock-in-trade	21,000	17,500
Sundry debtors	31,500	26,250
Loan and advances	14,000	14,000
Cash and bank	1,750	1,750
Total Assets	**1,24,250**	**1,05,000**
EQUITY AND LIABILITIES		
Capital accounts	71,750	59,500
Bank loans	14,000	10,500
Sundry creditors	38,500	35,000
Total Equity and Liabilities	**1,24,250**	**1,05,000**

Summarized Income Statement of Kumar and Jyothi

Particulars	Amount (₹)	
	2020	2019
Net sales	42,000	38,500
Less: Cost of sales	31,500	29,750
Gross margin	10,500	8,750
Operating expenses	8,750	7,000
Net profit before tax	1,750	1,750

Solution

Comparative Balance Sheet of Kumar and Jyothi

No.	Particulars	Amount (₹)		Absolute Increase or Decrease (₹)	Percentage Increase or Decrease (%)
		2019	2020		
I	**SOURCES OF FUNDS**				
	1. Owner's funds	59,500	71,750	+ 12,250	+ 20.59
	2. Non-current liabilities (Bank loans)	10,500	14,000	+ 3,500	+ 33.33
	Total funds available (1 + 2)	70,000	85,750	+ 15,750	+ 22.50

II	APPLICATION OF FUNDS				
	1. Non-current assets (Fixed assets)	43,750	52,500	+8,750	+20.00
	2. Investments	1,750	3,500	+1,750	+100.00
		45,500	56,000	+10,500	+23.08
III	WORKING CAPITAL				
	(A) Current assets				
	Stock	17,500	21,000	+3,500	+20.00
	Debtors	26,250	31,500	+5,250	+20.00
	Loans and advances	14,000	14,000	0.00	0.00
	Cash/bank	1,750	1,750	0.00	0.00
		59,500	68,250	+8,750	+14.71
	(B) *Less:* Current liabilities				
	Creditors	35,000	38,500	+3,500	+10.00
	3 = (A – B)	24,500	29,750	+5,250	+21.43
	Total funds employed (1 + 2 + 3)	70,000	85,750	+15,750	+22.50

Comparative Income Statement of Kumar and Jyothi

No.	Particulars	Amount (₹)		Absolute Increase or Decrease (₹)	Percentage Increase or Decrease (%)
		2019	2020		
1.	Sales	38,500	42,000	3,500	9.09
2.	*Less:* Cost of sales	29,750	31,500	1,750	5.88
3.	Gross profit (1 – 2)	8,750	10,500	1,750	20.00
4.	*Less:* Operating expenses	7,000	8,750	1,750	25.00
5.	Net profit (3 – 4)	1,750	1,750	0.00	0.00

Comments related to the comparative balance sheet are as follows:

1. The capital of the firm has increased by ₹12,250 in 2020 as compared to 2019. Out of this amount, ₹1,750 is due to profits of the firm during the year. This amount is assumed to be retained by the firm and remaining amount of ₹10,500 (12,250 – 1,750) is due to additional capital contributed by the partners.
2. Loan funds have increased by ₹3,500 or by 33.33% over the year. The firm has taken additional loans from the bank.
3. As a result of items (1) and (2), long-term source of funds has increased by ₹15,750 or by 22.50%.
4. Additional sources are used for
   (a) Buying fixed assets during the year   ₹8,750
   (b) New investments during the year   ₹1,750
   (c) Additional money blocked in working capital   ₹5,250
                                                      ₹15,750
5. Stock and debtors have increased by 20%, that is, by ₹3,500 and ₹5,250. This leads to a total increase in the current assets.
6. Increase in the current assets is partly financed by the increase in current liabilities (creditors) by ₹3,500. The remaining amount is financed by long-term sources of funds (₹5,250).

Comments related to the comparative income statement:

1. Sales increased by ₹3,500 or by 9.09%.
2. The cost of sales has also gone up by 5.88% in 2020.

3. An increase in sales is higher than increase in the cost of sales. As a result, gross profit has gone up by 20%.
4. Operating expenses have increased by 25%, that is, by ₹1,750.
5. There is no change in the amount of net profit earned. The net profit is constant at ₹1,750. An increase of 20% in the gross profit has not resulted in an increase in net profit because of a proportionate increase in operating expenses.
6. Profit in absolute terms remained constant. This translates into lower returns to partners on their increased capital.

■ **ILLUSTRATION 16.6** From the balance sheet of VJ Ltd as at 31 December 2019 and 2020, you are required to prepare a comparative balance sheet.

Balance Sheet of VJ Ltd as at 31 December 2019

Particulars	Amount (₹)	
	2019	2020
ASSETS		
Non-current assets (Fixed assets)	7,00,000	10,00,000
Investments (at cost)	1,00,000	1,20,000
Stock	1,50,000	1,80,000
Debtors	2,36,000	2,44,000
Cash	24,000	2,500
Total Assets	12,10,000	15,46,500
EQUITY AND LIABILITIES		
Preference share capital	0	4,00,000
Equity share capital	5,00,000	5,00,000
Reserves and surplus	1,35,000	1,71,500
12% Debentures	2,00,000	0
Bank overdraft	50,000	80,000
Sundry creditors	1,50,000	1,25,000
Provision for taxation	75,000	1,20,000
Proposed dividend	1,00,000	1,50,000
Total Equity and Liabilities	12,10,000	15,46,500

Solution

Comparative Balance Sheet of VJ Ltd

No.	Particulars	Amount (₹) 2019	Amount (₹) 2020	Absolute Increase or Decrease (₹)	Percentage Increase or Decrease (%)
I	SOURCES OF FUNDS				
	1. Shareholders funds:				
	Equity share capital	5,00,000	5,00,000	—	—
	Preference share capital	—	4,00,000	4,00,000	—
	Reserve and surplus	1,35,000	1,71,500	36,500	27.04
		6,35,000	10,71,500	4,36,500	68.74
	2. Non-current liabilities (Loan funds)				
	12% Debentures	2,00,000	—	(–) 2,00,000	(–) 100.00
	Total funds available (1 + 2)	8,35,000	10,71,500	2,36,500	28.32
II	APPLICATION OF FUNDS				
	1. Non-current assets (Fixed assets)	7,00,000	10,00,000	3,00,000	42.86
	2. Investment at cost	1,00,000	1,20,000	20,000	20.00
	3. Working capital				
	A Current assets:				
	Debtors	2,36,000	2,44,000	8,000	3.39
	Cash	24,000	2,500	(–) 21,500	(–) 89.58
	Stock	1,50,000	1,80,000	30,000	20.00
		4,10,000	4,26,500	16,500	4.02
	B Less: Current liabilities:				
	Sundry creditors	1,50,000	1,25,000	(–) 25,000	(–) 16.67
	Provision for taxation	75,000	1,20,000	45,000	60.00
	Proposed dividend	1,00,000	1,50,000	50,000	50.00
	Bank overdraft	50,000	80,000	30,000	60.00
		3,75,000	4,75,000	1,00,000	26.67
	Working capital (A – B)	35,000	(–) 48,500	(–) 83,500	(–) 238.57
	Total funds employed (1 + 2 + 3)	8,35,000	10,71,500	2,36,500	28.32

■ **ILLUSTRATION 16.7** Prepare the comparative statements of Viva Ltd by ascertaining the missing balances.

No.	Particulars	Amount (₹) 2019	Amount (₹) 2020	Absolute Increase or Decrease (₹)	Percentage Increase or Decrease (%)
A	Sales	x	x	(+) 4,00,000	+ 25.00
	Cost of goods sold				
	Opening stock	80,000	1,20,000	x	x
	Purchases	x	x	(+) 2,00,000	+ 20.00
	Wages	2,40,000	4,40,000	x	x
	Less: Closing stock	x	1,60,000	x	x
B	Cost of goods sold	x	x	x	x
C	Gross profit (A – B)	x	x	x	x
	Operating expenses				
	(a) Administrative	x	x	(+) 20,000	+ 20.00
	(b) Selling	50,000	60,000	x	x
	(c) Finance	x	x	(+) 4,500	+ 22.50
D	Total operating expenses	x	x	x	x
	Net operating profit (C – D)	x	x	x	x
	Add: Non-operating income	20,000	1,00,000	x	x
	Net profit before tax	x	x	x	x
	Less: Provision for tax	x	x	x	x
	Net profit after tax	2,10,000	2,35,500	x	x

Solution

Comparative Income Statement of Viva Ltd

No.	Particulars	Amount (₹) 2019	Amount (₹) 2020	Absolute Increase or Decrease (₹)	Percentage Increase or Decrease (%)
A	Sales	16,00,000	20,00,000	(+) 4,00,000	+ 25.00
	Cost of goods sold				
	Opening stock	80,000	1,20,000	(+) 40,000	+ 50.00
	Purchases	10,00,000	12,00,000	(+) 2,00,000	+ 20.00

	Wages	2,40,000	4,40,000	(+) 2,00,000	+ 83.33
	Less: Closing stock	1,20,000	1,60,000	(+) 40,000	+ 33.33
B	Cost of goods sold	12,00,000	16,00,000	(+) 4,00,000	+ 33.33
C	Gross profit (A – B)	4,00,000	4,00,000	—	—
	Operating expenses				
	(a) Administrative	1,00,000	1,20,000	(+) 20,000	+ 20.00
	(b) Selling	50,000	60,000	(+) 10,000	+ 20.00
	(c) Finance	20,000	24,500	(+) 4,500	+ 22.50
D	Total operating expenses	1,70,000	2,04,500	(+) 34,500	20.29
	Net operating profit (C – D)	2,30,000	1,95,500	(–) 34,500	(–) 15.00
	Add: Non-operating income	20,000	1,00,000	80,000	400
E	Net profit before tax	2,50,000	2,95,500	45,500	18.20
	Less: Provision for tax	40,000	60,000	20,000	50.00
F	Net profit after tax	2,10,000	2,35,500	25,500	12.14

COMMON SIZE STATEMENTS

Generally financial statements show odd amounts such as ₹67,689.92 and ₹57,324.96. It is difficult to compare such odd amounts, especially if the financial statements run into many pages. Accountants have devised common size statements for a quick comparison of the items in the financial statements shown in odd amounts.

Sales

For the purpose of comparing items in the income statement, sales revenue is taken as the base and treated as equal to 100. All the amounts of other items in the income statement are compared to sales and expressed as a percentage of sales. Thus, if the sales revenue is ₹1,29,980 and the cost of goods sold is ₹97,485, the cost of goods sold will be ₹75 (97,485/1,29,980 × 100). This clearly brings out the fact that the cost of goods sold is 75% of sales. This relationship between the cost of goods sold and sales is not readily evident from the absolute figures of ₹97,485 and ₹1,29,980.

Total Assets or Total Liabilities

For the purpose of comparing items in the balance sheet, the amount of total assets or total liabilities is treated as equal to 100. The individual items of assets or liabilities are expressed as a percentage of such total assets or total liabilities.

Horizontal and Vertical Analyses

Common size statements are used for both horizontal analysis (comparisons among firms or over a number of years) and vertical analysis (comparisons of items within the same financial statement).

Limitations

However, common size statements ascertain the relationship of all the items in the income statement with a single item of sales. It ignores the inter-relationship among the different items themselves. A common size balance sheet takes only total assets (or total liabilities) as the base for the other items in the balance sheet. This restricts the scope of analysis. In fact, this may be irrelevant because a particular item of assets (such as cash) has no relation with total assets. Such a comparison may not reveal any significant information.

Common size statements do not establish the relationship between the items in the income statement and the items in the balance sheet. Thus, a common size statement can make a separate analysis of the items in the income statement and the balance sheet, but cannot help in analysing the relationship between sales and capital employed. Such advanced analysis is done by means of ratio analysis which clearly reveals the relationship between any two items in the financial statements or between one item in the income statement (such as sales) and another item in the balance sheet (such as total assets employed).

■ **ILLUSTRATION 16.8** Prepare a common size financial statement based on the details provided.

Balance Sheet
as at 31 March 2020

Particulars	Amount (₹)
ASSETS	
Non-current assets (Fixed assets)	1,58,750
Cash	6,750
Debtors	27,750
Prepaid expenses	55,000
Stock	25,000
Other current assets	2,500
Total Assets	**2,75,750**
EQUITY AND LIABILITIES	
Capital	1,64,500
Reserves	25,000
Loans	56,250
Sundry creditors	10,500
Outstanding expenses	19,500
Total Equity and Liabilities	**2,75,750**

Income Statement
for the year ended 31 March 2020

Particulars	Amount (₹)
INCOME	
Net sales	3,17,250
Other income	3,000
Total	**3,20,250**
EXPENSES	
Cost of goods sold	1,77,750
Selling overheads	90,000
Administration and general expenses	23,000
Tax	8,500
Loss on sale of investmnents	12,000
Net Income	**9,000**
Total	**3,20,250**

Solution

Common Size Balance Sheet
as at 31 March 2020

No.	Particulars	Amount (₹)		%	%
I	SOURCES OF FUNDS				
	Shareholders' funds				
	Capital	1,64,500		66.94	
	Reserves	25,000		10.17	
			1,89,500		77.11
	Non-current liabilities		56,250		22.89
	(Loan funds)				
	Total funds available		2,45,750		100.00
II	APPLICATION OF FUNDS				
	Non-current assets (Fixed assets)	1,58,750			64.60

	Particulars	Amount		%
	Working capital			
	A. Current assets			
	Cash	6,750		2.75
	Debtors	27,750		11.29
	Other current assets	2,500		1.02
	Stock	25,000		10.17
	Prepaid expenses	55,000		22.38
		1,17,000		47.61
	B. *Less:* Current liabilities			
	Creditors	10,500		4.27
	Outstanding expenses	19,500		7.93
		30,000		12.21
	(A – B)		87,000	35.40
	Total funds employed		**2,45,750**	**100.00**

Common Size Income Statement
for the Year Ended 31 March 2020

No.	Particulars	Amount (₹)	%	%
1.	Net sales	3,17,250		100.00
2.	*Less:* Cost of goods sold	(1,77,750)		(56.03)
3.	Gross profit (1 – 2)	1,39,500		43.97
4.	*Less:* Operating expenses			
	Administration and general expenses	23,000	7.25	
	Selling overheads	90,000	28.37	
		(1,13,000)		35.62
5.	Operating income	26,500		8.35
	Add: other income	3,000		0.95
6.	Net Operating profit (3 – 4 + 5)	29,500		9.30
7.	*Less:* Non-operating expenses			
	Loss on sale of investments	(12,000)		(3.78)
8.	Net profit before tax (6 – 7)	17,500		5.52
9.	*Less:* Taxes	(8,500)		(2.68)
10.	Net profit after tax (8 – 9)	9,000		2.84

■ **ILLUSTRATION 16.9** The summarized balance sheets of two companies are as follows:

Balance Sheet
as at 31 March 2020

Particulars	Amount (₹)	
	Top Ltd	**Ten Ltd**
ASSETS		
Non-current assets (Fixed assets)	2,45,000	4,10,000
Current assets	2,90,500	3,32,800
Preliminary expenses	10,000	6,000
Total Assets	**5,45,500**	**7,48,800**
EQUITY AND LIABILITIES		
Equity share capital	1,20,000	3,50,000
10% Preference share capital	1,00,000	50,000
Reserves	1,40,000	56,000
15% Debentures	50,000	50,000
Current liabilities	1,35,500	2,42,800
Total Equity and Liabilities	**5,45,500**	**7,48,800**

Revenue Statements
for the Year Ended 31 March 2020

Particulars	Amount (₹)	
	Top Ltd	**Ten Ltd**
Sales	10,00,000	12,00,000
Less: Cost of sales	6,00,000	8,00,000
	4,00,000	4,00,000
Less: Operating expenses (including interest)	1,40,000	2,05,000
Less: Non-cash operating expenses (depreciation)	10,000	20,000
	2,50,000	1,75,000
Less: Taxes	1,00,000	70,000
Less: Dividend	70,000	75,000
Retained earnings	80,000	30,000

You are required to prepare the following:

(a) Common size balance sheets (in vertical form)

(b) Common size income statement (in vertical form)

(c) Comments in brief

(d) The statement of working capital funds generated before tax from operations of both the companies

Solution

Common Size Income Statement
for the Year Ended 31 March 2020

No.	Particulars	Top Ltd		Ten Ltd	
		Amount (₹)	%	Amount (₹)	%
1.	Sales	10,00,000	100.00	12,00,000	100.00
2.	*Less:* Cost of sales	6,00,000	60.00	8,00,000	66.67
3.	Gross profit (1 – 2)	4,00,000	40.00	4,00,000	33.33
4.	*Less:* Operating expenses (including interest)	1,32,500	13.25	1,97,500	16.45
	Depreciation	10,000	1.00	20,000	1.67
5.	Operating profit (before interest and tax) (3 – 4)	2,57,500	25.75	1,82,500	15.21
6.	Less: Interest on debentures	7,500	0.75	7,500	0.63
7.	Net profit before tax (5 – 6)	2,50,000	25.00	1,75,000	14.58
8.	*Less:* Taxes	1,00,000	10.00	70,000	5.83
9.	Net profit after tax (7 – 8)	1,50,000	15.00	1,05,000	8.75
10.	*Less:* Dividend	70,000	7.00	75,000	6.25
11.	Retained earnings (9 – 10)	80,000	8.00	30,000	2.50

Common Size Balance Sheet
as at 31 March 2020

No.	Particulars	Top Ltd		Ten Ltd	
		Amount (₹)	%	Amount (₹)	%
	SOURCES OF FUNDS				
1.	Shareholders' funds				
	A. Share capital				
	10% Preference share capital	1,00,000	25.00	50,000	10.00
	Equity share capital	1,20,000	30.00	3,50,000	70.00
		2,20,000	55.00	4,00,000	80.00
	B. *Add:* Reserves	1,40,000	35.00	56,000	11.20
	C. *Less:* Fictitious assets (Preliminary expenses)	(10,000)	(2.50)	(6,000)	(1.20)
		3,50,000	87.50	4,50,000	90.00
2.	Non-current liabilities (Loan funds)				
	15% Debentures	50,000	12.50	50,000	10.00
	Total funds available (1 + 2)	4,00,000	100.00	5,00,000	100.00
	APPLICATION OF FUNDS				
1.	Non-current assets (Fixed assets)	2,45,000	61.25	4,10,000	82.00
2.	Working capital				
	A. Current assets	2,90,500	72.63	3,32,800	66.56
	B. *Less:* Current liabilities	1,35,500	33.88	2,42,800	48.56
	(A – B)	1,55,000	38.75	90,000	18.00
	Total funds employed (1 + 2)	4,00,000	100.00	5,00,000	100.00

Working Capital Fund Generated before Tax

Particulars	Amount (₹)	
	Top Ltd	Ten Ltd
Net profit before tax	2,50,000	1,75,000
Add: Depreciation	10,000	20,000
Working capital fund from operations	2,60,000	1,95,000

Comments

Common size income statement:

(a) The cost of sales of Top Ltd is 60% of the sales revenue. The cost of sales of Ten Ltd is 66.67% of the sales revenue. The gross profit ratio is 40% for Top Ltd and 33.33% for Ten Ltd.

(b) Top Ltd spends only 13.25% of the sales revenue on operating expenses and Ten Ltd spends 16.46% of the sales revenue on operating expenses.

(c) Top Ltd earns ₹25.75 as operating profit out of every ₹100 earned. Ten Ltd earns ₹15.20 as operating profit out of every ₹100 earned.

(d) Top Ltd seems to be saving in cost as compared to Ten Ltd and hence its net profit ratio is also higher.

(e) Top Ltd has provided 10% of sales as taxes and Ten Ltd has provided 5.83% of sales as taxes.

(f) Top Ltd paid 7% of sales as dividend and retained remaining 8% of sales, whereas Ten Ltd paid 6.24% of sales as dividend and retained remaining 2.5% of sales.

Common size balance sheet:

(a) Out of total funds of ₹100, shareholders have contributed 87.50% in Top Ltd and 90% in Ten Ltd.

(b) Borrowed funds form 12.50% of the total funds available in Top Ltd and 10% of the total funds available in Ten Ltd. Both the companies have not taken advantage of trading on equity.

(c) Top Ltd has invested 61.25% of total resources in fixed assets, whereas Ten Ltd has invested 82% of total funds in fixed assets.

(d) 38.75% of the funds of Top Ltd and 18% of the funds of Ten Ltd are blocked in the working capital.

(e) Both the companies enjoy long-term financial stability.

TREND ANALYSIS

Comparative statements and common size statements compare the figures of the second year with those of the first year, the figures of the third year with those of the second year, and so on. Trend analysis, on the other hand, treats the first year as the base and compares the figures of all the other years against it. Thus, trend analysis of sales will reveal whether as compared to the base year, the sales show a trend of increase or decrease in subsequent years.

Trend analysis is useful because—(a) while comparative statements show the size of change, trends show the direction (up or down) of the changes; (b) trends are easy to calculate and interpret; (c) it is a quick method of analysis; and (d) it is more accurate because it is based on percentages and not absolute figures.

Limitations

The trend may change if a different year is chosen as the base year. Further, the total number of years covered should not be too large (such as 20 years) or too small (such as two years). Figures for a large number of years show large variations due to inflation and figures for a few years are not representative enough. The trend will give a distorted figure if the accounting policies, with respect to depreciation, valuation of closing stock, etc. have changed during the period under study.

■ **ILLUSTRATION 16.10**　Interpret the trend percentage based on the following information provided by Lilavati Ltd.

Comparative Balance Sheet

as at 31 December 2015–2020　　　　　　　　　　　　　　　(₹ in '000)

Assets	31 December, Amount (₹)						Trend % Base Date: 31/12/2015				
	2015	2016	2017	2018	2019	2020	2016	2017	2018	2019	2020
Current assets											
Cash	15.4	18.2	16.0	14.3	14.5	11.8	118	104	93	94	77
Marketable securities	7.2	5.5	4.4	5.6	6.9	2.7	76	61	78	96	37
Debtors	30.3	29.7	28.8	25.1	29.4	29.7	98	95	83	97	98
Stock-in-trade (FIFO)	39.4	37.4	35.9	36.2	42.6	41.8	95	91	92	108	106
Other current assets	1.8	0.5	3.4	4.4	2.6	0.6	28	189	244	144	33
Total current assets	94.1	91.3	88.5	85.6	96.0	86.6	97	94	91	102	92
Long-term investments	1.2	4.9	5.3	6.8	1.3	11.6	408	442	567	108	967
Property, plant, etc.	121.6	141.1	156.9	170.2	187.3	206.7	116	129	140	154	170
Less: Accumulated depreciation	49.7	58.4	63.4	70.3	72.3	80.9					
Net	71.9	82.7	93.5	99.9	115.0	125.8	115	130	139	160	175
Total assets	167.2	178.9	187.3	192.3	212.3	224.0	107	112	115	127	134

Solution

The interpretation of the trend percentage is as follows:

(a) The total assets show an increasing trend from 107 in the first year to 134 in the last year.

(b) The fixed assets also show a rising trend from 115 in the first year to 175 in the last year.

(c) The long-term investments show wide fluctuations due to new purchases and disposal of investments. Thus, a major purchase has been made in the first year and a major sale has been made in 2020.

(d) The current assets show a decreasing trend in all years except 2019. This is not a healthy trend at all.

(e) However a complete analysis would require ascertaining the trend in current liabilities, long-term liabilities, and equity funds as well as the trends in the items in the income statement in order to arrive at the overall trend of the business as a whole.

■ **ILLUSTRATION 16.11** Sudha and Vijay are partners in a business firm. Their position as on 31 December 2018, 2019, and 2020 is given here. You are required to work out the trend percentage and give your interpretations on the same.

Summarized Balance Sheet

Particulars	31/12/2020	31/12/2019	31/12/2018
ASSETS			
Non-current assets (Fixed assets)	4,00,000	3,60,000	2,80,000
Stock	1,60,000	1,50,000	1,35,000
Debtors	2,00,000	1,60,000	1,40,000
Loans and advances	1,00,000	80,000	60,000
Cash and bank balances	20,000	20,000	20,000
Total Assets	**8,80,000**	**7,70,000**	**6,35,000**
EQUITY AND LIABILITIES			
Partners' capital	4,00,000	3,40,000	3,00,000
General reserve	1,00,000	1,00,000	1,00,000
Secured loans	60,000	60,000	50,000
Unsecured loans	1,60,000	1,80,000	1,40,000
Sundry creditors	1,60,000	90,000	45,000
Total Equity and Liabilities	**8,80,000**	**7,70,000**	**6,35,000**

Summarized Income Statement

Particulars	31/12/2020 (₹)	31/12/2019 (₹)	31/12/2018 (₹)
Sales	40,00,000	36,00,000	30,00,000
Less: Cost of sales	28,00,000	24,00,000	20,00,000
Gross profit	12,00,000	12,00,000	10,00,000
Less: Expenses	8,00,000	8,00,000	7,00,000
Net profit	4,00,000	4,00,000	3,00,000

Solution

Balance Sheet

No.	Particulars		2018 (₹)	2019 (₹)	2020 (₹)	2018 (%)	2019 (%)	2020 (%)
	SOURCES OF FUNDS							
1.	Partners funds							
	Capital account		3,00,000	3,40,000	4,00,000	100.00	113.33	133.33
	Reserve funds		1,00,000	1,00,000	1,00,000	100.00	100.00	100.00
			4,00,000	4,40,000	5,00,000	100.00	110.00	125.00
2.	Non-current liabilities (Loan funds)							
	Secured loans		50,000	60,000	60,000	100.00	120.00	120.00
	Unsecured loans		1,40,000	1,80,000	1,60,000	100.00	128.57	114.29
			1,90,000	2,40,000	2,20,000	100.00	126.32	115.79
	Funds available (1 + 2)		5,90,000	6,80,000	7,20,000	100.00	115.25	122.03
	APPLICATION OF FUNDS							
1.	Non-current assets (Fixed assets)		2,80,000	3,60,000	4,00,000	100.00	128.57	142.86
2.	Working capital							
	A. Current assets							
	Debtors		1,40,000	1,60,000	2,00,000	100.00	114.29	142.86
	Loans and advances		60,000	80,000	1,00,000	100.00	133.33	166.67
	Cash and bank		20,000	20,000	20,000	100.00	100.00	100.00
	Stock		1,35,000	1,50,000	1,60,000	100.00	111.11	118.52
		(A)	3,55,000	4,10,000	4,80,000	100.00	115.49	135.21
	B. Current liabilities							
	Creditors	(B)	45,000	90,000	1,60,000	100.00	200.00	355.56
		(A – B)	3,10,000	3,20,000	3,20,000	100.00	103.23	103.23
	Funds employed (1 + 2)		5,90,000	6,80,000	7,20,000	100.00	115.25	122.03

Income Statement

No.	Particulars	2018 (₹)	2019 (₹)	2020 (₹)	2018 (%)	2019 (%)	2020 (%)
1.	Sales	30,00,000	36,00,000	40,00,000	100.00	120.00	133.33
2.	*Less:* Cost of sales	20,00,000	24,00,000	28,00,000	100.00	120.00	140.00
3.	Gross profit (1 – 2)	10,00,000	12,00,000	12,00,000	100.00	120.00	120.00
4.	*Less:* Expenses	7,00,000	8,00,000	8,00,000	100.00	114.29	114.29
5.	Net profit (3 – 4)	3,00,000	4,00,000	4,00,000	100.00	133.33	133.33

Comments on the balance sheet:

(a) Capital contributed by partners has increased from 100 in 2018 to 113.33 in 2019 and to 133.33 in 2020.

(b) There is an increase in secured loans taken by the firm in 2019. It has gone up from 100 in 2018 to 120 in 2019 and thereafter shows no change.

(c) When compared to the base year 2018, unsecured loans went up to 128.57 in 2019 and due to repayments came down to 114.29 in 2020.

(d) There is no change in the retained earnings of the firm.

(e) Non-current assets (Fixed assets) have gone up to 128.57 in 2019 and 142.86 in 2019. This seems to have been financed by capital contributed by partners and increased inflow of non-current liabilities (loan funds).

(f) Total current assets have increased from 100 in 2018 to 115.49 in 2019 and 135.21 in 2020. This increase is due to increase in debtors and loans and advances. Cash and bank balance has not changed.

(g) The position of creditors has changed drastically. Creditors have gone up from 100 in 2018 to 200 in 2019 and 355.56 in 2020. Working capital has not changed much over years from 100 in 2018 to 103.23 in 2019 and 2020.

The interpretation of the trend percentage with respect to the income statement is as follows:

(a) Sales for the past three years have increased from 100 in 2018 to 120 in 2019 and 133.33 in 2020.

(b) Increase in sales is accompanied by an increase in the cost of sales as a result of which profit could not increase in the same proportion. Profit has gone up from 100 in 2018 to 120 in 2019 and has remained constant in 2020.

(c) Expenses increased from 100 in 2018 to 114.29 in 2019. Expenses have not increased in 2020.

(d) In 2019, net profit increased by 33%. However, in 2020 it has remained constant.

RATIO ANALYSIS

Ratio analysis is a very powerful and the most commonly used tool for analysis and interpretation of financial statements. It concentrates on the inter-relationship among the figures appearing in the financial statements. Ratio analysis helps to analyse the past performance of a firm and to make future projection. It allows various interested parties like management, sharcholders, potential investors, creditors, government, and other analysts to make an evaluation of the various aspects of a firm's performance from their own point of view and interest. For example, management and shareholders may be interested in the company's profitability while creditors and debenture holders may be interested in the solvency of the company.

Accounting ratios are considered an important tool for the analysis of financial statements. A mathematical relational value is calculated by establishing the relationship between two or more numbers from the financial statements. The calculated mathematical value is widely known as a *ratio*. Ratios can also be expressed in terms of proportions, number of times, percentages, and fractions. As the calculation is made by establishing the relationship between two accounting numbers obtained from the financial statement, it is known as an *accounting ratio*.

A ratio shows the relationship between two numbers. Accounting ratios show the relationship between two accounting figures. Ratio analysis is the process of computing and presenting the relationship between the items in the financial statements.

Financial Ratios as Tools of Analysis

The analysis of financial statements aims to study the relationship among various factors in a business as disclosed in the financial statements for a particular period. A trend in these factors can be studied through the examination of such financial statements over a period of time. This study can be done from various angles for a number of different end users of the financial data of a company. These end users may include shareholders, creditors, management, government, and financial analysts. The end users are interested in the company's financial information due to various objectives.

Shareholders are interested in the yield and safety of their capital invested in the company. Creditors view the company's financial data from the angle of judging its repayment capacity and ability to service debts. Short-term creditors are interested in the company's liquid position which is estimated by equating the current assets and current liabilities. The management is interested in efficient fund generation and profitability of the company. In this way, end users strive to analyse the data to fulfil their own objectives.

Ratio analysis presents the relationship between the items in financial statements.

Forms

Accounting ratios can be expressed in three different ways—(a) proportion, (b) percentage, and (c) rate.

Proportion

A proportion is a simple division of one number by another. The relationship between current assets and current liabilities is expressed in this way. If the current assets are ₹2,00,000 and the current liabilities are ₹1,00,000, the ratio is derived by dividing ₹2,00,000 by ₹1,00,000. It will be expressed as 2:1.

Percentage

The relationship between profit and sales is expressed as a percentage. For example, if sales are ₹4,00,000 and gross profit is ₹2,00,000, gross profit is expressed as being 50% of sales.

Rate

Ratios are also expressed as rates over a certain period. The relationship between stock and sales is expressed in this way. If the stock turnover rate is eight times in a year, it means that the stock is converted into sales eight times in that year.

Interpretation of Ratios

Broadly speaking, ratios may be interpreted in four different ways, which are as follows:

1. An individual ratio may have significance of its own. For example, a ratio of 25% of net profit on capital employed shows a satisfactory return.
2. Ratios may be interpreted by making comparison over time. For example, ratio of net profit on capital employed is 25%. This ratio may be compared with the same ratio of a number of past years. Such is a comparison of the profitability.
3. Ratio of any one firm may be compared with ratios of other firms in the same industry. This is known as inter-firm comparison. Such a comparison shows the efficiency of a firm as compared to another firm. Suppose, return on capital employed is 20% for Alpha Ltd but is 12% for Beta Ltd. Thus, Alpha Ltd is more profitable.
4. Ratio may be interpreted by considering a group of several related ratios. For example, the utility of current ratio is enhanced if it is used along with other related ratios like acid test ratio, stock turnover ratios, etc. Similarly, various profitability ratios may be considered in relation to each other.

Classification of Ratios

Accounting ratios are classified into two categories—traditional and functional.

Traditional classification

Under the traditional classification, ratios are calculated based on the information contained in the financial statement. On this basis, a ratio can be further classified as follows:

Income statement ratios   Under this category, ratios are calculated based on the items of the income statement. For example, the *gross profit ratio* is calculated by establishing the relationship of gross profit with the base to the sales, both of which figures are taken from the income statement.

Balance sheet ratios   Balance sheet ratios are calculated only on the basis of the figures in the balance sheet. For example, the proportion of the current assets to current liabilities is known as the *current ratio*. In this ratio, both figures are taken from the balance sheet. These ratios help determine the liquidity, solvency, and capital structure of a firm.

Composite ratios   When the ratios are calculated on the basis of the figures obtained from an income statement as well as the balance sheet, such ratios are known as *composite ratios*. For example, *debtors' turnover ratio* is calculated by establishing the relationship between credit sales and the sum of debtors and bills receivable. This ratio is calculated using the value of credit sales from the income statement and the sum of debtors and bills receivable obtained from the balance sheet.

Functional classification

In the case of functional classification, ratios are classified by considering the purpose they serve. It means that classification is performed from the users' perspective such that it aids the users of the accounting ratio in decision making. Functional ratios are further classified into the following categories:

- Profitability ratios
- Liquid ratios
- Coverage ratios or solvency ratios
- Turnover ratios or efficiency ratios
- Financial ratios, structural ratios or leverage ratios

Profitability ratios   It comprises ratios that help establish the analytical study and view with respect to profits, in relation to the sales turnover or revenue of the firm or funds or assets deployed in the business to achieve the sales turnover or revenue. These ratios are calculated to meet the objective of the profitability study. They show the relationship between profit and sales or profit and investment.

Liquid ratios   *Liquid ratios* show the relationship between the current assets and the current liabilities of a firm. It is similar to the current ratio in the traditional classification.

Coverage ratios or solvency ratios   The ability of a firm to meet its contractual obligations towards providers of funds, goods on credit, services on credit, etc. is determined with the *solvency ratios*. The providers of funds, goods on credit, service on credit, etc. are widely known as external stakeholders. As the ratio helps measure the solvency, it is also known as *coverage ratio*. These ratios show the relationship between the profits and the claims of outsiders in the form of dividends, interest, etc.

Turnover ratios, efficiency ratios, or activity ratios   *Turnover ratios* are calculated to determine the efficiency of a firm in operating the resources utilized by it. Such ratios show the relationship between sales and assets. Stock turnover ratio, debtors' turnover ratio, etc. are examples of activity ratios.

Financial ratios, structural ratios, or leverage ratios   *Financial ratios* indicate the capital structuring or financial position of a company. These ratios measure the firm's capacity to carry out its business smoothly; to meet, without problems, its obligations, both short- and long-term, with the provider of funds. It generally shows the relationship between owners' funds and debts used in financing the assets of the firm.

Users

Debt–equity ratio, return on capital employed, and proprietary ratios are used by long-term creditors for making credit decisions. Short-term creditors use ratios such as current ratio, liquidity ratio, and stock working capital. Return on proprietors' funds and return on equity capital are ratios useful to the shareholder. Return on capital employed, turnover ratio, operating ratio, and expenses ratio help the management in making business decisions.

Management use of ratio analysis

The management of a company at all levels—top to middle and at operations level—makes use of ratio analysis for evaluating

achievements and making decisions. The following cases illustrate the management use of ratio analysis.

Production manager   Production managers require data regarding output of the various divisions of the firm in a form that facilitates comparison both with the production of the previous period and the results of the same period in the previous year. This data may be for a month, quarter, or week as per the requirement. Production at different levels may be related to the number of employees, number of hours, production per hour per worker, production per unit of capital employed, etc. Any increase or decrease in output can be investigated for taking appropriate decisions in each circumstance.

Sales manager   Sales managers can use ratio analysis for making sales decisions by comparing past sales performance with present sales and projecting sales for the future. Changes in sales may be observed by comparing sales to total industry sales, sales per division to total sales of the firm, output to sales, current sales to sales, sales to selling expenses, sales to debtors, sales to assets, etc.

In services industries such as hospitality, transportation, and banking, ratio analysis by sales managers constitutes the following:

1. In hotels, stress is laid on comparing income from rooms with the number of rooms, income from rooms with the cost of sales, income from the restaurant with respect to the capacity, income from restaurant with the cost, etc.
2. In the transportation industry, sales managers analyse income from carriage with respect to the total carrying capacity, income from carriage to cost of sales, etc.
3. Traders may analyse income from sales to operating sales, and sales to cost of goods.
4. The ratio of loans to deposits and income to operating expenses are important to evaluate the success of services in the banking industry.

Financial manager   The finance manager is more concerned with the supervision of a company's financing on a current basis as distinct from the other members of the management. The finance manager is involved with the analysis of current payments to current income, financial ratios, cost flow data, etc., in order to plan the company's future financial requirements. This analysis also helps in determining the credit facilities to be availed from the money market or capital market.

General manager   The responsibility of the general manager is to oversee the entire management of the company and analyse the relative position of marketing or sales, production, finance, inventory position, personnel planning, etc. The general manager, also known as executive manager, has to take strategic decisions by studying the relative position of performance in all departments through ratio analysis of past and present performance, and future projections.

Investor use of ratio analysis

Shareholders are investors of a company. The major interest of a shareholder in a company is not the day-to-day management of its affairs, but in the net results of its functioning in terms of profitability and reduction in the degree of risk. Ratios used by investors may be divided into three main forms—(a) profitability ratios; (b) risk ratios; and (c) analysing the market performance of shares.

Profitability ratios   Shareholders are interested in the profits earned by the company and the profits accrued on their own investments. Profitability ratios can be divided into the following forms:

- Profitability of the total investment, that is, gross profits earned on total funds invested in the company irrespective of the capital structure.
- Profits earned from normal business activity as a percentage of sales.
- Ratio of profits after payment of interest to shareholders equity. (This ratio indicates the actual earnings per share for investors).
- Dividend per share or dividend as a percentage of profits. (Dividend ratios can be computed to analyse a trend over a number of years).

All the sets of ratios discussed earlier can be used to compare the performance of the company in the previous period, quarterly, half-yearly, annually, or with other firms in the same industry.

Risk ratios   When making investments in a company, investors pay specific attention to these risks—(a) capital loss due to decline in share price because of lower profitability of the company or general economic depression; (b) bankruptcy of the company; and (c) non-payment of dividends. Ratio analysis serves as an indicator of the impending risk to shareholders. The dividend coverage ratio, utilized for this purpose, is calculated by dividing profit after tax by the number of equity shares.

Share performance   The main interest of shareholders is the market performance of the shares by capital gains realization. Earnings per share and market price per share can be analysed for the inter-firm comparison of two firms in the same industry.

Creditors' use of ratio analysis

Creditors frequently make use of ratio analysis to assess a firm's financial position. These creditors include financial institutions, banks, debenture holders, and investment institutions. Creditors assess a company's financial position with reference to its capacity to repay loan and interest charges. When creditors execute conversion rights, they remain interested in capital gains like ordinary shareholders through appreciation in the stock price and dividend rate.

Utility of ratios

Ratios can be analysed for the following purposes:

Inter-company and inter-firm comparisons   Inter-company comparison involves comparing a company's performance with other firms in the same industry. The reasons for any difference in efficiencies can be ascertained with the help of such comparisons. Accounting ratios are extensively used for evaluating financial performance. Important accounting ratios that may be used for inter-company comparisons are as follows:

Return on investment It is a key profitability and productivity ratio. Return on investment (ROI) can be broken down to components and sub-components for further analysis. A company with a high ROI is considered an efficient company.

Debt–equity ratio It analyses the financial policy of a company. A change in the debt–equity ratio reflects the change in a company's capital structure. This ratio also indicates a company's long-term stability. Every industry has a standard debt–equity ratio as per norms. A company which attains that standard is considered to be financially sound. Such a company ensures good returns to equity shareholders by proper utilization of debts.

Current ratio This ratio indicates the efficiency with which the company would be able to meet its short-term commitments. In other words, current ratio reflects a company's short-term solvency. A company having a current ratio 2:1 or the acceptable ratio as per industry norms is considered to be a solvent company with a good working capital position.

These three ratios evaluate the performance of a company and compare it with the performance of the other companies. However, there are certain limitations of ratio analysis for inter-company and inter-firm comparisons.

1. Inter-company comparison is practical only if the accounting policies followed by the companies are uniform.
2. Companies must be of same size and age. Old companies cannot be compared with the new firms because of the effect of inflation.
3. The most important condition is that companies should be willing to disclose the information necessary for calculating various ratios.

Inter-period comparison Ratio analysis has been widely used as a tool for analysing the performance of a company over the years. An analysis of the ratios indicates whether the company is moving in the right direction or not. There are certain ratios without any standard available to compare the performance with. For example, gross profit ratio, operating ratio, etc. do not have a standard. These ratios can be studied and interpreted only when they are compared with the company's previous years' ratios. Such a comparison is known as inter-period comparison of the same company.

Exhibit 16.3 shows the functional classification of ratios. It is useful in deciding which ratios are to be studied for what purpose, and how to compare actual ratios with the industry standard.

Calculation of Ratio Analysis

Ratios are calculated by adopting the functional classification, which are classified by considering the purpose they serve. The description and usefulness of these ratios are explained here.

Profitability ratios

Every firm should earn sufficient profit to survive and grow over a long period of time. In fact, efficiency of a business is measured in terms of its profit. Profitability ratio is calculated to measure the efficiency of a business. Profitability of a business may be measured in two ways:

1. Profitability in relation to sales
2. Profitability in relation to investment

Profitability in relation to sales indicates the amount of profit per rupee of sales. Similarly, profitability in relation to investment indicates the amount of profit per rupee invested in assets. If a firm is not able to pay a reasonable return to its investors, then the survival of the company may be threatened.

Different profitability ratios are explained in this section.

Gross margin ratio or gross profit ratio (GPM) This ratio helps calculate the percentage of sales income or revenue income available after fulfilling the requirement of the cost of goods sold from the net sales. It helps calculate the percentage of sales income available to meet the overhead expenses, return to the provider of the funds, and the retained profit of the firm.

The comparison of a firm's gross margin or gross profit ratio with competitors of similar businesses will indicate the relative strengths or weaknesses of the firm's activities. The gross margin ratio is calculated as follows:

$$\text{Gross Margin Ratio} = \frac{\text{Gross Profit}}{\text{Net Sales}} \times 100$$

Gross Profit is the net sales minus the cost of goods sold net sales are the gross sales minus the sales returns.

Operating ratio It indicates the relationship between the net sales and the total cost of sales. The cost of sales includes the cost of goods sold (COGS) and various operating expenses. The operating efficiency of management, expressed as a percentage, is revealed through this ratio.

$$\text{Operating Ratio} = \frac{\text{COGS} + \text{Operating Expenses}}{\text{Net Sales}} \times 100$$

Operating net profit ratio It is the ratio between the net operating profit or the net operating income and sales. It denotes the firm's earning capacity from its main line or core business activities. The net operating income refers to the earnings before interest and taxes, and unusual profit or loss. It means that profit or loss on non-business or non-usual activities such as profit or loss on sales of assets or long-term investments is excluded, along with interest and tax provisions. Interest expenses and provision for income tax are excluded from the calculation of the operating net profit because these items do not directly affect the earnings of the firm.

$$\text{Operating Net Profit Ratio} = \frac{\text{Operating Net Profit}}{\text{Net Sales}} \times 100$$

Expenses ratio Expenses ratio is calculated to analyse the relationship of each group of expenses, such as administrative expenses, selling and distribution expenses, and financial expenses with the net sales of the firm. Inter-year comparisons among expenses ratios are possible with the ratios of the current period in order to identify the problem areas and to initiate actions to improve upon the performance of the firm. These ratios can be calculated separately for each group of expenses or also in a combined view, depending on the need of the users of the financial statement.

$$\text{Expenses Ratio} = \frac{\text{Expenses}}{\text{Net Sales}} \times 100$$

Net profit margin ratio or net profit ratio (NPM)   NPM is the percentage of sales income left after subtracting the cost of goods sold and all overhead expenses, including the depreciation, interest on borrowed funds, and income tax provisions.

It provides a good indicator for comparison of the firm's return on sales with the performance of the past period, the projections, and the competitors. The net profit margin ratio is calculated as follows:

$$\text{Net Profit Margin Ratio} = \frac{\text{Net Profit After Tax}}{\text{Net Sales}}$$

Return on capital employed ratio (ROCE) or return on investment (ROI)   This measures the efficient utilization of the firm's assets to generate profits through proper comparisons with competitors or with the industry average. If the firm's ROCE is lower than that of the industry average or the competitor, then it indicates that the firm is not efficient in the use of its assets. The return on capital employed is calculated as follows:

$$\text{Return on Capital Employed} = \frac{\text{Profit before Interest and Tax}}{\text{Average Capital Employed}} \times 100$$

The profit before interest and tax is also known as the operating profit or the primary ratio. It compares the profit, that is, return, made by the firm with the amount of average funds invested, that is, its long-term capital and borrowed funds. The advantage of this ratio is that it relates the profit to the size of the firm. For the purpose of calculating this ratio, it is a standard practice to define the operating profit, that is, profit before tax and interest, as earnings before interest and tax (EBIT). Tax is ignored because it is determined by government regulations and is therefore beyond the control of the firm. Interest is excluded because it is not related to the firm's ordinary trading activities.

The average capital employed is the average of the opening and the closing long-term capital employed. The capital employed refers to the sum of long-term borrowed funds and long-term equity funds. Long-term equity funds include the share capitals, reserves, and surpluses, that is, retained profit of the firm also.

Return on proprietors' funds (ROPF)   ROPF indicates the return on the money contributed by, and belonging to, shareholders. Shareholders provide funds to a firm in the form of equity share capital and preference share capital. The proprietors' fund also includes, in addition to the share capital, the reserves and surpluses. ROPF is calculated using the following formula.

$$\text{Return on Proprietor's Funds} = \frac{\text{Net Profit (profit after tax)}}{\text{Average Proprietor's Funds}} \times 100$$

The average proprietors' fund is the average of the opening and the closing proprietors' funds.

Return on equity capital (ROE)   ROE indicates the earnings gained against per rupee of the owner's investment in the fund. The owners' investment in the firm includes the equity or ordinary shareholders' capital plus reserves and surpluses. The owners' investment in the firm is also known as owners' funds. Profit after tax as reduced by preference dividend including dividend tax on preference dividend, which is also known as equity earnings, is used to work out the ratio.

$$\text{Return on Equity} = \frac{\text{Equity Earnings}}{\text{Owner's Funds}} \times 100$$

Earnings per share (EPS)   An investor buys and retains a share with the idea of gaining a return in the future either in the form of dividends or in the form of capital gains. As earnings form the basis for dividend payments by a firm as well as for any future increase in the value of shares, investors are always interested in the firm's reported earnings per share.

An earnings per share (EPS) is the measurement of the net income per share of ordinary or equity shareholders of a corporate during a given period. A corporate whose shares are subscribed by public at large (public limited company) or whose subscribers include members outside the family of the corporate (private limited company) must report the earnings per share in their income statement.

The net income available to equity share holders is known as equity earnings. Profit after tax as reduced by preference dividend, including dividend tax on preference dividend, which is also known as equity earnings, is used to work out the ratio. When the number of equity shares outstanding has been changed during the period, a weighted average number of shares outstanding are used in the denominator.

An earnings per share is calculated using the following formula:

$$\text{Earnings per Share} = \frac{\text{Equity Earnings}}{\text{Number of Equity Shares Outstanding}} \times 100$$

It is used for comparing business performance and for valuation purposes. It is also used to reveal the market's evaluation of the firm's future earning capacity.

Diluted earnings per share   As a result of a growing tendency among firms to issue convertible securities of various types, such as preferred shares, or convertible bonds that carry a conversion feature allowing the investor to convert the holding into common or ordinary or equity shares at a future time, the American Institute of Certified Public Accountants has taken the stand that convertible securities should be treated in both their present and their prospective forms (Ray 1976). This requires the presentation of two earnings per share, that is, EPS, assuming no conversion of securities, and diluted EPS, assuming full conversion of convertible securities into equity shares.

Diluted EPS is calculated using the following formula:

$$\text{Diluted Earnings per Share} = \frac{\text{Equity Earnings}}{\text{Number of Equity Shares Originally Outstanding plus Converted Shares}} \times 100$$

Dividend per share Dividend per share is the net income distributed among the equity shareholders per share during a given period. The ordinary shareholders are very concerned about the position taken by the firm with respect to payment of cash dividend. If a firm pays insufficient dividends, the share will not be attractive to investors desiring some current income from their investment. If the firm pays excessive dividend, it may not be retaining adequate funds to finance the firm's future growth.

Dividend yield ratio Dividend yield ratio is a ratio of the dividend per share to the market price per share. It indicates the current return to the investor as a percentage of the investment. The dividend yield ratio is of interest to potential shareholders who are considering a purchase of the firm's share and who desire dividends as a source of income. It is calculated as follows:

$$\text{Dividend Yield Ratio} = \frac{\text{Dividend per Share}}{\text{Market Price per Share}} \times 100$$

Liquidity ratios or liquid ratios or short-term solvency ratios

The liquidity ratio, therefore, tries to establish a relationship between current assets and liabilities. The current assets indicate the level of funds available to meet the obligations in the nature of current liabilities. The said proportion of availability of current assets to current liabilities is indicated in the form of a ratio, that is, the number of times current assets are available in comparison to current liabilities. In other words, the liquidity ratios answer the question: 'Will the firm probably be able to meet its obligations when they are due?' The failure of a firm to meet its obligations due to lack of adequate liquidity will result in bad credit ratings, loss of creditor's confidence, or even in lawsuits against the company.

Different liquid ratios are discussed in this section.

Current ratio The current ratio is an indicator of the financial strength of a firm. It indicates the capacity of a firm to meet its short-term liabilities and in turn, to achieve technical solvency. Current ratio is defined as the number of times current assets are available with the firm to pay off the current liabilities. It is also known as the working capital ratio. It can be expressed with the following formula:

$$\text{Current Ratio} = \frac{\text{Total Current Assets}}{\text{Total Current Liabilities}}$$

Current assets refer to the cash or those assets that are convertible or expected to be converted into cash within the accounting period. Current liabilities are the liabilities that have to be paid within the accounting period.

Current assets include mainly cash in hand, cash at bank, marketable securities, realizable investments, bills receivable, book debts, inventories, and prepaid expenses. Current liabilities consist of outstanding or accrued expenses, sundry creditors, bills payable, pre-received or advance income, bank overdraft, provision for taxation, etc.

Bank overdraft, unless specifically stated as a permanent arrangement, should be included as a current liability. The long-term liabilities, repayable within the accounting period, should be treated as a current liability.

The bills receivable (whether discounted or not) should be treated as a current asset, and at the same time, the discounted bills receivable should be treated as a current liability.

Quick ratio or acid-test ratio The quick ratio is one of the best measurements of liquidity. Liquidity ratio may be defined as the ratio of the liquid assets to the liquid liabilities or the current liabilities.

Current assets can be classified into two categories: liquid assets and deferred assets. In the same way, current liabilities are classified as liquid liabilities and deferred liabilities. As per accepted commercial practices, current assets and liabilities are considered to be liquid if they are expected to be realized or paid within a month; otherwise, they are treated as deferred assets and liabilities.

Liquid assets normally include cash in hand, cash at bank, marketable securities, realizable investments, bills receivable, and book debts. Liquid liabilities consist of outstanding or accrued expenses, sundry creditors, bills payable, provision for taxation, etc.

The inventories and prepaid expenses are treated as deferred current assets, and in the same way, bank overdraft and income received in advance are treated as deferred current liabilities.

The ratio is determined as shown in the following text:

$$\text{Quick Ratio} = \frac{\text{Liquid Current Assets}}{\text{Liquid Current Liabilities}}$$

The quick ratio is a much more exact measurement of liquidity than the current ratio. Through the exclusion of inventories and prepaid expenses, it indicates the liquid assets whose realizable value is fairly certain.

Absolute liquid ratio Absolute liquidity of a firm is always equal to the cash and near cash items. Hence, in computation of the absolute liquid ratio, only the absolute current assets are compared with the liquid current liabilities. Current assets such as cash in hand, cash at bank, and marketable securities are only considered as absolute liquid current assets. This ratio is calculated using the following formula:

$$\text{Absolute Liquid Ratio} = \frac{\text{Cash + Bank Balance + Marketable Securities}}{\text{Liquid Current Liabilities}}$$

Coverage ratios or solvency ratios or long-term solvency ratios

Another important component of any financial analysis is examination of solvency. Solvency refers to a firm's ability to satisfy its short-term as well as long-term obligations. If a firm cannot satisfy its obligations and becomes insolvent, it can fall into bankruptcy, which can result in significant losses to investors and creditors.

Different coverage ratios or solvency ratios are discussed here:

Dividend payout ratio This is a ratio of the dividend per share to the earnings per share. It indicates what percentage of a firm's earnings is being paid to the common or ordinary shareholders in the form of dividends. The percentage not paid out is retained for the firm's future needs.

This ratio is calculated as follows:

$$\text{Dividend Payout Ratio} = \frac{\text{Dividend per Share}}{\text{Earnings per Share}} \times 100$$

Price earnings ratio   The price earnings ratio is calculated by dividing the market price of a share by the earnings per share. It is an important measure of value used by investors in the market place before making purchases.

It is calculated as follows:

$$\text{Price Earnings Ratio} = \frac{\text{Market Price per Share}}{\text{Earnings per Share}}$$

If a share has a low price earnings ratio (P/E), it may be considered as an undervalued share. However, if the ratio is higher, it may be considered to be overvalued.

$$\text{Debt Service Coverage Ratio} = \frac{\text{Operating Income} + \text{Lease Rental Payments} + \text{Hire Purchase Payments}}{\text{Interest} + \text{Lease Rental Payments} + \text{Hire Purchase Payment} + \{\text{Preference Dividend}/(1\text{-}t)\} + \{\text{Principal Loan Repayment}/(1\text{-}t)\}}$$

where t = tax rate in decimal

The debt service coverage ratio is also known as the fixed charge coverage ratio. This ratio is very important from the viewpoint of lenders of funds. It gives an idea of the number of times the fixed financial commitments are covered by the earnings. It is an index of the financial strength of a firm and indicates the margin of safety for long-term creditors or pro viders of funds.

Book value per share   The book value of a firm's common, equity, or ordinary share is calculated by dividing the share-holders' funds, that is, net worth, by the number of shares outstanding. The owners' investment in the firm includes the equity or ordinary shareholders' capital plus reserves and surpluses, which is also known as the net worth. Book value is useful for potential investors as well as for shareholders.

The book value is a reflection of the accounting records of a firm rather than a strong measure of the real value of the firm's assets. If two otherwise identical firms used different depreciation schedules, the book value of their assets would be different. As a general rule, the book value results from the use of conservative accounting techniques and is considerably lower than the market value of the stock. It is calculated as follows:

$$\text{Book Value per Share} = \frac{\text{Net Worth}}{\text{Number of Equity Shares Outstanding}}$$

Turnover ratios or efficiency ratios or activity ratios or performance ratios

Turnover ratio is used to indicate the efficiency with which assets and resources of a firm are being utilized. These ratios

Interest coverage ratio or time interest earned   A useful measure of profit that does not link returns to resources is the times interest earned ratio. It is calculated by dividing the firm's operating income, that is, earnings before interest and tax, by the interest it must pay on its debt. It is calculated as follows:

$$\text{Interest Coverage Ratio} = \frac{\text{Operating Income}}{\text{Interest}}$$

It relates the operating profits to the fixed charges created by the firm's borrowings. This ratio provides an indication of the margin of safety between the financial obligations and the net income before interest and tax.

Debt service coverage ratio   This ratio relates fixed interest charges, fixed committed dividend payments, lease and hire purchase rental payments, and principal loan repayment to the income earned by the firm. It indicates whether the firm has earned sufficient profits to fulfil its financial commitments. It is calculated as follows:

are known as turnover ratios because they indicate the speed with which assets are being converted or turned over into sales. These ratios, thus, express the relationship between sales and cost of the goods sold, with various assets. A higher turnover ratio generally indicates better use of capital resource, which in turn has a favourable effect on the profitability of the firm. Different turnover ratios are discussed hereunder.

Capital turnover ratio   This ratio measures the efficiency of a firm with respect to utilization of the total capital of the firm employed in revenue generation. It is calculated using the following formula:

$$\text{Capital Turnover Ratio} = \frac{\text{Net Sales}}{\text{Capital Employed}}$$

Stock to working capital ratio   The liquidity of a firm can be measured with respect to the proportion of stock or inventory in the total investment in the net working capital. The higher the ratio, the lower the level of hard liquidity with the firm. This ratio would normally be quite lower in a seasonal and perishable goods industry in comparison with the white goods industries. It is calculated as follows:

$$\text{Stock to Working Capital Ratio} = \frac{\text{Stock or Inventory}}{\text{Net Working Capital}}$$

The net working capital refers to the sum of the current assets less the current liabilities.

Working capital turnover ratio   The management of a firm might want to determine the velocity, that is, turnover, with which funds move through the various current asset forms.

Ratios such as working capital turnover support the firm's management to measure the overall effectiveness. This ratio indicates how well the firm is managing its assets and is calculated using the following formula.

$$\text{Working Capital Turnover Ratio (times)} = \frac{\text{Sales Revenue}}{\text{Average Working Capital}}$$

Sales revenue refers to the sales value less the sales returns from the customers. The average level of working capital is calculated by taking the average of the period beginning working capital and the period end working capital.

Stock velocity ratio, stock turnover ratio, or inventory turnover ratio This ratio measures how many times a firm's inventory has been sold during the year. It is computed by dividing the cost of goods sold by the average level of inventory on hand. The cost of goods sold refers to the sales value less the gross profit of the firm. The average level of inventory on hand is calculated by taking the average of the period beginning inventory and the period end inventory.

$$\text{Inventory Turnover Ratio (times)} = \frac{\text{Cost of Goods Sold}}{\text{Average Inventory}}$$

The number of days that it takes to sell the entire inventory can be determined by dividing 360 or 365 by the inventory turnover in times. This is known as the inventory holding period in days. It can also be calculated in terms of the number of months or weeks by taking 12 or 52 in the numerator, respectively.

$$\text{Inventory Holding Period (days)} = \frac{365}{\text{Inventory Turnover Ratio (times)}}$$

If a firm has a turnover that is much lower than the industry's average, then there may be obsolete goods on hand, or inventory stocks may be higher than needed. At the same time, if the inventory turnover in times is higher than the industry's average, then it is an indication that inventory levels maintained by the firm are inadequate.

Inventory turnover ratio varies significantly with the nature of the business. It is generally high for a firm that sells fresh products, but very small for a firm that sells jewelry. It is also influenced by the seasonality of sales. It indicates the velocity with which merchandise moves through a business.

Debtors' velocity ratio or debtors' turnover ratio, or accounts receivable turnover ratio The debtors' velocity ratio provides a rough gauge as to how well debtors or receivables are turned into cash. The debtors' turnover ratio is calculated by dividing the netcredit sales by the average accounts receivable balance during a period. The debtors include the book debts receivable in the form of debtors and also the bills receivable. The debtors' velocity ratio, when calculated in terms of days, is known as average collection period. This ratio represents the average member of days for which a firm has to wait before

its debtors are converted into cash. The formula for average collection period is as follows:

$$\text{Debtors' Velocity (times)} = \frac{\text{Net Credit Sales}}{\text{Average Debtors + Bills Receivable}}$$

$$\text{Average Collection Period (days)} = \frac{360}{\text{Debtors Velocity Ratio}}$$

where, 360 refers to the number of working days in a year.

The average level of debtors and bills receivable is calculated by taking the average of the period beginning debtors and the period end debtors.

Creditors' velocity ratio or creditors turnover ratio This ratio is similar to the debtors' velocity ratio. It compares the accounts payable with the total credit purchases. The accounts payable include the creditors for raw materials, components, and supplies, in addition to the bills payable. It signifies the credit period employed by the firm in paying creditors and bills payable. The creditors' velocity ratio, when calculated in terms of days, in known as average payment period. This represents the average number of days taken to pay the amount to the supplier by the firm. It is calculated as follows:

$$\text{Creditors' Velocity (times)} = \frac{\text{Credit Purchases}}{\text{Average Creditors + Bills Payable}}$$

$$\text{Average Payment Period (days)} = \frac{360}{\text{Creditors Velocity (times)}}$$

The average level of creditors and bills payable is calculated by taking the average of the period beginning creditors and the period end creditors.

Financial ratios, structural ratios or leverage ratios or long-term solvency ratios or gearing ratios or capital structure ratios

Capital structure ratio is also known as gearing ratio or solvency ratio or leverage ratio. These are used to analyse the long-term solvency of any particular firm. There are two aspects of long-term solvency of a firm: (i) ability to repay the principal amount when due, and (ii) regular payment of interest. In other words, long-term creditors like debenture holders, financial institution, etc. are interested in the security of the loan amount as well as the ability of the firm to meet the interest cost. Gearing ratios also consider the earning capacity of the firm to know whether it will be able to pay off the interest on loan amount. Liquidity ratio discussed earlier indicates short-term financial strength whereas solvency ratio judges the ability of a firm to pay off its long-term liabilities. The important solvency ratios are discussed below:

Debt to equity ratio Long-term creditors look primarily towards prospective earnings and budgeted cash flows in attempting to gauge the risk of their position. They cannot ignore the importance of keeping a reasonable balance between the portion of assets being provided by creditors and the portion of assets being provided by shareholders or owners of the

firm. This balance is measured by the debt to equity ratio, as shown in the following text:

$$\text{Debt to Equity Ratio} = \frac{\text{Total Liabilities}}{\text{Proprietor's Funds}}$$

The total liabilities include the long-term liabilities and also the current liabilities of the firm. The proprietors' fund includes the equity share capital, the preference share capital, and the reserves and surpluses.

Capital intensity ratio The capital intensity ratio focuses only on the long-term assets, that is, property, plant, and equipment items. It is calculated using the following formula:

$$\text{Capital Intensity Ratio (times)} = \frac{\text{Net Sales Revenue}}{\text{Property, Plant, and Equipment}}$$

Firms that are capital intensive such as steel plants have a lower capital intensity ratio in comparison with non-capital intensive firms such as the service sector. A comparison of the firm's capital intensity ratio with competitors or with the industry average indicates the efficiency in the use of the long-term assets of the firm.

Proprietary ratio This ratio is a variant of the debt–equity ratio. It relates the proprietors' fund by the total assets of the firm, and indicates the long-term or the future solvency position of the firm. It is calculated using the following formula:

$$\text{Proprietary Ratio} = \frac{\text{Proprietor's Funds}}{\text{Total Assets or Total Liabilities}}$$

Proprietors' funds include preference and equity share capital plus all reserves and surplus items. Total assets include all assets including goodwill. As the total assets are always equal to the total liabilities of the firm, the total liabilities may also be used as the denominator in the formula discussed earlier.

Capital gearing ratio or leverage ratio The capital gearing ratio is also closely related to the solvency ratio, which is used mainly to analyse the capital structure of a firm. The term capital gearing refers to the proportion between the fixed interest and dividend-bearing funds and the non-fixed interest or non-dividend-bearing funds. The fixed interest or dividend-bearing funds include the funds supplied by banks, financial institutions, debenture holders, public deposit holders, preference shareholders, etc. The non-fixed interest or non-dividend-bearing funds include the equity share capital and reserves and surpluses only. It is calculated as follows:

$$\text{Capital Gearing Ratio} = \frac{\text{Equity Share Capital and Reserves and Surpluses}}{\text{Fixed Interest and Dividend-bearing Funds}}$$

Exhibit 16.3 summarizes the important ratios and the points for comments in addition to the standard value of the ratio if any, available or used by industry players.

Advantages of Ratio Analysis

Ratio analysis and its indications provide a number of advantages to the users. The advantages offered by ratio analysis are summarized in this section.

Evaluation of the efficiency of decisions of a firm It helps evaluate the decision-making ability of a firm in terms of the correct decisions taken with respect to the management of operating activities, investment in fixed assets and current assets, and also managing finances to support the activities. These are known as operating, investing, and financing decisions, respectively. It, in turn, supports effective decision making to improve the firm's performance.

Simplification of a group of complex and multifaceted figures through proper establishment of relationships Ratios help simplify complex and multi-level accounting figures, which in turn helps one to establish meaningful relationships between different sets of data contained in the financial statement. It summarizes the financial information in such a way that it clearly supports the measurement and assessment of a firm's managerial efficiency, credit worthiness, earning capacity, etc.

Basis for comparative analyses Ratios of a particular year can be compared with the past years' data, projected data, and competitor's data. Such comparisons help determine the firm's achievements and highlight the strengths and weaknesses of the firm. Such analytical studies help the firm establish achievable projections with regard to the future course of activities to be undertaken by the business.

Identification of problem areas The critical study of ratios helps a firm to identify the weak areas as well as the strong areas of the business. The firm can establish the course of actions to cope with the weak or problem areas, and also improve upon or maintain their strong areas through proper monitoring and control.

Useful in improving future comparison Ratio analysis indicates the weak spots of a firm. This helps the management in overcoming such weaknesses and improving the overall performance of the firm in future.

Useful in judging the efficiency of a business As stated earlier, accounting ratio helps in judging the efficiency of a firm. Liquidity, solvency, profitability, etc. of a firm can be easily evaluated with the help of various accounting ratios like current ratio, liquid ratio, debt to equity ratio, and net profit ratio. Such an evaluation enables the management to judge the operating efficiency of the various aspects of the firm.

Useful in simplifying accounting figures Complex accounting data presented in profit and loss accounts and balance sheets is simplified and summarized with the help of ratio analysis so as to make it easily understandable. For example, gross profit ratio, net profit ratio, operating ratio, etc. give a more stable picture of the profitability of a firm rather than the absolute profit figure.

Accounting ratios are calculated based on the information and data contained in the financial statements, and hence, any mistakes made in the preparation of the financial statement or window-dressing of financial statements will be evident in the ratios. Thus, in brief, the limitations of financial statements are also applicable for accounting ratio analyses.

EXHIBIT 16.3   Functional Classification of Ratios

Objective of Analysis	Ratio to be Computed	Formula	Standard Ratio	Actual Ratio	Points for Comments — Higher than Standard	Points for Comments — Lower than Standard
1. Immediate liquidity	Quick ratio	Quick assets/Quick liabilities QA/QL	1:1	₹XX of liquid assets available for each ₹ of quick liability	1. Very good day-to-day liquidity solvency 2. Idle cash balances 3. Under-investment	1. Unsatisfactory day-to-day liquidity solvency 2. Low cash balances 3. Over-investment
2.1. Short-term liquidity	(A) Current ratio	Current assets/Current liabilities CA/CL	2:1	₹XX of current assets available for each ₹ of current liability	1. Very good short-term liquidity solvency 2. Excess stocks, bad debts, and idle cash 3. Under-trading	1. Unsatisfactory short-term liquidity solvency 2. Shortage of stocks, less credit sales, shortage of cash 3. Over-trading
2.2. Liquidity of stock	(B) Stock working capital	Stock/Working capital × 100(CST/WC) × 100	100%	% WC blocked in stock	1. More other current assets available to pay current liabilities	1. Less other current assets available to pay current liabilities
	(C) Stock velocity	COGS/Average stock COGS/[OST + CST]/2	Company standard	Stock holding period is XX	1. Stock is sold out fast 2. Same volume of sales from less stock 3. More sales from same stocks 4. Working capital requirement is less Too high ratios show stock-outs or over-trading	1. Stock is sold out at a slow speed 2. Same volume of sales from more stocks 3. Less sales from same stocks 4. Working capital requirement is less 5. Too low ratios show obsolete stocks or under-trading
2.3. Liquidity of debtors	(D) Debtors' velocity	Debtors + BR/[Daily credit sales]/(DR + BR)/CRS	Normal credit allowed	Debt collection period is XX	1. Debts are collected at a slow speed 2. More credit is given to debtors 3. More chances to bad debts	1. Debts are collected fast 2. Less credit is given to debtors 3. Less chances to bad debts
2.4. Liquidity of creditors	(E) Creditors' velocity	Creditors + BP/[Daily credit purchases]/(CD + BP)/CRP	Company standard	Debt payment period is XX	1. Creditors are paid late	1. Creditors are paid fast
3. Long-term solvency and stability	(A) Proprietary ratio	(Proprietors fund/Total assets) × 100 PF/TA × 100	65% to 75%	% of total assets financed by owners' fund	2. More credit is available from creditors 3. Working capital requirement is less 1. Very good solvency position	2. Less credit is available from creditors 3. Working capital requirement is more 1. Unsatisfactory solvency position
	(B) Debt-equity ratio	Borrowed funds/Proprietors' funds BF/PF	3:1	₹X obtained from debt, for each ₹1 from shareholders	2. No trading on equity 1. Low safety margin for lenders 2. More interest payments 3. Less scope for more loans 4. Trading on equity	2. Trading on equity 1. High safety margin for lenders 2. Less interest payments 3. Scope for more loans 4. No trading on equity
4. Operating or trading efficiency	(A) Gross profit ratio	(GP/Net sales) × 100	Company standard	1. Margin of ₹XX on sale of ₹100 2. ₹XX is available to meet other expenses	1. High efficiency in managing purchases, production, labour, sales, and inventory 2. High productivity	1. Low efficiency in managing purchases, production, labour, sales and inventory 2. Low productivity

Objective of Analysis	Ratio to be Computed	Formula	Standard Ratio	Actual Ratio	Points for Comments	
					Higher than Standard	Lower than Standard
	(A) *(continued)*				3. Large amount available to meet other expenses	3. Small amount available to meet other expenses
	(B) Operating ratio	COGS + Operating Exp. × 100 Net sales[(COGS + OE)/S] × 100	Company standard	1. Operating cost of ₹XX on sale of ₹100 2. ₹(100 – XX) is the operating profit	1. Low efficiency in managing purchases, production, labour, sales, and inventory 2. Low productivity 3. Small amount available to meet other expenses	1. High efficiency in managing purchases, production, labour, sales, and inventory 2. High productivity 3. Large amount available to meet other expenses
	(C) Operating net profit ratio	Operating net profit/Net sales × 100 = (OP/S) × 100	Company standard	1. Operating margin of ₹XX on sale of ₹100 2. ₹XX is available to meet non-operating expenses/losses	1. Good control over direct and indirect costs 2. High productivity 3. Large amount available to meet non-operating expenses/losses	1. Less control over direct and indirect costs 2. Low productivity 3. Small amount available to meet non-operating expenses/losses
	(D) Expenses ratio	Expenses/Net sales × 100 = (AE or SE or FE/S) × 100	Company standard	1. Expenses of ₹XX on sale of ₹100 2. ₹(100 – XX) available to meet other expenses	1. Less control on specific expenditure 2. Low productivity 3. Small profit available to meet other expenses	1. Very good control on specific expenditure 2. High productivity 3. Large profit available to meet other expenses
	(E) Net profit ratio	(Net profit/Net sales) × 100 = (NP/S) × 100	Company standard	1. Net margin of ₹XX on sale of ₹100 2. ₹XX is available for appropriations	1. Good control over all expenses 2. Unusual gains 3. Large amount available for appropriations 4. High increase in net worth 5. Strong capacity to face bad economic situation	1. Less control over all expenses 2. Unusual losses 3. Small amount available for appropriations. 4. Less increase in net worth 5. Weak capacity to face bad economic situations
5. Overall profitability	(A) Return on capital employed	(Net profit (before interest and tax)/Average Capital employed) × 100 = (PBIT/CE) × 100	Company standard	1. Return of ₹XX on each ₹100 of capital 2. ₹XX is available for tax, interest, and appropriations	1. Good profit ratios (more profit on each rupee of sales) 2. Good turnover ratios (more sales on each rupee of assets used) 3. Large amount for appropriations 4. High increase in net worth 5. Scope to attract fresh funds from owners or lenders	1. Unsatisfactory profit ratios (less profit on each rupee of sales) 2. Unsatisfactory turnover ratios (less sales on each rupee of assets used) 3. Small amount for appropriations 4. Low increase in net worth 5. Less scope to attract fresh funds from owners or lenders
	(B) Return on proprietor's fund	(Net profit after tax/Proprietor's funds) × 100 = (NPAT/PF) × 100	Company standard	1. Return of ₹XX on each ₹100 of owners' funds 2. ₹XX is available for appropriations	1. Large amount for appropriations 2. Scope to attach fresh funds from owners	1. Small amount for appropriations 2. Less to attach fresh funds from owners
	(C) Return on equity capital	Net profit after tax and preference dividends/(Equity capital + Reserves)] × 100 = PAES/EF × 100	Company standard	1. Return of ₹XX on each ₹100 of equity shareholders' funds 2. ₹XX is available for appropriations	1. Large amount for appropriations 2. High increase in net worth	1. Small amount for appropriations 2. Low increase in net worth

Objective of Analysis	Ratio to be Computed	Formula	Standard Ratio	Actual Ratio	Points for Comments	
					Higher than Standard	**Lower than Standard**
6. Capital structure	(A) Capital gearing	(Pref. capital + Debentures + Loan)/(Equity capital + Reserves) = (PC + BF)/EF	Company standard	For every ₹XX from funds with fixed returns, ₹1 is from equity shareholders	Higher returns for equity shareholders if rate of fixed returns is less than ROI 3. Scope to attract fresh funds from equity shareholders 4. High price for each equity share on stock exchange or in a merger	Low returns or loss to equity shareholders if rate of fixed returns is more than ROI 3. Less scope to attract fresh funds from equity shareholders 4. Low price for each equity share on stock exchange or in a merger
	(B) Debt/Equity	Debt/Equity	3:1	Refer 3 (B)	Refer 3 (B)	Refer 3 (B)
	(C) Proprietary ratio	(Proprietors' fund/Total assets) × 100	65% to 75%	Refer 3 (A)	Refer 3 (A)	Refer 3 (A)
7. Over-trading or under-trading	(A) Proprietary ratio	(Proprietors' fund/Total assets) × 100	Low ratio: Over-trading high ratio: under-trading	Refer 3 (A)	Refer 3 (A)	Refer 3 (A)
	(B) Stock turnover	Cost of goods sold/Average stock × 100	High ratio: Over-trading low ratio: Under-trading	Refer 2.2 (C)	Refer 2.2 (C)	Refer 2.2 (C)
	(C) Current ratio	Current assets/Current liabilities	Low ratio: Under-trading	Refer 2 (A)	Refer 2 (A)	Refer 2 (A)
8. Coverage	(A) Dividend payout	(Equity dividend/Profit for equity shareholders) × 100 = ED/PAES × 100	Company standard	1. ₹XX is paid as dividend out of each ₹100 available for distribution 2. Balance (100 – XX) can be transferred to reserves	1. Very high dividends make short-term equity shareholders very happy 2. Scope to issue fresh equity shares at high price 3. High price on stock exchange or in merger for equity shares 4. Less reserve may mean low growth in future and no bonus issue	1. Very low dividends make short-term equity shareholders unhappy 2. Less scope to issue fresh equity shares 3. Low price on stock exchange or in merger for equity shares 4. If transfers to reserves are more, it may mean high growth or bonus issue in future
	(B) Interest coverage	PBIT/Interest	Company standard	Earnings are XX times the interest	1. Strong capacity to pay interest as and when due 2. Large balance profits left for tax and dividends 3. Good scope to get more loans at low rate of interest 4. But less benefits of trading on equity, if assets are financed less by debt and more by equity	1. Weak capacity to pay interest as and when due 2. Small balance profits left for tax, dividends 3. Less scope to get more loans 4. More loans only at high rate of interest 5. But more benefits of trading on equity, if assets are financed more by debt and less by equity

List of abbreviations used:
Quick assets (QA)
Quick liabilities (QL)
Current assets (CA)
Current liabilities (CL)
Closing stock (CST)
Working capital (WC)
Cost of goods sold (COGS)
Opening stock (OST)
Debtors (DR)
Bills receivables (BR)
Daily credit sales (CRS)
Creditors (CD)
Bills payable (BP)
Credit purchases (CRP)
Proprietors fund (PF)
Total assets (TA)
Borrowed funds (BF)
Gross profit (GP)
Operating expenses (OE)
Operating net profit (OP)
Administrative expenses (AE)
Sales and distribution expenses (SE)
Financial expenses (FE)
Net profit (NP)
Net sales (S)
Net profit before interest and taxes (EBIT or PBIT)
Average capital employed (CE)
Net profit after tax (NP or NPAT)
Net profit after taxes and preference dividend (PAES)
Equity share capital plus reserves and surpluses known as equity funds (EF)
Preference share capital (PC)
Equity dividend (ED)

Limitations of Ratio Analysis

Ratio analysis is widely used to interpret a firm's financial statements. Ratios are no doubt useful but they also have their limitations. Interpretations of ratios after understanding the limitations would be more meaningful. Some of the important limitations of accounting ratios are as explained in this section.

Unreliable accounts

Accounting ratios are based on financial statements. Financial statements should be absolutely reliable so that the ratios derived from them could also be relied upon. For example, if contingent liabilities are treated as actual liabilities and are debited to the income statement, the profit as shown in the income statement would reduce. This figure would give a wrong interpretation of a company's profitability.

Inter-firm comparisons

Ratios are used for inter-firm comparison, as no two firms are similar in age, size, or accounting policies. For example, one firm may charge depreciation on the straight-line basis, while another firm may charge it on the basis of diminishing value. Different policies may be adapted for stock valuation. Due to such differences, a comparison of such ratios might not be feasible.

Meaningless ratios

Except a few cases, an accounting ratio may by itself be meaningless and acquire significance only when compared with relevant ratios of other firms or of the previous years. In fact, ratios yield their best advantage either on comparison with other similar firms or for a year compared with ratios in the previous years. Comparison is the essential requirement for using ratios for interpreting a given situation in a firm or industry.

Incomparable ratios

When the ratio of two firms is compared, it should be remembered that different firms may follow different accounting practices. For example, one firm may charge deprecation on straight line basis and the other firm on diminishing value. Similarly, different firms may adapt different methods of stock valuation. Such a difference may not make some of the accounting ratio strictly comparable. However, use of accounting standards make ratio comparable.

Misleading picture

Suppose, a firm produces 500 units in one year and 1,000 units the next year. The progress here is 100%. Another firm produces 4,000 units in one year and 5,000 in the next year. The progress here is 25%. The second firm will appear to be less efficient than the first firm, if only the rate of increase is compared. It will appear to be less active than the first firm, if only the rate of increase or ratio is compared. It will be much more useful if absolute figure is also compared along with the rate of increase, unless the firms being compared are equal in all respects. In fact, one should be extremely careful while comparing the result of one firm with that of another firm if the two figures differ in any significant manner, say in size, location, degree of automation, or mechanization.

Ignoring qualitative factor

Ratio is, as a matter of fact, a tool of quantitative analysis. It ignores qualitative factors which are sometimes either equally or more important than the quantitative factors. As a result of this, conclusions from ratio analysis may be distorted. For example, despite the fact that credit may be granted to a customer on the basis of information regarding the financial position of a prospective customer as disclosed by a certain ratio, the grant of credit ultimately depends upon the credit standing, reputation, and managerial ability of the customer, which cannot be expressed in the form of ratio.

No single standard for comparison

The ratios of a firm have meaning only when they are compared with some standard ratio. Circumstances differ from firm to firm as also nature of each industry. Therefore, the standard will differ for each industry. Hence, the circumstance of each firm will have to be kept in mind. In the absence of a proper basis of comparison, the performance of one industry may not be properly comparable with that of another. Usually, it is recommended that ratio should be compared with the average of the industry. But the industry average is not easily available.

Ratio based on past financial statements

Accounting ratio is calculated on the basis of financial statements of past years. Ratio thus indicates what has shaped in the past. Since past is quite different from what is likely to happen in future, it is difficult to use ratio for forecasting purpose. Financial analysts are more interested in what will happen in the future. The management of a firm has information about the firm's future plans and policies and is, therefore, able to predict future to a certain extent. But an outsider analyst has to rely only on the past ratio, which may not necessarily reflect the firm's future financial position and performance.

Changing prices

A change in the price levels can affect the validity of ratios calculated for various years. For example, turnover of fixed assets, that is, sales/fixed assets will be higher in 2007 than in 1985 because of rising prices. Fixed assets are always expressed at cost whereas sales price increases over the years. Inter-period comparison is affected by price level changes.

Similarly, in the case of two companies, one company may have purchased the asset at a lower price many years ago and another may have purchased it at a higher price recently. The return on investments of these companies is bound to differ. The company which purchased the asset at a lower price in the past will have a higher rate of return than the company which has purchased the same asset at a much higher price now. Inter-company comparisons are also affected by changes in the price level.

Different terms

Various terms such as capital employed, opening net profit, and quick assets should be properly defined. Otherwise, the comparison may become meaningless. Similarly, there can be many ways to calculate the same ratio. For example, quick ratio is calculated as per any of the two formulae mentioned in the following text:

> Quick Ratio = Quick Assets/Quick Liabilities
> Quick Ratio = Quick Assets/Current Liabilities

Different standard ratios

It is very difficult to decide the standard ratio against which the actual ratio should be compared. Some companies may be capital intensive, while some may be labour intensive. Some companies may believe in keeping a large stock of materials, while others may prefer to maintain a small inventory. The standard ratio has to be adjusted for each company so that ratios become comparable.

Deeper analysis

Ratio analysis is a tool of financial management. Ratios point out the area that needs investigation. For example, if the present year's gross profit ratio is lower than last year's ratio, the reasons may be poor sales, increase in cost of sales, wastages and losses, or bad purchasing. The analyst should try to locate the cause behind the decline in the gross profit ratio.

Year-end data

Ratio analysis is based on the financial statements prepared on the accounting year-end date. Seasonal factors may influence the figures of the closing stock. Financial statements can be manipulated to cover up a company's bad financial position. Therefore, ratios based on such figures are not reliable. Ratios should be based on average figures and not on the year-end date.

Related Concepts

Ratio analysis is useful for financial analysis but to get better results, ratio analysis should be done with care as several factors affect efficiency ratios. These factors are discussed in this section.

1. The type of the business a company is involved in affects its ratios and the conclusions drawn from them. For example, a public utility sector company with large fixed assets, but social benefit considerations, may have a high ratio of debt to net worth.

2. Seasonal characters of the business environment affect ratios of a particular type of industry or business enterprise. For example, inventory to sales ratio for a merchant during the peak season is higher than during any other period of the same year.

3. The quality of assets also affects ratio analysis. A current assets to current liabilities ratio of 2:1 is considered satisfactory for assessing a company's liquidity. However, a 2:1 ratio may depict the unsatisfactory position of liquid funds with the company to meet its most urgent and pressing obligations.

4. Adequacy of data is another consideration for comparison of factors with each other. For example, the average collection period for bills receivable for a particular month may differ from other months or the yearly average. Another consideration would be whether bills receivable have been properly valued for a particular period as over valuation may render the ratios incomparable.

5. Modification of ratios reflect only a company's past performance and must be modified by future trends of business.

6. Interpretation of ratios should not be relied upon in isolation. Ratios should be analysed along with accounting documents.

7. Non-financial data ratios based on financial data of firms should be considered with non-financial data to supplement the financial ratios and give a better interpretation.

It is desirable to analyse a group of ratios rather than studying only one ratio in isolation. Ratio analysis should not be considered as the ultimate test but it may be carried further depending upon the results and revaluations of the causes of variations. Many times, these variations are the direct result of accounting deficiencies or unreliability of financial data. In order to make sure that the results of ratio analysis are economically significant, it is necessary to make certain that the firms or items examined are comparable to each other.

Percentage ratios should be taken in their context to assure that the trends shown reflect true patterns and significant changes. These ratios should also be compared with other comparable factors such as percentage growth in profit, investment, export, employment, etc. Empirical studies have shown that firms operating in different industries tend to have different financial ratios. Inter-industry differences flow from two different factors—technology and degree of risk.

DuPont Analysis

Profit is indispensable for the survival and growth of both profit making and not-for-profit firms. Financial and business analysts are interested in identifying the driving forces that led to the generation of required amount of profit, that is, excess of income over expenses. Basic sources of profit are sales of goods or services provided to customers. Profit in the residual of sales over the cost incurred to earn such sales. These residuals are the accomplishments of the efforts made in the firm. The well-known measure of profitability is known as return on investment (ROI). ROI indicates the overall measurements of profitability and requires detailed analysis in several stages.

DuPont control chart

The DuPont control chart, which is also widely known as DuPont analysis, is named after the first user of ratios, that is,

the DuPont company of the United States. According to this chart, the return on investment (ROI) represents the earning power of a firm. It depends on two ratios: (a) net profit ratio and (b) capital turnover ratio. A change in any one of the two ratios will change the firm's earning power (i.e., ROI) and is affected by many factors. Figure 16.2 shows the DuPont chart.

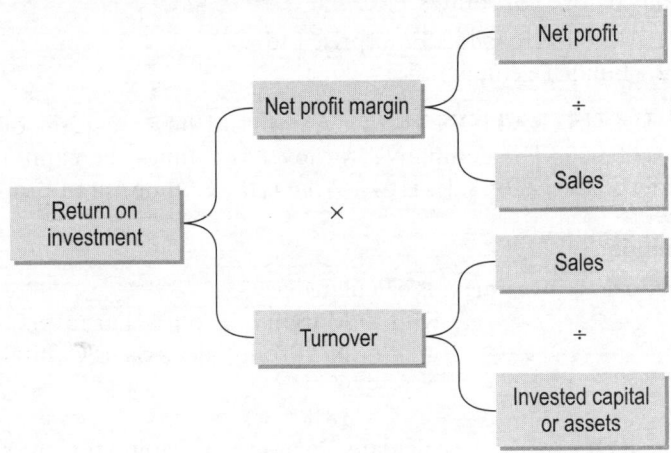

FIG. 16.2 The DuPont chart

The financial ratios of a company in a given year may not help in the complete assessment of its performance. To interpret the financial health of a company, it is crucial to analyse and compare the ratios for a given year with the ratios in the previous years and the industry ratios. DuPont has pioneered a system of financial analysis which has received widespread recognition and acceptance. The analysis takes into account important inter-relationships based on the information available in a company's financial statements. The usefulness of the DuPont chart lies in the fact that it presents an overall view of a company's performance (Fig. 16.3). It enables the management to identify the factors which have a bearing on the company's profitability.

The left hand side of the chart shows the details underlying the net profit margin ratio. An in-depth analysis of the ratio reveals the areas in which cost reduction can be achieved to improve the overall net profit margin.

The right hand side of the chart reveals the determinants of the total assets turnover ratio. The analysis can be extended to cover various turnover ratios such as inventory turnover ratio,

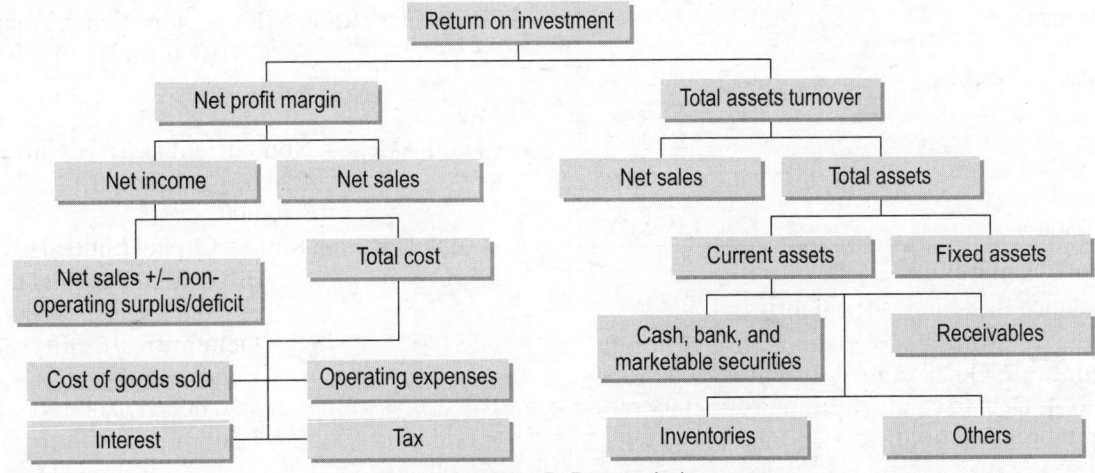

FIG. 16.3 DuPont analysis

receivables turnover ratio, and fixed assets turnover ratio. The analysis reveals the efficiencies or inefficiencies in the utilization of a company's assets. The ROI gives the overall picture by taking into account both profitability of investment and profitability on sales.

Exhibit 16.4 indicates the financial ratios and their presentations by two corporates:

1. Apollo Hospitals Enterprise Ltd
2. Balaji Telefilms Ltd

■ **ILLUSTRATION 16.12** Aarya Ltd has a capital of ₹10,00,000. The company's turnover is 3 times the capital and the margin on sales is 6%. What is the ROI of Aarya Ltd?

Solution

Return on investment is calculated as

$$\text{ROI} = \text{Margin of Profit} \times \text{Turnover}$$
$$= \text{Net Profit/Sales} \times \text{Sales/Capital}$$
$$= 6\% \times 3$$
$$= 18\%$$

The ROI can also be calculated by using the capital turnover ratio.

$$\text{Capital Turnover Ratio} = \text{Sales/Capital}$$
$$3 = \text{Sales/10,00,000}$$
$$\text{Sales} = ₹30,00,000$$
$$\text{Net Profit} = 6\% \text{ of } ₹30,00,000$$
$$= ₹1,80,000$$
$$\text{ROI} = (\text{Net profit/Investment}) \times 100$$
$$= (1,80,000/10,00,000) \times 100$$
$$= 18\%$$

■ **ILLUSTRATION 16.13** The following is the balance sheet of Manco Ltd as at 31 March 2020.

Summarized Balance Sheet

Particulars	31/12/2020
ASSETS	
Land and building	1,40,000
Plant and machinery	3,50,000
Stock-in-trade	2,00,000
Sundry debtors	1,00,000
Bills receivables	10,000
Cash at bank	40,000
Total Assets	**8,40,000**
EQUITY AND LIABILITIES	
Share capital	2,00,000
Profit and loss account	30,000
General reserve	40,000
12% Debentures	4,20,000
Sundry creditors	1,00,000
Bills payable	50,000
Total Equity and Liabilities	**8,40,000**

Answer the following questions:

(a) Convert balance sheet into vertical form.
(b) Calculate the following ratios
   1. Current ratio, 2. Quick ratio, 3. Inventory to working capital ratio, 4. Debt to equity ratio, 5. Proprietary ratio, and 6. Capital gearing ratio.

Solution

Vertical Balance Sheet of Manco Ltd
as at 31 March 2020

Particulars	Amount (₹)		
SOURCES OF FUNDS			
Equity share capital		2,00,000	
Profit and loss account	30,000		
General reserve	40,000		
Reserves and surplus		70,000	
Proprietor's funds			2,70,000
12% Debentures borrowed funds			4,20,000
Capital employed			6,90,000
APPLICATION OF FUNDS			
Non-current assets			
Land and building		1,40,000	
Plant and machinery		3,50,000	
			4,90,000
Current assets:			
Debtors	1,00,000		
Bills receivable	10,000		
Cash at bank	40,000		
Quick assets	1,50,000		
Closing stock	2,00,000		
		3,50,000	
Less: Current liabilities			
Sundry creditors	1,00,000		
Bills payable	50,000		
		1,50,000	
Working capital			2,00,000
Capital employed			6,90,000

The ratios are calculated as follows:

1. Current Ratio = Current Assets/Current Liabilities
   $$= 3,50,000/1,50,000$$
   $$= 2.33 : 1$$

2. Quick Ratio = Quick Assets/Quick Liabilities
   $$= 1,50,000/1,50,000$$
   $$= 1 : 1$$

3. Inventory to Working Capital = (Closing Stock/Working Capital) × 100
   $$= (2,00,000/2,00,000) \times 100$$
   $$= 100\%$$

4. Debt to Equity Ratio = Borrowed Funds/Proprietors' Funds
   = 12% Debentures/Proprietors' funds
   $$= 4,20,000/2,70,000$$
   $$= 1.56 : 1$$

5. Proprietary Ratio = (Proprietors' Funds/Total Assets) × 100
   $$= (2,70,000/8,40,000) \times 100$$
   $$= 32.14\%$$
   Where,
   Total Assets = Non-current assets + Current Assets
   $$= 4,90,000 + 3,50,000$$
   $$= 8,40,000$$

6. Capital Gearing Ratio = Capital Entitled to Fixed Interest or Dividend/Capital not so entitled to fixed interest or dividend
   = Debentures/Equity Shareholders Funds
   $$= 4,20,000/2,70,000$$
   $$= 1.56 : 1$$

EXHIBIT 16.4   Financial Ratios and their Presentations by Two Corporates

Apollo Hospitals Enterprise Limited

Sustained growth

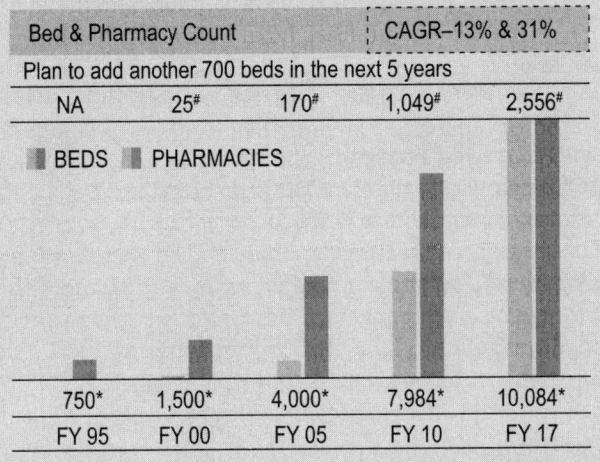

Bed & Pharmacy Count — CAGR–13% & 31%

Plan to add another 700 beds in the next 5 years

	NA	25#	170#	1,049#	2,556#

■ BEDS ■ PHARMACIES

	750*	1,500*	4,000*	7,984*	10,084*
	FY 95	FY 00	FY 05	FY 10	FY 17

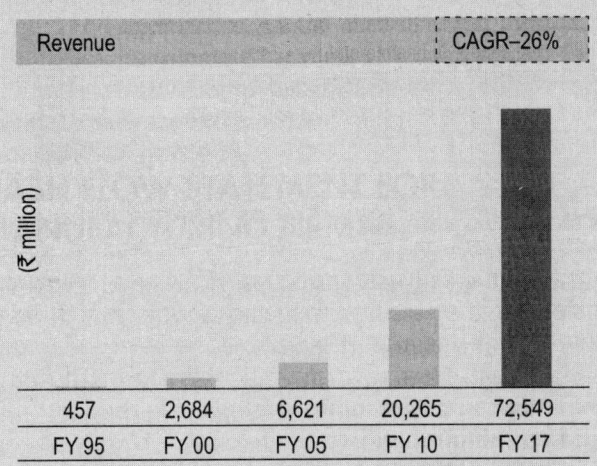

Revenue — CAGR–26%

(₹ million)

	457	2,684	6,621	20,265	72,549
	FY 95	FY 00	FY 05	FY 10	FY 17

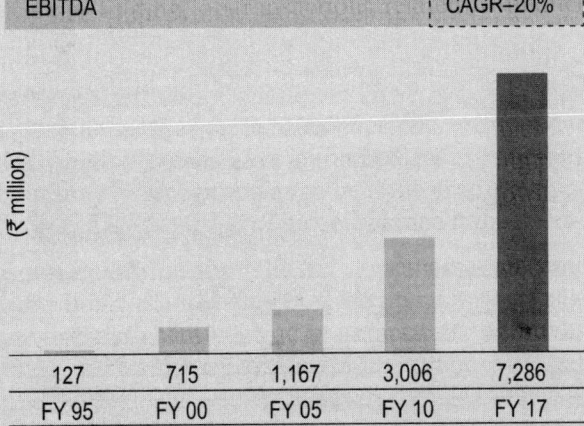

EBITDA — CAGR–20%

(₹ million)

	127	715	1,167	3,006	7,286
	FY 95	FY 00	FY 05	FY 10	FY 17

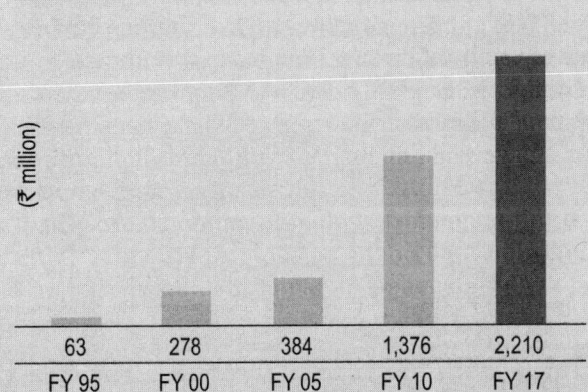

PAT — CAGR–17%

(₹ million)

	63	278	384	1,376	2,210
	FY 95	FY 00	FY 05	FY 10	FY 17

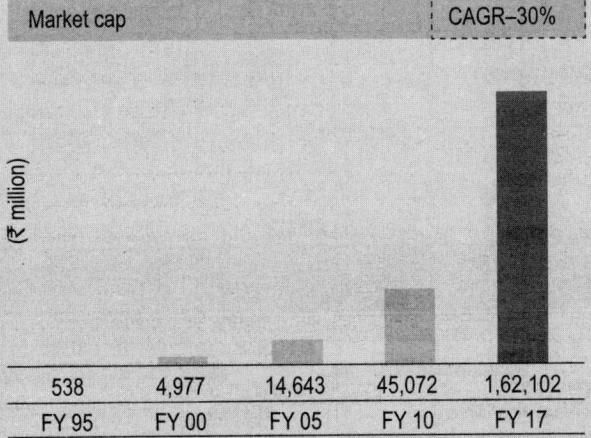

Market cap — CAGR–30%

(₹ million)

	538	4,977	14,643	45,072	1,62,102
	FY 95	FY 00	FY 05	FY 10	FY 17

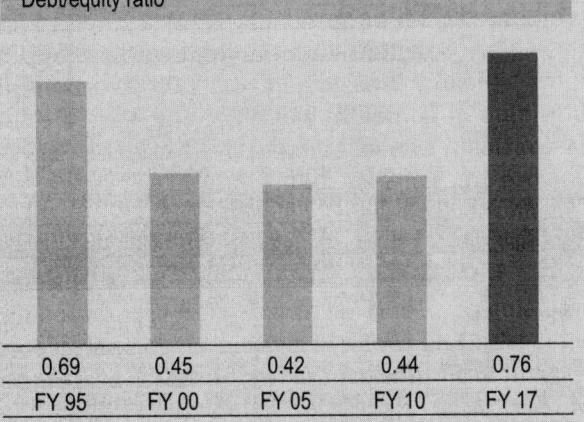

Debt/equity ratio

	0.69	0.45	0.42	0.44	0.76
	FY 95	FY 00	FY 05	FY 10	FY 17

* Bed includes both owned & managed hospitals;
\# Number of standalone pharmacies.

Note: FY17 figures have been presented on the basis of Ind AS.

Strong operational performance

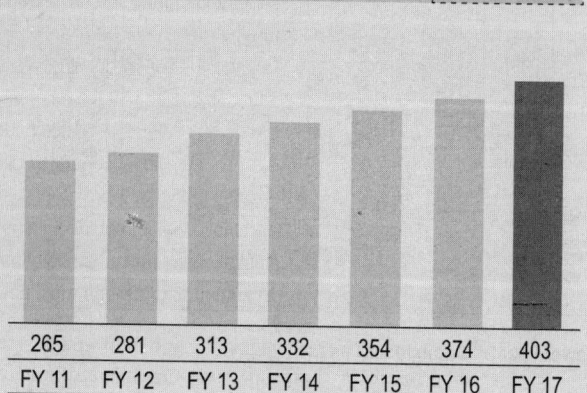

Discharges (in '000s) — CAGR–7%

	FY 11	FY 12	FY 13	FY 14	FY 15	FY 16	FY 17
	265	281	313	332	354	374	403

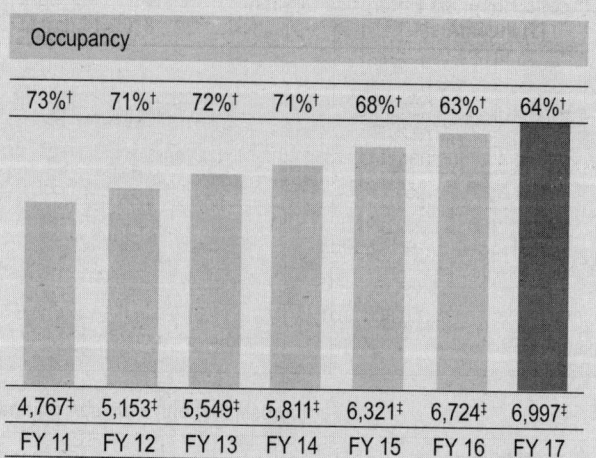

Occupancy

	73%†	71%†	72%†	71%†	68%†	63%†	64%†
	4,767‡	5,153‡	5,549‡	5,811‡	6,321‡	6,724‡	6,997‡
	FY 11	FY 12	FY 13	FY 14	FY 15	FY 16	FY 17

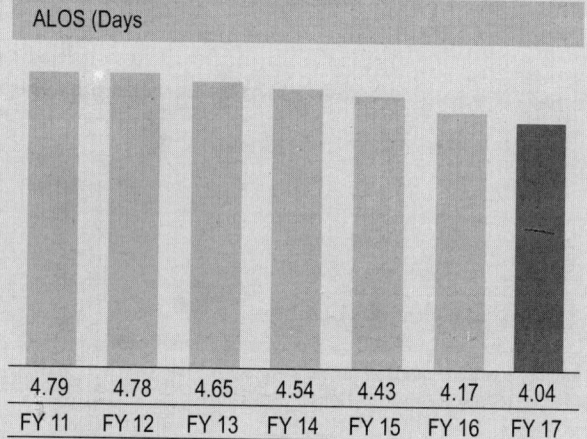

ALOS (Days

	FY 11	FY 12	FY 13	FY 14	FY 15	FY 16	FY 17
	4.79	4.78	4.65	4.54	4.43	4.17	4.04

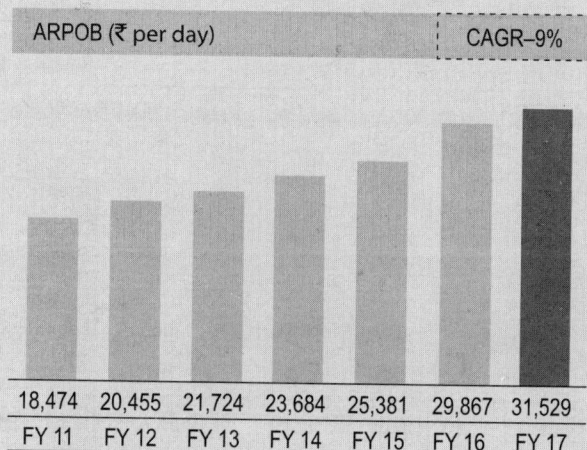

ARPOB (₹ per day) — CAGR–9%

	FY 11	FY 12	FY 13	FY 14	FY 15	FY 16	FY 17
	18,474	20,455	21,724	23,684	25,381	29,867	31,529

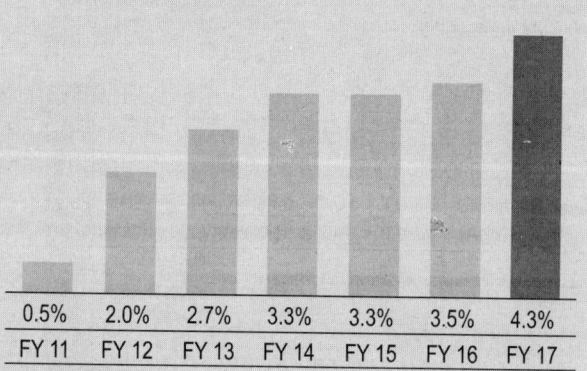

SAP EBITDA Margins

	FY 11	FY 12	FY 13	FY 14	FY 15	FY 16	FY 17
	0.5%	2.0%	2.7%	3.3%	3.3%	3.5%	4.3%

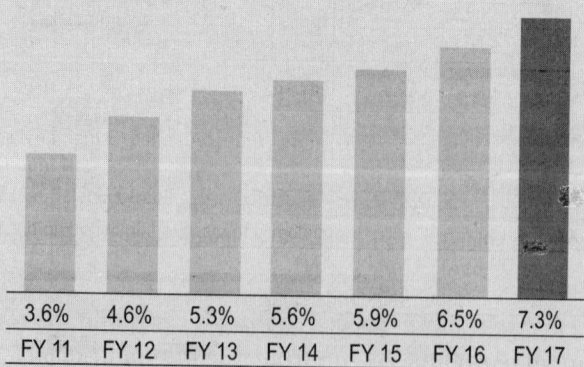

Mature Stores (Pre FY08) EBITDA Margins

	FY 11	FY 12	FY 13	FY 14	FY 15	FY 16	FY 17
	3.6%	4.6%	5.3%	5.6%	5.9%	6.5%	7.3%

ALOS – Average Length of Stay;
ARPOB – Average Revenue per Occupied Bed.
† Occupancy rate. ‡ Operating beds.

Note: FY17 figures have been presented on the basis of Ind AS.

Balaji Telefilms Limited: Financial Momentum

HOURS OF PROGRAMMING — Hrs

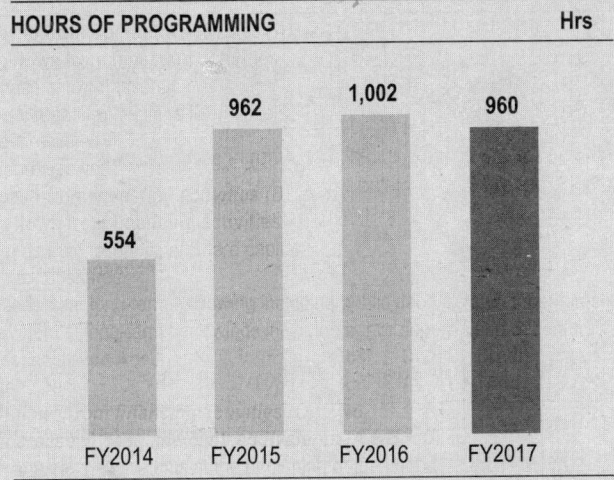

FY2014	FY2015	FY2016	FY2017
554	962	1,002	960

REALISATION PER HOUR — ₹ in Lacs

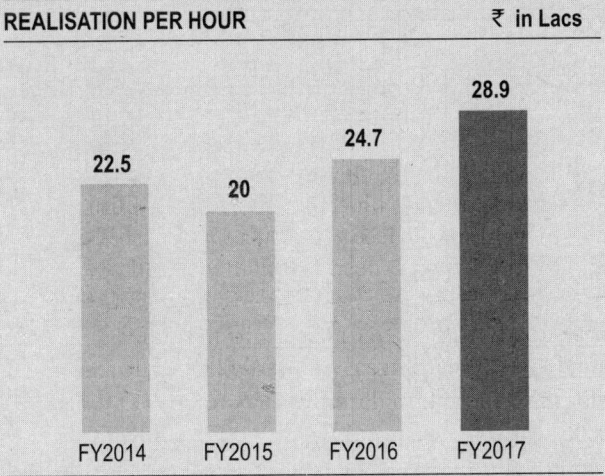

FY2014	FY2015	FY2016	FY2017
22.5	20	24.7	28.9

INCOME FROM OPERATION — ₹ in Lacs

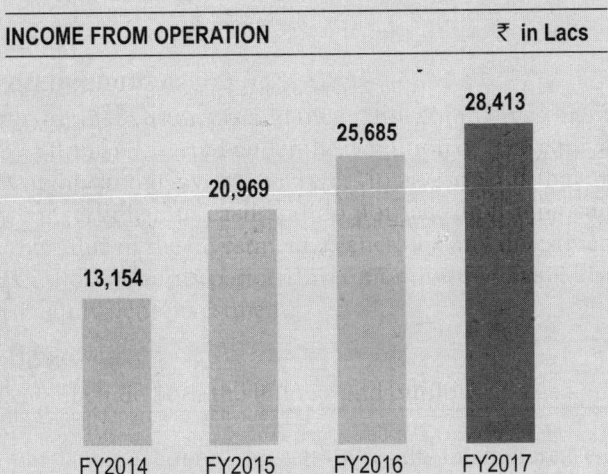

FY2014	FY2015	FY2016	FY2017
13,154	20,969	25,685	28,413

EBITDA — ₹ in Lacs

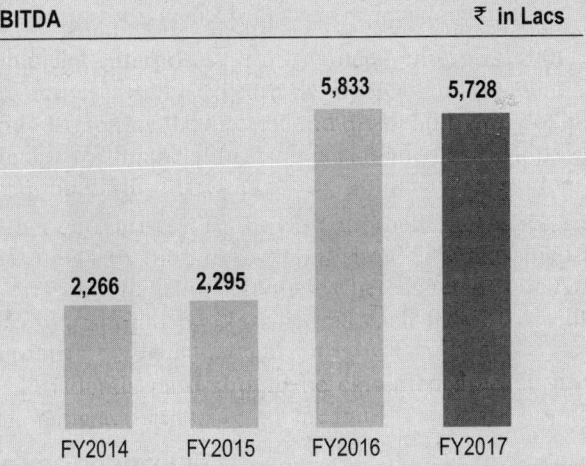

FY2014	FY2015	FY2016	FY2017
2,266	2,295	5,833	5,728

EBITDA MARGIN — %

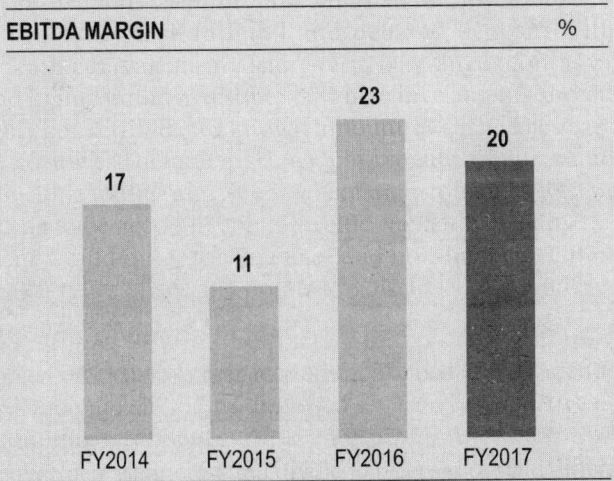

FY2014	FY2015	FY2016	FY2017
17	11	23	20

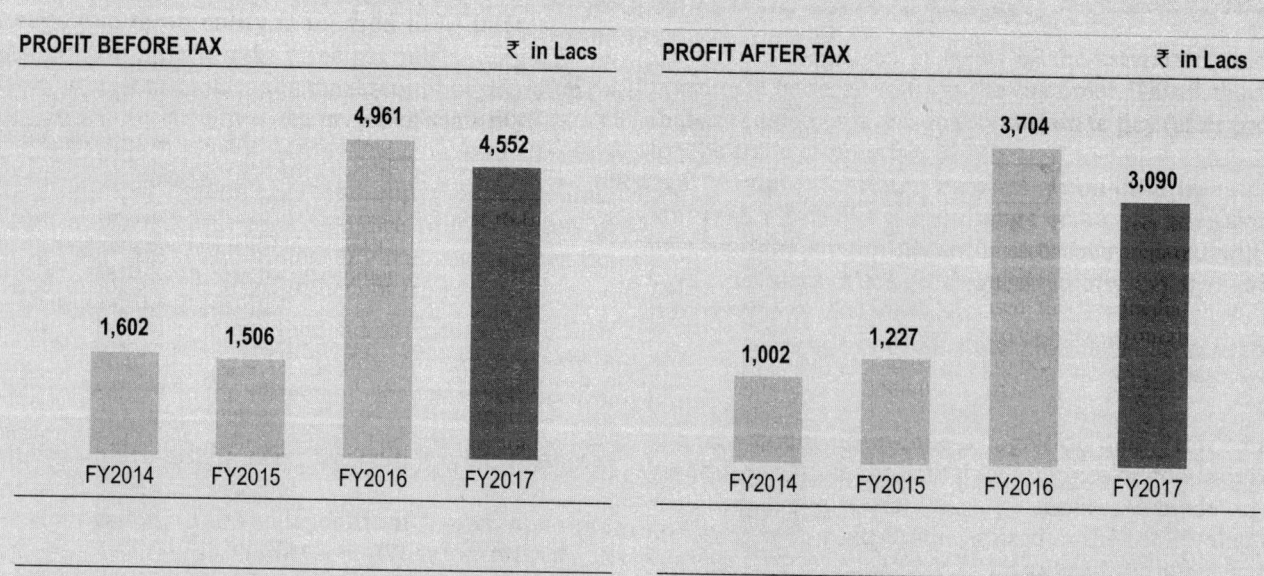

PROFIT BEFORE TAX — ₹ in Lacs

FY2014	FY2015	FY2016	FY2017
1,602	1,506	4,961	4,552

PROFIT AFTER TAX — ₹ in Lacs

FY2014	FY2015	FY2016	FY2017
1,002	1,227	3,704	3,090

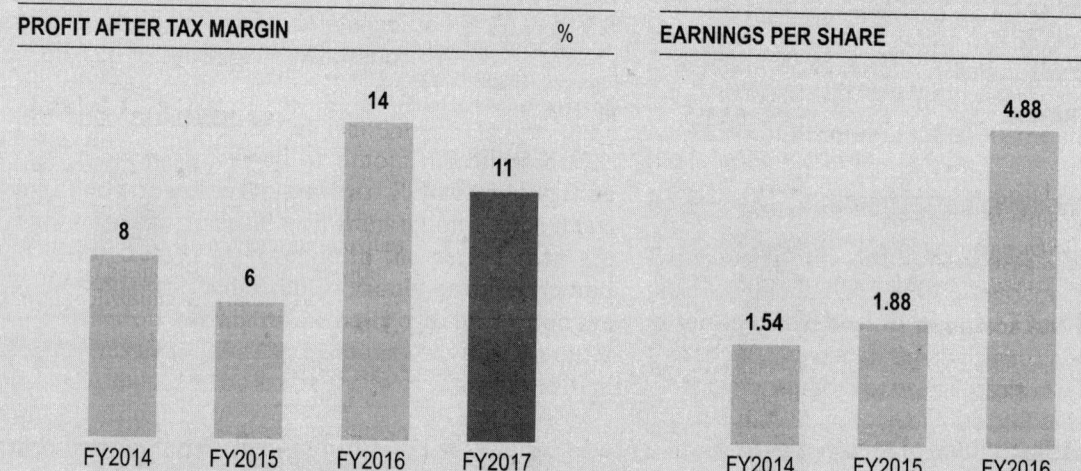

PROFIT AFTER TAX MARGIN — %

FY2014	FY2015	FY2016	FY2017
8	6	14	11

EARNINGS PER SHARE — ₹

FY2014	FY2015	FY2016	FY2017
1.54	1.88	4.88	4.07

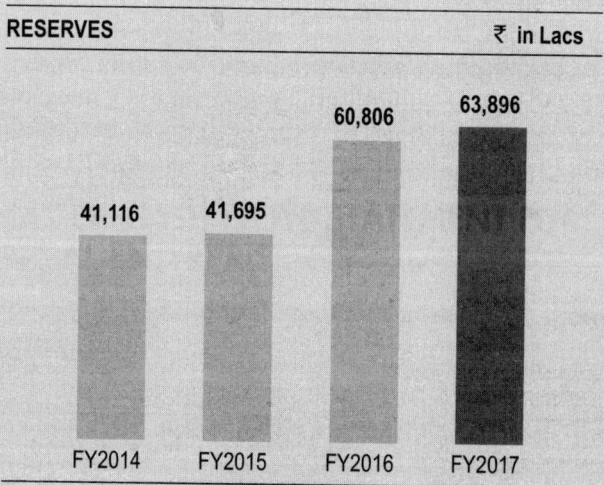

RESERVES — ₹ in Lacs

FY2014	FY2015	FY2016	FY2017
41,116	41,695	60,806	63,896

Note: *FY 2016 and FY 2017 numbers are as per IND-AS accounting standards. FY 2014 and FY 2015 numbers are as per IGAAP Based on Standalone numbers

Sources: Apollo Hospitals Enterprise Limited Annual Report 2017–18, pp. 54–55; Balaji Telefilms Limited Annual Report 2016–17, pp. 18–19

■ **ILLUSTRATION 16.14** Bansal Ltd has drawn up the following income statement for the year ended 31 March 2020.

Income Statement of Bansal Ltd
for the Period Ended 31 March 2020

Particulars	Amount (₹)
INCOME	
Sales	1,60,000
Closing stock	38,000
Total	**1,98,000**
EXPENSES	
Opening stock	26,000
Purchases	80,000
Wages	24,000
Manufacturing expenses	16,000
Gross profit	52,000
Total	**1,98,000**
Other Income	
Gross profit	52,000
Compensation for acquisition of land	4,800
Total	**56,800**
Other Expenses	
Selling and distribution expenses	4,000
Administration expenses	22,800
General expenses	1,200
Furniture lost by fire	800
Net profit	28,000
Total	**56,800**

Answer the following questions:

1. Convert the income statement of Bansal Ltd into vertical form and compute the following ratios.
   1. Operating ratio, 2. Operating net profit ratio, 3. Net profit ratio, 4. Gross profit ratio, and 5. Stock turnover ratio.

Solution

Income Statement of Bansal Ltd in Vertical Form

Particulars	Amount (₹)	Amount (₹)
Sales		1,60,000
Less: Cost of goods sold		
Opening stock	26,000	
Add: Purchases	80,000	
Add: Wages	24,000	
Add: Manufacturing expenses	16,000	
	1,46,000	
Less: Closing stock	38,000	
Cost of goods sold		1,08,000
Gross profit		52,000
Less: Operating expenses		
Selling and distribution expenses	4,000	

Particulars		
Administrative expenses	22,800	
General expenses	1,200	
		28,000
Operating profit		24,000
Add: Non-operating income		
Compensation for acquisition of land	4,800	
Less: Non-operating expenses		
Furniture lost by fire	(800)	4,000
Net profit		28,000

1. Operating Ratio = [(Cost of Goods Sold + Operating Expenses)/Sales] × 100
   = [(1,08,000 + 28,000)/1,60,000] × 100
   = (1,36,000/1,60,000) × 100
   = 85%

2. Operating Net Profit Ratio = (Operating Net Profit/Net Sales) × 100
   = (24,000/1,60,000) × 100
   = 15%

3. Net Profit Ratio = Net Profit/Net Sales × 100
   = (28,000/1,60,000) × 100
   = 17.5%

4. Gross Profit Ratio = (Gross Profit/Net Sales) × 100
   = (52,000/1,60,000) × 100
   = 32.5%

5. Stock Turnover Ratio = Cost of Goods Sold/Average Stock
   = 1,08,000/32,000
   = 338%

   Average Stock = (Opening Stock + Closing Stock)/2
   = (26,000 + 38,000)/2
   = 32,000

■ **ILLUSTRATION 16.15** The following is the balance sheet of Amit Ltd as at 31 March 2020.

Balance sheet of Amit Ltd
as at 31 March 2020

Particulars	Amount (₹)
ASSETS	
Non-current assets (Fixed assets)	6,10,000
Stock-in-trade	1,60,000
Sundry debtors	1,20,000
Bills receivables	25,000
Cash in hand and at bank	35,000
Total Assets	**9,50,000**
EQUITY AND LIABILITIES	
Equity share capital	4,00,000
1000 12% Preference shares of ₹100 each	1,00,000
Reserve and Surplus	1,00,000
12% Debentures	2,00,000
Creditors	1,20,000
Bank overdraft	30,000
Total Equity and Liabilities	**9,50,000**

Revenue Statement
for the Year Ended 31 March 2020

Particulars		Amount (₹)
Net sales (credit)		7,30,000
Cost of sales		6,20,500
Gross profit		1,09,500
Administrative expenses	18,250	
Selling and distribution expenses	36,500	54,750
Operating profit (before tax)		54,750
Taxation		25,550
Operating profit (after tax)		29,200

From the given information, you are required to compute the following ratios:

1. Current ratio
2. Liquidity ratio
3. Gross profit ratio
4. Debtor's velocity
5. Net profit ratio
6. Capital gearing ratio
7. Proprietary ratio
8. Stock working capital ratio
9. Administrative expenses ratio
10. Debt–equity ratio

Solution

1. Current Ratio = Current Assets/Current Liabilities
   = 3,40,000/1,50,000
   = 2.27:1

2. Liquid Ratio = Quick Assets/Quick Liabilities
   = Current Assets Less Stock/Current Liabilities Less Bank Overdraft
   = 1,80,000/1,20,000
   = 1.5:1

3. Gross Profit Ratio = (Gross Profit/Net Sales) × 100
   = (1,09,500/7,30,000) × 100
   = 15%

4. Debtor's Velocity = [(Debtors + Bills Receivable)/Total Credit Sales] × 365
   = [(1,20,000 + 25,000)/7,30,000] × 365
   = 73 days

5. Net Profit Ratio = [Net Profit (After Tax)/Net Sales] × 100
   = (29,200/7,30,000) × 100
   = 4%

6. Capital Gearing Ratio = Capital Entitled to Fixed Interest or Dividend/Equity Capital + Reserves
   = Preference Capital + Debentures/Equity Capital + Reserves
   = 1,00,000 + 2,00,000/4,00,000 + 1,00,000
   = 3,00,000/5,00,000
   = 0.6:1

7. Proprietary Ratio = (Proprietors' Funds/Total Assets) × 100
   = (Equity Capital + Preference Capital + Reserves/Total Assets) × 100
   = (4,00,000 + 1,00,000 + 1,00,000/9,50,000) × 100
   = 63.16%

8. Stock Working Capital Ratio = (Stock/Working Capital) × 100
   = 1,60,000/1,90,000 × 100
   = 84.21%

9. Administrative Expenses Ratio = (Administrative Expenses/Net sales) × 100
   = (18,250/7,30,000) × 100
   = 2.5%

10. Debt–equity Ratio = Borrowed Funds/Proprietor's Funds
    = Debentures/(Equity shares + Reserves = + Preference Capital)
    = 2,00,000/(4,00,000 + 1,00,000 + 1,00,000)
    = 2,00,000/6,00,000
    = 0.33

■ **ILLUSTRATION 16.16** A company has a current ratio of 2.5 and ₹60,000 as its working capital. Calculate the amount of current assets and current liabilities.

Solution

Current Ratio = Current Assets/Current Liabilities = 2.5
Current Assets – 2.5 × Current Liabilities = 0 (1)
Current Assets – Current Liabilities = 60,000 (2)
Subtracting Equation (2) from (1)
1.5 Current Liabilities = 60,000
Current Liabilities = 60,000/1.5
= ₹40,000
Current Assets = 40,000 × 2.5
= ₹1,00,000

■ **ILLUSTRATION 16.17** From the following information, calculate the stock at the end of the year.

Particulars	Amount (₹)
Opening stock	62,000
Purchases	4,20,000
Sales	6,00,000
Rate of gross profit on cost	33.33%

Solution

Let cost of goods sold be equal to 3, then gross profit is 1, which is 33.33% of sales.

Sales = Cost of Goods Sold + Gross Profit
= 3 + 1
= ₹4

If sales are ₹6,00,000, then the cost of goods sold is as follows:

Cost of goods sold = (3 × 6,00,000)/4
= ₹4,50,000
Closing Stock = Opening Stock + Purchases – Cost of Goods Sold
= 62,000 + 4,20,000 – 4,50,000
= ₹32,000

■ **ILLUSTRATION 16.18** Carmel Ltd has a liquidity ratio of 1.5. Its net working capital is ₹1,20,000 and its stock amounts to ₹80,000. Calculate the value of current assets.

Solution

Liquid Ratio = Quick Assets/Current Liabilities
= (Current Assets – Stock)/Current Liabilities
= (Current Assets – 80,000)/Current Liabilities
= 1.5

Current Assets – 1.5 Current Liabilities = 80,000   (1)
Current Assets – Current Liabilities = 1,20,000   (2)
Subtracting Equation (2) from (1)
0.5 Current Liabilities = 40,000

> Quick assets = Current assets – Stock.

Current Liabilities = 80,000
Thus, Current Assets = 1,20,000 + 80,000
= ₹2,00,000

■ **ILLUSTRATION 16.19** Calculate detailed working capital from the following information:

1. Current ratio	2.5
2. Liquid ratio	1.5
3. Stock turnover ratio (Cost of sales/Closing stock)	6 times
4. Debtors collection period	2 months
5. Gross profit ratio	20%
6. Net working capital	₹3,00,000
(there is no bank overdraft or prepaid expenses)	

Solution

Detailed Working Capital

Statement of Detailed Working Capital	Amount (₹)	
A. Current assets:		
Quick assets		
Debtors	2,50,000	
Cash	50,000	
	3,00,000	
Add: Non-quick assets (stock)	2,00,000	5,00,000
B. Current liabilities		2,00,000
WORKING CAPITAL		3,00,000

1. Current Ratio = Current Assets/Current Liabilities
= 2.5
Working Capital = Current Assets – Current Liabilities
= 3,00,000
Current Assets = Working Capital + Current Liabilities
= 3,00,000 + Current Liabilities
2.5 = (3,00,000 + Current Liabilities)/Current Liabilities
2.5 Current Liabilities = 3,00,000 + Current Liabilities
1.5 Current Liabilities = 3,00,000
Current Liabilities = 2,00,000

Working Capital = Current Assets – Current Liabilities
3,00,000 = Current Assets – 2,00,000
Current Assets = 5,00,000

2. Liquid Ratio = Quick Assets/Quick Liabilities
= 1.5
Since it is given that there is no bank overdraft, we will assume that quick liabilities are equal to current liabilities.
1.5 = Quick Assets/2,00,000
Quick Assets = 3,00,000

3. Stock = Current Assets – Quick Assets
= 5,00,000 – 3,00,000
= 2,00,000

4. Cost of Goods Sold = Stock × Stock Turnover Ratio
= 2,00,000 × 6
= 12,00,000
Sales = Cost of Goods Sold + Gross Profit (1/5 of Sales)
= 12,00,000 + 3,00,000 (1/4 of Cost) = 15,00,000
Debtors Collection Period = Credit Sales/Average Debtors
= 2 months
Debtors = (Credit Sales/Collection Period) × 2
= (15,00,000/12) × 2
= 2,50,000

5. It is stated that there are no prepaid expenses. Hence, it is assumed that the balance quick asset is nothing but cash.

> Quick liabilities = Current liabilities – Bank overdraft.

Cash = Quick Assets – Debtors
= 3,00,000 – 2,50,000
= 50,000

■ **ILLUSTRATION 16.20** From the following information, prepare a summarized balance sheet as at 31 March 2020.

Particulars	Amount (₹)
Working capital	1,20,000
Reserves and surplus	80,000
Bank overdraft	20,000
Fixed assets proprietary ratio	0.75
Current ratio	2.50
Liquid ratio	1.50

Your working notes should form a part of the answer.

Solution

Summarized Balance Sheet
as at 31 March 2020

Particulars	Amount (₹)
ASSETS	
Fixed assets	3,60,000
Stock-in-trade	1,10,000
Other current assets	90,000
Total Assets	**5,60,000**
EQUITY AND LIABILITIES	

Capital	4,00,000
Reserve and surplus	80,000
Bank overdraft	20,000
Other liabilities	60,000
Total Equity and Liabilities	**5,60,000**

Working Notes:

1. Current liabilities
   Let current liabilities be a
   So current assets will be 2.5a
   Hence, Working Capital = 2.5a – a = 1.5a
   1.5a = ₹1,20,000
   Current Liabilities = ₹80,000
   Other Current Liabilities = Current liabilities – Bank
   Overdraft
   = 80,000 – 20,000
   = ₹60,000

2. Current Assets = 2.5a
   = 2.5 × 80,000
   = ₹2,00,000

3. Quick Assets = 1.5a = 1.5 × [80,000 – 20,000]
   = ₹90,000

4. Stock-in-trade = Current Assets – Quick Assets
   = 2,00,000 – 90,000
   = ₹1,10,000

5. Fixed Assets

   > *Fixed assets to proprietary funds is expressed as Fixed assets/Proprietary funds.*

   Fixed assets to proprietary funds = 0.75
   So, working capital to proprietary funds = 0.25
   Working capital is ₹1,20,000
   Hence, fixed assets would be (1,20,000/0.25) × 0.75 = ₹3,60,000

■ **ILLUSTRATION 16.21** From the following information, prepare a summarized balance sheet as at 31 March 2020.

Current ratio	1.75
Liquid ratio	1.25
Stock turnover ratio (cost of sales/closing stock)	9
Gross profit ratio	0.25
Debt collection period	1.5 months
Reserves and surplus to capital	0.2
Turnover to fixed assets (COGS/FA)	1.2
Capital gearing ratio	0.5
Fixed assets to net worth	1.25
Sales for the year	₹12,00,000

Note:
COGS means cost of goods sold, and FA means fixed assets.

Solution

Balance Sheet

Particulars	Amount (₹)	
ASSETS		
Fixed assets		7,50,000
Stock-in-trade	1,00,000	
Debtors	1,50,000	

Cash and bank balance	1,00,000	
Current assets		3,50,000
Total Assets		**11,00,000**
EQUITY AND LIABILITIES		
Share capital	5,00,000	
Reserves	1,00,000	
Net worth		6,00,000
Long-term liabilities		3,00,000
Current liabilities		2,00,000
Total Equity and Liabilities		**11,00,000**

Working notes:

1. Sales = ₹12,00,000
   Less: Gross Profit (25%) = ₹3,00,000
   Cost of Goods Sold = ₹9,00,000

2. Closing Stock
   Stock Turnover Ratio = Cost of Goods Sold/Closing Stock
   Hence, Closing stock = ₹1,00,000

3. Current Assets and Current Liabilities
   Current Ratio = 1.75
   Current Assets = 1.75
   Current Liabilities = 1
   Liquid Assets = 1.25
   Current Assets – Liquid Assets = Stock
   Or, 1.75 – 1.25 = 0.5
   Stock = 0.5 = ₹1,00,000
   Hence, Liquid Assets = (1,00,000/0.5) × 1.25
   = ₹2,50,000
   Current Liabilities = (1,00,000 × 1.00)/0.5
   = ₹2,00,000
   Current Assets = (1,00,000 × 1.75)/0.5
   = ₹3,50,000

4. Debtors
   Debt Collection Period = 1.5 months or 3/2 months
   (Debtors × 12)/12,00,000 = 3/2
   Debtors = (3 × 12,00,000)/(12 × 2)
   = ₹1,50,000

5. Fixed Assets
   Fixed Assets Turnover Ratio = Cost of Goods Sold/Fixed Assets
   or, 1.2 = 9,00,000/Fixed Assets
   Fixed Assets = ₹7,50,000

6. Net Worth
   Fixed Assets to Net Worth = 1.25
   or, 1.25 = ₹7,50,000/Net Worth
   = ₹6,00,000

7. Capital and Reserves
   Reserves and Surplus to Capital = 0.2

   > *Reserves and Surplus to capital is expressed as Reserves and surplus/Capital + Reserves.*

   Share Capital + Reserves = ₹6,00,000
   1 + 0.2 = ₹6,00,000
   1 = ₹5,00,000
   Share Capital = ₹5,00,000
   Reserves and Surplus = ₹1,00,000

8. Cash and Bank Balance = Current Assets – (Debtors + Stock)
   = 3,50,000 – (1,50,000 + 1,00,000)
   = ₹1,00,000

SUMMARY

- Accounting is the recording and reporting of all activities of the management.
- The income statement and balance sheet together are called final accounts or financial statements.
- Financial statements reflect a combination of recorded facts, accounting principles, and personal judgement.
- Horizontal analysis moves over a number of years or across many firms. It is also known as dynamic analysis. Vertical analysis involves finding out the relationship between two items of the same firm and in the same year. It is also known as static analysis.

- The horizontal format of the balance sheet is designed from the point of view of the owner of the firm. The vertical format of the balance sheet is more useful for financial analysis.
- Common size statements, trend analysis, comparative statements, and ratio analysis techniques are useful for the interpretation of financial statements.
- Accounting ratios show the relationship between two accounting figures.
- Accounting ratios are classified based on financial statements, functions, and users.

KEYWORDS

Analysis The process of breaking up a large mass of raw data into a manageable form is referred to as analysis of financial statements.

Dynamic analysis It moves over a number of years or across many firms. It is also known as horizontal analysis.

Horizontal analysis See dynamic analysis.

Static analysis See vertical analysis.

Vertical analysis It involves finding out the relationship between two items with respect to the same firm and in the same year.

QUESTIONS

I. Answer the following questions in detail.

1. What is a financial statement? Define and explain how it reflects the activities of the management.
2. 'Financial statements reflect a combination of recorded fact, accounting principles, and personal judgment.' Explain this statement.
3. Describe the various users of financial statements.
4. Illustrate and explain the vertical form of the balance sheet.
5. What are the uses of comparative financial statements?
6. What are common size statements? Explain and illustrate.
7. What are accounting ratios? How can accounting ratios be classified? Enumerate any two ratios covered by each classification.
8. Distinguish between rate, proportion, and percentage. How are they used in ratio analysis? Give two illustrations of each.
9. Which ratios will you consider for measuring liquidity, profitability, and capital structure?
10. Write a note on the uses of ratio analysis.
11. What is an accounting ratio? State its main advantages.
12. Explain any two of the following ratios.
    1. Gross profit ratio
    2. Debtors' ratio
    3. Stock turnover ratio
13. Explain the limitations of ratio analyses.
14. Briefly explain the various profitability ratios.
15. Briefly discuss the uses of ratio analysis.
16. What do you mean by ratio analysis? Discuss the advantages and limitations.
17. Discuss the role of accounting ratio in judging the liquidity position of a business.

18. Briefly explain the meaning and significance of any two of the following ratios:
    (i) Operating ratio;
    (ii) Liquidity ratio;
    (iii) Stock turnover ratio.
19. Write short notes on
    (i) Price–Earnings ratio;
    (ii) Debt–Equity ratio.
20. 'Ratio analysis is only a technique for making judgement and not a substitute for judgements.' Examine.

II. State with reasons whether the following statements are True or False.

1. Horizontal analysis involves analysis of two items in the financial statements of the same firm and in the same year.
2. For an oil company, stock of oil is a liquid asset.
3. In a vertical balance sheet, fictitious assets are included under fixed assets.
4. Owed funds is an internal source of finance.
5. Intangible assets such as goodwill are shown under 'application of funds' in the vertical balance sheet.
6. Advances to suppliers for goods are classified as quick assets.
7. Advances to contractors for construction of building are classified as loans and advances under current assets.
8. Unclaimed dividends are classified as current liabilities.
9. Penalty for late payment of sale tax on sale of trading goods is an operating expenditure.

10. Common size statements are used for both horizontal and vertical analysis.
11. While a comparative statement shows the size of change, a trend statement shows the direction of change.
12. Proprietary ratio is classified as a liquid ratio.
13. Stock turnover ratio is a composite ratio.
14. A liquid ratio of 0.5:1 indicates over-investments.
15. Capital gearing ratio helps to ascertain whether a firm is trading on equity.
16. Operating ratio compares operating expenses with sales.
17. Net profit ratio compares net profit after tax to sales.
18. A debtors' turnover ratio of 7.3 indicates that, on an average, debtors pay after 7.3 weeks.
19. Turnover ratio helps to compute the period of the operating cycle.
20. Preference capital is treated like debt in the capital generating ratio.

III. Solve the following problems.

1. From the following data of the balance sheet as at 31 December 2020, calculate the following ratios:

    1. Shareholder's funds to total assets
    2. Shareholder's funds to fixed assets
    3. Receivable turnover ratio
    4. Net profit to sales
    5. Net profit to total capital employed
    6. Net profit to net capital employed
    7. Net profit to shareholders' funds
    8. Net profit to share capital
    9. Capital gearing as expressed by debt–equity ratio
    10. Book value per share.

    For the year under consideration, the total sales were ₹1,20,000. The net profit for the year was ₹20,000. The face value of each share is ₹10.

Balance Sheet
as at 31 December 2020

Particulars	Amount (₹)
ASSETS	
Land	4,000
Building	8,000
Machinery	28,000
Investment	6,000
Inventory	6,000
Receivables	12,000
Cash	6,000
Total Assets	**70,000**
EQUITY AND LIABILITIES	
Share capital	30,000
Retained earnings	10,000
Long-term loans	16,000
Accounts payable	6,000
Creditors	8,000
Total Equity and Liabilities	**70,000**

2. The balance sheet and supplementary data for Swanson Corporation are as follows:

Balance Sheet of Swanson Corporation
as at 31 December 2020

Assets		Amount (₹)
Cash		50,000
Marketable securities		30,000
Accounts receivable		70,000
Inventory		1,50,000
Building	4,00,000	
Less: Accumulated depreciation	(1,00,000)	3,00,000
Total Assets		**6,00,000**

Liabilities and Equity	Amount (₹)
Liabilities and Stockholder's Equity	
Accounts Payable	30,000
Bank loan payable (current liabilities)	20,000
Mortgage notes payable, Due in 2023	30,000
Bonds payable - 10 % due 31 December 2023	1,00,000
Equity share - ₹10 per value	3,00,000
Reserves and surplus	1,20,000
Total Liabilities and Stockholders' Equity	**6,00,000**

Additional Information	Amount (₹)
Net income: 2020	60,000
Cost of goods sold: 2020	5,40,000
Sales: 2020	9,00,000
Inventory, 31 December, 2019	1,00,000
Interest expense	20,000
Net Income before interest and taxes: 2020	1,30,000

Compute the following ratios:

1. Current ratio,
2. Net income to shareholders equity,
3. EPS,
4. Times interest earned ratio,
5. Net income to total assets,
6. Acid-test ratio.

3. Kopal & Co. reports the following data relative to hte accounts receivable:

	Amount (₹)	
	2020	2019
Average accounts receivable	4,00,000	4,20,000
Net credit sales	28,00,000	31,00,000

The terms of sale are net 30 days.

1. Compute the accounts receivable turnover and the collection period.
2. Evaluate the results. Assume a year has 360 days.

4. Playpen Company's net accounts receivable were ₹2,50,000 on 31 December 2019 and ₹3,00,000 on 31 December 2020. Net cash sales for 2020 were 1,00,000. The accounts receivable turnover for 2020 was 5.0. What were Playpen's total net sales for 2020?

5. On 1 January 2020, Moonlight Ltd's beginning inventory was ₹5,00,000. During 2020, the company purchased ₹18,00,000 of additional inventory. On 31 December 2020, the ending inventory was ₹4,00,000.

    1. What is the inventory turnover and the age of inventory for 2020?

2. If the inventory turnover in 2019 was 3.5 and the age of the inventory was 100 days, evaluate the results for 2020.

6. The following account balances are taken from the ledger of Goldfish Company:

Particulars	Amount (₹)	
	31 December 2020	31 December 2019
Allowance for doubtful accounts	40,000	30,000
Prepaid expenses	20,000	30,000
Accrued liabilities	1,40,000	1,20,000
Cash in Bank A	7,00,000	6,50,000
Bank overdraft in Bank B (credit balance)	0	25,000
Accounts payable	4,70,000	3,95,000
Merchandise inventory	8,95,000	9,50,000
Bonds payable, short duration	4,20,000	3,90,000
Marketable securities	1,00,000	90,000
Accounts receivable	5,00,000	4,85,000

1. Compute the amount of working capital for both the years.
2. Compute the current ratio for both the years.
3. Compute the acid-test ratio for both the years.
4. Comment briefly on the company's short-term financial position.

7. The data for Dawn Ltd is given here.

Balance Sheet of Dawn Ltd
as at 31 December 2020

Particulars	Amount (₹)
Assets	
Cash	40,000
Accounts receivable	80,000
Inventory	1,20,000
Prepaid expenses	3,000
Machinery	1,60,000
Building	20,000

	Amount (₹)
Total assets	4,23,000
Liabilities and Owner's Equity, that is, Capital	
Retained earnings	92,000
Equity capital	2,25,000
Long-term liabilities	30,000
Accounts payable	26,000
Notes payable	50,000
Total liabilities and owner's equity	4,23,000

Income Statement of Dawn Ltd
for the Year Ended 31 December 2020

	Amount (₹)	
Sales		10,00,000
Less: Cost of sales		
Opening stock	1,00,000	
Purchases	7,90,000	
Cost of goods available for sale	8,90,000	
Less: Closing stock	(1,20,000)	
Gross Margin		7,70,000
Operating expenses		2,30,000
Selling expenses	90,000	
Administrative expenses	80,000	1,70,000
Net Income or Net Profit		60,000

Calculate the following ratios:
1. Current ratio
2. Quick ratio
3. Receivable turnover
4. Average collection period
5. Net income to sales
6. Net income to total assets
7. Return on investment
8. Inventory turnover
9. Gross profit margin

8. The financial data for two companies, Edson Ltd and Teague Ltd, are as follows:

Particulars	Amount (₹)	
	Edson Ltd	Teague Ltd
Current assets		
Cash	12,500	19,500
Short-term investments	3,000	6,500
Accounts receivable	94,500	82,000
Inventory	1,05,500	91,500
Prepaid expenses	9,500	7,500
Total current assets	2,25,000	2,07,000
Fixed assets	2,62,000	2,62,000
Total Assets	4,87,000	4,69,000
Current liabilities	1,83,000	1,69,000
Other liabilities	1,50,000	1,77,000
Equity shares: ₹10 per value (7,500 shares) ₹5 Par value and (10,000 Shares)	75,000	50,000
Reserves and surplus	79,000	73,000
Total Liabilities and Shareholder's Equity	4,87,000	4,69,000
Market price per share of equity stock	14	24

Selected Income Statement Data for the Current Year

Net sales (all on credit)	3,01,500	2,59,000
Cost of goods sold	2,27,000	1,93,000
Other expenses	40,000	30,000
Profit before interest and taxes	34,500	36,000
Interest expense	6,500	17,000
Net Income	**28,000**	**19,000**

The investment strategy is to purchase the shares of companies that are financially strong and have low price earning ratio.

Calculate the following ratios for both the companies for the current year and decide which company's stocks are better for an investment strategy.

1. Current ratio
2. Quick ratio
3. Debtors turnover
4. Inventory turnover
5. Debt–equity ratio
6. Times interest earned ratio
7. Return on total assets
8. Return on shareholder's equity
9. Earnings per share of equity shares
10. Price earnings ratio

9. Following are the data from the balance sheet of Amir Limited.

Particulars	Amount (₹)
Current liabilities	2,80,000
Bonds payable @ 15%	1,20,000
Preferred stock, @13%, ₹100 par value	2,00,000
Equity shares - ₹25 par value, 16,000 shares	4,00,000
Premium on equity shares	2,40,000
Retained earnings	2,00,000

Income before taxes is ₹1,60,000. The tax rate is 45%. Shareholder's equity in the previous year was ₹8,00,000. The market price share of one equity share is ₹35.05. Calculate

1. net income,
2. preferred dividends,
3. return on net worth,
4. times interest earned,
5. earnings per share,
6. price earnings ratio, and
7. book value per share.

10. Ella Corporation's equity stock account for the years 2020 and 2019 showed ₹50,000 of equity stock of ₹10 par value. Additional data is provided in the following text:

Particulars	Amount (₹)	
	2020	**2019**
Dividends	2,250.00	3,600.00
Market price per share	20.00	22.00
Earnings per share	2.10	2.70

1. Calculate the dividends per share, dividend yield, and dividend payout.
2. Evaluate the results.

11. Following are the two balance sheets on two different dates. Rearrange them in a vertical form and prepare common size statements.

Balance Sheet
as at 31 December 2020

Particulars	2019	2020
ASSETS		
Goodwill	45,000	35,250
Machinery	67,500	1,43,250
Building	75,000	56,250
Long-term investments	7,500	26,250
Stock	63,750	58,500
Debtors	45,000	67,500
Bank balance	12,750	21,000
Cash	11,250	13,500
Total Assets	**3,27,750**	**4,21,500**
EQUITY AND LIABILITIES		
Equity share capital	2,25,000	2,62,500
General reserve	15,000	22,500
Capital reserve	0	18,750
Profit and loss account	13,500	20,250
Creditors	33,000	48,750
Provision for tax	21,000	**24,000**
Proposed dividend	20,250	24,750
Total Equity and Liabilities	**3,27,750**	**4,21,500**

12. Given here are the incomplete comparative income statements for the years 2018, 2019, and 2020.
You are required to find the missing figures.

No.	Particulars	Amount (₹) in lakh			% of trend		
		2018	**2019**	**2020**	**2018**	**2019**	**2020**
1.	Net sales	700	xx	xx	100	120	140
2.	*Less:* Cost of goods sold	560	xx	xx	100	110	×
3.	Gross Profit	140	xx	xx	100	160	150
4.	*Less:* Operating expenses	84	xx	xx	100	125	175
5.	Operating Profit	56	xx	xx	100	xx	xx
6.	*Add:* Non-operating income	xx	xx	5	100	120	50
		66	xx	xx	100	xx	xx
7.	*Less:* Non-operating expenses	(–)6	xx	xx	100	100	200
8.	Net profit	60	125	56	100	208.33	93.33

13. Complete the following balance sheet from the information given in the following text:

Balance Sheet
as at 31 December 2020

Particulars	2020
ASSETS	
Fixed assets	xx
Stock	xx
Debtors	xx
Other current assets	xx
Total Assets	**xx**
EQUITY AND LIABILITIES	
Equity share capital of ₹100 each	xx
Reserves and surplus	xx
10% Debentures	4,00,000
Current liabilities	
Sundry creditors	xx
Other current liabilities	2,00,000
Total Equity and Liabilities	**xx**

The following information is available:
(a) Sales for the year is ₹48 lakh
(b) Gross profit ratio is 25%
(c) Net profit after tax is ₹2,00,000
(d) Purchases and sales on credit basis
(e) Debtors turnover ratio is 12:1 (Sales/Debtors)
(f) Creditors turnover ratio is 12:1 (Cost of sales/Creditors)
(g) EPS is ₹20 per share
(h) Stock turnover ratio is 10
(i) Debt–equity ratio is 0.25:1
(j) Current ratio is 1.6:1

14. The balance sheet of Aavaya Ltd as at 31 December 2020 is as follows:

Balance Sheet of Aavaya Ltd
as at 31 December 2020

Particulars	Amount (₹)
ASSETS	
Machinery	8,40,000
Stock	2,70,000
Debtors	75,000
Bills receivable	15,000
Bank balance	1,50,000
Prepaid expenses	90,000
Preliminary expenses	9,000
Total Assets	**14,49,000**
EQUITY AND LIABILITIES	
Equity share capital	6,00,000
General reserve	45,000
Profit and loss	24,000
Debentures	2,70,000
Secured loans	30,000
Creditors	4,38,000
Proposed dividend	30,000
Provision for taxes	12,000
Total Equity and Liabilities	**14,49,000**

Additional Information

Particulars	Amount (₹) 31/12/20
Sales (credit sale is three times the cash sale)	7,20,000
Purchases	5,10,000
Purchase expenses	30,000
Office expenses	1,20,000
Sales distribution expenses	96,000

The book value of stock on 31/12/19 was ₹2,40,000, and its market value was ₹2,10,000. Find out the following ratios on the basis of the information given:
(a) Gross profit ratio
(b) Net profit ratio
(c) Liquid ratio
(d) Stock ratio
(e) Debtors' ratio (assume 360 days)
(f) Debt–equity ratio
(g) Operating ratio

15. Following is the income statement and balance sheet of Edward Ltd.

Income Statement

Sales		10,00,000
(including credit sales ₹7,00,000)		
Less: Cost of goods sold:		
Opening stock	1,20,000	
+ Purchases	+ 3,80,000	
	5,00,000	
– Closing stock	– 1,30,000	– 3,70,000
Gross profit		6,30,000
Less: Operation expenses		– 2,30,000
Net profit		4,00,000

Balance Sheet of Edward Ltd

Partculars	Amount (₹)
ASSETS	
Fixed assets	6,00,000
Debtors	2,00,000
Stock	1,30,000
Bills receivable	70,000
Total Assets	**10,00,000**
EQUITY AND LIABILITIES	
Equity share capital	5,00,000
Reserves and surplus	3,00,000
Creditors	1,00,000
Bills payable	50,000
Bills overdraft	50,000
Total Equity and Liabilities	**10,00,000**

Calculate the following:
(a) Net profit ratio
(b) Stock turnover ratio
(c) Liquid ratio
(d) Debtors ratio (No. of days in a year, 360)
(e) Operating ratio

 **CASES**

Conceptual Application Case

A company has just sold one of its buildings at a price equal to its book value, and has used the proceeds from the sale to retire long-term bonds payable. The price paid to retire the bonds was equal to the amount at which they were shown on the balance sheet. Upon selling the building, the company entered into a lease with a new owner.

Questions

1. If the new lease is treated as an operating lease, not requiring lease capitalization, how will this series of transactions affect.
   (a) Debt–equity ratio
   (b) Current ratio
   (c) Asset turnover ratio
2. If the new lease is treated as a repurchase of the property (requiring lease capitalization), how will this series of transactions affect these three ratios?

Business Application Case

1. The following data has been taken from the financial statements of a manufacturing company:

Particulars	Amount (₹)
Total assets	₹1,00,000
Interest expense	₹2,000
Tax rate	45%
Return on common equity	7.2%
Debt–equity ratio	0.25

The company had no preferred stock outstanding.

Questions

1. Calculate the overall rate of profitability (return on assets).
2. Did the company use the capital successfully?

2. Companies Gautam, Padma, and Chakra are three of the largest merchandising companies in India. We have the following data on these companies for 2020 (Rupees in thousands):

Particulars	Company Gautam	Company Padma	Company Chakra
Rank (by sales) among merchandising firms	26	11	2
Sales revenues (₹)	6,27,349	12,93,765	54,58,824
Assets (₹)	1,20,363	2,74,603	8,84,001
Shareholders' equity (₹)	43,554	1,63,317	6,27,366
Net income (₹)	11,477	8,327	55,897
Interest expense (₹)	3,994	5,342	13,088

Questions

1. Calculate income as a percentage of sales, asset turnover, return on assets, return on equity, and debt–asset ratio for each company. You should assume a 50% income tax rate.
2. For return on common equity, Company Gautam ranked first, Company Padma ranked 46th, and Company Chakra ranked 39th among the merchandising companies on the list. On the basis of your analysis of the financial statement data alone, explain the reasons for difference between the relative sales ranking and the relative return on common equity ranking.

 REFERENCES

Garrison, Ray, H. (1976), *Managerial Accounting—Concepts for Planning, Control, Decision Making*, Irwin-Dorsey, USA, p. 604.

Shah, Paresh (2009), *Management Accounting*, 1st edition, Oxford University Press, pp. 359–409.

Shah, Paresh (2009), *Financial Management*, 2nd edition, Biztantra, pp. 809–827.

Cash Flow Statement

Learning Objectives

After studying this chapter, you will understand

- role of cash flow statements
- methodology to prepare a cash flow statement
- cash flow statement for a manufacturing firm
- cash flow statement for a financial enterprise
- to calculate free cash flows

INTRODUCTION

An income statement provides information about a firm's financial performance during the period under review. A balance sheet highlights the information about assets and liabilities owned and owed by the firm. In other words, the income statement indicates the earnings of a firm using the accrual method of accounting, and the balance sheet provides information about the way the financing of assets took place. The earnings reported in the income statement need not be the same as the cash generated by the firm. There are instances when a firm may have reported a significant amount of profit during the period, but may still be unable to pay the suppliers of goods and services in time.

An accrual-based accounting statement considers items that have no effect on a firm's cash flow, such as depreciation, amortization of preliminary and pre-operative expenses, etc. Accrual-based accounting statements also consider the revenue that has not been received in cash during the period.

Hence, there is a need for a third type of financial statement, in the form of a cash flow statement.

Cash consists of cash in hand and demand deposits with banks. *Cash equivalents* consist of short-term, highly liquid investments that are readily convertible into known amounts of cash that are subject to insignificant risk of change in value. *Cash flows* are inflows and outflows of cash and cash equivalents for the preparation of cash flow statement. Movements within the constituents of cash or cash equivalents are excluded. *Cash management* includes investment of excess cash in cash equivalents.

Information about the cash flow of an enterprise is useful in providing users of financial statements a basis to assess the ability of the enterprise to generate cash and cash equivalents, and the needs of the enterprise to utilize those cash flows. The economic decisions that are taken by users require an evaluation of the ability of an enterprise to generate cash and cash equivalents and the timing and certainty

of their generation. The statement deals with the provision of information about the historical changes in cash and cash equivalents of an enterprise by means of a cash flow statement, which classifies cash flows during the period from operation, investing, and financing activities. This applies to (a) enterprises having an annual turnover of more than ₹50 crore and (b) listed companies (for which only the indirect method is to be adopted). The enterprises should prepare a cash flow statement and present it along with financial statements for each period.

CASH FLOW STATEMENTS AS PER COMPANIES ACT, 2013

The Companies Act, 2013 brought about many changes which directly impact the preparation of financial statements and require understanding of some new definitions and provisions. The Companies Act, 1956 did not include cash flow statement in its definition of financial statement. The Companies (Accounting Standards) Rules, 2006 controls the applicability of cash flow statements. However, according to the Companies Act, 2013, a cash flow statement shall be prepared and included in the financial statements subject to certain exemptions specified in the Act.

Definition of Financial Statement as per Companies Act, 2013

According to Section 2(40) of the Companies Act, 2013, a 'financial statement', in relation to a company, includes the following:

(i) a *balance sheet* as at the end of the financial year;
(ii) a *profit and loss account*, or in the case of a company carrying on any activity not for profit, an *income and expenditure account* for the financial year;
(iii) *cash flow statement* for the financial year;
(iv) a statement of *changes in equity*, if applicable; and
(v) any *explanatory note annexed* to, or forming part of, any document referred to in sub-clause (i) to sub-clause (iv).

Exemption from Applicability of Cash Flow Statements

As per the Companies Act, 2013, the financial statement of a one-person, small, and dormant company may not include the cash flow statement. As per Section 2(62) of the Act, a 'one person company' has only one person as its member. A 'dormant company' is formed and registered under this Act for a future project or to hold an asset or intellectual property and has no significant accounting transaction. Such an inactive company may make an application to the Registrar in such manner as may be prescribed for obtaining the status of a dormant company. According to Secion 2(85) of the Act, a 'small company' means a company, other than a public company,

(i) paid-up share capital of which does not exceed ₹50 lakh or such higher amount as may be prescribed which shall not be more than ₹5 crore or
(ii) turnover of which as per its last profit and loss account does not exceed ₹2 crore or such higher amount as may be prescribed which shall not be more than ₹20 crore.

However, this clause does not apply to (i) a holding company or a subsidiary company; (ii) a company registered under Section 8; or (iii) a company or body corporate governed by any special Act.

Format for Preparing Cash Flow Statement

Since no format is prescribed in Schedule III to the Companies Act, 2013, the cash flow statement shall be prepared in the format prescribed in the AS 3: Cash Flow Statement.

In listed companies, the listing agreement requires indirect method for preparing cash flow statements. Under AS 3 of the Companies Act, 2013, non-listed companies have the choice of applying between direct and indirect methods to prepare the cash flow statement. Due to the listing agreement requirement, such a choice is not provided to listed companies.

In other words, a private limited company with paid-up share capital of less than ₹50 lakh or such higher amount as may be prescribed (not exceeding ₹5 crore) or with a turnover of less than ₹2 crore or such higher amount as may be prescribed (not exceeding ₹20 crore) is not required to prepare cash flow statements while preparing financial statements at the end of the financial year. Cash flow statement is not applicable to such companies.

CASH FLOWS

Cash flows are from (a) operating activities, (b) investing activities, and (c) financing activities.

Operating Activities

Operating activities are the principal revenue-producing activities of the enterprise and other activities that are not investing and financing activities. Operating activities consist of inflows and outflows of cash resulting from transactions that affect a firm's net profit or loss. Examples are

- cash receipts from the sale of goods and the rendering of services;
- cash receipts from royalties, fees, commission, and other revenues;
- cash payments to suppliers for goods and services;
- cash payments to and on behalf of employees;
- cash receipts and payments of an insurance enterprise for premiums, claims, annuities, and other benefits;
- cash payments or refunds of income tax unless they are specifically identified with financing and investing activities; and
- cash receipts and payments relating to future contracts, forward contracts, option contracts, and swap contracts when the contracts are held for dealing or trading purpose.

Investing Activities

Investing activities are the acquisition and disposal of long-term assets (not held for resale) and other investments not included in cash equivalents. Examples are

- cash payments to acquire fixed assets, including intangibles (these payments include those relating to capitalized R&D costs, and self-generated fixed assets);
- cash payments to acquire shares, warrants, or debt instruments of the enterprises and interests in joint ventures (other than payment for those instruments considered to be cash equivalents and those held for dealing or trading purposes);
- cash receipts from disposal of fixed assets (including intangibles);
- cash receipts from disposal of shares, warrants, or debt instruments of the enterprises and interest in joint ventures (other than receipt from those instruments considered to be cash equivalents, and those held for dealing or trading);
- cash advances and loans made to third parties (other than those made by financial enterprises);
- cash receipts from the repayment of advances and loans made to third parties; and
- cash receipts and payments relating to future contracts held for dealing, trading, or transactions related to financing activities.

Financing Activities

Financing activities are activities that result in changes in the size and composition of the owner's capital (including preference share capital in case of a company) and borrowings of the enterprise. Examples are

- cash proceeds from the issue of shares or other similar instruments;
- redemption of debentures and preference shares, buyback of equity shares, and repayment of loans; and
- payment of dividend and interest.

Table 17.1 shows the classification of cash flows.

TABLE 17.1 Classification of cash flows in a nutshell

Operating Activities	
Inflows	*Outflows*
Cash collected from customers	Cash paid to employees and suppliers
Sale proceeds from trading securities	Cash paid for other expenses
	Acquisition of trading securities
	Taxes paid
Investing Activities	
Inflows	*Outflows*
Sale proceeds from fixed assets	Acquisition of fixed assets
Sale proceeds from debt and equity investments	Acquisition of debt and equity investments
Principal received from loans made to others	Loans made to others
Interest and dividends received	

TABLE 17.1 Classification of cash flows in a nutshell (contd.)

Financing Activities	
Inflows	*Outflows*
Principal amounts of debt issued	Principal paid on debt
Proceeds from issuing stock	Payments to reacquire stock
	Interest and dividends paid

CASH FLOW STATEMENT FOR MANUFACTURING FIRM

Transactions that increase cash are classified as inflows (sources) of cash, and transactions that decrease cash are classified as outflows (use or applications). In a nutshell, it provides the explanation with respect to changes in the cash position of a firm. The ICAI has issued Accounting Standard No. 3 for the preparation of a cash flow statement. The Ind AS 7 requires the cash flow statement to distinguish the cash flows occurring during a given period into three categories: *operating, investing*, and *financing*.

The activities that are revenue producing for the firm are named as *operating* activities. The acquisition and disposal of fixed assets, that is, long-term assets and other investments that are not included in the calculation of cash and cash equivalents are treated as *investing* activities. Changes in the size and composition of the capital and borrowings of a firm are treated as *financing* activities.

A firm can determine cash flows from operating activities by either a direct or an indirect method. In the direct method, the major classes of receipts and payments for operating activities are considered. In the indirect method, the net profit or the net loss of the firm is adjusted for the effect of a transaction of a non-cash nature, or deferrals or accruals of past or future operating cash receipts or payments, and items of income or expenses associated with investing or financing activities.

Ind AS 7 also issues guidelines on the presentation of the cash flow statement as part of the annual reporting by a company registered with the Companies Act, 2013.

The ICAI'S Ind AS 7 has explained in detail the cash flow information by way of notes and illustration in the appendix of the Ind AS 7. Ind AS 7 has not provided any specific format for preparing a cash flow statement. Some widely used formats of cash flow statements are given in Exhibit 17.1.

The *cash flow from operations* can be calculated by the direct method or the indirect method. The most commonly used method in the Indian corporates is the indirect method (refer Annexure A: Balaji Telefilms; Annexure B: Mahindra Finance; Annexure C: RPG Life; and Annexure D: SpiceJet).

EXHIBIT 17.1 Formats of Cash Flow Statements

(A) The Calculation of Cash Flows from Operating Activities (Direct Method)

Particulars	Amount (₹)	
Cash flow from operating activities		
Cash receipts from customers	XXX	
Cash paid to suppliers and employees	(XXX)	
Cash generated from operations		XXX
Income tax paid	(XX)	
Income tax refunds received	XX	
Cash flow before extraordinary Items		XXX
Proceeds from extraordinary events	XX	
Payment made for extraordinary events	(XX)	
Net cash from operating activities (A)		**XXX**

(B) The Calculation of Cash Flows from Operating Activities (Indirect Method)

Particulars	Amount (₹)	
Cash flows from operating activities		
Net profit as reported in profit and loss account	XXX	
Add:		
Tax provisions	XX	
Extraordinary expenses	XX	
Less:		
Extraordinary incomes	XX	
ADJUSTMENTS FOR::		
Depreciation	XX	
Foreign exchange loss	XX	
Interest income	(XX)	
Dividend income	(XX)	
Interest expenses	XX	
Operating profit before working capital changes		XXX
Increase in sundry debtors	(XX)	
Decrease in sundry debtors	XX	
Increase in inventory	(XX)	
Decrease in inventory	XX	
Increase in sundry creditors	(XX)	
Decrease in sundry creditors	XX	
Cash generated from operations		XXX
Income tax paid	(XX)	
Income tax refund orders	XX	
Cash flow before extraordinary Items		XXX
Proceeds from extraordinary events	XX	
Payment made for extraordinary events	(XX)	
Net cash from operating activities (A)		**XXX**

The final cash flow statement incorporating the cash flow results from operating, investing, and financing activities is prepared as per Exhibit 17.2.

Cash and cash equivalents shown in the cash flow statement include cash in hand, balances with banks, and short-term investments. This total is restated by adjusting the effect of exchange rate changes.

The meanings of specific terms, as supported by Ind AS 7, are given in this section.

Cash

The meaning of cash includes the hard cash kept in hand and also the balances lying with the bank on behalf of the firm, which can be withdrawn by demand.

EXHIBIT 17.2 Proforma of Cash Flow Statement (Ind AS 7) (for manufacturing firm)

Particulars		Amount (₹)
Net cash from operating activities (A)		XXX
Cash flows from investing activities		
Purchase of fixed assets	(XX)	
Sale proceeds from sale of fixed assets	XX	
Interest received	XX	
Dividend received	XX	
Net cash from investing activities (B)		XXX
Cash flows from financing activities		
Proceeds from Issuance of Share capital	XX	
Buy back of shares	(XX)	
Proceeds from long-term borrowing including public deposits and debentures issuance	XX	
Repayment of long-term borrowings including public deposits and debentures	(XX)	
Interest paid	(XX)	
Dividend paid	(XX)	
Cash flows from financing activities (C)		
Net increase in cash and cash equivalents (A + B + C)		XXXX
Cash and cash equivalents at the beginning of the period		XXX
Cash and cash equivalents at the end of the period		XXX

Cash equivalents

The short-term investments and the highly liquid investments made by a firm are covered under the definition of cash equivalents. A highly liquid investment refers to investments that are readily convertible into cash and do not face any significant risk in the value of the investment. Generally, any investment that has a short maturity period (three months or less) qualifies as a cash equivalent investment.

Cash flows

Cash flows include both the inflows and outflows of cash and cash equivalents.

If a particular event or transaction results in an increase in the value of cash or cash equivalents, then it is treated as an inflow (source); the reverse would result in case of a decrease in total cash, and is therefore treated as an outflow (use).

Cash includes cash in hand and demand deposits with banks. Cash equivalents are short-term (say three months or less) and highly liquid investments. These investments should be readily convertible into known amount of cash. These are subject to lowest default risk, which provides regular and timely income to the firm. Such type of an income received or paid needs to be accounted in a specific way, additionally the treatment would differ for financial and non-financial enterprise. Such types of specific points are discussed hereunder.

Interest and dividend

The impact on cash flows on account of interest and dividends received and paid should be disclosed separately respective of the accounting treatment.

The treatment of interest and dividend received or paid differs only in case the nature of the enterprise is different. For this purpose, firms are classified as (i) financial enterprises and (ii) other enterprises.

Financial enterprises For financial enterprises, the operating activity itself is to earn the interest and dividend income, and also to pay the interest and dividend by way of expenses. Hence, for financial firms, it is classified as cash flow arising from operating activities.

Other enterprises In the case of other enterprises, cash flow arising from the *interest paid* should be classified as cash flow from financing activities, whereas *interest and dividends received* should be classified as cash flows from investing activities.

Dividends paid should be classified as cash flow from financing activities.

Taxes on income

The payment of taxes is one of the major social responsibilities of a firm; hence, the cash flow arising on account of taxes on income should be disclosed separately. It is also generally reported as cash flow from operating activities. If the taxes on income are specifically identified with financing and investing activities, then those are treated as cash flow from financing and investing activities, respectively.

Acquisition and disposal of subsidiaries and other business units

The acquisition and disposal of subsidiaries and other business units should be considered as investing activities, and should be reported separately in the cash flow statement, so that readers can easily acquaint themselves with such activities. In aggregate, a firm should disclose the following details with respect to both acquisition and disposal of subsidiaries or other business units during the period:

- the total purchase or disposal consideration, and
- the portion of the purchase or disposal consideration discharged by means of cash and cash equivalents.

Differences in presentation style

The following table indicates the differences in the presentation of the cash flow statement as per the Indian Accounting Standards, IFRS or International Accounting Standards, and US Generally Accepted Accounting Practices.

Ind AS	IFRS/IAS	US GAAP
Cash flow is divided into three broad categories: operating, investing, and financing. Both direct and indirect methods are used in the preparation of cash flow from operating activities.	Similar to Ind AS.	Similar to IFRS. Both direct and indirect methods are used in the preparation of cash flow from operating activities. If the direct method is used, then reconciliation of the net income to cash flow from the operating activities is to be disclosed. Similar to IAS.
Cash includes cash and cash equivalents. Cash equivalents refer to investments with short-term maturities of less than three months. The bank overdrafts are excluded.	Cash equivalents include investments with short-term maturities of less than three months, and may also include the bank overdrafts repayable on demand, but do not include short-term borrowing as they are considered as a financing term.	
Cash flows from interest and dividends received and paid should each be disclosed separately for a financial enterprise and for other enterprises.	IFRS allows more flexibility in the classification of cash flows. Under IFRS, interest and dividends received may be classified as either operating or investing activities. Dividends paid to the company's shareholders and interest paid on the company's debt may be classified as either operating or financing activities.	Dividends paid to firm's shareholders are reported as financing activities, while interest paid is reported in operating activities. Interest received and dividend received from investments are also reported as operating activities.
Cash flows arising from taxes on income should be separately disclosed and should be classified as cash flows from operating activities unless they can be specifically identified with financing and investing activities.	Similar to Ind AS.	All the taxes paid are reported as operating activities, even the taxed related to investing and financing activities.

Foreign currency cash flows

Transactions that are denominated in a foreign currency should be recorded in the cash flow statement in the reporting currency of the firm only. For the said purpose, the value in reporting currency is calculated through the application of the exchange rate between the reporting currency and the foreign currency on the date of transaction of the foreign currency amount.

FORMAT OF CASH FLOW STATEMENT FOR FINANCIAL ENTERPRISE

The format of the cash flow statement for a financial enterprise is as given in Exhibit 17.3.

ADVANTAGES OF CASH FLOW STATEMENT

The following are the advantages of a cash flow statement.

1. The reasons and causes for changes in cash balances between two balance sheet dates can be easily traced.
2. It helps the management and readers of the statement to evaluate a firm's capacity to meet its obligations in the form of payment to creditors for raw materials, services, supplies, etc. It also helps evaluate the capacity to pay off a bank loan and for the payment of interest, taxes, dividend, etc. at the agreed and scheduled time.
3. It helps understand the causes for poor liquidity when the reported profit of a firm is high. It also helps determine the reasons for the availability of liquidity in spite of only a small amount of profit or if a firm has suffered losses.
4. Proper analysis of the cash flow statement will help the management to understand the cash cycle and the ways to control it.
5. A forecasted cash flow statement helps the management plan out repayment of loans, replacement of assets, etc.
6. It helps the management to work out the short-term financial requirements, based on which the firm can make temporary arrangements for the same.
7. It helps financial institutions, bankers, and investment advisors to decide about the lending of funds to a firm.
8. It discloses complete details about the movement of cash within a firm.
9. A cash flow statement provides information on all the operating, investing, and financing activities separately.

EXHIBIT 17.3   Cash Flow Statement (for financial enterprise)

Particulars	Note	Amount (₹)	
Cash flows from operating activities:			
Interest and commission receipts	√		
Interest payments (less)	√		
Recoveries on loan previously written off	√		
Cash payments to employees and suppliers (less)	√		
Operating profit before changes in operating assets	√		
(Increase) decrease in operating assets:			
Short-term funds	√		
Deposits held for regulatory or monetary control purpose	√		
Funds advanced to customers	√		
Net increase in credit card receivables	√		
Other short-term securities	√		
Increase (decrease) in operating liabilities:			
Deposits from customers	√		
Certificates of deposits	√		
Net cash from operating activities before income tax	√		
Income taxes paid (less)	√		
Net cash from operating activities		√	
Cash flows from investing activities:			
Dividends received	√		
Interest received	√		
Proceeds from sales of permanent investments	√		
Purchase of permanent investments (less)	√		
Purchase of fixed assets (less)	√		
Net cash firm investing activities		√	
Cash flows from financing activities:			
Issue of shares			
Repayment of long-term borrowings (less)			
Net decrease in other borrowings (less)			
Dividends paid (less)			
Net cash used in financing activities			
Net increase in cash and cash equivalents			
Cash and cash equivalents at the beginning of the period			
Cash and cash equivalents at the end of the period			

10. It provides infor mation regarding the sources and utilization of cash during a particular period. Thus, it helps the management to plan carefully for the cash requirements in the future, for the purpose of redeeming long-term liabilities or/and replacement of fixed assets.

LIMITATIONS OF CASH FLOW STATEMENT

The following are the limitations of the cash flow statement.

1. The real liquid position of a firm may not be indicated by the cash flow statement as it is prepared for a particular period of time and not at a particular date.

2. At the time of calculating the cash flow from operating activities, the non-cash changes are ignored; hence, it does not include the correct profitability.

3. The cash flow statement can provide meaningful information if it tallies with the income statement of the firm. However, the net cash flow disclosed by a cash flow statement rarely tallies with the net income (profit) of the business.

4. A cash flow statement is based on cash accounting. It is in contravention to the basic accounting concept of accrual.

5. It is practically very difficult to define the term cash in a precise manner. A specific problem that accountants often face is to define *near cash items,* such as cheques, stamps, postal orders, etc., and to decide whether an item is to be included in cash or not.

■ **ILLUSTRATION 17.1** From the following trading and profit and loss account, compute the cash from operations.

Trading and Profit and Loss Account
for the year ended 30 June 2020

Particulars	Amount (₹)
INCOME	
Gross profit	50,000
Profit on sale of land	9,000
Income tax refund	7,000
Total Income	**66,000**
EXPENSES	
Salaries	10,000
Rent	3,000
Depreciation	5,000
Discount	1,000
Loss on sale of plant	2,000
Goodwill written off	8,000
Proposed dividends	10,000
Provision for tax	10,000
Total Expenses	**49,000**
Net Profit	**17,000**
Total	**1,15,000**

Solution

Computation of Cash from Operations

		Amount (₹)
Net profit as per Profit and Loss Account		17,000
Add: Non-cash/ non-operating charges:		
Depreciation	5,000	
Loss on sale of plant	2,000	
Goodwill written off	8,000	
Proposed dividends	10,000	
Provision for tax	10,000	35,000
		52,000
Less: Non-cash/non-operating income:		
Profit on sale of land	9,000	
Income tax refund	7,000	16,000
Cash from operations		36,000

■ **ILLUSTRATION 17.2** Following are the condensed balance sheets of Sophia Ltd.

Particulars	2019 (₹)	2020 (₹)
Equity share capital	4,00,000	4,00,000
Reserves and surplus	2,82,000	3,46,000
Depreciation reserve	20,000	28,000
Secured loans	40,000	60,000
Creditors for goods	1,29,000	1,06,000
Outstanding expenses	17,000	3,000
	8,88,000	9,43,000
Plant and equipment (cost)	5,70,000	6,00,000
Inventories	1,96,000	2,26,000
Debtors	79,000	57,000
Cash at bank	43,000	60,000
	8,88,000	9,43,000

Work out figures of cash from operations.

Solution

Computation of funds from operations

	Amount (₹)
Reserves and surplus in 2020	3,46,000
Less: Balance in 2019	2,82,000
Profit added during the year	64,000

Computation of Cash from Operations

		Amount (₹)
Profit earned		64,000
Add: Depreciation	8,000	
Decrease in debtors	22,000	30,000
		94,000
Less: Decrease in creditors	23,000	
Decrease in outstanding expenses	14,000	
Increase in inventories	30,000	67,000
Cash from operations		27,000

■ **ILLUSTRATION 17.3** Transactions of Omni Cab Company for the year ended on 31 December 2020 include the following:

		Amount (₹)
1.	Borrowed from a bank and purchased land	4,00,000
2.	Sold investment securities	7,00,000
3.	Paid dividends	3,00,000
4.	Issued 500 equity shares	3,50,000
5.	Purchased machinery and equipment	1,75,000
6.	Bank loan paid	6,50,000
7.	Paid accounts receivable outstanding	1,00,000
8.	Accounts payable increased	1,90,000

Calculate the company's net cash flow used in investing and financing activities.

Solution

Investment and Financing Cash Flow Statement of Omni Cab Company

Particulars	Amount (₹)	
1. Investing activities:		
Cash inflows		
Sales of investment securities		700,000
Less: Cash outflows		
Purchase of fixed assets	400,000	
Purchase of machinery and equipment	175,000	575,000
Net cash flow from investing activities		125,000
2. Financing activities:		
Cash inflows		
Borrowed from bank to purchase fixed assets		400,000
Issued equity shares		350,000
		750,000
Less: Cash outflows		
Paid dividends	300,000	
Paid bank loan	650,000	950,000
Net cash flow from financing activities		(200,000)

■ **ILLUSTRATION 17.4** The income statement of Snow White Ltd is as follows:

Income Statement of Snow White Ltd

Particulars	Amount (₹)	
Sales		50,00,000
Cost of goods sold:		
Beginning inventory	12,50,000	
Purchases (net)	30,00,000	
Goods available for sale	42,50,000	
Ending inventory	13,00,000	
Cost of goods sold		29,50,000
Gross margin from sales		20,50,000
Operating expenses:		
Sales and administrative salaries	11,00,000	
Other sales and administrative expenses	6,24,000	
Total operating expense		17,24,000
Income before income taxes		3,26,000
Income taxes		70,000
Net income		2,56,000

Prepare a schedule of cash flows from operating activities using both the direct method and the indirect method.

Solution

Cash Flows from Operating Activities of Snow White Ltd
Direct Method

Particulars	Amount (₹)	
Cash from sales		50,00,000
Total operating cash inflow		50,00,000
Cost of goods sold	29,50,000	
Add: Increase in inventory	50,000	
Cash purchases	30,00,000	
Cash sales and administration expenses	17,24,000	
Income taxes	70,000	
Total operating cash outflow		47,94,000
Net cash flow from operating activities		2,06,000

Indirect Method

Particulars	Amount (₹)	
Net profit	2,56,000	
Less: Increase in inventory	50,000	
Cash flow from operating activities		**2,06,000**

■ **ILLUSTRATION 17.5** Balance sheets of Rehman and Sons on 1/1/2020 and 31/12/2020 were as follows:

Balance Sheet of Rehman and Sons
as at 1/1/2020 and 31/12/2020

Particulars	Amount (₹) 31/12/2019	Amount (₹) 31/12/2020
ASSETS		
Cash	10,000	7,000
Debtors	30,000	50,000
Stock	35,000	25,000
Machinery	80,000	55,000
Land	40,000	50,000
Building	35,000	60,000
Total Assets	**2,30,000**	**2,47,000**
EQUITY AND LIABILITIES		
Creditors	40,000	44,000
Mrs Rehman's loan	25,000	0
Loan from bank	40,000	50,000
Capital	1,25,000	1,53,000
Total Equity and Liabilities	**2,30,000**	**2,47,000**

During the year, a machine costing ₹10,000 (accumulated depreciation ₹3,000) was sold for ₹5,000. The provision for depreciation against machinery was ₹25,000 as on 1/1/2020, and ₹40,000 as on 31/12/2020. The net profit for the year 2020 amounted to ₹45,000. Prepare a cash flow statement.

Solution

Cash Flow Statement of Rehman and Sons

Particulars	Amount (₹)	
Cash balance as on 1/1/2020		10,000
Add: Cash inflows:		
Cash from operation	59,000	
Loan from bank	10,000	
Sale of machinery	5,000	74,000
		84,000
Less: Cash outflows:		
Purchase of land	10,000	
Purchase of building	25,000	
Mrs Rehman's loan repaid	25,000	
Drawings	17,000	77,000
Cash balance on 31/12/2020		7,000

Working Notes:

		Amount (₹)
Cash from operations		
Profit made during the year		45,000
Add: Depreciation on machinery	18,000	
Loss on sale of machinery	2,000	
Decrease in stock	10,000	
Increase in creditors	4,000	
	34,000	
		79,000
Less: Increase in debtors		20,000
Cash from operations		59,000

In the Books of Rehman and Sons
Name of Account: Machinery
Type of Account: Asset

Reference Account	Note No.	Dr. (Add)	Cr. (Less)
To Balance b/d		1,05,000	
By Bank			5,000
By Loss on sale of machinery			2,000
By Provision for depreciation			3,000
By Balance c/d			95,000
Total		**1,05,000**	**1,05,000**

Name of Account: Provision for Depreciation
Type of Account: Reduction in Asset

Reference Account	Note No.	Dr. (Less)	Cr. (Add)
By Balance b/d			25,000
To Machinery		3,000	
By Added profit and loss account			18,000
To Balance c/d		40,000	
Total		**43,000**	**43,000**

Note:

It may be observed that the increase/decrease in current assets has been adjusted to cash from operations. Alternatively, those items may also be shown in the cash flow statement.

■ **ILLUSTRATION 17.6** Prepare a cash flow statement from the following balance sheet of Excel Ltd:

Balance Sheet of Excel Ltd
as at 1 January 2020 and 31 December 2020

Particulars	Amount (₹) 31/12/2019	Amount (₹) 31/12/2020
ASSETS		
Buildings	8,00,000	10,00,000
Plant and machinery	2,50,000	3,70,000
Furniture	5,000	6,000
Cash	2,000	2,200
Debtors	1,00,000	45,000
Bills receivables	8,000	9,000
Stock	4,00,000	3,43,700
Prepaid expenses	3,000	3,100
Investments	1,64,000	1,70,000
Goodwill	3,00,000	3,43,700
Preliminary expenses	10,000	2,000
Total Assets	**20,42,000**	**22,94,700**
EQUITY AND LIABILITIES		
Share capital	17,00,000	18,35,000
Reserves	40,000	83,700
Profit and loss appropriation account	1,00,000	1,30,000
Provision for dividends	70,000	50,000
Creditors	1,00,000	95,000
Bank overdraft	8,000	18,000
Bills payable	14,000	13,000
Mortgage loan	10,000	70,000
Total Equity and Liabilities	**20,42,000**	**22,94,700**

1. Depreciation is charged at 3% p.a. of the cost of ₹9,00,000 for buildings, at 8% p.a. of the cost of ₹4,00,000 for plant and machinery, and at 5% p.a. of the cost of ₹8,000 for furniture.
2. Investments were purchased and ₹3,000 interest received was used in writing down the book value of investments.
3. The declared dividends for ₹70,000 were paid, and the interim dividend for ₹20,000 was paid out of the profit and loss appropriation A/c.

Solution

Cash Flow Statement (Indirect Method)

	Amount (₹)
I. **Cash Flows from Operating Activities:**	
Net profit before tax and extraordinary items	1,43,700
Adjustments for depreciation on furniture	400
Adjustments for depreciation on plant and machinery	32,000
Adjustments for depreciation on buildings	27,000
Preliminary expenses written off	8,000
Operating profit before working capital changes	2,11,100
Decrease in debtors	55,000

Decrease in stock	56,300	
Decrease in creditors	(5,000)	
Increase in bills receivable	(1,000)	
Decrease in bills payable	(1,000)	
Increase in prepaid expenses	(100)	
Net cash flow from operating activities		3,15,300
II. **Cash Flows from Financing Activities:**		
Interest on investments	3000	
Purchase of investments	(9,000)	
Purchase of buildings	(2,27,000)	
Purchase of machinery	(1,52,000)	
Purchase of furniture	(1,400)	
Purchase of goodwill	(43,700)	(4,30,100)
Net cash flow from investing activities		
III. **Cash Flows from Financing Activities:**		
Issue of shares	1,35,000	
Mortgage loan	60,000	
Dividend paid for 2019	(70,000)	
Interim dividend paid	(20,000)	
Net cash flows from financing activities		1,05,000
Net increase (decrease in cash and cash equivalents)		(9,800)
Cash and cash equivalents opening balance (Bank O/D – Cash)		(6,000)
Cash and cash equivalents closing balance (Bank O/D – cash)		(15,800)

Note:
Figures given within brackets represent cash outflows.

Working Notes:

	Amount (₹)
Net profit as per profit and loss account	
Closing balance of profit and loss appropriation A/c	₹1,30,000
Add: Transfer to reserves	43,700
Provision for dividends for 2020	50,000
Interim dividend paid	20,000
	2,43,700
Less: Opening balance of profit and loss appropriation A/c	1,00,000
Net profit before tax and extraordinary items	1,43,700

Name of Account: Investment
Type of Account: Asset

Reference Account	Note No.	Dr. (Add)	Cr. (Less)
To Balance b/d		1,64,000	
By Bank			3,000
To Bank (Purchase of investment)		9,000	
By Balance c/d			1,70,000
Total		**1,73,000**	**1,73,000**

■ **ILLUSTRATION 17.7** A company finds on 1 January 2020 that it is short of funds with which it intends to implement its expansion programme. On 1 January 2019, it had a credit balance of ₹1,80,000. From the following information, prepare a statement for the Board of Directors to show how the overdraft of ₹68,750 as on 31 December 2019 has arisen.

Figures as per the Balance Sheet (as at 31 December 2019)

Particulars	2018 (₹)	2019 (₹)
Fixed assets	7,50,000	11,20,000
Stock and stores	1,90,000	3,30,000
Debtors	3,80,000	3,35,000
Bank balance	1,80,000	68,750 (overdraft)
Share capital (Shares of ₹10 each)	2,50,000	3,00,000
Bills receivable	87,500	95,000
Creditors	3,40,000	4,20,000

The profit for the year ended 31 December 2019 amounted to ₹2,40,000 before charging depreciation and taxation. On 1 January 2019, 5000 shares were issued at a premium of ₹5 per share. ₹1,37,500 were paid in March by way of income tax. Dividends were paid as follows:

2018 (final) on the capital on 31 December 2018 at 10% less tax at 25%, 2019 (interim) 5% free of tax.

Prepare a cash flow statement by the indirect method.

Solution

Working Notes:

1. The final dividend works out to
   ₹2,50,000 × 10%   = ₹25,000
   Less tax deducted at source at 25% on, ₹25,000 = 6,250
   Net dividends amount paid   = 18,750
2. Interim dividends at 5% on ₹3,00,000 = ₹15,000
3. Interim dividend is free of tax; hence, nothing is deductible from the ₹15,000 on account of tax. However, a sum of ₹5,000, that is, ₹15,000 × 25/75, is payable to the government on account of tax.
4. It is assumed that the income tax of ₹1,37,500 paid includes ₹11,250 (₹6,250 + 5,000) with respect to the final and the interim dividends.
5. It is assumed that fixed assets are appearing at cost.
6. It is obvious therefore, that the profit for the year 2019, of ₹2,40,000 is before charging the final dividends and the interim dividends.

The cash flow statement as per the indirect method is as follows:

Cash Flow Statement (Indirect Method)
for the year ended 31/12/2019

Particulars	Amount (₹)	Amount (₹)
1. Cash flows from operating activities:		
Net profit before tax and extraordinary items	2,40,000	
Add: Decrease in debtors	45,000	
Increase in creditors	80,000	
Increase in stock and stores	(1,40,000)	
Increase in bills receivable	(7,500)	
Income tax paid	(1,37,500)	
Net cash flows from operating activities:		80,000
2. Cash flows from investing activities:		

Purchase of fixed assets	(3,70,000)	
Net cash flows from investing activities		(3,70,000)
3. Cash flows from financing activities:		
Issue of shares	50,000	
Share premium	25,000	
Final dividend paid	(18,750)	
Interim dividend paid	(15,000)	
Net cash flows from financing activities		41,250
Net increase (decrease) in cash and cash equivalents		(2,48,750)
Cash and cash equivalents at the beginning of the year		1,80,000
Cash and cash equivalents at the end of the year (overdraft)		(68,750)

FREE CASH FLOW

Free cash flow is the measure of cash that is available for discretionary purposes. This is the cash flow that is available once the firm has paid its capital expenditures. Free cash flows are often used for evaluating a company or firm. Two of the more common measures of free cash flows are free cash flow to firm and free cash flow to equity.

A valuable tool for evaluating the cash position of a firm is free cash flow. Free cash flow is a measure of operating cash flow available to a firm's purposes after providing sufficient funds for additions of fixed assets to maintain the current productive capacity and dividends. The free cash flows are measured through two perceptions: (i) free cash flow to a firm and (ii) free cash flow to equity.

Free Cash Flow to Firm

Free cash flow on the firm (FCFF) is the cash available to all investors, both equity owners and debt holders. FCFF can be calculated by starting with either net income or operating cash flow. FCFF is calculated from net income as:

> Net Income + Non Cash Charges (Depreciation and Amortization) + Interest Expenses × (1 – Tax Rate) – Net Capital Expenditure – Working Capital Expenditure = Free Cash Flow to Firm

Interest expenses is added back to net income because FCFF is the cash available to stockholders and debt holders. Since interest is paid to debtholders, it is always added back.

Free Cash Flow to Equity

Free cash flow to equity (FCFE) is the cash flow that would be available for distribution to common shareholders. FCFE is calculated from net income as:

> Net Income + Non Cash Charges (Depreciation and Amortization) – Net Capital Expenditure + Net Borrowing (Debt Issued – Debt Repaid) = Free Cash Flow to Equity

ANALYTICAL MEASUREMENT

An additional measure of liquidity that is based in part on information from the statement of cash flows is the ratio of cash flows from operations to current liabilities. This measure provides evidence of the firm's ability to cover its currently maturing liabilities from normal and recurring operations.

> Cash Flow from Operations to Current Liabilities = Cash Flow from Operating Activities/Current Liabilities

Another important ratio that is commonly used to assess a firm's cash is the cash flow adequacy ratio. The cash flow adequacy ratio compares free cash flow to the average amount of debt maturing in the next five years or long-term debt maturing on the balance sheet date. It represents a firm's ability to generate enough cash to pay its debt.

> Cash Flow Adequacy Ratio = Free Cash Flow/Long-term Outstanding Loan

■ ILLUSTRATION 17.8 Shah Brothers' transactions for the year ended 31 December 2020 included the following:

1. Cash sales ₹33,30,000.
2. Taxes and other compulsory payments ₹70,000.
3. Sold investment securities ₹9,00,000.
4. Cash borrowed from a bank ₹4,30,000.
5. Cash paid for inventory ₹8,00,000.
6. Issued 10,000 equity shares for land with a market value of ₹6,50,000.
7. Purchased equipment ₹1,00,000.
8. Purchased land ₹5,00,000.
9. Paid ₹2,50,000 towards a bank loan.
10. Sold 600 of its 12% debenture bonds due in the year 2022 for ₹7,20,000.

Calculate Shah Brothers' net cash inflows for (a) operating, (b) investing, and (c) financing activities. Explain the transactions that are not reported as part of the operating, investing, or financing activities of Shah Brothers, but are rather reported separately in the statement of cash flows.

Solution

Calculation of Three Types of Cash Flow Statement of Shah Brothers

(a) Cash Flows from Operating Activities

Particulars		Amount (₹)
Cash Sales		33,30,000
Less: Purchased goods in cash	8,00,000	
Income taxes	70,000	8,70,000
Cash flow from operating activities		**24,60,000**

(b) Cash Flows from Investing Activities

Particulars		Amount (₹)
Sale of investment securities		9,00,000
Less: Purchase of equipment	1,00,000	
Purchase of land	5,00,000	6,00,000
Cash flow from investing activities		**3,00,000**

(c) Cash Flows from Financing Activities

Particulars		Amount (₹)
Cash borrowed from a bank	4,30,000	
Issued debentures	7,20,000	
Less: Payment of a bank loan	(2,50,000)	9,00,000
Cash flow from financing activities		**9,00,000**
Total cash flow/net increase (decrease) in cash flow		**36,60,000**

Note:
Issue of 10,000 equity shares for land with a market value of ₹6,50,000 will not affect the cash balance.

■ ILLUSTRATION 17.9 Ajay Sales completed its calendar year 2020 operations. The comparative balance sheet of Ajay Sales as at 31 December is as follows:

Comparative Balance Sheets of Ajay Sales

Assets	2020 (₹)	2019 (₹)
Cash	73,000	32,000
Accounts receivable	85,000	66,000
Inventories	1,80,000	1,89,000
Land	85,000	1,00,000
Equipment	2,60,000	2,00,000
Accumulated depreciation	(66,000)	(42,000)
Total	**6,17,000**	**5,45,000**

Liabilities and Shareholder's Equity	2020 (₹)	2019 (₹)
Accounts payable	44,000	47,000
Bonds payable	1,60,000	2,00,000
Equity shares (₹10 par)	2,14,000	1,64,000
Retained earnings	1,99,000	1,34,000
Total	**6,17,000**	**5,45,000**

Additional Information:

1. Net income for 2020 is ₹1,50,000
2. Declared and paid cash dividends of ₹60,000.
3. Bonds payable of ₹40,000 were redeemed for cash of ₹50,000.
4. Equity shares was issued for ₹50,000.
5. Depreciation is ₹24,000.
6. Sales for the year are ₹8,50,000.

Prepare a statement of cash flow for the year 2020 using the indirect method.

Solution

Calculation of Three Types of Cash Flow Statement of Ajay Sales Using Indirect Method

Particulars	Amount (₹)	
(a) Cash flows from operations		
Net profit	1,50,000	
Depreciation	24,000	
	1,74,000	
Decrease in inventories	9,000	
Increase in accounts receivable	(19,000)	
Decrease in accounts payable	(3,000)	
Cash flow from operations		1,61,000
(b) Cash flow from investing activities		
Land Sold	15,000	
Equipments Purchased	(60,000)	
(c) Cash flow from investing activities		(45,000)
Equity shares issued	50,000	

Bonds redeemed	(50,000)
Bonds issued	10,000
Dividends paid	(60,000)
Interim dividend paid (Note)	(25,000)
Cash flow from financing activities	**(75,000)**
Total cash flow/net increase (decrease) in cash flow	**41,000**

Verification: The above statement indicates that cash balance should have increased by ₹41,000. If we refer the data given in the question, it directly indicates that cash is increased by ₹41,000 (₹73,000 – ₹32,000)

Note:

The retained earnings as per information given in the question is increased by 65,000. From the net profit of ₹1,50,000, dividend of ₹60,000 is paid as per information given in (c).

Hence, the increase should be ₹90,000. The actual increase is ₹65,000 as retained earnings, implying that Ajay Sales must have paid interim dividend of ₹25,000 during the year.

■ **ILLUSTRATION 17.10** Summarized balance sheets of Roshan & Co. for the years ended 31 March 2019 and 31 March 2020 are reproduced as follows:

Balance Sheets of Roshan & Co.

Particulars	Year Ended 31 March 2019 (₹)	Year Ended 31 March 2020 (₹)
Liabilities		
Equity capital	60,00,000	60,00,000
General reserve	30,90,000	34,10,000
Profit and loss account	1,50,000	1,80,000
9% Debentures	-	15,00,000
Sundry creditors	1,30,000	3,70,000
Proposed dividend	1,80,000	-
Total	**95,50,000**	**1,14,60,000**
Assets		
Land and building less depreciation	14,20,000	17,50,000
Plant and machinery less depreciation	31,00,000	37,50,000
Furniture and fixtures less depreciation	8,40,000	9,80,000
Investment	50,000	60,000
Stock	3,40,000	4,20,000
Debtors	30,00,000	36,00,000
Cash and bank	8,00,000	9,00,000
	95,50,000	1,14,60,000

Additional information for the year ended 31 March 2020:

1. Dividend of ₹1,80,000 for the year ended 31 March 2019 was paid during 2020.
2. Investment costing ₹10,000 was sold for ₹12,000.
3. Depreciation on assets for the year ended 31 March 2020 was charged to profit and loss accounts as follows:

Particulars	Amount (₹)
Land and building	42,000
Plant and machinery	4,74,000
Furniture and fixtures	1,84,000

4. Sales of fixed assets:

Machinery sale value ₹1,00,000 (WDV ₹2,20,000)	
Furniture sale value ₹30,000 (WDV ₹20,000)	

Prepare the cash flow statement for the year ended 31 March 2020 together with the relevant ledger accounts.

Solution

Income Statement of Roshan & Co.
for the year ended 31 March 2020

Particulars	Amount (₹)
Available	
By Balance b/d	1,50,000
Income	
By Net profit after tax	3,50,000
Total available	5,00,000
Expenses or uses	
To General reserve	3,20,000
Total uses	3,20,000
To Balance c/d	1,80,000
Taxation	0
Net profit before tax	**3,50,000**

Name of Account: Land and Building
Type of Account: Asset

Reference Account	Note No.	Dr. (Add)	Cr. (Less)
To Balance b/d		14,20,000	
To Bank (Purchase)		3,72,000	
By Depreciation			42,000
By Balance c/d			17,50,000
Total		**17,92,000**	**17,92,000**

Name of Account: Plant and Machinery
Type of Account: Asset

Reference Account	Note No.	Dr. (Add)	Cr. (Less)
To Balance b/d		31,00,000	
To Bank (Purchase)		13,44,000	
By Bank (Sale)			1,00,000
By Profit and loss account (Loss on sale)			12,0000
By Depreciation			4,74,000
By Balance c/d			3,75,0000
Total		**44,44,000**	**44,44,000**

Name of Account: Furniture and Fixtures
Type of Account: Asset

Reference Account	Note No.	Dr. (Add)	Cr. (Less)
To Balance b/d		8,40,000	
To Bank (Purchase)		3,44,000	
To Profit and loss account (Profit on sale)		10,000	
By Bank (Sale)			30,000
By Depreciation			1,84,000
By Balance c/d			9,80,000
Total		**11,94,000**	**11,94,000**

Name of Account: Investment
Type of Account: Asset

Reference Account	Note No.	Dr. (Add)	Cr. (Less)
To Balance b/d		50,000	
To Bank (Purchase)		20,000	
To Profit and loss account (Profit on sale)		2,000	
By Bank (Sale)			12,000
By Balance c/d			60,000
Total		72,000	72,000

Cash Flow Statement of Roshan & Co.
for the year ended 31 March 2020

Particulars	Amount (₹)	
Cash flow from operating activities (a)		
Net profit before tax and extraordinary items		3,50,000
Adjustment for depreciation	7,00,000	
Loss on sale of plant and machinery	1,20,000	
Profit on sale of furniture	(10,000)	
Profit on sale of investment	(2,000)	8,08,000
Operating profit before working capital changes		11,58,000
Adjustment for:		
Increase in stock	(80,000)	
Increase in debtors	(6,00,000)	
Increase in creditors	2,40,000	(4,40,000)
Net cash from operating activities (a)		7,18,000
Cash flow from investing activities (b)		
Purchase of land and buildings	(3,72,000)	
Purchase of plant and machinery	(13,44,000)	
Purchase of furniture	(3,44,000)	
Purchase of investments	(20,000)	
Sale of machinery	1,00,000	
Sale of furniture	30,000	
Sale of investments	12,000	
Net cash from investing activities (b)		(19,38,000)
Cash flow from financing activities (c)		
Issue of 9% debentures	15,00,000	
Dividends paid	(1,80,000)	
Net cash from financing activities (c)		13,20,000
Net increase in cash and cash equivalents (a+b+c)		1,00,000
Cash and cash equivalents as on 31 March 2019		8,00,000
Cash and cash equivalents as on 31 March 2020		9,00,000

■ **ILLUSTRATION 17.11** Prepare a cash flow statement from the following data of String Limited.

Income Statement and Reconciliation of Earnings of String Limited
for the year ended 31 March 2020

Particulars	Amount (₹)	
Net Sales		40,32,000
Less: Cost of sales	31,68,000	
Depreciation	96,000	
Salaries and wages	3,84,000	
Operating expenses	1,28,000	
Provision for taxation	1,40,800	39,16,800
Net operating profit		1,15,200
Non-recurring Income:		
Profit on sale of equipment		19,200
Profit for the year		1,34,400
Retained earnings (balance in profit and loss account brought forward)		2,42,880
		3,77,280
Dividend declared and paid during the year		1,15,200
Profit and loss account balance as on 31 March 2020		2,62,080

Comparative Balance Sheets of String Limited

Assets and Liabilities	As at 31/3/2019 Amount (₹)	As at 31/3/2020 Amount (₹)
Fixed assets:		
Land	76,800	1,53,600
Building and equipments	5,76,000	9,21,600
Current Assets		
Cash	96,000	1,15,200
Debtors	2,68,800	2,97,600
Stock	4,22,400	1,53,600
Advances	12,480	14,400
Total	14,52,480	16,56,000
Capital	5,76,000	7,10,400
Surplus in Profit and Loss A/c	2,42,880	2,62,080
Sundry creditors	3,84,000	3,74,400
Outstanding expenses	38,400	76,800
Income tax payable	19,200	21,120
Accumulated depreciation on building and equipments	1,92,000	2,11,200
Total	14,52,480	16,56,000

Cost of equipment sold was ₹1,15,200.

Solution

Cash Flow Statement of String Ltd (Direct Method)
for the year ended 31 March 2020

Particulars	Amount (₹)	
Cash flows from operating activities (a)		
Cash receipts from customers	40,03,200	
Cash paid to suppliers	(29,08,800)	
Cash paid for expenses	(4,75,520)	
Cash generated from operations	6,18,880	
Income tax paid	(1,38,880)	
Net cash from operating activities		4,80,000
Cash flows from investing activities (b)		
Purchase of land	(76,800)	
Purchase of building and equipment	(4,60,800)	
Sale of equipment	57,600	
Net cash used in investing activities		(4,80,000)
Cash flows from financing activities (c)		
Issue of share capital	1,34,400	
Dividend paid	(1,15,200)	
Net cash from financing activities		19,200
Net increase in cash and cash equivalents (a + b + c)		19,200
Cash and cash equivalents at the beginning		96,000
Cash and cash equivalents at the end		1,15,200

Working Notes:

Particulars	Amount (₹)	
1. Cash receipts from customers		
Sales		40,32,000
Add: Debtors at the beginning		2,68,800
		43,00,800
Less: Debtors at the end		2,97,600
Receipt from debtors		40,03,200
2. Calculation of purchases		
Cost of goods sold		31,68,000
Add: Closing stock		1,53,600
		33,21,600
Less: Opening stock		4,22,400
Purchases during the year		28,99,200

Particulars	Amount (₹)
3. Cash paid to creditors	
Opening balance of creditors	3,84,000
Add: Purchases	28,99,200
	32,83,200
Less: Closing balance of creditors	3,74,400
Cash paid to creditors	29,08,800
4. Expenses paid	
Salary and wages	3,84,000
Operating expenses	1,28,000
Add: Opening outstanding	38,400
Less: Closing outstanding	(76,800)
Add: Closing advances (prepaid)	14,400
Less: Opening advances (prepaid)	(12,480)
Expenses paid	475,520
5. Income tax paid	
Income tax payable at the beginning	19,200
Add: Provision for taxation	140,800
	160,000
Less: Tax payable at the end	21,120
Tax paid during the year	138,880
6. Accumulated depreciation written off on equipment sold	
Accumulated depreciation at the beginning	192,000
Add: Depreciation for the year	96,000
	288,000
Less: Accumulated depreciation at the end	211,200
Depreciation for equipment sold	76,800
7. Sale price of equipment	
Cost price	1,15,200
Less: Accumulated depreciation	76,800
	38,400
Add: Profit on sale	19,200
Sale price	57,600
8. Purchase of building and equipments	
Balance at the beginning	5,76,000
Less: Cost of equipments sold	1,15,200
Balance	4,60,800
Balance at the end	9,21,600
Purchase of building and equipments	4,60,800

Cash Flow Statement of String Ltd
for the year ended 31 March 2020
Indirect Method

Particulars	Amount (₹)	
Cash flows from operating activities (a)		
Net profit before taxation and extraordinary items	2,56,000	
Adjustment for depreciation	96,000	
Operating profit before working capital changes	3,52,000	

Increase in debtors	(28,800)	
Decrease in stock	268,800	
Increase in advances	(1,920)	
Decrease in creditors	(9,600)	
Increase in outstanding expenses	38,400	
Cash generated from operations	6,18,880	
Income tax paid	1,38,880	
Net cash from operating activities		4,80,000
Cash flows from investing activities (b)		
Purchase of land	(76,800)	
Purchase of building and equipment	(4,60,800)	
Sale of equipment	57,600	
Net cash flow from investing activities		(4,80,000)
Cash flows from financing activities (c)		
Issue of share capital	1,34,400	
Dividend paid	(1,15,200)	
Net cash from financing activities		19,200
Net increase in cash and cash equivalents (a + b + c)		19,200
Cash and cash equivalents at the beginning		96,000
Cash and cash equivalents at the end		1,15,200

■ **ILLUSTRATION 17.12** Prepare a cash flow statement as per proforma given in Ind AS 7 for Star Steel Ltd, whose balance sheets for the year 2019 and 2020 are as follows:

Comparative Balance Sheet of Star Steel Ltd
as at 1 January 2019 and 31 December 2020

Particulars	Amount (₹)	Amount (₹)
	31/12/2019	31/12/2020
ASSETS		
Land and building	5,00,000	4,75,000
Machinery	7,00,000	10,00,000
Investments	8,00,000	8,50,000
Current assets	39,50,000	46,50,000
Cash	50,000	25,000
Total Assets	**60,00,000**	**70,00,000**
EQUITY AND LIABILITIES		
Preference share capital	10,00,000	5,00,000
Equity share capital	10,00,000	12,00,000
Share premium	3,00,000	2,70,000
Capital redemption reserve	-	3,00,000
General reserve	5,00,000	3,00,000
Profit and loss account	3,20,000	4,30,000
Secured loan	8,80,000	9,70,000
Current liabilities	16,00,000	25,00,000
Proposed dividend	4,00,000	5,30,000
Total Equity and Liabilities	**60,00,000**	**70,00,000**

Additional information:

1. During the year, machinery costing ₹95,000 with WDV ₹17,000 was sold for ₹35,000.
2. Preference share capital was redeemed at a premium of 10% partly out of proceeds of issue of 20,000 equity shares of ₹10 each issued at 10% premium and partly out of profits otherwise available for dividends.
3. Depreciation on machinery for the year is ₹3,00,000.

Solution

Cash Flow Statement of Star Steel Ltd
for the year 2020

Particulars	Amount (₹)	
1. Cash flows from operating activities		
Profit before tax for the year	7,22,000	
Add: Depreciation on land and building	25,000	
Depreciation on machinery	3,00,000	
Increase in current liabilities	9,00,000	
Less: Increase in current assets	(7,00,000)	
Cash flows from operating activities		12,47,000
2. Cash flows from investment activities		
Sale of plant	35,000	
Purchase of investment	(50,000)	
Purchase of machinery	(6,17,000)	
Cash flows from investment activities		(6,32,000)

3. Cash flows from financing activities		
Issue of shares at premium	2,20,000	
Increase in secured loans	90,000	
Payment of dividends	(4,00,000)	
Redemption of preference shares at premium	(5,50,000)	
Cash flows from financing activities		(6,40,000)
Increase/(decrease) in cash during the year		(25,000)
Opening cash balance		50,000
Closing cash balance		25,000

Working Notes:

	Amount (₹)
Profit before tax for the year has been ascertained as follows:	
Increase in profit and loss account (4,30,000 – 3,20,000)	1,10,000
Add: Transfer to general reserve	1,00,000
Add: Proposed dividends	5,30,000
Less: Profit on sale of plant (35,000 – 17,000)	18,000
Profit for the year	7,22,000
Purchase of machinery during the year:	
Opening balance	7,00,000
Less: Sale of plant (WDV)	17,000
Less: Depreciation for the year	3,00,000
Closing balance should be	3,83,000
But, closing balance is	10,00,000
Therefore, purchase of machinery (10,00,000 – 3,83,000) = ₹6,17,000	

 ## SUMMARY

- Cash flow statements provide a base to the user to assess the ability of the enterprise to generate cash and cash equivalents, and the needs of the firm to utilize those cash flows.
- Cash flows may be from (a) operating activities; (b) investing activities; and (c) financing activities.
- The activities that are revenue producing for a firm are named as operating activities. The acquisition and disposal of fixed assets, that is, long-term assets and other investments that are not included in the calculation of cash and cash equivalents, are treated as investing activities. Changes in the size and composition of the capital and borrowings of the firm are treated as financing activities.
- The cash flow from operations can be calculated by the direct method or the indirect method. The most used method in Indian corporates is the indirect method.
- For financial enterprises, the operating activity itself is to earn the interest and dividend income, and also to pay the interest and dividend by way of expenses.

 ## KEYWORDS

Cash It consists of cash in hand and demand deposits with banks.

Cash equivalents They consist of short-term, highly liquid investments that are readily convertible into known amounts of cash and which are subject to insignificant risk of change in value.

Cash flows These are inflows and outflows of cash and cash equivalents.

Free cash flow to the firm (FCFF) is the cash available to all investors, both equity owners and debt holders. FCFF can be calculated by starting with either net income or operating cash flow.

Free cash flow to equity (FCFE) is the cash flow that would be available for distribution to common shareholders.

QUESTIONS

I. Solve the following problems.

1. From the following data, calculate the cash flow from operating activities for 2020.

Particulars	2020 (₹)	2019 (₹)
Cash	15,000	20,000
Accounts receivable	40,000	36,000
Inventories	38,000	50,000
Accounts payable	18,000	20,000
Accrued expense	9,000	4,000
Net income of the year	63,000	70,000
Depreciation of the year	12,000	10,000

2. From the following balances, you are required to calculate cash from operations.

Particulars	31/12/2019 Amount (₹)	31/12/2020 Amount (₹)
Debtors	50,000	47,000
Bills receivable	10,000	12,500
Creditors	20,000	25,000
Bills payable	8,000	6,000
Outstanding expenses	1,000	1,200
Prepaid expenses	800	700
Accrued income	600	750
Income received in advance	300	250
Profit made during the year		1,30,000

3. From the following information, work out the cash from operations:

Particulars	Amount (₹)
Profit made during 2020	50,000
Transfer to general reserve	10,000
Depreciation provided	20,000
Profit on sale of furniture	5,000
Loss on sale of machinery	10,000
Preliminary expenses written off	10,000

Additional information:

Particulars	2019 (₹)	2020 (₹)
Debtors	10,000	15,000
Bills receivable	7,000	5,000
Stock	15,000	18,000
Prepaid expenses	2,000	3,000
Creditors	20,000	18,000
Bills payable	15,000	25,000
Outstanding expenses	3,000	4,000

4. The following summary cash account has been extracted from the Doe Company's accounting records.

Particulars	Amount (₹ in '000)
Balance on 1/1/2019	35
Receipts from customers	27,83

Particulars	Amount (₹ in '000)
Issue of shares	300
Sale of fixed assets	128
	32,46
Payments to suppliers	20,47
Payments for fixed assets	230
Payments for overheads	115
Wages and salaries	69
Taxation	243
Dividends	80
Repayments of bank loan	250
	(3,034)
Balance on 31/12/2019	212

Prepare the cash flow statement of Doe Company for the year ended 31 December 2019 in accordance with Ind AS 7. Note that the company does not have any cash equivalents.

5. From the following details relating to the accounts of Grow More Ltd, prepare a cash flow statement.

Particulars	31/3/2020 Amount (₹)	31/3/2019 Amount (₹)
Liabilities and Capital		
Share capital	10,00,000	8,00,000
Reserve	2,00,000	1,50,000
Profit and loss account	1,00,000	60,000
Debentures	2,00,000	-
Provision for taxation	1,00,000	70,000
Proposed dividend	2,00,000	1,00,000
Sundry creditors	7,00,000	8,20,000
	25,00,000	20,00,000
Assets		
Plant and machinery	7,00,000	5,00,000
Land and building	6,00,000	4,00,000
Investments	1,00,000	-
Sundry debtors	5,00,000	7,00,000
Stock	4,00,000	2,00,000
Cash in hand/bank	2,00,000	2,00,000
	25,00,000	20,00,000

1. Depreciation @ 25% p.a. was charged on the opening value of plant and machinery.
2. During the year, one old machine costing 50,000 (WDV ₹20,000) was sold for ₹35,000.
3. ₹50,000 were paid towards income tax during the year.
4. Building under construction was not subject to any depreciation.

6. The balance sheets of Sun Ltd for the year ended 31 March 2020 and 2019 are summarized as follows:

Balance Sheets of Sun Ltd

Liabilities and Assets	2020 (₹)	2019 (₹)
Equity share capital	60,000	50,000
Reserves:		
Profit and loss account	5,000	4,000
Current liabilities:		
Creditors	4,000	2,500
Taxation	1,500	1,000
Proposed dividends	2,000	1,000
Total	**72,500**	**58,500**
Fixed assets (at written down value)		
Premises	10,000	10,000
Fixtures	17,000	11,000
Vehicles	12,500	8,000
Short-term investments	2,000	1,000
Current assets:		
Stock	17,000	14,000
Debtors	8,000	6,000
Bank and cash	6,000	8,500
Total	**72,500**	**58,500**

The income statement for the year ended 31 March 2020 disclosed the following:

Particulars	Amount (₹)
Profit before tax	4,500
Taxation	(1,500)
Profit after tax	3,000
Proposed dividends	(2,000)
Retained profit	1,000

Further information is available:

Particulars	Fixtures Amount(₹)	Vehicles Amount (₹)
Depreciation for the year	1,000	2,500
Disposals:		
Proceeds on disposal		1,700
Written down value		(1,000)
Profit on disposal		700

Prepare a cash flow statement for the year ended 31 March 2020.

7. M/s Jyoti Star Oils Limited has collected the following information for the preparation of cash flow statement for the year 2019.

Particulars	Amount (₹ in lakh)
Net profit	25,000
Dividend (including dividend tax) paid	8,535
Provision for income tax	5,000
Income tax paid during the year	4,248
Loss on sale of assets (net)	40
Book value of assets sold	185
Depreciation charged to profit and loss account	20,000

Amortization of capital grant	6
Profit on sale of investments	100
Carrying amount of investment sold	27,765
Interest income on investments	2,506
Interest expenses	10,000
Interest paid during the year	10,520
Increase in working capital (excluding cash and bank balance)	56,075
Purchase of fixed assets	14,560
Investment in joint venture	3,850
Expenditure on construction work-in-progress	34,740
Proceeds from calls-in-arrear	2
Receipt of grant for capital projects	12
Proceeds from long-term borrowings	25,980
Proceeds from short-term borrowings	20,575
Opening cash and bank balance	5,003
Closing cash and bank balance	6,988

Prepare the cash flow statement for the year 2019 in accordance with Ind AS 7 cash flow statements issued by the ICAI. (Make necessary assumptions).

8. The balance sheets of New Light Ltd for year ended 31 March 2019 and 2020 are as follows:

Balance Sheets of New Light Ltd
as at 31 March 2020 and 31 March 2020

Particulars	Amount (₹) 31/03/2019	Amount (₹) 31/03/2020
ASSETS		
Fixed assets	32,00,000	38,00,000
Less: Depreciation	9,20,000	11,60,000
Net fixed assets	22,80,000	26,40,000
Investments	4,00,000	3,20,000
Cash	10,000	10,000
Other current assets	11,10,000	13,10,000
Preliminary expenses	80,000	40,000
Total Assets	**38,80,000**	**43,20,000**
EQUITY AND LIABILITIES		
10% Preference share capital	4,00,000	2,80,000
Equity share capital	12,00,000	16,00,000
Capital reserve	-	40,000
General reserve	6,80,000	8,00,000
Profit and loss account	2,40,000	3,00,000
9% Debentures	4,00,000	2,80,000
Current liabilities	4,80,000	5,20,000
Proposed dividend	1,20,000	1,44,000
Provision for tax	3,60,000	3,40,000
Unpaid dividend	-	16,000
Total Equity and Liabilities	**38,80,000**	**43,20,000**

Additional information:

1. The company sold one fixed asset for ₹1,00,000, the cost of which was ₹2,00,000 and the depreciation provided on it was ₹80,000.
2. The company also decided to write off another fixed asset costing ₹56,000 on which depreciation amounting to ₹40,000 has been provided.
3. Depreciation on fixed assets provided ₹3,60,000.
4. Company sold some investment at a profit of ₹40,000 which was credited to the capital reserve.
5. Debentures and preference share capital redeemed at 5% premium.
6. Company decided to value stock at cost, whereas previously the practice was to value stock at cost less 10%. The stock according to books on 31/3/2019 was ₹2,16,000. The stock on 31/3/2020 was correctly valued at ₹3,00,000.
7. Prepare a cash flow statement as per revised Ind AS 7 by indirect method.
9. A store had the following transactions in 2019.
   (i) It bought merchandise on account for ₹10 lakhs.
   (ii) It sold merchandise on account for ₹15 lakhs.
   (iii) It used the services of its employees; these employees earned ₹3 lakh by providing these services.
   (iv) It received invoices worth ₹1 lakh from the electricity supplier, the telephone company, and other outside firms for services it used during 2019.
   (v) It paid ₹10,50,000 to merchandise suppliers, utility companies, and other outside service companies.
   (vi) It paid its employees ₹2,80,000.
   (vii) It collected ₹16 lakh in cash from its customers.
   (viii) It bought display cabinets and other store equipments for ₹40,000, paying ₹25,000 in cash, and promising to pay the balance early in 2020.
   (ix) It counted the merchandise on hand on 31 December 2019. The cost of that merchandise was ₹2 lakh. A similar count on 31 December 2018 had identified merchandise on hand at that time with a cost of ₹1,40,000.
   (x) It estimated that depreciation of store fixtures and equipment during the year amounted to ₹18,000.
   (xi) The owners withdrew ₹10,000 in cash for their own use.
   (a) Identify the effects of each of these transactions and other events on the company's assets, liabilities, and owners' equity. For each change, state both the amount in rupees and the direction of the change (+ or –).
   (b) Prepare an income statement for the year.
   (c) Prepare a statement of cash flow for the year.

REFERENCES

Ind AS 7 of MCA
AS-3 of ICAI
Provisions of the Companies Act, 2013.

Shah, Paresh 2015, *Financial Management*, 2nd edition, Wiley-Biztantra.

ANNEXURES

Annexure A: Cash Flow Statement for the Year Ended 31 March 2018—Balaji Telefilms Limited

Amount (₹ in lakh)

Particulars	For the Year Ended March 31, 2018		For the Year Ended March 31, 2017	
(A) Cash flow from operating activities				
Profit before tax		4,671.90		226.00
Adjustments for:				
Depreciation and amortisation	1,389.93		1,226.97	
Advances written off	199.52		-	
Provision for doubtful debts (net)	113.13		49.35	
Loss on sale of fixed assets	26.63		22.75	
Profit on sale of current investments (non-trade) (net)	(660.83)		(605.50)	
Exceptional items considered in income-tax	905.07		-	
Gratuity asset written off	30.62		-	
Creditors written back	-		(248.56)	
Advances written back	(67.29)		-	
Amortisation of prepaid rent element of rental security deposit	74.38		74.65	
Loss on fair valuation of non current investments (net of tax)	-		205.29	
Unwinding of discount on security deposit	(74.42)		(67.48)	
Profit on fair valuation of investments (net of tax)	(716.05)		-	
Service tax CENVAT credit write-off	153.57		-	
Interest income on fixed deposits	(16.76)		(10.89)	
Interest income on income-tax refund	(41.61)		(124.74)	
Interest income on loan to subsidiary	(24.40)	1,291.49	(21.03)	500.81
Operating profit before working capital changes		5,963.39		726.81
Adjustments for:				
Decrease/(Increase) in trade receivable	1,559.68		(1,395.46)	

Annexure A: Cash Flow Statement for the Year Ended 31 March 2018—Balaji Telefilms Limited (contd.)

Amount (₹ in lakh)

Particulars	For the Year Ended March 31, 2018		For the Year Ended March 31, 2017	
Decrease in other current financial assets	14.56		282.60	
Decrease/(Increase) in other current assets	4,470.21		(2,407.12)	
(Increase)/Decrease in other non current financial assets	(48.01)		386.74	
(Increase)/Decrease in loans	(18.69)		146.93	
(Increase) in other non current assets	(2,173.55)		(2,717.30)	
Decrease in inventories	2,349.50		2,469.51	
(Decrease)/Increase in trade payables	(2,368.51)		3,607.12	
Increase/(Decrease) in other financial liabilities	0.34		(8.79)	
(Decrease)/Increase in other current liabilities	(3,075.12)	710.41	808.98	1,173.21
Cash from operations		6,673.80		1,900.02
Income-tax (paid)		(1,469.34)		(432.22)
Net cash flow from operating activities (A)		5,204.46		1,467.80
(B) Cash flow from investing activities				
Payments for property, plant and equipment	(1,016.08)		(1,714.03)	
Proceeds from sale of property, plant and equipment	39.30		-	
Payments for purchase of current investments	(73,732.04)		(4,650.00)	
Proceeds from sale of current investments	45,969.10		4,507.63	
Payments for purchase of non current investments	(15,025.00)		-	
Proceeds from sale of non current investments	497.24		-	
Loans to related parties	(603.85)		(135.72)	
Interest Income	82.77		156.66	
Net cash (used in) investing activities (B)		(43,788.56)		(1,835.46)
(C) Cash flow from financing activities				
Proceeds from issue of equity share capital	41,328.00		-	
Share issue costs	(1,653.87)		-	
Dividend paid to company's shareholders (including DDT)	(486.87)		-	
Net cash flow from financing activities (C)		39,187.26		-
Net increase/(decrease) in cash and cash equivalents (A + B + C)		603.16		(367.66)
Cash and cash equivalents at the beginning of the year		70.48		438.14
Cash and cash equivalents at the end of the year		673.64		70.48

(i) Components of cash and cash equivalents include cash and bank balances in current and deposit accounts (Refer note 14).

(ii) Cash and cash equivalents above comprises of	₹ In Lacs	₹ In Lacs
— Cash and cash equivalent as per note 14 (excluding balance in unpaid dividend account & Fixed deposits kept in lien against bank guarantee.)	1,034.98	1,049.14
— Temporarily overdrawn book balances as per note 20	(361.34)	(978.66)
Cash and cash equivalents at the end of the year as per cash flow statement	**673.64**	**70.48**

The above statement of cash flows should be read in conjunction with the accompanying notes
This is the statement of cash flows referred to in our report of even date

| For Price Waterhouse Chartered Accountants LLP
Firm Registration No. 012754N/N500016

Mehul Desai
Partner
Membership No. 103211
Place: Mumbai
Date: May 19, 2018 | For and on behalf of the Board of Directors

Jeetendra Kapoor
Chairman
DIN: 00005345

Ekta Kapoor
Joint Managing Director
DIN: 00005093

Simmi Singh Bisht
Group Head Secretarial
Place: Mumbai
Date: May 19, 2018 | **Shobha Kapoor**
Managing Director
DIN: 00005124

D.G. Rajan
Director
DIN: 00303060

Sanjay Dwivedi
Group CFO |

Source: Balaji Telefilms Limited Annual Report 2017–18, pp. 110–111.

Annexure B: Cash Flow Statement for the Year Ended 31 March 2018—Mahindra Finance

₹ in lakhs

Particulars	Year Ended 31 March 2018	Year Ended 31 March 2017
Cash flow from operating activities		
Profit before exceptional items and taxes	1,30,777.65	62,006.83
Add/(Less):		
Non-cash expenses		
Depreciation and amortisation expense	4,419.21	4,602.14
Provision for non-performing assets	13,697.64	44,233.45
Bad debts and write offs	1,05,763.10	84,500.16
Provision for standard assets	3,208.00	2,180.00
Higher provision &. provision for diminution in the fair value of restructured advances	[9.27]	(0.94)
Employee compensation expense on account of ESOP Scheme	755.03	879.82
	1,27,833.71	1,36,394.63
Less:		
Income considered separately		
Income on investing activities	(7,516.92)	(6,686.96)
Profit on sale of assets	(51.28)	(15.24)
Profit on sale of current investments	(59.56)	(88.48)
Income from Assignment/Securitisation transactions	(14,199.95)	(11,936.72)
	(21,827.71)	(18,727.40)
Operating profit before working capital changes I	2,36,783.65	1,79,674.06
Less: Working capital changes		
(Increase)/Decrease in interest accrued - others	(76.62)	2,740.80
Increase in Trade receivables	(160.16)	(71.46)
Increase in Loans and advances	(10,28,408.68)	(6,90,503.93)
	(10,28,645.46)	(6,87,834.59)
Add: Increase in current liabilities	62,884.18	60,220.71
II	(9,65,761.28)	(6,27,613.88)
Cash used in operations [I + II]	(7,28,977.63)	(4,47,939.82)
Advance taxes paid	(55.099.29)	(42,750.27)
Net Cash Used in Operating Activities [A]	(7,84,076.92)	(4,90,690.09)
Cash flow from investing activities		
Purchase of fixed Assets/software	(5,246.53)	(4,546.05)
Proceeds from sale of fixed assets	133.53	93.96
Purchase of investments Other than investments in Subsidiaries and Joint Venture	(6,66,982.93)	(5,36,755.05)
Investments in Subsidiary Companies	(15,900.00)	(14,455.00)
Investments in Joint Venture Company	(1,662.44)	(3,111.84)
Maturity proceeds from term deposits with banks	12,191.81	12,452.00
Proceeds from sale of investments	6,84,592.13	5,14,150.35
Income received from investing activities	7,501.71	6,525.24
Increase in Earmarked balances with banks	(23.26)	(0.53)
Proceeds from sale of long-term investments [in equity shares of Mahindra Insurance Brokers Limited]	6,500.00	-
Net cash generated from/(used in) investing activities [B]	21,104.02	[25,646.92]
Cash flow from financing activities		
Issue of Equity shares [net of issue expenses]	2,09,789.87	-
Expenses incurred on issuance of Non-convertible debentures	(1,858.14)	[1,653.42]
Proceeds from long-term borrowings	11,31,951.88	10,46,022.59
Repayment of long-term borrowings	(5,44,966.50)	(6,28,104.76)
Proceeds from short-term borrowings	43,30,648.60	48,12,018.46
Repayment of short-term borrowings	[42,67,966.09]	[46,51,002.97]
(Decrease)/Increase in loans repayable on demand and cash credit/overdraft facilities with banks [net]	(37,284.09)	[19,744.55]
Decrease in Fixed deposits (net)	(1,24,559.01)	[40,130.21]

Annexure B: Cash Flow Statement for the Year Ended 31 March 2018—Mahindra Finance (Cont.)

₹ in lakhs

Particulars	Year Ended 31 March 2018	Year Ended 31 March 2017
Proceeds from Assignment/Securitisation transactions	69,360.66	45,708.90
Dividend paid [including tax on dividend]	[16,097.30]	[27,126.87]
Net Cash Generated From/(Used In] Financing Activities (C)	**7,49,017.88**	**5,35,987.17**
Net Increase/(Decrease) in Cash and Cash Equivalents (A+B+C)	**[13,955.02]**	**19,650.16**
Cash and Cash Equivalents at the Beginning of the year	**41,145.40**	**21,495.24**
Cash and Cash Equivalents at the End of the year (Refer Note 19 (A))	**27,190.38**	**41,145.40**
Components of Cash and Cash Equivalents		
Cash and cash equivalents at the end of the year		
- Cash on hand	904.46	1,723.81
- Cheques and drafts on hand	1,264.80	1,258.49
- Balances with banks in current accounts	24,996.12	38,163.10
-Term deposits with original maturity up to 3 months	25.00	-
Total	**27,190.38**	**41,145.40**

Notes:

The above Cash Flow Statement has been prepared under the 'Indirect method' as set out in Accounting Standard 3 'Cash Flow Statements'.

As per our report of even date attached.
For B S R & Co. LLP
Chartered Accountants
Firm's Registration No:101248W/W-100022

Venkataramanan Vishwanath
Partner
Membership No: 113156

For and on behalf of the Board of Directors
Mahindra & Mahindra Financial Services Limited

Dhananjay Mungale	**Ramesh Iyer**	**M. G. Bhide**	**Piyush Mankad**
Chairman	*Vice-Chairman &*	*Director*	*Director*
[DIN: 00007563]	*Managing Director*	[DIN: 00001826]	[DIN: 00005001]
	[DIN: 00220759]		
C.B. Bhave	**Rama Bjjapurkar**	**V. S. Parthasarathy**	**Dr. Anish Shah**
Director	*Director*	*Director*	*Director*
[DIN: 00059856]	[DIN: 00001835]	[DIN: 00125299]	[DIN: 02719429]

Place: Mumbai
Date: 25 April 2018

V. Ravi
Executive Director &
Chief Financial Officer
[DIN: 00307328]

Arnavaz Pardiwalla
Company Secretary

Source: Mahindra & Mahindra Financial Services Limited Annual Report 2017–18, pp. 150–151. Used by permission.

Annexure C: Cash Flow Statement for the Year Ended 31 March 2018—RPG Life Sciences Limited

(All amounts in Indian Rupees lakhs, unless otherwise stated)

	Note	Year Ended March 31, 2018	Year Ended March 31, 2017
(A) Cash Flow from operating activities			
Profit before income tax including discontinued operations		2,036	2,346
Adjustments for			
Add:			
Depreciation and amortisatian expenses	19	1,434	1,178
Finance costs	18	380	253
Loss on disposal of property, plant and equipment	20/15	-	2
Unrealised exchange rate difference	15	(29)	21
Provision for Doubtful Debts and Advances (Net)	20	22	23
Interest received	15	(1)	(40)
Provisions no longer required and written back	15	(69)	(4)
Gain on sale of business	25	-	(738)
		3,773	3,041

Annexure C: Cash Flow Statement For The Year Ended 31 March 2018-RPG Life Sciences Limited (Cont.)

(All amounts in Indian Rupees lakhs, unless otherwise stated)

	Note	Year Ended March 31, 2018	Year Ended March 31, 2017
Working capital adjustments:			
(Increase) in trade receivables	5(c)	(2,846)	(884)
(Increase)/decrease in financial assets - Loans	5(a)(b)	(4)	1
Decrease in other non-current assets	6	4	3
Decrease/(Increase) in other financial assets	5(b)	137	(124)
(Increase)/decrease in other current assets	6	(1,146)	140
(Increase) in inventories	7	(791)	(889)
Increase/(decrease) in trade payables	10(b)	2,361	(210)
Increase/ (decrease) in other financial liabilities	10(c)	295	(64)
Increase/ (decrease) in provisions	12	142	(33)
(Decrease)/Increase in other current liabilities	11	(87)	179
Cash generated from operations		1,838	1,160
Income taxes paid	24(e)	(370)	(427)
Net cash inflow from operating activities		1,468	733
(B) Cash flow from investing activities:			
Acquisition of property, plant and equipment and Intangible assets	3/4	(1,548)	(5,587)
Proceeds from sale of property, plant and equipment and Intangible assets		2	71
Bank deposits	5(e)	(9)	(17)
Proceeds from sale of discontinued operation		-	2,487
Interest received	15	1	40
Net cash (outflow) from investing activities		(1,554)	(3,006)
(C) Cash flow from financing activities			
Proceeds from long term borrowings		27	2,067
Repayment of long term borrowings		(470)	(34)
Proceeds from/(Repayment of) Short-term Borrowings (Net)		1,385	553
Dividend paid including dividend distribution tax thereon	9	(553)	-
Proceeds from share allotment under employee stock option plan		-	3
Interest paid	18	(378)	(253)
Net cash inflow from financing activities		11	2,336
Net increase/(decrease) in cash and cash equivalents		(75)	63
Add: Cash and cash equivalents at the beginning of the financial year	5(d)	86	23
Cash and cash equivalents at the end of the year		11	86
Cash and cash equivalents	5(d)	11	86
Bank overdrafts		-	-
Balances as per statement of cash flows		11	86

The above Cash Flow Statement has been prepared under the 'Indirect Method' as set out in the Accounting Standard (IND AS) 7 - "Cash Flow Statements".
The notes referred to above and other notes form an integral part of the financial statements.

In terms of our report of even date attached.
For **B S R & Co. LLP**
Chartered Accountants
Firm's Registration No: 101248W/W-100022

Bhavesh Dhupelia
Partner
Membership No. 042070

Mumbai, May 2, 2018

H. V. Goenka
Chairman
DIN: 00026726

C. L. Jain
Director
DIN:00102910

Mumbai, May 2, 2018

For and on behalf of the Board of Directors
RPG Life Sciences Limited
CIN: L24232MH2007PLC169354

CT. Renganathan
Managing Director
DIN: 02158397

Mahesh Narayanaswamy
Vice President - Finance

Rajesh Shirambekar
Company Secretary

Source: RPG Life Sciences Limited Annual Report 2017–18, pp. 52–53.

Annexure D: Cash Flow Statement for the Year Ended 31 March 2018—SpiceJet Limited

(All amounts are in millions of Indian Rupees, unless otherwise stated)

		Year Ended 31-Mar-2018	Year Ended 31-Mar-2017
Cash flow from/used in operating activities			
Profit before tax and exceptional items		**5,572.06**	**3,886.72**
Adjustments to reconcile profit before tax and exceptional items to net cash flows:			
Depreciation and Amortisation expense		2,313.18	1,986.14
Provision for doubtful claims/advances		103.07	-
Loss/(profit) on disposal of PPE (net)/assets written off		52.16	9.06
Provision for litigations		-	82.69
Advances/debts written off		36.54	79.35
Share-based payment expense		13.01	1,796.89
Provision for aircraft maintenance		2,823.63	122.81
Provision for aircraft redelivery		102.46	-
Liabilities/provision no longer required written back		489.08	(517.58)
Profit on sale of engine under sale and lease-back arrangement		(47.55)	(23.70)
Net (Gain)/Loss on financial assets measured at fair value through profit or loss ('FVTPL')		26.85	(34.83)
Finance income		(497.22)	(316.96)
Finance costs		923.30	650.40
Translation loss/(gain) on monetary assets and liabilities		115.04	(500.25)
Operating profit before working capital changes		**12,025.61**	**7,220.75**
Movements in working capital:			
(Increase)/Decrease in trade receivables		(258.39)	(184.26)
(Increase)/Decrease in inventories		(433.20)	(320.05)
(Increase)/Decrease in other financial assets		(1,258.25)	361.23
(Increase)/Decrease in other current assets		(1,677.16)	(481.77)
Increase/(Decrease) in trade payables		(2,359.70)	(784.52)
Increase/(Decrease) in other financial liabilities		1,619.10	(275.41)
Increase/(Decrease) in other liabilities		1,934.12	1,543.41
Increase/(Decrease) in provisions		1,241.45	(4,026.80)
Cash generated from operations		**10,833.58**	**3,052.58**
Income taxes received/(paid) (net of refunds)		(79.03)	81.23
Net cash generated from operating acitivities before exceptional items		**10,754.55**	**3,133.81**
Cash inflow from exceptional items (refer note 35)		-	1,658.32
Net cash flow from/(used in) operating activities	A	**10,754.55**	**4,792.13**
Cash flow from/used in investing activities			
Purchase of PPE and capital work in progress (including capital advances)		(5,611.65)	(2,492.17)
Proceeds from sale of PPE		18.73	4.26
Purchase of investments		358.04	(1,158.28)
Investments in bank deposits		214.74	(185.74)
Margin money deposits placed		(6,320.07)	(2,561.21)
Margin money deposits withdrawn		2,365.54	1,212.53
Finance income		303.56	252.52
Net cash from/(used in) investing activities	B	**(8,671.11)**	**(4,928.09)**
Cash flow from/used in financing activities			
Proceeds from short-term borrowings		1,051.93	1,472.45
Repayment of long-term borrowings		(1,229.55)	(1,255.72)
Finance costs		(902.49)	(650.24)
Net cash (used in)/from financing activities	C	**(1,080.11)**	**(433.51)**
Net increase/(decrease) in cash and cash equivalents	(A + B + C)	**1,003.33**	**(569.46)**
Effects of exchange difference on cash and cash equivalents held in foreign currency		(0.13)	6.75
Cash and cash equivalents at the beginning of the year		196.31	759.02
Cash and cash equivalents at the end of the year		**1,199.51**	**196.31**

Annexure D: Cash Flow Statement for the Year Ended 31 March 2018—SpiceJet Limited (Cont.)

(All amounts are in millions of Indian Rupees, unless otherwise stated)

	Year Ended 31-Mar-2018	Year Ended 31-Mar-2017
Notes:		
Components of cash and cash equivalents		
On current accounts	1,122.41	157.67
On deposit accounts	55.63	16.23
Cash on hand	21.47	22.41
Total cash and cash equivalents (Note 13)	**1,199.51**	**196.31**

See accompanying Notes forming part of the Financial Statements.
As per our report of even date.

For S.R. BATLIBOI & ASSOCIATES LLP   For and on behalf of the Board of Directors
Chartered Accountants
ICAI Firm Registration No.: 101049W/E300004

per Aniruddh Sankaran	**Ajay Singh**	**Kiran Koteshwar**	**Chandan Sand**
Partner	*Chairman &*	*Chief Financial*	*Company Secretary*
Membership No: 211107	*Managing Director*	*Officer*	
Place: Gurugram	Place: Gurugram	Place: Gurugram	Place: Gurugram
Date: May 11, 2018	Date: May 11, 2018	Date: May 11, 2018	Date: May 11, 2018

Source: SpiceJet Limited Annual Report 2017–18, pp. 150–151.

Special Topics

Foreign Exchange Accounting

Learning Objectives

After studying this chapter, you will understand

- currency exchange rates and foreign currency transactions
- the accounting methodology for foreign currency transactions and its impact on the account of changes in exchange rates
- different types of hedging transactions
- foreign branch accounting

INTRODUCTION

When a transaction takes place between two parties, both the parties record the transaction in their books of accounts in the same currency when they are located in the same country and express transactions in the same currency. However, when parties in different countries enter into transactions, each of them has to enter the transaction in his/her respective currency. Transactions are represented in the currency of one of the parties; hence, the other party needs to record the same in its own currency. Thus, when a need to translate currency arises, it is met by using currency exchange rates (the rate of exchange between two currencies). From the point of view of an enterprise, the currency used for presenting the financial statements is referred to as *reporting currency*. Exchange rate is the rate of exchange of two currencies.

> Reporting currency is the currency used for presenting financial statements.

Currency exchange rate is the amount required to purchase one unit of currency with that of another currency. Thus, the exchange rate may be viewed as the 'price' of buying one unit of a foreign currency, stated in terms of the domestic currency (Indian rupees in case of India). Exchange rates fluctuate daily, based on worldwide demand and supply for a particular currency. The current exchange rate between Indian Rupee and foreign currency (predominantly US $, Euro, Sterling Pound, Japanese Yen, etc.) are published daily in the financial and business newspapers.

Exchange rate may be used to determine how much one currency is equivalent to a given amount of another currency. Assume that an Indian company owes to a foreign company a US$10,000. How will Indian Rupees be needed to settle this function, assuming that the current exchange rate is ₹72? To restate an amount of foreign currency in terms of an equivalent amount of Indian Rupees, multiply the foreign currency (FX) amount by the exchange rate, which is as follows:

> Amount Stated in FX × Exchange Rate in Indian ₹
> = Equivalent Value in Indian ₹
> = $10,000 × 72 = ₹7,20,000

FOREIGN DENOMINATED TRANSACTIONS

In purchase or sale transactions, if the contract, either explicit or implicit, between the buyer and the seller can be denominated or expressed in foreign currency units, that is, other than the reporting currency of the party involved, then the transaction is known as a foreign-denominated transaction. For example, if Prince Ltd of India entered into transactions with Amey Corp of America to buy goods, and the contract is denominated in US dollars, then the said transaction is considered as a foreign-denominated transaction for Prince Ltd. This is because Prince Ltd's reporting currency, that is, local currency, is the Indian rupee, but the transaction is not considered as a foreign-denominated transaction for Amey Corp.

Here, the transaction is denominated in a foreign currency, that is, dollars, and hence, Prince Ltd will have to convert US dollars into Indian rupees to pay its bill and to record in the books of accounts. In order to convert foreign currency units into Indian rupees, a conversion rate or exchange rate must be used.

If the transaction is denominated in foreign currency, the Indian firm either receives foreign currency units (in a sale transaction) or pays in foreign currency (in a purchase transaction).

■ **ILLUSTRATION 18.1** Aiyaa & Co., Mumbai, buys some materials from Johnson & Co. of London. The invoice for the same by Johnson & Co. is in pound sterling (£) while accounting by Aiyaa & Co. will be in Indian currency (₹). What is the reporting currency of Aiyaa & Co.?

Solution

The amount in pound sterling is to be converted into rupees at the appropriate exchange rate. In such a case, from the point of view of Aiyaa & Co., '₹' is the reporting currency, and '£' is the foreign currency. From the point of view of Johnson & Co., '£' is the reporting currency, and '₹' is the foreign currency.

The rate of exchange between the pound sterling and the rupee is the exchange rate.

EXCHANGE RATES AND CURRENCY TRANSACTIONS

Foreign currency transactions include

- buying or selling of goods or services whose price is denominated in a different currency;
- borrowing or lending funds when the amounts payable or receivable are denominated in a different currency;
- unperformed foreign exchange contract; and
- acquisition or disposition of assets and incurring of liability by way of foreign currency loan.

In case of transactions with foreign countries, there arises the problem of which country's exchange currency they should transact in. In whatever currency they decide to transact in, the country whose currency is not selected (for the transaction to be dealt in) will have to account for the transaction by converting the cost/value in its own currency. For example, if an Indian company Ashes Ltd enters into a sale of goods with Vita Ltd of the USA and the price of the goods is fixed in US dollars (US $) 5,00,000 (not in Indian rupees (Indian ₹)), the exchange rate at which this is done has to be fixed, and the later events such as payments, or treatment at an intervening balance sheet date, etc. have to be converted into the domestic currency, accounting properly for the differences arising due to the different exchange rates prevailing at that time.

From the perspective of any given country, foreign currencies may be viewed as commodities that have specifiable prices in terms of the domestic currency. These prices, or rates of exchange, express the relative values of the two currencies. Historically, these rates purported to equate the gold content of the different currencies. However, this is no longer a significant relationship. Presently, two principal types of exchange rates are important.

- Free rates, which reflect the fluctuating market prices of the currency as an economic good (a function of supply and demand)
- Official rates, which are established by the governments for varying purposes

A given country may have several official rates, each of which pertains to a designated type of economic and financial activity and which reflects governmental policies in respect to desired economic development. For example, one rate may apply to the conversion of a country's currency for the purpose of importing new capital goods into the country, and a less favourable rate for conversion of its currency—for example, in order to make dividend payments to its country's company's shareholders domiciled in another country. The existence of a multiple rate structure requires the choice of a rate for financial accounting purposes by individuals doing business with, or holding ownership interests in, companies located in such a country. Once this is done, the particular accounting problems lie in (a) accounting for foreign currency transactions (the deals entered into terms of foreign currency and not the domestic currency that is the accounting basis), and in the (b) proper presentation and valuation of these at the year end in the financial statements and the translating of foreign currency financial statements/data so as to incorporate the same into the enterprise's consolidated financial statements.

DIRECT AND INDIRECT METHODS OF EXCHANGE RATES

Following are the two normally accepted methods of determining exchange rates:

Direct Method

Under the direct method, the foreign exchange rate of a foreign currency is expressed as the number of units of home currency (local, domestic currency, i.e., Indian Rupees for Indian sub-continent, US $ for USA, etc.). Under this method, the number of units of foreign currency is kept constant (normally a unit, with exceptions, namely Japanese Yen, in which Yen is taken as 100 if Yen is foreign currency) and any change in the exchange rate will be made by changing the value of local currency or home currency or domestic currency. For

> *Direct quote means one unit of foreign currency equals to number of units of local currency.*

example, Indian ₹72/US$1 means US dollar 1.00 = Indian Rupees 72 would be a direct exchange rate for the US dollar in India, and US$1.00 = Japanese Yen 93.25 is a direct quote for Japan.

Indirect Method

Under the indirect method, the foreign exchange rate is quoted as the number of units of foreign currency for a unit of local currency. Under this method, the number of units of the foreign currency is stated in exchange of a unit of local currency. Thus, in the indirect method, the number of units of the local currency is kept constant and the number of units of the foreign currency changes. Under the indirect method, any change in the exchange rate is stated as a change in the number of units of the foreign currency. For example, US$1.3889/Indian ₹100 means US dollar 1.3889 = Indian Rupees 100 is an indirect quotation in India for the US dollar.

Majority of countries in the globe use direct quote in the local domicile area. Table 18.1 is an example of both types of quotations for illustrative understanding.

TABLE 18.1 Direct and indirect quotations (for Indian sub-continent)

Country (Currency)	Direct Quotation	Indirect Quotation
USA (US $)	₹72/US $	US$1.3889/₹100
UK (Sterling Pound; £)	₹89/£	£1.1236/₹100
France (Euro; €)	₹75/€	€1.3333/₹100

If the exchanged currencies are to be delivered immediately, the exchange rate is referred to as the *spot rate*. In addition to immediate delivery, a market also exists for future delivery of exchanged currencies (for example, in 30, 90, or 180 days). A

> *Indirect quote means one unit of local currency equals to the number of units of foreign currency.*

future rate or *forward rate* expresses the rate of exchange that is presently agreed upon for a future date. The futures market allows a company to hedge against fluctuations in the spot exchange rate.

At present, certain accounting translations are based upon exchange rates in effect at different points in time. A current exchange rate is a rate prevailing at a balance sheet date, and a historical exchange rate is a rate that existed at the time a particular transaction or event took place.

TRANSLATION

Translation is the process of restating recorded financial data from one currency to another. This effort is necessary in several different situations. First, an Indian entity may either be selling to or buying from a foreign entity. The currency of settlement, if other than Indian rupee, until paid, results in a receivable or payable which will require conversion to Indian currency

at the date of the initial transaction and again at the date of the financial statements for the Indian entity. Strictly and technically, this may not be regarded as translation because the basic transaction is converted before recording. It may be referred to as *foreign exchange transaction*, and would require accounting to the extent of recording transactions termed in foreign currency and to be settled later in foreign currency and other related and allied issues.

Second, an Indian entity may be either a borrower or lender of foreign currency. When this happens, the resulting payable or receivable if denominated (payment required in) in foreign currency and foreign currency holdings, if any, must be restated in Indian currency at the date of the transaction and again at the date of subsequent financial statements.

Third, whenever a domestic entity (Indian entity) is doing business in a foreign country through a branch, division, investee, or subsidiary, the financial records of the foreign operation are normally kept in terms of the local currency. The resulting financial and operating results will have to be restated in terms of the Indian rupee before they can be combined with those from Indian corporations.

As already stated earlier, one of the important accounting problems of foreign operations relates to transactions between enterprises that are located in two different countries having different currencies. Figure 18.1 depicts such transactions.

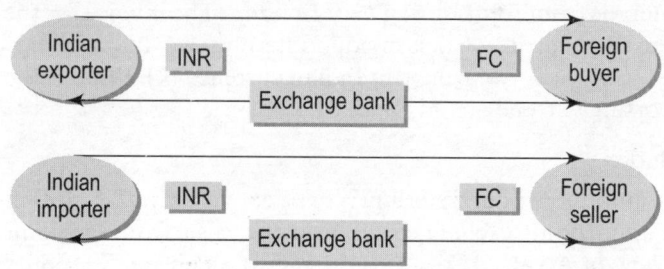

FIG. 18.1 Foreign transactions

Note:
FC = Foreign currency
INR = Indian rupee

In such instances, one of the parties to the transaction must accept its obligation (or receive its payment) in terms of a foreign currency. The party that undertakes this frequently incurs an exchange gain or loss, depending upon the direction and amount of the fluctuation in exchange rates between the date of billing and the date of payment. For example, if a domestic importer who purchases merchandise abroad is billed in a foreign currency, the invoice amount may be translated into domestic currency through the current rate of exchange (free or official) at the billing date. To extinguish the created debt, the domestic importer must acquire foreign currency within the billing date and the due date for payment. In the event exchange rates have fluctuated in the period between the date of purchase and the subsequent acquisition of foreign currency, gain or loss clearly results and identifies with, that is, confers or falls upon, the domestic importer. If the billing has

been expressed in domestic monetary units, the exchange risk would have been with the foreign exporter. A parallel may be easily drawn for a domestic exporter and a foreign importer. This has to be properly accounted for.

ACCOUNTING STANDARDS

The Institute of Chartered Accountants of India, which is the sole authority to issue the Accounting Standards, has issued Accounting Standard 11 (Ind AS 21) to cover the area of foreign exchange transactions. This applies for accounting of transactions in foreign currency and for converting statements of foreign branches to be included in head office accounts. The terms relevant to Ind AS 21 are explained in this section.

Relevant Business Terms

At present times, which is an era of borderless trading and business, the knowledge of foreign currency and international business terms helps a lot. Let us now discuss these important terms in this section.

Reporting currency   It is the currency used in presenting the financial statements. In the case of an Indian company, the Indian rupee is the reporting currency.

Foreign currency   It is a currency other than the reporting currency of an enterprise. In the case of an Indian party, all other currencies are foreign currencies.

Exchange rate   It is the ratio for exchange of two currencies as applicable to the realization of a specific asset, the payment of a specific liability, the recording of a specific transaction, or a group of inter-related transactions.

Average rate   It is the mean of the exchange rates in force during a period.

Forward rate   It is the exchange rate established by the terms of an agreement for exchange of two currencies at a specified future date.

Closing rate   It is the exchange rate at the balance sheet date.

Exchange difference   It is the difference resulting from reporting the same number of units of a foreign currency in the reporting currency at different exchange rates.

Monetary items   Money held and assets and liabilities to be received or paid in fixed or determinable amounts of money, for example, cash, receivables, and payables are referred to as monetary items.

Non-monetary items   Assets and liabilities other than monetary items, for example, fixed assets, inventories, and investments in equity shares are referred to as non-monetary items.

Settlement date   It is the date at which a receivable is due to be collected or a payable is due to be paid.

Recoverable amount   It is the amount which the enterprise expects to recover from the future use of an asset, including its residual value on disposal.

Specific rate   It is the exchange rate as defined in the financial statement with reference to a specific asset, liability, or transaction, or a group of inter-related transactions.

Inter-related transactions   Two or more transactions are considered inter-related if, by virtue of being set off against one another or otherwise, they affect the net amount of reporting currency that will be available for settlement of those transactions.

Foreign currency bank account   It is the bank account where realizations are deposited into and disbursements are made from.

Independent transactions   Where transactions cannot be considered inter-related as specified before, the receivables and payables are reported at the rates applicable to the respective amounts even where there are receivable from or payable to the same foreign party.

Spot/average rate   A transaction in foreign currency is recorded in the books of accounts on the date on which the transaction occurs at the exchange rate on that date. This exchange rate is referred to as the spot rate.

■ **ILLUSTRATION 18.2**   Krishna Corporation, an Indian company, sold merchandise worth US$1,000 to East-West Company of New York when the rate of exchange between rupees and dollars was ₹70.00. The billing is expressed in rupees/dollars as follows:

(a) ₹70,000
(b) US$1,000

Krishna Corporation purchased merchandise from Amita Company, which is based in USA, when the rate of exchange between the rupee and the US$ was ₹69.50. The billing is expressed in rupees/dollars as follows:

(a) ₹62,550
(b) US$900

Ignoring the effects of commissions and other service charges, show the entries in the books of Krishna Corporation for these transactions.

Solution

Particulars		(a) Where Billing is in Domestic Currency (Rupees)		(b) Where Billing is in Foreign Currency (Dollars)	
1. East-West Co. A/c (*Add*)	Dr.	70,000		70,000	
To Sales A/c (*Add*)			70,000		70,000
2. Purchases A/c (*Add*)	Dr.	62,550		62,550	
To Amita Co. A/c (*Less*)			62,550		62,550

EXCHANGE GAIN/LOSS

When the transaction is to be settled on a future date, the exchange rate on the date of transaction (purchase/sale) and on the date of settlement may be different. This difference results in accounting of two transactions at different conversion rates. The difference is termed as exchange loss or gain. This initial recognition's accounting is embodied in Ind AS 21 as 'A foreign currency transaction should be recorded on initial recognition in the reporting currency by applying to the foreign currency amount the exchange rate between the reporting currency and the foreign currency at the date of the transaction'.

■ **ILLUSTRATION 18.3** The payment of the East-West Company account with Krishna Corporation was received when the exchange rate was ₹70.50. Krishna Corporation made remittance to Amita Company when the exchange rate was ₹69.75. Ignoring the effects of commissions and other service charges, show the entries in the books of Krishna Corporation for these transactions.

Solution

Particulars		(a) Where Billing is in Domestic Currency (Rupees)		(b) Where Billing is in Foreign Currency (Dollars)	
1. Bank A/c (*Add*)	Dr.	70,000	—	70,500	
To Exchange gain A/c (*Add*)					500
To East Indies Co. A/c (*Less*)			70,000		70,000
2. Amita Co. A/c (*Less*)	Dr.	62,550		62,550	
Exchange loss A/c (*Add*)	Dr.			225	
To Cash A/c (*Less*)			62,550		62,775

These entries illustrate two important features of accounting for foreign currency transactions. First, on the date of sale or purchase, the transaction is measured and recorded in rupees in the books of Krishna Corporation (an Indian company using rupee as its unit of measure) at the same value under the two alternative billing assumptions. If the billing is in units of foreign currency, the rupee measure is obtained by multiplying the units of foreign currency by the prevailing spot exchange rate. In either case, the rupee amount recorded presumably reflects the value (in rupees) of the merchandise purchased or sold. Second, the billing terms place the risk of foreign currency exchange rate fluctuations on one company or the other. If the billing is in domestic currency units, Krishna Corporation is not exposed to any risk from exchange rate fluctuations. Regardless of the exchange rate prevailing on the date the transaction is settled, the amount of rupees received or paid is fixed in the contract, and is equal to the amount recorded on the date of sale or purchase. Therefore, no exchange gain or loss can occur. This situation is illustrated in column (a) for transactions (1) and (2).

On the other hand, if the billing is in foreign currency units, Krishna Corporation assumes the risk of foreign currency fluctuations. Herein, the reporting currency is Indian rupees (₹) and for US dollars ($). For example, in the sale to East-West Company, billing alternative (b) specifies a contract price of 1,000 dollars. On the date this transaction is settled, East-West Company discharges its obligation by remitting US$1,000, regardless of the exchange rate on that date. In transaction (1), it is assumed that Krishna Corporation immediately converts these foreign currency units into Indian rupees at the prevailing exchange rate US$1,000 × ₹70.50 = ₹70,500. The exchange gain of ₹500 results from the collection of ₹70,500 in full settlement of amount valued at ₹70,000.

The risk of exchange gains or losses can be hedged by buying or selling foreign currency for future delivery on the same date a company purchases or sells merchandise with payment terms denominated in foreign currency units.

When an Indian business sells its products to a foreign buyer, the transaction will be paid for either in a foreign currency or in Indian rupees. If the transaction is to be settled in Indian rupees, the Indian business will not incur any gain or loss on currency exchange. In this case, any change in the exchange ratio between Indian rupee and the foreign currency between the date of sale and date of payment will result in an exchange gain or loss to the foreign buyer. If, on the other hand, the transaction is to be paid for in units of the foreign currency, the Indian business will incur an exchange gain or loss.

■ **ILLUSTRATION 18.4** To illustrate the earlier discussions, assume that the original sales/purchase transaction for US$2,000 was recorded as follows. When the exchange rate was 1 unit of foreign currency (FC) to ₹70 with payment to be made in dollars.

Solution

Indian Seller			
Accounts receivable (in ₹) A/c (*Add*)	Dr.	1,40,000	
To Sales (in ₹) A/c (*Add*)			1,40,000
Foreign Purchaser			
Purchases (in US$) A/c (*Add*)	Dr.	2,000	
To Accounts payable (in US$) A/c (*Add*)			2,000

Suppose this transaction is paid for 30 days later when the exchange ratio has changed to 1 FC units to ₹67.60, the journal entry will be as follows:

Indian Seller (in ₹)			
Bank A/c (*Less*)	Dr.	1,35,200	
Loss on currency exchange A/c (*Add*)		4,800	
To Accounts receivable A/c (*Less*)			1,40,000
Foreign Purchaser (in US$)			
Accounts payable A/c (*Less*)	Dr.	2,000	
To Bank A/c (*Less*)			2,000

PROVISION FOR CHANGES IN EXCHANGE RATES

Until now, we have concentrated on the accounting aspects of recognition of the revenue (sale) and its settlement of account. However, if there were an intervening balance sheet date, the question arises as to the accounting position of the related items, that is, how they should be valued/presented in the balance sheet. The receivables or payables denominated in foreign currency are valued at the current exchange (spot) rate resulting in exchange gain or loss, which should be recognized as a separate item.

The Ind AS 21 stipulates the following.

Monetary Items

Foreign currency (e.g., foreign currency notes, balances in bank accounts denominated in a foreign currency, and receivables, payables, and loans denominated in a foreign currency) should be reported using the closing rate. However, in certain circumstances, the closing rate may not reflect with reasonable accuracy the amount in reporting currency that is likely to be realized from, or required to disburse, a foreign currency monetary item at the balance sheet date. For example, where

there are restrictions on remittances or where the closing rate is unrealistic and it is not possible to effect an exchange of currencies at that rate at the balance sheet date, in such circumstances, the relevant monetary item should be reported in the reporting currency at the amount that is likely to be realized from, or required to disburse, such item at the balance sheet date.

Non-monetary Items

Such items other than fixed assets, which are carried in terms of historical cost denominated in a foreign currency, should be reported using the exchange rate on the date of the transaction (e.g., investments or inventories carried at cost).

Non-monetary Items Other than Fixed Assets

The non-monetary items other than fixed assets, which are carried in terms of fair value or other similar valuation, for example, net realizable value, denominated in a foreign currency (e.g., inventories carried at market value being lower than cost), should be reported using exchange rates that existed when the values were determined, that is, in other words, the 'closing rate' (e.g., inventories). If the said values were determined on the balance sheet date, then the rates on the balance sheet date is the closing rate.

Exchange Differences

The exchange differences arising from foreign currency transactions should be recognized as income or as expense in the period in which they arise.

The exchange difference arising on repayment of liabilities incurred for the purpose of acquiring fixed assets, which are carried in terms of historical cost, should be adjusted in the carrying amount of the respective fixed assets. The carrying amount of such fixed assets should, to the extent not already so adjusted or otherwise accounted for, also be adjusted to account for any addition or decrease in the liability of the enterprise, as expressed in the reporting currency by applying the closing rate, for making payment towards the whole or a part of the money borrowed by the enterprise from any person, directly or indirectly, in foreign currency specifically for the purpose of acquiring those assets.

The carrying amount of fixed assets, which are carried in terms of revalued amounts, should also be adjusted in the manner described earlier. However, such adjustment should not result in the net book value of a class of revalued fixed assets exceeding the recoverable amount of assets of that class. The remaining amount of the increase in liability, if any, is debited to the revaluation reserve, or to the profit and loss statement in the event of inadequacy or absence of the revaluation reserve.

An exchange difference results when there is a change in the exchange rate between the transaction date and the date of settlement of any monetary items arising from a foreign currency transaction. When the transaction is settled within the same accounting period as that in which it occurred, the entire exchange difference arises in that period. However, when the transaction is not settled in the same accounting period as that in which it occurred, the exchange difference arises over more than one accounting period, or is spread over two accounting years.

> Carrying amount means the balance to be carried forward in the accounts.

■ **ILLUSTRATION 18.5** Sheeji Ltd imported goods worth of US$4,00,000 from a company in USA on 10 August, when the exchange rate was US$1 = ₹72.90. Sheeji Ltd agreed to pay its creditors in four equal instalments, on 10 September, 10 October, 10 November, and 10 December. The exchange rates on the settlement dates were as follows.

10 September	₹72.75
10 October	₹73.50
10 November	₹74.80
10 December	₹73.90

Prepare the ledger account of the US company in the books of Sheeji Ltd.

In the example considered, Sheeji Ltd sustained a net exchange loss of ₹3,35,000 (60,000 + 1,90,000 + 1,00,000 – 15,000).

Solution

Ledger Account of Sheeji Ltd

US Company Account

Type of Account: Liability   Normal Balance: Credit

Date	Reference Account	Voucher Type	Post Ref No.	Dr. (Less)			Cr. (Add)		
				US $	Rate (₹)	Amount (₹)	US $	Rate (₹)	Amount (₹)
10 Aug	By Purchase A/c						4,00,000	72.90	2,91,60,000
10 Sep	To Bank A/c			1,00,000	72.75	72,75,000			
	To Exchange fluctuation A/c					15,000			
10 Oct	To Bank A/c			1,00,000	73.50	73,50,000			
10 Oct	By Exchange fluctuation A/c								60,000
10 Nov	To Bank A/c			1,00,000	74.80	74,80,000			
10 Nov	By Exchange fluctuation A/c								1,90,000
10 Dec	To Bank A/c			1,00,000	73.90	73,90,000			
10 Dec	By Exchange fluctuation A/c								1,00,000
	Total			4,00,000		2,95,10,000	4,00,000		2,95,10,000

Note:

Exchange fluctuations account represents the difference in value in local currency at the time of realizing the transaction as receivables and payables.

As per Ind AS 21, the net loss arising due to fluctuation in the exchange rate should be charged to the income statement. If there is an exchange fluctuation loss in one account and a gain in another account, only the net gain/loss is shown in the income statement.

■ **ILLUSTRATION 18.6** Jasmin Ltd purchased a machine costing US$4,00,000 for which credit was provided by a financial institution. The terms of the financing arrangement were to repay the principal in five equal instalments together with the interest on the outstanding amount at 15% p.a. The machine was installed by the end of the first year. The exchange rates are given in the following text.

At the time of purchase (Year 0)	$1 = ₹71.50
At the end of 1st year (Year 1)	$1 = ₹73.00
At the end of 2nd year (Year 2)	$1 = ₹72.50
At the end of 3rd year (Year 3)	$1 = ₹73.50
At the end of 4th year (Year 4)	$1 = ₹73.50
At the end of 5th year (Year 5)	$1 = ₹72.75

You are required to state the carrying amount of fixed assets as at the end of year 1, year 2, year 3, year 4, and year 5. Ignore depreciation on the machine.

Solution

At the end of year 1 (T1):	
Price paid for the asset	$4,00,000
Interest paid during installation period @ 15% for one year	$60,000
	$4,60,000

	Amount (₹)
$4,60,000 translated to exchange rate of $1 = ₹71.50, that is, 4,60,000 × 71.50	3,28,90,000
Add: Loss on foreign exchange liability $4,60,000 × (₹73.00 – ₹71.50)	6,90,000
Carrying cost of the asset	3,22,00,000
At the end of year 2 (T2):	
Carrying cost at T1 as calculated before	3,22,00,000
Less: Gain on foreign exchange liability Outstanding $3,20,000 × (₹73.00 – ₹72.50)	1,60,000
Carrying cost at T2	3,20,40,000
At the end of year 3 (T3):	
Carrying cost at T2 as calculated before	3,20,40,000
Add: Loss on foreign exchange liability Outstanding $2,40,000 × (₹73.50 – ₹72.50)	2,40,000
Carrying cost at T3	3,22,80,000

At the end of year 4 (T4):	
Carrying cost at T3 as calculated before	3,22,80,000
There is no change in the carrying cost as there is no fluctuation in the exchange rate. Therefore, the carrying cost at T4 will also be	3,22,80,000
At the end of year 5 (T5):	
Carrying cost at T4 as calculated before	3,22,80,000
Less: Gain on foreign exchange liability Outstanding $80,000 × (₹73.50 – ₹72.75)	60,000
Carrying cost at T5	3,22,20,000

Instalment payment is assumed to be made after year end and interest is assumed to be charged on opening balance.

Note:

Instalment payment is assumed to be made after year end.

Working Note:

$4,00,000 is repayable in five equal instalments. Repayment schedule will be as follows:

Year		Amount ($)
1	Principal	4,00,000
	Less: Repayment	80,000
2	Principal	3,20,000
	Less: Repayment	80,000
3	Principal	2,40,000
	Less: Repayment	80,000
4	Principal	1,60,000
	Less: Repayment	80,000
5	Principal	80,000

■ **ILLUSTRATION 18.7** Pass journal entries for the following foreign exchange transactions in the books of Soham Ltd of Pune. Soham Ltd exported goods worth US$1,00,000 on 12 January 2019 to Universal Traders of USA. The payment for the same was received as follows:

15 February 2019	$50,000
2 March 2019	$10,000
12 April 2019	$40,000

The company follows the financial year as its accounting year.

The exchange rate for US$1 was as follows.

12 January 2019	₹71
15 February 2019	₹73
2 March 2019	₹70
31 March 2019	₹74
12 April 2019	₹75

Solution

Journal Entries in the Books of Soham Ltd

Date	Particulars		Dr. (₹)	Cr. (₹)
2019	Universal Traders A/c (*Add*)	Dr.	71,00,000	
12 Jan	To Export sales A/c (*Add*)			71,00,000
	(Being export of goods, exchange rate is $1 = ₹71)			
15 Feb	Bank A/c (*Add*)	Dr.	36,50,000	
	To Universal Traders A/c (*Less*)			35,50,000
	To Foreign exchange fluctuation A/c (*Add*)			1,00,000
	(Being amount received $50,000 @ ₹73 fluctuation $50,000 × (73 – 71))			
2 Mar	Bank A/c (*Add*)	Dr.	7,00,000	
	Foreign exchange fluctuation A/c (*Less*)	Dr.	10,000	
	To Universal Traders A/c (*Less*)			7,10,000
	(Being amount received $10,000 @ ₹70, fluctuation $10,000 × (70 – 71))			
31 Mar	Universal Traders A/c (*Add*)	Dr.	1,20,000	
	To Foreign exchange fluctuation A/c (*Add*)			1,20,000
	(Being difference in foreign exchange accounted for at the end of the year $40,000 × (74 – 71))			
31 Mar	Foreign exchange fluctuation A/c (*Less*)	Dr.	2,10,000	
	To Profit and loss A/c (*Add*)			2,10,000
	(Being profit on foreign exchange fluctuation transfer to profit and loss A/c)			
12 Apr	Bank A/c (*Add*)	Dr.	30,00,000	
	To Universal Traders A/c (*Less*)			29,60,000
	To Foreign exchange fluctuation A/c (*Add*)			40,000
	(Being amount received $40,000 @ ₹75, fluctuation $40,000 × (75 – 74))			

FORWARD EXCHANGE RATE

When an enterprise has to receive or pay foreign currency on a future date, it may enter into a forward contract to be sure of the amount receivable or payable in terms of the home currency. For example, if an enterprise has to receive US$1,00,000 on 30 April on the account of export made on 1 January, in order to be sure of the amount, it may sell dollars forward on 1 January at US$1 = ₹72.50. On that day, the spot rate may be US$1 = ₹73, whereas the forward rate agreed is US$1 = ₹72.50.

The Ind AS 21 stipulates the following:

- An enterprise may enter into a forward exchange contract, or another financial instrument that is in substance a forward exchange contract, to establish the amount of the reporting currency required or available at the settlement date of a transaction. The difference between the forward rate and the exchange rate at the date of the transaction should be recognized as income or expense over the life of the contract, except in respect of liabilities incurred for acquiring fixed assets, in which case, such difference should be adjusted in the 'carrying' amount of the respective fixed assets.

- The difference between the forward rate and the exchange rate at the inception of a forward exchange contract is recognized as income or expense over the life of the contract. The only exception is in respect of forward exchange contracts related to liabilities in foreign currency incurred for acquisition of fixed assets.

- Any profit or loss on cancellation or renewal of a forward exchange contract should be recognized as income or as expense for the period, except in the case of a forward exchange contract relating to liabilities for acquiring fixed assets, in which case, such profit or loss should be adjusted in the 'carrying' amount of the respective fixed assets.

In the illustration discussed earlier, when the dollars are received, the enterprise would receive ₹72,50,000 in terms of the forward exchange contract. The advantage of such an agreement is that the enterprise stands to gain if the spot rate is, say, $1 = ₹71. However, if the spot rate on 30 April is more than the forward rate, the enterprise stands to lose. In relation to future liabilities also, forward contracts can be entered into in order to be sure of the liability in terms of the home currency.

The standard requires recognition of the difference between the forward rate and the exchange rate at the date of transaction as income or expense over the life of the contract. In the example given earlier, there is a loss of 50 paise on every dollar sold forward since the spot rate is more than the forward rate. Therefore, the total loss of ₹50,000 should be recognized over the contract period. If the contract period is not confined to one accounting period, it should be allocated to the accounting periods concerned on a time basis. Likewise, any profit or loss arising on cancellation of a forward contract should be recognized as income or expense for the period.

■ **ILLUSTRATION 18.8** Acharya & Co. exported goods worth US$10,000 on 1 January 2020, and for the sake of security on exchange rate differences, entered into a forward exchange contract @ US$1 = ₹72.50 on the date of sale, when the spot rate was US$1 = ₹73.00. The money was due 4 months after the date of sale.

Pass the necessary journal entries in the books of Acharya & Co.

Solution

Journal Entries in the Books of Acharya & Co.

Date	Particulars		Dr. (₹)	Cr. (₹)
2020 1 Jan	Customer Co. A/c (*Add*) To Sales A/c (*Add*) (Being export of goods)	Dr.	7,30,000	7,30,000
1 Jan	US dollars (Receivable) A/c (*Add*) Loss on forward exchange contract A/c (*Add*) To Contractor's A/c (₹ payable) (*Add*) (Being amount payable to the contractor)	Dr. Dr.	7,25,000 5,000	7,30,000
31 Mar	Profit and loss account (*Add*) To Loss on forward exchange contract A/c (*Less*) (Being the loss on forward exchange contract transferred to profit and loss account) 5,000 × ¾	Dr.	3,750	3,750
30 Apr	Contractor (Payable) A/c (*Less*) To US dollars (Receivable) A/c (*Less*) To Bank A/c (*Less*) (Being payment made to the contractor)	Dr.	7,30,000	7,25,000 5,000
30 Apr	Profit and loss account (*Less*) To Loss on forward exchange contract (*Less*) (Being the loss on forward exchange contract transferred to profit and loss account) (5,000 × ¼)	Dr.	1,250	1,250

■ **ILLUSTRATION 18.9** On 1 January 2020, an Indian importer contracts with a customer to sell for ₹4,00,000 equipment that will be manufactured by a German firm. Delivery is to be in 18 months. On 1 January 2020, the spot rate for the euro (EUR) is ₹0.40 and the cost to the Indian importer is 8,00,000 euros. Since 8,00,000 euros are equivalent to ₹3,20,000, the contract sales price of ₹4,00,000 promises a gross margin to the seller of ₹80,000 (at spot rates). In order to ensure this potential margin, the importer enters into a forward commitment to purchase 8,00,000 euros in 18 months from Rico & Clay, foreign exchange brokers, at the forward rate of ₹0.41. (There is a premium on the euro because the consensus is that the euro will advance relative to the Indian rupee.) Assume further that the following spot rates for euros exist at subsequent dates.

30 June 2020	₹0.44
31 December 2020	₹0.46
30 June 2021	₹0.53

Give journal entries to summarize the transactions in the books of the Indian importer.

Solution

Journal Entries in the Books of the Indian Importer

Date	Particulars		Dr. (₹)	Cr. (₹)
2020	Forward currency purchased A/c (€8,00,000 × ₹0.40) (*Add*) Premium on futures contract (*Less*) To Due to exchange broker (*Add*) (Being import of goods)	Dr. Dr.	3,20,000 8,000	3,28,000
31 Dec	Forward currency purchased A/c (*Add*) To Deferred exchange gain A/c (*Add*) (€8,00,000 (₹0.46 – ₹0.40))	Dr.	48,000	48,000
2021 30 June	Forward currency purchased A/c To Deferred exchange gain A/c (*Add*) (€8,00,000 (₹0.53 – ₹0.46))	Dr.	56,000	56,000
	Due to exchange broker A/c (*Less*) To cash in bank A/c (*Less*)	Dr.	3,28,000	3,28,000
	Merchandise inventory A/c (*Add*) To Voucher payable A/c (*Add*) (€8,00,000 × ₹0.53)	Dr.	4,24,000	4,24,000
	Foreign currency A/c (*Add*) To Forward currency purchased A/c (*Less*) (₹3,20,000 + ₹48,000 + ₹56,000)	Dr.	4,24,000	4,24,000
	Vouchers payable A/c (*Less*) To Foreign currency (₹) A/c (*Less*)	Dr.	4,24,000	4,24,000
	Deferred exchange gain A/c (*Less*) (₹48,000 + ₹56,000) To Premium on futures contract A/c (*Add*) To Merchandise inventory A/c (*Less*)	Dr.	1,04,000	8,000 96,000
	Accounts receivables A/c (*Add*) To Sales A/c (*Add*)	Dr.	4,00,000	4,00,000
	Cost of goods sold A/c (*Add*) To Merchandise inventory A/c (*Less*) (₹4,24,000 – ₹96,000)	Dr.	3,28,000	3,28,000

Working Notes:

1. The foreign currency receivable (foreign currency purchased) is adjusted at each balance sheet date to reflect the current spot rate. The calculated exchange gains and the premiums on the futures contract are deferred to the date of the transaction; they are then recognized as adjustments to the recorded acquisition cost of the merchandise. An alternative treatment of discount or premium on such a futures contract is to amortize the cost against operations over the contract life.

2. In summary, the importer paid a total of ₹3,28,000 to acquire equipment for which the customer was invoiced ₹4,00,000. The importer has achieved a gross margin of ₹72,000, which equals the desired margin of ₹80,000 less the premium on the futures contract of ₹8,000. If the importer had not obtained a forward currency commitment, its cost on 30 June 2013 would have been ₹4,24,000, and thus it would have sustained a loss of ₹24,000.

HEDGING TRANSACTIONS

To guard against the hazards of loss from exchange rate fluctuations, a domestic importer, concurrent with the purchase of merchandise abroad, may also purchase foreign currency for future delivery. Billing and settlement are thereby made in terms of the same rate of exchange. A similar precaution may be taken in respect to a domestic exporter, who may elect to sell foreign currency for future delivery where the settlement of the

> *Hedging means guarding the firm against risk of loss on account of foreign exchange rate fluctuations.*

accounts receivable is to be made in foreign monetary units. This is known as hedging.

Under currency policy measurement and reporting principles applicable to forward contracts, the following sequence has to be adopted to account for the exchange price fluctuations.

- Hedge of a foreign currency commitment
- Hedge of a foreign currency exposed to net asset or liability position
- Speculation in foreign currency exchange price fluctuations

■ **ILLUSTRATION 18.10** The use of a forward exchange contract in the futures market to hedge an operating transaction is illustrated in the context of Krishna Corporation's transaction with Amita Company. Assume the following transactions.

- Krishna Corporation purchased merchandise from Amita Company for US$900 when the exchange rate between rupee and dollar was ₹72.50. Concurrent with the purchase of merchandise, Krishna Corporation also purchased US$900 for future delivery (on a date coinciding with the due date of the obligation to Amita Company) at ₹72.50.
- On the due date of the obligation to Amita Company, Krishna Corporation took delivery of the US$900 on the futures contract and remitted these to Amita Company in full settlement of its account. On this date, the exchange rate between rupee and a dollar was ₹72.75.

Ignoring the effects of commissions and other service charges, record the entries in the books of Krishna Corporation for these transactions.

Solution

Journal Entries in the Books of Krishna Corporation

Particulars		Merchandise Purchase Transaction (₹)		Hedging Transaction (₹)	
1. Purchases A/c (*Add*)	Dr.	65,250			
To Accounts payable (Amita company) A/c (*Add*)			65,250		
Dollars receivable from exchange broker A/c (*Add*)	Dr.			65,250	
To Rupees payable to exchange broker A/c (*Add*)					65,250
2. Foreign currency (Dollars) A/c (*Add*)	Dr.			65,475	
To Exchange gain or loss A/c (*Add*)					225
To Dollars receivable from exchange broker A/c (*Less*)					65,250
3. Rupees payable to exchange broker A/c (*Less*)	Dr.			65,250	
To Cash A/c (*Less*)					65,250
4. Accounts payable (Amita company) A/c (*Less*)	Dr.	65,250			
Exchange gain or loss A/c (*Less*)	Dr.	225			
To Foreign currency (dollars) A/c (*Less*)			65,475		

The entries related to the hedging transactions are displayed separately to distinguish the effects of currency exchange rate fluctuations on this forward exchange contract from the same effects on the account payable to the supplier (Amita Company). Since the spot and forward exchange rates were assumed equal (although there is usually a small difference), the exchange gain on the forward contract exactly offsets the exchange loss on accounts payable denominated in dollars.

This is precisely the desired effect when a forward exchange contract is purchased to hedge an open account payable (or receivable). It is achieved because the hedge eliminates the risk of future currency rate fluctuations on the payable denominated in units of foreign currency through the purchase of the required number of dollars for delivery on the date the account is to be settled. Thus, on the settlement date, Krishna Corporation receives US$900 from the exchange broker at the

previously agreed price in rupees (₹65,250), and these dollars are remitted to Amita Company. Whatever the exchange rate on the settlement date, it has no economic impact (favourable or unfavourable) upon Krishna Corporation.

DEPRECIATION

According to Ind AS 21, where the carrying amount of a depreciable asset has undergone a change, the depreciation on the revised unamortized depreciable amount should be provided in accordance with the Accounting Standards (Ind AS 16, depreciation accounting).

■ **ILLUSTRATION 18.11** Sunil Technologies Ltd purchased fixed assets costing ₹35 lakhs on 1 April 2020. The purchase was fully financed by a foreign currency loan in US dollars repayable in five equal annual instalments. The loan was obtained when the dollar was equal to ₹70. On 31 March 2021, the first instalment was repaid and the dollar rate at the time of payment moved to ₹72. The entire loss on exchange was included in the cost of goods sold. Sunil Technologies Ltd provides depreciation on fixed assets at 20% on written down value basis.

> Foreign currency loan in foreign currency = Amount of loan received in local currency/Exchange rate applicable on the date of loan

How would you deal with these items in the financial statements for the year 2021?

Solution

As per Paragraph 10 of Ind AS 21, exchange loss/gain arising on repayment of liabilities incurred for the purpose of acquiring assets, which are carried in terms of historical cost, should be adjusted in the carrying amount of fixed assets. The carrying amount should also be adjusted for any increase or decrease in the outstanding liability of the foreign currency loan on account of fluctuations in the foreign exchange rate.

Therefore, the entire loss on exchange should be added to the carrying amount and further depreciation should be provided in accordance with Ind AS 16 on depreciation accounting.

$$\text{Foreign currency loan} = \frac{₹35,00,000}{₹70}$$

$$= \$50,000$$

Exchange loss as on
31/3/2021 $= \$50,000 (₹72 – ₹70)$

$= ₹1,00,000$

In the balance sheet, the carrying amount of fixed assets (before depreciation) will be as follows:

₹35 lakhs + ₹1 lakh = ₹36 lakhs

Foreign currency loan will appear as:

$\$40,000 \times ₹72 = ₹28,80,000$

Further depreciation at 20% on ₹1,00,000 will have to be provided. Since exchange loss has been included in cost of goods sold by way of rectification, fixed assets must be debited with the amount and credited to the cost of goods sold account.

TRANSLATIONS OF FOREIGN CURRENCY

Multinational firms required to prepare consolidated financial statements incorporating the results of both domestic and foreign operations often face a problem when the components of financial statements are denominated in different currencies. Hence, the need arises to change the financial statements of subsidiary denominated in foreign currency (FC) to local currency (LC) or home currency (HC). For this, the following points need to be concentrated upon.

Translation of independent transactions Independent transactions are translated at the exchange rate prevailing on the date of the transaction. The exchange rate is known as spot rate. Average rate is applied for all the transactions during the concerned week or month.

Translation of inter-related transactions In the case of inter-related transactions, the net amount due is translated and reported at the rate of exchange applicable. Deposits and payments in the foreign currency bank account are also inter-related transactions. They are translated at the average rate during the period, that is, a week or a month.

Translation of balances at year end After the initial recognition, balances are translated for preparing the balance sheet at the end of the year. The balances of the following items in foreign currency are to be translated into rupees.

Monetary items Monetary items are money held and assets or liabilities to be settled in fixed amount of money, that is, foreign currency notes included in cash, bank balance, debtors, creditors, loans, etc.

Non-monetary items Non-monetary items are assets and liabilities other than monetary items, that is, fixed assets, stock, and investment in equity shares.

Rate of translation Translation of various items is done as per the following rates.

Monetary items Balances of various monetary items such as cash, debtors, and creditors should be translated at the closing rate. Wherever closing rate is not realistic, such items should be translated at the expected realizable value.

Non-monetary non-fixed assets carried at historical cost Balances of non-monetary items other than fixed assets, namely inventory, valued at historical cost and denominated in a foreign currency should be translated at the historical cost, that is, at the exchange rate on the date of the original transaction.

Non-monetary non-fixed assets carried at fair value The balances of non-monetary items other than fixed assets which are carried at fair value should be translated at the exchange rate that existed when such value was decided.

Purchase of fixed assets out of foreign currency loans According to the revised Ind AS 21, the foreign currency difference occurred will be debited or credited to the income statement arising on long-term foreign currency monetary items, whether they are assets or liabilities. Till 31 March 2011, the firm was allowed to capitalize the asset linked foreign currency difference in the asset account, and to modify the depreciable value of the asset accordingly.

NET INVESTMENT IN FOREIGN EQUITY

After the foreign subsidiary company's account balances as per its trial balance are translated into domestic currency, the net difference in the trial balance as translated should be dealt with as follows:

Exchange differences arising on a monetary item that forms part of an enterprise's net investment in a foreign entity should be classified as separate components of equity in the reporting enterprise's financial statements until the disposal of the net investment at which time they should be recognized as income/expense.

Exchange differences arising on a foreign currency/liability accounted for as a hedge of an enterprise's net investment in a foreign entity should be classified as equity in the enterprise's financial statements until the disposal of the net investment at which time they should be recognized as income/expense.

The separate component, which is attributed to the net investment of the holding domestic company in its foreign subsidiary, should be adjusted against the paid capital and retained earnings. Of this, the paid-up capital should be converted at the historical exchange rate and the balance should be adjusted in the retained earnings.

■ **ILLUSTRATION 18.12** Adidas sold goods to Monte Carlo payable in euros. The invoice amounted to €19,800, the rate of exchange being €13.20 to the pound. Upon remittance, the banker credited Adidas with the proceeds of the euros, the sterling equivalent being £1,506.85, that is, 19,800 euros at 13.14 to £. No arrangement had been made for forward exchange. Show the ledger account of Monte Carlo in the seller's books.

Solution

Ledger Account of Adidas

Monte Carlo A/c
Type of Account: Asset

Normal Balance: Debit

Date	Reference Account	Voucher Type	Post Ref No.	Dr. (Add)			Cr. (Less)		
				Euro	Rate (Pound)	Amount (Pound)	Euro	Rate (Pound)	Amount (Pound)
	To Sales A/c			19,800	13.2	1,500			
	By Remittances A/c						19,800	13.14	1,506.85
	To Profit and Loss on Exchange A/c					6.85			
	Total			19,800		1,506.85	19,800		1,506.85

■ **ILLUSTRATION 18.13** Consider the same facts as discussed earlier, except that Monte Carlo pays by two remittances of €8,000 at 13.25 and €11,800 at 13.18. Show the ledger account of Monte Carlo in the seller's books.

Solution

Ledger Account of Adidas

Monte Carlo A/c
Type of Account: Asset

Normal Balance: Debit

Date	Reference Account	Voucher Type	Post Ref No.	Dr. (Add)			Cr. (Less)		
				Euro	Rate (Pound)	Amount (Pound)	Euro	Rate (Pound)	Amount (Pound)
	To Sales A/c			19,800	13.2	1,500.00			
	By Remittances A/c						8,000	13.25	603.77
	By Remittances A/c						11,800	13.18	895.30
	By Profit and Loss on Exchange A/c								0.93
	Total			19,800		1,500.00	19,800		1,500.00

If the difference in exchange was transferred on the occasion of each remittance, the foregoing account would show the following:

1. Loss of £2.29
2. Profit of £1.36

Similar principles apply when the English trader is a debtor.

FOREIGN BRANCH ACCOUNTS

When a branch of a business is located in a foreign country, it is known as a foreign branch. Such a branch will keep its books of accounts in the foreign currency. The main problem that the head office has to face under this type of branch is to convert the branch trial balance from the foreign currency

> When the branch of a business is located in a foreign country, it is known as a foreign branch.

to the currency of that country where the head office is working in order to incorporate the branch trial balance in the books of the head office. Otherwise, for all purposes, this branch is treated as an independent branch.

Rules for Converting Branch Trial Balance into Books of Head Office

The following are the main rules which should be taken into consideration while converting the figures of the foreign trial balance in the books of the head office for the purpose of their incorporation in the books of the head office.

1. If the fluctuations in the rate of exchange are neither frequent nor violent, then the branch trial balance should be converted at a fixed rate of exchange.
2. If the rate of exchange is subject to frequent and violent fluctuations, then the following rules should be adopted for converting the branch trial balance.

Fixed assets and fixed liabilities   Fixed assets should be converted at the rate of exchange prevailing on the day when these assets were purchased or on the date of contract. Similarly, fixed liabilities should be converted at the rate of exchange ruling on the day when such liabilities were incurred or the payment was received.

Floating assets/liabilities   These should be converted at the rate of exchange prevailing on the last day of the year.

Revenue items   These items should be converted at the average rate of exchange ruling during the period under review. If fluctuations are violent, then these should be converted each month at the average rate prevailing during that month.

Head office account   It is converted at the same figure at which branch accounts appear in the head office books.

Remittances   These are converted at the figures at which they appear in the head office books.

Opening and closing stock   The opening stock should be converted at the rate of exchange prevailing in the beginning of the period and closing stock should be converted at the rate prevailing on the last day of the period.

After converting the various items of the branch trial balance according to the rules discussed earlier, a new trial balance can be prepared but such trial balance will seldom tally. In order to make it agree, sometimes the difference is put in a separate account known as 'Difference in exchange account'. If the difference is small, it is closed by transfer to an income statement, but if the difference is big, it should be put under a separate account known as 'Exchange fluctuations account' and will be shown in the balance sheet either as an asset or as a liability depending on whether its balance is debit or credit. If the rate of exchange fluctuates mildly, there is less chance of a big difference.

■ **ILLUSTRATION 18.14**   Bombay Company Ltd has a branch in New York. On 31 March 2020, the trial balance of the branch was as given in the following text.

Trial Balance of New York Branch
as on 31 March 2020

Particulars	Dr. ($)	Cr. ($)
Head office account		8,500
Sales		61,000
Goods from head office A/c	44,000	
Stock on 1 April 2019	8,500	
Furniture	9,000	
Cash in hand	250	
Cash at bank	1,250	
Salaries	2,800	
Rent	1,200	
Insurance	150	
Owing for expenses		800
Sundry debtors	3,150	
	70,300	70,300

The branch account at the head office showed a debit balance of ₹3,06,500 and goods sent to branch, a credit balance of ₹18,57,000. Furniture was purchased in 2012 when US$1 = ₹60. The exchange rates were:

1 April 2019	$1 = ₹68
31 March 2020	$1 = ₹70
Average rate	$1 = ₹69

Convert the branch trial balance into rupees and prepare the branch trading and profit and loss account for the year ended on 31 March 2020, and the balance sheet on that date in the head office books. Depreciation is to be written off on furniture at 10%. The stock at branch on 31 March 2020 was valued at US$7,500.

Solution

Trial Balance of New York Branch
as on 31 March 2020

Account Name	Exchange Rate	Dr. ($)	Cr. ($)	Dr. (₹)	Cr. (₹)
Head office	Given		8,500		3,06,500
Sales	69		61,000		42,09,000
Goods from head office	Given	44,000		18,57,000	
Stock 1/4/2019	68	8,500		5,78,000	
Furniture	60	9,000		5,40,000	
Cash in hand	70	250		17,500	
Cash at bank	70	1,250		87,500	
Salaries	69	2,800		1,93,200	
Rent	69	1,200		82,800	
Insurance	70	150		10,500	
Owing for expenses	70		800		56,000
Sundry debtors	70	3,150		2,20,500	
Difference in exchange				9,84,500	
Total		**70,300**	**70,300**	**45,71,500**	**45,71,500**
Closing stock	70	7,500		9,66,500	

Trading Account of New York Branch of M/s Bombay Company Ltd
for the year ended as on 31 March 2020

Particulars	Amount (₹)
REVENUE	
By Sales	42,09,000
By Closing stock	9,66,500
Total Revenue	**51,75,500**
EXPENSES	
To Opening stock	5,78,000
To Goods (Head office)	18,57,000
Total Expenses	**24,35,000**
Gross Profit (Total Revenue − Total Expenses) (Transferred to Profit and Loss A/c)	**27,40,500**

Profit and Loss Account of Bombay Company Ltd
for the year ended 31 March 2020

Particulars		Amount (₹)
REVENUE		
By Gross profit (Transferred from Trading A/c)		27,40,500
Total Revenue		27,40,500
EXPENSES		
To Salaries		1,93,200
To Rent		82,800
To Insurance		10,500
To Depreciation	(9,000 x 60 = 5,40,000 x 10% = 54,000)	54,000
To Difference in exchange		9,84,500
Total Expenses		**13,25,000**
Net profit *(Total Revenue − Total Expenses)* (Transferred to head office A/c)		**14,15,500**

Balance Sheet of Bombay Company Ltd
as on 31 March 2020

Particulars	Amount (₹)	Amount (₹)
I. EQUITY AND LIABILITIES		
Head office		17,22,000
Expenses outstanding		56,000
Total Equity and Liability		**17,78,000**
II. ASSETS		
Furniture	5,40,000	
Less: Depreciation at 10% p.a.	54,000	4,86,000
Cash in hand		17,500
Cash at bank		87,500
Stock		9,66,500
Debtors		2,20,500
Total Assets		**17,78,000**

In the Books of Head Office of Bombay Company Ltd
New York Branch A/c

Account No:
Normal Balance: Debit   Account Type: Asset

Date 2020	Reference Account	Voucher Type	Post Ref No.	Dr. (Add)	Cr. (Less)	Balance (₹)
	To Balance b/d			3,06,500		(3,06,500)
	To Net profit (Transferred from Profit and Loss Account)			14,15,500		(17,22,000)
	By Balance c/d				17,22,000	0
	Total			**17,22,000**	**17,22,000**	
	To Balance b/d			17,22,000		

■ **ILLUSTRATION 18.15** Madura Coats Limited has a branch in London. On 31 December 2020, the trial balance of the branch was as given in the following text.

Trial Balance of London Branch
as on 31 December 2021

Particulars	Dr. (£)	Cr. (£)
Head office account		9,000
Sales		60,000
Goods from head office A/c	45,000	
Stock on 1 January 2020	7,500	
Furniture and fixtures	10,000	
Cash in hand	50	
Cash at bank	950	
Owing for expenses		1,000
Salaries	3,000	
Taxes, insurance, etc.	250	
Rent	1,000	
Sundry debtors	2,250	
	70,000	70,000

The branch account in the head office showed a debit balance of ₹5,62,500 and the 'goods sent to branch account' a credit balance of ₹40,37,500. Furniture and fixtures were acquired in 2000 @ £1 = ₹67.50.

The exchange rates were:

1 January 2020	£1 = ₹87.50
31 December 2020	£1 = ₹92.50
Average	£1 = ₹90.00

The stock at branch on 31 December 2020 was valued at £4,500.

Convert the branch trial balance into rupees and prepare the branch trading and profit and loss account for 2020, and the branch account in the head office books. Depreciation is to be written off furniture and fixtures at 10%.

Solution

Trial Balance of London Branch
as on 31 December 2020

Account Name	Exchange Rate	Dr. (£)	Cr. (£)	Dr. (₹)	Cr. (₹)
Head office	Given		9,000		5,62,500
Sales	90.00		60,000		54,00,000
Goods from head office	Given	45,000		40,37,500	
Stock 1/1/2020	87.50	7,500		6,56,250	
Furniture & fixtures	67.50	10,000		6,75,000	
Cash in hand	92.50	50		4,625	
Cash at bank	92.50	950		87,875	
Expenses outstanding	92.50		1,000		92,500
Salaries	90.00	3,000		2,70,000	
Taxes and insurance	90.00	250		22,500	
Rent	90.00	1,000		90,000	
Sundry debtors	92.50	2,250		2,08,125	
Difference in exchange				3,125	
Total		**70,000**	**70,000**	**60,55,000**	**60,55,000**
Closing stock	92.50	4,500		4,16,250	

Trading Account of New York Branch of M/s Bombay Company Ltd
for the year ended as on 31 March 2020

Particulars	Amount (₹)
REVENUE	
By Sales	54,00,000
By Closing stock	4,16,250
Total Revenue	**58,16,250**
EXPENSES	
To Opening stock	6,56,250
To Goods (Head office)	40,37,500
Total Expenses	**46,93,750**
Gross Profit (Total Revenue − Total Expenses)	**11,22,500**
(Transferred to Profit and Loss A/c)	

Balance Sheet of Bombay Company Ltd
as on 31 March 2020

Particulars	Amount (₹)	Amount (₹)
I. EQUITY AND LIABILITIES		
Head office		12,31,875
Expenses outstanding		92,500
Total Equity and Liability		**13,24,375**
II. ASSETS		
Furniture and fixtures	6,75,000	
Less: Depreciation at 10% p.a.	67,500	60,7,500
Cash in hand		4,625
Cash at bank		87,875
Stock		4,16,250
Debtors		20,8,125
Total Assets		**13,24,375**

Profit and Loss Account of Bombay Company Ltd
for the year ended 31 March 2020

Particulars	Amount (₹)
REVENUE	
By Gross profit	11,22,500
(Transferred from Trading A/c)	
Total Revenue	**11,22,500**
EXPENSES	
To Salaries	2,70,000
To Taxes and insurance	22,500
To Rent	90,000
To Depreciation	67,500
To Difference in exchange	3,125
Total Expenses	**4,53,125**
Net Profit (Total Revenue − Total Expenses)	**6,69,375**
(Transferred to Head Office A/c)	

In the Books of Head Office of Bombay Company Ltd
New York Branch A/c

Account No:
Normal Balance: Debit
Account Type: Asset

Date 2020	Reference Account	Voucher Type	Post Ref No.	Debit (Add)	Credit (Less)	Balance (₹)
	To Balance b/d			5,62,500		(5,62,500)
	To Net Profit (Transferred from Profit and Loss Account)			6,69,375		(12,31,875)
	By Balance c/d				12,31,875	0
	Total			**12,31,875**	**12,31,875**	
	To Balance b/d			12,31,875		

Exhibit 18.1 indicates the practices adopted by Indian companies for recording of foreign currency transactions in the books of accounts.

EXHIBIT 18.1 Foreign Exchange and Currency Transaction Practices Adopted by Indian Companies

Let us see how various Indian companies treat foreign exchange and currency transactions in the books of accounts.

Pharmaceutical Industry: Cadila Healthcare Limited
Foreign currency transactions

The Company's financial statements are presented in Indian Rupees [INR], which is the functional and presentation currency.

A. The transactions in foreign currencies are translated into functional currency at the rates of exchange prevailing on the dates of transactions.
B. Foreign Exchange gains and losses resulting from settlement of such transactions and from the translation of monetary assets and liabilities [except as covered in "E" below] denominated in foreign currencies at the year end exchange rates are recognised in the Statement of Profit and Loss.
C. Foreign exchange differences regarded as an adjustment to borrowing costs are presented in the Statement of Profit and Loss within finance costs. All the other foreign exchange gains and losses are presented in the Statement of Profit and Loss on a net basis.
D. Investments in foreign subsidiaries and other companies are recorded in INR [functional currency] at the rates of exchange prevailing at the time when the investments were made.
E. The net gain or loss on account of exchange rate differences either on settlement or on translation, of long term foreign currency monetary items recognised on or after April 1, 2016, is recognised as income or expense in the Statement of Profit and Loss in the year in which they arise. The net gain or loss on long term foreign currency monetary items recognised in the financial statement for the period ended on March 31, 2016 is recognised under 'Foreign Currency Monetary Items Translation Difference Account' [FCMITDA], except in case of foreign currency loans taken for funding of Property, Plant and Equipment, where such difference is adjusted to the cost of respective Property, Plant and Equipment. This is as per the exemption given under Ind AS 101 to defer/capitalize exchange differences arising on long-term foreign currency monetary items. The FCMITDA is amortised during the tenure of loans but not beyond March 31, 2020.

Financial Reports

Financial Services Industry: Vistaar Financial Services Private Limited
Foreign currency transactions

Initial recognition Foreign currency transactions are recorded in the reporting currency, by applying to the foreign currency amount the exchange rate between the reporting currency and the foreign currency at the date of the transaction.

Conversion Foreign currency monetary items are reported using the closing rate. Non-monetary items which are carried in terms of historical cost denominated in a foreign currency are reported using the exchange rate at the date of the transaction.

Exchange differences Exchange differences arising on the settlement of monetary items or on reporting Company's monetary items at rates different from those at which they were initially recorded during the year, or reported in previous financial statements, are recognized as income or as expenses in the year in which they arise.

Media and Entertainment Industry: Balaji Telefilms Ltd
Foreign currency transactions

In preparing the financial statements of entity, transactions in currencies other than the entity's functional currency (foreign currencies) are recognised at the rates of exchange prevailing at the dates of the transactions. At the end of each reporting period, monetary items denominated in foreign currencies are retranslated at the rates prevailing at that date. Non-monetary items carried at fair value that are denominated in foreign currencies are retranslated at the rates prevailing at the date when the fair value was determined. Nonmonetary items that are measured in terms of historical cost in a foreign currency are not retranslated.

Airline Industry: SpiceJet Limited
Foreign currencies

The standalone financial statements of the Company is presented in Indian Rupees (₹) which is also the Company's functional currency.

Initial recognition Transactions in foreign currencies entered into by the Company are accounted at the exchange rates prevailing on the date of the transaction or at the average rates that closely approximate the rate at the date of the transaction.

Conversion Foreign currency monetary items are translated using the exchange rate prevailing at the reporting date. Non-monetary items which are measured in terms of historical cost denominated in a foreign currency are translated using the exchange rate at the date of the transaction; and non-monetary items which are carried at fair value denominated in a foreign currency are translated using the exchange rates that existed when the values were determined.

Exchange differences Exchange differences arising on settlement or translation of monetary items are recognised in profit or loss except to the extent it is treated as an adjustment to borrowing costs.

The Company has opted to avail the exemption under Ind AS 101 to continue the policy adopted for accounting for exchange differences arising from translation of long term foreign currency monetary items recognised in financial statements for period ended immediately before beginning of first Ind AS financial reporting period as per Indian GAAP (i.e. till March 31, 2016) (Refer to note 53 for Ind AS 101 exemptions adopted).

Consequent to which:

- Exchange differences arising on long term foreign currency monetary items related to acquisition of certain Bombardier Q400 aircraft are capitalized and depreciated over the remaining useful life of the asset.
- Exchange differences arising on other long-term foreign currency monetary items are accumulated in the "Foreign Currency Monetary Item Translation Difference Account" and amortized over the remaining life of the concerned monetary item.

Sources: Cadila Healthcare Limited Annual Report 2017–18, p. 102; Vistaar Financial Services Pvt. Ltd Annual Report 2017–18, p. 107; Balaji Telefilms Limited Annual Report 2016–2017, p. 110; SpiceJet Limited Annual Report 2016–2017, pp. 91–92.

SUMMARY

- Reporting currency is the currency used for presenting the financial statements. The rate of exchange between two currencies is known as the exchange rate.
- Foreign currency transactions include
  (i) buying and selling of goods or services whose price is denominated in a different currency;
  (ii) borrowing or lending of funds denominated in a different currency;
  (iii) unperformed foreign exchange contract; and
  (iv) acquisition and disposition of assets and liabilities in a different denominated currency.
- Two principal types of exchange rates are (a) free rates, and (b) official rates.
- Transaction is the process of restating recorded financial data from one currency to another

KEYWORDS

Exchange rate It is the ratio for exchange of two currencies.
Foreign currency It is a currency other than the reporting currency of an enterprise.
Forward rate It is the exchange rate established by the terms of an agreement for exchange of two currencies at a specified future date.

Reporting currency It is the currency used in presenting the financial statements.
Spot rate It is the exchange rate applicable on the date of transaction

QUESTIONS

I. Answer the following questions.

1. What are currency exchange rates?
2. What is a forward exchange contract?
3. What are hedging transactions?

II. Solve the following problems.

1. M/s Sun International, an Indian exporter, sells goods to a foreign purchaser, Ramon Co., and invoices US$10,000 on 31 December 2020. The exchange rate at the time of invoice was ₹68. M/s Sun International received a remittance of US$9,995 45 days later. The rate of exchange at the time of remittance was ₹69. The local bank deducted their charges of ₹500 while crediting the amount in the account of M/s Sun International. Record the transactions discussed in the books of M/s Sun International.

2. A foreign currency loan was obtained for US$1,00,000 to purchase plant and machinery and to acquire technical know-how, which was purchased 3 months before the year end. The rate was US$1.0526 = ₹100. On closing date of the year, the rate became US$1.0417 = ₹100. How will you deal with the above?

3. Pass the necessary journal entries in the books of Nutan Ltd of Nagpur on the basis of the following information. A machine was imported on 20 January 2020 from Jackie Corp. of China for US$2,00,000. The payment for the same was made as follows.

   US$1,50,000 on 27 February 2020
   US$50,000 on 15 March 2020

   The exchange rate for US$1 was as follows:

20 January 2020	₹67.00
27 February 2020	₹66.50
15 March 2020	₹68.00

   The company follows the financial year as the accounting year.

4. Stock at cost of Popular Impex on 31 March 2020 was valued at the cost of US$2,000 being purchased on 31 December 2019. The rates of exchange were US$1 = ₹69 (31 March 2020) and US$1 = ₹65 (31 December 2019). The market value on 31 March 2020 of the stock was higher than its cost, when Popular Impex paid half the amount due on the purchases. Show the calculations and entries passed by Popular Impex on relevant dates.

5. Xena Ltd, dealer in leather goods, exports on 1 January 2020 goods worth US$1,00,000 to ABC Co. in New York. The payment was received on 31 March 2020. On the date of invoice, the exchange rate was US$1 = ₹67, and when the dollars were received it was US$1 = ₹68. Record the transactions in the books of Xena Ltd in accordance with Ind AS 21.

6. On 1 June 2020, the Andrus Corporation sold goods to Basel Company of Switzerland for 1,00,000 Swiss francs (SwF) due on 30 July. On the same day, Andrus sold 1,00,000 Swiss francs for delivery in 60 days in order to hedge its exposed net asset position. The Andrus Corporation operates on 30 June fiscal year. The receivable from Basel was collected on 30 July and turned over to the foreign exchange department of the Lincoln National Bank.

   Selected foreign exchange rates for the Swiss franc were as follows.

	June 1	June 30	July 30
Spot Rate	US$0.600	US$0.605	US$0.608
30-Day Forward	US$0.595	US$0.598	US$0.600
60-Day Forward	US$0.592	US$0.596	US$0.598

   Give the journal entries for the foregoing events from 1 June through 31 July.

7. The Paris agents of a London firm, having collected a certain amount of money on behalf of their principals from French debtors, have in hand a sum of 66,000 francs. In the London books, this amount of currency is converted into sterling at 13.20

francs to £1. On instructions, the agents purchase 1,600 French 8% bonds of 37.50 francs each (nominal) at 99.5% of which they sell 960 bonds at 102%, remitting the proceeds to their principals, the rate of exchange being 13.18 francs to £1. Shortly afterwards, the London firm makes up its books, the then current rate of exchange being 13.22 francs to £1.

Show the accounts the London firm would keep to record these transactions, disclosing the profits and losses on the investment and on the foreign exchange fluctuations. Ignore the expenses.

8. Vineeta Exports Limited exports business through its overseas branch whose currency is Khushbu. The trial balances of the head office at Mumbai and of the overseas branch as on 31 March 2020 were as under:

Particulars	Dr. Head Office	Cr. Head Office	Overseas Dr. (Khushbu)	Branch Cr. (Khushbu)
Freehold building (at cost)	2,800		12,000	
Debtors/creditors	1,780	1,900	7,200	312
Sales		20,800		86,400
Components sent to branch		7,000		
Share capital		8,000		
Head office/branch	12,020			1,00,352
Branch cost of sales			72,000	
Provision for depreciation on machinery		300		11,340
Head office cost of sales (including goods sent to branch)	11,800			
Administrative expenses	3,040		3,000	
Stock on 31/3/2020	5,780		2,304	
Profit and loss account		400		
Machinery at cost	1,200		25,200	
Remittances		5,600	54,400	
Cash at bank	920		15,840	
Selling and distribution expenses	4,660		5,750	
	44,000	44,000	1,98,904	1,98,904

The following adjustments were desired to be made.

(a) The cost of sales includes depreciation charge of 10% p.a. on cost of machinery.

(b) A provision of ₹60 for unrealized profit in the branch stock is to be made.

(c) On 15 March 2020, the branch remitted 3,200 khushbus. This amount was received by the head office on 4 April 2020 and realized ₹398.

(d) During January 2020, a customer of the branch by mistake paid the head office for goods supplied by the branch. The amount due from him was 64 khushbus which realized ₹10. It has been correctly dealt with by the head office but has not yet been entered in the branch accounts.

(e) Provide commission at 5% of the net profits of the branch after charging such commission which is payable to the branch manager.

You are informed of the following exchange rates, which are always expressed equivalent to ₹1. On 1 April 2019, 10 khushbus were equal to ₹1, while on 31 March 2020, ₹1 was equivalent to 2 khushbus less than it was on 1 April 2019. The average rate was 1 khushbu more than it was on 31 March 2020, and on the date of purchase of building and machinery, it was 3 khushbus less than it was on 1 April 2019.

You are required to prepare the trading and profit and loss account of the head office and of the branch office in the currency of the head office for the year ended 31 March 2020, and the consolidated balance sheet of the company as at 31 March 2020.

 # REFERENCES

Guidance notes by Institute of Chartered Accountants of India.
Indian Accounting Standards (Ind AS) released by Ministry of Company Affairs.

Shah, Paresh (2015), Forex Management, Wiley_Biztantra, India, pp. 82–83.

Regulatory Framework on Accounting and Reporting

Learning Objectives

After studying this chapter, you will understand

- importance of generally accepted accounting principles
- importance of accounting standards and their implementation
- significance of IFRS and its implementation

INTRODUCTION

The American Institute of Certified Public Accountants (AICPA) opines that the word principle refers to 'a general law or rules adopted or proposed as a guide to actions, a settled grounds or basis of conduct of practice'. These principles have evolved over decades of accounting practice. The Generally Accepted Accounting Principles (GAAP) give creditability to financial statements which are drawn and prepared on the basis of such principles. These principles, when adopted by the makers and users of the financial statements, give meaning to the information contained in these statements.

Accounting principles are not rigid like the principles of physics, chemistry, or natural sciences. Accounting principles are the result of practice and experiences. Any rule or law that offers a solution to the problem being faced and accepted by accounting professionals becomes an accounting principle.

DEVELOPMENT OF FINANCIAL REPORTING

Financial reporting is developed the world over based on two broad models: the fair value statement of financial position (FVSP) model and the Anglo-Saxon Financial Reporting (ASFR) model (Epstein and Jermakowicz 2009).

The FVSP is the earliest systematized form of accounting regulation developed in continental Europe, starting in France in 1673. The requirement of an annual fair value statement of financial position was introduced by the government to protect the economies from bankruptcies (Epstein and Jermakowicz 2009).

The ASFR arose in the end of the nineteenth century as a consequence of the industrial revolution. Industrialization resulted in the need for a large capital to undertake industrial and social projects, and also to reduce spreading the risk among other providers of funds (Epstein and Jermakowicz 2009). ASFR provided a means of monitoring the activities of large government undertakings, businesses, and corporate houses. It also informs other stakeholders, such as the shareholders and capital providers, about the economic activities undertaken by the firm in question (Epstein and Jermakowicz 2009).

The concept of development and establishment of international accounting standards emerged initially in the first International Congress of Accountants held at St. Louis in 1904 (Rathore 2009).

The need for harmonization through comparisons was recognized by most accountants across the globe in the 1960s (Rathore 2009).

With the growing internationalization of trade, business, and capital markets, financial information prepared according to the national accounting system of one country no longer satisfied the needs of users from other countries. The users of accounting information of other countries needed more information to make informed decisions with a global scope. The International Accounting Standards Committee (IASC) was formed in the year 1973, with the intention to become the original international standards setter, and is headquartered at London. The IASC is the outcome of the 1972 World-Accounting Congress after an informal meeting between representatives of the Institute of Chartered Accountants of England and Wales (ICAEW) and the American Institute of Certified Public Accountants (AICPA) (Epstein and Jermakowicz 2009).

In the US, the Financial Accounting Standards Board (FASB), AICPA, and Securities and Exchange Commission (SEC) provide guidance about accounting and financial statements.

In the year 2001, the International Fraternity of Accountants constituted the International Accounting Standards Board (IASB) to evolve and prescribe norms for the treatment of several events and accounting transactions in the preparation and reporting of financial statements. The IASB issues International Financial Reporting Standards (IFRS) that identify preferred accounting standards in addition to the International Accounting Standards (IAS).

The FASB and the IASB are in the process of creating harmony among different types of accounting practices among different countries and in turn eliminating a few accounting standards. The European Commission, the UN, the International Federation of Accountants (IFAC), and the Organization for Economic Cooperation and Development (OECD) are some of the international accounting bodies who form the IASB with other member countries. IFRS is an example of the capital market-oriented and investor-oriented systems of financial reporting rules.

The IASC was established in London, where its successor, the IASB, remains today (Epstein and Jermakowicz 2009).

The historical Anglo-Saxon standard setting model, where professional accountants set rules for themselves, had largely been abandoned in the twenty-five years since IASC has been formed, and the standards were mostly being set by dedicated and independent national boards such as the FASB, and not by profession-dominated bodies such as the AICPA (Epstein and Jermakowicz 2009).

GENERALLY ACCEPTED ACCOUNTING PRINCIPLES (GAAP)

Accounting is more an art than a science. GAAP stands for Generally Accepted Accounting Principles. It refers to the various methods, rules, practices, and procedures that have evolved over a period of time in response to the need for some form of regulation over the preparation of financial statements.

Accounting principles become 'generally accepted' by agreement; such agreement is not influenced solely by format and logical analysis. Experience, custom, usage, and practical necessity contribute to the set of principles. Astoundingly, it might be better to call them conventions, because principles suggest that they are the product of airtight logic.

Accounting is the language of business. It makes sense only when it is understood by many in the same way. Setting 'Accounting standards' is a step taken in that direction. Hence, it can be said that the logic of standard setting is based on the necessity of harmonizing the diverse policies and practices adopted by different enterprises. Accounting standards ensure consistency in the reported information of an enterprise from year to year so that users of financial statements are in a position to understand and make proper use of the financial statements for decision-making purpose.

GAAP in Different Nations

India

Organizations like Institute of Chartered Accountants of India (ICAI), Accounting Standards Board (ASB), Ministry of Corporate Affairs (Govt. of India), Securities and Exchange Board of India (SEBI), Institute of Cost Accountants of India, stock exchanges and the literature, each of these published are instrumental in the development of most accounting principles.

Accounting standards are specified by ICAI under Section 211 of the Companies Act, 1956. The Accounting Standards Board (ASB) was formed in April 1977 by ICAI. The ASB is the autonomous council with the objective of formulating accounting standards in India. It rolls out new accounting standards as and when there are any changes in the applicable laws, customs, business environment, and the International Accounting Standards.

USA

GAAP is largely the work of the Financial Accounting Standards Board (FASB). The FASB consisting of seven full time members is an independent creation of the private sector. International GAAP is set by the International Accounting Standard Board (IASB). By federal law, the Securities and Exchange Commissions (SEC), a government agency, has the ultimate responsibility for specifying GAAP for US companies whose stock is held by the general investing public.

UK

The Accounting Standards Board (ASB) issues all accounting standards for UK companies.

Canada

Accounting Standards Committee (ASC) lays down accounting standards for most entities in Canada.

Finally, an accounting organization must conduct an audit before it can render an opinion. An audit is an 'examination' or in-depth inspection of financial positions, records made accordance with generally accepted in auditing standards, which have been developed by the American Institute of Certified Public Accountants (AICPA).

ACCOUNTING STANDARDS

Accounting standards comprise a set of statements of code of practice set by the regulatory accounting bodies, which are to be followed in the preparation and presentation of financial statements. Accounting standards are the written documents issued by the regulatory bodies covering various aspects of guidelines, treatment, and disclosure of accounting transactions. It may be in the form of a written statement of accounting practice issued by an authority or an institution of accounting profession or an institution, established expressly for the purpose.

An accounting standard is a guideline for financial accounting, such as how a firm prepares and presents its business income and expense, assets, capital and liabilities. International Accounting Standards Board (IASB) has been created 'to formulate and publish, in the public interest, basic standards to be observed in the presentation of audited accounts and financial statements and to promote their worldwide acceptance and observance.'

Objectives of Accounting Standards

The following are the broad objectives of accounting standards:

1. To harmonize the diverse accounting policies
2. To eliminate variations in the treatment of several accounting aspects
3. To provide inference and guidelines on accounting standards
4. To bring uniformity in the presentation of accounting aspects
5. To facilitate inter-firm and intra-firm comparison
6. To make credibility, reliability, and acceptability of accounting
7. To make usefulness by informing the rules and regulations of financial statements' preparation
8. To improve the transparency in financial statements
9. To help in determining corporate accountability and managerial effectiveness

Significance of Accounting Standards

Financial statements are prepared to summarize all business activities by an organization during an accounting period in monetary terms and disclose the results in terms of performance and financial position. It is mandatory according to the Companies Act, 2013 and previously by the Companies Act, 1956 that the profit and loss account and balance sheet should be prepared as per the accounting standards. Adherence to the accounting standards provides the following benefits:

1. Accounting standards establish the credibility, reliability, and acceptability of accounting.
2. They are useful to accountants in informing the rules and regulations of preparation of financial statements.
3. They improve transparency in financial statements.
4. They improve corporate governance.
5. They help in determining corporate accountability and managerial effectiveness.
6. They help in developing accounting theory.

Advantages of Accounting Standards

Following is the illustrative list of advantages offered by accounting standards for the society at large:

1. Accounting standards increase the investors' confidence in the business by ensuring that the documents reviewed are accurate and genuine.
2. Government regulators have made accounting standards mandatory, that is, accounting standards have to ho adhered by all companies. This is beneficial to the investors or customers since it protects them from frauds in business.
3. Accounting standards eliminate variations in the accounting treatments.
4. Accounting standards promote transparency in the business transactions, which in turn improves efficiency of the financial and commercial markets.
5. Accounting standards facilitate inter-firm and intra-firm comparison.
6. Outsiders such as shareholders, suppliers, customers, employees, and banks can use the financial statements for making sound decisions.
7. Accounting standards provide guidelines and framework within which financial statements can be produced. Since accounting standards are regulations to be followed, it becomes easy to compare the results and financial positions of different firms. Thus accounting standards protect users of financial information by providing them with data on which they can rely.
8. All chartered and certified accountants necessarily have to subscribe to the accounting standards. This ensures that individual accountants and chartered accountancy firms are cautious and alert while auditing and signing the financial statements. In cases of undetected fraud and of audited accounts, which are held to be misleading due to insufficient disclosure or use of inappropriate accounting principles, the accountant stands at risk in terms of uncovered financial exposure to liability or adverse effects on personal reputation. It is here that accounting standards become useful.
9. Accounting standards help in determining specific corporate accountability and regulation of the company. They assess managerial skills in maintaining and improving the position of profitability, liquidity, and solvency of the business. They also ensure consistency and comparability in place of uniformity in financial reporting.

Accounting Standards Board of India

The Institute of Chartered Accountants of India (ICAI), recognizing the need to harmonize the diverse accounting policies and practices at present in use in India, constituted the Accounting Standards Board (ASB) on 21 April 1977. The main role of ASB is to formulate accounting standards from time to time. The Board will take into consideration the usage, conventions, and applicable law and due consideration will be given the International Accounting Standards issued by IASC.

IND AS ISSUED BY MINISTRY OF CORPORATE AFFAIRS

Ind AS are the accounting standards notified by the Ministry of Corporate Affairs (MCA) in line with the Interpretation Financial Reporting Standards. Ind AS has a wider coverage as compared to accounting standards notified by Institute of Chartered Accountants of India (ICAI) in past. The Ind AS are more principal based as compared to the existing AS.

Objectives of Ind AS

The objectives of Ind AS are as under:

i. To ensure reliable and uniform financial reporting
ii. To enhance the credibility of the businesses in the eyes of investors to take informed investment decisions
iii. As per India's G-20 commitment, the process of synchronization of Indian standards of corporate affairs with IFRS through extensive consultative exercises with all the stakeholders.

How are Ind AS different from IFRS?

Ind AS are different from IFRS in the following ways:

1. In order to maintain uniform accounting policies and procedures, almost all the countries have agreed to apply International Financial Reporting Standards (IFRS).
2. India has also agreed to apply IFRS. But the name of this IFRS has been changed to Ind AS.

Comparative Analysis of Ind AS and Existing Accounting Standards

Appendix B at the end of the book indicates the linkages between accounting standards as issued by ICAI (AS) and Indian Accounting Standards (Ind AS) as notified by MCA.

IND AS

A brief explanation of significant and applicable Ind AS on day to day life is followed hereunder.

Ind AS 101: First-time Adoption of Indian Accounting Standards

The objective of this Ind AS is to ensure that an entity's first Ind AS financial statements, and its interim financial reports for part of the period covered by those financial statements, contain high quality information that: (a) is transparent for users and comparable for all periods presented; (b) provides a suitable starting point for accounting in accordance with Indian Accounting Standards (Ind ASs); and (c) can be generated at a cost that does not exceed the benefits.

An entity shall apply this Ind AS in: (a) its first Ind AS financial statements; and (b) each interim financial report, if any, that it presents in accordance with Ind AS 34, Interim Financial Reporting, for part of the period covered by its first Ind AS financial statements.

An entity's first Ind AS financial statements are the first annual financial statements in which the entity adopts Ind ASs, in accordance with Ind ASs notified under the Companies Act, 2013 and makes an explicit and unreserved statement in those financial statements of compliance with Ind AS.

(*Adapted from* http://mca.gov.in/Ministry/pdf/INDAS101.pdf; https://taxguru.in/company-law/applicability-indian-accounting-standard-ind.html; https://accountingstandardsindia.wordpress.com/2015/08/29/first-time-adoption-of-ind-as-ind-as-101/)

Ind AS 102 to Ind AS 114 are same as the IFRS 2 to IFRS 14.

Ind AS 1: Presentation of Financial Statements

1. The objective of financial statements is to provide information that is useful in making economic decisions. This Standard prescribes the basis for the presentation of general-purpose financial statements in order to ensure comparability both with the entity's financial statements of previous periods and with those of other entities.

Financial statements are prepared on a going concern basis, and under the accrual basis of accounting. There are minimum disclosures to be made in the financial statements and in the notes. This Standard does not apply to the structure and content of condensed interim financial statements prepared in accordance with *Ind AS 34: Interim Financial Reporting*.

An entity shall present, with equal prominence, all of the financial statements as a complete set of financial statements. Financial statements disclose corresponding information for the preceding period, unless a standard or interpretation permits or requires otherwise.

2. **A complete set of financial statements comprises**

   (a) Balance sheet as at the end of the period;
   (b) Statement of profit and loss for the period;
   (c) Statement of changes in equity for the period;
   (d) Statement of cash flows for the period;
   (e) Notes, comprising a summary of significant accounting policies and other explanatory information.

3. **Explanation of terms**

Material items   The nature and amount of items of income and expense are disclosed separately where they are of material nature. Disclosure may be in the statement or in the notes. Such income and expenses might include restructuring costs; write-downs of inventories or property, plant and equipment; litigation settlements; and gains or losses on disposals of property, plant and equipment, etc.

Presentation of true and fair view Financial statements shall present a true and fair view of the financial position, financial performance and cash flows of an entity. The application of Ind AS, with additional disclosures when necessary, is presumed to result in financial statements that present a true and fair view.

Going concern and accrual basis of accounting An entity shall prepare financial statements on a going concern basis unless management intends to either liquidate the entity or cease trading, or has no realistic alternative but to do so. An entity shall prepare its financial statements, except for cash flow information, using the accrual basis of accounting.

Offsetting An entity shall not offset assets and liabilities or income and expenses, unless required or permitted by other Ind AS.

4. Balance sheet

The balance sheet presents an entity's financial position at a specific point in time. Subject to meeting certain minimum presentation and disclosure requirements, management may use its judgment regarding the form of presentation, such as sub-classifications and disclosure of information on the face of the statement or in the notes.

Ind AS 1 specifies that the following items, as a minimum, are presented on the face of the balance sheet:

Assets Property, plant and equipment; investment property; intangible assets; financial assets; investments accounted for using the equity method; biological assets; deferred tax assets; current tax assets; inventories; trade and other receivables; and cash and cash equivalents.

Equity Issued capital and reserves attributable to the parent's owners; and non-controlling interest.

Liabilities Deferred tax liabilities; current tax liabilities; financial liabilities; provisions; and trade and other payables.

Assets and liabilities held for sale The total of assets classified as held for sale and assets included in disposal groups classified as held for sale; and liabilities included in disposal groups classified as held for sale.

Current and non-current assets and liabilities are presented as separate classifications in the statement, unless the presentation based on liquidity provides reliable and more relevant information.

5. Statement of profit and loss

The statement of profit and loss presents an entity's performance over a specific period. The statement of profit and loss includes all items of income and expense and includes each component of other comprehensive income classified by nature.

Items to be presented in statement of profit and loss Additional line items or sub-headings are presented in this statement when relevant to an understanding of the entity's financial performance. The expenses are classified in the statement of profit and loss based on the nature of expense.

Other comprehensive income An entity shall present items of other comprehensive income grouped into those that will be reclassified subsequently to profit or loss and those that will not be reclassified. An entity shall disclose reclassification adjustments relating to the components of other comprehensive income.

An entity presents each component of other comprehensive income in the statement either as (i) net of its related tax effects, or (ii) before its related tax effects, with the aggregate tax effect of these components shown separately. An entity needs to also disclose reclassification adjustments relating to components of other comprehensive income.

6. Statement of changes in equity

The following items are presented in the statement of changes in equity:

Total comprehensive income for the period, showing separately the total amounts attributable to the parent's owners and to non-controlling interest.

For each component of equity, the effects of retrospective application or retrospective restatement recognized in accordance with Ind AS 8, 'Accounting Policies, Changes in Accounting Estimates, and Errors'.

For each component of equity, reconciliation between the carrying amount at the beginning and the end of the period, separately disclosing changes resulting from the following:

1. Profit or loss
2. Other comprehensive income
3. Transactions with owners in their capacity as owners, showing separately contributions by and distributions to owners and changes in ownership interests in subsidiaries that do not result in a loss of control
4. Any item recognized directly in equity such as capital reserve on bargain purchase in a business combination transaction
5. The amounts of dividends recognized as distributions to owners during the period, and the related amount of dividends per share, shall be disclosed.

7. Statement of cash flows

Cash flow statements are addressed in a separate summary dealing with the requirements of Ind AS 7.

8. Notes to the financial statements

The notes are an integral part of the financial statements. Notes provide information additional to the amounts disclosed in the 'primary' statements. They also include accounting policies, critical accounting estimates and judgments, disclosures on capital and financial instruments classified as equity.

(*Adapted from* https://www.readyratios.com/.../ifrs/ias_1_presentation_of_financial_statements.html; https:// www.pwc.in/assets/pdfs/publications/2016/ind-as-pocket-guide-2016.pdf; https://inform.pwc.com/inform2/s/IAS_1_Presentation_of_financial_statements/informContent/0902225504094676)

Ind AS 2: Inventories

1. The objective of this Standard is to prescribe the accounting treatment for inventories. A primary issue in accounting for inventories is the amount of cost to be recognized as an asset and carried forward until the related revenues are recognized. This Standard deals with the determination of cost and its subsequent recognition as an expense, including any write-down to net realizable value. It also provides guidance on the cost formulas that are used to assign costs to inventories.

2. This Standard applies to all inventories except financial instruments, biological assets (e.g., living animals, or plants), agricultural produce at the time of harvesting, minerals and mineral products (to the extent they are measured at net realizable value), and commodity brokers.

3. **Inventories are assets**

   (a) held for sale in the ordinary course of business;

   (b) in the process of production for such sale; or

   (c) in the form of materials or supplies to be consumed in the production process or in the rendering of services.

   Inventories encompass goods purchased and held for resale including merchandise purchased by a retailer and held for resale, or land and other property held for resale. Inventories also encompass finished goods produced, or work in progress being produced, by the entity and include materials and supplies awaiting use in the production process.

4. **Cost of inventories**

   The cost of inventories shall comprise all costs of purchase, costs of conversion, and other costs incurred in bringing the inventories to their present location and condition.

   a. Cost of purchase: The costs of purchase of inventories comprise the purchase price, import duties, and other taxes (other than those subsequently recoverable by the entity from the taxing authorities), and transport, handling, and other costs directly attributable to the acquisition of finished goods, materials, and services. Trade discounts, rebates, and other similar items are deducted in determining the costs of purchase.

   b. Costs of conversion: The costs of conversion of inventories include costs directly related to the units of production, such as direct labour. They also include a systematic allocation of fixed and variable production overheads that are incurred in converting materials into finished goods. Fixed production overheads are those indirect costs of production that remain relatively constant regardless of the volume of production, such as depreciation and maintenance of factory buildings and equipment, and the cost of factory management and administration. Variable production overheads are those indirect costs of production that vary directly, or nearly directly, with the volume of production, such as indirect materials and indirect labour. The allocation of fixed production overheads to the costs of conversion is based on the normal capacity of the production facilities. Normal capacity is the production expected to be achieved on average over a number of periods or seasons under normal circumstances, taking into account the loss of capacity resulting from planned maintenance. The actual level of production may be used if it approximates normal capacity. The amount of fixed overhead allocated to each unit of production is not increased as a consequence of low production or idle plant. Unallocated overheads are recognized as an expense in the period in which they are incurred. In periods of abnormally high production, the amount of fixed overhead allocated to each unit of production is decreased so that inventories are not measured above cost. Variable production overheads are allocated to each unit of production on the basis of the actual use of the production facilities.

   c. Other costs: Other costs are included in the cost of inventories only to the extent that they are incurred in bringing the inventories to their present location and condition.

   d. Exclusion of costs: Examples of costs excluded from the cost of inventories and recognized as expenses in the period in which they are incurred are

      (a) abnormal amounts of wasted materials, labour, or other production costs;

      (b) storage costs, unless those costs are necessary in the production process before a further production stage;

      (c) administrative overheads that do not contribute to bringing inventories to their present location and condition; and

      (d) selling costs.

5. **Recognition of value as an asset**

   Inventories are initially recognized at the lower of cost and net realizable value (NRV). Cost of inventories includes import duties, non-refundable taxes, transport and handling costs and any other directly attributable costs, less trade discount, rebates, and similar items. Costs such as abnormal amount of wasted materials, storage costs, administrative costs, and selling costs are excluded from the cost of inventories.

   NRV is the estimated selling price in the ordinary course of business, less the estimated costs of completion and estimated selling expenses.

   Techniques for the measurement of the cost of inventories, such as the standard cost method or the retail method, may be used for convenience if the results approximate cost.

   'Inventories' requires the cost for items that are not interchangeable or that have been segregated for specific contracts to be determined on an individual-item basis. The cost of other inventory items used is assigned by using either the first-in, first-out (FIFO) or weighted average cost formula. Last-in, first-out (LIFO) is not permitted. An entity uses the same cost formula for all inventories of similar nature and use to the entity. A different cost formula may be justified where inventories have a different nature or use. The cost formula used is applied on a consistent basis from period to period.

An entity may purchase inventories on deferred payment terms. When the arrangement effectively contains a financing element, that element, for example, a difference between the purchase prices for normal credit terms and the amount paid, is recognized as interest expense over the period of the financing.

6. Recognition as an expense

When inventories are sold, the carrying amount of those inventories shall be recognized as an expense in the period in which the related revenue is recognized. The amount of any write-down of inventories to net realizable value and all losses of inventories shall be recognized as an expense in the period the write-down or loss occurs. The amount of any reversal of any write-down of inventories, arising from an increase in net realizable value, shall be recognized as a reduction in the amount of inventories recognized as an expense in the period in which the reversal occurs.

Some inventories may be allocated to other asset accounts, for example, inventory used as a component of self-constructed property, plant, or equipment. Inventories allocated to another asset in this way are recognized as an expense during the useful life of that asset.

(*Adapted from* http://www.mca.gov.in/Ministry/pdf/Ind_AS2.pdf; http://ebook.mca.gov.in/Childwindow1.aspx?pageid=25407&type=RU&ChildTitle=The%20Companies%20(Indian%20Accounting%20Standards)%20Rules,%202015; https://www.readyratios.com/reference/ifrs/ias_2_inventories.html)

Ind AS 7: Statement of Cash Flow

1. The objective of this Standard is to require the provision of information about the historical changes in cash and cash equivalents of an entity by means of a statement of cash flows which classifies cash flows during the period from operating, investing, and financing activities.

2. What are cash flows, cash, and cash equivalents?

Cash flows are inflows and outflows of cash and cash equivalents. Cash is cash on hand and held in demand (at call) deposits. Cash equivalents are short-term, highly liquid investments readily convertible to cash and subject to an insignificant risk of changes in value.

An investment will generally be short-term if it is purchased and sold as part of the entity's cash management activities and has a maturity of three months or less from the date of acquisition, for example, short-term money market investments and fixed-term deposits with a maturity period of less than three months. Equity investments are excluded from cash equivalents unless they are, in substance, cash equivalents, for example, in the case of preference shares acquired within a short period of their maturity and with a specified redemption date.

3. Preparation of statement of cash flows

The statement of cash flows shall report cash flows during the period classified by operating, investing, and financing activities.

An entity presents its cash flows from operating, investing, and financing activities in a manner which is most appropriate to its business. Classification by activity provides information that allows users to assess the impact of those activities on the financial position of the entity and the amount of its cash and cash equivalents. This information may also be used to evaluate the relationships among those activities.

Operating cash flows   The amount of cash flows arising from operating activities is a key indicator of the extent to which the operations of the entity have generated sufficient cash flows to repay loans, maintain the operating capability of the entity, pay dividends, and make new investments without recourse to external sources of financing. Cash flows from operating activities are primarily derived from the principal revenue producing activities of the entity. Therefore, they generally result from the transactions and other events that enter into the determination of profit or loss.

An entity shall report cash flows from operating activities using either

- (a) the direct method, whereby major classes of gross cash receipts and gross cash payments are disclosed; or
- (b) the indirect method, whereby profit or loss is adjusted for the effects of transactions of a non-cash nature, any deferrals or accruals of past or future operating cash receipts or payments, and items of income or expense associated with investing or financing cash flows.

Investing cash flows   The separate disclosure of cash flows arising from investing activities is important because the cash flows represent the extent to which expenditures have been made for resources intended to generate future income and cash flows. Only expenditures that result in a recognized asset in the balance sheet are eligible for classification as investing activities.

Financing cash flows   The separate disclosure of cash flows arising from financing activities is important because it is useful in predicting claims on future cash flows by providers of capital to the entity.

A single transaction may include cash flows that are classified differently. For example, when the instalment paid in respect of an item of Property, Plant, and Equipment acquired on deferred payment basis includes interest, the interest element is classified under financing activities, and the loan element is classified under investing activities.

Cash flows arising from transactions in a foreign currency shall be recorded in an entity's functional currency by applying to the foreign currency amount the exchange rate between the functional currency and the foreign currency at the date of the cash flow.

4. It focus on the user-need for information about the changes in cash and cash equivalents of an enterprise by means of a cash flow statement which classifies cash

flows during the period into operating, investing, and financing activities. Both the Standards permit usage of either Direct Method or Indirect Method for presenting cash flows from operating activities.

5. **Cash and cash equivalents:** Ind AS 7 takes note of the fact that in some countries, bank overdraft which are repayable on demand form an integral part of an entity's cash management. A characteristic of such banking arrangements is that the bank balance often fluctuates from being positive to overdrawn. Thus, to the extent that, in substance, such an arrangement forms a part of an entity's cash management, the overdraft can be treated as cash and cash equivalents.

6. **Extraordinary items:** The disclosure of cash flows associated with extraordinary items has been dispensed with under the revised version of Ind AS 7, as adopted by IASB (a corresponding amendment to AS 3 is on the anvil)

7. **Interest and dividends:** In addition, dividends paid may be classified either as financing cash flows or as operating cash flows. Ind AS 7 concedes that there is no consensus on the classification of these cash flows for other entities. Item relating to (i) interest paid and (ii) interest and dividends received may be classified as operating cash flows because they enter into the determination of profit or loss. Ind AS 7 also permits an alternative approach of interest paid, and interest (and dividends) received, being classified as financing cash flows and investing cash flows respectively, because they are costs of obtaining financial resources or returns on investments.

(*Adapted from* https://www.iasplus.com/en/standards/ias/ias7; http://mca.gov.in/Ministry/pdf/INDAS7.pdf; https://www.aasb.gov.au/admin/file/content105/c9/AASB107_07-04_COMPjul07_07-07.pdf)

Ind AS 8: Accounting Policies, Changes in Accounting Estimates, and Errors

1. The objective of this Standard is to prescribe the criteria for selecting and changing accounting policies, together with the accounting treatment and disclosure of changes in accounting policies, changes in accounting estimates, and corrections of errors.

2. **Terms**

Accounting policies are the specific principles, bases, conventions, rules, and practices applied by an entity in preparing and presenting financial statements.

A *change in accounting estimate* is an adjustment of the carrying amount of an asset or a liability, or the amount of the periodic consumption of an asset, that results from the assessment of the present status of, and expected future benefits and obligations associated with, assets and liabilities. Changes in accounting estimates result from new information or new developments and, accordingly, are not corrections of errors.

Omissions or misstatements of items are *material* if they could, individually or collectively, influence the economic decisions that users make on the basis of the financial statements. Materiality depends on the size and nature of the omission or misstatement judged in the surrounding circumstances. The size or nature of the item, or a combination of both, could be the determining factor.

Prior period errors are omissions from, and misstatements in, the entity's financial statements for one or more prior periods arising from a failure to use, or misuse of, reliable information.

Retrospective application is applying a new accounting policy to transactions, other events, and conditions as if that policy had always been applied.

Retrospective restatement is correcting the recognition, measurement, and disclosure of amounts of elements of financial statements as if a prior period error had never occurred.

3. **Changes in accounting policies**

An entity shall change an accounting policy only if the change

(a) is required by an Ind AS; or

(b) results in the financial statements providing reliable and more relevant information about the effects of transactions, other events, or conditions on the entity's financial position, financial performance, or cash flows.

4. **Changes in accounting estimates**

As a result of the uncertainties inherent in business activities, many items in financial statements cannot be measured with precision but can only be estimated. Estimation involves judgements based on the latest available and reliable information. For example, estimates may be required of (a) bad debts; (b) inventory obsolescence; (c) the fair value of financial assets or financial liabilities; (d) the useful lives of, or expected pattern of consumption of the future economic benefits embodied in, depreciable assets; and (e) warranty obligations.

The use of reasonable estimates is an essential part of the preparation of financial statements and does not undermine their reliability. An estimate may need revision if changes occur in the circumstances on which the estimate was based or as a result of new information or more experience. By its nature, the revision of an estimate does not relate to prior periods and is not the correction of an error.

5. **Errors**

Errors can arise in respect of the recognition, measurement, presentation or disclosure of elements of financial statements. Financial statements do not comply with Ind ASs if they contain either material errors or immaterial errors made intentionally to achieve a particular presentation of an entity's financial position, financial performance or cash flows. Potential current period errors discovered in that period are corrected before the financial statements are approved for issue.

However, material errors are sometimes not discovered until a subsequent period, and these prior period errors are corrected in the comparative information presented in the financial statements for that subsequent period.

6. Changes in financial statements

To the extent that a change in an accounting policy or estimate or errors gives rise to changes in assets and liabilities, or relates to an item of equity, it shall be recognized by adjusting the carrying amount of the related asset, liability, or equity item in the period of the change.

7. An entity shall correct material prior period errors retrospectively in the first set of financial statements approved for issue after their discovery by

   (a) restating the comparative amounts for the prior period(s) presented in which the error occurred; or

   (b) if the error occurred before the earliest prior period presented, restating the opening balances of assets, liabilities and equity for the earliest prior period presented.

(*Adapted from* https://www.researchgate.net/publication/50310791_IAS_8_Accounting_Policies_Changes_in_Accounting_Estimates_and_Errors_-_A_Closer_Look; https://www.iasplus.com/en/standards/ias/ias8; https://taxguru.in/chartered-accountant/accounting-adjustment-prior-period-errors-omissions.html)

Examples/Comments

1. The adoption of an accounting policy for events or transactions that differ in substance from previously occurring events or transactions.
   Example: Introduction of formal retirement gratuity scheme by an employer in place of ad-hoc ex-gratia payment to employees on retirement.

2. In many cases it could be difficult to distinguish between a change in accounting policy and change in accounting estimate. In such a situation, the change is treated as a change in an accounting estimate.

3. Vivaan company has a fleet of 20 diesel buses which are operating in Delhi. New legislation on pollution will ban them for use in Delhi from 1st April 2018, reducing their useful lives. The company will need to accelerate depreciation and review their residual values. This is a revision of estimates and will have no impact on prior periods, but the depreciation of current year and subsequent years will increase.

4. While preparing the accounts for the year ended 31.03.2019, Rainbow Limited created a provision for bad and doubtful debts at 2% on trade debtors. A few weeks later, the company found out that the payments from some of the major debtors were forthcoming. Consequently, the company decided to increase the provision to 10% on the debtors as on 31.03.2019 as the accounts were still open awaiting approval of the Board of Directors. Is this to be considered as an extraordinary item or prior period item?
   This is a change in accounting estimate. It is not considered as an extraordinary item or prior period item.

5. During the year 2019–2020, a medium-sized company wrote down its inventories to net realizable value by ₹5,00,000. Is a separate disclosure necessary?

This is an ordinary activity. Ordinary activities which are usually, frequently or regularly, undertaken by an enterprise as part of its business.

Expenses or incomes which are exceptional on account of size (large or small) and/or incidence (extent or frequency of occurrence) that arises from the ordinary activities of a business should be separately disclosed. Therefore, writing down inventories to net realizable value by ₹5 lakh has to be disclosed separately.

Ind AS 10: Events after the Reporting Period

1. The objective of this Standard is to prescribe

   (a) when an entity should adjust its financial statements for events after the reporting period; and

   (b) the disclosures that an entity should give about the date when the financial statements were authorized for issue and about events after the reporting period.

2. **Terms**

Events after the reporting period are those events, favourable and unfavourable, that occur between the end of the reporting period and the date when the financial statements are authorized for issue.

3. **Adjusting and non-adjusting events**

   Two types of events can be identified:

   (a) Those that provide evidence of conditions that existed at the end of the reporting period (*adjusting events after the reporting period*); and

   (b) Those that are indicative of conditions that arose after the reporting period (*non-adjusting events after the reporting period*).

   Events after the reporting period include all events up to the date when the financial statements are authorized for issue, even if those events occur after the public announcement of profit or of other selected financial information.

4. The process involved in authorizing the financial statements for issue will vary depending upon the management structure, statutory requirements, and procedures followed in preparing and finalizing the financial statements.

   In some cases, an entity is required to submit its financial statements to its shareholders for approval after the financial statements have been issued. In such cases, the financial statements are authorized for issue on the date of issue, not the date when shareholders approve the financial statements.

   In some cases, the management of an entity is required to issue its financial statements to a supervisory board (made up solely of non-executives) for approval. In such cases, the financial statements are authorized for issue when the management authorizes them for issue to the supervisory board.

5. **Recognition and measurement**

   (i) *Adjusting events after the reporting period* An entity shall adjust the amounts recognized in its financial statements to reflect adjusting events after the reporting period.

   (ii) *Non-adjusting events after the reporting period* An entity shall not adjust the amounts recognized in its

financial statements to reflect non-adjusting events after the reporting period.

(iii) *Dividends* If an entity declares dividends to holders of equity instruments after the reporting period, the entity shall not recognize those dividends as a liability at the end of the reporting period. If dividends are declared (i.e., the dividends are appropriately authorized and no longer at the discretion of the entity) after the reporting period but before the financial statements are authorized for issue, the dividends are not recognized as a liability at the end of the reporting period because they do not meet the criteria of a present obligation in Ind AS 37. Such dividends are disclosed in the notes in accordance with Ind AS 1: *Presentation of Financial Statements.*

6. Exceptions

An entity shall not prepare its financial statements on a going concern basis if management determines after the reporting period either that it intends to liquidate the entity or to cease trading, or that it has no realistic alternative but to do so.

Deterioration in operating results and financial position after the reporting period may indicate a need to consider whether the going concern assumption is still appropriate. If the going concern assumption is no longer appropriate, the effect is so pervasive that this Standard requires a fundamental change in the basis of accounting, rather than an adjustment to the amounts recognized within the original basis of accounting. Ind AS 1 specifies required disclosures if:

(a) The financial statements are not prepared on a going concern basis; or

(b) Management is aware of material uncertainties related to events or conditions that may cast significant doubt upon the entity's ability to continue as a going concern. The events or conditions requiring disclosure may arise after the reporting period.

7. Disclosure

Date of authorization for issue An entity shall disclose the date when the financial statements were authorized for issue and who gave that authorization. If the entity's owners or others have the power to amend the financial statements after issue, the entity shall disclose that fact.

Updating disclosure about conditions at the end of the reporting period If an entity receives information after the reporting period about conditions that existed at the end of the reporting period, it shall update disclosures that relate to those conditions, in the light of the new information.

Non-adjusting events after the reporting period If non-adjusting events after the reporting period are material, non-disclosure could influence the economic decisions that users make on the basis of the financial statements. Accordingly, an entity shall disclose the following for each material category of non-adjusting event after the reporting period:

(a) the nature of the event; and

(b) an estimate of its financial effect, or a statement that such an estimate cannot be made.

The following are examples of non-adjusting events after the reporting period that would generally result in disclosure:

(a) a major business combination after the reporting period (Ind AS 103: *Business Combinations* requires specific disclosures in such cases) or disposing of a major subsidiary;

(b) announcing a plan to discontinue an operation;

(c) major purchases of assets, classification of assets as held for sale in accordance with Ind AS 105: *Non-current Assets Held for Sale and Discontinued Operations*, other disposals of assets, or expropriation of major assets by government;

(d) the destruction of a major production plant by a fire after the reporting period;

(e) announcing, or commencing the implementation of, a major restructuring (Ind AS 37);

(f) major ordinary share transactions and potential ordinary share transactions after the reporting period (Ind AS 33: *Earnings per Share* requires an entity to disclose a description of such transactions, other than when such transactions involve capitalization or bonus issues, share splits, or reverse share splits all of which are required to be adjusted under Ind AS 33);

(g) abnormally large changes after the reporting period in asset prices or foreign exchange rates;

(h) changes in tax rates or tax laws enacted or announced after the reporting period that have a significant effect on current and deferred tax assets and liabilities (see Ind AS 12: *Income Taxes*);

(i) entering into significant commitments or contingent liabilities, for example, by issuing significant guarantees; and

(j) commencing major litigation arising solely out of events that occurred after the reporting period.

(*Adapted from* https://www.iasplus.com/en/standards/ias/ias10; https://www.wirc-icai.org/material/IAS-%2010%20Events%20after%20Reporting%20Period.pdf; http://mca.gov.in/Ministry/pdf/INDAS10.pdf)

Examples/Comments

1. A trade customer, for whose balance, a full specific provision has been made at 31st March 2019, paid the full amount of ₹84,000 before the date if final approval of financial statements by Board of Directors.

   It is an adjusting event. Provision for bad debts is to be reduced by ₹84,000 in the financial statements, by increasing the profit in profit and loss account.

2. In April 2019 a fire destroyed part of a company's warehouse, with an uninsured loss of inventory worth ₹10 lakh and damaged the building, also uninsured of ₹25 lakh. The going concern status of the company is not affected. It is a non-adjusting event. The profit of the period under consideration will not be altered. However, a detailed note should be given stating the fact and its impact.

3. Jeeyansh Limited has prepared its account for the year ended 31st March 2019 in the usual manner. Jeeyansh

Limited's only plant has been destroyed by fire on 15th May 2019. The plant was not insured. Now it is certain that the company will be liquidated.

The financial statements to 31st March 2019 should be produced on a liquidation basis, not a going concern basis.

4. The professional valuation of a fixed asset one month after the balance sheet date at a figure of ₹3 lakh below the current book value. The diminution in value is considered to be permanent.

This is an adjusting event, because the valuation provides information about a condition existing at the balance sheet date. if it could be established that the decline in value occurred after the balance sheet date, it would become a non-adjusting event.

5. The destruction of the company's warehouse two weeks after the balance sheet date. The loss on the building and stock it contained amounted to ₹6 lakh; due to administrative error neither was insured.

This is a non-adjusting event which concerns a condition which did not exist at the balance sheet date. Moreover, this event does not indicate that the application of going concern concept is not appropriate. Therefore, it should be disclosed in the notes to the financial statements.

Ind AS 12: Income Taxes

1. The objective of this Standard is to prescribe the accounting treatment for income taxes. The principal issue in accounting for income taxes is how to account for the current and future tax consequences of:

    (a) the future recovery (settlement) of the carrying amount of assets (liabilities) that are recognized in an entity's balance sheet; and

    (b) transactions and other events of the current period that are recognized in an entity's financial statements.

For the purposes of this Standard, income taxes include all domestic and foreign taxes which are based on taxable profits. Income taxes also include taxes, such as withholding taxes, which are payable by a subsidiary, associate or joint arrangement on distributions to the reporting entity.

2. Terms

Accounting profit is profit or loss for a period before deducting tax expense.

Taxable profit (tax loss) is the profit (loss) for a period, determined in accordance with the rules established by the taxation authorities, upon which income taxes are payable (recoverable).

Tax expense (tax income) is the aggregate amount included in the determination of profit or loss for the period in respect of current tax and deferred tax.

Current tax is the amount of income taxes payable (recoverable) in respect of the taxable profit (tax loss) for a period.

Deferred tax liabilities are the amounts of income taxes payable in future periods in respect of taxable temporary differences.

Deferred tax assets are the amounts of income taxes recoverable in future periods in respect of

    (a) deductible temporary differences;

    (b) the carry forward of unused tax losses; and

    (c) the carry forward of unused tax credits.

Temporary differences are differences between the carrying amount of an asset or liability in the balance sheet and its tax base. Temporary differences may be either:

    (a) *taxable temporary differences*, which are temporary differences that will result in taxable amounts in determining taxable profit (tax loss) of future periods when the carrying amount of the asset or liability is recovered or settled; or

    (b) *deductible temporary differences*, which are temporary differences that will result in amounts that are deductible in determining taxable profit (tax loss) of future periods when the carrying amount of the asset or liability is recovered or settled.

Tax base of an asset or liability is the amount attributed to that asset or liability for tax purposes.

Tax expense (Tax income) comprises current tax expense (current tax income) and deferred tax expense (deferred tax income).

3. Recognition and measurement

Current tax expense for a period is based on the taxable and deductible amounts to be used for the computation of the taxable income for the current year. An entity recognizes a liability in the balance sheet in respect of current tax expense for the current and prior periods to the extent unpaid. It recognizes an asset if current tax has been overpaid.

Current tax assets and liabilities for the current and prior periods are measured at the amount expected to be paid to (recovered from) the taxation authorities, using the tax rates and tax laws that have been enacted or substantively enacted by the balance sheet date.

Tax payable based on taxable profit seldom matches the tax expense that might be expected based on pre-tax accounting profit. The mismatch can occur because Ind AS recognition criteria for items of income and expense are different from the treatment of items under tax law.

Management only recognizes a deferred tax asset for deductible temporary differences to the extent that it is probable that taxable profit will be available against which the deductible temporary difference can be utilized. This also applies to deferred tax assets for unused tax losses carried forward.

Current and deferred tax is recognized in profit or loss for the period, unless the tax arises from a business combination or a transaction or event that is recognized outside profit or loss, either in other comprehensive income or directly in equity in the same or different period.

The accompanying tax consequences, for example, a change in tax rates or tax laws, a reassessment of the recoverability of deferred tax assets or a change in the expected manner of recovery of an asset are recognized in profit or loss, except to

the extent that they relate to the items previously charged or credited outside of profit or loss.

4. Disclosure

The major components of tax expense (income) shall be disclosed separately.

Components of tax expense (income) may include

(a) current tax expense (income);

(b) any adjustments recognized in the period for current tax of prior periods;

(c) the amount of deferred tax expense (income) relating to the origination and reversal of temporary differences;

(d) the amount of deferred tax expense (income) relating to changes in tax rates or the imposition of new taxes;

(e) the amount of the benefit arising from a previously unrecognized tax loss, tax credit, or temporary difference of a prior period that is used to reduce current tax expense;

(f) the amount of the benefit from a previously unrecognized tax loss, tax credit, or temporary difference of a prior period that is used to reduce deferred tax expense;

(g) deferred tax expense arising from the write-down, or reversal of a previous write-down, of a deferred tax asset; and

(h) the amount of tax expense (income) relating to those changes in accounting policies and errors that are included in profit or loss in accordance with Ind AS 8, because they cannot be accounted for retrospectively.

The following shall also be disclosed separately:

(a) the aggregate current and deferred tax relating to items that are charged or credited directly to equity;
  (i) the amount of income tax relating to each component of other comprehensive income;

(b) a changes in the tax status of an entity or its shareholders;

(c) an explanation of the relationship between tax expense (income) and accounting profit in either or both of the following forms:
  (i) a numerical reconciliation between tax expense (income) and the product of accounting profit multiplied by the applicable tax rate(s), disclosing also the basis on which the applicable tax rate(s) is (are) computed; or
  (ii) a numerical reconciliation between the average effective tax rate and the applicable tax rate, disclosing also the basis on which the applicable tax rate is computed;

(d) an explanation of changes in the applicable tax rate(s) compared to the previous accounting period;

(e) the amount (and expiry date, if any) of deductible temporary differences, unused tax losses, and unused tax credits for which no deferred tax asset is recognized in the balance sheet;

(f) the aggregate amount of temporary differences associated with investments in subsidiaries, branches, and associates and interests in joint arrangements, for which deferred tax liabilities have not been recognized;

(g) in respect of each type of temporary difference, and in respect of each type of unused tax losses and unused tax credits:
  (i) the amount of the deferred tax assets and liabilities recognized in the balance sheet for each period presented;
  (ii) the amount of the deferred tax income or expense recognized in profit or loss, if this is not apparent from the changes in the amounts recognized in the balance sheet;

(h) in respect of discontinued operations, the tax expense relating to
  (i) the gain or loss on discontinuance; and
  (ii) the profit or loss from the ordinary activities of the discontinued operation for the period, together with the corresponding amounts for each prior period presented;

(i) the amount of income tax consequences of dividends to shareholders of the entity that were proposed or declared before the financial statements were approved for issue, but are not recognized as a liability in the financial statements;

(j) if a business combination in which the entity is the acquirer causes a change in the amount recognized for its pre-acquisition deferred tax asset, the amount of that change; and

(k) if the deferred tax benefits acquired in a business combination are not recognized at the acquisition date but are recognized after the acquisition date, a description of the event or change in circumstances that caused the deferred tax benefits to be recognized.

An entity shall disclose the amount of a deferred tax asset and the nature of the evidence supporting its recognition, when

(a) the utilization of the deferred tax asset is dependent on future taxable profits in excess of the profits arising from the reversal of existing taxable temporary differences; and

(b) the entity has suffered a loss in either the current or preceding period in the tax jurisdiction to which the deferred tax asset relates.

(*Adapted from* http://www.mca.gov.in/Ministry/pdf/Ind_AS12.pdf; https://www.wirc-icai.org/material/IAS%2012%20Income%20taxes.pdf; https://www.iasplus.com/en/standards/ias/ias12)

Ind AS 115: Revenue from Contracts with Customers

1. This Standard deals with methods of accounting for construction contracts. Type of contract recognized are fixed price contracts and cost plus contracts.

2. Two types of accounting treatment have been prescribed: completed contract method (CCM) and percentage

completion method (PCM). The Standard permits a choice between PCM and CCM for accounting purpose.

3. Where two or more contracts bear similar characteristics, the accounting should be by the same method, PCM or CCM.

4. Revenue from construction contracts is measured at transaction price, i.e., the amount of consideration to which an entity expects to be entitled in exchange for transferring promised goods or services to a customer, excluding amounts collected on behalf of third parties.

5. Revenue is recognized when the outcome of a construction contract can be estimated reliably, and contract revenue should be recognized by reference to the stage of completion of the contract activity at the reporting date.

6. The disclosure requirement pertains to the method adopted, changes in the method, progressive payments received, WIP (work-in-progress), money retained by clients, contingent losses, etc.

7. This Standard deals with timing and amount of revenue to be recognized in the profit and loss account.

8. This does not apply to construction contracts.

9. Revenue is the gross inflow of cash, receivables or other consideration arising in the course of the ordinary activities. Revenue is measured by the charges made to customers or clients for goods supplied and services rendered to them and by the charges and rewards arising from the use of resources by them.

10. This Standard recognizes the flow of revenue from the following sources: sale of goods, rendering of services, and use of resources by others (interest, dividend, and royalty).

11. If consideration is not measurable, postpone recognition of revenue.

12. If there is uncertainty in collection, postpone to the extent of uncertainty. If uncertainty arises after recognition, then recognize revenue but make a provision.

13. In the case of sale of goods, revenue is recognized if the seller has transferred to the buyer the property in goods for a consideration, or significant risk and rewards of ownership has been transferred to the buyer and no uncertainty exists regarding collectibility of consideration.

14. For rendering of service, the Standard suggests two methods: completed service method (when the final act is done) and proportionate service method.

15. The disclosure requirement is that the amount of turnover less excise duty is disclosed on the face of profit and loss account.

Ind AS 16: Property, Plant, and Equipment

1. Introduction

The objective of this Standard is to prescribe the accounting treatment for property, plant and equipment so that users of the financial statements can discern information about an entity's investment in its property, plant and equipment and the changes in such investment.

This Standard does not apply to:

(a) property, plant and equipment classified as held for sale;

(b) biological assets related to agricultural activity other than bearer plants. This Standard applies to bearer plants but it does not apply to the produce on bearer plants;

(c) the recognition and measurement of exploration and evaluation assets; and

(d) mineral rights and mineral reserves such as oil, natural gas, and similar non-regenerative resources.

2. Terms

The following terms are used in this Standard with the meanings specified:

Bearer plant is a living plant that

(a) is used in the production or supply of agricultural produce;

(b) is expected to bear produce for more than one period; and

(c) has a remote likelihood of being sold as agricultural produce, except for incidental scrap sales.

Carrying amount is the amount at which an asset is recognized after deducting any accumulated depreciation and accumulated impairment losses.

Cost is the amount of cash or cash equivalents paid or the fair value of the other consideration given to acquire an asset at the time of its acquisition or construction or, where applicable, the amount attributed to that asset when initially recognized in accordance with the specific requirements of other Indian Accounting Standards, e.g. Ind AS 102: *Share-based Payment*.

Depreciable amount is the cost of an asset, or other amount substituted for cost, less its residual value.

Depreciation is the systematic allocation of the depreciable amount of an asset over its useful life.

Entity-specific value is the present value of the cash flows an entity expects to arise from the continuing use of an asset and from its disposal at the end of its useful life or expects to incur when settling a liability.

Fair value is the price that would be received to sell an asset or paid to transfer a liability in an orderly transaction between market participants at the measurement date.

An *impairment loss* is the amount by which the carrying amount of an asset exceeds its recoverable amount.

Property, plant, and equipment are tangible items that:

(a) are held for use in the production or supply of goods or services, for rental to others, or for administrative purposes; and

(b) are expected to be used during more than one period.

Recoverable amount is the higher of an asset's fair value less costs to sell and its value in use.

Residual value of an asset is the estimated amount that an entity would currently obtain from disposal of the asset, after deducting the estimated costs of disposal, if the asset were already of the age and in the condition expected at the end of its useful life.

Useful life is

(a) the period over which an asset is expected to be available for use by an entity; or

(b) the number of production or similar units expected to be obtained from the asset by an entity.

3. Recognition and measurement

Property, plant, and equipment (PPE) is recognized when the cost of an asset can be reliably measured and it is probable that the entity will obtain future economic benefits from the asset.

PPE is measured initially at cost. Cost includes the fair value of the consideration given to acquire the asset (net of discounts and rebates) and any directly attributable cost of bringing the asset to working condition for its intended use (inclusive of import duties and non-refundable purchase taxes).

Directly attributable costs include the cost of site preparation, delivery, installation costs, relevant professional fees, and the estimated cost of dismantling and removing the asset and restoring the site (to the extent that such a cost is recognized as a provision).

Items of PPE may be acquired for safety or environmental reasons. The acquisition of such PPE, although not directly increasing the future economic benefits of any particular existing item of property, plant, and equipment, may be necessary for an entity to obtain the future economic benefits from its other assets. Such items of property, plant, and equipment qualify for recognition as assets because they enable an entity to derive future economic benefits from related assets in excess of what could be derived had those items not been acquired.

Classes of PPE are carried at historical cost less accumulated depreciation and any accumulated impairment losses (the cost model), or at a revalued amount less any accumulated depreciation and subsequent accumulated impairment losses (the revaluation model). The depreciable amount of PPE (being the gross carrying value less the estimated residual value) is depreciated on a systematic basis over its useful life.

Subsequent expenditure relating to an item of PPE is capitalized if it meets the recognition criteria. PPE may comprise parts with different useful lives. Depreciation is calculated based on each individual part's life. In case of replacement of one part, the new part is capitalized to the extent that it meets the recognition criteria of an asset, and the carrying amount of the parts replaced is derecognized.

An entity does not recognize in the carrying amount of an item of PPE the costs of the day-to-day servicing of the item. Rather, these costs are recognized in profit or loss as incurred. Costs of day-to-day servicing are primarily the costs of labour and consumables, and may include the cost of small parts. The purpose of these expenditures is often described as for the 'repairs and maintenance' of the item of PPE.

The cost of a major inspection or overhaul of an item occurring at regular intervals over the useful life of the item is capitalized to the extent that it meets the recognition criteria of an asset. The carrying amounts of the parts replaced are derecognized.

A condition of continuing to operate an item of PPE (for example, an aircraft) may be performing regular major inspections for faults regardless of whether parts of the item are replaced. When each major inspection is performed, its cost is recognized in the carrying amount of the item of PPE as a replacement if the recognition criteria are satisfied. Any remaining carrying amount of the cost of the previous inspection (as distinct from physical parts) is derecognized.

4. Self-constructed asset

The cost of a self-constructed asset is determined using the same principles as for an acquired asset. If an entity makes similar assets for sale in the normal course of business, the cost of the asset is usually the same as the cost of constructing an asset for sale (Ind AS 2). Therefore, any internal profits are eliminated in arriving at such costs. Similarly, the cost of abnormal amounts of wasted material, labour, or other resources incurred in self-constructing an asset is not included in the cost of the asset.

5. Exchange of asset

One or more items of property, plant, and equipment may be acquired in exchange for a non-monetary asset or assets, or a combination of monetary and non-monetary assets. The cost of such an item of PPE is measured at fair value unless (a) the exchange transaction lacks commercial substance or (b) the fair value of neither the asset received nor the asset given up is reliably measurable. The acquired item is measured in this way even if an entity cannot immediately derecognize the asset given up. If the acquired item is not measured at fair value, its cost is measured at the carrying amount of the asset given up.

6. Revaluation

After recognition as an asset, an item of PPE whose fair value can be measured reliably shall be carried at a revalued amount, being its fair value at the date of the revaluation less any subsequent accumulated depreciation and subsequent accumulated impairment losses.

Revaluations shall be made with sufficient regularity to ensure that the carrying amount does not differ materially from that which would be determined using fair value at the end of the reporting period.

When an item of PPE, the carrying amount of that asset is adjusted to the revalued amount, at the date of the revaluation, the asset is treated in one of the following ways:

(a) the gross carrying amount is adjusted in a manner that is consistent with the revaluation of the carrying amount of the asset. For example, the gross carrying amount may be restated by reference to observable market data or it may be restated proportionately to the change in the carrying amount. The accumulated depreciation at the date of the revaluation is adjusted to equal the difference between the gross carrying amount and the carrying amount of the asset after taking into account accumulated impairment losses; or

(b) the accumulated depreciation is eliminated against the gross carrying amount of the asset.

If an item of property, plant, and equipment is revalued, the entire class of property, plant, and equipment to which that asset belongs shall be revalued.

7. Depreciation

Each part of an item of PPE with a cost that is significant in relation to the total cost of the item shall be depreciated separately. An entity allocates the amount initially recognized in respect of an item of PPE to its significant parts and depreciates separately each such part. For example, it may be appropriate to depreciate separately the airframe and engines of an aircraft, whether owned or subject to a finance lease.

Similarly, if an entity acquires PPE subject to an operating lease in which it is the lessor, it may be appropriate to depreciate separately amounts reflected in the cost of that item that are attributable to favourable or unfavourable lease terms relative to market terms.

The depreciable amount of an asset shall be allocated on a systematic basis over its useful life. The depreciable amount of an asset is determined after deducting its residual value.

In practice, the residual value of an asset is often insignificant and therefore immaterial in the calculation of the depreciable amount.

The residual value and the useful life of an asset shall be reviewed at least at each financial year-end and, if expectations differ from previous estimates, the change(s) shall be accounted for as a change in an accounting estimate in accordance with Ind AS 8: *Accounting Policies, Changes in Accounting Estimates and Errors.*

Depreciation is recognized even if the fair value of the asset exceeds its carrying amount, as long as the asset's residual value does not exceed its carrying amount. Repair and maintenance of an asset do not negate the need to depreciate it.

A variety of depreciation methods can be used to allocate the depreciable amount of an asset on a systematic basis over its useful life. These methods include the straight-line method, the diminishing balance method, and the units of production method. Straight-line depreciation results in a constant charge over the useful life if the asset's residual value does not change. The diminishing balance method results in a decreasing charge over the useful life. The units of production method result in a charge based on the expected use or output. The entity selects the method that most closely reflects the expected pattern of consumption of the future economic benefits embodied in the asset. That method is applied consistently from period to period unless there is a change in the expected pattern of consumption of those future economic benefits.

8. Impairment

To determine whether an item of PPE is impaired, an entity applies Ind AS 36: *Impairment of Assets.* That Standard explains how an entity reviews the carrying amount of its assets, how it determines the recoverable amount of an asset, and when it recognizes, or reverses the recognition of, an impairment loss.

(*Adapted from* http://mca.gov.in/Ministry/pdf/INDAS16.pdf; https://www.readyratios.com/reference/ifrs/ias_16_property_plant_and_equipment.html; https://inform.pwc.com/inform2/show?action=informContent&id=0904082003182692)

Ind AS 17: Leases

1. Introduction

The objective of this Standard is to prescribe, for lessees and lessors, the appropriate accounting policies and disclosure to apply in relation to leases.

This Standard shall be applied in accounting for all leases other than

(a) leases to explore for or use minerals, oil, natural gas and similar non-regenerative resources; and

(b) licensing agreements for such items as motion picture films, video recordings, plays, manuscripts, patents, and copyrights.

However, this Standard shall not be applied as the basis of measurement for

(a) property held by lessees that is accounted for as investment property;

(b) investment property provided by lessors under operating leases;

(c) biological assets within the scope of Agriculture held by lessees under finance leases; or

(d) biological assets within the scope of Agriculture provided by lessors under operating leases.

2. Terms

Lease is an agreement whereby the lessor conveys to the lessee in return for a payment or series of payments the right to use an asset for an agreed period of time. The definition of a lease includes contracts for the hire of an asset that contain a provision giving the hirer an option to acquire title to the asset upon the fulfilment of agreed conditions. These contracts are sometimes known as hire purchase contracts.

Finance lease is a lease that transfers substantially all the risks and rewards incidental to ownership of an asset. Title may or may not eventually be transferred.

Operating lease is a lease other than a finance lease.

Non-cancellable lease is a lease that is cancellable only

(a) upon the occurrence of some remote contingency;

(b) with the permission of the lessor;

(c) if the lessee enters into a new lease for the same or an equivalent asset with the same lessor; or

(d) upon payment by the lessee of such an additional amount that, at inception of the lease, continuation of the lease is reasonably certain.

Inception of the lease is the earlier of the date of the lease agreement and the date of commitment by the parties to the principal provisions of the lease.

As at this date,

(a) a lease is classified as either an operating or a finance lease; and

(b) in the case of a finance lease, the amounts to be recognized at the commencement of the lease term are determined.

Commencement of the lease term is the date from which the lessee is entitled to exercise its right to use the leased asset. It is the date of initial recognition of the lease (i.e. the recognition of the assets, liabilities, income or expenses resulting from the lease, as appropriate).

Lease term is the non-cancellable period for which the lessee has contracted to lease the asset together with any further terms for which the lessee has the option to continue to lease the asset, with or without further payment, when at the inception of the lease it is reasonably certain that the lessee will exercise the option.

Minimum lease payments are the payments over the lease term that the lessee is or can be required to make, excluding contingent rent, costs for services and taxes to be paid by and reimbursed to the lessor, together with:

(a) for a lessee, any amounts guaranteed by the lessee or by a party related to the lessee; or

(b) for a lessor, any residual value guaranteed to the lessor by (i) the lessee; (ii) a party related to the lessee; or (iii) a third party unrelated to the lessor that is financially capable of discharging the obligations under the guarantee.

However, if the lessee has an option to purchase the asset at a price that is expected to be sufficiently lower than fair value at the date the option becomes exercizable for it to be reasonably certain, at the inception of the lease, that the option will be exercised, the minimum lease payments comprise the minimum payments payable over the lease term to the expected date of exercise of this purchase option and the payment required to exercise it.

Fair value is the amount for which an asset could be exchanged, or a liability settled, between knowledgeable, willing parties in an arm's length transaction.

Economic life is either

(a) the period over which an asset is expected to be economically usable by one or more users; or

(b) the number of production or similar units expected to be obtained from the asset by one or more users.

Useful life is the estimated remaining period, from the commencement of the lease term, without limitation by the lease term, over which the economic benefits embodied in the asset are expected to be consumed by the entity.

Guaranteed residual value is

(a) for a lessee, that part of the residual value that is guaranteed by the lessee or by a party related to the lessee (the amount of the guarantee being the maximum amount that could, in any event, become payable); and

(b) for a lessor, that part of the residual value that is guaranteed by the lessee or by a third party unrelated to the lessor that is financially capable of discharging the obligations under the guarantee.

Unguaranteed residual value is that portion of the residual value of the leased asset, the realiza tion of which by the lessor is not assured or is guaranteed solely by a party related to the lessor.

Initial direct costs are incremental costs that are directly attributable to negotiating and arranging a lease, except for such costs incurred by manufacturer or dealer lessors.

Gross investment in the lease is the aggregate of

(a) the minimum lease payments receivable by the lessor under a finance lease, and

(b) any unguaranteed residual value accruing to the lessor.

Net investment in the lease is the gross investment in the lease discounted at the interest rate implicit in the lease. Interest rate is the difference between

(a) the gross investment in the lease, and

(b) the net investment in the lease.

Interest rate implicit in the lease is the discount rate that, at the inception of the lease, causes the aggregate present value of (a) the minimum lease payments and (b) the unguaranteed residual value to be equal to the sum of (i) the fair value of the leased asset and (ii) any initial direct costs of the lessor.

Lessee's incremental borrowing rate of interest is the rate of interest the lessee would have to pay on a similar lease or, if that is not determinable, the rate that, at the inception of the lease, the lessee would incur to borrow over a similar term, and with a similar security, the funds necessary to purchase the asset.

Contingent rent is that portion of the lease payments that is not fixed in amount but is based on the future amount of a factor that changes other than with the passage of time (e.g., percentage of future sales, amount of future use, future price indices, future market rates of interest).

3. Asset plus services agreement

Ind AS 17 also applies to agreements that transfer the right to use assets that also contain substantial service elements.

Example: Entity A may enter into an agreement to rent photocopiers from entity B. As part of that agreement, entity B agrees to provide maintenance services in respect of the copiers. The fact that entity B has agreed to provide maintenance services does not change the fact that the part of the agreement that deals with the provision of the copiers should be treated as a lease.

A lease gives one party (the lessee) the right to use an asset over an agreed period of time in return for payment to the lessor. Leasing is an important source of medium and long-term financing; and accounting for leases can have a significant impact on lessees' and lessors' financial statements.

4. Finance lease and operating lease

Leases are classified as finance or operating leases at inception, depending on whether substantially all the risks and rewards of ownership transfers to the lessee. Under a finance lease, the lessee has substantially all of the risks and rewards of ownership. All other leases are operating leases. Leases of land and buildings are considered separately.

Finance lease A lease that transfers substantially all the risks and rewards incidental to ownership of an asset. Title may or may not eventually be transferred.

Finance lease indicators

1. Transfer of ownership to lessee
2. Option to purchase asset at a price that is expected to be sufficiently lower than the fair value

3. Lease term equals to major part of the economic life of the asset

4. Present value of the minimum lease payments amounts to at least substantially all of the fair value of the leased asset (Note: No hard line defined for 'substantial' – can be taken to be at least 90%).

5. Specialized nature such that lessee can only use

Under a finance lease, the lessee recognizes an asset held under a finance lease and a corresponding obligation to pay rentals. The lessee depreciates the asset. The lessor recognizes the leased asset as a receivable. The receivable is measured at the 'net investment' in the lease–the minimum lease payments receivable, discounted at the internal rate of return of the lease, plus the unguaranteed residual that accrues to the lessor.

Operating lease A lease other than a finance lease—in effect it is a lease where substantially all the risks and rewards incidental to ownership of an asset are not transferred.

Under an operating lease, the lessee does not recognize an asset and lease obligation. The lessor continues to recognize the leased asset and depreciates it. The rentals paid are normally charged to the income statement of the lessee and credited to that of the lessor on a straight-line basis unless another systematic basis is more representative of the time pattern of the user's benefit or if the payments to the lessor are agreed to increase in line with expected general inflation to compensate for the lessor's expected inflationary cost increases.

5. Inception and commencement of the lease

Lease classification (whether operating or finance) is made at the inception of the lease. The inception of the lease is the earlier of the date of lease agreement or parties' commitment to the lease's principal provisions. The commencement of the lease term is the date from which the lessee is entitled to exercise its right to use the leased asset

Example: A lessee may sign an agreement to lease a car on 31 March, but does not take delivery of the car until 30 June. The classification of the lease and the measurement of the related assets and liabilities will take place on 31 March, but the recognition in the financial statements of the lease assets and liabilities will not take place until 30 June.

6. Lease term

Non-cancellable period Period for which the lessee has contracted to lease the asset together with any further terms for which the lessee has the option to continue to lease the asset, with or without further payment.

Non-cancellable lease A non-cancellable lease is defined by the Standard as a lease that is cancellable only

1. upon the occurrence of some remote contingency
2. with the permission of the lessor
3. if the lessee enters into a new lease for the same or an equivalent asset with the same lessor

Break and exit clause If a lease contains a clean break clause, that is, where the lessee is free to walk away from the lease agreement after a certain time without penalty, then the lease term for accounting purposes will normally be the period between the commencement of the lease and the earliest point at which the break option is exercizable by the lessee.

Renewal clauses and lease term Where the terms of renewal are significantly below a fair market rental then it is reasonable to assume that the lessee will extend the lease. Then the lease term would include both the minimum period and the renewal period.

Where the rentals in the secondary period are based on a fair market basis, then the lease term will normally exclude the secondary period.

Changes in lease classification Changes in estimates or changes in circumstances should not result in a change in classification. Lease renegotiation results in reclassification of operating lease as a finance lease.

Lease involving land & buildings For classifying a lease involving land and buildings, land and buildings elements are required to be separated.

1. The minimum lease payments are allocated between the land and buildings elements in proportion to their relative fair values.

2. The land element of lease is normally classified as an operating lease; however, when the title of land passes to the lessee at the end of the lease term it is classified as finance lease.

3. A long-term lease of land should be classified on the basis of its substance and not only based on its legal form.

4. In the case of long-term land agreements, the risks and rewards would be automatically transferred to the lessee, even though the title is not transferred in such a case, the lease for the land should be treated as a finance lease.

5. The buildings element is classified as an operating or finance lease by applying the classification criteria specified in the Standard.

7. Accounting for finance leases—by lessees

Accounted in lessee's balance sheet both as an asset and as an obligation to pay future rentals:

Amount to recognize = Lower of fair value of the leased asset or the present value of the minimum lease payments

Initial direct costs of the lessee are added to the amount recognized as an asset.

Discount factor is the interest rate implicit in the lease.

Interest rate implicit in lease It is the discount rate that, at the inception of the lease, causes the present value of a) the minimum lease payments b) the unguaranteed residual value = c) Fair value of the leased asset + Initial direct costs of the lessor.

Examples/Comments

1. A company leases an item of equipment whose useful life is 10 years. Lease payments are ₹15,580 per year payable at the end of each of the next 10 years. This is a capital lease because the lease term exceeds 75% of the asset's life. The fair value of the equipment is ₹1 lakh. When the equipment is acquired, the entry is

Equipment account ...(Add)... Dr. .... ₹1,00,000

To Capital lease (Financial lease) obligation A/c (Add) ₹1,00,000

Assume that the firm's annual lease payments consist ₹9,000 of interest expense and ₹6,580 to reduce the liability. The entry for this payment is as follows:

Interest Expenses account (Add)   Dr....₹9,000
Capital lease (Financial lease) obligation a/c (Less) Dr....₹6,580
To Cash account (Less)   ₹15,580

Also, depreciation on the asset would be charged as an expense each year, just as if the entity had bought the asset for cash. Assuming the straight-line method is used, the entry is

Depreciation expense account (Add)   Dr.... ₹10,000
To Equipment account ... (Less)   ₹10,000

At the end of the 10 years, all of the ₹1,00,000 asset cost will have been charged to Expense via depreciation mechanism. Also, the capital lease obligation will have been reduced to zero, and the annual interest expense will have been recognized in each of the 10 years via entries such as the one shown above. Note that once the lease item is acquired and the initial equipment asset and lease obligation liability entry is made, accounting for the leased asset and for the lease obligation are separate, unrelated processes.

(*Adapted from* http://www.mca.gov.in/Ministry/pdf/Ind_AS17.pdf; https://library.croneri. co.uk/cch_uk/dgaap/appc4-8-3; https://assets.kpmg/content/dam/kpmg/xx/pdf/2017/09/ leases-discount-rate.pdf)

Ind AS 19: Employee Benefits

1. It deals with accounting treatment for retirement benefits and applies to defined contribution schemes and defined benefit schemes.
2. As per the accounting treatment, the provident fund (PF) and other defined contribution schemes should be charged to profit and loss on accrual basis. In case of defined benefit schemes, benefit is to be met out of own funds or creation of trust or insurance premium. It should be debited to profit and loss account. Actuarial valuation should be made at least once in three years.
3. Shortfall in actuarial valuation is charged to profit and loss account and excess be treated as prepayment.
4. There should be disclosure of the method of calculation of retirement benefit, date of actuarial valuation, and method of actuarial valuation.

Ind AS 20: Accounting for Government Grants and Disclosure of Government Assistance

1. Introduction

This Standard shall be applied in accounting for, and in the disclosure of, government grants and in the disclosure of other forms of government assistance.

This Standard does not deal with

(a) the special problems arising in accounting for government grants in financial statements reflecting the effects of changing prices or in supplementary information of a similar nature;

(b) government assistance that is provided for an entity in the form of benefits that are available in determining taxable profit or tax loss, or are determined or limited on the basis of income tax liability. Examples of such benefits are income tax holidays, investment tax credits, accelerated depreciation;

(c) government participation in the ownership of the entity; and

(d) government grants covered by Ind AS 41: Agriculture.

Government grants are sometimes called by other names such as subsidies, subventions, or premiums.

2. Terms

Government refers to government, government agencies, and similar bodies whether local, national, or international.

Government assistance is action by government designed to provide an economic benefit specific to an entity or range of entities qualifying under certain criteria. Government assistance for the purpose of this Standard does not include benefits provided only indirectly through action affecting general trading conditions, such as the provision of infrastructure in development areas or the imposition of trading constraints on competitors.

Government grants are assistance by government in the form of transfers of resources to an entity in return for past or future compliance with certain conditions relating to the operating activities of the entity. They exclude those forms of government assistance which cannot reasonably have a value placed upon them and transactions with government which cannot be distinguished from the normal trading transactions of the entity.

Grants related to assets are government grants whose primary condition is that an entity qualifying for them should purchase, construct, or otherwise acquire long-term assets. Subsidiary conditions may also be attached restricting the type or location of the assets or the periods during which they are to be acquired or held.

Grants related to income are government grants other than those related to assets.

Forgivable loans are loans which the lender undertakes to waive repayment of under certain prescribed conditions.

Fair value is the price that would be received to sell an asset or paid to transfer a liability in an orderly transaction between market participants at the measurement date. (See Ind AS 113: *Fair Value Measurement*)

3. Recognition and measurement

A forgivable loan from government is treated as a government grant when there is reasonable assurance that the entity will meet the terms for forgiveness of the loan.

The benefit of a government loan at a below-market rate of interest is treated as a government grant. The loan shall be recognized and measured in accordance with Ind AS 109: *Financial Instruments*. The benefit of the below market rate of interest shall be measured as the difference between the initial carrying value of the loan determined in accordance with Ind AS 109, and the proceeds received. The benefit is accounted for in accordance with this Standard. The entity shall consider the conditions and obligations that have been, or must be, met when identifying the costs for which the benefit of the loan is intended to compensate.

Once a government grant is recognized, any related contingent liability or contingent asset is treated in accordance with Ind AS 37: *Provisions, Contingent Liabilities and Contingent Assets.*

Government grants shall be recognized in profit or loss on a systematic basis over the periods in which the entity recognizes as expenses the related costs for which the grants are intended to compensate.

There are two broad approaches to the accounting for government grants: the capital approach, under which a grant is recognized outside profit or loss, and the income approach, under which a grant is recognized in profit or loss over one or more periods.

Government grants are recognized when there is reasonable assurance that the entity will comply with the conditions related to them and that the grants will be received.

Grants related to income are recognized in profit or loss on a systematic basis over the periods necessary to match them with the related costs that they are intended to compensate. They are either offset against the related expense or presented as separate income. The timing of such recognition in profit or loss will depend on the fulfilment of any conditions or obligations attached to the grant.

Grants related to assets are presented as deferred income in the balance sheet. Profit or loss will be affected by deferred income being recognized as income systematically over the useful life of the related asset.

Cash movements related to purchase of assets and receipt of related grants are disclosed as separate items in the statement of cash flows.

A government grant that becomes receivable as compensation for expenses or losses already incurred or for the purpose of giving immediate financial support to the entity with no future related costs shall be recognized in profit or loss of the period in which it becomes receivable.

A government grant may take the form of a transfer of a non-monetary asset, such as land or other resources, for the use of the entity. In these circumstances, the fair value of the non-monetary asset is assessed and both grant and asset are accounted for at that fair value.

A government grant that becomes repayable shall be accounted for as a change in accounting estimate (see Ind AS 8: *Accounting Policies, Changes in Accounting Estimates and Errors*). Repayment of a grant related to income shall be applied first against any unamortised deferred credit recognized in respect of the grant. To the extent that the repayment exceeds any such deferred credit, or when no deferred credit exists, the repayment shall be recognized immediately in profit or loss. Repayment of a grant related to an asset shall be recognized by reducing the deferred income balance by the amount repayable.

Examples/Comments

1. M/s Dilemma Ltd received a grant of ₹100 lakh for acquisition of machinery costing ₹1,200 lakh on 1.04.2015.

The useful life of the machinery is 10 years. On 1.4.2015, the grant was credited to differed income. On 1.4.2018 the company had to refund the whole grant of ₹100 lakh to the government due to non-compliance of condition laid down in the grant agreement. On 1.4.2018, the balance in deferred income was ₹70 lakh, and book value of machinery was ₹840 lakh.

a. What should be the treatment of the refund of the grant and the effect on cost of the fixed asset and the amount of depreciation to be charged during the year 2018–19 in profit and loss account?

b. What should be the treatment of the refund if the grant was deducted from the cost of machinery on 1.4.2015?

Answer:

a. Reverse of ₹70 lakh lying in deferred credit account. Increase cost of asset by ₹30 lakh. Deprecation during 2018–19 shall be ₹124.28 lakh.

   {Based on up to last 3 years : ((1,200 − 840)/3) = ₹120 p.a. + (₹30/7 years) = ₹4.28}

b. At the time of refund, increase value of machinery by ₹100 lakh.

2. M/s Dilemma Ltd has received from Government of India a subsidy of 20% of the cost of machinery. Having fulfilled all the conditions under the sanction, the company on its acquisition of machinery of ₹50 crore received ₹10 crore from the government in the year 2015−16. Give the accounting treatment.

Answer:

As per Ind AS, there are two alternative methods of presentation of government grant relating to specific fixed assets. Under the first method, the grant is shown as a deduction from the gross value of the asset concern in arriving at its book value. Thus, in the case the machinery may be recorded at ₹40 crore. In this manner the grant is recognized in the profit and loss account over the useful life of the depreciable asset by way of reduced depreciation charge.

Under the second method, grant related to depreciable assets are treated as a deferred income which is recognized in the profit and loss account on a systematic and rational basis over useful life of the asset. Such allocation to income is usually made over the periods and in the proportions in which depreciation of related assets is charged. Thus, the government grant of ₹10 crore will be treated as deferred income to be recognized in the profit and loss account on a systematic and rational basis over the useful life of the asset.

3. M/s Dilemma Ltd received subsidy from the central government on installation of anti-pollution equipment. Give the accounting treatment in respect of subsidy.

Answer:

The amount of subsidy is to be deducted from the cost of anti-pollution equipment or it may be credited to deferred income account.

4. M/s Dilemma Ltd received subsidy from the central government for setting up a factory in a backward area. Give the accounting treatment in respect of subsidy.

Answer:

The amount of subsidy is to be credited to the capital reserve account.

(*Adapted from* https://www.readyratios.com/reference/ifrs/ias_20_accounting_for_government_grants_and_disclosure_of_government_assistance.html; https://www.ifrs.org/issued-standards/list-of-standards/ias-20-accounting-for-government-grants-and-disclosure-of-government-assistance/; http://mca.gov.in/Ministry/pdf/INDAS20.pdf)

Ind AS 21: The Effects of Changes in Foreign Exchange Rates

1. Introduction

The objective of this Standard is to prescribe how to include foreign currency transactions and foreign operations in the financial statements of an entity and how to translate financial statements into a presentation currency.

This Standard shall be applied

(a) in accounting for transactions and balances in foreign currencies, except for those derivative transactions and balances that are within the scope of Ind AS 109: *Financial Instruments*;

(b) in translating the results and financial position of foreign operations that are included in the financial statements of the entity by consolidation or the equity method; and

(c) in translating an entity's results and financial position into a presentation currency.

This Standard does not apply to hedge accounting for foreign currency items, including the hedging of a net investment in a foreign operation. Ind AS 109 applies to hedge accounting.

2. Terms

Closing rate is the spot exchange rate at the end of the reporting period.

Exchange difference is the difference resulting from translating a given number of units of one currency into another currency at different exchange rates.

Exchange rate is the ratio of exchange for two currencies.

Fair value is the price that would be received to sell an asset or paid to transfer a liability in an orderly transaction between market participants at the measurement date.

Foreign currency is a currency other than the functional currency of the entity.

Foreign operation is an entity that is a subsidiary, associate, joint arrangement or branch of a reporting entity, the activities of which are based or conducted in a country or currency other than those of the reporting entity.

Functional currency is the currency of the primary economic environment in which the entity operates.

A *group* is a parent and all its subsidiaries.

Monetary items are units of currency held and assets and liabilities to be received or paid in a fixed or determinable number of units of currency.

Net investment in a foreign operation is the amount of the reporting entity's interest in the net assets of that operation.

Presentation currency is the currency in which the financial statements are presented.

Spot exchange rate is the exchange rate for immediate delivery.

3. Benefits of Ind AS 21

- This reduces the risk of foreign activities being incorrectly accounted for and the functional currency being determined incorrectly.
- This could have a major impact on the financial statements.
- This improves efficiency when dealing with foreign activities.

4. How to determine functional currency

The functional currency is determined separately for individual entities. There is no such thing as a 'group functional currency'.

It cannot be chosen freely by an entity. Once determined, it is not changed unless there is a change in those underlying circumstances.

Following are the factors that help in determining the functional currency of an entity:

1. The currency that mainly influences sales prices for goods /services, i.e., sales prices are denominated/settled.
2. The currency of the country whose competitive forces and regulations mainly influence the pricing policy.
3. The currency that mainly influences labour, material, and other costs of providing goods or services.
4. The currency in which finance is generated (i.e., issuing debt and equity instruments).
5. The currency in which receipts from customers are retained by the entity.

5. Importance of functional currency

1. Incorrectly determining the functional currency can have a major impact on the financial statements.
2. If it is determined incorrectly, transactions in the correct functional currency will be recorded as if they were foreign currency transactions.
3. Exchange differences will be recognized on transactions for which no foreign exchange difference should have arisen.
4. Similarly, transactions that should have led to recognition of foreign exchange differences will not be provided for.
5. This may have a significant impact on both the statement of comprehensive income and the statement of financial position.

6. What is foreign operation?

Foreign operation is an entity that is a subsidiary, associate, joint venture, or branch of a reporting entity, the activities of

which are based or conducted in a country or currency other than those of the reporting entity.

7. Presentation currency

The currency in which the financial statements are presented is defined as the presentation currency. Unlike the functional currency, the presentation currency can be any currency of choice.

8. Differences between functional currency and presentation currency

Functional Currency	Presentation Currency
Application of the factors in *Ind AS 21* to a set of facts and circumstances	Flexible choice The presentation currency can be any currency of choice
Selected currency may have a big impact on net profit for the period	Selected currency has no impact on net profit for the period

9. Monetary and non-monetary items

Monetary items   The essential feature of a monetary item is a right to receive (or an obligation to deliver) a fixed or determinable number of units of currency.
Examples:

1. Pensions and other employee benefits to be paid in cash
2. Provisions that are to be settled in cash
3. Cash dividends that are recognized as a liability
4. Investment in debt instruments held with the objective of collecting contractual cash flows

Non-monetary items   The essential feature of a non-monetary item is the absence of a right to receive (or an obligation to deliver) a fixed or determinable number of units of currency.
Examples:

1. Amounts prepaid for goods and services (e.g. prepaid rent)
2. Goodwill and inventories
3. Intangible assets
4. Property, plant, and equipment
5. Provisions that are to be settled by the delivery of a non-monetary asset
6. Investment in equity instruments

10. Foreign currency transactions

A foreign currency transaction is one that is denominated or requires settlement in a foreign currency.

For example, an entity may

1. buy or sell goods or services in a foreign currency;
2. borrow or lend funds when the amounts payable or receivable are in a foreign currency;
3. acquire or dispose of assets, or incur or settle liabilities, in a foreign currency

Recording of foreign currency transactions   An entity must convert foreign currency items into its functional currency for recording in its books of account. A foreign currency transaction is entered into directly by an entity. They often occur on a day-to-day basis. They involve cash flows and increase or decrease the net assets of the entity.

Initial recognition   A foreign currency transaction is one denominated or requiring settlement in a foreign currency.

These transactions are recorded in the functional currency by applying to the foreign currency amount the spot exchange rate between the functional currency and the foreign currency at the date of the transaction.

For practical reasons, a rate that approximates the actual rate at the date of the transaction is often used, for example, an average rate for a week or a month might be used for all transactions in each foreign currency occurring during that period. However, if exchange rates fluctuate significantly, the use of the average rate for a period is inappropriate.

Subsequent measurement at subsequent reporting periods   The treatment of foreign currency items at the end of the reporting period depends on whether the item is

1. monetary or non-monetary, and
2. carried at historical cost or fair value

Items	Measurement Basis	Exchange Rate
Monetary items	NA	Closing rate
Non-monetary items	Historical cost	Exchange rate at the data of transaction
Non-monetary items	Fair value	Exchange rate at the date at which fair value was determined

The carrying amount of an item—Monetary items   The carrying amount of an item is determined in conjunction with other relevant standards.

Example: Property, plant, and equipment may be measured in terms of fair value or historical cost in accordance with Ind AS 16: Property, Plant and Equipment.

Whether the carrying amount is determined on the basis of historical cost or on the basis of fair value, if the amount is determined in a foreign currency it is then translated into the functional currency in accordance with Ind AS 21 only.

Comparison of two amounts   The carrying amount of some items is determined by comparing two or more amounts.

Examples: The carrying amount of inventories is the lower of cost and net realizable value in accordance with Ind AS 2: Inventories. Similarly, as per Ind AS 36: Impairment of Assets, the carrying amount of an asset for which there is an indication of impairment is the lower of its carrying amount before considering possible impairment losses and its recoverable amount.

Carrying amount—Non-monetary assets   When an asset is non-monetary and is measured in a foreign currency, the carrying amount is determined by comparing the cost or carrying amount, as appropriate, translated at the exchange rate at the date when that amount was determined (i.e., the rate at the date of the transaction for an item measured in terms of historical cost); and the net realizable value or recoverable amount, as appropriate, translated at the exchange rate at the date when that value was determined (e.g., the closing rate at the end of the reporting period).

The effect of this comparison may be that an impairment loss is recognized in the foreign currency but would not be recognized in the functional currency, or vice versa.

Several exchanges rates   When several exchange rates are available, the rate used is that at which the future cash flows represented by the transaction or balance could have been settled if those cash flows had occurred at the measurement date. If exchangeability between two currencies is temporarily lacking, the rate used is the first subsequent rate at which exchanges could be made.

11. Financial statements

The results and financial position of an entity whose functional currency is not the currency of a hyperinflationary economy shall be translated into a different presentation currency using the following procedures:

(a) assets and liabilities for each balance sheet presented (i.e. including comparatives) shall be translated at the closing rate at the date of that balance sheet;

(b) income and expenses for each statement of profit and loss presented (i.e. including comparatives) shall be translated at exchange rates at the dates of the transactions; and

(c) all resulting exchange differences shall be recognized in other comprehensive income.

For practical reasons, a rate that approximates the exchange rates at the dates of the transactions, for example, an average rate for the period, is often used to translate income and expense items. However, if exchange rates fluctuate significantly, the use of the average rate for a period is inappropriate.

(*Adapted from* http://www.mca.gov.in/Ministry/pdf/Ind_AS21.pdf; https://www.iasplus.com/en/standards/ias/ias21; https://www.aasb.gov.au/admin/file/content105/c9/AASB121_07-04_COMPfeb07_02-07.pdf)

Ind AS 23: Borrowing Costs

1. Introduction

An entity shall apply this Standard in accounting for borrowing costs. The Standard does not deal with the actual or imputed cost of equity, including preferred capital not classified as a liability.

An entity is not required to apply the Standard to borrowing costs directly attributable to the acquisition, construction or production of

(a) a qualifying asset measured at fair value, for example, a biological asset; or

(b) inventories that are manufactured, or otherwise produced, in large quantities on a repetitive basis.

2. Terms

Borrowing costs are interest and other costs that an entity incurs in connection with the borrowing of funds.

A *qualifying asset* is an asset that necessarily takes a substantial period of time to get ready for its intended use or sale. Borrowing costs may include

(a) interest expense calculated using the effective interest method as described in Ind AS 109: *Financial Instruments*;

(b) finance charges in respect of finance leases recognized in accordance with Ind AS 17: *Leases*; and

(c) exchange differences arising from foreign currency borrowings to the extent that they are regarded as an adjustment to interest costs.

With regard to exchange difference required to be treated as borrowing costs in accordance with point (c), the manner of arriving at the adjustments stated therein shall be as follows:

(i) the adjustment should be of an amount which is equivalent to the extent to which the exchange loss does not exceed the difference between the cost of borrowing in functional currency when compared to the cost of borrowing in a foreign currency.

(ii) where there is an unrealized exchange loss which is treated as an adjustment to interest and subsequently there is a realized or unrealized gain in respect of the settlement or translation of the same borrowing, the gain to the extent of the loss previously recognized as an adjustment should also be recognized as an adjustment to interest.

3. Qualifying and non-qualifying assets

Depending on the circumstances, any of the following may be qualifying assets:

(a) inventories

(b) manufacturing plants

(c) power generation facilities

(d) intangible assets

(e) investment properties

(f) bearer plants

Financial assets and inventories that are manufactured, or otherwise produced, over a short period of time, are not qualifying assets. Assets that are ready for their intended use or sale when acquired are not qualifying assets.

4. Recognition and measurement

An entity shall capitalize borrowing costs that are directly attributable to the acquisition, construction, or production of a qualifying asset as part of the cost of that asset. An entity shall recognize other borrowing costs as an expense in the period in which it incurs them.

Borrowing costs that are directly attributable to the acquisition, construction or production of a qualifying asset are included in the cost of that asset. Such borrowing costs are capitalized as part of the cost of the asset when it is probable that they will result in future economic benefits to the entity and the costs can be measured reliably.

Borrowing costs eligible for capitalization The borrowing costs that are directly attributable to the acquisition, construction, or production of a qualifying asset are those borrowing costs that would have been avoided if the expenditure on the qualifying asset had not been made. When an entity borrows funds specifically for the purpose of obtaining a particular qualifying asset, the borrowing costs that directly relate to that qualifying asset can be readily identified.

It may be difficult to identify a direct relationship between particular borrowings and a qualifying asset and to determine the borrowings that could otherwise have been avoided. Such a difficulty occurs, for example, when the financing activity of an entity is coordinated centrally. Difficulties also arise when a group uses a range of debt instruments to borrow funds at varying rates of interest, and lends those funds on various bases to other entities in the group. Other complications arise through the use of loans denominated in or linked to foreign currencies, when the group operates in highly inflationary economies, and from fluctuations in exchange rates. As a result, the determination of the amount of borrowing costs that are directly attributable to the acquisition of a qualifying asset is difficult and the exercise of judgment is required.

To the extent that an entity borrows funds specifically for the purpose of obtaining a qualifying asset, the entity shall determine the amount of borrowing costs eligible for capitalization as the actual borrowing costs incurred on that borrowing during the period less any investment income on the temporary investment of those borrowings.

In some circumstances, it is appropriate to include all borrowings of the parent and its subsidiaries when computing a weighted average of the borrowing costs; in other circumstances, it is appropriate for each subsidiary to use a weighted average of the borrowing costs applicable to its own borrowings.

Commencement of capitalization An entity shall begin capitalizing borrowing costs as part of the cost of a qualifying asset on the commencement date. The commencement date for capitalization is the date when the entity first meets all of the following conditions:

(a) It incurs expenditures for the asset;
(b) It incurs borrowing costs; and
(c) It undertakes activities that are necessary to prepare the asset for its intended use or sale.

The activities necessary to prepare the asset for its intended use or sale encompass more than the physical construction of the asset. They include technical and administrative work prior to the commencement of physical construction, such as the activities associated with obtaining permits prior to the commencement of the physical construction. However, such activities exclude the holding of an asset when no production or development that changes the asset's condition is taking place. For example, borrowing costs incurred while land is under development are capitalized during the period in which activities related to the development are being undertaken. However, borrowing costs incurred while land acquired for building purposes is held without any associated development activity do not qualify for capitalization.

Suspension of capitalization An entity shall suspend capitalization of borrowing costs during extended periods in which it suspends active development of a qualifying asset. An entity may incur borrowing costs during an extended period in which it suspends the activities necessary to prepare an asset for its intended use or sale. Such costs are costs of holding partially completed assets and do not qualify for capitalization. However, an entity does not normally suspend capitalizing

borrowing costs during a period when it carries out substantial technical and administrative work. An entity also does not suspend capitalizing borrowing costs when a temporary delay is a necessary part of the process of getting an asset ready for its intended use or sale. For example, capitalization continues during the extended period that high water levels delay construction of a bridge, if such high-water levels are common during the construction period in the geographical region involved.

Cessation of capitalization An entity shall cease capitalizing borrowing costs when substantially all the activities necessary to prepare the qualifying asset for its intended use or sale are complete. An asset is normally ready for its intended use or sale when the physical construction of the asset is complete even though routine administrative work might still continue. If minor modifications, such as the decoration of a property to the purchaser's or user's specification, are all that are outstanding, this indicates that substantially all the activities are complete.

Examples/Comments

1. The notes to accounts of M/s Dilemma Ltd for the year 2019–2020 include, inter alia, the following:

   'Interest on loan from financial institutions attributable to new project amounting to ₹430.60 lakh has been capitalized during the year which includes ₹82.40 lakh capitalized irrespective of the utilization of loan for the said purpose.' – Comment.

   Answer: ₹82.40 lakh has been wrongly capitalized.

2. M/s Dilemma Ltd has obtained a secured loan of ₹1,366 lakh for acquisition of plant and machinery. As on 31.3.2019, the plant and machinery acquired amounts to ₹942 lakh. Advances to suppliers amounts to ₹125 lakh and balance loan has been utilized for working capital purpose. The total interest for the above loan amounted to ₹136.60 lakh during the year 2019–20. Advise how the interest on secured loan is to be accounted for the year 2018–19.

   Answer: Interest amounting to ₹94.20 lakh to be capitalized as a part of plant and machinery. ₹12.50 lakh to be capitalized as capital work in progress and ₹29.90 lakh to be charged as expense.

3. M/s Dilemma Ltd has raised the following borrowings during the year 2018–19 for a new project:

Borrowings	Date of Borrowing or Issue	Amount (₹ in lakh)	Purpose
18% term loan	1.4.2018	3,500	General
11% deposits	1.4.2018	130	Plant and machinery
14% debentures	30.9.2018	3,500	General
Total		7,130	

The qualifying assets are as follows:

Assets	Amount (₹ in lakh)	Status as on 31.3.2019
Building	900	Not complete
Plant and machinery	430	Not complete
Other fixed assets	800	Not complete

Earnings from temporary investments ₹0.70 lakh (Against specific borrowings).

Find out the borrowing cost to be capitalized on qualifying assets for the year 2018–19.

Answer:

Borrowing cost to be capitalized:

On Building	₹112.52 lakh
On Plant and machinery	₹ 51.11 lakh
On Other fixed assets	₹100.02 lakh

4. M/s Dilemma Ltd is engaged in the manufacturing of sugar. The quantity to be sold in the market is regulated by the central government and the release orders in this regard are issued by the central government on monthly basis. Due to seasonal nature of production, the company has to carry large inventories throughout the year, the average period of holding generally exceeds 12 months (i.e., substantial period of time). The government reimburses the carrying charges for the inventory to be carried, which includes interest. M/s Dilemma Ltd incurs high interest cost to meet working capital specifically for payment to sugarcane producers. Raw materials and interest costs are two major expenditure of the company. Comment on treatment of borrowing costs.

Answer: Interest cannot be capitalized. Inventory of sugar is not qualifying assets.

(*Adapted from* http://www.mca.gov.in/Ministry/pdf/Ind_AS23.pdf; https://www.aasb.gov.au/admin/file/content105/c9/AASB123_08-15.pdf; https://www.ucetni-portal.cz/stahnout/ias-23-en_858.pdf)

Ind AS 24: Related Party Disclosures

1. Introduction

This Standard shall be applied in

(a) identifying related party relationships and transactions;

(b) identifying outstanding balances, including commitments, between an entity and its related parties;

(c) identifying the circumstances in which disclosure of the items in (a) and (b) is required; and

(d) determining the disclosures to be made about those items.

This Standard requires disclosure of related party relationships, transactions and outstanding balances, including commitments, in the consolidated and separate financial statements of a parent or investors with joint control of, or significant influence over, an investee. This Standard also applies to individual financial statements.

2. Terms

Related party is a person or entity that is related to the entity that is preparing its financial statements (in this Standard referred to as the 'reporting entity').

(a) A person or a close member of that person's family is related to a reporting entity if that person

(i) has control or joint control of the reporting entity;

(ii) has significant influence over the reporting entity; or

(iii) is a member of the key management personnel of the reporting entity or of a parent of the reporting entity.

(b) An entity is related to a reporting entity if any of the following conditions applies:

(i) The entity and the reporting entity are members of the same group (which means that each parent, subsidiary and fellow subsidiary is related to the others).

(ii) One entity is an associate or joint venture of the other entity (or an associate or joint venture of a member of a group of which the other entity is a member).

(iii) Both entities are joint ventures of the same third party.

(iv) One entity is a joint venture of a third entity and the other entity is an associate of the third entity.

(v) The entity is a post-employment benefit plan for the benefit of employees of either the reporting entity or an entity related to the reporting entity. If the reporting entity is itself such a plan, the sponsoring employers are also related to the reporting entity.

(vi) The entity is controlled or jointly controlled by a person identified in (a).

(vii) A person identified in (a) (i) has significant influence over the entity or is a member of the key management personnel of the entity (or of a parent of the entity).

(viii) The entity, or any member of a group of which it is a part, provides key management personnel services to the reporting entity or to the parent of the reporting entity.

Related party transaction is a transfer of resources, services or obligations between a reporting entity and a related party, regardless of whether a price is charged.

Close members of the family of a person are those family members who may be expected to influence, or be influenced by, that person in their dealings with the entity including

(a) that person's children, spouse, or domestic partner, brother, sister, father, and mother;

(b) children of that person's spouse or domestic partner; and

(c) dependants of that person or that person's spouse or domestic partner.

Compensation includes all employee benefits. Employee benefits are all forms of consideration paid, payable or provided by the entity, or on behalf of the entity, in exchange for services rendered to the entity. It also includes such consideration paid on behalf of a parent of the entity in respect of the entity.

Key management personnel are those persons having authority and responsibility for planning, directing, and controlling the activities of the entity, directly or indirectly, including any director (whether executive or otherwise) of that entity.

Government refers to government, government agencies, and similar bodies whether local, national, or international.

Government-related entity is an entity that is controlled, jointly controlled, or significantly influenced by a government.

3. Not related parties

In the context of this Standard, the following are not related parties:

(a) two entities simply because they have a director or other member of key management personnel in common or because a member of key management personnel of one entity has significant influence over the other entity.

(b) two joint venturers simply because they share joint control of a joint venture.

(c) (i) providers of finance, (ii) trade unions, (iii) public utilities, and (iv) departments and agencies of a government that does not control, jointly control, or significantly influence the reporting entity, simply by virtue of their normal dealings with an entity (even though they may affect the freedom of action of an entity or participate in its decision-making process).

(d) a customer, supplier, franchisor, distributor, or general agent with whom an entity transacts a significant volume of business, simply by virtue of the resulting economic dependence.

4. Disclosures

Management discloses the name of the entity's parent and, if different, the ultimate controlling party. Relationships between a parent and its subsidiaries are disclosed irrespective of whether there have been transactions with them.

Where there have been related party transactions during the period, management discloses the nature of the relationship, as well as information about the transactions and outstanding balances, including commitments, necessary for users to understand the potential impact of the relationship on the financial statements. Disclosure is made by category of related party and by major type of transaction. Items of a similar nature may be disclosed in aggregate, except when separate disclosure is necessary for an understanding of the effects of related party transactions on the entity's financial statements.

Management only discloses that related party transactions were made on terms equivalent to those that prevail in arm's length transactions if such terms can be substantiated.

An entity is exempt from the disclosure of transactions (and outstanding balances) with a related party that is either a government that has control, joint control, or significant influence over the entity or is another entity that is under the control, joint control, or significant influence of the same government as the entity. Where the entity applies the exemption, it discloses the name of the government and the nature of its relationship with the entity. It also discloses the nature and amount of each individually significant transaction and the qualitative or quantitative extent of any collectively significant transactions.

Examples/Comments

1. M/s Dilemma Ltd, a listed company, owned 57% of shares of M/s Visual Ltd. Ear Ltd, a listed company, owned the remaining 43 per cent of the ₹10 ordinary share in Visual Ltd. The holding on shares were acquired on 1 April 2019. Visual Ltd sold a factory outlet site to Ear Ltd at a price determined by an independent surveyor on 18 February 2020.

   On 1 June 2020, M/s Dilemma Ltd purchased a further 29% of the ₹10 ordinary shares of Visual Ltd from Ear Ltd and purchased 22% of ordinary shares of ₹10 of Ear Ltd. On 30 September 2020 Visual Ltd sold the machinery to Ear Ltd at a price determined by an independent valuer. Explain the implications of the above transactions for the determination of related party relationships and disclosure of such transactions in the financial statements of M/s Dilemma Ltd, M/s Visual Ltd, and M/s Ear Ltd for the years ending 31 March 2020 and 2021.

   Answer:
   Disclosure in the following cases is required:

   Year ended 31.3.2020:
   In financial statements of M/s Dilemma Ltd: M/s Vision Ltd has control relationship; transactions NIL.
   In financial statements of M/s Vision Ltd: M/s Dilemma Ltd has control relationship; transactions NIL; and M/s Ear Ltd has significance influence relationship; transaction has taken place.
   In financial statements of M/s Ear Ltd: M/s Vision Ltd has significance relationship; transactions have taken place.

   Year ended 31.3.2021:
   In financial statements of M/s Dilemma Ltd: M/s Vision Ltd has control relationship; transactions NIL.
   In financial statements of M/s Vision Ltd: M/s Dilemma Ltd has control relationship; transactions NIL.
   In financial statements of M/s Ear Ltd: NIL

2. M/s Dilemma Ltd has 10 directors and M/s Vision Ltd has 7 directors. 5 of the directors of M/s Dilemma Ltd are directors of M/s Vision Ltd. There are business transactions between the two companies. For the year ended 31.3.2020 there are no business transactions between these two companies. Discuss on reporting requirements.

   Answer:
   Alternate 1:
   If the directors happen to be common directors because of professional reasons and in their individual capacity, then there is no related party relationship.

   Alternate 2:
   If the persons happen to be common directors, appointed by M/s Dilemma Ltd, for the purposes of either controlling or significantly influencing the operational and financial decisions of M/s Vision Ltd, then a related party relationship shall arise.

3. M/s Dilemma Ltd is a company which deals with the manufacturing of transformers, and it buys its raw

materials wholly from M/s Vision Ltd. Will M/s Vision Ltd be a related party to M/s Dilemma Ltd?

Answer:

No.

4. M/s Dilemma Ltd sold to M/s Vision Ltd goods having a sales value of ₹31.45 lakh during the financial year that ended on 31.3.2020. Mr Raju, the Managing Director and Chief Executive of M/s Dilemma Ltd, owns nearly 100% of the share capital of M/s Vision Ltd. The sales were made to M/s Vision Ltd at the normal selling price of M/s Dilemma Ltd. The chief accountant of M/s Dilemma Ltd does not consider that these sales should be treated any differently from any other sales made by the company despite being made to the controlled company, because the sales were made at normal and, that too, at arm's length prices. Discuss the above issue from the view of Ind AS 24.

Answer:

Control relationship exists. The following disclosure is required accordingly:

1. Name of the related party
2. Relationship
3. Description of nature of transaction
4. Volume of transaction—amount or proportion
5. Any other elements of related party transactions necessary for understanding the financial statements
6. Outstanding items pertaining to related party as on balance sheet date (amount or proportion);
   Provisions for doubtful debts due from related parties as on balance sheet date (amount or proportion)
7. Amount written off or written back during the period in respect of debts from or to related parties.

(*Adapted from* http://www.mca.gov.in/Ministry/pdf/Ind_AS24.pdf; https://library.croneri.co.uk/cch_uk/dgaap/b33-4-2; https://www.iasplus.com/en/standards/ias/ias24)

Ind AS 27: Separate Financial Statements

1. This Standard lays down principles and procedures for preparation and presentation of consolidated financial statements and accounting for investment in subsidiaries.
2. Consolidated financial statements comprise balance sheet, profit and loss account, notes to account, and cash flow statement.
3. It does not apply to accounting for amalgamation, investment in associates, investment in joint venture, subsidiary where control is temporary, or where there is restriction in transfer of funds to parent company.
4. The disclosure requirement requires a list of all subsidiaries including name, country and proportion of ownership, comparative figures for previous year, and all other items requiring disclosure under schedule VI.

Ind AS 28: Investments in Associates and Joint Ventures

1. This Standard is mandatory for all such entities that prepare CFS. It sets out principles and procedure for recognizing the effect of investment in associates in CFS.
2. An associate is an enterprise, other than a subsidiary, where the investing company has a significant influence.
3. Significant influence is the power to participate in the financial or operating decisions. Significant influence is linked with control of 20% or more of voting power.
4. Investment in associates should be accounted for under equity method only, except where investment is required for temporary period and where there is constraint in transfer of fund to the investor company. Under equity method, investment is initially recorded at cost, identifying any goodwill or capital reserve at the time of investment. Carrying amount of investment is adjusted thereafter, for post-acquisition changes in the net assets of associates.
5. The disclosure requirement includes investment in associates, which are not accounted for under equity method, component of goodwill or capital reserve, extent of holding in associates, etc.

Ind AS 29: Financial Reporting in Hyper-inflationary Economies

1. This Standard shall be applied to the financial statements, including the consolidated financial statements, of any entity whose functional currency is the currency of a hyperinflationary economy.
2. In a hyperinflationary economy, reporting of operating results and financial position in the local currency without restatement is not useful. Money loses purchasing power at such a rate that comparison of amounts from transactions and other events that have occurred at different times, even within the same accounting period, is misleading.
3. This Standard does not establish an absolute rate at which hyperinflation is deemed to arise. It is a matter of judgement when restatement of financial statements in accordance with this Standard becomes necessary. Hyperinflation is indicated by characteristics of the economic environment of a country which include, but are not limited to, the following:
   (a) the general population prefers to keep its wealth in non-monetary assets or in a relatively stable foreign currency. Amounts of local currency held are immediately invested to maintain purchasing power;
   (b) the general population regards monetary amounts not in terms of the local currency but in terms of a relatively stable foreign currency. Prices may be quoted in that currency;
   (c) sales and purchases on credit take place at prices that compensate for the expected loss of purchasing power during the credit period, even if the period is short;
   (d) interest rates, wages and prices are linked to a price index; and
   (e) the cumulative inflation rate over three years is approaching, or exceeds, 100%.

4. It is preferable that all entities that report in the currency of the same hyperinflationary economy apply this Standard from the same date. Nevertheless, this Standard applies to the financial statements of any entity from the beginning of the reporting period in which it identifies the existence of hyperinflation in the country in whose currency it reports.

(*Adapted from* http://mca.gov.in/Ministry/pdf/INDAS29.pdf; https://www.icaew.com/technical/financial-reporting/ifrs/ifrs-standards/ias-29-financial-reporting-in-hyperinflationary-economies; https://www.iasplus.com/en/standards/ias/ias29)

Ind AS 31: Interests in Joint Ventures

1. This Standard applies to accounting for interest in joint venture assets, liabilities, income and expenses in the financial statement of ventures, and consolidated financial statements.
2. Joint venture (JV) refers to contractual arrangement whereby two or more parties undertake an economic activity which is subject to joint control.
3. This classifies JV in three broad types: jointly controlled operations, jointly controlled assets, and jointly controlled entities.
4. In jointly controlled operations, the venturer should recognize in its separate financial statements the assets that it controls, share of liability, share of income and expenses.
5. In jointly controlled assets, the venture should recognize in its separate financial statements share of the assets, income from the sale or use of the assets, and corresponding expenses.
6. In jointly controlled entities, the venture should recognize in its separate financial statement its interest as per AS-13.
7. In consolidated financial statement, a venture should report its interest using proportionate consolidation method.

Ind AS 32: Financial Instruments: Presentation

1. This Standard comes into effect for accounting periods commencing on or after 1 April 2009, and is recommendatory for an initial period two years, thereafter it becomes mandatory from 1 April 2011 for all commercial, industrial, and business entities (except for small and medium sized entities).
2. The issuer of a financial instrument should classify it or its component parts, on initial recognition as a financial liability, a financial asset, or an equity instrument in accordance with the substance of the contractual arrangement and the definitions of a financial liability, a financial asset, and an equity instrument.
3. In case of compound financial instruments, the issue should evaluate the terms of the instrument to determine whether it contains both a liability and an equity component.
4. The issuing entity will recognize separately the components of a financial instrument that creates a financial liability of the entity, and grants an option to the holder of the instrument to convert it in to an equity instrument of the entity. For example, a convertible debenture issued by an entity is an example of a compound financial instrument.
5. When an entity acquires own equity instruments, it is known as 'treasury share'.
6. Treasury shares should be deducted from the equity value of a balance sheet of an entity.

Ind AS 33: Earnings Per Share

1. Introduction

This Standard shall apply to companies that have issued ordinary shares to which Indian Accounting Standards (Ind ASs) notified under the Companies Act apply.

2. Terms

Antidilution is an increase in earnings per share or a reduction in loss per share resulting from the assumption that convertible instruments are converted, that options or warrants are exercised, or that ordinary shares are issued upon the satisfaction of specified conditions.

Contingent share agreement is an agreement to issue shares that is dependent on the satisfaction of specified conditions.

Contingently issuable ordinary shares are ordinary shares issuable for little or no cash or other consideration upon the satisfaction of specified conditions in a contingent share agreement.

Dilution is a reduction in earnings per share or an increase in loss per share resulting from the assumption that convertible instruments are converted, that options or warrants are exercised, or that ordinary shares are issued upon the satisfaction of specified conditions.

Options, warrants, and their equivalents are financial instruments that give the holder the right to purchase ordinary shares.

An *ordinary share* is an equity instrument that is subordinate to all other classes of equity instruments.

Potential ordinary share is a financial instrument or other contract that may entitle its holder to ordinary shares.

Put options on ordinary shares are contracts that give the holder the right to sell ordinary shares at a specified price for a given period.

3. Recognition and measurements

Basic earnings per share Basic EPS is calculated by dividing the profit or loss for the period attributable to the equity holders of the parent by the weighted average number of ordinary shares outstanding (including adjustments for bonus and rights issues).

An entity shall calculate basic earnings per share amounts for profit or loss attributable to ordinary equity holders of the parent entity and, if presented, profit or loss from continuing operations attributable to those equity holders.

Basic earnings per share shall be calculated by dividing profit or loss attributable to ordinary equity holders of the parent entity (the numerator) by the weighted average number of ordinary shares outstanding (the denominator) during the period.

Earnings For the purpose of calculating basic earnings per share, the amounts attributable to ordinary equity holders of the parent entity in respect of

(a) profit or loss from continuing operations attributable to the parent entity; and

(b) profit or loss attributable to the parent entity shall be the amounts in (a) and (b) adjusted for the after-tax amounts of preference dividends, differences arising on the settlement of preference shares, and other similar effects of preference shares classified as equity.

Where any item of income or expense which is otherwise required to be recognized in profit or loss in accordance with Indian Accounting Standards is debited or credited to securities premium account/other reserves, the amount in respect thereof shall be deducted from profit or loss from continuing operations for the purpose of calculating basic earnings per share.

For the purpose of calculating basic earnings per share, the number of ordinary shares shall be the time-weighted average number of ordinary shares outstanding during the period.

Diluted earnings per share Diluted EPS is calculated by adjusting the profit or loss and the weighted average number of ordinary shares by taking into account the conversion of any dilutive potential ordinary shares. Potential ordinary shares are those financial instruments and contracts that may result in issuing ordinary shares such as convertible bonds and options (including employee share options).

An entity shall calculate diluted earnings per share amounts for profit or loss attributable to ordinary equity holders of the parent entity and, if presented, profit or loss from continuing operations attributable to those equity holders.

For the purpose of calculating diluted earnings per share, an entity shall adjust profit or loss attributable to ordinary equity holders of the parent entity, and the weighted average number of shares outstanding, for the effects of all dilutive potential ordinary shares.

Basic and diluted EPS for both continuing and total operations are presented with equal prominence in the statement of profit and loss for each class of ordinary shares. Separate EPS figures for discontinued operations are disclosed in the same statement or in the notes.

Examples/Comments

1. From the following data in respect of M/s Dilemma Ltd, compute the weighted average number of shares outstanding during 2019–2020.

Date	Particulars	No. of Shares	Nominal Value (₹)	Paid up (₹)
1 April 2019	Opening balance	2500	10	10
30 November 2019	Shares issued for cash	300	10	5

Answer:
Weighted average number of shares: 2,550
Calculation:

Opening	2,500
New issue (of equivalent ₹10 paid up) = (300 × 5)/10 = 150	150
Proportionate time period (150/12) × 4	50
TOTAL	2,550

2. From the following data in respect of M/s Dilemma Ltd, compute the basic EPS for the year 2019–2020 along with previous year figures to be reported in the financial statements of 2019–2020:

Net profit for the year 2018–19	₹13,75,000
Net profit for the year 2019–20	₹15,00,000
Number of equity shares outstanding prior to rights issue	5,00,000 shares
Rights issue (1 equity share for each 5 equity shares outstanding)	Exercise price = ₹15 per share
Date of exercise of right	1 June 2019
Fair value of one equity share immediately prior to exercise of rights	₹21

Answer:
Year 2018–19
Basic EPS = Net Profit/Number of Shares
$\qquad$ = 13,75,000/5,00,000 = ₹2.75

Year 2019–20
Basic EPS = Net Profit/Number of Shares
$\qquad$ = 15,00,000/5,00,000 = ₹3.00
Diluted EPS = Net Profit/Number of shares including exercises
$\qquad$ = 15,00,000/5,71,429 = ₹2.625
Number of shares including exercises:

Original shares	5,00,000
Add: Number of new shares by way of right (5,00,000/5 × 1)	1,00,000
Less: Cost of Right (1,00,000 shares × ₹6 = ₹6,00,000 ₹6,00,000/fair value of share ₹21)	28,571
TOTAL	5,71,429

3. From the following data in respect of M/s Dilemma Ltd, compute the basic EPS to be reported in the financial statements of 2019–20.

Net profit	₹46,00,000
12% cumulative preference shares of ₹100 each	50,000 shares
Number of equity shares outstanding on 1 April 2019	10,00,000 shares
Bonus shares issued on 1 September 2019	4,00,000 shares

Answer:
Basic EPS = ₹2.86
Basic EPS = (PAT – Preference Dividend)/ (No of Original Shares + Bonus Shares)
$\qquad$ = (46 lakh – 6 lakh)/(10 lakh + 4 lakh) = 2.86

4. From the following data in respect of M/s Dilemma Ltd, compute the the basic EPS to be reported in the financial statements of 2019–20.

Net profit for the year	₹9,50,000
Number of equity shares outstanding on 1 April 2019	3,00,000 shares
Average fair value each equity share during the year	₹20
Shares under option to employees (option price = ₹15)	1,00,000 shares

Answer:

Basic EPS = Net Profit/Number of Shares

= 9,50,000/3,00,000 = ₹3.17

Diluted EPS = Net Profit/Number of Shares Including Exercises

= 9,50,000/3,75,000 = ₹2.53

Number of shares including exercises:

Original shares	3,00,000
Add: Number of new shares by way of ESOP	1,00,000

Less: Cost of ESOP

(1,00,000 shares x ₹20 = ₹20,00,000

Less: Amount recovered ₹15,00,000

= Cost of ESOP ₹5,00,000

Equivalent number of shares of Cost of ESOP

₹5,00,000/Fair value ₹20   25,000

TOTAL   3,75,000

(*Adapted from* http://mca.gov.in/Ministry/pdf/INDAS33.pdf; https://www.iasplus.com/en/standards/ias/ias33; http://eirc-icai.org/admin_panel/background_Material/IndAS%2033.pdf)

Ind AS 34: Interim Financial Reporting

1. This Standard applies to such an enterprise which is required to prepare and present interim financial statements (IFS). This does not prescribe which enterprise should prepare it and how frequently.

2. IFS contain either a complete set of financial statements or a condensed statement prepared prior to annual financial statements. It includes balance sheet, profit and loss account, cash flow statement, and notes on account. An enterprise is free to prepare the statement either in full detail or in condensed form.

3. If condensed statement is prepared, it should include, at a minimum, each of the headings and sub-headings that were included in the last annual financial statement.

4. An IFS should normally disclose the following:

   (a) That there is no change in accounting policies

   (b) Nature and amount of items affecting assets, liabilities, equity, cash flow, etc.

   (c) Changes in the estimate of amount reported in earlier IFS

   (d) Issue, buy-back, repayment, restructuring of debt, and equity

   (e) Dividend declared

   (f) Changes in the composition of an enterprise—amalgamation, acquisition, etc.

5. In preparing interim financial statements, comparative figures of the previous period in last year and cumulative figures should be given.

Ind AS 36: Impairment of Assets

1. Introduction

This Standard shall be applied in accounting for the impairment of all assets, other than

   (a) inventories;

   (b) contract assets and assets arising from costs to obtain or fulfil a contract;

   (c) deferred tax assets;

   (d) assets arising from employee benefits;

   (e) financial assets that are within the scope of Ind AS 109: *Financial Instruments*;

   (f) biological assets related to agricultural activity;

   (g) deferred acquisition costs, and intangible assets, arising from an insurer's contractual rights under insurance contracts; and

   (h) non-current assets (or disposal groups) classified as held for sale.

This Standard does not apply to inventories, assets arising from construction contracts, deferred tax assets, assets arising from employee benefits, or assets classified as held for sale (or included in a disposal group that is classified as held for sale) because Indian Accounting Standards applicable to these assets contain requirements for recognizing and measuring these assets.

2. Terms

Carrying amount is the amount at which an asset is recognized after deducting any accumulated depreciation (amortization) and accumulated impairment losses thereon.

Cash-generating unit is the smallest identifiable group of assets that generates cash inflows that are largely independent of the cash inflows from other assets or groups of assets.

Corporate assets are assets other than goodwill that contribute to the future cash flows of both the cash-generating unit under review and other cash generating units (CGU).

Costs of disposal are incremental costs directly attributable to the disposal of an asset or cash-generating unit, excluding finance costs and income tax expense.

Depreciable amount is the cost of an asset, or other amount substituted for cost in the financial statements, less its residual value.

Depreciation (Amortization) is the systematic allocation of the depreciable amount of an asset over its useful life.

Fair value is the price that would be received to sell an asset or paid to transfer a liability in an orderly transaction between market participants at the measurement date.

Impairment loss is the amount by which the carrying amount of an asset or a cash-generating unit exceeds its recoverable amount.

Recoverable amount of an asset or a cash-generating unit is the higher of its fair value less costs of disposal and its value in use.

In the case of an intangible asset, the term 'amortization' is generally used instead of 'depreciation'. The two terms have the same meaning.

3. Recognition and measurements

Nearly all assets—current and non-current—are subject to an impairment test to ensure that they are not overstated on the balance sheet.

The basic principle of impairment is that an asset may not be carried on the balance sheet above its recoverable amount.

Recoverable amount is defined as the higher of the asset's fair value less costs of disposal and its value in use. Fair value less costs of disposal is the price that would be received to sell upon disposal of an asset in an orderly transaction between market participants at the measurement date, less costs of disposal. Guidance on fair valuing is given in Ind AS 113: 'Fair value measurement'. Value in use requires management to estimate the future pre-tax cash flows to be derived from the asset and discount them using a pre-tax market rate that reflects current assessments of the time value of money and the risks specific to the asset.

All assets, subject to the impairment guidance, are tested for impairment where there is an indication that the asset may be impaired. Certain assets (goodwill, indefinite lived intangible assets, and intangible assets that are not yet available for use) are also tested for impairment annually even if there is no impairment indicator. This impairment test may be performed any time during the annual period, provided it is performed at the same time every year.

When considering whether an asset is impaired, both external indicators (for example, significant adverse changes in the technological, market, economic or legal environment or increases in market interest rates) and internal indicators (for example, evidence of obsolescence or physical damage of an asset or evidence from internal reporting that the economic performance of an asset is, or will be, worse than expected) are considered.

Recoverable amount is calculated at the individual asset level. However, an asset seldom generates cash flows independently of other assets, and most assets are tested for impairment in groups of assets described as cash-generating units (CGUs). A CGU is the smallest identifiable group of assets that generates inflows that are largely independent from the cash flows from other CGUs. The carrying value of an asset is compared to the recoverable amount (being the higher of value in use or fair value less costs of disposal). It is not always necessary to determine both an asset's fair value less cost of disposal and its value in use. If either of these amounts exceeds the carrying amount, the asset is not impaired and it is not necessary to estimate the other amount.

An asset or CGU is impaired when its carrying amount exceeds its recoverable amount. Any impairment is allocated to the asset or assets of the CGU, with the impairment loss recognized in profit or loss.

Goodwill acquired in a business combination is allocated to the acquirer's CGUs or groups of CGUs that are expected to benefit from the synergies of the business combination. However, the largest group of CGUs permitted for goodwill impairment testing is an operating segment before aggregation. An impairment loss recognized in prior periods for an asset other than goodwill shall be reversed if, and only if, there has been a change in the estimates used to determine the asset's recoverable amount since the last impairment loss was recognized. An impairment loss recognized for goodwill is not reversed in a subsequent period.

Examples/Comments

1. Decide whether there is any indication as to the impairment of machinery in the following case:
   As on 31.3.2016, M/s Vision Ltd estimated the useful life of the machinery to be 3 years henceforth, instead of remaining 6 years because of technological changes.

   Answer: Yes, decline due to technological changes.

2. Decide whether there is any indication as to the impairment of assets in the following case of M/s Vision Ltd:
   The book value of net assets of Vision Ltd is ₹10 lakh and the market capitalization of the company is ₹7,70,000.

   Answer: Yes, market capitalization is less than carrying amount.

3. M/s Vision Ltd acquired an equipment for ₹85 lakh on 1.7.2017. The equipment has 10 years' life. The salvage value at the end of useful life is estimated at ₹7 lakh. Vision Ltd follows the straight-line method of depreciation. On 31.3.2020 a test for impairment reveals that the present value of future cash flow from the use of equipment and its ultimate disposal value is ₹59,40,000 and net selling price is ₹57,10,000 on the same date. Compute the impairment loss to be recognized as on 31.3.2020.

   Answer: ₹4,15,000

   Book value on 31.3.2020:

Purchase value	₹85,00,000

   Less: Depreciation of 2 years and 9 months period
   {(85 lakh – 7lakh)/10 years = per year ₹7,80,000
   Depreciation for 2 years and 9 months:

$(7,80,000 + 7,80,000 + (7,80,000/12 \times 9)) =$	₹21,45,000
= Book Value of Assets	₹63,55,000

   Fair value based on present value of future cash flow

	₹59,40,000
Hence impairment loss =	₹4,15,000

4. Dilemma Ltd has estimated the cash flow relating to equipment on 31.3.2018.

Year Ended	Cash Flow (₹)
31.3.2019	25,000
31.3.2020	28,500
31.3.2021	35,000
31.3.2022	42,000
31.3.2023	48,500

   The equipment was purchased on 1.4.2016 for ₹2,11,200. The estimated useful life of equipment was 8 years. The residual value of the equipment is estimated at ₹1,200 at the end of its useful life. The net selling price of the equipment as on 31.3.2018 is ₹1,25,000. The discount rate is 14%. Compute the following as on 31.3.2018:

   a. Carrying amount as on 31.3.2018
   b. Value in use on 31.3.2018
   c. Recoverable amount on 31.3.2018
   d. Impairment loss to be recognized for the year ended 31.3.2018
   e. Revised carrying amount as on 31.3.2018
   f. Depreciation charge for the year ended 31.3.2019

Answer:

Carrying amount as on 31.3.2018	₹1,58,700
Value in use on 31.3.2018	₹1,18,164
Recoverable amount on 31.3.2018	₹1,25,000
Impairment loss to be recognized for the year ended 31.3.2018	₹33,700
Revised carrying amount as on 31.3.2018	₹1,25,000
Depreciation charge for the year ended 31.3.2019	₹24,760

(*Adapted from* https://www.iasplus.com/en/standards/ias/ias36; https://www.ifrs.org/issued-standards/list-of-standards/ias-36-impairment-of-assets/; https://www.ey.com/Publication/vwLUAssets/Impairment_accounting_the_basics_of_IAS_36_Impairment_of_Assets/$FILE/Impairment_accounting_IAS_36.pdf)

Ind AS 37: Provisions, Contingent Liabilities, and Contingent Assets

1. Introduction

This Standard shall be applied by all entities in accounting for provisions, contingent liabilities, and contingent assets, except

(a) those resulting from executory contracts, except where the contract is onerous; and

(b) those covered by another Standard.

This Standard does not apply to financial instruments (including guarantees) that are within the scope of Ind AS 109: *Financial Instruments*.

Executory contracts are contracts under which neither party has performed any of its obligations or both parties have partially performed their obligations to an equal extent. This Standard does not apply to executory contracts unless they are onerous.

When another Standard deals with a specific type of provision, contingent liability, or contingent asset, an entity applies that Standard instead of this Standard.

2. Terms

Provision is a liability of uncertain timing or amount.

Liability is a present obligation of the entity arising from past events, the settlement of which is expected to result in an outflow from the entity of resources embodying economic benefits.

Obligating event is an event that creates a legal or constructive obligation that results in an entity having no realistic alternative to settling that obligation.

Legal obligation is an obligation that derives from

(a) a contract (through its explicit or implicit terms);

(b) legislation; or

(c) other operation of law.

Constructive obligation is an obligation that derives from an entity's actions where

(a) by an established pattern of past practice, published policies, or a sufficiently specific current statement, the entity has indicated to other parties that it will accept certain responsibilities; and

(b) as a result, the entity has created a valid expectation on the part of those other parties that it will discharge those responsibilities.

Contingent liability is

(a) a possible obligation that arises from past events and whose existence will be confirmed only by the occurrence or non-occurrence of one or more uncertain future events not wholly within the control of the entity; or

(b) a present obligation that arises from past events but is not recognized because:

(i) it is not probable that an outflow of resources embodying economic benefits will be required to settle the obligation; or

(ii) the amount of the obligation cannot be measured with sufficient reliability.

Contingent asset is a possible asset that arises from past events and whose existence will be confirmed only by the occurrence or non-occurrence of one or more uncertain future events not wholly within the control of the entity.

Onerous contract is a contract in which the unavoidable costs of meeting the obligations under the contract exceed the economic benefits expected to be received under it.

Restructuring is a programme that is planned and controlled by management, and materially changes either

(a) the scope of a business undertaken by an entity; or

(b) the manner in which that business is conducted.

3. Provisions vs liability

A provision is a liability of uncertain timing or amount. A liability is a present obligation of the entity arising from past events, the settlement of which is expected to result in an outflow from the entity of resources embodying economic benefits.

The Standard distinguishes provisions from other liabilities such as trade creditors and accruals. This is on the basis that for a provision there is uncertainty about the timing or amount of the future expenditure. Uncertainly is also present in the case of certain accruals but the uncertainty is generally much less for liabilities than for provisions.

A provision should be recognized as a liability in the financial statements when an entity has a present obligation (legal or constructive) as a result of a past event. It is probable that an outflow of resources embodying economic benefits will be required to settle the obligation. A reliable estimate can be made of the amount of the obligation.

4. Constructive obligation

An obligation that derives from an entity's actions where

- By an established pattern of past practice, published policies, or a sufficiently specific current statement the entity has indicated to other parties that it will accept certain responsibilities; and

- As result, the entity has created a valid expectation on the part of those other parties that it will discharge those responsibilities.

Example: An oil company may have an established practice of always making good any environmental damage caused by drilling, even though it is not legally obliged to do so. In this way, it has created a valid expectation that it will do this and it will have to recognize the constructive obligation and make a corresponding provision each time it drills a new well.

X Ltd is engaged in the manufacture of fertilizers. Effluents from the plant polluted a river near the plant. Residents of the locality were agitated against the pollution. X Ltd agreed to give in to their demands by reducing pollution discharge and installing an effluent treatment plant (ETP). After 1 year, no ETP has been installed and there is no legislation mandating such an installation. X Ltd has created a valid expectation on the part of the public that it will discharge its responsibilities.

5. Contingent assets

An entity shall not recognize a contingent asset. Contingent assets usually arise from unplanned or other unexpected events that give rise to the possibility of an inflow of economic benefits to the entity.

An example is a claim that an entity is pursuing through legal processes, where the outcome is uncertain.

Contingent assets are not recognized in financial statements since this may result in the recognition of income that may never be realized. However, when the realization of income is virtually certain, the related asset is not a contingent asset and its recognition is appropriate.

Contingent assets are assessed continually to ensure that developments are appropriately reflected in the financial statements. If it has become virtually certain that an inflow of economic benefits will arise, the asset and the related income are recognized in the financial statements of the period in which the change occurs. If an inflow of economic benefits has become probable, an entity discloses the contingent asset.

6. Probable transfer of resources

A transfer of resources embodying economic benefits is regarded as 'probable' if the event is more likely that not to occur. This appears to indicate a probability of more than 50%. However, the Standard makes it clear that where there is a number of similar obligations, the probability should be based on considering the population as a whole, rather than one single item.

Example: If a company has entered into a warranty obligation then the probability of transfer of resources embodying economic benefits may well be extremely small in respect of one specific item. However, when considering the population as a whole, the probability of some transfer of resources is quite likely to be much higher. If there is a greater than 50% probability of some transfer of economic benefits, then a provision should be made for the expected amount.

7. Measurements

Measurement of provisions The amount recognized as provision should be the best estimate of the expenditure required to settle the present obligation at the end of the reporting period. Estimates determined by the judgment of the management are supplemented by the experience of similar transactions. Where provision involves a large population of items, obligation is estimated by weighing all possible outcomes by their associated probabilities, i.e., expected value. Where provision involves a single item, such as the outcome of a legal case, provision is made in full for the most likely outcome.

Where the effect of the time value of money is material, the amount of a provision should be the present value of the expenditure required to settle the obligation. An appropriate pre-tax discount rate should be used. The discount rates(s) should not reflect risks for which future cash flow estimates have been adjusted.

Future events/disposal of assets Future events which are reasonably expected to occur (e.g., new legislation, changes in technology) may affect the amount required to settle the entity's obligation and should be considered.

Gains from the expected disposal of assets should not be considered in measuring a provision. Some or all of the expenditure needed to settle a provision may be expected to be recovered from a third party, then reimbursement should be recognized only when it is virtually certain that reimbursement will be received if the entity settles the obligation.

Reimbursement Reimbursement should be treated as a separate asset, and the amount recognized should not be greater than the provision itself. The provision and the amount recognized for reimbursement may be netted off in profit or loss.

Changes in provisions Provisions should be reviewed at the end of each reporting period and adjusted to reflect the current best estimate. If it is no longer probable that a transfer of resources will be required to settle the obligation, the provision should be reversed.

Onerous contracts For onerous contracts, the present obligation under the contract should be recognized and measured as a provision. For example, leasehold property may be vacant with an entity. The entity holding the lease is under an obligation to maintain the property but receives no income or benefit from it.

Warranties These are argued to be genuine provisions as on past experience it is probable, i.e., more likely than not, that some claims will emerge. The provision must be estimated, however, on the basis of the class as a whole and not on individual claims. In this case there is a clear legal obligation.

Major repairs Companies usually provide for expenditure on a major overhaul to be accrued gradually over the intervening years between overhauls. Now this is no longer possible as this may be a mere intention to carry out repairs, not an obligation. The entity may also sell the asset in the meantime.

Examples/Comments

1. Dilemma Ltd, a software development company, has given counter guarantees for ₹85 lakh to various banks in respect of guarantees given by the said banks in favour of government authorities. The counter guarantees outstanding as on 31.3.2020 were ₹48,75,000. Advise accounting treatment in the financial statement of Dilemma Ltd for the year ended 31.3.2020.

   Answer:
   ₹48,75,000 to be reported as contingent liability. No provision is required.

2. Dilemma Ltd has entered into a sale contract of ₹48 lakh with Vivaan Ltd during the financial year 2019–20. The profit on this transaction is expected to be ₹4.80 lakh. The delivery of the goods is to take place in the month of May

2020. In case of failure by Dilemma Ltd, to deliver within the schedule, a compensation of ₹2.40 lakh is to be paid to Vivaan Ltd. Dilemma Ltd planned to manufacture the goods during March 2020. As on the balance sheet date, i.e., 31.3.2020, the goods were not manufactured and it was unlikely that Dilemma Ltd would be in a position to meet the contractual obligation. Advise.

Answer:
Provide for expected compensation of ₹2.40 lakh in the financial statements for the year ended 31.3.2020.

3. During the year 2019–2020, few people died of food poisoning from products sold by an enterprise. The legal proceedings are started seeking damages from the enterprise but the enterprise disputes the liability. Up to the date of approval of the financial statements for the year ended 31.3.2020, the enterprise's lawyer has advised that it is probable that the enterprise will not be found liable. However, when the enterprise was in the process of preparing the financial statements for the year ended 31.3.2021, its lawyer advised that owing to developments in the case, it is probable that the enterprise would be found liable. Advise.

Answer:
31.3.2020: No provision is required. Disclosure as contingent liability is required.
31.3.2021: Provision of expected liability is required to be made.

4. Dilemma Ltd is in the process industry causing water pollution. It discharges residual in the river adjacent to the factory. The river has been contaminated over a period of time. At present, there is no legislation requiring cleaning up. As on 31.3.2020, it is virtually certain that a law requiring a clean-up of river already contaminated will be enacted shortly after year end. Advise an accounting treatment.

Answer:
Provide for expected loss (cost of clean-up).

(*Adapted from* https://www.oreilly.com/library/view/ifrs-essentials/9781118501344/ OEBPS/9781118501344_epub_c_26.htm; https://www.iasplus.com/en/ standards/ias/ias37; https://www.ifrs.org/issued-standards/list-of-standards/ ias-37-provisions-contingent-liabilities-and-contingent-assets/)

Ind AS 38: Intangible Assets

1. Introduction

This Standard shall be applied in accounting for intangible assets, except
   (a) intangible assets that are within the scope of another Standard;
   (b) financial assets;
   (c) the recognition and measurement of exploration and evaluation assets; and
   (d) expenditure on the development and extraction of minerals, oil, natural gas, and similar non-regenerative resources.

If another Standard prescribes the accounting for a specific type of intangible asset, an entity applies that Standard instead of this Standard. For example, this Standard does not apply to
   (a) intangible assets held by an entity for sale in the ordinary course of business
   (b) deferred tax assets
   (c) leases
   (d) assets arising from employee benefits
   (e) financial assets
   (f) goodwill acquired in a business combination
   (g) deferred acquisition costs, and intangible assets, arising from an insurer's contractual rights under insurance contracts
   (h) non-current intangible assets classified as held for sale (or included in a disposal group that is classified as held for sale), *Non-current Assets Held for Sale and Discontinued Operations*
   (i) assets arising from contracts with customers that are recognized as *Revenue from Contracts with Customers*

2. Terms

Amortization is the systematic allocation of the depreciable amount of an intangible asset over its useful life.
   Asset is a resource
   (a) controlled by an entity as a result of past events; and
   (b) from which future economic benefits are expected to flow to the entity.

Carrying amount is the amount at which an asset is recognized in the balance sheet after deducting any accumulated amortization and accumulated impairment losses thereon.

Cost is the amount of cash or cash equivalents paid or the fair value of other consideration given to acquire an asset at the time of its acquisition or construction, or, when applicable, the amount attributed to that asset when initially recognized in accordance with the specific requirements of other Indian Accounting Standards.

Depreciable amount is the cost of an asset, or other amount substituted for cost, less its residual value.

Development is the application of research findings or other knowledge to a plan or design for the production of new or substantially improved materials, devices, products, processes, systems, or services before the start of commercial production or use.

Entity-specific value is the present value of the cash flows an entity expects to arise from the continuing use of an asset and from its disposal at the end of its useful life or expects to incur when settling a liability.

Fair value is the price that would be received to sell an asset or paid to transfer a liability in an orderly transaction between market participants at the measurement date.

Impairment loss is the amount by which the carrying amount of an asset exceeds its recoverable amount.

Intangible asset is an identifiable non-monetary asset without physical substance.

Monetary assets are money held and assets to be received in fixed or determinable amounts of money.

Research is original and planned investigation undertaken with the prospect of gaining new scientific or technical knowledge and understanding.

Residual value of an intangible asset is the estimated amount that an entity would currently obtain from disposal of the asset, after deducting the estimated costs of disposal, if the asset were already of the age and in the condition expected at the end of its useful life.

Useful life is

(a) the period over which an asset is expected to be available for use by an entity; or

(b) the number of production or similar units expected to be obtained from the asset by an entity.

3. Intangible assets

An intangible asset is an identifiable non-monetary asset without physical substance. The identifiable criterion is met when the intangible asset is separable (that is, when it can be sold, transferred or licensed), or where it arises from contractual or other legal rights.

Entities frequently expend resources, or incur liabilities, on the acquisition, development, maintenance, or enhancement of intangible resources such as scientific or technical knowledge, design and implementation of new processes or systems, licences, intellectual property, market knowledge, and trademarks (including brand names and publishing titles).

Common examples of items encompassed by these broad headings are computer software, patents, copyrights, motion picture films, customer lists, mortgage servicing rights, fishing licences, import quotas, franchises, customer or supplier relationships, customer loyalty, market share, and marketing rights.

4. Recognition and measurements

Separately acquired intangible assets Separately acquired intangible assets are recognized initially at cost. Cost comprises the purchase price, including import duties and non-refundable purchase taxes and any directly attributable costs of preparing the asset for its intended use. The purchase price of a separately acquired intangible asset incorporates assumptions about the probable economic future benefits that may be generated by the asset.

Internally generated intangible assets The process of generating an intangible asset is divided into a research phase and a development phase. No intangible assets arising from the research phase may be recognized. Intangible assets arising from the development phase are recognized when the entity can demonstrate the following:

1. Its technical feasibility
2. Its intention to complete the developments
3. Its ability to use or sell the intangible asset
4. How the intangible asset will generate probable future economic benefits (for example, the existence of a market for the output of the intangible asset or for the intangible asset itself)
5. The availability of resources to complete the development
6. Its ability to measure the attributable expenditure reliably

If an intangible asset is acquired in a business combination, both the probability and measurement criteria are always considered to be met. An intangible asset will therefore always be recognized, regardless of whether it has been previously recognized in the acquiree's financial statements.

Subsequent measurement Intangible assets are amortized unless they have an indefinite useful life. Amortization is carried out on a systematic basis over the useful life of the intangible asset. An intangible asset has an indefinite useful life when, based on an analysis of all the relevant factors, there is no foreseeable limit to the period over which the asset is expected to generate net cash inflows for the entity. Intangible assets with finite useful lives are considered for impairment when there is an indication that the asset has been impaired. Intangible assets with indefinite useful lives and intangible assets not yet in use are tested annually for impairment and whenever there is an indication of impairment.

Some intangible assets may be contained in or on a physical substance such as a compact disc (in the case of computer software), legal documentation (in the case of a licence or patent), or film. In determining whether an asset that incorporates both intangible and tangible elements should be treated under Ind AS 16: *Property, Plant and Equipment,* or as an intangible asset under this Standard, an entity uses judgment to assess which element is more significant.

For example, computer software for a computer-controlled machine tool that cannot operate without that specific software is an integral part of the related hardware and it is treated as property, plant, and equipment. The same applies to the operating system of a computer. When the software is not an integral part of the related hardware, computer software is treated as an intangible asset.

Examples/Comments

1. Dilemma Ltd has got the license to manufacture particular medicines for 4 years at a license fee of ₹91 lakh. The expected pattern of production and operating cash flows is as under:

Year	No. of Tables (in lakh)	Cash Flows (₹ in lakh)
1	800	8,000
2	1,000	10,500
3	1,200	13,200
4	1,200	13,800

Compute the license fee to be amortized every year.

Answer:

Amortization as per the pattern of economic benefits (operating cash flows):

Year	No. of Tables (in lakh)	Cash Flows (₹ in lakh)	Amortization of License Fee (₹)
1	800	8,000	16,00,000
2	1,000	10,500	21,00,000
3	1,200	13,200	26,40,000
4	1,200	13,800	27,60,000
Total	4,200	45,500	91,00,000

2. On 1.4.2019, M/s Vivaan Ltd purchased M/s Dilemma Ltd at a cost of ₹95 lakh which resulted in recognition of

goodwill of ₹4,50,000 having an expected benefit period of 10 years. During the year 2019–2020, Vivaan Ltd incurred an additional cost amounting to ₹1,25,000 which is likely to enable the asset to generate future benefits in excess of originally assessed standards of performance. On 31.3.2020, Vivaan Ltd, based on its best estimate, assessed the benefit period of goodwill to be 15 years. Give the accounting treatment, assuming Ind AS 103 not applicable in this case.

Answer:
Additional cost of ₹1,25,000 is to be capitalized. Amortization should be as per best estimate of useful life of 15 years.

3. M/s Vivaan Ltd has spent ₹67 lakh for publicity and research expenses on one of its new products which has marketed in the accounting year 2019–2020 but proved to be a failure. State how you will deal with the same in the accounts of M/s Vivaan Ltd for the year ended 31.3.2020.

Answer:
The expenditure on research should be recognized as an expense when it is incurred. Hence, the entire amount of ₹67 lakh should be recognized as an expense in the accounting year 2019–2020.

4. M/s Vivaan Ltd is engaged in the business of stock broking. Its NSE and BSE broking activities are handled through two stock exchange cards for which it has paid a consideration of ₹200 lakh. Can the stock exchange card be treated as an intangible asset in the books of the company? If yes, can the life of the card be treated as infinite as the company has the right to use the card even after 10 years?

Answer:
Yes, the stock exchange cards can be treated as intangible assets. M/s Vivaan Ltd can treat the useful life of the stock exchange cards more than 10 years by disclosing the reasons as to why the presumption of useful life of 10 years is rebutted and the factors that played a significant role in determining the useful life of the asset.

(*Adapted from* http://mca.gov.in/Ministry/pdf/INDAS38.pdf; https://www.iasplus.com/en/standards/ias/ias38; https://www.readyratios.com/articles/ifrs/ias-38-intangible-assets.html)

Ind AS 39: Financial Instruments: Recognition and Measurements

1. This Standard comes into effect for accounting periods commencing on or after 1 April 2009, and is recommendatory for an initial period of two years, thereafter it becomes mandatory from 1 April 2011 for all commercial, industrial, and business entities (except for small and medium sized entities).
2. An entity should recognize a financial asset or a financial liability on its balance sheet when the entity becomes a party to the contractual provisions of the instrument.
3. A financial asset should be derecognized only where the contractual rights to the cash flows have expired, or a financial asset's contractual rights are transferred to the other party.
4. A financial liability should be removed from the firm's balance sheet only when it is extinguished.
5. An exchange between an existing borrower and lender of debt instruments with substantially different terms, or a substantial modification of the terms of an existing financial liability or part thereof, should be accounted for as extinguishment of the original liability and recognition of a new one.

Ind AS 40: Investment Property

1. An investment property is a real estate property that has been purchased with the intention of earning a return on the investment (purchase) either through rent (income), the future resale of the property or both.
2. An investment property is like any other investment, the goal is to generate a profit. The way in which a property is used has a significant impact on its value. Investors sometimes conduct studies to determine the best and most profitable use of a property. This is often referred to as its highest and best use.
3. The Standard applies to the measurement in a lessee's financial statements of investment property held under a finance lease and to the measurement in the lessor's financial statements of investment property leased out under an operating lease. However, this Standard does not apply to the matter covered in Ind AS 17: Leases, biological assets related to agricultural activity (Ind AS 41), or mineral rights and mineral reserves such as oil, natural gas, and similar non-regenerative resources.
4. **Classification of property**
   Investment property: It is a land and/or building, or part of a building, or both, held by the owner or the lessee under a finance lease to earn rentals and/or for capital appreciation, rather than for use in production or supply of goods and services or use in administrative purposes or sale in the ordinary course of business.
   Owner-occupied property: It is a property held (by the owner or by the lessee under finance lease) for use in the production or supply of goods or services or for administrative purposes. One of the distinguishing characteristics of investment property (compared to owner-occupied property) is that it generates cash flows that are largely independent from other assets held by an entity. Owner-occupied property is accounted for under Ind AS 16: Property, Plant and Equipment.
5. Examples: Land held for long-term capital appreciation rather than for short-term sale; A building owned by the entity and leased out under one or more operating leases; a building that is vacant but is held to be leased out under one or more operating leases; property that is being constructed or developed for future use as investment property.
6. Recognition criteria: Investment property shall be recognized as an asset if and only if it is probable that future

economic benefits will flow towards entity; and the cost of the investment property can be measured reliably.

7. Initial measurement: An investment property shall be measured initially at cost including transaction charges. However, property held under a finance lease shall be measured initially using the principles contained in Ind AS 17: Leases—at the lower of the fair value and the present value of the minimum lease payments.

8. Cost of purchased investment property: It comprises its purchase price and any directly attributable expenditure. Directly attributable expenditure includes, for example, professional fees for legal services, property transfer taxes, and other transaction costs. However, cost of an investment property does not include start-up costs, operating losses incurred before the investment property achieves the planned level of occupancy, or abnormal amounts of wasted material, labour or other resources incurred in constructing or developing the property Interest cost in case of deferred payment.

9. Measurement after recognition: An entity shall also measure subsequently after initial recognition all its investment property at cost. This Standard requires all entities to measure the fair value of investment property, for the purpose of disclosure even though they are required to follow the cost model. An entity is encouraged, but not required, to measure the fair value of investment property on the basis of a valuation by an independent valuer who holds a recognized and relevant professional qualification and has recent experience in the location and category of the investment property being valued.

10. Transfers: Transfers to, or from, investment property shall be made when, and only when, there is a change in use, evidenced by: commencement of owner-occupation, for a transfer from investment property to owner-occupied Property; commencement of development with a view to sale, for a transfer from investment property to inventories; end of owner-occupation, for a transfer from owner-occupied property to investment property; commencement of an operating lease to another party, for a transfer from inventories to investment property. Transfers between investment property, owner-occupied property and inventories do not change the carrying amount of the property transferred and they do not change the cost of that property for measurement or disclosure purposes.

11. Derecognition: An investment property shall be derecognized on disposal or when no benefit is expected from future use or disposal. Any gain or loss is determined as the difference between the net disposal proceeds and the carrying amount is recognized in the income statement.

12. Disclosure requirements: Classification criteria (to distinguish owner-occupied investment property, property held for sale in situations where classification is difficult) to be explained.

(*Adapted from* http://mca.gov.in/Ministry/pdf/INDAS40.pdf; http://www.focusifrs.com/content/view/full/5200; https://www.ifrs.org/issued-standards/list-of-standards/ias-40-investment-property/)

Ind AS 41: Agriculture

1. It applies to the following when they relate to agriculture activities:

   (a) Biological assets
   (b) Agriculture produce at the point of harvest
   (c) Grant related to biological asset

2. 'Agriculture activities' is the management by an entity of the biological transformation and harvest of biological assets for sale or for conversion into agricultural produce or into additional biological assets which essentially means that there should be some managed services before it being qualified as agricultural activities. For example, there are some fish which are in the sea water and apparently the sea cannot be managed by any entity (it is rather managed by government); hence these activities will not fall into agriculture activities for such entity.

3. This Standard wanted majorly to focus on 'living' plants and /or animals which are being used either to produce some harvested products or grow any biological assets further.

4. As per this Standard, all biological assets at the initial recognition level and subsequently will be measured at its fair value less cost to sell and all harvested produce (products which usually come out from biological assets) at the point of harvest (only at the harvest point) whereas in the current accounting system these types of products are being measured at cost or at its NRV.

5. This Standard says that after the point of harvest (i.e., a product which is to be sold by the entity) it will then be treated as inventories (if not sell) and hence Ind AS 2: 'Inventories' will be applicable.

6. As per this Standard, there should be some transformation of biological assets (defined above) and should be managed (as discussed above) by the entity for its sale or for producing harvested product.

7. Land which is normally being used for the purpose of such agriculture activities is not in the scope of this Standard and will continue to be governed with either Ind AS 16: 'Property, Plant and Equipment' or Ind AS 40: 'Investment Property' as the case may be.

8. Any intangible asset that meets recognition criteria will be governed by Ind AS 38: 'Intangible Assets' and will not be covered within this Standard.

9. One has to carefully note that while transiting from current accounting practice to Ind AS regime, there would be deemed cost exemption available for all assets that are being carried over and hence entity will have gain/loss by valuing such biological assets at fair value soon after the date of such transition.

10. There are some practices available where an entity makes a policy to capitalize some of the directly attributable expense incurred on such biological assets; however it will not make any difference by capitalizing such expenses in such assets as all such assets will be fair valued at each reporting date

with corresponding effects in P&L (difference between previous carrying value and reporting date fair value).

11. There are some situations where fair value of such biological assets cannot be reliably measured because of non-availability of active market. This Standard then gives an alternative to account at cost till the time its fair market value is available.

12. There are many situations where government provides grants to such activities. This Standard states as per its para 34: '*An unconditional government grant related to a biological asset measured at its fair value less costs to sell shall be recognised in profit or loss when, and only when, the government grant becomes receivable*', which means that when there is no pending condition (where some grants requires an entity to fulfil certain conditions) which is to be fulfilled by the entity, then only it will be recognized in profit and loss account. However, para 37 of the Standard specifically excludes its applicability in case the grants are being given to the assets measured at cost, and in those cases it will be governed by Ind AS 20: 'Government Grants'.

(*Adapted from* http://mca.gov.in/Ministry/pdf/INDAS41.pdf; https://www.iasplus.com/en/standards/ias/ias41; https://www.ifrs.org/issued-standards/list-of-standards/ias-41-agri-culture; https://taxguru.in/finance/agriculture-accounting-indas-ifrs.html)

INTERNATIONAL FINANCIAL REPORTING STANDARDS (IFRS)

International Financial Reporting Standards (IFRS) are a set of international accounting standards that lay guidelines on reporting of certain types of transactions and other events in financial statements. These standards are issued by the International Accounting Standards Board (IASB). Each country has its own set of rules, which makes international comparisons difficult. The primary objective of IFRS is to make such comparisons easy and to synchronize accounting standards across different nations. For example, US GAAP is different from Canadian GAAP. IFRS plays an important role here.

Assumptions of IFRS

There are four underlying assumptions in IFRS:

Economic entity Economic activity can be identified with particular unit of accountability. That means, a company must separate its activity from the owners and other businesses.

Going concern The company will have a long life and will be in operation for foreseeable future.

Monetary unit assumption Money is used as a common denominator of economic activity and provides appropriate basic accounting measurement and analysis. It ignores price-level changes such as inflation and deflation because it assumes that the unit of measurement of currency remains stable, except for dramatical changes like hyperinflation.

Accrual basis The transactions in accounting are recorded when the events are recognized as they occur, not when cash is paid or received.

Objectives of IFRS

The objectives of IFRS are as follows:

1. To develop, in the public interest, a single set of high quality, understandable, enforceable, and globally accepted financial reporting standards based upon clearly defined principles.
2. To ensure high quality, transparent, and comparable information in financial statements and other financial reporting to help investors, other participants in the world's capital markets, and other users of financial information make economic decisions.
3. To promote the use and rigorous application of those standards.
4. To promote and facilitate adoption of IFRS, being the standards and interpretations issued by the IASB, through the convergence of national accounting standards and IFRS.
5. To make a common platform for better understanding of accounting, internationally.
6. To synchronize accounting standards across the globe.
7. To create comparable, reliable, and transparent financial statements.
8. To facilitate greater cross-border capital raising and trade.
9. To have company-wide one accounting language which has subsidiaries in different countries.

Advantages of IFRS

The advantages of IFRS are as follows:

1. IFRS provides better financial information for the shareholders and regulatory system in India.
2. IFRS enhances global ability and improves transparency of results.
3. IFRS users can increase ability to secure cross-border listing of their companies.
4. With the help of IFRS one can improve management of global operations and better access the capital market.
5. Business houses having presence in both India and outside India had to go for multiple reporting, which got eliminated with the introduction and implementation of IFRS.
6. IFRS facilitates global investment opportunities inbound and outbound and also reduced cost of capital.
7. IFRS reduces barriers to enter global market and lowers the risk associated with dual filings of accounts.
8. IFRS provides new and enhanced services especially in the field of business process outsourcing and professional services firms.
9. With the help of IFRS one can conduct only review of financial reporting and information system for control.
10. Uniform accounting standards enable investors to understand investment opportunity as against two different sets of national standards.
11. With the help of IFRS corporates and investors would know its true worth because fair valuation is mandated for many balance sheet items.

Disadvantages of IFRS

The disadvantages of IFRS are as follows:

1. Indian GAAP is different from US GAAP, because of which it becomes difficult to synchronize the financial statements of two GAAPs.
2. IFRS implementation brings change in new standards, because of which it becomes complex for users to decide how to finalize the old and new accounting data.
3. When preparing financial statements by the use of IFRS, old and new standards may create confusion.
4. In India, there are no separate committees for implementation, follow-up, and feedback process of IFRS.
5. Lack of proper training and guidance programme in India delays the process of IFRS implementation.
6. IFRS implementation involves the cost over a period of time; hence, it becomes mandatory for companies to make cost-benefit analysis.
7. The taxation system also gets impacted after implementation of IFRS in India.
8. GAAP and respective regulatory body of each country has different sets of rules, which is the biggest hurdle for companies to adopt uniform accounting standards across the globe.
9. IFRS is simply a set of principles laid down by IASC but it does not provide detailed rules to follow up.
10. IFRS mainly focuses on presenting financial statements of companies and focus is very less on the users of accounting standards.
11. Lack of awareness between users about the international financial reporting practices is a major drawback.
12. IFRS uses fair value and market value as the measurement base before its assets are valued as per book value. Due to this financial statements of any company get impacted significantly.
14. Lack of proper data impact the effective implementation of IFRS process.
15. For comparison purpose IFRS needs to convert historical data into market value. Due to this IFRS becomes more subjective.
16. Coordination with different countries for IFRS implementation is a challenging task.
17. Lack of proper resources also affects successful implementation of IFRS.

Appendix A at the end of the book gives a list of comparative study of IFRS and Ind AS.

IFRS-1 First-time Adoption of International Financial Reporting (Accounting) Standards

An entity, which is operating transnationally, is required to present the opening balance sheet according to the IFRS. In other words, adopting IFRS implies that the entity has to use the same accounting policies, practices, and procedures as explained through the IFRS and IAS. There are some concepts which are to be given effect to as given in the following text:

1. The date of transition refers to the beginning of the accounting period for which an entity presents the full comparative information according to the IFRS.

   A set of financial statements as per IFRS-1 includes the following information.
   (i) Statement of the financial position (i.e., balance sheet)
   (ii) Comprehensive income statement (i.e., profit and loss account)
   (iii) Statement of cash flows
   (iv) Statement of changes in equity
   (v) Notes including a summary of accounting policies and explanatory notes

   Comparative financial figures are to be provided for one previous year for the balance sheet, the income statement (profit and loss account), and the cash flow statement.

2. IFRS does not prescribe any specific format for the presentation of the balance sheet and the income statement, but it indicates the minimum line items. It also specifies that the balance sheet is to be presented in the increasing order of liquidity, and in addition, the assets and liabilities are to be classified as current and non-current items. For example, in case of the balance sheet, the items to be presented include property, plant and equipment, investment property, intangible and financial assets, etc. In case of the income statement, disclosure includes revenue, finance charges, share of post-tax results of joint venture, associates using the equity method, etc. IFRS-1 does not make it compulsory to consolidate the financial statements of subsidiaries.

3. The significant events that occur between the balance sheet date and the Board of Directors' meeting date are to be reported. These are of two types.
   (i) Events that provide further evidence of conditions that existed on the date of the balance sheet
   (ii) Events that provide only indications of the happening of such conditions as a probable event

Such events have to be provided at the time of preparation of financial statements.

■ ILLUSTRATION 19.1

A: On 13 April, due to the destruction of the factory by a fire (the fire broke out on 28 March), one customer of the company declared himself as insolvent. He owed ₹5.50 lakh to M/s Parshwa Company.

Solution: In this situation, it is an event that occurred after the balance sheet date. Hence, provisions for bad debts to the tune of ₹5.50 lakh are to be created in the financial statement for the year ended 31 March.

B: While preparing the final accounts for the year ended 31 March, M/s Parshwa Company made a provision of bad debts at the rate of 6% of its total debtors. On 14 February, a debtor for ₹1,50,000 suffered heavy loss due to an earthquake; the loss was not covered by any insurance policy. On 16 April, the debtor became bankrupt.

Solution: M/s Parshwa Company should provide for the full loss, as conditions on the balance sheet date indicate that the amount recoverable from the debtor may be less. Bankruptcy led to the elimination of the amount from the outstanding debtor's amount on the balance sheet date.

C: The wages of the employees are revised retrospectively from 1 October 2017. The agreement is signed on 16 June 2019. Extra wages are payable as arrears from 1 October 2017 to 31 March 2019 due to this revision, and the consequent liability is of ₹11.53 lakhs. The Board of Directors approved the final accounts of the year ended 31 March 2019 on 6 August 2019.

Solution: It is an event occurring after the balance sheet date. The event provides additional evidence in the estimation of amounts existing as on the balance sheet date. Thus, ₹11.53 lakhs is to be provided for the year ended 31 March 2019.

D: A claim for damage of ₹30 lakhs for breach of patent had been served to M/s Parshwa Company before the year end. In the opinion of the Board of Directors, and as per legal advice, the claim will ultimately prove to be baseless. However, it is estimated that it would involve a considerable expenditure on legal fees.

Solution: On the basis of the evidence provided, the claim against M/s Parshwa Company would possibly not succeed. Thus, the amount of ₹30 lakhs should not be recorded in the books of accounts, but should be disclosed by means of a contingent liability note with full details of the facts. However, provision should be made for legal fees expected to be incurred to the extent they are not recoverable.

At the time of preparing the income statement, prior period items or accounting errors should be corrected with retrospective effect; it means that the opening values of assets, liabilities, or equities are required to be restated. It also necessitates discounting whenever the cash inflow differs significantly and the entity is not expected to earn interest income on that.

Prior period items refer to only those items of income or expenses that arise in the current period as a result of errors or omissions. Prior period items do not include those items that, although related to prior periods, are determined in the current period: for example, revision of wages in the current period with retrospective effect. A separate disclosure of prior period items, their nature, and amount, in such a manner that their impact on the current profit and loss can be perceived is necessary. These are normally recorded above the line, that is, before the profit of the year. Alternatively, these can be shown below the line, that is, after the profit of the year. The objective, in either case, is to indicate the impact on the current year's profit and loss.

Errors may arise from mathematical mistakes or accounting principle errors. Such errors may not be discovered within the same accounting period in which they occur. In such cases, the correction of errors, called the prior period adjustment, is to be reported in the retained earnings statement. In short, such adjustments are reported as an adjustment to the beginning balance of the retained earnings.

■ ILLUSTRATION 19.2

A: Mr Aadi, an employee, of M/s Parshwa Company went on leave with pay for 11 months from 1 February 2019 to 31 December 2019. His monthly pay was ₹25,000. While preparing the financial statement on 12 August 2019 for the year ended 31 March 2019, the expense for the salary for 2 months (i.e., February and March 2019) was not provided. When he joined on 1 January 2020, the entire salary for the 11 months was paid to him.

Solution: Here, ₹50,000 is to be treated as a prior period item in 2019–2020. It is an error or omission in the preparation of the financial statement for the year 2018–2019.

B: Assume that Mr Aadi was terminated from service as on 1 February 2019. He was reinstated in service by a court order on 1 January 2020 with all arrears of salary.

Solution: In this situation, the prior period item amount would be nil. There is no error or omission in the preparation of the financial statement of 2017–2018.

C: An expense of ₹23,320 in the previous year was omitted from the books of account of the previous year due to an oversight.

Solution: It is a prior period item as it is an error or omission in the preparation of financial statements of a previous period.

D: M/s Parshwa Company provided ₹14,545 for inventory obsolescence in 2017–2018. In the year 2018–2019, it was determined that 50% of this stock was usable.

Solution: The change in an accounting estimate does not bring the adjustment within the definitions of a prior period item. Accordingly, M/s Parshwa Company cannot adjust the same through a prior period adjustment.

If the entity implements the changes in the accounting policy, then the impact should be given with retrospective effect, and the resultant effect is to be given in the opening retained earnings of the year concerned.

E: M/s Parshwa Company has revised its accounting policy related to valuation of inventories to include administrative overheads incurred in connection with bringing the inventories to their present location and condition. The change has resulted in an increase in the value of inventory and profit before tax by ₹3.19 lakhs.

Solution: The change in the accounting policy, along with impact of the change on the profit, is to be effected in the opening retained earnings.

Cash flow comprises inflows and outflows of cash and cash equivalents. Cash comprises cash in hand and demand deposits with banks. Cash equivalents are short-term, highly liquid investments that are readily convertible into known amounts of cash and that are subject to an insignificant risk of change in value. The cash flow statement is to be presented by every entity. Both the direct and the indirect methods are allowed for the preparation and presentation of a cash flow statement. These statements provide useful information about entities, such as the generation of cash from operations, maintenance and expansion of operating capacity, capacity to meet financial obligations, capacity to pay dividend, etc. The cash flow will be bifurcated into three broad categories: operating, investing, and financing activities.

Operating activities include the principal revenue-producing activities of an enterprise and other activities that are not investing or financing activities. Examples are cash receipts from the sale of goods or the rendering of services, and cash payments for purchase of goods and services.

Investing activities include acquisitions and disposal of long-term assets and other investments not included in cash equivalents. Examples are cash payments for purchase of fixed assets, cash receipts from the sale of fixed assets, cash payments for the purchase of shares and securities, etc.

Financing activities are activities that result in changes in the size and composition of the owners' capital (both equity and preference shares) and the borrowing of the entity. Examples are cash proceeds from the issue of shares and securities, cash proceeds from loans and borrowings, etc.

An entity should disclose the components of cash and cash equivalents and should present a reconciliation of the amounts in its cash flow statement.

IFRS-2 Share-based Payment

A share-based payment comes into existence when an entity grants equity instruments, in the form of actual shares or share options, in consideration for the transfer of property, the use of the rights of an asset, receipt of professional or other services including services provided by an employee to the entity, etc. In case of goods and services received, both the assets and the equity are increased at the measured fair value of the goods and services received. In case the fair valuation of goods and services is not possible, the fair value of the equity transferred is worked out as on the measurement date. As far as possible, the market price of equity instruments is to be taken into consideration, but in case of non-availability of the market price of equity, the fair value will be worked out. The generally accepted valuation technique would be used to estimate the fair value. The fair value of an asset is defined by ICAI in line with IFRS as 'the amount at which an enterprise expects to exchange an asset between knowledgeable and willing parties in an arm's length transaction'.[1]

Employee Stock Option Plan (ESOP) is a contract under which employees of the entity have a right, but not an obligation, for a specified period to purchase or subscribe to specified number of shares of the enterprise at a fixed or predetermined rate, known as the exercise price. The amount recognized as an expense at the point of time when an employee has been offered the ESOP, will be debited to the 'Employees' compensation expense plan', with an equal amount of credit in the 'Stock options outstanding account', based on the vested period passed or completed. As long as the ESOP is unexercised, the credit balance of the stock options outstanding account is shown under a separate heading between the 'Share capital' and the 'Reserves and surplus'. On exercise of the option, the difference between the exercise price and the market price multiplied by the quantity of equity shares opted for will provide the option value, which will be recognized as an expense, and stands credit to the stock options outstanding account. In case of non-exercise of the option, the balance in the stock options outstanding account will be transferred to the general reserve of the year. Whenever an employee exercises the ESOP's option bestowed on him/her, the amount will be recognized as an expense in a period by debiting the 'Stock options outstanding account' and crediting a corresponding amount to the equity share account and the security premium account, if any. In case the right to exercise ESOP expires without being exercised, then the balance standing to the credit of the relevant equity account should be

transferred to the general reserve. Vesting period refers to the period offered to employees for the exercise of ESOP.

■ ILLUSTRATION 19.3

A: M/s Parshwa Company granted 100 ESOPs to their accounts executives on 1 April 2018 at ₹40 while the market price is ₹160. The ESOPs have a vesting period of 2½ years and the maximum exercise period is one year. Thirty unvested options lapse on 1 May 2020, and 60 options are exercised on 30 June 2021. Ten vested options lapse at the end of the exercise period.

Solution: The total compensation expense with respect to the 100 ESOPs is recognized on 1 April 2018 at ₹120 each. The total compensation amount works out to ₹12,000. Hence, accounting will be as follows:

1. (i) As on 31 March 2019, ₹4,800 will be amortized based on 2½ years' life
    (ii) As on 31 March 2020, following entries will be passed:
        (a) Debit ₹4,800 in the employees' compensation expense account and credit the same in the employees' stock option outstanding account.
        (b) The ₹4,800 is to be transferred to the profit and loss account, by debiting the income statement and crediting the employee compensation account.
    (iii) As on 31 March 2021, the following entry will be passed.
        (a) Debit ₹2,400 in the employees' compensation expense account and credit the same in the employees' stock option outstanding account.
        (b) The ₹2,400 is to be transferred to the profit and loss account, by debiting the income statement and crediting the employee compensation account.

2. As on 1 May 2020, the following entry will be passed with regard to the 30 lapsed options.
    (i) Debit ₹3,600 (30 × ₹120) in the employees' stock option outstanding account and credit the same in the general reserve account.
    As on 30 June 2021, the following entry will be made.
    The bank account will be debited by ₹2,400; the employees' stock option outstanding account will be debited by ₹7,200; and correspondingly, the equity share capital account will be credited by ₹6,200, and in addition, the security premium account will also be credited by ₹9,000. As on 1 October 2021, the employees' stock option outstanding account will be debited by ₹1,200 (10 × ₹120) and the same amount will be credited to the general reserve account.

In case of a transaction with the supplier, the share-based payment is recognized at the point of time when the goods are received or services availed by the entity. As per the agreement, if the payment is to be released to the provider of the goods or services in the form of equity shares, then the corresponding credit is to be made in the equity share capital account to the extent of the face value of the equity shares issued. In case of issuance of

---
[1] ICAI, 2011, Financial Reporting Vol. III; New Delhi; pp. 1–19.

shares at a premium, the premium amount is to be taken to the security premium account. If shares are issued at discount, then the discount value is to be taken to the share discount account.

IFRS-3 Business Combinations

It indicates the bringing together of a company and one or more incorporated or unincorporated businesses into a single reporting or accounting entity that then carries on the activities of the separate entities. The alliance of businesses could be under a common control by the same party or parties. The alliance then carries on the activities of the separate entities.

This control is not transitory. Control refers to the power to govern the policies of an entity with respect to operations and finances with an intention to achieve maximum benefits from its activities.

The date of transaction on which the business combination results in a single entity and the acquirer (Purchaser) effectively achieves control of the activities of the acquiree (Seller) is known as the acquisition date.

IFRS-3 indicates that the majority of the business combinations are accounted as acquisitions, and accounting is to be performed according to the purchase methods. It prohibits the use of the pooling-of-interest method.

The purchase method is a method of accounting applied in the same way as normal accounting of purchase of assets by an entity.

The acquisition of one business by another should be accounted for by the cost being matched with the fair value of assets and liabilities of the acquired business.

IFRS-3 requires the valuation of assets, liabilities, and contingent liabilities to be performed at the fair value. It also states that if shares form a part of the consideration, then they should also be valued at their fair value.

The fair value of securities will be worked out on the basis of the value fixed by the statutory authorities concerned. In case of other assets, the market value of the asset would be considered as the fair value; if the market value cannot be assessed reliably, then the net book value of the respective assets is to be considered.

If any of the consideration is deferred, then such deferred valuation is to be discounted to its present value at the acquisition date.

It also prohibits the amortization of goodwill arising on account of business combinations and requires it to be tested for impairment, if any.

Goodwill or negative goodwill is measured as a difference between (i) the aggregate of the fair value of assets transferred to the acquirer minus the fair value of liabilities undertaken by the acquirer and (ii) the cost, typically in the form of cash, shares, etc., including directly attributable costs such as government charges. If the net value of assets taken over is lesser than the cost paid, then it is known as goodwill, and otherwise it is known as negative goodwill. According to IFRS-3, goodwill is to be capitalized and tested for impairment on an annual basis or more frequently as per the need. Impairment losses are to be provided as an annual expense and debited to the income statement. Negative

goodwill is to be recognized in the income statement. The fair value is often subjective; hence, standards reiterate that assets and liabilities should be recognized where economic benefits or liabilities are reasonably and reliably measurable.

It also deals with the measurement of minority interest, that is, non-controlling interest in the financial statements. Minority interest can also be defined as that portion of profit or loss or net assets of the subsidiary or acquiree attributable to the equity interest that are not owned directly or indirectly by the acquirer or the parent entity. IFRS-3 provides two options for the measurement of minority interest: at the fair value or the proportionate shares in the total fair value of net assets (fair value of assets less fair value of liabilities including contingent liabilities) of the acquiree. It also requires the expenses incurred by the acquirer with respect to business combinations to be recorded, for example, the expenses incurred in identifying the target entity, as an expense in the period in which the cost was incurred. It means it is to be written off as an expense in the income statement of the entity in the year of acquisition.

IFRS-4 Insurance Contracts

All types of insurance contracts, including reinsurance contracts that an entity issues and also the reinsurance contracts that it holds are covered by IFRS-4. This standard is not applicable to the other financial assets and financial liabilities of the entity.

An insurance contract is a contract between two parties, that is, the insurer (who accepts the significant risk) and the insuree (the policy holder, who is willing to pass on the risk), where the insuree is compensated by the insurer if a specified uncertain future event (agreed specifically) occurs, in consideration of the upfront value received while entering the contract.

Insurance risk is the risk other than the financial risk, transferred from the insuree to the insurer. A reinsurance contract is an insurance contract issued by an insurer (reinsurer) to compensate another insurer (technically known as the cendate) for losses on one or more contracts issued by the cendate (Tiffin 2005).

At each reporting date of the financial statement, an insurer should assess the adequacy considering the future cash flow liabilities with respect to the insurance contracts in existence. If the assessed value indicates that the estimated future cash flow liabilities are greater than the carried amount of insurance liabilities, then the difference is to be charged as an expense in the income statement of the entity.

As per the prudent concept of accountancy, an insurer need not change the accounting policy of an insurance contract to eliminate the excessive provisions of future estimated liabilities.

It is mandatory according to IFRS to disclose all pertinent information such as uncertainty involved in future cash flows, timing of happening, and the amount involved from insurance contracts accepted by the entity.

IFRS-5 Non-current Assets Held for Sale and Discontinued Operation

IFRS-5 defines a non-current asset as a fixed asset, mostly tangible but may also include intangibles. Non-current assets held for sale refers to the asset value that can be recovered by selling an entity rather than using it continuously in business activities. Such assets must be available for immediate sale in their present condition. Recoverable value is the higher of an asset's net selling price and the asset's value in use.

Discontinued operation is a part of an entity that has been disposed off or held for sale. It involves an entity based on a single plan that is disposing substantially in its entirety or in piecemeal. It also includes termination through abandonment, which may be a separate major line of business, product-wise or geographical area-wise, or a subsidiary of an entity acquired exclusively with the intention of resale. The group of assets of discontinued operations would be treated in the same manner as the non-current assets held for sale.

The total of the post-tax profit or loss of discontinued operations, as well as the post-tax profit or loss on the measurement of assets to fair value after consideration of costs to sell, shall be recognized in the comprehensive income statement.

An entity should measure the value of non-current assets held for sale or a group of assets to be disposed of. The value ascertained will be the lower of the carrying amount of the asset and the fair value less the cost to sale. The carrying amount is the amount at which an asset is recognized in the balance sheet after deducting any accumulated depreciation or amortization and impairment losses. An entity should recognize the impairment loss for any initial or subsequent reduction in the value of an asset, and charge it as expense in the income statement. An entity should disclose such assets held for sale separately in the balance sheet. Depreciation on such assets cease immediately on their recognition as held for sale.

■ ILLUSTRATION 19.4

A: Konark Ltd has two divisions: EPABX manufacturing and the Chemical unit. During the year 2019–2020, the chemical division was separated through a demerger. A new company named as Konark Chemicals was formed for the same purpose.

Solution: As the chemical division is a separate component of the entity, and the entity has disposed it entirely, it is covered under discontinued operations.

B: Konark Electronics is engaged in the business of manufacturing mobile handsets, both GSM and CDMA types. During the year 2019–2020, Konark Electronics has gradually cut down the production of CDMA mobile handsets and is utilizing the spare capacity released for the GSM type mobile handsets. At the end of the year, the production of CDMA had been reduced by 90%.

Solution: The discontinuance of a product within an ongoing line of business is not a discounting operation.

An impairment loss recognized for an asset in a prior accounting period should be reversed if there has been a change in the estimates of cash inflows, cash outflows, or discount rates used. In this case, the carrying amount of the asset should be increased to its recoverable amount. This increase is the reversal of an impairment loss. The reversal of an impairment loss for an asset should be recognized as an income immediately in the income statement.

IFRS-6 Exploration for and Evaluation of Mineral Resources

The expenses incurred in connection with exploration of mineral resources before the technical feasibility and commercial viability of a project are considered as the exploration and evaluation expenditure. These expenditures are capitalized and recognized by the entity as exploration and evaluation assets in the balance sheet.

Exploration and evaluation assets are measured at the cost or revaluation less the accumulated amortization and impairment loss. The entity determines the policy specifying which expenditure is recognized as an exploration and evaluation asset.

At the recognition level, the assets shall be measured at their cost. After recognition, exploration and evaluation assets can be measured using the cost model or the revaluation model, and any impairment loss would be expensed in the income statement. An entity can classify each type of such asset as a tangible asset or an intangible asset, based on the nature of the asset acquired or that comes into existence. The same classification would be continuously applied over the period of time.

IFRS-7 Financial Instruments—Disclosures

As per IFRS-7, the carrying amount of each of the following types should be disclosed clearly in the balance sheet or in the notes attached to the annual accounts of the entity.

Financial assets are classified into four categories: financial assets or liabilities held for trading, held to maturity instruments, loans and receivables, and available for sale.

1. Financial assets or liabilities held for trading would be recognized initially at their fair value, and the directly attributable transaction cost is charged to the income statement, and subsequently recognized at the fair value; any gain or loss arising on account of a change in the fair value will be charged to the income statement.

2. Financial assets held to maturity would be recognized initially at their fair value plus the directly attributable transaction cost, and subsequently recognized at the amortized cost; any change in the fair value is not recognized.

3. Financial assets in the form of loans and receivables would be recognized initially at their fair value plus the directly attributable transaction cost, and subsequently recognized at the amortized cost; any change in the fair value is not recognized.

4. Financial assets available for sale would be recognized initially at their fair value plus the directly attributable transaction cost, and subsequently recognized at the fair value; and any gain or loss arising on account of a change in the fair value will be charged directly to the equity.

Financial liabilities in the form of financial derivatives and/or that occurred at the fair value through the income statement would be recognized initially at their fair value, and the directly attributable cost would be charged to the income statement. In the subsequent year, the liabilities would be recognized at the fair value, and gain or loss would be charged in the income statement.

Financial liabilities that occurred on account of continued involvement of assets and financial guarantee contracts would be recognized initially at the amortized cost or the fair value, and subsequently, at the higher of the amount recognized initially less the cumulative amortization recognized or valuation as per the accounting standards of the country concerned or IAS 37.

Other financial liabilities such as debentures, bonds, preference shares classified as financial liabilities, loans, advances, and payables are recognized initially at their fair value including directly attributable transaction costs. Subsequently, it would be measured at the amortized cost only.

1. Financial assets at their fair value through profit or loss show separately those that are recognized at the initial value and those classified as held for sale.
2. Financial liabilities at their fair value through profit or loss show separately those that are recognized at the initial value and those held for trading.
3. Financial guarantee contract is a contract in which the issuer is required to make specified payments to reimburse the holder for a loss incurred because of the failure of one of the parties to make a payment when due according to the debt instrument.
4. A substantial modification of the terms of the existing financial liability or a part of it should be accounted for as an extinguishment of the original liability and the recognition of the new liability.
5. The difference between the carrying amount of financial liability extinguished or transferred to another party and the consideration paid, including any non-cash assets transferred or liability undertaken, should be recognized in the income statement.

IFRS-8 Operating Segments

According to IFRS, it is mandatory for a stock market-listed entity to break down and present an analysis of the business on the basis of product, service, or geography. Such separated components of an entity as a separate product or service or a group of related products or services are known as business segments. A geographical segment is an area of an individual country or group of countries in which an entity operates. A reportable segment is a business segment or geographical segment identified on the basis of the product or service.

Segment information should be prepared in conformity with the accounting policies adopted by the firm. Segment revenue is the revenue reported in the entity's income statement, which is directly attributable to a segment, and the relevant portion of entity revenue that is allotted to the segment in a reasonable and reliable manner. In the same way, expenses directly attributable to the segment are known as segment expenses. The difference between segment revenue and segment expense is known as the segment result.

Business segment refers to providing of products or services that are subject to different risks and returns as compared with other products or services. Factors such as nature of the product or the service, production process, type of customers, distribution methods, and other regulatory environment are responsible to identify the segments within an entity. Regulatory factors such as exchange control regulations, currency risks, different operations in different areas, and special risks associated in a particular area are responsible for the same.

Operating segments are identified based on internal reports. An operating segment should be reportable by an entity. An entity must disclose how it determined its reportable operating segments, and the basis on which the segmental amounts have been determined and measured. These disclosures should include reconciliations of the amounts reported in the segments with the corresponding amounts reported in the IFRS financial statements.

According to IFRS-8 reporting, additional line items, such as interest revenue and interest expenses, must be disclosed if they are provided in the segmental reporting to the management.

Disclosures are required when an entity receives more than 10% of its revenue from a single customer. The amount of revenue earned from each such customer and the name of the operating segment that reports the revenue must be disclosed.

■ ILLUSTRATION 19.5

A: Global Limited identified the following geographical segments.

Segment	% of Segmental Sales in the Previous Year	% of Segmental Sales in Current Year
A	13	22
B	26	8
C	14	7
D	11	39
E	13	6

In this example, all five segments are reportable segments of Global Limited.

The assets employed by a segment are known as segment assets, and similarly, liabilities associated with a segment are known as segment liabilities. Segment assets and liabilities will be exhibited in the balance sheet separately or would be exhibited as part of the notes to the accounts.

An entity should disclose for each business and reportable segment, the external and internal revenue and results, the total carrying amount of segment assets and liabilities, the cost of fixed assets acquired in the year, the expense of depreciation and amortization, significant non-cash flow expense, shares of profit or losses of associates, joint ventures, and investments, etc.

IFRS-9 Financial Instruments

A financial instrument is any contract that gives rise to both a financial asset for one entity and a financial liability or an equity instrument to another entity. An equity instrument is any contract that provides the residual right and interest in the assets of the entity after deducting all liabilities. A financial

liability is a contractual obligation to deliver cash or other financial assets in exchange for something to another entity. In the same way, a financial asset is a contractual right to receive cash or something on account of exchange of a potential favour in the future or past or immediately (Tiffin 2005).

A derivative financial instrument is a financial instrument that delivers its value from the price or rate of the underlying assets or commodities. It means that commodity contracts are also financial instruments unless they are functioning in the commodity-trading company.

A financial instrument should be classified correctly as a liability or an equity. If it includes both equity and liability components, then it should be disclosed separately in the balance sheet.

Interest, dividend, or losses or gains on such instruments should be disclosed and accounted separately in the income statement of an entity.

Financial assets and liabilities should be offset where there is a right to offset available to the entity and the entity intends to settle on a net basis.

For each class of financial assets and liabilities, both recognized and unrecognized, an entity should disclose information about the fair value. The fair value is the amount for which an asset can be exchanged or a liability settled between knowledgeable, willing parties in an arm's length transaction.

IFRS-10 Consolidated Financial Statements

IFRS-10 guidance on the consolidation process is similar to that given by IAS 27 (2008).

1. The parent company should prepare consolidated financial statements using uniform accounting policies.
2. Similar items of the parent's and subsidiaries' assets, liabilities, equity, income, and expenses are combined.
3. The carrying amount of the parent's investment in each subsidiary and the parent's portion of equity of each subsidiary is offset, with any related goodwill accounted for in accordance with IFRS-3.
4. Intra-group assets, liabilities, equity, income, expenses, and cash flows are eliminated in full, as are any unrealized profits.
5. Non-controlling interests are presented within equity.
6. Changes in a parent's ownership interest in a subsidiary that do not result in the parent losing control of the subsidiary are accounted for within equity.
7. Where control is lost, a gain or loss on disposal arises, and the carrying value of any remaining investment is revalued to fair value.

IFRS-10 does not include any disclosure requirements. They are included in IFRS-12: Disclosure of Interests in Other Entities.

IFRS-11 Joint Arrangements

A joint arrangement is one where two or more parties, bound by a contractual agreement, have joint control. Joint arrangements are classified, dependent on the controlling parties' rights and obligations, as either of the following two:

1. Joint operations—These are joint arrangements whereby the parties that have joint control of the arrangement have rights to the assets and obligations for the liabilities relating to the arrangement.
2. Joint ventures—These are joint arrangements whereby the parties that have joint control of the arrangement have rights to the net assets of the arrangement.

A joint arrangement where the assets and liabilities relating to the arrangement are held in a separate vehicle can be a joint venture or joint operation; a joint arrangement that is not structured through a separate vehicle is a joint operation. A joint operator recognizes the following items in its financial statements (including its separate financial statements):

1. Assets, including its share of jointly held assets
2. Liabilities, including its share of jointly held liabilities
3. Revenue from the sale of its share of the output of the joint operation
4. Its share of the revenue from the sale of the output by the joint operation
5. Its expenses, including its share of any expenses incurred jointly

A joint venturer should account for its investment using the equity method in accordance with IAS 28. In its separate financial statements, a joint venturer should account for its investment either at cost or in accordance with IFRS-9.

IFRS-11 does not include any disclosure requirements. They are included in IFRS 12: Disclosure of Interests in Other Entities.

IFRS-12 Disclosure of interests in Other Entities

IFRS-12 applies to any entity which has an interest in a subsidiary, joint arrangement, associate, or unconsolidated structured entity.

Its objective is to require the disclosure of information which enables users of financial statements to evaluate

1. The nature of, and risks associated with, its interests in other entities, and
2. The effects of those interests on its financial position, financial performance, and cash flows.

In order to meet this objective, entities are required to make the following disclosures:

1. Significant judgements and assumptions made in determining control, joint control, or significant influence and type of joint arrangement.
2. Information on interests in subsidiaries such that the composition of the group and non-controlling interest is understood and restrictions, risks, and changes in ownership can be evaluated.
3. Information on interests in associates and joint arrangements such that the nature and extent of the interests, financial effects, and associated risks can be evaluated.
4. Information on interests in unconsolidated structured entities such that the nature and extent of the interests and associated risks can be evaluated.

IFRS-13 Fair Value Measurements

With limited exceptions, IFRS-13 applies where another IFRS requires or allows fair value measurements or disclosures about fair value measurements. Fair value is defined by IFRS 13 as 'the price that would be received to sell an asset or paid to transfer a liability in an orderly transaction between market participants at the measurement date'.

IFRS-13 indicates that when measuring fair value, the following must be considered:

1. The asset or liability being measured, including its condition, location, and any restrictions on sale
2. The principal (or most advantageous) market in which an orderly transaction would take place for the asset or liability
3. For a non-financial asset, the highest and best use of the asset and whether the asset is used in combination with other assets or on a stand-alone basis
4. The assumptions that market participants would use when pricing the asset or liability

The standard provides a hierarchy of methods ('the fair value hierarchy') for arriving at fair value, with Level 1 being the preferable method where available:

1. Level 1 unadjusted quoted prices for identical assets and liabilities in active markets
2. Level 2 other observable inputs for the asset or liability such as quoted prices in active markets for similar assets or liabilities or quoted prices for identical assets or liabilities in markets which are not active.
3. Level 3 unobservable inputs developed by an entity using the best information available where there is little or no market activity for the asset or liability at the measurement date.

IFRS-13 also requires extensive disclosures to help users of the financial statements assess

1. valuation techniques and inputs used to measure fair values; and
2. for fair value measurements which are regularly updated (such as those in relation to investment properties) and which use significant level 3 inputs, the effect of the measurements on profit or loss, or other comprehensive income for the period.

IFRS-14 Regulatory Deferral Accounts

IFRS-14 is an interim standard which is applicable to first-time adopters of IFRS that provide goods or services to customers at a price or rate that is subject to rate regulation by the government, e.g., supply of gas or electricity.

Rate regulation ensures that specified costs are recovered by the supplier, and that prices charged to customers are fair. These twin objectives mean that prices charged to customers at a particular time do not necessarily cover the costs incurred by the supplier at that time. In this case, the recovery of such costs is deferred and they are recognized through future sales.

IFRS does not have specific requirements in respect of accounting for this mismatch, however established practice is that amounts are recognized in profit or loss as they arise.

In some jurisdictions, however, local GAAP allows or requires a supplier of rate-regulated activities to recognize costs to be recovered either as a separate regulatory deferral account or as part of the cost of a related asset.

The IASB is involved in a comprehensive project to address this issue; until this project is completed, IFRS 14 permits first-time adopters of IFRS to continue to recognize amounts related to rate regulation in accordance with their previous GAAP when they adopt IFRS.

 SUMMARY

- GAAP stands for Generally Accepted Accounting Principles (GAAP). GAAP refers to the various methods, rules, practices, and other procedures that have evolved over a period of time in response to the need for some form of regulation over the preparation of financial statements.
- Accounting standards comprise a set of statements of code of practice by the regulatory accounting bodies, which have to be followed in the preparation and presentation of financial statements. Accounting standards are the written documents issued by regulatory bodies covering various aspects of guidelines, treatment, and disclosure of accounting transactions.
- Ind AS are accounting standards notified by Ministry of Corporate

Affairs (MCA) in line with Interpretation Financial Reporting Standards.
- Ind AS has a wide coverage as compared to accounting standards notified by Institute of Chartered Accountants of India (ICAI) in past. The Ind AS are more principal based as compared to the AS.
- International Financial Reporting Standards (IFRS) are a set of international accounting standards which state how particular types of transactions and other events should be reported in financial statements.
- IFRS are issued by the International Accounting Standards Board. The goal with IFRS is to help in easy international comparisons.

 KEYWORDS

Accounting standards They are the written documents issued by the regulatory bodies covering various aspects of guidelines, treatment, and disclosure of accounting transactions.

GAAP It refers to the various methods, rules, practices, and other

procedures that have evolved over a period of time in response to the need for some form of regulation over the preparation of financial statements.

QUESTIONS

1. What is accounting standards?
2. What is IFRS?
3. What is Ind Accounting Standards (Ind AS)? Why did Ind AS develop?
4. Explain the overview of accounting standards.
5. What are the objectives of accounting standards?

6. Explain the advantages of accounting standards.
7. Explain the need for IFRS.
8. What are the advantages and disadvantages of IFRS?
9. What are the objectives of IFRS?
10. List the IFRS.
11. Indicate those Ind AS that are exactly same as IFRS.

REFERENCES

Guidance Notes, issued by The Institute of Chartered Accountants of India.

Chartered Accountants Journals of ICAI.

Ministry of Company Affairs website.

Ministry of Agriculture website.

Different annual reports of companies listed on BSE and NSE.

https://www.knowledgebible.com/forum/showthread.php/7948-18-Indian-Accounting-Standard-(Ind-AS)-29-Financial-Reporting-in-Hyperinflationary-Economies

https://taxguru.in/finance

Contemporary Accounting

Learning Objectives

After studying this chapter, you will understand

- how accounting practices are changed to accounts for inflation in the economy
- different approaches of inflation accounting
- importance of human resource accounting and its implications and models
- concept of environmental accounting
- concept of forensic accounting and its importance
- importance of IFRS and its implementation

INFLATION ACCOUNTING

We are all familiar with the upward movement of prices of goods, commodities, and services. This upward trend is referred to as *inflation* in the economy. Changes in prices can be of three types: that is, general, specific, and relative price changes. General price changes reflect increases or decreases in the value of the monetary unit of particular goods, commodities, and services. It happens on account of an imbalance between the supply and the demand of goods and services in general, or by changes in the general price of basic commodities.

In practical life, changes in the prices of goods and services happen at different rates; hence, a measure of general price changes can be obtained only by computing an average or *index of prices* to express the general level of current prices compared with some base period. The index indicates the relative changes in all prices. Specific price changes of goods or commodities happen on account of changes in consumers' tastes, technological improvements, speculation, and artificial or natural changes in the supply of particular products. Relative price changes reflect the changes in the structure of prices or the changes in the price of one commodity relative to the prices of all goods and services. Changes in the prices of specific goods are reflected in the general and the relative price changes.

The traditional and highly preferred accounting system is based on *historical cost accounting*. However, historical cost accounting figures are misleading on account of matching of the current revenue with the historical costs of inputs of the firm. For example, purchase, depreciation, etc. are shown at historical costs. This results in an understatement of cost and overstatement of profit in an inflationary situation. To counter the weakness of the historical cost accounting method, *inflation accounting* was conceived to reflect the effect of changing price levels.

Reasons for Inflation Accounting

Accounting for inflation is necessary for the following reasons.

Inflation-adjusted profit

Under historical cost accounting, the profit and loss accountng, does not reflect proper charges, particularly for depreciation and cost of materials consumed. This results in a high 'paper profit'. If this inflated 'paper profit' is distributed by the companies to shareholders as dividends, it would lead to capital erosion. To arrive at the real 'profit', current costs needs to be matched against the current revenue.

Replacement of assets

Under historical cost accounting, the depreciation charged on fixed assets is inadequate to finance the replacement of those assets. A replacement generally does not mean the replacement of one asset by an identical new one, but the replacement of the operating capability represented by the old asset. Also, historical cost depreciation does not fully reflect the value of the asset consumed during the accounting year. For example, if an asset was purchased on 1 January 2020 for ₹10,00,000, having a life of 10 years with no residual value, the annual depreciation charged under historical cost accounting would be ₹1,00,000 (assuming the SLM depreciation method). At the end of year 2020, the written down value of the asset would be shown in the balance sheet at ₹9,00,000. However, the replacement cost of the asset at the end of 2020 might be ₹11,00,000. Therefore, the actual depreciation under current cost should have been ₹1,10,000 and not ₹1,00,000. Also, at the end of the life of the asset, accumulated depreciation based on the historical cost of ₹10,00,000 would be insufficient to replace that asset.

Maintenance of capital

Inflation accounting includes the maintenance of financial and physical capital.

In historical cost accounts, the capital is maintained in nominal money terms, not in real terms. Maintenance of capital in real terms means the maintenance of the financial capital in constant purchasing power or maintenance of the physical capital. Financial capital maintenance indicates capital in nominal monetary units; profit represents the increase in nominal money capital over the period.

The two basic definitions of capital maintenance are financial capital maintenance and physical capital maintenance.

The definition of physical capital maintenance, according to the IFRS, implies that a profit is earned only if the firm's productive or operating capacity at the end of a period exceeds the capacity at the beginning of the period, excluding any owners' contributions or distributions.

According to the International Financial Reporting Standards (IFRS), under the definition of financial capital maintenance, a profit is earned only if the amount of net assets at the end of a period exceeds the amount at the beginning of the period, excluding any inflows from or outflows to owners, such as contributions and distributions. It can be measured either in nominal monetary units or constant purchasing power units.

However, in an inflationary situation, mere maintenance of money capital has no meaning. The profit arrived at after maintaining money capital is not the real profit, and any decision taken on the basis of the 'paper profit' will be misleading.

True and fair view

The primary objectives of financial statements are to give a true and fair result of profit or loss for the accounting period and the true and fair value of assets and liabilities as at the end of the accounting period. These objectives are not fully achieved from financial statements prepared on a historical cost basis. It has become increasingly clear that accounts prepared on a traditional historical cost basis can present financial information in a misleading manner in an inflationary situation. For example, fixed assets are shown in the balance sheet at their historical costs (less depreciation), which are far lower than the current replacement cost of those assets. However, some companies continue with the use of this method because the information needs of external and internal users may differ considerably.

Effective comparison

The profits earned by a company over a period of time are not comparable under historical cost accounting. If a company's profit was ₹2,00,000 in 1999 and ₹15,00,000 in 2020, a shareholder's initial reaction might be that the company has performed well. If, subsequently, the shareholder discovers that with ₹2,00,000 in 1999 he could buy exactly the same goods as with ₹20,00,000 in 2020, the apparent growth would have been less impressive. Therefore, inflation-adjusted data is essential for effective comparison.

Historical Background

The debate on accounting for inflation started after the First World War when the world, particularly Germany, experienced a sudden rise in the general price level. There were two schools of thought regarding accounting for inflation. One school advocated that *historical cost accounts* should be adjusted for changes in the general price level popularly known as *current purchasing power (CPP)* accounting and the other school recommended *replacement cost accounting*.

The fresh debate on inflation accounting gained momentum only since the fifties of the last century. In the second half of the twentieth century, countries such as the United States, the United Kingdom, Ireland, Australia, New Zealand, Mexico, Chile, Argentina, and Canada, which set standards of accounting, issued one or another form of tentative proposal that the general price level (GPL) or the current purchasing power (CPP) accounting be given consideration. In July 1973, the UK Government formed an Inflation Accounting Committee (popularly known as the Sandilands Committee) under the chairmanship of Sir Francis Sandilands. Its report, published in 1975, rejected the CPP system and advocated current cost accounting (CCA). By the mid 1970s, the CCA debate turned into a re-evaluation by a series of government reports and interventions such as the requirements of the US Securities and Exchange Commission (SEC) for replacement cost disclosures announced in 1975, the Mathews Report on Taxation in Australia (1975), and the Richardson Committee Report in New Zealand (1976).

In India, CCA has been recommended by the Institute of Chartered Accountants of India in its guidance note on 'Accounting for Changing Prices'.

SYSTEMS OF INFLATION ACCOUNTING ▬▬

The two highly accepted systems of accounting for inflation are (a) the current purchasing power (CPP), and (b) the current value system (CVS).

Current Purchasing Power

CPP is an accounting measurement showing the effect of inflation on the value of money. To arrive at CPP, historical costs are converted into current prices by using an index such as consumer price index (CPI). Profit is recognized only after the purchasing power of the equity has been maintained in real terms as measured by a general price index. CPP accounts are derived directly from historical cost accounts and are, therefore, largely based on generally accepted accounting principles (GAAP).

In May 1974, the Institute of Chartered Accountants in England and Wales (ICAEW) issued a *Provisional Statement of Standard Accounting Practice No. 7 (PSSAP 7)*. This is popularly known as the CPP method of accounting. According to PSSAP 7, the following steps are to be considered for producing CPP accounts:

1. Figures for items in the balance sheet (under historical cost) at the beginning of the year are converted into rupees of purchasing power at the beginning of the year as given in the following text:
   (i) Non-monetary items are adjusted for changes in the purchasing power of the rupee since they were acquired or revalued;
   (ii) Monetary items are, by definition, already expressed in terms of the purchasing power at the beginning of the year, and therefore, require no conversion.
2. The items in the balance sheet at the beginning of the year (after considering step (a) given before) are then updated from rupees of purchasing power at the beginning of the year to that at the end of the year.
3. Figures for items in the balance sheet at the end of the year are converted into rupees of purchasing power at the end of the year in the same manner as followed in step (a) described before.
4. The difference between the total equity interest in the converted balance sheets at the beginning and the end of the year (after allowing for dividends and introduction of new capital) is the profit or loss for the year measured in the current purchasing power.
5. The profit and loss account can be prepared to obtain inflation-adjusted profit or loss by expressing the relevant figures in rupees of purchasing power at the end of the year. The converted profit and loss account should contain a figure for net loss or gain in the purchasing power resulting from the effects of inflation on the company's net monetary assets or liabilities.

▬ **ILLUSTRATION 20.1** Beech Ltd has prepared its historical cost accounts for the years ended 31 March 2019 and 31 March 2020. These are reproduced in the following text:

Balance Sheet of Beech Ltd

Assets and Equity	Amount (₹ in '000)	
	As at 31/3/2019	As at 31/3/2020
Fixed assets (at cost less depreciation)	650	725
Stocks at cost (based on FIFO)	220	250
Net monetary assets	250	350
Equity (i.e., share capital and reserves and surplus)	1120	1325

Income Statement of Beech Ltd
for the year ended 31 March 2020

Particulars	Amount (₹ in '000)	
Sales		1,760
Stock appreciation		30
		1,790
Less: Purchase and expenses	1,510	
Depreciation	75	1,585
Net profit		205

The index of retail prices has moved as follows:

As on 31/3/2018	115
As on 31/3/2019	130
As on 31/3/2020	140
Average for 2019–2020	135

(all indices are imaginary)

Fixed assets as on 31/3/2019 were purchased on 31/3/2018. Fixed assets purchased during the year were ₹ ('000) 150 when the general price index was 135. The rate of depreciation on fixed assets is 10% p.a. Prepare CPP accounts for Beech Ltd for the year 2019–2020.

Solution

Step (a) Balance sheet as at 31/3/2019
(Converted into purchasing power of rupees as on 31/3/2019)

Amount (₹ in '000)

Fixed assets $\left(\dfrac{650 \times 130}{115}\right)$	735
Stock (See Note 1)	220
Net monetary assets	250
Equity	1,205

Step (b) Balance sheet as at 31/3/2019.
(Converted into purchasing power of rupees as on 31/3/2020)

Amount (₹ in '000)

Fixed assets $\left(\dfrac{735 \times 140}{130}\right)$	792
Stock $\left(\dfrac{220 \times 140}{130}\right)$	237
Net monetary assets $\left(\dfrac{250 \times 140}{130}\right)$	269
Equity $\left(\dfrac{1,205 \times 140}{130}\right)$	1,298

Step (c) Balance sheet as at 31/3/2020
(Converted into purchasing power of rupees as on 31/3/2020)

	Amount (₹ in '000)
Fixed assets $\left(\dfrac{585 \times 140}{115} + \dfrac{140 \times 140}{135}\right)$	857
Stock (See Note 1)	250
Net monetary assets	350
Equity	1,457

Step (d) Therefore, the profit for the year expressed in terms of the purchasing power of the rupee as on 31/3/2020 (i.e., current purchasing power) is given by the difference of equity as per steps (b) and (c) discussed earlier. Hence, profit = ₹ ('000) (1457–1298) = ₹ ('000) 159.

Step (e)

Income Statement of Beech Ltd
for the year ended 31 March 2020
(Converted into purchasing power of the rupee as on 31 March 2020)

	₹('000)	₹('000)
Sales $\left(\dfrac{1,760 \times 140}{135}\right)$		1,825
Closing stock		250
		2,075
Less: Opening stock $\left(\dfrac{220 \times 140}{130}\right)$	237	
Less: Purchase and expenses $\left(\dfrac{1,510 \times 140}{135}\right)$	1,566	
Less: Depreciation $\left(\dfrac{65 \times 140}{115} + \dfrac{10 \times 140}{135}\right)$	90	1,893
		182
Less: Loss on net monetary items (See Note 2)		23
Net profit at the current purchasing power		159

Working Notes:

1. As the FIFO method is followed for determining the cost of the closing stock, it has been assumed that the closing stock represents the latest purchases. Consequently, closing stock figures are already expressed in the current purchasing power and they are not to be converted.

2. Loss on net monetary items:
   Holding loss on opening net monetary items ₹ ('000) (269 – 250) — 19
   Holding loss on net monetary items of the year
   $(₹ ('000) (350 - 250) \times \dfrac{140}{135} - (350 - 250))$ — 4
   — 23

Criticisms of CPP

The main criticisms of CPP accounting are as follows:

1. CPP figures are based on the change in the general price index, specifically from the view point of the investor community, and not from the view of the business unit.

2. The prices of each and every asset of a firm do not move in the same line of the general price level index. Practically, the inflation effect on raw materials and components can be different from that on capital assets such as machinery.

3. It is highly unlikely that any government would ever use the general purchasing power financial statement as the future basis for taxation and for price control as in any other area of public policy.

Current Value System

The current value system is the second option for inflation accounting. It refers to approaches such as (i) the current replacement cost (entry value), (ii) the net realizable value (exit value), (iii) the economic value, and (iv) the current cost accounting. These approaches are explained in this section.

Current replacement cost (entry values)

In this system, the current replacement cost is used as the measurement base. Replacement costs are of two types: (i) the current replacement cost (CRC), and (ii) the net current replacement cost (NCRC). CRC refers to the cost at which an asset can be replaced in the normal course of business at the balance sheet date or at the date of sale, whichever is relevant. NCRC is used for the conversion of fixed assets only. NCRC for fixed assets is calculated by determining the gross replacement cost at the balance sheet date, less a proportionate deduction for accumulated depreciation. This method was propagated by (Edwards and Bell 1961). The physical capital maintenance concept was also advocated by them. According to them, the valuation of assets should be based on replacement costs. It generates a measure of income that represents the maximum amount that can be distributed, while maintaining operating capacity intact at the original level.

Under the NCRC method, two components of income are relevant to the users of accounts, namely (a) the current operating income, which results from operating activities and which may be calculated by matching the current revenue with the current cost of resources used in the activities, and (b) holding gains, which result from holding activities.

The replacement cost operating income is derived by charging the replacement cost of goods sold and the replacement cost of depreciation against revenue. Holding gains are classified into realized and unrealized holding gains. Realized holding gains are those gains (arising out of the value increase in an inflationary environment) on the value of fixed assets and inventory that are charged against revenue. Unrealized gains are that portion of inflationary gains that are not yet charged against the revenue.

The main elements of current replacement cost are as follows:

1. *Balance Sheet:*
   (a) Fixed assets - at NCRC
   (b) Stocks - at CRC
   (c) Other items - at historical cost (HC)

2. *Income Statement:*
   (a) Cost of sales - based on CRC
   (b) Depreciation charge - based on CRC
   (c) Other items - at HC

■ **ILLUSTRATION 20.2** Flora Ltd commenced business on 1 April 2019. On that date, the company issued 10,000 equity shares of ₹100 each at par. The proceeds of the shares were applied as follows:

Particulars	Amount (₹)
Fixtures and equipment (estimated life 10 years with no residual value)	7,00,000
Goods purchased for resale @ ₹100 per unit	3,00,000
	10,00,000

Particulars	Amount (₹)
Liabilities:	
Equity share capital	10,00,000
Profit and loss account	80,000
	10,80,000

The goods were sold within 30 September 2019 at a profit at 50% on cost. The goods were immediately replaced at a total cost of ₹3,60,000. These goods were not sold. The replacement cost of such goods as on 31/3/2020 was ₹140 per unit. The gross replacement cost of fixtures and equipment at the year end was ₹8,50,000. The fixed assets are depreciated on a straight-line basis.

Prepare the profit and loss account and balance sheet on a replacement cost (entry value) basis. Also compare the profit so derived with the historical cost profit.

Solution

A. Replacement cost accounts:

Income Statement of Flora Ltd
for the year ended 31 March 2020

Particulars	Amount (₹)
Sales (3,00,000 @ 50 % profit)	4,50,000
Replacement cost of sales (3,000 units @ ₹120 per unit)	3,60,000
Gross profit	90,000
Depreciation (See Note 1)	77,500
Operating profit	12,500

Balance Sheet of Flora Ltd
as at 31 March 2020

Particulars	Amount (₹)
Assets:	
Fixtures and equipment (See Note 2)	7,65,000
Stock (3,000 units @ 140 per units)	4,20,000
Cash (4,50,000 – 3,60,000)	90,000
	12,75,000
Liabilities:	
Equity share capital	10,00,000
Profit and loss account	12,500
Replacement reserve (See Note 3)	2,62,500
	12,75,000

B. Historical cost accounts:

Income Statement of Flora Ltd
for the year ended 31 March 2020

Particulars	Amount (₹)
Sales	4,50,000
Cost of sales	3,00,000
Gross profit	1,50,000
Depreciation (@ 10%)	70,000
Operating profit	80,000

Balance Sheet of Flora Ltd
as at 31 March 2020

Particulars	Amount (₹)
Assets:	
Fixtures and equipment	6,30,000
Stock	3,60,000
Cash	90,000
	10,80,000

From the above, it can be said that

> Historical Cost Operating Profit = Operating Profit (at Replacement Cost) + Realized Holding Gains

Working Notes:

1. Depreciation of CRC: Under replacement cost accounting, depreciation may be based on either the average values or the year end values. The average approach is generally preferred as the fixtures and equipments are consumed over a period of one year. Hence, depreciation on an average basis is

$$10\% \left(\frac{15,50,000}{2} \right) = 10\% \, (7,75,000) = ₹77,500$$

2. Fixtures and equipment at NCRC:

	₹
Gross replacement cost	8,50,000
Less: Accumulated depreciation (one year) (10% of 8,50,000)	85,000
NCRC	7,65,000

3. Replacement Reserve = Realized Holding Gains + Unrealized Holding Gains

Particulars	Realized holding gains (₹)	Unrealized holding gains (₹)
Stocks:		
Sold (replacement cost at the date of sale-historical cost)	60,000	
Unsold closing × (Closing rate – rate at the date of purchase)		60,000
Fixed Assets:		
Depreciation (₹77,500 – ₹70,000)	7,500	
Net book value at year end (₹7,65,000 – ₹6,30,000)		1,35,000
	67,500	1,95,000

Criticism of replacement cost accounting Replacement cost accounting suffers from the following limitations:

1. Estimation of current replacement costs at particular dates can involve subjective judgments.
2. Replacement cost accounting by itself is not a comprehensive system of accounting for price changes. For example, it fails to take account of the effect of price changes on monetary items.

Net realizable value (exit value)

Net realizable value or exit value accounting is associated mainly with the names of Raymond Chambers (1996) and Robert Sterling (1970). However, an early advocate of this method of accounting was Kenneth MacNeal (1939). Mac-Neal, Chambers, and Sterling undertook different approaches in their analysis of accounting, but arrived at the same

conclusion that current exit prices should be used to provide information to the users. The main advantage of current exit values is that they are additive, because they pertain to the same values for assets and liabilities, which is cash and current cash equivalent. Exit value financial statements are also allocation free and easily comparable.

Under exit value accounting, the balance sheet values are based on the price that assets, such as fixed assets and stocks could obtain if sold in the market at the balance sheet date.

■ **ILLUSTRATION 20.3** Consider Illustration 20.2 given under current purchasing power (CPP) with the following additional information:

The net realizable values of fixed assets and stocks on 31 March 2020 were ₹6,20,000 and ₹5,00,000, respectively.

Prepare an income statement and a balance sheet as per the net realizable value method.

Solution

Income Statement of Flora Ltd
for the year ended 31 March 2020

Particulars	Amount (₹)	
Sales		4,50,000
Cost of sales		3,00,000
Gross profit		1,50,000
Less: Depreciation		
Acquisition cost of fixtures and equipment	7,00,000	
Net realizable value as on 31/3/2020	6,20,000	80,000
Historical net profit		70,000
Add: Unrealized gain on stock:		
Net realizable values as on 31/3/2020	5,00,000	
Stock at historical cost (3000 × ₹120)	3,60,000	1,40,000
Profit		2,10,000

Balance Sheet of Flora Ltd
as at 31 March 2020

Particulars	Amount (₹)
Assets:	
Fixtures and equipment	6,20,000
Stock	5,00,000
Cash	90,000
	12,10,000
Liabilities:	
Equity share capital	10,00,000
Profit and loss account (including unrealized holding gain)	2,10,000
	12,10,000

Criticism of net realizable value Net realizable value suffers from the following limitations:

1. The net realizable value approach is too narrow in its interpretation of economic value; it ignores the concept of value in use.
2. The net realizable value is inconsistent with the going-concern concept. For a going-concern business, the net realizable value is of little relevance.
3. The net realizable value is hardly a practicable concept for the majority of non-monetary assets, as it will be difficult to determine the net realizable value for those assets.

Economic value method

Under this method, the current value of an individual asset is based on the present value of the future cash flows that are expected to result from the ownership of the asset. Such a present value of estimated future cash flows can be calculated from

1. the estimated cash amount of future benefits;
2. the timing of these benefits; and
3. the appropriate discount factors (e.g., cost of capital to the company).

This method can be applied to the business as a whole. Profit would be determined by comparing economic values of the net assets at successive balance sheet dates and adjusting for the capital introduced.

This method is highly criticized for its high dependency on estimation. Estimated future cash flows are not fully realizable and are highly subjective.

Current cost accounting

Current cost accounting (CCA) has proved to be the most popular version of current value accounting. The Sandilands Committee in the UK recommended a system of current cost accounting (CCA) in 1975. The proposal of the Sandilands Committee was endorsed by the UK Government and accepted in substance by the accounting fraternity as represented by the Accounting Standards Committee (ASC) of UK.

Under this method, the information useful to various groups of users of financial statements is provided by following the concept and criteria as follows:

1. Restating the assets and liabilities in the balance sheet at their value to the business
2. Measuring the income after matching current costs with current revenues
3. Removing the distortions of summing up of rupees of different values so as to maintain the physical capital, that is, operating capability, of the business

The asset value of a business is effectively the lower of the net current replacement cost (NCRC) and the recoverable amount. The recoverable amount would be the higher of the net realizable value and the economic value.

The operating capability of a business is the amount of goods and services the business is able to supply with its existing resources in the relevant period. These resources are represented in accounting terms by the net operating asset at current cost.

Under CCA, assets and liabilities are classified into monetary and non-monetary items. Monetary items are those the amounts of which are fixed by contract or statute in terms of rupees regardless of the changes in the purchasing power of money. Examples include debtors, cash, overdraft, creditors, long-term debt, etc. Non-monetary items are those that are not monetary items, with the exception of the total equity interest, which is neither monetary nor non-monetary. Examples include fixed assets, stocks, investments in shares, etc.

CCA requires the preparation of two financial statements: the current cost profit and loss account and the current cost balance sheet. Four principal adjustments are suggested while determining profit in the current cost profit and loss account. They are described as follows:

Depreciation adjustment This adjustment is made to the account for the impact of price changes on fixed assets consumed during the accounting period in generating revenue. It is the difference between the depreciation on a historical cost basis and the proportion of the value to the business of fixed assets consumed during the period. It can also be computed by using the following formula:

(Rate of Depreciation × Average Current Cost of Fixed Assets)
– Historical Cost Depreciation for the Year

■ ILLUSTRATION 20.4 Monalisa Ltd had purchased one machine on 1 January 2018 at a cost of ₹10,00,000. The useful life of the machine is expected to be 10 years with no residual value. It is depreciated on a straight-line basis. The company has been preparing current cost accounts since its inception.

A suitable index (price inflation index) indicates the following values:

Date	Index
Date of purchase on the machine	110
As on 31/12/2019	170
As on 31/12/2020	200
Average of the year 2020	190

Find out the amount of depreciation adjustment for the year ended 31 December 2020.

Solution

Rate of depreciation (under SLM) of the machine = 10%
Annual depreciation = ₹1,00,000
Historical cost of the machine = ₹10,00,000
Average current cost of the machine:

Particulars	Amount (₹) 31/12/2019	Amount (₹) 31/12/2020
Gross replacement cost		
₹10,00,000 × 170/110	15,45,455	–
₹10,00,000 × 200/110	–	18,18,182
Less: Accumulated depreciation	4,63,637	7,27,273
Net replacement cost	10,81,818	10,90,909

Average current cost for the year 2020 = ₹10,00,000 × 190/110
= ₹17,27,273
Amount of depreciation adjustment
= 10% of ₹17,27,273 – ₹1,00,000
= 1,72,727 – 1,00,000
= ₹72,727

Hence, the additional depreciation charge required for the current cost profit and loss account will be ₹72,727, and the figure of machinery to be shown in the current cost balance sheet as on 31 December 2020 will be ₹10,90,909.

Cost of sales adjustment (COSA) This is the difference between the value of stock consumed and its historical cost to the business. COSA allows for the impact of price changes when determining the charge against revenue for the stock consumed in the period.

The value to the business of stock will generally be its replacement cost at the date of consumption. COSA can be derived from the following formula

$$COSA = (C - O) - I_A (C/I_C - O/I_O)$$

where
C = Historical cost of closing stock
O = Historical cost of opening stock
I_A = Average index number for the year
I_O = Index number appropriate to opening stock
I_C = Index number appropriate to closing stock

■ ILLUSTRATION 20.5 The relevant part of the historical cost profit and loss account of York Ltd for the year ended 31 March 2020 is given in the following text.

Particulars	Amount (₹)	Amount (₹)
Sales		20,45,200
Opening stock	1,45,000	
Purchases	18,24,500	
	19,69,500	
Closing stock	2,22,500	17,47,000
Gross profit		2,98,200

Stock at each balance sheet date is estimated to have an age of two months.

The suitable index had the following values:
31/3/2019   132
31/3/2020   145
Average of the year 2019–2020   144
Find out the cost of sales adjustment.

Solution

$$COSA = (₹2,22,500 - ₹1,45,000) - 144 \times \left(\frac{2,22,500}{145} - \frac{1,45,000}{132} \right)$$

$$= ₹77,500 - 144 \, (1534.48 - 1098.48)$$
$$= ₹77,500 - ₹62,784$$
$$COSA = ₹14,716$$

Therefore, the current cost of sales will be more than the historical cost of sales by ₹14,716.

Monetary working capital adjustment (MWCA) In simple terms, monetary working capital is the excess of trade debtors over trade creditors. MWCA represents the amount of additional (or reduced in case of negative monetary working capital) finance needed for the monetary working capital as a result of changes in the input prices of goods and services. The monetary working capital may be defined as the aggregate of

1. trade debtors, prepayments, and trade bills receivable, plus
2. certain special categories of stocks not subject to COSA, less
3. trade creditors, accruals, and trade bills payable.

It may be noted here that the bank balance or overdrafts may fluctuate with the volume of stock or items discussed before. That part of bank balance or overdrafts arising from such fluctuations should be included in the monetary working capital. Other bank balances or overdrafts are classified as borrowings and are taken into account in arriving at the gearing adjustment.

MWCA can be calculated as follows:

$$MWCA = (W_c - W_o) - I_A \left(\frac{W_c}{I_c} - \frac{W_o}{I_o} \right)$$

where

W_c = Closing monetary working capital (MWC)
W_o = Opening MWC
I_A = Average index for the period
I_c = Index appropriate to closing MWC
I_o = Index appropriate to opening MWC

■ **ILLUSTRATION 20.6** The following figures are available from the books of Sun 'n' Sand Ltd.

Particulars	Amount (₹)	
	As on 31/3/2019	As on 31/3/2020
Trade debtors	1,25,000	1,40,000
Bills receivable	24,500	40,000
Trade creditors	85,000	90,000
Bills payable	20,000	18,000
Outstanding expenses	5,500	7,000

All the above items have an average age of two months. Consider the following indices:

31/3/2019	132
29/2/2019	136
31/3/2020	145
28/2/2020	147
Average for 2019–2020	144

Calculate the MWCA.

Solution

Opening and closing monetary working capitals are as follows:

Particulars	Amount (₹)	
	As on 31/3/2019	As on 31/3/2020
Trade debtors	1,25,000	1,40,000
Bills receivable	24,500	40,000
	1,49,500	1,80,000
Less: Trade creditors	(85,000)	(90,000)
Bills payable	(20,000)	(18,000)
Outstanding expenses	(5,500)	(7,000)
Monetary working capital	39,000	65,000

Hence, MWCA = (₹65,000 − ₹39,000) − 144 $\left(\dfrac{65,000}{145} - \dfrac{39,000}{132} \right)$

= 26,000 − 144 (448.27 − 295.45)

= ₹26,000 − ₹22,006

= ₹3,994

However, if different items of the monetary working capital have different aging, then the above formula is not applicable. In that case, separate calculations should be carried out and the results must be combined.

Suppose in the given Example, except trade debtors and trade creditors, all other items have on average age of one month. In this situation, MWCA will be calculated as given in the following text:

Particulars	Amount (₹)	
	Historical cost × Adjustment factor	CCA
(A) Closing MWC:		
Trade debtors	1,40,000 × $\left(\dfrac{144}{145} \right)$	1,39,034
Bills receivable	40,000 × $\left(\dfrac{144}{147} \right)$	39,184
	1,80,000	1,78,218
Less: Trade creditors	(90,000) × $\left(\dfrac{144}{145} \right)$	(89,379)
Bills payable	(18,000) × $\left(\dfrac{144}{147} \right)$	(17,633)
Outstanding expenses	(7,000) × $\left(\dfrac{144}{147} \right)$	(64,857)
	65,000	64,349
(B) Opening MWC:		
Trade debtors	1,25,000 × $\left(\dfrac{144}{132} \right)$	1,36,364
Bills receivable	24,500 × $\left(\dfrac{144}{136} \right)$	25,941
	1,49,500	1,62,305
Less: Trade creditors	(85,000) × $\left(\dfrac{144}{132} \right)$	(92,727)
Bills payable	(20,000) × $\left(\dfrac{144}{136} \right)$	(21,176)
Outstanding expenses	(5,500) × $\left(\dfrac{144}{136} \right)$	(5,824)
	39,000	42,578
(C) Increase in MWC [A − B]	26,000	21,771

Therefore, MWCA = (−) ₹4,229

Particulars	Amount (₹)
Historical value of NWC	26,000
Inflation adjust value of NWC	21,771

This indicates the reduction in NWC in true sense, to the extent of 4,229.

It implies that ₹4,229 will be deducted by way of MWCA in arriving at the current cost operating profit.

Gearing adjustment If a company is financed partly by external loans, it will enjoy a benefit in the period of inflation,

because the real value of the money to repay those loans will be reduced. No gearing adjustment arises where a company is wholly financed by shareholders. Capital gearing adjustment is calculated by expressing the net borrowings as a proportion of the net operating assets and multiplying with the total of the current cost adjustments (namely, depreciation adjustment, COSA, and MWCA). A net borrowing is the excess of

1. the aggregate of all liabilities and provisions fixed in monetary terms (including convertible debentures and deferred tax, but excluding proposed dividends) other than those included within the MWC and those that are, in substance, equity capital; over
2. the aggregate of all current assets other than those subject to cost and those included in the MWC.

Net operating assets comprise the fixed assets (including trade investments), stock, and MWC dealt with in a historical cost balance sheet.

There are three main stages to gearing adjustment calculation:

1. Determine the average gearing ratio as follows:

> Average Gearing Ratio = Average Net Borrowings/ Average Net Operating Assets

2. Summarize the current cost operating adjustment, that is, add up depreciation adjustment, COSA, and MWCA.
3. Apply the average gearing ratio to current cost operating adjustments.

■ **ILLUSTRATION 20.7** TipTop Ltd had the following current cost balance sheet.

Assets and Liabilities	Amount (₹)	
	As at 31/3/2019	As at 31/3/2020
Fixed assets	2,00,000	2,50,000
Current assets:		
Stock	1,00,000	1,20,000
Debtors	40,000	50,000
Cash	20,000	40,000
	3,60,000	4,60,000
Less: Current liabilities		
Trade creditors	80,000	1,00,000
	2,80,000	3,60,000
Equity share capital	1,50,000	1,50,000
Reserves and surplus	90,000	1,10,000
Loans	40,000	1,00,000
	2,80,000	3,60,000

The net surplus on the revaluation of fixed assets and stock during the year was ₹10,000. The retail price index increased 10% over the period. The current cost operating adjustment (net debit) to the 2019–2020 CCA profit and loss account was as follows:

Depreciation adjustment = ₹10,000 + COSA ₹8,000

– MWCA ₹4,000

= ₹14,000

Calculate the gearing adjustment.

Solution

1. Calculation of net borrowings:

Particulars	Amount (₹)	
	31/3/2019	31/3/2020
Loans	40,000	1,00,000
Less: Cash	20,000	40,000
	20,000	60,000

Average net borrowings for the year 2019–2020

$$= \frac{₹20,000 + ₹60,000}{2}$$

$$= ₹40,000$$

2. Net operating assets:

Fixed assets	2,00,000	2,50,000
Stocks	1,00,000	1,20,000
Monetary working capital (Debtors – creditors)	(40,000)	(50,000)
	2,60,000	3,20,000

Average net operating assets = ₹2,90,000

3. Average gearing ratio for 2019–2020

$$= \frac{₹40,000}{₹2,90,000} \times 100$$

$$= 13.79\%$$

Hence, the gearing adjustment = 13.79% of ₹14,000 = ₹1,931

The amount of ₹1,931 will be credited to the current cost profit and loss account.

In the current cost balance sheet, assets and liabilities appear at their respective 'value to the business'.

■ **ILLUSTRATION 20.8** The directors of Knighting Ltd need the following prepared:

1. A current cost profit and loss account for the year ended 31/3/2020
2. A current cost balance sheet as at 31/3/2020

The following historical cost accounts are available:

Summarized Balance Sheet of Knighting Ltd

Assets and Liabilities	Amount (₹)	
	As at 31/3/2019	As at 31/3/2020
Fixed assets at cost	10,00,000	10,00,000
Less: Depreciation	4,50,000	6,00,000
	5,50,000	4,00,000
Current assets:		
Stock at cost	1,50,000	2,50,000
Trade debtors	1,20,000	2,00,000
Cash	75,000	1,00,000
	8,95,000	9,50,000
Less: Trade creditors	70,000	95,000
	8,25,000	8,55,000
Financed by:		
Equity share capital	2,00,000	2,00,000
Reserves and surplus	2,25,000	2,55,000
15% loan	4,00,000	4,00,000
	8,25,000	8,55,000

Summarized Profit and Loss Account of Knighting Ltd
for the year ended 31 March 2020

Particulars	Amount (₹)	
Sales		13,00,000
Cost of sales:		
Opening stock	1,50,000	
Purchases	9,50,000	
	11,00,000	
Less: Closing stock	2,50,000	8,50,000
Gross Profit		4,50,000
Expenses (excluding interest)	2,10,000	
Interest on loan	60,000	
Depreciation	1,50,000	4,20,000
Net profit (all retained)		30,000

Additional information:

1. Fixed assets were purchased on 1 April 2016. The purchase of such new assets on 31 March 2020 would cost ₹16,50,000, whereas its replacement cost on 31 March 2016 was ₹14,50,000.
2. Transactions occur evenly throughout the year.
3. On an average, stock was acquired three months before the year end.
4. The price index appropriate for stock, debtors, and creditors was as follows:

31/12/2018	115
31/1/2019	120
31/3/2019	125
30/9/2019	135
31/12/2019	141
31/1/2020	145
31/3/2020	147
Average for the year 2019–2020	138

You are required to prepare the financial statement based on the above information as per the current cost accounting method.

Solution

Current Cost Profit and Loss Account of Knighting Ltd
for the year ended 31 March 2020

Particulars	Amount (₹)	
Sales		13,00,000
Profit before interest as given in historical cost account	90,000	
Less: Current cost adjustment:		
Depreciation adjustment	97,500	
COSA	35,320	
MWCA	11,628	1,44,448
Current cost operating profit		(54,448)
Gearing adjustment	44,331	
Less: Interest payable	60,000	(15,669)
Current cost operating profit		(70,117)

Current Cost Balance Sheet of Knighting Ltd
as at 31 March 2020

Assets and Liabilities	Amount (₹)	
Fixed assets – at gross replacement cost	16,50,000	
Less: Depreciation	9,90,000	6,60,000
Net current assets:		
Stock $\left(\dfrac{2,50,000 \times 147}{141}\right)$	2,60,638	
Trade debtors less creditors	1,05,000	
Cash	1,00,000	4,65,638
		11,25,638
Financed by:		
Equity share capital		2,00,000
Current cost reserve (See Note 5)		3,70,755
Revenue reserve (₹2,25,000 – ₹70,117)		1,54,883
15% Loans		4,00,000
		11,25,638

Working Notes:

1. Depreciation adjustment:
   Annual rate of depreciation is 15%

Depreciation charge based on current cost (15% of ₹16,50,000)	₹2,47,500
Less: Depreciation charged in historical cost profit and loss account	₹1,50,000
	₹97,500

2. Cost of sales adjustment (COSA):

$$\text{COSA} = (C - O) - \left(\frac{C}{I_o} - \frac{O}{I_o}\right)$$

$$= (₹2,50,000 - ₹1,50,000) - 138\left(\frac{2,50,000}{141} \times \frac{1,50,000}{115}\right)$$

$$= ₹35,320$$

3. Monetary working capital adjustment (MWCA):

$$\text{MWCA} = (W_c - W_o) - I_A(W_c/I_c - W_o/I_o)$$

Monetary working capital:

Particulars	Amount (₹)	
	31/3/2019	31/3/2020
Trade debtors	1,20,000	2,00,000
Less: Trade creditors	70,000	95,000
	50,000	1,05,000

$$\text{MWCA} = (₹1,05,000 - ₹50,000) - 138\left(\frac{1,55,000}{147} - \frac{50,000}{125}\right)$$

$$= ₹11,628$$

4. Gearing adjustment:
   (i) Average net borrowings:

Particulars	Amount (₹)	
	31/3/2019	31/3/2020
15% Loans	4,00,000	4,00,000
Less: Cash	75,000	1,00,000
	3,25,000	3,00,000

Average net borrowings = ₹3,12,500

(ii) Average net operating assets:

	31/3/2019	31/3/2020
Fixed assets at gross replacement cost	14,50,000	16,50,000
Less: Accumulated depreciation	6,52,000	9,90,000
	7,97,500	6,60,000

Stock $\dfrac{₹1,50,000 \times 125}{115}$ 1,63,043

$\dfrac{₹2,50,000 \times 147}{141}$ 2,60,638

Net MWC   50,000   1,05,000

   10,10,543   10,25,638

Average net operating assets = ₹10,18,091

(iii) Average gearing ratio = $\dfrac{₹3,12,500 \times 500}{₹10,18,091}$

= 30.69%

(iv) Gearing adjustment = 30.69 % of ₹(97,500 + 35,320

+ 11,628)

= ₹44,331 (approximate)

5. Current cost reserves :

Particulars	Amount (₹)	
Surplus arising on revaluations:		
Fixed assets:		
Net replacement cost	6,60,000	
Net book value	4,00,000	
Surplus	2,60,000	
Depreciation adjustment	97,500	3,57,500
Stock		
Replacement cost	2,60,638	
Historical cost	2,50,000	10,638
COSA		35,320
MWCA		11,628
Gearing adjustment		(44,331)
		3,70,755

Criticism of CCA   Following are the major criticisms of current cost accounting:

1. CCA systems rely on subjective judgments to an unreasonable extent.
2. Logically, it may not be acceptable to work out the MWCA and gearing adjustment.
3. Under CCA, successive balance sheets are stated in terms of rupees of different purchasing power and are thus not directly comparable.

HUMAN RESOURCE ACCOUNTING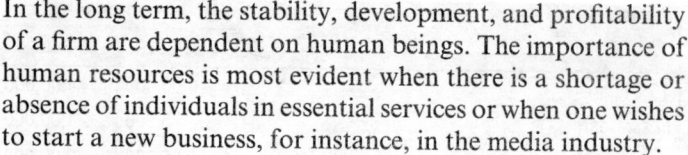

In the long term, the stability, development, and profitability of a firm are dependent on human beings. The importance of human resources is most evident when there is a shortage or absence of individuals in essential services or when one wishes to start a new business, for instance, in the media industry.

Definitions

Human resource accounting has been variedly defined by academicians.

Eric Flamboltz said, 'Human resource accounting is the process of identifying and measuring data about human resources and communicating this information to interested parties.'

According to Woodruff Jr. R.L., Vice President of R.C. Barry Corporation, 'Human resource accounting is an attempt to identify and report investments made in human resources of an organization that are presently not accounted for under conventional accounting practice. Basically it is an information system that tells the management what changes over time are occurring to the human resources of the business'.

In simple words, human resource accounting is the art of evaluating the worth of human resources of an organization in a systematic manner. This evaluation is relevant for the organization and the society. It is essential to record the data for presenting the information in a significant manner in the financial statement. Through this information in the financial statement, the worth of the human resources in the organization is communicated to the users of such data. The recordings would also include changes over the period and results obtained from their utilization.

Human resource accounting covers three aspects: valuation of human resources, recording of such values in the books of accounts, and communicating and presenting the said information in financial statements.

Development of Concept

The economic and political history of every civilization has witnessed and has been impacted by the importance of human resource.

Sir William Petty in the year 1691 made the first attempt to estimate the value of human beings in monetary terms. Petty considered labour as the father of wealth, and felt that labour must be included in any estimate of national wealth. For this purpose, he estimated the value of human capital by capitalization of the wage bill with the assumption of perpetual life at the applicable market interest rate.

On the same guidelines and thought, further efforts were made by William Farr in 1853 and Earnest Engle in 1883. Since the 1960s, human behavior has been considered as a significant factor affecting the performance of a firm and society at large. A few names that worked on it and produced models include Schuliz (1960), Hermanson (1964), Rensis Likert (1967), Hekimian and Jones (1967), Bummet, Flamholtz, and Pyal (1969), Likert and Pyle (1971), Levand Schwartz (1971), Flamholi (1971, 1972, 1975), Likert and Bowers (1973), Morse (1973), Jaggi and Day (1974), Pekin Ogan (1976), and Kenneth Sinclair (1978). All the studies discussed earlier relate to the valuation of human resources.

Approaches to the Human Valuation Methodology

The following are a few major approaches on human valuation.

Cost-based models

Under this model, the measurement of human resource costs is performed through the application of historic cost, standard cost, and opportunity cost concepts. The human resource costs are bifurcated into two broad parameters, acquisition costs and development costs.

Value-based methods of capitalized earnings approach

This method relates to the investigation of the determinants of the value of human resources as a group or of individual employees based on the capitalization of salary method; that is, the economic value method, the net benefit method, and the certainty equivalent benefit method come under this category.

Non-monetary approach

The techniques used in this method include listing the credentials of the key personnel for installing a computer-based information system. Lickert and Flamhdtz (1973) developed tentative correlations between casual variables, such as managerial behavior, organization structure, and subordinate-peer behavior, and intervening variables, such as perception, motivation, and decision-making processes, as indicators to the management systems of companies, and the attainable status of productivity of a firm.

Methods of Human Valuation

The important methods of valuation created till date are explained here briefly.

Acquisition cost method

Under this method, the valuation of human resources and its recording in the books of accounts, is based on the cost of recruiting, hiring, training, familiarization, and development of an employee. These cost based valuations are capitalized and written off over the expected length of service of an individual employee. It is also known as the deferred revenue expenditure of the historic cost method.

The unamortized portion of cost is shown as investment in human assets. If an employee leaves the firm (i.e., the human asset expires or resigns) before the expected service life, the net asset value to that extent is charged to the current revenue.

Replacements cost method

It is a measure of the cost to replace a firm's existing human resources by a new one. It indicates the value of sacrifice that a firm has to make to replace a human resource by an identical one. It indicates what it would cost the firm to recruit, hire, train, and develop human resources to their present level of technical proficiency and familiarity with the organization and its operations. It has the advantage of adjusting the human value to the current market value.

Standard cost

Under this method, the human resource valuation is performed based on the standard costs of recruiting, hiring, training, and developing for each grade of employee, and it is made up to date every year. The standard costs thus derived for all human beings of a firm are treated as the value of human resources for accounting purposes.

Current purchasing power method

Under this method, the capitalized historic cost of investment in human resources is converted into the current purchasing power of money with the help of index numbers.

Opportunity cost method

Hekimian and Jones, in 1967, suggested the use of the opportunity cost concept. Under this method, the valuation of an employee is based on the alternative use of the particular employee. There is no opportunity cost for employees who can easily be hired externally. To determine the opportunity cost, the competing bidding method is used. Bidding takes place only for those assets that are scarce. It means that the opportunity cost is linked with scarcity. Only scarce human resources will have an opportunity cost, and in case of a scarce resource, the division, department, or firm with the highest bid would acquire the particular human resource and would include its price in its investment base.

Capitalization of salary method

This method was suggested by Lev and Schwartz (1871). It is also known as the present value method or the present value of future earnings model.

In this method, the present value of the expected future earnings of the employees is worked out, assuming that the employee will work with the firm up to his or her retirement, and these values are discounted by the rate of the cost of capital. Each and every employee of a firm is analysed according to age and skill. The annual average earning per employee in each group is determined for various ranges of age, and based on the same, the total earning for each group will be estimated. This is then discounted at the rate of the cost of capital as in the capital budgeting decisions. This value is known as the value of human assets.

Human assets multiplier method

A variation of the capitalization of salary method is the human assets multiplier method. Instead of using the cost of capital as a discount factor, here, the present salary is directly multiplied by a factor called the human assets multiplier. A multiplier is developed based on the job grading and the skill of each person individually. The multiplier is applied to the remuneration received by each to arrive at an asset value for the balance sheet. The multipliers are determined rather arbitrarily based on the importance of the person (the more important the person, the higher the multiplier). The person is valued on the basis of the remuneration received and his importance to the firm. If, by chance, his importance decreases or disappears, the multiplier decreases or disappears respectively.

Economic value method

This method has been suggested by Brummet, Flamholtz, and Pyle (1969). They have proposed that a group of human resources should be valued by estimating their contribution to the total economic value of the firm. The present value of a portion of the firm's future earnings attributable to human resources will be the value of the human resources.

Net benefit method and certainty-equivalent net benefit method

Another variation of the economic value method that has been suggested by Morse (1973) and Ogal (1976) is that instead of the total future services, net benefits from the services rendered should be considered to calculate the value of human resources.

The net benefit method has been suggested by Morse. He says that the value of human resources will be equal to the present value of the gross value of services to be rendered in future by individuals both in an individual capacity and in a collective capacity minus the present value of the future payments (direct and indirect) to the individual.

Residual income concept

This method has been proposed by Kenneth Sinclair (1978). Its main purpose has been to suggest as to how human resources accounting can help in decision making using the residual income concept. The method of valuation of human resources suggested under this method is the same as that suggested under the acquisition cost method. The use the residual income derived after deducting a capital charge based on the total assets (human and non-human) from the total income operation has been suggested to help in decision making.

Dr S.K. Chakraborty model

Dr S.K. Chakraborty is the first Indian to suggest a method for human resource valuation and accounting. Under this method, the average tenure of employment of employees is estimated on the basis of past experiences of the firm. By taking into consideration the salary grade structure, the average salary of each group is determined, and then the future total remuneration costs of employees are worked out. The said future total remuneration cost is discounted at an appropriate rate, that is, the cost of capital to arrive at the present value of human resources. Then, the expenditure incurred on recruitment, training, and development is added to this present value to work out the final value of human resources. This value should be shown as investment on the assets side of the balance sheet, and is added to the capital employed.

ENVIRONMENT ACCOUNTING

Environment accounting is also referred to as 'green accounting' because it accounts for the use or the depletion of natural resources in the books of national accounting.

The term environment includes all tangible and intangible items that may be available beneath the earth's surface, on the earth's surface, and above the earth's surface.

All business organizations, non-profit organizations, and service firms use social and ecological resources to maximize their wealth. The functioning of a firm or a unit may impact the environment directly or indirectly. This impact may be positive or negative from the broader view of the society. Hence, it has become important to record the effects of the firms' activities on the environment in the books of accounts.

As per ICWAI (Final RTP Notes p. 104) 'Environmental accounting can be defined as a system (methodology) for measuring environmental performance and communicating the results of these measurements to users. It helps in presenting the utilization of natural resources by an enterprise, the costs incurred to use them and the income earned there from in a transparent manner.'

Environment accounting is a newly emerged concept of accounting. It tries to identify and work out the resources used by a firm and the cost incurred for the society at large on account of its activities. Largely, it involves the determination of the effectiveness of the use of the resources of nature, with an intention to comply with the environmental and societal needs. It also involves accounting for the expenses or costs incurred by a firm to manage the safety and quality control of their products, in the wider interest of the society.

This would in turn support the firm to use the database, and decide future course of actions for correcting any adverse impact on the society.

The parameters discussed seem to work on an academic basis, but practically, it seems to be quite illogical on account of subjective tools for the measurement and recording of the damage to environment.

Following are a few examples that will facilitate the understanding of environment accounting measurement and reporting.

1. Any expenditure incurred by a firm can be recorded primarily as a business expenditure and then as an environmental expenditure. For example, the purchase of a highly automatic machine will result in capital costs, and their running and maintenance cost can be treated as an expenditure that is to be partly paid for the benefit of the society in the form of preventing and/or controlling the resulting air pollution, noise pollution, etc.

2. A firm may establish an effluent treatment plant, which can be treated as capital costs. When the firm uses the effluent treatment plan for protecting the environment surrounding the unit, then it is considered as a revenue expense. It is very difficult to work out all such expenses, and report them separately.

3. Some contingent liabilities may also arise on account of social awareness about future prospective problems which are remote and difficult to measure. For example, presently in India, the society at large is protesting against the establishment of nuclear plants in a few places.

FORENSIC ACCOUNTING

The word forensic is derived from the Latin word 'forum', which means of, or relating to, the legal system or court. The broader definition of forensic simply means applying scientific knowledge to legal issues. Forensic accounting blends special scientific and mathematical skills in auditing, accounting, risk analysis, quantitative methods and research with law, investigative techniques, courtroom procedures, and digital forensics. Technology and greed have been combined to change the corporate landscape and environment and business crime over the past few decades.

Frauds happen through misrepresentation of data and financial information in the financial statements. The financial accountant has to undertake necessary care at the time of submission of information through financial statements to the public at large, that it should not result in losses to the stakeholders associated with the firm. Hence, the financial

accountant assumes the role of a forensic accountant. A forensic accountant has to provide all types of support and take care of financial dealings within the firm or between firms, or has to deal with government agencies.

The term 'forensic accounting' indicates accounting information in a court of law, while dealing with cases related to financial scams, money laundering, insufficient securitization, etc. This concept and word was first used by Maurice E. Peloubet in the year 1946.

Forensic Accounting Practices

Forensic accounting is the validation of the accounting principles, concepts, and government guidelines during the time of preparation and maintenance of financial books of accounts, by taking into consideration the ethical, moral, and legal needs. For this purpose, all the steps of accounting, like vouching proper verification and justification, should be done for every economical event that take place within a firm and/or inter firms. This results in the use of forensic accounting practices during the time of investigation for criminal matters and also in the court of law, to resolve disputes and provide support for unbiased judgements.

Forensic Accountants

A forensic accountant is different from a financial auditor. A financial auditor normally works as a watchdog, while a forensic accountant performs like a bloodhound. However, both behave with the impression in mind that frauds, reported financial scams in public sector units, inability of corporate borrowers to repay the loans taken by them, the overall corrupted systems, etc. could happen.

Financial accountants are accountants specially trained as financial investigators and fraud experts. Fraud is theft by deceit, misrepresentation, and trickery. Financial accountants develop profiles of individuals and groups, conduct interviews of subjects and witnesses, gather evidences, and prepare affidavits for use in the court of law. They often conduct a detailed financial analysis of businesses and personal records in a never-ending quest to follow the money. They summarize their findings and conclusions in financial investigative reports and exhibits, and frequently testify about their financial investigations before the judicial authorities and act as a fact or expert witness at criminal and civil trials.

The forensic accountant and the team develop the methodology of compilation, measurement, and recording of events, with an intention to safeguard the firm, against any possible intentional or unintentional fraud.

Application of Principles of Forensic Accounting to an Enterprise

The following are the illustrative principles of application of financial accounting in practical working of an enterprise:

1. Identify and trace out for indications of abnormal occurrences in the accounting and financial reporting systems.
2. Design the accounting processes in such a way so that it will provide an opportunity to identify and support

for verification of key assumptions and data while also providing the opportunity for identifying possible fraud.
3. Develop routine check of all documentary evidences through standardization of audit procedures.
4. Undertake forensic audits on a concurrent basis; thus help detect frauds at an early stage and provide support for the completion of statutory audit in time.
5. Forensic audit should try to cover each and every function and department working within the firm, including intra-branch, intra-plant transactions, etc.
6. Conduct constant review of operational transactions for compliance with standard operating procedures and approvals.
7. Undertake thorough and complete analysis of financial disbursement transactions in the accounting system to determine their normality as per enterprise policy and, thus, find out possible fraudulent transactions.
8. Conduct review of general ledger and financial reporting system transactions for possible improper classification or manipulation of data or accounts and its impact on the resulting financial reports.
9. Examine all warranty claims or returns from customers or returns to suppliers for patterns of fraud or abuse.
10. Estimate the economic damages and the resulted insurance claims that stem from calamities such as fire or other natural disasters.
11. Evaluate or confirm business valuation in case of mergers and acquisitions or reconstruction of enterprise.

Forensic Accounting in India

Forensic accounting is an emerging need for the country. It is still under the development phase. No specific and detailed guidelines are available from any government authority or professional accountant institutions. In India, financial accounting is required on account of increasing fraud occurrences by corporates as well as non-performing asset problems faced by financial institutions at large.

COMPUTERIZED ACCOUNTING

A computer is an electronic device, which senses or accepts input data, performs operations or computations on the data in a prearranged sequence of programmes, and provides the results as an output of action. Computers are used to handle a large volume of complex data and to provide information with speed and high accuracy.

A computer has different units such as an input unit, the main memory, an arithmetic logic unit, a control unit, an output unit, etc.

Computers may be classified into three types, namely digital, analog, and hybrid. There can also be special-purpose and general-purpose computers.

In business, financial accounting is of paramount importance, whereby the accounting of all business transactions is maintained. The accounting of small-scale businesses may be maintained easily without the help of computers, but

large-scale businesses have wider transactions, and hence require computerized records to carry out the business successfully.

Computers are used in financial accounting for processing day-to-day transactions and to prepare ledgers, trial balances, income statements, and balance sheets. Computers play a vital role in decision support systems and provide analysis-based information to the managers in different decision areas.

To use computerization in a business, one will require at least the following:

- PC AT (80286 to Pentium – 133 MHz)
- DOS (disk operating system software)

Financial Accounting Software

For the sake of financial accounting, it is not required for one to have a thorough knowledge about computers. Only a general knowledge about DOS is sufficient. For financial accounting, the user should know the following commands of a disk-operating system software (DOS):

- Copy command
- Ren command
- Del command
- CLS command
- DIR command

The Copy command is an important internal command to copy any type of files into the computer's hard disk or on a floppy to transfer the data to another computer. Indeed, it is an input–output command.

The Ren command allows users to rename any file. The Del command is used to delete unnecessary files. The DOS Erase command may be used as an alternative of the DEL command. The CLS command is used to clear the monitor. The DIR command is used to view the files stored in a computer.

Computers and Financial Accounting

The core of any financial accounting system is a *'General Ledger'* system. General ledger accounts are supported by detailed subsidiary ledgers. Most of the business firms require financial information for daily operations, planning, and control.

The most common statements comprise income and expenditure statements and balance sheets. Quite often, these statements are generated weekly or monthly to provide information to the management for managing day-to-day operations. A typical general ledger system will interface with all other financial accounting systems.

General ledger

The basic characteristics of a computer-based general ledger are mentioned in the following text:

1. A chart of accounts flexible enough to take care of a variety of requirements
2. Provisions for adding, deleting, and modifying master file records
3. An automatic interface during the end-of-period processing, with other modules such as accounts receivable, accounts payable, etc.

4. Generation of reports such as trial balance, balance sheet, etc.
5. Control producers involving an interactive system, self-instructing documentation, and automatic back-ups at the end of the month

The fixed procedure of accounting is shown in the following text:

- Making a voucher
- Maintaining a day-book
- Making a ledger
- Making a trial balance
- Making balance sheets, profit and loss account, and an annexure of balance sheet
- Making vouchers

The accounting voucher is prepared for every business event. Example are cash voucher, bank voucher, journal voucher, sale voucher, purchase voucher, debit note. credit note voucher, etc.

Cash voucher

A cash voucher is prepared in the following references:

- Cash expenses voucher
- Cash payment voucher
- Cash receipt voucher
- Cash deposit in bank voucher
- Cash withdrawal from bank voucher
- Cash expenses voucher

Bank voucher

A bank voucher is required to maintain the accounts of payments made or received by a user through bank cheques or demand drafts.

Journal voucher

A journal voucher is generally used for rectification of technical mistakes and accrued transactions.

Purchase voucher

A purchase voucher is of two types: (a) cash purchase voucher and (b) credit purchase voucher.

Sales voucher

A sales voucher is of two types: cash sales voucher and credit sales voucher.

Cash book

A cash book helps maintain records of all business transactions so that any related information will be easily obtainable. The four basic elements of a day book are mentioned in this section:

Opening balance   It is the cash amount in hand at the start of a financial year. The opening balance of a cash book is always on the debit.

Cash receipt section   All matters related to receipt of cash are written under this column of the cash book.

Cash payment section   All matters related to expenses are written under this column of the cash book.

Closing balance   When the business of a particular day closes, then the cash in hand after closure of business of that particular

day is the closing balance of that day, which is expressible as follows:

(Opening Balance + Receipt) − (Payment) = Closing Balance

A day book is written by combining all the four elements stated earlier.

Bank book

Like the cash book, a bank book also consists of four elements. The only difference here is that in case a cheque deposited in a bank is bounced, then the same is again entered into the payment column with specific narration. Similarly, in the case of a cash book, it is certain that the balance amount is always on the debit, but in the case of a bank book, it may also be kept on the credit as the cash balance of a bank book is put on the credit.

Sales book

A sales book may be written in two ways. If the user does not require detailed information about the article being sold, it can be recorded by the single-entry system; in case the user requires detailed information about the article being sold, then the double-entry system must be used to write this book.

Purchase book

Like the sales book, a user may also write the purchase book in two ways. In this book, all information regarding transactions is written.

Journal book

A journal book is of paramount importance in accounting. This book is virtually used to modify entries made earlier, and the closing balance of this book always remains zero.

Ledger writing

Usually, the voucher is written first, followed by the day book, and based on the entries made in the day book, an individual ledger is written. While writing a ledger, one first writes the name of the ledger, followed by the column date, the opening balance, a description, the debit and credit, and then the balance. All entries pertaining to the concerned party are recorded in the ledger, whether it belongs to the cash book or to the sale purchase book or to the bank and journal book (including debit–credit note book).

Making a trial balance

The trial balance is written after the ledger is completed. This is probably the most complicated work in accounting, the major difficulty being that the sum total of the debit and the credit of a trial balance should always be the same.

Making a balance sheet

The preparation of a balance sheet is one of the final steps of accounting. Here, the user gives different groupings of the balance sheets to all the trial balance items. These groupings are prescribed in advance; presently, two types of balance sheets are being used: the bridge way method and the column method.

The bridge way balance sheet is divided into two parts. The first part is assets and the second part is liabilities.

Both these parts have their sub-parts in which the amount is written. There sub-parts are known as schedule or annexure. Preparing a balance sheet is primarily based on these annexures, and these annexures are made as a result of the ledgers given in the trial balance.

Income statement

A balance sheet also takes the income statement in the form of an annexure. However, a user may utilize the income statement differently. While preparing a balance sheet with the help of a computer, one has to perform the coding in such a way that the entire schedule and the income statement are also automatically prepared along with the balance sheet. This coding shall become very clear from the following example.

XYZ Press
Balance Code List

Account code

A	Assets
A1	Fixed assets
A2	Stock in hand
A3	Cash & bank balance
A4	Sundry debtors
A5	Loans & advances
L	Liabilities
L1	Capital account
L2	Unsecured loans
L3	Interest payable
L4	Salary payable
L5	Sundry creditors
L6	Profit & loss
L61	Opening stock
L62	Purchases
L63	Manufacturing expenses
L64	Administrative expenses
L65	Sales
L66	Closing stock

With the help of the above-mentioned coding, a user will be able to process the balance sheet easily.

SUMMARY

- Historical cost accounting method is the traditional and highly preferred accounting system.
- The historical cost accounting figures are, however, misleading as it results in an understatement of cost and overstatement of profit in an inflationary situation.

- To counter the weaknesses of the historical cost accounting method, inflation accounting has been conceived as a realistic system which reflects the effect of changing price levels.
- The two highly accepted systems for accounting of inflation are (a) the current purchasing power (CPP) method and (b) the current

value system (CVS). The current purchasing power method is an accounting measurement showing the effect of inflation on the value of money. The current value system refers to approaches such as the current replacement cost (entry value) approach, the net realizable value (exit value) approach, the economic value, and the current cost accounting approach. Human resources accounting is the process of identifying and measuring data of costs/investments incurred on human resources in an organization.

- In a global economy, financial information reported by an entity needs to be realigned in such a way that international financial analysts can understand it easily.

- Accounting is the procedural methodology used to record and present business events in financial statements in such a manner that it can help the users of financial statements to take well-informed decisions. The adoption of accounting rules, conventions, concepts, and practices means that business events will always be recorded correctly and presented correctly and fairly.

- The financial information should be presented in the language, currency, accounting principles, and authentication in which the foreign investors can have trust and confidence.

- Environment accounting, also referred to as 'Green accounting', accounts for the use or the depletion of natural resources in the books of national accounting.

- Environment accounting includes all tangible and intangible items available beneath, on, and above the earth's surface.

- Forensic means something that is suitable for use in a court of law. Forensic accounting is the practice of applying accounting, auditing, and investigative skills in assisting legal matters.

- Forensic accounting blends special scientific and mathematical skills in accounting, auditing, risk analysis, quantitative methods and research with investigative techniques, law, courtroom procedures, and digital forensics.

- Forensic accountants along with prosecutors, attorneys, and other investigators plan and guide financial aspects of investigations in legal cases.

- Forensic accountants investigate complex financial crimes involving different types of frauds.

KEYWORDS

Current purchasing power (CPP) It is an accounting measurement showing the effect of inflation on the value of money. To arrive at CPP, historical costs are converted into current prices by using an index such as consumer price index (CPI).

Current replacement cost (CRC) It refers to the current cost of replacing an asset or property with the same quality and utility in the normal course of business at the balance sheet date or at the date of sale, whichever is relevant.

Environment accounting (green accounting) It is a modified system of accounting, which accounts for the use or the depletion of natural resources in the books of national accounting.

Human resource accounting It is an attempt to identify, assign, budget, and report costs/investments incurred on human resources

in an organization, including wages, and salaries and training expenses. Basically it is an information system that tells the management what changes over time are occurring to the human resources of the business.

Index of prices The index indicates the relative changes in all prices.

Monetary items It refers to those amounts of assets (such as cash and amounts receivable) and liabilities (such as notes and amounts payable) which are fixed by contract or statute in terms of rupees unaffected by inflation or deflation.

Non-monetary items It refers to those amounts of assets that are not monetary items, with the exception of the total equity interest, which is neither monetary nor non-monetary. Examples include fixed assets, stocks, investments in shares, etc.

REFERENCES

Brummet, R.L., E.G. Flamholtz, and C.P. William 1968, 'Human Resource Management: A Challenge for Accountant', *The Accounting Review*, 43(2), pp. 217–224.

Brummet, R.L., E.G. Flamholtz, and W.C. Pyle 1968b, March, 'Accounting for Human Resources', *Michigan Business Review*, pp. 20–25.

Brummet, R.L., E.G. Flamholtz, and W.C. Pyle 1969, August, 'Human Resource Accounting: A Tool to Increase Managerial Effectiveness', *Management Accounting*, pp. 12–15.

Chakraborty, S.K. 1976, *Human Asset Accounting: The Indian Context in Topics in Accounting and Finance*, Oxford University Press, New Delhi.

Dasgupta, N.D. 1978, *Human Resource Accounting*, Sultan Chand and Sons, New Delhi.

Edwards, E.O. and P.W. Bell 1961, *The Theory and Measurement of Business Income*, University of California Press.

Lev, B., and A. Schwartz 1971, January, 'On the Use of the Economic Concept of Human Capital in Financial Statements', *Accounting Review*, pp. 103–112.

Likert, E. and E.G. Flamholtz 1973, 'HRA: Measuring Positional Replacement Costs', *Human Resource Management*, 12 (Spring), pp. 8–16.

Likert, R.M. 1961, *New Patterns of Management*, McGraw–Hill, New York.

Likert, R.M. 1967, *The Human Organization: Its Management and Value*, McGraw-Hill, New York.

'Accounting Standards and Corporate Accounting Practices', *Miller GAAP Guide Level A* 2006.

Morse, W.J. 1973, 'A Note on the Relationship between Human Asset and Capital', *The Accounting Review*, 37 (3), pp. 589–593.

Ogan, P.A. 1976', 'Human Resource Value Model for Professional Service Organizations', *The Accounting Review*, 51(2), p. 306.

Rathore, Shirin 2009, *International Accounting*, 2nd Edition, PHI, New Delhi, pp. 257, 258, 269–274.

Samuelson, Paul A. and William D. Nordhaus 2004, *Economics*, 18th edition, McGraw-Hill, Irwin.

Shah, Paresh, 'Forensic Accounting as a Tool for Fraud and Corruption Detection', *An International Multidisciplinary Half Yearly Research Journal, Royal*, December 2017–May 2018, Vol VI, Issue 2, ISSN 2278-8158, pp. 21–26 (Proceeding of National Conference New Horizons in Accounting, Taxation and Management, Savitribai Phule Pune University).

Sinclair, Kenneth 1978, March, *Accountancy*, Vol. 89, Issue 1015, p. 48.

Tiffin, Ralph 2005, *The Complete Guide to International Financial Reporting Standards*, Thorogood, London, pp. 150–155, 203.

http://www.iasplus.com/standard/ias14.htm, accessed on 1 May 2012.

http://www.masb.org.my/index.php?option=com_content&id=1138 %3Amasb28-discontinuing-operations-pgl&catid=7%3Amasb-for-private&Itemid=15, accessed on 1 May 2012.

www.fasb.org, accessed on 1 May 2012.

www.iasb.org, accessed on 1 May 2012.

Comparative Study of IFRS and Ind AS

Appendix A below indicates a comparative study of IFRS and Ind AS.

SI No.	Name (International Financial Reporting Standards)	Issued (Reissued)	IFRS	Corresponding Indian Accounting Standard (Ind AS)
1	First Time Adoption of International Financial Reporting Standards	2008	IFRS 1	Ind AS 101
2	Share-based Payment	2004	IFRS 2	Ind AS 102
3	Business Combinations	2008	IFRS 3	Ind AS 103
4	Insurance Contracts	2004	IFRS 4	Ind AS 104
5	Non-current Assets Held for Sale and Discontinued Operations	2004	IFRS 5	Ind AS 105
6	Exploration for and Evaluation of Mineral Assets	2004	IFRS 6	Ind AS 106
7	Financial Instruments: Disclosures	2005	IFRS 7	Ind AS 107
8	Operating Segments	2006	IFRS 8	Ind AS 108
9	Financial Instruments	2014	IFRS 9	Ind AS 109
10	Consolidated Financial Statements	2011	IFRS 10	Ind AS 110
11	Joint Arrangements	2011	IFRS 11	Ind AS 111
12	Disclosure of Interests in Other Entities	2011	IFRS 12	Ind AS 112
13	Fair Value Measurements	2011	IFRS 13	Ind AS 113
14	Regulatory Deferral Accounts	2014	IFRS 14	Ind AS 114

Comparative Analysis of Ind AS and Existing Standard

Appendix B indicates the linkages between Accounting Standards as issued by ICAI (AS) and Indian Accounting Standards (Ind AS) as notified by MCA.

		Indian Accounting Standards [Ind Existing Accounting Standards AS]		
1	Ind AS 101	First-time Adoption of Indian Accounting Standards	---	
2	Ind AS 102	Share-based Payment	---	
3	Ind AS 103	Business Combinations	AS 14	Amalgamations
4	Ind AS 104	Insurance Contracts	---	
5	Ind AS 105	Non-current Assets Held for Sale and Discontinued Operations	AS 24	Discontinuing Operations
6	Ind AS 106	Exploration for and Evaluation of Mineral Resources	---	
7	Ind AS 107	Financial Instruments: Disclosures	AS 32	Financial Instruments: Disclosures
8	Ind AS 108	Operating Segments	AS 17	Segment Reporting
9	Ind AS 1	Presentation of Financial Statements	AS 1	Disclosure of Accounting Policies
10	Ind AS 2	Inventories	AS 2	Inventory Valuation
11	Ind AS 7	Statement of Cash Flows	AS 3	Cash Flow Statements
12	Ind AS 8	Accounting Policies, Changes in Accounting Estimates and Errors	AS 5	Net Profit or Loss for the Period, Prior Period Items and Changes in Accounting Policies
13	Ind AS 10	Events after the Reporting Period	AS 4	Contingencies and Events Occurring after the BS date
14	Ind AS 11	Construction Contracts	AS 7	Construction Contracts
15	Ind AS 12	Income Taxes	AS 22	Accounting for Taxes on Income
16	Ind AS 16	Property, Plant and Equipment	AS 10	Property, Plant and Equipment
17	Ind AS 17	Leases	AS 19	Leases
18	Ind AS 18	Revenue	AS 9	Revenue Recognition
19	Ind AS 19	Employee Benefits	AS 15	Employee Benefits
20	Ind AS 20	Accounting for Government Grants and Disclosure of Government Assistance	AS 12	Accounting for Government Grants
21	Ind AS 21	The Effects of Changes in Foreign Exchange Rates	AS 11	The Effects of Changes in Foreign Exchange Rates
22	Ind AS 23	Borrowing Costs	AS 16	Borrowing Costs
23	Ind AS 24	Related Party Disclosures	AS 18	Related Party Disclosures
24	Ind AS 27	Consolidated and Separate Financial Statements	AS 21	Consolidated Financial Statements

25	Ind AS 28	Investments in Associates	AS23	Accounting for Investment in Associates in the Consolidated Financial Statements
26	Ind AS 29	Financial Reporting in Hyper-inflationary Economies	----	
27	Ind AS 31	Interests in Joint Ventures	AS 27	Financial Reporting of Interests in Joint Ventures
28	Ind AS 32	Financial Instruments: Presentation	AS 31	Financial Instruments: Presentation
29	Ind AS 33	Earnings Per Share	AS 20	Earnings Per Share
30	Ind AS 34	Interim Financial Reporting	AS 25	Interim Financial Reporting
31	Ind AS 36	Impairment of Assets	AS 28	Impairment of Assets
32	Ind AS 37	Provisions, Contingent Liabilities, and Contingent Assets	AS 29	Provisions, Contingent Liabilities and Contingent Assets
33	Ind AS 38	Intangible Assets	AS 26	Intangible Assets
34	Ind AS 39	Financial Instruments: Recognition and Measurements	AS 30	Financial Instruments: Recognition and Measurements
35	Ind AS 40	Investment Property	---	
36	Ind AS 41	Agriculture	---	

Index

Related Titles

MANAGEMENT ACCOUNTING [9780195695250]

Paresh Shah, *Visiting Professor, G.H. Patel Post Graduate Institute of Business Management (SP University), IIPM, EDII, SLIMS (GTU), United World, and IBS and Director, Fenil Institute*

Management Accounting explores core concepts of management accounting through managerial applications and supplements them through numerous solved problems and case studies.

Key Features

- Focuses on the uses of accounting information to resolve different managerial issues emerging in different organizations
- Provides numerous illustrative problems for better understanding and application of management accounting tools and techniques
- Contains real-world cases to stimulate students' interest and to provide a springboard for classroom discussions

FINANCIAL MANAGEMENT, 2/E [9780198072072]

Rajiv Srivastava, *Professor, Indian Institute of Foreign Trade, New Delhi*; **Anil Misra**, *Associate Professor, Management Development Institute, Gurgaon*

This new edition provides a detailed coverage of the core concepts of financial management and has been updated thoroughly with additional sections and improved explanations.

Key Features

- New sections on corporate debt restructuring and regulation of working capital finance
- Revised content related to corporate governance, economic value added, venture capital and private equity, long-term and short-term sources of funds
- Finding yields and portfolio risk
- Computation of EVA, WACC, and BEP
- Determination of Beta

ACCOUNTING FOR MANAGEMENT [9780198093312]

S. Ramanathan, *Visiting Professor, Institute of Chartered Accountants of India, Institute of Cost Accountants of India, and Institute of Management Studies (Kanpur University)*

Accounting for Management is a comprehensive textbook specially designed for postgraduate students of business management. It follows a practice-oriented approach to explain the core concepts of accounting, with the help of numerous illustrations and solved examples.

Key Features

- Covers important contemporary accounting concepts of product life cycle costing, target pricing, activity-based costing, among others
- Presents interesting and engaging case studies at the end of every chapter
- Includes appendices that provide useful analysis of IFRS, Indian GAAP, and US GAAP guidelines

MARKETING: ASIAN EDITION [9780198079446]

Paul Baines, *Reader in Marketing, Cranfield School of Management, Cranfield University*; **Chris Fill**, *Director of Fillassociates, and formerly Principal Lecturer, University of Portsmouth*; **Kelly Page**, *Lecturer in Digital Media Marketing, Cardiff Business School*; **Piyush K. Sinha**, *Director, CRI Advisory and Research, Ahmedabad*

Marketing is an exciting new textbook packed with learning features, combining authority with a lively and engaging writing style; and a diverse range of resources, available online.

Key Features

- Separate chapters on Digital Marketing, Relationship Marketing, Not-for-Profit Marketing, Postmodern Marketing, and Marketing, Sustainability, and Ethics
- Deals with contemporary marketing practices with relevant examples drawn from international as well as Asian markets including India
- Case Insights: Accounts of real-life situations faced by top marketers from leading organizations, including Adani Wilmar, Oxfam, DLF, HMV, MOLLY MAID, and Crompton Greaves, encouraging the reader to consider possible solutions.

Other Related Titles

- 9780198066903 Khatua: *Project Management and Appraisal*
- 9780198064343 Srivastava: *Derivatives and Risk Management*
- 9780198064510 Aurora, Shetty, & Kale: *Mergers and Acquisitions*
- 9780198074113 Jyothi and Venkatesh: *Human Resource Management, 2/e*
- 9780198095170 Banerjee: *Financial Management*
- 9780198094739 Mishra: *Business Research Method*
- 9780198098621 Ghosh: *Business Environment*
- 9780199463169 Albuquerque: *Legal Aspects of Business, 2/e*
- 9780195690873 Bedi: *Production and Operations Management, 2/e*
- 9780198070795 Chandrasekaran: *Strategic Management*